West London colleges specialise in helping overseas students with internationally recognised qualifications leading to a professional career or to university. Tutors combine practical experience with the highest academic honours and have at their disposal an impressive range of advanced teaching aids. Special care is taken to introduce students to the wealth of cultural and leisure opportunities with which London and the UK are so richly endowed.

BUSINESS TRAINING We offer a Basic Business Course and training for the examinations leading to the Association of Business Executives' qualification. The Diploma of the Association of Business Executives is designed for students who wish to achieve executive positions in commerce or industry. The course lasts one year and successful completion of the examinations means you will be entitled to put the letters MABE after your name. On completion of the Advanced Diploma of the ABE you are then eligible to progress to an MBA at a British University.

MARKETING A marketing professional is essential to every progressive company and a Certificate or Diploma from the Institute of Marketing qualifies you for this important position.

ACCOUNTANCY
The Association of Certified Accountants (ACCA)
In modern business and industry, the person who really matters is the qualified accountant. The success of the business can depend on him.

BANKING We train you for the Institute of Bankers' examinations which are recognised internationally—so you will be able to work in any part of the world.

... London ... opportunity to ... upon which all others are increasingly dependent: the computer industry. The course prepares you for the internationally recognised Association of Computer Professionals. On completion of the Advanced Diploma of ACP you are then eligible to progress to an MSc.

COOKERY AND CATERING The aim of the course is to provide a sound technical education to people who are keen to pursue a career in the catering industry, in particular hotels and restaurants.

TOURISM AND HOTEL MANAGEMENT More and more people are travelling overseas and the growth industry of the developing world is Tourism and Hotel Management. At West London College, we train you for the internationally recognised examinations and qualifications of the Confederation of Tourism, Hotel and Catering Management.

MANY OTHER SUBJECTS are available.

We have been inspected and are recognised as efficient by the Association for the Recognition of Business Schools (ARBS).

SEND FOR HELPFUL PROSPECTUS Provided you have the necessary educational qualifications or are willing to let us prepare you for them, we shall be happy to send you the very informative prospectus giving you full details of careers, opportunities and examinations. Or call in NOW!

WEST LONDON COLLEGE WLC

51 Avon House, 360–366, Oxford St., London W1 Tel: 01-491 1841/2

Careers Encyclopedia

Careers Encyclopedia

12th Edition

Audrey Segal

CASSELL

Cassell Educational Ltd: Artillery House, Artillery Row, London, SW1P 1RT

First edition 1952
Second edition 1958
Third edition 1963
Fourth edition 1965
Fifth edition 1967
Sixth edition 1969
Seventh edition 1970
Eighth edition 1975
Eighth edition, second impression 1977
Ninth edition 1978
Tenth edition 1980
Eleventh edition 1984
Eleventh edition, second impression 1985
Twelfth edition 1987

British Library Cataloguing in Publication Data
Careers encyclopedia. —— 12th edition.
   1. Vocational guidance —— Great Britain
   2. Great Britain —— Occupations
   I. Segal, Audrey
   331.7'02'0941   HF5382.5.G7

ISBN 0 304 31139 1

Typeset by Millford Reprographics International Ltd., Luton, Beds.
Printed and bound in Great Britain by Mackays of Chatham Ltd

Contents

Introduction   vii

Academic and Vocational Qualifications   1
School and pre-vocational qualifications – further and higher education

Academic and Vocational Studies and Where They Can Lead   63
Arts qualifications and careers – creative and performing arts – engineering and technology – land use – science – social sciences

The World of Work   334
The future of employment – choosing and pre-vocational preparation – alternatives to, and self, employment

The Information Society   356
Information technology and computing – library work and information science

Commerce, Administration and Finance   397
Administration and management – finance – marketing (including advertising, market research and public relations) – purchasing and buying, selling and retailing

Creative, Cultural and Entertainment Work   527
Art, design, photography, etc. – media careers – museums, art galleries and archive work – performing (including sport) – recreation and leisure industries

Land- and Environment-related Work   654
Agriculture, fishing, forestry and horticulture – conservation and the environment – the construction industry – the land use professions – mining, prospecting and quarrying – the water industry

Central and Local Government and the Armed Forces   734
The Armed Forces – central government – local government – politics

Manufacturing and Production   813
How industry works – employment in manufacturing industry – manufacturing sectors

Professional, Scientific and Social Services   913
Education – health and medical services – the legal system – management services – religious organisations and services – social work – translating and interpreting, working with languages

The Service Industries   1069
Communications systems/services – hotels and catering, and institutional management – personal and domestic service – protective services – the tourist industry – transport and travel

Working Overseas   1161
Working abroad permanently – short-term opportunities

Appendix I: Organisations Providing Further Information   1175

Appendix II: Higher and Further Education Institutions   1209

Index to Advertisers   1229

Index   1231

Introduction

Change, as predicted in this *Encyclopedia* in 1980, has indeed become endemic. The changes brought about by the recession of the first half of the decade are now almost – already – historic, yet the pace and scope of change continue, if anything, to accelerate. Change is now increasingly structural, brought about by a complex mesh of political, economic, technological, social, and now demographic factors. The evidence throughout this edition of the *Encyclopedia* shows the effects of the rising pressure of 'market forces' and intensifying competition on individual jobs and career opportunities.

While new jobs are emerging and older – and some not so old – vanishing, the nature of a great many jobs, and the kind and mix of skills, know-how and experience needed to do them, are continuing to undergo far reaching and all-pervasive changes.

The level of unemployment has, at last, flattened out and may even be falling, with some distinct indicators of improving opportunities. However, there are still not enough reasonable career starts for all the young people leaving the education system, even with the now rapidly-falling numbers of sixteen- to eighteen-year-olds. While the range of opportunities available to school-leavers (especially) depends to a considerable extent on the accident of where they live, the balance of opportunities has – so far at least – continued to swing in favour of those who are better educated, who have appropriate skills, aptitudes, qualifications. As industry and commerce recover from recession, the skill shortages grow steadily, made worse by the widespread failure to train, to the extent that they could affect firms' ability to compete.

But while paper qualifications – school-leaving, degree – count, personal skills and attitudes, work experience – almost above all the ability to cope in a competitive environment whether that environment is profit-oriented or not – are increasingly seen as crucial.

Now a new, and probably major factor is about to affect the employment market, and is likely to have dramatic effects on opportunities for young people, possibly to the extent of giving them some advantage over recruiters once again. By the early 1990s numbers leaving the education system will have halved. Aptly called a 'demographic time bomb' by the nursing profession, the first to quantify its (potentially dire) effects on their recruitment, this has to mean there will be rising and considerable shortages – in straight numbers let alone quality – of new entrants for careers, occupations, jobs of all kinds. Some YTS schemes already cannot find enough trainees to fill their agreed number of places.

Exactly how much brighter the opportunities will be is difficult to predict. Much depends on how employers react to the problems as they grow. At present, most aim to keep up a reasonable level of recruitment, even when cutting overall numbers, to provide for the future – especially of young people able to work on and with new technologies. The total number of jobs is not expected – as of 1987 – to increase by anything like enough to mop up the millions at present unemployed, so employers may yet decide to (re-)train more adults to help make up the shortfall – and find they prefer them. It can be expected that technology, in the form of automation where possible, and probably 'expert' and other new easier-to-use computer-based systems, will help to solve manpower problems. Although the case for 'de-skilling' tasks and jobs is far from proved, employers can be expected to try this too. Hopefully, employers will also have to move back into those areas of the country where unemployment is highest, to give career opportunities there once again.

But despite the improving employment market, full employment – or anything close to it – is still probably not achievable for the foreseeable future, at least not without some form of job-creating central intervention. The consensus of economic opinion appears to be that growth will not be high or fast enough for long enough to create the number of jobs needed for full employment. 'Market forces' – even in the service industries such as tourism – alone apparently cannot deliver them.

New, 'information' technology is helping to generate – as well as destroy – jobs, but cannot be expected to produce the millions that are needed for everyone who wants to work. Since much automation is justified because it cuts labour costs, new technology cannot help but contribute to unemployment. The main hope has to be that greater (industrial) efficiency – using information and other new technology as well as more skilled management etc – will generate enough wealth for jobs to be created (or re-created) elsewhere – in education, health, social services, the arts, etc.

There is no shortage of ideas both for ways of creating, or helping to create, new jobs and for radical alternative work, leisure and learning patterns. It is not the role of this *Encyclopedia* to argue the case for or against any of them, but we have to sympathise with careers advisers who must cope daily with the fears and frustrations of young people and their parents rightly seriously concerned that more is not being done. Continuing high unemployment, as well as wasting a major resource – the potential of so many people – is a serious social problem.

As page after page of this edition of the *Encyclopedia* shows, work opportunities are changing and will go on doing so, frequently quite dramatically, and in ways that are difficult to predict. Technology, mainly information technology, and intense competition now both rival each other in forcing change, and in many instances are working together, both to create and destroy opportunities. It is difficult to know whether it would be a good or bad thing if what has been happening in the financial world since mid 1986 were to be the precursor of changes in other sectors – noting as we go to press in late 1987 that a rising number of so-recently created City jobs are being lost. Certainly what is happening in the financial world is having considerable effect in the financial offices of most major organisations – see, for instance, CORPORATE TREASURY.

Many unskilled, particularly manual, jobs have been lost partly through recession, partly technology. Skilled and semi-skilled jobs, automatable by existing, or recently-developed, technology, up to craft, and at least technician

INDEPENDENT ASSESSMENT AND RESEARCH CENTRE

CAREERS GUIDANCE
For students and adults who desire help
with choosing or changing a career
EDUCATIONAL GUIDANCE
for the younger student

Services offered by professional psychologists

I.A.R.C., (ref. CCE), FREEPOST 11, LONDON W1E 2JZ 01 486 6106

(eg draughting) level have gone. Even some of the newer, computer-based skills are now outdated, and job opportunities in eg lower-level applications programming look likely to fall. Where jobs are not actually lost, they are changing, often out of all recognition. The pace of office automation is now increasing, with less and less routine work, and jobs here are changing in character too.

Coming developments in computer-based technologies will be felt by people in more and more occupations, right through management and the professions. While the paperless society may still be a very long way off, the whole thrust of information technology – speeding and sophisticating the flow of information – cuts the amount of paper that has to be generated and pushed around. This is already affecting a whole range of executive/middle-manager level jobs, especially where people have (up to now) laboriously compiled, assessed and presented data collected from others for decision-making managers. For example, spread-sheet and accounting packages for micros (at one end of the scale) and financial information systems (at the other) already allow managers to control their budgets and accounts rapidly and directly and do many other financial management tasks for themselves quite easily. As more and more efficiently-packaged information of all kinds is presented to managers via electronic systems, decision-making is being devolved to smaller, localised units, whose managers may become less specialised in function, and therefore need a wider range of skills and understanding. It is here that the radical re-structuring of financial institutions and the breakdown in the traditional division of interests between them, made possible by information technology, has to be an indicator of the kind of changes to come in many sectors.

The traditional, very separate and distinct professions – law, banking, medicine, accountancy, architecture, surveying, librarianship etc, and the 'technician-level' people who work with them – each controlling highly-specialised sets of information, are now beginning to be changed by information technology and the competitive environment. Some, like lawyers, already have highly sophisticated data bases to give them faster and more efficient access to the specialised information (eg case law) they work with. 'Expert systems' (see IT/COMPUTING) are now being developed which will turn all kinds of skills, including professional skills in assessing, analysing and exploiting specialised information, into computer programs which can be used by people with little or no expertise in the field. The professions as we know them today could then look very different by the end of the century – now less than fifteen years away. Professions are having to come to terms with progressive loss of monopoly in specific skill areas and develop new, competitive skills – just as craft workers have had to already. There is already growing competition for areas of work between professions – eg architecture and surveying, banking and building society management – where traditional boundaries of responsibility are breaking down. It is clearly government intention – as shown by decisions on conveyancing and spectacle supply – to encourage inter-professional competition.

Education, vocational preparation and training for this very different future are clearly crucial for both individuals and the organisations which will employ them. Here too there are problems, not least of which is the near-impossibility of deciding what is actually needed. Certainly, most authorities agree that most people will need to be better educated, to be more skilled and skilled in different ways – probably multi-skilled – and better prepared for work to be able to cope with the jobs of the future. Beyond that, there is just as much uncertainty as there is about what jobs will be like. Demand for many traditional skills is declining sharply, but the exact shape and content of the skill packages people will need in future are not easy to define.

A leading industrialist, Sir Kenneth Corfield, then chairman of both a high-technology company and the Engineering Council, has said, 'In the world into which we are now moving, those employed will be those with a basic framework of education on to which skills can be grafted and regrafted... The ability to be trained and retrained, a pattern which is intrinsic to careers today, increasingly depends upon length and levels of initial educational attainment, and access to continuing education and training...' Which implies a 'steady integration of the education and training systems'.

The difficulties of developing such an education and training system which will cope with the future needs of both individuals and employers cannot be underestimated. Demographic changes, political theories and financial restrictions compound the problems of trying to anticipate those needs. Many long-established traditions and structures need to be re-thought. More vocational education and preparation, both within education (schools and non-advanced further education) and immediately after was long overdue; too much weight probably has been given to purely academic study and norm-rather than criterion-referenced examinations. Mastery of basic core skills is now essential for all, and these need to be taught, tested and recorded in ways which will show everyone's positive achievements, rather than negatively divide into success and failure against a sterile statistical yardstick.

While GCSE is now finally replacing O levels and CSE, albeit in a rather unsatisfactory way, the problems of what should be taught at school are still not resolved, after nearly ten years of debate. The government, though, is now (1987) proposing to implement a tightly-defined 'national curriculum', to be followed by pupils at all state-maintained schools. It is clearly sensible to insist on all pupils studying English, maths, science and technology up to sixteen. But in terms of what is likely to be needed for 21st-century careers, the consultative document appears to put too great an emphasis on circumscribed subject-based learning, and is weak on skills such as how to learn and re-learn; analyse, assess and manage information; problem solve, and so on. The benefits of schemes such as TVEI are in danger of being marginalised. At a time when young people should be prepared for change, flexibility and adaptability, the national curriculum seems set on taking them back to the rigid subject-divisions of the beginning of the century.

A balanced and unified education/training system, giving young people the necessary and maximum flexibility still seems as far off as ever. Part of the problem is that education and training continue to be treated as separate processes, when in fact they are both part of a single, learning, process, and should be considered as such.

The 1981 White Paper, 'New Training Initiative' set out plans for widespread changes in both pre-vocational preparation and training systems, designed to give a better trained work-force, and to create forms of training – in skills from craft through to professional – based on defined standards ('standard led') rather than time serving and age related, and therefore more suited to today's – and tomorrow's – changing work opportunities. Following this, government has been pushing through major national changes (described fully in the first two chapters following) concentrating heavily so far on pre-vocational preparation – the Youth Training Scheme (YTS), the Certificate of Pre-Vocational Education (CPVE), and the Technical and Vocational Educational Initiative (TVEI) – almost to the extent of suggesting that such preparation can of itself create jobs for the recipients.

The danger here is still that the pendulum may swing too far towards schemes directly and totally 'relevant' to work (however relevance may be defined). It is questionable how far pre-vocational schemes designed specifically to help young people into work, or to train them in very narrowly-based 'competencies' (the latest jargon word for work-related skills) – can help them prepare for the periods when there are no jobs for them, to improve their education/training base, or change occupation. If, for some, there are no jobs at all, the effects could be catastrophic. One professional body, the Institute of Chartered Secretaries and Administrators, writing in response to BTEC's 1983 discussion document on educational policy, suggested that 'The emphasis on job-related skills that is currently required has probably gone too far. There may now be danger of losing the benefits which accrue from the provision of a broader-based (business) education ... to encourage concentration on the development of highly job-specific skills is not in the wider interests of students, employers or British industry and commerce as a whole.' There is also the risk of teaching young people specific skills which will be redundant all too soon. The newly-created (1986) National Council for Vocational Qualifications (NCVQ) appears to be in danger of accepting narrow-based 'competencies' too, although it is very early days. NCVQ has yet to start tackling the major problems of progression, via acceptability of lower-level qualifications, and the sensitive issue of bringing professional qualifications within a national framework.

Major changes of the kind introduced by the government since 1981 were bound to attract criticism, especially as they involved giving progressively more influence to the training side, as represented by the Manpower Services Commission, and have been accompanied by cuts in educational expenditure which have adversely affected eg opportunities for young people to go on into higher education (although this is now being at least partly reversed). Industrialists like Sir Frank Corfield have questioned whether schemes such as YTS – however admirable they may be in their own right – are the best way of making use of the available resources, especially when there are shortages of people with high-level, high-technology skills.

Such a heavy emphasis on training-led initiatives make it difficult to achieve the integration of education and training and the flexibility needed to allow young people to acquire educational/vocational-skill packages which cross the conventional academic-vocational divide, both as the basis for new jobs and to

help them through times when they may not be in work. YTS has the inevitable rigidities of any scheme that attempts to be all things to over a quarter of a million young people, when flexibility ought to be the dominant factor. For example, it is difficult both to provide a broad enough base to allow them to transfer into other areas of employment and at the same time meet the rising standards of first-stage training in specific industries so that trainees can go on straight on to second-stage skill training. YTS will clearly have to be further sophisticated and have more flexibility built into it if it is to become the intended all-purpose bridge from school to employment for so many. Other new initiatives have similar problems – young people following a TVEI scheme as presently organised risk closing off options at sixteen- and eighteen-plus, for instance. CPVE as so far developed is too tightly restricted to one age group and to full-time study (although it is now being piloted for YTS). Disagreements on the ability range for which it caters – and the conflict between CPVE and BTEC First awards – illustrate the still-serious problems to be solved in the pre-vocational field.

Progression is a problem generally. Increasingly, YTS schemes are becoming the first stage of longer-term training in a growing range of industries (eg engineering, agriculture). However, it is still generally difficult for people coming out of pre-vocational schemes to have their training formally accepted for entry to more advanced levels of education and/or training. Especially for those for whom there may be no job at the end of a YTS year, more links and bridges are needed. The growing and confusing complexity of educational and training provision for the sixteen-plus age group, which is compounded by the varying financial support (or lack of it) which goes with the various schemes, still makes logical choices and progression even more difficult to achieve.

Concern for the poor employment prospects of the majority of sixteen/seven-teen-year-olds leaving the education system means that most pre-vocational schemes have so far been developed mainly for the average and less able academically. While this has obviously been a necessary priority, vocational preparation and its essential role in preparing young people for change is just as crucial for the more and most able. Until vocational preparation (including work experience) is built in to their course and training structures right through to eighteen- and twenty-one-plus too, the charge that vocational preparation schemes are being used mainly to reduce youth unemployment figures will be difficult to avoid (although government long-term policy is to provide vocational preparation for all, no firm date for this has been set). Evidence suggests that if a scheme is successful enough to persuade employers to keep – or take on – YTS trainees permanently, some of the most able of them will actually take up places which would have gone to school-leavers with A levels but no work experience. Their opportunities for work have been adversely affected by the plentiful supply of graduates and they have suffered from cuts in the number of higher education places. Instead, then, of creating separate academic and non-academic schemes for the over sixteens still in education, some form of modular provision which would enable young people to gain a 'basket' of academic and pre-vocational qualifications best suited to individual needs would probably be a better preparation. It is increasingly accepted that A-level studies should be broadened, beyond the (optional) provision of AS levels.

Careers experts – advisers and teachers – are therefore working today in a setting where not only are employment prospects changing, uncertain and difficult, but preparation for work is also changing and becoming more complex to assess.

They now have a massive task in helping understandably-anxious young people (and their parents) come to terms with this very different future. Young people and their parents have quite naturally reacted to a worrying employment scene by competing even harder for what they believe is the security of very traditional-style careers – even though life-long job security is probably no longer possible and the opportunities within some of these occupations are declining sharply. Careers advisers have to counter this, and instead must get over to them that they have look forward and accept that the main opportunities will probably be with the new, unfamiliar and different. Young people from professional families no less than those from families with long traditions of craft skills, will have working lives quite different in content, form, pattern, style, and environment from those of their parents. The conventional view of a career – as the 'upward movement of an individual to clearly-defined stratified stages within a profession and the associated norms, expectations and life styles, and necessarily involving a long-term commitment to an occupation' – is becoming less and less accurate.

Young people starting out today are being told that they will probably have to think in terms of and be prepared for change, for the high probability that their 'careers' will not be in a single occupation; that the clearly-defined stratified stages may no longer be there; that movement may be in any direction – sideways, in, out, and perhaps even what might appear to be downwards; and that above all, a long-term commitment to one occupation may be the greatest possible mistake. It is, of course, easy to say (or write) all this, but an entirely different matter to have to learn to live with it. Any kind of change which affects people so fundamentally as does change in the way in which they gain a living, is painful, difficult, disruptive and stressful. It is asking a very great deal of people to live with regular and perhaps frequent changes in the work they do, to live without long-term job security or all the expectations, life styles and stabilities that go with it. Much better preparation, support and counselling for this new way of life will be needed if the problems people will face are to be minimised.

Although it has been a convention that a career, once chosen, is a career for life, in fact this has never been completely true. Far more people than is generally realised have always made quite radical changes of occupation once, twice or even more often during their working lives. Declining opportunities in particular occupations and areas of employment have always played their part, but for many people it has been a matter of lucky accident and choice – quite deliberately to change occupation or because a new opportunity has presented itself. If change of occupation is now likely to become, for many more people, a regular and necessary feature of their working lives, with periods spent in re-education/training and doing something else other than a 'regular' job, they will have to be prepared for it.

Learning to be flexible and adaptable enough to survive and do well in the employment conditions of the next forty years could involve today's young people in some radically different thinking. They are being asked to be very open-minded and unprejudiced in their views of what is, and what is not, acceptable work – yet employers want them to be 'well-motivated'. They are being encouraged to start out by seeing 'what opportunities there are to learn skills, acquire know-how and get practical experience' and then to ask where these opportunities lead, rather than to begin by asking what jobs there are. It makes sense for young people to take their education as far as they are capable and willing to do so – the better educated generally seem better able to ride change, and are far less likely to be unemployed or unemployable. But, in the conditions likely to apply through the 1980s and into the 1990s too, even the most able must learn that to take advantage of the available opportunities they may still have to put a great deal of effort into making themselves employable. This makes pre-vocational preparation essential for all. They cannot rely on being able to walk into a job just because they have a qualification such as a degree.

All this obviously has many implications for young people. It has implications for the way in which choosing a career and deciding what to *be* plays a part in young people's search to discover who they 'are' – for an identity. It appears to make sense, and help to make them less vulnerable to change, to suggest that young people see themselves in terms of the range of skills, knowledge and experience they have instead of the actual job they do because, as MSC's Director, Geoffrey Holland says, skills are 'portable' from occupation to occupation, and are always with them. In this context, 'skills' are defined in the widest possible sense, as anything of value in employment, ranging from basic literacy and numeracy through to professional/managerial-level know how. Ironically, perhaps, some of the most 'portable' of skills in future may be those taught via the apparently least 'work-relevant' subjects – the intellectual training claimed for their subjects by history teachers, for example, where some of the more up-to-date syllabuses actually help pupils to understand change.

There are implications for the decisions young people must make about their futures. In a difficult world, experts will obviously try to show young people what they think are the most likely routes to the most reasonable employment opportunities – but must guard against the risk that young people will be over-pressured or panicked into decisions which are wrong for them as individuals. Motivation – being keen and interested in the course, the training opportunity, or the occcupation – is just as, if not more, important than ever, to the course admissions tutor and the recruiter no less that than the candidate. Young people must remain as free as possible to decide for themselves how they will come to terms with the working world as it is developing now – and be allowed to opt for alternatives if they so wish.

CAREERS EDUCATION AND ADVICE

But young people need increasingly sophisticated and expert support, counselling and accurate, up-to-date information to cope with all this and on which to base their decision making. They need both to understand what is happening in the employment market place and in the ways they can prepare for it, and to be trained in the techniques of learning about themselves and how to make decisions.

This puts an increasing load on schools' careers guidance and teaching, on the careers service, and on parents. It is a complex partnership, in which parents and careers advisers are there to help young people make their own decisions and choices – which they must do if they are to develop fully and be able to cope with the increasingly complex and frequent decisions and adjustments they will probably have to make in future.

Research shows that most young people are strongly influenced in their career and course choices by their parents, more strongly than by their teachers, advisers or friends. They need the positive support of their parents, parents who will always be ready to listen, be interested and encouraging, but who will not interfere too much, or be dictatorial or prejudiced in their attitudes to particular occupations or education/training opportunities, or try to persuade the young to make up for their own personal frustrations or ambitions or let them follow unquestioningly in their own footsteps. It is a very difficult balance for parents to achieve, especially as communication between the generations is so often at its worst at this stage.

But the expertise of careers teachers and advisers is also crucial. It is difficult enough for career experts to keep up to date with the changing opportunities; parents have to recognise that their own experiences of the transition from school are not likely to be relevant now for their sons/daughters. (They can, though, make considerable contributions to the school's careers effort – from helping to keep the careers library up to date through giving talks on their present work to helping arrange visits and possibly work experience.) They, like their sons and daughters, have to look to careers experts to help them discover what the possibilities now are.

Schools and careers services have been steadily improving their provision, but it is still patchy, varies greatly from school to school and in too many is still inadequate, rather too often in some of the schools which are amongst the strongest academically. Although a recent (1986) survey by the National Association of Careers and Guidance Teachers (NACGT) showed that 71% of schools had a careers education policy, 59% of LEAs careers-education advisors/inspectors, the majority of pupils still have less than half an hour per week of careers education, and careers teachers reported a lack of training, not enough time, and not enough money to do the job properly.

With tightening resources schools are expected to prepare pupils for a radically-new sixteen-plus (GCSE) examination, raise academic standards, increase 'relevance', add pre-vocational preparation to the syllabus, and generally improve schooling for all pupils. This is involving them in many new approaches to learning, some of which are not, as is traditional, based on individual subjects. It is on top of this that they must also find the resources to give students the kind of careers education, advice and counselling they need, and stay abreast of the bewildering (even to the most expert) pace of change and the increasingly more complex range of study/training and work opportunities.

The government has made regular public commitments to careers *education* (as opposed to individual, one-to-one *advisory work*), culminating (in April 1987) in the widely-welcomed document *Working together for a better future* which stressed the government's wish to see careers education given a higher priority and a better environment for careers work. The initiative instructed LEAs to submit (by late 1988) plans and policies for their careers education programmes, and they should by then be on the way to providing a well-co-ordinated, professional range of services for all young people. The careers world has therefore been greatly dismayed that the 1987 consultative document on the national curriculum omits any mention of careers education, and of the social and personal – 'life skills' – courses into which some of the best careers education programmes are set. It has subsequently been suggested that careers education should, when the national curriculum is introduced, be 'woven' into the main (examination) subjects as a 'cross-curricular' theme. This, research has shown, is the most difficult to achieve effectively and efficiently, and would require extra resources, and close co-operation and co-ordination between subject and careers teachers. Once schools are committed to meeting a legally-prescribed curriculum, it could be difficult for them to find the teaching and other resources needed for careers education if this, too, is not part of their legal obligation.

Schools also have problems in adjusting to new and different opportunities which means they must be prepared to question their traditional attitudes to what is or is not 'suitable' work, training or higher/further education for their pupils – or even what they should study at school. On the other hand, they have to learn to assess realistically the value of the latest 'initiative' very quickly if they are to advise their pupils properly.

The broad pattern of careers education and guidance in schools is, or should be, firmly established now as an essential and established component of young people's general preparation for adult life, and should therefore be an integral, fully-timetabled part of secondary education for pupils of all abilities, aptitudes and interests, from thirteen-plus on. Endemic change, though, means that schools have always to be ready to adapt their careers programmes to changing circumstances – so flexibility has to be built in now.

Careers education and guidance has several major strands –

Accurate, up-to-date and carefully assessed information about opportunities is obviously even more crucial than ever.

However, so also is teaching young people to understand and analyse themselves; to recognise their own specific aptitudes and abilities, interests, weaknesses and problems; to help them look ahead to think about what they want and can expect from life generally; to see what opportunities are open to them, and to show them how to analyse these in terms of their own priorities.

Within this framework, young people have now to focus more on skills – to find out what skills they already have; what other skills they may need, can gain – and how; where particular skills can take them and what is meant by the whole idea of skill transfer. The practical techniques of decision making – how best to go about it, what criteria to use, and so on – also have to be taught. Within their decision making, young people have to know how to make alternative plans, to decide what they will do if things go wrong, and where to go for help.

Exploring and preparing for the working world – and what it is possible to do outside paid employment – is the other major element of careers education. In as imaginative and realistic way as possible, the adult world of employment – and unemployment – must be brought into the classroom, and classes taken as much as possible out into the working world. Mainly this is, obviously, to give young people the information on which to base their choices, but it should also help familiarise them with the quite different environment they face when they leave school/college, and so both ease the transition for them and make them more acceptable to employers.

And so they should learn about life in the work place, the day-to-day routines, what the working conditions are like in different jobs and how to compare them; how people work together; how organisations are structured and managed; the place of unions; health and safety, etc.

A career programme has to give young people a general understanding of employment patterns in relation to the country's economic, social and political structure, why and how employment and training opportunities change, as well as introducing them to the full range of possibilities open to them. It also has to focus in on individual occupations and on local opportunities, but must now also constantly open up young people's ideas by discussing related occupations at the same time – the whole para-medical field and not just, for example, physiotherapy, so getting across the need to be flexible and to think in broad occupational terms. Here, occupational groups will have to be linked in to the concept of skills and skill packages as methods for demonstrating these are developed.

Since pupils' decision making starts with the choices, made at thirteen-plus, of what to study to sixteen, some form of preparation has to begin before then. And because what pupils choose to study between thirteen and sixteen can restrict their later choices, of courses and job opportunities, this preparation has to include some grounding in the importance of keeping options open and what effects dropping particular subjects has. In a growing number of schools, of course, this is the point at which some pupils now have the option to choose a TVEI or other pre-vocational scheme, and guidance has to take this into account. Between fourteen and sixteen, careers education and guidance has to explain all the possible routes – new and old – through the sixteen to nineteen period, and similarly, seventeen-year-olds should have all the different choices now open to them clearly explained. Even students in higher or further education need to know what is happening in the job market, what additional training is available and may be needed, how best they can exploit the available opportunities, and (as discussed under DEGREES AND VOCATIONAL PREPARATION), what they can do to improve their chances of a reasonable start to their careers.

Time, and plenty of it is, in any case, an essential ingredient of career preparation. It is not only time to explore the opportunities in all their complexity and to absorb all the necessary information that is needed, but the time that it takes young people to work through the necessary stages from the point at which they are still fantasising about what they want to be to a more mature and realistic picture of themselves and their likely futures. No two teenagers develop at the same rate, and it is not unreasonable for some to need much longer than others to make firm decisions. For them, it is a positive advantage to be able to put off some choices until eighteen or even twenty-one and to complete pre-vocational or academic courses first.

Careers education and guidance/counselling is given in many different forms. It may be an entirely separate scheme in some schools, but in many it forms part of a more general community education/education for life programme, so that learning about working life is not separated completely from studying other life skills. Other subjects may contribute – it may be convenient to teach the changing industrial scene as part of history, for example; what biotechnology is in a science class. Careers education may vary in format at different stages, and subject choices for exams, or degree-course study (for example) may be dealt with by form or year teachers. Within schools and sixth forms/sixth-form colleges, it is being integrated into programmes of pre-vocational study for those pupils who choose this. Career guidance/counselling is supposed to be built in to YTS schemes too. In higher education careers advisory work is run quite separately from teaching, and is voluntary.

Careers education needs trained staff – who have preferably had the chance to gain experience outside the school – who will work as a team, often with one or more LEA-based careers officers. Space for activities, exhibitions etc is essential, and so is a well-stocked, up-to-date library/information centre.

Careers education should use all the modern teaching methods, and have the hardware and other resources to make it interesting and lively – audio-visual aids such as films, videos etc; projects and 'games' of all kinds in which young people can act out working roles or compete with each other in teams to see who can invest or run a company most successfully; quizzes, and computer-based material. The range of possible activities is extensive. Discussions and carefully-chosen speakers who can talk well about the courses or training

schemes they run, or the work they do should be part of every programme. Young people should spend time observing people doing particular jobs (perhaps in parents' work places), and go on visits to colleges, universities, polytechnics as well as to other working environments. They should be able to talk to young and older workers, students and trainees, and compare their findings. Familiarisation courses, such as those run by universities to let girls find out more about engineering, are also invaluable. Wherever possible, but not always easy to arrange, young people should have some real work experience, although bringing local employers into the school may help. In some schools, pupils run their own small businesses on a project basis to simulate work experience, some with support from local firms.

Careers education has also to teach young people the practicalities – applying for jobs and courses, filling in application forms, making a *curriculum vitae*, being interviewed, and so on. Within a school's careers programme, pupils need special support – and individual help – at the major decision points – choosing subject options at thirteen-plus, deciding between opportunities at sixteen, seventeen-plus. The careers officer may be involved here, and the LEA careers service continues to provide information and guidance after school. Career guidance for older students is usually provided at the university, college or polytechnic, where services are also on tight budgets but are improving.

THE ENCYCLOPEDIA
In this twelfth edition of the *Careers Encyclopedia* we continue to try to map as

many occupations, areas of work and preparation for them as possible, and to show how these are changing in the 1980s. As in the last four editions, we attempt a broad general survey of the working world with education and training as they relate to work, and try to show how economic and social conditions, technological developments, political decisions and events generally are affecting employment and occupations. The *Encyclopedia* deals with work and occupations in the widest possible sense, and is not limited in any way by type or level of work – although we have probably not caught every single job in our net. Occupations are examined against the background of the relevant sector of employment. The *Encyclopedia* gives an outline sketch of each occupation and area of employment; what is happening to them and any available information on employment trends; what the work is like and what kinds of skills are needed. It describes recruitment and entry patterns, and the relevant education and training. Wherever possible, we try to look ahead, and to sketch in the possible prospects within each occupation, but this – as must be apparent – is becoming increasingly difficult.

This edition of the *Encyclopedia* has been written as the economy comes out of major recession, so it is still too soon to be sure (if it ever can be again) which are the permanent, long-term job losses and changes, and which are still the effects of recession. On top of the widespread upheavals in many areas of employment, there have also been major organisational changes – in, for example, educational/training structures, amongst employers (eg many state enterprises which have been 'privatised'). Virtually every chapter of this edition of the *Encyclopedia* has examples of such changes. Many of the changes are so recent that it is impossible to make any assessment of their possible long-term effect.

We print such statistics as are available, because figures can often illustrate a situation more clearly and economically than long descriptions. However, statistics on many aspects of employment have always been difficult to obtain and are only too frequently very out-of-date, incomplete, or inadequate. Official, and other cost-cutting exercises – and the demise of bodies such as sixteen (out of twenty-four) training boards which previously kept detailed employment figures – have further reduced the range of useful, reliable figures at a time when rapid change makes them more rather than less important.

While a great many organisations have provided much useful information, information-gathering on career, employment and especially training opportunities is also becoming increasingly difficult, especially where changes are involved. In particular, although Youth Training Schemes are increasingly designed to be the main entry route to a growing number of occupations, MSC still has not published a comprehensive guide showing which occupations are (best) entered via YTS. We have, therefore, been totally dependent on very busy training organisations, many with very limited resources, telling us whether or not they have established a YTS entry route. We hope we have not missed too many as a result.

As in the last four editions, the *Encyclopedia* begins with the educational base from which young people start out, and with the qualifications (educational and other) and the newer pre-vocational schemes which for them form the main bridge between the educational world and the world of work. Here the changes are such as to warrant a new shape to the first chapter which as in the last edition deals with the changing academic and vocational preparation of the sixteen to nineteen age group. The following chapter relates subjects studied to work opportunities. Between this and the chapters on broad areas of employment, we examine the the way the working world is developing and the reasons for it, before discussing young people's choices and pre-vocational preparation in contemporary employment conditions. Because so much importance is being given to information technology, and its influence is clearly so all pervasive, it has, as in the last edition, a separate chapter.

This edition of the *Encyclopedia* carries revisions and new information received through to June 1987. In an era of such frequent change it is, however, essential to check on factual information given – entry requirements, courses, forms of entry etc.

CAREERS INFORMATION AND SOURCE MATERIAL

This *Encyclopedia* can, in a single volume, give only the broadest possible sketch of what is happening across the spectrum of employment and in the general and specific preparation and routes into work. In earlier editions we included titles for further reading on specific occupations, areas of work, subjects for study, etc. Aside from the problems of space, we now prefer to suggest that readers to look for more in-depth reading material which is as up to date as possible – and with few exceptions that means books no more than two years old now. In most instances, the contact organisation under *Further information* will be able to suggest up-to-date literature also. Most LEA careers services have information officers who will generally be happy to help. The Careers and Occupational Information Centre (COIC) publishes a monthly bulletin, *Newscheck*, which reviews new literature, as does the Independent Schools Careers Organisation (ISCO) in its termly *Careers Bulletin*; both also print articles bringing careers information up to date.

While the range of straight, independent careers material written for young people is not at present very extensive, it is generally of reasonable quality, factually accurate, lively and well-presented. Most careers material comes from a small number of publishers – careers literature lends itself easily to series. The main publishers are –

Careers and Occupational Information Centre (part of the Manpower Services Commission): publishes the official annual *Occupations* (which deals in a traditional way with careers which mostly need formal school-leaving qualifications); a wide range of more informal series, illustrated, in colour, and lively in style, including short profiles of people at work; and a number of 'one-off' books including some for classroom use. COIC also provides a literature distribution service, maintains registers of locally-prepared and other career information.

Address: Careers and Occupational Information Centre, Manpower Services Commission, Moorfoot, Sheffield S1 4PQ

CRAC/Hobsons Press Ltd publishes a wide range of careers and related literature. It includes reference works such as the annual *Directory of Further*

Education; books and other material designed for classroom use in teaching decision-making etc; the *Your choice* series (13/14-plus, 15/16-plus, 17/18-plus, choice of A levels, degrees etc); quite a number of one-off books.
Address: Hobsons Press, Bateman Street, Cambridge CB2 1LZ

Association of Graduate Careers Advisory Services (AGCAS) publishes a range of careers information booklets designed primarily for students studying at university, polytechnic, and CHE, but useful also for people taking A levels. Also publishes a *Register of Graduate Employment and Training* (ROGET), and acts as a central information point on careers information for students.
Address: Association of Graduate Careers Advisory Services, Central Services Unit, Crawford House, Precinct Centre, Oxford Road, Manchester M13 9EP

Kogan Page Ltd publishes the most extensive series of books on careers. Two series – *Careers in* ... aimed at those expected to gain at least O levels (or equivalent); and *Jobs in* ... pitched at occupations up to craft/technician level. Also publishes a standard annual reference work, *British Qualifications*.
Address: Kogan Page Ltd, 120 Pentonville Road, London N1 9JN

Careers should not, though, be treated as though they are in a watertight compartment. Some of the best introductions to the working world and to individual occupations are not written as careers literature at all. Biographies and memoirs, surveys and reports, even newspaper and magazine articles, can all help to give a more rounded picture – provided they are not dated. Recruiting literature from prospective employers (and some from other interest groups, eg professional bodies, too) should be treated with caution, and never used as a first introduction to a specific career. It can, though, form a useful basis for critical project work on careers literature.

Up-to-date information is crucial for a good career start, and it is somewhat surprising that more databases, giving on-line computer access has not developed faster.

The only fully-operative, public-access system so far, ECCTIS (Educational, Counselling and Credit Transfer Service), deals almost entirely with all higher-education, and a growing number of further education courses – where they are, what the entry requirements are etc.
Address PO Box 88, Walton Hall, Milton Keynes MK7 6DB. Telephone: 0908 368921.

However, further systems are being developed, in particular –
TAPS (Training Access Points) – an MSC project, with (computer) terminal access points in a steadily rising number of locations, including job centres and libraries. (Further information from careers offices etc.)

Finally, for those who are interested in studying the development of areas of employment and occupations seriously, there are numerous sources. The Institute of Manpower Studies at Sussex University, and the Institute of Employment Research at Warwick University (Coventry), are two of the major research centres. The National Economic Development Office (NEDO) (which provides the professional staff for the National Economic Development Committee and the Economic Development Committees) has produced a range of detailed publications on a number of sectors of the economy which have considerable relevance to employment, but the future of these is now in doubt. The remaining training boards (and especially the EITB), produce very useful studies. The annual reports and journals of any organisation (training board, employers' federation, professional body, trade union etc) with interests in employment are generally fruitful sources of information and statistics. Finally, government – the Departments of Education and Science (and especially the Further Education Unit), Employment, and Industry – still provides some useful information. The Manpower Services Commission itself is another possible source.

Audrey Segal
September 1987

The author would like to thank the several hundred organisation who have, as for previous editions, so willingly provided information, answered questions and solved problems. Without them, it would have been impossible to produce.
The author also has to thank Mr D Wilson, orthopaedic surgeon, of the Royal Free Hospital, and his team, without whose intervention she might never have completed this edition.

Notes

†   **O-level equivalent at 16-plus:** the change-over from O level and CSE to GCSE (and a similar transition in Scotland) as the main educational qualification at sixteen-plus, with the widening range of alternatives, will mean some years of transition. Many of the bodies setting entry requirements to individual occupations, careers etc have, to date (1987), not finally decided on what (if any) changes they will make in the qualifications they require. Once they have actual experience of GCSE (etc) changes are possible. At this stage, it is only possible for the *Encyclopedia* to indicate that candidates offering GCSE, or alternatives, will be expected to achieve results which are deemed to equate with O-level passes at grades A-C. See also pages 9-10.

††   **BTEC entry requirements:** see page 32.

†††   **SCOTVEC entry requirements:** see pages 33-4.

Course information: some abbreviations are used in course lists.
f-t: full-time   p-t: part-time   yr/yrs: year(s)
fte: full-time equivalent
yr-s: sandwich-based course (ie year in industrial/commercial training)

Late information

Manpower Services Commission: to become the Training Commission in 1988.

Academic and Vocational Qualifications

Introduction   1
School and pre-vocational qualifications   6
Vocational qualifications   24
Further and higher education   35

INTRODUCTION

If evidence were needed that qualifications matter, the speed with which recruitment of graduates recovered from recession provides it. Even the government, in restoring the number of undergraduate places in universities, accepted that graduates are half as likely to be unemployed as non-graduates. The proportion of 1986 graduates still looking for work at Christmas was the lowest for eight years. The employment market has fewer and fewer places for those with the least qualifications or none at all. Statistically, it is again proved that better educational qualifications generally mean a better chance of a reasonable career start.

And so the cycle starts again, and it begins to look as though the people who predicted that this time round there would never again be enough jobs were at least to some extent wrong. Partly, perhaps, because we all forgot about the 'demographic timebomb', quietly ticking away through the 1980s – having done its worst to teacher training in the 1970s – the dramatic one-third fall in the numbers born in and after 1968. It is, though, too soon to tell how far down the qualification scale recovery will go, but there is little doubt now that the horizon is rather brighter for most young people than seemed possible back in 1983 and 1984.

Only the nursing profession seems to have had its sums done properly, but there are few people involved in recruiting intelligent young adults for courses, professions, high tech, jobs, who have not pulled out their calculators – and then ordered a glossy new revamp for the prospectus, the recruiting literature, the career brochure. If the shortages are beginning to show now, in 1987, what will it be like in 1990? The admissions tutors and public relations experts are girding themselves for the marketing battle of the century.

What will this do to the fragile start that has been made on giving UK Ltd a highly-trained workforce? Will the young be able to dictate their terms in interview rooms far from the City? Will recruiters still be able to ask for (not now demand), even get, all the other, personal, qualities they want to see in their ideal employees? Will accountancy practices still be able to afford to look at graduates' A-level results? Will the academic requirements for popular degree courses start spiralling down again?

Or will recruiters start wooing the young graduate mothers at home with crèches? Will such shortages at long last force UK employers to tempt recruits with *real training*? Or will they reach for the expert systems, the robots, the FMS factory – and if they do, who will design and manufacture the automated equipment and software? Or will companies start to migrate to where populations are still rising, and workers still plentiful and not too expensive? The possible scenarios are many and varied, but the real one is just as serious as mass youth unemployment. UK Ltd looks like having to compete with the rest of the world with both declining oil revenue and an older workforce – when the technological changes will need bright young brains. Employers in all sectors are demanding people who are more highly skilled, and who are also multi- and flexibly-skilled, able to change jobs much more easily. Everyone, from craft- through to professional-level employee has to be able to understand much more complex equipment; everyone, and not just professionals, will need better training in the skills of reasoning, communicating, diagnosing faults and problem-solving. When a numerically-controlled machine tool goes wrong it needs a faster, more intelligent response from the skilled operator than the traditional kind. The HITECC group already trying to bring people with arts A levels into crash maths and physics courses to turn them into engineers want people who actually want to be *thinkers*, not engineers. There's a belief around that businesses won't get their IT strategy right till both computer-illiterate general manager and the backroom boffin-type dp manager retire.

Are all the manifold 'initiatives', started back in 1981 partly in response to the problems of mass youth unemployment, now sufficiently in place to solve a major skill crisis over the next decade? Will Kenneth Baker's prescriptive and dated national curriculum – right as it is to insist on compulsory science, maths and technology – create the flexible, adaptable, practical, fast thinkers needed by pushing Lord Young's TVEI – co-incidently going national in September 1987 – into a ghetto called 'curriculum development'?

The proposed national curriculum looks like more of the same heavy academic emphasis, with non-academic – practical/creative subjects, training and vocational preparation again having only second-class status. Only TVEI has begun to change an education systems which NEDO said was 'predominantly a filtering system for identifying the academically most able', with industry's needs having very low priority.

Nor have British employers moved very far on training, as report after report shows. Whatever criticisms are made of them, the seven remaining statutory training boards have a far better record – and three out of four of the first NCVQ awards it should be noted – than the majority of the voluntary training organisations which have so far lamentably failed to fill the gap. Only now, five years after the Boards went, is MSC able to bring enough pressure to bear to get the most basic 'competences' identified and proper certification underway. Cuts in finance for education have been administered in such a way that the needs of industry and commerce appear to have been ignored.

It is worth repeating what the Task Force Group which prepared the plans for the Manpower Commission's Youth Training Scheme wrote (in 1981) –

'Prosperity and growth require invention, innovation, investment and exploitation of new technologies. They require the exploitation of new and growing markets to replace those that are declining. They require standards of production and service every bit as competitive, effective and reliable as those of our competitors.'

'This cannot be achieved with an under-qualified, under-trained or immobile workforce. It cannot be achieved if people resist change or cannot cope with it. Increased productivity means doing things in new ways. This will require training and for young people entering work it requires proper vocational preparation.'

'Britain has one of the least-trained workforces in the industrial world... In total only just over half our young people receive any systematic vocational or educational preparation compared with more than 90% in West Germany and more than 80% in France. Around 35% of 16-year-olds entering jobs receive no training at all, and a further 18% receive hardly any training.'

'In recent years, despite major public provision, our training performance has tended to get worse, not better. In the 1960s, 40% of 16-year-old boys leaving education got apprenticeships. By the 1980s this proportion had halved.'

Five years on, has
The government's New Training Initiative (NTI), 'modernised' the country's training system?
Have the main objectives for the future of industrial training been met? They were –

to develop skill training including apprenticeship to allow young people entering at different ages and with different educational attainments to acquire agreed standards of skill appropriate to the jobs available and to provide them with a basis for progress through further learning;

to move towards a position where all young people under the age of eighteen can either continue in full-time education or have a period of planned experience combined with work-related training and education;

to open widespread opportunities for adults, whether employed or returning to work, to acquire, increase or update their skills and knowledge during their working lives.

How has the 'programme for action' done? What about
the Youth Training Scheme (described fully later in the chapter);
increased incentives for employers to provide better training (?);
replacing time-serving and age-restricted apprenticeships for all the main craft, technician and professional skills with 'recognised standards', by 1985 (?);
better preparation for working life in initial full-time education (see Technical and Vocational Education Initiative below);
more opportunities for vocationally-relevant courses for those staying on in full-time education;
closer co-ordination of training and vocational education provision nationally and at local level.

The Task Force report quoted above said that public policy would have to reflect young people's longer term needs because
'their future employment destination is uncertain, more than job- or firm-specific training is required;
unskilled work is declining, a basis for higher levels of competence needs to

be laid;
the context of work is changing and more and more people are involved in
processes, rather than the repeated performance of a single task, training has
increasingly to meet the needs of a variety of industries, firms and
occupations;
the labour market is highly competitive, basic knowledge of the world of
work, job search and other skills is essential;
young people may well experience spells of unemployment, personal and life
skills are needed to help them survive and benefit from change;
young people have their own expectations and aspirations, opportunities
must be designed for their benefit as well as those of the economy.'
Has it?

MSC has, at least to some extent modified its attitude to college-based learning, since growing numbers of YTS trainees (130,000 at the last count), spend
time in the broader environment of FE now. But MSC is still clearly convinced
that training schemes for young people should be employer-led, and wherever
possible employer-based, even though the Task Force report made plain that it
is not possible for individual firms to meet the scale of what is required. MSC
believes that many young people, especially the less able, learn best in the
practical environment of the work-place, that 'only learning in the work
situation is real, relevant and worthwhile... work-based assignments are good,
classroom learning is bad... education-driven learning is teacher-centred,
work-driven learning is trainee-centred, motivating and useful, etc'. Yet as a
report from the Tavistock Institute (commissioned by MSC) says, 'There is no
right way of running all schemes of learning.'

There is still a need to develop nationally-agreed criteria on a balanced,
comprehensive and integrated 'preparation for life' for young people from
fourteen to nineteen. The first, cautious step – AS levels – to broadening and
liberalising sixth-form studies for abler students starts only in September 1987,
and is hardly good enough. Education and vocational preparation are both
necessary and should be seen as a closely linked and overlapping rather than
separate processes. Relatively specific vocational, as well as generic, skills can
often be best learned by also studying underlying principles and on an even
broader front, just as a training course can improve students' motivation and
add to their general educational background.

Obviously there has to be a greater recognition in the curriculum of the real
world outside the school. As the Royal Society of Arts (RSA) said in a report
on the future of technological higher education, the education system should
be producing people who are technologically and economically literate, and
the traditional academic bias inhibits this. The RSA wanted to see greater
value put on the level of achievement whether the field of achievement is
academic or not, and greater emphasis on teaching pupils to produce practical
solutions to real problems, without losing the emphasis on high standards of
numeracy or literacy. It is, however, also crucial that young people are encouraged and helped to develop talents and skills other than those they may need in
the work place, and are given greater opportunities to be culturally and
politically literate. GCSE is clearly a major step in the right direction.

In the 1980 edition of the *Encyclopedia* we quoted Sir Ieuan Maddock on the
future of work, and the new-style preparation for life that this will entail. It has

not been difficult to get over the concept that a single lifelong skill or craft is no longer valid, or that people from semi-skilled to professional will need to be taught new skills and additional knowledge to enable them to cope with the greater demands which will be made on them, and to change jobs. The need to be adaptable is accepted, but the education system has still to find ways to prepare young people for this, and has still not found ways to avoid early specialisation, especially for the more able.

Sir Ieuan would be pleased to see that Kenneth Baker's national curriculum recognises that 'an appreciation of the arts, a sense of history, and a wish to be creative are essential if a stable society is to be sustained in the future'. But he might wonder what happened to 'an understanding of how society works, an interest in other people'.

NTI's longer term and even more far-reaching aims were designed to change entry to and education/training for all occupations, and not just lower-level work entered via traditional apprenticeships. NTI aimed to 'replace time-serving and age-restricted apprenticeships for all the main craft, technician *and professional* skills with "recognised standards", by *1985* [our italics], to create a more flexible and open system'. Elsewhere (eg in the March 1983 *Youth Training News*), MSC expanded on this: it 'means introducing the concept of training to agreed and tested standards as opposed to time serving; and it means opening up entry to training according to ability and experience rather than operating existing rigid age barriers or arbitrary educational qualification. By 1985, MSC expects to restrict financial support to schemes which meet these requirements'. Since presumably the National Council for Vocational Qualifications is part of this strategy, it is under way, although the timetable seems to have slipped a bit. But the bodies representing eg the professions, such as law and engineering, which have been able to decide for themselves what their academic entry requirements, age limits and periods of training should be, are being drawn into the net. It is yet possible that the rigid barriers to entry to many occupations, professional and other, may be relaxed. As some engineers now acknowledge, this has excluded people whose expertise and experience could be essential.

MSC's aim, then, is clearly twofold. Firstly, to allow able people once again to come through even up to the most expert, professional-level, occupations without having to go through the stiff academic hoops of university entry and a once-and-for-all three/four-year full-time degree course. Second, MSC obviously considers that entry to professional- and graduate-level occupations direct from school may have to be re-vamped, to allow for unforeseen and rapidly changing employment prospects for the professions as well as craft and technician people. Allowing professional and other bodies controlling entry to particular occupations to make restrictive changes in entry requirements without reference to the employment position generally, and solely to control numbers, has to be changed. But, as MSC officials admit, engineering is a priority, law probably is not.

To cope with the changes and developments in working life in the future, young people of all abilities and aptitudes will need preparation of far greater sophistication and flexibility than has ever been delivered before. There is a long way to go before this is achieved.

In the future, educational qualifications will have to change, to widen, and become more flexible. They will not be important just for for the level of attainment they show or because they open specific occupational doors, but are also needed to provide a sound basis for radical and possibly several changes of direction, in occupation, in leisure pursuits (which may themselves become 'occupational' in the sense that there may be more time to spend on them), and even in total life-style. Up to now, the education process has been treated as though it were in a watertight compartment, and as having a finite end – it stops when the young recipient leaves school, college, polytechnic or university. Now the pace of technological, social, economic, industrial, vocational change is going to be such that 'continuing' or 'recurrent' education becomes essential, with everyone able to return to the educational system whenever necessary, to improve on their vocational opportunities, to enable them to change occupation, or simply to learn more. This too argues against early specialisation in secondary and tertiary education and should mean more concern with teaching fundamentals of subjects rather than specific techniques.

SCHOOL AND PRE-VOCATIONAL QUALIFICATIONS

Despite the changes both already under way, and planned, for the education system (see below) over the coming years, the subject and course choices students make at school will continue to be crucial for their futures. Whatever the long-term effects of developments in training and vocational qualifications, the subjects studied at school, and examination results, are still going to be used in selection by recruiters, and inevitably by admissions tutors for degree and other higher-level courses.

Certainly from fourteen – and perhaps in future even earlier – on, pupils (and their parents) are faced with a series of complex and difficult decisions, all of which must be based on accurate and very up-to-date information, because prospects and the consequences of these decisions are changing all the time. Difficult as it may be, schools, with the help of careers officers, have to keep pace with the changes, and the effects they have on pupils' choices. Time has to be spent ensuring that pupils and their parents understand the importance and significance of their choices.

The choices, and decisions, that pupils must make at various stages in their school lives should be part of the process of careers education, preparation and counselling as discussed in the Introduction. Pupils must have all the necessary information. They need to know, for example –
  what choices the school offers;
  how their choice of school, and subjects for school examinations will affect, even limit, any choice of subject for study after school, or entry to particular institutions (as, eg Cambridge University requires at least an O-level-equivalent pass in a language), or particular occupations;
  which subjects will give them the greatest choices;
  what the advantages are of the various 'programmes' being offered.

ELEVEN TO SIXTEEN

The state-maintained secondary-school system is going through major upheaval, partly with the intention of raising standards, broadening and 'balancing' the subject base and making sure that all pupils study right through to sixteen what are considered essential subjects.

Until 1987 LEA-maintained schools had considerable freedom in what to teach and how. A growing consensus, though, means that most secondary schools already insist that all pupils study English (often as two subjects – literature and language), and mathematics through to sixteen. Most now also take a 'balanced' range of subjects including at least one science, at least one 'humanities' subject (such as history, geography, economics, social studies), a creative subject (art, music, drama etc), and in many comprehensive schools at least, a practical subject (eg home economics, or craft, design and technology). Some schools expect pupils to study a language, at others it is optional. Beyond this, from fourteen on, they have a choice of subjects – limited by resources now in some schools – from (further) languages, additional humanities subject(s), one or two more sciences, creative/practical subjects.

In most schools at present, students in the top ability band take up to seven or eight subjects in the two years fourteen to sixteen. In some academically-selective schools it is often more. Pupils may also have a choice of new kinds of 'programmes of study', such as TVEI (below).

Schools have been moving towards this less specialised and better-balanced curriculum at 14 to 16 for some time now. But since the future needs people who are flexible and adaptable in outlook, rather than specifying subjects too tightly, HMI have recently described the curriculum in terms of the areas of 'learning and experience' they think important for all pupils – aesthetic and creative, human and social, linguistic and literary, mathematical, moral, physical, scientific, spiritual, technology. This is in line with a growing view that traditional subjects should not be divided into such watertight compartments and need, at very least, to be linked by cross-curricular courses. Educationalists also suggest that young people facing a fast-changing future will not need to learn so many facts, but should instead be helped to develop concepts, skills, and values. Schools are putting greater emphasis on active, practically-oriented learning, linking what is learned to real-life situations, and – under the influence of the Manpower Services Commission's TVEI (below) – are giving greater emphasis to the world of work.

The choices that young people have to make at thirteen plus, on what they will study from fourteen to sixteen, have always been difficult ones. In making subject choices, pupils are generally encouraged to aim for the broadest spread of subjects they can cope with. Theoretically, the range of post-sixteen options and greater opportunities to go on from vocational qualifications to more advanced academic or other study should make these choices less critical in the future. In practice, this is probably some time away. Entry to many training schemes, professions, and courses can still be a minefield, and is likely to remain so for some years. Sciences, particularly physics and chemistry, are hard to catch up on if not studied from fourteen to sixteen, and are often unexpectedly crucial for some career starts. It is not so difficult to start a second language later on, although two may be needed for a language degree course. Some professional bodies, and academic institutions, limit the number of 'non-academic', ie practical and/or creative subjects like art, CDT, music, needlework etc, they will accept, although this should not prevent any pupil taking one or two of these.

However, the government now proposes some radical changes which will, progressively from about 1989, require state schools to teach to a national curriculum, which is set out in a very prescriptive way, as conventional water-tight subjects. While most accept the need for at least a common 'core', at first sight the proposed curriculum appears to lack any of the flexibility and adapt-ability which experts suggest will be needed as the basis for life and work in the future.

Maths, English and science are to form the core of the national curriculum, and schools will be required to spend 30-40% (ie with the option of 10 or 20% on science) of curriculum time on them. Most of the rest of the curriculum (45-55% depending on how much time is spent on science) is to be devoted to technology (10%), a modern language (10%), history and/or geography (10%), a combined art, music, drama, design course (10%), and physical education (5%). Choice will be limited to 10-20% of curriculum time, and some subjects (eg health education and use of information technology) will be taught through other subjects. Programmes of study are to be based on the recommendations of (national) subject groups. 'Attainment targets' are to be set for the three core and some other 'foundation subjects', and these are to be tested (at ages 7, 11 and 14, and 16 if not taken for GCSE).

The government is also establishing (with industry) a new type of school – 'city technology colleges' – but they too will be required to keep to the 'substance' of the curriculum. Independent schools are expected to follow the curriculum principles as one of the conditions of registration. LEA-maintained schools are also to be allowed to 'opt out' of LEA control, and become (directly) maintained by the DES.

These changes are important to parents and pupils, because they will affect the choices they make, both of school at 11-plus, and in what options, programmes (eg TVEI), schools are able to offer at 14-16. Some schools, for example, may not be able to offer certain subject options because they have to increase staffing for the mandatory foundation subjects. If a school 'opts-out' of its LEA it may lose the many supporting services, and links with other schools and FE colleges, which enable it at present to offer a more varied programme for their pupils. The consultative document does not state how the curriculum will be kept in line with expected rapid technological and other developments which are certain to require changes – possibly frequently – in what the curriculum should be like in the 1990s and beyond.

It is somewhat ironic that the Secretary of State should make such proposals, including extra formal testing, at a time when a substantial number of educa-tionalists are questioning the need for formal 'public school-leaving' examin-ations at 16-plus at all, given that few sixteen-year-olds will go straight into full employment, and the government has agreed to introduce 'records of achieve-ment' for all pupils leaving school by 1990.

The government's new plans come as the school system is trying to cope with the problems of adapting to new 16-plus examinations.

GCSE and SCE are designed to be taken by all sixteen-year-olds. In fact, by 1984-5, only 11.3% of school-leavers (98,000) had no GCE/SCE/CSE qualifications at all (against 44% in 1970-1); 32.7% (283,000) had one or more O-level/grade passes at grades D-E and/or CSE grades 2-5 (against only 10% in 1970-1), 26.8% (232,000) had one to four GCE/SCE O level/grade (grade C or above) and/or CSE grade 1 passes (against 17% in 1970-1), and 10.7% (93,000) five or more O-level-equivalent passes.

The General Certificate of Secondary Education is replacing, in England and Wales, both GCE O level and CSE with a single set of examinations. Courses began in September 1986, and all sixteen-year-olds will take GCSE examination from June 1988.

The subject range of GCSE examinations is similar to O level and CSE, although the number of available exams in each subject have been reduced, as there are now only five (regional) examining groups. But GCSE differs from O level and CSE in that there are published criteria which provide a nationally-agreed framework. General criteria set out principles governing all GCSE syllabuses and examinations, eg specifying that candidates across the ability range must be given the opportunity to 'show what they know, understand and can do'. Syllabuses should be designed to 'help candidates understand the subject in relation to other areas of study and its relevance to the candidate's own life'. Subject criteria are nationally-agreed statements about the objectives, content and assessment methods to be used in any syllabuses. Grade criteria are being developed to show the knowledge, understanding and competencies needed by candidates to gain a particular grade in each subject. What is taught and how is supposed to be matched to students' abilities and aptitudes.

GCSE is to have a single scale of grades, from A through to G. A, B and C will be treated as equivalent to the same grades at O level and CSE grade 1. D and E are the same as the equivalent O-level grades and CSE grades 2 and 3 (but O-level D and E were never equated with CSE 2 and 3), and CSE grades F and G equal CSE grades 4 and 5. For, eg university entry and the entry requirements for many professional bodies, grade C in GCSE will continue, as with O level, to be the lowest grade accepted as a 'pass'. There is unlikely to be any (immediate) change either in the number of such passes needed to gain entry to courses/training schemes post-sixteen, so four or five grade C or above passes will still be the minimum generally needed for direct entry to technician-level occupations, or to go on to further academic study. CSE grades 2-5 or O levels at grade D or below never really gained any currency with employers, but the new GCSE grades will hopefully be acceptable for some training schemes.

In some subjects all students will take the same examinations, and be graded on the result, in others separate questions may be set, and in others different examinations will be set for different ability groups, and the range of possible grades will be limited for each set of examinations. Almost all GCSE syllabuses also have a requirement for assessment (by teachers) of students 'coursework', eg essays, oral work in languages, lab or other practical work. This, and 'criteria referencing' should help to give a fairer picture of individual students' actual achievements, rather than (as with O levels) their achievements relative to other students taking examinations in the same subject at the same time.

The Scottish Certificate of Education The Scottish (approximate) equivalents of O level are also being replaced, but the new examinations are being phased in, rather than changing over completely in one year.

The old O grades (now grades 1 to 5 instead of A to E with C or 3 as the accepted minimum to be counted as a 'pass'), are being replaced by a new 'Standard' or S grade. Full, two-year, S grade courses are designed for a wider ability range, and there are three course 'levels' – foundation, general and credit. Awards are graded on a single scale of 1 to 7, and there is some overlap to allow credit for higher than expected achievement at any one level. New forms of teaching and assessment, as for GCSE, are being developed, and it is also possible to take multidisciplinary and short courses. For university and similar entry, grade 3 or better is needed, but the acceptability of S grades in particular subjects must be checked with the institution/body concerned.

The Technical and Vocational Education Initiative (TVEI) is not a new examination, but a major effort to 'shift the curricular emphasis for the fourteen to eighteen age group towards a more work-oriented philosophy', to 'stimulate more technical and vocational education at school level'. 'Managed' by the Manpower Services Commission, TVEI is designed to produce schemes which will –

attract more young people to try for and gain qualifications/skills of direct value in work;

equip them better for the world of employment and help them to think realistically about jobs and employment prospects and assess their own potential;

give them a more direct appreciation of the practical application of qualifications for which they are working;

give them experience of using their skills and knowledge to solve the real-world problems they will meet at work;

give greater emphasis to developing initiative, motivation and enterprise as well as problem-solving skills and other aspects of personal development, encouraging young people to become progressively responsible for this;

build a bridge from education to work rather earlier via training/work experience;

involve close collaboration with local industry/commerce/public service.

TVEI started with fourteen pilot schemes in September 1983, and has expanded each year since, to include over 600 schools/colleges and 65,000 students in 1986-7. Originally designed with a limited five-year life, TVEI 'goes national' in 1987-8, when some 90% of LEAs are expected to be taking part, providing 90-100 schemes nation-wide, and involving 83,000 students under sixteen. Funding is committed to the scheme for at least ten years.

The aim is to keep a 'broad and balanced' education, but to make learning a practical process, learning by doing, with real tasks to do, practical problems to solve, and actual work experience. Schemes are supposed to cater for all levels and types of abilities, and it is stressed should not exclude the most able. Guidelines say 70% of pupils' time should still be spent on general education, and 30% on TVEI from fourteen to sixteen, and the reverse from sixteen to eighteen. While each scheme is supposed to be a four-year 'all-through' programme, in practice it has to be possible for students to choose to opt in or out at sixteen, and perhaps at other points too.

There is no standard TVEI scheme. Each can be, and most are, completely different, designed either by the local education authority with school and college staff, by schools/FE colleges jointly, by 'consortia' of schools and colleges, or by individual schools or colleges. A high proportion of schemes are, though, run on an area basis or by groups of schools/colleges, to make a wider range of activities and choice possible, since developing the curriculum has to depend on available experience, expertise etc. Schemes involve local firms, and some universities/polytechnics.

While scientific, technological and business-related activities form the basis of many schemes, others are designed round sport/leisure, and creative arts. Schemes cutting across conventional subject boundaries are encouraged.

TVEI schemes are not 'certificated' as such. They are designed to allow students to take existing recognised awards – not only GCSE, but also BTEC, RSA, CGLI etc (see below). BTEC and CGLI have, however, been piloting a new pre-vocational programme, which all schools can take up in 1987-8, and some other examination bodies/boards are introducing new qualifications to meet a growing demand for examinations/assessment specially tailored to TVEI. For instance, some are to certificate or give an accreditation to modules or units of study for which no other examination exists.

But although schemes are expected to link effectively with subsequent training/educational opportunities, any occupational element is intended to relate only broadly to potential employment opportunities and TVEI is not designed as a simple 'mechanistic' route into work. Programmes are supposed to be flexible enough to make sure there are alternative routes, to allow genuine choices as pupils gain experience, to allow for different ability levels, and provide for those who want to continue into further education and training as well as those who want to go straight into work.

TVEI is still an experimental scheme and it will be some years before its full value can be properly assessed, although there seems to be little doubt that well-designed and -delivered schemes are proving useful. Pupils offered the choice of a TVEI scheme, should though, make quite sure it does not restrict their later choices and that they have the opportunity to gain qualifications which will allow them to go on to further study after school if they wish.

The education minister's plans for state schools (see above), have implications for TVEI. The 'National Curriculum' document does specifically state that legislation will allow scope for such 'curriculum development programmes' to 'build on the framework offered by the national curriculum and to take forward its objectives'. But it is not clear how some TVEI schemes will be able to continue in their present form if, for example, TVEI-based business studies, sport, or creative arts take up 30% of curriculum time. Allowing individual schools to become state-, rather than LEA-maintained, could also jeopardise multi-school/college schemes.

SIXTEEN TO EIGHTEEN-PLUS

At sixteen, school leavers have an increasingly complex set of choices to make. Provision for the age group is getting more, rather than less, fragmented, uneven, complicated and hard to understand. It is difficult for young people to decide on their best course of action. The different schemes put them firmly into separate categories.

There is a strong argument for a fully-integrated, comprehensive but flexible programme of education and training, with appropriate work experience for all sixteen- to eighteen-year-olds regardless of ability and where they are based (school, college, even workplace). It needs to have built into it 'bridges and ladders' which would allow young people to change direction more easily at this stage, and to move in and out of education/training/work experience. The 'academic' student, no less than the YTS trainee, needs to learn about the all-important generic life and vocational skills, and to gain work experience.

At sixteen-plus, then, a young adult can/has to choose between –

Employment or a training scheme

While an improving job market and a falling number of sixteen-year-olds have started (1986-7) making it easier to find jobs, in January 1987 only 17% of sixteen-year-olds were working (in addition to the 27% on YTS schemes), and 11% were still unemployed. The combined total of sixteen-year-olds working and on YTS schemes, at 44% is, however, somewhat better than the 39% of 1983.

Employers are free to decide whether to take on trainees as full employees or under YTS, but they are being encouraged to take all new entrants via YTS and a growing number are clearly doing so. By 1984 about half of all first-year apprenticeships had, MSC estimates, been brought within YTS.

Although there is no hard evidence, it is probable that YTS has not, as least yet, had any significant effect on entry qualifications to individual occupations. If anything, entry requirements have been rising. However, where YTS1 is treated as 'diagnostic' by employers, trainees who show they don't have the stipulated school-leaving qualifications are taken on if they show aptitude during the year. The clearing banks, for example, consider entrants who do not have their 'normal' requirement of at least four (and more usually five or six) O levels, but will expect them to pass a literacy and numeracy test which is likely to be close in standard to O-level grade C or CSE grade 1. Some firms, though, do expect even YTS trainees to have appropriate GCE/GCSE/CSE passes for training in some occupations.

Occupations/areas of employment with no formal qualifications/some lower grade passes at 16-plus† ie, 'a good general education'. This list has to be qualified. First, direct entry to jobs which carry training, formal traineeships or training courses without any, or a minimal number, of exam passes at 16-plus is likely to be extremely difficult, since competition for places means recruiters can usually ask for considerably more. Second, entry to some sectors is now increasingly via YTS training and there is no statistical data on how this is affecting entry requirements (the occupational areas involved, which also have approved qualifications/preferred national schemes as of mid-1987, are asterisked). Note also that the lower age limit for some occupations is seventeen or eighteen. See also under individual occupations.

AGRICULTURE etc:	manual and craft farm work*, forestry, horticultural worker*; farrier; gamekeeper/warden; gardener.
ANIMAL WORK:	kennel, stable work; jockey.
ART/DESIGN:	possible, but most art/design schools require some academic qualifications; signwriting.
BUSINESS/COMMERCE:	junior office/clerical/reception/telephonist.
CRAFT:	eg book binding, cabinet making, ceramics, dressmaking; jewellery; upholstery;
CONSTRUCTION*:	manual and craft eg brickwork and masonry, carpentry and joinery, electrical work, machine woodworking, painting and decorating, plastering, plumbing, roof work, shopfitting.
ENGINEERING*:	manual and craft eg assembly, electrical installation and maintenance, fitting, foundry work, maintenance, patternmaking, welding.
HEALTH SERVICES:	manual and craft eg cleaning, portering, ward orderly; ambulance work
HOTELS & CATERING*:	manual and craft, eg food preparation and cooking, waiting, possibly some clerical.
LEISURE/RECREATION:	manual and craft eg baths attendant; groundsman/woman; stage hand/wardrobe.
MINING etc:	manual and craft;
PERFORMING:	eg acting, dancing, music – possible to perform without academic qualifications, but most reputable training schools require some; sportsman/woman.
PRINTING*:	all skills.
RETAILING etc:	sales, cashier etc; crafts eg butcher; floristry; modelling.
SERVICES:	armed forces eg junior entry; fire service (England/Wales); hairdressing* and beauty therapy; postal services; prison officer.
TRANSPORT:	driver/delivery; merchant navy rating; coastguard; traffic warden; vehicle maintenance*.

Occupations for which at least four or five O-level equivalent passes needed As above, direct entry to jobs which carry training, formal traineeships or training courses with the minimum stated exam passes at 16-plus is likely to be extremely difficult, since competition for places means recruiters can usually ask for considerably more. Second, entry to some sectors may be via YTS training, or for technician training, a 'diagnostic' period effectively on YTS (the occupational areas involved, which also have approved qualifications/

preferred national schemes as of mid-1987, are asterisked). Note also that the lower age limit for some occupations is seventeen or eighteen. See also under individual occupations.

AGRICULTURE etc	technician occupations.
ANIMAL WORK:	nursing; technician work.
ART/DESIGN:	craft and technician entry to eg graphic design, display/exhibition design, furniture/other crafts, textile and fashion design; photography
BUSINESS/COMMERCE:	eg secretarial and clerical work.
COMPUTING:	computer operating.
CONSTRUCTION*:	architectural technician, draughtsman/woman, engineering technician.
ENGINEERING*:	technician-level work.
FINANCIAL WORK:	eg accounting technician, banking, building society work, insurance work.
GOVERNMENT:	Civil Service eg administrative officer, technician engineering apprentice, assistant scientific officer; local government eg clerical work.
HEALTH SERVICES:	dental auxiliary/hygiene/technician; dispensing optician; laboratory work; nursing; pharmacy technician; junior administration/clerical work.
HOTELS & CATERING:	eg receptionist, clerical work, trainee manager.
LAND USE etc:	cartography or surveying technician.
LAW:	legal executive, barrister's clerk.
LEISURE/RECREATION:	junior administration.
MEDIA:	camera work; engineering technician.
RETAILING:	sales/administrative trainee; travel agency work*.
SCIENCE:	eg animal and laboratory technician.
SERVICES:	armed forces eg technician entry; police; postal officer.
SOCIAL:	care work; nursery nursing.
TRANSPORT/TRAVEL:	eg air cabin crew/maintenance engineering; freight forwarding/ship broking; merchant navy cadet/engineer cadet; operations management trainee; travel agency*

Youth Training Scheme (YTS) is designed to provide the main route into employment for all sixteen- and seventeen-year-olds who do not go on to full-time study or other schemes, and not just those who cannot find work. This, though, depends on persuading employers to recruit via the scheme, as well as young adults that it provides the best-available opportunities. Young people who unreasonably refuse a place on a scheme will, in future, lose their unemployment benefit.

YTS started in September 1983 (replacing the Youth Opportunities Programme and some other schemes), as a one-year scheme. In April 1986, it was extended to a fully-structured two-year work experience/training programme for sixteen-year-olds (one year for seventeen-year olds), with at least twenty weeks off-the-job training (eg in a training centre or FE college) on the two-year scheme.

YTS has changed considerably in its first four years (1983 to 1987), and especially with the extension to a two-year programme. It is, perhaps, unfortunate that Manpower Services had to take an 'evolutionary' approach, starting with fairly minimal standards but a high profile. As a result, the scheme gained a reputation which it is proving hard to change, although substantial efforts are now going into raising standards and 'feeding good practice' into the guidelines (the Tavistock Institute suggested 'Good learning opportunities will not be provided by adopting items of "bolt on" good practice...'). The scheme is vast, and to get it established so rapidly on a national basis it had to be heavily sold. The early literature relied too heavily on 'jargon' which, together with some rather naive descriptions of skills and suggestions for assessment techniques, gave critics rather too much ammunition.

The scheme has been greatly simplified, both organisationally and in the way guidelines, etc are presented. The language has been toned down. The 'occupational families' so heavily marketed in 1983 have been quietly transformed into a straightforward 'training and occupational classification' (which has, though, to be called TOC). The statistical and factual information provided is getting harder and coming out more frequently, which suggests growing confidence.

With an extra year available, the drive behind YTS is now focusing harder on giving trainees basic 'competence'-based vocational training in all industrial sectors and occupations linked to nationally-recognised qualifications, or credits towards them.

MSC is attempting to move as rapidly as possible (target date April 1988) to the point where all training programmes are 'delivered' and arranged by organisations with 'approved training' status, although this is clearly only a first step in pushing up the quality level, since YTS teams are next to agree 'quality development programmes' with ATOs. By June 1987, 3266 organisations – managing agents – had applied for ATO status. Just 1294 were fully approved, 1546 provisionally approved – which meant they did not meet all the ten stipulated criteria – twelve had been rejected and 68 had withdrawn. While some of these last had merged, some felt they could not meet the criteria, and some did not have the necessary financial resources.

In a rather less publicised operation, MSC is clearly putting some very heavy pressure – using the carrot and stick principle – on industries and sectors to set up (or get an existing body to agree to be) an acceptable training organisation (called a 'lead industry body'), to develop their 'nationally-preferred training schemes', with qualifications, as rapidly as possible. As of June 1987, as a result, the YTS Certification Board was able to approve qualifications in agriculture and commercial horticulture, engineering, retail travel, road transport, hotel and catering, printing, electrical contracting, and the building sector of construction. (It is notable that four of these are based on remaining statutory training boards.) A 'nationally-preferred training scheme' had been agreed for hairdressing, and others – eg in retailing – are well under way.

Since in each case this involves identifying, agreeing and codifying a large number of 'competences' (70 in one instance), designing training modules and packages, assessments and certification (with a reputable national certifying body such as CGLI or RSA), the amount of work which has been going on behind the scenes is clearly considerable. Once an industry-preferred scheme has been adopted and the qualification approved, all ATOs in that industry/sector must give their trainees an opportunity to gain it. Otherwise they must be able to try for an existing relevant qualification, eg a BTEC or CGLI award.

MSC now sets just four 'outcomes' for YTS schemes –
   competence in a job or range of occupational skills;
   competence in a range of transferable core skills;
   ability to transfer skills and knowledge to new situations; and
   personal effectiveness.

While YTS is a national scheme, all programmes under two-year YTS are devised, designed and run by individual managing agents, now ATOs. These may be individual employers, groups of firms, local authorities, voluntary organisations, industrial training boards, colleges and commercial training organisations, and former 'mode B' providers, eg ITeCs. Some organisations act solely as managing agents, organising employer-based training and where necessary buying expertise for, eg the off-the-job training, or they may supervise, organise and co-ordinate group programmes carried out by others. Within national guidelines, recommendations, and illustrative schemes, ATOs are free to develop programmes as they see fit, but MSC is working towards agreed 'preferred model' recommendations and establishing a modular, standards-based system of accreditation. The guidelines suggest that, while some basic competence objectives must be agreed, programmes should be flexible enough to meet the needs of individual trainees. No two programmes will therefore be the same. MSC started piloting 'enterprise training' schemes in mid-1987, and hopes to have at least 1000 schemes offering enterprise modules by 1989.

ATOs who are national bodies, eg the Engineering and Construction Industry Training Boards, the Association of British Travel Agents, and the Footballers Further Education and Vocational Training Society, have devised and supervise national programmes carried out locally (but perhaps with some local variations) by employers within their industries and in industry training centres. Other schemes may be designed by local ATOs. The largest companies may have up to a dozen separate schemes running in different parts of the country, and one area training council runs five schemes with a total of nearly 1400 places.

Some 318,000 trainees were on YTS programmes at the end of March 1987 (against 265,000 in March 1986). Some 482,000 starts were notified between April 1986 and March 1987 compared with 399,000 in the year before. Up to the end of March 1987, MSC had been notified of 208,000 YTS1 completers of whom 70,000, or 35% (MSC had anticipated one in two continuing) had gone on to a YTS2 continuation place. A further 35% went on to a full-time job with a scheme employer, about 20% went to a job with a different employer, and just over 10% were still unemployed three months after completing their YTS year.

In December 1986, over 20% of places/trainees were in administrative/clerical work, about 15% each in selling/storage and construction, about 12% in health and personal services, under 10% in each of mechanical engineering and vehicle repair, about 5% in catering and food preparation, agriculture, and electrical engineering, and under 5% (but a significant number) in each of clothing/textiles, creative and educational work, transport operation, non-metal process industries, printing, scientific work, and fishing.

Recruitment for YTS is via 'normal' routes, ie the careers service, MSC job centre or, if ATOs want to, by direct advertising. The level of allowances alone means that trainees will generally have to be home based. The number and range of schemes varies in different parts of the country, and the choices are probably more limited in areas of high unemployment. Some undoubtedly good-quality schemes (eg in the City of London) have difficulty in finding the high-calibre recruits they want, so it is always worth considering YTS.

Entrants to one-year YTS, according to MSC's study of the first three years, generally had the same levels of qualification as other sixteen-year-old school-leavers, excluding those going on to full-time education. Getting on for two-thirds of trainees had middle and lower grade CSEs on entry, nearly as many had CSE grade 1 passes, O levels/grades with and without other CSE grades. Only 25% of entrants had no qualifications at all on entry. MSC's study does not give any statistics on correlation of school-leaving qualifications with what happened to trainees when they left YTS.

Sixteen-year-olds should weigh up very carefully the schemes offered to them and what they can provide, and take independent advice on them. The training – and the length and type of off-the-job training (130,000 YTS trainees were enrolled at FE colleges in 1984-5, 70% on day-release courses) – the qualifications which it is possible to take (and how many have gained them), the proportion of former trainees still with the ATO and the proportion in work elsewhere (doing what and where), are all factors to take into account. MSC surveys show that, in 1985-6, 81% of trainees gained a place on the scheme they wanted.

Some 24% of trainees stayed with their managing agent/employer when they finished their 1985-6 scheme. About 31% found a full-time job with another employer (down from 37% in 1984-5), 3% went on to a full-time course, 8% went on to another YTS, and 32% were unemployed (down from 35% in 1984-5). Some 52% of trainees left their schemes before the end of the year in 1985-6, according to MSC follow-up surveys, but this was a fall from 89% in 1984-5. Their reasons for leaving included getting a full-time job (46%), not happy on the scheme (24%), not getting the training needed (13%), joined another YTS (8%), dismissed (7%), and ill (5%).

While YTS is now the accepted (and in some cases now the only) route into formal training in a number of sectors and industries, eg AGRICULTURE, HORTICULTURE, CONSTRUCTION, ENGINEERING, THE MOTOR TRADE/VEHICLE REPAIR, these figures show that the problems to be solved are still quite extensive. In addition to continuing concern about quality, some experts suggest YTS is not turning out people with the level and types of skills needed – particularly craftworkers and workers for the new-technology industry – and industry claims it cannot complete their training.

The education service fears that its expertise and resources are not being fully utilised (because of cost) – and that it is being excluded from MSC consultative and decision-making procedures. FE colleges are under pressure from MSC to work in new ways – and rather faster than local government does traditionally – at a time when local-authority funding is being 'capped' by Whitehall. FE colleges expect to participate fully in YTS, and do not want merely to provide teaching for a programme which has been decided by someone else without any college involvement.

Much depends on individual staff running programmes, and particularly the trainees' tutors, although management is also crucial. Many staff have had to learn new skills and techniques – including negotiation. While MSC has recognised the need for staff development, critics suggest that the Commission did not realise the scale or character of what was needed – or how many training staff have suffered redundancies. It asks a great deal for so many firms to have workplace personnel able to help trainees to learn.

But the success or failure of YTS in the eyes of the client young people may be outside the control of the scheme's organisers. Much depends on what happens to trainees when they have completed the scheme. At the moment, a significant proportion become unemployed, simply because there are still not enough jobs for them all, however well prepared for work by YTS. There are so far no plans for any formal provision to help these young people to hold on to and continue to improve their skills, or to add to their YTS qualifications. Ex-YTS trainees entitled to unemployment benefit can use the '21-hour' rule which allows them to go to college for 21 hours a week to study, but contingency plans which will allow ex-YTS students to keep up their education/training appear to have low priority.

Staying on in full-time education

Given there are financial advantages in leaving full-time education, a remarkably high proportion of young people now choose not to do so – in 1986 a record 30% of 16-year-olds decided to stay at school – against only 16% in 1966-7.

A steadily-rising number/proportion of 16-year-olds stay on at school or further education college to improve their qualifications to help them find work, with no intention of going on to advanced academic study. In 1985, over 23% of pupils (about 72,500) over school-leaving age studying in maintained schools were not taking A-level courses, against around a sixth (about 37,000) fifteen years earlier. In addition, over 315,600 students study full time at this level in further education colleges (but this includes those studying for A levels).

The majority of 16-year-olds staying on at school and not starting a two-year A-level course were studying for O-level-equivalent/CSE exams (as above), adding to such passes as they gained at sixteen. In sixth-form colleges and FE colleges catering for the age group they have also had the option to choose from a range of pre-vocational courses, and these are now also available in schools. Many pre-vocational and vocational courses also include elements of general education too, though. Effectively, there is a growing convergence between school- and college-based provision for the age group. About 108 sixth-form 'colleges' now teach 17% of all pupils studying post-sixteen. More education authorities would like to reorganise in this way, but face problems of eg parental opposition and in finding resources.

Sixteen-year-olds staying on at school can take –

The Certificate of Pre-Vocational Education (CPVE) is a new national qualification, designed to help in the transition from school to work by equipping students with basic skills, experiences, attitudes, knowledge and personal and social competences needed for life generally. The award of a CPVE is designed to show that students are prepared to –

  start on specific vocational courses;

  transfer into more specifically academic studies;

  gain credit towards or exemption from parts of the requirements for some vocational courses;

  respond and perform effectively at work (preferably with further specific training);

CPVE is designed mainly for sixteen-year-olds, who would work for it in the year immediately after completing compulsory education, though it can be suitable for other students. While CPVE caters for all ability levels, in practice most schemes are designed for 'new' sixth form/college students who are not generally likely to go on to A levels.

The CPVE framework is made up of a 'core' and vocational studies which must take up at least 75% of course time, and should be co-ordinated and integrated as a coherent whole rather than separate subjects, and 'additional' studies.

The 'core competences' are personal and career development; industrial, social and environmental studies; communication; social skills; numeracy; science and technology; information technology: creative development; practical skills; and problem solving. Schemes may include 'additional studies' time, eg to take an (extra) GCSE exam, or do more work on core and vocational studies.

In vocational studies, students are expected to 'explore' and develop broad vocational skills, including at least four modules from eg business and administrative services (control of organisations, services to business), technical services (IT and microelectronic systems, service engineering), production (manufacture, craft-based activities), distribution (retail and wholesale), services to people (health and community care, recreation services, hospitality including food and accommodation). No specific guidelines are set for the 'additional studies'. Activity-based learning (including eg work assignments and projects), and work experience are essential components. Within this framework, LEAs, schools and colleges put together their own schemes.

Nearly 1180 CPVE schemes had been approved by May 1987, involving 2314 centres and over 35,000 students. About 60% of centres are in 'consortia', and most FE colleges are now involved in CPVE.

'Progression', says the DES's Further Education Unit (FEU), 'is still an unresolved issue' (in mid 1987). FEU's findings are that CPVE is not yet fully understood and/or accepted by employers, academics or students themselves. Many YTS managing agents had not heard of it, even though it is now possible for CPVE to be used in YTS programmes. It appears, according to FEU, to be

in danger of becoming the 'last option for students of lesser ability' unless it is given greater support. BTEC's First awards will compete with the CPVE, and may 'cream off' the more motivated sixteen-year-olds (some LEAs do not allow sixteen-year-olds to do First awards as a result). Students who stay on for CPVE are now only entitled to a year on YTS, and may be too late to get into better schemes. Much depends on how NCVQ (see below) treats CPVE. FEU surveyed what happened to a sample of students completing CPVE in 1985. About 30% found work, 35-40% went on to (further) full-time education, 20% went on to YTS, and 10% became unemployed. (When the study was extended to 1986 leavers, only 26% found work, 24% went on to YTS – and 25-30% left the course early, some for jobs or further training.)
(CPVE has replaced a number of other schemes and awards run by CGLI, BTEC, and RSA.)

GCE A-level examinations are (still) predominantly designed to form the second half of the university entrance requirement. Full A-level examinations are taken after an intensive two-year course, in a school sixth-form, 'sixth-form' or FE college, at 17 or 18. The standard of the examinations is consistent with the specialist study of two or three (some students take four) subjects for two years. AS levels are of the same *standard* as full A levels, but cover only some 50% of the syllabus in that subject – they are not, therefore, at an intermediate level between O and A level.

Proposals to replace A levels with a broader, more flexible scheme have been rejected several times over the last ten years or so, and yet another review is at present (1987) under way, theoretically though with a fairly narrow brief. A new set of examinations, AS levels, will be examined for the first time in the summer of 1988 (with courses starting in September 1987), but they still leave A-level students very isolated from the rest of the 16-18 age group.

A-level courses have changed little for many years. It is generally agreed that they force the most able students to specialise too early – and this it is hoped AS levels will at least help to improve. But the changes in GCSE, and the new forms of study and assessment that these entail, will mean that A/AS-level students starting their courses in September 1988 will find them very old-fashioned and probably very restrictive. A/AS level courses are almost all very 'academic', when the general trend is bring the real world into education, A/AS-level courses do not, either, give students time or any real opportunity to study anything else, or to spend time on pre-vocational and/or work experience programmes – which they need just as much any other young adult.

As the number of young people of this age group falls, and with tight and tightening resources, LEAs and schools are having increasing problems giving students a wide enough choice of A-level subjects, and some will not be able to afford to offer AS levels at all. The problems are only solved by teaching A-levels in sixth-form or tertiary colleges, or grouping schools with or without FE colleges in A-level 'consortia' – in remoter areas where distances would make travelling to different colleges/schools impossible, 'distance learning' packages are being mooted. If schools are allowed to leave their LEA to become independently 'state maintained', these complex arrangements could collapse.

Choice of A/AS-level subjects begins to narrow further later choices – of subjects to study in full-time higher or advanced further education, and of entry to particular careers. Before choosing their A/AS level subjects, students must have clear information on what their choices will mean, in terms of the courses and careers open to them. They must, then, have already been introduced to the subjects they can study with given sets of A levels and/or AS levels, especially subjects that are not taught at school (or which are rather different to study), and to the possible careers which follow on directly from these A levels or from specific degree subjects. Again, they should be clearly advised on the consequences of choosing to drop particular subjects, and helped to keep their options as wide open as is possible given the level of specialisation required at A/AS level.

Students themselves are clearly keen to study as broadly as possible – the pattern of A-level/H-grade choices has been changing for some years now, with a steady trend to 'mix' subjects. The ratio between students gaining all science/maths, arts and/or social science, and mixed science and arts/social science was 28: 38: 35 in 1984-5, against 33: 51: 15 in 1970-1. The proportion with a mathematics A level/H grade rose to 43% in 1984-5 (53% of girls gaining A levels, and 79% of boys) from 31% in 1970-1. Over 20% of the age group now gain one or more A levels (against under 10% in 1962-3), nearly 16% two or more (against 7.6%), and nearly 11% three or more (against only 5%).

In Scotland, courses leading to H-grades are rather broader, and most students study four or more subjects. Nearly 30% of boys and over 35% of girls gain some H grades, and some 15% of boys, 16% of girls gain four or more.

University entrance requirements stipulate two or three A-level passes (depending on the number of O-level-equivalent† passes gained) – the number of H-grade passes required varies from university to university. Universities say they will accept two AS levels in place of a third A level. This is, however, only the general requirement. In practice the course requirement (set by individual faculties or departments) overrides this, so that if the course requirement asks for three subjects at A level the number of O levels gained cannot reduce this. Course requirements can be extremely complex, but efforts are being made to simplify them, as in the new *University Entrance: the Official Guide* (published annually by the Association of Commonwealth Universities, and available from Sheed & Ward, 2 Creechurch Lane, London, EC3A 5AQ).

Universities, up to 1987 entry gave their requirements for individual courses in terms of 'required' and 'preferred' subjects in the *Compendium*, which the new *Guide* has replaced, but this has now been dropped. Departments or faculties may still ask for two or three A-level subjects, and may specify exactly what subjects should be offered for a particular course, or stipulate only one or two, either leaving free choice of the other(s) or asking for one or two passes in one or two ranges of appropriate subjects. The pattern varies from subject to subject, and between universities within a single subject. The number of subjects stipulated often depends on the continuity between sixth-form studies and university courses, although there are some A-level subjects (art, for example) which are not considered a good grounding for the study of the same subjects at university. In the sciences, particularly physical and applied sciences, relevant A levels are seen as most important, and languages are normally required if they are to be read at university.

The new *Guide* gives the course requirement in a greatly simplified form. While some admissions tutors have actually simplified their course requirements in line with what the *Guide* says, there is no guarantee of this. It is, therefore, crucial to check either in the prospectuses, but better with the admissions tutors themselves, what the specific course requirements are. It is important not to rely on old editions of the *Guide* (or the *Compendium*), out-of-date prospectuses, or someone's memory.

The new *Guide* does, though, now also give the 'typical' A-level grade offer(s) made by universities for their courses. A-level passes are graded from A down to E, and universities usually express their offers of places as conditional on gaining certain grades. The basis on which the grade required is decided varies according to the criteria adopted by the individual department, mostly depending on the level of competition in particular subjects and/or for places in particular departments. Against this is given the range of grades gained by accepted candidates for the preceding year's entry (based on UCCA statistics). Most departments now make fairly standard offers, although some still vary them, depending on whether or not they want to encourage a candidate, or consider that the candidate has suitable qualities regardless of examination grades.

CNAA degrees at polytechnics and C/IHEs The Council for National Academic Awards is 'liberalising' the entry requirements for its degree courses, and is encouraging polytechnics and colleges to accept a widening range of qualifications. However, at present the great majority of those going on to degree courses do so with A levels. The 'normal minimum requirement' in terms of (full) A-levels/O-level-equivalent passes is the same as for universities, but CNAA says polytechnics and colleges may accept four AS levels instead of two A levels. Polytechnics and colleges are generally also more 'liberal' in their course requirements, and rarely require more than one 'set' A level. The grades required, which are not at present (1987) published officially, have been rising steadily, especially for very popular subjects. In law, for instance, most polytechnics can ask for the equivalent of three grade Cs.

(Entry to some CNAA degree courses, eg in art and design, may depend more on eg completing a foundation course and a portfolio, than on A levels.)

BTEC Higher National award (diploma and certificate) courses are open to those who have studied two subjects to A-level but have passed only one (although students may have to do a short preliminary 'bridging' course designed to introduce them to the industrial/business world).

Other opportunities at 18-plus with A levels Formal entry to the majority of professional-level careers is now, with few exceptions, a degree. Even where a direct A-level entry route is kept open, most entrants are now graduates. In engineering- and science-based higher-technician-level work, there are now shortages of *good* entrants with A levels. Elsewhere, 18-year-olds are just as affected as anyone else in the age group by unemployment (worst affected are those with poor exam results), which have been aggravated to some extent by graduates moving into occupations for which people with A levels were recruited previously. If, as seems likely, the supply of graduates does not keep pace with demand, opportunities for people with A levels may improve again.

Choices at 18-plus Once again at eighteen, young adults have a choice between employment – preferably with training – and further full-time study, either directly for a vocational (higher-technician or a decreasing number of professional qualifications) or to a degree course. Over 80% of those who qualify (ie get two or more A levels), go on to full-time study. For the rest, the work situation is probably improving now. Eighteen-year-olds do not have YTS to help them into work, although they can qualify for the Job Training Scheme.

Occupations requiring two/three GCE A-level passes for direct entry

ART/DESIGN: higher technician work eg in graphic design, display/exhibition design, furniture/other crafts, textile and fashion design; photography.

BUSINESS/COMMERCE: eg advertising*; company secretarial work; marketing; personnel work; purchasing/buying; secretarial work.

COMPUTING: (applications) programming.

CONSTRUCTION: higher technician/engineer.

ENGINEERING: higher technician/engineer.

FINANCIAL WORK: eg accountant*, actuary*, banking, building society work, insurance work.

GOVERNMENT: Civil Service eg executive officer, student apprentice engineer; local government eg administrative trainee, environmental health, housing management, trading standards.

HEALTH SERVICES: administration, chiropody**, occupational therapy**, physiotherapy**, radiography*.

HOTELS & CATERING: trainee management††.

LAND USE ETC: cartographic draughting††, estate agency, land management; landscape design*; surveying*.

LAW: justice's clerk, solicitor*.

LEISURE/RECREATION: administration††.

MEDIA: advertising*, journalism.

RETAILING: administrative trainee.

SCIENCE: eg animal, laboratory, medical-laboratory higher technician††.

SOCIAL: some areas of social work.

TRANSPORT/TRAVEL: air traffic control; aircraft engineering technician; pilot.

* majority of entrants are graduates.

** normally via a full-time training course (but not necessarily a degree).

†† entry as for BTEC Higher awards (or equivalent) ie two subjects studied to A level but one pass usually acceptable.

VOCATIONAL QUALIFICATIONS

In the past, qualifications and awards have been introduced as needed, mainly to meet a particular demand. The result has always been a maze of qualifications of Byzantine complexity. Attempts at rationalisation have been made several times over the past twenty years, but change has become endemic, with reorganised examining bodies being overtaken by events and having to react to unexpected developments. The overwhelming problem now, of course, is to provide sets of qualifications flexible enough to cope with rapidly-changing conditions and needs, to raise standards, and to give people qualifications on which they can base further 'progression'.

Constant attempts were made to impose some kind of 'order'. Successive reorganisations tried to create a coherent and stable structure of awards, as well as firm and clearly-recognisable identities, for broad levels of skills – 'craft', 'technician', and professional-level. But the effect was to produce increasingly rigid divisions, chasms, between the career levels, making progression from one to another virtually impossible.

Technician courses developed very haphazardly, each designed to meet a specific need, as and when identified, and at first mainly gave promotion to the best craft workers. In 1969, Haselgrave tried to create 'a national pattern of courses, examinations and qualifications which, while sufficient to meet all reasonable requirements, can be easily understood and kept reasonably compact'. The result, nearly ten years later, was the Technician and Business Educational Councils (TEC and BEC) – which have since themselves merged. TEC, too, helped to tidy up and establish a range of now widely-accepted design courses.

Effectively, this meant four main sets of vocational examining bodies – TEC and BEC for technician-level awards, the City and Guilds of London Institute with the regional examining bodies for lower-level courses. Less-commonly mentioned, but important for students in employment, were the training board awards at all levels. At the top of the structure (as it were), the Council for National Academic Awards (CNAA), validating courses for and awards degrees and postgraduate and supervisory/management qualifications (see HIGHER EDUCATION below).

Of course there are many others. Although professional bodies (of which there are some 250) have, even if unintentionally, contributed to rationalisation by accepting national awards (eg BTEC, degrees) as exempting from all or part of their own exams, a significant number still set them, and almost all are 'qualifying bodies'. Amongst others are the Royal Society of Arts and the Pitmans Institute, the GCSE examining boards. In all, one estimate suggests over 1.75 million awards are offered each year by around 300 different examining bodies (and over 40% of the workforce as of 1984 had no recognised qualification at all). This is hardly a 'rationalised' system.

MSC has been certain for some time that the arcane qualifications structures – from craft right through to professional – needed a major shake-up if an adaptable workforce trained to the levels necessary to compete with the rest of the world was to be forged. A working group to review vocational qualifications was set up, its report – that changes to the present system of vocational qualification are needed for a better-trained workforce, to bridge the 'unhelpful' divide between so-called academic and vocational qualifications, and to improve the status of vocational qualifications – accepted, and implemented, all in under two years.

THE NATIONAL COUNCIL FOR VOCATIONAL QUALIFICATIONS (NCVQ), set up in 1986, is the result of this review. NCVQ is to establish a simpler, clearer and better-linked system, a 'national vocational qualifications framework' to meet the employment needs of industry, commerce and the professions, working with interested bodies to define the 'competence' requirements – skills, knowledge, understanding and ability in application – on which the qualifications within the framework are to be based.

NCVQ will not, itself, be an examining or validating body. Existing examination bodies (see below) will continue to develop their own qualifications and, if they satisfy the NVQ criteria, will be accepted.

The NVQ objectives will also provide –

vocational qualifications based on employment-led standards of competence;

levels of award which enable clear routes of progression and are relevant to employment;

minimum constraints on access to vocational qualifications;

clarification of the relationships between vocational qualifications.

Each approved qualification will be assigned to a 'level' within the framework. Initially the framework will have four levels. Levels of award do *not* equate with 'craft', 'technician' etc, or with (eg) BTEC levels. They indicate different attainments of competence and the ability to perform defined work-related activities to set standards. People can increase their competence by extending the range of work-related activities, mastering more complex tasks, specialising, etc. All forms of progression developing individual potential are encouraged.

The higher the level of a qualification, the more it may indicate the range, breadth and complexity of the competences attained; the degree of skill and flexibility; and combinations of other factors such as the ability to –

undertake specialist activities;

organise and plan work;

transfer competences from one context or work environment to another;

innovate and cope with non-routine activities;

supervise and train others.

The levels do not indicate any set period of learning, but relate to attainment of competence, irrespective of the time it takes to do so.

The levels would typically (and not prescriptively) show eg –

Basic level 1 ability to perform a limited number of work activities within realistic time constraints, under supervision, to match a minimum employment requirement or for training programmes preparing for employment (eg YTS). Competence should be based on a foundation of broad-based vocational education training, emphasising core skills, personal effectiveness and planned work experience. CPVE may 'contribute' to meeting the requirements for level 1.

Standard level 2 Appropriate to many routine jobs and occupations of a predictable character. The minimum standard should ensure a competent performance under normal and difficult working conditions, with minimum guidance and induction, allowing the individual to demonstrate a degree of flexibility in adapting to new situations.

Advanced level 3 Suitable for many non-routine skilled jobs and occupations, denoting a broad range of work-related activities, including many that are complex and difficult, and showing the ability to sustain regular output to set standards. Awards at this level may also indicate capability for supervisory and junior management roles, or progression into advanced further education and learning.

Higher level 4 Appropriate for specialist, supervisory or professional occupations requiring adaptability to major job role changes, while maintaining full accountability and responsibility for outputs. Awards may indicate ability to perform a range of complex and difficult tasks, appropriate to designing and planning products, services, operations and processes to meet employers' and customers' needs. Relates to occupations which currently carry Higher National awards.

Professional level(s) NCVQ does not (yet) have the remit to award qualifications above level 4, but the Council is consulting with professional bodies on how higher levels of professional qualifications can best be 'articulated' within the NCVQ framework.

NCVQ has only just started on its task, which is a massive and difficult one. The Council has a number of major problems to solve –
  the framework has to be further developed by being considered in the context of specific areas of employment – which includes examining existing awards and seeing how far they meet the requirements;
  the NVQ has to be implemented fully up to level 4 by 1991;
  the professional bodies and their awards have to be negotiated into the framework;
  the present qualification system has to be simplified by finding ways to reduce the number of separately-recognised awarding bodies, especially in occupational areas where there are a large number of them;
  national arrangements to allow NVQs to be awarded by a process of credit accumulation have to be set up;
  NVQs have to be classified, mainly to simplify the present arrangements and to make sure the whole vocational field is appropriately and uniformly covered;
  NCVQ and MSC have to clarify the ways they will work together to improve training and qualifications;
  establish an open-access national data base of (existing) vocational qualifications – by the end of 1987.

NCVQ made its first four awards in mid-1987. The level 2 awards have been certificated by the YTS Certification Board (which will at some point be subsumed into NCVQ). They are –
  Electrical installation (construction) – level 3 – CITB skills assessment in

achievement measure tests AM1/2 plus CGLI 236 parts I/II.

Light/heavy vehicle mechanic national craft certificate – level 3 – RTITB post-foundation modules in set range plus CGLI 361 part II or BTEC National in motor vehicle engineering.

Travel skills certificate – level 2 – joint ABTA/CGLI competence test: COTAC I, plus 18 months' relevant experience.

Food preparation and cooking – level 2 – Caterbase modules (22 set and 7 optional) plus CGLI 706/1.

FEU has sounded a small warning. 'There is a danger ... that an over-emphasis on free-standing tests of competence, irrespective of how, when or where the necessary learning has taken place, may affect the quality of the learning process.'

EXAMINING BODIES not so long ago had a clear and firm brief, covered a particular segment of the educational field, and led fairly quiet lives.

Today, their position is quite different. They are, in effect, operating in a tough and competitive market and have to be almost entrepreneurial themselves. There are no longer any 'gentlemen's agreements' to stay out of each other's territory. They have to react, as quickly as anyone else, to fast-moving changes, to be ready to develop a new scheme, a new 'package', or curriculum, whenever a need is identified. Almost all have, for example, moved into the pre-vocational preparation field. CGLI helps firms and other organisations to develop assessment and quality assurance systems ('skill tests') for their proposed youth training programmes. The Institute has been helping MSC to test the suitability of profile reporting for the new training initiative over a wide range of courses. BTEC has gone into 'continuing education'.

Now the future is even more difficult to read. They have to gain NCVQ's imprimatur. But this now appears to mean working very closely with training organisations they may never have met before, and perhaps competing with each other for the 'business' of a particular industry. Most redesigned their main-stream schemes in anticipation of what they thought NCVQ would do and want. It may be that some have not got it quite right.

It is, then, only possible to describe examination schemes as they are in 1987. In 1988, or 1989, they could be quite different.

The City and Guilds of London Institute, CGLI, has long been the main qualifying body at craft (and operative) level (CGLI, of course sharing responsibility for schemes with regional examining bodies), and for some years awarded technician level qualifications too.

When the Technician Education Council was formed in 1973, CGLI was asked to transfer its formal technician-level courses to the new body (and SCOTEC in Scotland). Since the late 1970s, however, CGLI has adopted an increasingly 'entrepreneurial' attitude to the examinations business, and has moved in to provide examinations/testing and qualifications wherever the need arises, rather than restricting itself along formal and traditional lines. The restriction on CGLI technician qualifications being awarded in the UK was withdrawn in 1983-4, so that people with CGLI craft-level awards can progress more easily through the 'increasingly blurred' craft-technician divide. Since, CGLI has been providing joint certification with EITB at all levels of training.

CGLI has, then, been steadily widening rather than narrowing the schemes it provides. CGLI's policy is to provide assessment and accreditation of learning wherever it takes place, and for all kinds and levels of vocational preparation. CGLI pioneered the first 'pre-vocational', so-called foundation courses, in the 1970s, and now has schemes in professional, and 'high technology' areas. Major schemes are being developed in information technology, for instance on one level, and in Asian cookery on another. CGLI has identified what it sees as an important gap in British qualifications – the German 'meister' and the Japanese 'team leader', and has started a certificate scheme for gauge and toolmakers and plans more in other industrial sectors.

Despite the transfer of technician schemes and the declining number of candidates for craft schemes in traditional industries, the number of candidates sitting for CGLI exams has continued to go up, to over 562,400 in 1985-6. Of those taking 'specific vocational' schemes, over 31% took examinations in engineering (against almost 36.5% in 1981-2), 12.7% in construction, furniture etc (against 13.7%), nearly 11% in professional and scientific services, 9.6% in vehicle work (against 12.5% in 1981-2), 6.4% in personal services and community care, 5% agriculture, and 2.6% in information technology.

CGLI schemes are designed for maximum and increasing flexibility: to make it possible for students to move with reasonable ease from level to level and to make transfer easier from one skill to another and from one course to another, and making provision for re-training also easier. Specialisation is delayed as long as possible, teaching increasingly emphasises fundamental principles, and modular schemes, in which 'common core' units are used to teach fundamental material, with specialist units added as and where needed, help to keep the total number of courses to a minimum and make it possible to enter courses with a wide variety of qualifications.

All courses are regularly reviewed and revised as necessary, and with increasing frequency – thirty out of 238 schemes in 1985-6. The Institute is moving increasingly to a 'competence-based' system, providing clear statements of physical, mental and attitudinal skills which a typically-successful candidate ought to show. The system identifies in detail the skill and knowledge needed in all occupations, and these can be grouped in various ways to give a flexible curriculum.

CGLI works increasingly – and closely – with organisations responsible for training in a growing range of sectors, both statutory training boards and voluntary training organisations, providing 'joint certification'.

CGLI's present pattern of certification (introduced in 1978) is designed to relate to the significant stages of career development, to link attainment in industrial training and experience, and to create a clear and progressive route through technical education, and to create opportunities for progressive transfer to other appropriate courses and qualifications.

The main body of CGLI schemes is designed to meet the needs of skilled workers in any area of employment where there is an identifiable need – specific vocational preparation. Many are, of course, still for craft skills, but they also include some schemes for skilled operatives, for technicians, and for people needing to acquire newer skills.

Specific vocational preparation schemes are generally in three stages; career extension awards are used to mark attainment of a position of responsibility; and senior awards are at a professional level. There is less and less emphasis on specific periods of study.

Major schemes begin with basic level-1 training, broadly-based and, where possible centring on elements common for all, or a number of, entrants to a particular industry – eg first-year engineering crafts or general catering. In some sectors there may be a bias towards a particular trade or trade group, eg general and mechanical, electrical and electronic, fabrication and welding, shipbuilding, and vehicle body work in engineering.

After completing level 1, trainees go on to a more specialised level 2 course, normally spread over two years. Again the courses are designed to complement training in industry, and colleges do not normally provide training in practical skills. Schemes are usually made up of courses in principles and applications, associated studies, workshop or laboratory activity and college-devised technical studies and project work. This gives the main qualification.

The level 3 of a complete scheme is more advanced work but continues to complement industrial training. Level 3 syllabuses are designed to provide specialised studies, a treatment in greater depth of an aspect of level 2, a sideways step introducing another set of skills, or studies appropriate to more technically-demanding work; many level 3 courses are planned to prepare abler employees for supervisory, design or planning posts.

Once qualified at this level, it is possible to go on to the CGLI 'career extension' level, which trains, via schemes such as that in organisational studies, for supervisory work. Alternatively, abler trainees who have completed craft training with above-average performance can go on to technician training. While this can mean technician training does not begin until the age of 20 or 21, trainees who do well may be allowed to transfer from craft to technician training at 18 or 19.

The Business and Technician Education Council BTEC (pronounced Be-TEC) started (in 1974) as two separate organisations (in response to an earlier attempt to boost training and qualifications), merging effectively in 1983.

Technician-level qualification occupies the middle ground between craft and full professional training. Qualifications, careers etc, at this level are often described in terms of what they are *not*, rather than of what they are. Technician-level qualifications lead to work that lies between craft- and graduate-professional. Traditionally, technician-level training followed on after craft training, as a form of promotion. As this pattern of entry changed, at the same time the part-time route to professional qualification was steadily down-graded, and the resulting broad band of people trained to this level began to develop some kind of identity of their own as special qualifications and training were developed for them. Largely, perhaps, because the word 'technician' rarely appears in a job specification (many people working in these grades prefer 'officer'), and it applies in so many sectors of employment and to so many different jobs now, it still is not widely used, despite the rewards, job satisfactions and responsibility gained by many 'technicians'. Now the boundaries between craft-technician and technician-professional are becoming less rigid, as flexibility becomes increasingly important.

'Technician-level' covers a very wide band of qualification. Technician is often, in turn, divided into lower and higher level, as indicated by the two levels of qualification (see below), and in some occupations, eg engineering, this is formalised (in this case into technician and technician engineer, although this may become 'incorporated' engineer). The lower level is, otherwise, often treated as a training grade, eg in laboratory sciences. Technician-level is supposedly more expert and technical than 'craft', but less demanding than graduate-professional. It usually means training initially for an assistant's-style job but for a fairly broadly-based qualification (in eg sciences), but for the well-qualified and able, experience can take them progressively up to quite high levels of supervisory or middle-managerial responsibility.

BTEC courses cover a wide, and steadily-widening, range of subject areas. The main areas now are – with percentages of students registered in 1985-6 – agriculture (1%), business and finance (36%), computing and information systems (5%), construction (8%), design (7%), distribution, hotel and catering and leisure services (4%), engineering (30%), public administration (2%), and science (6%). Caring and leisure studies were introduced in 1985-6.

Nearly 186,000 students were registered with BTEC in 1985-6, about 56% for National awards, about 30% for Higher awards and the rest for the last year of the General. The majority of students are in the 16-20 age range, and about 50% of students are in employment, and so study part-time. Comparisons with previous years are not really valid since there have been so many changes, and BTEC is also affected by the falling numbers of school leavers. Courses for the main BTEC awards are taught mainly in FE colleges (National awards mainly but Higher Nationals in some larger colleges), and in polytechnics and colleges of higher education (Higher National awards mainly).

BTEC kept two quite distinct and separate types of courses and awards until 1986-7 (but withdrew the General Certificate and Diploma at the end of 1985-6). A new integrated, standard 'framework' only finally came into force for almost all schemes and awards from September 1987.

BTEC's new framework is designed to give recognition of achievement for formally-structured courses of study which are inevitably education-based, although they focus on learning through a mix of both education and vocational experience. While the framework is flexible, and there is provision for students to gain 'certificates of achievement' for unit(s) gained etc, a full BTEC qualification is only given on completion of a total scheme.

Some schemes are unit based, with progression depending on success in each and credit given for each unit achieved whether or not the whole course is completed. Some are integrated 'grouped' courses, so that each stage has to be passed in its entirety before going on to the next. Both types of courses must be structured so that they have 'overall coherence' and must be 'delivered' so that interrelationships are emphasised. Required periods of study are also set for each award.

Within the new framework, a minimum percentage of the available/required study time is to be spent on 'core' studies. The concept of the 'core' has been extended to include core 'skills' – inter-personal and other general skills needed to be successful at work as well as skills needed for the specific award – and core 'themes' – which are interdisciplinary and are used to 'integrate' core skills with course content. A range of units, in eg languages, business skills, computing skills, etc can be included as options in almost any schemes.

The number of different 'levels' for units in the new framework is down to three (under the old TEC system it was five), corresponding to the main qualification levels, and so there is no longer any requirement for students to include a minimum number of units at a higher level. The minimum 'learning support time' for a unit in the new framework is most commonly 60 hours for a part-time course (because it is complemented by work-based 'experiential' learning), with up to 90 hours more usual on a full-time course. Students who already have appropriate qualifications and/or experience over and above the basic entry qualifications may be exempted from up to 50% of the study/ assessment requirements at any level.

BTEC no longer allows candidates on Diploma courses to gain a Certificate just because their marks are not good enough to be awarded a Diploma; BTEC says that Certificates are now to be awarded on the basis of a combination of college-based study and on-the-job training. Diploma students do not gain this on a full-time course, so to be awarded a Certificate instead, they will have to prove, or add, appropriate on-the-job training.

The Council's three main qualifications, designed as nationally-recognised 'benchmarks' against which student achievement can be judged are now –

BTEC First Certificate and Diploma A completely new qualification, designed to provide an initial vocational qualification for those who, at or after sixteen, have already chosen the area of work/employment for which they are being prepared, and who may 'realistically' expect to go on to technician- or equivalent-level studies at a later date.

The 'mainstream' route to a First Certificate is a one-year part-time course including at least five units (or the equivalent) with at least 50% of learning support time on core studies. The 'mainstream' routes to a Diploma are a one-year full-time or two-year part-time course, including at least eight units or the equivalent, with at least 33% of learning support time on core studies. Units are designated *F* level, and are equivalent in standard to old TEC level-1 units. For entry: no formal academic requirements. It is possible to work for a first award on some YTS schemes.

BTEC National Certificates and Diplomas The 'mainstream' routes are similar to the old BEC nationals, namely two years part-time for a Certificate and two years full-time, three-year sandwich or part-time for a Diploma. Certificate courses must include at least ten units or their equivalent, with at least 50% of learning support time on core studies. (The first year of the old TEC National is now effectively the new First award and the length of a National course is fixed.) Diploma courses must include at least 16 units with at least 33% of learning support time on core studies. Units are designated *N* level, equivalent to old TEC level II and III units.

For entry: a First Certificate or Diploma, four O-level-equivalent passes†, full CPVE certification with an equivalent level of attainment, or a certificate of achievement from a BTEC/CGLI 14-16 preparatory programme. On YTS schemes in a few areas (eg COMPUTING) trainees with the necessary entry qualifications may be able to take a BTEC National.

BTEC Higher National Certificates and Diplomas The 'mainstream' routes remain very similar to the old awards at this level, ie two years' part-time study for a Certificate and two years full-time, three years' sandwich or part time for a Diploma. Certificate courses must include at least ten units or their equivalent with at least 50% of learning support time on core studies. Diploma courses must include at least 16 units with at least 33% of learning support time on core studies. Units are designated *H* level, equivalent to old TEC level-IV and V units.

For entry: a BTEC National, at least one GCE A-level pass plus appropriate supporting O-level-equivalent† passes, BTEC certificates of achievement at appropriate levels and in relevant subjects, and/or appropriate on- or off-the-job training.

BTEC has also added a fourth qualification –

BTEC Continuing Education Certificate and Diploma is designed for adults who want to extend and develop previous education and experience. Courses must include at least five units of study, but the route and period of study is left flexible. Students should be over 21 or have at least three years' experience of responsible work. For the certificate, students should have a level of proficiency of at least BTEC National, for a diploma 'intellectual capacity' of

BTEC Higher National level.

BTEC is also involved in pre-vocational preparation schemes (see above).

The Scottish Vocational Education Council (SCOTVEC) is the equivalent of BTEC. Formed, like BTEC, by an amalgamation of the Scottish Business Education Council (SCOTBEC) and the Technician Education Council (SCOTEC) in 1985, SCOTVEC is responsible for developing, administering and assessing courses for awards across the vocational spectrum. The main awards are –

The National Certificate This is a completely new scheme and is quite different from BTEC's design. It is designed mainly to –

  encourage more 16-18-year-olds to take up further education;
  make the provision more responsive to the needs of employers and students;
  take account of the growth of new technology and the changing business scene;
  integrate education and training into a more structured framework to prepare young people for their first job and help them form the flexible attitudes to deal with life in an increasingly complex society.

The new scheme is intended to be completely comprehensive and gradually take in the whole range of non-advanced further education provision in Scotland, and so covers traditional craft/technical qualifications as well as technician. It also includes general vocational provision in schools, as well as the 'off-the-job' component of training schemes. It is not replacing existing (Scottish) Higher or post-Higher studies, although students can supplement their Higher courses with NC modules, if they want to.

The National Certificate has a very flexible 'framework'. 'Programmes of study' are made up of a series of modules – course building blocks, each consisting of a self-contained unit of 40 hours' study. Such programmes can be biased towards particular vocational areas, taking employers' needs into account, and including where relevant, eg communication, numeracy, and personal and social development. Although it is unlikely that students can have unlimited choice of modules, students are allowed to put available modules together to make up programmes tailored to their personal needs. Custom-designed programmes can still be nationally-recognised and -certificated. All students' achievements are recorded on the National Certificate.

However, a fixed programme may be necessary if a student is to be able to go to a more advanced course, but wherever possible they should be able to choose a programme with a mix of set core and elective optional modules.

Students may study for the National Certificate on a full- or part-time basis. A full-time course will cover some 20 modules a year, a day-release course normally about six, but other flexible part-time arrangements are allowed for re-training, for special needs, and for YTS off-the-job training. Evening, and some distance-learning, programmes are possible, and a National Certificate can be gained by almost any combination of full- and part-time study. A completely full-time, vocational programme might last one year, a day-release programme typically two or three. Students do not, however, have to complete their NC programme in a single 'burst' of study – they can complete modules as and when they wish, building up to a Certificate over a number of years.

National Certificate modules and modular programmes can be taken in FE colleges, Scottish central institutions, secondary schools, and other centres, so long as the student is sixteen or over.

Higher National Diploma/Certificate schemes are more 'conventional' with a centrally-set broad syllabus. The subject range is greater than BTEC's – eg there is a scheme in legal studies. Certificates are normally taken over one year full-time or two-years part time, Diplomas over two years full-time.

Entry requirements: set individually for each scheme, but the broad requirement is normally a National Certificate with at least 12 appropriate modules (usually including communication 4), or three SCE Higher grade passes and not less than two other SCE O grade passes, normally including Higher English but a subject showing use of English may be accepted instead.

Royal Society of Arts The Society (with the London Chamber of Commerce) has a long history of providing vocational qualifications and single-subject certificates.

The main vocational areas are clerical and administration, business and financial, secretarial, reception, retail distribution, warehousing, storage and distribution, road freight and passenger transport. The awards can be taken at four successive levels – certificate, diploma, advanced diploma, and higher diploma. RSA itself sets no formal entry qualifications, although colleges may do so. The schemes can be taken either at college or at work.

Subject certificates can be taken at elementary, intermediate, and advanced levels in a range of commercial subjects (eg audio-transcription, information technology, law, office practice, shorthand-typewriting, word processing) and in languages for eg secretarial work, catering, export etc.

Over 600,000 candidates (in the UK and overseas) take RSA examinations (above and others) each year.

National Examinations Board for Agriculture, Horticulture and Allied Industries see AGRICULTURE.

Professional qualifications The number of professional institutes setting their own examinations fell steadily for many years, many phasing them out and replacing them – totally or in part – replacing them with or by giving exemptions for national qualifications including degrees and BTEC awards. The trend slowed in the late 1970s/early 1980s, and more recently a few professional bodies have gone back to setting (some) of their own examinations again, although still allowing exemptions. A number have also introduced awards which allow mature entrants (eg to insurance, banking, building society work) to gain a qualification which is useful in its own right, but also allow the holder to go on to 'professional' level exams without the academic entry requirements set for school-leaver/graduate entrants.

One of the more sensitive problems facing NCVQ (above) is that of bringing professional qualifications, awarded by bodies which have always been extremely independent, into the NVQ framework. The problem has two dimensions. Firstly, some professional bodies award qualifications – or have an interest in what happens to qualifications related to their own (eg as entry qualifications) – which come within the four levels which NCVQ aim to have established by 1991. Here NCVQ has to gain their co-operation if this deadline is to be met. Secondly, NCVQ has to find a way of persuading professional bodies, many with their own royal charters, to accept the extension of the framework to higher professional qualifications. By implication this could also involve professional bodies awarding competing and overlapping qualifications agreeing to some form of co-operation (at very least), if the framework is to produce a 'simpler, clearer and better-linked' system of vocational qualifications.

Training boards/organisations Since the majority of the statutory boards were abolished, there has been a large vacuum in many sectors of employment. 'Voluntary training organisations' were set up in most sectors, but their level of activity and effectiveness varied tremendously. At least four of the remaining statutory training boards continued to work hard at developing training, and with it certification for trainees, and some voluntary organisations developed strongly. Since the start of two-year YTS, MSC has been working hard to 'activate' the other sectors, with some success already. A number of brand new training organisations – called 'lead industry bodies' in MSC jargon – have started up and some that appeared completely defunct have had new life pumped into them. These organisations are now hard at work, with expert trainers and educationalists, identifying their sector's 'core competencies', and designing 'preferred national training schemes' and certification. As many of these organisations as have been identified are included in the main section of the book, but many are working on very tight budgets which do not allow them to provide any careers information service.

Further information from the City and Guilds of London Institute, and the Business and Technician Education Council.

FURTHER AND HIGHER EDUCATION
Further education   35
Higher education   39
Further and higher education provide, between them, for most of the educational, and many of the vocational-preparation, needs of young adults, and adults. Together they form a sometimes-overlapping spectrum of provision, stretching from (increasing) involvement in and with the schools, in many instances from sixteen and even fourteen for FE, through to high-level postgraduate training and research at universities.

The broad pattern of education after eighteen, entry to careers post eighteen, and training at eighteen and after have still, up to 1987, and despite many changes and reorganisations, seemingly continued the trends of the preceding twenty to thirty years.

As of 1987, the government plans major changes in the organisation of further and higher education. The consequences are difficult to predict.

FURTHER EDUCATION
Further education has always been hard to describe. FE is quite different to both school and higher education, at least as they are now. While schools and higher education traditionally provide set courses and expect students to choose between them, further education does the opposite – trying to tailor

the courses offered to the needs of their 'customers', and to respond and adapt to the many and often conflicting demands made upon it, from student, employer, professional body, training board, Manpower Services Commission, trade unions, government departments, examination bodies, voluntary training authorities, and so on.

The result has been a pyramid of about 750 colleges – of further education, technical colleges, colleges of technology, and specialist colleges, of agriculture, art, or building, for example. Polytechnics and some colleges of higher education, although technically part of the further education sector, are generally nowadays called advanced further education – AFE – and treated as part of higher education (see below). However, there has been no neat division, and many larger colleges offer both non-advanced and advanced courses.

The numbers and status of FE colleges change regularly in response to government policy and local and even national need. The falling birth rate had a sharp effect on further education many years before the actual numbers of students were likely to decline, because the numbers of teachers being produced had to be cut. The consequent re-organisation of colleges training teachers led education authorities to re-organise all their colleges, with many amalgamations and more multi-purpose colleges. At one end of the FE spectrum colleges teaching at advanced levels have moved into the higher education sphere. At the other end the changing needs of the fourteen/sixteen to eighteen age group means growing convergence between school- and college-based provision, resulting in the development of 'tertiary' colleges especially designed for the age group, extending the comprehensive principle into post-compulsory education, by providing both academic and pre-vocational courses. FE pre-vocational and academic provision for the sixteen to eighteen year old age group is discussed in the preceding section.

The government now (1987) plans to split the FE sector in England firmly into 'advanced' and 'non-advanced'. Polytechnics and the larger C/IHEs whose students study mainly advanced courses are to be taken out of LEA control (see HIGHER EDUCATION below), and some advanced courses in the remaining colleges will also be nationally funded. In England, this will leave LEAs controlling some 400 colleges catering for over 1.8 million students, 93% of them on non-advanced courses.

FE colleges put on a constantly changing and very complex structure of overlapping courses, operating as a series of interconnecting ladders, with 'bridges' to fill in the gaps between one set and another, creating various routes to similar educational goals, generally shorter and straighter for the conventionally qualified, and longer, more tortuous for others. Further education has to take account of, for example, the need –

for far fewer courses for traditional manufacturing and construction industries which have trained fewer and fewer apprentices for more than a decade;
to develop courses for an ever widening range of new technologies, which are generally more demanding on teachers and students, for rather fewer people;
to meet increasing demand for vocational education in business and allied services;
to meet increasing demand for better and continuing education;
for new pre-vocational courses for young people including CPVE, TVEI, and YTS.

A major problem for further education is that no one, least of all employers or training organisations, any longer knows with any certainty what skills will really be needed in the future. This means designing courses for uncertainty, a whole new situation for everyone concerned.

Further education has continued to grow, at least in some sectors, despite tight funding. Any growth has largely been funded from outside the local authority, and means that colleges have to respond to different paymasters and to reconcile conflicting and changing demands. The industrial training boards had a major effect on college courses. While the training programmes the defunct boards developed may continue in some form, a source of funding has been lost.

For some while now, colleges have been involved in teaching and training for many MSC schemes. By 1985-6 the numbers of MSC-sponsored and -funded students studying in FE had risen to 130,000, 70% of them YTS trainees. Now MSC has direct control over some of the funds provided for work-related non-advanced FE (WRNAFE) – an estimated 12.5% of total NAFE funding in 1986-7, excluding the sums spent by MSC directly on their own schemes. Before these funds are released, LEAs have to agree with MSC a three-year 'forward' plan, and a firm plan for the next year. Their plans have to be in linked with MSC's current policies and plans, which are designed to see that FE responds to the needs of both the market-place and individual students.

Further education has to try to meet as closely as possible the needs of both the student – for preparation and qualifications which will best help them to get, and get on at, work; and of employers for staff with specific skills. Given the lack of financial support for training, employers are not unnaturally less willing than ever to fund students' more general personal development, however vocationally useful that may be. It is not easy for FE to match the demands of Manpower Services for schemes which are extremely cost-effective and matched even more closely to employers' needs, and of employers for specific, yet flexible, skill training, with the broader-based training people must have if they are to be able to cope with rapidly-changing employment conditions. Life for the further education sector is changing ever-more rapidly, and in ways that are less predictable. One answer seems to be a steady increase in 'modular' syllabuses, with the units or 'building bricks' covering smaller areas or topics which can be put together to make up a programme to suit the employer and the student.

The extent to which further education has had to respond to changing demand is demonstrated by the statistics. Total enrolments at FE colleges (including polytechnics) rose to nearly 2.1 million in 1985-6 – 1.66 million non-advanced and 428,000 advanced. In non-advanced further education (ie all courses below BTEC higher awards), the number of full-time/sandwich-based students is rising again (after a sharp fall between 1980 and 1983) to 340,000. Numbers on day-release schemes are still well down on 1980, at 363,000. Evening-only enrolments were well up to 669,000. Figures for advanced FE are given with higher education, below.

On non-advanced courses some 30% of all students (17% in 1979), 24.5% of full-time students (27% in 1979) were studying for GCE/SCE/CSE in 1984-5.

About 17% were studying engineering and technology (29% in 1979); about 20% social, administrative and business studies (9%); about 17.5% 'other' professional and vocational subjects; about 4.65% subjects related to health; nearly 2% agriculture etc; 6.25% music, drama, art and design; 2.6% sciences, and barely 1.5% 'arts' subjects.

Just because further education is so sensitive to influence and change, the courses and qualifications that it offers are constantly being reorganised. One problem has been the multiplicity of bodies responsible for supervising courses in the further education sector. The complexity is not so great as might appear, since representatives of any one such body will sit on the relevant committees of others in the field, but to date no one body has had any 'overview' of developments, so conflicting interests make management difficult.

FE expects to provide successful students with a paper qualification. Where possible, this will be an award from an 'outside' body (see *Examining bodies* above), whose standing and standards will be recognisable by and acceptable to an employer, or give entry to a higher-level course at another college, or university. If there is no external qualification, then the college itself will make an award.

Qualifications and courses in further education Further education aims to provide sets of clearly defined courses and qualifications to meet specific needs, but courses are becoming increasingly flexible – and therefore not so easy to document – to allow students to pick up their studies and/or training at a level matched to the qualifications and skills they already have (or don't have).

FE has to try to provide courses which are both relevant to possible areas of employment, usually within a locality (eg a college in a town where the major employer was a now-closed steel works has to make radical changes), and which allow students eventually at least, to reach their full potential. FE has to work in the knowledge that there is widespread uncertainty on the future requirements of employers and students.

Students must be able to retrain when necessary, and to study on whatever basis best suits their circumstances, whether full- or part-time, by block release (in bursts of some six weeks at a time), on a sandwich-based course (where a year or six months of study is interspersed with similar periods of work experience and training), or by 'distance learning', studying mainly at home. (For this, FE now has a new organisation, 'Open Tech', which is developing schemes to make it easier for people to go on developing their skills and qualifications, even though they are unable to study at a college.)

Traditionally, further education courses had set syllabuses, depending on the area of study and the end qualification. Increasingly, a student's programme of study is made up of a set of 'units' on specific topics, depending on the level already reached and the objective. A typical programme or scheme will involve a set number of units for the award concerned, made up of a mixture of set 'core' units – eg numeracy or maths to a certain level, and a selection of other units chosen to meet the student's and employer's needs – and to try to cope with the uncertainty on the future requirements of both. Students on widely differing programmes in terms of specific skills may share units in, eg maths, communication skills, or computer literacy. 'Common' core courses, for eg all students in the finance field, whether they are working in banking, insurance, accountancy or public finance, help to ensure that skills are more easily transferable from job to job.

HIGHER EDUCATION

Higher education is the generic term used as a convenient label to describe universities, polytechnics, Scottish higher institutions, and other colleges offering degree-level courses, and are mostly called colleges or institutes of higher education.

It used to be a convention that higher, as opposed to further, education is relatively stable and does not change that much. The events of the past twenty-five years have disproved this, and change now constantly affects the setting in which students now read for degrees and related qualifications.

For a decade or so, starting in the early 1960s, all sectors of higher education expanded, under the impetus of the Robbins Committee's recommendation that higher education should be available to all who qualify, and the sharply-rising numbers of eighteen-year-olds. New universities and colleges of education were founded, older ones grew out of all recognition; the polytechnics were formed; courses were developed in new subject areas, and new types of courses developed.

Since the start of the 1980s, higher education has been living in a quite different climate. The main factors have been the dramatic fall in the birth rate since

---

Southampton Institute of Higher Education

Full-Time and Sandwich Courses

2 A-level entry
Accountancy Foundation; Institute of Cost and Management Accountants; Association of Certified Accountants; Royal Institute of Chartered Surveyors (Chattels); Communications, Advertising and Marketing Foundation Diploma.

1 A-level entry
BTEC HND Business and Finance, Public Administration, Computer Studies, Building Studies, Engineering (Computer Systems and Information Engineering, Mechanical, Production, Computer Aided Engineering, Marine, Naval Architecture); Institute Diploma Yacht and Boat Design, Yacht & Boatyard Management; RSA Secretarial Linguist's Certificate; RSA Personal Assistant's Diploma; LCCI Private and Executive Secretary's Certificate.

5 O-level entry
ISVA (Estate Management, Auctioneering, Valuation and Fine Arts and Chattels).

4 O-level entry
Institute Diploma in Creative Communication Studies; BTEC HNC Engineering (Electronics and Communications); BTEC HND Engineering (Marine), BTEC ND Engineering (Marine), Nautical Science, Maritime Technology.

3 O-level entry
BTEC ND Design (Print Design and Production, Graphic Design, Technical Illustration, Fashion, Crafts); Foundation Course in Art and Design.

The Academic Registrar,
Southampton Institute of Higher Education,
East Park Terrace,
Southampton,
SO9 4WW.
Telephone (0703) 229381

1964, and an economic/political situation which has resulted in retrenchment and cuts. The role of higher education has been under intense scrutiny, and long-accepted traditions questioned – especially (as far as prospective students are concerned) academic work and courses in subject areas with no apparent direct vocational or practical value.

The future of higher education has been (and still is), being debated against the background of the declining number of young people, which alone produces complex problems. The general effects of the declining birth rate have already been discussed, but they have major implications for higher education. Teacher training was in fact the first to suffer – the falling birth rate and lack of government investment made the 1970s reorganisation of teacher training – upgrading and integrating it into the rest of HE – a very disruptive, and destructive, process.

The future of higher education as a whole has been discussed exhaustively since 1974 – nearly fourteen years. Even though the numbers of eighteen-year-olds are known some seventeen years in advance, predicting how many will want to go on to higher education, and will qualify, is a statistical nightmare. The numbers of eighteen-year-olds rose until 1982, peaking at 939,000. Numbers will continue to fall steadily at least until 1994, to under 640,000.

In 1981, the government decided on a 10% cut in the size of of the higher education sector (in terms of staff and students). In this exercise, university cuts were made with such speed that the 'surgery' was extremely crude, and was very damaging for some universities, including one or two with the strongest technological provision. It appeared then that further cuts were highly probable as the number of eighteen-year-olds fell and the proportion of unemployed graduates rose.

But as of spring 1987, the position looks somewhat brighter. The number of students in higher education has, in fact, increased since 1979 – to 693,000 in 1985 – although virtually all the extra numbers are in the polytechnic/college sector, with university numbers almost static (so for the first time, more than half of all HE students are studying in polytechnics and colleges). The increase in numbers since 1982 has been made up from –

a rise in the 'age participation rate' (the number of young initial entrants to full-time HE expressed as a percentage of half the total number of 18 and 19 year olds) from 12.4 in 1979 to an estimated 14.2 in 1986, despite rising entry qualifications – the mean A-level 'score' for university entrants was 11.1 in 1984-5 which is at least two Bs and a C;

a 25% increase in the number of mature students, and

more women in HE (44% in 1986 against under 40% in 1979).

The government has (in the White Paper, *Higher education: meeting the challenge*), on this evidence – and taking into account projected increasing demand for highly-qualified people from employers of all kinds – accepted the need to use the higher projections of future demand. On current (1987) projections numbers are planned to rise to 726,000 in 1990, fall slightly (to under 700,000) in 1996, with a subsequent increase to 723,000 by 2000. These figures imply a further rise in the age participation rate, to 18.5, a further rise in demand from young women, and an increase in the proportion of young people gaining sub-degree/HND vocational qualifications and then wanting to go on to higher education.

However, the government is to monitor the evidence of actual demand for places and undertake a major review of employers' needs. On the basis of these government will 'adjust' – up or down – their 'planning framework' and number of places. The universities believe that the government has considerably underestimated demand from employers. Their figures suggest employers want 2-5% extra graduates every year for the foreseeable future, rather more that the 8% planned by the government over the thirteen years from 1987. They also question how the increased numbers will be funded, since government plans a (further) fall in total expenditure on higher and further education, at least to 1989-90. Average expenditure per student fell in real terms between 1980-1 and 1986-7 by 5% in universities, and by 15% in polytechnics and other LEA colleges. Government clearly expects a greater proportion of funding to come from alternative sources, and students are likely to find resources of all kinds tight.

The government plans other changes, which are set out in the 1987 White Paper. Some of the most significant for prospective students are –

The government expects higher education to 'achieve greater commercial and industrial relevance', and will encourage and reward institutions which bring them closer to the world of business – and also expects industry and commerce to work more closely with HE. While at least now acknowledging the importance of encouraging scholarship in arts, humanities and social sciences, the government wants to increase further the proportion of students studying sciences and technology. This rose from 50% to 53% for universities, and 36% to 41% in polytechnics and colleges between 1979 and 1985, and funding is being geared to a total increase of 35% in science graduates and 25% engineering for 1990 over 1980. But shortages of candidates interested in and qualified to study science and engineering are already serious, and special programmes have been set up to try and improve numbers.

Widening access to higher education. The government has modified the Robbins' principle – to 'places should be available for all those who have the necessary intellectual competence, motivation and maturity to benefit from higher education, and who wish to do so', and this appears slightly more restrictive. However, it has also accepted the arguments for giving greater access to people who have qualifications other than the traditional A levels/H grades (or even no qualifications at all). These include vocational qualifications, and successful completion of 'access' courses. This should mean it is less crucial to gain a place in higher education at eighteen-plus, although employers will have to adjust their recruitment policies to accept more older new graduates for main-stream career development if the policy is to be credible. It will probably mean that course design and teaching methods will have to change also.

Major organisational changes are also proposed, but it is impossible to predict at this stage what practical effect these will have on students, their chances of a place in higher education, and their courses should they get one. While universities and the 'public/voluntary' sector (polytechnics etc) will continue to be funded separately, and (probably) keep their distinctive features, the main effect will be to increase centralised – governmental – control over the system. Polytechnics, and most of the larger C/IHEs (ie those with over 350 fte home and EEC HE students), which are currently controlled by their local education authorities, are to become 'free-standing', independent corporate bodies, funded (more or less directly) by central government. They would be expected to continue to meet both national and local/regional needs for HE, and local authorities will be able to use the polytechnics (etc) for other course provision, on contract.

Funding and planning for the two sectors are to remain separate, and universities will clearly continue to have greater autonomy than the public sector institutions, although it could be less than they have now. Government itself will provide 'global' funds and set guidelines, but says it will play no part in decisions on how funds are divided between institutions. The White Paper proposes a new funding body for each sector, and these will allocate funds, according to the White Paper on a 'contractual' basis, which would give them greater control over how funds are spent.

The higher-education 'institutions'

Higher education is 'delivered' in the UK via a comparatively large number of institutions, each with an identity and characteristics of its own. They are, though, divided into distinctly separate sectors –

THE UNIVERSITIES are the oldest and most traditional form of higher education in Britain. Oxford and Cambridge were the only universities in England for 600 years, although Scotland already had four. The 19th century brought the first secular higher educational institution (University College, London), and over the next hundred or so years a range of foundations emerged in all the major industrial and commercial centres, to become university colleges (regulated by the University of London) and, eventually, universities in their own right. Even so, despite 13 'civic' universities, and London and Wales with their satellite university colleges, higher education was available to very few. These were then very small institutions by today's standards.

Large-scale expansion began even before the 1963 Report of the Robbins Committee on Higher Education. Between 1958 and 1963 seven new universities were founded, two more following on from Robbins, and nine colleges of advanced technology were subsequently 'promoted' to university status. Two existing universities released satellite university colleges to become full universities in their own right, to give a total of 44 universities, two of which, London and Wales, are still federations of semi-autonomous colleges.

At the same time, almost all the older civic and ancient universities also expanded, so that student numbers rose from 113,150 in 1961-2 to a peak of 333,380 in 1981-2 – falling subsequently to some 291,000 full-time students in 1984-5, although the number of part-time students rose to 36,000. First figures for 1985-6, however, show an upturn again in full-time numbers, to 294,700, and part-time up another 1100 (but still only 6500 studying for first degrees). In 1963-4, only sixteen universities and semi-autonomous university colleges had student populations of over 2500: twenty-four years later all but a few university colleges are larger than this.

The result is a university system which, with the exception perhaps of the more traditionalist older English universities, is barely recognisable from that of 25 years ago. Categorising universities by image – 'civic' or 'red-brick', technological, 'new' or 'plate glass' – is now more or less forgotten, for instance, although Oxford and Cambridge continue to dominate.

The financial cuts of the 1980s changed the overall picture of the university sector somewhat, although hardly as drastically as some feared. London University has been forced to rationalise, and amalgamate colleges (eg Bedford with Royal Holloway; King's, QEC and Chelsea; QMC and Westfield). Ulster's New University and Polytechnic have amalgamated, and Cardiff's University College and UWIST are also merging. Quite a number of universities have, though, had to close departments. Future funding problems threaten more changes but it is not yet certain what these may be.

The first modern privately-funded university, Buckingham, gained its royal charter in 1983. Cranfield Institute of Technology also has university status, and was, and still is mainly a postgraduate institution. However, Cranfield incorporates the former National College of Agricultural Engineering, 'manages' (under contract to the Ministry of Defence) the Royal Military College (Shrivenham), awarding RMC graduates' degrees (RMC has extended its range of courses and admits 'civilian' students), and has a 'satellite' IT centre.

THE POLYTECHNICS, although most are now coming up to their twentieth birthdays, form a comparatively young sector of higher education, located between the further education sector from which they evolved and the universities, combining the vocational ethos of the former, but at a higher level, with some of the traditional academic ideals of higher education. It is not an easy position, since the education system in Britain remains so strongly divisive, traditionally separating vocational and academic study into watertight compartments. The polytechnics have always fought to avoid any suggestion that they should follow tradition and behave, and be treated, as apprentice universities.

While they have long wanted to gain independence from LEA control (as now proposed), and have the right to award their own degrees (as now being negotiated with CNAA below), they want to maintain and develop the roles they have already established. They attempt this in the face of considerable difficulties, not least of which are the problems of combating traditional attitudes which see polytechnics as second-class universities rather than the unique institutions they are.

But despite the problems, the polytechnics do now have recognisable identities, and a generally-accepted role. Formed post-Robbins largely as a way of providing a massive expansion of higher education, it made economic and academic sense to concentrate 'public-sector' degree and degree-level work in a smaller number of institutions. These 'new' polytechnics 'were not to be confused or merged with the universities: the two types of institution would co-exist ... with assurances that the polytechnics would not suffer what was seen as the "fate" of the colleges of advanced technology' (which became 'technological' universities and have had problems with their 'images' and status ever since). The polytechnics were intended to protect students on advanced, non-degree, part-time courses, which previously had been moved out to other colleges.

By 1986-7, some 320,000 students were at polytechnics. Half of them were on full-time and sandwich courses, a 22% increase on 1981-2, and more than double 1974's 76,800. Some 75% of full-time students were studying for first degrees. Numbers of students studying on a part-time basis are still rising, if more slowly, to nearly 61,000 in 1986-7. The other 100,000 took short courses.

The size of individual polytechnics varies, although they are now all large institutions. In terms of full-time and sandwich students, one now has over 9600, two nearly 8000 and none less than 3000. Five have between 6000 and 7000, five between 5000 and 6000, thirteen between 4000 and 5000, and four between 3000 and 4000. Their part-time student numbers have evened out – only one teaches more than 4000, only two under 1000 – the rest between 1100 and 3400 each.

Polytechnics are mostly located in industrial or commercial towns/cities, mostly regional centres, many in towns/cities with universities too. Eight are in and around London, with major groups in the Midlands, the north, industrial Yorkshire and the north-west, plus three in the south/south-east (only one of them in the south-west), and one in Wales. Wales, East Anglia, Kent, east Yorkshire and the far north-west are still poorly served.

In terms of their advanced-level academic work, the polytechnics have already changed and evolved considerably over their comparatively short lives, and are likely to go on doing so. The balance of enrolments (1986-7) on full-time and sandwich courses have been tilting towards engineering, science etc – accounting for 41.6%, with almost 30% on administrative, business and social studies, over 13% on 'other' professional and vocational studies (including 6% training to be teachers), and 15.4% on creative arts (7.6%), languages and literature (3.4%), and arts other than languages (4.4%).

COLLEGES/INSTITUTES OF HIGHER EDUCATION mostly developed as a result of the reorganisation of teacher training in the mid-1970s, but a number were simply designated by their local authorities to do advanced level work.

Teachers were, traditionally, educated and trained in specialist colleges of education, which grew and expanded with the birth rate and demand for improved and longer teacher training. At peak in 1972, they numbered just over 150 with virtually 110,000 students. Some were founded and administered by local education authorities, others were voluntary and, although partly state-supported through student fees and grants, administered by their founding bodies, the largest group belonging to the Churches.

Reorganisation began with government acceptance of the 1972 James Committee's proposal that teacher training should be integrated with the rest of higher education, so that students could study with students studying other subjects, and that all teachers should have degrees. Orderly reorganisation plans were, though, turned upside down by the unexpected and continuing fall in the birth rate, which forced successive, and increasingly large, cuts in the numbers of teachers in training, and although numbers are now being increased again (see EDUCATION), the college sector remains dramatically smaller.

The successive reorganisations left 59 institutions involved in training teachers outside the universities. Of these 16 are polytechnics (see above) and just three remaining 'monotechnics' which continue to specialise solely in teacher training. About 56 colleges make up the 'CHE sector' including the 43 teacher-training colleges/institutes plus some which, although they were originally colleges of education no longer train teachers, and about half-a-dozen other colleges which have simply adopted the 'of higher education' title and/or status.

Some colleges of higher education developed from a single former college of education, some are based on an amalgamation of two or more such colleges, some are the result of mergers between one or more colleges of education with one or more FE colleges. Around 40 of these colleges/institutes in England are to become 'free-standing' under the 1987 White Paper proposals (see above), ie those with more than 350 students and with more than 55% of their work in HE. This includes (with the polytechnics) almost all colleges training teachers in England. Some of the larger colleges/institutes may become polytechnics as a result of the new proposals.

It is difficult to describe colleges of higher education collectively, since they are still relatively new, are still changing and developing, and have had so little time to establish their identities. In any case, there has been no central guidance as to what a college of higher education should be or do – although this could change when they become free standing – and they have developed, to some extent, differently. Some concentrate on degree courses for prospective teachers with a parallel – possibly partly 'integrated' – liberal arts degree, based on the disciplines taught to prospective teachers. Some provide other forms of vocational preparation: the administration and planning, and media studies alternatives to the professional teaching streams at Trinity and All Saints' in Leeds are an example. Colleges (such as Humberside in Hull), which incorporate former FE institutions, of course, are able to provide more vocational training, mainly in business/commercial studies, while other colleges have started courses in, for instance, social work, have absorbed schools of, eg physiotherapy or formed links with dance schools. Only those with an FE background are able, at present, to teach engineering or other technologies to advanced, degree, level, and few have major provision for science. In terms of student numbers, C/IHEs are almost all smaller than polytechnics. Of the C/IHEs listed in the 1987 White Paper, only one English CHE has more than 3000 full-time equivalent students, nine have between 2000 and 3000, sixteen have between 1000 and 2000, and the rest less than 1000. This excludes, though, those with under 55% of their students on HE courses – and they include some of the largest.

SCOTTISH HIGHER EDUCATION INSTITUTIONS are differently organised from those of England and Wales. Scotland has a number of 'central institutions', most of which are equivalent in status to the polytechnics of England and Wales, although they are not quite so 'comprehensive', plus just five colleges of education.

NAPIER COLLEGE
EDINBURGH

FULL-TIME DEGREE COURSES (CNAA)

BA Accounting
BSc Applied Chemistry
BSc Biological Sciences (Hons/Ord)
BA Business Studies (Hons/Ord)
BA Catering and Accommodation Studies
BSc Communication and Electronic Engineering

BA Commerce
BSc Computing & Data Processing
BSc Industrial Design (Technology)
BSc Science with Industrial Studies (Hons/Ord)
BEng Technology with Industrial Studies (Hons/Ord)
BEng Energy Engineering

HIGHER NATIONAL DIPLOMA COURSES

Acounting
Applied Physics with
  Electronics
Applicable Mathematics
Biology
Book and Periodical
  Publishing
Building

Business Studies
Business Studies with
  Languages
Catering and Hotel
  keeping
Chemistry
Civil Engineering
Commerce

Communication Studies
Computer Studies
Electrical and Electronic
  Engineering
Engineering (Mechanical/
  Production)
Interior Design
Music

Photography
Printing Administration
  and Production
Secretarial Studies
Secretarial Studies with
  Languages

PROFESSIONAL/POST GRADUATE COURSES

Accounting (ACA/ICMA)
Chemistry (GRSc)
Computer Studies (Advanced Diploma)
Careers Guidance (Diploma)
European Marketing & Languages (CNAA)
Graduate Secretaries
Physics (Grad Inst P)
Industrial Administration (DIA)

Information Technology (Computer Aided
  Engineering)
Management Studies (DMS/CNAA)
Photography (IIP)
Personnel Management (IPM)
MSc Biology of Water Management
Transportation Planning in Developing Countries

FOR INFORMATION WRITE TO:
Information Office, Napier College, Freepost, Edinburgh EH10 0PA

THE COLLEGE IN THE CAPITAL

OTHER INSTITUTIONS are treated as part of higher education because they mainly concentrate on work at degree level and above, but the trend to merge smaller colleges into larger institutions means fewer all the time.

A number are specialist colleges/schools – of agriculture, art, speech and drama, and music mainly. One (Camborne) specialises in mining, and Watford College of Technology serves the needs of the printing industry at degree and managerial level, but is otherwise mainly an FE college. About a dozen of these colleges/schools are to become 'free-standing' under the 1987 White Paper (see above), and another eleven have the option to transfer.

Finally, a few independent colleges also offer degree courses. They include University College Buckland, which is the one institution allowed to continue full-time courses for London University external degree, some specialist colleges (for example, Spurgeon's College, the London Bible College), and some 'closed-entry' colleges, such as the Royal Naval Engineering College at Maradon (Plymouth).

Higher-education awards and awarding bodies
The range of different kinds of qualifications (degrees etc) offered by the higher education sector has narrowed, particularly for those who cannot gain at least two GCE A levels. The major professions have moved away from setting their own examinations, requiring special courses, for school-leavers, and instead ask for either a specialist degree in a relevant subject, or recruit

graduates from many disciplines and provide professional examinations for them.

DEGREES, then, are the main qualifications available to school-leavers, in higher education.

The pace of innovation and radical ideas and thinking about subjects to be taught and ways to study them has slowed noticeably in the last few years, particularly in 'pure' arts/humanities, social sciences, creative arts etc. Course development is largely concentrated in subject areas with some direct vocational value. The main examples are – upgrading ENGINEERING courses to make courses more closely geared to professional needs, and to produce graduates trained for INFORMATION TECHNOLOGY. Sciences, too, are moving in line with developments in eg molecular biology and physical electronics. Some new courses are starting in agriculture but mainly to provide sound business skills for a problem industry. BUSINESS/MANAGEMENT STUDIES is currently a growth area, and so is vocationally-, and particularly business-oriented LANGUAGE studies, especially those not widely taught in the UK, eg Chinese, Japanese.

Universities offer only degree courses mainly on a full-time and sandwich basis, still mainly to school-leavers who can meet their entry requirements (see above), although they are slowly 'liberalising' and so admitting more students with other than conventional academic backgrounds. The whole ethos of university education is still academic excellence, training in intellectual, and especially analytical skills, to a very high level indeed. Aside, therefore, from the professional disciplines traditionally taught by universities (architecture, engineering, law, medicine, for instance), which are considered to have the academic status appropriate to university study, the range of courses which have direct vocational relevance in areas other than research and teaching is still comparatively small, although expanding. Universities have been developing quite substantial numbers of courses in eg accountancy and finance, and business studies/management generally. Traditionally, university study is concentrated on the 'single honours' course, in which students study in considerable 'depth' a single subject, with only subsidiary and supporting studies outside their main field. However, many universities offer a widening range of two-subject honours courses, and some kind of 'modular' scheme developed outside the university sector (but pioneered by universities) which enables students to make a much more flexible choice between various levels of specialisation.

The pressure to increase numbers studying science and technology has not so far changed the balance of subjects taught in universities very much, although the available figures are dated and still show the effects of the 1981-2 cuts. Figures are not now strictly comparable with earlier years because the categories have been changed. But, in 1985-6, excluding those on 'multidisciplinary' courses, 24% of first degree students were reading science (against 23% in 1981-2), 14.66% engineering and technology (against 14.5% in 1981-2), 13.9% medicine, dentistry and health-related subjects (11.2% in 1981-2), and 2.2% agriculture, forestry, and veterinary science – almost 55% in total (against under 51% in 1981-2). For the rest, the breakdown was 21% social, administrative and business studies (down 2.7% on 1981-2) of whom a third were on business-related courses, 12.6% language, literature and area studies (almost as 1981-2), 8.4% other arts subjects (against 9%), 1.8% architecture, planning etc, and 1.3% education. Only one in eighteen university students were on sandwich courses (down from one in sixteen in 1981-2).

Polytechnic teaching increasingly centres on courses leading to degrees too, but with greater emphasis on work-related training. By 1986-7, 73.5% of all full-time and sandwich-based students enrolled in the polytechnics were reading for first degrees (almost all validated by CNAA – below), with 13.4% following courses leading to BTEC higher awards or their equivalents. Just 8.5% were studying for professional and 'other' qualifications, and 1% for the DipHE. About 2.5% were postgraduates. The proportion of science- and technology-based full-time and sandwich students, at 41% of the total, is still far lower than that of the universities, although a 36% increase on 1981-2, with particularly large increases in science and maths numbers. A higher proportion than in universities study administrative, business and social studies, but it is down to under 30% from 36% in 1981-2. 'Other' professional and vocational subjects account for 6.7% (against 4.7%), and education 6.5% (against 3.7%). Of course, far fewer polytechnic students study arts/humanities – and the proportion has fallen to 15.4%, of which nearly half are studying music, drama and visual arts. One in three (double the 1981-2 figure) of all polytechnic students are on sandwich courses.

Colleges of higher education, and colleges of education, have mainly built their degree and degree-level work on the basis of the academic disciplines previously taught, mainly to teachers in training, although some have an FE base too. Most offer students a fairly broad range of subject studies, either for a BEd or a 'liberal arts' degree which usually includes two or three subjects. Most options are at present, in the 'academic' arts/humanities, creative arts, media studies, human movement, environmental studies, with some broadly-based sciences. Comparatively few colleges have the facilities to offer degree courses in subjects which have vocational value outside the field of teaching. Colleges can have their degree courses validated by universities or the CNAA. Some of the larger colleges with an FE base also offer courses leading to BTEC Higher awards.

No statistical breakdown of subjects being studied in these colleges is published separately. However, the 'First destination' figures published by AGCAS for 76 C/IHEs with an output of at least 100 graduates (degree and HND) gives some clues. Of degree graduates, as might be expected, over 29% studied education for a teaching qualification, over 25% arts/humanities (but only 4% of them languages/literature), over 17% art/design/music, over 12% social and business studies, under 10% pure science, 3% 'other' professional/vocational studies, and only 1% engineering/technology. For HND, the picture is somewhat different – almost 26% had studied social and business studies, almost 25% engineering and technology, 14.5% art, design and music, almost 10% 'other' professional/vocational studies, 7.5% science, and 6.7% agriculture. Only one in five of degree students are on sandwich courses (although BEd courses do include work experience in the form of 'school practice'), but for HND students it is more than one in three.

Universities award their own degrees, under their own royal charters. Public-sector polytechnics, Scottish central institutions and other colleges and institutions do not (as yet), and degrees gained by their students are awarded by a single, similarly chartered body. This is

The Council of National Academic Awards (CNAA) which also 'validates' – approves – their degree, and some other, courses.

CNAA's royal charter requires its degrees to be comparable in standard with university awards. Institutions have always designed their own courses, but the CNAA's extremely rigorous validation process, conducted by subject boards with both academic and working-professional members, has been extremely cautious and rather slow. These boards scrutinise the proposed syllabus, and inspect both the quality of the teaching and facilities needed for the course itself, 'the environment in which the course is conducted, and the breadth of personal education which the student can be expected to receive'. So the quality of the library and the number of tutorial rooms are also taken into account.

Polytechnics, in particular, have been trying to gain greater and more direct control over their own academic development for some time.

Like most other educational organisations at present, CNAA is changing rather more radically than ever before. CNAA is now (1987) –

Devolving some of its responsibilities to the polytechnics, colleges and institutions running CNAA-approved courses. They can become 'accredited' institutions if CNAA agrees they have 'appropriate arrangements for validating and monitoring their own courses' to make sure they are achieving academic standards comparable with other institutions. Eventually, institutions educating some 75% of CNAA students are expected to be accredited, but CNAA is to maintain its validating role for the rest, who will be called 'associated' institutions. CNAA is maintaining a range of ways to ensure standards in accredited institutions do not fall. Nine polytechnics and one CHE already have special agreements with CNAA which give them a measure of independence on course validation.

Developing a 'credit accumulation and transfer scheme' (CATS). This allows students to gain maximum possible credit for any qualifications they already have and learning they have done, including 'experiential' learning, and lets/helps them put together a programme of study to suit their own particular needs. They can choose to study at university and/or public sector institutions. The scheme only started in 1985-6 and is still in its 'pilot' stage, but some 200 students were 'placed' by September 1986. As an extension of this, CNAA is accrediting 'non-traditional' programmes of study. This includes giving approval/credits to companies' in-house training schemes and professional bodies' continuing professional development programmes. As of mid-1987, a small number of linked company-polytechnic schemes were approved, including a three-year work-based degree programme being developed jointly by IBM and Portsmouth Polytechnic.

In its early years, most CNAA degree schemes were in the more obvious fields of engineering, science and technology. However, for a variety of reasons the subjects taught diversified rather faster than expected. These included the swing away from science and technology amongst candidates which meant unfilled places (which is still a problem), and polytechnics wanted to develop their own (rather than London-external) courses in arts and social studies. Although the original stated aim of the CNAA was to combine vocational with academic study, schemes in 'purely' academic subjects have never been excluded.

And so, in its twenty-second year, 1985-6, the CNAA recorded nearly 200,000 students studying on nearly 1380 (first) degree courses (against 41,000 on 532 courses in 1973-4). Another 16,000 students were studying for postgraduate awards, and small numbers on a range of other types of courses.

CNAA statistics give a picture of a large segment of higher education – over a third of all degree students are on CNAA-approved courses.

In terms of mode of study, the picture has been fairly steady for some years now, with around 60% of degree students studying full-time, 28-29% on sandwich-based courses, and 10-11% on part-time courses (the number of courses has increased by 186% over ten years, and is now over 300).

CNAA now gives a detailed breakdown of the subjects students are reading for degrees, and these too have been fairly steady for a while now. The largest group, 18% study sciences; 15% study social sciences; 12% engineering; 11% each art/design, arts/humanities, and business/management studies; 7% 'built environment' (architecture etc); 10% education (teacher training), and 5% were on 'interdisciplinary' courses. This gives 37% studying scientific and technological subjects, slightly down on 1982 and 26% arts/social sciences (down 2% on 1982). Art/design is also down 1%, business/management studies up 1%.

CNAA schemes cover the full spectrum of disciplines studied at first-degree level, with the exception of medicine. Growth levelled off after 1982, and the number of new courses is comparatively small – 28 in 1985-6.

Science now (1985-6) has 286 courses. The largest numbers are in computing and data processing (41), maths/statistics/computing (38), biological sciences (34), chemistry (32), combined sciences 31, but physics has only 16. The 26 health and paramedical studies courses include 12 in nursing, with another five in environmental and occupational health, six in pharmacy and two in pharmacology. Catering and food sciences number 18, with four in dietetics. Agriculture has two courses and archaeology one.

In engineering, the largest numbers are still in electrical/electronic (46), mechanical (44), civil/structural (33), and broad-based engineering (24). The number of courses in other branches of engineering and technology is quite small. The 'built environment' is a major subject area for CNAA. Quantity/building surveying etc has 29 courses, estate management 24, and architecture 23. Planning has 13 and building/building services 16.

In arts/humanities, the largest group is combined studies (English, history, drama etc), now up to 68. Language courses (mostly with some vocational linguistic-training component) are also up, to 24. The number of specialist English courses is 14, theological/religious studies 8, and creative/performing arts 7 (no increase).

Business studies courses now number 71, with 24 in accountancy and four in marketing. The steady growth in popularity of professional and vocational disciplines has increased the number of courses in law to 39, public and social administration to 24, recreation/sports studies 15, but the number of librarianship/information science courses has fallen to 11. Combined social science degrees are up to 38, economics 22, but the numbers of single-subject courses in geography (14) and politics (six) have not changed, and in sociology have fallen to 11.

In art and design, while most courses are still in the 'traditional' main areas of study – 68 in three-dimensional design, 46 in fine art, 41 in textile/fashion design, and 31 in graphic design – there are now eight multidisciplinary courses, eight in history of art and design, and 11 in photography, film and TV.

CNAA validates some 55 initial teacher training courses, and a further 41 in-service courses.

QUALIFICATIONS OTHER THAN DEGREES can be gained mainly in the public sector of higher education: universities concentrate almost entirely on degrees at post-school level (with rare exceptions like the licentiate in theology at St Andrews) and primarily on higher degrees at postgraduate level, although many universities do provide professional training, and qualifications for areas like education, management, social work, law, architecture, and some technologies.

In the public sector it is possible to choose from a rather wider range, even though the underlying trend is to incorporate professional training into degrees (as has happened in eg TEACHING and DIETETICS) or into BTEC programmes. Polytechnics, and colleges of higher education which incorporated former LEA FE colleges which had previously taught at advanced level, provide a wide range of courses which include BTEC Higher National awards (see above), and courses for professional qualifications in areas such as ACCOUNTANCY, CHARTERED SECRETARYSHIP, ENVIRONMENTAL HEALTH, HOTEL, CATERING AND INSTITUTIONAL MANAGEMENT, PARA-MEDICAL STUDIES, SECRETARIAL AND BI-LINGUAL SECRETARIAL WORK and SOCIAL WORK, although it is possible to study many of them at other FE colleges also. Most of these institutions also have, often for historic reasons, one or two unique non-degree courses of their own. Colleges of higher education whose constituent colleges were all colleges of education have not diversified quite so far, although some have developed courses leading to social work qualifications (eg at Reading: Bulmershe), para-medical studies (eg occupational therapy at Canterbury: Christ Church).

Degrees and vocational preparation

Faced with graduates unable to find jobs which fully employ and extend their capabilities and education, it was hardly surprising that many started to question the value of three or more years spent reading for a degree. However, even in the depths of recession, at worst probably no more than one in eight of all graduates had real problems, while up to one in two of school leavers, at sixteen, seventeen and eighteen could not find work – and in some areas still (in 1987) the situation is nearly as bad for them.

Graduate recruitment, though, recovered from the effects of recession extremely fast, and by December 1986, only one in fourteen of university graduates whose 'first destination' was known was still looking for work, one in twelve of polytechnic graduates, and one in eleven of C/IHE graduates. This is the lowest level for eight years, and Labour Force Survey data confirms that graduates generally are less than half as likely as non-graduates to be unemployed. Moreover, a separate survey has shown that nearly 70% of the 9.5% of 1984 graduates who had not found work by that December, were in employment by the end of the following year. Another follow-up survey of 1982 polytechnic graduates showed that only 4% were unemployed after three years.

This survey also showed that over two-thirds of the graduates also thought their studies had made a 'useful', even 'essential' contribution to the quality of their work. But some 30% of graduates thought their degree courses had not given them sufficient opportunity to develop oral communication skills, 13% felt the same about written communication, and 41% about computing skills.

For 1987 graduates the prospects – as shown by a sharply-rising number of reported vacancies – looked increasingly bright, and the majority of graduates in most age groups continue to earn more than non-graduates. Prospects for full-time research and/or study are also better than for many years (see below).

To a large extent, however, the evidence is that increasing numbers of organisations of all kinds now believe that to operate in today's conditions, young and highly-intelligent, trained, minds – graduates – are essential in almost every 'function'. This extends from the largest multinationals through to some of the smallest companies, especially those which are innovating, moving over from older to new technologies, and/or adopting the latest managerial/production techniques. It also includes public-sector organisations – the Civil Service, the NHS, and local authorities among them. Although most organisations are holding down hard the total numbers they employ, they expect to maintain, and even increase, the proportion of graduate recruits. Even with the recently-announced increase in degree places, all the evidence suggests that output is unlikely to keep pace with demand. Even during recession, output of graduates, particularly in eg electronic engineering, was never enough. Teaching alone needs to recruit a huge percentage of maths and physics graduates. The shortages are likely to get much worse unless more young people can be persuaded to study scientific and technological subjects. A small but growing number of recruiters are trying out schemes to 'convert' graduates in non-technological subjects to fully-professional engineers, and special schemes are available for students with arts/social science A levels to spend a year upgrading their maths and physics to the level needed to study degree-level engineering.

But graduates, like everyone else searching for a career, will still have to be more open-minded about the kind of work they will accept. The movement of graduates into new areas of employment is a continuous process which has been going on for as long as the supply of graduates has been growing, but particularly since 1960. Then even experts could not conceive that there were more than 1000 organisations large enough to be capable of fully employing graduate skills. As recently as 1980 it was predicted that output of graduates would outstrip demand by 1986, and the fact that during recession graduate careers advisers were forced to 'sell' the products of their institutions, seemed to bear this out. But even during the recession employers were actually taking on more new graduates than they did in the 1970s, and demand is now rising rapidly. From 1987 on, employers will be competing ever more fiercely for graduates whatever their disciplines.

However, those 1000 large organisations have shrunk in size considerably, and the new opportunities will continue to be in areas of employment which may not have recruited (many) graduates before, and in totally new areas of work. The employment sectors, and the jobs, requiring graduates will be changing, often swiftly and fundamentally. Graduates will almost certainly have to be as flexible, adaptable and innovative as the rest of the workforce.

That the pattern of graduate recruitment is changing can be shown by the dramatic increase since about 1984 in the number and percentage of jobs open to graduates 'of any discipline'. For many years it remained fairly static at about a third of all vacancies. By 1985 it had risen to 40%, and the latest figures show that in 1986 it was nearer 50%. Partly this is due to firms – especially in the City – looking for numerate graduates, and graduates with computing experience, and so recruiting scientists and engineers. It could be that this trend is not therefore so helpful to arts and social science graduates as might at first appear. However, it is also probably partly because recruiters are interested mainly – and increasingly – in the intellectual abilities and training graduates have had, and so the subject-content of their degree courses is only crucial for a declining number of first jobs.

Professions and other occupations too are still moving towards graduate entry, although rather more slowly than in the 1960s and 1970s. More young people, then, have to go on to higher education, just to get into jobs which, in a previous generation, they would have been able to start as school-leavers.

Most degree courses at least at university, are not intended to have direct, practical vocational value, except for the minority of graduates who go on to an academic career (and even they have to do further training via a postgraduate degree) or who choose a subject which is otherwise vocational in content, and is taught by universities almost by historical accident. There are advantages, however, in any degree course. A degree course provides a better base for the career changes which face even the highly qualified in the future. A degree gives considerably wider career choice than lower-level qualifications, and generally shortens the time needed to complete professional qualifications. It also lets young people put off final decisions about what occupation to start with in working life until graduation or after, which means they are likely to know themselves better and be more mature, be better informed about the possibilities and can take account of the most recent changes in the labour market.

But graduate careers advisers still continue to emphasise that '[Graduates] are not offered employment as a reward for their academic achievement. They are rather *considered* for employment because they can be presumed to be of high intellectual intelligence, and to have the capacity to apply that intelligence to the problems of industry, commerce or other sectors of activity. Graduates receive offers of jobs if they can demonstrate some understanding of these problems, and some evidence of that capacity ...' (W P Kirkman in the *Financial Times*).

For most graduates, certainly most university graduates, the major problem is coping with the dramatic switch from being 'driven' above all else to try for the highest-possible level of intellectual and academic excellence, to the ever-tightening drive for cost-benefit and meeting targets and schedules out in the real world. Graduates have to recognise that 'UK employers' willingness to take on people regardless of academic discipline is not at all the same thing as willingness to be bemused by uncritical addiction to the cult of the omnicompetent amateur. Attitude and aptitudes matter' (ibid).

Since the statistics alone show a degree is still a worthwhile qualification, there really is no point in any eighteen-year-old who really wants to go on studying – and has the aptitudes needed for a degree course – turning down the opportunity of a degree place in favour of a job in hand. Such a decision, in any case, ought to be made for positive rather than negative reasons. Not only are most graduates more likely to find work, but it is more likely to be responsible and interesting work too, than that available to many school-leavers.

A degree is an advantage. A degree, even a good degree, is not enough. In today's tough market conditions, even a good degree will not automatically ensure graduates a good job, rapid promotion, managerial status, or a high salary.

Graduates, though, like everyone else, have to prepare, plan, plot, research, and use all their skills and intelligence to compete effectively in the job market. It still seems to be conventional wisdom that there is nothing to be done, that can or even should be done, between the day students start at university, polytechnic or college, and finals. More students seem to be working harder, in the belief (rightly in most cases), that a good degree is important. But most students could easily benefit so much more than they do, and give themselves a better chance in the labour market, by taking advantage of the services the university or polytechnic offers, and by using some of their spare time productively.

It makes sense for students to think about life post-university or -polytechnic, rather earlier than they have in the past. Without going to extremes, it is worth mapping out a broad general personal strategy, starting to look at the broader possibilities, and finding out about employers' broad demands of graduates sometime during the first year.

By the middle of their final year, well-prepared students should have done a lot of research. They will know a great deal about the graduate job market in general and about particular career opportunities and employers, as well as having a fair idea of what they want and what they have to offer employers. They will know what skills, academic and other, are needed for specific openings, and have some idea of what jobs involve. They know something about firms or organisations in the areas that interest them, their successes and problems, facts and figures on them. They may have spent time adding to the skills and experience learnt on their courses.

Well-prepared students have a plan which either keeps their options as wide open as possible, or allows for alternatives, since they will know that it is very unrealistic to be too single-minded. They have taken the trouble to learn how to sell themselves to employers, how to fill in application forms to the best advantage, and how to handle an interview.

All this takes time, and cannot be done in a rush in the few short weeks at the start of the final year. The process ought nowadays to begin much earlier, especially for the very many students who have little idea of what they want to do. The alternative, which is increasingly popular with many students, is to leave career-searching until they have completed their final examinations.

Employers generally take a reasonable academic record for granted. They will also tend to assume that university or polytechnic will have taught all graduates to think logically, to search out relevant information, marshal facts and arguments systematically and analyse them properly, be able to see what information is important in a given situation, and have the basic skills needed for problem solving, whatever subject they may have studied.

They also want qualities and skills not necessarily taught on a degree course. They expect the graduates they recruit to be capable of developing organisational, supervisory, planning and administrative skills. They want graduates who can learn quickly, apply their intelligence and contribute early. They want their graduate recruits to fit in; to be able to work with people at all levels, as part of a team; to be able to communicate easily and clearly, both in talking and listening to people and making verbal reports, and on paper; to be 'self-starters', and to adapt quickly to the 'real' world where solutions inevitably involve compromises.

It is also useful for students to have some kind of real work experience at least once between sixteen and twenty-one, if only to convince employers they can do it. The more responsible the job and the more 'relevant' it can be, though, the better.

Many employers also like graduates to show they have taken on some kind of real responsibility – and most universities and polytechnics are ideal places to gain this in real situations, where the consequences of mistakes can be learnt without major disaster. It is possible to edit a student newspaper – and so learn to co-ordinate a team of voluntary journalists and meet tight set schedules, to organise printing the paper within budgets set by a management committee, to see that advertising space is sold, and often sell the paper itself too. Here students can learn fast that meeting deadlines is difficult, that printers charge a lot for overtime if copy is late or has to be re-edited, that journalists have to be able to count words if a story is to fit into the space allocated to it, that in even a creative business careful planning is needed, that being organised is important, as is communicating well with staff.

Alternatively, it is possible to gain 'work experience' on a voluntary or full-time basis in the student union, organising student entertainments or welfare, 'managing' student facilities such as bars, shops and cafeterias. Being secretary of a departmental society, organising student social/community work effort, putting on plays, or running sports programmes all give the right kind of experience. Getting involved in student activities, voluntary work etc can help students to see that there are skills other than those learnt on a formal course, and these are just as important for their careers as their academic abilities.

University and polytechnic are also good places to improve on 'numeracy', and to find out what IT systems/computers can do and learn how they work – recruiters would like their graduate recruits to have some business-related IT training on both the user and 'computer professional' sides. For most engineers and scientists this usually all comes as part of the course package. Arts students may also have a free choice of some kind of subsidiary study, which could be in maths or statistics, and the computer centre generally puts on spare-time IT/computer appreciation and/or elementary programming courses for anyone who wants them. If it proves difficult to do either, there is usually a nearby technical college with evening classes. CGLI provide a certificate which can useful be taken by students (see INFORMATION TECHNOLOGY AND COMPUTING).

University and polytechnic language centres/labs mostly give undergraduates the chance to keep up their languages, or start them from scratch, in their spare time – and these too are useful 'add-on' skills.

Students aiming to prepare themselves properly will use their careers advisory service reasonably early in their second year. Despite tight resources, advisory work has improved sharply in response to the difficulties graduates have had. Advisers will help graduates to come to an informed decision, and organise their thinking about themselves and their futures, to help them assess themselves realistically. University careers services collect a wide range of literature and information about all kinds of careers, statistics, directories, data on areas of employment and individual employers. Careers advisers both sell graduate skills and try to stay ahead of developments in graduate employment.

University and polytechnic/college careers services co-operate to produce their own directory of graduate employers – called ROGET, their own careers literature, statistics on what happens to graduates, and vacancy lists. Careers services put on talks and seminars, and courses, like short introductions to aspects of management – a week spent playing business games with people from industry, commerce and public service; give practice interview sessions, and help with filling in forms and making up a curriculum vitae.

Subject choice and careers In some subject areas, of course, a degree combines the educational base required for particular careers – for example, medicine, dentistry and architecture – but for these the practical training is integrated into the degree course, lengthening it appropriately, to some five or more years. The need for engineering graduates with greater understanding of industry's needs is also lengthening a considerable proportion of engineering courses, to four (and even more) years. Courses in some other subjects provide a large measure of the educational requirements and specialist knowledge needed for entry to particular professions, for example, law, and some sciences (including, for instance, pharmacy), but practical training is needed before the graduate is considered fully 'professional'. Sandwich courses, in which students spend some part of his or her degree course gaining relevant work experience, go some way towards meeting the need for a practical component for some degrees, but again the period of study has to be lengthened to allow for this, to four or five years.

As an approximate guide, therefore, a graduate with a degree in a subject which is relevant to a profession or function should expect to spend two years in addition to the three for the degree in completing vocational training. The graduate who has read a subject which has no direct vocational value, or who enters a career unrelated to his or her degree subject must, in general, be prepared to spend rather longer training, although this depends to some extent on the occupation or function. (And many training schemes are geared to getting graduates into interesting and responsible work as early as possible.) There are, of course, exceptions. Teaching, for example, where the study of the subject(s) to be taught is considered far more important than learning teaching skills, still requires only one year's formal training on top of a degree.

School-leavers can, of course, choose to read subjects at university or polytechnic which are more specifically vocationally-orientated. Demand for such courses has been rising sharply since 1970, but there are possible pitfalls. Very narrow vocational specialisation makes it difficult to move into a different career if the choice proves wrong for the individual – or the job vanishes as a result of competition or technological change. Law is an example of a subject which has both direct vocational value in a legal career, but is also appreciated by employers in many other sectors, so its vocational 'value' has held up remarkably well, until now at least. Accountancy, as a degree subject, may not have such currency because it tends to be rather narrow. Neither the legal nor the accountancy profession restricts entry to graduates with relevant degrees – because they would rather recruit from amongst the best graduates than from people with degrees in appropriate subjects but poor results. One of the best routes to management consultancy is via an engineering degree, a professional accountancy qualification, and an MBA – not a route often recommended to candidates. Similarly the computing world does not particularly like graduates with specialist computer studies degrees as preparation for work on the business-applications side – because they don't learn about the needs of business and how to supply them.

The answer, though is as it always has (or should have) been – to encourage candidates to study the subject – or subjects – that really interest them, and interest them most. A good degree is almost essential, and gaining a good degree means enjoying the subject. There are plenty of ways of improving career prospects which are better than choosing a subject which can easily prove boring in pursuit of what may be an illusory career three or four years hence. A CNAA follow-up survey of 1982 polytechnic/college graduates showed that the proportion of graduates in arts/humanities and social sciences in 'preferred' jobs had actually risen during the three years since they graduated, from 44% to 54% and 49% to 59% respectively, despite all the evidence that graduates in these subjects have more difficulty in finding work they want.

Occupations requiring degrees Not that many careers have an absolute requirement for a specific degree, although a degree is needed for many.

Relevant/specific degree essential for ACADEMIC/RESEARCH WORK, ARCHITECTURE, DENTISTRY, DIETETICS, ENGINEERING, GEOLOGY, MATHEMATICS, MEDICINE, OCEANOGRAPHY, OPHTHALMIC OPTICS, PATENT WORK, PHARMACY, PSYCHIATRY, PSYCHOLOGY, RESEARCH (INDUSTRIAL/OTHER), SCIENTIFIC WORK, SPEECH THERAPY, TEACHING (SECONDARY), VETERINARY SCIENCE.

Degree demanded, not necessarily a relevant degree, but probably an advantage ARCHAEOLOGY, LEGAL PROFESSION (BARRISTER), MANAGEMENT SERVICES, MUSEUM WORK, OPERATIONAL RESEARCH.

Degree needed but subject not important CHURCH OF ENGLAND PRIESTHOOD, LIBRARY/INFORMATION WORK, PSYCHOTHERAPY, PUBLISHING, TEACHING (PRIMARY).

Degree not demanded but intake mainly/almost entirely graduate (non-graduate entry now very small and/or extremely difficult) ACCOUNTANCY, ACTUARIAL WORK, LEGAL PROFESSION (SOLICITOR), MARKET RESEARCH, PLANNING (TOWN/ COUNTRY), SURVEYING.

Degree can be (major) career advantage COMPUTING, JOURNALISM, MARKETING, PERSONNEL WORK, PUBLIC ADMINISTRATION, PURCHASING/SUPPLY, SOCIAL WORK.

Relevant degrees exist but career advantage 'variable' ART/DESIGN, COMPUTER SCIENCE, DRAMA/THEATRE STUDIES, MEDIA STUDIES, MUSIC, PHOTOGRAPHY.

Relevant degree courses exist but (not yet) necessarily career advantage NURSING, OCCUPATIONAL THERAPY, PHYSIOTHERAPY, RADIOTHERAPY.

Graduates are recruited for particular, and a widening range, of 'functions' by firms and other organisations in almost all sectors of employment now. Most organisations recruiting graduates expect the majority to develop as future managers, some to become the senior managers in 2010-20. The 1987 edition of 'ROGET' listed 1959 known graduate recruiters, and this is certainly a conservative figure. Graduates are being encouraged to think of working for small firms, and to set up businesses of their own.

Graduate entry In most occupations/functions/professions it is usual to have special entry arrangements for graduates, with exemptions from parts of the professional examination according to the relevance of their degree, or shorter, more intensive, and specially-designed training courses. While the proportion of graduates in many areas of employment is steadily increasing, it is very unlikely that many will now change to all-graduate entry in the foreseeable future, although in some the professional examinations (eg ACCOUNTANCY) are becoming increasingly difficult hurdles for A-level entrants. The competition for places on graduate training schemes in popular occupations, eg THE MEDIA, is likely to go on being stiff, since the number of actual places per year is very small.

While many major firms and other organisations still have formal graduate recruitment programmes the numbers taken on each year have fallen sharply, and some may never go back to their 1970s levels. Others, particularly in the public sector, look likely to find it hard to compete for the kind of graduates they are after. The trend is increasingly away from taking on graduates on a once-a-year basis, to recruiting more as and when needed, although the CIVIL SERVICE, BANKS, the BBC, and larger firms still keep to the older system.

'First destination' figures do not, obviously, reflect the very latest trends, since they are inevitably somewhat out of date. However, the latest available (for 1985-6, published 1987) are at least some indication of trends.

	1985-6 (%)			1977-8 (%)		
	univ	poly	C/IHE	univ	poly	C/IHE
research/further study	10.0*	4.6	3.1	10.5	5.0	n/a
training	22.1	12.7	14.4	15.6	15.1	n/a
teacher	4.1	2.7	6.1	8.6	4.4	n/a
'believed' unemployed Dec 31	6.2	8.7	8.5	11.7	5.4	n/a
permanent UK employment	49.5	49.3	50.0	45.0	42.4	n/a
employers						
industry –	29.2	4.1	8.7	35.5	36.4	n/a
commerce	32.0	27.3	17.1	22.0	20.0	n/a
public service	25.2	18.7	12.6	26.0	19.3	n/a
education	5.6	10.5	48.9	5.2	17.4	n/a
functions –						
personnel/social work	21.1	10.3	6.7	21.0	9.5	n/a
financial work	18.1	13.3	5.5	15.0	9.1	n/a
admin/op management	9.3	9.6	8.4	7.8	3.5	n/a
marketing etc	7.9	8.8	6.9	6.5	6.5	n/a
management services	8.0	8.0	1.2	7.9	6.3	n/a
eng R&D etc	11.1	9.5	1.1			
scientific R&D etc	4.5	2.6	0.5	13.0	8.1	n/a
scientific/eng support etc	2.1	2.7	0.6	3.5	3.9	n/a
teaching/lecturing	3.2	8.9	47.2	2.9	5.0	n/a
environmental planning	3.4	9.3	1.4	5.0	12.4	n/a
creative, entertainment	2.2	6.6	8.7			
information/advisory etc	1.9	1.9	1.6	2.9	2.4	n/a
legal work	0.4	0.4	0.3	3.7	1.0	n/a

*16% in 1969-70

The polytechnics and colleges also analyse the destinations of students gaining a BTEC Higher National award –

	1985-6 (%)		1977-8 (%)	
	polytechnic	C/IHE	polytechnic	C/IHE
further education/training	25.0	10.5	18.1	n/a
first-degree course	14.7	3.8	5.6	n/a
professional qualification	3.9	1.9	4.8	n/a
research/further study	0.7	1.0	2.1	n/a
'other' vocational	5.7	3.0	5.3	n/a
'believed' unemployed Dec 31	8.1	6.6	4.1	n/a
permanent UK employment	40.0	50.6	38.0	n/a
employers –				
industry/commerce	79.6	77.2	79.5	n/a
engineering etc	35.0	34.1	25.6	n/a
construction etc	8.7	2.4	10.5	n/a
public service	12.4	9.0	14.1	n/a
education	2.1	2.0	153.0	n/a

Postgraduate qualifications

Nearly 20% of university graduates, 11% of polytechnic graduates, and over 14% of C/IHE graduates go straight on to further study when they have completed their degree courses. Some 52,600 full-time and 30,600 part-time postgraduate students were studying in universities in 1985-6 (the highest numbers ever and 3-4% up on the previous year), and over 5000 full-time and more than 7000 part-time in polytechnics (CNAA registered over 12,000 postgraduate students altogether in 1985-6). They do –

RESEARCH TRAINING involves a further three years full-time (or an equivalent in part-time work), studying/researching a topic – normally developing out of the student's first-degree subject – under supervision. The topic is studied/researched 'in depth', to the extent that the researcher is expected to produce something new and original which is a real 'contribution to knowledge'. The results have to be written up as a thesis, generally the length of a short book. This is assessed (and the researcher questioned on it), and a doctorate (PhD, DPhil etc) awarded if the work is of high enough standard. The time spent working for a PhD is treated as research 'training', although not all supervising departments give formal tuition.

It is also possible to spend a (calendar) year on a research project, which is a rather more modest effort, for an 'intermediate' master's degree. Some universities require students intending to work for a doctorate to register first for a master's degree, as a form of probationary period.

PhDs and other research degrees are awarded, like first degrees, either by universities or the CNAA. It is possible to work for a PhD in a university or polytechnic with the appropriate facilities, or in one of the research institutes of one of the research councils, some of which are based at universities. Universities, or CNAA, may also allow a PhD student to carry out their research elsewhere (eg in industry, a government research establishment), if the arrangements for supervision etc are suitable.

In theory it is possible to do research in almost any subject. In practice the problem is one of funding, and this is much easier to find to do research which has 'practical' value for industry. Some awards are tied to work at particular universities/polytechnics, either because the research/training being done there is approved by the grant-awarding body and/or, in social sciences, because they are successful at getting students to complete their thesis to time. After some very lean years, the number of available research grants did increase in 1986. It is still, though, probably essential to have a first-class honours degree to gain a research grant.

FURTHER ACADEMIC STUDY It is also possible to continue studying on what is called a master's degree by 'taught course' (to distinguish it from a research degree). If this is within the subject area of the student's first-degree course the course normally lasts a (calendar) year including up to three months spent on research or other project work. If the subject is new to the student the teaching institution may require a preliminary year, or only award a diploma.

Taught courses are available in almost every subject, and for a number of quite different purposes. Some allow students to study a topic from their first-degree subject in considerable 'depth'. Some are designed to give students high-level training in an applied area of their original degree subject, eg medical bio-chemistry. Some are designed as 'conversion' courses, eg to train physics graduates as electronics specialists, chemists as chemical engineers or in control and instrumentation, mathematicians as engineers. Extra awards may be available to increase the number of specialists in crucial subjects eg, bio-technology and information technology. Some courses, eg an MBA (Master of Business Administration), are mainly designed for graduates who have worked for some time. Master's degrees awarded on the results (usually an examination plus thesis) of a taught course are awarded also either by universities or the CNAA, which had 246 approved master's courses and 115 postgraduate diploma courses running in 1985-6 in a very wide range of subjects.

VOCATIONAL TRAINING Even for graduates, full-time training is normally essential for some occupations, eg ARCHIVE WORK, CAREERS ADVISORY WORK, CONSERVATION, LEGAL PROFESSION, LIBRARIANSHIP/INFORMATION SCIENCE, MUSEUM WORK, PLANNING, PSYCHOLOGY (CLINICAL AND EDUCATIONAL), SOCIAL WORK, TEACHING. For some other occupations it may be an advantages to have completed a course before looking for vacancies. Examples are ARTS ADMINISTRATION, BUSINESS STUDIES, COMPUTING/IT, JOURNALISM, LANGUAGES FOR BUSINESS, MARKETING, PERSONNEL WORK, SECRETARIAL AND SECRETARY-LINGUIST WORK. Some courses are 'taught' higher degrees (as above) at university or polytechnic; others are certificate or diploma courses at university, polytechnic or other colleges: yet others lead to the exams of professional bodies. Competition for some places, at eg law schools, can be considerable.

CAREER PROSPECTS for people with postgraduate qualifications vary, although the percentage of postgraduates who are still unemployed six months after completion of their studies has always been very low.

Because awards for most 'taught courses' are as tightly targeted as possible to potential demand from employers these, together with other vocational courses – which again are unlikely to run or attract grants if there are no jobs at the end of them – the career advantages are generally good.

Prospects are more problematic with a research degree. There are at present (1987) comparatively few vacancies for permanent teaching/research posts in higher education (it may be slightly easier to get a short-term contract) or other research organisations, for which a research degree is virtually essential. Industrial firms are increasing the proportion of first-degree graduates they take on for research, and reducing their intake of PhDs. There are very few other careers for which a research degree is actually needed. For work outside research, employers tend to be somewhat wary of people who have spent so long in a fairly 'rarified' academic environment. The answer seems to be to do research in an area likely to interest a potential employer – which is hard on arts and most social-science graduates, and even some scientists.

'First employment' percentages for postgraduates are

	1985-6 (%) university only	1977-8 (%) university only
further research/study/training	9.4	11.5
'believed' unemployed Dec 31	1.6	1.0
permanent UK employment	40.3	25.5
employers –		
education	40.6	31.0
public service	20.5	22.6
industry	24.2	33.3
commerce	8.7	6.8

[Nearly a third of postgraduates are overseas as students returning home.]

Academic and Vocational Studies and Where They Can Lead

Introduction   63
Arts/humanities   64
Creative and performing arts   84
Engineering and technology   94
Land use   205
Science   211
Social sciences   294

INTRODUCTION

The problems that even some of the most able young people have been having in finding career starts which match their ambitions have made them, with their parents, commentators, and politicians, increasingly and insistently question the value of even the most hallowed of academic subject studies. They want to know how a given qualification in a particular subject will, or will not, help them to achieve their goals. Pressure continues from all sides to make degree courses, traditionally purely intellectual training, more relevant to graduates' future employment needs, to increase numbers studying subjects with obvious vocational value, and reduce intake and output for the rest.

This may seem to make sound sense, given the economic needs of the country and the steadily-rising, even chronic, shortages of people with the needed technological training. But critics say there are severe risks in going too far along this road, and most recently (1986) there has been some recognition of this in the speeches of education ministers.

Academics have always claimed much for the general vocational value of the intellectual training they give to all graduates, whatever subject(s) they study, and the recruiting policies of many employers bear this out, in that so many career starts (almost 50% as of 1986) are open to graduates whatever their discipline. More, expert opinion suggests that, when 'fifth generation' information technology begins to take over, even before the end of the century, demand for some specific, graduate, skills could well decline sharply, both because the systems will probably provide much of the expertise and because the skills will date so rapidly. Recruiters are then likely to want graduates who are flexible and quick thinking, who can cope with and manage change; graduates with the abilities to select, assess and use complex information; who will analyse complex issues and report on them clearly and succinctly, and identify and solve problems. Detailed subject knowledge may become much less relevant.

However, it is only reasonable that students should be aware of the career implications of the subject they are considering, even if only to discover careers for which it is not a suitable qualification (as with conventional language degrees for careers in interpreting and translating), and to understand the need for further training after graduation.

Every qualification has two components: the level of the award and the subject in which it is awarded. For some careers the two must go together (an English degree to lecture in English), but for others one or other may be irrelevant – a professional entry requirement specifying two A-level passes (or their equivalent) but not the subjects, for example. With qualification in some subjects it is possible to follow a career developing out of that subject or to branch out in other directions – a chemistry graduate may go on to teaching or research in chemistry, or become any one of a number of other things, related or unrelated – a chemical engineer or an information scientist, for example. Just because of this, and because the connections are so difficult to make, the *Encyclopedia* examines academic qualifications in individual subjects with the occupations for which they are the main entry route, and tries to indicate the range of other occupations for which they are also suitable.

ARTS QUALIFICATIONS AND CAREERS

Introduction	64
Archaeology	65
Classics	71
English	72
History	73
Languages	76
Philosophy	81
Regional studies	82
Religious studies and theology	82

INTRODUCTION

The subjects defined as arts or humanities – English, Classics, history, languages, philosophy and so on – are 'academic' subjects, studied largely for their own 'sake', in a completely disinterested way. Except where studying languages means learning to use them in some way in daily life, or where any of these subjects are studied as a preliminary to a teaching or academic career, they have no obvious direct value in preparing people for work. Most academics, however, claim that studying one or two of these subjects for three years for a degree will give graduates intellectual skills which are valuable to employers (see also HIGHER EDUCATION above).

For most people, serious, formal study of these subjects ends at age sixteen. Only 19.5% of school leavers, just over 20,600, with two or more A-levels gained them both/all in arts subjects in 1983-4, down from 25.9% in 1973-4. A further 18.6%, 19,680, combined arts with social studies, also down from the 20.6% of 1973-4. Beyond O and A level arts subjects are, with few exceptions – mainly languages – studied full time only for degrees.

Some 59,100 students – postgraduate and first-degree – were studying arts subjects in UK universities in 1984-5. The numbers have been falling steadily since 1979-80 (the 1981-2 figure was nearly 62,600) but it is still is about 20% of the total. First degree students reading arts subjects at university numbered

51,700 in 1984-5 (down from 57,500 in 1981-2) – just over 21% of the total (against 22% in 1981-2). Of just over 15,400 students who started degree courses in arts in 1984-5 (down nearly 1400 on 1981-2), almost 76% had gained three or more A levels (against under 71% in 1981-2), about 7.4% had two A levels (against over 11% in 1981-2), just under 6% five or more SCE H grades, and 3% three or four H grades; 7.2% held 'other' qualifications. The mean grade point 'score' for A-level entrants was 11.3 for languages, 10.4 for other arts subjects.

In advanced further education – polytechnics and colleges – there were about 49,000 students (mostly working for degrees or similar qualifications) studying arts subjects (including music, drama, art and design) in 1984-5, making up almost 18% of the total. This is a major increase on the 37,600 of 1980-1, but numbers on courses in humanities other than languages have fallen recently.

What has been said earlier on graduate careers (under HIGHER EDUCATION), applies generally to arts graduates. However, it is probably not so easy for graduates who have read arts subjects than – say – for engineering graduates, to find a reasonable career start, despite a more buoyant market for high-calibre people. Of 15,671 people who graduated in arts subjects at universities in 1984-5, 1536 or 9.8% of the total, were 'believed' to be still unemployed six months after graduation (against 8.6% of all graduates), well down on the worst years of 1981-3. From polytechnics (same year), there were 4446 graduates in arts subjects, of whom about 11% were 'believed' unemployed six months after graduation, against 9.9% for all polytechnic graduates – again a very substantial improvement on the preceding years. For the immediate future, the position is expected to improve even further. Even during recession arts graduates fared better than school-leavers (see preceding chapter).

Even so, arts graduates must expect to graft vocational skills on to their academic achievements, in other words to gain training, either by further full-time study, or on the job with part-time study for a professional qualification. People reading arts subjects must still expect to face greater competition for the best first jobs, must be ready to consider a wider range of different kinds of work than graduates have accepted in the past, and must prepare for their careers much more carefully than was necessary in the 1970s.

ARCHAEOLOGY

Archaeology is, theoretically, both an academic subject to study for a degree and a possible career. However, there is only enough work in professional archaeology for at best one in ten of those who want it, and so very few who read archaeology at university can expect to become archaeologists. Luckily, many do not even plan to do so.

Archaeology does rather more than hunt for and save what is left of the past, even though much excavation today is so-called 'rescue' archaeology, which means working fast and in weeks rather than months or years under the shadow of bulldozers and concrete mixers before the remains vanish for ever under deep concrete foundations.

Archaeologists look for almost anything that is left of the past, from the rare royal burial to the more common – and often more valuable archaeologically

– rubbish dumps of ordinary people, to help build up a picture of life of the time.

Although much archaeological work concentrates on prehistoric and classical times, many archaeologists study later periods. They find and map lost medieval villages, chart the physical changes of historic towns – eg Winchester, York, and London – through the ages, or track down early industrial sites. Marine archaeology – eg raising Henry VIII's *Mary Rose* – is also expanding.

What archaeologists find tells them not only something new about the place they have excavated, but also produces evidence to fill gaps in, for example, our understanding of the way that Vikings lived, and may also help answer the larger question of how economic, technological and social changes took the human race from primitive hunter to astronaut in so short a time.

Archaeologists are scholastic detectives. Their evidence comes from the ground, from caves, from buildings and ruins. Like police detectives, they look for clues, not only amongst the objects which are conventionally considered 'archaeological', but also from their surroundings. Here are the 'fingerprints' of the past, in the state and different levels of soil, and all the minute particles, like long-preserved seeds and pollen, in it. Even plants now growing can hint at long-forgotten disturbance of the ground. The archaeologist's task, though, is tougher than the police detective's – the trail is often very old and the clues harder to find.

Archaeology has changed dramatically in the last thirty years, mainly due to new scientific techniques and methods, but also through new thinking on human history and what archaeology should be doing. The first major breakthrough came with radiocarbon dating, which uses the known rate of decay of the carbon-14 isotope to work out the age of the remains of living things. Finds are also dated by dendrochronology which can go back over 8000 years via the yearly growth rings in tree trunks, thermoluminescence, and magnetic methods.

Physical and chemical techniques are used to decide on the properties of finds, so helping to identify and date artefacts and where they came from. Physicists, for instance, can bombard ancient beads with neutrons in an atomic reactor to show the tiny chemical differences in their make-up, making it possible to work out where they were made. Macroanalysers use x-ray beams to identify what and how much of each metal is in an object without damaging it. Gas-liquid chromatography can identify animal fats left in prehistoric cooking pots. Very high resolution microscopes analyse the 'scars' on prehistoric flints and other tools, to work out what they were used for.

Biological techniques are used to study visible or microscopic plant or animal remains – scanning-electron microscopy, for instance, to identify stray seeds trapped in a clay pot, and do pollen counts. Soils, sediments, rocks can be analysed to show (for example), where the blue stones of Stonehenge came from (but not so far how they were moved there).

Aerial photography, scanning magnometers, soil-sounding radar and even satellites can detect not only hidden 'treasure', but also soil disturbances, so indicating where it would be most productive to dig. Computers help map, classify, sort out and analyse finds or soil measurements to help decide where or what to dig next, and to test theories on, for example, trading patterns, based on the numerical distribution of particular tools, or domestic items like pots. Computers are used to produce a three-dimensional picture of a building from the remaining ruins.

Long-held theories on how civilisation developed – based on the belief that agriculture, metal working, building technology etc, first developed in the Middle East, and only then spread out along trade routes, by migration and invasion into Europe – were shown by scientists and anthropologists to be inaccurate. Europe's prehistoric people, we now know, were quite capable of working out for themselves how to build tombs, grow plants, domesticate animals, and work metals.

Archaeological method was not, clearly, scientific or rigorous enough, so archaeologists have now sharply improved techniques for collecting and interpreting evidence. They conduct experiments, and use mathematical and statistical analytical techniques and much tougher testing methods for better thought through hypotheses. It may seem just fun for archaeologists to make flint axes (and try to cut up dead elephants with them), farm with primitive tools, grow early wheat or sail in primitive boats, but by so doing they can find out what the tools can and cannot do, test the fertility and measure the harvest of wheat, and so make more realistic calculations about prehistoric economies.

This so-called 'new' archaeology also tries to decide what questions to ask, eg why sheep and goats were domesticated and not deer, and what information is needed to answer them. In other words the emphasis is less on describing finds and more on building 'models' of life in the past, and on why, for instance, cave paintings, were made. Some archaeologists, for example, have been looking for evidence of what prehistoric people ate – were they totally meat-eating or did they also eat plant-crops earlier than has been thought? 'New' archaeologists try to make deductions about, and explain the minds of, the people of the past.

Scientific and anthropological thinking have produced more breeds of archaeologist. Environmental archaeologists take a much wider view of the past than is traditional, by studying the way people have exploited and manipulated the area in which they live, and the way they interacted with the environment: for example, did men and women first deliberately plant wheat as a crop, or did wild wheat seed itself in the first man-made woodland clearings?

There are always disagreements – between, for archaeologists, the scientific and historical approaches. At the extreme, some scientists want to treat Stonehenge as a prehistoric computer, while traditional archaeologists continue to believe it to be a religious site. In Britain, anyway, historically-thinking archaeologists outnumber the newer breeds. There are also archaeologists who want a social purpose for their work, like the British excavators of an Inca valley in Peru who hunted for the crops the Incas grew, and how to help the people living there now.

Preserving historic sites and objects is a popular cause today, but does not necessarily produce jobs – archaeological work is mostly paid for from public funds and so the number of posts is mostly linked to government economic priorities rather than to public interest in the past (although property developers are now contributing more than they did). Archaeologists find it difficult, therefore, to decide on priorities on a logical and long-term basis. A high proportion of available resources has to go into 'rescue' archaeology, finding out as much as possible about a site before it is developed. Long-term studies do continue, as in York, but there has been no really serious expansion in this kind of work for some time. Increasingly, archaeologists must try to catch the public imagination – the York re-creation of Viking life is successfully helping to fund posts.

Of course excavations go on in other parts of the world – Africa and South America as well as Europe and the Mediterranean basin. Despite some major projects, eg re-creating an Inca city in Peru (financed by British industry), it has been said that British archaeology tends to be too inward-looking and insular, although of course work overseas has to be shared with archaeologists from other countries.

Working in archaeology

Excavating, though, is only part of archaeological work. As much, if not more, time is spent analysing and assessing the evidence, writing reports, etc, as well as on planning projects and trying to raise the finance for them. Some archaeologists spend all their time assessing and re-assessing the finds of over a century, without ever excavating anything themselves.

Archaeological research involves close collaboration between experts and digging teams. The excavation (which can last years or be a race against developers) team may include several archaeologists, since most specialise, at least one of them being a conservationist. With them can be, on a large party, a geologist, an ecologist, a botanist, a plant geneticist, a zoologist, an anthropologist, even a geographer and a sociologist. Other experts may be needed – civil engineers, skilled divers, for example.

After first-aid treatment on site, finds go to laboratories, where cleaning, recording, dating, analysing, and classifying is supervised by archaeologists, but since they cannot acquire all the necessary expertise, they need other specialists, particularly scientists.

Archaeology combines the scholastic life of the desk, library and laboratory with a variable amount of what is usually quite rugged field work. Conditions on 'digs' can be difficult, even dangerous, with a lot of mud and extremes of weather. Excavations can be in remote areas where archaeologists live in a caravan or tent, or on an inner-city building site. On site, most painstaking manual work is done by volunteers and supervised directly by trained people, but all archaeologists expect to do their share of patient extraction of a fine fragment from the bottom of a deep, wet hole, although mostly they plan, direct, observe, measure, and supervise.

Most professional archaeologists combine research with university teaching: there are, though, probably no more than 175 posts in departments of archaeology – the staff of the London Institute of Archaeology is the largest at about 30, but six or so is the average; there are also a few posts in, eg classics, history and oriental studies departments. Others work for MUSEUMS, where their time is divided between being a museum keeper or curator and an archaeologist.

The main permanent, full-time archaeological posts are in local authority or university field units, some of which double as regional units (of which there are eight) and/or 'rescue' units. The GLC's unit had some 350 staff, the City of London about 50, but Leicestershire's unit has only nine full-time people, and Lancashire and Cumbria's, based on Lancaster University, only two. Most counties have archaeological officers who (with their staff) decide what work to do with available funds, record archaeological discoveries, try to protect known sites, and get something done where a site is going to be disturbed for some reason.

Rescue archaeology has produced the most work recently, but is very vulnerable to cuts in public expenditure. There are some 150 full-time rescue organisations, which at peak employed over 1600 people, but only 40% of them were estimated to have any kind of job security at all, and only about 15% an effective career structure or real security.

The small number of posts in the CIVIL SERVICE are in national museums, and the Ordnance Survey. The English Heritage Commission administers government grants for rescue archaeology (currently being spent mainly on study and publication of past work though), houses the ancient monuments laboratory, and has an archaeological 'flying squad' (see also CONSERVATION).

Many archaeologists, particularly those who specialise in excavation work, 'freelance', moving from project to project. Several hundred are believed to support themselves throughout the year in this way, although the 'pay' many receive is described as expenses and is often barely a living wage. With unemployment still high, the Manpower Services Commission supports staff on particular excavations, but these are only short-term contracts.

Science-based archaeology is supported by the Science and Engineering Research Council (SERC). About 20 university-based research projects are under way at any one time, and SERC offers around nine research and two or three university-museum/government department co-operative studentships each year.

PUBLISHING, JOURNALISM, and BROADCASTING have occasional vacancies but they are rare and normally filled by established archaeologists.

Archaeologists are generally pessimistic about career prospects. There was certainly a modest increase in the number of jobs during the 1970s, mainly in local authorities, but several hundred have been lost since.

Archaeology employs quite a number of technicians. They work on conserving and repairing objects, as draughtsmen and women, in surveying and photography, and as laboratory assistants. In all except the first of these they usually start out as surveyors, photographers or laboratory technicians, and go into archaeological work later.

Recruitment and entry is normally via a good honours degree, not necessarily in archaeology, although one is increasingly useful. People do, though, find their way into archaeology, normally via a postgraduate course at some stage, from a surprisingly wide range of other subjects – not only history, anthropology, classics, but also the sciences, and even art history and geography.

Archaeologists have to be academically very able, good at – and interested in – intellectual problem solving, to work on and interpret what is found in the field. Reasonable numeracy and some scientific background are needed to be able to use scientific method and interpret results. Working knowledge of at least one language, German rather than French, is an advantage. Archaeologists need imagination, and to be painstaking, meticulous and careful, patient and practical, good at observing and detailed work.

Studying archaeology/qualifications and training This can be formal or informal. Mainly at –
Professional/graduate level Most archaeologists study archaeology at university and/or complete postgraduate courses. Some 275 students gained places in 1985-6. The mean grade point 'score' at A level was 9.2 in 1984-5.

Although there are not that many courses, the choice is considerable. Many emphasise scientific aspects, and a few specialise in conservation. Some courses are biased to environmental and 'new' archaeology. Others concentrate on the classical period.
Degree courses, all at university (with one exception), are at –
Belfast[1], Birmingham[2], Bradford[1], Bristol[1][2], Cambridge (with anthropology – and option to specialise in Assyriology or Egyptology in Oriental studies), Cardiff: UC (conventional archaeology course and one specialising in conservation; includes environmental archaeology); Durham (archaeology with environmental option, also option in Egyptology); Edinburgh[3]; Exeter[3]; Glasgow[3]; Leicester; Liverpool[3] (specialising in eastern Mediterranean, the middle ages, or Egyptian); London: UCL/Institute of Archaeology (several courses: can emphasise Roman, prehistoric, or human environment studies, conservation, classical or western Asia) – with KQC, QMC, and with SOAS African archaeology; Manchester[2]; Newcastle; Nottingham; Reading; Sheffield (emphasises prehistory); Southampton (emphasises role in understanding human development); York (emphasises principles and method).
At polytechnic: North-East London[1] (evening only).
Archaeology can also be combined with another subject at most of the above, and at Bangor and Lampeter.
[1]   stresses scientific aspects   [2]   classical   [3]   mainly historical
'First destination' figures are –

	1984-5 university only	1977-8 university only
total graduating	322	238
research/further study	49	43
teacher training	6	10
'other' training	12	10
'believed' unemployed Dec 31	38	26
short-term employment	23	44
permanent employment	135	52
employers –		
local government[1]	26	15
commerce	30	8
industry	11	3
civil service	21	8

	1984-5 university only	1977-8 university only
university	12	2
cultural/leisure etc	1	13
functions –		
research/information etc	58	29
admin/operational management	15	7
personnel/social work	14	nil
marketing etc	15	1
financial work	9	6
management services	2	1

[1] still well up on 1974-5 (when it was only seven), and probably showing the growth of local-authority rescue units and museum work.

Professional qualification The Council for British Archaeology (CBA) sets examinations for a diploma in archaeological practice. At sub-degree level, the diploma exams consist of seven separate certificate papers, four of which must be passed for an ordinary-level diploma, all seven for the higher. Candidates must be at least 18, but there is no formal academic entry requirement.

For technicians, London: Institute of Archaeology has a three-year course in conservation of archaeological materials (A-level physics or chemistry needed). Dorset IHE (Bournemouth) has a BTEC HND course in practical archaeology.

Further information from the Council for British Archaeology (free leaflets, priced books, journal etc), and 'Rescue', the British Archaeological Trust (sixth-form conferences etc).

CLASSICS

Although a purely academic subject, with teaching, academic or museum work, or perhaps archaeology offering only a few openings which are directly relevant, much has always been claimed for a classical education as a preparation for high-level careers. Classics has been one of the traditional entry routes to a career in government administration, and the computer industry considers a degree in Classics evidence of the right kind of intellectual ability for programming, systems analysis etc.

Studying Classics Classics (Greek and/or Latin in varying proportions but usually both) can be studied at many universities but the number of courses is falling. Academics have radically reformed degree-course syllabuses to bring them closer to the modern courses being taught in schools. Many universities teaching Classics now also offer courses for complete novices, since so many schools no longer teach Greek or Latin. They also provide courses on classical civilization and literature which can be taken by those who do not wish to study the languages in any depth. Classics are not taught at all by polytechnics or colleges of higher education.

'First destination' figures are –

	1984-5 university only	1977-8 university only
total graduating	526	383
research/further study	42	37
teacher training	37	65
'other' training (eg law)	74	26
'believed' unemployed Dec 31	63	16
short-term employment	24	22
permanent UK employment	192	45
employers –		
commerce (excl finance)	39	12
accountancy	34	37
banking/insurance	31	17
industry	20	24
civil service	16	12
local government	13	12
culture/leisure etc	9	8
universities	7	3
functions –		
financial work	54	60
admin/operational management	27	31
marketing etc	27	6
personnel/social work	18	8
management services	18	10
legal work	nil	11

Entry: conventional Classics courses require A-level Latin and Greek if possible. Nearly 620 students were accepted to read Classics in 1985. The mean grade A-level 'score' for 1984 entry was 11.6.

ENGLISH

Most English degree courses centre on critical analysis of literary (and some linguistic) texts, ideas and theories with endless discussion and essay work. It is a training, through reading and practice, in personal critical judgement. Some courses teach creative writing, but except for TEACHING, and the rare openings for literary editors, or academic work in higher education, English is not a direct preparation for any career other than academic work/teaching.

Studying English English can be studied at all but seven universities; English as a single-subject is taught at seven polytechnics and it is a major field of study in arts/humanities courses in well over a dozen, as well as a major option in many 'liberal arts' degrees at colleges of higher education. The range and variety of courses is considerable, with plenty of choice between different approaches. English can be studied alone or in combination with any one of number of other subjects, studied comparatively with European or American literature; mostly courses emphasise literature, but it is possible to specialise in linguistic aspects.

'First destination' figures are –

	1984-5 university	1984-5 polytechnic	1977-8 university	1977-8 polytechnic
total graduating	2755	338	2894	105
research/further study	215	25	280	4
teacher training	297	25	560	14
'other' training (eg law)	297	28	232	2
'believed' unemployed Dec 31	295	59	161	11
overseas employment	74	1	94	1
short-term UK employment	140	36	235	10
permanent UK employment	839	81	725	23
employers –				
commerce (excl finance)	263	24	140	3
industry	94	11	100	2
local government	83	10	121	3
civil service	68	6	53	3
banking/insurance	67	7	26	nil
accountancy	52	nil	3	1
higher/further education	48	3	40	1
culture/leisure	42	3	154	8
schools	24	4	28	2
functions –				
marketing etc	147	12	104	1
financial work	127	5	58	1
admin/ops management	115	11	150	2
personnel/social work	103	nil	87	1
research, advisory etc	54	4	73	1
management services	15	4	22	2

Entry: English at A level is usually required, and some departments like a language. Some 2800 students were accepted for university degree courses, about 480 for CNAA courses in 1985. The mean grade A-level 'score' for universities was 11.8 in 1984.

HISTORY
Very few people who read history can, or even want, to become professional historians, and opportunities to become one are now at an all-time low. History, though, is generally seen as a reasonable basis for many non-academic careers.

Working as a historian
Professional historians never expect to discover the whole 'truth' about any aspect of the past, and are never really satisfied that the last word has been said. They can usually work on any aspect of the past that interests them, such as European trade in the later middle ages, the English working classes, modern Sino-Japanese relations, early Islamic history – all examples of topics being researched by individual historians. They may try to find answers to questions other historians failed to answer, or re-examine the answers given by

others in the light of new evidence, make new analyses of older evidence, or just try to show greater insight.

Historians work on factual evidence, and first try to discover as nearly as possible what actually happened. But they are just as, if not more, interested in causes, effects, and trends. They not only chart political events, wars, kings and governments and their struggles for power, but also how people of all kinds lived, worked and thought; they are interested in social structures, eg the feudal system – in fact the whole complex interplay of cultural, political, economic, social, technological and religious development over the centuries, to analyse, for instance, the many strands which caused the industrial revolution to happen when it did.

Historians work where possible from original and other documentary sources, such as the state papers of king and their chancellors; government records, and parliamentary papers and reports; church records (eg parish registers and the reports of medieval inquisitors on heretical villages); Norse sagas and medieval chronicles; memoirs and papers of individuals; the output of contemporary biographers and diarists; political and other pamphlets and records of speeches; even the work of playwrights, novelists and poets. The records of trade, agricultural and industrial output, of employers and trade unions; statistics of all kinds – from how many people were born and died to migration figures and so on, popular literature and broadsheets, are all used in historical evidence.

Documentary evidence is, however, often incomplete, and not only in the distant past: the telephone has created great gaps in the written evidence of the 20th century. Documentary evidence can often be one-sided or actually biased – people who could write rarely put down anything about the majority who could not; many of the people who wrote official records documented their own views (so historians usually treat this kind of evidence as opinion not fact). Records may only be made years after the event when memories have faded, and so on.

Historians must, then, look elsewhere for other evidence, or evidence to prove or disprove doubtful records – from ARCHAEOLOGY; from philology (which, by analysing the language of English place names can chart the spread of Danes and Norsemen through Britain). Historians take into account the work of scholars in other disciplines, eg economists (on, for example, early 19th century industry and working conditions), and anthropologists. Like other scholars, historians use statistical techniques and the computer, to analyse evidence on, for instance, the age at which women first marry in studies of population changes.

While historians make up their own minds on topics they are researching – and at least one contemporary historian admits relying on intuition as much as on documentary research – they usually test their own findings against those of other historians, and deliberately look for flaws in the arguments. Historians spend a lot of time in libraries; read many books, articles, reports, opinions, discussions, and get involved in debates, disagreements and controversy about past events.

Most professional historians combine historical research with teaching in university or polytechnic, and since communication is an important part of history, it is generally a happy combination. Just a few historians can make a living editing books or journals. Most historians specialise in teaching a particular period of history.

Studying history History is taught at first degree level at all but five universities and all but six polytechnics, and is a major option in some liberal arts degrees in colleges of higher education. Almost all courses are based on European and British history (because it is easier to teach methods and analysis through material that is familiar and dealing with a culture which is easily understandable). Even so, so it is possible to bias studies to ancient, mediaeval or modern history. Some courses include options in non-European history, but only London, Oxford (in Oriental studies) and Sussex offer courses which concentrate on other parts of the world.

'First destination' figures are –

| | 1984-5 | | 1977-8 | |
	university	polytechnic	university	polytechnic
total graduating	2484	142	2482	52
research/further study	184	11	210	1
teacher training	208	8	460	1
'other' training (eg law)	269	8	200	1
'believed' unemployed Dec 31	242	24	136	7
overseas employment	56	nil	66	2
short-term UK employment	130	11	201	13
permanent UK employment	929	41	773	10
employers –				
commerce (excl finance)	182	8	140	2
accountancy	156	2	70	nil
banking/insurance	142	4	77	3
industry	111	3	127	1
local government	102	7	100	2
civil service	81	8	8	nil
higher/further education	33	1	50	1
cultural/leisure	13	1	80	nil
schools	12	nil	11	nil
functions –				
financial work	299	9	179	2
admin/ops management	154	2	182	1
marketing etc	114	4	92	1
personnel	96	nil	63	1
research/advisory etc	56	5	81	nil
management services	25	2	22	1

Entry: Most candidates have history at A level, but in fact many universities do not actually require it. Many do want students to have language qualifications at least to at least 16-plus† and preferably A level. Nearly 2800 students were accepted for university degree courses in 1984-5, about 280 started CNAA degree courses. The 1984 mean A-level grade 'score' for universities was 11.3.

LANGUAGES

A language qualification does not, by or in itself, qualify for a career as a linguist. The section on TRANSLATING, INTERPRETING AND WORKING WITH LANGUAGES explains that rather more is needed. Language courses after school range across the spectrum from purely academic to completely practical.

Degree courses There are two different kinds of degree courses in languages. By far the larger group consists of traditional-style courses which concentrate on literature and literary language; the much smaller group is made up of courses which teach the kind of language used in everyday working life, and links this to subjects other than literature which could form the basis of a career 'using' the language(s) learnt.

Generally the standard of 'practical' language teaching on degree courses, training graduates to communicate with people who use the language all the time, has been rising steadily. Most universities and polytechnics now have language laboratories, and on most courses students are expected to (or can) spend a year in the country (or countries) where the language(s) they are studying are spoken.

Traditional-style courses are, though, not designed to provide the level of linguistic competence needed to work in the language and so are still rarely high enough (and standards of fluency that students reach vary considerably from department to department) without additional training and experience. Further, a career which 'uses' languages demands a second set of skills and knowledge of use to an employer, and courses that concentrate on literature do not and cannot provide this. The exceptions are TEACHING, and possibly literary translation – although this demands other skills too, and the number of openings is infinitesimal. However, some employers now need people who can use specific languages (a current example is Japanese in the financial sector), so badly that they will recruit graduates from the most academically-biased courses, if they have the right aptitudes.

Typical, traditionally academic-style modern language degree courses involve studying one or two languages and their literature, or one language and its literature combined with another subject. It cannot be emphasised too strongly that these courses inevitably concentrate largely on teaching the language of literature – the language of the playwright, the novelist, and the poet, and more often than not the language of the very best writers, who will usually have written not only in a literary style but in an earlier century. This language is always very different from that used by today's business men and women, lawyers, accountants, industrialists, journalists, economists, scientists and engineers. While these courses can obviously bring the graduate to a reasonable level of competence in one or more languages, they cannot be more than a useful back-up skill.

Robbins pinpointed the need for a new kind of language course as long ago as 1963: 'the traditional honours course is not designed to meet the more practical needs and interests of many young people who would like to be able to speak and read languages fluently'. The report recommended courses involving the study of two or three modern languages, with the emphasis on oral fluency, translation and interpreting combined with the study of the relevant background of the countries concerned.

In the twenty-three years since Robbins, universities, polytechnics and colleges have produced a variety of different kinds of courses – although perhaps not so many as Robbins would have liked.

Some of these courses concentrate almost entirely on the skills needed by a professional translator or interpreter, teaching at least two languages and appropriate background studies. Some courses integrate languages with business studies. Some combine linguistic training with a subject like law which is studied with reference to Western Europe as a whole, or with the technological background to particular industries. These courses are all based on language departments, so the emphasis is on language.

Since Britain joined the EEC, courses have also been developed which integrate a professional subject with a language, and in some instances providing training in the professional subject which allows the graduate to practise in two countries. Law is a major example of this, offering pre-professional training in English and French (or German, Italian or Spanish) law with the language to the level of practical competence, but it does mean reading law with a language rather than the other way round.

Graduates who have taken such a 'practical' language course usually have no problems in finding relevant work, and their skills are generally in considerable demand, not least among Europe-based companies. However, these courses are not 'soft' options. Learning techniques like interpreting and translating, or studying the law of England and another country in sufficient depth to practise in them as well as learning the language, can be very hard work, and requires high-level aptitude for languages.

Between the two extremes are a range of language courses, at both university and polytechnic, where there is a greater emphasis than is traditional on achieving real competence in the day-to-day use of languages, but which do not train in interpreting and translating techniques; some of these still concentrate on literary or social studies, but others have broader syllabuses, particularly in the less commonly taught languages – a higher proportion of Russian courses, for example, study the USSR as it is today than do those in French or German.

Virtually any language, with the possible exception of Icelandic, can be studied on a first degree course. Obviously many students prefer the languages they know best, and in the context of life in the EEC French and/or German are likely to be of increasing value for the foreseeable future. But there are other languages which can usefully be studied. Holland, for example, is also a member of the EEC, yet few people study Dutch (which is taught at only three universities). Arabic, Chinese and Japanese are languages now in demand from employers; African languages in contemporary use are rarely considered. Anyone who has studied the languages not now regularly learnt in Britain could hold highly-marketable skills, whichever type of degree is chosen. Demand for language teachers in schools or higher/further education is at present fairly low, but this may change.

There is no disadvantage in beginning a new language at university or polytechnic. Anyone showing real aptitude for language study at A level should not find it too tough. Where languages are not normally taught at school, most universities and polytechnics have specially-designed and intensive first year courses for beginners. Otherwise, candidates are normally expected to have A-level passes in the language(s) they plan to study, sometimes also English literature or history, and Classical languages at O level.

Most universities and some polytechnics teach some languages, more usually French, and German, but quite a few Italian and Spanish too. There is still a significant number of Russian courses, even though some have been closed. There has been a modest expansion in the number of 'applied' courses recently.

Courses providing the basis for a language-related career include, at

Universities –

Bangor:	German language & modern Germany
Bath:	European studies (French and/or German, French and Spanish, plus subsidiary Italian or Russian)
Birmingham, Aston:	Modern languages (French and/or German with option to include Japanese as a subsidiary) or International business with French or German
Bradford:	European studies (French or German); Modern languages (two of French, German, Russian, Spanish); or Management studies and French
Canterbury, Kent:	European management studies (France or Germany)
Edinburgh:	Business studies & French, German or Spanish
Edinburgh, Heriot-Watt:	Languages (interpreting/translating) – two of French, German, Russian, Spanish
Glasgow, S'clyde:	Marketing with modern languages
Guildford, Surrey:	Linguistic & international studies (French, German, or Russian, with special study of economics, international relations or law, and for some, subsidiary language which may be Swedish)
Lancaster:	Accounting or marketing with French, German or (accounting only) Spanish
Loughborough:	Business administration with a foreign language
Manchester, UMIST:	Computational linguistics or European studies & modern languages (two of, French, German, Spanish)
Norwich, E Anglia:	French & German with business studies or interpreting & translating
Salford:	Modern languages (two of French, German, Hispanic studies or Spanish, Italian)
Stirling:	French or German & accountancy, management science or marketing

| Swansea: | Two languages (from French, German, Italian, Russian, Spanish, Welsh) with business studies; European business studies (France or Germany) |

Polytechnics/colleges –

Brighton:	Applied language (emphasises French)
Bristol:	Modern languages (2 from French, German, Spanish), or Modern languages with information systems
Coventry:	Modern languages (2 from French, German, Spanish)
Leeds:	European languages & institutions (main language from French, German, Spanish, with complementary from these or Dutch, Italian, Portuguese), or European finance & accounting (German only)
Liverpool:	Modern language studies (2 of French, German, Russian, Spanish)
London, Ealing:	Applied language studies (3 from French, German, Russian, Spanish, with English option for non-native speakers)
London, PCL:	Modern languages (2 of Arabic, Chinese, French, German, Italian, Russian, Spanish)
London, Middx:	European business administration (French, German or Spanish based)
London, NLP:	Contemporary European studies (French or German)
London, S Bank:	Modern languages with international studies (2 of French, German, Spanish)
Newcastle:	Modern languages & economic or political studies (2 from French, German, Russian, Spanish)
Nottingham, Trent:	European business (French or German based)
Portsmouth:	French &/or German studies, Hispanic & French studies, Latin-American studies, Russian & Soviet studies, Russian & French or German, Spanish or Spanish & Latin-American studies
Wolverhampton:	Modern languages (2 from French, German, Russian, Spanish with introductory Italian, Portuguese or Swedish), or Languages for business

As an alternative, a growing number of universities and polytechnics let students combine another vocationally-'useful' subject, such as engineering, a science, economics, with one or more languages.

'First employment' figures, for all language graduates, are –

| | 1984-5 | | 1977-8 | |
	university	polytechnic	university	polytechnic
total graduating	5790	864	5385	475
research/further study	275	23	200	14
teacher training	617	53	700	50

| | 1984-5 | | 1977-8 | |
	university	polytechnic	university	polytechnic
'other' training (eg law)	719	97	500	52
'believed' unemployed Dec 31	522	103	235	55
overseas employment	516	86	235	41
short-term UK employment	243	43	342	40
permanent UK employment	1913	235	980	132
employers –				
commerce (excl finance)	477	73	150	27
industry	332	49	218	27
banking/insurance	266	21	123	12
accountancy	185	8	78	1
civil service	164	36	120	10
local government	129	18	86	7
university/FE	64	8	79	3
(school) teaching	50	2	32	4
functions –				
financial work	431	25	207	12
marketing etc	376	47	176	25
admin/operational man	314	54	194	26
personnel, social work	149	5	52	10
information, library work	119	13	130	10
management services	87	3	52	4

Entry: most language departments want evidence of aptitude, usually via at least one, and preferably two, languages at A level. About 4080 students were accepted for university modern language courses in 1985, nearly 2000 for CNAA degrees.

Other courses Most other courses concentrate on teaching the hard practicalities of using – speak, write, work in – one or more languages. While there are many useful 'ad hoc' courses concentrating on just one language in both public-sector and private colleges, some leading to formal examination and qualification, the most valuable in career terms combine language training with other skills, usually some form of business training, which may be secretarial, although at least one university business school now provides intensive tuition in a wide range of languages for managerial people.

Qualifications for which courses are widely available include –

Institute of Linguists' examinations in a wide range of languages at five different levels from preliminary (beginner/learning for pleasure) through to final, which is at degree-level but with a practical/vocational bias. Courses put on by FE colleges throughout the country.

BTEC HND in business studies with language option at polytechnics: Hatfield, London: City, S Bank, Newcastle, Plymouth, Pontypridd: Wales, Preston: Lancs, Sheffield, Teesside; colleges: Chelmsford: Essex IHE, Derby CHE,

Gloucester CA&T, High Wycombe: Bucks CHE, Hull: Humberside CHE, Newport: Gwent CHE, Norwich CF&HE, Richmond C, Salford CT, Southampton CHE, Swansea: W Glam IHE.

Royal Society of Arts/London Chamber of Commerce: set range of examinations mainly for secretary-linguistics but also now more generally for office staff.

See also INTERPRETING AND TRANSLATING

PHILOSOPHY

As taught in British universities, philosophy does not just study the work of individual philosophers and schools of philosophy, it also aims to train students to think for themselves, and to examine critically the ideas used outside philosophy, either in everyday life or in specialist fields. Although philosophy has no direct value in career preparation, like other arts subjects, it is supposed to train in independent thinking, critical analysis and logical thought and should allow graduates to offer a trained mind.

Studying philosophy Philosophy is taught for first degrees in a majority of universities, either as a single honours subject or combined with another, which can (for instance) be a science, so teaching how to apply philosophical techniques to scientific thinking.
'First employment' figures are –

	1984-5 university only	1977-8 university only
total graduating	454	400
research/further study	58	54
teacher training	6	15
'other' training (eg law)	25	12
'believed' unemployed Dec 31	65	47
overseas employment	12	9
short-term UK employment	20	28
permanent UK employment	114	103
employers –		
commerce/industry	50	50
local government	16	20
accountancy	9	15
civil service	9	9
education	7	9
culture/leisure	5	10
functions –		
financial work	25	23
personnel/social work	16	13
marketing	15	10
creative/entertainment	13	nil
admin/ops management	9	14
management services	8	19
research/information	2	4

No school subjects prepare for a degree course in philosophy and so rarely any specific course requirements, although a language (and possibly logic) can be useful. Some 385 UK students were accepted for university degree courses in 1985. The mean A-level 'score' was 9.7 in 1984-5.

REGIONAL OR AREA STUDIES

There was great enthusiasm in the 1960s for developing courses which allowed students to make integrated studies of coherent areas of the world, although London University has had two schools specialising in studies of particular areas – the Schools of Oriental and African Studies, and Slavonic and East European Studies – since the early 1900s. Most courses introduced in the 1960s continue, but it is no longer an expanding area of study.

The vocational value of these degrees is probably no greater than that of traditional modern language courses, but in some areas the number of graduates is so small that some should be able to find posts related to their degree subject if they so wish, especially if one or more languages are studied to complete fluency.

Examples of these courses are European studies at a number of universities and polytechnics, some of which are biased to industrial or technological studies (for example, Bradford); African studies (at Birmingham and the London School of Oriental and African Studies, and the 'contextual' studies in the Sussex University School of African and Asian Studies); East European Studies (BSocSc or BCom in Russian studies at Birmingham; Russian studies at Sussex, in addition to the courses at London: SSEES); Hispanic studies at twelve universities and one polytechnic; Latin American studies at Essex, London (UCL) and Portsmouth Polytechnic; Scandinavian studies at Norwich; E Anglia, Hull, London: UC; South East Asian studies at Hull, Kent and the School of Oriental and African Studies (London); and Middle East Studies at Durham.

RELIGIOUS STUDIES AND THEOLOGY

For anyone seeking ordination to the Christian ministry, theology is a vocational training, but theology and the wider discipline of religious studies are also said to have a great deal to offer (to those who are interested) in terms of a deeper understanding of particular cultural traditions.

Until relatively recently studies at undergraduate level were restricted to Christianity and the theology associated with it, but in the 1970s the boundaries of the discipline were expanded to take in other major religions too. However, the influence of Christianity has been so all-pervasive for so long that the major part of almost all courses is devoted to its study, but in more general religious studies degrees it is set into historical and comparative perspective. Joint honours courses frequently link the two subjects studied – for example, at Leeds, students taking Arabic specialise in Islam in the religious studies half of their course.

One result of the expansion of religious studies courses has been that not all exempt from the general bible paper for Church of England ordination examinations. Those which do are theology courses at Birmingham, Bristol, Cambridge, Cardiff, Durham, Exeter, Hull, Kent, Lampeter, Leeds, London, Manchester, Nottingham, and Oxford, and biblical studies at Bangor, Manchester and Sheffield.

Broader courses in religious studies (and variants thereof) are taught at Bristol, Cardiff, Lampeter, Lancaster, Leeds, London: KQC, Manchester, Newcastle, and Stirling Universities.

Outside the universities, there are now degree courses for those training for particular ministries – mainly at specialist colleges (Bristol: Trinity, London Bible, Oak Hill, Oxford: Westminster, Spurgeon's), and in Jewish studies at Jews' College (London). Many colleges of higher education and several polytechnics also include religious studies in their BEd and liberal arts degree courses which have developed from courses provided for teachers in training.

All graduates gain some exemption from the training requirements of their particular churches according to the subject read (see under RELIGIOUS ORGANISATIONS AND SERVICES). Most theological colleges are affiliated to a nearby university, and their qualifications are university awards. Where feasible, theological colleges make use of the facilities of their 'parent' universities, and students can usually study right through to a higher degree.

'First employment' figures are –

	1984-5 university only	1977-8 university only
total graduating	659	600
research/further study	45	80
teacher training	97	133
'other' training		
(eg for the ministry)	105	121
'believed' unemployed at Dec 31	34	18
overseas employment	19	14
permanent UK employment	227	165
employers –		
commerce	29	11
civil service	19	6
local government	14	14
education	13	11
industry	11	10
functions –		
pastoral/social work etc	129	97
admin/ops management	19	13
marketing etc	18	4
financial work	17	4
research/advisory etc	3	27

Entry: Institutions do not normally set particular A-level subjects, but a classical language, preferably Greek, is the most useful. Membership of a particular church, or indeed any church, is not normally needed, although some college courses are based on the teachings of one of them. Some 625 students were accepted for university degree courses in 1985, about 140 for CNAA courses. The mean A-level 'score' for university was 9.7 in 1984.

See also RELIGIOUS ORGANISATIONS AND SERVICES

CREATIVE AND PERFORMING ARTS QUALIFICATIONS AND CAREERS

Introduction   84
Art and design   85
Dance   87
Drama   87
Media and communication studies   89
Music   91

INTRODUCTION

Formal courses devoted to the academic study (in addition or as opposed to the practice) of the creative and performing arts – art, dance, drama, music, and the related areas like media studies, are a relatively recent phenomenon. Training for careers in these arts has, traditionally, been given in colleges and schools specialising in them, and so completely separately from universities and even polytechnics.

However, since the 1970s the trend has been to bring them into the 'mainstream' of higher and further education. The diploma in art and design became a degree (of the Council of National Academic Awards) in 1974 – to some extent as a result of the earlier incorporation of many major art schools into the then new polytechnics. Colleges of higher education and polytechnics, in developing degree-level work from redundant teacher training resources, have not unnaturally tried to stay with the strongest and most popular subjects taught to teachers in training – and these always included dance, drama, human movement, creative arts and music.

Courses in these subjects now range from the purely theoretical and critical (at degree level only) to the most practical, with every permutation of both in between. In the late 1970s and early 1980s they developed quite rapidly, but the end of expansion in higher and further education has also meant that new developments in the creative and performing arts have virtually halted, although some areas of training have been given more formal educational standing, eg technician-level awards in (art and) design, as part of the drive to improve vocational preparation for skills seen to be crucial to modern industry and commerce.

While most courses in the performing and creative arts specialise – in music, or drama, there are some which combine and integrate the study of more than one, in varying weights and combinations. They include –

At university
Birmingham: Music, drama & dance
Canterbury, Kent: Visual & performed arts (integrates study of drama, film, and history and theory of art)

At polytechnic
Brighton: Expressive arts (main study visual art, with historical studies, and a subsidiary from theatre, dance, music)
Leicester: Performing arts (specialisation in dance, drama, music or arts administration with joint performance workshops)

London, Middx:	Performance arts (core course on all aspects of performance but with in-depth study of one of music, dance or drama)
Newcastle:	Creative arts (major in drama, music or visual arts, plus arts, society and community, community project)
Nottingham, Trent:	Creative arts (includes studies in art, dance, drama and music)
At other colleges	
Chichester, W Sussex:	Related arts (core component studies the relation between the arts), with a subject study from art, dance, English, music
Crewe & Alsager CHE:	Creative arts (core course on integrated arts, with two of: dance, drama, music, visual arts, writing)
Wakefield, B Hall:	English/inter arts (builds on study of literature and practice of writing by work on relations between publications, performances and other arts)

The vocational value of these courses, both those described above and the more specialist ones in the sections following, is difficult to assess and it is probably safer to treat them as interesting and worthwhile, but with not much more vocational value than more conventional arts degrees, particularly those that are more historical, analytical and theoretical than practical. Moreover, the occupations for which even the most practical are apparently a preparation are extremely overcrowded, and a degree is not necessarily going to carry any advantage. Even with a degree, it is still necessary to have exceptional performing talent, well above average drive, and the knack of being in the right place at the right time, although a degree can help if it becomes necessary to find an alternative career.

See also CREATIVE, CULTURAL AND ENTERTAINMENT WORK

ART AND DESIGN

To study art means, to most people, learning how to paint, sculpt, etc, professionally. However, art can also be a critical, historical and theoretical study, without the student ever becoming involved with paint brushes, canvases, oil or clay at all.

There are three kinds of courses, then: those which prepare students to be practising artists (for which see under CAREERS IN ART); those which study the history, theory and criticism of art; and thirdly, courses in which the two can be combined.

Art as a vocational subject, but including history and theory, is studied in art schools (many of them in polytechnics), where the main qualification is the CNAA BA in art and design (formerly DipAD). Art as a theoretical and historical study, with some training in artistic techniques in some cases, is taught by some universities, and some polytechnic and colleges.

Art can be studied for a degree at –

Universities Some 25, but more than half of these concentrate on history, theory and criticism. Only ten offer training in artistic techniques to a professional level in some media (see under ART), combining this with historical and

theoretical studies. They are –
Aberystwyth, Edinburgh, Exeter, Lancaster, Leeds, London: UC (Slade), Loughborough, Newcastle, Oxford (Ruskin) and Reading.

In art history and theory, most courses concentrate on the post-classical period of Western European art, emphasising major periods.

With the exception of the ten courses mentioned above, a university degree course is clearly not suitable preparation for the intending professional artist. These courses are limited in their vocational value, and the areas for which they are most suited are very overcrowded (for example, MUSEUM AND GALLERY WORK, THE MEDIA, PUBLISHING); many graduates continue with further academic training or research. As the figures show, more graduates with degrees in art are now prepared to work in commerce and industry.

Other art schools Eight have degree courses in history of art and design. They are –
Brighton, Leicester, London: Middx, Manchester, Newcastle, N Staffordshire and Sheffield Polytechnics, and London: Camberwell. Their courses are rather different from university courses in that they concentrate mainly on the modern (post-1750) period, and most emphasise design (Camberwell concentrates on drawing and printmaking and Middx and Sheffield include film).

Options in all kinds of visual arts, history, etc are taught on polytechnic arts/humanities and multidisciplinary degree courses, and in 'liberal arts' degrees in colleges of higher education.

'First employment' figures are –

	1984-5 university only[1]	1977-8 university only
total graduating	655	376
research/further study	46	44
teacher training	21	42
'other' training	73	31
'believed' unemployed Dec 31	83	58
short-term UK employment	24	40
permanent UK employment	246	82
employers –		
commerce	84	16
industry	35	15
entertainment, cultural etc	16	21
education	14	5
local government	13	11
functions –		
creative etc	103	nil
marketing etc	45	18
research/information etc	22	13
admin/ops management	21	8
teaching, lecturing	12	6
financial work	3	5

[1] For polytechnic graduates see under CAREERS IN ART AND DESIGN.

Entry: Universities prefer candidates to have studied European history and history of art to A level, but do not usually ask for A-level art (some will not even accept it as meeting the A-level requirement unless it includes history of art); a language is also commonly wanted. Universities which train in artistic skills usually want to see a portfolio also. Just 302 UK students were accepted for university courses in art history in 1985, about 240 for CNAA courses. The mean A-level 'score' for university was 9.8 in 1984-5.

At sub-degree level, there were for many years a large number of courses, collectively described as 'vocational', but which developed on a very ad hoc basis (although many had quite considerable reputations). These practical, technician-level training courses have now been taken over by the Business and Technician Education Council. See under CAREERS IN ART AND DESIGN.

DANCE AND HUMAN MOVEMENT STUDIES
Although not widely accepted as subjects suitable for study for a degree, except in preparation for teaching, a few courses have been developed. They include –

Bedford, Dance/Dr:	Dance (BEd)
Guildford, Surrey:	Dance in society, with 'an element' of performance, plus choreography, management etc
London, Laban:	Dance theatre – broadens dancers' training to include history of dance and related arts, aesthetics and critical studies, production, music accompaniment and composition for dance, to widen career opportunities

Dance is also major options in degree courses in performing arts (at Brighton, Leicester, Middlesex, and Trent Polytechnics, and at Crewe & Alsager and West Sussex colleges). Other colleges have formed links with dance schools – eg West London Institute with the Ballet Rambert's Academy, but these are courses solely for potential performers (see DANCE under PERFORMING CAREERS).

Other courses Dance and human movement, sometimes linked to sports, PE and recreation studies, can also be studied at a number of polytechnics and colleges of higher education as part of BEd courses and 'liberal arts' degrees, developed from physical education training courses for teachers. Career opportunities for graduates are difficult to assess, but there has to be some room in the LEISURE AND RECREATION industries and dance-in-exercise.

Training courses, for which see DANCING under PERFORMING CAREERS are co-ordinated by the Committee for Dance Education and Training.

DRAMA
Purely academic study of drama generally happens within literary degree courses – in eg English, French, German – where the emphasis is usually on textual studies (style, structure, theme) and their relation to the literary and cultural life of the day, some also examining the theatrical setting, but not including any practical drama. On these courses drama is only one theme in the study of literature.

Specialist drama departments, in universities, polytechnics and colleges of higher education, treat all aspects of drama, ranging from purely theoretical and historical study of texts right through, in many cases, to practical involvement in play-making – acting, directing, technical aspects, backstage crafts, and writing for the stage. Courses vary considerably, though, in the proportion of time they give to performing plays, and some university courses offer little or no practical theatre.

Strictly vocational training for, eg acting, is generally given by drama schools (see ACTING under CREATIVE CAREERS), and the theatre world is not keen on degree courses. Nevertheless, there are

Vocationally-oriented courses at –
Sidcup, Rose Bruford: Theatre arts emphasising acting and performance
Totnes, Dartington: Theatre (covers all aspects of play production including acting, directing, writing)

Other degree courses These rarely provide a career basis, and are more academically oriented.
At university Some 16 teach drama as a degree-course subject. Most combine academic study with practical training – the proportion varies from course to course, but there is no practical drama on two, and it is limited in some others. 'Theatre' is interpreted broadly, often to include film and broadcast drama, opera and ballet. They are at –
Aberystwyth, Bangor, Birmingham, Bristol, Canterbury: Kent, Exeter, Glasgow, Hull, Lancaster, London: Goldsmiths', London: RHB, London: Westfield, Loughborough, Manchester, Norwich: E Anglia, Warwick.
Polytechnic and college of higher education courses in drama (many of which are options within 'liberal arts' degrees) may be biased rather more to practical aspects. Many link together drama, dance, movement, film etc. (Drama is also available within a number of BEd courses) –
Colleges: Chester, Crewe/Alsager, Exmouth: Rolle, Liverpool IHE, London: Roehampton, St Mary's, W London, Newport: Gwent, Northampton: Nene, Ormskirk: Edge Hill, Reading: Bulmershe, Ripon/York St John, Wakefield: Bretton Hall, Warrington: N Cheshire, Winchester: King Alfred's, Worcester.
Polytechnics: Brighton, Huddersfield, Leicester, Liverpool, London: Middlesex, Manchester, Newcastle, Nottingham: Trent, Pontypridd: Wales.

However great the proportion of training in theatrical skills, though, most drama courses are still not intended to give a full vocational training, and particularly not in acting. A significant proportion of graduates from some departments do go into directing, production management and theatrical administration generally, and broadcast drama/film, however.

'First employment' figures are –

| | 1984-5 | | 1977-8 | |
	university	polytechnic	university	polytechnic
total graduating	213	302	77	n/g
research/further study	8	5	3	n/g
teacher training	6	33	10	n/g
'other' training	31	12	7	n/g
'believed' unemployed Dec 31	17	35	3	n/g

| | 1984-5 | | 1977-8 | |
	university	polytechnic	university	polytechnic
short term UK employment	12	16	12	n/g
permanent UK employment	76	208	24	n/g
employers –				
entertainment, cultural etc	30	26	18	n/g
education	3	4	1	n/g
commerce/industry	13	25	3	n/g
local government	4	13	2	n/g
functions –				
creative etc	43	34	20	n/g

Entry: most universities prefer English literature and language at A-level; some advise history and languages. Just 233 students were accepted for university degree courses in 1985, about 100 for CNAA courses. The mean A-level grade 'score' for university was 10.4 in 1984-5.

MEDIA AND COMMUNICATION STUDIES

The popularity of careers in the media could have produced degree courses at any time in the 1960s. In fact it was not until the mid-1970s that there was any major development, largely outside the university sector.

Following academic tradition, most degree courses in this field do not just give a narrow preparation in the skills needed for broadcasting, journalism or film work. They set the study of the media into the wider context of the theory and problems of human communication in all its complexities, and the role of communication generally (and the media in particular) in society. Communication is studied as a 'linguistic, cultural and social process', as an aspect of human behaviour. This means courses at least partly consist of, for example, the appropriate aspects of linguistics, psychology, sociology, human biology, perhaps literature. Courses vary in the extent to which they also train in the use of the media, and the media they study. Few cover media 'management' skills such as budgeting and forecasting.

Few courses are intended to prepare graduates directly for careers in the media, although there are some whose graduates consistently get media jobs. Graduates from these courses are also well placed to take advantage of the newer media employment opportunities, such as video, audio-visual resource work for the education sector – see also CAREERS IN THE MEDIA. However, none give any exemptions from professional training requirements, and graduates going into, for example, JOURNALISM, must normally complete the same training as any other graduate.

Course titles can be misleading – communication or media studies can mean something quite different to different colleges and polytechnics (there are very few university courses). In particular, it is quite hard to find out just how much practical experience is given.

Courses which emphasise vocational training include –

Bournemouth, Dorset IHE: Communication & media production (academic, practical, technical and professional

	aspects, specialisation in audio, video or computer graphics; major production in year 3)
Farnham, W Surrey:	Photography, film & video, animation (studio based, 70% practical, workshop, project work; work experience included)
London, PCL:	Film & photographic arts (equal theory and practice, specialising in film or photography in last two years; includes extensive project work)
London, PCL:	Media studies (specialising in journalism or media arts – writing and production skills – in last two years: third of course practical)
London, Harrow:	Applied photography, film & TV (specialisation in cultural and commercial or scientific and industrial applications of photography, film and TV, or in photography)
London, Printing:	Media & production design (practical, sandwich-based, with two terms work experience, biased to design, specialises in publishing, information, or media design; includes business skills)
London, Printing:	Photography, film & TV (very practical, biased to design and production; specialises in photography or film and TV in last 2 years; final year includes production planning and budgeting, director's role and responsibility, writing for film and TV, individual and group productions; practical business skills)

Courses focusing on academic study of communication but with strong practical elements include –

Birmingham U:	Communication & cultural studies with another subject (stress on useful practical skills)
Cant'bury, Ch Ch:	Radio, film & TV studies with art, English, geography, history, maths, movement studies, music, religious studies or science (includes researching, writing and production techniques: two weeks work experience)
Coventry P:	Communication studies (studies work of media eg film, photography, print, journalism, broadcasting, media policy)
Glasgow/S'clyde:	Film & TV studies with another subject ('strong practical element')
Leeds, Tr/AS:	Communication arts & media can be taken with professional study of public media, with 12 weeks' relevant work experience
London, Goldsmiths':	Communication studies & education or sociology (combines practical units – eg graphic design, CCTV, film and photography, print

media, film animation, computer-aided communication – with theoretical studies)

Ripon/York St John: Drama, film & TV (possible major with options in eg practical TV, recording reality, TV and the dramatist, visual communication, film studies, and drama for TV production)

Warrington N Ches: Media & communication can be studied for 50% of course; combines theory and practice, can include business and management

Winchester, K Alf: Drama, theatre & TV studies (though strongly practical emphasises drama in theatre and TV)

Courses which are primarily academic with little or no practical or vocational training include –

Canterbury, Kent: Film studies can make up half course

Edinburgh, QM: Communication studies (workshops illustrate, consolidate and inter-relate theoretical material)

Glasgow CT: Communication studies (some 'practical studies' in years 1-2)

Lancaster U: Human communication

Nottingham, Trent: Communication studies

Pontypridd, Wales: Communication studies ('some' practical work in eg film, TV studio or electronic field production)

Sheffield P: Communication studies ('studio workshop' sessions on techniques and media skills eg editing audio and video tape, in year 1; final-year option applied media studies

Stirling U: Film & TV studies (can gain some practical experience)

Sunderland P: Communication studies (specialising in communications aspects of technology, visual arts, or language, but year-1 units on basic techniques of radio and video; final year options include practical experiments with film and video; work on local radio)

Ulster U: Human communications (includes work experience which may be in media agency)

MUSIC

It is possible to study music either to become a professional musician, or as an academic subject, that is emphasising analysis, history and theory. Traditionally there is a firm division between the two – musicians train in separate music schools ('conservatoire') and music is studied academically at university.

To a large extent this is still so – music schools teach practical skills, universities still tend to be very academic in their approach. However, over the last twenty years many university music departments have widened the scope of their courses, and in particular most have increased very substantially the amount of instrumental teaching and training that they do, and also spend more departmental time on performing – in orchestras, groups of all kinds, and choirs. Composition, as a creative skill and not just a formal academic exercise, and conducting, are also taught now. There are also some unusual courses, including Tonmeister studies at Surrey (Guildford) which teaches electronics and recording engineering as well as more conventional music subjects, the BSc at City (London) which also combines traditional with scientific aspects, and the 'project-based' course at York.

No university, polytechnic or college degree course, however, is even now intended to train professional musicians. In some departments it is possible to gain enough teaching and experience on an instrument (some university departments arrange for music students to study their instruments at the nearest music school), to use it as the basis for a performing career, but further training is normally needed for even the most talented.

Music is taught as a first degree subject by about 40 universities and university colleges, by several polytechnics and other colleges. It is an integral part of several performing arts degrees (listed above), and an option in about twenty liberal arts degrees. At a number of universities it is possible to read music for either a BMus or a BA (there is no difference in the status of the degrees, but the syllabuses may differ); at all but two of the rest, music is read for a normal BA, either as a single honours subject or in combination with a second.

'First employment' figures are –

| | 1984-5 | | 1977-8 | |
	university	polytechnic	university	polytechnic
total graduating	622[1]	47	588	25
research/further study	44	nil	55	6
teacher training	145	15	210	7
'other' training	122	9	77	1
'believed' unemployed Dec 31	44	4	16	2
short-term UK employment	13	2	26	nil
permanent UK employment	158	10	116	5
employers –				
education	35	2	7	2
commerce/industry	33	3	21	1
cultural etc	24	nil	37	2
local government	12	1	12	nil
civil service	11	nil	6	nil
functions –				
creative etc	38	1	nil	nil
teaching, lecturing etc	34	4	17	2
admin/ops management	15	1	14	nil
personnel/social work	12	nil	8	nil

	1984-5 university polytechnic		1977-8 university polytechnic	
financial work	12	1	14	nil
marketing etc	11	2	9	1
research, information work	10	1	8	nil

[1] down from 743 in 1983-4

Entry: Music is taught as though it were a language, and students are expected to be able to read, understand and write music as well as they do English before they are accepted for most degree courses. Music at A level is normally essential for entry to a degree course, and some departments also want a language. Most departments now want candidates to be able to play at at least one and preferably two instruments (including a keyboard), one to Associated Board grade VIII (a distinction may be assumed).

Other courses There are nine major music schools –
Birmingham (closely linked with the Polytechnic), Cardiff (College of Music and Drama), London (Guildhall, London College, Royal Academy, Royal College and Trinity College), Manchester (Royal Northern College of Music) and Glasgow (Royal Scottish Academy). Eight of these (not Cardiff) offer music degrees or graduate diploma courses with the same standing and academic entry requirements as university degree courses. The standard of performance, though, usually has to be rather higher, and a distinction at grade VIII in Associated Board examinations, or an equivalent, on at least one instrument, and a good grade on the second, in addition to A levels, plus evidence of high musical ability and achievement are usually needed.

These three-year courses teach all-round musicianship and scholarship as well as training students to a very high standard of performance. As at university, all students are normally expected to take part in the corporate musical life of the college, in orchestral, choral and ensemble work. Most courses include the practical subjects associated with music and also background studies and options in particular kinds of music.

All nine colleges also have non-graduate courses for associateship or licentiateship. These last two or three years, but the academic entry requirements are just GCE O-level passes. Although similar in content to the graduate diploma courses, they are usually more practical, and biased to either teaching or performing.

Some colleges (ie the Guildhall, Royal Academy and Royal College) provide for students who wish to, or can only, study on a part-time basis, and for students who want to study externally, at other colleges. They mainly examine instrumental performance, but it is possible to study conducting, speech and drama, harmony and counterpoint, composition, orchestration and choral arranging. Courses for these examinations are available at a number of further education colleges.

See also MUSIC under PERFORMING AS A CAREER.

QUALIFICATIONS AND CAREERS IN ENGINEERING AND OTHER TECHNOLOGIES

Introduction   94
Engineering as a career   95
Engineering functions   108
Engineering courses, qualifications and training   117
The branches of engineering   134

INTRODUCTION

The term 'engineering' serves several purposes: it defines the *career* of engineering, the *academic subject* engineering, and the *industries* which employ engineering techniques. All too often the three are confused and the distinction between them blurs: the career is seen to follow on logically, and inevitably, from the academic study, and just as inevitably, as being pursued in the engineering industry.

In fact engineering is an academic discipline in its own right, just like science and arts subjects. A career in engineering is no more the inevitable outcome of a degree course in engineering than a career as a mathematician or physicist is for graduates in those subjects. To emphasise that engineering can be studied as an independent academic subject, and to demonstrate the possibilities emerging from such a study, engineering is described here as an academic discipline and as a career; engineering as an industry is dealt with under MANUFACTURING.

Engineering is constantly being re-defined nowadays, largely as part of all the attempts to promote it both as a subject study and as a career, and to improve the professional engineer's image.

Traditional definitions (all going back to engineering's military origins) tended to play down the subject's originality and creative aspects, making it sound dull, repetitive and mechanical. Describing it (rightly) as an applied subject using scientific principles implied (wrongly) that the 'principles' were discovered by others and the engineer simply took them over – which inevitably made the engineer seem a second-class brain, someone not quite bright enough to be an original scientist-researcher. (In fact engineers have always worked out many of the scientific principles needed for themselves.)

Describing engineering as designing practical solutions to real-life problems, and developing imaginative ideas into novel working products, devices, processes, structures, systems which serve human needs, perhaps redresses the balance, coming closer to a fair definition, at least when a trained engineer is being fully and properly employed. All that is lacking is to make clear the vast range of products which result from engineers' skills – from tiny silicon chips to giant power stations, from static structures like dams to mobile machinery like cars, and not forgetting all kinds of industrial processes from refining oil and sugar to turning raw materials into anything from cakes to glue.

It is still too soon to assess the success of the great many efforts – some of which are in any case designed with the longer term in view – still underway to improve engineering's image and end the misconceptions which make it such an under-rated subject and profession. It is crucial that they are. To be competitive in world markets, industry needs to make the most of existing technologies and develop and exploit new ones. This will demand high-calibre people able to conceptualise, research, design, develop, and manage in a tough and frequently-changing environment.

ENGINEERING AS A CAREER
Introduction — definitions (professional engineer — technician engineer — engineering technician — craft worker) — where engineers work — future of engineering

Introduction
If the definition of the term 'engineering' is confused, then so is the meaning of the title 'engineer'. Strictly, 'engineer' means 'professional' and perhaps 'technician engineer', but too many people still lump all engineers together, as manual workers in dirty overalls working deep inside oily machines. Even journalists still tend to write about 'engineers' on strike, when they (usually) mean the craft engineering worker or engineering technician (albeit skilled) members of a particular union – toolmakers, fitters, maintenance people, people on the assembly line – and not professional or technician engineers. Leaving aside the fact that modern electronic technology is fast removing much of the muck from most machines, professional and technician engineers work with their brains and imaginations rather than their hands.

As a 1984 survey commissioned by the Engineering Council noted, 'The actual occupations of professional engineers – the jobs they do as distinct from the qualifications they hold – do nothing to present a clearer image to those intent on allocating status ... The fields in which the professional engineer applies his expertise can appear to the layman to be totally dissimilar... To the layman at least how can there be a single concept of status attached to a widely differing group operating within a technology of which he understands little? ... The world of the professional engineer presents to the public a picture which is far from clear.'

Yet the lack of clear distinction between one kind of engineer and another is only a realistic picture of the position as it actually is in the real working world (with some exceptions, most notably construction) in Britain. The Engineering Council realistically accepts that there is no hard and fast line between the kind of work undertaken by those in the different grades, unlike the medical and para-medical professions (for example). The greater flexibility being promoted by employers and education/training initiatives alike mean that the distinctions are likely to blur even further.

Engineering, then, covers a very wide spectrum of activity indeed, from the most creative and cerebral to the most practical and repetitive.

Professional engineering obviously equates with the most complex end of the spectrum, craft work with the most practical, but there is a very wide area in between where the role of professional, technician engineer, engineering technician and even craft worker is not so easily defined in practice. The divisions probably vary from branch to branch of engineering, and from industry to industry, to some extent depending on the complexity of the product being made or whatever is being built – it may even vary from firm to firm.

Some professional engineers work on projects which take them to – or even beyond – the boundaries of existing knowledge or put them in control of massive and/or potentially highly-dangerous resources (eg nuclear power stations). But others may well be doing work which makes little demand on their professional skills. In one situation, the technician engineer may be doing the

kind of work given to a chartered engineer in another (and vice versa), or the engineering technician work similar to craftworkers elsewhere and vice versa.

Moreover, graduate and other professionally-qualified engineers have, it would seem from Engineering Council surveys anyway, been moving away from their traditional roles in research, development and design, into other functions.

In the 1985 Engineering Council survey of professional and technician engineers, for example, 58.5% of chartered engineers working in maintenance and repair were graduates and nearly 6% postgraduates (against 41.5% and nearly 5% in 1977), in an area not traditionally considered to need such a high level of qualification. Conversely, technician engineers (9% of whom, according to the survey, are in any case graduates) are not excluded from professional-level work: just over 4% of technician engineers answering the questionnaire in 1985 worked in R&D (against 3.7% in 1977), 7.9% in design (against only 6.5% in 1977) and 7.7% in teaching.

Definitions

Engineering Council defines an engineer as 'one who acquires and uses scientific, technical and other pertinent knowledge and skills to create, operate and maintain efficient systems, structures, machines, plant, processes and devices of practical and economic value'.

The official definitions of professional and technician engineers, as agreed by the Engineering Societies of Western Europe and the USA, but more recently 'refined' by the UK Engineering Council, show where the theoretical boundaries are –

'Professional engineers are concerned with the progress of technology through innovation, creativity and change. They should be able to develop and apply new technologies, promote advanced designs and design methods, introduce new and more efficient production techniques, marketing and construction concepts and pioneer new engineering services and management methods. They may also be involved with the effective direction of advanced existing technology involving high-risk and capital-intensive projects.

The work of a professional engineer is predominantly intellectual and varied. It requires the exercise of original thought and judgement and the ability to supervise the technical and administrative work of others, and ... to assume responsibility for the direction of important tasks, including the profitable management of industrial and commercial enterprises. [They] have a responsibility to society with regard to the ethical, economic and environmental impact of technical need and changes.

Professional engineers must be competent...

to apply scientific methods and outlook to the analysis and solution of engineering problems;

to develop a thorough understanding of ... a branch of engineering, including interdisciplinary aspects, and continuously following progress on a world-wide basis, assimilating such information and applying it independently, so as to be in a position to make contributions to the development of engineering science and its applications;

to assume personal responsibility for the development and application of engineering science and knowledge in research, design, construction, manufacture, marketing, managing, and in the education and training of engineer...'

In more everyday language, professional engineers are scientifically trained to solve problems, in a practical way. They *design and develop* devices (such as computers or machine tools), plant and processes (to refine petrol or produce beer), or structures (such as bridges and dams), which solve problems (as in extracting oil and gas from the North Sea), improve existing products (using microprocessors to build ever smaller but more powerful and sophisticated computers), or create new ones (such as space satellites). They use exact scientific methods and their work is based on scientific principles, physical – as work in solid-state physics lead eventually to the silicon chip; chemical – the basic principles for chemical engineering, and even biological – for genetic engineering and biotechnology. The solutions, machines, processes etc, have to be designed so as to take account of all kinds of often conflicting technical, economic, commercial, social and even political factors. Where professional engineers work in actual manufacturing or construction, it is in a *managerial* capacity, which usually means working with a team of other people.

Employed according to their training and capability (which does not always happen), professional engineers have to be able to use ingenuity, original thinking and judgement. They ought to be able to look ahead, foresee problems and plan to meet or forestall them. They must keep up to date with technological developments, know how to take advantage of them, and how to manage change. They must learn how to negotiate – on contracts for instance – to write reports, and to manage, both people and resources.

Professional engineering is mostly a desk- and/or laboratory-based job, but also normally involves much liaison and team work, with customers, with the company's marketing staff, with other engineers, and with support people. It will, usually, mean using and/or working on all kinds computer-based systems. Many professional engineers, though, make regular visits to the site or the factory floor, especially in their earliest years (when they may, as part of their training, actually work as a foreman or supervisor). Some – especially in large-scale construction – may work on site, as part of the 'resident' engineer's team, and later, perhaps, as resident engineer.

Professional engineers can expect to move on from direct involvement in an engineering 'function' (see below) into management, especially if they have gained in-depth training and experience in, for instance, contract negotiation, financial control. Technological sophistication and complexity, the vast scale of many engineering projects, and the financial investment involved, means there are signs that more engineers are (once again) being groomed for senior, general, management (see, eg, the new Ministry of Defence engineering service, under CIVIL SERVICE).

The Engineering Council's 1985 survey showed that over 73% of chartered engineers are now qualified to graduate level or above, rising from 58-59% of those over the age of 50, to nearly 98% of those under 30.

The technician engineer 'performs technical duties of an established or novel character either independently or under the general direction of more senior engineers. They require the power of logical thought and, when in a management role, the qualities of leadership and effective control.

Fundamentally the nature of posts occupied ... is such as to demand a practical approach and a detailed understanding of a particular technology. They require specific and detailed knowledge of the bases and practices of current technology and are concerned with maintaining and managing existing technology efficiently. They also need communication skills and awareness of the environment beyond the limits of their specific responsibility.

Technician engineers provide, either independently or as leaders, the most satisfactory service possible through existing resources and so exercise a significant influence on the general effectiveness of the organisation in which they work.

Technician engineers must therefore –

be competent to exercise technical judgement in and assume responsibility for duties in the engineering field;

understand, by the application of general principles and established techniques, the reasons for and the purposes of the operations for which they are responsible;

be aware of the business, management, safety, social and economic context of their work both within the organisation and in the wider environment.'

Engineering technicians 'are competent ... to apply proven techniques and procedures to the solution of practical problems with an element of personal responsibility usually under the guidance of chartered or technician engineers'.

Technician engineer and engineering technician are really blanket terms referring to qualifications rather than job specifications for a wide variety of different occupations at varying skill levels between, and overlapping with, craft work at one end and professional engineering at the other. Technician engineers are generally senior to engineering technicians (because they have more advanced-level technical qualifications and experience), but there is often some overlap in the kind of work they do, and the level of skills needed can vary from branch to branch of engineering.

Technician engineers normally hold the senior position in a team of technicians, as in the drawing office, usually under a professional engineer, or give direct assistance to professional engineers, for instance in R&D or project engineering. In production, the manager's functions may be subdivided, with someone of technician-engineer status (or a young professional engineer) deputising in each of the functions. There is nothing to prevent a technician engineer moving up into more senior and even general managerial positions – and the indications are that a significant proportion do so – although there may be problems in gaining relevant experience early enough.

Engineering technicians often lead teams of craft workers, in technical after-sales service, for example. They, too, can gain promotion to what is defined as technician-engineer-level work, and beyond.

Like professional engineers, engineering technicians and technician engineers normally work within one branch of engineering, and further within one kind of occupation. There are a great many areas of work for technicians and technician engineers, many now (becoming) computer-based jobs. Examples include –

design/drawing office work – which ranges from preparing detailed scale drawings of components for individual products, to component and assembly design with responsibility for relevant engineering calculations, preparing materials and parts lists, and supervisory work;

testing, for research and development or inspection – for example, setting up and even making test equipment, and then running the test programme;

production – where technician engineers deputise for the production manager in larger firms;

estimating – for example, costing standard components, or one-off projects;

installing and 'running in' new equipment or plant;

scheduling production – deciding when raw materials should be delivered, keeping checks on lists of materials, preparing information for production planning, and analysing the work content of orders;

programming numerically-controlled (automatic) machine tools – analysing what the machine is expected to do in a given operation, and then writing, checking and 'de-bugging' the specifications for the control tapes;

maintaining and repairing machinery and other equipment and services – for example, in broadcasting or telecommunications;

after-sales service or sales engineering maintaining and repairing equipment, eg machine tools or computers, for customers;

applications engineering finding and promoting uses for a company's products, and working with a (professional) project engineer on design, development and testing of new products or modifications.

Technician engineers and technicians are expected to show ingenuity, to be able to diagnose and solve problems, identify and analyse faults, use a variety of sophisticated tools and measuring devices and processes, be able to organise their own and others' work, understand the processes involved in making or building products, and be able to make technical reports, both verbally and in writing.

The Engineering Industry Training Board's 1985-6 annual report shows that the *number* of technicians employed in the engineering industries rose steadily until 1978-9, to 218,000 – but then fell to barely 179,000 in 1984-5. However, the *proportion* of technicians has continued to rise to 9% of total employment (about a quarter of them draughtsmen/women), as has the ratio of technician to craft trainees under first-year basic training. In 1981-2, about 35% of all technicians in the industry were described as technician engineers. About 51% were working in production-related jobs, 32% in research, development and design, 11% in commercial activity, and 6% in central services (eg computer services, finance, management services, personnel etc).

The 1983 survey showed the first jobs technicians had taken after training. Some 19% became draughtsmen and women, 15% went into production planning or other production jobs; 11% started work in development and design work, and another 11% in test and quality assurance. Some 8% gained central service type jobs, 7% became lab technicians; 6% became service engineers and another 6% went into other customer- or supplier-related jobs.

The engineering craft worker 'specialises in a specific, normally practical, skill; craft workers are expected to be able to understand the principles underlying the work they do; they must be able to read a complex engineering drawing and turn it into a practical reality; they must be able to order the right materials in the correct quantities to make a piece of equipment or machinery, plan the order in which the job is done, set it up and then carry it out, frequently to very high degrees of accuracy and precision; they must be able to solve basic problems. Promotion is to supervisory work, to quality control and inspection.'

Examples of craft work include –
machine shop crafts – toolmaking, turning (on a lathe), milling (where the component is fixed and the machine moves to produce flat or curved surfaces, slots, grooves, gears or cam-forms);
jig-boring and grinding;
electrical, electronic or mechanical fitting – assembling components which may need preparation to make them fit together and therefore need accurate measurement and marking, and use of hand tools;
maintenance – of cars, electrical plant, electronic equipment, lifts, instruments, machine tools, etc;
'setting' machines for semi- or unskilled workers.

Craft workers traditionally work with a minimum of direction and supervision and are expected to be able to read and interpret complicated engineering drawings, and make the component or product or wiring system correctly from it. This means they must also be able to order the right materials in the correct quantities, plan for themselves the order in which the job is done, set it up, and then carry it out, very often to a high degree of accuracy and precision. They also solve basic problems.

Over 352,000 craft workers were still employed in engineering industries in 1985-6, 17.7% of total employment (down from 19% in 1983).

Where engineers work
Most people going into engineering usually begin their working lives specialising in one of the so-called 'branches' (see THE BRANCHES OF ENGINEERING). They are employed in a number of sectors –
Industry, both manufacturing and other sectors such as construction, has traditionally employed the majority of engineers, but with the decline of MANUFACTURING INDUSTRY, the proportion has been falling for some time. In 1985, just about 41% of both professional and technician engineers were working for industrial companies (against nearly 47% and 42% in 1983), but a further 10% of professional engineers, 12% of technician engineers worked for nationalised industries, where the decline has been less. In industry, they start out in one of several different types of work (see ENGINEERING FUNCTIONS), although later many engineers change the area of engineering in which they work, and also their 'function'.
Local authorities are also major employers of engineers – over 19.5% of all professional engineers and over 13% of all technician engineers in 1985. They manage and organise road building, planning, and maintenance; traffic systems (planning and organising eg new one-way systems, and all that goes with them, like islands, intersections); sewage and refuse disposal, and street cleaning; local-authority building and housing; building controls and inspec-

tion; parks, playing fields and cemeteries; sometimes public transport. See also LOCAL GOVERNMENT.

The Civil Service employs a sizeable number – in 1985, 5.3% of all professional and technician engineers. They work in R&D, project management, construction and installation, and even (but less and less) production.

Civil and structural engineers work for the PROPERTY SERVICES AGENCY, looking after government property and land from airfields and dockyards to office buildings and royal palaces.

Mechanical, electrical and electronic, and marine engineers, naval architects etc work for the Ministry of Defence, mainly on the design, development, and production (in government ordnance factories but these are being 'contracted out' to private managers), but increasingly they supervise defence contracts. See also CENTRAL GOVERNMENT.

Education employs some 7% of chartered/professional engineers, 6.4% of technician engineers – several thousand perhaps. They work in universities, where they combine teaching with research, development, consultancy etc, and in further education. A SERC study (on chemical engineering) suggests that teaching and research in universities and polytechnics right across engineering and technology could collapse in the next ten to fifteen years, for lack of suitably motivated and qualified academic staff.

Other employers Nearly 9% of professional engineers are consultants, and 6.6% self-employed (for technician engineers the equivalents are 3.1% and 4.9%). Only 1.6% of professionals, but 4.8% of technician engineers are in the ARMED FORCES.

The future of engineering
Engineering as a career is changing. First, there are the effects of new technology itself, and of economic and industrial conditions. Second, but closely bound up with this, are the changes that engineers are making to their own futures.

Changing patterns of employment Predicting future levels of employment for engineers is as difficult as for any other occupation. With even only a relatively modest recovery from recession, however, shortages of skilled professional and technician engineers, technicians and skilled workers, have already been reported. The shortages have been made worse by the disastrous fall in the levels of apprentices/trainees taken on in the early 1980s and by the now-falling numbers of young people coming out of the education system, compounding the problems created by the failure to recruit and train enough people even before the recession.

The problems are particularly acute in electronics, instrumentation, office machinery and aerospace, the sectors on the leading edge of technology, but there are also reportedly shortages in a widening range of industries, even the more traditional (eg machine tools and motor vehicles). At least one major recruiter has been piloting a scheme to convert graduates in non-technical/scientific subjects into full professional engineers; the Engineering Industry Training Board (EITB) is promoting programmes to up-grade the skills of technician engineers and engineering technicians, particularly in areas such as software engineering; and students with arts/social science A levels can now (from 1987-8) take a one-year 'conversion' in preparation for a degree or HND course in engineering, technology, or science/CDT teacher training.

Radically-changing technology, the drive for greater efficiency and competitiveness, has already resulted in a steady change in the balance between skilled and unskilled workers. The engineering industry, which employs most engineers, increased the proportion of professional engineers and technologists by 15% over the years in which it contracted by nearly 25%. Future needs may not be met – output of engineering and technology graduates was sharply down in 1986, 9.4% on 1985, when there had already been a slight fall on the peak of 1984.

The proportion of technicians employed in engineering went up from 7.4% to 9% between 1980 and 1985, and estimates suggest the engineering industries will still need over 162,000 in 1989. Skilled craft workers still make up nearly 18% of the engineering workforce, and the number of craft jobs is not expected to fall below 300,000 at least in this decade. Current recruitment of craft and technician trainees, although now running (1984-5 and 1985-6) at about 9100 a year (having bottomed out at some 8000 in 1983-4), is not anything like enough to maintain industry's skill base at even those comparatively low levels. A further indicator is that apprentice redundancies (some 6300 lost their jobs between 1980 and 1984) had slowed to a trickle by the start of 1985. (EITB figures)

In this situation, it is unlikely that any job losses resulting from automation or other technological developments will adversely affect general career opportunities for skilled people overall, at least for the immediate future. Of course actual jobs, even for skilled engineers, will go as new technology makes them obsolete – as digital-electronic telephone exchanges cut the number of production jobs dramatically even for technicians. Computer-aided design (CAD) is steadily automating away routine drawing-office work. But the increased efficiency made possible by new technologies looks set only to help ease skill shortages, and of course engineers also design, develop and make the new machinery and products, which makes them somewhat less vulnerable.

But the corollary is that even skilled engineers will need to be flexible both in their approach to what work they will do and in their training. The evidence says engineers will also need to have broader-based skills, even to be multi-skilled, and to have skills which cross traditional barriers. A major example here is the growing need for integrated electro-mechanical skills (now rather unfortunately being labelled 'mechatronics' by some), and of course 'information technology' – or 'engineering' – is itself a complex amalgam of what have been treated as independent disciplines.

Engineers will need to have skills which will transfer, and there will have to be more systematic arrangements for up-dating and converting engineer's skills through continuing education and training, just as in all other sectors of employment, both for their personal futures and to make their employers more competitive.

Jobs will obviously go on changing in character with all kinds of new technology, as they have been for some time now. Sophisticated computer-based technology is now routinely in use throughout industry – in research and development, in design, in manufacture, in stores, in distribution, in administration, to be used by people of all skill levels, but with many more revolutionary developments, particularly in robotics and automation, to come. Other technologies have been developing and have come in to use more quietly and are set to make even more dramatic changes.

Lasers are an example. They are already commonly in use for drilling, welding and cutting, increasingly in areas like printing and copying, and the basis of a growing range of new and redeveloped products (such as navigational gyros, defence equipment and compact discs). A new generation of efficient 'free-electron' lasers (which can be 'tuned' to different radiation frequencies) could be extremely useful in a range of chemical processes. Optical fibres may be able to carry laser-light energy powerful enough to melt even metal, scientists believe. Computers using laser beams could be a thousand times faster than any produced up to now.

The level and range of skills needed for specific jobs may change, and so may the levels of responsibility. In a fully automated cement factory, central control can be supervised by a single operator (in place of several technicians for less sophisticated systems), but automated machine tools tend to require higher-level skills: they have to be programmed, and the operator has to be able to react appropriately to problems. The skills may change – in maintenance, when electronic equipment replaces mechanical, for example.

Recruiters suggest they will in future be looking for higher-calibre people for engineering functions, right through from management level – to be able to get people working in teams and getting greater efficiency and productivity; amongst technician and technician engineer grades, and to craft levels where high-grade, flexible skills and the ability to tackle problems will be of increasing importance.

In the longer term, however, early signs are that the demand for some technological skills could decline. The crucial factor will be whether or not the next generations of computers and software can deliver effective 'expert' systems which will enable many people to do tasks of increasing technical sophistication without necessarily being a fully-qualified specialist engineer/technologist. If, when, this happens, the skills needed will change yet again, probably to (even) more broadly-based intellectual training, and even greater emphasis on flexibility, adaptability, problem-solving and trouble-shooting.

A changing profession The engineering profession has been through a period of intense self-analysis and criticism, with a full-scale official enquiry into the profession (1978-80), under Sir Montague Finniston. The enquiry's terms of reference spelt out the problems –

to examine the needs of British industry for professional and technician engineers, the extent to which these needs were being met, and the use made of engineers in industry;

the role of the engineering institutions in relation to the education and qualification of engineers at professional and technician level;

the advantages and disadvantages of statutory registration and licensing of engineers in the UK;

the arrangements in other major industrial countries, particularly in the EEC, for handling such problems.

The major factor which led to the enquiry was the recognition that there were serious weaknesses, probably very long-standing, in Britain's industrial performance: the poor record of economic growth, low productivity compared with major competitors and Britain's declining share of world trade. Although the causes were (and still are) obviously very complex and involve many factors, the provision, education and training of engineers, the nature and attitudes of the education system, and the treatment of engineers by society in general (in terms of status etc) and by industry (status, pay etc) are generally considered central.

The Finniston Committee Report, *Engineering Our Future* (1980) made a valuable analysis of engineering, manufacturing and national economic needs. It confirmed the decline in British manufacturing competitiveness and output, and made suggestions for reversing the trend (see MANUFACTURING).

The Report confirmed the view that, unlike their counterparts in other industrial countries, British engineers lacked the special social standing which attracts young people to engineering careers, that engineers did not achieve the levels of management and involvement in policy-making (either in the firm or at national level), and that their pay levels generally reflected this. Finniston suggested that the confusion caused by the image of even a professional engineer as some kind of manual worker and the tendency to regard engineering as a subordinate branch of science might be contributing factors. (Another view traces the problems back to Arnold, and the fact that the educational system is modelled on the public-school emphasis on education as a humanising process, resulting in a continuing bias in schools against engineering, against industry. It could also be because teachers, and many parents, themselves products of 'humanising' education, have little experience of, or know much about, industry.)

Whatever the reasons, the Report endorsed the view that the profession urgently needed to find ways of attracting high-calibre men and women into engineering, but said that improved standing for engineers and greater career attractiveness would only come with greater recognition of the nature and importance of engineering. Finniston suggested that one key factor in Britain's failure to invest in marketable innovation might be the predominantly non-technical background from which senior decision-takers in British industry, finance and government are drawn. The Report said that employers must consider improved salary and career structures for engineers, and that engineers must be recognised as key assets within the engineering 'dimension'. Finniston was sure that many more engineers than are currently available will be required by both manufacturing and other sectors of employment in the future.

Finniston accepted criticisms that –
    the education of engineers was unduly scientific and theoretical;
    newly-graduated engineers lacked awareness of 'real life' constraints to text-book solutions;
    they were oriented too much towards research and development work and uninterested in working in production or marketing functions; and
    they lacked understanding of the factors in the commercial success of their employing organisation.

Finniston noted that the amount of formal training given to engineers had progressively fallen over the previous 20 years, largely with the decline in the part-time route to qualification. Further, the Committee considered that the machinery for the qualification and registration of engineers failed to give engineers the necessary standing with employers.

Finniston proposed both a radical revision of the way engineers were educated and trained – even using a new word, 'formation' to describe the process – and a new professional structure, with an independent, statutory authority.

Finniston's new model of engineering 'formation', was designed to provide an integrated mix of theory, application and experience, and cater for the differing requirements of the main body of engineers, those who demonstrate exceptional potential for leadership, and for a large group of supporting engineers. Finniston made a great many recommendations, including detailed proposals for routes to professional status; the way engineering courses should be revised; and the role and activities of the new engineering authority. The proposals inevitably met with some controversy (most notably, the government rejected statutory powers for the new authority). Nevertheless, many of the Committee's intentions have been and are being implemented, as is clear in the following paragraphs and pages.

The first, and most major, change was to create (in 1981) the Engineering Council (EC) replacing (effectively from 1983) the Council of Engineering Institutions (CEI), which a decade earlier had set up (and tried to get employers' recognition of) a three-tier system of registration for professional and technician engineers and technicians, with an Engineers Registration Board. Although still only a voluntary not a statutory body and with limited funding (which do to some extent limit its possible effect from the start), EC differs from its predecessor in that it involves employers as well as the profession. All the member institutions of CEI have joined the Engineering Council, and more will do so if they can meet EC standards for their qualifications. The Council would like to see fewer separate institutions (by 1988 there could be over seventy members), but wants this to happen 'naturally'. A number of amalgamations are, in fact, under way or in the pipeline.

The Council sees two aspects to its role. The first is to be the 'engine of change', projecting what Finniston called the 'engineering dimension' in industry. The second is setting the standards for qualifications, education, and training of chartered engineers and technicians. It does not, however, see these two activities as separate, because the right type of qualification policy is, says the Council, of immense importance in developing the 'engine for change' role.

In setting new standards for qualification etc, the Council has kept a three-tier register, with the designations Chartered (professional) Engineer (CEng), Technician Engineer (TEng), and Engineering Technician (EngTech), but the form is somewhat different from that of the old CEI/ERB register. (A search is currently – 1986–7 – under way for a more suitable title for technician engineers.)

First, the new Board for Engineers' Registration (BER) insists that, for all three sections, study and training programmes must emphasise *relevance* to developing industrial, commercial and national needs, and *integration* of theory and practice.

Second, each section has a three-stage registration. At each stage the standards must meet the Council's requirements, which includes arrangements to assess training, accreditation of courses etc. The stages are –

Stage 1 educational qualification – registers those who have passed an examination or other academic test in the principles of engineering.

Stage 2 training qualification – registers people who have been trained for the profession, or have held position(s) which have given such training. Entrants must have satisfied the stage 1 requirement.

Stage 3 experience – registers people who have gained responsible engineering experience, and have met both stage 1 and 2 requirements.

These clearly-defined stages of registration are designed to put greater emphasis in future on training and experience. The new standards are being introduced progressively, but will be in force for all new applicants at all stages on 1st January 1992.

For each section of the register –

Chartered engineer (CEng) The stage 1 main route is via an accredited enhanced, honours BEng or an enhanced and extended MEng (see ENGINEERING COURSES AND QUALIFICATIONS below). Alternative routes are via EC part 2 examinations, a part-accredited course or an accredited ordinary or unclassified degree plus extra engineering studies.

For stage 2, entrants must normally go through a two-year approved training programme (of which at least six months must be postgraduate), but other routes are possible, eg scientists and mathematicians can qualify if they complete a longer training.

Stage 3 requires at least two years' responsible experience, and (from 1988) a professional review including a report and an interview. The minimum age for CEng is 25.

People with appropriate qualifications can apply direct to go on the professional register, but must be members of a qualifying institution to gain 'chartered' status.

Technician engineer (TEng) The stage 1 main route is via an accredited BTEC/SCOTVEC HNC/D (see ENGINEERING COURSES, QUALIFICATIONS AND TRAINING below). Alternative routes are an equivalent qualification (eg CGLI) or an accredited ordinary or unclassified degree.

For stage 2, entrants must normally have had at least two years' approved training.

Stage 3 requires at least two years in a post of increasing responsibility. The minimum age is 23.

Engineering technician The stage 1 main route is via an accredited BTEC/SCOTVEC NC/D; alternative routes are an equivalent qualification (eg CGLI).

Stage 2 requires at least two years' approved training programme or scheme.

For stage 3, entrants must show competence in relevant skills and be responsible for work where proven techniques and procedures are used, but no time is set. The minimum age is 21.

By 1986, there were some 200,000 chartered engineers; 60,000 registered technician engineers, and 20,000 engineering technicians on the new register.

These numbers have hardly changed since 1983, and for chartered engineers, are slightly down. Engineers are not legally required to join a professional institution or to be registered as such with the Engineering Council to practice/ work as a professional. But chartered status may sharply improve promotion prospects, especially with major employers and for consultancy work. At present, though, many new graduates clearly do not join. Engineering Council is determined to change this, by getting employers voluntarily to require professional registration. It may, therefore, be a worthwhile precaution for newly-qualified people to register straightaway. Because, if EC is successful at some future date, the academic and/or training standard may well have been raised in the intervening years (as EC expects), making it impossible for people who qualified at a previous standard then to go on the register.

Further information from the Engineering Council and individual engineering institutions (see sections following).

ENGINEERING FUNCTIONS
Introduction — design — research and development — draughtsmanship — production planning and management

Introduction
Careers in engineering divide in two ways – into BRANCHES (see following section) and into occupations or 'functions' which are common to all or most of the branches, although the proportions employed in the various functions vary from branch to branch.

The main engineering functions are design, research and development; production (which may be construction or manufacture), planning and management; commissioning, installation, maintenance and servicing. Terms used sometimes vary between industries and branches. Increasingly, especially where contracts are very large and complex – for multi-million pound chemical or other plant, major civil engineering projects like dams, even defence projects (like the Tornado plane) 'project' engineers oversee them from start to finish. A high proportion of professional, and some technician, engineers become managers.

In industries where the product is technologically-sophisticated – computers, or chemical plant – MARKETING and sales employ qualified engineers too.

Professional and technician engineers, sometimes engineering technicians, do also go into engineering-related functions like PURCHASING, PATENT WORK, TRAINING. Some go on to train to become ACCOUNTANTS, which is a useful stepping stone into MANAGEMENT CONSULTANCY – and FINANCE generally has been showing greater interest in people with technological backgrounds lately. A few go into PERSONNEL WORK. The proportion of chartered engineers working in non-engineering functions has risen recently (1985) to 2.4% (against a steady 1.6-1.7% for earlier years). The proportion of technician engineers working outside engineering has similarly gone up, to 2% from 1.1-1.2%.

Engineering design
Engineering designers turn ideas into plans or specifications for a real product

– its performance, shape and size, the materials from which it will be made, and so on. Engineering designers work on 'products' which range from a completely new bridge or dam (which is civil engineering), down to a new microprocessor, which is electronic engineering. Chemical engineers design new processes and plant to make a new detergent, naval architects design ships, mechanical engineers cars or machine tools. In some industries, eg aircraft, a completely new design is a comparatively rare event – although new modifications may be made, to take advantage of a new technical development (which could, perhaps, improve fuel consumption), to meet a competitor's design modification, or to improve materials. In other industries, like civil engineering, each new project usually means a completely new design.

'Design' is a word which implies 'creating' something that looks good. But in engineering, design has first and foremost to come up with a product that does the job for which it is intended, which actually works. Aesthetic appeal and visual impact may be built in, but the priority for this varies from product to product. In civil engineering, for example, a bridge or a dam is expected first and foremost to be strong enough for the traffic it must carry or the water held, but they are also expected to 'fit' aesthetically into the environment. Car designers must make a car's appearance appeal to the customer, but within the constraints of a vehicle that is fast, safe, fuel efficient, and so on. Aesthetics barely rate in designing machine tools or electronic components.

The creativity of a design engineer lies in the ability to make critical judgements on what will be the best design in the circumstances. This means trying to balance the customer's ideal with the very many constraints set by technical, manufacturing, and marketing – including pricing – factors. A dam must meet specific stresses and strains for a given weight of water, taking into account all the factors of terrain, soil etc, yet be technically possible to build with a minimum of materials of a given strength, at a price the customer will pay – and still fit into its surroundings. To improve sales, a company's designers worked out a completely new set of principles for garden secateurs, giving them a more efficient hammer action with which even the least green fingered cannot bruise plant stems, with few parts to rust or lose – and therefore also easier to manufacture, with a better grip and balance, and better looking too.

These designers worked to specifications set by MARKETING, who commissioned MARKET RESEARCH to survey gardeners' needs. They took into account all the manufacturing problems, and designed it to be as economical to produce in terms of time, labour, tools, and machinery as they could. They ironed out problems which could have resulted in a part snapping under certain stresses by changing the material used, and made some modifications at the request of service staff. They discussed with packaging whether or not the standard box could be used or whether it needed strengthening, and how much this would cost.

Most engineering design offices handle very large amounts of information, much of it in number form. Here other departments may be involved – research and development may be asked for reports and tests on possible materials for a product and how they behave, if they need any strengthening, and if so how it can be done, and whether or not the material can be produced economically in the right amounts. Marketing researches customers and retailers and feeds back the information, and designers do their own searches of the technical literature, or get the library to do it.

Designers have to make a great many calculations, not only of sizes and shapes of both the finished product and the parts, but also of how best to achieve the result the customer wants in many other ways. A chemical engineer has to calculate how strong a chemical reactor vessel must be to withstand given pressures, for instance. The design process may involve several modifications, and all the other calculations then have to be re-checked. The final 'design' translates all these parameters into a tight specification, expressed in engineering and mathematical terms and with working drawings etc, with the balance between all the factors right.

Reconciling all the conflicting demands, yet finding a satisfactory result is not simple, but designers do now have computer-aided design (CAD) systems which handle the data and do most of the calculations, with VDUs on which they can see the design in three dimensions and considerable detail, so it can be modified using a light pen. These systems, widely in use now in many industries, help designers to work out, for example, the best way to route pipes round an oil refinery, lay out electronic circuits, or the most aerodynamically-efficient shape for a car.

CAD systems save the designers a great deal of time, cut the amount of testing that has to be done – in a wind-tunnel for example, on aerodynamic shaping – and so keep down costs. They drive automatic draughting machines, and in the more sophisticated systems, the same 'tapes' are used to make special machine tools to exact specifications, and control parts of manufacture, eg cutting car body panels. CAD systems can give greater consistency, and the best design practices can be selected, coded and stored in the machine, to be adapted for the next related project. They cannot (yet) replace designers, but allow more sophisticated thinking, save valuable time, and give more time for making decisions. In some sectors, though, CAD has become crucial to future development – further miniaturisation of integrated circuits would be impossible without CAD systems.

Engineering designers work mostly in teams, of qualified engineers supported by technicians, such as draughtsmen and women (who produce the final specifications in working drawings again increasingly using CAD systems rather than drawing boards). Since most engineering products are complicated and have many parts, the design work is divided between them according to the complexity and sophistication of the design and the individual engineer's level of experience. They may work directly for a manufacturer, or work for (or be) a design consultant.

The proportion of qualified professional engineers working in design has been falling steadily, down to 7.7% of the total in 1985, against over 18% in 1966. There seems to be no satisfactory explanation for this, except the possibility that a significant proportion of those working as designers are not registering as chartered engineers. The proportion of registered technician engineers in design has risen to around the 8% mark lately, against only 6.5% in 1977. In 1981, some 63% of all chartered engineers working in design had degrees (against under 56% in 1977), and a further 10.5% had higher degrees (10% in

1977). By 1985, 5% of technician engineers working in design were graduates too.

The Institution of Engineering Designers surveyed its members (most of whom are qualified as technician engineers) in 1985.

In terms of the work they do, just 20% described themselves as design engineers, 14% as design draughtsmen/women, almost 11% as project engineers, and 10% as design managers. Over 9% were teaching, and nearly 6% had moved into general management with another 4% in technical administration. Over 53% were working for private companies, nearly 9% for local authorities (including those teaching etc in polytechnics and FE colleges), over 7% were self-employed, about 7% were employed by nationalised industries, public corporations or regional authorities, and over 4% were working for consultancies.

Almost 60% were working on industrial products (including 7% on electronics or telecommunications equipment, 5.6% on vehicles and components, and 4.3% on aircraft and aero-engines), 4% in construction, and almost 3% for research bodies.

Qualifications and education/training Engineering design work is technologically very sophisticated and designers need a high-level of engineering know how, so at most levels it is more usual to start by gaining a qualification in one of the BRANCHES OF ENGINEERING.

At first degree level the design content of all engineering degree courses is now being substantially increased, and some now give considerable emphasis to design. Examples include –
Universities
Glasgow: Product engineering design (BEng 4 yrs)
Hull: Engineering design & manufacture (BEng 4 yrs)
Liverpool: Mechanical systems & design engineering (BEng 3 MEng 4 yrs)
Loughborough: Design & manufacture (BSc 3/BSc/dip 4 yr-s)
Warwick: Engineering design & appropriate technology BSc* 3/MEng 4 yrs)
Polytechnic
Leicester: Engineering technology (BEng* 3/4 yr-s) includes option in mechanical engineering design and design management

At technician-engineer and engineering-technician level, design and/or draughtsmanship is most frequently a stream/option within BTEC courses, which can be linked to formal training as a draughtsman/women or design technician with an employer. However, there is at least one scheme specialising in engineering design (but based on mechanical/production engineering) at the Polytechnic of Wales.

'Professional' qualifications Most design engineers usually qualify for membership of the professional body which covers their 'branch' of engineering. However, one body specialises in design –
The Institution of Engineering Designers, with a membership (1986) of about 6,400 (down lately in line with members' age profile). The main route to fully-qualified associate membership of the Institution is with a BTEC HNC with two years' training and three years' experience in design or drawing office (another four years' experience for full membership), which qualifies for

TEng, but a significant proportion of members qualify with a BTEC national plus two years' training and seven years' experience (including two in a design or drawing office). Only an estimated 25% are graduates, but the Institution can nominate the suitably qualified for chartered status.

Further information from the Institution of Engineering Designers (leaflets).

Research and development

These frequently go together for engineers. Most engineers who are researchers are employed in industry, where they work mainly on solving specific and actual problems which are often fairly routine. They support design (above), particularly in testing prototypes, finding and/or testing new and/or cheaper materials. But as often it is practical problem-solving on an existing range of products. Research engineers look for ways of using research done elsewhere in the company's products or processes; try to solve production problems – perhaps by modifying a tool, iron out snags in processes, or try to improve and simplify them, and so make them more efficient and cheaper. They may search for ways to cut fuel consumption, eg by using heat exchangers.

Massive technological leaps in industry are infrequent and there is only rarely any really original research – in the very new fields of biotechnology, for example, most research is being done in universities, research-council labs, or small science companies (which may be university or polytechnic based), and the results 'sold' to multinationals interested in exploiting it. A major exception was the first work in fibre optics which was done in the labs of a telecommunications company.

Chances to work on more fundamental problems, to use very advanced theoretical and experimental methods, are found mainly in universities and polytechnics (generally combined with TEACHING), or in government or industrial research establishments. In the latter, research workers may do some very fundamental work – such as how aircraft wings behave at different speeds and under different conditions.

However, major efforts are under way to step up more industrially-useful research in universities, via collaborative ventures with industry. Universities and polytechnics now need more financial support from industry, and the government, mainly via SERC, is looking for more effort in this direction. SERC is increasing the proportion of its budget spent on engineering to 29% by 1989-90 (from 10% in 1975), which put nearly £49 million into engineering research in 1985-6. A large proportion of SERC's engineering budget goes into 'high tech' lead areas like information technology, biochemical engineering (for biotechnology), the application of computers to manufacturing engineering (including robotics), and (bio)medical engineering. Other 'growth' points are fundamental concepts in design, space technology, and control of large scale systems. But research is also supported in areas which, though less glamorous, are still crucial to industry – on eg combustion engines, construction management, design of high-speed machinery, and process engineering.

Defence, via joint research council/Ministry contracts, is another expanding area of more practical research for university/polytechnic engineers.

Engineers in both universities and industry develop new equipment for science too. Much new scientific research depends on engineering developments – progress in particle and nuclear physics, for instance, usually follows closely on new, ever more sophisticated particle accelerators; astronomy and astrophysics depend on refinements in mirror technology, highly-sophisticated computer-based machines to record and analyse observations, as well as space problems and satellites.

Engineering R&D is multidisciplinary team work, with engineers from more than one 'branch' working alongside and closely with materials specialists, physicists, chemists and even doctors (on eg medical equipment). They are supported by technicians whose work includes running experiments and tests, operating things like wind tunnels, test beds, building equipment etc.

While much of the research that engineers do is still based on the traditional lab, a lot also goes on in 'labs' which look more like factory workshops or areas which have, or are, 'models' of real life – the river to be dammed, the wind tunnel etc. Increasingly, though, both lab- and model-based research, especially in the early stages and on areas like wind-tunnel testing, computer modelling and simulation/emulation are being used. They are faster and cheaper, but involve researchers in writing programs, of eg offshore gas or oil production processes.

The proportion of chartered engineers working in R&D stayed fairly static between 1979 and 1983, at just under 10% of the total, but this was down on the 12.5% of 1966, and in 1985 the proportion fell again, to only 7.3% (including software development, 6% without). Even though industrial research effort is known to have declined, once again, this suggests people working in engineering R&D are not seeking chartered status. Some 4% of technician engineers work in this area, including software development, 3.5% without, showing little change since 1966.

Some 51% of all chartered engineers working in R&D in 1985 held first degrees (the percentage has fluctuated between 50% and the peak of 58% in 1977), and a further 31% (25% in 1977) held higher degrees. Some 13.5% of technician engineers working in R&D in 1985 were also graduates, and 1% also had higher degrees.

Qualifications and training Virtually all engineers going into R&D are now graduates, who generally read for a degree in an appropriate BRANCH OF ENGINEERING or (general) engineering science followed by research training for a higher degree. Support staff normally qualify via a BTEC award in an appropriate branch of engineering.

Draughtsmanship

Draughtsmen and women produce the necessary drawings in any area of work which involves making or building anything.

It is common to think of draughtsmen and women as working only in the ENGINEERING INDUSTRY, but CONSTRUCTION in general and ARCHITECTURE in particular are among those employing many in their drawing offices; map makers (see CARTOGRAPHY) use draughtsmen and women trained in cartographic techniques. BRITISH TELECOM, as one example, is one of the largest employers.

This is, then, a 'function' and a career stage rather than a career in its own right. It is an area of work which has been changing for some years, but is doing so particularly rapidly just now, mainly with the introduction of computer-aided design (CAD) systems (see ENGINEERING DESIGN).

CAD systems produce drawings in two or three dimensions, 'compiling' them either from data entered in 'real-time', or from information stored in a linked database. Drawings can be modified electronically, usually on a VDU screen using a 'light pen'. CAD has been a viable proposition for most engineering firms and design practices since about 1978, so they can produce both new and modified products, much faster than by traditional drawing methods. Firms can also improve their service – offering more elaborate drawings with tender documents, for example, or meeting demand for special features – with CAD systems. Typically, drawing office productivity can be raised by a factor of three using CAD systems, after 9-12 months' training and experience. CAD automates drawing rather than design, which still needs an expert brain instructing/guiding the system, so it is drawing office jobs that are most at risk.

Employers identify two levels of draughtsmanship –

At the upper level, the technician engineer works directly under a design (or other) engineer, and probably prepares 'general-arrangement' rather than detail drawings. Higher-level draughtsmen/women may supervise the work of detail draughtsmen/women, and are often qualified to BTEC/SCOTVEC Higher award (or equivalent) level.

Lower-level draughtsmen/women may work under a design draughtsman/woman or other technician engineer, probably doing component or part drawings from general-arrangement drawings prepared by the technician engineer draughtsman or women, and probably qualified to, BTEC National level (or equivalent).

(Technical changes in drawing materials, reprographics and microfilming have now virtually eliminated tracing work.)

In engineering, about three-fifths of draughtsmen/women at present work at the higher level. CAD is likel to affect lower-level draughtsmen/women rather more than at the higher level, because it automates 'pure' routine and repetitive drawing, so fewer draughtsmen/women reliant on drawing, rather than engineering, skills may be needed.

Traditionally, the drawing office was the bright apprentice's route to professional qualification, standing etc. The closing-off of the part-time route to professional qualification and the increased intake of young graduates with whom the draughtsmen/women had to compete for promotion, has altered this, rather than any automated system. CAD, however, does threaten the supply of higher-level draughtsmen/women, if it cuts the number of lower-level jobs, because training is still largely on-the-job.

The numbers of draughtsmen/women employed in the engineering industry alone have more than halved in the last two decades, from nearly 92,400 in 1964 to 45,500 in 1985, and the proportion of total employment from 2.69% in 1964 to 2.3% (a slight recovery from the 1.08% of 1978 though). Much of this fall is attributed to the parallel decline in firms' R&D activity, particularly in mechanical engineering, which employs about half of all draughtsmen/women working in engineering. There were shortages of draughtsmen/women until about 1980-1, but from then to 1985, the main impact on jobs was recession rather than CAD.

In engineering, most draughtsmen/women work (1982 figures) in MACHINERY AND MACHINE TOOL MANUFACTURE (about 15,000), in 'other' MECHANICAL ENGINEERING (9000), and in VEHICLE MANUFACTURE (up to 12,000). While ELECTRICAL ENGINEERING employs substantial numbers (some 13,500), ELEC-TRONICS tends to employ engineers rather than draughtsmen/women in design. Other sectors employing draughtsmen/women include METAL GOODS MANUFAC-TURE (under 6000), and MARINE ENGINEERING (around 1000).

The other main area of employment for draughtsmen/women is CONSTRUCTION (where they may have a somewhat broader job specification which can include brief preparation through to account settlement). Professional SURVEYORS, ARCHITECTS and CARTOGRAPHERS, whether themselves in employment or in private practice, generally have drawing office staff.

Qualifications and training There is no separate education or training for draughtsmen/women as such. Learning drawing office skills is part of techni-cian-level training within a particular field of employment. The evidence suggests that in future it is essential to gain a broadly-based engineering (or building/construction) training which leans more heavily on basic engineering skills than on straightforward drawing ability – indeed the ability to draw on paper is likely to become less and less important.

Most draughtsmen/women in training are office- rather than college-based and in engineering normally serve an trainee/apprenticeship, or its equivalent. College courses are taken on a release basis. Qualification should normally be via appropriate BTEC/SCOTVEC courses (see individual branches of engin-eering etc), preferably starting with four passes at 16-plus† (or the equivalent), or even one or two A levels.

Institution of Engineering Designers' membership: see ENGINEERING DESIGN.

Draughtsmen/women need a solid background in the principles of the particu-lar industry in which they are working and of the manufacturing and produc-tion processes through which the product must go, and the materials and components from which it will be made. Mathematical skills are very import-ant, as is scientific/technological understanding, and an interest in how things are made. They must obviously understand the new computer-based systems with which they will increasingly work. Draughtsmen/women need imagina-tion to help them understand what the designer intends and visualise the finished product or construction, but actual drawing skills are not now crucial.

Further information from professional bodies with technician-level entry, or specific technician organisations in the areas in which draughtsmen/women work, eg the Royal Aeronautical Society, the Institution of Civil Engineers, the Institution of Structural Engineers, the Society of Architectural and Associated Technicians, or the Institution of Engineering Designers.

Production planning and management (including project engineering, con-struction, installation, inspection)
These are functions in which engineers plan, organise and control production in manufacturing industry – from sophisticated single aircraft through to mass

production of cars or home computers – or the site in civil or chemical engineering construction. There are some variants, for example –

Project engineers are increasingly put in charge of very large contracts, particularly in civil and chemical engineering, starting from the time when the contract is signed, through construction, installation, and commissioning, to the final handing over of the facility to the customer.

Production engineers are normally the people who plan and try to improve productivity, who see that the plant produces the right number of cars or cans of soup at the right quality, at the right cost, on time. Planning production means breaking down the manufacturing or construction process into stages, deciding (for mass production) what the most efficient batch size is. They prepare flow charts and from them production plans and work schedules, which are at their most complicated when many different components have to come together in sub- and main-assemblies from different places (stores, machine shop, forge etc), with each part arriving at the right time. They have to work closely with other departments, such as PURCHASING and stores.

At the planning stage, too, production engineers work out, whether in the factory or out on the site, what plant, machinery and tools are needed (and if necessary have them made or purchased), estimate the people (numbers and types of skills), needed to produce the goods, and cost the operation.

Production engineers organise the assembly, product or flow lines, work out the machine loadings, arrange materials handling, and see that progress is monitored and controlled. Production engineers try all the time to improve on their systems: they may look for simpler (ie cheaper and faster) ways of making the product (with designers), more economical ways of using materials, assess new machinery (including automated production systems such as numerical machine tools, continuous processing, or robot equipment) for viability. If new systems and equipment are purchased, they must be planned for, installed and run in. Different production methods may be needed, and incentive systems worked out, with MANAGEMENT SERVICES staff.

Traditionally, production is part of the promotion ladder for skilled craft workers and technicians, but simpler production lines (making biscuits, chocolate, etc), often employ people (eg any graduate) who are not technologically trained at all, as part of their management training, but under the supervision of qualified engineers. The more complex and sophisticated the product and/or production process, the closer to the line or the site qualified engineers are employed, but scientists (usually physicists or chemists, depending on the product) are often 'converted' to production.

Production itself employs (EC 1985 figures) only 2.5% of chartered engineers (down from 9.4% in 1966) and about 3% (down from 4%) of technician engineers. But a further 12.6% of chartered engineers, 10.3% of technician engineers are 'project' engineers. Almost 50% of chartered production engineers were graduates, over 60% of chartered project engineers. Nearly 6% of technician engineers in production were graduates, over 6% in project engineering.

Inspection and quality control are part of the production process. Routine inspection is based on statistical sampling, and it is not only the finished product which has to be inspected, but everything that goes to making a particular product – the raw materials coming into a plant, or onto a construction site. Tests have to be made to see that processes have been completed properly, that there are no flaws in the material from which the product is made (possibly using sophisticated techniques like ultrasonic testing). Inspection and quality control teams are constantly trying to improve and if possible simplify their methods – if only to cut hold-ups in production. In science-based industries, quality control is a lab function – see SCIENTIFIC LABORATORY WORK. Some 2% of chartered engineers, 5.6% of technician engineers work (1985) in inspection.

Maintenance is a carefully organised programme of cleaning, inspection, testing, adjusting, and replacing parts, etc, designed to see that production is not interrupted any more than can be avoided. Maintenance must also solve any problems as fast as possible when machinery and equipment develop faults. Maintenance is more a technician engineer (nearly 17% of all registered technician engineers in 1985 up from 14% in 1966) than a chartered engineer (just 4% of the total) function, and the latter are generally only employed as managers etc, where the machinery and/or equipment is particularly sophisticated, or where there can be problems of keeping major installations running continuously, eg nuclear power plant, and where there has to be a particularly large team of maintenance engineers.

Qualifications and training See PRODUCTION ENGINEERING under BRANCHES OF ENGINEERING below.

ENGINEERING COURSES, QUALIFICATIONS AND TRAINING
Introduction — professional/graduate — technician engineer — engineering technician — craft

Introduction
The pattern of education and training in engineering is going through a period of considerable change right through from professional to craft level. Partly this is due to radically-changing technology and structural changes in employment which need higher-grade professional, technical and craft skills; partly because, perhaps for many years, education and training for engineers may not have properly matched the needs of employers (*pace* Finniston above); partly because the future needs of industry are likely to demand different, more flexible and even more sophisticated preparation. There is, for example, the problem of ensuring that engineers at all levels gain sufficient training in software disciplines, so that they do not lose work to people whose main expertise is in computing.

Engineering is at the lead edge in the revision of vocational preparation set out in the White Paper, *New Training Initiatives*, to a large extent because change is seen to be so crucial for the future of manufacturing industry if it is even to survive in competitive world markets. It also happens to have organisations – such as Engineering Council, the Engineering Employers' Federation, and the Engineering Industry Training Board (EITB) – in place which are able at least to attempt to push through change, even though the problems they face in so doing are considerable.

Engineering Council has, from the first, seen it as crucial to develop a national strategy for engineering education and training at all levels. The Council said (1983), '... there is no doubt that the engineering education and training system is a complex jigsaw in which the pieces do not quite fit, and may in some respects show the wrong pattern'. It suggested that the developments of the last twenty years – Robbins, CNAA, the creation of the 'colleges of advanced technology' and their rapid conversion into universities, the separate creation of the polytechnics, the replacement of national certificates and diplomas by TEC, and Dainton's enhanced degree courses – all 'admirable' in themselves, represented a string of uncoordinated developments which neglected to consider (because they were not asked to) the effect of change in one part of the system on others. Only the Finniston Committee 'began to get it right' by looking across the spectrum.

The Engineering Council wants 'initial' training for engineers of all levels treated as an integrated whole, with the needs of industry in mind, and with the professional institutions' 'benchmarks' defining the three grades of engineer.

The Engineering Council published its requirements for all three stages to registration in 1984, and the new standards are being progressively introduced from January 1986.

The educational stage 1 of all three sections of the register must meet Council criteria. Qualifications must have –

sufficient engineering subject content, although courses may be in specific disciplines (eg mechanical, aeronautical etc); unified, interdisciplinary or other broadly-based engineering; or joint, combined and modular schemes which include engineering-related options;

educational objectives: every course should embody and integrate theoretical, practical and project work, and convenient, familiar, traditional examining methods should not be allowed to inhibit course development or dictate teaching methods and syllabuses; and courses should enable students to progress as fast as possible towards defined roles and responsibilities, with particular regard to the present and future needs of industry and other employers.

an *academic standard* that satisfies EC-set criteria; considerable weight is put on course content, with special emphasis on –
  'integration' and 'relevance';
  the impact of new technologies and exclusion of obsolete material;
  teaching fundamentals and engineering applications;
  experimental project and design work offering intellectual challenge;
  appropriate examining methods;
  maintenance of output standards;
  preparing engineers for work in interdisciplinary teams.

The training stage 2 requirements emphasise again the need to integrate training and academic work and the practical application of analysis and theory. They also signal an end to 'time serving' and the traditional 'round all the departments' time-based schemes (although minimum training periods are suggested), and an emphasis on gaining specific knowledge and skills via recognised schemes of monitored and structured training under qualified supervision. Trainees are expected to gain practical knowledge and experience by taking part in useful work, and to be given supporting general education so they can apply new developments and techniques from other areas of technology, science, economics and sociology to their own speciality or in management.

Entrants will normally follow a training scheme and/or register with an EC member institution (called a nominated body for this purpose) approved by the Council to set and implement standards.

The experience stage 3 general requirements for all sections also emphasise performance in the job and, for potential chartered and technician engineers, early responsibility. Again this means less concern with the actual formal period of experience, so any minimum length of time given is only a guideline.

The Engineering Industry Training Board, in parallel with the Engineering Council (and in consultation), also believes 'that the time had come to take a broader view of all the well-established training patterns for separate areas of skill (operator, craft, engineering technician, technician engineer and professional engineer).' EITB is now placing these within a 'flexible and coherent system of training extending across the whole spectrum of skill levels'. The Board wants engineering training to be able to accommodate changes in technology swiftly, react quickly when skill shortages appear, and deliver the objectives of MSC's new training initiative so as to meet the industry's needs as well as the overall objectives of the initiative (see preceding chapter).

EITB, in line with MSC thinking, is moving further away from all reference to length of training, at least at craft and technician level, to a standards-based system. The Board is also working closely with the Engineering Council and BTEC on more flexible training recommendations for technicians and graduates in engineering. Clearly there is at last movement towards more co-ordination in provision for education and training in this area, and other organisations, like the National Advisory Board for Local Authority Higher Education (NAB), the UGC and CNAA, are also working with Engineering Council, EITB, BTEC, SCOTVEC and CNAA on this.

Progression For the past twenty or so years, education and training for engineering have become more rigidly stratified and divided between craft, technician and professional levels. Although never really reflecting the actual pattern of career movement in industry itself, the chances to go on from technician to professional qualification have been cut considerably, particularly as the part-time routes to professional qualification were lengthened and became tougher, as the academic requirements for membership of many professional bodies were raised sharply.

Moving from craft to engineering technician and thence to technician engineer qualification never became quite so difficult – progression routes have stayed open and even become more flexible.

While for the present at least, this pattern remains, it looks possible that routes through will open up again. The commitment of NCVQ to base qualification on competency and to allow people to build on their competencies instead of having to meet rigid formal examination requirements, and so go step-by-step into different levels must result in this if it is to be credible. EITB has already a common first year via YTS for all craft/technician entrants to engineering training – although those aiming from the start for professional levels (who would normally continue to go through a sixth form) are still excluded.

However, Engineering Council has committed itself to preserve, and if possible supplement the existing education 'bridges' (transfers between academic courses, eg from BTEC/SCOTVEC HNC/D to a degree) and 'ladders' ('bolt-on' modules taken during or after some training and experience). Students graduating from part-accredited degree courses may gain CEng status by undertaking extra study to raise their formation to BEng equivalent, and people registered as TEng may go on to take Engineering Council part 2 exams to complete the academic requirement for CEng. It is also possible to be entered in different sections of the professional register at the same time. For example, someone qualified at stage 3 TEng may also be entered at stage 1 CEng if he or she has the appropriate qualifications.

Engineering Council also sees 'due recognition of engineering talent, at whatever stage it can be identified, as an important contribution... and is anxious that individuals who achieve a high standard of professional competence during their careers should not be handicapped by lack of early educational opportunities.' The mature-candidate route to registration does allow direct entry to stage 3 (at age 35) and EC says a conventional examination to satisfy stage 1 requirements would not be appropriate . However, entry to chartered (as opposed to registered) status is still subject to the requirements of individual engineering institutions, and it is stressed that the 'burden of proof' on the individual is stringent.

Professional/graduate courses, education and training

For some time now, the great majority of professional engineers have started on the route to their careers with full-time or sandwich-based study for a degree in engineering. While an engineering degree course can be treated as a purely academic/intellectual education, giving the graduate a wide range of possible careers, in fact most engineering graduates do go on to become professional engineers.

Traditionally, engineering degree courses have been heavily academic and theoretical in bias. Whatever changes are needed, it is still certainly essential that every course gives a solid foundation of basic engineering sciences ie thermodynamics, fluid dynamics, electrical science and technology, materials science, measurement principles, chemistry and mathematics. However, culminating in Finniston (see above), there has been growing pressure to make courses more 'relevant' to the needs of industry.

Finniston wanted courses with the main emphasis on the 'synthesis of basic subjects', with greater emphasis on developing design and problem-solving skills taught mainly through project work and incorporating only enough engineering science and mathematics as needed to provide the foundations for teaching practice and applications. Finniston also wanted to see more time spent on fabrication and use of materials, and thought courses should also include relevant business techniques, again to be taught mainly via case studies and worked projects, so that engineers learn from the start to work within the limits of time (schedules), cost market factors and budgets, to work with others and cope with the problems of relationships in industry.

There is, though, no general agreement on what should go into an engineering degree course. As a result, engineering departments have become much more 'creative' in their syllabus design, bringing increasing variety and diversity into degree courses. But by no means all employers want engineering students taught 'management' on a first degree course, for example – they prefer graduates who are fully trained in fundamental sciences, basic skills and practices on a degree course, leaving management training until they have had reasonable work experience.

Finniston also wanted as many students as possible to gain their initial industrial experience via a sandwich-based degree course, and failing that, for departments to have well-equipped workshops where students can learn to use the very latest in computer-controlled machine tools, for example. In fact, a mix of experience of real working life in factories and learning to use machinery in a university or polytechnic workshop, where the student is not constrained by the production line, has to be valuable.

The Engineering Council has now laid down firm guidelines on what it requires for accreditation of degree courses (in its 1984 policy statement, *Standards and routes to registration* – SARTOR), even though it earlier agreed that it is difficult to find out what industry really wants. The guidelines try also to tidy up the confusion of new terminology – between so-called 'enhanced' and 'extended' courses, for example – which resulted from the uncoordinated response to the so-called 'Dainton' initiative which set up 'extended' courses in a few universities.

Engineering Council recommendations can be summarised as follows –
All courses should adopt an integrated approach to theoretical and practical teaching related to the needs of industry.
Such courses will be known as 'enhanced' (but not necessarily 'extended'). 'Enhanced' means remodelled courses which are in line with the subject content described below. 'Extended' courses should be broad courses (ie not an in-depth study of a specialist area), with entry (for students with both high academic ability and potential for success in an engineering career) mainly after a two-year course in common with the 'enhanced' course (preferably after assessment which should include performance on the engineering applications elements), but with the possibility of either direct entry, or transfer after a year only.
Accredited degree courses should be designated as Bachelor of Engineering (BEng) or if 'extended' MEng, and Engineering Council 'strongly discourages' the use of these titles for other courses. Places which cannot introduce them at once for accredited courses are expected to do so within a reasonable time (ie five years).
From 1992 (year of graduation), BEng courses must be of honours standard and classified to gain accreditation. This appears to mean that anyone starting an unclassified degree course in 1987 (four-year courses), 1988 (three-year courses), and those who gain only a pass or ordinary result on an honours course, will not be accepted automatically for stage 1 chartered register when they graduate in 1992. In practice, there would seem to be some latitude on Engineering Council's part, and once again all chartered engineering institutions are making their own rules within these guidelines. Thus the Civil

Engineers have already given notice that an honours result on an accredited honours course will be required from 1992 on, while the Mechanical Engineers say they will continue to accept an ordinary or pass result on an accredited honours course, and may continue to accredit unclassified BEng courses if the content and standard are very close to honours.

MEng courses need not be classified, but anyone gaining an MEng should be capable of at least a second class BEng.

Subject content: at least two-thirds of the content of accredited courses should be on engineering subjects. All students should be introduced to good engineering practice and be involved in a 'significant' amount of relevant, individually-assessed, project work.

Courses are expected to have the following features ('enhancement') –

Technical content in appropriate depth and breadth, emphasising fundamentals and including relevant maths and sciences.

Application of scientific and engineering principles to the solution of practical problems of engineering systems and processes; emphasis on the relevance of theory and analysis (including training in developing and using theoretical models from which the behaviour of the physical world can be predicted). Courses should embody and integrate theoretical, practical and project work.

Introduction to good engineering practice, and the properties, behaviour, fabrication and use of relevant materials and components.

Design studies (including manufacturing, reliability, maintainability, quality assurance and economic aspects): 'Engineering should be taught in the context of design, so that design is a continuous thread running through the teaching... exposing the student to a proper mixture of analysis, synthesis, conceptual design and other wider issues.'

Emphasis on methods of practical problem-solving using the latest technology, excluding obsolete methods and topics – computers should mean a more, not less, fundamental approach because real systems can be modelled more closely, so fewer assumptions need be made and many possibilities can be rapidly investigated.

Technical decision-making and its commercial implementation; use of technical information services; relevant government legislation; management and industrial relations principles; engineers' responsibility to the profession, the community and the environment.

Specific measures, eg teaching methods, to encourage students to find out and learn for themselves, eg communication skills, oral and written expression, and a critical approach to problem solving, with appropriate methods of examination and assessment.

Significant industrial involvement in the preparation of the course.

Engineering Council is also to 'part-accredit' courses which do not include enough of the above (especially engineering content). Graduates from these will be entitled to entry on a special 'holding' list, for chartered engineers. These must still be honours degrees, and no course can be part-accredited unless graduates can clearly make good the academic gaps within a year of full-time (or equivalent part-time) study.

Ordinary- and unclassified degree courses in engineering not accredited for direct entry to stage 1 of the chartered engineers' register (applicable to those graduating from 1992 on), will be for stage 1 of the technician engineers' section. But graduates with accredited ordinary and unclassified degrees will be entitled to entry on the same special 'holding' list, 1(H) as graduates with part-accredited degrees, and the same conditions for full registration apply.

It must be made clear that Engineering Council requirements are a *minimum*. Individual engineering institutions are still free to ask for still-higher standards (eg second-class honours) – see sections following.

Studying engineering for a degree Engineering at degree level is taught by universities and polytechnics, but only a very few other colleges. Over 41,600 first degree and postgraduate students were studying engineering in UK universities in 1984-5 (down from 44,100 in 1981-2), over 14% of the total (slightly up on 1981-2). Some 34,600 were studying for first degrees in engineering (against 37,800 in 1981-2), 14.3% of the total (against 15% in 1981-2). Another 38,400 students were on advanced engineering courses full-time in polytechnics and other colleges in 1984-5 (against 34,000 in 1981-2), about 13% of the total (15.5% in 1981-2), including 25,600 on first-degree courses.

Most people reading engineering choose to specialise in one of the main branches (see following sections), most from the start of their course, but it is possible to choose courses which are more broadly-based, or which start broadly-based, letting students defer specialisation until the second or third year, when they have a better idea of what each branch is about. This is not always easy to organise, because it can be difficult to get agreement between, say, electrical and mechanical engineering staff, on how much of what subjects should go into the 'common' part of the course. However,

Broadly-based or engineering science courses (* EC-accredited at July 86) are at

Universities –

Aberdeen:	Engineering BEng* (4 yrs) common course for two years, with specialisation in final years
Bath:	Engineering BSc/BEng* (3/4 yrs) common course for 4-5 terms, then specialisation in aero, computer-aided, mechanical, production or systems engineering
Birmingham, Aston:	Engineering BEng (3 yrs) basic engineering theory and practice throughout, but with some specialisation in final two years
Brighton, Sussex:	Engineering BSc* (3 yrs) all courses start with common four terms; specialisation thereafter
Brunel:	Special engineering programme BSc* (4 yrs) integrates mechanical, electrical, electronic and production engineering with business/management studies (including marketing and financial aspects)
Cambridge:	Engineering BA* (3/4 yrs) engineering sciences in year 1, then increasing specialisation
Durham:	Engineering BSc* (3 yrs) common course for five terms, then either interdisciplinary course or specialisation in one branch; can also be combined with management

Edinburgh:	Engineering BEng* (4 yrs) broadly based for a year, specialisation thereafter
Exeter:	Engineering science BSc (3 yrs)/BEng (4 yrs) common year 1 for all main branches, but not chemical, then specialisation (BEng*), or engineering science (BSc or BEng)
Guildford, Surrey:	Engineering with industrial management BEng (3/4 yrs) principles, practice, management and applications throughout
Lancaster:	Engineering BSc (3 yrs) common course for five terms, then specialisation*, or broad-based engineering
Leicester:	Engineering BSc* (3 yrs) common course for two years, then either specialisation or interdisciplinary course in final year
Liverpool:	Engineering science, or engineering science with industrial management BEng* (3 yrs)/MEng (4 yrs) both broad-based throughout, emphasising solution of real problems
Liverpool:	Engineering science & manufacture BEng (3 yrs)
London, QMC:	Engineering or engineering science BSc(Eng) (3 yrs) part of flexible degree scheme in engineering with considerable choice between broad-based scheme or specialising* later in course
Loughborough:	Engineering science & technology BTech* (4 yrs) interdisciplinary throughout)
Oxford:	Engineering science BA (4 yrs) common course for two years, followed by two years' specialisation*(not all options)
Reading:	Engineering science BEng* (3 yrs) broadly-based throughout, emphasising creative design and project work
Warwick:	Engineering science BSc* (3 yrs) BSc/MEng* (4 yrs) common, broadly-based year 1 continued into year 2 for most; then flexible choice of progressive specialisation or engineering science continued
Polytechnics – Birmingham:	Engineering BEng (3 yrs) integrates study of engineering principles with microprocessor and computer technology – strong emphasis on industrial applications
Coventry:	Combined engineering studies BEng* (3/4 yrs) common year 1, then flexible choice of units to give possible specialisation
Leicester:	Engineering technology BEng* (3/4 yrs) first half broadly based, second half specialisation in design, operations, systems, or energy utilisation
London, Thames:	Engineering BEng (3 yrs) common year 1, then mechanical or electronic/electrical engineering

Manchester:	Engineering BEng (3 yrs) broadly based throughout centring on industrial applications engineering
Nottingham, Trent:	Engineering & business studies BSc/BA* (5 yrs), or Industrial studies BSc* (4 yrs) both broadly based throughout
Oxford:	Engineering BEng* (3 yrs) broadly-based for two years with final year bias to electrical and/or mechanical engineering
Portsmouth:	Engineering with business studies BSc* (4 yrs) interdisciplinary throughout
Sheffield:	Engineering BEng* (4 yrs) broadly based throughout with choice of options in final year
	Engineering with business studies BEng* (4 yrs) broadly based throughout
Colleges –	
Aberdeen: RGIT:	Engineering technology BSc (4 yr-s) combines engineering science and technology covering electrical and mechanical engineering
Glasgow CT:	Engineering BEng* (3/4 yr-s)
Hull, Humberside:	Engineering BEng (4 yr-s) basic principles of electrical and mechanical engineering, and engineering practice
Plymouth, RNEC:	Engineering BEng (3 yrs) years 1-2 basic grounding in electrical and mechanical engineering sceince, properties of substances and engineering field theory; specialisation in year 3

'First destination' figures for general and combined engineering subjects, and general technology are –

	1984-5		1977-8	
	university	polytechnic	university	polytechnic
total graduating	1640	595	1660	400
research/further study	160	39	121	21
'believed' unemployed Dec 31	79	64	18	9
permanent UK employment	1129	310	774	150
employers –				
engineering	430	202	332	86
'other' manufacturing	107	38	112	19
oil, chemicals etc	106	8	61	10
construction	67	4	81	25
public utilities	75	9	47	9
accountancy	22	3	29	nil
'other' commerce	98	19	32	7
armed forces	35	3	23	3
civil service	18	13	12	3
local authorities	23	9	24	7

	1984-5		1977-8	
	university	polytechnic	university	polytechnic
functions –				
R&D/design	571	167	371	52
scientific R&D, design	84	9		
admin/op management	82	35	85	49
management services	74	25	49	16
financial work	73	6	32	2
eng etc support	67	21	33	11
environmental planning	56	26	93	2
marketing etc	35	11	17	9

Entry to engineering degree courses normally requires full A levels in maths and at least one science (physics or chemistry as appropriate) and for university, preferably two (but two AS levels may be accepted for the third). The overall 'mean' A-level score for all university engineering and technology first years was 11.1 in 1984-5 (10.3 with Scottish H-grades), but 12.4 for general and combined engineering subjects.

Students with A levels in arts/social science subjects can take a one-year 'conversion' course, designed to give them the maths and physics needed for entry to an engineering degree (or HND), at a number of polytechnics and CHEs.

Alternative to a degree The Engineering Council has taken over responsibility for administering the direct-entry examinations in engineering from the now-defunct Council of Engineering Institutions. The Council is continuing the examinations in roughly their present form but suitably 'enhanced' with course and project work, design etc, to bring them into line with the requirements for degree courses. Entry to courses for these examinations for professional qualification is still possible direct from school (via the same qualifications as for entry to a degree course), or an appropriate technician-level course with credit-standard results. But this two-part examination is the *minimum* requirement for registration as a professional engineer, and may not meet the requirements of some individual institutions; additional study may be necessary (see individual sections following) for chartered status.

Part 1 covers mathematics, mechanics, properties of materials, presenting engineering information, and two options (in eg electrotechnics, electronics, chemistry, thermodynamics). However, candidates who must choose this route (and the advice must always now be to read for an honours degree) are generally recommended to take a BTEC HND (entrants are discouraged from taking HNC and only exceptional candidates can follow this with part 2 examinations) instead of part 1 (but only 135 UK candidates took part 1 in 1986, the other 2000 being from overseas).

Part 2 consists of a compulsory subject, 'the engineer in society' and five others chosen from some 40 options in fields such as thermodynamics, fluids and fuels; materials and structures; electrical and electronic; systems and control; geotechnics and mining. In theory there is no restriction on choice of subjects, but in practice candidates normally also want membership of an institution, and each institution sets some restrictions and has some requirements on subjects which may or may not be taken to meet its specific entry qualifications. Total entries for Part 2 were about 4600 in 1986, but barely 1100 from UK candidates.

Qualifying for chartered status (EC stage 2 and 3) Set training, experience and a period spent holding down a responsible job have long been a requirement for full professional qualification, but under Engineering Council the required standards are being raised and vetting improved. While the requirements vary between individual institutions (see sections following), the Engineering Council has laid down minimum standards –
For stage 2, training must –

extend the scope of engineers' knowledge beyond their degree studies, to applying principles and theory to solving real problems, in design, manufacture, construction, marketing, operation and maintenance of their employers' products or services;

include a structured, supervised introduction to a range of practical assignments with as wide a range of engineering and management activities as possible, while learning to apply available practical and analytical techniques in practical situations;

develop sound judgement and critical abilities (with reference to factors eg technical, managerial, financial, commercial, relevant to engineering projects), flexible attitudes (to cope with rapidly-changing technology and materials, techniques and processes not yet fully developed);

teach broad engineering practice relevant to a trainee's branch of engineering including familiarity with design, materials, techniques and processes in that and related branches;

include a working knowledge of general factors such as financial, economic and commercial constraints; limitations imposed by available manpower and materials; operational and maintenance requirements.

For stage 3, responsible experience is defined as employment requiring an engineer to develop and prove fully technical competence and demonstrate a range of functions and characteristics, such as –

independent technical judgement requiring both practical experience and application of engineering principles;

direct responsibility for management or guidance of technical staff and other resources;

innovation in technical matters via eg design, development, research, manufacturing technology;

creation of systems and procedures and proving their cost-effectiveness;

design, development and manufacture of products, equipment and processes to a competitive level of cost, safety, quality, reliability and appearance.

Postgraduate study Far fewer graduate engineers (under 8%) than scientists (nearly 20%) go on to further academic study or research (training) – and over 50% of the 7000 postgraduate students studying engineering full-time in universities in 1984-5 came from overseas. However, it is probable that more engineers return to postgraduate study after a period in employment.

Graduate engineers can choose to go on, or return, to further study for a variety of purposes. They can decide to train for research, normally by completing a three-year PhD; they can choose to do a one-year full-time course either to specialise in one area of their first-degree subject, or to 'convert' their basic engineering training to another area (eg chemical engineering to bio-technology, broad-based electronics to software engineering), or add on extra skills, eg management. They can return to study to upgrade or update their original training.

The Science and Engineering Research Council (SERC) gives grants for conventional forms of postgraduate study – one-year advanced courses leading to a master's degree or higher diploma (about 490 awards in 1985-6), three-year schemes for a PhD (about 350). SERC's engineering board sees all advanced courses as vocational preparation for industry (and only continues to approve courses if a 'substantial' proportion of students find jobs in industry), but SERC also tries to encourage more industry-related training via 'directed' awards. These include (as of 1986) –

Co-operative Awards in Science and Engineering (CASE) scheme (200 engineering awards in 1985-6).

The 'industrial studentship' scheme, under which students holding any (other) type of SERC award stays in employment, receiving their normal salaries, part of which SERC repays to their employer – but this was taken up by only 68 in 1985-6.

The 'integrated graduate development' scheme, designed to attract high-quality graduates into key engineering functions in industry, giving them in their first year in industry short courses to broaden their technical knowledge and to widen their understanding of the part it plays in the wider context of their firm's business. In 1985-6, 135 students joined such programmes.

Further information Engineering Council (which publishes a definitive list of accredited courses); Science and Engineering Research Council (for postgraduate awards).

Technician-engineer courses, education and training

Traditionally, senior or higher technicians came through, via promotion and/or additional qualification, from technician level and frequently still do (see Engineering technician below). But for a decade or more now a direct education/training route to technician engineer has been developing, largely to accommodate those who could no longer qualify for professional status. When the Engineering Council restricts direct entry from the education system to graduates with honours-standard degrees (or equivalent), more people with unclassified and ordinary/pass degrees will follow this route too.

But the Engineering Council wants to see the education and training routes for technician engineers expanded, and has set standards for academic qualifications, training and experience which seek to give technician engineers a much more definitive, positive identity, rather than negatively describing them in terms of failed chartered engineers.

However, Engineering Council has also kept open clear routes through from technician- to professional-engineer qualification and, with rising shortages of professionals, the number of courses and training schemes designed for this is expected to increase.

Engineering Council's key educational objective for technician engineers is a high level of technical proficiency, with sufficient knowledge of modern technology to relate to operating practice in a specific field. This must be based on a fundamental understanding of relevant basic principles, and curricula must be designed with this in view. Maths, physical sciences and appropriate engineering theory should be included and the relevance of basic principles to a specific field should be the major factor in selecting subject material.

Engineering Council sets the 'mainstream' academic route to stage-1 technician-engineer registration as via Council-accredited BTEC/SCOTVEC courses. For the time being the minimum is an accredited HNC (so equivalent and higher qualifications are accepted, if accredited for the purpose). But Engineering Council envisages that within five years (ie by 1990) HND 'may well' be the minimum (and at least two professional bodies are implementing this). As of 1987-8 entry, Engineering Council requires eight units at BTEC's new H level relevant to engineering, normally as an integral part of a Higher-award course, but some may be completed as supplementary studies. The H-level units package must include an engineering project of at least one unit which integrates work within the course.

Unclassified and ordinary degrees are also listed, but must be specifically accredited as being specially designed for technician-engineer preparation (albeit at the 'highest levels of activity'), and are not just lower-grade qualifications for people who have failed to achieve honours.

The distinctive features required of all courses for accreditation include –
treatment of physical laws needed to understand the particular field of engineering and training to apply them to the design and conduct of experiments to provide design data;
mathematics (equivalent to at least one unit at NIII level) needed to understand the derivation of commonly-used major design criteria and training to interpret the criteria for variations from the norm, to use (and so understand) computer applications and calculation methods likely to be met (including at least one computing unit, with assignment work related to engineering applications at NII level);
study of materials needed to understand relevant properties and problems met in adequately defining and measuring them; to design equipment and structures with appropriate materials and components, and to be sure that externally-imposed criteria have been met;
specialist technology needed to understand techniques (eg in reliability, maintainability and qualify control) normally used, or being developed, in the field of engineering being studied;
technical communication topics, eg normal drawing office practice (including computer-based methods), interpreting engineering drawings and significance of standard symbols, dimensions etc, writing clear memoranda and more extended detailed reports, formulating clear and unambiguous instructions, effective speaking;
professional and general topics including economic factors affecting the specific industry, its financial structure and significance of costs on work and freedom of choice.

Technician-engineer level qualifications The main courses for technician engineers are those leading to BTEC and SCOTVEC Higher National Diplomas and Certificates, although as indicated earlier, after 1992 ordinary and unclassified degree courses may no longer qualify for chartered status without additional study, and so may progressively become technician-engineer qualifications too.

Courses (part time only from 1987-8 for HNC, full time, sandwich based or part time for HND) for BTEC and SCOTVEC higher awards are taught at polytechnics (England and Wales), central institutions (Scotland), and larger FE colleges. As for all other BTEC courses, HND/C in all branches of engineering are being revised. Guidelines for 1987 on have not yet (spring 87) been issued but will (as all BTEC schemes) be unit based and modular, take into account developments in technologies, evolving needs of employers and professional recognition. BTEC expects the number of units required in future for an HND in engineering is likely to be more than the minimum stated in the new general guidelines (see TECHNICIAN-LEVEL QUALIFICATIONS).

Over 21,500 people registered for BTEC Higher awards in all branches of engineering in 1985-6 (still up from the low of 19,500 in 1983-4 although slightly down on 1984-5), with an increasing proportion studying for Diplomas (over 30% in 1985-6). The great majority of people who study engineering for an award at this level specialise in a branch of engineering (see sections following) relatively few registering for general engineering.

BTEC general engineering courses teach students to apply analytical concepts beyond certificate level, or whose occupations involve personal responsibility for broad-ranging, cross-disciplinary activity where the emphasis is more on synthesis than analysis. The list of possible options from which courses can be built is lengthy, and has included mathematics, computer applications and theory, terotechnology, work study, manufacturing technology, control theory, materials science, logic and drive systems, product design, economics, languages, supervisory studies, construction and materials, industrial organisation, instrumentation and systems, measurements, properties and uses of materials, electronics, and project work.

Higher National courses (full time/sandwich based) are at – High Wycombe: Bucks CHE; London, S Bank P, Willesden CT; Manchester P; Newcastle P; Northampton: Nene C; Norwich CCF&HE; Pontypridd, Wales P; Swindon C; part-time: at 24 polytechnics and colleges.

Entry to HND/C is as for all BTEC Higher awards††, if via A-level with the pass in maths or physics, and the other studied to A level.

SCOTVEC general engineering (HND only) is built around mechanical, plant and production engineering, training for relatively senior work. Design and industrial studies are integral, and final-year options include agricultural engineering and offshore petroleum technology.

Entry is as for all SCOTVEC higher awards†††, the H grades to include maths and physics or engineering

Qualifying as a technician engineer The new requirements for full EC registration as a technician engineer are –

For stage 2, training should develop the skills needed to use equipment, instruments, apparatus and techniques; give familiarity with as wide a range of good engineering practice as possible, and show how available practical and analytical techniques can best be applied. Training should cover materials, components, techniques and processes used in both trainees' own and related engineering branches. They must learn a flexible attitude to meet rapidly-changing technology, and so training must be as deep and broad as possible. Special emphasis should be given to –

using and communicating information;

choosing materials and components and understanding materials processing; practical design work;

organisation of engineering work and associated financial and economic practice;

using diagnostic skills and applying technical and analytical techniques;

organising and giving direction to the work of other people.

For stage 3, appropriate experience is similar to that for chartered engineers, but with a different emphasis and more limited depth and range. Functions and characteristics will normally include –

exercising independent technical judgement;

designing, developing and manufacturing products, equipment and processes to a competitive level of cost, safety, quality, reliability and appearance;

understanding of and involvement in financial, statutory and commercial considerations;

communication skills and human/industrial relations;

a responsible attitude to engineering and changes in technology.

Engineering-technician courses, qualifications and training
As for technician engineers, engineering technicians used mainly to come through from skilled craft level, but direct entry routes to engineering-technician training and qualification have been developing for some years now. However, more recently there has been some return to older patterns via, mainly, EITB's common first year training scheme for craft and technician entrants at 16 plus.

While Engineering Council is establishing a firm educational and training basis for engineering-technician status in its own right, it says courses, and training, should still be designed so students can go on directly to technician-engineer level studies.

Engineering Council's mainstream route to stage 1 engineering-technician registration is, at least an accredited BTEC or SCOTVEC national certificate (so a BTEC national diploma also qualifies).

The EC looks for distinctive features in accredited courses. They include –

treatment of scientific laws needed to understand design and operation of components and systems and their applications in a particular field of engineering; units of measurement, principles and methods of measurement and sources of error; calibration requirements and techniques;

mathematics needed to understand, interpret and apply the above in a particular engineering specialisation, and modern computing techniques at an appropriate depth;

study of working practices and materials needed to understand basic properties of relevant materials; measurement methods and equipment; appropriate standards and specifications; codes of practice; technical and economic factors affecting selection of materials;

enough engineering technology for a basic understanding of the techniques used in a particular field;

topics in technical communication, eg reading and interpreting engineering drawings; making engineering sketches; using technical manuals effectively; writing technical reports: giving technical instructions to craft workers and operators; interpreting technical activities to non-technical people;

emphasis on practical problem solving; covering latest technology and excluding obsolete material and methods.

Engineering-technician level qualifications The main courses for engineering technicians are those leading to BTEC National Diplomas and Certificates, and SCOTVEC National Certificates.

BTEC courses (part time only from 1987-8 for National Certificates, normally two-year full time or three-year sandwich based for National Diplomas) and SCOTVEC courses for National Certificates are taught by many FE colleges. As for all other BTEC courses, National Certificate and Diploma courses in all branches of engineering are being revised, and the National Diploma in Technology (engineering) has been withdrawn, leaving just the National Diploma in engineering.

Some 34,000 people registered for BTEC National awards in engineering in 1985-6 (still up from the low of 33,000 in 1983-4 although down from nearly 35,700 in 1984-5), with about 31% (1985-6) studying for Diplomas.

BTEC National engineering courses are being revised along new guidelines mostly from 1987-8 entry (some colleges may run existing schemes for a year or two).

The new courses are unit-based, or modular (see TECHNICIAN-LEVEL QUALIFI-CATIONS), with specific aims in line with EC requirements (above). Six (of the required ten) units for a Certificate and 7.5 (of the required eighteen) for a Diploma must now be 'common core studies' – engineering applications of computers, industry and society, scientific principles, and applications/technology (which can be biased to a particular branch), and within these must be taught materials, communication, information/developing technologies, and systems/diagnostic skills. Student-centred investigation/design work (including projects and problem solving) is a central requirement for core skills. The remaining units can be chosen from a steadily-lengthening, and regularly-changing, list of BTEC-devised (or, but only if there is a clear, locally-identified need, centre-developed) options either to give further broad-based studies or be designed for a specific field of engineering. Diploma students can take a special maths 'package' which will give the necessary qualification to go on to an engineering degree course.

Full-time (diploma) students must also gain at least 300 hours' structured vocational experience (which can be met via EITB-approved basic training). For an integrated BTEC/EITB award, a further 450-500 additional hours of learning support time is required.

Entry to a BTEC National-award engineering course is (from 1987 entry) only as listed in TECHNICIAN-LEVEL QUALIFICATIONS, via 16-plus† normally including mathematics and a suitable science.

BTEC First engineering courses The new First Certificate (one-year part time) and Diploma (one-year full or two years' part time) courses, effectively replacing the old (National) Certificate/Diploma level 1, start in 1987-8. Modular and unit based, all five units for the Certificate and six (of eight) for the Diploma are required core studies – engineering fundamentals, maths, science, information technology studies and, for the Diploma, vocational assignments. Diploma unit options include engineering drawing, built environment, metals technology, microelectronic systems, motor vehicle engineering, instrumentation and process measurements, communications systems, or may be centre-devised.

Entry to BTEC First-award courses is as listed in TECHNICIAN-LEVEL QUALIFI-CATIONS††.

SCOTVEC National Certificate courses the modular structure of the new Certificate (see TECHNICIAN-LEVEL QUALIFICATIONS) means that there is no set curriculum for engineering courses – but as students can choose modules so as to gain an endorsement 'equivalent to the Certificate in multidisciplinary engineering'.

Entry to SCOTVEC National courses is as listed in TECHNICIAN-LEVEL QUALIFI-CATIONS.

Qualifying as an engineering technician The new requirements for full EC registration as an engineering technician are –

For stage 2 training, the aims are more or less the same as for technician engineer, as are the points for emphasis, leaving out application of technical and analytic techniques, and organising and directing other people.

At stage 3, entrants should show full responsibility in their own right for work where proven techniques and procedures are used, and should be competent at, eg –

constructing accurate models and special equipment;
safe working practices;
leadership at supervisory level;
effective oral and written communication in English;
interpreting technical drawings and specifications;
capabilities, limitations and possibilities of tools, materials, equipment and operations;
design and operation of systems and related mathematical skills;
industrial relations principles.

Craft courses, education and training

Gaining engineering skills has traditionally meant a three- or four-year apprenticeship, straight from school at sixteen, learning on-the-job but with release to study at college on craft courses, usually for CGLI awards. The engineering apprenticeship system has a history going back a hundred or more years, and has survived many attempts to modernise it, but has lately been going through substantial changes under the Engineering Industry Training Board, to the extent that the term 'apprentice' has now been replaced by 'trainee'.

Recession, and the particularly sharp decline in employment in MANUFACTUR-ING INDUSTRY since 1979, led firms to cut drastically the numbers of engineering craft trainees recruited, even though this has resulted in skill shortages. EITB's 1985-6 figure was barely 6400 (numbers 'bottomed out' at 6300 the year before) – against nearly 17,000 in 1979-80.

Engineering craft training schemes, courses and qualifications are designed co-operatively by the Engineering Industry Training Board, CGLI, FE and industry. EITB has completely revised craft training since 1983. Training is now standards and competency based, and increasingly 'modular' with far less emphasis on rigid patterns and periods of training, and no artificial time-serving requirement. Most trainees still start before their seventeenth birth-day, and usually complete normal training by the time they are 20.

First-year training in basic engineering skills involves 46 weeks (shorter for trainees who have successfully completed an acceptable technical/practical option at school or on a YTS scheme), off-the-job in a training centre, with day- or block-release to study, normally for CGLI exams. Thereafter, trainees are taught specific craft skills on a 'modular' basis, the choice of modules depending on company need and the trainee's potential. Time spent on each module depends on progress, content, availability of training opportunities. Each trainee takes either two stage II modules or one stage II and one stage III module as a minimum. Extra 'endorsement' modules can be added at any time. All trainees should have day- or block-release to continue to study for CGLI exams.

CGLI engineering craft schemes match the EITB training pattern and are also, therefore, 'modular'. The schemes begin with –
Engineering craft studies part I (CGLI 200): has a core of common craft units, but is combined with units in a specific craft area – mechanical or electrical engineering, for instance. From this basic level, trainees go on to a scheme in a specific job area (see BRANCHES below). Free-standing supplementary studies, in eg engineering drawing, workshop maths, systems units in eg micro-electronics, can also be taken.

Entry to craft traineeships is now generally set at a *minimum* of three suitable subjects (eg maths, physical science, English) at CSE (any grade) standard†, plus (for preference) one or more practical subjects (eg technical drawing, CDT, metalwork, woodwork) but employers are likely to prefer rather more. Entry is also possible via a YTS scheme, but the 'foundation' units only contribute to the basic stage, and so YTS entrants have to complete further basic training to gain a certificate and go on to module training, after their YTS year. This can defer entry to a traineeship until seventeen-plus.

Further information from the Engineering Industry Training Board.

THE BRANCHES OF ENGINEERING
Introduction — aeronautical — agricultural — automobile — biomedical — building services — chemical — civil and structural — computer/infor-mation — control and measurement — electrical and electronic — environmental — fuel — mechanical — mining and mineral — naval architecture and marine — production

Introduction
Most engineers qualify initially in a 'branch' of engineering, and careers

literature tends to emphasise the divisions between them. But these 'branches' evolved by historical accident, and in the real working world the distinctions are much less hard and fast. In a fast-changing technological environment they can look rather artificial. All the major growth points in engineering R&D are interdisciplinary, and the trends in modern technology increasingly mean a cross-, interdisciplinary or 'systems' approach to problems, so the distinctions between them are blurring even further. Machinery – conventionally designed by mechanical engineers – is now being given sophisticated electronic, frequently computer-based, control systems which must be closely integrated into the design. One result is a growing demand for people skilled in electronic/mechanical engineering, which one group of academics is trying to label 'mechatronics', but electronics and computing, 'software engineering', are now essential ingredients for all branches.

Engineers also change their specialisations during their career, often because they find themselves applying their initial skills in a different industry. They mostly work in multidisciplinary teams, alongside engineers from 'other' disciplines, and often with scientists too.

Aeronautical engineering
This is one of the most technologically-advanced branches of engineering, often involving quite original research and high-level development work in solving design problems. Real technological 'leaps' may be needed, to exploit new materials (eg lithium) and find the aerodynamically-perfect wing, for example, to slash fuel consumption. Aero engineers are already working on 'proof of concept' studies for an earth-to-orbit vehicle, and in France and the US design teams are working on second-generation 'transatmospheric' supersonic planes, for which further technological breakthroughs, especially on engines, will be needed.

Designing and building civil and military aircraft is not only technologically demanding. Aeronautical engineers must also meet customers' other, often tight, specifications. It is, for example, pointless producing a technological miracle (eg Concorde), if it cannot be operated economically. New civil aircraft must meet market requirements: they must be capable of carrying a certain number of passengers, at certain altitudes, at certain speeds, over certain distances; they must be as economic as possible in their use of fuel; they must be straightforward to maintain, and above all, safe to fly. It is not a simple job to make an aircraft completely safe and also ensure that it is profitable to operate. Planes must also be structurally strong, and comfortable for passengers and crew, but also as light and as aerodynamically streamlined as possible – all of which cause design conflicts and make decisions difficult, with no room for error. Military aircraft, loaded with armaments and electronic equipment, demanding higher speeds and manoeuvrability and flexibility, are even more difficult to design.

Fortunately, computer-aided design now helps to solve many problems, and its sophistication also makes possible substantial improvements, in wing design to give better aerodynamic efficiency, for example. CAD also helps to cut design costs, because less time has to be spent in wind-tunnel testing for example, and also makes the whole design process faster.

What aero engineers do This varies according to qualification –

Professional aeronautical engineers usually specialise in one of the main aspects of aeronautical design. These are aerodynamic systems – hydraulic, fuel, pneumatic; and avionics, which involves designing the very sophisticated navigational, communication and radar systems which are now based on airborne minicomputers (see also ELECTRONICS). Aeronautical engineers are more usually employed in R&D and design, less in production and related functions than other engineers. There is more team work, liaison and consultation in aeronautical R&D/design than in other branches of engineering.

Technician engineers and engineering technicians work in design or project work (eg as draughtsmen or women), in jig and tool or layout offices, as planning or project engineer in a production office, as inspectors or foremen who need technical knowledge.

Where they work Aeronautical engineers (qualified professional, technician engineer, engineering technician) work mainly in AIRCRAFT MANUFACTURING and for firms supplying them, some for firms in the space industry, which uses them in R&D, design and production of commercial and other satellites, rockets, missiles and so on. About 2.4% of all chartered engineers were working in aircraft or aeroengine manufacture in 1985, against 3.5% in both 1983 and 1979, and 4.2% in 1966. Some 2.5% of all registered technician engineers were working in aerospace in both 1985 and 1983, against 1.6% in 1966.

Some aeronautical engineers work for firms designing/manufacturing other vehicles where aerodynamic principles are useful, eg hovercraft, high-speed and linear motor systems, and even the auto industry, although generally the very exacting techniques of aeronautical engineering are too expensive for other industries.

Quite a few aeronautical engineers work for airline companies. Professionals work with manufacturers on plans for the next generation of aircraft, and manage and administer (and try to improve) the airline's service and repair operations. The servicing and repair is actually done by technicians and craft workers (see also AIR TRANSPORT).

Aeronautical engineers are also employed by the Ministry of Defence, both on R&D and design, and on contractual work. See CIVIL SERVICE.

The RAF recruits some professional and technician engineers, the latter as radio officers or supervising repairs and maintenance (see also ARMED FORCES). Some (normally technician engineers) become test pilots, or instructors.

The cost of designing and building military and large civil aircraft has cut the number of companies able to do so, and the UK now has only one major firm, although others make smaller and lightweight planes, helicopters etc, as well as aeroengines and components. Aircraft manufacturing is now an international business, and so aeronautical engineers may have to think internationally in future, spending part of their working lives abroad. Demand for aeronautical engineers at all levels fluctuates, largely depending on work in progress, but is expected to rise in the next few years.

Qualifications, courses and training differ between levels –

Professional: normally via a first-degree course in aeronautical engineering, although it is possible to convert to aeronautical at postgraduate level from, eg mechanical engineering or electronics. In 1985, 49% of all chartered aero engineers were graduates, and a further 26.5% had second degrees, so only 24.5% were non-graduates. Degree courses are at (* EC-accredited July 86) Universities (all honours courses) –

Bath:	Engineering BScBEng*(3/4 yrs), specialising in aeronautical engineering; option to include French or German
Belfast:	Aeronautical engineering BEng*(3 yrs) options in air transportation, advanced aerodynamics, stability and control, aircraft production
Bristol:	Aeronautical engineering BEng* (3 yrs) final year options include wind tunnels, the atmosphere, astronautics, systems, instrumentation, and aircraft production
City (London):	Aeronautical engineering BSc* (3 yrs), BSc (4 yrs), MEng (5 yrs) BSc/MEng common first six terms; options include aerodynamics, aircraft structures and propulsion
	Air-transport engineering BSc* (4 yrs) includes airline economics and administration
Glasgow:	Aeronautical engineering BEng* (4 yrs) course partly in common with other branches of engineering; choice of options in final year
	Avionics BEng (4 yrs) entry via Aero or Electronics and electrical engineering
London, Imperial:	Aeronautical engineering BSc(Eng)* (3 yrs)/BEng (4 yrs) specialising in aeronautics or fluid and structural mechanics
London, QMC:	Aeronautical engineering BSc(Eng)* (3 yrs) option to specialise in aircraft production or propulsion
	Avionics BSc(Eng)* (3 yrs)
Loughborough:	Aeronautical engineering & design BSc (3 yrs), BSc/DIS* (4 yrs) or BSc/BEng/MEng* (5 yrs)
Manchester:	Engineering (aeronautical) BSc (3 yrs) final year options eg helicopters, aerodynamics, heat transfer and high-speed flight, turbulence
Salford:	Aeronautical engineering BEng* (3 yrs) or BEng (4 yrs) first part of course common with mechanical engineering, then aerodynamics, aircraft structures, flight systems engineering and aircraft design
Southampton:	Aeronautics & astronautics BSc* (3 yrs)/MEng (4 yrs)
	Aerospace systems engineering BSc (3 yrs)/MEng (4 yrs)

Polytechnics (both can lead to honours)–

Hatfield:	Aeronautical engineering BEng* (4 yrs) first part common with mechanical engineering; includes flight

dynamics, aerodynamics, aerospace structures and materials, control/instrumentation, and design.

Kingston: Aeronautical engineering BEng* (4 yrs) design-based including flight dynamics, lightweight structures, aircraft power plant, aerodynamics, aeronautics.

Numbers graduating in aeronautical engineering rose slowly for fifteen years, peaking (for universities) at 371 in 1983-4, with few apparent problems in finding employment even in recession –

| | 1984-5 | | 1977-8 | |
	university	polytechnic	university	polytechnic
total graduating	329	47	245	35
research/further study	32	1	38	2
'believed' unemployed Dec 31	14	nil	5	nil
permanent UK employment	220	29	136	14
employers –				
engineering	141	19	94	13
armed forces	29	3	18	1
commerce	17	1	nil	nil
public utilities	8	2	9	nil
civil service	8	2	8	nil
'other' industry	7	1	5	nil
education	6	nil	nil	nil
functions –				
R&D/design	156	24	82	5
admin/ops management	24	2	42	3
management services	8	2	2	nil
marketing etc	8	nil	2	nil
financial work	8	nil		
scientific/eng support	7	4	5	5

Entry to degree courses in aeronautical engineering normally requires three A-levels (or at least five H grades) including maths, physics (physical or engineering science). Some 347 students began university courses in 1984-5, with a mean A-level grade 'score' of 12, H grade of 9.8.

After graduating, professional aeronautical engineers normally complete their practical training on the job. Membership of a professional body and registration as a chartered engineer is optional. The two professional bodies are now (1987) in process of amalgamating –

The Royal Aeronautical Society, with approx 14,000 members, of whom about 9000 are full 'corporate' members (an increase, from 13,200 and 7800 respectively in 1978). The Society has always accepted CEI examinations as meeting academic requirements for entry, but prefers a degree. The Society accepts EC academic-entry standards, but will continue, for the immediate future at least, to require at least eight years' experience for membership (but training periods during degree study can be counted).

The Society of Licensed Aircraft Engineers and Technologists' members work mainly in civil aircraft maintenance and airworthiness. Only a small proportion of members are registered chartered engineers (see Technician engineer qualifications below).

Technician-engineer qualification is normally via a BTEC or SCOTVEC Higher National award.

BTEC HND/C engineering (with aeronautical specialisation): new guidelines (to bring courses into line with the new framework) have not yet (1987) been issued. The old aerospace studies schemes gave specialisation in either avionics or mechanical options, and mechanical/production engineering could be studied with a aeronautical bias. Numbers taking these schemes have always been very small.

HND/C-level aerospace/aeronautical engineering is taught at –
Polytechnics: Bristol, Hatfield, Kingston, Preston: Lancs; colleges: Bedford CHE, Belfast CT, Connah's Quay: NE Wales IHE, Crawley CT, Croydon C, Fareham TC, Farnborough CT, Southall CT, Stockport CT, Witney: W Oxon TC.

Entry to HND/C is as for all BTEC Higher awards††, with the A-level pass in maths or physics, and the other studied to A level.

SCOTVEC provides only an HNC in aeronautical engineering (aircraft engineering) including design or advanced propulsion technology.

Entry is as for all SCOTVEC Higher awards†††.

See also Civil Aviation Authority examinations, under TRANSPORT.

Technician engineers will be able to join the new professional body –
The Royal Aeronautical Society has more than 3000 associate or technician engineers and technicians members, who must have at least a BTEC higher national award or CGLI FTC, plus at least six years' experience.

The Society of Licensed Aircraft Engineers and Technologists accepts as qualifications for associate membership awards which meet the requirement for EC engineering technician registration, but requires at least three years' experience. Total membership is well over 7000, with probably about a third registered as technician engineers and engineering technicians (probably about a third).

Engineering-technician qualifications are also BTEC and SCOTVEC awards, at National level.

BTEC National Certificate and Diploma engineering courses, under the new guidelines (see under ENGINEERING QUALIFICATIONS, COURSES AND TRAINING above) must have a common core of basic engineering skills, but the two required 'applications/technology' units can be biased to the aero field, as can some or all of the optional four (Certificate), 10.5 (Diploma) units. Further details of option units are not yet (1987) published. Numbers taking these schemes have always been quite small.

National Certificate/Diploma-level aerospace/aeronautical engineering is taught at –
Barry CFE, Bedford CHE, Belfast CT, Bristol: Brunel TC, Connah's Quay: NE Wales IHE, Crawley CT, Croydon C, Fareham TC, Farnborough CT, Macclesfield CFE, Milton Keynes CT, Preston: W R Tuson CFE, St Albans C, Southall CT, Yeovil C (and at Service colleges).

Entry to a BTEC National-award engineering course is (from 1987 entry) only as listed in TECHNICIAN-LEVEL QUALIFICATIONS.

BTEC First Certificate/Diploma, see ENGINEERING QUALIFICATIONS, COURSES AND TRAINING.

SCOTVEC National Certificate courses: the modular structure of the new Certificate (see TECHNICIAN-LEVEL QUALIFICATIONS) means that there is no set curriculum for engineering courses – but students can choose to take modules which give them specialisation in aeronautical engineering.
Entry is as listed in TECHNICIAN-LEVEL QUALIFICATIONS.

Engineering technicians can qualify for associate membership of SLAE&T (as Technician engineer qualifications above).

Craft-level qualifications are awarded by CGLI –
Aeronautical engineering craft studies (scheme 208) is for trainees working on aircraft maintenance and production, and who are being given training based on EITB and Air Transport and Travel Industry Training Board recommendations. Much of the level 1 syllabus is common with the mechanical engineering craft course. Level 2 is more advanced and can be entered via mechanical or electrical engineering craft studies. Level 3 syllabuses are college-devised to meet local requirements.

Further information from The Royal Aeronautical Society.

Agricultural engineering
This is one of the several technologies and sciences on which the post-world war II revolution in agriculture has been based (see also AGRICULTURE). An interdisciplinary study which applies engineering principles to the needs and problems of the industry, it needs a fully-integrated training in the theory and practice of both engineering and agriculture, horticulture and forestry.

Mechanisation and automation have been central to increasing food production and making it more efficient and cost-effective both in Britain and overseas in developing countries. Every stage in crop and livestock production can be made more effective and economic using more sophisticated and complex equipment, but more efficient systems and equipment still are needed even in developing countries where high technology is not appropriate.

Firms making agricultural machinery and equipment suffered quite badly from recession, and EEC cut-backs in agricultural output will continue to affect them. Signs are that they may have over-estimated the ability and readiness of customers in both the developed and developing worlds to pay for machinery and equipment of increasing sophistication, and therefore cost. Agricultural engineers now have to develop and design buildings, machines and equipment which take account of the realities of the farming business. Demand for agricultural engineers, though, is unlikely to fall.

What agricultural engineers do The three main areas of work for agricultural engineers are –
Designing, developing, producing and marketing agricultural vehicles and machinery of all kinds – tractors and harvesters for farms, horticultural holdings, and forestry operations – based on mechanical engineering principles.
Planning, designing and laying out farm and horticultural buildings which

incorporate advanced control systems – milking parlours, glass houses, crop dryers, buildings where poultry or pigs (for example) are reared intensively – which involves environmental control engineering.

Field engineering of systems for, eg irrigation, drainage, roads and water supplies, which depend on civil engineering principles. Soil conservation, land clearance and reclamation – planning, designing and managing soils and water resources efficiently – increasingly involve agricultural engineers.

Agricultural engineers must work closely with others. With farmers, for instance, to understand what they want (such as tractors which cope with anything farm workers do with them), with plant breeders (for easier-to-harvest plants) on harvesting machines, with civil engineers on irrigation systems.

This is not a highly-structured area of employment, and there are no hard-and-fast divisions between the work of professionals and technicians or between technicians and mechanics.

There are many posts for both professional and technician engineers overseas, especially in developing countries, and particularly for field engineers.

Professional agricultural engineers The relatively small numbers work mainly in R&D, design, technical management, and field engineering, in MANUFACTURING. They also do research (often industry linked or sponsored) in one of the four major centres (Silsoe College, and the National Institute based there; the Scottish Institute at Penicuik, and Newcastle University) and/or AFRC units. They do advisory work (for the Ministry of Agriculture and Fisheries, ADAS and the Food and Agricultural Organisation) eg on suitable systems and machines for particular situations. Some work in marketing and sales. Some teach in university or technical/agricultural college.

Engineering technicians and technician engineers are also employed in R&D and development as support staff, but more often in manufacture, advisory work, technical writing and sales, demonstrating and also field engineering. They also work in distribution, in management or at foreman level and on installation of, for example, field systems, grain dryers and automatic feeders.

Craft workers Mechanics (rather than technicians or professional engineers) look after maintenance and repair – crucial when animals' lives or the survival of crops may be dependent on very sophisticated control systems. On the land, mechanics are generally employed only on the largest farm or horticultural units where there is enough machinery to use their time economically, and therefore they must be able to service and repair a variety of different kinds of machinery. Rather more work for dealers, manufacturers, and contractors.

Qualifications and training While it is possible to train and qualify in agricultural engineering straight from school, a significant proportion of people become agricultural engineers – professional, technician or craft workers – after training and experience in a related occupation, eg mechanical engineering or agriculture. Direct entry is via –

Professional/graduate qualifications Demand for graduate agricultural engineers is relatively small.

First degrees – only three courses (all at universities) at (*EC-accredited at July 1986) –

Cranfield/Silsoe: Agricultural engineering BEng* (3 yrs) with final-year specialisation in machinery engineering, environmental control or field engineering.

Newcastle: Agricultural engineering BSc* (3 yrs) final-year choice from eg quantitative mechanisation management, soil mechanics, dynamics and control, environmental thermodynamics, fluid flow engineering, advanced design.
Agricultural mechanisation management BSc (3 yrs) emphasises organisation, management and marketing machinery systems.

Entry to all three is with A-level passes in physics (or engineering science) and mathematics, or via technician-level awards at credit standard plus appropriate industrial experience.

Postgraduate courses (for conversion after a degree in agriculture or engineering) for an MSc/diploma are put on by both universities, at
Cranfield/Silsoe: with options in machinery, crop storage and processing (with separate tropical stream), irrigation water management, land resource planning, manufacturing for agricultural and industrial development mechanisation, soil and water engineering.

The Institution of Agricultural Engineers has a rising percentage of professional members: over 60% of 1986 membership (fairly static since 1983 at some 2400) are academically qualified to be chartered or technician engineers, and Institution members can register. The top corporate grade of fellow requires a degree plus eight years' appropriate experience (including full-time training).

Technician-engineer qualifications are now BTEC/SCOTVEC Higher National awards.
BTEC Higher National award agricultural-engineering courses will be revised for 1987 entry in line with the new framework (see TECHNICIAN-LEVEL QUALIFICATIONS), but engineering guidelines are not yet (spring 1987) published.
HND courses at – Chelmsford: Writtle AgC, Newport: Harper Adams AgC, Thame: Ryecotewood C.
HNC courses at – Chippenham: Lackham AgC, Grantham: Lincoln CAgH, Thame: Rycotewood C.
Entry is as for all BTEC Higher awards†† (A level in maths or a science with the other studied to A level).
SCOTVEC's HND in engineering (see ENGINEERING COURSES, QUALIFICATIONS, AND TRAINING) has a major option in agricultural engineering and a minor in agricultural building and services engineering. It is taught at –
Ayr/Glasgow: WScot AgC/Bell CT, Cupar: Elmwood AgTC.
Entry is as under ENGINEERING COURSES etc.

Institution of Agricultural Engineers' membership is possible with HND/C plus appropriate training, etc.

Engineering-technician qualifications are also now BTEC and SCOTVEC National awards.
BTEC National Certificate and Diploma engineering courses, under the new guidelines (see ENGINEERING QUALIFICATIONS, COURSES AND TRAINING) must have a common core of basic engineering skills, but the two required 'applica-

tions/technology' units can be biased to agricultural engineering, as can some or all of the optional four (Certificate), 10.5 (Diploma) units. Further details of option units are not yet (spring 87) published.

National Diploma courses (although theoretically allowed, no certificate courses have so far been offered) are at –

Carmarthen T&AgC, Chippenham: Lackham CAg, Grantham: Lincoln CAg&H, Nantwich: Cheshire CAg, Thame: Rycotewood.

Entry is as for all BTEC Nationals††; with 16-plus†, passes should include maths and a physical science. Pre-entry experience (eg on a YTS scheme) is useful.

Alternatively, the

BTEC National Diploma course in farm mechanisation is agriculture based. It can be taken at – Chippenham: Lackham CAg, Maidenhead: Berks CAg.

Entry is as all BTEC Nationals†† (with 16-plus†, passes to include maths and a physical science), plus twelve months' experience in the industry (eg on a nationally-preferred YTS scheme).

SCOTVEC's National Certificate with agricultural-engineering modules can be taken at – Broxburn: Outridge AgC, Cupar: Elmwood Ag&TC, Dumfries: Barony AgC, Kinellar: Clinterty AgC.

Entry is as under ENGINEERING QUALIFICATIONS etc.

First Certificate/Diploma: see ENGINEERING QUALIFICATIONS etc.

Craft-level qualifications For mechanics, CGLI administers –

National Certificate in agriculture specialising in farm machinery and mechanisation (an appropriate level-1 award needed for entry).

Scheme 015 teaches basic knowledge of agricultural machinery and workshop processes and of maintenance and repair of farm tractors, implements and machinery, complementing industrial experience by introducing a wider range of practice and problems than is normally met in daily work.

Scheme 018 gives more specialised training in tractors, power units and mechanisms, or machinery maintenance and repair. No specific entrance requirement but some colleges prefer students to have done first-year engineering. Available at a number of colleges across the country, courses last three years day- or block-release, but can be taken full-time.

See also AGRICULTURE and MECHANICAL ENGINEERING.

Further information from Institution of Agricultural Engineers (leaflets).

Automobile engineering

This is not a fully-fledged branch of engineering in its own right but has always been a specialisation within its parent branch, mechanical engineering.

The car industry appears to need very few people who have specialised straight from school in automobile engineering, although one major manufacturer is sponsoring a part-time MSc course (at Loughborough) to bring together essential elements of car electronics, mathematical modelling, aerodynamics etc.

Professional engineers Most of the small proportion (only 2.3% in 1985), who work mostly in vehicles design and production, are probably mechanical engineers with some increase in electrical/electronic engineers. The industry does comparatively little R&D, which is estimated to use under 30% of those qualified engineers the industry does employ. Of course, there have recently been significant developments in, for example, integrated wiring for cars, increasingly sophisticated control and information systems, engines for greater fuel economy, etc. The work for this is, however, done increasingly on a multi-national, European basis, and is unlikely to increase demand for professional engineers in the UK.

Technician engineers, engineering technicians and craft workers in manufacturing (as of 1985, 2.2% of registered technician engineers worked in the industry, down from 3.9% in 1983), and mechanics in the service industry, do specialise in trades associated with automobile engineering. Technicians supervise, work in the drawing office, and inspect. Automation in both manufacturing and servicing is now making heavy inroads into craft work.
See MANUFACTURING and SERVICE INDUSTRIES.

Qualifications and training Most training specifically for car manufacture is done within the industry.

At professional level, most engineers going into the industry have degrees in MECHANICAL ENGINEERING, although ELECTRONICS is increasingly useful.

Only one specialist degree course exists, at –
Loughborough U: Automotive engineering and design BSc (3 yrs), BSc/Dip* (4 yrs), BSc/BEng* (5 yrs) choice of specialised topics in final year.
Other mechanical engineering courses include options in automotive engineering, eg at Coventry (Lanchester) and Hatfield Polytechnics. Most mechanical engineering courses include relevant topics, eg the internal combustion engine.

Postgraduate engineering courses giving useful specialisation at –
Bath U: Diesel engine technology MSc/dip
Cranfield IT: Automotive product design MSc
London, RCA: Industrial design MDes specialising in automotive design
Southampton U: Automotive engine and vehicle design technology MSc/dip

The Institution of Mechanical Engineers has an automobile division. See MECHANICAL ENGINEERING.

Technician-engineer qualification is normally via BTEC and SCOTVEC Higher National awards.
BTEC HND/C courses in Motor vehicle management combine technological subjects with, eg management, financial, commercial and marketing studies. Courses are at –
HND – London: Willesden CT; Norwich CF&HE
HNC (part time only from 87 entry) nearly 50 colleges country-wide
BTEC HND/C engineering (with motor vehicle engineering specialisation): new guidelines have not yet (spring 87) been issued. Courses are at –
HND – Bromsgrove: N Worcs C, London: Waltham Forest C
HNC (part time only from 87 entry) at some 20 centres countrywide
Entry to HND/C is as for all BTEC Higher awards††, with the A-level pass in maths or physics, and the other studied to A level.

SCOTVEC's HNC in Motor vehicle engineering also combines managerial and technical studies. Entry is as for all SCOTVEC Higher awards†††.

Engineering-technician qualifications are also BTEC and SCOTVEC awards, at National level.

BTEC National Certificate and Diploma engineering courses, under the new guidelines (see ENGINEERING QUALIFICATIONS, COURSES AND TRAINING) must have a common core of basic engineering skills, but the two required 'applications/technology' units can be biased to motor vehicle engineering, as can some or all of the optional four (Certificate), 10.5 (Diploma) units. Further details of option units are not yet (spring 87) published.

National Certificate/Diploma-level motor-vehicle engineering is taught at at nearly 140 colleges country-wide, full-time at over 50.

Entry to a BTEC National-award engineering course is as for all BTEC Nationals††.

BTEC First Certificate/Diploma, see ENGINEERING QUALIFICATIONS, COURSES AND TRAINING.

SCOTVEC National Certificate courses: the modular structure of the new Certificate (see TECHNICIAN-LEVEL QUALIFICATIONS) means that there is no set curriculum for engineering courses – but students can choose to take modules which give them specialisation in motor-vehicle engineering. Entry is as ENGINEERING QUALIFICATIONS etc.

Craft qualifications are linked closely to on-the-job training, either in MANUFACTURING, or servicing (see TRANSPORT SERVICES).

Biomedical engineering
Here engineering, biological and physical sciences come together in a highly-interdisciplinary way to solve all kinds of practical medical problems. Although scientists and engineers have been designing and producing devices, instruments, equipment, etc for use in medicine for over a hundred years, biomedical engineering has only quite recently been recognised as a discipline in its own right (SERC only began making grants in 1978).

Biomedical engineers design 'prosthetic' devices and materials to replace, support or repair parts of the body which have been lost or damaged by trauma or disease. Many are now in everyday use – heart pacemakers and valves, joint replacements, and kidney dialysis machines, for example. Work on refining and improving them, however, is continual. Prostheses, particularly those which go inside the body, must be extremely reliable – maintenance and repair is impossible once they are in place yet they must stand up to very hard wear, be made of materials that the body will tolerate, and must often be extremely small.

Biomedical engineering also develops instruments of increasing complexity and sophistication. They measure analyse, monitor, diagnose, and even operate.

In the clinical laboratory, elaborate and intricate machinery, computer-controlled, accurately and exactly measures and analyses body fluids, like blood, often doing many tests at the same time, separating samples, and so on.

Doppler measurement of blood velocity has opened up research into an ever-wider range of uses for ultrasonics for both monitoring and diagnosis.

In monitoring, biomedical engineers have produced a wide range of equipment which can watch patients continuously, in intensive care, under surgery, or even in day-to-day life, and can be programmed to signal crucial changes. Ultrasonic scanning has replaced x-rays in monitoring the developing foetus more efficiently and less dangerously than x-rays. Instruments will soon monitor the body's ions and molecules so that eventually closed-loop control and treatment in anaesthetics, dialysis, intensive care and post-operative recovery may be possible.

In diagnosis, equipment in common use includes the whole-body ultrasonic scanner (linked to computer-based analysis of multiple readings which would take a lifetime to calculate manually).

Nuclear magnetic resonance (nmr) and measurement of electrical resistance distribution in the body are being developed for even more sophisticated imaging. Delicate, hairline tubes and optical fibres can take miniature instruments in to explore and even operate inside the body on, for instance, lung, heart or vein unreachable by other means. Use of biosensors and cheap, disposable diagnostic 'kits' (increasingly making use of developments in biotechnology) is expected to grow rapidly. Simple enough to use at home, the readings from such kits can be transmitted automatically via the phone to the monitoring hospital.

Surgeons can have scalpels which seal blood vessels as fast as they are cut. Lasers are almost routine in some forms of surgery, and scientists have devised a 'weapon' which combines the power and penetration of radiation therapy with the pin-point precision of the surgical laser.

Biomedical engineering is developing computer programs to analyse the information collected by the new medical instrumentation or see what can be discovered from the case histories of many patients with a particular disease – its epidemiology, or the success rates of specific forms of treatment, for instance. Computer programmes have been designed which can begin the process of asking a patient about the symptoms which have brought them to the doctor or hospital.

Research and development in biomedical engineering is often extremely expensive, and so can be the resulting equipment. Much of the R&D is done to meet a specific need in a particular hospital or unit, and only if and when it is successful is it developed for wider use and commercial sale – if investment can be found. There is, though, now some systematic research – SERC funded over 100 projects (costing over £3.5 million), between 1981 and 1986, and some firms (especially in ELECTRONICS), have long-term development programmes.

Advances in biomedical engineering depend not only on developments in the technologies which go to create devices and techniques, but also on complete understanding of how the body works and the medical problems which researchers are trying to solve, and on other basic sciences, especially MATERIALS SCIENCE.

Working in biomedical engineering The numbers employed are relatively small. There is no clearly-defined career structure or a formal educational ladder.

Rarely does any one person have all the necessary expertise on a project, so there has to be close team work and collaboration between, for example the scientists, engineers, and the medical people, and through this scientists and engineers often gain the extra skills they need.

Most people working in this field are in universities, medical schools, polytechnics, some in non-teaching hospitals, a few in the Department of Health, some in research organisations and firms, some specialist medical equipment manufacturers and others for whom this is a small part of a business mainly concerned with scientific instruments generally, or even electronics generally.

The career as described is a professional one, and there is no formal equivalent for technicians. However, technicians are employed, probably coming through the SCIENTIFIC or MEDICAL LABORATORY route (see ACADEMIC QUALIFICATIONS AND CAREERS IN SCIENCE, and HEALTH SERVICES).

Qualifications and training Most people go into professional-level biomedical engineering after qualifying in another subject, usually via a degree. Almost any branch of engineering is useful, but ELECTRONICS is one of the most useful today. Alternatives are materials science, medicine, physics, computer science, or a life science – especially physiology. (50% of BES members are engineers, 15% physicists, 10% medically qualified, 6.5% biologists, 12% chemists, computer specialists, materials scientists etc.)

A full, first-degree course in one of these basic subjects is probably more useful than early specialisation in biomedical engineering, although it is possible to include it in some courses, at eg (*EC-accredited at July 86) –
Canterbury, Kent: Electronic engineering with medical electronics BSc* (3 yrs)
Cardiff, UWIST: Electronics BSc/BTech* (3/4 yrs) includes medical electronics option.

Many people go into biomedical engineering without any further formal training, learning any necessary additional skills 'on-the-job' from colleagues. It is, though, possible to take a specialist postgraduate course, eg –
Biomedical engineering (MSc/dip) – at Dundee U, Guildford, Surrey U
Medical electronics/physics (MSc) – at London, St Barts Hosp MC.

The Biological Engineering Society (1986 membership c600) can now nominate suitably-qualified members (membership requires a degree in an appropriate subject and suitable experience) for chartered-engineer registration. A certification scheme for clinical engineers was introduced in 1986.

Further information from the Biological Engineering Society.

Building services engineering

This is a relatively new term for what used to be called – and often still is – heating, air-conditioning and refrigeration engineering (design, construction and maintenance of sewage- and waste-treatment systems generally stay with the civil engineer). The new term is used to show that these systems are increasingly designed and built in a single operation rather than separately, so that they can be integrated where possible and give maximum effectiveness and efficiency, and to see that systems which now have to take in the needs of the electronic office and other new technology too, fit into the building as compactly and neatly as possible, and do not conflict.

Building services engineers look at the environmental needs of buildings as a coherent problem, solving them by using engineering principles. However, many engineers who actually work on building services probably still think of themselves as electrical, mechanical (or whatever their original specialisation was).

What building-services engineers do Working alongside, and with or for, architects, civil engineers and building contractors, building-services engineers plan and design mechanical, electrical/electronic, and electro-mechanical systems. These range from the commonplace heating and ventilating systems, plumbing and lighting, through the increasing use of air-conditioning in larger buildings, to the sophisticated systems needed by some industries to create particular kinds of environment (eg refrigeration for food storage, low-temperature areas for liquifying gases and other industrial processes, dust-free atmospheres for firms manufacturing electronic equipment, special ventilation to clear factory fumes and sprinkler systems to douse fires).

Such systems have to be both efficient and economic, to give comfortable, hygienic and safe conditions. Building services engineers often need to know a great deal about other aspects of advanced building technology – to design and construct air-conditioning and heating systems for glass-clad buildings for example, or they may have to be very well briefed on a product to be stored, or on industrial processes which a building will house. They may influence the design of a new building – to get service piping, ducts, cables and so on in a central 'core', and on access for maintenance. They also tackle the problems of creating better systems for older buildings which are being redeveloped or upgraded. Building services engineers will even be needed to work on the design, construction and maintenance of space stations.

Building services engineers also work on the development of novel systems, such as solar heating, or attempt to improve existing systems, for instance developing computer-controlled data collection from heating systems, to give more efficient use of fuel.

Some 17,000 are estimated to work at varying levels on the engineering problems of designing and installing the mechanical and electrical services that go into buildings. Employers include manufacturers of environmental control equipment of all kinds, building services groups, lighting and heating contractors, refrigeration firms, major building and civil engineering contractors, and larger architectural/civil engineering practices. Major users of particular types of environmental control (eg food and computer manufacturers) may employ their own resident engineers, mostly to develop, design and improve systems. Significant numbers work for CENTRAL GOVERNMENT in the Property Services Agency, and for LOCAL GOVERNMENT, the HEALTH SERVICES etc. Some professional engineers work as independent consultants.

There is no really firm division between the work done by professional and technician engineers, or between technician engineers and engineering technicians. Much depends on the employer and the technical sophistication of the system and the work involved. Technician engineers are expected to be able, with experience, to design quite complex systems and they can go on to contract management. Engineering technicians are trained to be skilled draughtsmen and women, to work-up and design less complex systems, and help design more advanced schemes. Craft workers install and maintain systems, and have to be skilled fitters, and sometimes welders, to assemble all the various components. They must be practical, but must also be able to understand the principles involved, and how systems work.

Demand for building services engineers at all levels is largely dependent on conditions in the CONSTRUCTION INDUSTRY. It is increasingly necessary to be prepared to work abroad.

Qualifications and training vary between levels –

Professional engineers increasingly qualify via a degree course, either specialising (as below) or reading MECHANICAL or ELECTRICAL ENGINEERING. Course titles can be rather confusing, and each specialist course is tailored to meet a specific demand. They include (all lead to honours/* CE accredited at July 86), at –

Universities

Bath:	Building engineering BSc (4 yrs) option to specialise in environmental/building services engineering
Edinburgh, H-Watt:	Building services engineering BEng (4 yrs)
Glasgow, S'clyde:	Environmental engineering BSc (4 yrs)/BScMEng (5 yrs) biased to building aspects of environmental control, but includes some public health engineering and environmental hygiene; options in design and control, environmental biology, and fuel and combustion technology
Liverpool:	Building services engineering BEng* (3 yrs)
London, City:	Mechanical engineering specialisations BSc (3/4 yrs) option in building services engineering
Loughborough:	Civil engineering BSc* (3 yrs)/BSc/dip* (4 yrs)/BSc/BEng (5 yrs) includes building services engineering stream
Manchester, UMIST:	Building services engineering BSc (3 yrs)
Ulster U:	Building services engineering BEng (4 yrs)

Polytechnics

Brighton:	Building BSc (4 yrs) includes environmental science and building services
Leeds:	Building BSc (4 yrs) includes environmental science and building services
Newcastle:	Building services engineering BEng (4 yrs) integrates environmental studies, building technology and administration
Wolverhampton:	Building services engineering BEng (3/4 yrs)

Postgraduate study It is also possible to convert to building services engineering after a degree in another branch of engineering, a related technology or eg architecture. The only MSc course is at Brunel University.

'Professional' qualification is via –

The Chartered Institution of Building Services Engineers (CIBSE) has over

6000 members. Usually new (corporate) members qualify via an appropriate degree, plus technologist training and at least three years' responsible work. Corporate membership can, at present (1987), also be gained by passing the Institution's own examinations, but these are being withdrawn with effect from 1991, though the Institution will then accept EC part 2 (in appropriate papers) instead. Students and newly-qualified graduates can become 'probationary' members.

The Institute of Refrigeration requires for fellowship an honours degree in environmental engineering or its equivalent plus at least five years in a position of special responsibility in the refrigeration or an allied field.

Technician-engineer qualification is now normally via a BTEC Higher National award.

BTEC HND/C syllabuses for building engineering will continue to follow existing guidelines for 1987-8, but will be revised in line with the new framework for all courses from 1988-9. At present, all students take appropriate core studies, and then specialise in one of –

Controls – no courses approved to run (as at end 86)

Electrical installations HNC only – Birmingham: M Boulton TC; Bridgend CT; Carlisle TC; Kingston CFE; London: S Thames C, Tottenham CT; Manchester: Central C

Gas distribution HNC only – London: E Ham CT; Trafford: North CFE;

Gas utilisation HNC only – Croydon C; Leeds: Building C; London: E Ham CT; Trafford: North CFE

HVAC (heating, ventilating and air conditioning) HNC only – Bath CFE; Belfast CT, Birmingham: Garrets Green; Cardiff: S Glam IHE; Colchester I; Croydon C; Leeds: Building; London: E Ham CT, Newham CC, S Thames C; Newcastle CA&T; Nottingham: Basford Hall CFE, Trent P; Salford CT; Slough CHE; Southampton IHE

Plumbing HNC only – Birmingham: Hall Green TC; Ewell: NE Surrey CT; London: S Bank P; Nottingham: Basford Hall CFE, Trent P; Salford CT; Slough CHE; Southampton IHE

Refrigeration HND/C – London: Willesden CT; HNC only – Grimsby CT, Hull: Humberside CHE; Nottingham: Basford Hall CFE, Trent P; Salford CT;

Surveying HNC only – London: S Bank P.

Entry to HND/C is as for all BTEC Higher awards††, with the A-level pass in maths or physics, and the other studied to A level.

'Professional' bodies accepting technician engineers as members include –

CIBSE: Associate membership is a technician-engineer grade, for which the Institution sets its own diploma examinations, although approved awards (eg HND/C) exempt.

The Institute of Refrigeration requires, for corporate membership, an FTC in the science and technology of refrigeration or an appropriate HNC, plus at least three years' experience in the field in a technical or scientific capacity.

The Institute of Domestic Heating Engineers: full membership depends on completing a two-part examination, the BTEC equivalent, or an acceptable alternative.

Training arrangements for technician engineers: see CONSTRUCTION.

Engineering-technician qualification is via BTEC National awards or a SCOTVEC National Certificate.

BTEC National courses in building services engineering follow the same pattern as HND/C above, but at a lower level. As with HND/C, National syllabuses will be revised for 1988 entry, but the length of courses and entry requirements will as be in the new framework from 1987 entry. At present, all students take appropriate core studies, and then specialise in one of –

Controls NC only – Stockport CT;

Electrical installations NC/D – Bournemouth/Poole CFE; Manchester Central C; NC only – Birmingham: M Boulton TC; Carlisle TC; Croydon C; Huddersfield TC: Kingston CFE; Leeds: Kitson CT; London: Brixton C, C&E London C, Hackney C, Paddington C, S Thames C, Tottenham CT; Merton C; Newcastle CA&T; Salford CT; Wigan CT;

Gas distribution NC only – Bristol: Filton TC; Cardiff: Rumney CT; Chatham: Mid-Kent CH&FE; Connah's Quay: NE Wales IHE; Coventry TC; London: E Ham CT; Newcastle CA&T; Nottingham: Basford Hall CFE; Stockton-Billingham TC; Swansea: W Glam IHE; Trafford: N CFE; Walsall CT;

Gas utilisation NC/D – London: SE C; NC only – Cardiff: Rumney CT; Connah's Quay: NE Wales IHE; Coventry TC; Croydon C; Leeds: Building C; Leicester: S Fields CFE; London: E Ham CT, Paddington C; Nottingham: Basford Hall CFE; Plymouth CFE; Preston: W R Tuson C; Reading CT; Southampton: Highbury CT; Stoke-on-Trent: Cauldon CFE; Stockton-Billingham TC; Swansea: W Glam IHE; Trafford: N CFE; Walsall CT;

HVAC NC/D – London: S Thames C; NC only – at colleges in most large centres;

Plumbing NC/D – Birmingham: Brooklyn TC, Hall Green TC; NC only – Bournemouth/Poole CFE; Bridgwater C; Chatham: Mid-Kent CH&FE; Cleveland TC; Coventry TC; Ewell: NE Surrey CT; Hartlepool TC; Leeds: Building C; Liverpool: Central CFE; London: E Ham CT, Vauxhall CB&FE; Northampton: Nene C; Nottingham: Basford Hall CFE; Salford CT; Sheffield: Shirecliffe; Southampton: Highbury CT, Soton TC; Stoke-on-Trent: Cauldon CFE; Swansea: W Glam IHE; Wigan CT;

Refrigeration NC only – Bath CFE; Cardiff: S Glam IHE; Eastleigh CFE; Grimsby CT; Hull: Humberside CHE; London: SE C; Manchester: Central C; Newcastle CA&T; Nottingham: Basford Hall CFE; Solihull CT; Wigan CT.

Entry to a BTEC National-award building-engineering course is as for all BTEC Nationals††.

BTEC First Certificate/Diploma, see CONSTRUCTION.

SCOTVEC National Certificate courses: the modular structure of the new Certificate (see TECHNCIAN-LEVEL QUALIFICATIONS) means that there is no set curriculum for engineering courses – but students can choose modules which give them specialisation in building-services engineering.

Entry is as ENGINEERING QUALIFICATIONS etc.

'Professional' bodies accepting engineering technicians as members include –
CIBSE: engineering technicians who have completed appropriate exams (eg BTEC NC/D), training and experience can become licentiate members.

Institute of Refrigeration associate membership requires a CGLI technician's certificate in an approved subject, a BTEC national certificate, or equivalent, and active engagement in science or practice relating to refrigeration.

The Institute of Domestic Heating Engineers: technician level is intended for senior operatives, but although at a practical level requires a technological background. Students planning to take the two-year part-time technician training course and examination should normally have previously studied and completed another craft course, eg CGLI advanced craft certificate in plumber's work. Associate membership emphasises design, commissioning, setting up and trouble-shooting; entry requirements are normally a CGLI technician-level qualification, a BTEC national, or a related qualification. The course lasts up to a year, part-time.

Training for engineering technicians: see CONSTRUCTION

Craft qualifications are awarded by CGLI. Schemes include –

Refrigeration and air-conditioning (scheme 207): level 2 and 3 for installation and service mechanics (who should have taken a preliminary engineering craft certificate).

Gas studies (scheme 598): extended studies for craft workers qualified at advanced level in plumbing or heating and ventilating, extending the gas-work-related technology and further develops skills in fault diagnosis and rectification and their application to domestic, commercial and industrial installations.

Heating & ventilating fitting (scheme 604): level 2 and 3 techniques for installing and testing water, gas and oil heating systems, air-conditioning systems and domestic heating systems (appropriate welding techniques are studied in scheme 599).

Mechanical services skills-testing certificate is awarded on completion of nine practical tests specialising in plumbing or heating and ventilating.

See also BUILDING TECHNOLOGY, CIVIL ENGINEERING and CONSTRUCTION

Further information from the Construction Industry Training Board and the above professional bodies.

Building technology

The building industry is traditionally craft-based and fragmented into a comparatively large number of small units. It has not therefore, in the past, employed highly trained professionals in any numbers. Lately there has been some regrouping to give larger units which need them. Many of the industry's problems can only be solved by more efficient management, to ensure greater economy in the use of resources and of building time, and thereby reduce costs, and by making greater use of technology and technological skills. The industry itself recognises this, and is now said to be 'screaming' for graduate building technologists.

What building technologists do Some 60% are believed to work for contractors (usually the larger ones) in the building/construction industry. Very few work for non-building firms. Firms manufacturing building equipment, especially of the more sophisticated 'industrial' kind, also employ technologists, and some work for property developers. Over a fifth work in the public sector, a high proportion of them in local government, relatively few in central government. A significant proportion work for consultancies, and quite a few teach.

Nearly a quarter are managers – two-thirds general managers and a third project managers. Over a fifth become surveyors, two thirds of these quantity surveyors. Much smaller proportions work in estimating; design; property development, maintenance and management; site supervision; quality control; production planning and control, and very small proportions in training, work study, purchasing, sales. Very few work in R&D.

Studying building technology The use of modern technologies in the construction industry means the building technologist must learn much more about the fundamental sciences. Modern building techniques depend heavily on the right, and often new, materials, so materials science and technology is also part of building courses. Structural and environmental engineering are also major subjects of study. Surveying, building economics, contract work, and managerial and site-control techniques are also taught.

Many qualifications in this field complement, and have indeed developed from, those in CIVIL AND STRUCTURAL ENGINEERING. A related area is BUILDING SERVICES.

At professional level, it is increasingly useful to study for a degree. The construction industry would like to recruit more specialist graduates, but the number of courses has been cut. Courses (all can lead to honours) are available at –
Universities

Edinburgh, H-W:	Building BSc (4 yrs)
	Building economics & quantity surveying BSc (4 yrs)
Liverpool:	Building technology BA (3 yrs)
London, UCL:	Building BSc (3 yrs) linked to architecture, planning and environmental studies
Manchester, UMIST:	Building technology BSc (3 yrs)
Reading:	Building construction & management BSc (3 yrs)
Salford:	Building surveying BSc (4 yrs) includes a building production option

Polytechnics/colleges
Brighton, Bristol, Coventry, Leeds, Liverpool, London: PCL, S Bank, Nottingham: Trent, Pontypridd: Wales, Sheffield; Glasgow CB.

The professional body is the
Chartered Institute of Building. Broadly-based, the CIOB created a route to professional status for construction technicians. The licentiate examination is designed for people with a technician's certificate (and can therefore become technician members) who want to qualify for more responsible administrative posts in the industry. Students with an acceptable BTEC Higher award in building are exempt from this exam, and if they also pass supplementary subjects, are also exempted from these in the final part 1. Associate membership provides for those who have passed or are exempted from associate examinations (parts 1 and 2) and is an intermediate step to full membership; most degrees in building exempt graduates from part 1 and also from part 2, once the graduate has three years' appropriate experience. Full membership is

via a part 3 'examination' which is, in fact, a written report on the candidate's personal training and experience and an interview, plus a further two years' appropriate experience. Institute membership is under 30,000 (out of an estimated 60,000 qualified to be members).

Building technicians at higher level qualify via BTEC and SCOTVEC Higher National awards.

BTEC HND/C building studies courses, from 1988-9, will be revised in line with BTEC's new framework. For 1987-8, programmes continue to follow the old guidelines. They are grouped, sharing common units with the SURVEYING, ARCHITECTURAL WORK, and CIVIL ENGINEERING SERVICES programmes, to ensure flexibility.

HNC/D programmes at present include building technology to level 5, building services and equipment, and contractual procedures and legislation to level 4, with a choice from a wide range of advanced units in eg mathematics, measurement, site surveying, economics of the industry, maintenance and adaptation, site studies (personnel and production), tendering and estimating. HND courses involve 20 units (with additional units including at least 16 at level 4 or above), HNC ten.

HND courses at – Ulster U; polytechnics: Bristol, Huddersfield, Leeds, Leicester, Liverpool, London: S Bank, Newcastle, Nottingham: Trent, Oxford, Pontypridd: Wales, Preston: Lancs, Sheffield, Wolverhampton; colleges: Bexley: Erith CT; Bolton IHE; Chelmsford: Essex IHE; Ewell: NE Surrey CT; Gloucester: Glos CA&T; Guildford CT; London: Hammersmith & WL C, Willesden CT; St Albans: Herts CB; Southampton IHE;

HNC courses are at over 100 polytechnics and other colleges.

Entry as is for all BTEC Higher National awards††; if via A levels, the pass should be in maths or a science, with the other studied to A level.

SCOTVEC HND/C courses in building have a set syllabus, HND courses going to a higher level (management) than HNC (site supervision). Entry is as for all SCOTVEC Higher awards†††; for HND, H grades to include maths or physics.

Institute of Building: see professional/graduate above.

Building technicians at the lower level qualify via BTEC National awards, SCOTVEC national certificate.

BTEC National Diploma and Certificate courses in building studies are being revised in line with the new framework. Courses will continue in their present form for 1987-8, with new guidelines for 1988-9. The National Diploma in building studies is being merged with that in civil engineering studies in a new common National Diploma in construction, including the core studies of Certificate courses in building and civil engineering studies. Further details had not been published at end-86.

In their present form, certificate/diploma courses also share common units as at higher level. Units in construction technology are studied throughout, mathematics to level 2, science and materials, measurement, site surveying and levelling at level 2, and options from further mathematics, design procedures and other level 2 subjects at level 3. The diploma course must include 25 units (15 for the certificate) including at least six at level 3 (only two for the certificate).

National Certificate/Diploma courses are given at over 160 colleges countrywide.

Entry is as for all BTEC National awards††; with 16-plus† normally including maths, applied science and English language.

SCOTVEC National Certificate courses offer a wide choice of building studies modules. Entry is as for all SCOTVEC NC courses.

Craft-level qualifications are those set by CGLI. Schemes include courses for individual crafts agreed with the Construction Industry Training Board (see CONSTRUCTION). Advanced courses include

Construction site supervision (scheme 628) dealing with organisational skills needed by a senior site supervisor.

See also CONSTRUCTION, BUILDING SERVICES ENGINEERING, CIVIL ENGINEERING and ENVIRONMENTAL ENGINEERING.

Further information from the Institute of Building (careers booklets and leaflets) and the Construction Industry Training Board.

Chemical, or process, engineering

Increasingly process engineering, since for many years chemical engineering has treated all kinds of materials, not just chemicals. Even the 'processes' need not involve chemical changes but can be any kind of physical transformation. They are, though, mostly large scale.

Chemical engineers design, construct, commission, control and operate plant and equipment capable of yielding a steadily-widening range of products. They turn crude oil into petrol and plastics, concentrate sulphuric acid and sugar, convert minerals into fertilisers and iron into steel, desalinate water, refine copper and aluminium, produce drugs and paper, and treat waste. They are even involved in producing energy from atomic reactions.

Biochemical engineering, which processes biological rather than other materials, is a branch of chemical engineering. It combines traditional fermentation techniques with the principles used in chemical engineering to produce pharmaceuticals like antibiotics and vitamins, some foodstuffs, in brewing and, increasingly, in treating waste products. It links closely with biotechnology (see BIOLOGICAL SCIENCES).

But whatever the material being treated or the product being made, the fundamental principles and problems are similar for them all: the equipment used to concentrate sulphuric acid is very like that used by refiners to concentrate sugars. The central problem is to turn what is a satisfactory process on the laboratory bench to the vastly greater scale of a commercially-viable plant, generally via an intermediate stage, a 'pilot' plant to see what the problems will be in 'scaling up' the process. The chemical engineer cannot simply enlarge the laboratory equipment: a giant reactor vessel cannot be shaken like a test tube, so other ways of getting a proper mix of the materials must be used. Similarly, separating, filtering, distillation heat exchange etc, become much more complex operations on a large scale, which means being expert on both the theory and the practical side of gas, liquid and fluid flow, heat and mass transfer, temperature measurement, and control. Ways – transport systems – have to be found to get raw 'feedstock' and intermediate and end products to flow evenly through a sequence of these 'unit' operations. Plant cannot be made of glass, but must be built of materials which will withstand extreme temperatures, high pressures, corrosion, etc.

Traditionally, processes and plant were designed as a series of separate, but linked 'unit' operations, and the unit operation is still the basis of most processes. Now, however, the computer – both as a design tool and as the basis for automatic control systems for the processes themselves – makes 'continuous' processes more common. Chemical engineers therefore try to design 'all through' processes and plant with control systems fully integrated into them.

It isn't too difficult to design a process to convert materials into useful products. The real expertise in chemical engineering lies in designing processes and plant which work as economically as is feasible, produce as much as possible of any given product at the least possible cost, and at the same time waste as little of the raw feedstock and energy used as is practical. A chemical engineer may have to find a marketable use for a by-product of distillation or a new process where the existing one has become too expensive, or has unwanted effects on the environment. The petrochemical industry can find a use for every single fraction of the end-products of a barrel of crude oil, for example, and can change the balance between products (more petrol, less domestic heating fuel and petrochemicals for plastics, for instance) to match changing market demand. Computers aid substantially in designing processes and systems which give optimum performance and efficiency. Some of the most difficult problems have been solved via a single computer programme; others, previously thought too complex ever to be solved, can now be analysed.

Chemical engineering involves complex problem-solving using logical and mathematical techniques, and finding answers in which economics is often just as important as technology. Chemical engineers more often than not work as members of a team.

What chemical engineers do The IChemE's 1986 employment survey gives the most up-to-date picture –
In terms of the work they do –

Engineering development and design employs by far the most – over 33% of chartered engineers, over 36% of technician engineers.

Design engineers turn the data produced at pilot-plant stage into plans for full-scale equipment. This may mean working on an entire process or plant, or on, for instance, the size, working temperatures, pressures and flow rates for individual units; or designing the pipework, valves and pumps that transport materials from operation to operation, or the complex layout of reactors, distillation columns, pipes, pump houses and control rooms. Some design engineers specialise in the detailed design of the sophisticated, mostly computer-controlled control systems.

Design technicians mostly prepare flow charts and layout drawings, and work on details.

Manufacturing and production employ the next largest group – 16.5% of chartered engineers, 22.6% of technician engineers. Chemical plant is extremely expensive, and even to recoup the cost – let alone make a profit – plant must run continuously (twenty-four hours a day, seven days a week if possible). The plant manager's job, keeping everything – controlling raw materials and fuel supplies, energy consumption, staffing and labour relations, maintenance etc – running smoothly, is crucial. Plant engineers 'trouble shoot', check equipment performance and look for ways to improve efficiency.

Technician engineers work mostly as members of the teams which, under the managers, keep the plant running to schedule, often as day supervisor or shift superintendent.

Instrumentation and control employs just 1% of chartered engineers, 2.8% of technician engineers, while analytical work and quality control employ barely 1% of either group. Only 1.2% of chartered engineers, 1% of technician engineers work in maintenance and servicing.

Research employs only 7% of chartered engineers, nearly 9% of technician engineers, and as elsewhere, has been declining, although perhaps not on the same scale as in some other areas of engineering. SERC, for example, supports research in process engineering, especially on less energy-intensive methods.

Research ranges from the most theoretical study of basic phenomena to practical work on full-scale plant. It involves developing new techniques and processes for new products (liquid fuel from coal for example); designing and evaluating pilot plant (and producing data from which profit forecasts can be made); looking for methods to cut down the impurities in a product, and technical service work (often for customers).

Technicians work mainly as assistants, eg constructing and running pilot plant, model building etc.

Construction and installation of plant employs 5% of chartered engineers, 3.3% of technician engineers.

Engineers can specialise in, eg site supervision or commissioning, usually working for a contractor. Project engineers oversee and co-ordinate the teams involved in constructing and commissioning a new plant from start to finish, which can take several years. Project engineers have to be able to 'deliver' a plant, in working order, on time and within budget. Any engineer working for chemical plant contractors can expect to work overseas.

Marketing and sales employs a growing percentage of chemical engineers – 7% of chartered engineers (against 5% in 1977), and 5.3% of technician engineers. They work in teams negotiating sales of plant, equipment, servicing etc. Some go into buying or purchasing – raw materials, equipment, fuels – which, as elsewhere today, demands sophisticated skill, shrewdness and business sense.

Management services employ 2.8% of chartered engineers, 1.7% of technician engineers. Specialist chemical engineers are usually part of WORK STUDY, OPERATIONAL RESEARCH and ORGANISATION AND METHOD teams in the chemical industry, and may also work in computing. Chemical engineers also go into PATENT WORK.

General administration right up to senior management, has absorbed 9.3% of chartered engineers, 2.6% of technician engineers. A high proportion of chemical engineers eventually become administrators and managers, and most large employers, especially the oil companies, see almost all their chemical engineering intake as potential managers, although obviously most start in one of the technical 'functions'.

Teaching, lecturing and other educational work, mostly in higher and further education, employs 5.6% of chartered engineers, 1.9% of technician engineers.

In terms of where chemical engineers work –

Industry employs the majority – over 63% of chartered engineers, over 70% of technician engineers. They work in virtually all industries.

Not surprisingly, the largest group still works in the CHEMICAL INDUSTRY itself – 19.1% of chartered engineers, 20.5% of technician engineers – despite the fact that industry world-wide was hard hit by recession and cut back hard on jobs. Included in that figure is the 4.7% of chartered engineers, 5.1% of technician engineers, who work for pharmaceutical companies, the rest for companies making detergents and soaps, cosmetics and toiletries, fertilisers, dyes and dyestuffs, and a wide range of basic chemicals.

Not far behind are the 17.4% of chartered engineers, 15.2% of technician engineers, who work for the OIL INDUSTRY – right through from extraction to refining and production of petrochemicals. Some chemical engineers are 'converted' by the industry into petroleum engineers, to work in, eg drilling and reservoir engineering, secondary recovery of oil fields by gas- and water-injection.

The FUEL INDUSTRIES take over 8% of chartered engineers, over 12% of technician engineers. Included are nearly 4% of chartered engineers, 5.4% of technician engineers who work for the nuclear fuel industry. Around 3% of chartered engineers, 6% of technician engineers work in GAS production and distribution – the remaining few in coal processing. Here some are already working on new forms of synthetic natural gas (eg analysing feedstock from gas and oil), and on processing coal to produce liquid fuel and/or gas. MINING AND QUARRYING employ almost 4% of chartered engineers but barely any technicians.

Other industries employing significant proportions include FOOD AND DRINK (4.5% of chartered, over 7% of technician engineers), especially where traditional fermentation methods can be used in process plant, eg brewing. PLASTICS, RUBBER, POLYMERS employ 5.2% of chartered engineers, over 6% of technician engineers). GLASS, CERAMICS etc, PAPER AND PRINTING, ELECTRICAL AND ELECTRONICS, TEXTILES, all take some.

Process contractors, the firms which build chemical plant, employ 16.3% of chartered engineers, 11.6% of technician engineers. Most operate on an international basis, so most engineers can expect to work abroad, wherever plant is being built. Virtually 3% of chartered engineers, 2% of technician engineers work for consulting engineers.

The education sector employs nearly 7% of chartered engineers, 3% of technician engineers, most of them working in universities.

Other employers include water supply, river purification, sewage and waste disposal (about 2% of both chartered and technician engineers), research institutes/stations (1.4% of both chartered and technician engineers), and central and local government (1% of chartered engineers). BANKS, and other financial institutions use chemical engineers as advisers (on development finance, investment etc), but they normally have to add ACCOUNTANCY or BANKING qualifications. INSURANCE companies specialising in industrial plant train chemical engineers as surveyors.

Qualifications and training/studying chemical engineering vary between levels.

Professional chemical engineers mostly qualify via a degree course (in 1985, 69.6% of all chartered chemical engineers were graduates, and a further 27.6% held second degrees, so under 3% were not graduates), normally in chemical engineering. While it is possible to become a chemical engineer via a degree in chemistry, physical sciences or mechanical engineering followed by postgraduate training in chemical engineering, a first degree in chemical engineering is preferable.

Chemical engineers need training which integrates and closely dovetails relevant theoretical principles and practical training from chemistry and engineering. It is no use adding some engineering to chemistry, or vice versa.

The Institution of Chemical Engineers' guidelines on what degree courses should involve assumes a full-time course lasting at least three years. It sets a 'core curriculum' of at least 1000 hours, divided into 250 hours on basic sciences (maths, chemical, computer applications, and some physics); 250 hours on process principles and analysis, thermodynamics, chemical kinetics and reactor design; 250 hours on transfer and separation processes and particle technology; and 250 hours on measurement and control, industrial and business principles, process, equipment and plant design, including at least 60 hours on a design project. This leaves 500 hours for 'additional studies' which the Institute does not specify, but 'expects' they will be well-balanced and in most cases include a fuller treatment of chemical engineering topics. The Institution says courses should include some industrial experience.

Degree courses at (all lead to honours/* CE-accredited at July 86)
Chemical engineering
Universities
Bath (Chemical and bio process engineering BEng* 4 yrs option to specialise in process management and economics, biochemical engineering, or computing in process design and control), Belfast (BEng* 3 yrs) Birmingham (BEng* 3 yrs/MEng 4 yrs), Birmingham, Aston (Chemical process engineering BEng* 3/4 yrs, MEng 4/5 yrs), Bradford (BEng* 4 yrs/BEng-MEng* 5 yrs), Cambridge (BA* 3/4 yrs: years 1-2 natural sciences or general engineering), Edinburgh (BEng* 4 yrs), Edinburgh, H-Watt (BEng* 4 yrs), Exeter (BEng* 4 yrs), Glasgow, Strathclyde (BEng* 3/4 yrs, BScMEng 5 yrs), Guildford, Surrey (BEng* 4 yrs), Leeds (BEng* 3 yrs/MEng* 4 yrs), London, Imperial (BEng* 4 yrs), London, UC (BSc(Eng)* 3 yrs/BEng 4 yrs), Loughborough (BSc* 3 yrs/BSc/dipl* 4 yrs: also management-based version), Manchester, UMIST (BSc* 3 yrs), Newcastle (BEng* 3/4 yrs, MEng* 4 yrs), Nottingham (MEng* 4 yrs), Salford (BEng* 3/4 yrs), Sheffield (Chemical process engineering BEng 3 yrs/MEng 4 yrs), Swansea (BEng* 3 yrs/MEng* 4 yrs)

Polytechnics (all 4-year sandwich BEng*)
London: NE London, S Bank; Middlesbrough: Teesside; Pontypridd: Wales.

Related subjects
Universities
Belfast: Chemical & food engineering BEng (3 yrs)
Birmingham: Chemical engineering with biochemical or minerals engineer-
                 ing BEng (3 yrs)/MEng (4 yrs) year 1 common with chem eng
London, UC: Biochemical engineering BSc(Eng)* (3 yrs)
Reading: Biotechnology BSc (4 yrs)
Salford: Natural gas engineering BEng* (4 yrs)
Sheffield: Chemical process engineering BEng (3 yrs)/MEng (4 yrs) bio-
                 technology option
Swansea: Biochemical engineering BEng* (3 yrs)
                 Process biotechnology BSc (3 yrs)

'First destination' figures are –

	1984-5		1977-8	
	university	polytechnic	university	polytechnic
total graduating	700[1]	119	552	69
research/further study	46	13	106	4
'believed' unemployed Dec 31	53	19	8	2
permanent UK employment	224	41	293	25
employers –				
oil & chemicals	190	15	150	11
'other' industry	83	8	13	5
public utilities	61	3	24	1
engineering	55	7	83	8
commerce	54	1	30	nil
construction	6	nil	8	nil
civil service	3	2	2	nil
local government	2	nil	1	nil
functions –				
R&D/design	280	24	179	9
admin/op management	48	2	79	11
financial work	33	1		
sci/eng support	30	2	5	4
management services	20	1	12	nil
marketing etc	21	nil	2	nil

[1] down from a peak of 909 in 1982-3

Chemical engineering is a more self-contained branch of engineering than most others with much less in common ground with the rest. It is, then, rather more important to be sure of a strong interest in chemical engineering since there is less chance of transferring into other areas of engineering, though chemical engineering is just as good a basic discipline for careers in many areas outside professional engineering. Typical entry requirements are A-level passes in chemistry, maths and physics, but some places will accept biology, engineering or physical science, or economics. Some 715 students started university courses in 1984-5; their mean A-level 'score' was 11.

Professional qualification The Institution of Chemical Engineers' members are mostly professional engineers, or student or trainee professional engineers. Membership has risen steadily for some years from under 9000 in 1967 to nearly 16,800 (12,400 in the UK), of whom 7200 were chartered (UK 5300) at end 1985. IChemE accepts EC examinations as the academic entry qualifications for corporate membership. The 'normal' training period required is four years, but this may be reduced, eg to three years for those who have completed a 'sandwich' degree course, or increased, to five years to allow those who have not gained an honours degree to show they are capable of becoming a professional engineer.

Postgraduate training in chemical engineering for graduates in other, but related, subjects is available at a number of universities and one or two polytechnics. Graduates in chemical engineering can go on to specialise, for instance, in biochemical engineering, biotechnology, integrated design of chemical plant, plant engineering in the process industry, and desalination technology.

Technician-engineer qualification is via BTEC Higher awards and SCOTVEC Higher National Certificate.
BTEC HND/C courses in engineering (chemical engineering specialisation): new guidelines have not yet (end-86) been issued. HND/C level chemical engineering is taught at –
Grimsby CT, Hull: Humberside CFE, London: S Bank P, Manchester P, Middlesbrough: Teesside P, Neath TC, Pontypridd: Wales P, Southampton CHE, Wallasey: Wirral MC.
Entry is as for all BTEC Higher awards††; if via 16-plus† and A levels, passes to include chemistry, maths and physics, with at least one of these at A level.

Only 42 people gained HND in chemical engineering in polytechnics in 1984-5 (down from 62 in 1980-1). Some 21 went on to study full-time for degrees, one for a professional qualification, and two into 'other' training. Two were 'believed unemployed' in December 1985. The destinations were known of only three others: one went into the oil and chemical industry, one into the Civil Service, and one into short-term employment.

Technician engineers can become associate members of the IChemE (see above), but comparatively few do.
BTEC HND/C courses in engineering (plant engineering specialisation): new guidelines have not yet (end-86) been issued. HND/C level plant engineering is taught (mainly part-time, therefore for HC only from 87 entry) at –
Bradford/Ilkley CC; Chesterfield CT; Coventry TC; Derby-Lonsdale CHE; Durham: Consett TC; Grimsby CT; Hull: Humberside CFE; Leeds: Kitson CT; London: E Ham CT, Richmond C, S Thames C, SE C, Southall CT; Newcastle P; Plymouth CFE; Port Talbot CFE; Rotherham CA&T; Salford

CT; Scunthorpe: N Lindsey CT; Southampton CHE; Stoke on Trent: N Staffs P; Taunton: Somerset CA&T; Wakefield MC; Wallasey: Wirral MC; Watford C; W Bromwich CC&T; Workington: W Cumbria C.

Entry is as chemical engineering above.

SCOTVEC sets only an HNC in chemical engineering. Entry is normally via a National Certificate which includes appropriate modules, or the equivalent.

Engineering-technician qualification: There is, at present, no BTEC National scheme in chemical engineering as such. The options to date have been plant engineering (below), general engineering, or general science (with appropriate option), depending on the job and industrial training scheme.

BTEC National Certificate and Diploma engineering courses, under the new guidelines (see under ENGINEERING QUALIFICATIONS, COURSES AND TRAINING above) must have a common core of basic engineering skills, but the two required 'applications/technology' units can presumably be suitably biased for trainees working in any capacity in any of the process industries, as can some or all of the optional four (Certificate), 10.5 (Diploma) units. A long list of options in plant, process and control engineering is already available, and BTEC has produced training scheme guidelines for process plant technicians. Plant engineering is taught at this level, on a full-time/sandwich basis, at – Bristol: S Bristol TC; Grimsby CT; Hornchurch: Havering TC; Leicester: Ch Keene CFE; Rugby: E Warwicks CFE; Salford CT; Taunton: Somerset CA&T; Watford C; Wirral MC; Yorks CA&T; part-time/block-release certificate only – courses at 40 centres.

Entry is as for all BTEC National courses in engineering (see ENGINEERING QUALIFICATIONS etc).

BTEC First Certificate/Diploma: see ENGINEERING QUALIFICATIONS etc.

SCOTVEC's National Certificate can include modules appropriate to chemical/process plant engineering. Entry is as for all SCOTVEC National Certificate courses†††.

Craft qualifications CGLI administers –

Process plant operation (scheme 060) for chemical, food, petroleum, pharmaceutical, and related industries. Part 1 includes process equipment, instrumentation and services; part 2 specialisation in each of: solids, sedimentation, evaporation and distillation.

Further information from the Institution of Chemical Engineers.

Civil and structural engineering

These disciplines underpin the design and construction of many different kinds of structures. They include highway and railroad systems (including bridges, flyovers and tunnels), airports, harbours, docks and canals, dams and barrages, coastal protection systems, sports stadia, irrigation systems, and structures and systems for services such as water, gas, sewerage and electricity, and for mining. Traditionally, civil engineering dealt only with unroofed structures, but civil engineering principles and techniques have to be used in designing and constructing very large buildings which need very deep foundations and steel or stressed concrete frames. This has led civil engineers to be closely involved right from the design stage in projects like the Sydney Opera House and Lloyd's new building in the City of London.

Many civil engineering structures today are increasingly massive in scale, and get more adventurous all the time, which means extremely complex problems have to be solved. Currently most frequently quoted are the bridge over the Bosphorus in Turkey, the Tarbela dam in Pakistan, the Humber bridge which has the world's largest single span (4500 feet) 100 feet above the river, the Thames barrage, oil and gas drilling and production platforms, and many hydro-electric and massive irrigation schemes overseas. The Channel tunnel is probably one of the most ambitious civil engineering projects ever planned.

Civil engineering has a number of sub-branches and most civil engineers eventually develop their expertise in one of these and/or in working in particular areas of construction. But it is usual to qualify and gain plenty of broad-based experience before specialising. The main sub-branches are –

Structural engineers deal with stresses and strains, and ensure that structures are safe. It involves learning about structural materials and mechanics, local and national regulations, and British Standards specifications in just about the full range of civil engineering construction work.

Municipal engineers work for LOCAL AUTHORITIES and are legally responsible for eg planning, highways, sewage disposal, lighting, building and housing, traffic engineering, transport, parks, playing fields, cemeteries, building control, cleansing and refuse collection.

Water engineers, who may also be municipal engineers, either specialise in water conservation and work on the construction of dams, water towers, pumping stations and supply, or work for river or other water authorities, or help to develop hydroelectric schemes.

Public health engineers specialise in designing, constructing and maintaining sewage and waste treatment and disposal systems, sanitation, heating, lighting and ventilating (see also BUILDING SERVICE ENGINEERING).

Highway and traffic engineers mainly deal with road and bridge design, construction, planning and maintenance, but increasingly also with traffic control systems and planning.

Working in civil engineering The civil-engineering design process has to be based on extensive information about the site, which often involves younger engineers in making ground and soil surveys, and the way it relates to and affects the surrounding area. Accurate measurement for all projects is crucial – for pinpoint accuracy the most modern electro-magnetic instruments are used (but before that long satellites will take over). Roads, bridges and tunnels built from both ends must meet exactly in the middle; complex road intersections must be fitted into the smallest possible site.

Every project involves laboratory analysis (of soil and rock samples, for instance), model testing and computer simulation and analysis before the designers start work, and throughout the process. A great many calculations have to go into working out forces and stresses, resistance to wind, water (or other pressures), and choice of materials, etc. Computer-aided design systems now play a major part – most of the routine drawing work is done on computer-driven plotters.

Designers look for an optimum solution, which takes into account economy, safety and environmental factors as well as more obvious design criteria, and they use computer-based analysis for this too. The size and sophistication of modern structures, the new techniques and materials available to them, mean that civil engineers depend increasingly on close co-operation with other experts.

In any case, civil engineers have to work very closely with everyone else concerned in the project, from the authority or firm commissioning it (which means politicians, planners and other officials) to the contractor and other land-use experts, eg ARCHITECTS, BUILDING managers, SURVEYORS.

Once the design is complete, materials etc, have to be specified in detail, costings made, tenders put out, and contractors briefed. On site, professional engineers are responsible for 'setting-out' and general preparation (such as seeing that safety precautions are taken), and go on – as 'resident' (increasingly project) engineer – to monitor and supervise, organising the work so that people, materials and machines are there as needed, that work is kept on schedule (often just as difficult in a busy city centre as in the depths of a vast desert), anticipating and solving the inevitable day-to-day problems, and trying to see that normal activity in the area can go on with minimal interruption.

What civil engineers do The majority of civil engineers work in or close to their branch of engineering.

For *professional engineers*, the Institution of Civil Engineers 1986 survey gives a breakdown –

In terms of the type of work, the largest group (23% of chartered civil engineers, 33% of 'others' – graduates not yet chartered and technician engineers) actually do construction and installation work. Nearly as large is the group (also 23% of chartered engineers, 24% of others) working as consultant engineers. Roughly 20% of chartered engineers and over 26% of the others work in development and design (for consultants or contractors). Very few – 1.2% of chartered engineers and 2.3% of the others – do research work (mostly in research stations, but with some posts in industry. Examples of their work include problems of corrosion, or the strength of water-retaining structures).

Over 7% of chartered engineers have become general administrators or managers. Nearly 6% of chartered engineers, 1.8% of the others work in maintenance and servicing. Over 3% of chartered engineers, 1.3% of others teach/ lecture. Very small percentages of both groups are in manufacturing and production, quality control, management services, or marketing and sales. However, a sizeable 11.6% of chartered engineers, 8.2% of the others are doing 'other' work.

Not surprisingly, almost 41% of chartered engineers, nearly 59% of the others work in the civil engineering 'industry', with a further 12% of chartered engineers, 16.6% of the others employed in building. Municipal engineering employs 15.4% of chartered engineers, but only 7.3% of the others. Water supply – nearly 7% of chartered engineers, under 2% of the others – and transport – 6.3% of chartered engineers, 5.9% of others – are the other major areas.

The largest employers of civil engineers are local authorities – 31% of chartered engineers, 22.4% of the others. Independent engineering consulting practices employ 22% of chartered engineers, 31% of the others (mainly on design, project engineering, and supervisory work). Some 18.7% of chartered engineers, 30% of the others, work for civil engineering contractors (mainly in planning or project engineering, contract work, site management, organisation and administration generally). Just 11% of chartered engineers, 7.7% of the others work for central government, public corporations and nationalised industries, and 6.2% of chartered engineers, 2.5% of the others are employed by water authorities. A few work for manufacturers who design and build large industrial plant (eg power stations, chemical and petrochemical complexes). There is structural design work for a few in, eg the aircraft and steel industries.

Civil engineers have always moved around a lot in their work, but recent recession has pushed constructors into a greater than ever effort to sell themselves abroad. Which means many more civil engineers have to be prepared to work on projects overseas.

Technician engineers and technicians Team work, say the professional institutions, is the keystone of civil engineering. Professional engineers depend considerably on the support of technician engineers and engineering technicians.

They work in design offices, as draughtsmen and women (but more often than not now using computer-driven equipment), preparing general arrangement and layout drawings, and detail structural elements, working details and schedules, formwork and other temporary works.

They help to make calculations; select materials, components, and plant; collect technical data on different construction methods, etc; make routine specification clauses and decide on quantities; work out the best way to organise a construction project; look after safety measures, and so on.

On site, technicians and technician engineers provide the support in eg project management, site supervision, with possible promotion to clerk of works, site agent, contract work, etc.

Technician engineers, as in all branches of engineering, are expected to be able to exercise independent technical judgement, assume personal responsibility (to management level) and carry out technical duties.

Qualifications and training vary between levels –

Professional engineers normally qualify via a first degree. The Institution of Civil Engineers' guidelines for first-degree courses define broad requirements, and assume a three-year full-time course –

'... there must be adequate mathematics, appropriate to engineering subjects... studied at least until the end of the second year... four hours per week of lectures and tutorials combined...'

'Of the time remaining... at least two-thirds should be taken up by subjects in which, by calculation, or by observation and deduction, students are encouraged to build on basic scientific principles learned at A level, and to produce numerate answers to problems... There must be an acceptable civil engineering content and standard ... and finals would be expected to include structures, soil mechanics and hydraulics, surveying, engineering materials and design projects...'

'In the remaining one-third of the time the subjects studied should be relevant to civil engineering, but need not lead to easily quantifiable concepts, and might include economics, politics, law taught within an engineering context, management ..., planning and languages... emphasis should be given to courses which demonstrate the interaction of the engineer with the environment...'

'There should be a content of design, practical laboratory work, and suitable field studies. Curricula should not be overloaded, but should encourage exploratory learning... Attention should be given to improving communication... site visits are to be encouraged, and counselling by practising engineers.'

Last entry to unclassified or ordinary degree courses which will be accepted for ICE corporate membership is 1987 for four-year courses, 1988 for three-year courses. Civil engineering degree courses approved by the Institution are at (all can lead to honours/*EC-accredited as at July 86) –

Universities –

Aberdeen (BEng* 4 yrs), Bath (Civil/structural BSc* 4 yr-s), Belfast (BEng* 3 yrs/MEng* 4 yrs), Birmingham (BEng* 3 yrs/MEng 4 yrs), Bradford (Civil/structural BSc* 3 yrs/BEng 4 yr-s), Brighton, Sussex (Structural BSc 3 yrs), Bristol (BEng* 3 yrs), Cambridge (BA* 3 yrs), Cardiff, UC (Civil/structural BSc* 3 yrs), Cardiff, UWIST (BEng* 4 yr-s), City (BSc* 3/4 yr-s/MEng* 4/5 yr-s), Dundee (BSc* 4 yrs or with building management, economics, or management accounting or law), Durham (BSc* 3/MEng* 4 yrs), Edinburgh (BEng* 4 yrs), Edinburgh, H-Watt (BEng* 4 yrs), Exeter (BEng 4* yrs), Glasgow (BEng* 4 yrs), Glasgow, Strathclyde (BEng* 4/BScMEng* 5 yrs), Guildford, Surrey (BEng* 4 yr-s), Lancaster (BSc* 3/4 yr-s), Leeds (BEng* 3/MEng* 4 yrs; also with architecture), Leicester (BSc* 3 yrs), Liverpool (BEng* 3/MEng 4 yrs; also with environmental, maritime or structural MEng 4 yrs), London, Imperial (BSc(Eng)* 3 yrs), London, KQC (BSc(Eng)* 3 yrs), London, QMC (BSc(Eng)* 3 yrs), London, UCL (BSc(Eng)* 3 yrs), Loughborough (BSc* 3/4 yr-s/BSc/BEng 5 yr-s), Manchester/UMIST (BSc*3 yrs/MEng 4 yrs), Newcastle (BEng* 3/4 yrs/MEng* 4 yrs; option with environmental), Nottingham (BEng* 3/MEng* 4 yrs), Oxford (Engineering science BA* 4 yrs), Salford (BEng* 3/4 yr-s), Sheffield (Civil/structural BEng* 3 yrs/MEng* 4 yrs), Southampton (BSc* 3 yrs/MEng 4 yrs), Swansea (BSc* 3 yrs/BEng* 4 yrs), Ulster (BEng/MEng* 4 yr-s), Warwick (BSc* 3 yrs/BScMEng 4 yrs).

Polytechnics/colleges (all EC accredited; all BEng, 3-yr f-t or 4-yr sandwich, unless shown otherwise) –

Bolton IHE (4 yr-s); Brighton (3 yrs); Coventry; Dundee CT (4/5 yr-s); Hatfield; Kingston; Liverpool (4 yr-s); London: Middx, NELP, PCL, S Bank, Thames; Middlesbrough: Teesside (4 yr-s); Nottingham: Trent (4 yr-s); Oxford (4 yr-s); Paisley CT (5 yr-s); Plymouth; Pontypridd: Wales; Portsmouth; Sheffield (4 yr-s); Shrivenham, RMCS (BSc 3 yrs); Sunderland (4 yr-s).

Some of the more specialised branches may be studied as optional subjects in many of these courses.

'First destination' figures are –

	1984-5 university	polytechnic	1977-8 university	polytechnic
total graduating	1570[1]	681	1900	800
research/further study	136	45	146	30
'believed' unemployed Dec 31	51	51	44	15
permanent UK employment	786	278	1151	382
employers				
construction	494	190	760	250
commerce	73	9	25	1
local government	67[2]	58	174	89
engineering	37	5	52	12
public utilities	30	9	78	17
oil & chemicals	17	1	17	2
overseas	17	10	42	12
armed forces	16	2	7	3
civil service	13	3	26	3
education	8	3	6	2
functions				
environmental planning	552	243	730	208
eng R&D/design	95	14	154	22
management services	27	5	12	3
financial work	51	3	21	1
marketing etc	16	5	7	2
admin/ops management	15	3	7	20

[1] down from 2014 in 1980-1 [2] down from 300 in 1973-4

Entry requirements normally include maths and physics at A level, but departments may take account of Institution requirements (see below). Only 1285 students started university courses in civil engineering in 1984-5. Their mean A-level grade 'score' was 10.2.

Postgraduate studies Higher-degree/diploma courses in advanced civil and/or structural engineering at a number of universities, but most postgraduate courses are designed to give graduates more specialised training. Examples include foundation engineering at Birmingham; civil engineering (highways and transport) at City; soil mechanics at Cambridge, Heriot-Watt, Newcastle (with foundation engineering), and London (Imperial); engineering hydrology at London (Imperial); geotechnical engineering at Newcastle; irrigation engineering at Southampton; bridge engineering at Surrey; and water resources engineering at Birmingham, London (QMC) and Newcastle.

Professional qualification More people join their professional organisations in civil engineering and related branches than in any other. The main bodies are –
The Institution of Civil Engineers (which has merged with the Institution of Municipal Engineers) has (1986) some 71,250 members (including c48,000

chartered, of whom over 71% are graduates, and a further 15.5% have higher degrees leaving only 13.4% non graduates).

The Institution has set membership requirements rather more stringent than those of the Engineering Council. A complex point system is used to assess academic qualifications, with 40 points effectively needed for corporate membership. Of these –
at least 20 must be gained via an approved first degree in civil engineering or its equivalent. An MEng gives 32 points, a first- or upper second-class honours degree 30 points, lower second or third class honours 25 points, and a pass or ordinary degree (accepted until 1991 only) 20 points. Points can also be gained for higher degrees and diplomas.
Each pass at O-level/GCSE grades A-C counts as one point, but A-/AS-level passes are awarded points according to grade (A-level: six for A down to two for E; AS level: three for A, two for B or C, one for D or E). No subject can be counted twice.
With, for example, 25 points for a lower second degree, it would be necessary to have GCE passes in at least six different subjects, including three at grade C (four points each) at A level, or higher grades at A level if fewer subjects are taken.
Points (up to twelve) can be gained for an appropriate BTEC National but marks must average at least 65%, and/or for an HND/C (maximum five points).
Candidates for full membership/chartered status must take a further two-part professional examination, the first (PE1) after at least three years' approved training, PE2 after at least three years' experience in a responsible post.

The Institution of Structural Engineers (of corporate members 52.6% are graduates and 15.7% have higher degrees): accepts EC parts 1/2 or an approved degree, but for full corporate membership also requires at least three years' training, plus a pass in the part 3 examination, a seven-hour paper in structural engineering design and practice.

The Institution of Public Health Engineers is amalgamating (July 1987) with the Institution of Water Engineers and Scientists and the Institute of Water Pollution Control to form the Institution of Environmental Management and Control; see WATER INDUSTRY.

Technician-engineer qualification is normally via a BTEC or SCOTVEC Higher National award, taken on a full-time/sandwich or part-time basis.
BTEC Higher National Certificate and Diploma courses in civil engineering studies: new guidelines have not yet been issued. Under present (1986) guidelines all programmes must include a common core of advanced civil engineering construction, contract administration, geotechnics and a project, but for the other units there is a wide range of choice (depending largely on local needs) in, for instance, road transport operation, highway design, highway technology, science and materials, site surveying, transportation, concrete technology, design of structural elements, hydraulics, hydrology, foundation engineering, project management, or temporary works.
HND courses (full time and/or sandwich only from 87 entry), are at Ulster U; polytechnics/colleges – Birmingham; Bolton IHE; Hatfield; Kingston; Leeds;

Liverpool; London: NELP, S Bank, Thames, Willesden CT; Middlesbrough: Teesside; Nottingham: Trent; Oxford; Pontypridd: Wales; Plymouth; Portsmouth; Reading CT; Sheffield; Stockport CT; Wigan CT; Wolverhampton.

HC (part-time only from 87), at over 60 centres including polytechnics.

Entry requirements are as for all BTEC Higher awards††; if with A levels, normally a pass in maths or physics with the other studied to A level.

'First destination' figures are –

	1984-5 polytechnic only	1977-8 polytechnic only
total gaining HND	289	550
overseas students going home	27	24
first degree course	94	31
full-time study for prof qual	nil	17
'believed' unemployed Dec 31	10	16
permanent employment (UK)	90	211
employers –		
construction	46	144
local government	20	38
engineering	3	6
'other' industry	4	4
public utilities	3	5
civil service	1	3
functions –		
environmental planning	57	113
eng/science support	16	28
R&D/design	5	9
admin/op management	1	9
management services	1	5

A joint training scheme for technician-engineers and engineering technicians (promoted by the Institution of Civil Engineers, the Association of Consulting Engineers and the Society of Civil Engineering Technicians, with the Federation of Civil Engineering Contractors), combines study for academic qualifications with required practical training (four years for engineering technicians, six for technician engineers, under indenture, against five and seven years respectively without) and an interview; certificates are awarded under the scheme with BTEC awards.

SCOTVEC provides both HNC and HND courses in civil engineering. Entry is as for all SCOTVEC Higher awards†††.

'Professional' qualifications: The Society of Civil Engineering Technicians requires a BTEC HNC for membership, and further training followed by an interview for fellowship.

The Institution of Structural Engineers has associate membership for technician engineers with qualifications equivalent to a BTEC Higher National award in appropriate subjects, plus experience in a responsible post.

Engineering-technician qualification is normally via BTEC National award, or a SCOTVEC National Certificate.

BTEC National awards are to be revised in line with the new framework from 1987 entry, but in civil engineering (and building studies) will continue in their present form for 1987-8 only. From 1988-9, the National Diploma (full-time or sandwich-based only) will be merged with the building studies course, to form a new, common National Diploma in Construction, including the core studies of both associated National Certificate courses. The National Certificate in civil engineering studies will continue, with a revised syllabus.

Civil engineering studies as presently (1986-7) organised, have some features in common with BUILDING studies and cover the core studies and appropriate options needed not only for civil engineering technician-level work, but also for structural, highway, traffic, water and public health engineering. Diploma programmes have the same core studies as the Certificate, but colleges have greater freedom in the choice of options.

Full-time/sandwich-based courses are at present at nearly 90 colleges country-wide; part-time courses are at about 140.

Entry requirements are as for all BTEC National awards††; if via 16-plus†, passes to include maths, physics, and English.

BTEC First National awards: see CONSTRUCTION.

SCOTVEC's National Certificate can include modules in civil engineering. Entry requirements are as for all SCOTVEC National Certificate courses†††.

Training: see technician engineering training above.

See also CONSTRUCTION.

Further information from the Civil Engineering Careers Service.

Computer/information engineering/technology
Despite all the major developments in this field, despite the millions of computers built and in use, despite the crucial nature of information technology generally and computer engineering in particular, they have not – at least as yet – gained formal status as a 'branch' or 'branches' of engineering, nor have they their own, separate professional institution.

Definitions of 'information technology' (see separate chapter) are so open-ended that, as one commentator put it, they encompass everything from carrier pigeons to the latest in supercomputers. Information technology is used to describe both design and manufacture of systems, the uses to which they can be put, and almost every job that touches upon any system which can be remotely described as IT based. It is not (at least yet) possible to analyse the work involved or what people with qualifications in this field do – it is all still too new, although all reports suggest there are intensifying shortages of people with IT skills and an IMS report suggests that 84% of people gaining postgraduate qualifications in IT found jobs, the majority using their IT skills. The main aim of this chapter is to map a way through the multiplicity of courses which deal with the set of technologies which concentrate on the design, development and manufacture of IT-systems in general, and computers and computer-based systems specifically.

Information technology, as a term to describe a subject for research and study, has not gained universal approval from academics, and this adds to the minefield of confusion. Equally confusing, too, is the term 'software engineering', which attempts to put programming onto a more scientific footing, injecting some rigorous rules and techniques into making computers work efficiently and effectively. Information and computer engineering, then, although they are clearly still firmly based in their 'enabling' discipline, electronics, are becoming multi-disciplinary, in that the separate 'science' of computing, until recently treated quite separately, has now to be included.

For most people, the way into work on the engineering side of design, development and manufacture of IT, computer-based, and computer systems, will continue to be via a broadly-based electronics course (see ELECTRICAL AND ELECTRONIC ENGINEERING). Some courses specialising in development and design of computers have been available for a while now, with a few in software engineering. But authorities such as SERC have identified a clear need for some graduates to become hybrid, multi-skilled electronic engineers-cum-computer scientists to develop and design full-scale IT systems, including both hard- and software, and to manage their development.

There is, though, no common agreement on what courses should cover and, worse, what they should be called. One very confusing side-effect of this is that courses entitled 'Information technology' can either be about design, development – 'engineering' – or can be for people who will go on to work, most probably as some kind of systems analyst in the first place, at the 'interface' between manufacturer/software house and user, often for users. These latter courses are covered in the INFORMATION TECHNOLOGY chapter.

Courses of study The dividing line between courses which deal with IT systems, with computer systems, and in software engineering, is not hard and fast, and many of the schemes listed here overlap – the differences are mainly of emphasis.

First-degree courses
In information technology: this is a route designed for high-calibre school-leavers. Given their completely unco-ordinated development, courses are developing along remarkably similar lines. Most bring together the analytic and experimental skills of a computer scientist with the development and design skills of an electronic engineer. These skills are 'integrated' in the design and implementation of IT systems. The main elements are computer science, electronics and communications engineering, with a strong mathematical content. But while these courses are often out on the very forefront of the technology, the emphasis is also on developing a good 'interface' between the highly-sophisticated systems and their human users.
Courses include (all lead to honours/* EC-accredited at July 1986 but many courses are too new to have got through the accreditation process by that date) –
Universities

Bangor:	Computer systems engineering (BSc* 3 yrs)
Birmingham, Aston:	Electronic engineering & computer science (BSc 3/4 yr-s)
Bradford:	Electronic, communication & computer engineering (BEng* 4/MEng* 5 yr-s)
Brunel:	Information technology (BSc 4 yr-s)

Cambridge:	Engineering: electrical & information science (BA* 3-4 yrs)
Canterbury, Kent:	Computer systems engineering (BSc* 3 yrs)
Chelmsford, Essex:	Electronic engineering (computers & communications or microprocessors)(BSc/BEng* 3 yrs)
Durham:	Information systems engineering (BSc 3 yrs)
Edinburgh, H-Watt:	Information systems engineering (BEng 4 yrs)
Glasgow, S'clyde:	Information engineering (BSc/BEng 4 yrs)
Guildford, Surrey:	Information systems engineering (BEng 4 yr-s)
Lancaster:	Information engineering (BSc* 3 yrs)
Loughborough:	Information technology & human factors (BSc/dip 4 yr-s)
Manchester: UMIST:	Microelectronic systems engineering (BScBEng 4 yrs)
Oxford:	Engineering & computer science (BA 4 yrs)
Sheffield:	Electronic engineering (information & systems) or Electronic, control & systems engineering (BEng 3 yrs)
Southampton:	Integrated information engineering (MEng 4 yrs)
York:	Electronic systems engineering (BEng* 4 yrs)
Polytechnics	
Brighton:	Microelectronics & information processing (BSc* 4 yr-s)
Coventry:	Information systems engineering (BEng 4 yr-s)
Leicester:	Information technology (BSc 4 yr-s)
London, S Bank:	Computer & information engineering (BEng 4 yr-s)
Manchester:	Information technology (BSc 4 yr-s)
Sheffield:	Information technology (BSc 4 yr-s)
College	
Shrivenham, RMCS:	Information technology (BSc/BEng 3/4 yr-s)

In Computer engineering (may be called computer systems engineering, but there are other variants) –
Universities – Brighton, Sussex (BSc 3 yrs), Bristol (BEng 3 yrs), Canterbury, Kent (BSc* 3 yrs), Cardiff, UC (BSc* 3 yrs), City (BSc 3 yrs), London, QMC (BSc(Eng)* 3 yrs), Manchester (BSc* 3 yrs), Norwich, E Anglia (BSc* 3 yrs), Salford (BEng* 3 yrs), Sheffield (BEng* 3 yrs), Swansea (Computer science/electronics BSc* 3 yrs), Warwick (BSc 3/MEng 4 yrs), York (Computer systems & software engineering MEng 4 yrs)
Polytechnics – Middlesbrough: Teesside (BEng* 4 yr-s), Sunderland (Digital systems engineering BEng 3/4 yr-s)

In software engineering: Universities – Bath (Computer software technology BSc 3 yrs), Birmingham (BSc 3 yrs), London: Imperial (BEng 4 yrs), York (with computer systems MEng* 4 yrs)

Entry to all these courses is mostly with very good grades in three A levels/two A and two AS levels to include A-level maths and physics.

Postgraduate study The SERC administers a greatly-increased IT training budget (but which covers the 'soft' computing subjects as well as 'hard' engineering), which currently (1986) provides over 1000 extra advanced-course studentships (mostly 'conversion' awards), about 400 research students and 25 research fellowships a year. There is a growing range of one-year diploma and master's degree courses both in information technology, and in the various contributing technologies, as well as schemes designed for more specific purposes, eg information technology for manufacture at Warwick University.

Technician-engineer qualifications BTEC named information technology schemes are designed mainly to train people to work at the 'user' end. On the engineering/computer science side, BTEC does approve 'hybrid' type courses which 'integrate' electronics, communications technology and computer science, but suggests that the new framework allows schemes in eg electronic/ electrical engineering to include the necessary units.

At HND level, technology-biased courses include –

Computer technology: polytechnics – Birmingham (with electronics), London: PCL, Middlesbrough: Teesside

Engineering (computer studies): polytechnic – Coventry

Information technology: polytechnics – Brighton, Hatfield (for industrial applications), Leeds, Leicester, Middlesbrough: Teesside, Preston: Lancs, Stoke on Trent: N Staffs

Entry requirements are as for all BTEC Higher awards††, straight from school exam passes to include (mostly) maths and a suitable science.

See also ELECTRICAL AND ELECTRONIC ENGINEERING, COMPUTER SCIENCE, and the chapter on INFORMATION TECHNOLOGY.

Control and measurement engineering, instrumentation

These are closely linked. Control depends on accurate measurement, because control systems operate by continuously monitoring, or measuring, the difference between the actual and the required value of each parameter or variable concerned (such as the speed of flow of a liquid, or the temperature in a building, or the pressure in a reactor), and, also continuously, as a result of this 'feedback', taking action to make any necessary correction. Measurement also depends on accurate and reliable instruments, both where they are used in control systems and in devices used solely for measuring, for instance industrial, laboratory and scientific instruments for research of all kinds, and those used in clinical diagnosis.

Even windmills used the basic principles of control, but real development came with world war II when electro-mechanical ('wired') control systems were adopted to increase the speed and accuracy of training and firing guns to combat rockets, to steer radar and searchlights following highly manoeuvrable aircraft, and to guide naval vessels automatically onto submarine tracks. Computers and microprocessors brought increasingly sophisticated, fast and efficient control systems (robots are now even added to them), made it feasible to automate many more activities, and to 'manage' all kinds of services – such as the heating system for a hospital complex to both improve conditions and save energy. Future advances in solid-state electronics and computers will make possible on-line, complex non-linear control and filtering strategies, and adaptive control, with machines capable of learning from experience and adapting themselves to new and changing conditions.

Control systems are used in particular machines – automatic pilots, telescopes, radar trackers, generating equipment, gas turbines, and machines tools – and in production processes, particularly in chemicals, food and textile manufacture, where accurate, high-speed and sensitive control saves labour, raw materials, and energy. Sophisticated central heating systems and grain dryers use automatic control. Continuous crop production is possible in computer-controlled environments that provide plants with their optimum growing conditions automatically. Medical diagnosis and treatment uses control technology.

Working in control engineering Most control engineers are employed by firms making the machinery, equipment and systems in which control systems are installed – for defence, navigation, signalling, air-traffic control, computing, communications and so on. Chemical engineers who have specialised in control systems are employed by chemical-plant manufacturers. Large manufacturers, especially in process industries, employ their own – to identify areas where new control equipment can be used profitably; monitor the design and manufacture of the system; help with installation; supervise maintenance, and trouble shoot. Many millions of pounds-worth of control systems are being installed in British industry alone every year.

Professional control engineers can work in –
Research – into developing more sophisticated principles of measurement and new approaches to automatic control. This can involve finding out first which measurement will produce the information needed, or what controls will give a particular result, often using mathematical modelling.
Design and development – of new systems and instrumentation, modifying, adapting and upgrading systems and sub-systems, and looking for new applications;
Instrument manufacture or production, installation and maintenance – complex and sophisticated control and instrumentation systems, often costing many hundreds of thousands of pounds, need very careful maintenance and fast, well-organised repair systems, or a lot of money could be lost – or risk a serious disaster;
Marketing/sales – sophisticated systems need professional engineers to sell them.

People with first-degree and postgraduate qualifications in control engineering are in considerable demand, but many employers still 'grow their own' control engineers by training new graduates from almost any branch of engineering or even maths or physics.

Technicians and technician engineers solve problems in measurement and control instrumentation using established techniques and principles; provide suitable instrumentation, either by ordering or by adapting existing devices; produce sketch drawings of details so that craft workers can construct 'one-off' devices for special applications; compile schedules of routine procedures for instrument craft workers; and see that calibration of electrical and physical parameters is done correctly and recorded.

Craft workers are also employed. Skilled production, installation, and maintenance craft workers can gain promotion to eg prototype production, supervisory posts.

Qualifications and training/studying control engineering courses are available at several levels –

For a first degree, although it is a multidisciplinary subject, control engineering is most often studied as a specialised option or aspect of electrical and electronic engineering adding, eg control systems, the theory and practice of feedback and measurement, instrumentation, communication and information theory, and design of computer systems, logic and hardware as well as programming and systems analysis. A few courses take a 'systems' approach, training control engineers to design control systems and strategies for almost any process. It is also possible to combine control with another engineering subject, which may mean specialising in control systems within that branch (notably chemical) or with related subjects such as computing.

Control engineering is taught as a full honours subject at (*EC-accredited as at July 86) –

Universities

Birmingham:	Electronic & control engineering BEng * (3 yrs)/MEng (4 yrs)
Brighton, Sussex:	Control engineering BSc* (3 yrs)
Brunel:	Electrical/electronic engineering BSc* (4 yr-s) major option in control/instrumentation
City:	Control, instrumentation & systems engineering BSEng* (3/4 yr-s)/MEng* (4 yrs)
Hull:	Electronic control & robot engineering BSc*/dip/MEng (4 yrs)
Kent:	Chemical systems automation engineering BSc (3 yrs)
Leeds:	Electrical/electronic engineering BEng* (3 yrs)/MEng* (4 yrs) major option in control/instrumentation
Nottingham:	Electrical control engineering BEng (3 yrs)/MEng (4 yrs)
Reading:	Cybernetics & control engineering BSc* (3 yrs)
Sheffield:	Control engineering BEng* (3 yrs)/MEng (4 yrs)
Southampton:	Electronic engineering BSc* (3/4 yr-s)/MEng (4 yrs) with major control option

Polytechnics

Coventry:	Computer & control systems BEng* (3/4 yr-s)
Huddersfield:	Engineering systems & control BSc* (4 yr-s)
London, PCL:	Control & computer engineering BEng (3 yrs)
Manchester:	Engineering BEng (3 yrs) emphasises interfacing between digital control methods and production and process equipment
Middlesbrough, Teesside:	Instrumentation & control engineering BEng* (3/4 yr-s)

Sheffield: Electronic systems & control engineering
                                 BEng* (4 yr-s)

Postgraduate study Control engineering can usefully be added to a first-degree in any branch of engineering. It is possible to go on to study control after a first degree in another branch of engineering at –
Universities: Bradford, Cambridge (with OR), Cranfield, London (Imperial), Sheffield (with information technology).

Professional qualification The (chartered) Institute of Measurement and Control normally requires a degree in science or engineering for corporate membership (plus four years' experience), but will accept EC part 2 (in set papers). Nearly 60% of the 2854 corporate members are graduates (1986) – total membership (at 5700) has varied little for ten years.

Technician-engineer qualification is normally via a BTEC Higher National award or a SCOTVEC HNC.
BTEC HND/C engineering (with instrumentation and control specialisation): new guidelines (to bring courses into line with the new framework) have not yet (end-86) been issued. Existing programmes have core units in analytical instrumentation, process sampling systems, fault diagnosis, and process control or control engineering, with additional units chosen from use of computers, electronic instrumentation systems, further analytical instrumentation, monitoring systems and sequential control, data-handling, terotechnology, industrial relations and work study, and college-devised units for local needs.
Courses are at –
Birmingham and Teesside Polytechnics; Bolton IHE; Bournemouth: Dorset IHE; Bridgwater C; Cardiff: W Glam IHE; Chelmsford: Chelmer IHE; Connah's Quay: NE Wales IHE; Grays: Thurrock TC; Halton CFE; Lincoln CT; London: SE London C; Manchester: Central C; Newbury CFE; Newport: Gwent CHE; Plymouth CFE; Redruth: Cornwall CF&HE; Rotherham CA&T; Scunthorpe: N Lindsey CT; Stevenage C; W Cumbria C.
Entry is as for all BTEC Higher awards††; via A levels, maths and physics should have been studied to A level with a pass in one.

SCOTVEC sets an HNC course in industrial instrumentation and process control. Entry is as for all SCOTVEC Higher awards†††.

The Institute of Measurement and Control accepts HNC/D, plus five years' experience for Licentiate (TEng) membership, and has (1986) over 1600 licentiates.

Engineering-technician qualification is via BTEC National awards and SCOTVEC National Certificate.
BTEC National Certificate and Diploma engineering courses, under the new guidelines (see under ENGINEERING QUALIFICATIONS, COURSES AND TRAINING above) must have a common core of basic engineering skills, but the two required 'applications/technology' units can be biased to instrumentation and control, as can some or all of the optional four (Certificate), 10.5 (Diploma) units. Further details of option units are not yet (end-86) published. The

existing model programme includes, eg instrumentation systems and fluid dynamics, and later studies in measurement of process variables, instrument drawing, transmission of measurement signals, and plant and process control. National-level industrial measurement and control is taught at about 36 colleges.

Entry is as for all BTEC National awards††, via 16-plus† with passes in mathematics, a science subject with a bias towards physics, and a non-technical subject demonstrating use of English.

First Certificate/Diploma: see ENGINEERING QUALIFICATIONS, COURSES AND TRAINING.

SCOTVEC's National Certificate allows choice of modules which can bias a course to industrial measurement and control. Entry is as for all SCOTVEC National Certificate courses.

The Institution of Measurement and Control accepts a BTEC National (plus five years' experience) for Associateship (TEng), but has (1986) barely 250 associates.

Craft-level qualification is via CGLI awards. After basic engineering craft studies (scheme 200), apprentices/trainees can go on to –

Instruction production craft studies (scheme 206) levels 2 and 3: techniques of instrument production in light engineering and instrument trades; or

Maintenance craft studies in measurement and control (scheme 225) levels 2 and 3: installation and maintenance of instruments used in process and production measurement and control in industrial plant; or

Industrial control systems technology (special scheme 226) levels 2 and 3: a new multidisciplinary approach to control systems with a bias to either mechanical (hydraulics, pneumatics, electrics/electronics) or electronic (including control microprocessors and fluid power).

Further information from the Institute of Measurement and Control.

Electrical and electronic engineering

Based on common principles, both electrical and electronic engineering make use of the way moving electrons produce energy. They have been so successful in so doing that modern industrial societies are largely dependent on the results, from the power which provides heat, light and energy through to electronics in communications and dissemination of information.

Electrical engineering is the basis of power production in generating plants, the transmission systems which take the power to factories, homes, hospitals etc, that use it, the electrical installations in buildings, domestic and industrial equipment to exploit it, and electric traction systems (such as trains). Electricity is produced from large quantities of irreplaceable and relatively expensive raw materials (oil and coal), or from hydraulic or nuclear power, wastes a lot of them, and uses complicated and often very large moving machinery which has many parts to break and wear out. However, phosphoric acid fuel cells (PAFC), which can convert fuel directly into power without wasting any of it, could revolutionise generation, and supply space- and industrial process-heating by the turn of the century.

Electronics produces devices which work on extremely small amounts of power, and use it economically. They have fewer and fewer parts, let alone moving ones, and so are increasingly reliable, longer lasting and need less maintenance. They get smaller all the time.

It is hardly surprising then, that electronic engineering is a growth area of enormous potential. With the microprocessor, opto-electronics and fibre optics (so messages can be sent, by laser light rather than electrical energy, faster and more efficiently), not only can electronic devices and control systems replace the less efficient electrical and many electro-mechanic ones in so many areas, but they also have more and more new applications in every walk of life.

The only limitations on electronic systems are apparently social (eg whether or not people want a 'cashless or chequeless' society), and the problems and cost of organising and instructing (ie efficient systems and programs for) computers and computer-based systems.

Electronics is now the dominant technology in telecommunications (including not only telephone systems, but also TV and radio transmission and reception, radar and navigational systems). Computers are sophisticated electronic systems, and so are the automated control systems used in industrial and other processes. More and more industrial, scientific and medical instruments are electronics based. Microelectronic technology makes it possible to improve existing electronic systems and devices (eg industrial automation), replace electromagnetic equipment (eg cash registers and navigational gyros), create new products (eg video machines and computer-aided design systems), or put new-style controls into electrical products (eg timers for cookers). Opto-electronics, which has major potential as a more efficient alternative to integrated circuit technology, and is expected to be incorporated into many telecommunications, computing, control and instrumentation systems in the next ten years, is now a major area of R&D.

What electrical and electronic engineers do The range of work and employment is extensive and widening steadily.

Professional engineers The Institution of Electrical Engineers regularly surveys its members (1986 figures) –

Research, development and design employ the largest proportion of electrical and electronic engineers. In the private sector, 42% were working in development and design (against under 40% in 1978) – nearly two-thirds of them as managers – and 4.4% in research. In the public sector, only 18.4% were working in development and design (and down from 21.5% in 1978), with just 5.5% doing research only.

The figures show that the proportion doing just research is relatively small, although the dividing line between research and development is very fine in such an advanced field. Much of the theoretical work which produces new ideas may be done by scientists. Electrical and electronic engineers take the ideas and do further work to develop them into possible products and systems, although, as in opto-electronics, this can be very advanced-level work. Electrical and electronic engineers may do research work that is fundamental and basic if needed to develop particular products – they may then have to study the structure and properties of materials, for instance. Electrical and electronic engineers in research and development, and design, work in teams, often with other engineers, eg mechanicals, and scientists, eg physicists and materials scientists.

In research, development and design, the kind of work involved in the 'heavy' electrical end differs somewhat from the 'light' electronic.

There is (probably) rather less really advanced research and development work at the 'heavy' end, on generators and motors, switchgear, power transmission lines and equipment, transformers, lighting and heating equipment, and traction equipment. There is, however, research into new methods of generating electricity, eg using wind (technological versions of the windmill) and sea waves. Development concentrates to some extent on improving existing equipment and systems, on solving and preventing causes of breakdown, and improving efficiency. In the generating field, the CEGB (see ELECTRICITY SUPPLY) and the ELECTRICAL ENGINEERING INDUSTRY do most of the research, development, and design between them. Designing a new power station is a one-off project. Electrical engineers also develop and design new components, for eg a new design of car, or small motors for a host of uses. Some research is done in universities and polytechnics, in industrial research associations, and in government, especially Ministry of Defence, establishments (see CIVIL SERVICE).

Electronic engineers work on new systems, devices etc, for computers, telecommunications, broadcasting, radar, satellite systems, etc. They are employed by both the manufacturers, ELECTRONICS firms of all kinds, and by the larger users, such as British Telecom (see TELECOMMUNICATIONS), broadcasting organisations, eg the BBC and IBA, and the CIVIL SERVICE (again mainly the Ministry of Defence), and ARMED FORCES.

In production, electrical and electronic engineers plan, manage, and trouble shoot. Production may mean being a member of the management team of a CEGB power station, supervising the assembly of a cathedral-sized generator, or controlling the production of printed-circuit boards. With more industries installing sophisticated automated production systems, eg CHEMICALS, OIL, FOOD, PAPER etc, recruitment of electronic engineers has increased. In the private sector, only 5.4% of chartered engineers worked in production in 1986, with another 2.4% in quality control, and 4.2% in maintenance and servicing. In the public sector, some 3.8% worked in production, under 1% in quality control, and 10.4% in maintenance and servicing.

Construction and installation work includes, for professional engineers, being on the management team building a new power station, or a major new telecommunications facility. Some 3.5% of electrical/electronic engineers working in the private sector, 11.5% in the public sector, were employed in construction and installation in 1986.

Marketing and selling some of the highly sophisticated equipment produced in the electrical and electronic industries, and large-scale generating, transmission and computing equipment often requires people who have a good technological understanding of what they are selling. In the private sector, some 12.3% were doing this kind of work (against over 10% in 1978), 1.7% in the public sector.

Many electrical and electronic engineers move up and out into general management – some 19% of those working in the private sector (against only 17%

in 1978), and over 24% in the public sector (up from 21% in 1978). Another 10% of engineers working in the private sector had become consultants, 3% in the public sector.

Some electrical/electronic engineers teach/lecture, mainly in universities, polytechnics and FE colleges – over 20% of those working in the public sector, but under 1% in private-sector employment.

In terms of where they work, in 1986, of the fully-qualified and experienced chartered engineers, the largest group, 47.7%, were employed in private industry or commerce – a sharp increase on the 36% of eight years earlier. The second largest group, hardly 19%, worked for nationalised industry or public corporations (down from 27.6% in 1978). Just about 6% (against between 7% and 8% in 1978) worked for central and local government. Under 4% work in universities (slightly down on 1978), about 4.5% teach in polytechnic or technical college, against 6.5% in 1978. Around 4.7% are self-employed, 3.7% in consulting practice (both slightly up) and 2.7% in the armed forces (slightly down). About 1% work for each of the UKAEA and associated companies, and the health authorities (again similar to 1978). Only 0.5% were unemployed in 1986 (the same as 1978 and slightly down on 1983).

In 1986, 27.4% of all chartered electrical and electronic engineers worked in electronic or telecommunications equipment development or manufacture (against under 21% in 1983). Under 15% were working in electricity generation or distribution, against 22% in 1978. The proportion working in electrical machinery or equipment development or manufacture fell further, to 5.9%, from just over 9% in 1978. Over 7% worked on computer control systems and instrumentation. Just over 5% worked in broadcasting, telecommunications etc, roughly as eight years earlier. Some 5.6% worked in building services, rather more than in 1978. Some 3.6% were employed in chemical or allied manufacture or processing, as in 1978 but down on 1983. Just over 4% worked in 'all other' development, manufacturing or processes. Smaller percentages were working in transport (3%), research organisations (1.8%), 'other' engineering services (3%).

For *technician and technician engineers*, there has always been steady demand. The range of occupations is extensive and immensely varied, and many posts carry considerable responsibility. In the private sector nearly 17% (but only 6.7% in the public sector) of IEEIE members have 'full, unsupervised managerial responsibility for budgets and long-range planning with full control over senior staff'. Nearly 23% (22% in the public sector) 'undertake long- and short-term planning and supervision of projects and decisions on work programmes, with budgetary control ...'. Almost 43% (over 51% in the public sector) 'plan, conduct and co-ordinate projects of some complexity, are responsible for technical matters, work to general objectives and priorities, and supervise qualified and other staff'.

Within the various specialisations, for instance telecommunications, electronic and data-handling systems, electrical plant, radio and TV, electrical contracting, illuminating engineering, or electricity supply, technician engineers and engineering technicians work in (figures from the Institution of Electrical and Electronics Incorporated Engineers' (IEEIE) 1986 survey) – Maintenance and servicing employ the largest group – over 18%.

Research, development, and design – 15.3% work in development and design, under 1% in research only.

Construction and installation (including commission and testing), employ over 13%.

Education and training occupy 10.6%, while 9.4% are consultants.

Marketing and sales employ 8.2%.

Manufacturing and production employ only 4.2%, with a further 2.3% working in quality control.

Management services – work study, OR etc – employ 2.2%.

In terms of employers, by 1986 –

Just 34% of technician engineers were working in industry and commerce (against 28% in earlier surveys), some 27% for nationalised industry and public corporations (down from over 35%), 7.8% for universities, polytechnics etc, 5.5% for local government, 4.9% for central government, 3.8% in consulting practice, and 3.4% in the armed forces.

For technicians, nearly 47% were working in industry or commerce (up from 34%), 16.7% in nationalised industry or public corporations (down from 28%), 5.7% in the armed forces, over 5% each for health authorities and central government, and some 3% for each of local government and education.

The survey does not give a breakdown by industry or commercial sector, but these are probably similar to the kind of firms employing professional engineers, with some in RETAIL service organisations and departments, TV rental and relay companies, and the MERCHANT NAVY.

By field of employment, in 1986 –

Some 21.5% of technician engineers work in electricity generation or distribution (down from over 25%), over 10% in electronic or telecommunications equipment development or manufacture, and almost 7% in manufacture and development of electrical machinery or equipment. Some 17.6% work in building services (up from 16%), 7% in broadcasting, telecommunications and postal services; 6.4% in technical college teaching. Nearly 6% work on computer control systems and instrumentation, with just under 1% in software engineering. Some 2.5% work in chemical or allied manufacturing or processing (and 2.1% in 'other' manufacturing or processing), and 2% in transportation.

Building services now absorb the largest group of technicians (over 19% against only 14.6% earlier). Some 14% (against an earlier 17%) work in broadcasting, telecommunications and postal services. Just 15.5% in electronic or telecommunications equipment development or manufacture, another 4% on electrical machinery or equipment development or manufacture. Some 9.5% work on computer control systems and instrumentation, and only 5.2% in electricity generation or distribution.

Qualifications and courses in electrical and electronic engineering Electrical and electronic engineering are studied at first-degree, postgraduate, technician and craft levels.

First-degree courses are taught by almost all universities with engineering faculties, and most polytechnics. There is more and more variety in courses with increasing emphasis on electronics, although it is still most common, and sensible, to start with a broadly-based scheme covering the fundamentals of both electrical and electronic engineering, with a choice of specialisation/options later in the course. Courses are at (all can lead to honours/*EC-accredited at July 1986) –

Electrical/electronic (broad-based schemes)
Universities – Aberdeen (BEng* 4 yrs), Aston (BSc* 3/BEng* 4 yr-s), Bath (BEng* 3/4 yr-s/BScMEng* 4 yr-s), Belfast (BEng* 3/MEng* 4 yrs), Birmingham (BEng* 3/MEng 4 yrs), Bradford (BEng* 4 yrs/BEngMEng* 4 yrs), Brunel (BSc* 4 yr-s), Cambridge (BA* 3 yrs), Cardiff: UC (BSc* 3/BEngMEng 4 yr-s), Cardiff: UWIST (BEng* 3/BEng(Tech)* 4 yr-s), City (BSc* 3/4 yr-s/MEng 4 yrs), Durham (BSc* 3 yrs), Edinburgh (BEng* 4 yrs), Edinburgh: Heriot-Watt (BEng* 4/MEng* 5 yrs), Exeter (BEng* 4 yr-s), Glasgow (BEng* 4 yrs), Glasgow: Strathclyde (BEng* 4/BScMEng 5 yrs), Guildford: Surrey (BEng* 4/MEng 4 yr-s), Leeds (BEng* 3/MEng* 4 yrs), Leicester (BSc* 3 yrs), London: Imperial (BSc(Eng)* 3/BEng* 4 yrs), KQC (BSc(Eng)* 3 yrs), UCL (BSc(Eng)* 3/BEng 4 yrs), Loughborough (BSc* 3 yrs/BScdip* 4/MEng* 5 yr-s), Manchester (BSc* 3/BScBEng* 4 yrs), Manchester: UMIST (BSc* 3 yrs), Newcastle (BEng* 3/MEng 4 yrs), Nottingham (BEng* 3/MEng* 4 yrs), Oxford (BA* 4 yrs), Salford (BEng* 3/4 yr-s), Swansea: UC (BSc* 3 yrs/BEng 4 yrs), Warwick (BSc* 3/BScMEng 4 yrs)
Polytechnics (all BEng)
Brighton (*3/4 yr-s), Coventry: Lanchester (*4 yr-s), Hatfield (*4 yr-s), Huddersfield (*4 yr-s), Liverpool (*3/4 yr-s), London: NELP (4 yr-s), S Bank (BEng* 4/MEng* 4 yr-s), Manchester (*4 yr-s), Newcastle (*4 yr-s), Nottingham: Trent (*4 yr-s), Pontypridd: Wales (BEng* 3/4 yr-s/MEng* 4 yr-s), Preston: Lancs (BSc* 4 yr-s), Stoke: N Staffs (3/4 yr-s), Plymouth (*3/4 yr-s), Portsmouth (*3/4 yr-s), Sunderland (*3/4 yr-s)
Colleges – Aberdeen: RGIT (BEng* 4 yrs), Dundee CT (BEng* 5 yr-s), Paisley CT (BEng* 5 yr-s), Shrivenham: RMCS (BSc* 3 yrs)
Communication(s) engineering
University – Canterbury: Kent (BSc* 3 yrs)
Polytechnics – Leeds (BSc* 4 yr-s), Plymouth (BEng* 4 yr-s)
Electrical engineering (only)
Universities – Bangor (BSc* 3 yrs), Brighton: Sussex (BSc* 3 yrs), Bristol (BEng* 3 yrs), Liverpool (BEng* 3/MEng 4 yrs), London: QMC (BSc(Eng)* 3 yrs), Sheffield (BEng* 3/MEng 4 yrs), Southampton (BEng* 3/MEng* 4 yrs)
Polytechnic – Stoke: N Staffs (BEng* 3/4 yr-s)
Electrical/mechanical engineering
Universities – Brighton: Sussex (BSc* 3 yrs), Edinburgh (BEng* 4 yrs), London: QMC (BEng* 4 yrs)
Electromechanical (power) engineering
Universities – Birmingham: Aston (BEng* 4 yr-s), Loughborough (BSc 3 yrs/BScdip 4 yr-s)
Electronic engineering (only)
Universities – Bangor (BSc* 3 yrs/BEngMEng* 4 yr-s), Brighton: Sussex (BSc* 3 yrs), Bristol (BEng* 3 yrs), Canterbury: Kent (BSc* 3 yrs), Cardiff: UWIST (BSc(Tech)* 4 yr-s), Chelmsford: Essex (BEng* 3 yrs), Dundee (BSc* 4 yrs), Lancaster (BSc* 3/4 yr-s), Liverpool (BEng* 3/MEng 4 yrs),

London: QMC (BSc(Eng)* 3 yrs), Manchester: UMIST (BSc* 3 yrs), Newcastle (BEng* 3/MEng 4 yrs), Reading (BEng* 3 yrs), Salford (BEng* 3 yrs), Sheffield (BEng* 3/MEng 4 yrs), Southampton (BEng* 3/4 yr-s/MEng* 4 yrs), Warwick (BSc* 3 yrs), York (BSc* 3 yrs)

Polytechnics (all BEng) – Birmingham (4 yr-s), Leicester (*4 yr-s), London: Middx (4 yr-s), PCL (3 yrs), Stoke: N Staffs (*3/4 yr-s)

Electronic/communications engineering
Universities – Bath (BEng 4 yr-s), Birmingham (BEng* 3/MEng 4 yrs), Hull (BScMEng* 4 yrs), Salford (BEng* 3 yrs), Sheffield (BEng* 3/MEng 4 yrs)
Polytechnics – London: NLP (BEng* 3 yrs), Plymouth (MEng* 4 yr-s)

Electronic/communications/computer engineering
Universities – Bradford (BEng* 4/BEngMEng* 5 yr-s), Chelmsford: Essex (BEng* 3 yrs)

Electronic/computer engineering (science)
Universities – Birmingham (BEng* 3/MEng 4 yrs), Edinburgh (BEng* 4 yrs), London: UCL (BSc(Eng)* 3 yrs), Nottingham (BEng 3/MEng 4 yrs), Swansea: UC (BSc* 3 yrs)

Electronic/computer/microprocessor engineering
University – Chelmsford: Essex (BEng* 3 yrs)

Electronic/computer/systems engineering
University – Loughborough (BSc* 3 yrs/BScdip* 4 yr-s)

Electronic/control engineering – see CONTROL ENGINEERING

Electronic/manufacturing engineering
University – Birmingham (BEngMEng 4 yrs)

Electronic/mechanical engineering
University – Lancaster (BScMEng 4/5 yr-s)

Electronic systems engineering
Universities – Birmingham, Aston (BEngMEng 4 yr-s), Bradford (BEngMEng 5 yr-s), York (MEng* 4 yrs)
Polytechnic – Kingston (BEng* 4/MEng 4 yr-s)

Electronic/telecommunication engineering
Universities – Chelmsford, Essex (BEng* 3 yrs), London, QMC (BSc(Eng)* 3 yrs)

'First destination' figures (electrical/electronic) are –

| | 1984-5 | | 1977-8 | |
	university	polytechnic	university	polytechnic
total graduating	2695	991	2071	584
overseas students	281	109	85	95
destination unknown	231	179	155	144
research/further study	235	44	200	25
'other' training	15	4	8	nil
'believed' unemployed Dec 31	95	52	34	9
short term employment	16	15	14	4
overseas employment	33	6	34	4
permanent employment (UK)	1823	537	1247	263
employers –				
engineering	1252	427	900	223

	1984-5		1977-8	
	university	polytechnic	university	polytechnic
public utilities	161	36	121	16
oil & chemicals	77	19	33	6
commerce	76	14	24	1
entertainment/leisure*	51	22	58	7
'other' manufacturing	39	18	20	4
civil service	35	16	22	nil
armed forces	29	4	10	1
higher/further education	17	11	5	2
construction	12	2	8	3
local government	6	5	3	1
functions –				
eng R&D/design	1439	450	820	166
scientific/eng support	65	53	50	15
scientific R&D/design	51	19		
admin/ops management	36	16	270	69
management services	27	27	70	5
marketing etc	27	5	14	3

*includes BBC/IBA

Entry requirements normally include A levels in maths and physics. Over 2600 UK students started university courses in 1984-5. Their mean A-level 'score' was 11.9.

Postgraduate study The number of postgraduate courses in electrical and electronic engineering has risen considerably in recent years. Some help graduates who have read related subjects (eg applied physical sciences or physics), to convert to electrical and/or electronic engineering at postgraduate level. Graduates in related fields may also be accepted for some of the more specialised courses, although they may have to study for a longer period.

Professional qualifications These are awarded by –
The Institution of Electrical Engineers (IEE) (total 1986 membership well up, to nearly 90,500, of whom over 40,000 are corporate members) requires (from January 1988) at least a second-class on an *accredited* honours degree in electrical/electronic engineering for corporate membership. Graduates who gain a lower class can meet the requirement by passing set examinations at second-class standard or by gaining a master's degree. All entrants must have at least two years' industrial training and two years' career development in a responsible position, and pass a professional test.

The Institution of Electronic and Radio Engineers (IERE) (total 1986 membership down slightly to about 13,200, of whom 8260 are chartered) continues for now to accept appropriate EC examinations or an exempting degree (but over 81% of all members are graduates) plus at least two years' practical training and experience.

These two institutions are to amalgamate in October 1988.

Technician-engineer qualification is via a BTEC or SCOTVEC Higher award. BTEC Higher National Diploma/Certificate engineering with specialisation in electrical, electronic, communications etc: new guidelines (to bring courses into line with the new framework) have not yet (spring 87) been issued. Under existing programmes it has been possible to study electrical and/or electronic engineering, and a wide range of units can be put together to give many different specialisations, in, eg communications or telecommunications engineering.

HND/C courses at –

Communications engineering full-time/sandwich – Ulster U; polytechnics: Hatfield, Leeds, Leicester, Liverpool, Newcastle, Plymouth; colleges: Chelmsford: Essex IHE, Crosskeys C, Ebbw Vale CFE, Liverpool: Riversdale, Lowestoft CFE, Newport: Gwent CHE, Newport CFE, Pontypool C, S Shields M&TC, Swansea: W Glam IHE (part-time at about 50 centres)

Electrical/electronic engineering full-time/sandwich – polytechnics: Bristol, Coventry (Lanchester), Leeds, Liverpool, London: NELP, S Bank, Newcastle, Nottingham: Trent, Plymouth, Portsmouth, Sheffield, Stoke on Trent: N Staffs, Sunderland; colleges: Bolton IT (part-time at about 40 centres)

Electrical engineering (only) full-time/sandwich – polytechnics: Liverpool, Newcastle (part-time at over 60 centres)

Electronics (only) full-time/sandwich – polytechnics: Bristol, Coventry (Lanchester), Hatfield, Kingston, Leicester, Liverpool, London: S Bank, Thames, Middx, Newcastle, Nottingham: Trent, Pontypridd: Wales, Preston: Lancs, Sheffield, Stoke on Trent: N Staffs; colleges: Bournemouth: Dorset IHE, Bristol: Brunel TC, Cambs CA&T, Croydon C, Doncaster MIHE, Liverpool: Riversdale CT, Loughborough TC, Newcastle CA&T, Plymouth CFE, S Shields M&TC, Swansea: W Glam IHE, Weston-super-Mare TC (part-time at nearly 60 centres)

Electronics/communications engineering full-time/sandwich – Ulster U; polytechnic: Liverpool, London: NLP; colleges: Bangor: Gwynedd TC, Bristol: Brunel TC, Hull: Humberside CHE, Liverpool: Riversdale, Llandaff: S Glam IHE, Loughborough TC, Lowestoft CFE, Plymouth CFE, Reading CT, S Shields M&TC (part-time at about 30 centres)

Electronics/telecommunications, part-time only – Bangor: Gwynedd TC, Canterbury TC, London: S London C

Telecommunications, full-time (only) – Ulster U

Entry is as for all BTEC Higher awards††; via A levels, maths and physics studied with a pass in one.

SCOTVEC sets both HNC and HND courses in electrical/electronic engineering, with a wide range of options at level V. Entry is as for all BTEC Higher awards†††.

'First destination' of HND graduates –

	1984-5 polytechnic only	1977-8 polytechnic only
total gaining HND	650	260
destination unknown	192	70
overseas students going home	22	18
first degree course	39	7
full-time study for prof qual	3	13
'believed' unemployed at Dec 31	51	16
permanent employment (UK)	309	106

	1984-5 polytechnic only	1977-8 polytechnic only
employers –		
engineering	249	76
entertainment/leisure	13	5
'other' manufacturing	8	4
local government	6	2
public utilities	4	16
functions		
eng R&D/design	180	31
eng/science support	100	8
management services	14	nil
marketing etc	8	nil
admin/ops management	3	66

'Professional' qualifications: The 'professional' bodies for technician engineers are –

The Institution of Electrical and Electronic Incorporated Engineers (IEEIE), which has some 20,000 members (1986). Minimum requirement for membership is at present (1986) BTEC HNC (in a coherent group of units with at least six units at level IV/V including at least four with a 'substantial' electrical/electronic engineering content; at least two at level V, one related to electrical/electronic engineering; and at least one full maths unit at level III). From 1990 the requirement will be an HND in appropriate subjects, or an equivalent, and so people seeking to qualify via an HNC will normally have to gain supplementary units. The Institution publishes a list of approved training schemes.

The Institution of Electronic and Radio Engineers (see also Professional level above) accepts for associate membership a BTEC HNC in electrical/electronic engineering (or equivalent) plus at least five years training/responsible experience.

The Society of Electronic and Radio Technicians (membership some 8000), also at present accepts a BTEC HNC in an appropriate subject, but, as the IEEIE, will require an HND or equivalent from 1990.

Engineering-technician qualification is via a BTEC National award or a SCOTVEC National Certificate.

BTEC National Certificate and Diploma engineering courses, under the new guidelines (see ENGINEERING QUALIFICATIONS, COURSES AND TRAINING) must have a common core of basic engineering skills. The two required 'applications/technology' units can be biased to electrical/electronic engineering, as can some or all of the optional four (Certificate), 10.5 (Diploma) units. Guidance suggests four main streams – in electrical and electronic, electronic, communications, or computer engineering, but courses will continue to be designed to meet local needs, and the communications stream, for example, can be adapted for telecommunications trainees. All four streams are expected to include electrical and electronic principles at NII and NIII, electronics at NII and NIII. A wide range of option units will be made available.

Under current guidelines, the programme in electrical engineering has specialised options for eg general electrical technicians, practical electrical technicians biased to electrical services, technicians in illuminating engineering, electrical draughtsmen, technicians in electricity supply, and maintenance technicians; other programmes are in electronics and telecommunications, in audio and TV servicing, etc. The various programmes share many common courses, and students can switch from, eg telecommunications to electrical engineering, at various levels. At Certificate level, electrical technicians should, for example, study both light- and heavy-current applications.

Courses in all these subjects are available at many centres throughout the country.

Entry requirements are as for all BTEC National courses††; via 16-plus†, passes should include mathematics, physics (preferably) and a non-technical subject testing use of English.

SCOTVEC's National Certificate courses can include a large proportion of modules in electrical/electronic engineering and/or related subjects. Entry is as for all SCOTVEC National Certificate courses†††.

'Professional' qualification for engineering technicians can be with –
The Institution of Electrical and Electronics Incorporated Engineers (see also Technician engineer level above). IEEIE accepts, for associate membership, BTEC National awards in electrical engineering, electronics, telecommunications, and building services (electrical). The award must be in a coherent group of units at pass standard with at least three relevant level III units, two electrical/electronic-related.

The Society of Electronic and Radio Technicians (membership around 8000), which accepts any BTEC National awarded under the electronics and communication engineering programme committee.

Craft qualifications are set by CGLI, which tries to provide for the many and varied needs within the various industries. It is closely linked into EITB training schemes. Craft training may begin with –
Engineering craft studies (scheme 200), the basic modular course, which can be taken with an electrical bias. But some schemes are specialised from the start, eg –
Telecommunication and electronic mechanics (scheme 221), levels 1-3 on installation, maintenance or operation of telecommunication, electronic or data-handling systems, with two main options – telephone switching systems, and data communication and control systems.

Electronics servicing (scheme 224) of radio, TV and electronic equipment, domestic, professional or industrial, at levels 1-3.

Electrical and electronic craft studies (scheme 232) a range of level 2 and 3 syllabuses for advanced craft workers, all emphasising heavy plant and switchgear.

Electrical installation (scheme 235) of wiring and equipment in all types of building (eg offices, homes, factories) at levels 1-3 (the national qualification for the electrical contracting industry with level 3 for electricians who plan and supervise installation).

Further information from all the above professional institutions, all of whom publish a range of leaflets and booklets on careers in electrical and electronic engineering.

Environmental engineering

This is an academic's course title rather than a career. Most of the courses so called deal with BUILDING SERVICES ENGINEERING and are described under it, or are linked with CIVIL ENGINEERING.

Fuel/energy engineering and technology

'Fuels' traditionally meant those coming from conventional sources, and more specifically, fossil fuels like coal and oil. Today, the subject covers the whole spectrum of energy including nuclear power, energy policy and management.

At one point in the 1970s it seemed that a replacement for oil was the major priority. Recession cut not only oil, but all other fuel consumption, and the urgency is no longer there, at least for now – although supplies are still finite and the problem has only receded, not gone away altogether. Fuel technologists are still working on the more efficient and economic use of energy, and on new sources of energy and fuel, including substitute natural gas from coal, wind- and seapower, and the possibility of unlimited, safe energy created by harnessing nuclear fusion. Such research, however, employs scientists, engineers and technologists in multidisciplinary teams, rather than fuel technologists *per se*.

Research is both fundamental, into materials and the laws which govern their behaviour, for example, and applied, where as well as trying to find replacements, synthetic or otherwise, for hydrocarbons, research looks for better and more sophisticated methods for controlling, utilising, conserving and recovering fuels already in use. Research also has to solve specific technological problems for fuel suppliers, appliance manufacturers and consumers.

Fuel technology deals with the preparation of raw (fossil) materials, processing both natural and derived fuels (converted by carbonisation, gasification, hydrogenisation, distillation, reaction and so on) for solid liquid or gaseous fuels, and recovery of by-products. It involves designing and developing whole systems, processes, plant and equipment, eg boilers, heat-exchangers and pumps, and burners, ranging in size from the giant boilers for massive power stations, down to domestic boilers. Control systems (see also CONTROL AND MEASUREMENT ENGINEERING) of increasingly sophistication are now an essential part of energy supply and systems. Fuel technologists have to see that the right kinds of fuel are produced to meet specific demands, in the correct amounts and at the right cost. They also try to solve technical and economic problems in transporting fuels, according to bulk, weight, state (liquid, solid, gaseous) and safety.

Energy management is an expanding area of work now, but except in organisations where the problems are extremely complex, does not necessarily involve expert fuel technologists.

It is usual to specialise in a particular branch of fuel engineering –

The GAS INDUSTRY, for instance, employs specialised gas engineers, to work on distribution, in contracting, appliance and industrial gas-burning equipment manufacture, in exploration, and in areas of advanced technology.

ELECTRICITY SUPPLY normally employs ELECTRICAL ENGINEERS.

Although nuclear engineering is not necessarily confined to power production, future career opportunities are likely to be in mainly constructing and/or operating electricity-producing reactors, working for organisations ranging from those carrying out basic research, such as the UKAEA, to the electricity generating board, and consortia designing, developing and building power plant.

See also ENERGY INDUSTRIES.

Studying fuel/energy engineering/technology At one time it looked as though fuel and energy would expand as a first-degree subject in its own right, but this has not happened to any real extent. Courses at present (1987) available include (all lead to honours/*EC-approved at July 86) –
Universities
Birmingham, Aston: Chemical process engineering (BEng 3/MEng 4 yrs) fuel option
Glasgow, S'clyde: Chemical engineering (BEng 4/MEng 5 yrs) fuel option
Leeds: Fuel & energy engineering (BEng* 3/MEng 4 yrs)
Fuel & combustion science (BSc* 3 yrs) can also be combined with another science
London, Imperial: Chemical engineering (BSc(Eng) 3 yrs) options in energy, combustion and pollution, nuclear technology
London, KQC: Mechanical engineering (BSc(Eng) 3 yrs) energy option
Manchester: Engineering (nuclear) (BSc 3 yrs)
Salford: Natural gas engineering (BEng* 4 yr-s)
Sheffield: Fuel technology (BEng 3/MEng 4 yrs)
Polytechnics
Leicester: Engineering technology (BEng* 3/4 yr-s) specialisation possible in energy utilisation
London, S Bank: Chemical engineering (BEng 3/4yr-s) includes energy engineering
Pontypridd, Wales: Chemical engineering (BEng 4 yr-s) includes energy studies

See also CHEMICAL ENGINEERING.

At postgraduate level it is possible to convert from a first degree in any science or engineering via, for instance, courses in fuel engineering and science, or in combustion and energy.

Professional bodies: these are –
The Institute of Energy (1986 membership 5200): requires, for full membership, an honours degree in fuel technology or in a technology, engineering or science with either special reference to fuel technology or postgraduate training in fuel technology (eg a higher degree or diploma), or CEI part 2 in fuel and energy, and combustion and propulsion engineering. Candidates must also normally have four years' relevant training and responsible experience. About 60 people join each year.
The Institution of Gas Engineers (1986 membership 5764 – down from 1982's near 6100): requires, for full membership, a degree-level qualification in engineering, science or a related subject, plus 'substantial' training and experience in the gas industry (age at least 25).

Technician-engineer and engineering-technician qualification is via BTEC/SCOTVEC Higher awards for technician engineers, National awards for engineering technicians. Student technician engineers and engineering technicians take courses specific to their industry and/or work: for the electrical industry the schemes are in ELECTRICAL/ELECTRONIC ENGINEERING; gas services is taken in distribution or utilisation.

'Professional' qualification: both the above institutions have membership grades for technician engineers with a relevant BTEC/SCOTVEC Higher National award plus appropriate training experience (five years for the Institute of Energy). IGE also has an engineering technician grade for people with BTEC or SCOTVEC Nationals.

See also relevant industries under MANUFACTURING.

Further information from the above institutions.

Mechanical engineering

Applies basic scientific/engineering principles to designing, developing, manufacturing, installing, operating and maintaining machinery of all kinds. Mechanical engineering is not just about completely mechanical systems – levers, inclined planes, pulleys, wheels, axles, screws – although some or all of these may be involved. The same principles are used in designing and developing (etc), any kind of moving machinery, whatever actually makes it move or work – gas or steam (turbines), electricity, petrol, compressed air, or hydraulics – or even if it is manually operated.

'Machinery' stretches from dentists' drills to giant cranes, and includes cars, turbines, refrigerators, and machine tools which process materials. Today's electronic devices and systems, being 'solid-state' and therefore having no moving parts, do not theoretically involve mechanical engineering, but although inevitably some equipment stops being 'mechanical' or even 'electro-mechanical', and becomes totally 'electronic' – eg telephone exchanges – much equipment with solid-state control systems, eg robot arms which paint or weld, still has moving parts. Some products, eg cars and trucks, are still predominantly mechanical. It is not, then a 'dying' discipline, but mechanical engineers do have to extend their know-how across the subject's traditional boundaries into areas more commonly associated with other disciplines. They must stay abreast of electronic technology, learning, for instance, about the new kinds of control systems which go into moving machinery, whether it is a gas turbine or sewing machine.

Whatever the machinery, common mechanical principles are involved, common types of components – gears, wheels, bearings – are used, and common problems have to be solved. Stresses and strains in structures and between moving parts must be calculated; appropriate materials of the right strengths etc, chosen; tolerances allowed for. Vibration, lubrication (tribology), noise, and weight-support considered.

Mechanical engineers also plan complete plants and factories, choose and supervise installation of equipment, develop operating systems and manufacturing processes, and organise and administer whole plants etc. Mechanical engineers design and manufacture the equipment used to process and refine basic materials into metals and plastics, and the machine tools which shape them. Here mechanical engineering meets production engineering (following).

Accepting that most systems are now designed, made and operated by multi-disciplinary teams, mechanical engineers work increasingly closely with other engineers, eg electrical/electronic engineers in the development and design of equipment which is 'electro-mechanical' and/or computer based, but see themselves in a pivotal role in such teams, and as interfacing with other technologies.

Working in mechanical engineering Mechanical engineers work in most industrial sectors and in a wide range of functions –

Professional engineers (with percentages from the IMechE 1986 survey of members): the largest group (almost 32%) work in engineering development and design. Manufacturing and production planning and management takes the next largest group, just over 10%, with a further 7.8% working in maintenance and servicing, 2.9% on quality control and standards, 1% in instrumentation and control. Just 5.5% work in construction and installation (including testing and commissioning) of new plant and machinery. Nearly 7% work as consultants, 5.7% in marketing and technical sales. Only 4.4% do research. Some 7.7% have moved into general administration (more than half of all mechanical engineers are believed to become managers within a few years of graduating, and most do so eventually). Over 6% work in the educational field, 2.3% are in management services.

Mechanical engineers work in most industries and throughout most sectors. Industry employs most. Just under 22% of chartered mechanical engineers, over 25% of 'others' (graduates, technician engineers etc) work in the mechanical engineering industry (making agricultural machinery, metal-working equipment, machine tools, pumps, valves and compressors, industrial engines, textile machinery and accessories, construction and earth-moving equipment, mechanical handling equipment, industrial plant and steelwork, etc). Over 6% of chartered engineers, over 11% of the 'others' work for the aerospace industry; 3.4% of chartered engineers and over 7% of others for auto manufacturers. Some 5.6% of both groups are employed by the oil industry. About 4.5% of chartereds, 5.5% of others work in the electrical and electronic sector, 4% of each group for manufacturers of military equipment, and 4% of chartered engineers but barely 2% of the others in chemicals.

Metal industries now take only around 2% of both chartered and others. Small percentages work in other industries such as food and drink (about 2%), plastics etc (just under 2%), glass and ceramics etc, and paper/printing (under 1% each of each group). Docks, harbours, shipbuilding, marine engineering employ under 2% of both groups.

Beyond manufacturing industry, public utilities employ substantial numbers, mostly in electricity generation distribution – over 7% of chartereds, nearly 6% of the others, with another 1.7% of chartereds, 2.4% of the others working in the nuclear fuel industry – only 1.5% of each group are employed in gas. Mining and quarrying – including coal – take barely 1%. Some 3.6% of chartereds, 3.1% of the others, work in building services (heating, ventilating etc), with a very small number (under 1% of each group) working on mechanical and electrical services in construction.

The proportions working in very high-tech areas are still small – just under 1%

of chartereds, just over 1% in computer control systems and instrumentation; less than half a percent in robots and robotics, and only half a percent of chartereds, but over 1% of the others in software engineering.

About 3.6% of chartereds, but only 2.3% of the others, work for consultancy firms. Research institutions/stations (including government ones) employ just under 2% of both groups; universities and polytechnics, where they may combine research with teaching, 4.6% of chartereds, 1.9% of others (2.2% of chartereds work for technical colleges). Just under 2% of each group are in the armed forces. 'Other' services – patents, information, insurance, banking, health and safety – employ just 1.5% of chartereds (only 0.5% of the others) altogether. Central and local government administration have only 1% of chartereds and hardly any others, but getting on for 6% of both groups work in other non-mechanical fields.

By type of employer, chartered mechanicals work mainly for industrial or commercial organisations – nearly 60% in 1986. Of the rest, 13.5% work for nationalised industries, UKAEA etc, plus 5.4% for central government (including research councils). Over 8% work for educational establishments (mostly universities). Some 3.5% are principals or partners of consulting practices, and another 2.3% are self employed.

Technician engineers and engineering technicians work throughout industry in support functions, mostly in production and in the drawing office, but also in, eg marketing. Technicians also work on installation, maintenance etc.

They are expected to develop and use skills in communicating technical information, in measuring and making use of measurement and components and understanding the materials processing, in understanding manufacturing activities and the general commercial organisation and practice of the company, in diagnosing problems, and in organising, and sometimes supervising, the work of others.

Craft workers in mechanical engineering are tool-makers, fitters, machinists, mechanics etc. They are not only employed in manufacturing, but also in service industries for maintenance, as eg garage mechanics.

Qualifications, courses and training Mechanical engineering can be studied at a number of levels.

First-degree courses, through which most professional engineers now qualify, are taught at some 35 universities and almost all polytechnics. Most courses concentrate on the broad basic principles of mechanical engineering, but have also now to include increasingly large elements of, for instance, electrical/ electronic engineering. IMechE's latest (1986) guidelines expect courses to cover basic materials, solid mechanics, dynamics and control, fluid mechanics and thermodynamics. Alongside, IMechE wants included the principles and applications of manufacturing systems, measurement and instrumentation, electrical power and machines, electronics and microprocessors, and computer-aided engineering. Maths, statistics and computing are studied to a level needed to underpin the engineering subject and with a bias to application. Finniston's engineering applications – materials, manufacture and design – should be 'woven' into courses. Design has to be treated in its widest sense, from identification of need, through concept evaluation to manufacturing method and including aesthetics where it affects marketability.

IMechE encourages the use of project work throughout, and at least one 'significant' project is mandatory. IMechE wants at least two subjects studied in greater depth in the final year. Most courses give a choice of options in the final year(s), which range from advanced work in areas such as control, energy conversion, applied mechanics, fluid mechanics, reactor engineering, tribology, auto engineering, through to 'broadening' studies like human factors in engineering, languages, environmental engineering.

More mechanical engineering courses are now biased to manufacturing (see PRODUCTION ENGINEER/MANUFACTURING below), and a small, but increasing number of courses combine mechanical with electrical/electronic engineering (see ELECTRICAL/ELECTRONIC ENGINEERING above). Courses in mechanical engineering are at (all courses lead to honours/* EC-accredited at July 1986) –

Universities

Aberdeen (BEng* 4 yrs), Bath (BSc* 3/BEng* 4 yr-s), Belfast (BEng* 3/MEng* 4 yrs), Birmingham (BEng* 3/MEng* 4 yrs), Birmingham: Aston (BEng* 3 or 4 yr-s/MEng 4 or 5 yr-s), Bradford (BEng* 4/BEngMEng 5 yr-s), Brighton: Sussex (BSc 3 yrs), Bristol BEng* 3/MEng 4 yrs), Brunel (BEng* 4 yr-s), Cambridge* (BA 3 yrs), Cardiff: UC (BSc* 3/BEngMEng 4 yrs), Cardiff: UWIST (BEng* 3/BEng(Tech)* 4 yr-s), City (BSc* 3 or 4/4 yr-s/MEng* 4 yrs), Durham (BSc* 3 yrs), Edinburgh (BEng* 4 yrs), Edinburgh: Heriot-Watt (BEng* 4/MEng 5 yrs), Exeter (BEng* 4 yrs), Glasgow (BEng/BSc* 4 yrs), Glasgow: Strathclyde (BEng 4/BScMEng 5 yrs), Guildford: Surrey (BEng 4 yr-s), Lancaster (BSc* 3/4 yr-s), Leeds (BEng* 3/MEng* 4 yrs), Leicester (BSc* 3 yrs), Liverpool (BEng* 3/MEng* 4 yrs), London: Imperial (BSc(Eng)* 3/5 yr-s/BEng 4 yrs), KQC (BSc(Eng)* 3 yrs), QMC (BSc(Eng)* 3/BEng* 4 yrs), UCL (BSc(Eng)* 3/BEng 4 yrs), Loughborough (BTech* 4/BTechBEng* 5 yr-s), Manchester (BSc* 3 yrs), Manchester: UMIST (BSc* 3 yrs), Newcastle (BEng* 3/MEng 4 yrs), Nottingham (BEng* 3/MEng* 4 yrs), Oxford (BA 4 yrs), Reading (BEng* 3 yrs), Salford (BEng* 3/4 yr-s), Sheffield (BEng* 3/MEng 4 yrs), Southampton (BSc* 3/MEng* 4 yrs), Swansea (BSc* 3 yrs), Warwick (BSc* 3/MEng 4 yrs).

Polytechnics (all BEng)

Brighton (*3/4 yr-s), Coventry (*4 yr-s), Hatfield (BEng*/MEng 4 yr-s), Huddersfield (*4 yr-s), Kingston (*4 yr-s), Liverpool (*3/4 yr-s), London: PCL (*3 yr-s), Middx (*3/4 yr-s), NELP (*4 yr-s), S Bank (*3/4 yr-s), Thames (4 yr-s), Manchester (*4 yr-s), Middlesbrough: Teesside (*4 yr-s), Newcastle (BEng 4/MEng 4 yr-s), Nottingham: Trent (*4 yr-s), Plymouth (*3/4 yr-s), Pontypridd: Wales (*4 yr-s), Portsmouth (*3/4 yr-s), Preston: Lancs (*4 yr-s), Stoke: N Staffs (*4 yr-s), Sunderland (*3/4 yr-s), Wolverhampton (*4 yr-s).

Colleges

Dundee CT (BSc* 4/5 yr-s), Shrivenham: RMCS (BSc* 3 yrs)

'First destination' figures are –

| | 1984-5 | | 1977-8 | |
	university	polytechnic	university	polytechnic
total graduating	1854	734	1440	580
overseas students	242	84	528	91
research/further study	119	34	171	24
'believed' unemployed Dec 31	84	60	23	7
permanent employment (UK)	1197	404	780	247
employers –				
engineering	744	342	530	205
oil, chemicals etc	107	10	33	11
public utilities	77	19	64	10
'other' manufacturing	61	27	30	10
armed forces	46	5	13	1
civil service	38	3	12	1
commerce (not accountancy)	34	11	2	nil
accountancy	31	nil	3	1
construction	13	2	18	2
local authorities	5	4	5	1
functions –				
eng R&D/design	935	320	390	112
eng etc support	65	48	22	14
admin/ops management	63	30	40	28
financial work	37	1	6	2
management services	32	10	74	2
marketing etc	29	9	14	2

Entry requirements normally include A levels in maths and physics. Over 1700 UK students started university courses in October 1985. The 1984-entry mean A-level 'score' was 10.6.

Postgraduate study Graduates in mechanical engineering, whether they have specialised or not, can usefully go on to postgraduate study, where there is an equally varied range of courses to be taken by graduates in either mechanical engineering or related subjects. The range of courses available in any one year should demonstrate the type and kinds of advanced techniques which industry wants at the time.

Professional qualification is via
The Institution of Mechanical Engineers (1986 total membership 76,000, over 50,000 chartered): requires an accredited degree (but also accepts EC examinations) to meet the academic requirements for corporate membership. The Institution will continue to accept a pass or ordinary result from an honours course, but may not continue to accredit unclassified degrees if the standard is significantly lower than the parallel honours course.
The training requirement must also be met, this (including career-directed experience) must be in line with the Institution's aims and objectives – no actual period is now specified but candidates must be at least 25.
The 'monitored professional development scheme' is an alternative route to membership – the student engineer works for four years (normally two years' professional training then two years' planned career development) under the

general supervision of a principal industrial mentor (who must be a chartered engineer).

Technician-engineer qualification is via BTEC or SCOTVEC Higher National awards.

BTEC Higher National Diploma/Certificate engineering with specialisation in mechanical engineering etc: new guidelines (to bring courses into line with the new framework) have not yet (end-86) been issued. Under existing programmes it has been possible to bias courses to, eg aeronautical or auto engineering, refrigeration and air-conditioning, marine engineering, fuel technology, and a wide range of units can be put together to give many different specialisations.

Courses are available at well over 100 centres including all but one polytechnic.

Entry is as for all BTEC Higher-award courses††; if via A-level, maths and physics (or engineering science) should have been studied, with a pass in at least one.

SCOTVEC provides an HNC course in mechanical/production engineering. Entry is as for all SCOTVEC Higher Nationals†††.

'First destination' figures HND (mechanical/production engineering) are –

	1984-5 polytechnic only	1977-8 polytechnic only
total gaining HND	400[1]	281
destination unknown	114	78
overseas students going home	21	12
research/further study	7	16
first degree course	44	21
full-time study for prof qual	nil	4
'believed' unemployed Dec 31	34	7
permanent employment (UK)	151	141
employers –		
engineering	123	97
'other' industry	20	14
functions –		
eng R&D/design	87	34
eng/science support	32	5
admin/ops management	10	74
environmental planning	4	nil
marketing etc	4	3

[1] down from 596 in 1980-1

Technician-engineer level 'professional' qualification is via –
The Institution of Technician Engineers in Mechanical Engineering (formed only 1978 but by 1986 5000 members): minimum academic requirements for corporate membership is a CGLI FTC in an appropriate subject or a BTEC HNC/D (or equivalent) plus at least two years' practical training and at least three years' engineering experience; age at least 23.

Engineering-technician qualification is via BTEC or SCOTVEC National awards.

BTEC National Certificate and Diploma engineering courses, under the new guidelines (see ENGINEERING QUALIFICATIONS, COURSES AND TRAINING) must have a common core of basic engineering skills, but the two required 'applications/technology' units can be biased to mechanical/production engineering, as can some or all of the optional four (Certificate), 10.5 (Diploma) units. Further details of option units are not yet (end-86) published.

Under current guidelines courses are expected to have a minimum core of essential units; these include mathematics to level 2, engineering science to level 3, level 2 courses in manufacturing technology and in engineering drawing and design. Other units are chosen according to the needs of particular groups or of individual students – examples of possible additional units include level 3 manufacturing technology, control of manufacture, electrical science, mechanical science, mathematics, engineering drawing and design, and project work. The diploma course is intended to be broader than the certificate.

Courses are available at a large number of centres.

Entry requirements are as for all BTEC National awards††; if via 16-plus†, passes to include mathematics, physics and English language.

First Certificate and Diploma: see ENGINEERING QUALIFICATIONS, COURSES AND TRAINING.

SCOTVEC's National Certificate courses can include a substantial number of modules in mechanical, production and related areas of engineering. Entry is as for all SCOTVEC National Certificate courses†††.

Engineering-technician 'professional' qualification: The Institution of Technician Engineers in Mechanical Engineering accepts these BTEC/SCOTVEC awards for associate membership.

Craft-level qualifications are set by CGLI, whose courses conform to the standards set by the Engineering Industry Training Board. Schemes are modular, providing courses which complement industrial training rather than incorporating practical work in college courses. Schemes include –

Basic engineering craft studies (scheme 200) has a special mechanical engineering craft bias.

Mechanical engineering & mechanical engineering maintenance craft studies (scheme 205) at levels 2 and 3, follows on scheme 200 and is for those students training or employed in fitting and machining, or learning mechanical engineering skills for mechanical maintenance.

Further information from the above institutions.

Mining and mineral engineering

These subjects deal with all aspects of extracting ores and other minerals and materials from the ground.

For over a century, until the mid-1970s, mining and mineral exploration in Britain meant almost solely coal production (pre-1870 the British Isles was a major mineral- and metal-producing area and a net exporter of coal and many base metals; see MINING). The coal industry was (and now is again) contracting too, so education and training in mining engineering was cut and university departments closed, though there has always been a small but steady demand for expertise in mining and mineral extractive training for those prepared to work overseas. Since the mid-1970s there has been some increased investment in mining minerals and ores.

Working in mining engineering The problems of mining have always been great, and as easier reserves are worked out, they become steadily worse. The effort to make mines more efficient and cost-effective is continuous, and fully-mechanised, even automated systems, are now common.

Professional mining engineers work in prospecting and surveying, in test drilling, designing and planning both underground and opencast workings, sinking shafts and making them safe – from gas, dust, and flood – with ventilation and pumps. Mining engineers manage mines once they are operating.

The Coal Board is the only major employer of mining engineers in the UK. Although the UK is a major producer of industrial minerals, eg clays, salt, fuller's earth, the number of jobs is quite small.

Most mining engineers become managers – all colliery managers are mining engineers, responsible for the safety and efficiency of the mine, and they have mining engineers on their staff. Only a few work in research and development.

British-trained engineers are also employed by international, mainly metal, mining companies. Here mining engineers usually begin in mine management, but can go on to planning, assessing new projects, dealing with contractual or financial work, or investigating and starting new technological developments. Some go on to consultancy work, or mining finance. Mining overseas is likely to mean working in increasingly harsh conditions, as the less remote mines are worked out.

Qualifications, courses and training Professional engineers normally qualify via –

First-degree courses Mining engineers study not only mining operations such as drilling and blasting, support and excavation, but also the origin and nature of ore deposits, structural geology, and applied geophysics. It also involves studying mechanisation and automatic control (since automated mining machinery is now some of the most sophisticated around), power supply and transmission, transportation, ventilation and air-conditioning, etc. Basic engineering and geological principles, management, organisation and economics are also taught.

Minerals engineering and technology covers similar ground, but also deals with the treatment of mined ores by chemical and physical processes, to separate valuable minerals from others and from the rocks and soil.

Courses include (*EC-accredited at July 1986) –

Mineral processing (engineering/technology), at universities – Birmingham (with chemical engineering BEng* 3/MEng 4 yrs), Cardiff, UC (BSc* 3 yrs), Leeds U (BEng 3* yrs), London: Imperial (BEng* 3/MEng 4 yrs); other – Camborne (BEng* 3 yrs).

Mining (engineering) at universities – Cardiff: UC (BSc* 3 yrs), Glasgow: Strathclyde (with petroleum engineering BEng* 4 yrs), Leeds (BEng* 3 yrs), London: Imperial (BEng* 3/MEng 4 yrs), Newcastle (BEng* 3 yrs), Nottingham (BEng* 3/MEng 4 yrs); other – Camborne (BEng* 3 yrs), Stoke on Trent: N Staffs P (BSc* 4 yrs).

Mining geology at universities (all BSc 3 yrs) – Cardiff: UC*, Leicester*, London: Imperial.

Petroleum engineering at universities – Glasgow: Strathclyde (with mining engineering BEng* 4 yrs), London: Imperial (BEng* 3/MEng* 4 yrs).

'First destination' figures (all male) –

| | 1984-5 | | 1977-8 | |
	university	polytechnic	university	polytechnic
total graduating	217	33	193	7[1]
research/further study	24		31	
'believed' unemployed Dec 31	24		7	
overseas	27	5	26	
permanent employment (UK)	82	27	88	
employers –				
oil, chemicals	42[2]	24	14	
construction	6		5	
engineering	10		9	
public utilities	1		50[2]	
functions –				
eng R&D/design	42		25	
eng etc support	16		7	
admin/ops management	6		6	

[1] All already in employment [2] including NCB

At postgraduate level there are currently few courses specifically in mining. Most train for oil exploration and exploitation. Related courses are in engineering mechanics, excavation engineering, mineral process design, production management, coal preparation and ore dressing.

Other courses: Camborne School of Mines trains engineers for the whole world and particularly for metal mines overseas, including gold, copper, tin, zinc and lead mines. The School has a three-year full-time diploma course (entry qualifications two appropriate A levels and three other subjects at 16-plus†) leading to associateship, and one-year postgraduate diploma courses in applied geochemistry, mineral dressing, and mining geology.

Professional qualification The professional bodies are –

The Institution of Mining Engineers (membership about 5000), requires all candidates for full membership either to have a degree or to have passed EC examinations, and at least two years' appropriate experience in the industry. The Institution has also associate membership for technician engineers, for which the entry requirements are an appropriate HNC or its equivalent, and at least five years' appropriate experience including two years' practical training. The Institution of Mining and Metallurgy (membership 5000-plus) requires all entrants to be of graduate standard, with either an appropriate degree in science or technology, or EC examinations; at least seven years' training and experience is also required.

(Both Institutions accept as members anyone working in mining or an allied industry – not just qualified mining engineers but those qualified in other professions, for example, other branches of engineering and surveying, and research scientists.)

The Association of Mining Electrical and Mechanical Engineers (total membership c4000) requires members to have passed its own certificate examination (entry is via a BTEC national certificate or equivalent), or an equivalent examination. The Association's certificates exempt from MQB written examinations. Candidates for membership must normally have had appropriate training and at least five years' engineering experience and four years' employment in a responsible position.

Technician-engineer, engineering-technician and craft-level qualifications
These are closely linked to training for the National Coal Board and the examinations of the Mining Qualifications Board: see MINING.

See also GEOLOGY, MINING and MATERIALS SCIENCE AND TECHNOLOGY.

Further information from the above Institutions.

Naval architecture, marine engineering and shipbuilding
These cover between them the expertise used in designing and building ships.

Shipbuilding is a complex problem in engineering design and production, but traditionally the 'ship' and the 'engine' have been treated separately, although 'they have common and overlapping interests requiring a common identity of thought and purpose for their common pursuit'.

Ships have to be designed to meet the tight specifications of their owners – to carry a certain cargo, to have a certain capacity, to travel in particular seas and dock at specific ports, to sail at set speeds, and to be built to budget and schedule. Technical considerations include stability, vibration, hydrodynamics, and fuel and general operating economy. Giant tankers have one set of manoeuvrability problems, naval vessels another. Particular cargoes need special care – eliminating all fire risks for crude oil and chemicals, for instance.

Naval architects, who are engineers, design, build, rebuild, maintain and repair the ship and its components, excluding the machinery. In theory, they are trained to design and construct every kind of vessel from a dinghy to a massive oil tanker, a submarine or an oil rig, but in practice few work on small, unpowered craft. Some do design the unconventional, eg hovercraft, and naval architects are involved in designing off-shore oil rigs.

Marine engineers design, construct, operate and maintain ships' machinery, including the engines.

Naval architects and marine engineers must, obviously, work closely together, not only on how a ship is to be powered and on the new and very sophisticated control systems she is likely to have, but also on plumbing, electrical systems, perhaps refrigeration and air conditioning.

Working as naval architects and marine engineers Both naval architects and marine engineers have been suffering from the problems of the industry (see SHIPBUILDING).

Professional naval architects are relatively few in number with only about 4500 qualified people. A relatively small proportion of these, some hundreds only, work in the shipbuilding and repair industry itself, as designers and/or managers, and some work for oil-rig constructors. Some work for ship-owning companies which have their own marine technical departments where they not only design ships, but also solve problems in eg cargo handling. Others work for one of the several firms of marine consultant employing naval architects as ship designers, and supervising ships under construction.
Lloyd's Register of Shipping and the Department of Trade both recruit naval architects and marine engineers as ship surveyors. Lloyd's surveyors, of whom there are over 400, assess ships' structural strength, while those working for the DOT mainly enforce safety regulations, but both have research sections.
The Ministry of Defence employs about 200, most of whom are members of the Royal Corps of Naval Constructors (now part of the new integrated Defence Engineering Service), and a small number work for the Royal Naval Scientific Service (see ARMED FORCES and CIVIL SERVICE).
About 100 naval architects do research, and teach (mainly in universities and polytechnics). The major research units are Marine Technology Ltd, and the ship division of the National Physical Laboratory. Ministry of Defence establishments also do research on naval vessels, and there are naval architects working in other fluid dynamics laboratories on ship research and development and for shipbuilders and ship-owners. There is some university- and polytechnic-based research.

Professional marine engineers work for the same range of employers, and also for inland engine manufacturers. They also go to sea as ships' engineering officers.

Technicians and technician engineers within the industry work in design (drawing offices), and in supervisory/managerial capacities.

Qualifications, courses and training Naval architecture and marine engineering can be studied at professional/degree, technician and craft ('technical') level.

First degree courses traditionally specialise in naval architecture or marine engineering, although it is possible to combine them. Marine engineering is closely allied to mechanical engineering. Courses include (all lead to honours/* EC-accredited at July 86) –
Universities

Edinburgh, H-Watt:	Off-shore engineering (with chemical & process, civil, electrical & electronic, or mechanical engineering)(BEng* 4 yrs)
Glasgow:	Naval architecture & ocean engineering (BEng* 4 yrs)
Glasgow, S'clyde:	Naval architecture (BEng* 4/BScMEng* 5 yrs)
Guildford, Surrey:	Mechanical engineering (BEng* 4 yr-s) includes option in marine engineering

London, UCL:	Naval architecture & ocean engineering (BSc(Eng) 3/BEng 4 yrs) shares common core of studies and options with mechanical engineering
Newcastle:	Marine engineering (BEng* 3 yrs) or Marine technology (MEng 4 yrs) Naval architecture & shipbuilding (BEng* 3 yrs) with options in marine engineering, and in marine transport and operations
Southampton:	Ship science (BSc* 3/MEng* 4 yrs) biased to naval architecture
Ulster:	Engineering (BEng 4 yr-s) includes ship design and production option
Polytechnics	
Liverpool:	Mechanical engineering (BEng* 3/4 yr-s) with marine option
Plymouth:	Fishery science or Nautical studies (BSc 3 yrs) both include naval architecture option
Sunderland:	Nautical studies (BSc* 3 yrs) includes marine vessel design
College	
Plymouth, RNEC:	Naval engineering (BSc* 3 yrs)

Sea-going marine engineer officers must meet the same requirements of the Department of Trade as other sea-going personnel (see TRANSPORT).

Postgraduate courses include (1987) –
Marine engineering at – London: UC, Newcastle U, Plymouth (RNEC)
Marine technology at – Glasgow: Strathclyde, Newcastle U
Maritime civil engineering – Liverpool U
Naval architecture – Glasgow, London: UC, Newcastle U
Ocean engineering – Glasgow U, London: UC
Ship/ship production technology – Glasgow: Strathclyde U

Professional qualification The professional bodies are –
The Royal Institution of Naval Architects (1986 membership about 6700 of whom some 4360 chartered): deliberately keeps its statements on entry requirements unspecific and so changes are always possible. The requirement is at present for 'an academic qualification of degree standard' which allows entry via EC examinations, plus a set period of formal training and responsible experience.
The Institute of Marine Engineers (1986 about 19,500 members, a third overseas, about two-thirds chartered): also accepts EC examinations or Department of Trade extra first class certificate as meeting the academic requirement for membership, but practical training and responsible experience are also required.
The Institution of Mechanical Engineers: has marine engineer members.

Technician-engineer qualification is via a BTEC or SCOTVEC Higher award. BTEC Higher National Diploma and Certificate programmes are due to be revised in line with the new framework, but as yet (spring 1987) new guidelines have not yet been published. Existing programmes are –

Marine engineering for both sea-going (including RN personnel) and land-based technician engineers. Full time/sandwich courses are at –
Hull: Humberside CFE, Liverpool: Riversdale CT, London: Hackney C, Plymouth P, S Shields M&TC, Southampton: Highbury CT, Wallasey: Wirral MC.
Shipbuilding and naval architecture, sandwich-based: Sunderland P; part-time: Barrow CFE, Bath TC, Chatham: Mid-Kent CH&FE, London: City P, Plymouth CFE, Southampton CHE, Wallasey: Wirral MC.
Entry for both courses is as for all BTEC Higher awards††.

SCOTVEC also sets HNC/D syllabuses for marine engineering, and HNC only for shipbuilding. Entry is as for all SCOTVEC Higher awards†††.

Technician-engineer 'professional' qualification is via –
The Royal Institution of Naval Architects (see also above) admits to non-corporate membership with an appropriate HNC/D
The Institute of Marine Engineers gives associate membership to people with any of a number of qualification at HND/C level, including appropriate CGLI FTC and DOT first-class certificate.

Engineering-technician qualification is via a BTEC or SCOTVEC National award.

BTEC National Certificate and Diploma engineering courses, under the new guidelines (see ENGINEERING QUALIFICATIONS, COURSES AND TRAINING) must have a common core of basic engineering skills, but the two required 'applications/technology' units can presumably be biased to marine engineering or shipbuilding, as can some or all of the optional four (Certificate), 10.5 (Diploma) units. There is also to be a new National Diploma course in maritime technology. Further details of option units are not yet (end-86) published.
Marine engineering, courses are at about a dozen centres.
For shipbuilding, under the existing guidelines, courses start with basic engineering science, marine and shipbuilding technology and technical communications, plus optional modules in naval architecture, basic ship materials, materials and mechanical science. Part-time only courses are at about a dozen centres.
Entry is as for all BTEC National awards††; if via 16-plus† passes to include mathematics, a science biased to physics and English language.

See also ARMED FORCES, SHIPBUILDING and TRANSPORT.

SCOTVEC's National Certificate course can include a substantial number of modules in marine engineering, shipbuilding etc. Entry is as for all SCOTVEC National Certificate courses.

Engineering-technician 'professional' qualification: engineering technicians can become non-corporate members of both the RINA and IME with appropriate BTEC National awards and training/experience.

Craft-level qualifications are CGLI awards. Craft workers in the industry can start with –
Basic engineering studies (scheme 200), with a shipbuilding bias;
Shipbuilding craft studies (scheme 240) is at levels 2 and 3, following on from

scheme 200. It is for loftsmen, platers, shipwrights, welders;
Marine craft fitting (scheme 244), levels 1-3 for boatyard fitters who install machinery in small craft;Yacht and boat building/joinery (scheme 245) at levels 1-3 on materials and techniqued used to fit equipment and accommodation in small craft.
See also MANUFACTURING, ARMED FORCES and TRANSPORT.

Further information from the above institutions (both publish careers booklets).

Production engineering

The *branch* of engineering called production is not easy to separate from the production *function*, or production management (discussed earlier in this section), and in fact it is probably indistinguishable.

The professional production engineer is the technological expert of the production team as well as a trained manager, and so the chartered production engineer usually works where the product being made, or the machinery and equipment which is used to make it, is the most technologically-sophisticated and complex.

In any manufacturing firm, production engineers plan and design new production facilities, revamp or revise existing equipment or arrangements, look for ways to improve production methods, speed production, cut costs, or counter new competition. Production engineers assess the potential and check the specifications of new machines and machine tools, and may manage any switch to automation or other use of computer-based technology. They plan the layout of production lines for maximum efficiency. Some production engineers design and produce new manufacturing equipment.

The production engineer is an expert in the economics as well as the technology of production, and must be able to justify changes or new machinery in terms of saved costs or improved production. Production engineers also deal with the problems of industrial relations on the shop floor, especially when systems are being changed.

Production engineers do also manage production facilities, especially early in their careers (many spend their first training periods working as foremen), but their special expertise is designed to take them into more senior posts reasonably quickly. But production still suffers from the poor image of engineering, and industry is short of them.

Production technician engineers, working under the production engineer, control known manufacturing techniques and give detailed instructions to the workshops as well as, in many cases, supervising the work of skilled craft workers.

Production engineering technicians provide support for the senior staff and work in specific areas of production.

Qualifications and courses in production engineering Courses are available at several levels.

First degree courses The number of degree courses relevant to production engineering has increased lately, with pressure to improve both the expertise of engineers going into production, and indeed to increase the number of such graduates. It is not always called production engineering – there are numerous variants including manufacturing management, industrial engineering, plant engineering, production technology. Production engineering is also frequently taught as part of mechanical engineering courses (which see). For production engineering subjects studied include basic sciences, mathematics, engineering principles (many courses are common in their early years with mechanical engineering), and then extensive studies of production/manufacturing (examining production, processes, methods, machine tools, assemblies, accessories etc), planning and control (including, increasingly, automation), economics and economics of production, industrial relations and management sciences (eg work study and operational research).

Relevant courses include, at (all courses lead to honours/*-EC accredited at July 86) –

Universities

Bath:	Manufacturing (BSc/BEng* 4 yr-s)
	Production engineering (BSc/BEng 3/4yr-s)
Birmingham:	Engineering production (BEng* 3/MEng 4); can also be studied with economics (for BEngBCom*)
Birmingham, Aston:	Production technology & management (BEng* 3/4 yr-s/MEng* 4/5 yr-s); manufacturing systems can also be studied as part of a two-subject course
Brunel:	Manufacturing engineering (BEng* 4 yr-s)
Cambridge:	Production engineering (BA* 4 yrs) yrs 1-2 on Engineering course
Cardiff, UWIST:	Engineering production & production management (BEng* 3/BEng(Tech)* 4 yr-s)
Coventry, Warwick:	Manufacturing (MEng* 4 yrs)
Glasgow, S'clyde:	Engineering, production & management (BEng* 4/BScMEng* 5 yrs)
Hull:	Engineering design & manufacture (BEng* 4 yrs)
Loughborough:	Manufacturing engineering & management (BSc* 3/BScdip 4 yr-s/MEng* 5 yr-s) manufacturing engineering can also be taken with electronics
Manchester/UMIST:	Engineering manufacture & management (BSc/BEng* 4 yrs)
Nottingham:	Production engineering & management (BEng* 3/MEng* 4 yrs)
Ulster:	Manufacturing engineering (BEng 4 yr-s)

Polytechnics

Coventry, Lanchester:	Production engineering (BEng* 4 yr-s)
Hatfield:	Manufacturing systems engineering (BEng* 4 yr-s)
Kingston:	Production engineering (BEng* 4 yr-s)
Leeds:	Manufacturing systems engineering (BEng* 4 yr-s)
Liverpool:	Manufacturing engineering (BEng* 3/4 yr-s)
London, NELP:	Manufacturing studies (BSc 4 yr-s) trains managers rather than experts in production
Nottingham, Trent:	Manufacturing engineering (BEng* 4 yr-s)
	Plant engineering (BEng* 4 yr-s)

Sheffield: Manufacturing systems engineering (MEng* 4 yr-s)
'First destination' figures are –

| | 1984-5 | | 1977-8 | |
	university	polytechnic	university	polytechnic
total graduating	232	214	192	58
research/further study	5	18	4	8
'other' training	25	20		
'believed' unemployed Dec 31	5	14	2	1
permanent employment (UK)	160	132	52	37
employers –				
engineering	114	102	39	35
oil, chemicals etc	8	4	1	nil
'other' manufacturing	13	7	3	1
construction	nil	1	nil	nil
commerce (not accounting)	7	4	nil	nil
accountancy	5	1	nil	nil
public utilities	2	3	nil	nil
civil service	1	3	1	1
functions –				
eng R&D/design	93	84	41	35
admin/ops management	20	8	3	1
eng etc support	11	16	nil	nil
financial work	7	1	nil	nil
marketing etc	3	3	nil	nil
management services	17	6	nil	1

At postgraduate level a number of courses leading to higher degrees and diplomas, but industrial experience and/or sponsorship is usually necessary.

The professional body is – The Institution of Production Engineers (total membership nearly 19,000 of whom some 13,000 are chartered): accepts EC examinations as satisfying the academic requirement, but full membership also requires at least two years' experience and a position of 'technological responsibility in production engineering'.

Technician-engineer and engineering-technician qualification is combined with MECHANICAL ENGINEERING (which see).

Further information from the Institution of Production Engineers.

QUALIFICATIONS AND CAREERS IN LAND USE

Introduction   205
Architecture   207
Geography   208
Planning   211
Surveying   211

INTRODUCTION
Land, particularly in the relatively crowded British Isles, is an increasingly

scarce resource. Many, and often conflicting, demands are made on the land: it must produce food; it must give up the minerals which lie beneath it; it must provide space for housing, industry, transport facilities; it must be kept looking as attractive as possible. More people care about how land is used, and are increasingly passionate in their advocacy of what should or should not happen whenever a significant decision has to be made. Land-owners, industry and public authorities are all now expected to take wide environmental and social issues into account when developing and building, and all decisions are subjected to rigorous scrutiny.

This has considerable impact on the people whose work is concerned with land and land use, with the decision-making process, with responsibility for control in land development, with planning, designing, building or even preserving the existing environment. The quality of performance expected of them has increased sharply in recent years, in parallel with the rise in demand for a pleasant and humane environment in which to live and work. These professions frequently find themselves at the centre of controversy, tensions and even conflict; they must take greater care over decision-making on problems which grow ever more complex, and must be ready to justify their decisions; they must meet demands for greater economy in terms of use of land, building resources, and even time; they must protect the environment as far as possible; they must meet changing aesthetic, health and anti-pollution demands; they must use technologies of growing sophistication and potential hazard.

All these disciplines, as subjects of study, have therefore developed and changed quite considerably over the past 30 years, and will probably have to continue to do so. In particular, this has meant steadily-rising standards of education and training; almost all the professions involved in the land are now at least partly educated to degree level, and many almost entirely so.

Studies must involve deeper appreciation and knowledge of the fundamental principles; they must keep up with technological advances; include business methods, relevant economics and understanding of, for instance, the demands imposed by cost-benefit analysis. Courses must now cover behavioural and social sciences, so-called social accounting, to give graduates understanding of individual, family and community human needs in terms of their environment. Since most of the people who go on to practice in these professions must work in integrated multi-disciplinary teams, they are growing less insular, more aware of the influences they have, and of the need for architects, planners, building developers, transport experts and so on to be aware of what others are taught. The boundaries between the various disciplines have blurred somewhat, with common areas identified and taught as part of an interdisciplinary scheme on some courses.

All the subjects in this area can be considered as education and training for careers well outside the disciplines themselves. People qualified in architecture, planning and land uses in general can find posts away from their own professions, in advising all kinds of organisations and authorities on land and building development, and in generally influencing policy and decision-making. There is also considerable interchange between these disciplines: architects may become planners or landscape architects, for example.

ARCHITECTURE

While architecture is, for most people, a vocational training for a specific career, it is also an interesting subject for study in its own right. Degree courses have been broadened, and while they are still strongly design based (and primarily studio taught), studying aesthetics and architectural history in depth, courses have also to give plenty of time to building science and technology, and the construction process. Schools are being urged also to train architectures to use computer-aided design. Courses also cover the environmental setting of architectural design, via urban planning and the planning process, behavioural and social sciences.

Working as an architect see LAND USE PROFESSIONS under LAND AND ENVIRON-MENT-RELATED CAREERS.

Studying architecture Architecture is now studied almost entirely on degree courses, full-time. The number of places is being cut, and courses closed.

Degree courses in architecture traditionally lasted for five years, but most now have two-part structures to give a first degree in architecture after three years, and a postgraduate award after a further two. Within these courses, syllabuses are designed to let anyone whose interests change during the first three years take options suitable to another careers.

Architecture is taught at –

Universities – Bath (emphasising environmental technology), Belfast, Cambridge (emphasising history), Cardiff: UWIST, Dundee, Edinburgh, Edinburgh: H-Watt, Glasgow, Glasgow: Strathclyde, Liverpool (special year-3 options for those not wishing to continue in architecture after graduation), London: UC (linked to planning, building, environmental studies), Manchester, Newcastle, Nottingham, Sheffield (with special stream for those planning careers in eg public administration, commerce or industry).

Polytechnics – Birmingham, Brighton, Kingston, Leeds, Leicester, Liverpool, London: NELP, NLP, PCL, S Bank, Thames, Manchester, Oxford, Plymouth, Portsmouth; colleges – Aberdeen: RGIT, Canterbury CA, Hull: Humberside CHE.

Entry requirements normally include mathematics or a science subject.

'First destination' figures are –

	1984-5		1977-8	
	university	polytechnic	university	polytechnic
total graduating	488[1]	974[2]	579	726
research/further study	19	10	48	6
'other' training	85	115	127	53
'believed' unemployed Dec 31	10	36	6	18
destination unknown	62	157	51	137
permanent employment	271	542	305	426
employers –				
architecture etc	212	272	228	197
local authorities	27	122	46	134
commerce	4	66	2	2
civil service	2	26	16	23

	1984-5		1977-8	
	university	polytechnic	university	polytechnic
oil, chemicals etc	nil	2	1	nil
functions –				
environmental planning	255	415	299	332
marketing etc	3	41	1	14
admin/ops management	nil	30	1	nil
financial work	nil	25	nil	18
management services	nil	4	1	1

[1] down from 582 in 1983-4   [2] includes planning

Entry: architecture schools vary in the A-level subjects named, but a mix of arts and science subjects is most useful, including maths and art. 595 UK students were accepted for university courses in 1985, about 890 for CNAA degrees. The mean A-level 'score' for university entrants in 1984 was 11.1.

Professional qualification All students who plan to qualify as architects must, legally, complete a full five-year course of training. This means that after a three-year first-degree course, graduates must study for a further two years. All courses listed above award a degree after three years, a postgraduate diploma or a master's degree after a further two (a year in between is usually spent in an architects' office). In the final two years courses are generally more heavily biased to professional studies with advanced work in architectural design and building technology as well as office practice. To satisfy the educational requirements for registration an examination in professional practice must be passed, and appropriate professional experience, normally two separate years, gained, making seven years in training altogether.

The Royal Institute of British Architects (RIBA) sets its own examinations, but all architects must, by law, register with the Architects' Registration Council of the United Kingdom (ARCUK), and the RIBA examinations are only one of the qualifications (which include those from overseas schools) recognised by the Council. Both ARCUK and RIBA list schools and courses they approve, ARCUK as qualifying holders for registration and the RIBA as exempting from its own examinations for corporate membership. Corporate membership of the RIBA is not, therefore, a requirement.

The RIBA sets a three-part examination; the structure is similar to that of degree courses. Most architects take courses which exempt them from the RIBA examinations (which include those listed above) but it is possible to take full-time courses leading to RIBA examinations at –
Glasgow SA, London: AA, S Bank P.
It is also still possible to take RIBA examinations by part-time study, but it takes at least seven years and is discouraged by the Institute.

Further information from the Architects' Registration Council of the United Kingdom, the Royal Institute of British Architects (leaflets and a list of recognised schools), and the Royal Incorporation of Architects in Scotland.

GEOGRAPHY

At degree level, geography is not just descriptive, but is far more analytical and interpretive. The main theme is relationships, or the interaction between human activities – economic, political and social – and the physical environment. Geography has extended its scope and content enormously over the past thirty to forty years, and also developed in method and purpose. During this time the world has become even more crowded, competition for space and resources fiercer, which makes it even more important to understand how the physical environment has evolved and how it is affected – by weather, by human activity, etc.

Geography courses have changed too. Traditionally, geography students specialised in human or physical geography, but today they have a wide ranging and flexible choice of topics. The traditional divisions still exist, but the possible 'mix' is less rigid.

'Systematic' studies form a substantial proportion of most courses –
Physical geography studies the earth's natural features, how they were formed and change, what changes them, which means it includes studies of atmosphere and climate, water resources and soils etc, including the energy chain and the ecosystem, and their relevance to human society.

Human geography ranges widely over the interaction of people and the environment, and is increasingly concerned with human and social problems with a 'spatial' context – the conflicts caused by changes in transport policy, for instance. It covers economic geography, studying the geographical reasons for industrial development, trading patterns and long-term effects of development. Human geography has many modern aspects – land use and resource studies, urban geography (the patterns of towns and suburban development, decay and renewal), medical geography (where, for instance, geographers mapped the spread of diseases), and even recreational geography.

What used to be called regional studies, particular places or areas are examined, places with distinctive geographical 'identities' – such as 'functional' regions, a city and the area it serves, an industrial region, or places with cultural and climatic identity. They are studied as living, changing, developing organisms, in critical analyses of them at a particular point in time.

Geography uses scientific methods of collecting information, statistics, storing data and analysing it by computer, but still also working with maps, diagrams and photos.

Opportunities for geographers Smaller proportions of geography graduates now find posts in careers traditionally associated with the subject – such as TEACHING and PLANNING (about half did so in the early 1970s) – although substantial numbers do still go on to teach. Geography is relevant (according to AGCAS) for careers in SURVEYING, LAND VALUATION, CARTOGRAPHY, ENVIRONMENTAL PROTECTION or CONSERVATION, LANDSCAPE ARCHITECTURE, LEISURE INDUSTRIES, TRANSPORT AND TOURISM, government resource planning (see CIVIL SERVICE).

Geographers' understanding of spatial/human relationships are exploitable in areas like locational planning for large RETAILERS, MARKET RESEARCH, international trade. Although otherwise geography graduates have to compete for a career start with other graduates whose degree subject is not of direct relevance to work, the 'multi-faceted' nature of most courses, the numeracy needed do, according to AGCAS, give them a reasonable basis to do so.

Studying geography Geography, as a single honours subject, in combination with another, and as part of a broader-based and/or modular scheme is taught at most universities and at a number of polytechnics. At most universities it is possible to read for an arts, social science or science degree. The courses do not necessarily differ – usually it is the entry requirements and the subsidiary subjects studied which differentiate them.

'First destination' figures are –

| | 1984-5 | | 1977-8 | |
	university	polytechnic	university	polytechnic
total graduating	1958[1]	486	2078	299
research/further study	160	28	23	11
teacher training	163	38	408	46
'other' training	119	28	22	5
'believed' unemployed Dec 31	192	61	93	34
destination unknown	185	74	152	52
permanent employment (UK)	911	182	758	97
employers –				
accountancy	162	4	76	1
banking & insurance	100	11	53	3
'other' commerce	176	49	109	18
local authorities	94	34	10	24
civil service	66	24	66	6
public utilities	46	14	76	2
engineering	35	8	2	13
oil, chemicals etc	34	6	28	1
other manufacturing	51	12	4	4
armed forces	35	4	19	5
higher/further education	27	16	16	nil
construction etc	10	4	10	5
functions –				
financial work	279	25	163	10
admin/ops management	149	50	209	29
marketing etc	129	27	139	14
personnel/social	70	16	48	6
management services	56	11	56	3
environmental planning	20	17	37	12

[1] down from 2120 in 1982

Entry normally requires A-level geography. Just 2238 students were accepted for university degree courses for 1985 entry, about 640 for CNAA degree courses. The mean A-level 'score' for 1984 university entry was 11.1.

Postgraduate study Advanced courses in geography most frequently extend a specialised part of a first-degree courses, often of a region, for example, geography of Africa and the Middle East or monsoon Asia at London (SOAS), Middle East and Mediterranean studies at Durham, polar studies at Cambridge. Some, though, specialise in techniques, eg geographical information systems at Edinburgh, photogrammetry at Glasgow.

Further information from the Royal Geographical Society (leaflets on careers and degrees in geography).

GEOLOGY & EARTH/ENVIRONMENTAL SCIENCES
See under QUALIFICATIONS AND CAREERS IN SCIENCE.

PLANNING
See LAND USE PROFESSIONS under ENVIRONMENT-RELATED CAREERS.

SURVEYING
See LAND USE PROFESSIONS under ENVIRONMENT-RELATED CAREERS.

QUALIFICATIONS AND CAREERS IN SCIENCE

Introduction	211
Agricultural, horticultural and forest sciences	220
Astronomy	225
Biological sciences and biology	227
Chemistry	245
Computer science	252
Ergonomics	257
Food science and technology, dietetics and nutrition	258
Geology and earth sciences	261
Materials science and technology	266
Mathematics and statistics	272
Medical sciences	276
Meteorology	279
Oceanography	281
Ophthalmic optics	282
Pharmacology and pharmacy	283
Physics	287
Veterinary science	292

INTRODUCTION
The sciences explore the natural world in all its complexity and variety, probing ever more deeply into the make-up of both living and non-living things, from the smallest nuclear sub-particle to the giant supernova star, from the most minute microbe to the dinosaur.

In investigating the natural world, in endless experiment, careful observation and inspired speculation, scientists try to discover the reasons for what happens in the natural world, and the common patterns and underlying principles, attempting to set up a network of logically-connected theories which represent current thinking about the natural world.

But science has a practical side too and, either deliberately or incidentally, plays a major part in solving problems, such as the causes of a crippling disease, or of a fault in a metal structure. Scientists may choose to work directly in 'applied' research, but more often than not more fundamental, 'pure', research work is needed first to solve practical problems of this kind – discovering how a particular part of the body works or a metal is made up, for instance, before it is possible to see what has gone wrong. Pure and applied work, therefore, do not always go into separate, watertight compartments, and most scientific discoveries, however theoretical and irrelevant, however speculative they may seem, soon or later turn out to have some practical value, simply because science is about the real world.

The tools and techniques developed for scientific research, both the very exacting methods of experiment and testing, and the sophisticated equipment like electron microscopes, oscilloscopes and computers, have also found uses outside the lab – in industry, for example, in measuring chemicals as they go through a conversion process, or in hospitals, monitoring patients' conditions in intensive care.

Science stretches from the most abstract and theoretical thought (eg proving mathematically the existence of 'black holes' in space), to the most practical (eg developing a new moth-proofer for wool). And even scientific thinking and the rigorous and exact methods by which scientists observe, experiment, test, prove and quantify are now adapted for use outside the sciences, from ARCHAE-OLOGY to SOCIAL SCIENCES, and MANAGEMENT.

Although it is common to talk and think about chemistry, biology, and physics (for example), as separate 'branches' of scientific knowledge, 'real' science cannot be rigidly divided into such neat and watertight compartments. They are no more than convenient labels. There is no rule of nature which dictates the divisions between 'branches', and more often than not they have come about by accident. As a quick definition, we describe chemistry as the science of materials, biology as the science of life. But living thing – plants, animals, people – are also materials, so here chemistry and biology meet and merge in a common interest in living materials – and is called 'biochemistry'.

Chemistry and physics also supply the rest of the scientific world with instruments, techniques, even ways of thought. For example, oceanographers use chemical techniques to analyse the make-up of sea water and any increase or fall in oxygen content (which can affect marine life). All scientific labs, whether technically working in chemistry, biology or physics have, for a long time now, been full of equipment developed by physicists.

Science as a career
It is common to think of studying science in order to become a scientist of some kind. But science graduates do not have to become scientists, and nowadays it is not always possible anyway. Financial cuts – in the number of posts in government-supported research labs and services, in university funding – and a long decline in investment in research in industry generally, mean there is not, just now (1987), a science slot for every science graduate. But with fewer science graduates coming out of higher education, some shortages are already apparent – of physics teachers, for example – and if industry were to increase investment in research and development, the situation could change dramatically.

In any case, a higher proportion of people with science qualifications find work which 'uses' their degrees than do, say, philosophy graduates, and they probably have a wider choice of non-scientific work too, simply because they understand scientific 'language', and have to be very numerate. It is also easier to acquire technological skills from a science base, and so go into occupations when particular shortages emerge.

Supposedly, there are the 'professional' scientists and the 'technician' scientists, but the line between them is increasingly blurred, for a variety of reasons, including the fact that, to stay in science, science graduates are going into what has been considered technician-level work. This is only one example, but a major one, of the changing pattern of scientific careers.

OPPORTUNITIES FOR PROFESSIONAL SCIENTISTS There is no such person as 'the' scientist. 'Among scientists', wrote Nobel-Prize winner Sir Peter Medawar, 'are collectors [eg geologists], classifiers [eg zoologists], and compulsive tidiers-up [of theories, ideas, etc]; many are detectives by temperament, and many are explorers, some are artists and others are artisans.'

Most scientists at least begin their careers in a particular 'branch' of science, as physicists or chemists or biologists, and this dictates to some extent what their working lives are like, or at least how they start. Many, though, are recruited more for their broad scientific training than for their specialist skills, and many will move on into jobs which cannot be easily labelled as, eg 'physicist'. Many work in multi-disciplinary 'teams' – in research labs, in design and development, in analytical work and control – and over the years their skills become more multi-disciplinary too. Multi-skilled scientists are in demand – advertisements such as 'experienced physicist with a considerable depth of software experience' (or 'life sciences training backed by research degree on topic related to animal health – and practical experience in handling farm animals') are common.

What professional scientists do 'Being a scientist' is generally equated with doing scientific research work, and most people who call themselves scientists probably do start their careers here, or (in some disciplines) analytical work.

'Research' is mostly lab based, although some scientists, eg geologists, may spend more of their time 'in the field', while others eventually become scientific managers. Many scientists in all 'branches' spend working time at a computer terminal.

Research ranges from (for relatively few), the most abstract, which at present probably means working out on the theoretical frontiers of, for example, particle physics, to the most practical, largely working for, with, or in support of industry. In the academic world they talk of 'pure' and 'applied' for either end of the spectrum, which generally means that 'pure' research is totally speculative, investigating something for its own sake, while 'applied' has a definite aim, which may or may not turn out to have a practical use. Many universities and most polytechnics now work more closely with industry, encouraged by SERC's current grants policy, doing research work on contract or collaboratively with firms, and this will usually have a totally practical aim. Research on applied and industrial problems – in advanced fields like biotechnology for instance – can be just as taxing, and interesting, as more theoretical work, although in industry scientists are not always stretched to their full potential and the work can be routine.

In industry, they tend to talk about 'basic' or 'fundamental' and 'product-directed' research – fundamental, or basic research (of which is now much less than in the 1960s), looks at areas within a company's scope (eg chemicals, electronics), to see if there is anything new which could be exploited. Even within the strict confines which companies set on this kind of research, though, scientists working out on the frontiers of materials science or electronics – for example – can find themselves in some very speculative work. Electronics firms, particularly, still do some pioneering – eg combining a sophisticated lab technique, nuclear magnetic resonance, with computer technology to produce a radiation-free method to replace x-raying in medical diagnosis, even analysing the chemicals inside the body. A soap manufacturer has a major research project studying the molecular and macro-structure of toilet soaps and relating this to the bars' physical appearance.

Scientific research has very precise methods of working. Based on existing knowledge, scientists suggest draft theories or 'hypotheses' to begin to fill in the gaps in their knowledge of a particular area, and then by very exact observation, experiments and endless testing try to prove or disprove the theories, modify them, or come up with a new theory.

It can take a long time. Astronomers and physicists battled over the 'big bang' theory of the origins of the universe for many years. In the 1970s they became fairly convinced that this was how it happened, and went on to try and decide whether the still-expanding universe will go on doing so for ever, or whether it will collapse back into itself. Lately, though, 'big bang' has come under suspicion again. Space probes like the 'Voyagers' produce some of the evidence, but knock down theories almost as fast as they are set up.

Some problems have to wait for techniques and apparatus to be developed before they can be solved, and some scientists spend years developing techniques of, say, chemical analysis before they can get down to the problem that really interests them – mapping the structure of a protein, for example. Computers, electron and field-ion microscopes, space probes, cyclotrons and bubble chambers have made possible many of the major discoveries of the last twenty years. The equations now used to forecast the weather numerically (with one of the most sophisticated computers there is), were invented over 60 years ago, but it would have taken 64,000 mathematicians working day and night just to forecast one day ahead.

Scientific research, then, is a mixture of hard and logical thinking and desk-calculating, observing, doing experiments, and then trying to decide what it all means. Some of it can be very exciting, much is very routine, and it all involves a lot of rather boring repetitive work – although automated and computer-driven equipment has eased this.

Once there is something to show for all the hard work, researchers have to write up their results, present them at seminars and conferences, and get them published in the right scientific journals, for other scientists to argue over, scrutinise, and compare with their own work.

Analytical work Closely allied to research, scientific analysis takes things apart for practical purposes. This can be to check that a drug is correctly formulated, in a pharmaceutical firm, and is part of quality control. It can be to see what is wrong with a patient's blood (for example), which means working for the HEALTH SERVICE. It can be examining physical clues from a crime, working for

POLICE forensic labs. It can be analysing food to see if it is infected with bacteria, in LOCAL GOVERNMENT environmental control labs, or in the public analyst's office.

Other science-based work While not strictly scientific work, a number of occupations require a scientific training/background.
TEACHING, of course, is one. In schools, scientists rarely get a chance to do anything else, but in universities and polytechnics they can combine teaching with research work. PATENT WORK is another. A few may find work in CONSERVATION or other ENVIRONMENTAL WORK.

Related occupations A scientific training is also a useful basis for work in technical JOURNALISM, COMPUTING and other MANAGEMENT SERVICES, scientific PUBLISHING or BROADCASTING, MUSEUM WORK, LIBRARY/INFORMATION WORK, technical TRANSLATING.

Non-scientific work Partly because there has been a shortage of openings for research scientists, partly because other employers have become more interested in people with numerate, scientific backgrounds, increasing numbers of graduate scientists are accepting work in, and accepted for, non-scientific careers. A science degree can be treated as a non-vocational qualification and as the 'first employment' figures (below) show, FINANCIAL WORK, including ACCOUNTANCY, BANKING and INSURANCE; MANAGEMENT SERVICES, and all kinds of COMMERCE generally, are taking on science graduates.

Where scientists work No firm statistics on the employment of scientists have been produced for nearly twenty years. Estimates suggest, however –

Industry employs the largest group – perhaps a third. They work in research and development, mainly in traditional science-based industries (making, for instance, drugs, processed food and drinks, or chemicals), but also in high-technology areas such as biotechnology, and engineering, such as electronics. Others manage production or quality control and testing in a great many industries from electricity generating to brewing, or work in specialised, technical marketing, sales, and even purchasing in, eg pharmaceuticals or the food industry. See MANUFACTURING INDUSTRY.
Industrial research associations also employ research scientists.

Education probably employs up to 25%. Some 33,500 teach in schools (1984-5). At least 13,000 (including mathematicians and scientists teaching in pre-clinical medicine) are academics (teaching and researching) in universities and nearly 10,000 in polytechnics and FE colleges (1984-5), but several thousand more are financed by other organisations (mainly research councils), many of them as full-time researchers and so not teaching. See EDUCATION.

Central government employs quite large numbers. Most (close to 13,000 in 1986) work in the scientific civil service. They mainly do research in government research units, which range from the massive National Physical Laboratory, which looks after national standards of measurement, to freshwater fisheries labs studying salmon and trout. Some government labs, though, are being 'privatised', and there is tight control on the number of jobs. The government also has analytical labs, eg the forensic science lab. Scientists are also advisers in most areas of government, for example, the Ministry of

Defence's chief scientific adviser (with staff) keeps the government abreast of the impact of scientific and technological advances in future weapons and equipment, and on defence policy. Other government work which needs a scientific background includes, eg the Factory Inspectorate. See CIVIL SERVICE. Government-funded research councils (Agricultural and Food, Medical, Natural Environmental, and Science and Engineering), employ several thousand scientists, in their own research units, but most are funded to work in universities, medical schools, polytechnics and other colleges.

In *local government*, scientists work in, for instance, the public analyst's office, or in environmental control.

The health service is also a major employer of scientists.

OPPORTUNITIES FOR TECHNICIANS IN SCIENCE Professional scientists wouldn't get very much done if they had to do all the work needed to, for example, set up research experiments, constantly monitor drug production, operate quality control machinery, or do all the tests for a trial chemical. (Although automated lab equipment has eased the problems it seems largely to have increased productivity rather than reduce the number of technician-level jobs.) Nor would a science teacher, or university lecturer, do much teaching if he/she had to prepare all the frogs needed for dissection, or care for all the rats, rabbits and insects, or set up or make the equipment for an experiment.

And so most large labs, and many small ones too, most groups and teams of scientists, have assistants to do much of the technical/scientific work that takes skilled, often very skilled, training, but does not necessarily need a fully-qualified/experienced scientist or teacher to do it. Lab technicians, lab officers, assistants, scientific assistants – there are many different names and titles – are not 'dogsbodies' to fetch and carry or clean and sterilise test tubes (they have unqualified or trainee assistants to do that). It is a practical job, though, and some of the work is repetitive and routine, especially at the beginning. It is, however, skilled and, at the top, the very experienced technician will be in charge of much of the day-to-day work that goes in the lab, and may also be doing full-scale research (but part-time) every bit as intellectually demanding as that of the lab's fully-professional scientists, and hoping for a higher degree out of it.

There are probably nearly as many different jobs for technicians as there are labs. One large university employs four scientific-glass blowers, just to make the needed complex equipment. Met Office weather forecasters (civil servants) are scientific technicians. All the research councils employ lab technicians in some numbers. Lab technicians in the police forensic units actually analyse the blood, sweat and saliva taken from murder victims, and operate the laser microspectral analyser which can tell whether or not a coin is a genuine gold sovereign.

In universities and polytechnics, lab staff work for particular departments, eg microbiology, genetics, or physics, and specialise in the kind of experimental work, for research and teaching, that the department does. They do most of the endless sampling, measuring, testing and analysing which is the basis of so many experiments. Much equipment, from electron microscopes to x-ray diffraction and fluorescence machines, is highly sophisticated, and more often than not computer-controlled and automated, so lab staff do not spend as much time as they once did actually remembering to take and write down regular readings – this comes automatically as computer printout. There is still a lot of routine, though. In microbiological labs, bacteria have to be grown, as do plants (for studies of eg virus diseases) in botany labs. Technicians prepare microscopically-thin sections and slices of rocks for geologists, and animal tissue for zoologists. Technicians breed and care for animals used in experimental work, and do tests on them.

In industry, which employs many thousands, technicians also work in research labs, but more often in areas like quality control, where much of the work is analytical. Raw material, whether metal, sugar or plastic, coming into any factory has to examined and analysed to see that it is up to specification. If the plant is a CEGB electricity generating station, that will include the water to see what impurities there are to foul the steam boilers; if it is the Milk Marketing Board, the job is to make sure the milk coming in from the farm is fresh, that the fat 'solid-not-fat' content is right, and that there are no traces of, for instance, antibiotics. Throughout production, of everything from cheese to paper, drugs to plastics, petrol and chemicals, lab technicians test and analyse regular samples, and make sure the mix is correct and has the right qualities.

The HEALTH SERVICES employ very large numbers of 'technicians' – now officially called 'officers'.

Studying sciences
After school, sciences can be studied for a first degree, or for a BTEC award.

First-degree courses in science Most specialise in one, sometimes two, of the main 'branches' of science (see individual sections following). However, most courses include other sciences as well, partly because techniques or background material from other subjects may be essential to a proper study of the main subject, and partly to provide a broad base. For those interested in studying two sciences, the range of choice is enormous.

Nearly 65,500 students were reading for first degrees in sciences in 1984-5 in universities. Over 39,900 were studying advanced sciences full-time in FE.

Science faculties vary in the way they organise courses. Some decide quite firmly what the syllabus should be, and believe quite strongly that if the subject is to be studied seriously, then there are elements which must be included. Others give a flexible range of choices which allow students to change direction in their studies. Some begin broadly based and increase specialisation as the course continues – example are the Natural sciences tripos at Cambridge University, single entry for sciences at Kent and Sussex. Most polytechnic science degrees are 'modular', and give a reasonably flexible range of choices. Studying broadly across several sciences is, however, relatively rare.

'First destination' figures are –

	1984-5		1977-8	
	university	polytechnic	university	polytechnic
total graduating	19745	3467	15134	2089
overseas students	480	100	305	
destination unknown	1909	501	1157	475
research/further study	3522	337	3165	235
teacher training	948	134	1312	100
'other' training	576	97	285	30
'believed' unemployed Dec 31	1562	435	716	135
short-term work	456	175	778	183
permanent overseas work	285	38	150	17
permanent UK work	9448	1564	6172	828
employers –				
commerce (non-fiscal)	2219	684	557	91
engineering	1411	475	1505	195
oil/chemicals	1096	318	813	117
accountancy	1016	66	554	14
NHS/local government	931	441	625	115
banking/insurance	658	104	284	17
higher/further education	451	146	341	75
'other' manufacturing	440	136	400	80
civil service	437	82	316	34
public utilities	78	115	286	29
agriculture, etc	247	10	31	3
entertainment/leisure	79	40	107	13
construction	32	24	38	8
functions –				
management services	1967	882	1351	249
financial work	1672	141	944	31
scientific R&D	1430	331	1407	129
medical/personnel/social	1177	459	232	18
admin/operational management	769	193	651	49
marketing etc	575	151	325	50
scientific support	553	259	745	190
eng R&D	490	132		
teaching/lecturing	116	46	74	5
information/library etc	98	27	117	4

Entry to a science degree course generally needs three sciences at A level (although two, plus one A or two AS levels in other subjects may be accepted for some subjects or courses), the combination depending on the subject(s) chosen. The personal qualities needed to study science and to become a scientist professional are very similar. Scientists need to be of above-average intelligence (although genius level is not necessary even for research). They need the kind of mind that always wants to know, and is always curious about the natural world. Scientists like to have an explanation for what happens, and why things are as they are. Imagination, and some creativity, concentration and tenacity are useful. Scientists need to be methodical, good at observing and making deductions, and logical thinking. They need to be, at least, numerate enough to be able to use maths, statistics etc in problem solving. It is useful, also, to be able to pick up new information, skills, or a supporting subject easily, as needed. Inventiveness (in designing new experimental apparatus, for example) and some practical skills also help. Scientists need to be prepared to work as part of a team. They must learn to communicate results clearly and concisely, both verbally and in written reports.

Postgraduate study A higher degree is virtually essential for research work. But the decline in research activity generally, and in the number of posts in higher education in particular, means there are too many graduates with higher degrees in pure science. This creates even more severe problems, because other potential employers do not always want to take on people with highly-specialised doctorates, since the extra high-level training they have had may actually make them unsuitable for the available posts.

The Science and Engineering Research Council, which supports students studying for higher degrees, tries to see that, while postgraduate study and training continues at a reasonable level, an increasing proportion of graduates studying in scientific as well as technological disciplines do so in ways which can be of more use to a wider range of employers than the traditional research degree, concentrating its support for advanced courses which provide vocational education and training which is relevant to everyday needs. The SERC supports schemes of training for qualifications of PhD status with a greater content of taught and project work more directly concerned with the needs of industry, and courses which convert pure science degrees into higher degrees via studies more directly concerned with applied research. More studentships are allocated to collaborative university or polytechnic and industry schemes. SERC also operates 'integrated graduate development' schemes, set up by universities and polytechnics with firms interested in the programme: one trains 30 graduates to MSc level in information systems design, with a high practical content. The SERC is also encouraging more part-time courses, post-experience and short courses.

Professional qualification There is no 'umbrella' professional body for all scientists in the way engineers have the Engineering Council (although there are the 'learned societies'), or any scientific registration board. Each 'branch' of science has its own professional body (see sections following).

Technician-level qualification is via BTEC and SCOTVEC awards, at Higher National and National levels. All BTEC science programmes are being revised in line with BTEC's new framework (SEE TECHNICIAN-LEVEL QUALIFICATIONS).

BTEC Higher awards (HNC two years' part-time only, HND two years' full time, three years sandwich only from 87 entry) New guidelines for science have not yet (spring 87) been issued. Existing guidelines build in flexibility by avoiding narrow subject titles and watertight syllabuses. However, a lengthening list of model programmes within science and technology recognise that students will specialise – in chemistry or physics, electronics, medical laboratory sciences, laboratory science and administration, applied biology etc.
About 4900 students were registered for Higher awards in sciences in 1985-6 (against just over 5000 in 1983-4); the ratio between certificate and diploma courses was 60: 40. Broad-based science courses leading to BTEC Higher awards are at, full-time – Nottingham: Trent P; part-time – Bristol P, London: S Bank P, Swansea: W Glam IHE; see also individual sections

following.

Entry requirements are as for all BTEC Higher awards††.

SCOTVEC Higher awards These include a broad-based HNC course in science laboratory technology. Other Higher award schemes are in individual sciences. Entry requirements are as for all SCOTVEC awards†††.

'Professional' qualification for technicians: Awards at this level in the various sciences have never had general currency in terms of entry to professional careers. They have always been an alternative, but extremely difficult, route and it has always been necessary to complete a professional examination after gaining a higher award. Some institutions, eg the Institute of Physics, have closed even this route.

The Institute of Science Technology (membership about 4000), is the 'professional' body for technicians. A BTEC Higher National Certificate (or equivalent) and seven years' experience is required for full membership, but there are other grades.

BTEC National programmes are also being revised for 87 entry. The old guidelines are for a flexible scheme, designed to serve the needs of technicians in a wide variety of employment. Diploma schemes are broader based than those for the certificate. They divide into science- and technology-based programmes. Model science-based programmes include a core of mathematics, and at least two of physics, chemistry and biology at level 1, and then allow for options designed for, for instance, chemistry or medical laboratory technicians. The technology-based schemes include at least two units of science, in eg a physical science. More model programmes are being added for 1987, eg in dental technology, pharmacy and food technology.

Numbers registering for the certificate rose to a peak of nearly 4600 in 1984-5, but fell back slightly, to 4330 in 1985-6. Diploma registrations had been rising steadily reaching almost 6650 in 1984-5, only to drop back to 6500 in 1985-6. Broad-based science schemes are available on a full-time basis at over 90 colleges, part-time at over 140.

Entry requirements are as for all BTEC National awards††, via 16-plus† passes should include mathematics, a subject showing proficiency in English and two sciences.

SCOTVEC National awards include a broad-based scheme for a Diploma in science and technology with options in biology, chemistry, physics etc. The National Certificate scheme allows students to put together a programme of study suited to their individual needs, including science modules.

BTEC First Certificate/Diploma Schemes in science were being piloted from September 1986, and were expected to be more widely available from 1987 entry. Guidelines were not published by spring 87.

Technician training is normally laboratory based with some form of release for study. See also individual sciences below, and (eg) MEDICAL LABORATORY WORK under HEALTH SERVICES.

AGRICULTURAL, HORTICULTURAL AND FOREST SCIENCES

Agricultural scientists are not scientifically-qualified farmers. While a degree in agriculture may be a useful qualification to have for a contemporary farmer, university degrees, particularly, are intended to produce agricultural scientists who will be research workers, advisers and so on. (Farmers generally train in agricultural colleges, taking national awards – see AGRICULTURE.)

Scientists have made an enormous contribution to the increased productivity of the agricultural and horticultural industries in the past forty years. This has largely been the result of extensive research – into improving crop yields, into new ways of growing crops, into making soils more fertile (eg greatly-improved fertilisers), matching crops more closely to soil types, finding better ways of controlling pests and making crops disease resistant, breeding fruit trees and bushes which can be harvested mechanically, improving animal stock through genetic studies.

The direction of R&D in agriculture is now changing, partly as a result of its own success – which has brought overproduction – partly due to financial cutbacks. More 'straightforward' research, on eg arable crops and animal diseases and production, is being cut back, and more complex, 'modern' interdisciplinary studies, on eg the molecular biology of crops and livestock, 'genetic engineering', will expand. Seeds are being improved with work in plant biochemistry and genetics; 'cloning' is producing plants with the most useful characteristics; more highly-selective pesticides are being made by biocatalytic syntheses and isomer separation; new complex 'plant growth regulators' promise major improvements in crop yields, plants that are easier to manage and tailored to fit their purpose and available growing space, and even to open up new markets – miniature carrots, for instance, as health-food 'snacks'.

What agricultural scientists do The number of jobs is never large, but the range of possibilities includes –

In research, agricultural scientists work in universities, for research establishments (eg government-controlled animal health and pest-infestation control laboratories, Agricultural and Food Research Council units), and for manufacturers of animal feedstock, and pest control and drugs and other veterinary products. Most of the work is very practical – the most fundamental is in areas like growth and genetics – and in industry is likely to be concerned with the development or improvement of specific products. Most agricultural research involves both lab work and field and farm tests and trials, and yields, weights, output, etc, all have to be recorded and analysed statistically.

In advisory work, mainly in the government's Agricultural Development and Advisory Service (ADAS) – see under AGRICULTURE. Larger farm-supply manufacturers and wholesalers also employ qualified advisers, but they may not give such a comprehensive service.

In industry, large farm-supply manufacturers also employ specialist graduates in marketing and sales. Food companies purchasing large quantities of produce, eg cereals for bread etc, vegetables for freezing, take agricultural scientists to train as buyers.

For overseas, agricultural scientists with a background of tropical agriculture are recruited by the Overseas Development Administration for the British aid programme to developing countries; by the Commonwealth Development Corporation for similar programmes; and by some large companies for man-

agerial and technical work on their crop operations in other countries. See also
WORKING OVERSEAS.
TEACHING, mainly in agricultural college but with a small number of posts in
universities.
See also AGRICULTURE.

Studying agricultural sciences Almost all courses are at degree level. Most
courses in agriculture are biased to scientific aspects; few include any practical
farming, and all begin with a substantial grounding in biological sciences,
chemistry, some physics and mathematics. There have been several cuts in the
number of university courses since the mid-1960s. Even so, there is a wide
range of different kinds of courses, but at a relatively small number of institutions. While there are many different course titles, it is generally possible at
any one university to put off finally choosing a particular specialisation until
the end of the first year. Courses available (as for 1987 entry) are –

Agriculture
Universities – Aberdeen (general or biased to animal or crop sciences),
Aberystwyth, Bangor (where agriculture can also be studied with agricultural
botany, applied zoology, biochemistry, forestry, marine biology or soil science), Belfast, Edinburgh, London: Wye (biased to farm business management, or animal or crop production), Newcastle (general, or biased to animal
or crop production), Nottingham, Reading.
Polytechnics/colleges – Plymouth with Seale-Hayne; Wolverhampton with
Harper Adams (agricultural technology).

Agricultural science courses specialising entirely in scientific aspects –
Universities
Aberystwyth: Agricultural biochemistry or botany, or Plant breeding
Bangor: Agricultural botany, Applied animal biology, Applied biology (crop
protection), or Pest science
Bath: Applied biology (specialising in crop protection).
Belfast: Agricultural botany or zoology, Agricultural & food microbiology,
Crop protection science, or Mycology and plant pathology.
Brunel: Medicinal, agricultural & environmental chemistry.
Edinburgh: Agricultural science (with wide choice of specialisation).
Glasgow: Agricultural botany, chemistry or zoology, or Animal developmen-
tal biology.
Leeds: Agricultural chemistry or zoology, Agricultural science (animal sci-
ence or crops), Animal physiology & nutrition, or Plant biology (includes
agricultural botany).
London, Wye: Animal sciences, Applied plant sciences (includes agricultural
botany), or Soil & plant nutrition
Newcastle: Agricultural biochemistry & nutrition, Agricultural biology (crop
protection, plant science or zoology).
Nottingham: Agricultural biochemistry or botany, Animal or plant & crop
science, or Environmental biology
Reading: Agricultural botany, or Physiology, biochemistry & nutrition of
farm animals

Soil science studies ways of making, and keeping, soil as fertile as possible, and
involves understanding soil types and their suitability for particular crops –

soil-plant relationships generally, and the effect of weather and different methods of cultivation on the soil. While scientists with varying backgrounds work on research, soil analysis, etc, specialised degree courses include –
Universities – Aberdeen, Bangor (with another science only), Edinburgh, London: Wye (with plant nutrition), Newcastle (with land resources science), Nottingham, Reading.

Agricultural economics Managing both the industry generally and the individual farm is a sophisticated business today, especially as both are directly affected day-to-day by, for instance, EEC agricultural policies. This range of degree courses is designed to produce both advisers and managers. It is possible to approach agricultural economics in two ways, ie –
Based on departments of agriculture, mainly agricultural emphasis, at –
Universities – Aberdeen, Bangor, Edinburgh, London: Wye (agricultural economics or business management), Newcastle, Reading; or
Taught mainly in economics departments, emphasising economics, at –
Universities – Aberystwyth, E Anglia (in Development studies), Exeter, Glasgow, Manchester, Nottingham.

Horticulture courses are based on the relevant sciences, especially botany and chemistry, deal mainly with both theory and practice of horticultural technology, including crop protection, but also cover economics, and modern management methods (including marketing), essential for all sectors of the industry (see HORTICULTURAL INDUSTRY). Courses are at –
Universities – Bath, Glasgow: Strathclyde, London: Wye, Nottingham, Reading.
'First destination' figures (agriculture/agriculture sciences) are –

	1984-5 university	1977-8 university
total graduating	857[1]	762
destination unknown	41	45
research/further study etc	103	120
teacher training	16	22
'other' training	34	21
'believed' unemployed Dec 31	63	40
temporary work	22	5
permanent overseas work	58	59
permanent UK work	539	347
employers –		
agriculture etc	174	116
commerce	67	38
industry other than chemical	43	43
civil service	42	48
chemicals	38	43
local government	31	18

	1984-5 university	1977-8 university
higher/further ed functions – admin/operational	22	45
management	134	129
marketing etc	82	64
scientific R&D	62	13
financial work	34	20
medical/personnel/social	25	5
scientific support services	23	33
teaching/lecturing	12	5
management services	2	55

[1] against a peak of 999 in 1982-3

Forestry involves the study of biological characteristics of tree and forest growth, forests as 'raw material' for the timber industry, and the role trees and forests play in ecology and rural economy, as well as forest management. Only three universities now teach forestry (but see also FORESTRY INDUSTRY) – Aberdeen, Bangor (or agroforestry or wood science), Edinburgh.

'First destination' figures (forestry) are –

	1984-5 university	1977-8 university
total graduating	142[1]	88
research/further study etc	26	12
training	4	4
'believed' unemployed Dec 31	9	1
temporary work	9	12
permanent overseas work	9	6
permanent UK work	64	46
employers –		
forestry, agriculture etc	24	26
commerce	13	5
civil service	6	3
industry	5	6
local government	4	4
functions –		
admin/operational management	35	31
scientific R&D	8	1
financial work	6	nil
medical/personnel/social	1	1
scientific support services	nil	1
environmental planning	nil	9

[1] down from a peak of 152 in 1983-4

Entry: A-level requirements vary from course to course, but two, preferably three, sciences normally needed, with chemistry most frequently named; the other(s) from biological subjects, physics, maths. A year's practical farming experience may be required/an advantage. About 800 people were accepted for university courses in 1985, only 82 for CNAA courses. The mean A-level 'score' for 1984 university entrants was 8.6-9.

Postgraduate study A few higher-degree and diploma courses courses both allow those have graduated in agricultural or horticultural sciences to continue their studies to a more advanced level, and give graduates with suitable degrees in related disciplines the opportunity to convert to an applied special- isation in this area. Mostly the opportunities follow the same pattern as for first degrees, eg forestry at Bangor, horticulture at Bath, some institutions offer wider ranges of courses than others.

See also AGRICULTURE and HORTICULTURE AND FORESTRY.

ASTRONOMY

Sir Bernard Lovell has said this is an age of great astronomical excitement. He suggests 'it has become quite reasonable to ask again the fundamental ques- tions about how our solar system came into existence, where life on earth as we know it is unique, and how the entire cosmos came into existence. It is reasonable to ask these questions because it may be that we are in the process of lifting the questions from the realm of theory to a state where experimental evidence, which will lead to some definitive ideas about the answers, may now be in process of emerging.' Sir Bernard says this is because astronomers are no longer limited to the very narrow and localised view of the universe which can be studied by optical observation from the earth, but they now have far more powerful tools – radio telescopes (which listen to and analyse the sounds of space), space probes and satellite investigations. Which, says Sir Bernard, implies they are coming closer all the time to answers on the fundamental questions of the origins of time, space and the universe.

Astronomy is almost all pure research of the most original and fundamental kind – and working alongside the astronomers are people doing theoretical work, such as astrophysics.

The weather and atmospheric distortion in Britain make observational astron- omy difficult, so the largest telescopes have moved to La Palma in the Canary Islands. Built jointly with other countries, los Muchachos' observatory has the Isaac Newton from Herstmonceux, and three new reflectors. In Hawaii, the Edinburgh Royal Observatory runs the UK infra-red telescope, and a 15-metre millimetre-wave radio telescope with the Dutch. A small infra-red telescope is on Tenerife. UK astronomers also use major telescopes at Sidings Springs in Australia, and in South Africa, and some university departments have arrangements with European and US observatories – but they have always to compete for time.

The UK regularly has experiments on space missions, one of the most recent being a pair of coded mask x-ray telescopes, built by Birmingham University, on NASA's space lab 2; UK astronomers were involved in the European 'Giotto' space craft which sent back data on comet Halley; a UK space craft observed cosmic x-ray sources for some five years. The 'Voyager' space probes told astronomers a great deal about the planets. A big observational telescope is to go into orbit when Challenger flights resume, making it possible to 'see', and work on, even more distant parts of the universe.

Although there are only smaller and/or older telescopes in the UK now, British astronomers do not spend all their time abroad. Astronomers at Edinburgh already have remote control of their IRT 7000 miles away in the Pacific, the La Palma telescopes will also go on-line, and at least one US telescope can be used from Britain.

As important as telescopes to astronomers now are the computer-controlled 'star machines' which extract and analyse data from astronomical observations on a level of sophistication not possible with 'manual' techniques. Yet today's – and tomorrow's – telescopes are themselves only possible because of major technological advances in glass and mirror technology. Instrumentation took over in large observatories a long time ago, so professional astronomers need never actually look through a telescope themselves. A 'Starlink' computer network, made up of ten VAX mainframes, serves radio, x-ray, optical and infra-red astronomers in the UK and abroad. Senior astronomers are as much 'project managers' of complex teams of scientists and equipment as they are research workers.

Astronomy is very expensive (SERC spent £51 million in 1985-6 but is switching about 1% of its resources to other areas of research), the number of posts for professional astronomers getting fewer. The 'Greenwich' Royal Observatory at Herstmonceux is to close by 1990, and most of its work moves to Cambridge. Herstmonceux's current (1986) scientific work includes the astronomy-based public services (eg preparing navigational almanacs and the time service), astrometric and astrophysical research (eg working out the distance of nearby stars or more remote clusters and galaxies, and quantitative chemical analysis of stars and nebulae to try to trace their past history and future evolution), and internal services in engineering, electronics, physics and instrument development.

The move to Cambridge is likely to cut the 1986 total staff of about 195 (down from 1983's 233), to around 120. A small but increasing number, 20 or so as of 1986, work permanently on La Palma. Even in 1986, Herstmonceux employed barely 90 professional scientists, who included not only astronomers, but also computing and instrumentation experts, physicists, mathematicians, and engineers. About 50 are technicians, most of the rest administrators (who may have been astronomers). Around 110 work at the Edinburgh observatory. Royal Observatory staff are part of the CIVIL SERVICE science group.

In addition, there are (probably) about 80 university posts, but the emphasis is equally on teaching.

Everyone going into astronomy now is a graduate. While there are first-degree courses in astronomy and astrophysics (see below), it is generally suggested that intending astronomers should study physics and/or mathematics, largely because there are so few astronomy posts. However, an astronomy or astrophysics degree involves extensive mathematics and physics, and so graduates can go into a number of related fields, for example geodesy, upper-air research, rocket and satellite studies and, for those who have studied radio astronomy, telecommunications and electronics. The developing European space research programme may bring more technological posts.

Studying astronomy/astrophysics first-degree courses are available at –
Astronomy & astrophysics Universities – Newcastle, St Andrews

Astronomy Universities – Brighton: Sussex[2] ; Cardiff[1] ; Glasgow; Leicester[1] ; London: QMC[2] , UCL; Sheffield[3]

Astrophysics (which is far more theoretical), Universities – Birmingham[2] ; Cardiff; Edinburgh; Kent[2] ; Leeds[2] ; Leicester[2] ; London: KQC[2] , QMC, RHB[2] ; Manchester [2] ; Newcastle
[1] with maths   [2] with physics   [3] with another science
Entry normally requires very good grades in A-level maths and physics.

BIOLOGICAL SCIENCES AND BIOLOGY
Introduction — branches of biology — opportunities for biologists — studying biological sciences

Introduction
The biological sciences evolved very rapidly after world war II from straight-forward, descriptive natural history of living organisms – plants, animals, bacteria, microbes, etc – to a highly-experimental study of the common principles and processes of life itself. At one end of the scale, biologists now probe into the most fundamental structures at sub-cellular and molecular levels; at the other, they do research on complete animal and plant communities and habitats, how animals and plants live and behave in them, what affects the ecology of communities, and their conservation.

Biology, today, studies the basic similarities and common features of living systems – the cells and cellular structure; how living organisms acquire and use energy through chemical changes; how they reproduce themselves, grow and develop. It treats life as a series of processes with characteristics to be observed, described and analysed, studying the origins of living organisms and how they are made.

The current emphases in biology can be seen from the seven 'themes' SERC has chosen for the main thrust of future research. These are – genetics and biological engineering, microbes, plant science and productivity, developmental biology (gene expression; control of cell growth, division and shape; pattern formation, and cell signalling); neurobiology and cognitive science, animal function, and biological macromolecules, structure, function and engineering.

These 'modern' biological sciences only became possible with modern technology – eg the electron microscope which can examine the fine detailed structure of plants and animal tissue – and advances in other sciences. Real understanding of the complex chemical order and functioning of living cells was impossible until chemists had developed both the necessary theories, and the sophisticated experimental, analytical and other techniques needed to do the research. Other scientists have contributed – physicists, with both new scientific techniques and ideas, developed as biophysics (see below).

Biologically-based processes have been in practical use for many centuries – in fermenting yeast for bread-making and brewing, for example   long before they were properly understood. Modern developments in the biological sciences have given many more ways in which they can be exploited. Biologists make regular contributions to medical advance, for instance helping to stop transplants being rejected, and work on controlling neurological disorders and pain. Agriculture – and agricultural research – and the food-processing and -preserving industries depend in many ways on biological work. So-called pure research almost always has practical value eventually – biochemical research on how substances are 'transported' from stomach to bloodstream helps to find ways of neutralising toxic substances, and research in physiology could show how to prevent diabetes, for example.

Biological sciences are the basis for one of the major technologies of the future – *bio*technology. Much existing industrial technology is based on exploiting mineral (and non-renewable therefore) resources, using techniques from the physical and engineering sciences. Industrial systems will have to change over to biological (and therefore renewable) resources and use biological systems, in other words 'growing' resources, as much in the lab as on the land. But estimates suggest that already over 40% of manufacturing output is biological in nature or origin. See also BIOTECHNOLOGY below.

But biological sciences are becoming even more widely 'applicable' – and interdisciplinary. Two major SERC 'initiatives' demonstrate this. One is the study of image interpretation – how the human brain recovers useful information from a retinal image to guide a response to a changing scene – detecting, discriminating and interpreting intensity changes, surface features, edges and two- and three-dimensional features. Such biological information is needed to underpin advances in *engineering* systems, such as designing high-resolution TV displays and developing 'intelligent' machines able to recognise and assemble components. The neuroscience initiative, ranging from molecular and cellular to behavioural and psychological, crosses biology, chemistry and physics.

The 'branches' of biology
Biochemistry — biophysics/molecular biology — biotechnology — botany — ecology — marine biology — microbiology — parasitology — physiology — zoology

Biology is a huge subject, and one in which the traditional subjects into which it has been divided have become less and less relevant, and indeed are frequently quite artificial. 'A major difference between biochemistry and molecular biology', according to one professor, 'has been that the latter has attracted a much more varied group of scientists [he is referring to physicists] than would ever have been drawn to biochemistry alone.' Research work increasingly crosses the traditional frontiers, and often takes multidisciplinary teams – biochemists and molecular biologists, as well as crystallographers and computer graphics experts to design new enzymes, for example, which can function at higher temperatures and acidity.

Scientists who may describe themselves as physiologists use *chemical* methods to find out how pain is passed to the brain and processed by it to produce a reaction to the pain. There are, conversely, chemists whose main interest is in the chemical changes which happen in biological systems, such as the brain. The difference between a physiologist and a zoologist, once they are well into their careers, may be difficult to define. In research on, say, cats' muscles, the physiologist is probably more interested in muscle systems generally and how they differ, what it is about cat muscles that enables them to jump so well, when dogs (for example) cannot. The zoologist, on the other hand, may be interested in what effect such muscle power has on a cat's development etc.

Nevertheless, it is still common, at least for school-leavers starting out, to think in terms of studying one branch of biology, if only because they have to choose a named course. Biology can be divided in several ways, but however it is done, the emphasis today is on seeing the relationships and common features between the branches. These 'branches' are not watertight compartments, but rather themes running through all biological studies.

Traditionally, the main 'branches' of biology studied particular *types* of living things – plants, animals, microbes. These were then just 'descriptive' sciences, concentrating on classifying types of (for example) animals, their anatomy and how their 'gross' organs and systems work. With all the recent rapid developments in studies at cellular level, subjects like botany, zoology and microbiology have become much more experimental in their approach, and more concerned with basic biological principles.

The other way of dividing biology, therefore, is to study particular *aspects* or *levels* of living systems, regardless of the type of organism. While there always were scientists interested in physiology, or genetics (for example), once again the developments in the biochemical field – creating a whole new discipline – have given a considerable impetus to these subjects. Other aspects of the biological sciences have also developed into studies in their own right – ecology, for example, which links biological sciences with environmental.

Biology has, also, always been an applied subject, but the tendency has been to think in terms of applications of particular branches – applied biochemistry, or microbiology, for example. Now scientists are developing ways of turning basic biological principles to practical, medical, industrial use, they are thinking in more general terms, of applied biological sciences, or biotechnology.

The main divisions of the biological sciences are –

Biochemistry
Studies the way in which biological systems of all kinds are organised, and function, at molecular and atomic levels. This means that biochemists see all living things – animals, plants, microbes, parasites, viruses – in terms of their basic chemical substances and processes – and have demonstrated the basic similarities of life systems at these levels. Biochemists are more interested in living cells, rather than the organ or system, or the kind of body it comes from, although in practice biochemists have tended to be more interested in the cells and chemical processes of animals and microbes rather than plants – for example, many of the chemical reactions by which yeast produces alcohol from sugar are almost identical with those by which muscles derive the energy needed for their concentration. Photosynthesis has been one exception, and SERC is now giving priority to work in plant science and productivity, including the biochemistry of plant systems.

Biochemistry began by identifying, analysing and synthesising the chemicals, such as complex proteins, which make up living cells. It then moved on to draw maps of cells and the place of each chemical within them, and to work out the major pathways by which chemical changes take place inside the cell, and the mechanism of different reactions. Biochemists mapped the 'metabolic pathways' which allow living cells to synthesise and break down, for example, sugars, fats and amino acids, and worked out how cells keep a balance between energy-producing and -demanding reactions.

Once enough was known about the mechanisms of enzyme reactions, about their energy needs, and how enzymes worked in series in metabolic pathways, they went on to examine how the cell controls and regulates its own metabolism. This led to the solution of the problem of how giant molecules are copied accurately to reproduce themselves on cell division, how coded genetic messages contain the instruction on synthesising cells – to operate kidneys and muscles, nerves and brain, and how the nerve-cell network communicates with muscle or other nerve cells.

The work of biochemists is, then, fundamental and crucial to understanding the fundamental processes of living systems, crucial in any attempts to improve and exploit them.

Biophysics/molecular biology
Both apply the methods developed by physicists to establish laws and theories about the rest of the natural world to the study of living things, and contribute experimental physical techniques, including actual instruments, to biological research.

The distinctions between biophysics and molecular biology – and between molecular biology and biochemistry – are not easily explained in a few words. *Biophysicists* look at biological systems and processes and try to fit them into the system of models of the physical world that physicists have already built, and then try to see if there are any general rules to be made about the living world. It was a physicist who saw, long before it was proved experimentally, that a living gene could not have more than a few thousand atoms, and that according to the *physical* laws of thermodynamics, the gene must represent a code specification.

Examples of biophysical studies are – the electrical and mechanical properties of cells and tissues, and the methods of energy conversion that take place between a living organism and its environment, and within the organism itself. Biophysicists do research on enzyme, protein and nucleic acid structure and mechanism. They study the transmission of nerve signals.

Molecular biology specifically studies the three-dimensional structure, forms, physical properties, behaviour and mechanism of molecules in all kinds of living systems and their evolution, exploitation and ramification in the 'ascent to higher and higher levels of organisation'.

The work of molecular biologists is critical to breakthroughs in genetic engineering. It can take years – even using computer-aided design systems – to build a three-dimensional 'model' of an enzyme which genetic engineers want to change. An enzyme can be made up of up to 1000 aminoacids, generally in an 'array' of side chains arranged along a spine. Making changes to just one side chain can alter the enzyme's surface chemistry, and its properties. 'Modelling' is needed to show the effects of each minute change.

Biotechnology

Not particularly new – brewing can be described as biotechnology. It first became a modern technology in the 1940s with new fast-fermentation techniques to produce, eg antibiotics and steroids. Oil companies have been trying to exploit the fact that yeasts thrive on the waxy fraction of some crude oils, multiplying to make a protein-rich animal feed and raising the quality of the oil fraction itself, since the late 1950s.

The present phase of development began in the mid-1970s with the discovery that living organisms can be modified genetically to make substances not known in nature or too scarce to be used commercially, and to modify and improve existing substances.

Biotechnology is not, though, based on a single, clearly-identified product like the silicon chip. Biotechnology involves processes, processes whereby living organisms are 'cosseted' so that they grow and multiply efficiently, to the point where they can yield a product – beer, penicillin, interferon, hormones.

Biotechnology is not, either, a branch of biological sciences. Biotechnology is a convenient label to use for the application of fundamental biological research in industrial processes – and eventually it will be used by many different, often existing, industries (food, agriculture, chemical, pharmaceutical, medical, etc), not by a new, or separate 'biotechnology' industry (see MANUFACTURING INDUSTRY). It has become a major interest in the scientific and industrial world because the right discoveries and ideas from the frontiers of 'bio-science' can be turned into practical processes, process aids, and routes to new products and devices, which industry can exploit for a profit. But although there have been considerable successes already, the long-term future is still not absolutely certain yet.

A growing range of products are already being made, or are in the pipeline. First of the genetically-engineered drugs is insulin, and human-growth hormone. Gene probes – highly sensitive single DNA strands which can recognise specific gene sequences – are coming which will detect viruses etc, faster from smaller samples. A 'cocktail' of enzymes and microbes has been developed to boost farmers' silage production. Inoculating plant roots with mycorrhizal fungi can increase yields and improve resistance to disease.

Biotechnology is not the result of research in any one area of biology – it is multidisciplinary. Molecular biology and the well-publicised techniques of genetic engineering – recombinant DNA technology – are certainly central. SERC gives other priority areas – such as biocatalysis, including immobilised enzymes and cells; plant genetics and biochemistry, and large-scale growth of mammalian and plant cells.

To exploit biological processes technology is needed – 'scaling up' from the lab to an industrial process is a major problem (see CHEMICAL ENGINEERING) – as well as science. SERC is financing work in fermentation technology (especially new reactor design and microbial physiology), new concepts in 'downstream' processing, and the control aspects – sensors and bioelectronics generally. Specialised 'back-up' technologies are major growth points for better separation and purification of products like proteins, faster speeds and greater purity.

Botany/Plant science

Botany has developed from a purely descriptive study of the morphology, anatomy and taxonomy of living and fossil plant forms, into a much more experimental subject, increasingly called plant science. It studies plants of all kinds, from the so-called lower plants with the simplest structures (such as mosses and algae), and the invisible phytoplankton in the sea, through to the highest forms, such as trees and cactus.

But botanists now study plants as biological systems, right down to the cellular level (where their interests cross those of the biochemists, especially in photosynthesis), and in their relationships with the rest of the living world (where their studies link into those of ecologists). They study them as sources of food and energy for animals and people (for example), and their place in the natural environment. Plant ecology is not just the study of plant communities but is analytical in that it tries to record accurately the dynamics of vegetation.

Botanists study how plants have evolved and breed new strains. They study plant growth, development, demography (measuring plant birth and death rates to study factors determining the size of natural plant populations), and reproduction, and the physiological and biochemical mechanisms involved. Botanists do research on particular plants, such as trees – trees suitable for coniferous plantings, and intensive culture of poplars for wood fibre. One department studies nitrogen-fixation in lichens to assess their contribution to the nitrogen economy of their environment.

But despite all the years of research, according to SERC, understanding of the fundamental processes involved in plant growth and development is in 'urgent need' of further work even to bring it to the level of understanding in comparable animal sciences, certainly if plant activities are to be manipulated. The work to be done is interdisciplinary, at the interface of biochemistry, cytogenetics and molecular genetics, but still needing a 'strong research base' in taxonomy. To 'engineer' genetically the new and improved plants that food-hungry countries need means there is a lot of work to be done first on characterising plant genes. Botanists are using the techniques of biotechnology to produce saffron (which, as harvested now, costs about £5000 a kilo because the quantities are so small) commercially.

Crucial are the major plant processes, like photosynthesis – the only real system known to convert the energy of sunlight directly into the energy of chemical bonds. Understanding photosynthesis will make it possible to create even more efficient plant systems, and 'mimic' photosynthetic systems for other uses, ultimately to cut dependence on non-renewable mineral resources. A great deal is still not known about photosynthesis. How do plants split water molecules and so produce the electrons needed to assimilate carbon dioxide into carbohydrate, for instance? How do they adapt the photosythesis process to environmental conditions – how can some photosynthesise at quite low temperatures while others must have greater heat, how can some live in shade and others not?

SERC is also pushing research into the physiology and biochemistry of plant development – how plant metabolism is biochemically regulated, how plants take up and assimilate nitrate, plant growth regulating substances, and the biochemical mechanisms underlying plant responses to their environment;

into plant molecular genetics; into taxonomy and genetic diversity, and into plant biophysics – the structure, isolation and function of cell membrane systems and the transport of nutrients through them.

Ecology
Studies animals, plants, microbes, parasites, etc, in their natural settings, and especially the way they interact with each other and with the non-living world around them. Ecologists model the environment, and try to build a scientific but 'living' picture of the real natural world. They try to discover why there are 'x' numbers of mice, 'y' numbers of foxes, and 'z' numbers of particular plants, what the factors and processes are which produce these figures, what happens to change the numbers and the balance between them.

Ecologists work by dividing the environment into clearly-defined units of study – 'ecosystems' – all the living things and their physical surroundings in a homogeneous geographical unit – an island, a rain forest, a lake, or a desert area – which is self-sustaining given enough sunlight. Studying an ecosystem involves all the living things within it, how they are adapted to each other and to the environment, and their effect on the geographical and geological nature of the land, the climate, etc.

In this way, ecologists can use strict scientific rules to collect information, and exact statistical and mathematical techniques in measuring, weighing, counting, comparing and analysing. Understanding and analysing an ecosystem depends on the rules which dictate the food chains or webs, and the 'flow' of energy through it, starting with the plants which fix the sun's radiant energy in photosynthesis (which obeys the first and second laws of thermodynamics).

Genetics
Studies how living organisms of all kinds, from the relatively simple (eg viruses, bacteria and fungi) to the most complex higher animals and man, acquire and pass on their own individual and distinctive characteristics from one generation to another. Genetics deals with the physical and chemical properties of genetic material and how the information it contains is expressed in the growth and development of the organism.

'Classical' genetics began simply with experiments to show that, in sweet peas, it was possible to predict whether the flowers would be red or white. The experimental work led to practical applications – improving wheat strains to increase crop per plant, for example.

With the discovery of how DNA copies itself, 'modern' genetics became more concerned with what actually happens inside living cells when new cells develop – the structure of chromosomes and the genes from which they are made, and how the genetic information – such as colour of hair or eyes – is transcribed and translated into the form of a protein.

Modern research in genetics has played a central part in formulating concepts which unify biology, crucial and fundamental to underpinning biological research and the exploitation of biological systems. Much of the success of modern genetics, according to SERC, has come from the analysis of genetic mechanisms at cellular and sub-cellular levels using sophisticated techniques from chemistry and physics to probe the structure and function of genetic material. From this, geneticists have developed techniques to 'splice' DNA (isolating a length which represents the gene for a particular protein), and implant it into a micro-organism so that it will be 'copied' as though it 'belonged' to the host cell. Geneticists use these experiments in 'pure' scientific research to identify and analyse the functioning of gene products and the effect of DNA change on them. But recombinant-DNA technology, as it is called, is also one of the biological techniques on which biotechnology is based (see above), and is now being further developed in protein engineering, which makes minute artificial changes – perhaps to one of 300 amino acids – to the genes before inserting them in the hosts, by 'site-directed mutagenesis'.

'Modern' genetics has other applications, for example making it possible to diagnose genetically-caused disease by identifying damaged genes in cell cultures or tissue samples in the foetus. Geneticists have recently developed genetic 'fingerprinting', capable of identifying everyone with absolute certainty by their DNA.

Other 'branches' of genetics include population genetics – studying changes, usually very long term, in the genetic make up of any group of individual living things that can interbreed, and their offspring, and the forces that can cause these changes. This involves geneticists in discussions and arguments on evolutionary theory, and as 'models' of genetic change become more sophisticated, genetics will help to refine and develop ideas on how evolution happens. More practically, population genetics isolates, for example, what causes the prevalence of diseases to vary in different parts of the country.

Research also looks into possible genetic origins of, eg diabetes and schizophrenia, and studies agents producing genetic damage in relation to environmental hazards. Geneticists isolate weaknesses in pests which can be used to control them biologically.

SERC policy is to concentrate research on genetic manipulation, structure and function, control of gene expression, and evolution and ecological genetics.

Marine biology

Brings together the study of life in the seas, from tiny algae and plankton to whales, which means it cuts across the interests of most other branches of biology. It studies their special structural, developmental, physiological, and behavioural problems, and adaptations needed to live in water. Studying the ecology of sea life has its own special aspects, and involves studying related sciences, eg oceanography. Marine biologists work with other scientists in practical research, in developing artificial rearing and farming of sea creatures, looking for new sources of food amongst sea organisms, showing how to conserve fish stocks, and solving the problems involved in pollution at sea, and waste disposal. The ecology of estuaries and coastal waters is important in seeing that they are properly 'managed', by understanding the basic properties and processes underlying these ecosystems, and the effect of, eg oil terminals or wave barriers.

Microbiology

Studies the smallest forms of life, the microbes, existing as single cells or at most very small groups of cells, so small that they cannot be seen without a microscope. Microbes – viruses, micro-algae, protozoa, bacteria, yeasts, and micro-fungi – can be animals or plants. Microbes are interesting in themselves, as the most widely and diversely adapted of any living organisms, and some microbiologists study their structure and metabolic processes, their physiology, biochemistry and ecology, variation and genetics, as well as classifying them.

However, practically microbes 'play unseen but critical roles' in all living systems, both for good and for ill. Microbes have been used for centuries, to produce beer and bread, to make yoghurt, and silage to feed farm animals, and they are being grown in attempts to produce a direct source of fats, proteins, and vitamins. New strains of microbes have been used in developing new enzymes, organic chemicals, etc. Microbes are used to recycle waste products and keep the soil fertile. Biotechnology is largely founded on the molecular genetics of a small group of bacterial species. But micro-organisms can also do great damage, spoiling food, for example, attacking timbers or textiles or damaging buildings, metal tools, pipelines, ships and aircraft through corrosion.

Current research is concentrating on the basic physiology of bacteria, filamentous fungi and yeasts, largely based on biochemical understanding; on their molecular genetics; on screening to find organisms, microbial systems or enzymic activity likely to be useful; and on developing faster methods to detect micro-organisms and stop spoilage.

Learning even more about microbes and what they can do, how to control and use them, should give many useful results. Microbial treatment could control 'nuisance' organisms such as those which cause food to spoil – one project is aimed at detecting rapidly and early small numbers of bacteria in yeast, meat and milk.

Within microbiology, *virology* studies viruses – and shows just how tightly the different aspects of biology link together, since viruses are both microbes and parasites which affect the cells of all living things. They are also the simplest form of life which can reproduce itself using a genetic code, and so are used to study the basic characteristics of living molecules. Virologists study the detailed make-up of virus particles, map how they reproduce themselves, observe and try to explain the changes a viral infection produces in cells, how viruses can become part of the hereditary material of a host cell, and what happens to viruses when the symptoms of an infection have gone. Virologists have developed very advanced vaccines to prevent some viral attacks, but a great deal more can still be done.

Parasitology
Specialises in life forms which live on or in other living creatures – they may be plants (mistletoe), animals (tapeworms), or microbes (protozoa). Interesting in their own right, they are important because they are involved in the transmission of so many serious diseases, particularly in the third world. Parasitology often involves studying ecology too, because parasites are part of all ecosystems. They have extremely complex life cycles. They can adapt their metabolisms to very different hosts and energy supplies. Parasites have developed very sophisticated ways of avoiding attempts to get rid of them, both by the host body's natural defences and by, for example, drugs.

Physiology

Studies the ways in which the systems which are part of all living things function – not just describing them, but probing how and why they function as they do, and researching into the underlying physical and chemical principles. Physiologists want to know how systems work. For example, how the heart beats; how the brain thinks; how a fertilised egg develops into an embryo; how bacteria, fish, birds, and people obtain food and convert it into energy; how the body regulates its own growth, metabolism, and reproduction. Physiologists are, like other biologists, interested in how the processes they study are regulated and controlled. Like other biologists, too, physiologists don't only study the 'gross' organs and systems – the heart, or muscles – but also investigate processes at the cellular level – how cell membranes, for example, function, and how substances get through them. Here they work closely with biochemists and pharmacologists.

While theoretically they study the functional processes of all living organisms, in practice physiologists are usually more interested in animals and especially the higher vertebrates, including humans. A great deal of interest is centred on neurophysiology, physiology of the cardio-vascular system, and electrophysiology.

Zoology

Today makes experimental studies of animals, as well as describing and classifying them. Animal development and behaviour, and ecological studies are the areas currently interesting many zoologists, although others still study structure and systems, cells and tissues.

Studies of reproductive physiology can help in saving rarer species. Ecological studies in Africa have helped to decide which areas are suitable for animal parks and reserves, as part of a growing interest in improving the 'management' of wild-animal communities. Studying patterns of fish migration may aid in conserving stock. Fauna surveys are made to assess levels and effects of pollution, and of herbicides and pesticides.

Insect-pest resistance to chemical control is now a major problem. Entomologists are studying insect physiology and neurobiology as part of the drive to develop new pesticides which are based on the biology of chemicals that their neuro-secretory cells produce.

Zoologists are interested in finding out how whales and dolphins avoid the 'bends' when they surface after diving. They study the ultra-sounds produced by insects, parasitic infections in wild mammals, the interactions between parasites, and host-parasite relations in domestic birds. In studying animal development and behaviour, zoologists' work overlaps with that of psychologists.

Opportunities for biologists

With biology probably the most popular of the sciences amongst school-leavers, output of graduates rose steadily for ten years or more up to 1982-3, outstripping the supply of 'relevant' jobs, especially as, at the same time, the number of posts in schools, higher education and research organisations was falling. To stay in biology-based careers, graduates have been taking posts previously considered non-graduate, largely in university and Health Service laboratories – to the extent that nearly everyone going into NHS labs is a graduate now.

The long-term future could look rather different as the number of biology graduates falls. Although on present evidence there are never likely to be directly relevant jobs for all, numbers recruited for scientific work did pick up considerably in 1984-5. Much depends on the extent, and speed, with which industry invests in, develops and exploits the latest biological advances, and the funding universities etc receive for relevant research, but the number of new jobs biotechnology directly creates is never likely to be very large. SERC has, however, been sufficiently concerned about shortages of expertise to monitor the scale of the 'brain drain' of biotechnologists, and has increased sharply the number of postgraduate awards (86 were taken up in 1985-6).

Employers tend to differentiate between biologists, between what are often termed 'harder' and 'softer' biological sciences. Biochemists and microbiologists have for some years been in greater demand than botanists or zoologists, particularly for R&D, and in analytical and other test labs. Biotechnology-based research reinforces this, but also takes graduates with training, usually to PhD level, in molecular biology, genetics etc – demand for people who have actually studied biotechnology as a biology-based first degree has not (yet) developed. Research and development mostly employs people with highly-specific training, working in teams, rather than all-rounders – the wide-ranging expertise needed is almost impossible for one scientist to gain. The main shortage is of people trained in engineering for biotechnology.

While SERC insists current research needs a strong taxonomic base, botanists and zoologists who have specialised in description and classification can be at a disadvantage in the employment market, and cuts in more straightforward agricultural/horticultural research can only make this worse. Work on pest and disease control, on producing better crops by the newer genetic methods – 'cloning' etc – is the exception, but needs a background of molecular/cellular studies.

What biologists do and where they work The range of possible employment includes –

Biotechnology jobs for scientists are mainly in research and development, but also in areas like quality control.

There are two kinds of employer in biotechnology. Firms planning to use biotechnology processes or make biotechnology-based products are not all doing the fundamental scientific research themselves, or even all of the development work involved in turning a lab technique into an industrial process. These they buy from 'research boutiques' – commercial research laboratories and university-based research centres. The majority are in the US, but by 1986 it was estimated that some 300 firms in the UK were involved in biotechnology in some way, including twenty or so university-based centres, which are jointly funded by industry and SERC. The largest specialist UK company in the field now (1986) employs 200 people, with a further 158 in joint ventures with other companies. One university-based centre alone has about 60 scientists doing research. At least two government research establishments

– the Laboratory of the Government Chemist and Warren Spring Lab – have biotechnology research groups. In companies exploiting biotechnology industrially, work specifically for biologists is likely to be in developing industrial processes, quality control, etc. This is more difficult to isolate at present, partly because it is still early days, and partly because the newer technologies are often replacing older ones, so it is difficult to know if these are new jobs. See also MANUFACTURING INDUSTRY.

Teaching While the largest single group of working biologists is almost certainly teaching, the proportion going into teaching has been falling steadily for some years. At secondary level this will continue for most of the 1980s, but primary-school recruitment could increase.

In higher and further education, recruitment improved somewhat in 1984-5. The number of university posts – mostly combining teaching with research – in biological sciences peaked at over 2000 in the late 1970s and has since fallen, although there may be some increase in the late 1980s. Most polytechnics also teach degree-level biological sciences, but the research opportunities are not so great. There are fewer posts in biology in further education, although more students do study for GCE exams and BTEC schemes in FE. A small number of biologists teach in agricultural and horticultural colleges. See also EDUCATION.

Civil service The government is traditionally a fairly large employer of biologists (about 1500 altogether). The Ministry of Agriculture takes the largest numbers, both for research (eg on animal health, fisheries, pest control, plant pathology) and advisory work (see AGRICULTURE), but there have been some cuts in both. Some work for the Home Office Forensic Science Service (biochemists, botanists and zoologists mainly, some microbiologists), the British Museum (Natural History), the Centre for Overseas Pest Research (mainly zoologists and entomologists), and the Tropical Products Institute, the Forestry Commission (small numbers), and the Ministry of Defence, in eg the Chemical Defence Establishment (mainly biochemists and physiologists), naval and aviation medicine. See also CENTRAL GOVERNMENT.

Research councils employ biologists, but research training and a higher degree are usually needed.

A significant proportion of the Agricultural and Food Research Council's 3000-plus scientists have degrees in biological subjects (including quite a large proportion of biochemists). They do directed research on improving quality and productivity of agricultural products working in some 30 or so research units, both AFRC-managed and university based. See also AGRICULTURE.

Many of the Medical Research Council's 800 non-clinical staff are biologists (including about 180 biochemists), working in one of about 50 units, many attached to hospitals or universities. Research ranges from very fundamental studies, in eg molecular biology, through to clinical work. See also MEDICAL SCIENCES.

The Natural Environment Research Council probably has over 200 biologists, including biochemists (out of a total 1400-plus scientists), working mainly for the Institute of Terrestrial Ecology, but also for, eg the British Antarctic

Survey, the Institute of Oceanography, and the marine and freshwater biological units. See CONSERVATION.

Other research organisations employing biologists include research associations serving individual industries (especially those mentioned below but mainly food); commercially-run contract organisations, some specialising in evaluation and testing of products such as drugs, others doing very-advanced 'seed corn' research in biotechnology. Privately-funded (eg by charities) research institutions specialise in areas like work on cancer.

The National Health Service employs graduate biologists, including a high proportion of biochemists, in relatively large numbers in medical laboratory work. Graduates now go in on two levels – first, as scientists supervising and checking diagnostic testing, carrying out the more sophisticated analyses, developing new analytical tests and methods, and going over results with medical staff. Second, new medical laboratory scientific 'officers' (who were, until very recently effectively 'technicians'), are now virtually all graduates, and most of the 200 taken on each year are at this level. They do the all the actual routine analyses of blood, tissue samples etc (much of it now computer-controlled and automated).

Most medical research is done in MRC units, but there may be some opportunities to do work on, eg the nature and mechanism of particular diseases, epidemiology and disease control, enzyme defects, etc.

Clinical biochemists working in the NHS also teach undergraduate medical students.

Geneticists are employed in advisory services on hereditary disease.

See also HEALTH SERVICES.

The public health laboratories – many housed in hospitals – and the blood transfusion service employ biologists too, but mainly microbiologists.

Industry employs biologists in some numbers, in 'traditional' production as well as biotechnology. The industries needing biologists are mostly those which process biological materials, use biological agents to make a product, or make agricultural or medical products (agriculture, horticulture and fishing are also effectively biology-based industries).

The PHARMACEUTICAL INDUSTRY takes the most biologists (microbiologists, biochemists, physiologists, pharmacologists mainly but with some demand for people who have specialised in immunology, bacteriology, virology and parasitology). They are needed mostly for (applied) research and development, working in multidisciplinary teams, on the steadily-widening range of biologically-based products from antibiotics and vaccines through to antibody diagnostic 'kits'. Biologists also evaluate and test products, with some posts in quality control, and in developing production techniques. Pharmaceutical companies, particularly, recruit biologists for MARKETING, technical SALES, and PURCHASING.

The FOOD AND DRINK INDUSTRY (which includes dairies and breweries) employs scientists, including biologists (mainly microbiologists, some biochemists), some for research (on standards, preventing contamination, and new products), but mostly in product development, quality control, technical management. The BREWING INDUSTRY recruits a small number of biochemists and some microbiologists most years. Biochemists can work in areas other than research using their specific expertise in, for example, control of fermentation or food-processing plant, or in developing industrial processes, and can train in production management.

The CHEMICAL INDUSTRY has always employed small numbers of biologists (including biochemists), largely in research and development on agrochemicals (insecticides, fungicides and weed killers), but chemical firms are also moving into biotechnology. Agrochemical firms also take on biology graduates for MARKETING and SALES. Some biologists work in areas like environmental protection in the oil industry.

The WATER INDUSTRY employs scientists (including biochemists), in fishery administration and management, pollution control, weed and insect control, marine ecology, toxicity testing, protozoology and virology.

Overseas, developing and other tropical countries still have major problems to solve in agriculture, forestry and health, for which biologists are employed. The majority of posts are either in government service or in overseas universities and are usually on a contract basis (see under OVERSEAS CAREERS). Some commercial organisations with interests overseas have research programmes on crop improvement and production. There may be short-term projects in countries too dependent on particular crops (sugar, for example) and which must diversity their economy to meet changing world markets.

Other biologically-relevant work Examples include –
The HORTICULTURAL INDUSTRY has always taken small numbers of biologists, mostly for practical management, but a few for research and development. Now the growing success of 'cloned' plants could create new opportunities – the major UK firm had a turnover of £7 million in 1985, and a team of 40 scientists experimenting with new techniques. Other possible growth areas include research to enhance, or find new uses for, arid-land plants with work in progress at, eg Kew Gardens.

Small numbers of biologists are employed by organisations involved in CONSERVATION AND THE ENVIRONMENT.

Biologists are just as well qualified as other scientists to go into areas such as INFORMATION/LIBRARY WORK, PATENT WORK, TECHNICAL WRITING etc.

Studying biological sciences

Biological sciences can be studied after school at degree or higher-technician level.

First-degree courses offer the student increasing variety, which makes choice hard. Given that this is one of the most rapidly developing of the sciences at present, there is a strong argument for choosing flexible courses which allow students to defer any choice of specialisation for as long as possible, which can be as late as the end of the second year. Anyone intending to teach is generally advised to study as broadly as possible, but it is usual for anyone planning to do research to specialise at some stage, although there is an argument for joint honours in two biological subjects, given the interdisciplinary nature of much current research. To gain the best chance (but it is only chance) to do research in a specific area, it is advisable to choose a course in a department doing advanced research in that field.

Although the boundaries between the 'traditional' divisions of biology have become increasingly blurred, it is still common to specialise at some stage in a named 'branch' of the subject. There are various choices to make, such as whether to specialise in a 'branch' of biology from the start of the course, with the alternative of a course which starts with a broadly-based introduction to biological sciences generally. Some courses continue broadly, but usually give a choice of topics for advanced study in the final year (and these may fall across the conventional boundaries). In other courses, students are given a thorough grounding in the common aspects of the biological sciences, then go on to specialise in one or two of the traditional branches. To benefit from a biology degree, a sound background in chemistry and/or physics and a reasonable level of mathematical skill are useful.

Broadly-based biological sciences/biology courses are at –
Universities – Aberdeen (reproduction and development); Aberystwyth; Bangor; Belfast; Birmingham[1]; Birmingham: Aston; Brighton: Sussex[1]; Bristol; Chelmsford: Essex[1]; Dundee[1]; Durham; Edinburgh[1]; Exeter; Glasgow: Strathclyde[1]; Hull[1]; Keele; Lancaster[1]; Leicester[1]; London: Imperial[1], KQC[1], QMC[1], RHB, UCL[1]; Loughborough (human); Manchester; Newcastle[1]; Norwich: E Anglia[1]; Nottingham; Oxford[1]; Reading[1]; St Andrews[1]; Southampton; Stirling; Swansea[1]; Ulster[1]; Warwick[1]; York[1]
Polytechnics – Leicester[1]; London: City; Oxford; Plymouth; Portsmouth; Stoke on Trent: N Staffs; Wolverhampton

Applied biology courses (courses above may include applied options) are at –
Universities – Bath[1]; Birmingham: Aston (and human); Brunel; Cardiff: UWIST[1]; Liverpool; London: Imperial; Salford (tropical/arid zone)
Polytechnics – Bristol; Coventry; Hatfield; Kingston; Liverpool; London: NELP, S Bank, Thames; Manchester; Nottingham: Trent; Sunderland
[1] Specialisation in a branch of biology in latter part of course

Biochemistry: most universities teaching both biological sciences and chemistry have degree courses in biochemistry. Because biochemistry requires a more thorough grounding in chemistry than other biological sciences, it is more usual to specialise from the start of the course, although it is possible to specialise after a year studying biology and/or chemistry. At some universities it is possible to study the applied options, eg industrial biochemistry, medical or clinical biochemistry, toxicology, and pharmaceutical biochemistry. In polytechnics, biochemistry is more usually taught as part of 'integrated', and mostly applied, broadly-based biology courses (see above).

Graduates can convert to biochemistry after a degree in another subject via a postgraduate course. Many graduate biochemists go on to more advanced postgraduate study, needed for most research posts, with the possibility of specialising in eg clinical, molecular, agricultural or analytical biochemistry, steroid endocrinology, and biochemical pharmacology. Heriot-Watt University specialises in brewing. Courses in biochemical – biological chemical –

engineering train biochemists in the engineering skills used by industry to exploit biological processes.

Biophysics and molecular biology are not taught extensively at first-degree level. Courses are at –
Universities – Durham (molecular biology & biochemistry); Edinburgh; Glasgow; Leeds; Leicester; Liverpool; London: KQC, QMC; Manchester: UMIST (applied molecular biology & biochemistry); Norwich: E Anglia
Polytechnics – London: NELP, Portsmouth.

Biotechnology courses are not intended to give directly vocational training, but do bring together relevant material from eg genetics, microbiology, biochemistry, and chemical engineering, to give an integrated introduction. To go on to research work in biotechnology will still need a very good degree, and postgraduate training. For the best chance of a research post in biotechnology, study somewhere with a major programme can be useful. Biotechnology is at present mostly taught as a specialised option after a broadly-based introduction to biological sciences. Courses are at –
Universities, as biological science – Birmingham (with biochemistry); Canterbury: Kent (with microbiology); Leeds; London: Imperial, KQC; Warwick; as engineering – Guildford: Surrey; London: UCL; Reading
Postgraduate 'conversion' courses are available.

Botany or plant biology/sciences is taught as a specialist honours subject at about 35 universities and university colleges, and is a possible specialisation in all the biology courses above. There are only one or two specialised postgraduate courses.

Ecology forms part of most biology courses. It is not common to specialise in it on biological sciences courses (but more usual in environmental studies), but is possible at –
Universities – Brighton: Sussex; Cardiff: UWIST; Lancaster; Leeds; Leicester; London: RHB, UCL; Norwich: E Anglia; Oxford; St Andrews; Stirling; Ulster; York

Genetics may be the basis of modern biological development, but courses have still been cut. Available at –
Universities – Aberdeen; Belfast (joint hons only); Birmingham; Brighton: Sussex; Cambridge; Edinburgh; Glasgow; Leeds; Leicester; Liverpool; London: QMC, UCL; Manchester; Newcastle; Norwich: E Anglia; Nottingham; Oxford; St Andrews; Sheffield; Swansea

Marine biology is taught in first-degree courses at –
Universities – Aberdeen (marine and fisheries), Aberystwyth (aquatic), Bangor (marine botany or zoology), Edinburgh: Heriot-Watt, Liverpool, London: QMC (and freshwater), Newcastle, St Andrews.

Microbiology either as a single or joint honours course, or as a major option within a biological sciences degree, is taught at most universities with science faculties, and as a major option in biological sciences at polytechnics. It is also possible to specialise, eg in bacteriology, at Edinburgh and Manchester (with virology); in applied microbiology at Glasgow: Strathclyde; in medical microbiology at Birmingham; in immunology at Glasgow, Glasgow: Strathclyde (with biochemistry), and London: KQC; in parasitology at Aberdeen (animal) and Glasgow; and in virology with microbiology at Warwick.

Physiology can be studied as a first-degree subject (but only 300 people a year specialise) at –
Universities – Aberdeen; Belfast; Birmingham; Bristol; Cambridge; Cardiff: UC, UWIST; Dundee; Edinburgh; Glasgow; Lancaster; Leeds; Leicester; Liverpool; London: KQC, QMC (animal), RHB, UCL; Manchester, Newcastle, Oxford, Reading (with biochemistry), St Andrews, Salford (with chemistry), Sheffield, Southampton, York (of organisms)

Zoology, or animal science/physiology is available at most universities teaching biological sciences. More unusual courses are –
Animal physiology and nutrition at Leeds.

'First destination' figures for all biological sciences –

	1984-5 university	1984-5 polytechnic	1977-8 university	1977-8 polytechnic
total graduating	4544[1]	837	4620	400
destination unknown	481	117	407	67
research, etc	1132	103	1242	55
teacher training	232	36	495	34
'other' training	153	18	128	8
'believed' unemployed Dec 31	484	110	297	43
temporary work	89	59	354	51
permanent overseas work	50	9	31	1
permanent UK work	1643	356	1517	133
employers –				
NHS/local government	309	128	439	43
commerce (excl accountancy)	269	36	118	10
chemicals[2]	209	44	176	25
higher/further ed	206	52	214	15
'other' industry	151	25	141	10
civil service	118	19	101	8
accountancy	85	7	93	nil
agriculture, etc	29	7	20	nil
functions –				
scientific R&D	396	100	356	20
scientific support services	280	125	327	63
financial work	201	19	128	5
admin/ops management	187	23	200	11
marketing, etc	166	38	132	19
medical/personnel/social	102	14	130	1
management services	97	5	120	5

[1] down from a peak of 4986 in 1982-3   [2] includes pharmaceuticals, agrochemicals, some other fermentation industries.

Entry is normally with at least two science A levels (three or two plus two AS levels for university – any permutation of A and AS levels for polytechnic) including an appropriate biological science and preferably maths. Over 5560 students were accepted for university degree courses, well over 1200 for CNAA degree courses in 1985-6. The mean A-level 'score' for 1984-5 university entry was 11 in biochemistry, 9.2 for botany, 10 for biology.

Professional qualification The Institute of Biology's membership examinations are an alternative route to an honours degree. The first stage is a BTEC Higher award (see below). The Institute's own examinations are in two parts: the first is divided between general biology and a special subject, with part 2 devoted entirely to the special subject; courses may be taken on a full- or part-time basis.

The Institute requires additional experience in responsible work in the field of biology for full membership, the requirement varying according to the entrant's initial qualification, eg with a first- or second-class honours degree in biology or biological subjects only three years, while via the Institute's examinations or a first- or second-class BEd five years. The Institute has an associate-membership class for those who have not yet completed the required work experience, and licentiate membership for those with initial qualifications below those required for associate membership.

Technician-level qualification is via a BTEC or SCOTVEC Higher National award, which is also the first stage to professional qualification (above) – but well over a third (1986) go on to a degree (against only a sixth in 1977-8).

BTEC HND/C Science (applied biology) schemes are to be revised in line with the new framework, but new guidelines were not (as of spring 87) yet available. All present schemes are different, each being designed by the polytechnic or college. Courses are available at –

HND (full-time or sandwich only) – Ulster U; Polytechnics: Bristol; Leicester; London: NELP, S Bank; Manchester; Nottingham: Trent; Plymouth; Preston: Lancs; Sheffield; Sunderland; Colleges: Brighton CT; Ewell: NE Surrey CT; Llandaff: S Glam IHE; Luton CHE.

HNC (part-time only) – at about 40 polytechnics, colleges etc.

Entry qualifications are as for all BTEC Higher National awards††; via A levels two sciences (preferably biology or chemistry) should have been studied with a pass in one.

'First destination' in Science (Applied biology) HND –

	1984-5 polytechnic only	1977-8 polytechnic only
total graduating	309	227
destination unknown	34	42
on to first-degree course	116	51
on to complete prof qual	31	32
'believed' unemployed Dec 31	29	18
temporary work	12	8
permanent UK work	77	69
employers –		
NHS/local government	26	15

	1984-5 polytechnic only	1977-8 polytechnic only
higher/further ed	12	17
civil service	3	3
chemicals[1]	8	6
'other' industry	13	2
commerce	5	2
functions –		
scientific support services	49	50
scientific R&D	4	5
admin/operational management	6	5
medical/personnel/social, etc	2	3

[1] includes pharmaceuticals, agrochemicals, some other fermentation industries

Further information from the Institute of Biology, the Biochemical Society, the Association of Clinical Biochemists, the Society for General Microbiology and the Society for Applied Bacteriology: all produce booklets.

CHEMISTRY

Almost all research in chemistry is of practical use to someone, somewhere. Any advance in chemistry – however disinterested in its applications the researcher may be – on, for instance, the structure of glass or the synthesis of compounds from plants, can have results which are useful. Whole industries have been built on chemistry and chemical research. They include agrochemicals (herbicides, fungicides, and fertilisers), cosmetics and toiletries, dyestuffs, fine and heavy chemicals, paints, pharmaceuticals, and petrochemicals. Chemical research made the petroleum industry the supplier of more than half the new materials used in the chemical industry – products made by separating and purifying crude oil include plastics, man-made fibres, drugs, solvents, detergents and fertilisers as well as fuels and lubricants.

The influence of chemistry extends well beyond the chemical industry. All manner of industries benefit if understanding the chemical characteristics of the materials being used can improve a product or make the production method more efficient, especially if this can also make the materials more suitable for the use to which they are being put. Chemists help to improve the qualities of fibres used in making textiles, work with metallurgists in reducing the 'fatigue' properties of metals by changing their crystal structures. There are applications for chemical research in work on electronic components needed for eg more advanced computing and IT systems, building materials, ceramics, food processing, and glass. Chemistry is fundamental to much medical research, for instance, in developing new chemical methods of treating or otherwise combating diseases.

There are always new substances to be found, developed and investigated. A central objective of modern chemistry, according to SERC, is the understanding and regulation of biological processes at the molecular level. This needs, says the Council, a strong input from synthesis, ranging from small molecules with specific isotopic labelling to study enzyme mechanisms and their inhibition, to the total synthesis of complex antibiotics and the peptide, saccharide and nucleotide building blocks of natural macromolecules. Current SERC 'special initiatives' include chemical sensors (to improve basic understanding of sensor systems and develop new devices), heterogeneous catalysis, controlled growth of semiconductors by metallo-organic chemical vapour deposition techniques, non-linear optical devices, and molecular electronics. Research continues on more complex bondings, the mechanisms of very fast reactions, and the detailed atomic and molecular properties of the more complex elements.

The analytical techniques and equipment that chemists have developed for their own research are now widely used elsewhere – in other sciences (biochemistry and geochemistry, for example), in industry for analytical and quality control, in diagnostic work in the Health Service, in ensuring clean water, in local government labs, and in forensic labs, amongst many others.

Opportunities for professional chemists
Demand for chemistry graduates in terms of chemistry-related work has been fluctuating for many years now, and is almost impossible to predict. The chemical industry (and that includes, eg agrochemicals and pharmaceuticals) still depends on a high rate of innovation – new products and better processes – and is, therefore, still research intensive, it is also affected by the economic situation. And so although the 'lead time' for new products and processes in chemicals, etc, is long, recruitment of chemists both for research and other work varies from year to year and from sector to sector (see MANUFACTURING INDUSTRY). Further, there are now far fewer posts in academic work in higher/further education, and in the public sector – the Civil Service, NHS etc. However, numbers graduating are now falling sharply, the number of vacancies going up (by 67% May 84-February 85, and by over 70% May 85-86, according to AGCAS), and there is a severe shortage of school-teachers in physical sciences.

An estimated 60,000 or more professional chemists work in Britain, about half of whom are members of the Royal Society of Chemistry. The Royal Society makes regular surveys of members; the 1986 results are incorporated below –

What chemists do The range of work done by professional, normally graduate, chemists, includes –
Research and development still employ the largest group of chemists. In 1986, 31% of chartered RSC members (just over half mainly as managers), were working in research and/or development (only slightly down on 1978).
Many chemists still start their careers in the laboratory. Fundamental research, going ever deeper into the nature of matter and of chemical processes, is not limited to universities, although in industry speculative research happens only in larger companies heavily involved in chemicals and pharmaceuticals. There is increasing emphasis on more applied work, which is not restricted to industry – random examples of university-based projects include chemical conversion and storage of solar energy (at Aston), application of analytical techniques to pollution control (Surrey), new refining processes for rarer metals (Brunel), ways to improve the properties of cement and concrete by modifying their composition, including reinforcement with polymers and fibres, especially for use in the North Sea. Research usually means team work, and chemists work particularly closely with biochemists and physicists.

In industry (and industrial research associations) most research is on possible new products, ways of improving existing ones, cheaper or more efficient raw materials, cheaper or more efficient routes to a new product, or replacing an existing product which (for example) may have some undesirable qualities. Chemical research is not as routine as in some other industries, and may involve much more original thinking, inspiration and speculative work than some other kinds of industrial research, but the researcher is usually working to a tight plan and budget, and cannot (as in eg university) investigate anything interesting that turns up.

Development chemists turn a new reaction into a commercially viable process, check for unwanted side-effects (in eg drugs) or pollution problems, and make sure that the qualities and process are the best possible, given available finances, potential profits, manufacturing methods, etc. Development work, which may be combined with research, involves a considerable amount of repetitive experimentation and testing. Some development chemists specialise in improving or designing new processes (for instance, increasing the yield from a particular raw material, or finding a better catalyst for a reaction), and work closely with CHEMICAL ENGINEERS.

Linked to R&D is formulation – formulation chemists work out a form for the product which is easy and economical to use, will store without breaking down or congealing, and can be safely packaged.

Chemists also do research in government departments and government-financed research establishments. The largest numbers work for, eg

The National Physical Laboratory, which maintains national standards of accurate measurement and works on developing reliable standards, with research ranging from the precise determination of fundamental physical constants to developing improved calibration methods, all using the most advanced techniques and facilities, including submillimetre and molecular spectroscopy and advanced microscopy techniques;

The Warren Spring Laboratory, which is a centre for industrial and environmental research, working on contract to government departments, industry, local authorities, etc. Research includes, eg physical and chemical methods of mineral concentration; treatment of domestic and industrial waste materials, particularly to recover metals which can be recycled; measuring and controlling atmospheric pollution, and evaluating methods of combating oil pollution;

The Chemical Defence Establishment, which continually assesses the threat of chemical and biological agents, and devises defensive equipment;

The Government Chemist's Laboratory (LGC), part of the Department of Trade and Industry, which does work in support of government policies, and does wide-ranging R&D designed to help both industry and government to innovate and exploit new technologies, eg biotechnology.

Explosives Research and Development, the Ministry of Defence Quality Assurance Directorate and the Naval Aircraft Materials Laboratory.

Other government departments employing chemists include the Home Office forensic laboratories, the British Museum's research laboratory, and the National Gallery (where they try to understand deterioration processes and especially the long-term effects of light, heat, humidity and atmospheric pollution, analysing old varnish and paint media using thin-layer and gas chromatography and infra-red analysis, and developing permanent picture varnish).

Analytical work employs (1986) just under 12% of professional chemists (similar to 1983), almost 75% of them mainly as managers and administrators. Quality control employs 5.7% of professional chemists, almost all of them as managers and administrators.

In industry, analytical work and quality control involve continuous checking for purity, quality, correct proportions, and safety. Elsewhere, analytical work is done by, eg local authority public analysts, the forensic services, and the Health Service, and employs about 5% of professional chemists in all. Much of this work is now fully automated, using all forms of chromatography and spectroscopy. The professional chemist manages and supervises, looks into problems, develops standards, and works out new techniques when needed. Larger industrial groups still have quite large laboratories working on longer-term problems.

In technical service, chemists work as members of liaison teams which deal with industrial and commercial customers. The chemist makes up technical specifications, discusses and agrees solutions to customers' problems and complaints, shows them how to make the best use of the firm's products, and generally gives technical back-up to sales and marketing.

Education employs just 19% of chartered chemists (down from over 21% in 1983) – teaching pupils in schools, trainee technicians in technical college, or degree and postgraduate students in polytechnic or university, where teaching is normally combined with research.

Other chemistry- or science-related occupations include PRODUCTION in the chemical and allied industries (employing 3.9% of professional chemists), PATENT WORK, TECHNICAL WRITING and INFORMATION AND LIBRARY WORK. About 9% of professional chemists have become general managers/administrators, and 4.2% work in SALES/MARKETING (up from 3.5% in 1983). Nearly 7% of professional chemists do 'other' (unspecified) scientific or technical work – mostly as managers or administrators. About 4% work in 'other' services (eg health and safety, patents and information), and 2.5% are consultants.

Where professional chemists work According to the 1986 RCS survey, professionally-active members (over 22% of members are fully or partly retired, and 1.1% unemployed) are employed in –

Industry and commerce employ 55%. Just over 48% work in manufacturing. The largest groups, not surprisingly, are in the chemical-related industries – 14.5% in pharmaceuticals (up from 12.8% in 1983), 8.2% on 'other' chemicals (slightly up from 1983), 5.5% in plastics and polymers (slightly down), 4.5% in each of food and drink and oil (both similar).

About 3% work in energy production, including over 1% for the nuclear fuel industry – nearly 2% actually work for UKAEA and associated companies. Some 3.5% work for the water, sewage and waste disposal industry.

As already described, most work in R&D, or analytical work, but some are employed in production, general management, marketing and sales etc.

Government, local and central, and the NHS employ the next largest group. Nearly 13% work for local government (down from over 14% in 1983), nearly 7% for central government, and just under 2% for the NHS.

Education employs most of those working for local government – nearly 7% of all professional chemists work in polytechnics and colleges, 5.5% in schools (both down slightly) – but over 9% work for universities.

Some 3.5% of those working for central/local government are employed in analytical, testing or service labs. Research units, government or otherwise, employ 5.6% (slightly down).

Opportunities for technician chemists

The work of chemistry-trained technicians is mainly as described in the general sector on scientific careers, but the figures show a high proportion are clearly working in jobs virtually indistinguishable from those of professionals – over 40% work in a managerial or administrative capacity. The RSC 1986 survey showed that, for licentiates –

The work technicians do Over 19% work in research and development, with over a third of them employed primarily as managers or administrators. More than 17% do analytical work, with about 40% employed mainly as managers or administrators. Another 14.5% work in quality control, over 70% of them as managers or administrators. Over 12% do other scientific or technical work, over half of them as managers or administrators.

Other types of work include – general management or administration (9.4%), marketing and sales (7.6% – up on 1983), education (6.7%), production (5.8%), other services, eg health and safety, patents, information work (3.2%).

Where technicians work Some 64% work in industry or commerce (up from 62.5% in 1983). Nearly 59.5% work for manufacturing, with the largest group in chemical-related industries – 11.6% in pharmaceuticals (up from 10%), 8.7% in 'other' chemicals (down 1%), 7.7% for plastics and polymers (up nearly 1%), 7% in food and drink (up slightly), 5.4% for oil companies, 1.2% in cosmetics and toiletries. Other manufacturing industries employing significant proportions include electrical and electronics (3.4%), and paper and printing (2.6%).

Water, sewage and waste employ 7.7%, and nearly 6% work in energy supply (mostly in electricity generation), with almost 3% working in ferrous and non-ferrous metals.

Central and local government, and the NHS, together employ nearly 14%. Almost 8% work for local government – 3.5% work in schools, 2.7% in polytechnics and FE colleges, with under 2% working for universities. Some 3.5% work for central or local government analytical, testing or service labs, with another 4.5% working for research units, government or otherwise.

Studying, and qualifying in, chemistry

After school, chemistry can be studied at first-degree and technician level. Most professional chemists today read for degrees, but the route to qualification via professional examinations remains open (see below), and there is a significant technician level entry.

As of 1986, over 32% of RSC members have doctorates, 7.7% masters degrees, over 21% first degrees only, 18% the Graduateship of the Royal Society of Chemistry (GRSC) – or earlier qualifications – only, and 16.4% RSC part 1 or equivalent only.

At first-degree level chemistry is taught at most universities and polytechnics, excluding only those with no science faculties. At degree level chemistry deals more with concepts, theories, laws and basic principles than processes and techniques. Many courses take a more 'unified' modern approach to the traditional divisions of physical, organic and inorganic chemistry, although courses obviously still spend more time on types and groups of elements and compounds, their synthesis and the reactions involved.

Because it is such a vast subject, chemistry degree courses generally try to reflect this broad span, and to cover it as widely as possible, concentrating largely on fundamental principles, concepts and methods in the early years. However, because there is always something new happening in chemical research, most courses also respond quickly to the latest advances, and give students at least a glimpse of current research – usually via research projects in their final year. There is normally a strong emphasis on experimental work.

There are a few exceptions to the conventional pattern – one example is the Sussex course which bases students' studies almost entirely on research (alongside postgraduates or senior members of the department), expecting them to learn principles, concepts and methods through experimental work, as they need them; examination is then entirely by thesis. Essex has started a similar scheme. Some courses are biased to applied chemistry at some universities and most polytechnics. There is, generally, wide choice of specialised, often applied, options in many courses – agricultural, analytical, environmental, industrial, mathematical, medicinal, pharmaceutical, polymer chemistry, forensic science, etc.

It is also possible to combine chemistry with a second subject, such as a second science, and some combinations of chemistry and physics are so closely integrated as to become a specialisation, chemical physics, in their own right. The same degree of integration is possible with biology – biochemistry – and geology (geochemistry). More unusual are the combinations of chemistry with languages, with education for a teaching qualification, with materials or metallurgy, and with management, business studies or economics.

'First destination' figures are –

| | 1984-5 | | 1977-8 | |
	university	polytechnic	university	polytechnic
total graduating	2254[1]	443	1845	193
overseas students	37	12	46	6
destination unknown	172	75	112	37
research, etc	679	77	578	31
teacher training	114	14	149	4
'other' training	44	5	34	4
'believed' unemployed Dec 31	198	54	84	18
temporary work	33	10	53	9
permanent overseas work	12	nil	12	1
permanent UK work	966	189	764	83
employers –				
chemicals[2]	334	93	277	29

	1984-5 university	1984-5 polytechnic	1977-8 university	1977-8 polytechnic
manufacturing industry	158	43	263	57
commerce (excl accountancy)	129	12	52	3
accountancy	112	4	58	nil
civil service	47	7	40	7
NHS/local government	46	9	24	1
higher/further ed	27	9	35	2
functions –				
scientific R&D	332	80	283	22
financial work	157	8	68	nil
admin/ops management	108	19	137	25
marketing etc	107	22	44	9
scientific support	86	31	112	24
management services	63	5	69	nil
medical/personnel/social	32	6	13	nil

[1] down from a peak of 2415 in 1983-4   [2] includes pharmaceuticals, agrochemicals, etc.

Entry: A-level chemistry and normally maths and another science needed. Almost 2400 students were accepted for university courses in 1985, about 740 for CNAA degree courses. The mean A-level 'score' for 1984 university entry was 11.6.

Professional qualification The Royal Society of Chemistry (1986 membership over 40,500) is the learned and professional body. Most chartered members qualify via an approved first or second class honours degree and at least two years' relevant experience. However, the RSC has a long tradition of maintaining an alternative route, and hopes to see the possibilities for progression improved.

Graduateship examinations are in two parts, although many candidates start by completing a BTEC Higher National award and then go on to part I GradRSC after another year's study (direct entry to part I requires an A level or equivalent in chemistry). The minimum study time for part II is 500 hours. It is possible to qualify in three or four years, but can take much longer on a part-time basis. Up to 500 people attempted each stage of the exams in 1986, and 360 passed part I, 340 part II.

Postgraduate study Research, posts in higher education, and some other areas of work normally require a higher degree. However, there are research and/or academic posts for only very few of those who gain PhDs, and such a degree is not always a suitable preparation for other areas of work. It is possible to avoid this 'trap' by finding work in industry, and combining this with part-time study for a higher degree. The majority of courses leading to higher degrees or diplomas (as opposed to research degrees) are very specialised – at present, a high proportion are in advanced analytical chemistry, but there are also options in, eg silicate and solid state chemistry, in surface chemistry and colloids, electrochemistry, nuclear and radiation chemistry. Many can be taken on a part-time basis.

Technician-level qualification is via a BTEC or SCOTVEC award.
BTEC Higher awards will be revised in line with the new framework. Schemes are now all to be called Science (Chemistry) or (Chemistry and computing) but

are designed individually by the polytechnic or college, so there is at present no 'standard' scheme, and a wide range of different options, eg in analytical chemistry, process technology, toxicology, pollution technology, and schemes can include physics, biology, computing etc.

HND (full-time or sandwich only from 87-8) is available at –
Polytechnics: Hatfield, Huddersfield, Kingston, Leicester, London: NELP, Thames, Manchester, Middlesborough: Teesside, Nottingham: Trent, Portsmouth (with computing), Pontypridd: Wales, Preston: Lancs, Sheffield, Stoke-on-Trent: N Staffs; Colleges – Blackburn C, Doncaster IHE, Halton CFE, Lancaster: Lancs/Morecambe CFE, London: E Ham CT.

HNC (part time only from 87-8) are available at over 70 centres.

Entry is as for all BTEC Higher National awards††; via A levels with a pass in chemistry, plus physics and maths studied for at least one year post 16-plus.

'First destination' in chemistry HND –

	1984-5 polytechnic only	1977-8 polytechnic only
total graduating	37	120
destination unknown	4	43
on to first-degree course	1	12
on to complete professional qual	22	33
permanent UK work	5	20
employers –		
chemicals[1]	4	10
'other' industry	nil	7
commerce	1	nil
functions –		
scientific support services	5	10
scientific/eng R&D	nil	8

[1] includes pharmaceuticals, agrochemicals, etc.

Further information from the Royal Society of Chemistry (leaflets etc).

COMPUTER SCIENCE

Computer science is an academic discipline (like physics or maths) which studies all aspects of computing from the most abstract theory through to the most practical applications. It is, of course, a fast-developing and -changing discipline, rife with new ideas, theories and systems. It is difficult even for computer scientists themselves to decide where the boundaries of the subject are at any one time, as computer systems increasingly become part of and are 'integrated' into other, 'information technology', systems.

Until quite recently, for example, there was a fairly firm distinction between the 'hardware' side – designing and making the circuits, machinery, memory, and so on – and the so-called 'software' side which concentrates on turning the hardware into a usable information-processing, control, or other computer system via sets of instructions, or programs. The former has commonly been described as electronic engineering, the latter as computer science. Now hardware and software aspects are being deliberately brought together, making design of systems an integrated discipline. Largely this is because there are alternative ways – via the soft- or hardware – to solve problems now, and more and more programs are 'written' into the hardware itself – into the chip. 'Hybrid' skills are needed – with equal understanding of the 'hard' electronics and 'soft' computer science, to be able to assess which is best, and to be able to plan systems coherently.

Software development has lagged seriously behind the colossal advances in hardware, and is holding up development of more advanced systems. Research – collaboratively between universities/polytechnics and industry – in the computing field is largely to concentrate in the immediate future on the so-called Alvey programme. This has four priority areas, which are –

Software engineering: developing more efficient and better ways of instructing computers, via software which is high quality, reliable and cheap. The emphasis here is on improving the basic routines, developing specially programmed computers which will produce better programs faster than can human programmers, and standard tools for developing and maintaining programs.

Very large-scale integration: developing even more advanced and minute silicon chips, with even more electronic circuits on them, which will be faster and more powerful than today's computers.

Human-machine interface: making computers more 'user-friendly', especially for people who are not computer experts, and especially making it possible for them to communicate with computers by voice, touch and sight.

Intelligent knowledge-based or expert systems: developing computer systems able to manipulate more sophisticated and complex factual data, the specialist information of professionals and experts, so that others can interrogate a system to gain access to their knowledge, for example diagnosing diseases, configuring optimum computer systems, analysing faults in telecommunication systems. At this stage, this is being done by developing new software (see also 'knowledge engineering' under COMPUTING). So-called 'fifth-generation', parallel-processing machines (today's operate sequentially) will use redeveloped architecture for even more sophisticated systems.

Other major areas of development include networking, distributed systems and computer-computer communication, and data bases. Computer scientists often work in teams with other experts. For example, the EEC's community-wide machine-translation research project employs about 100 computer scientists and linguists to develop computer systems for automatic translation between all EEC languages.

The Alvey programme alone is costing £350 million, so the research programmes are large scale. Research into all aspects of computing is done by very many organisations – the manufacturers, the software houses, and universities and polytechnics for the most high-level work, and Alvey aims to promote greater co-operation. See also COMPUTING.

Opportunities for computer scientists

There is very little firm information on what happens to people who gain high-level qualifications in computer science. Such a degree is obviously not intended to take graduates into the more routine areas of computer work, although to gain experience some go first into programming in eg software houses. There is a chronic shortage of top-level computer experts, especially in software design, and those who gain good degrees are likely to be in demand for both research work and development.

In future, what computer science graduates do may depend more on the kind of course (see below) they have taken, but it should be possible for them to get into advanced-level work ranging from research to the design and application of computer systems in industry, commerce and administration, and especially in software development. Computer scientists are in greatest demand for systems programming or design, which is mostly with manufacturers rather than users. Large users may, though, increasingly develop their own systems, eg adding a network of remote terminals to an existing range of computers. Government establishments also employ computer science graduates, mainly in research and development, but with some advisory work. The National Physical Laboratory studies human-computer interactions, and has developed a range of microprocessor-based devices for teaching and medicine. The Met Office has one of the most sophisticated computer systems in existence, to model the atmosphere and predict the weather (see METEOROLOGY). The Warren Spring Laboratory investigates the use of on-line computers in the control of industrial processes. In the Home Office both the Police Scientific Development Branch and the Scientific Advisory Branch employ computer experts. Government Communications HQ, the Institute of Naval Medicine, the Mapping and Charting Establishment, and the Royal Armament R&D Establishment, also have their own computer experts.

See also INFORMATION TECHNOLOGY/COMPUTING.

Studying computer science

Computing courses range from some of the most academic and theoretical degree and higher-degree courses, to very practical training in the techniques of programming, etc.

First-degree courses in computer science are changing and developing with the same speed as computing itself. There is also growing variety in the aims, approach and content of courses. Some, particularly at university, take a more theoretical, scientific approach. A growing number, at university and poly-technic, are developing an 'engineering' approach, which they define as con-structing practical solutions to real problems rather than analysing back to fundamentals, and more are now integrating the treatment of hard- and software as more programmes are 'written in' to systems. Some, particularly at polytechnics, are orientated to business and commercial needs – and are increasingly broadening out to deal with wider, user-oriented problem-solving for INFORMATION TECHNOLOGY. Some emphasise management services – oper-ational research, and some systems analysis.

The main areas of study generally include computer 'architecture' – how they are constructed and organised; software for systems of many types and sizes; and applications – commercial, industrial, scientific – again the emphasis may vary – and areas such as file organisation and updating. Programming is generally taught from the start and from basic level through to very advanced, including both machine and a range of high-level languages. The maths and numerical analysis content also depends on the approach, as does the amount of theory taught.

Computer science departments anticipate that most of their graduates will be doing work at the the the forefront of development in computing and information technology. Courses are, therefore, kept thoroughly up to date, dealing with the latest in research and development. And so syllabuses are full of the latest terminology – VLSI, 'parallel processing', artificial intelligence and 'intelligent' knowledge-based (expert) systems (IKBS).

Most courses include a substantial amount of practical and project work – all departments have their own computing facilities for students to use. Sandwich-based courses allow students to gain working experience. Courses aim to make sure that students can appreciate and adapt to changes and developments in computing.

Computer science or computing has conventionally been studied as a 'single subject', or in combination with mathematics, or a science. With the ever-widening range of applications the argument strengthens for combining computer science with another subject, for instance computing with accountancy or business studies, or with electronics/electronic engineering. Some courses now 'integrate' computing with an area of application, such as business. On top of this, the distinction between computing as a 'science', computing as an 'engineering' discipline and, indeed, computing as a 'business' subject, is becoming very blurred. A growing number of 'hybrid' courses are on offer.

Almost all universities and polytechnics now have straightforward degree courses in computer science/computing.

Additionally, there is a range of courses with less-usual slants, eg

Business computing systems: City University

Computerised accountancy: Norwich: E Anglia University

Computing/artificial intelligence: universities – Brighton: Sussex, Edinburgh

Computing in business: Huddersfield Polytechnic

Computing/informatics: Plymouth Polytechnic

Computing information systems: Birmingham Polytechnic

Computing for business: Newcastle Polytechnic

Computer science/cybernetics: Reading University

Computer science/digital electronics: universities – Dundee, London: KQC

Computer science/management studies: universities – Edinburgh, St Andrews, Stirling

Computer science/systems/software engineering: see Computer engineering

Computer science/electronics/engineering: see Computer engineering

Computing/information systems/informatics, at Manchester University, Sunderland Polytechnic.

Computer/microprocessor systems/micro-electronics, at universities – Chelmsford: Essex, Glasgow: Strathclyde, London: KQC, QMC

Computing/OR/statistics/management services, at universities – Canterbury: Kent, Lancaster, Leeds, Liverpool, London: QMC, UC, Reading, St Andrews, Warwick; polytechnic – Leeds

Computer software technology: Bath University

Computer systems: Cardiff: UC

Data processing, at universities – Leeds, Loughborough; polytechnic – Sunderland

Micro-electronics/information processing, at Brighton Polytechnic

Software engineering: see Computer engineering

Systems analysis: at Bristol Polytechnic
See also COMPUTER ENGINEERING/INFORMATION TECHNOLOGY and chapter on INFORMATION TECHNOLOGY (including COMPUTING).

Entry: Most departments want a reasonable mathematical background (up to A level in mathematics), but this depends to some extent on the course – the more theoretical it is, or biased to high-level systems design, the higher the mathematical skills needed. Over 1500 students were accepted for university courses in 1985, over 2000 for CNAA degree courses.

Professional qualification The main qualifying body is –
The British Computer Society (1986 membership over 25,000 against 18,000 in 1969). BCS examinations, useful but not essential, are in two parts: part I is at HND level (HND and above exempts) and the entry is via GCE passes including one at A level. Part 2 is at honours-degree level, and requires an honours degree in computer studies to exempt.

Postgraduate study An extensive range of postgraduate courses in advanced computer science and specialised aspects of computer is available, at both universities and polytechnics. Some provide additional specialisation, some introduce particular techniques or applications, and others are 'conversion' course for graduates in other disciplines.

'Technician'-level qualification is via a BTEC or SCOTVEC award in computer studies.

BTEC Higher-National course guidelines were revised in 1985 taking account of new policies, so are still 'relevant to market needs'. Schemes are very loosely intended for any students wanting to become 'computer practitioners'. Because the range and variety of tasks in computer work – both industrial and commercial – are continuously developing and expanding, BTEC says it is no longer realistic or desirable to specify closely courses which will be appropriate to everyone employed in computing. The structure therefore 'promotes the development of skills and abilities important to all "practitioners" irrespective of type of employing organisation'. The guidelines are capable of wide interpretation and centres can develop and expand their courses to give a special emphasis reflecting employers' needs in a variety of different applications.
The guidelines give three areas considered important for all students – the computer and its behaviour, methods for the design and implementation of computer-based systems, and the environment of computer-based systems. The amount of time and depth of treatment given to each may vary according to the bias of the course, but at least 75% of HNC, and 50% of HND courses must be devoted to them. Model programmes suggest courses can emphasise business or industrial data processing, or be more general.
Courses are also revised to keep up with modern developments – syllabuses include, eg distributed systems, database management, graphics, artificial intelligence, and software engineering.
Courses are available at most polytechnics and some other colleges.
Entry is as for all BTEC Higher awards††; via A levels/16-plus† passes to include mathematics at either level.

BTEC National course guidelines were also revised recently, so will not be changed again in the immediate future. The scheme is designed to meet the needs of 'computer practitioners', preparing for work in the areas of programming, computer systems maintenance, system analysis and design, and operations. All courses must include five 'core' units – introduction to programming, computer systems, information systems, quantitative methods, and communication skills. In addition, for the Certificate, students must complete one major stream or one minor stream with one option unit. For the Diploma, students must also complete one major stream and one option unit, one minor stream and two option units, or two minor streams. The possible streams (major and minor – students may not take major and minor in the same stream) are programming, small-business computer systems, and microprocessor-based systems, and (minor only) operations.

Entry is as for all BTEC National awards††.

For CGLI schemes and other courses, see INFORMATION TECHNOLOGY chapter (including COMPUTING).

Further information from the British Computer Society.

ERGONOMICS

Ergonomics studies, and applies scientific and technological principles to, the relationship between worker and machine, and between people and their environment. Its origins were military, used in world war II as aircraft manufacturers tried to design fighter planes around their pilots so that they 'interacted' with maximum efficiency. It became a technique for relating worker and working environment more closely to each other's needs, and now is applied wherever fitting people more comfortably and efficiently into what can be very complex environments has beneficial results, and designs can be practically improved.

Ergonomics is now used in all kinds of situations – in the design of factory and office layout, in matching machine or computer/word-processor to operator, and even in the detailed planning of kitchens for safety, convenience and efficiency. It is used in designing planes and ships, schools and hospitals. It can help solve problems for disabled people. It is used in systems design by, for example, suggesting which processes are best done by people and which by machine, and tailoring work to human skills rather than making people adapt themselves to the machine. It can also be used in preventing accidents and promoting safety. Increasing use of automation and much more sophisticated machinery in use everywhere adds to the possible applications.

Ergonomics is a very advanced field of study and as such generally requires a high level of education and training. It does not have any formal educational or careers structure. It is multi-disciplinary study and most people come to it having started out in something else.

Where the ergonomics expert works depends a great deal on personal interests. Many firms require these skills, from design work on buildings, factories, machines or consumer goods to analytical research and advisory work in personnel and industrial relations as well as industrial training. There is also some advance research on, for example, the contribution of experimental psychology to modern technological systems, and into new applications of ergonomics.

Studying ergonomics combines a range of basic sciences, including 'human' biology (ie anatomy, physiology and psychology) with mathematics, physics (including experimental design and instrumentation), and appropriate technological and social studies.

It is taught as a degree subject separately from related areas at only two universities –
Birmingham: Aston, where, linked to human psychology, it can be combined with one of a range of other subjects for a joint honours degree; and Loughborough.
It is sometimes a component of other related courses of study, for example, in the building technology course at Manchester (UMIST).

At postgraduate level it is possible to study ergonomics after a first degree in, for example, psychology, engineering, physiology, architecture.

FOOD SCIENCE AND TECHNOLOGY, DIETETICS AND NUTRITION

The food sciences, nutrition, and dietetics all focus on food in some way.

FOOD SCIENTISTS AND TECHNOLOGISTS (there is no firm division between them) concentrate on the food itself – its chemical/biological composition, and the role of eg microbiology. They analyse it; assess nutritional values; develop new ways of preparing and preserving food; develop and assess ways of controlling food spoilage and quality.
Food scientists make studies of, for instance, the distinctive properties of proteins and their response to processing. Some food scientists and technologists do research which seeks to protect consumers' interests, others work on maximising efficiency and effectiveness in food processing and production. Food technologists developed, for example, modern preservation methods, such as freezing, which (with new packaging methods) made it possible to store large harvests year round, and without which the increased production of agriculture and horticulture would have been largely pointless. The food processing industry actually invests in increasing growers' productivity and efficiency, as well as making its own production more cost-effective.

NUTRITION EXPERTS AND DIETITIANS measure people's food intake, promote healthy eating and balanced diets, plan menus for specific groups (eg patients in hospitals or children in school), and advise on special diets, for the overweight or diabetic (for instance).

Nutrition experts generally make scientific studies – on the effects of food processing, on practical ways to improve nutrition in elderly people, for instance.

Dietitians translate scientists' findings and doctors' recommendations into actual diets, taking into account all the factors – psychological, economic, etc – which affect people's choice of food. They assess the nutritional value of particular foods, and teach cooks and patients how to prepare and present them. They help people to solve what can be very difficult nutritional and dietetic problems, explain the reasons for a diet, and help them put it into practice, bearing in mind the shopping, cooking and budgeting problems most families have, as well as their food fads and fancies. They advise not only people with medical problems, but groups such as the elderly, or immigrants who must follow strict religious dietary rules, but cannot get or afford in Britain the food they are used to.

Opportunities in food sciences, nutrition and dietetics

Some 4000 people have qualifications in food science/technology, and about 2100 are fully-qualified dietitians.

The FOOD INDUSTRY – producing, processing and preserving vegetables, biscuits, pizzas, hamburgers, ice cream, fish etc – employs most food scientists and technologists (about 60% of IFST members), nutrition experts, and some dietitians (but they work mostly for firms making specialist dietetic products). They can work in product and process development – of new and improved ways of preserving, processing and packaging food, new products (especially pre-prepared meals), better flavours; trying out new raw materials and recipes, in experimental labs and kitchens. There is little fundamental research except in the largest companies, but some 'trouble-shooting', solving problems.

Most food scientists/technologists in the industry work in food (quality) control and production management. Mass food production demands both very high standards and maximum efficiency. Quality has to be checked continuously from the arrival of new raw materials through to finished products, via batteries of scientific tests and sample tasting, but has to interrupt production as little as possible. Purchasing has to be of such high standard that it is often supervised by food scientists or technologists.

Food scientist/technologists, and some dietitians also work in technical advisory and information services, for teachers, health workers, etc. They help prepare advertising material, technical information sheets, dietary notes, posters, etc.

The HEALTH SERVICE employs over 60% of dietitians. Mostly they advise on special diets – for patients who have, for example, renal failure and are on regular kidney dialysis, or supervise the diets of pregnant women. Others are health education officers. They can become catering managers.

RETAILING, MARKETING and PUBLIC RELATIONS employ a rising number of dietitians.

The CATERING industry employs mainly, but not very many, dietitians, but does also absorb some food scientists. Again, some dietitians become catering managers.

TEACHING, mainly in higher/further education, employs experienced food scientists, nutritional experts and dietitians. Some ten universities and polytechnics, plus a number of other colleges, do RESEARCH in food science/technology, on topics ranging from physiology of yeasts, and applications of protein engineering, through the effects of farming and processing methods on trout, to prison and army feeding, and use of food waste. People qualified in this area can, with extra training, become HOME ECONOMICS teachers, or education-authority advisers.

Some welfare organisations employ dietitians and food scientists, mainly as advisers. A few dietitians find work with the media, writing for magazines on diets, health foods, recipes etc, or for broadcasting or TV.

Studying food sciences, nutrition, and dietetics
Food science/technology can be studied at degree, postgraduate and technician levels. Dietitians must qualify via a degree, and increasingly specialise via postgraduate courses.

First-degree courses in all these subjects all start with basic sciences, like biochemistry, microbiology, physiology, and generally all include nutrition and food science. Dietitians who plan to work as professionals in the NHS must make sure they take a degree recognised by the Dietitians Board (titles vary). All approved dietitians courses include 28 weeks' practical experience. Courses include –

Brewing: Heriot-Watt University.
Dietetics: colleges – Aberdeen: RGIT (nutrition/dietetics), Cardiff: S Glam IHE, Edinburgh: Q Margaret, Glasgow: Queen's/Paisley CT; polytechnic – Leeds
Food manufacture: Manchester Polytechnic
Food marketing (sciences) university – Reading (with food science & economics); polytechnic – Sheffield
Food process technology: Ulster University
Food sciences: universities – Belfast, Glasgow: Strathclyde, Guildford: Surrey (with nutrition), Leeds, London: KQC, Nottingham, Reading (or with food economics/marketing); polytechnic – S Bank
Food studies: Edinburgh: Q Margaret
Food technology: university – Reading; college – Hull: Humberside (industrial)
Nutrition: universities – Guildford: Surrey, London: KQC, Nottingham, Southampton (with biochemistry/physiology); polytechnics – Huddersfield (catering & applied), London: NLP (with biology)
Entry is normally with appropriate sciences at A level or equivalent. About 190 students were accepted to read food science by universities in 1985, under 120 for CNAA dietetics (etc) degree courses (there are less than 200 places on dietetics/nutrition courses approved for state registration.

The professional bodies are –
The British Dietetic Association (1986) has c2100 members all but 300 in the UK. BDA is not a qualifying body, but members must have a recognised dietetic qualification, which has to be a degree in dietetics or nutrition.

The Institute of Food Science and Technology (1986 membership just over 2500) requires a relevant degree or equivalent for corporate members (1600 in 1986) – candidates following the BTEC Higher route must therefore also gain IFST's graduate diploma. All entrants must also have at least three or four years' (depending on initial qualification) relevant experience. A rising 200 a year join IFST.

Postgraduate study –
In *food sciences/technology*, there are 'conversion' courses for graduates in related subjects, and more advanced specialist courses at a number of universities, polytechnics and colleges. A postgraduate, post-experience qualification in food control (awarded jointly by the Institute of Food Science and

Technology, Royal Society of Chemistry and Institute of Biology) is useful for senior posts in industry.

In *dietetics*, graduates who have studied a related subject (including enough human biochemistry and physiology) can qualify via a two-year diploma course at Glasgow: Queen's College, or Leeds Polytechnic. Dietitians who want to specialise, eg in work with children, are increasingly doing postgraduate training.

Higher-technician qualification is via a BTEC or SCOTVEC Higher National award.

BTEC Higher (national) level awards are all science based. New guidelines will not be set for 1987 entry. At present, courses can be taken in food science or technology of food. It is possible to take options in eg dairy, bakery, and other specialist technologies, as well as quality control. Courses are at –
Science (food science) HNC: Reading CT
Science (technology of food) HND: polytechnics – Bristol (with Seale-Hayne), London: S Bank, Manchester; Colleges – Cardiff: S Glam IHE, Glasgow CFT, Grimsby CT/Hull: Humberside CHE, Loughry CA&FT.
Entry is as for all BTEC Higher awards††; via A level/16-plus† chemistry and another science studied to A level, one passed.
Professional qualification: a relevant HND qualifies for licentiate membership of the Institute of Food Science and Technology (see above).

Technician qualification is via BTEC or SCOTVEC National award.
BTEC Nationals are also science based. New guidelines are to be issued, but not for 1987 entry. Present technology of food courses train in basic sciences, food processing and preservation, and include elements of business studies. There is a special scheme in baking technology. Courses are available at –
Colleges – Birmingham CF&DA; Blackpool/Fylde CF&HE; Brackenhurst; Notts CA; Bridgwater: Somerset CA&H; Cardiff: S Glam IHE; Grimsby: Humberside CHE; Leeds: Th Danby; Liverpool: Colquitt; London: S London C; Loughry CA&FT; Lowestoft CFE; Nantwich: Ches CA; Portadown TC; Seale-Hayne; Southall CT; Polytechnics – Manchester.
Entry is for all BTEC National awards††; via 16-plus† passes to include chemistry and mathematics
See also HEALTH SERVICES, MANUFACTURING and SERVICE INDUSTRIES.

Further information from the British Dietetic Association, and the Institute of Food Science and Technology.

GEOLOGY AND EARTH SCIENCES

Geology is the science which studies the physical history of the earth – from its beginnings to the present day. What happens to the earth is largely controlled by changes deep inside it, and these obviously cannot be observed or recorded directly. However, what happens is recorded in the rocks which make up the earth's crust, and so geologists study earth's history using the crust as though it were a set of historical documents.

And so they study the make-up, arrangement and origins of the rocks which form the earth's crust, and the processes involved in the evolution of its present structure. To build a complete record of the sequence of events, geologists must disentangle what happened when rocks were originally formed from later events which may have changed them.

Geologically, 'rocks' are not the only 'hard' parts of the earth's crust: all natural, non-living, solid material found in or at the earth's surface is a 'rock' of some kind or another – peat and mud as well as granite and slate.

Geology involves much detective work, fitting hard-won evidence together, and theory building and testing based on the evidence. Geologists' model of the earth's history has grown enormously in the last two decades, from evidence confirming the theory of 'plate tectonics' and 'continental drift'. Geologists are sure that today's continents are drifting fragments of an ancient 'supercontinent', and that the outer layer of the earth is made up of rigid plates. They have plotted the pattern of drift in detail for the last 200 million years.

Geology is generally broken down into clearly defined topics –

Physical geology studies processes which shape the earth's surface – the work of gravity, the atmosphere, weathering, wind, water, ice, rivers, and the sea – the operations of denudation or erosion, and deposition or building up. Physical geology also studies rock structures.

Petrology studies the nature, make up, textures and origins of igneous (volcanic), metamorphic (formed below the earth's surface), and sedimentary rocks, and of mineral ores.

Mineralogy studies the make-up and physical characteristics (including crystal forms) of naturally-formed substances with definite chemical compositions and definite atomic structures (minerals), eg diamond and graphite.

Sedimentology studies the processes which form sedimentary rocks.

Stratigraphy is the historical study of the rocks that make up the earth's crust, their relationship to each other, their structure, how they are grouped chronologically, their lithology and the conditions involved in their formation, and their fossil contents. It is usual to study particular periods of geological time – 'Quaternary', 'Precambrian', etc.

Palaeontology and palaeobotany trace the history of life on earth and the structure and relationships between different kinds of organisms. Palaeontology studies them in fossil form.

Tectonics and structural geology specialise in rock structures.

Geology also has some relatively new sub-divisions. Like other sciences it uses techniques developed in chemistry and physics, which results in subjects which are mainly about methods – *geochemistry* and *geophysics*. The age patterns of continents can now be worked out using radio-isotopes, like dating the rings in a tree trunk.

Then there are the 'applied' aspects. Most geological studies give results which are useful somewhere, and a high proportion are very practical. Geological information and techniques are used in exploring for, finding and extracting ores for metals, fuels (eg coal), and hydrocarbons – oil and gas.

Engineering geology investigates and reports on conditions of sites, of ground to be built on, for dams, roads, tunnels, even offshore oil rigs. Geology is used in studies of soil and slope stability, and geological hazards like volcanoes and landslides.

Hydrogeology means water is involved.

Economic geology concentrates on aspects needed by mineral industries, the ore and other deposits, and their nature and origins. It includes, for example, assessing the economic values of particular reserves and the cost of mining them.

Opportunities for professional geologists

The main fields of employment for geologists, geophysicists and geochemists are the oil, mining and quarrying and civil engineering industries; government and government-supported scientific establishments, geological surveys (mostly overseas), specialist geological consultants and research companies; and teaching.

Demand for professional geologists is erratic and generally, so far as industry is concerned, tied to the availability of the enormous funds it takes to prospect and whether or not companies think they can recover the cost and make a profit within a reasonable period. Projects therefore close down if oil or mineral prices fall, re-open when they improve. Political and other events also affect policy. The 1986 slump in oil prices, and the tin crisis have recently had a very adverse effect.

Although the number of long-term, permanent posts abroad is now fairly small, most professional geologists still spend at least part of their working lives in the field, moving around the world a lot, in more and more remote areas, under difficult physical conditions. Generally this is in their earlier years, since promotion brings more desk and office work. But in, for instance, oil exploration and production, the amount of field work needed is falling – partly because geophysical techniques make it possible for geologists to do some of the analytical work in the lab and at a desk (from computer output), and partly because the search for new resources is moving more into offshore waters, so geologists are forced to use remote techniques.

In the oil, mining and quarrying industries geologists work in exploration – surveying and surface mapping in geologically promising areas of the world from the Arctic to the tropics, looking for new mineral deposits and working out the size of the reserves. In the oil industry, geologists analyse geological data and recommend which areas to bid for exploration licences and then try to pin-point the optimum place(s) to test drill. They log or analyse the material brought up by the test drills, decide whether to continue or abandon a test and, in production, work out where to site development wells. Geophysical, or seismic, surveying and well-logging is increasingly done by specialist service companies. Most oil firms have their own research labs though, which both provide analytical services for operating staff and do more theoretical studies to improve, for instance, ways of predicting where oil may be found.

Mining production has geologists not only advising on development and estimating reserves, but based on core drillings, suggesting the most economic way to mine, and advising on structural safety as the mine is dug or the open pit excavated. Most work is overseas – in the UK British Coal is the largest employer, of about 200, half in geological work and half on prospecting for reserves suitable for open-cast mining.

In construction, engineering geologists work mostly for consulting civil engineers, specialist site investigation consultants, and the small number of construction firms specialising in foundation or ground engineering. In addition to examining sites to see if they are suitable for buildings, dams, tunnels, underground storage etc, and checking on stability where slopes etc, are involved, geologists also assess rocks and soils for use as construction materials.

Government and government-financed organisations employing geologists include –

The Natural Environment Research Council: spends roughly 40% of its funds on geological sciences, nearly 49% all told on the 'solid earth'. Nearly 14% goes on geological survey work, including the British Geological Survey (BGS), formerly the Institute of Geological Sciences. Over half the 1400-plus scientists working for NERC are geologists or earth scientists (NERC also funds about 150 geology-based projects in universities). Most geologists – about 520 in the science group, 780 staff in total – work for BGS as of 1986. Changes in funding have meant considerable cuts in BGS staffing, and more are expected by 1990. BGS is divided into eight 'directorates' – four multidisciplinary, looking after geological survey and linked field work (two for mainland Britain, one for offshore work mainly Department of Energy projects, and one for overseas); three looking after basic scientific research – one for geochemistry, one for geophysics, one for geology itself; and the eighth covers information and central services. BGS is giving priority to complete the basic survey of the UK by the year 2000, and also studies the country's deep geology, attempting to build up a three-dimensional 'picture', as well as studying geological hazards, the earth's magnetic field, and remote sensing from aircraft and satellites. BGS also works on contract to government departments and industry. In addition to BGS, some geologists are employed by, for example, the Institute of Oceanographic Sciences (about 30) and the British Antarctic Survey (about a dozen permanently and up to 20 on short-term contract). See also ENVIRONMENT.

The Department of the Environment (minerals division and environmental protection, building research station and civil engineering lab), the Department of Energy, and Department of Transport (road research lab), but only in very small numbers and mainly as advisers.

EDUCATION employs geologists as lecturers etc in higher and (fewer) in further education, as technicians in universities, and as school teachers, although they generally have to teach another subject as well as geology.

LOCAL GOVERNMENT (in eg mineral planning), WATER AUTHORITIES (as hydrogeologists), scientific MUSEUMS, and ENVIRONMENTAL organisations like the Nature Conservancy Council employ geologists in very small numbers.

Recruitment and entry A degree in geology is normally needed, and a growing number of employers prefer a higher degree as well.

Potential professional geologists are not just scientists. They must be able to report results, etc, clearly and lucidly, both verbally and on paper. They have to be able to work with other people, have good academic potential, especially in maths. They must also be capable of standing up to tough conditions – self-sufficient and physically fit.

Opportunities for technicians

Geology is generally thought of as an all-graduate profession, but AGCAS suggests, from survey results, that getting on for 3500 people are doing work which could be described as 'technician', although some are qualified right up to PhD level. The work they do, according to AGCAS, includes full chemical analysis of a rock sample, cutting thin sections, running x-ray fluorescence or diffraction machines, preparing geological maps and diagrams, taking photos of microfossils, etc. This is all support work, carried out under supervision from a professional geologist.

Studying geology
Geology is studied almost entirely at degree and postgraduate levels, although there is now a technician qualification.

For a first degree Geology can be studied at most universities, four polytechnics (Kingston, Oxford, Plymouth, Portsmouth) and two CHEs (Derbyshire and Cheltenham: St Paul/St Mary). Most courses cover all the main areas of geology, as already described, in the first two years. It is not usual to specialise to any great extent in any branch of geology, although on some courses it is possible to opt for an applied bias. There are also some more specialist courses, for example (at universities unless otherwise indicated)
Engineering geology – Exeter (with applied geophysics); Portsmouth Polytechnic (with geotechnics)
Engineering geomorphology – London: QMC
Geochemistry – London: QMC, Manchester (with geology), Reading, St Andrews, Swansea (with geology)
Geophysics – Bath (with physics), Cardiff, Durham (with geology), Edinburgh, Lancaster, Leicester, Liverpool, London: Imperial, London: UCL (exploration), Newcastle (with planetary physics), Norwich: E Anglia, Reading (geological), Southampton
Mining geology – Leicester, London: Imperial
There may also be options in these within broader geological courses.
Entry requires 'above-average' chemistry, good physics and adequate mathematics.

'First destination' in geology –

	1984-5 university	1977-8 university
total graduating	909	750
destination unknown	107	65
research/further study, etc	196	169
training – teacher	15	45
'believed' unemployed Dec 31	102	42
temporary work	36	72
permanent overseas work	34[1]	48
permanent UK work[2]	372	269
employers –		
oil, mining, etc [3]	179[2]	120
commerce	72	32
manufacturing industry	42	48
NHS/local government	19	15

	1984-5 university	1977-8 university
higher/further ed	15	8
civil service	8	48
construction	4	11
functions –		
scientific/eng R&D	133[2]	121
management services	51	40
scientific support services	35	23
financial work	30	17
marketing etc	27	25
admin/operational management	21	25
personnel/social	16	9

[1] down from 112 in 1980-1   [2] down from 206 and 158 in 1980-1
[3] UK employers, especially in oil and mining, may also send geologists abroad (about half of all professional geologists work overseas at some time)

The professional body is the Institute of Geologists. Membership requires a degree in geology or a related subject and five years' experience including two in postgraduate training. Technician-associate grade requires an appropriate qualification to at least two A-level standard.

Postgraduate study Almost all postgraduate courses provide for further specialisation, but it is possible to gain entry to these on the basis of a degree in a subject other than geology, eg chemistry, physics or engineering. They cover subjects such as engineering geology, geotechnical engineering, exploration geophysics, structural geology and rock mechanics, hydrogeology, engineering geology, micropalaeontology, geodesy, geotechnics, geochemistry, geophysics, marine geology and geophysics, mining geostatistics, petroleum geology, remote sensing and image processing.

Technician-level qualification Only one course exists in geological technology at South London C, leading to a BTEC HND. Entry is as for all BTEC Higher awards††; straight from school, to include a science at A level.

See also ENVIRONMENT and MANUFACTURING.

Further information from the Institution of Geologists.

MATERIALS SCIENCE AND TECHNOLOGY (including ceramics, glass and refractories technology, metallurgy and plastics and polymers)
Many modern technological advances would be impossible without new and better materials. The process is two way: on one hand, design engineers need materials to meet more exacting specifications, for instance to withstand greater stress or higher temperature; to be more flexible to mould; to keep their shape and size under intensive radiation; or to replace materials which have become too scarce or expensive to use. On the other, research can result in new materials and by-products for which new uses can be found, and may even make possible advances in other areas of technology. Sometimes uses may be found for a new discovery – a plastic made by bacterial fermentation using sugar or other renewable material (as substrate), for instance, turns out to be 'biodegradable', and so possibly usable for controlled, or slow release of drugs or agrochemicals, or as sutures or temporary implants. Polymer, sturdier and easier to join, could replace glass in optical fibres in future.

In 1986, scientists working on materials made what could be the next techno-logical 'quantum leap', by discovering a group of ceramics which are 'super-conducting' – have zero resistance and exclude any magnetic field that comes near them – at room temperature. This means they can be cooled by liquid nitrogen, instead of the dangerous and expensive liquid hydrogen needed to cool earlier superconductors, and are usable. The possibilities are extensive, including extremely-fast computers, cheaper and more efficient medical equipment such as body scanners, trains hovering on magnetic tracks.

Most materials, whether metal, ceramic or polymer, have the same kind of microstructure. All are made up of innumerable fine crystals, and the dif-ferences between materials are due to the myriad different shapes, types, and size of crystals, the different structures which link up the crystals, and the impurities and defects in them. Creating new materials for particular pur-poses, adapting and improving materials to more exacting specifications are often only possible because materials scientists and technologists now know how to manipulate and create new crystal structures to meet demand. New composite materials combining the best characteristics of metals and poly-mers, or bonding them together efficiently, often for the first time, are needed and being developed. The silicon chip would have been impossible without a detailed understanding of the structure of materials, and further research on electronic materials, such as 'super lattices', will bring more novel devices. Modern medicine demands materials which will survive and work in the body – in heart valves, hip joints etc.

The long business of turning novel plastics with metal-like electrical properties to commercial applications involves scientists in trying to find out much more about the relation between crystal structure, chemical composition and physi-cal properties, studying films of materials only one molecule deep. This is but one instance of research on what are called 'low dimensional structures' which is, according to SERC, almost like a new science in its own right – and the shift towards its study is probably greater than any change in university research for over 30 years. Between 1984 and 1986, SERC committed £7.9m to it (plus £2m from industry), and will spend a further £10.5m by 1989. As a result, over 30 groups are now working in the field. It is a very multidisciplinary study, and one from which ideas and trained manpower can be rapidly transferred into industry.

New and improved materials come not only from the use of new substances or new mixes, but also from scientific methods which can improve and control more exactly the techniques and processes used to form, treat, shape and join materials. Ceramics looks set to become a real high-tech 'wonder' material with the discovery that copper-oxide ceramics are superconductors. It is the second largest group of man-made engineering material already, and can be such good heat resisters that they are used on the outside of space shuttles, in rocket nozzles, and nuclear fuel elements. Ceramics can cut steel at high speed and are used to line bullet-proof vests. Glasses and ceramics are being tried out for use in gas turbines, fuel-burning devices, hard-wearing jibs, and high-temperature chemical plant where existing metallic materials are near the limit of their performance. Ceramic engines for aircraft and cars are a real pos-sibility.

Scientists have produced strengthened glass, flexible glass and glass for use in laser technology. Glass optical-fibre cable, transmitting light rather than electrical signals, is replacing conventional copper wire in the telephone system – but the chemical purity of the glass had to be improved by a factor of about a thousand, with physical perfection to match. Glass-ceramic coatings as tough as steel are being tried to protect surfaces from abrasion.

But research also looks for new and better ways of working with and on materials. Areas of current interest include improving manufacturing methods using, for instance, 'near-net shaping' – making castings from powdered metals instead of solid shapes to cut waste and the number of manufacturing stages; improving surface and joining technology – increasing heat and wear resistance of tools by coating them with ceramics; and assurance of product performance, eg using automated methods to create new materials, new ways of evaluating materials, and assessing their likely operational life. Materials and methods of joining them have to be bettered constantly to cope with more difficult environments – from oil rigs in the North Sea to shuttles in space.

In academic study and research, 'materials' is increasingly treated as one subject, based on common scientific principles and benefiting considerably from a logical, collective study of all solids. However, integrated study of materials is still relatively young, and it is still common to think in terms of the individual branches.

Metallurgy deals with metals from their extraction from ores – chemical metallurgy (refining, mineral dressing, preparing ore concentrates), metal forming or process metallurgy (eg shaping by casting, rolling, forging, drawing), to physical metallurgy – structure and physical properties of metals including their behaviour under stress and temperature.

'Ceramics', to the technologist, is not the craft of producing pottery. Ceramic products range from the output of the traditional clay-based industry – building bricks, pipes, domestic china and pottery – through to the very many used in industry which depend on their physical hardness and heat and chemical resistance. The study of ceramics covers, of course, the various processes by which they are made. Modern bonding techniques and the use of temporary plastic binders during forming and firing produce a reaction-bonded ceramic, most commonly silicones.

Glass, although one of the oldest man-made materials, has only been studied scientifically for 50 years and the modern industry is almost entirely based on the results of 20th-century research. Glass technologists have developed completely-new products, new production processes, and even glass ceramics, with more to come. Nevertheless, the basic process remains the same: glass is produced from the fusion of one or more oxides of silicon, boron or phosphorus with basic oxides (eg, sodium, magnesium, calcium and potassium).

'Plastics' all have a common source. All are produced from chemicals whose feedstock is crude oil (for example, acetylene, benzene, butadiene, ethylene, propylene and ammonia), which are variously combined, with ancillary materials such as heat and light stabilisers, anti-oxidants and pigments, to form

bulk synthetic resins and polymers. The two groups of plastics are – thermoset (materials set under heat and pressure by an irreversible chemical reaction) and thermoplastic (softening with heat to become workable but resuming their former state on cooling) and there are, commonly, only twelve of the latter and six of the former. Plastics production is, therefore, mainly a chemical process, although forming them into semi-finished and finished products is more akin to metal-forming.

Opportunities for materials experts

Most metallurgists and ceramic, glass and plastic/polymer technologists (there are very few of the last three), work in their 'parent' industries – metallurgists in metal production, etc. Significant and probably rising numbers do work for firms making other materials, especially as 'composite' material production increases, and for the larger customer firms which use metals, plastics, glass etc in large quantities, particularly in sectors like ELECTRONICS, AEROSPACE, CAR MAKING, CHEMICALS and PLASTICS, ELECTRICITY GENERATION, and GAS. Numbers, however, tend to be small in any one industry, and they may recruit only occasionally. Demand for people with a broader, and more fundamental, materials training, is probably going up, and certainly gives graduates greater flexibility.

All kinds of factors affect employment for materials specialists. Recession, competition from overseas producers (both of materials and of the products, such as cars, from which they are made), and increasing competition from other materials (especially plastics), has adversely affected the METAL INDUSTRIES and especially STEEL, ALUMINIUM and GLASS.

In industry, materials experts are employed in –

Research and development employs all kinds of materials specialists, who usually work in multi-disciplinary teams with other materials specialists – eg polymer technologists in the steel industry trying to improve plastic coatings – and scientists, especially chemists. R&D ranges all the way from developing new materials for particular purposes, through working on new products, or improved versions of old ones, usually to meet customer demand, to finding ways of making production more efficient, faster, and less wasteful. The CEGB, for example, has had to develop metals capable of withstanding higher temperatures, so power stations can be run less wastefully. Some of the research may be done in industry research associations.

In engineering design, materials specialists make sure that the materials being specified are right for the product and the possible (manufacturing) processes, and/or that suitable materials are available. Manufacturing is the major employer, but in sectors like construction, too, major contractors and firms of contractors employ materials scientists as advisers.

Production employs materials specialists in a wide range of functions – senior managers of steel mills are all metallurgists, for example – including analytical and quality control.

Universities, and some polytechnics, employ rather more materials scientists than, eg metallurgists, in research combined with lecturing etc.

Government departments and establishments (but mainly in defence), also employ materials specialists, mostly in R&D but also in advisory work and contract administration.

Studying materials science and technology
Materials of all kinds are studied at degree, postgraduate, and sub-degree levels.

First-degree courses increasingly 'integrate' the study of materials, but some are 'integrated' throughout, and some give specialisation in particular materials in the latter part of the course. Some are science-based, others engineering biased. Course titles can be misleading and may not reflect what the course currently covers – separate courses in, eg materials science and metallurgy at the same university may start with common studies. Courses include –

Ceramics, science/technology of: Sheffield U (BEng 3/MEng 4 yrs)
Engineering metallurgy: Salford U (BEng 4 yrs)
Glasses, science/technology of: Sheffield U (BEng 3/MEng 4 yrs)
Materials engineering: Universities – Guildford: Surrey (BEng 4 yrs), Loughborough (BSc 4 yrs)
Materials process engineering: Sheffield U (MEng 4 yrs)
Materials science: Universities – Bath (BSc 3 yrs), Liverpool (BEng 3 yrs), Manchester/UMIST (BSc 3 yrs); polytechnics – London: Thames (BSc 4 yrs), Sunderland (BSc 3/4 yrs)
Materials science/engineering: Universities – Leeds (BEng 3 yrs), London: QMC (BSc(Eng) 3 yrs)
Materials science/technology: Universities – Brunel (BSc 4 yrs), Sheffield (BEng 3/MEng 4 yrs), Swansea: UC (BSc, 3 yrs)
Materials science/technology/engineering: Birmingham U (BEng 3/MEng 4 yrs)
Materials technology: Coventry: Lanchester P (BSc 3/4 yrs)
Metallurgical engineering: Leeds U (MEng 4 yrs)
Metallurgy: Universities – Glasgow: Strathclyde (BSc 4 yrs), Guildford: Surrey (BEng 4 yrs), Leeds (BEng 3 yrs), Liverpool (BEng 3 yrs), Manchester/ UMIST (BSc 3 yrs), Newcastle (BEng 3/MEng 4 yrs), Sheffield (BMet 3 yrs), Swansea: UC (BSc 3 yrs); polytechnic – London: City (BSc 3 yrs)
Metallurgy/materials engineering: Birmingham U (BEng 3/MEng 4 yrs)
Metallurgy/materials (science of): Universities – Cambridge (option in Natural sciences BSc 3 yrs), Cardiff: UC (BSc 3 yrs), London: Imperial (BSc(Eng) 3 yrs), Nottingham (BEng 3/MEng 4 yrs), Oxford (BA 3 yrs)
Metallurgy/microstructural engineering: Sheffield P (BSc 3/4 yrs)
Polymer science/engineering: Universities – London: QMC (BSc(Eng) 3 yrs), Manchester: UMIST (BSc 3 yrs)
Polymers, science/technology: Universities – Sheffield (BEng 3/MEng 4 yrs); polytechnics: London: NLP (BSc 3/4 yrs), Manchester (BSc 4 yrs)
Science of engineering materials: Universities – Glasgow: Strathclyde (BSc 4 yrs), Newcastle (BEng 3/MEng 4 yrs)

'First destination' figures (in metallurgy only) are –

	1984-5		1977-8	
	university	polytechnic	university	polytechnic
total graduating	275[1]	24	256	19
research/further study	65	1	48	2
'believed' unemployed Dec 31	21	1	4	1
permanent UK employment	153	15	146	15
employers –				
engineering	86	11	94	12
oil, chemicals, etc	16	nil	18	nil
public utilities	9	1	9	nil
'other' manufacturing	3	nil	8	nil
accountancy	13	nil	2	nil
'other' commerce	7	1	2	nil
civil service	6	1	12	3
armed forces	5	1	4	nil
functions –				
R&D/design	86	7	57	2
financial work	17	nil	3	nil
admin/operational				
management	15	5	45	11
eng/scientific support	12	1	22	1
management services	5	1	9	nil
marketing etc	4	nil	8	1

[1] down from 328 in 1980-1

Professional qualifications The Institute of Metals (formerly Metallurgy) – 1986 membership over 13,000 – for professional membership normally requires an accredited (honours) degree, plus four years' relevant training and at least four years' relevant, supervised training. An honours degree in another subject is accepted with additional evidence of appropriate training in materials/metallurgy. Entrants with ordinary/pass degrees in metallurgy or materials must take additional exams or undergo a longer period of training and experience. Technician-engineer membership requires a HNC/D or eg FTC in metallurgy plus at least two years' practical training and three years' appropriate experience.

The Plastics and Rubber Institute requires a science or engineering degree for full corporate membership, plus three years' industrial experience if the degree is in an appropriate subject, four if not. The Institute accepts an appropriate BTEC higher award plus further study for the graduate examination, with three years' industrial experience post-qualification.

Postgraduate study It is possible to convert to materials/metallurgy from a science or engineering degree, or go on to advanced study/research.

Technician and craft level qualification is still almost entirely based on the traditional industry-based materials disciplines.

In materials technology, BTEC will make awards at both national and higher national levels in engineering-biased schemes, and in materials science, science-based higher awards but to date (1986-7) no broad-based courses appear to have been approved.

See individual industries under MANUFACTURING.

Further information from the institutions cited above.

MATHEMATICS AND STATISTICS

Mathematics is a scientific 'language', a logical language for reasoning in, and a set of number-based tools and techniques which can be used to tackle all kinds of problems. Problems in scientific and technological research and development, and organisational problems – for governments, for industrial and commercial firms – have become more complex and difficult to solve.

Mathematics provides a scientific shorthand in which to describe complex situations relatively simply, concisely and precisely, making it easier to state and analyse problems, and then demonstrate – again in mathematical terms – the different effects of, for instance, a design change on the performance of a gas turbine, or a tax or mortgage rate change on families, both of which use well-tried and tested techniques. The problems may be such, however, that new techniques may have to be developed to formulate, for example, a new theory in particle physics. New mathematical techniques, being developed all the time (mathematics is a living and growing language), coupled with the use of sophisticated computers, make it possible to do research and solve real problems that would have been impossible only a few years ago.

Statistics is very closely related to mathematics, and it is very difficult to separate them, because statistics relies heavily on mathematical techniques. Statistics is mostly used in analysing complex data, and therefore means knowing how to ask the right questions, how to produce information which will help in decision-making and clear up problems of uncertainty. Statistics can be used to test hypotheses, to plan experiments, to chart changes in experimental results, to produce indices. Statistics is used to design a way of gathering the information needed to provide an exact picture in number form of, for instance, the use of a particular street by traffic at different times of the day, showing the ratio of cars to commercial vehicles, where they come from and go to, to help in planning new traffic systems. Statistics can give an accurate picture of, for example, voters' attitudes to a political policy, by sophisticated 'sampling' techniques, and can be very good at predicting ahead using, for instance, probability theory.

As mathematical and statistical techniques are refined, as computers make it possible to solve more complex problems via more highly-sophisticated calculations, and at enormous speed, more problems can be solved using mathematical and statistical analysis, and more organisations turn to maths to predict ahead and solve problems.

Opportunities for mathematicians and statisticians

Although it is common to talk about 'being' a mathematician, in fact most work which employs people trained in mathematics actually applies mathematical skills to solving someone else's problems. There are very few people indeed who do purely mathematical work – which generally means improving techniques and systems, or defining principles – without also working on the kind of problems they are intended to solve. And so most mathematicians have to develop an interest in another subject, or subjects, – which be almost anything from theoretical physics through life insurance to sewage. They must also learn to, for instance, communicate results, often to the mathematically semi-literate.

The balance of employment for mathematicians has been changing since the mid-sixties. Then, most mathematicians were academics or teachers. Today, probably at least half of all younger mathematicians, and over a third of the total, work in industry and commerce. Well under a third work in universities and polytechnics, about an eighth in other colleges, and only a tenth in schools (although this is much less than it should be).

Most graduate mathematicians begin their careers in one of the maths-based occupations, not as mathematicians 'per se'. They go into, eg ACCOUNTANCY, BANKING, COMPUTING, OPERATIONAL RESEARCH, INSURANCE including ACTU-ARIAL WORK, STATISTICS, FINANCE. Not nearly enough go into school TEACHING (8500 in state schools in 1984-5) – another 5000 work in universities, poly-technics and colleges.

In research and development work, for which postgraduate training is usually needed, there are opportunities in industry and in university or or govern-ment-supported research units, although even for mathematicians economic recession had some adverse effect.

In industry, the main employers are research-intensive firms in, for example, aero-engineering, electronics and telecommunications, chemicals, and firms making and using large-scale power equipment. Mathematicians here work as members of R&D or design teams, and have to become fairly expert in the field in which they are working. They make theoretical predictions of what will happen to a particular engineering design under given conditions, help to calculate complex stresses, analyse what has happened in the experimental test bed or wind tunnel, or make mathematical models of the possible behaviour of a liquid as it is processed. Examples include –

a study of the breakdown of sewage by micro-organisms,
models of polymer melt processing (eg film blowing),
an analysis of how cracks (in eg metals) grow,
work on problems in telephone traffic,
applications of micromagnetics to recording-head design,
predicting the aerodynamic performance of an aircraft wing, and
modelling the behaviour of a gas turbine.
In production, mathematicians work on machine and production scheduling, systematic stock provision, and developing new control systems.

Organisations of all kinds use mathematicians to help solve complex organisa-tional and business problems, eg the optimum places to site distribution depots. But here they are usually working as part of the MANAGEMENT SERVICES team on, for instance, OPERATIONAL RESEARCH.

Government establishments employing the largest groups of mathematicians include the DHSS – on NHS and medical problems: the Home Office scientific advisory branch; various units of the Ministry of Defence – eg the RAF department of the chief scientist, the mapping and charting establish-ment, and the Meteorological Office – where they help to model the atmosphere. See also the CIVIL SERVICE.

Statisticians also work as part of research teams, in both universities and industry, for the government (where there are statistics divisions in most major departments, co-ordinated by a central office for the whole statistical service), and for a great range of other employers.

Studying mathematics

Mathematics is most extensively studied for first degrees – in almost all universities and polytechnics, but also for higher degrees and technician-level awards.

First-degree courses Mathematics at university is becoming more abstract, although it also has (obviously) applications – and abstract mathematical ideas developed in one century or decade have a habit of turning into theories with a real existence – as wave equations accurately predicted radio waves. Abstract in the sense that mathematicians spend more of their time developing concepts, theories – and looking for underlying patterns which, for example, explain something about all prime numbers, rather than something about a single prime number; instead of studying, for instance, a single ring, rings are studied as classes.

Degree courses are on a different 'level' from sixth-form studies – tackling complete theories rather than formulae and single patterns. Much time is spent on basic rules – axioms, theorems, etc, and using logical argument (and intuition and even creative imagination), to devise and prove theorems, and then use these theorems to prove others.

The first, and usually the second year too, is a broadly-based study of what mathematicians see as the 'central' and most important areas of maths. On most courses this still means roughly equal time to 'pure' and 'applied' maths, although the distinctions between them are becoming blurred – as topics like differential equations and numerical analysis 'cross' the boundary and are important in both. Mathematicians are always creating new links between what are often thought of as separate parts of maths – as one mathematician said, 'it is commonplace to start with a problem in analysis, turn it into topology, reduce it to algebra, and solve it by number theory'.

Central to most mathematics courses on the pure side are areas like algebra and analysis (which continues calculus on a more theoretical level). Applied maths takes the ideas, theorems and techniques of pure maths and use them to solve problems in the real world. Applied maths traditionally deals almost entirely with applications in other sciences, and in engineering technology, but today it is also applied in areas like OPERATIONAL RESEARCH, games theory, linear programming and, newest of all, 'catastrophe' theory, otherwise called the theory of discontinuous processes.

Most courses include at least some statistics – and most professional statisticians study maths. Statistics covers basic theories and techniques – of probability, for example. Courses generally include some computer science.

Maths is a very large subject, and most courses offer a considerable choice of topics to study. The range of subjects which can be combined with mathematics for joint honours is now very wide and includes education, computer science, operational research, economics, experimental psychology, and management sciences, as well as the more conventional combinations with physics, chemistry and so on, all providing a useful basis for many careers.

'First destination' in mathematics –

	1984-5 university	1984-5 polytechnic	1977-8 university	1977-8 polytechnic
total graduating	4572	1228	2930	88
overseas students	258	40	113	4
destination unknown	366	148	183	11
research, etc	452	50	384	14
teacher training	305	13	256	4
'other' training	129	2	33	nil
'believed' unemployed Dec 31	243	82	66	4
temporary work	56	23	61	2
permanent UK work	2659	842	1728	48
employers –				
engineering industry	654	288	567	22
commerce (not finance)	579	260	173	9
accountancy	426	10	238	nil
banking/insurance[1]	377	48	180	nil
public utilities	113	50	90	nil
oil, chemicals etc	97	42	67	3
civil service	93	13	54	3
higher/further education	76	27	16	1
local government/NHS	65	25	59	3
'other' manufacturing	61	39	80	4
functions –				
management services[2]	1341	696	887	33
financial work	792	19	444	4
scientific/eng R&D	228	39	142	4
admin/op management	84	21	87	1
marketing etc	46	11	46	nil
personnel/social etc	34	1	17	nil
teaching/lecturing	29	12	40	1
scientific support	25	6	13	4

[1] includes actuarial training   [2] mainly computing, also OR, O&M

Entry: A levels should normally include maths – universities usually want two separate passes. Just 2740 students were accepted for university courses in 1985, over 600 for CNAA courses. The mean A-level 'score' for universities in 1984-5 was 12.2.

Professional qualification While mathematics is primarily a graduate career, it is possible to work in a mathematical environment without a degree, and there are a number of useful qualifications.

The Institute of Mathematics and its Applications has a graduateship examination, of honours-degree standard. The Institute has grades of individual membership ranging from fellow, through associate fellow and graduate member to licentiate, companion and student membership. Licentiateship needs a qualification of HND or ordinary-degree standard, while graduateship is honours-degree standard.

The Institute of Statisticians' examination is in four parts. GCE A level in statistics or maths exempts from part 1, and exemption from parts 1 and 2 is gained with a degree or equivalent which includes mathematics in the first year; full exemption is gained only with an equivalent degree. Membership also requires appropriate experience.

The Royal Statistical Society does not set any examinations.

Technician level qualification is via BTEC or SCOTVEC higher national awards.

BTEC Higher awards can be taken in mathematics with statistics, or with statistics and computing or physics. Entry is as for all BTEC Higher awards††, but qualifying exams must include maths (50% pure) at A-level or equivalent.

'First destination' in mathematics HND –

	1984-5 polytechnic only	1977-8 polytechnic only
total graduating	1081	121
destination unknown	201	28
on to first-degree course	90	22
on to complete professional qual	122	6
other training	51	7
research, etc	4	8
'believed' unemployed Dec 31	116	9
permanent UK work	425	29
employers –		
commerce	174	2
engineering	106	15
'other' industry	52	6
NHS/local government	48	4
higher/further ed	14	1
civil service	10	2
functions –		
management services[1]	341	20
financial work	18	1
admin/operational management	14	2
scientific/eng R&D	9	3
marketing, etc	8	nil
personnel/social, etc	5	nil
scientific support services	4	1

[1] Includes computer programming, etc

See also individual careers mentioned above, and MANAGEMENT SERVICES

Further information (careers booklets etc) from the Institute of Mathematics and Its Applications, the Institute of Statisticians, and the Royal Statistical Society

MEDICAL SCIENCES

Medicine is so much the vocational degree subject that it is rare to consider it as a purely scientific discipline in its own right as well, with career potential outside the strictly medical field. Yet the form and content of medical education are solidly scientific enough (and at most medical schools it is possible to complete a science as well as a medical degree with only an extra year), to be the basis of a number of scientific or other careers. Six years is a long time, and a medical training is very tough. It is unrealistic, therefore, to expect that every 18-year-old who begins a course in medicine will still want to practise medicine when he or she graduates at 24.

Working in medicine and dentistry See HEALTH SERVICES

Alternatives to a medical career Probably the closest alternative to a career as a medical practitioner is in research, either clinical, or in medical sciences, which usually means working in the laboratory. Other scientists (see eg BIOCHEMISTRY and GENETICS), have always played a major part in medical research, but medically-qualified people are also needed, both because of the multidisciplinary nature of their 'pre-clinical' training (see below), which matches the generally-interdisciplinary nature of the research, and because their clinical training gives the necessary practical slant.

Medical research takes two main forms: work on solving specific problems, and developing new techniques and instrumentation, with a great deal of overlap between them. Since medical research is multidisciplinary, medically-qualified researchers work alongside and/or in teams with other scientists. Research workers are employed either in hospitals (where the employer may be the NHS, the teaching university/medical school, the Medical Research Council, or even all three), or in research units in universities or government-sponsored laboratories. The Medical Research Council currently has some 56 units spread throughout the UK and employs (1986), 189 medically-qualified staff (and 818 other scientists) and funds over 1750 projects, thus paying another 1800 scientists, some of whom are medically qualified, mostly employed through universities. The main government agency for promoting research in medical and allied sciences, MRC funding has been tightened though, units have closed, and jobs cut.

Although all its work is medically oriented, MRC also supports fundamental research, believing that it will provide important leads – the Council has been deeply involved in promoting research in molecular biology, for example. MRC units either do long-term, multidisciplinary research on problems of public concern (eg AIDS), or build up research potential in subjects before they become fully established in universities. A new molecular neurobiology unit has been set up to concentrate on the molecular processes responsible for normal and abnormal behaviour of nerve transmitters and receptors, using the latest methods, including DNA cloning, to study brain and nervous system at genetic, molecular and cellular level. This research could be the basis for the design of new drugs and strategies to prevent and treat mental illness. Other examples of MRC research include working out the structure of the influenza virus, developing gene probes to diagnose inherited diseases, a possible vaccine against malaria, and studying the junction between nerve and muscle to learn more about autoimmune responses.

Other opportunities Medical qualifications, and preferably some experience as a GP, are a basis for work in advisory services, such as those run by local authorities, and the public health services (see under LOCAL GOVERNMENT and HEALTH SERVICES).

Beyond the strictly medical field, medically-qualified staff are employed by, eg pharmaceutical firms in research or advisory and consultancy work.

To TEACH any medically-related subject in medical school or university (eg PSYCHIATRY), a medical degree is also needed.

Social and related services employ medical graduates.

Otherwise a degree in medicine can be treated purely and simply as any other science degree.

Qualifying in medicine and dentistry

The pattern and content of medical courses have changed quite considerably over the past twenty years, although they still start with a firm grounding of relevant sciences. At least three kinds of change have affected medical teaching.

First, all the many developments in medical research mean that there is so much more to learn, and since many of the advances in understanding disease and in treatment are science-based, the emphasis is on understanding the scientific basis of medicine and on scientific method.

Second, most medical schools teach students more about the people they are treating – the 'whole person' and their family and community – and do not just concentrate on the body, how it works, what goes wrong with it and how to treat it.

Third, some schools no longer divide the basic scientific studies (called 'pre-clinical') quite so rigidly from the vocational, clinical stage, which means introducing students to the patients and the wards rather earlier than is traditional. In the traditional course, healthy lungs are studied and dissected in the first year (for example), and lung diseases (and patients with them) are not met until (say) the fourth. In the modern, more 'integrated' course, the chest and lungs in health and disease are studied at the same time.

Schools have also introduced a range of 'elective' studies as part of medical degree courses, giving students some opportunity to broaden or deepen their studies in ways that interest them individually. Intending medical students should, then, study syllabuses carefully, since the range and depth of such options varies between schools.

Whichever way the course is organised, studying medicine involves some solid science – physiology, biochemistry, anatomy, and so on, usually with some behavioural/social sciences. There is some variation in the balance between these – not all schools insist on so much dissection, for example. As we have seen, some schools introduce medical techniques and clinical work fairly early, others still do not start clinical studies until the third year. While the teaching of medical techniques is more integrated than it used to be, via a system of team teaching, the traditional clerkship – short periods attached to specialist teams in particular areas of medical and surgical practice – is still usual.

However, more time is now given to work in, for example, community medicine and general practice, geriatrics and psychiatry, with chances to specialise in some. One now common, and popular, 'elective' allows students to spend some weeks on a relevant 'project' almost anywhere in the world.

Medicine is taught at – Aberdeen; Belfast; Birmingham; Bristol[1]; Cambridge; Cardiff: UWCM[1]; Dundee[1]; Edinburgh; Glasgow; Leeds; Leicester; Liverpool; London: Charing Cross/Westminster, Guy's/St Thomas's, King's, London, RFH, St Bartholomew's, St George's, St Mary's, UCL/Middlesex; Manchester[1]; Newcastle[1]; Nottingham; Oxford; St Andrews (pre-clinical only: clinical at Manchester); Sheffield[1]; Southampton. There are about 3900 places.

Dentistry is taught at – Belfast; Birmingham; Bristol[1]; Dundee[1]; Edinburgh; Glasgow; Leeds; Liverpool; London: Guy's, King's, The London, UCL; Manchester[1]; Newcastle[1]; Sheffield. The number of places is down to under 850.

[1] Premedical or dental course – ie small number of candidates who do not have three science A levels (normally chemistry, physics, and biology, zoology or maths) admitted to preliminary year. For entry with three science A-levels, the mean A-level grade 'score' in medicine was 13.2 (13.9 with SCE H grades), 11.7 (11.9) for dentistry, in 1984-5.

Postgraduate study A second qualification is generally needed for advanced and specialised work in particular branches of medicine, surgery and dentistry, and for research. This may be via (university) higher degrees and diplomas following further medical-school training, and/or via membership and fellowship of one of the Royal Colleges (eg General Practitioners, Obstetricians and Gynaecologists, Pathologists, Physicians of Edinburgh and London, Physicians and Surgeons of Glasgow, Surgeons of Edinburgh or England, and Psychiatrists), or the Faculty of Radiologists. In most cases these qualifications require candidates to have practised in the appropriate branch for a set period and to pass an examination. Some candidates do take courses to prepare for these but formal study is not required. A great many other diplomas in specialist areas of medicine are awarded by universities, the Royal Colleges, etc, and for most of these full- or part-time courses of instruction are required. See also HEALTH SERVICES

METEOROLOGY

Meteorology is technically the physics of the earth's atmosphere, and a branch of geophysics – the science of the weather and forecasting is only an applied aspect of meteorology. Studying the atmosphere, and not just weather or climate, means work on eg the surface energy balance, fluid dynamics, radiation, cloud physics, turbulence, and the boundary layer.

Meteorological research and forecasting, however, go hand in hand, and both are done co-operatively, with the weather services of almost all countries working closely together. The global network of basic systems observes, collects, disseminates, stores and retrieves data. 'Systems' now range from the most modern satellites through 'radiosonde' instrument packages carried by balloons, to the more traditional weather ships, automatic weather stations, and the straightforward observations of ships at sea (8000 belong to the 'voluntary observing fleet') and coastguards. Methods are being improved all the time: at present, crews of civilian and military aircraft provide data on temperature and wind speed and direction at cruise levels, but in future new instrument systems will give automatic readings which can be transmitted to a data-collecting centre via a satellite. Automated regional and global communication networks exchange and distribute nationally-collected data rapidly and continuously.

Internationally, the 'world climate research programme' is studying the mechanisms that influence climate, especially the interactions between the atmosphere and the other components of the climate system (eg oceans, sea-ice and land surfaces, dust and carbon dioxide). The Met Office does research on forecasting – mainly trying to improve computer models and attempting to predict weather variations on smaller space and time scales. It also has research groups working on geophysical fluid dynamics, atmospheric chemistry, planetary boundary layer studies, and satellite meteorology. On the atmospheric boundary layer (the lowest kilometre), for example, where heat and moisture are transferred between the atmosphere and the earth's surface, the Met Office does research into the effects of hills on airflow, the dispersal of pollutants, and sulphur concentration in rain. A whole project is devoted to rain research, not only to understanding it, but recording it and its rate of fall using radar, so that rain belts can be mapped on a visual display screen. A 'flying laboratory' Hercules is used to study, for instance, radiative transfer through clear air and cloud to improve its representation in numerical forecasts and climate models.

Other research aims to improve and develop instruments of all kinds, the computer systems, and programs.

Modelling the atmosphere and forecasting the weather is a mathematical exercise, using one of the most advanced numerical-physical models there is. Data collected world wide is fed through a telecommunications network into one of the most powerful and complex computer systems operating, for analysis and model building. The Meteorological Office's weather service is one of the world's most sophisticated. Computers have relieved forecasting staff of routine work, but they must still monitor the basic data and computer analysis, and may have to modify the data, or adjust the computer's findings.

The Meteorological Office, which is part of the Ministry of Defence, provides a wide range of weather information. The daily general forecasts are a comparatively small part of the work. One of the main tasks is a weather service for the RAF, and another for shipping – helping them avoid hurricanes, for instance. Specialist weather information is sold commercially – to anything that flies, from pigeons to airlines, to the offshore oil and gas industries, to highway authorities (who want snow and ice warnings so they can grit roads), gas and electricity boards (to anticipate changes in demand), to farms and other crop sprayers, to the construction industry, and even ice-cream makers.

Working in meteorology
Most meteorologists work for the Meteorological Office – staff there number (1986) just under 2590 (down from about 3000 in 1983). Of these, 1695 are scientific officers, 33 are technical (including marine) staff, and 132 work in telecommunications. A small number research/teach in universities and a few private organisations employ meteorologists.

Scientific officers (normally graduates) in the Meteorological Office generally start with work in research, on computer and instrumental development, and then go on to weather forecasting. Forecasters prepare detailed forecasts from the computer output of charts and graphs. The intervention team of senior forecasters constantly monitors the basic data and computer analysis. Forecasters work at Bracknell or at civil and RAF airfields both in the UK and overseas. Those stationed on airfields may work exclusively for aircrew, while elsewhere general, or a range of special forecasts may be produced.

Junior grade staff make scheduled weather observations, code reports for transmission over international networks, and generally help forecasters. Some work in research – as the equivalent of technicians – or with computers and become programmers. Promotion, which depends on gaining a BTEC Higher award in physics or mathematics, is to scientific officer/forecaster.

The Meteorological Office operates round the clock and so there is shift work for everybody.

Recruitment and entry is to the scientific CIVIL SERVICE.

Assistant scientific officers must have at least four GCE passes including English language and maths or physics but preferably both. Most successful candidates have at least one science A level now. About 80 assistant scientific officers (down from 120) are recruited each year – and up to 1500 apply.

Scientific officers are normally expected to have a degree in maths or physics, meteorology, computing science or electronics, possibly physical chemistry or oceanography, but not single-subject geography, or a BTEC Higher award in mathematical or computing subjects, or applied physics. Currently (1986) about 30 vacancies a year (over 500 apply).

Qualifications and training The Meteorological Office gives all new entrants basic training, and more advanced skills are taught as needed. Staff are also released for outside training.

While meteorology is normally studied at postgraduate level (the Met Office recruits mostly mathematicians, computer scientists and physicists), and as a branch of geophysics, Edinburgh and Reading Universities offer first-degree courses. Postgraduate courses are available at Aberystwyth, Birmingham, Reading.

Further information from the Meteorological Office (leaflet).

OCEANOGRAPHY

Oceanographers study the seas: how waves, tides and water behave and why, and the effects they have on, for example, coasts. They study how the sea and the atmosphere interact, how the seas' behaviour affects weather and vice versa. They study the chemistry and composition of sea water. Some oceanographers also study the sea bed and the sediments covering it, but this is developing into a separate discipline, marine geology, linked closely with geology and geophysics – partly because ocean floors are important in studying how and why the earth's outer layer moves ('plate tectonics'), and partly because valuable minerals lie on the sea floor and beneath it. Some oceanographers also study life within the seas, for example, the relationships between the sea and the organisms living in them.

It can be difficult to be sure where the boundaries of oceanography are, because it links so closely with both physical (physics, chemistry, geology, meteorology), and biological sciences. As a result, oceanographers often work in teams with scientists from other disciplines, and even with engineers. Different organisations may have a common interest in the seas, but for different reasons, and they co-operate in joint research programmes; for instance, both meteorologists and fisheries research units are interested in just how salty particular parts of the Atlantic are. Collecting information about the seas can be very expensive, and so several countries may co-operate, using one fleet of ships and aircraft. But oceanographers also work in the lab, doing experiments on physical models of, for instance, estuaries, and in wave tanks, but also on computer-based mathematical 'models'.

The seas and sea floors are increasingly important – for the minerals there and the food the seas can provide. Oceanographers study the conditions fish and algae need to thrive, and how to avoid killing them (or their food) with pollution. Much research has practical value – a map of the sea floor shows telephone engineers where best to lay their cables, for example.

Oceanographic research helps to improve prediction of tides, which is used in weather forecasts and by engineers designing oil rigs or developing devices for generating electric power from sea waves. It is useful in preventing and solving coastal erosion. Defence uses oceanography work in developing underwater weapons and improving ways of detecting submarines, mines, etc, using sound equipment. Developing and improving instruments and equipment for use in research is part of the work.

Working in oceanography

There are few jobs in Britain for oceanographers. The main employers are the research units, such as the Institute of Oceanographic Sciences – which employs (1986) only 182 scientists (down on 250 in the early 1980s) – marine biologists, chemists and physicists as well as oceanographers, and the Institute for Marine Environmental Research, with under 70. Even fewer work for the Ministry of Agriculture on fishery research, a few in the national hydraulics laboratory, a few for the Admiralty (on weapons research), a few for the Navy, and a few for the Meteorological Office. Few universities employ oceanographers, but seven centres have marine technology research centres (working on off-shore oil and gas technology, mining, power generation from the sea and food production). There seem to be few posts in commercial firms, in Britain anyway, but the US has a large oceanographic research programme.

Studying oceanography Oceanography can be studied as a first-degree subject at Bangor, Liverpool (marine chemistry or physics), Southampton and Swansea (joint honours only), and at postgraduate level at Bangor, London: UCL, and Southampton.

Further information from the Institute of Oceanographic Sciences.

OPHTHALMIC OPTICS (OPTOMETRY)

Degree courses in ophthalmic optics are designed to give opticians a sound scientific training and provide a basis for research in the optical field. Research on ophthalmic optics itself is mainly clinical and in developing diagnostic techniques and new, computer-based equipment. In physics, though, there is also optical research in such areas as lens theory and design, optical instrumentation (including fibre optics), lasers and coherent optical techniques including holography and optical data-processing, and electron optics and optical design which also means developing new techniques using computers. Graduate ophthalmic opticians are also employed by, for example, glass and lens manufacturers in both production and research.

Ophthalmic work see HEALTH SERVICES

Studying and qualifying in ophthalmic optics Ophthalmic opticians must meet statutory education/training requirements.

First-degree courses in ophthalmic optics begin with physical and biological sciences, and some anatomy and physiology, since opticians must understand fully the structure and function of the eyes, nerves and muscles and how they work, in detail, and how they can go wrong. Optical principles are also introduced early, and courses go on to apply these, how to test eyes (including how to deal with patients), and how to recognise abnormalities which indicate injury or disease and must be referred to a doctor.

Courses cover the complex instruments (eg ophthalmoscopes and retinoscopes) and how to use them. They teach how to work out what lenses are needed to correct vision using trial lenses, how to fit contact lenses, and how to make them, how to advise on colour vision. There may be work on industrial needs, on problems of lighting and illumination, and safety in industry. More than half the time is spent in practical work, in labs and workshops, making lenses and frames and examining and testing 'real' patients.

Only six first-degree courses in ophthalmic optics exist, at –

Universities: Aston, Bradford, Cardiff: UWIST, City, Manchester: UMIST; college: Glasgow CT. The number of places is about 270.

Entry requirements vary. Only Manchester actually specifies physics at A level, but A-level subjects should include physics, biology or zoology, and another science or mathematics; for university schools at least 11 points needed.

Postgraduate courses which can be taken after a degree in a related subject, but which train for research rather than professional practice, are available at City, London: Imperial and Reading.

Professional qualification All ophthalmic opticians must register with the General Optical Council. To do so, they must have an approved degree, pass examinations set by the British College of Optometrists (ophthalmic opticians) and complete a year's experience under supervision. Over 6600 ophthalmic opticians are (1986) registered (against barely 5900 ten years earlier).

PHARMACOLOGY AND PHARMACY

Pharmacology studies the actions of all kinds of chemical and biological substances on living organisms, both the 'substances' used to treat diseases, and anything which can do damage to tissue, etc. Pharmacy is more applied – preparing and dispensing medicinal products, mainly drugs.

Pharmacy has to include pharmacology, but pharmacology does not normally include pharmacy, although it does extend to work on preparing new drugs, testing and developing them. Pharmacology also studies the ways the systems of the body (eg respiratory, nervous and blood), work, and the relation between the chemical structure of drugs and the way they affect body tissues.

'Drugs' grow steadily more complex and sophisticated, and pharmacology learns all the time from biochemists' and physiologists' work on cell, protein and genetic structures, making possible new ways of attacking disease. 'Drug' action generally interferes in some way with the body cells' communication systems, which operate via chemical substances, so that the most effective drugs intervene chemically. As more is learnt about the body's chemical-messenger system, so new drugs to block or stimulate messenger substances, can be developed. Equally, pharmaceutical research on the effects of particular substances can lead to the discovery of yet another chemical control system in the body. By the year 2000, pharmacologists predict that 40% of new, 'designer' drugs, genetically engineered, will be protein- and peptide-based.

Opportunities for pharmacologists and pharmacists

A degree in pharmacy qualifies for work as a pharmacist, a degree in pharmacology does *not*. Otherwise both pharmacology and pharmacy graduates are qualified to work in similar fields, although in practice close to 90% of working pharmacy graduates are in community/retail (nearly 74%) or hospital (nearly 16%) pharmacy work (1985 figures). But because so many more people qualify in pharmacy, that 'other' 10% virtually equals an entire year's output of pharmacologists, so a 'small' number of pharmacists may be equivalent to a 'large' group of pharmacologists.

Pharmacy work in both community/retail 'shops' and hospitals theoretically involves pharmacists in both preparing and supplying medicines and medical products from doctors' prescriptions. In practice, of course, most drugs are now prepared and pre-packaged by pharmaceutical companies, so there is little or no compounding to do. This does not, however, reduce or remove pharmacists' responsibility for making sure that the correct drugs are dispensed in the correct dosage. Most pharmacists also use their expertise to advise people on minor health problems. Beyond this, the work of the community/retail and hospital pharmacist does differ. See also HEALTH SERVICES and RETAILING.

In industry, PHARMACEUTICAL companies employ the largest group of pharmacologists, but only 5% of pharmacists – the figure is probably that low because pharmacists do not choose to work in industry and not due to any industry policy. The industry, indeed, has problems in recruiting high-calibre pharmacy graduates, and probably needs more of them, especially as licensing legislation is tightening.

Developing new and improved drugs mainly, but also some more-fundamental research, employs most pharmacologists, but relatively few pharmacists (possibly no more than 550 industry-wide), working in teams with other scientists. Product co-ordination (eg monitoring clinical trials, drug registration, and information) employs both groups (possibly around 300 pharmacists). Production itself, including developing new equipment, product support, controlling and supervising production and packaging, and quality assurance and control (with eg chemists) also employs both groups (perhaps 400 or so pharmacists).

MARKETING, SALES, ADVERTISING are 'technical' functions in pharmaceuticals, and so also employ pharmacists (perhaps about 300) and pharmacologists, as well as other life scientists, and people with medical qualifications.

Government employs both pharmacologists and, in very small numbers, pharmacists. Mostly they do research, working for eg, the chemical defence establishment, on compounds of high pharmacological activity, investigating synthetic routes and the relation between chemical structure and biological activity. Pharmacists also work for the health ministries, some in advisory capacities, and also for the Home Office, which include the forensic service. See also CIVIL SERVICE.

The NHS, in addition to the pharmacy service, employs pharmacists and pharmacologists in medical and physiological research, clinical trials etc (although some is done by pharmacists employed as such).

In higher education (universities, polytechnics, colleges) both pharmacologists and pharmacists (under 300 in pharmacy schools) combine teaching and research. See also EDUCATION.

Studying pharmacology and pharmacy

Both pharmacology and pharmacy courses generally start with a year of pure sciences – chemistry, physiology and some biology or biochemistry are the most usual, although some give a choice. Some pharmacology courses introduce pharmacology in the first year, but many leave it to the second. Some pharmacy courses also leave pharmacology and/or basic pharmacy until the second year.

Pharmacology courses, after the first year, continue basic sciences in the second, but increasingly they are biased to aspects relevant to pharmacology. Increasing time is spent on studying pharmacology in depth, and the final year is normally totally devoted to it – much of the year is usually spent on 'recent advances'. Pharmacology can also be studied with another subject, eg biochemistry, physiology, chemistry, or psychology.

Courses are at –

Universities – Aberdeen; Bath; Bradford: Bristol; Cambridge; Cardiff; Dundee; Edinburgh; Glasgow; Leeds; Liverpool; London: Chelsea, King's, School of Pharmacy, UCL; Manchester; Nottingham; Sheffield; Southampton; Strathclyde. Polytechnics – Portsmouth and Sunderland.

Entry requirements normally include A-level chemistry, and one or two other sciences; sciences not offered at A level should normally have been passed at 16-plus†.

'First destination' in pharmacology –

	1984-5 university	1977-8 university
total graduating	196	150
destination unknown	40	18
research, etc	58	63
training (incl teacher)	9	4

	1984-5 university	1977-8 university
'believed' unemployed Dec 31	13	6
permanent UK work	59	53
employers –		
chemical industry[1]	15	27
NHS/local government	12	9
higher/further ed	9	7
'other' industry	8	3
commerce	8	4
civil service	2	1
functions –		
scientific R&D	24	21
financial work	9	2
admin/op management	5	6
scientific support	5	7
medical/personnel/social	4	5

[1] includes pharmaceuticals

Postgraduate courses are mainly intended to give advanced training to graduates in related disciplines.

In pharmacy, the main body of the course generally covers pharmacognosy (studying crude drugs of plant and animal origin), pharmaceutical chemistry (the chemistry and analysis of naturally-occurring and synthetic substances used in medicine, including their structure and synthesis and the relation between chemical structure and biological action), pharmaceutics (how to formulate, prepare and test compounds for medical use) and chemotherapy. Basic sciences, like chemistry, continue. 'Professional practice' is taught, and options may prepare for work in, eg research on new drugs, quality control, etc.

The Nuffield Foundation report on pharmacy (1986) proposes some changes in degree courses, mainly by adding (more) pharmaceutical and behavioural sciences (dropping some basic science), bringing out the relevance of what is taught to later employment linked to vacation work experience, and giving greater attention to 'participatory' teaching (to improve communication skills) and problem solving. A new 'core' syllabus is proposed, breaking down the traditional groupings to make clearer the relations between subjects and how they are related to pharmacy practice.

Courses at –

Universities – Aston; Bath; Belfast; Bradford; Cardiff: UWIST; Glasgow: Strathclyde; London: KQC, School of Pharmacy; Manchester; Nottingham.

Polytechnics/colleges – Aberdeen: RGIT; Brighton, Leicester, Liverpool, Portsmouth, Sunderland.

Entry requirements normally include A-level chemistry, and one or two other sciences; sciences not offered at A level should normally have been passed at 16-plus†.

'First destination' in pharmacy –

	1984-5 university	polytechnic	1977-8 university	polytechnic
total graduating	706[1]	429	750	380
overseas students	7	5	18	3
destination unknown	39	17	21	28
research, etc	6	9	16	12
'believed' unemployed Dec 31	1	3	2	1
permanent UK work	641	393	667	320
employers –				
commerce[3]	304	271	239	233
NHS/local government	272	121	286	89
chemicals[2]	38	38	86	9
functions –				
medical services	636	371	657	319
scientific R&D	2	5	4	6
financial work	1	2	nil	nil

[1] down from 775 in 1982-3   [2] includes pharmaceuticals   [3] includes retail pharmacies

Qualifying in pharmacy Pharmacy graduates who wish to practise in either retail or hospital pharmacies must be registered pharmaceutical chemists and members of the Pharmaceutical Society of Great Britain (with 33,000 members as of 1986, including pharmacists working in industry and academic institutions).

Pharmacists must also gain a year's experience pre-registration. At present half has to be in hospital or community/retail pharmacy, the other half may be in industry, pharmacy school, or agricultural, veterinary pharmacy. In practice, over 54% spend the full year in retail/community pharmacy (nearly 55% of them in the major chain), and almost 40% in hospital pharmacy. Changes to the pre-registration year, proposed by the Nuffield Foundation Report (1986) are being discussed.

Postgraduate courses are mainly intended to give advanced training to graduates in related disciplines.

Technician-level qualification is now via BTEC National and Higher National Certificates in Science (pharmaceutical). Entry is as for all BTEC National/ Higher National awards††; qualifying exams taken should include appropriate sciences.

At present no formal route through from technician to professional qualification exists, but the Nuffield Report recommends making it easier to progress.

Further information from the Pharmaceutical Society of Great Britain.

PHYSICS

Physics, according to the dictionary, is the study of the properties of matter and energy. This is a very short definition for a subject which ranges so widely over the physical world, and tries to identify the laws which dictate the way it works, and how it is put together. It takes in space, time, motion, electricity, radiation, magnetism, heat, optics, sound, and mechanics. It studies the atom, and so extends from the level of invisible elementary and sub-nuclear and antiparticles right out to the entire universe. It takes in the most abstract of concepts, such as relativity, and the most practical, such as radiotherapy.

And so one physicist can be a very different kind of scientist from another. Some are theoretical physicists, for example, who use maths, logical thinking and intuition – even guesswork – to come up with possible new physical laws. Others spend all their time at the lab bench or the bubble chamber trying to prove the theoreticians right or wrong, and yet others find and develop applications of physics.

Despite the huge body of knowledge that physics has already accumulated, it is still developing new ideas and producing results, refining and revising theories in the light of new experimental data, and vice versa. The 'spin-off' from research in physics is phenomenal, and however theoretical the work may seem, it will inevitably have applications somewhere. Much of engineering depends on the laws of classical physics. Nuclear physics has applications not only in new ways of making energy, but also, very widely in medicine and engineering too. Low-temperature physics is the basis of a whole industry – cryogenics – which makes, for example, liquid helium for rocket fuels, and is also used in surgery. It is work in solid-state physics which results in so many more uses for electronics, and in the silicon chip – and is still producing results of enormous value. Optical electronics has already produced the optical fibres now replacing copper cables in telephone transmission systems and is now producing many more integrated optical devices to replace electronic circuits for many purposes. The possibilities of lasers are equally extensive.

The laws of physics, physicists' research techniques and equipment are now also used in research in many other areas, from materials science and the biological sciences, to geology and archaeology. Co-operation between physicists and other scientists has resulted in whole new areas of study with 'names' of their own, like chemical physics, biophysics and geophysics. Astrophysics investigates the physical laws of the universe, out in space with the astronomers (see ASTRONOMY).

Opportunities for physicists

There are probably around 30,000 physicists in the UK. Of these, just under a third are believed to work in industry, just under 40% in education (half in higher/further education, half in schools), and about a fifth in the public sector, including the Civil Service, the UKAEA (which alone employs some 400), the NHS and other research organisations.

Industry is, reportedly, taking increasing numbers. A high proportion of physics graduates begin their careers in research and development, many of them in industry. While there is no 'physical' industry is the same sense as there is a 'chemical' industry, in many industrial sectors products depend on applications of physics, and at present, especially in electronics where the most-commonly predicted growth area is optoelectronics, developing new semiconductor materials, devices and communication systems.

The range of work in which physicists are involved is extremely wide. Industry is, obviously, most interested in developing new products, so R&D is largely directed to this, but because fundamental research by physicists so often results in major practical developments, firms do get involved to some extent in carefully-chosen speculative research.

In electronics, for example, where the industry is developing the fruits of some very advanced research indeed (so even turning this into real products can be scientifically demanding), physicists work in multi-disciplinary teams, with eg electronic engineers, on (for instance), new solid-state infra-red lasers for range-finder systems, on the next generation of semiconductor devices, and on improving production methods to meet the technical demands of new processes in making semiconductors.

In telecommunications (both manufacturing and BT), now rapidly becoming all electronic, physicists work on developing automatic switching systems and optical-fibre networks. One group works on methods for producing – growing – specialised compound semi-conductors from which are made the lasers and photo-diodes that make up the transmitters and receivers for fibre-optic communication links.

In heavier engineering, physicists do experimental work with mechanical engineers on turbine aerodynamics, on vibration and stress problems, and develop testing techniques. Physicists work on developing, for instance, new designs of circuit breakers for the electricity boards.

In the chemical industry, physicists work with chemists and biologists on designing new measuring techniques, and with engineers and polymer chemists on developing improved methods to make, for instance, coated films. They work with instrument engineers and computer scientists to improve process control systems for chemical plant.

They may do basic studies on materials – eg fatigue studies on polymers, or in economic method for strengthening yarn fibres, or try to solve specific problems, overcoming technological problems which prevent advance in a particular field. They also study and measure such things as wear, investigate problems of noise (for example, in aircraft engines), and are generally involved in the design, construction and application of mechanical, optical and electronic instruments.

Particularly in industrial research, physicists generally develop expertise in the field in which they are working, and their original degree subject steadily becomes more irrelevant to their future careers.

Government is a major employer of physicists (although taking fewer than in the 1970s), in over 50 research units. These include –

The National Physical Laboratory, which specialises in measurement and, eg is developing super-conducting quantum devices to monitor electrical quantities, research into holographic methods of measuring exposure to potentially-harmful radiation. The Lab is making balloon-borne spectroscopic experiments for atmospheric analysis, and evaluating propagation of noise and its effects on human hearing.

Warren Spring Laboratory specialises in industrial and environmental research, with work on, for example, physical methods of mineral concentration, control of industrial processes, measuring and abating atmospheric pollution.

Weapons-research establishments – atomic (eg reproducing under lab conditions unusual states generated by a nuclear explosion and production of high temperatures and densities by high-energy lasers), surface weapons for the Navy (sophisticated surveillance, tracking and navigation radars and electro-optics) and underwater (eg acoustic research), gas turbines, etc.

United Kingdom Atomic Energy Authority, which does research both for the nuclear power programme and for industry.

See also CENTRAL GOVERNMENT and MANUFACTURING.

The Meteorological Office both employs physicists in atmospheric research and trains them in METEOROLOGY.

The medical and health sector employs significant numbers of physicists. All NHS radiation-protection advisers are physicists, and they also work on developing electronic aids and instruments for diagnosis and treatment.

See HEALTH SERVICES, and BIOMEDICAL ENGINEERING.

Education There is at present (1986) a chronic, and growing, shortage of physics teachers in schools. Opportunities in higher education – to lecture and/or do research – are down sharply, and likely to fall further as SERC cuts expenditure on expensive nuclear physics research.

See also EDUCATIONAL SERVICES.

Studying physics

Physics is studied mainly at degree level, although there are courses at higher-technician level too.

First-degree courses are available at almost all universities and most poly-technics offer degree courses, although two universities (Aston and Bradford) have recently closed theirs, for lack of applicants.

Because physics is such a vast subject, almost all courses try to give the widest possible picture, starting with and concentrating on fundamental principles, and going on to more advanced theories and experimental work. Courses go through more advanced studies of 'classical' physics – eg mechanics, electricity and magnetism, structure and properties of matter, vibrations and waves, thermodynamics. They may also start early on areas of 'modern' physics, such as relativity, quantum mechanics, nuclear and atomic or particle physics, optics, and solid state, and will also cover eg thermal physics, electromagnetism. But because there is always something new happening in physics research, most courses also respond quickly to the latest advances, giving graduates at least a glimpse of current research – usually in the final year.

Because there is so much to cover, there are not usually quite so many choices as in some other subjects before the final year, but a chance to specialise to some extent may be given, perhaps in theoretical or experimental aspects, or to pick out a variety of topics. Other choices can include atomic physics, astrophysics, theoretical physics, solid state; the physics of materials, or of the atmosphere, oceans, and solid earth; applied and practical aspects such as health or medical physics, radiation physics, acoustics, optics, etc.

Some give the chance to study physics in relation to another science, eg biophysics or geophysics, or to study advanced spectroscopy or instrument design. Some courses allow earlier specialisation in physical electronics, which deals more with the scientific principles of electronics and with developing new devices than electronic engineering, and which at some places can be studied with microcomputer electronics. Physics may be studied 'with' a linked subject, eg laser technology, computing, or management science.

Some courses are called applied physics, concentrating on this in the later years of the course, and even including an industrial training period. Generally, applied physics courses start with the same basic as a 'normal' physics course, but move on to more technological aspects – options may include eg vacuum technology, applied solid-state, microprocessors, macromolecules, applied acoustics, x-ray diffraction, and nuclear technology, energy in nature, human uses of energy, reactor physics, instrument physics, corrosion science, medical physics, computers in the lab, acoustics, optics.

Students are also thoroughly trained in the 'language' of physics, which means learning to use sophisticated mathematical methods, thinking and analysing mathematically. Most physics research nowadays uses computers, and students learn to use them, to process data for the computer, and interpret what comes out. Obviously, a great deal of time is spent in labs, learning the full range of modern experimental techniques, and ending in the final year with a small experimental project.

'First destination' in physics –

| | 1984-5 | | 1977-8 | |
	university	polytechnic	university	polytechnic
total graduating	2444[1]	123	1862	43
overseas students	32	2	23	nil
destination unknown	230	10	143	4
research, etc	557	15	496	9
teacher training	115	5	100	1
'other' training	52	2	21	nil
'believed' unemployed 31 Dec	198	17	72	1
temporary work	30	1	60	nil
permanent UK work	1127	67	893	28
employers –				
engineering industry	454	39	446	19
commerce (excl accountancy)	165	4	48	1
public utilities	105	5	60	1
accountancy	89	nil	52	nil
chemicals	70	3	60	2
civil service	65	2	31	nil
'other' manufacturing	43	4	28	1
NHS/local government	34	2	27	1
higher/further education	25	3	12	1
functions –				
scientific/eng R&D	561	47	458	1
management services	195	8	138	nil
financial work	114	nil	76	nil
admin/operations management	64	1	89	1
scientific/eng support	50	7	65	7

| | 1984-5 | | 1977-8 | |
	university	polytechnic	university	polytechnic
marketing etc	36	1	20	nil
medical/personnel/social	22	1	nil	nil
teaching/lecturing	9	12	11	1

[1] down from peak of 2521 in 1983-4

Entry normally requires three science A levels (but universities may accept two AS levels in place of one, polytechnics two A levels, a mix of A and AS levels, or all AS levels), normally including physics and maths. Over 2500 students were accepted for university courses in 1985, under 500 for CNAA courses. The mean A-level 'score' for 1984 university entry was 11.6.

Professional qualification The Institute of Physics (1986 membership almost 13,600) requires four to five years' (depending on degree class) appropriate postgraduate experience for full membership. The Institute has withdrawn its graduateship examination.

Postgraduate study Most courses in physics are specialised, for example, in medical physics, principles of instrument design, and semi-conductor physics and technology. Physics graduates can also qualify by postgraduate study in another discipline – astronomy, astrophysics, geophysics, engineering, for instance.

Technician-level qualification is via BTEC or SCOTVEC awards.

BTEC Higher awards will be revised in line with the new framework. Schemes are now all to be called Science (Physical science) or (Physics) but are designed individually by the polytechnic or college, so there is at present no 'standard' scheme, and a wide range of different options.

Courses are available at –

Science (physical science) HND (full-time only): university – Ulster; polytechnics – Bristol, London: S Bank, Manchester, Stoke: N Staffs;

Science (physics) HND (full-time only): polytechnics – Coventry: Lanchester, Kingston, London: Middx, Stoke: N Staffs; colleges – Bournemouth: Dorset IHE, Farnborough CT.

Entry as for all BTEC Higher awards††; with school-leaving qualifications, physics and maths studied to A level and a pass in one.

Only 47 people gained physics HNDs from polytechnics in 1984-5 (against 63 in 1980-1). Thirteen (against eight) went on to a first-degree courses, and one (six) to complete a professional qualification. Twenty (against 21) found permanent work. Nine (against sixteen) went into the engineering industry, five into 'other' industries, and one into the NHS. Nine gained R&D posts, four jobs in scientific support services, two in marketing.

Further information from the Institute of Physics (booklets).

VETERINARY SCIENCE

Caring for animals – preventing and treating diseases, treating injuries – is the most obvious purpose of veterinary science. However, veterinary scientists also look for ways of improving conditions for animals, and work with other scientists to develop more efficient methods of animal husbandry and stock-breeding.

Opportunities for veterinary scientists

Of some 11,000 veterinary surgeons on the RCVS register (an increase of only a few hundred over the last twenty years), under 8000 practice in the UK. Three quarters work in private practice, a high proportion looking after 'small animals' (ie pets) including almost all the vets who work in towns. If they work in the country they may look after pets too, but most of their 'patients' are farmed animals – which can include even fish. In some areas practices may have to specialise – in looking after (race) horses in the Newmarket area, for example. Three animal-welfare organisations also have their own clinics and hospitals, and employ some 200 vets.

On the farm, as much time is spent trying to prevent disease – through regular testing and inoculations – as in curing it, and in helping to 'manage' the animal stock, keeping them healthy and productive, checking on possible health reasons for failure to put on flesh or lay eggs, for example. Modern vets may have efficient, modern drugs to use, and scientific equipment. Farms may be cleaner and more hygienic than in the past, but animals still give birth or become ill at the most inconvenient times, the work can still be extremely messy, and animals still tend to bite or kick anyone trying to help them. Hours can be long and irregular in all practices.

Several hundred vets work for the Ministry of Agriculture, where they deal with government regulations and schemes to control and improve health standards for farm animals. Government vets run schemes designed to prevent and control notifiable diseases (eg foot-and-mouth disease in cattle), tuberculin test cattle, campaign to get rid of warble fly, inspect animals both on the land and in markets. In the Veterinary Investigation Service, veterinary surgeons work in the laboratory on the causes of diseases, identifying them from the carcasses and organs sent in by other vets. They do field investigations into outbreaks of disease among farm animals, advise on treatment and decide what needs to be done to prevent outbreaks spreading. They also monitor disease, providing information, advice etc for farmers.

Some 10% of veterinary scientists work in research, in universities (where they also teach), government-financed research establishments, and in firms in industries linked to farming, such as feedstuff manufacturers, drug companies, and firms making equipment used to feed animals and poultry kept indoors and control their environment. Research in university veterinary science schools is mostly on the clinical side, with some work on, for example, parasitology and pathology. But veterinarians also work on teams doing research in animal husbandry in agriculture departments, where research is more usually in areas like genetics linked to improving breeds (eg for meat production), or on better methods of nutrition, as well as in control parasite and basic animal physiology. Government-supported institutions include the Animal Health Laboratories where, as well as research and laboratory investigations, some biological products are made, for example, tuberculin and S19 vaccine to control brucellosis; these Laboratories also house the cattle breeding centre. The Agricultural Research Council supports a number of units too.

Many veterinarians are needed overseas. Small numbers are employed full time by horse breeders and racing stables, zoos and safari parks, and the Army.

Qualification and courses at first-degree level.
Courses last five years. The first two years cover basic sciences, such as

biology, chemistry, anatomy, physiology, pathology and biochemistry, with some genetics and microbiology. The final years concentrate on veterinary science, medicine and surgery with integrated studies in animal husbandry, pharmacology, public health etc.

Only six schools (approx 350 places: about 3 applications per place), at – Universities – Bristol, Cambridge, Edinburgh, Glasgow, Liverpool, London (Royal Veterinary College).

To practise as a a veterinary surgeon, graduates must register with the Royal College of Veterinary Surgeons.

Entry requirements are three science GCE A levels, to include biology and usually physics and chemistry (mean A-level/H-grade grade 'score' 14.2 for 84 entry). Prospective vets not only need the intelligence to study at an advanced level, but personal qualities which include an interest in and an intelligent concern for animals, and the ability to gain the confidence of both owners and animals.

Further information from the Royal College of Veterinary Surgeons.

QUALIFICATIONS AND CAREERS IN SOCIAL SCIENCES

Introduction	294
Anthropology	298
Applied social sciences	299
Business and management studies	300
Economics	308
Education	312
Home economics	313
Law	315
Politics/political science	320
Psychology	323
Sociology	330

INTRODUCTION

The social sciences study people, and how they behave, as individuals, to each other, and in groups. Social 'scientists' study how people live alongside and 'interact' with each other, as members of families, communities and other organisations; how they earn a living and decide how to spend the money they earn; what rules they use to govern their communities; how and why societies and communities change. They try to describe as accurately as possible what happens inside communities and the complicated network of relationships between the people who make up those communities. They also attempt to draw conclusions from their findings.

The social sciences are relatively new disciplines, and still somewhat controversial. Some people still think that the scientific study of something so unpredictable as human behaviour and forms of social organisation is impossible. Yet people from the ancient Greeks onwards have thought and written about human behaviour and ways of organising societies.

More systematic studies of income and wealth – the beginnings of economics – started in the 18th century, as did the statistical study of populations, without which it is impossible to study any other aspects of society. The foundations of political science, psychology, and sociology, were laid in the 19th century. However, it was not until world war II that psychologists, economists, and sociologists were able to show that their studies were accurate and could be useful – in providing, for instance, the basis on which to decide how to distribute scarce food and clothing through rationing; how to test recruits to the armed forces to see which jobs suited their capabilities best; to find ways of keeping up morale, and devise propaganda and counter-propaganda techniques.

The social sciences attribute their academic 'respectability' partly to this, partly to the importance of understanding more about large modern industrialised societies as they grow more complex and have more difficult social problems to solve, and partly to the fact that social scientists have adopted rigorous methods of observation and analysis from the sciences. They follow the same strict rules as scientists in collecting data and applying highly sophisticated and refined statistical and mathematical methods to analysing it, building mathematical models to test theories. Obviously, though, social scientists can only go so far in using the scientist's controlled experiments – it just is not possible to dissect human society on the lab bench. Instead, social scientists use techniques not available to 'pure' scientists – they interview and survey their human subjects, and so claim an advantage over the scientist, who can hardly expect atoms or molecules to answer questionnaires. Social scientists also use comparative techniques – comparing aspects of two, or several, societies to see if there is any similarity or difference and, by isolating the points of comparison, testing possible generalisations against different sets of evidence.

Even so, there are still many arguments about the validity of the social sciences – whether 'society' is a living organism like a microbe, and can be studied in the same way; whether it is possible for social scientists to establish 'laws' about the behaviour of society in the same way that physicists can establish 'laws' of behaviour for the physical world; whether it is possible to 'measure' accurately the information based on what people say to interviewers, and whether they even tell the 'truth'.

Although it is common to refer to them as social scientists, in fact people working in this field are generally economists, psychologists, sociologists and political scientists. These subjects developed more or less independently, and are not 'branches' of a 'tree' called social science. Indeed, it is only quite recently that this 'umbrella' term has been in general use, although it is commonly accepted that it is impossible to study society as, say, a sociologist, without being familiar with the work being done in psychology, economics, or politics.

The social sciences developed and expanded at an almost explosive rate up to the mid-1970s. Although expansion has more or less ended, a large and significant range of disciplines and courses exists.

The social sciences have taken proportionately higher cuts in government expenditure on research (and on teaching in higher education) than sciences, except where it is of 'practical' value, and so the number of openings for research and teaching has also fallen substantially. The Economic and Social

Research Council (ESRC), with less to spend annually now than in 1974, is concentrating on research which –

analyses and explains the major social and economic changes in the UK in the 1970s and 1980s;

provides theoretical frameworks which increase understanding of what is happening;

improves and develops research methods and techniques which can be applied to these problems.

Up to two-thirds of all ESRC 1986-91 funding will focus on change. The main initiatives are – functioning of markets; economic life and social change; young people in society; changing urban and regional systems; structure of public expenditure and revenue; impact and economic, social and managerial implications of information and communication technologies; adult and continuing education; information technology in education; transport needs, provision and management; the countryside; competitiveness of British industry; government and industry relations; policy for science and technology; new technology in industry; management, efficiency and organisational design in government; and race relations.

The Council also expects to develop research in, for example, cognitive science needed in developing advanced information technology; cost-benefit analysis as an aid to efficient choice; social consequences of high unemployment; drug addiction; mass communications and the implications of increased information; risk perception and its implications for policy making; social effects of rising material expectations if not matched by economic growth; international debt problem; multicultural education.

People with degrees in some disciplines, psychology and economics (for example), may be recruited for their specific academic skills by other employers, but in general people with social science degrees will not normally find work related to their disciplines.

There is some strength in the argument that a social science degree may provide some insight into the workings of society and the real world which is possibly a better preparation for some areas of employment than (say) an arts degree – trainee journalists, it has been suggested, are better off with a degree in economics or politics than history or English. Social scientists are, theoretically at least, rather more numerate than arts graduates, but social science degrees generally have to be treated as an intellectual training, not a strictly vocational preparation.

Studying social sciences The social sciences are mainly studied at university, in polytechnic or as 'background' studies in further education, although some are also taught in many schools (see preceding chapter).

The range and variety of social science degree courses is quite considerable, and students have a very flexible choice of subjects and of the depth to which they can be studied. It is possible to combine social science subjects with many others, including more vocationally-orientated professional studies (such as computer science or business studies) which may help them in preparing for careers in these areas.

Most universities and polytechnics recognise that many students starting social science degrees do not know very much about the subject or subjects they are going to study. Therefore, whatever subject or subjects students eventually choose for specialisation, the first year, or even two, of many courses is devoted to a broad general introduction to the social sciences in all their variety, emphasising common principles and methods, and demonstrating the overlapping territory between the individual disciplines. Courses of this type give students more time to discover which of the social sciences interest them most, and so make it possible to make a better choice of the one (or two) in which to specialise on a sounder understanding of what each social science involves.

Degree schemes beginning with broadly-based introductory courses at –
Universities – Aberystwyth, Belfast, Birmingham, Bradford, Brighton: Sussex, Canterbury: Kent, Cardiff, Chelmsford: Essex, City, Dundee, Edinburgh, Glasgow, Leicester, Liverpool, London: LSE, Manchester, Newcastle, Norwich: E Anglia, Reading, Salford, Sheffield, Swansea, Ulster.
Polytechnics – Bristol, Hatfield, Kingston, Liverpool, London: Middx, PCL, S Bank, Manchester, Middlesbrough: Teesside, Nottingham: Trent, Oxford, Sheffield, Wolverhampton. Colleges – Glasgow CT, Hull: Humberside CHE.
Examples of other broadly based courses include –
Cambridge: social and political sciences, with a wide range of choices, normally taken after a year or two spent studying another subject.
Oxford (and Keele), link philosophy, politics and economics (PPE) and allow students to choose two of these in the later part of the course.
At Brunel, government, politics and history are taught together.
'Human' science courses which integrate biological and social sciences at, eg London: UCL and Oxford.

'First destination' in social, administrative and business studies –

| | 1984-5 | | 1977-8 | |
	university	polytechnic	university	polytechnic
total graduating	18475	9207	16900	5200
destination unknown	2153	1750	1900	1300
research etc	1068	310	1360	250
teacher training	598	164	1200	200
law exams	2330	784	1142	8
other training	765	236	1001	85
'believed' unemployed Dec 31	1512	894	800	300
temporary work	585	457	1084	
permanent UK work	7939	4109	7158	1800
employers –				
accountancy	2052	438	1780	231
local government	1016	471	1330	450
banking/insurance	977	153	429	68
civil service	443	175	280	84
engineering	405	90	343	127
'other' manufacturing	383	81	249	72
oil & chemicals	201	36	200	2
higher/further ed	174	71	126	
armed forces	123	23	65	16

	1984-5		1977-8	
	university	polytechnic	university	polytechnic
construction	52	72	44	19
functions –				
financial work	3240	1288	2580	520
admin/operations management	1119	684	800	255
personnel/social etc	1053	506	880	265
marketing etc	829	1023	793	280
management services	383	153	300	73
research/information	170	47	210	21
legal work	84	38	974	55

Entry requirements: universities and polytechnics very rarely require social sciences at O or A level for entry to social science degree courses. In fact, some admission tutors prefer candidates to have a solid grounding in subjects such as mathematics, history and English rather than any inevitably simple introduction to social sciences. However, A-level social science can be quite useful for students who plan to go directly into vocational training, since they may give some examination exemptions.

ANTHROPOLOGY

Anthropologists study human cultural, social and biological development and adaptation from the earliest, primitive times up to today. Anthropology grew from an 18th-century interest in human origins and the differences between races, first noticed by European explorers. After Darwin, it developed as the study of human social, psychological and physical evolution, but in a rather fossilised way. Social, or cultural anthropology emerged in the 1920s, studying primitive peoples as living and growing societies, not just as accidental survivors of prehistoric times.

Archaeology and linguistics have since developed as studies in their own right (although they still have very close links, and anthropologists are again making a major contribution to archaeological research). This leaves social anthropology, and physical anthropology (which still studies human origins and evolution, heredity, the relation between primates and humans, and the differences between races), and the study of how human tool-making and technology developed. Some anthropologists include ecology, studying the relationship between people and their environment, and how they exploit it. Some scholars even treat social anthropology as a branch of sociology, teaching the two together.

Anthropologists do study modern societies – for example, one researcher has examined the organisational development of Japanese factories and their relation to Japanese society. Most, though, study societies which are very different from modern, industrialised ones – Pacific Island tribes, peasant societies in remoter parts of Europe and around the Mediterranean, Eskimos, Amerindians, South East Asian civilisations. Anthropologists do not just study, for instance, the meaning of myths or witchcraft, but also why and how they are important to the tribe involved.

Anthropologists draw conclusions from their findings, especially as they compile more detailed, statistical records, and make comparisons between different communities and cultures.

A major area of study is change, and the social and economic problems of adapting to the modern world, particularly for less sophisticated communities

– what happens to tribes when major highways are driven through the forests of South America; or to nomadic peoples when they have to settle in one place.

Opportunities for anthropologists

Anthropology is largely an academic career, combining research with teaching. Studying non-industrialised societies normally means spending long periods – possibly years – living with and among the people being studied, learning the language, and gaining the people's trust and friendship, since this is usually the only way to find out about their customs, etc. Once home, anthropologists write up their findings, and analyse them. Some government and international bodies employ anthropologists as advisers, but more usually they hire anthropologists working in universities as consultants, or contribute to their research funds. Many anthropologists seem able to produce both very scholarly works on their research and popular books on their lives amongst unusual peoples. It is a very small profession, and very dependent on public funds.

Studying anthropology Anthropology is studied mainly on first degree courses, and for higher degrees. Courses mostly concentrating on social and cultural aspects, is taught for a first degree at –
Universities: Belfast; Brighton: Sussex; Cambridge (linked with archaeology)[2] ; Canterbury: Kent; Durham[2] ; Edinburgh; Hull[1] ; London: LSE, SOAS, UC[2] ; Manchester; Stirling[1] ; Swansea.
[1] social anthropology integrated with sociology [2] also physical anthropology.

Postgraduate courses: at most of these universities (but not Hull) and at Oxford.

Further information from the Royal Anthropological Society.

APPLIED SOCIAL SCIENCES (including social administration)
While many students who read social sciences, particularly sociology, at university or polytechnic, intend to work somewhere in the field of the social services, their degree courses do not give the necessary training. However, one group of courses does deal more directly with social administration than, for example, courses in sociology. Since they take a very broad view of the social services and the disciplines used in developing them, they can prepare graduates for such careers, while still giving a broad enough education to allow them to opt for something different.

Social administration studies the human problems which can be dealt with by social work agencies. It examines the methods of solving such problems, and tries to analyse the causes, relating the problems to their wider social setting. This usually involves studying the disciplines which are designed to explain society and its mechanisms, as they impinge upon social problems. This type of course also gives a much wider view of social problems and their solution than would be the case otherwise – for example, through comparative studies of social service systems in other countries, and through the study of social policy, which relates the social services to the political and economic theories and practices on which they are based.

While graduates in social administration may still have to take further training and practical experience to become social workers (see SOCIAL SERVICES), these courses are also a preparation for research and teaching, more general administrative work, careers in local and central government, and personnel work in industry and commerce.

First-degree courses in social administration or applied social studies at –
Universities – Bangor, Bath, Birmingham, Bradford, Brighton: Sussex, Bristol, Canterbury: Kent, Cardiff, Dundee, Edinburgh, Exeter, Hull, Keele, Lancaster, Leeds, London: LSE, RHB, Manchester, Newcastle, Nottingham, Southampton, Stirling, Swansea, Ulster, Warwick, York.
Polytechnic – most degree courses in social sciences and sociology are to some extent biased to empirical studies. Courses specifically devoted to applied social science are at: Coventry, Hatfield, Leeds, London: Middx, NELP, NLP, Nottingham: Trent, Plymouth, Portsmouth, Preston: Lancs, Sheffield; colleges – Paisley CT.

Postgraduate courses include diploma courses intended to provide a professional qualification in social work (see under SOCIAL SERVICES), and postgraduate, post-experience advanced courses such as that in methods in applied social research at Essex University. In between is a range of courses aimed at providing higher degrees in social administration for graduates in other, but normally related, disciplines. Some of these are also recognised professional qualifications, but many are intended primarily as preparation for research or social policy administration.
See also SOCIAL SERVICES

BUSINESS AND MANAGEMENT STUDIES
'Academic' courses – degree and postgraduate – in business/management studies have been fully established for over twenty years now (and some universities had 'commerce' degrees well before that). Yet there are still many arguments about exactly how valuable they are, and they are still not as generally accepted by employers as perhaps might be expected.

The problems faced by firms of all kinds, the increasing complexity of the business world, the rapid changes, the intensified competition, and so on, appear to demand more expert and sophisticated business and managerial skills on the commercial and financial side of business, as well as in design and production. However, some still think the necessary skills, particularly for management, are best taught 'on-the-job' with integrated, preferably short, training courses.

Some firms still prefer to recruit their future managers from amongst graduates who have gone through the most rigorous intellectual training possible at university, consider this is best done through traditional and conventional courses in subjects like history, English, and Classics, and are not fully convinced that business studies courses are, for this purpose, sufficiently academically rigorous enough. Firms recruiting graduates for non-technical management training make certain assumptions about graduates' intellectual ability and achievement, and tend to be more concerned with their personal qualities rather than the subject they have read. They look for graduates who are well motivated, can work with other people and are potential leaders, who can think and act independently, solve problems, take on responsibility quickly, and so on. To be acceptable to prospective employers, graduates in business studies need these qualities too.

Nevertheless, a significant proportion of employers do see a business studies degree as an advantage, enough to ensure that business studies graduates have fewer problems in finding a first job than graduates in many other subjects. Such employers recognise that graduates in business studies have already tested their motivation to work in industry or commerce. What a degree in business studies may lack in high academic content should be counterbalanced by a realistic knowledge of what happens, and how, in the business world. Business studies graduates will normally understand the language of business before they start work, will know how to apply statistical and other management techniques, what kinds of problems may be met, how to work with other people, and so on. They are less likely to be against profit as a motive. Most business studies graduates, at least those who have studied at polytechnic or 'technological' university, will have had lengthy work experience as part of their sandwich-based courses.

First-degree courses in business studies generally give a broader base than can be gained by studying for a single professional qualification. They provide a foundation in the principles and techniques of modern business and management and the directions in which they are developing, training in one or more specialised aspects of business studies or management, contact with the business world (ideally via more forward-thinking concerns), and training in the sources and uses of information, and methods of investigation.

Courses mostly start with a firm basis of economic principles, the human and behavioural sciences such as sociology and psychology (generally emphasising the 'organisational' aspects relevant to industry and commerce), mathematics and statistics to an appropriate level, computing and relevant aspects of law. Most also put some emphasis on finance and/or accounting, but to varying levels. The first year may also include the opportunity to spend some time on a subject outside the business field, or to add a useful skill like languages.

Courses generally continue with a core of training in the skills needed in running any business to decide on and achieve set objectives, policy and decision making, developing systems and analysing information, generally covering also the setting in which business has to operate. Some continue the broad approach, teaching everyone functional skills like accounting, marketing, manpower and personnel management. Some give students the chance to specialise in some depth in one of these, or in (say) the management service skills like operational research. On other courses, students can choose a middle route and study to a fairly advanced level two subjects – accounting and systems analysis, or marketing and personnel.

Polytechnic courses are usually more directly vocational than those of most universities, and are normally sandwich based (most university and polytechnic courses, though, give graduates some exemptions from professional qualifications). Sandwich courses give students a full year (or the equivalent in two or more shorter periods) of training in the business world. Quite a few firms sponsor students for business studies courses.

Business studies are not taught just by conventional lectures and seminars. They usually also involve extensive project-based work, case studies, problem solving, business games and other simulations of the real business world.

Broadly-based business studies (in universities: may be called management sciences, or commerce), some including the option to specialise, are at – Universities – Bath, Birmingham, Bradford, Cambridge (after another subject), Cardiff: UC, UWIST, Dundee, Edinburgh, Edinburgh: Heriot-Watt, Kent, Liverpool, London: City, London U: LSE, Loughborough, Manchester: UMIST, Newcastle, St Andrews, Salford, Sheffield, Stirling, Ulster, Warwick; polytechnics – all 30; colleges – Aberdeen: RGIT, Bournemouth Dorset IHE, Dundee CT, Ealing CHE, Edinburgh: Napier, Glasgow CT, Hull: Humberside CHE, Paisley CT, Swansea: W Glam IHE.

More specialised courses include –
Accountancy: degree courses give students a broader base in business and financial studies and deal with advanced aspects of financial management. Courses are at –
Universities – Aberystwyth, Bangor, Birmingham, Canterbury: Kent, Cardiff: UC, Chelmsford: Essex, Dundee, Edinburgh: Heriot Watt, Exeter, Glasgow, Glasgow: Strathclyde, Hull, Lancaster, Liverpool, London U: LSE, Loughborough, Manchester, Newcastle, Norwich: E Anglia, Salford, Sheffield, Southampton, Stirling, Ulster; polytechnics – Birmingham, Brighton, Bristol, Huddersfield, Kingston, Leeds, Liverpool, London: City, Middx, NELP, NLP, Manchester, Newcastle, Nottingham: Trent, Oxford, Plymouth, Portsmouth, Preston: Lancs, Sheffield, Wales; colleges – Dundee CT, Ealing CHE, Edinburgh: Napier, Hull: Humberside CHE.

Banking and finance now a number of specialist courses, but also options in some of above general business studies courses –
Universities – Bangor, Birmingham, Cardiff: UWIST, Heriot Watt, London: City, Loughborough, Ulster; polytechnic – London: City; college: Bournemouth: Dorset IHE.

Business information systems/technology specialist courses slow to develop (but increasingly an option in general business studies), so only at –
Universities – Glasgow: Strathclyde, Norwich: E Anglia; polytechnics – Kingston, Preston: Lancs; colleges – Hull: Humberside CHE.

European business studies courses, training for careers in Britain and Europe, and including languages, have developed in some numbers. Courses come in two forms:
Some courses 'integrate' business studies and language(s), and students study for part of the time at a business school in Europe, sometimes gaining dual qualification, some providing work experience abroad also. These are at –
Universities – Birmingham: Aston, Bath, Bradford, Canterbury: Kent, Edinburgh: H-Watt, Swansea, Ulster; polytechnics – Leeds (specialising in finance), London: Middx, Nottingham: Trent; colleges – High Wycombe: Bucks CHE, Hull: Humberside CHE; other – London: EBS (private school diploma).

Others teach business/management studies and language(s) separately, and the period abroad is generally similar to a conventional language degree.

These are at –
Universities – Bangor (banking/finance), Belfast, Birmingham, Canterbury: Kent (accountancy), Durham (Chinese), Edinburgh (French, German or Spanish), Glasgow: Strathclyde, Lancaster (accountancy), Leeds, Sheffield (Japanese), Stirling, Swansea (two from French, German, Italian, Russian, Spanish, Welsh), Warwick (German).

Marketing can be studied for a degree in its own right (although it can be a specialisation in many of the above general business studies courses) at –
Universities – Glasgow: Strathclyde. Lancaster, Stirling; Polytechnics – Huddersfield (engineering or textile), London: City, and Thames (international).

'First employment' figures are –

	1984-5		1977-8	
	university	polytechnic	university	polytechnic
total graduating	1432	2503	788	1150
destination unknown	107	397	53	267
research etc	40	31	31	32
teacher training	5	11	11	3
other training	45	18	18	11
'believed' unemployed Dec 31	76	148	26	39
temporary work	22	95	37	42
permanent UK work	1018	1596	525	701
employers –				
accountancy	182	108	175	61
commerce (excl finance)	178	429	57	172
engineering	140	257	104	165
'other' manufacturing	112	166	61	86
banking/insurance	103	114	54	33
public utilities	73	122	24	35
local government	64	95	17	49
oil & chemicals	43	85	32	36
construction	16	77	2	12
civil service	42	54	4	28
higher/further ed	9	12	4	1
functions –				
financial work	313	432	252	210
marketing etc	273	545	121	209
admin/ops management	218	322	68	144
management services	98	98	52	36
personnel/social etc	54	22	20	41
'First employment' in accountancy –				
total graduating	1032	877	747	249
destination unknown	57	136	47	48

| | 1984-5 | | 1977-8 | |
	university	polytechnic	university	polytechnic
research etc	11	12	17	3
teacher training	2	1	4	2
'other' training	33	11	11	5
'believed' unemployed Dec 31	26	41	13	4
temporary work	7	9	4	3
permanent UK work	808	629	619	181
employers –				
accountancy	574	417	501	127
banking/insurance	90	23	18	1
industry	50	75	71	31
'other' commerce	20	38	10	6
local government	19	18	4	1
civil service	6	7	4	1
functions –				
financial work	746	578	582	175
marketing etc	16	11	8	nil
admin/operations management	16	197	nil	nil
management services	8	6	7	nil
personnel/social etc	8	3	1	1

Entry normally requires evidence of numeracy with an exam pass at A level or 16-plus†. Almost 1580 UK students were accepted for university business/management studies courses in October 1985 (1984 entry mean A-level 'score' 10.8), 824 for accountancy and financial management (1984 mean A level 'score 11.3').

Business and Technician Education Council (BTEC) courses are designed to give a coherent, national framework to business education and training for all sectors. The three main sets of awards provide for all levels of ability and entry qualification, stopping just short of degree standard, and with a strongly practical bias. Courses can be biased (via the option units) to, theoretically, virtually any business-oriented skill, but in practice colleges and polytechnics tailor their schemes to demand and the skills they are qualified to teach, so the range available at any one of them is fairly restricted. At some colleges and polytechnics students can put together their own choice of option modules, at others option modules are packaged to give a choice between groups biased to, eg distribution, public administration, marketing, banking, personnel work. Languages are also an option at some places.

Both National and Higher awards will, if the student has passed in appropriate units, give exemption from some or all of the equivalent professional examinations. Some professional and other training organisations have integrated these schemes into their examination structures, stipulating only that students must pass in certain required subjects. This way, students can both gain a broad general training giving them flexibility, and make a start on the route to professional qualifications. These awards can be treated as qualifications in their own right, or as steps *en route* to higher qualifications.

All BTEC business studies schemes are being revised both to up-date them and to bring them in line with the new BTEC framework (see TECHNICIAN-LEVEL QUALIFICATIONS AND COURSES).

BTEC Higher National awards – Diplomas (two-year full-time or three-year sandwich courses) and Certificates (at least two years' part-time) reach a level approaching a pass degree.

Under the new guidelines, 12 units are required for an HNC, 16 for an HND. For both, required 'core' studies take up eight units, options the rest. The business and finance scheme (there are slightly different versions for distribution studies and public administration) has six core study areas – work organisations, the external environment, operational techniques and procedures, organisational structures and operations, financial planning and control, and environment and enterprise. Colleges can use the core study areas as the basis for developing new cross-sector schemes.

'Core themes and skills' are integral parts of the core study areas – BTEC is promoting a problem-solving approach to develop them.

Four core themes are named – resources (the financial consequences of business decisions and how human and material resources are involved), people (the wider issues affecting the ways people contribute and interrelate in work organisations etc), technology (its general impact), and change (implications of work organisations' changing goals and objectives and effect of changing external factors on organisations).

Core skills are listed as – learning and studying, working with others, communicating, quantitative and numerate skills, information gathering, information processing and technology, and design and visual discrimination (these last two are completely new to BTEC business studies schemes).

Courses leading to BTEC Higher awards are taught by all polytechnics and a further 30 or so other larger colleges. Nearly 10,700 students registered for Higher National awards (ratio of 6: 4 diploma to certificate) in 1985-6.

Entry is as for BTEC Higher awards††; students who do not have a BTEC National in business studies, and so lack the 'knowledge, skills and understanding' it provides, must normally take a short preparatory basic business studies course.

'First destination' figures for business studies HND –

	1984-5 polytechnic only	1977-8 polytechnic only
total graduating[1]	2191	1411
destination unknown	515	359
overseas students leaving UK	41	94
first degree course	201	42
complete professional qual	24	26
other training	175	116
research etc	23	33
'believed' unemployed Dec 31	210	67
temporary work	103	74
permanent UK work	846	576

[1] Nearly 6000 people in all gained Higher National awards in 1984-85 and 1985-6.

	1984-5 polytechnic only	1977-8 polytechnic only
employers –		
commerce (excl finance)	253	181
banking/insurance	131	32
local government	66	35
'other' manufacturing	59	68
public utilities	55	45
accountancy practice	52	48
engineering	48	88
civil service	46	18
entertainment, leisure etc	22	14
oil & chemicals	22	20
construction	16	20
functions –		
marketing etc	262	130
financial work	178	148
admin/operations management	157	151
personnel/social etc	26	12
management services	20	31

BTEC National awards – Diploma (two-year full-time or three-year sand-wich-based courses) and Certificate (normally two years' part-time) courses – provide a broad business education for 16- and 17-year-old school-leavers with appropriate qualifications (see entry below).

Under the new guidelines, minimum total unit value for a Certificate must equal 12.5, for a Diploma, 16.5. For business and finance, the core element must equal 7.5 units for both Certificate and diploma. A further 2 units must be in business-related skills, leaving the remainder for options.

The core element, in addition to business-related skills, for business and finance, includes people in organisations and the organisation in its environment. Finance/accounting is a core subject for some streams. 'Cross-course' themes are money (the financial consequences of business decisions), the impact of technology, and the implications of change. 'Skill areas' are learning and studying, working with others, communicating, numeracy, information gathering, identifying and tackling problems, and design and visual discrimination.

Options are available in a wide range of commercial subjects (advertising, marketing, international trade), secretarial skills (available as single units or a package), general business (eg business law, information processing, industrial relations, languages), finance (banking, building society practice, insurance, investment etc), in addition to units and packages in public administration, travel and tourism, and distribution.

Courses are available at a large number of colleges country-wide. Over 24,800 students registered for Nationals in 1985-6, with certificate registrations outnumbering diplomas by nearly 2: 1.

Entry is as for all BTEC National awards†† with appropriate competence in English language and numeracy.

BTEC First award – Diploma (one-year full time) and Certificate (one-year part time) courses fully replaced BTEC General from September 1986. They provide both job-specific and business-related training as an alternative to, eg CPVE. The First Certificate has a minimum value of five units, the Diploma at least 8 units. Core studies take up three units for both. Core studies have three elements. A core unit is called working in organisations. Core, business-related and personal, skills essential to success at work, and core themes cover the same areas as the BTEC National at a lower level.

A wide range of option units is on offer, including units on finance, information processing, production, sales, secretarial skills, product design and packaging, and distribution. Students may take one or two 'sector study' units in eg banking, housing, insurance, travel and tourism.

Entry is as for all BTEC First awards††.

Postgraduate study A widening range of courses of all kinds are offered, by universities, polytechnics and FE colleges, and by independent schools, although the academic nature of some are under constant scrutiny, and not all employers consider lengthy full-time courses worthwhile. Business schools of all kinds, including university schools, are becoming more and more entrepreneurial, tailoring their programmes to the perceived needs of their market. The major qualifications available are, however –

Master of Business Administration (MBA or MBA-type): Over twenty universities, several independent schools and some polytechnics put on traditional-length full-time management studies courses (for an MBA at most universities), but quite a number now put on part-time courses too, and it is possible to study by 'distance' learning. MBA programmes emphasise an analytical approach to managerial problem solving, and much of the teaching is by case study. While covering the main managerial disciplines such as economics, quantitative methods, finance, behavioural studies and marketing, MBA programmes now give students increasing choice, in whether or not to specialise, and to put together their own 'package' of options.

Entry: for most MBA programmes, schools prefer students to have gained some working experience first, although they do accept new graduates. Graduates in unrelated disciplines, or with lower than a second-class honours degree; people with professional qualifications only; candidates with extensive business experience but no formal academic or professional qualification, may be accepted, but may have to take a two-, instead of a one-year course (possibly gaining a diploma at the end of the first year).

Diploma in management studies (DMS): awarded by CNAA, courses are put on at 127 centres – by most polytechnics, some higher education, and a large number of FE colleges, both on a full- and part-time basis. Mainly intended for the practising manager (and most people take it part-time), the DMS is a general introduction to management and the industrial/commercial background, introducing management processes, tools and techniques. The courses include quantitative methods, finance etc; behavioural studies; new technology and management; decision making and problem solving; the main business functions (including marketing), industrial relations and law, and policy making. Most courses give students a choice of specialist options, and these may be geared to the needs of local firms.

Entry is with a first degree or equivalent, HNC, or an appropriate professional qualification. Total enrolments were almost 5600 in 1984-5 (up over 500 since 1982-3).

Continuing Education Certificates/Diplomas (CEC/D): in management studies are being developed by BTEC.

See also INTRODUCTION TO ADMINISTRATION/MANAGEMENT.

ECONOMICS

Economics is based on the assumption that a society can never fully satisfy everybody, that however high living standards are, people will want to go on improving theirs, and that people's wants (as opposed to basic needs) – for food and clothing, houses and cars, holidays and entertainment, etc – are unlimited. Given that resources are finite, this is clearly an impossible goal. Economists therefore say that resources are 'scarce', not because there is necessarily any apparent shortage now, but because the potential level of demand cannot be met. 'Resources' can mean finance, raw materials, goods of all kinds, services, even people.

And so economists study the way available resources are allocated, by individuals and collectively – by businesses, by industries, by local communities, by the nation (government), even by families. They study the way such choices are, and can be, made – how to decide who should have what; what to produce and in what quantities; the most 'economic' way of providing goods and services, and the often wide-ranging effects of particular decisions.

Everyone makes economic decisions. Individuals may have to decide whether the cost of maintaining an ageing car is becoming so high that it would be more 'economic' to buy a new one, and whether it is more 'economic' to save up for it or to buy it on credit. Firms may have to decide, for example, at which point (if any) the cost of investment in new, automated machinery can be covered from extra sales and will improve profits, perhaps partly by cutting labour costs, or whether the price at which the goods would have to be sold would be 'uneconomic' for the consumer.

Governments, of course, make major economic decisions, presumably based on their interpretation of voters' views, and on whether they believe they will achieve greater economic success and their political goals by following free-market, or centrally-planned economic policies (or a mixture of both). One of the central economic problems of the 1980s is clearly whether it is possible to control inflation and unemployment at the same time, and if so, how.

Economists are not decision or policy makers. They are expert advisers, providing the information and analyses on which policy makers can work. Just as they do not try to suggest any limits to consumer demand, so they do not tell government, or firms, how to choose their priorities. Economists observe, chart and monitor the choices made, attempt to produce theories which explain economic behaviour, and use them to analyse and attempt to predict the consequences of the choices made, and what the alternatives are. They may also show how to achieve particular results.

Economics is a relatively young science, and the methods used are often still experimental with few agreed conclusions – not all the workings of economic systems are fully understood. Economists have to work on factual information, and they are always trying to obtain better and more exact information on which to build a picture of what actually happens in the economy, or one part of it, or to a firm's business affairs. The number of facts and 'influences' which economists can build into their 'models' of the economy or the firm is almost limitless, and a major problem is the sheer complexity of economic systems. They begin with very simple models of what happens in an economic system, and step by step add more proven facts to get closer to the real level of complexity. But it is difficult. In the sciences, a 'fact' (eg the speed of light), once established, stays constant. In economics, 'facts' may be variables and change frequently: a lower birth rate and rising number of older people, for example, is changing some of the criteria for allocating resources in health and social services. It is not always easy to decide what all the factors are in analysing a given economic problem – such as whether or not reducing benefits would reduce numbers unemployed.

Economics also involves making assumptions about the way people behave, which is obviously not so easily mapped or predicted as the behaviour of an atom of hydrogen. Economists also need time to test their theories: as it is clearly impossible to create lab conditions to test economic theories, they must either wait for real events to prove them right or wrong or work on a period in the past, and test them there.

Economists work, like scientists, by observing, by recording and analysing data, and by developing possible theories. They also build assumptions and try to work out logical consequences from their research. Economic analysis uses mathematical techniques extensively – theories can be expressed better in mathematical terms, and their meaning worked out mathematically. Statistical analysis is used to make sense of the data collected, and can help to decide the probability that certain economic events had particular causes – for instance, that increasing indirect taxes reduces consumption. Economists have to write up their results, sometimes in technical language for publication in academic journals and books, sometimes in language more readily understood by the lay reader, in reports for firms or government, for example. They may have to present a case personally, and be able to make a case for their arguments.

Opportunities for economists

Most professional economists combine research with teaching in a university or polytechnic. University and polytechnic economists can and do also act as advisers and consultants on economic affairs to outside bodies, some running their own intelligence units.

Many economists can, and do, though, work full-time as professional advisers, often in multi-disciplinary teams under the generic title of 'economic intelligence unit' for a wide range of organisations. Most public bodies (eg the Bank of England), and major utilities (British Coal, British Gas, and British Telecom) have their own economic intelligence units. And so do the larger commercial and merchant banks (with staff ranging from three up to 40) and stockbrokers, where information systems and/or forecasting are used to decide where investment should be made, and sophisticated computer-based analysis used. The City's recent 'big bang' has almost certainly made economic intelligence even more crucial.

Larger industrial and commercial firms may employ economists to advise on, for example, the effects of government policies, or trade trends, the implications of technological innovation, and to make detailed forecasts on marketing, or the economic advantages or disadvantages of, for example, changing production methods or sites, to provide intelligence reports and help analyse statistical data. Management consultants, CBI, the TUC and other major unions also employ economists.

Economists can become economic journalists on newspapers and magazines, and on radio and television (see under JOURNALISM) and in independent economic intelligence units, but numbers are small.

Professional economists move around and between, for example, government service or journalism to academic life and back again.

Government economic service, which gives expert advice to Ministers and senior civil servants, employs about 300 economists (1986). They work in nearly all the major departments, but the largest group is in the Treasury.

Treasury economists prepare short- and medium-term projections on how the economy may develop, mostly using a large computerised model of it. They also analyse the consequences (in terms of the growth of the economy, inflation, unemployment, the balance of payments, etc) of policy proposals (eg plans for public expenditure). Treasury economists advise on specific policy questions including domestic monetary policy, commercial policy, social service finance, and so on. They also provide general briefings for ministers and other officials.

Department of Employment economists advise on, for instance, incomes, employment, industrial relations, redundancies and productivity, keeping economic aspects under continuous review, and contribute to policy formation and conceptual developments, analysing implications of policy and doing supportive research. They make both short- and medium-term forecasts of the economy, with detailed assessments of employment. Economists also work in the manpower studies unit, preparing research reports on a wide range of manpower and labour-market issues. Economists are involved in developing a manpower intelligence system for the Manpower Services Commission, and analysing the Commission's policy options, as well as working on more fundamental research on future patterns of employment and the potential contribution of MSC.

In the Department of Energy, economists advise on problems of national and international energy policy, and in the management of these industries. They are involved in setting financial targets for nationalised corporations, devise performance indicators and monitor corporate plans. They work with engineers in appraising technological developments, and make short- and long-term analyses of fuel requirements.

In the Department of Health and Social Security a team of economists advises on all aspects of departmental activity and plans, but especially in analysing and reviewing policies affecting particular groups of beneficiaries, and assessing and monitoring the effects of social policies. They have made cohort studies of the unemployed, and an econometric analysis of retirement. They advise on finance problems, and assist in evaluating medical developments on a cost-benefit and -effectiveness basis.

In the Department of Industry and Trade, economists analyse changes in manufacturing industry; examine the economics of technology, research and development; analyse, and do case work on industrial subsidies and regional industrial policies, etc. Trade advises on the domestic economy and economic policy in terms of trade, competition, company policy etc. They also work on policy for international trade, civil aviation, shipping etc.

The Departments of Environment and of Transport share a common economics service with about 90 economists, who work on economic problems in local government, land use, transport, housing, urban and regional development and environmental protection. They apply new techniques of economic analysis to conceptually difficult problems, eg evaluating environmental costs and benefits, and analysing indirect effects of policy on income distribution. They advise on policy issues in local government expenditure, on house-purchase finance, and on all aspects of the construction industry.

Research officers (as opposed to economists) in the Civil Service may be involved in both economic and sociological research, industrial intelligence, and analyse and interpret data for policy planning.

International organisations such as the United Nations agencies, the World Bank, and the International Monetary Fund, which work extensively on the economic problems of developing countries; and the administrative offices and various organisations of the European Economic Community, all employ economic advisers.

Work in other organisations is mainly in economic intelligence and/or forecasting, linked to the interests of the particular employer. Few employers do primary economic research on anything like the scale of the government economic service or the universities. The economist mostly forecasts and makes predictions on published or unpublished data from other sources, and in some organisations the work shades off into a form of economic public relations.

An economics degree is, of course, a good basis for careers in related areas like OPERATIONAL RESEARCH and other MANAGEMENT SERVICES, ACCOUNTANCY, BANKING, INSURANCE, INVESTMENT ANALYSIS, MARKETING and MARKET RESEARCH, or indeed any career for which an understanding of economic affairs is useful.

Studying economics Economics is taught mainly at first and higher degree levels, but is also a significant element in a wide range of business studies and business-related professional training courses.

First degree courses are offered by the majority of universities and most polytechnics, either as a single honours subject, as the major subject after a broad introductory course in social sciences, or in a two-subject degree course. Some provide options within economics to give practical training for what may be considered related careers, eg integrating accountancy with economics to give some exemption from professional examinations, while others include less formal options in these subjects. Some courses are more rigorously mathematical or quantitatively-based than others, some specialising extensively in mathematical economics, or econometrics, but it is possible to take options in econometrics as part of most economics degree courses. Most polytechnic courses strongly emphasise applied economics.

'First destination' in economics –

	1984-5 university	1984-5 polytechnic	1977-8 university	1977-8 polytechnic
total graduating	2089	763	2150	420
destination unknown	235	104	270	112
overseas students	85	33	79	26
research etc	120	47	165	47
teacher training	43	23	127	25
law exams	8	2	7	1
'other' training	73	13	59	5
'believed' unemployed Dec 31	176	113	100	32
temporary work	58	31	120	23
permanent UK work	1018	377	1109	141
employers –				
accountancy	404	75	175	25
banking/insurance	260	65	137	33
'other' commerce	138	51	307	10
civil service	66	20	37	5
local government	65	44	17	19
'other' manufacturing	65	26	66	12
engineering	60	35	141	26
public utilities	40	18	45	10
oil & chemicals	31	5	41	4
higher/further education	19	10	15	nil
armed forces	13	6	8	4
entertainment, leisure	6	6	23	4
functions –				
financial work	697	167	612	69
marketing etc	142	64	140	16
admin/operations management	140	61	146	31
management services	87	25	65	7
personnel/social etc	37	19	30	1
research/information	21	1	64	nil

Entry: maths is the most common requirement at A level. Nearly 2100 UK students were accepted for university courses, about 1040 for CNAA courses in October 1985. The mean A-level 'score' for 1984 university entry was 11.

Postgraduate study Training for professional economists leads to specialisation, in eg development studies, econometrics, fiscal studies, industrial or regional economics, economic statistics, or economics of education.

EDUCATION

Education, until about fifteen years ago, was rarely taught as a conventional first-degree subject except in Wales, where education traditionally had a higher academic status than in the rest of Britain.

The majority of degree courses in education are designed to prepare graduates to teach: see TEACHING. However, a small number of courses treat education as a subject of purely academic study (normally combined with a second subject). Education is taught in this way at Aberystwyth, Bangor, Cardiff, Lancaster, Warwick and York Universities.

These courses are generally more theoretical, more analytical and fundamental in content than those designed as an initial professional qualification. They often include options and/or courses in areas such as educational research, the relationship between education and industry, and educational administration, and are generally rather broader in scope. Some courses include substantial options in educational psychology, for example, and form a basis for a career in this. These three-year courses do not give qualified teacher status: graduates must still complete a year's certificate course.

Postgraduate courses leading to higher degrees or diplomas are even more heavily biased to research, curriculum development, administration or specialist studies. For most advanced courses, students must be qualified teachers and have extensive teaching experience, however. There are such courses at virtually all universities.

See also EDUCATION.

HOME ECONOMICS

Officially defined as 'the study of the inter-relationship between the provision of food, clothing, shelter and related services and people's physical, economic, social and aesthetic needs in the home'. It has, then, evolved a long way from its origins in domestic-science teaching. Home economists have become, according to their Institute, 'professional advisers on food, clothing, management and design, household services and research related to home and community, acting as a link between producers and consumers of goods and services...' They are professional advisers both to consumers, and to the organisations who supply them with goods and services. Home economists do, of course, continue to teach.

Qualifications in home economics appear to be taking people into a number of different types of work, although such qualifications are not required for any except teaching. Personality and approach to the work are.
The possible areas of work include –

Industry The work may be in R&D on new and improved products, and testing and evaluating them. In market research they test new products on consumers and do surveys to see if there is a gap in the product range to be filled – both involve field work. In marketing/sales and public relations they may help prepare publicity material (for photographs of new food products or copy for leaflets, for instance) or instruction booklets; demonstrate products on promotional stands at exhibitions, in stores, at WI meetings, press conferences etc. The work is not always directly sales-oriented – home economists may advise consumers how to, for instance, save on fuel, or make best use of a particular appliance.
The main sectors employing home economists are domestic appliance manufacturers (see also ELECTRICAL INDUSTRY), the FOOD INDUSTRY, and fuel (ENERGY).

Consumer advisory services either directly for a manufacturer or supplier (as above), or in local-authority or independently run centres. Here they are expertly assessing and evaluating products and services for the customer. Closely related is consumer-advisory work for the media – radio, TV, newspapers and magazines – either writing and/or presenting consumer-oriented material, or testing, evaluating, and preparing material for the columnist or presenter. Advertising, public relations and market research agencies may also employ home economists if they have contracts with eg, food manufacturers.

Community services Social service departments employ home economists to, for example, help solve the problems of families in difficulty, show them how to budget, teach economic and nutritious cooking, family care etc. They also work in home help services, residential care, and other rehabilitation units. Home economists are qualified to train as NHS domestic services managers.

Retailing Large groups employ home economists in developing and evaluating new products, liaison with customers, demonstration and promotional work, and staff training. Home economics is an accepted qualification for trainee management.

Home economics courses and qualifications The study of home economics is now much broader and wider-ranging than old-style domestic science courses. It begins with basic sciences and social studies; goes on to specialist areas like nutrition, food science, practical studies of the home, equipping and caring for it, planning a family budget and menu, budgeting and caring for clothes and therefore studying textiles and their composition. They also extend more widely into the whole field of consumer affairs, the position of women in society, the problems of the family and deviance and delinquency, and even the whole field of community studies.

For first degrees there are two kinds of courses.
Broad-based courses at –
Universities – Cardiff: UC, Ulster; polytechnics – Leeds, Liverpool, Manchester, Newcastle (applied consumer science); colleges – Aberdeen: RGIT, Bath, Bradford, Edinburgh: Queen Margaret, Glasgow: Queen's, Leeds: Trinity/All Saints', London: Roehampton.
BEd courses (intended primarily to train teachers, but also a basis for other careers), at –
University – Cardiff: UC; polytechnics – Leeds, Liverpool, London: S Bank, Newcastle, Sheffield; colleges – Bath, Leeds: Trinity & All Saints', Worcester.

BTEC awards Home economics can be studied at both national and higher national levels, at both levels for certificates (two years' part time) and diplomas (two years' full time, three on a sandwich basis).
Entry is as for all BTEC awards at the appropriate level††. For higher awards via 16-plus/A levels, passes must include a biological or physical science.
HND/C courses are available at: polytechnics – London: PNL, Sheffield: colleges – Birmingham CF&DA, Croydon C, Salford CT.
Nationals are available at about 30 colleges.

Professional qualification The Institute of Home Economics (1986 about 1700 members) requires for full membership a degree or HND specialising in home economics plus two years relevant experience; with an ND, four years' experience is needed.

Further information from the Institute of Home Economics.

LAW

Law is both a vocational subject and a rigorous academic training, valuable as the basis for a wide range of non-legal careers. It is not necessary to plan to be a lawyer to choose to read law at university or polytechnic – in fact the output of law graduates is now certainly too great for the profession to absorb.

Law is no longer practised, or studied, as a series of rules operated in isolation from life around it, but is examined in its social and economic setting, particularly in its relation to the business world on the one hand and to the community on the other. Law is now defined as a social phenomenon which both affects and is affected by society and what goes on within it, and is influenced by, and influences, political thinking. The law is influenced by thinking in, for example, psychology, sociology, and even criminology. The law is more complex than it ever was, and has greater problems to solve.

The legal profession
Law is now almost entirely a graduate profession. Only a very small number of school-leavers with good grades at A level start training as solicitors each year. Theoretically, it is not necessary to have a law degree, but in practise competition for training places, for both the Bar and in the larger solicitors' offices, is now so great that a law degree is a strong advantage.
See LEGAL SERVICES

Studying law
Law is studied mainly on courses for first and higher degrees, although it is an element in most business-related courses at all levels.

A first degree in law is designed to be more than a straightforward vocational training, although the demands of the profession do mean that courses are mostly very specialised – at least in England and Wales. Law degrees in Scotland are usually more broadly based (but do not train in English law). Law degrees study the law in its historical and social context and give a rigorous training in logical and analytical reasoning.

Most law courses can deal with only some twelve subjects/topics in three years, four in each year. Six of these normally cover the essential 'core' subjects, needed for exemption from the pre-vocational stage of legal training (the so-called 'Common Professional Examination' – CPE, although it isn't common). These are contract, tort, criminal and property law, constitutional law, administrative law, and trusts. If only one of these is left out a prospective lawyer will have to spend a full year completing the CPE exam in it. Law courses do not even touch on the differences between the work of barrister and solicitor – both deal with the same law. All courses also cover the English, or Scots, legal system (they have to differentiate between Scots law and the law of England and Wales, since they are separate and quite different).

For the rest of the course, most law schools allow students a fairly wide choice of topics, but usually they are all legal. Some courses are still very traditional (at some universities, for example, Roman law is still compulsory), and stay with more conventional subjects, like conflict of laws, equity and trust, family law, labour law, jurisprudence, legal history, procedure and evidence, revenue (tax) law, and succession. A high proportion, though, have moved into newer areas of legal concern – EEC law, for example, and developing areas of legal practice, such as welfare law, consumer law, criminology, as well as socio-legal studies, and the law and medicine. Business and company law is another traditional area of study, but a few courses, particularly in polytechnics, give the option to specialise in business law.

The legal complexities of the Common Market, and the need to have lawyers who can cope with French, German, Italian, or Spanish law and legal procedures, has resulted in a number of courses training graduates to work in English, EEC, and French, German, Italian or Spanish law, teaching them also the language. African and Asian law can be studied at a small number of schools.

Beyond this, few strictly law courses find time to let students study non-legal subjects – Sussex and Warwick are the two main exceptions, although at, eg Kent the first year is broader. It is, however, possible to study law with another subject at some universities, although this does make it more difficult to qualify for the profession.

Law schools – English/Welsh law:
Universities – Aberystwyth[2] ; Birmingham[1 3] ; Brighton: Sussex[1] ; Bristol; Brunel (4 yrs); Buckingham (2 yrs); Cambridge; Canterbury: Kent[1 2] ; Cardiff: UC[2] , UWIST; Chelmsford: Essex[1] ; Durham[2] ; Exeter[1 2] ; Hull[2] ; Keele (no LLB)[2] ; Lancaster; Leeds; Leicester[1] ; Liverpool; London: KQC[2] , LSE[2] , QMC, SOAS, UCL; Manchester[3] ; Newcastle[2] ; Norwich: E Anglia[1] ; Nottingham[1] ; Oxford; Reading; Sheffield; Southampton[2 3] ; Warwick[1 2] .
Polytechnics – Birmingham; Bristol; Coventry[3] ; Huddersfield[3] ; Kingston; Leeds; Leicester; Liverpool; London: City, Middx, NELP, NLP, PCL, S Bank; Manchester[1 2] ; Newcastle; Nottingham: Trent; Pontypridd: Wales; Preston: Lancs; Stoke: N Staffs; Wolverhampton.
Colleges – Chelmsford: Essex IHE; Ealing CHE.
Law schools (Scots law): universities – Aberdeen[1 2] ; Dundee (includes English law)[2] ; Edinburgh[2 3] ; Glasgow; Glasgow: Strathclyde (includes English law)[2] ;
Law schools (N Ireland legal system): – Belfast: Queen's U.
[1]'European' variant also [2]law can be combined with other subjects [3]business law (polytechnic)/law & business studies option (university)
'First destination' in law –

	1984-5 university	1984-5 polytechnic	1977-8 university	1977-8 polytechnic
total graduating	3642	1271	3368[1]	805
destination unknown	320	204	170	154
overseas students	259	24	111	1
research etc	113	30	82	12

	1984-5 university	polytechnic	1977-8 university	polytechnic
law exams	2175	750	1022	453
other training	550	18	352	25
'believed' unemployed Dec 31	92	57	12	8
temporary work	41	23	58	16
permanent UK work	498	152	1249	110
employers –				
accountancy	123	11	93	4
banking/insurance	83	20	38	7
'other' commerce	51	75	39	12
local government[1]	48	15	54	12
industry	44	20	58	17
solicitors' office[2]	43	26	352	46
civil service	37	12	22	2
higher/further ed	12	12	18	3
armed forces	10	1	9	nil
functions –				
financial work	200	31	144	14
legal work	65	30	58	53
admin/operations management	66	26	53	13
personnel/social etc	61	19	32	7
marketing etc	26	14	21	6
management services	14	2	12	2
research/information	11	2	7	5

[1] 2600 in 1972-3   [2] includes those going into articles

Entry: no specific A-level subjects named. Over 3400 UK students were accepted for university degree courses in October 1985, nearly 2600 for CNAA degree courses. The 1984 university entry mean A-level 'score' was 12.3.

Professional/vocational training

A truly-common professional examination for both prospective barristers and solicitors (to make interchange between the two easier), has not been achieved, although they have come close to it. Under the post-Ormrod training arrangements, both require graduates to complete, or be exempt from, the same six core subjects, for instance.

THE BAR: prospective entrants must first to be admitted as a student member of one of the Inns of Court (which originated as medieval 'colleges') – Lincoln's Inn, Inner Temple, Middle Temple or Gray's Inn – which are all in London. The minimum entry requirement is a first degree in any subject, but *with second-class honours* (with very limited exceptions). Graduates in disciplines other than law must complete the academic-stage examination, via a full-time, one-year course for a diploma in law at either the City University or the Polytechnic of Central London. Law graduates whose degrees do not include all six core subjects are required to pass exams in the rest *before* beginning the vocational stage. Candidates, who may not be members of 'disqualifying' professions, must also offer two character references.

Only members of the Inns of Court can practise as barristers in English and

Welsh courts. To be 'called to the Bar' students must keep dining terms, ie dine in their hall three times during the term, 'keeping' four terms before sitting the vocational-stage examination, and eight before being called to the Bar. Students must also keep four further terms during pupillage if they intend to practise at the Bar of England and Wales, and must also pass the required Bar examinations and practical exercises in advocacy and drafting.

The academic stage covers the 'core' subjects, ie law of contract and of tort, criminal and land law, constitutional and administrative law, equity and trusts. There are no exemptions from the vocational-stage examination. This consists of two general papers (practitioners' problems in two selected areas of tort and criminal law, law of trusts and remedies of breach of contract), civil and criminal procedure and evidence, and three options (from eg revenue law, family law, landlord and tenant, hire purchase and sale of goods, local government and planning, practical conveyancing, conflict of laws, law of international trade, public international law, and Roman-Dutch law of property). All students must attend a one-year course at the Inns of Court School before taking the vocational examination and this also involves tutorial classes. Numbers are restricted, currently (1986-7 and 1987-8) to 900 places (over 1400 were admitted in 1982-3), but in fact 943 were accepted in 1985-6.

Once students have been called to the Bar, they must serve twelve months' 'pupillage', or apprenticeship in chambers with an experienced barrister as pupil master. It is usual to split pupillage between two sets of chambers, one specialising in common law and the other in chancery.

SOLICITORS: their professional body is the Law Society.

The Law Society has retained (in deference to members' views), a route into the profession for school-leavers, although graduate entry is now well over 90%.

School-leavers must have four or five 16-plus†/A-level passes in separate subjects, including three or two (respectively) at A level. The A-level passes must be at least grades B and C or three Grade Cs at one sitting. They must start with a full-time, one-year course at a polytechnic to take four of the eight papers in the first examination. After this, students must serve articles for at least five years (the third is spent preparing for finals), taking the remaining four first examination papers during the first two years after part-time study at polytechnic or by correspondence course.

Graduates in subjects other than law must complete the so-called common entrance examination – CPE (the syllabus at least is almost identical to the Bar Council's diploma). Law graduates who have not passed degree papers in any of the subjects set for the CPE must take the CPE equivalent. Full-time courses preparing for CPE are given by the College of Law (at Guildford, in London and in Chester), or students can study the subjects in a polytechnic law department alongside law-degree students.

All entrants, regardless of initial qualification, must take the final examination for which a year-long course is compulsory. This covers the solicitor and the practice, the solicitor and the business client, the solicitor and the private client, and litigation.

Graduates must also complete an uninterrupted period of two years' service under articles.

In Scotland, solicitors must serve under an indenture, which varies in length according to qualifications (up to five years), but only non-graduates have to pass the Law Society of Scotland's examinations.

BARRISTERS' CLERKS see LEGAL SERVICES

LEGAL EXECUTIVES (formerly called managing clerks) can take the examinations of the Institute of Legal Executives, which has substantial support from the Law Society, but they are not compulsory. ILE 1986 membership was over 14,900, against 13,000 in 1983.

Academic entry qualifications are either four passes at 16-plus†, or three including at least two at A level (or equivalent in AS levels); subjects must include English. The Institute is reviewing its list of approved subjects ('practical' subjects are not accepted). There are no age restrictions.

The Institute sets a two-part examination (about 4500 students took parts of these in 1986) –

Part I (a BTEC National award with law options exempts) introduces the legal system and covers elementary law and practice, with a practical approach. Students normally study part-time over two years at one of over 80 colleges, but full-time study is possible.

Part II (subject-for-subject exemptions for law graduates) requires candidates to take three 'substantive' law subjects (each with a 'pair' of linked law and practice papers), plus a specialist procedure paper and two further options, to qualify in civil or criminal litigation, matrimonial or company and partnership practice, probate practice or conveyancing. Candidates must have taken an approved course (which can be by home study), normally lasting two years' part time.

Full fellows of the Institute have to be qualified, have five years' qualifying employment, and be over 25. Institute examinations provide an entry route to the legal profession for a few 'late starters'.

LEGAL ACCOUNTANTS The Institute of Legal Executives has introduced a full scheme of training and qualification for finance staff employed in solicitors' offices.

Students must normally have four passes at 16-plus†, including English or maths. A two-part examination is set – part I covers general accounting principles and specialised aspects of solicitors' accounts, and the legal background. Part II deals with four specialist financial/legal subjects. Completion of the exams gives accountancy membership of ILE; at least five years' legal-accountancy experience entitles members to call themselves legal accountants.

LEGAL SECRETARIAL WORK see SECRETARIAL WORK.
See also LEGAL SERVICES.

Further information England/Wales: from the Council of Legal Education, the General Council of the Bar, the Under-Treasurers of the individual Inns of Court, the Law Society, and the Institute of Legal Executives. For Scotland: the Faculty of Advocates and the Law Society of Scotland.

LIBRARIANSHIP AND INFORMATION SCIENCE

These are now taught as degree and degree-level subjects, although not all

graduate entrants read librarianship. For courses, see LIBRARY AND INFOR-
MATION WORK.

POLITICS/POLITICAL SCIENCE/PUBLIC ADMINISTRATION

Political science makes objective studies of politics, politicians, government
and political life. It studies the function of government, how it operates, what
influences it, the causes of political changes, and theories on which political
systems and life are based. It is not intended to train people to take part in
politics or to be a civil servant or local government officer.

Political scientists observe, analyse and assess what happens and how people
behave in political life. They do not (normally) suggest what should happen in
political life or government, or whether or not changes should be made,
although politicians frequently take account of and use studies made by
political scientists of, for example, the reaction of voters to particular policies.

British government and the British political system are an obvious central
interest for political scientists. They study in detail the way the machinery of
central government works, how it changes and evolves, its problems, and
particularly the way in which policy and decisions are made, as well as the
policies and decisions themselves. They examine the complex tensions and
even conflict between elected members of government and permanent civil
servants, and the influences on policy- and decision-making of all the many
interests and pressure groups – farmers and fishermen, employers, industries,
trade unions, people for and against a particular reform – and the role of
factors such as social status, personal links, and class loyalty. They study the
effect of external factors, such as EEC decisions, on policy making.

They also study the electoral system and how it works, analysing problems
such as the way 'third' parties fail to gain the number of parliamentary seats in
line with voters' support. They study political parties and movements, and of
course, the voters and how they behave, both as individuals and groups (eg by
age, class, ethnic origins, social mobility) – which is called political sociology.
Political change is a theme running through much research, how people
change their voting behaviour with changing circumstances, for example.

Local government and public administration, and their relations with central
government, form another major area of study.

The political systems of other countries are all studied, both because they are
interesting in their own right, and because they can form part of comparative
studies so that political scientists can try to make generalisations good for all
political systems.

International relations studies not only relations between different states (this
started as diplomatic history) but also international bodies like the EEC and
United Nations. Strategic studies of war – and peace – are related.

But political science does not only study the practicalities of political systems.
A central theme is the theory and philosophy – of political thinkers and
philosophers, from Plato and Aristotle through to Marx and John Stuart Mill,
and beyond. This analyses key issues such as power and authority and what
rules are used to control those who hold them; freedom, democracy, and the
rule of law; the rights and obligations of the government and the governed;

how the governed give their consent to be ruled and how they withdraw it, and so on. Political science also studies the language of politics – what exactly is meant by democracy, totalitarianism, or participation?

Much of the raw material of political science comes from written papers – the reports and minutes of not only government and parliamentary assemblies, but all kinds of bodies and organisations. In some areas, though, political scientists also work on data acquired through surveys, for instance, in studying the attitudes and behaviour of voters.

Opportunities for political scientists/public administrators

The chances to become a professional political scientist are very few. Most combine research with teaching in university or polytechnic. Some also write popular books on political affairs, and/or provide expert commentary for the press, television or radio, although this is usually only a part-time possibility. The great majority of graduates in political science have to treat their degree subject as completely non-vocational. Graduates in public administration are at least part prepared for careers in central or local government, or related organisations, but as recruiters are looking as much, if not more, at personal qualities, they do not necessarily have an advantage over others.

Studying political science Politics is generally available only as a first, or higher, degree subject, although relevant aspects may be covered in some vocational courses. Vocational courses in public administration are available at all levels, although university courses may be rather more academic, oriented to the study of policy and policy making.

First-degree courses Government, politics, political studies or science, either as a single-subject honours course, or as a major option within a social science degree, or as a joint honours subject in either, is taught at the majority of UK universities, but only at eight polytechnics.

Public administration is taught at –

Universities – Birmingham, Canterbury: Kent, Durham[1] , Glasgow: Strathclyde[1] , London: RHB (with economics), Southampton[1] ; polytechnics – Leicester, Manchester, Middlesborough: Teesside, Nottingham: Trent, Pontypridd: Wales, Sheffield; colleges – Aberdeen: RGIT, Glasgow CT.
[1] with social administration.

'First destination' figures (politics/public administration) –

| | 1984-5 | | 1977-8 | |
	university	polytechnic	university	polytechnic
total graduating	893[1]	418	835	58
destination unknown	178	97	116	6
research etc	60	26	86	4
teacher training	7	6	60	1
law exams	14	1	15	nil
'other' training	54	14	53	3
'believed' unemployed Dec 31	130	63	61	5
temporary work	38	23	69	7

| | 1984-5 | | 1977-8 | |
	university	polytechnic	university	polytechnic
permanent UK work	362	158	245	31
employers –				
commerce (excl finance)	70	33	24	3
local government	60	41	46	16
banking/insurance	49	6	14	nil
industry	40	18	58	6
accountancy	37	2	20	2
civil service	32	14	22	1
armed forces	16	4	1	nil
higher/further ed	12	8	11	2
functions –				
financial work	92	11	40	6
admin/operations management	82	59	68	6
personnel/social etc	52	19	49	5
marketing etc	44	26	31	4
research/information	14	4	10	3
management services	11	2	6	2

[1] down from 994 in 1982-3

Entry qualifications: no specific A-level subjects normally needed. Just 814 UK students were accepted by universities for 1985 entry. The mean A-level 'score' for 1984 entry was 10.4.

Postgraduate courses in politics are mostly quite specialised, with a choice from a wide spectrum of topics, from the study of foreign governments and political systems to specialist study of, eg political behaviour or theory, social theory and public policy, modern political analysis. Courses in public administration are also available.

BTEC awards Public administration can be taken at both Higher National and National levels, and for Certificates and Diplomas at both levels. At both levels, courses share some core studies, core themes and skills, with other business schemes (SEE BUSINESS STUDIES).

Higher National courses – Diploma (two-year full-time or three sandwich-based) and Certificate (two-year part-time) – include core studies on work organisations, external environment, and operational techniques and procedures as other business studies, plus public sector organisations, structures and processes, and resource management in the public sector. Option units are designed by the centres.

Courses are available at over 30 polytechnics and colleges.

Entry is as for all BTEC Higher awards††.

National courses – Diploma (two-year full-time or three sandwich-based) and Certificate (two-year part-time) – include core studies in business-related skills, people in organisations, the organisation and the environment, and finance as other business studies, with one core unit on public administration. Public administration option units include housing studies, introductory practical administration, and the developing social structure of modern Britain,

but students can take other appropriate options in eg commerce, finance. Courses are available at a large number of colleges.
Entry is as for all BTEC National awards††.

PSYCHOLOGY
Psychology is both a subject for academic study, and a professional career. It is a very large field, and so is generally divided in various ways. The divisions can be confusing, because inevitably the interests of the various groups overlap. Further, the divisions of the academic subject are not necessarily the same as the career divisions.

Psychology as a discipline
Is officially defined as the scientific study of human and animal behaviour. Psychologists explore the way individuals act, behave, and think. They try to work out, describe and explain how people learn – to speak, to read, to find their way about, to become skilled at work, and even to walk. They want to know how people come to understand and apply mathematics, to appreciate art or poetry, and why they want to play or watch football or tennis, drink alcohol or smoke. They investigate what memory is, and how and why people remember, and forget. They try to understand what makes people feel different emotions, why and how they make choices, what affects their relationships with other people – as friends, in families, at school and work. They study the way human and animal brains process and interpret information fed into them by external senses – eyes, ears, nose – and the messages sent by other parts of the body, about pain and hunger, cold and stress. They question the reasons why humans and animals react as they do to particular circumstances. They study people and animals awake and asleep (and dreaming), happy and depressed, calm and aggressive, working and playing, as child and as adult.

Psychology is rather more scientific than can be politics or sociology, because science's experimental methods can be used, to some extent on people but rather more on animals, and the methods of measuring, analysing, and assessing results can be much more exact. It is also closely linked to BIOLOGICAL SCIENCES, since mind and body are inextricable from each other.

But psychology does study people, people in their social settings, so it is also a social science. Psychology has many controversial aspects, and the division between those who, to put it crudely, see all human behaviour in terms of scientific formulae, and those who stress the human personality, feelings and emotions – which cannot be expressed in scientific or mathematical terms – is only one example.

Although there is a very long way to go to anything like full understanding, psychologists know enough about human behaviour to be able to apply what they know in everyday life – to try to improve job satisfaction or productivity, to help find ways to teach particular skills, to design equipment that is easier to use, and to help people through crises in their lives.

Psychology should not be confused with psychiatry or psychoanalysis, although of course they have much in common. Psychiatry (which requires a medical qualification), and psychoanalysis specialise in diagnosing, explaining and trying to treat mental illness and behavioural problems, while psychology, although it does study so-called 'abnormal' behaviour, deals with behaviour of all kinds, and spends more time on normal than abnormal patterns.

Psychology as a discipline is divided into a number of clearly defined areas of study. First-degree courses usually provide a broad introduction to all of them, while professional psychologists usually specialise.

DEVELOPMENTAL PSYCHOLOGY studies how behaviour, skills and abilities, such as perception, learning, remembering, problem-solving and motivation, are passed on from generation to generation, and how they develop within individuals. It probes into, for example, which characteristics are inherited and what is the balance between heredity and the 'environment' (the family, the school, the estate, the town, and the country in which people have grown up), in trying to decide whether, for instance, people are more or less 'intelligent'.

Developmental psychologists try to decide what 'intelligence' is, and how it is best measured. They study the processes of learning – whether, for instance, babies have to reach a certain level of 'readiness' before they can be toilet trained, and whether or not the same applies to learning to read or ride a bicycle. They investigate the value of play in a child's development, the effect of separating child and mother, and the way childhood experiences influence adult attitudes, behaviour and relationships with other people. They also study, and help to solve, actual behaviour problems caused by failures in social training.

EXPERIMENTAL PSYCHOLOGY is a label used to describe any research which can use scientific, experimental methods, often in the laboratory, but also data collecting and statistical analysis. It specialises in finding better ways of doing controlled research in psychology, and then carrying it out, but experimental psychologists more usually develop and refine their techniques as part of their research rather than in isolation from it. Examples of experimental work range from studying the psychological aspects of car sickness, through working on ways in which the blind can use sound to detect obstacles, or methods to improve the layout of an instrument panel of, say, an aircraft.

PHYSIOLOGICAL PSYCHOLOGY studies the relation between behaviour/emotion and the body, to discover the physical basis of behaviour. Specifically, it investigates how the body transmits information and substances to the brain, what the brain does with them, and how the brain triggers a reaction – and what the reactions might be. It involves investigating how the brain, as one of the most sophisticated processors of information there is, and nervous system work in detail. It is an area where the work is largely experimental (see above), and involves psychologists in working closely with, for example, BIOCHEMISTS, PHARMACOLOGISTS, and PHYSIOLOGISTS.

SOCIAL PSYCHOLOGY studies the way behaviour of individuals is affected by groups – families, school, the firm, the community in general – and how individuals in turn influence the behaviour of the groups, how they interact with the other people in them, and the impact of social conditions (such as poor housing, or lack of transport) on individuals and groups.

Social psychologists study accepted social patterns of behaviour expected of, for example, English boys or German girls, the way parents influence their children – to become tennis stars or doctors, perhaps, but in more subtle ways too. They also study practical social problems – drug addiction, the effect of TV on children, and the relations between ethnic minorities and the community at large, or the police.

Social psychology has much in common with sociology and social anthropology, but the viewpoint is different – it deals with the relationship between individual personalities and behaviour, and the social rules within which people live.

ABNORMAL PSYCHOLOGY and the psychology of personality study the differences between one person and another in terms of temperament, intelligence, behaviour patterns, and personality structure.

ANIMAL PSYCHOLOGY specifically observes and studies animal behaviour, partly because it is interesting in its own right, but mainly because such studies can illuminate some patterns of human behaviour. In the laboratory, animal psychologists study animals under controlled experimental conditions, to clarify learning processes (for instance, how rats find their way through a maze) or to discover how conditional reflexes work (the famed Pavlovian dog). Animals are also studied in their natural settings – the efficient division of labour amongst insect communities, for example, or the 'pecking order' amongst hens.

COMPARATIVE PSYCHOLOGY compares and contrasts the behaviour of animal species with each other and with human behaviour.

Studying psychology Psychology is studied mainly at first and higher degree levels.

First-degree courses may be classed as science or social science. Science degrees tend to be biased to biological aspects, social sciences to behavioural aspects, but there are fewer hard and fast divisions than there used to be. Entry requirements, and supporting subjects are often the main difference. It is taught at –
Universities – Aberdeen; Bangor; Belfast; Birmingham: U, Aston; Bradford; Brighton: Sussex; Bristol; Cambridge; Cardiff: UC, UWIST; Dundee; Durham; Edinburgh; Exeter; Glasgow: U, Strathclyde; Hull; Keele; Leeds; Leicester; Liverpool; London: Brunel U, City U; London U: RHB, Goldsmiths', LSE, UCL; Loughborough; Manchester; Newcastle; Norwich: E Anglia; Nottingham; Oxford; Reading; St Andrews; Sheffield; Southampton; Stirling; Swansea; Ulster; Warwick; York.
Polytechnics – Hatfield; London: City, Middx, NELP, PCL; Manchester; Newcastle; Oxford; Plymouth; Pontypridd: Wales; Portsmouth; Preston: Lancs; Sunderland; colleges – Bolton IHE.
'First destination' figures are –

| | 1984-5 | | 1977-8 | |
	university	polytechnic	university	polytechnic
total graduating	1482[1]	412	1565	213
destination unknown	191	57	187	45

| | 1984-5 | | 1977-8 | |
	university	polytechnic	university	polytechnic
research etc	170	32	220	19
teacher training[2]	135	20	200	28
other training	79	16	85	10
'believed' unemployed Dec 31	190	60	102	13
temporary work	71	35	129	31
permanent UK work	555	172	470	57
employers –				
local government/NHS	180	58	161	16
commerce (excl finance)	82	38	139	7
industry	73	11	88	10
accountancy	33	1	27	2
banking/insurance	27	4	13	nil
civil service	27	11	27	4
higher/further ed	23	7	23	7
functions –				
personnel/social etc	241	73	188	25
marketing etc	66	18	57	6
financial work	62	5	46	4
admin/operations management	59	16	58	6
research/information work	23	8	21	4
management services	22	1	31	5
teaching/lecturing	19	5	22	1
scientific research	9	1	26	3

[1] down from 1590 in 1982-3 [2] needed for entry to educational psychology

Entry qualifications vary, to some extent, between science- and social-science-based courses, but most usefully A levels should include a science and/or maths. Some 1530 UK students were accepted for university courses, over 500 for CNAA courses in October 1985. The mean A-level 'score' for 1984 university entry was 10.1.

Postgraduate courses include advanced study and training courses in educational psychology (for which teaching experience is normally required), clinical psychology, occupational psychology, abnormal psychology, social psychology, applied psychology, computer applications in psychology, industrial psychology, psychology of mental handicap, organisational psychology, psychopathology, and child psychology. Competition for places on 'vocational' postgraduate courses is as intensive as for the more academic, and an upper second (class honours) degree is almost essential.

Professional qualification The British Psychological Society (BPS) requires an approved honours degree in psychology for graduate membership, but does accept other equivalent (or higher) qualifications on a complex points system. BPS approves post-graduate professional training courses, and itself offers a diploma in clinical psychology.

Psychology as a career
Not a very large profession: the British Psychological Society has (1986) about

9500 full and well over 1000 student members (but not every psychologist belongs). First-degree output of graduates in psychology has reached the point where there are neither enough professional posts nor training places for everyone who wants to be a psychologist. A higher proportion of psychology graduates will, therefore, have to find other careers in future.

Most psychologists specialise after graduation, normally as one of –

RESEARCH PSYCHOLOGISTS Most psychologists do at least some research as part of their work. Opportunities to do research full-time are limited. Even in university and polytechnic, most have to combine research with teaching. About 1200 psychologists work in universities, about 300 polytechnics, and 450 or so in colleges.

The research may be the kind of studies described earlier – and so a research psychologist may be called a social or developmental psychologist, if that is his or her area of research. It may have practical applications – looking at the reliability of identification evidence in courts, working on the language problems of immigrant children in schools, or fundamental problems in the nature of learning and memory. The impact of unemployment is now an important area of research. Research psychologists also work on problems of new technology, in areas ranging from, for instance, designing 'user-friendly' computers and other machinery, to looking at ways of getting information technology accepted in the work place and in the community.

Other organisations carrying out research include –

Some government departments employ research psychologists. Ministry of Defence establishments, for instance, for work on the design of military equipment, to take account of psychological factors in, for example, the layout of submarine or tank interiors. Research stations may need psychological input – in road research, for example, on psychological aspects of preventing road accidents via experiments on, for instance, drivers' reaction times.

A small number of independent centres exist, but they rarely employ more than one or two research psychologists.

Industry and commerce offer few research opportunities, although some large organisations, eg the Post Office, employ psychologists to do research on training schemes.

EDUCATIONAL PSYCHOLOGISTS work mostly with children and teenagers who have problems in learning, whose behaviour is causing concern, or who have emotional problems. They try to discover what has gone wrong, using established tests, looking into the child's background, and talking to parents, teachers and the child.

They may treat a child or teenager themselves, largely through personal counselling, and/or advise the parents and teachers on how to help, and say whether or not some form of remedial teaching is needed. Psychologists also work with handicapped children. They also advise schools on organisational problems, or help design programmes for particular groups of pupils. They also give talks or group counselling for teenagers

Educational psychologists in England and Wales work mostly for local authorities, either in child guidance clinics, or in the school psychological service (see EDUCATION), with a few posts in specialist assessment units, eg community schools, hospital paediatric units, or university or medical school research units. In Scotland, mostly they work for child guidance services which deal with both school assessment and clinical treatment. Estimates suggest about 1300 educational psychologist posts.

Qualification and training require, first, qualification in both psychology and teaching, and then at least two years' teaching experience. It is possible to start with either a teaching qualification or a psychology degree, but the latter route is two or three years' shorter, since a PGCE takes only one year. A training course in educational psychology (at one of about 17 universities/polytechnics etc) lasts at least one year full time, two part-time; competition for places can be considerable.

CLINICAL PSYCHOLOGISTS, of whom there are at least 1800, work alongside psychiatric and other medical staff mainly in NHS (and some Army and RAF) hospitals.

Clinical psychologists have been taking on a steadily-widening range of work. Forty years ago, they spent most of their time making routine tests on psychiatric and mentally-handicapped patients. Now many are directly involved in treatment, in one-to-one therapy for people who may be, for example, addicted to gambling, have a fear of open spaces, or who are severely depressed. They help patients who have been in hospital a long time to prepare to live in the community again. They use their detailed understanding of how people learn, develop and can change their patterns of behaviour, in helping to overcome, for instance, compulsive shop lifting. They work with patients' relatives, and teach them to understand and cope with the problems.

They do still do diagnostic work and test intelligence, skills and aptitudes, or for possible brain damage. They work on new methods of assessment and treatment, and may have the opportunity to do some research. They also train other health care staff. Senior staff are generally also involved in planning and administering psychology services, but there are no purely administrative senior posts. Work with the mentally handicapped and older people are the main growth areas.

A BPS survey of advertisements for basic grade posts showed 40% for work with adults with acute psychological problems, 25% with the mentally handicapped, 10% with children, and 10% for work with the elderly.

Qualifications and training via either a full-time two-year postgraduate course for a higher degree at a university or polytechnic, usually in association with a teaching hospital, or on a three-year 'in-service' training course, as a 'probationer' which leads to a diploma examination set by the British Psychological Society. Both routes are supposed to carry equal status. After qualifying, at least two years are spent in the 'basic' grade working under experienced supervision.

OCCUPATIONAL PSYCHOLOGISTS basically work on fitting people to jobs and jobs to people, but the scope of occupational psychology is now much wider than that. It includes 'industrial' and 'organisational' psychology, and can deal even more broadly with almost any aspect of the relation between people and their environment which can benefit from the expertise of psychologists.

There are probably only between 500 and 600 people working as occupational psychologists. A high proportion work in government service of some kind – the Civil Service employs some 200 all told, many of them occupational psychologists. Few industrial or commercial firms employ psychologists *per se*. Occupational psychologists give expert help and advice to people who need assessment and guidance in finding work to suit their aptitudes, abilities and interests. Such services are usually only publicly provided for people with problems – people in employment rehabilitation units who have some form of disability which makes finding work difficult, or who have been made redundant, or who may be leaving the armed forces for civilian life, for example.

Occupational psychologists may do the counselling, but more often work on developing methods, including assessment tests, and services. They work for the Manpower Services Commission (about 60), for whom some act as regional advisers, some are attached to some larger job centres, some advise on policy. Some are employed by local authority careers services. There is a single careers advisory work research unit, and a few commercially-run vocational guidance units.

Occupational psychologists also work in personnel selection, training, and career development programmes for staff. They design and evaluate tests and interview techniques for choosing people to match particular job requirements, or to re-assess the job to make it fit the type of people available in the employment market. Closely linked is work on developing and improving training programmes, based on the results of research on how people learn skills. Here again, they are employed by the Civil Service and the Ministry of Defence, the Manpower Services Commission, some industrial training boards, and by some larger employers. The Ministry of Defence employs psychologists on defining and assessing the abilities, skills and personal qualities needed for service jobs, experimental studies of operational or training performance, surveys of motivation and morale, or personnel selection and allocation, and with physiologists and designers on designing and evaluating equipment, basic work on performance criteria, numeracy tests, incentives and job satisfaction.

Fitting work to people, the other aspect of occupational psychology, overlaps with work study and ergonomics. Here psychologists look at office or factory layouts, the design of equipment and machinery, to see that they take into account psychological factors, and are therefore designed for maximum efficiency. This can mean finding ways to reduce stress factors, improve safety (ensuring that guards are so designed that people will use them), etc, and so increase productivity.

Occupational psychologists are involved when new technology is introduced – for instance, helping to redesign office jobs around word-processors. They also help to improve working methods, and advise on ways of organising a firm to make communication between, say, the shop floor and senior management more efficient.

Qualifications and training No formal training schemes exist, but there are some postgraduate courses, and some first-degree courses include an occupational psychology option, which can be useful in gaining a first post.

THE PRISON SERVICE employs about 80 psychologists, and about 30 psychological assistants. Psychologists work with individual inmates, particularly younger people and disturbed and aggressive prisoners, counselling and giving therapy, running group sessions and training in social skills etc. Some do psychological testing and assessment for the courts, and with probation officers, and in turn evaluate the tests and court reporting system. They help design, develop and evaluate the regimes/systems under which prisoners live, advise on security and control methods, and test the effects of, for example, industrial prisons on reconviction rates. There is increasing emphasis on helping to ensure good communication systems within prisons, and in helping other staff, mainly prison officers, with the problems of dealing with prisoners, working with them on training programmes and in advisory services. This means less time is spent with individual inmates.

OTHER PSYCHOLOGY-RELATED WORK Psychology graduates can go on to train to be PSYCHOTHERAPISTS, ANALYSTS and/or COUNSELLORS, or PSYCHIATRIC SOCIAL WORKERS.
A degree/qualification in psychology is a useful basis for PERSONNEL WORK, MARKET RESEARCH, MANAGEMENT CONSULTANCY, OPERATIONAL RESEARCH, etc.

Further information from the British Psychological Society.

SOCIOLOGY

This is the broadest of the social sciences, studying the whole of human society in all its many and varied aspects. Sociology and psychology obviously overlap, since they both deal with people and society, human behaviour and relationships. Psychology, though, focuses mainly on the behaviour of individuals, and is concerned with society only in relation to them. Sociology focuses mainly on society and the pattern and behaviour of people in and as groups.

Sociologists examine the behavioural norms or rules – called social 'institutions' – which society sets (consciously or unconsciously) so people can live close to each other. They study the characteristics of social groups – the family, social classes, religious groups, women, adolescents – and not individual personalities or intelligence as does psychology. They study social 'systems', or groups of related activities, like education, and the established social 'structures' – everything which relates to economic activity goes to form a country's economic structure, for example, which means sociologists also make their own critical studies of the work of economists or educationalists.

Sociologists examine the relations between social groups, between long-established citizens and recently-arrived minorities, between workers and employers, and between doctors and patients. They study the forms of communication society uses, such as newspapers, broadcasting, and their effects on young people, or the political system.

Sociologists study ideas, such as power and inequality. They study conflict and change in society today, class divisions, how and why people change their position in society, what happens in society to produce people who do well and people who are disadvantaged. They compare aspects of one society with another (training systems in England, Japan and Germany), study the role of trade unions in different industries and countries, or of international companies in developing countries.

Whatever sociologists study, they never isolate their research from its complex and ever changing social setting. There are no watertight compartments in society and so, in studying racial prejudice (for example), the sociologist has to take account of the effects of religious and political beliefs and behaviour, of social class, of educational background, of family attitudes, environment, and so on.

All sociological research, whether on the finer points of the British policeman's sub-culture, or the grand sweep of the social role of religion in India, is producing evidence for sociologists who specialise in building up a body of sociological theory. Here they may be trying to make generalisations about society, and test these against factual evidence – what is significant, for instance, about the fact that the family, in some form, appears to be common to all known societies?

Sociology is often confused with social work. Social workers are there to help people who have problems which can be described as 'social': sociologists may study the causes of such problems, or make analytical studies of the personal social services operated by local authorities, but as professional sociologists they do not work at the 'sharp end' with individuals.

People argue a great deal about the value and validity of sociology. Although it studies real, ordinary everyday situations and problems, it cannot provide easy answers to complicated issues. Some sociologists think they should just observe, analyse and report their findings, while others are prepared to make recommendations, and yet others want to take action themselves – but most sociologists probably want their work to make some contribution to improving the quality of life. There are even sociologists whose work can be described as 'interventionist' – with teenage girls, for instance, to see if it is possible to change the image they have of themselves and their interests, mainly to allow them to develop their full potential, academically and in their careers.

Sociological research, although about people, is increasingly based on statistical analysis. Whatever the problems, the sociologist studies it against the background of a 'working model' of the society – the number of people who live in, for example, Britain: how many are young, how many are old, how many are women, how many belong to trade unions and churches, how many own houses and videos, what people read and how they vote, and spend their leisure time. Sociologists may use statistics of crime rates, on the levels of substandard housing, on the distribution of wealth. The statistics themselves may pose questions – why, for example, has the birth rate been falling so dramatically in western industrialised countries?

Sociologists work largely through interviews and surveys, carefully designed to give the right 'mix' of people, and perhaps repeated with the same group over a period – for instance, a long-term investigation of how children are brought up interviewed the mothers of 700 Nottingham children on their first, fourth, seventh, eleventh and sixteenth birthdays. Using statistical analysis, such a study gives an account of what parents typically say and do in relation to seven year olds, and also charts the variations in views which differ (for example) according to social circumstances. Such a study involves, perhaps, two to four sociologists, two research assistants, and five interviewers.

Opportunities for sociologists
Most professional sociologists do research, and combine this with teaching in

higher or further education. Here they may choose their own studies, or work (as junior staff) on a senior colleague's project, or do research on contract to an organisation which wants information on which to base decisions or policy – such as government departments, political parties, religious bodies, or commercial firms.

There are few research posts outside the education system – in the Civil Service, in local authorities, in independent research organisations. In all these, research is usually directed at providing information for some kind of decision-making, and the sociologist is normally one of a team of experts.

There are now few opportunities to start work in sociological research – public expenditure cuts have been compounded by the very rapid expansion of sociology departments in the 1960s, giving a high proportion of younger staff and therefore fewer to retire. A very good first degree, plus a postgraduate qualification is needed and even then there is no guarantee of a post – and a higher degree may not be an advantage in the open employment market.

Studying sociology Sociology is studied mainly for first and higher degrees.

First degree courses in sociology are available over 40 universities, and with a more empirical and practical bias, at 14 polytechnics and one college of higher education. It is often also included in other social science degrees, notably those in applied social studies.

'First destination' figures are –

	1984-5 university	1984-5 polytechnic	1977-8 university	1977-8 polytechnic
total graduating	1406	1299	1500	2000
destination unknown	237	368	265	644
research etc	83	61	158	110
teacher training	56	27	106	208
'other' training	3	72	112	93
'believed' unemployed Dec 31	159	186	104	182
temporary work	67	99	132	218
permanent UK work	597	432	565	456
employers –				
local government	245	156	289	198
commerce	126	86	87	74
civil service	48	44	26	36
industry	47	33	86	54
higher/further education	32	25	17	22
functions –				
personnel/social etc	271	175	275	177
admin/operations management	84	72	80	75
financial work	55	27	41	31
marketing etc	39	39	44	28

	1984-5		1977-8	
	university	polytechnic	university	polytechnic
research/information	22	15	19	12
management services	7	5	24	16

Entry: specific A-level subjects are not normally needed. Only 734 UK students were accepted for university courses starting in October 1985, over 500 for CNAA courses. The mean A-level 'score' for 1984 university entry was 9.2.

Further information from the British Sociological Association.

The World of Work

The future of employment   334
Choosing and pre-vocational preparation   347
Alternatives to, and self, employment   352

Thirty years of comparatively full employment and widening job and career opportunities for young people came to an abrupt end, rather more sharply than even the experts predicted, in 1979-80. For several years the picture was one of intense competition for work of almost any kind, although all recruiters continued to report some shortages – especially of all-round high calibre people for management training and some specific skills. The overall job situation has only, and fairly slowly, begun to recover over 1986 and early 1987 (partly due to government 'special measures'), and it is by no means clear how far this will be sustained, or improve. The picture that is emerging, though, largely confirms the view that economic recovery provides expanding opportunities for the qualified and 'competent' with recent and relevant experience, and has much less to offer for the rest. But complicating all discussion of future prospects is the looming 'spectre' (for recruiters) of the so-called 'demographic time bomb' – the year in the early 1990s when the number of school-leavers falls to the point where nursing *alone* will need to recruit half of all young women who gain at least five O-level-equivalent passes.

THE FUTURE OF EMPLOYMENT
Changes in the type, range and variety of jobs and occupations which make up the world of employment are not new. Indeed, they have probably been near continuous since primitive people first began to cultivate the land as well as hunt for food. However, the nature of the changes, the number of the changes which have taken place in any one period of time, and the speed of change have, up to now, been such that they could be relatively easily absorbed by society, causing few long-term difficulties in themselves – even though for very many people work could be intermittent and so poorly paid that most effectively lived in perpetual poverty until well into the 20th century. Some of the necessary adaptations were obviously difficult and even painful for particular individuals and groups, especially in economic recession, but transitions have been made, new occupations and work have replaced the old.

But the pace and magnitude of change have both been accelerating over the past two centuries, and have now reached a stage where technological development, social, economic and political factors have interacted and combined to have a cumulative and massive world-wide impact on the pattern of employment in the 1980s and 1990s. In an industrialised, largely urbanised society, paid employment (or state benefit) is essential for physical survival, and for many, a psychological necessity too.

The changes are both quantitative and qualitative. There is considerable disagreement on the quantitative effects, ranging from predictions of continued massive and widespread unemployment for the rest of the century and discussions on whether or not attitudes to work should be completely re-thought, to assumptions that society will be able to continue to adapt to change as it always has in the past, that the needed jobs will reappear once the economy has recovered fully from recession. Few now disagree that the skill content of work is rising.

THE SIZE AND SHAPE OF THE LABOUR MARKET

Most realistic predictions suggest that for the immediate future, economic recovery will be modest and growth relatively low – unless there is a totally unexpected and major improvement in the country's manufacturing trading position. To reduce unemployment significantly, an average annual growth rate of at least 3% is needed, it is estimated. While a rate of 3.5% was reached in 1986, it is predicted to fall again, possibly to 1.75% by mid-1988 – some experts suggest it will be no more than 2-3% yearly, at least up to 1990. Meanwhile, industry has already reached peak productivity, so if the credit boom – on which much of the current growth is based – continues, an import surge is likely. This together with declining oil revenues probably means a worsening balance of payments.

Obviously it is impossible to be exact about jobs in the future, but attempts to predict ahead are made. Both the Institute of Manpower Studies (IMS) at Sussex University) and the Institute for Employment Research (IER) at Warwick University have both recently (1986 and 1985) produced some very similar estimates. IMS predicts 20.53 million in employment, IER 21 million in 1990, with 2.75 million self-employed according to IMS, 2.70 million by IER. Official figures suggest that the civilian labour force is likely to have increased by 600,000 between 1985 and 1991, to 27.2 million of whom 26.7 million will be of working age. On IMS/IER estimates, this still leaves at least 3 million unemployed in 1990. The population of working age will be much larger, rising by 500,000 to 34.3 million with a much greater proportion in the age groups 24-54 and especially 25-34, despite the much smaller under-24 age group. The fact that an unknown number of women not currently counted as part of the civilian labour force would work if work is available means that 3 million may be an underestimate – one estimate suggested 2.3 million extra jobs would be needed to bring unemployment down by 1.25 million, because so many people are not registered.

The world's labour force is still growing – exponentially. The world population was expected to pass 5000 million in July 1987, and had been predicted to reach 6000 million (just four times 1900's 1500 million) by 2000. By 1987, it looked as though the 6000 million figure will be reached by 1995. The developing nations need to create another 750 million jobs by 2006 is the World Bank's recently-revised projection (they had estimated 500 million). The United States needs a million new jobs a year, just to keep pace with population increases – and is currently achieving it. Britain needed some 2 million more jobs during the 1980s. *This is in addition to any new jobs for people at present unemployed.* But Britain now has to compete with the rest of the world, not just for business but for jobs too. Companies are, and will continue to, set up operations wherever they are most cost effective, freed from most currency restrictions, and able to transmit information with increasing ease around the globe.

All the major influences on trends in employment appear to be acting to reduce the number of jobs available, at least in the older industrialised countries of the Western world. These all centre on a process which is not new, but has been going on for a long time, namely the search for ways of doing more of the same thing, more efficiently, at less cost and greater profit. In the industrialised world this was to some extent slowed for 40 or so years by policies and legislation designed to give employees reasonable terms and conditions at work. Competition for jobs and markets with third-world countries which never had such laws has put pressure on the more expensive of them, and changes in work practices introduced with new technology are being used to reduce costs and increase productivity here too, further reinforcing job losses. Straight productivity agreements, negotiated now in the knowledge of high unemployment, are also changing work practices – eg demarcation between trades and working times – inevitably with more job losses.

The three main sectors of employment are –

The primary industries are agriculture, fishing and forestry.

The secondary sector covers firstly manufacturing, and secondly mining, quarrying, construction etc (figures for these are usually given separately).

The tertiary sector is made up of the so-called services, from education, health and science, through the professions like law and accountancy, to financial services, communications, transport, and the leisure and recreational industries.

At the beginning of the 19th century in the UK, employment was divided just about equally between the three sectors.

By the mid-1980s, employment in the primary sector had plummeted to under 2% of the work force.

In the secondary sector the proportion rose to well over 50% of the total by 1851. It remained relatively steady until the early 1960s (with a fall during the 1930s recession), but has since been declining, and by 1986 was barely 33% of the work force.

Tertiary-sector employment has continued to expand proportionately throughout the period, to 65% of the total by 1986. But this is not all new jobs. While the number of jobs in the service industries increased by 575,000 between 1979 and 1985, a significant proportion of these were simply transferred (by sub-contracting) from manufacturing. In 1975 some 15% of service-sector jobs depended on manufacturing (against 12% in 1972) and this is predicted to rise to 18% by 1990. The work being done in the estimated 300,000 jobs which switched sectors between 1979 and 1985 is, then, the same – probably eg in eg computing, business services, catering etc.

The significant factor about the primary sector is that, despite the massive decline in the proportion of the work force employed, both volume and quality of output have increased substantially, feeding a larger proportion of the British population each year. This is called 'jobless growth', and has been achieved largely by much greater capital investment in mechanical and electro-mechanical technology, by taking advantage of all the available and increasingly sophisticated scientific techniques, with sharply-increased expenditure on eg energy and chemicals, by integrating farms into larger, more economically-viable units, and by state financial support. All this in 150 years without a single silicon chip or even that many computers at all. Job losses came, though, slowly and the people so released were absorbed relatively easily by expansion of work elsewhere. IMS projects that employment in the sector will continue to fall at least up to 1990, to 328,000 employees (from 1985's 365,000) and 270,000 self-employed (from 291,000).

In the manufacturing sector, there is similar structural (ie long-term and fundamental) change in the pattern of employment which is not simply the result of short-term economic recession and low aggregate demand. The change is relatively new, and has to some extent been masked by the limits to economic growth. The Science Policy Research Unit at Sussex University has shown that, since 1965, any growth in industrial output has not been accompanied by growth in employment, and even that, since 1973, the reverse has been the case within the EEC. Even in the years 1965-73 when there was a relatively high growth rate (an annual average of 6%), there was virtually no parallel growth in the number of jobs.

The Sussex Science Policy Research Unit suggested that between 1963 and 1976 competition, mainly between developed countries, was the crucial factor in persuading industries into cost-reducing and therefore labour-saving and job-displacing technical change, and to a large extent this is still obviously the case. However, developing nations are also investing in their own manufacturing bases (and multinational companies are investing there), and are now increasingly competing with the developed countries, eroding the latter's share of world markets, and forcing an even higher level of international competition. Many developing countries have now reached levels of literacy and education which make it possible for them to absorb rapidly and efficiently technologies developed far more slowly and expensively by the industrialised nations – Brazil, for example, has built a trainer plane good enough for the RAF to prefer over all others. All their newly-installed plant is up to date and efficient, and the expectations of workers moving from rural-peasant occupations are not as high as those of the developed world, giving lower labour costs.

Industries can survive only by adapting to the new levels of competition. The alternative is to make a deliberate decision to move out of areas of production where competition with other countries is most intensive, and invest in industries, products, based on new, complex technologies and/or 'value-added' products. Evidence shows that, to date, industrialised nations of the West have preferred to adapt, while Japan and some other Far East countries make deliberate decisions to change the country's manufacturing base instead. Adaptation means speeding technical changes to rationalise, increasing thereby capital-intensity, but of course also reducing the number of jobs. Most of Britain's manufacturing industry has been under such pressure, both in overseas and domestic markets, and all have responded with labour-saving rationalisation. Failure to invest or rationalise results equally in loss of jobs through lack of competitiveness and loss of markets. And when and where the cost of capital intensity falls to or below the cost of labour, the move to capital-intensity, and further job losses, is likely to accelerate. At present, Britain still counts as a low-wage economy, and is still not as competitive as is needed.

Of course the effects of a very deep economic recession make it difficult to tell how many of the massive job losses in manufacturing (some 2 million, nearly 40% of jobs, between 1980 and 1986) are permanent, but IMS estimates that on present projections there will be a further loss of nearly a million by 1990.

Statistics show that since 1970 new industrial investment in Europe has moved away from new product development and towards increasing investment in job-reducing rationalisation. Recently, though, some sectors of British industry have begun to innovate, but this does not seem to be helping the job position much yet. IMS quotes the food manufacturing company – already highly automated – which closed an uneconomic plant, shedding 700 jobs, and opened a new one producing a greater volume of a more successful product using the latest technology, employing just 100, mostly skilled, workers.

Manufacturing, then, is unlikely to absorb more than a small proportion of those coming on to the labour market, unless policies and attitudes change in favour of greater innovation. Within the overall picture of continuing job losses, though, there are already shortages of technician and professional skills, and the larger, and permanent job losses are amongst the semi- and unskilled, and single-skilled craft workers (see also MANUFACTURING).

The secondary sector also includes construction, mining and quarrying. Numbers working in construction fluctuate with economic conditions, but the trend has been downwards – it is only comparatively recently that numbers fell for the first time below one million, and the percentage of the workforce in construction is down from 7.5% at the start of the century to only 4% in 1985. In mining and quarrying the proportion employed is now barely 1%, against 5.8% in 1901.

The tertiary sector divides into public service (central and local government administration, education, health etc), and private services (as above). In both public and private sectors, employment continued to rise sharply until the late 1970s.

In the public sector, since 1979, however, it has been government policy to cut numbers as far as possible, particularly in the Civil Service and local government. More and more services are being transferred to the private sector, but a significant proportion of jobs may disappear altogether. In fact, though, numbers rose between 1979 and 1986, if only slightly – by about 5% in medical and health, around 1% for educational and public administration. Further increases in numbers in health and personal social services are needed – just to cope with an ageing population alone – but cash-limited budgets are likely to hold this – and increases in eg police, prison service numbers – to a minimum. IMS predicts a slight fall in public-sector employment – to just under the 5 million mark from just over (24% of the workforce) by 1990. The sector's main problem, though, in the 1990s will be to recruit enough people to fill even the minimum.

Private tertiary-sector employment looks set to go on rising (it went up by 2% between 1982 and 1986) – by some 600,000 according to IMS, by 1990. The Sussex Science Policy Research Unit suggested in 1980 that employment had continued to rise because, by comparison with manufacturing, the tertiary sector has employed low-quality labour, has had lower *per capita* capital investment, and a slower rate of technological change (as well as a much higher proportion of part-time workers).

Of course some sectors, such as banking and insurance, have increased capital investment sharply, especially on computer-based systems eg directly labour-saving equipment such as autobanks and computerised cheque-clearing systems. But although the finance sector is trying to hold down numbers employed to stay competitive, expanding business increased employment by 30% over 1979-86, and is currently creating 30,000 new jobs a year.

The greatest increase in jobs is predicted to come in the leisure, tourist-related industries. Here employment rose by 3% between 1982 and 1986, although the increase in numbers was 30% short on government predictions (30,000 not 50,000) and a high proportion are part-time jobs. This is almost all as a result of expanding business, with little technology involved in job creation or loss. IMS estimates a further increase of about 200,000 in all leisure-based industries by 1990.

IER predicted in 1983 that any increase in jobs in communication up to 1990 would be more than offset by losses in transport. In fact the number of communication jobs appears to be levelling out (after an increase of about 3% over 1979-86), and IMS predicts a small fall in numbers by 1990.

The Science Policy Research Unit has suggested that the increasing availability of new technology suitable for other sectors of service industries may mean that fewer jobs are created in future, although again there is no way of estimating accurately the capacity or demand for innovation in new services. Jobs in the service industries are also vulnerable to replacement by equipment which consumers can use themselves, eg cars replacing public transport, and that new technology reinforces this trend (from more self-service equipment like petrol pumps, through to greater direct access to entertainment, information and education in the home, for instance).

THE IMPACT OF TECHNOLOGICAL DEVELOPMENT
In the long history of technological advance, change has been largely incremental, with one development building on others, and the effects therefore progressive and not immediately disruptive. But it is also possible to identify rare but real innovatory break-throughs which have rapid, and quite dramatic effects on human development – the wheel, the printing press, gunpowder, steam, radio, splitting the atom – and the computer. These major developments, moreover, are now happening more frequently.

From amongst the very many technological advances of the 20th century, semi-conductor technology – micro-electronics – was probably the most significant in terms of innovation at least up to 1986, with all the potential to make really fundamental changes throughout society in a relatively short space of time. Optical fibres and laser technology together are raising still further the potential of microelectronics, particularly in communications. Magnetic recording technology (used for computers' floppy discs as well as in audio and video) is also essential to the microelectronic revolution.

Other technologies, though, already promise more such changes in the future. Biotechnology is now having a growing impact in many areas and will probably have as great an impact as microelectronics in the long run. But 1986 saw yet another major 'leap' in technology – a (ceramic) material capable of 'superconducting' at temperatures which make it usable.

Superconductors are more than just a possible way of speeding up computers even further. They also make possible hovering transport and, probably most useful of the so-far identified potential applications, a way of making electricity generation and transmission 'super'efficient. But superconductors may have other implications too. They demonstrate that the day of the 'designer material' has fully arrived, and they are cheap to make. While it will be some, probably many, years before superconducting materials have a major impact on daily life they seem set to be as significant as microelectronics.

For the moment, though, microelectronics is the dominant technology, and its technological features are fairly common knowledge now. Its significance is so great because microelectronic devices are so tiny, can be produced in huge quantities and so are cheap. Standard microprocessors can be programmed to do so many and varied different tasks and so are immensely flexible. They are, being solid-state, totally reliable (if properly programmed). Future development of these devices seems near limitless.

Micro-electronic technology is seemingly all-pervasive, with actual or potential applications in almost all areas of employment and implications for virtually every job. It is now impossible to describe briefly all the innovations. Chapter after chapter throughout this edition of the *Careers Encyclopedia* demonstrates the revolutionary nature of micro-electronic technology – in INFORMATION TECHNOLOGY, in BROADCASTING and COMMUNICATIONS, in MANUFACTURING, and in FINANCE, are only some of the examples.

Micro-electronics makes possible faster, more efficient, reliable and usually less labour-intensive ways of doing progressively more tasks, and to do sophisticated tasks that were completely impossible, or not cost-effective, premicroelectronics. Micro-electronics brings together the previously separate technologies of (tele)communications, broadcasting and computing, to create many new ways of capturing, transmitting, managing and exploiting information, to analyse, monitor, present, and use it in many more and sophisticated ways. Used to convert voice and eg fax to the same digital signals that transmit computer data, it is integrating all forms of communication, so information can be transmitted flexibly between different kinds of equipment down the same (optical fibre) lines. Used with satellite and/or fibre-optic cable it makes communication around the world all but instantaneous. Micro-electronics can make computer-based systems as 'interactive' – communicating in both directions – as the telephone.

Microelectronics – with its supporting technologies –

has given a great many products microprocessor controls, making them smaller, neater, with fewer parts to assemble or go wrong.

cut out much routine, time consuming tasks like calculations and data transformation in engineering design, and put isometric drawings on a graphic-display screen – of the shape of a car, the detail of a component, the layout of pipes in a chemical plant.

created near-'intelligent' systems to do more sophisticated tasks – medical and scientific instruments to analyse, monitor and measure more efficiently and automatically; robots to paint, weld and assemble; in-car systems.

has already brought – almost – a single, global financial market through information systems.

will soon bring programmes from television stations round the world direct into everyone's home.

brings into prospect factories – widely spread across a continent – virtually controlled by designers at their CAD (computer-aided design) terminals telling robots what to make, and customers at their VDUs telling them how many of each product, with marketing, purchasing, stock-control, finance etc, working from the information the system generates.

will let people work and shop, deal with their bank, study, at home, as well as widen the range of available home entertainment.

Microelectronics has and is taking the computer and computer-based systems into almost every possible environment – the home, the school, the factory, the construction site, the shop, the artist/designer's studio, the salesman or woman's briefcase, the bank, the car, the doctor's surgery, the farm office, the airliner's cabin, the lawyer's and the journalist's desk, the hotel, the police station, the ship's bridge, the telephone exchange, the travel agent – the list could be endless.

But the 'enabling' technology, however clever, is not enough and never has been. Not every new technology has been a commercial success in the past – most recently, for instance, supersonic airliners and quadraphonic sound. There is no guarantee that all the possible applications of microelectronic technology will find a market either. Especially where the investment is high, it can be a major gamble. Cable TV, for instance, is developing only very slowly, and progress towards a 'cashless society' and 'paperless office' is far, far slower than the optimists have been predicting.

New technology – any technology not just microelectronics – is adopted to meet a perceived necessity, to combat or get ahead of competition (technological or cost), to cut costs (so the capital cost of the new equipment must be right), to meet an established or certain demand, to combat skill shortages, or to fill a gap in the market by innovating. Innovation for its own sake is a non-starter, especially in today's market conditions. Firms are reluctant to accept new technology if there is no apparent advantage in so doing, if the cost is too high (particularly for small firms), if they have already expensively re-tooled with an earlier technical advance and are still competitive, if resistance by key workers is too great, or they simply cannot afford it given high interest rates (or the ever-present risk of them) and, eg tight market conditions. Firms are also more likely to invest when market prospects are improving – and although silicon chips themselves may be cheap, they need software which is not, and the complete systems can have very expensive consequences.

But once new technology is in place in any market, the other firms in that market have very little option but to become 'players', or find other ways round the competitive advantage gained by the innovator – although sometimes there is an argument for letting someone else do the pioneering to pinpoint the hidden snags. But sooner or later, the majority of employing organisations will have to take on microelectronic, information, technology.

The consequences for jobs could be as bad, if not worse, if they do not than if they do. Most experts are now quite sure that IT, properly used, can provide most commercial and industrial firms with a greater competitive 'edge', and can give every organisation better control over eg costs while improving services. Not to invest in new technologies is to risk going out of business altogether, and so losing even more jobs than might go as a result of IT. The worrying factor for the future of employment is that too few employers in the UK have so far (1987) recognised IT as the key to future success.

Microelectronic technology, it is now clear, both creates and destroys jobs. In what proportion, and with what net effect, is probably impossible to calculate (even using IT systems), since so many different factors are involved. The most likely outcome is that in the immediate future adopting micro-electronic technology will tend to reinforce existing structural changes in the primary and secondary sectors, and produce similar changes in the tertiary sector.

IT can destroy quite quickly jobs it created earlier in the technological process – eg data preparation as a separate skill. (And once the major failure of IT technology – cheap and simple optical methods of 'capturing' data for the first time from printed/written documents – is solved, and/or voice recognition becomes practical, the number of clerical and secretarial workers is also likely to fall.) The need for large numbers of (applications) programmers has prob-ably peaked – or will do so quite soon. But the business world is looking for a new animal who doesn't even have a recognised job specification or title yet – IT staff who combine computer and business 'literacy' and can select, modify and implement software packages, and work on projects, inside the user-department or -organisation (see INFORMATION TECHNOLOGY).

In manufacturing, the most obvious job losses are in the increasing levels of automation, where because the technology is improving all the time even greatly increased sales do not create enough jobs to balance out the losses (the classic example is all-electronic telephone exchanges which need only one out of every 26 needed to make an electro-mechanical exchange). Automation is not the only job loser, however. Where and when microprocessors replace components in existing products, not only are there fewer parts to put together, and therefore fewer processes or assemblies (which then also become easier to automate), but fewer items have to be held in stock, and since the new components are smaller, less warehouse space and less transport are needed. Fewer stages in manufacturing mean fewer supervisory and admin-istrative staff to link them.

The next stages in developing IT business systems link manufacturer, or other supplier (eg tour and airline operators) directly to their retail outlet via what are called 'value added networks'. This is amongst the developments which let firms 'strip out' whole layers of staffing. Here, according to IMS, 'line' man-agers are becoming the point of contact rather than the travelling salesman/ woman. More, the information generated from direct, on-line ordering by customers (for eg chemicals), and/or retailers can be used to 'tell' automated stock-controllers how many of what components/raw materials are needed and the plant itself how many to make. An international car firm expects both to be able to generate sophisticated financial information almost to the nth degree *and* cut its financial staff by 50% in the not too distant future.

With some exceptions, maintenance and servicing of micro-processor based equipment needs fewer people. The next generation of cars may need only 40% of the servicing needed now, with extended intervals between services, because cars will have computerised systems which can diagnose their own faults, and by-pass them if necessary. Computers based at service outlets will take information from the car's computer memory to tell when parts need replacing.

Any new jobs, therefore, have to come from innovation, or a very significant expansion in demand. Factors other than technology play a part, too.

The financial sector has been the runaway success of the 1980s so far, and shows just how fast it is possible to move from the eighteenth to the twenty-first century. The financial sector's share of GDP has risen to nearly 20% (1985), from under 18% in 1980 and only 15% in 1970. More significantly, the numbers employed rose by 21% between 1978 and 1986, to a total of 759,000 (including estate agencies and business services). This despite a considerable amount of labour-saving 'automation' which lead to predictions of declining employment. Moreover, this is probably a fairly considerable underestimate of the expansion in the size of the financial sector. Most of the largest firms have, for example, effectively turned their corporate treasury departments into minibanks/investment houses (see ACCOUNTANCY AND FINANCIAL MAN-AGEMENT), but figures relating to them are incorporated with their business sector.

But this is not all down to IT. De-regulation to force competition was probably the trigger here, but helped by factors like the sale of nationalised industries on the stock market, relaxation of credit facilities, changes in financial regulations of all kinds, the need to create 'hedges' against fluctuating currency-exchange and interest rates, and the fashion for take-overs and mergers – although an element of some of these may be effect rather than cause.

Automating the office, it is generally agreed, is having considerable impact on employment. While there are few figures to go on, it seems clear that the effect, to date, has been greatest on clerical and secretarial staff, with greatest losses in un- and semiskilled jobs. Word-processing alone can increase office efficiency by up to 100%, suggesting a decline in employment of up to 50%. It is unlikely to be as high as this: offices with only one or two typists can hardly reduce their numbers, and existing secretarial staff are increasingly expected to handle a larger work load. An IMS survey showed most firms expecting no change in numbers, but larger firms do expect to be able to reduce staffing levels further, while smaller ones expect to have to take on more staff. Many firms expect to cope with increased work loads using temporary or part-time staff.

Any additional increase in efficiency in information flow within organisations, via the increasing use of software packages – which users can now modify for themselves with new programming languages – further automation and integration of office systems and telecommunications, will also make it possible to cut the number of managerial, administrative and even professional staff, although so far firms are only predicting 'nil growth'. Automating office work in manufacturing industry, reducing paperwork by collecting orders and taking payment 'on-line' for example, is expected to have even greater impact – on both productivity and employment – than automating the production line.

It seems that, since most organisations moving over to IT claim to be able to achieve any cuts in the number of jobs through natural wastage, it will be future, new jobs that just will not happen. To date, the brunt of job loss has, then, largely been borne by inexperienced school-leavers or would-be re-entrants to the labour market who are looking for jobs with relatively low skill content.

The complicating factor is the falling number of young people coming out of the education system. Shortages of people with all kinds of skills are apparently rising sharply – although studies suggest firms could solve at least some of their problems by being more open-minded on the qualifications they demand for particular jobs, and by doing more cross training themselves (and this they may be forced to do). While most firms prefer people with experience, they also need a constant and steady injections of 'new blood', people who have grown up with new systems and who can be trained for management in what will be a very different environment in the 21st century. How they will handle the shortages as they get worse is not clear. Some firms are just not expanding. Others are looking at ways of training and re-training, but in general the level of training in industry/commerce is abysmal, and developing training facilities may well take too long.

Another possible source of help is the development, and increasing success, of 'expert' systems (see INFORMATION TECHNOLOGY), which may prove a better way of 'deskilling' all kinds of tasks than has ever been possible before. They may just help solve the problem of skills shortages, they may make more innovation possible, they may make inroads into the number of jobs in professional and managerial work as well as other skilled jobs. The physical limits of what microelectronics can do may soon be reached, and exploiting it will increasingly depend on developing more sophisticated but cost-effective and 'user-friendly' software. A qualitative 'leap' seems to have begun, at last, here, but the likely effects on employment have not yet worked through to the analysts' models.

THE CHANGING PATTERN OF WORK

Under the impact of (mainly) technological change and competition – which interact to bring organisational and work restructuring – both the types of jobs and the work done are also changing in many ways.

Up to 1987, the effects of competition have probably been somewhat greater than the effects of (information) technology, largely because the number of organisations making maximum use of IT is still comparatively small and is concentrated amongst larger organisations – and competition has affected almost all to a greater or lesser extent.

While predicting ahead is increasingly difficult, it is possible to identify some of the trends.

Organisations of all kinds, reportedly, want to increase the flexibility of their workforces. The emerging pattern, according to an IMS study, is of a workforce clearly divided between permanent and part-time, temporary, contract and casual workers, as well as sub-contracting firms. The 'core' of permanent workers will be kept as small as possible, and as many functions as possible will be done by specialist sub-contractors – individuals or companies (eg caterers for staff restaurants/canteens, cleaning firms). Where special projects, or particularly heavy work-loads demand it, other staff will be taken on. This may be, eg systems analysts to work on a new IT system on short term contract; regular part-time staff to cope with Saturday trade in a store or casual staff for the summer tourist trade. Evidence for this is also coming from elsewhere – for instance, one secretarial agency predicts a massive increase in demand for temporary staff by the year 2000, and many computing staff reputedly find contract working attractive.

The computer terminal, VDU and keyboard, personal computer is now a major, and near ubiquitous feature of the work place – and if it isn't already soon will be – and being able to work with information – creating, organising, retrieving/receiving, and/or exploiting it – is already a growing component of a great many jobs, and will affect most of the rest in some way.

The balance between the different kinds of jobs is generally changing as has been predicted, and is likely to go on doing so. Professional, technician, multi-skilled craft, and part-time support/personal-service jobs will increase in numbers, full-time unskilled jobs will decline 'significantly', says the Institute of Manpower Studies. Employers want a 'major improvement' in the quality and breadth of skills amongst managers, professionals of all kinds (but especially IT staff). IMS evidence confirms that –

In production industries, the occupation(s) which have expanded most recently (1983-5) are engineering, science and technology (by 23%), and that work for operatives and support services (eg clerical/secretarial/sales) has contracted most (by 35% and 27% respectively). Here the shift is clearly in favour of occupations with a higher skill or knowledge content, and this the Institute expects to continue at least up to 1990. Large firms expect to employ more managers, engineers, scientists, technologists, 'other' professions, but smaller companies will increase intake of all occupations – including the less skill-intensive – if demand for their products increases.

In the service industries, according to IMS, the different sectors have only one feature in common – the relatively low proportions of managerial and professional groups. In distributive, financial and business services, sales assistants and clerical employees predominate. In leisure it is 'personal services' staff, in transport and communications, operatives, technicians and craftworkers. Recent expansion has benefited most support services, especially sales (31%), professions (28%), operatives, technicians and craftworkers (17%), and managers (17%). Contraction has been greatest in clerical and related jobs (45%), and operatives, technicians and craftworkers (29%). Growth in jobs has been due almost entirely to expansion in business. Up to 1990, IMS expects expansion across the occupation spectrum, except in transport/communications, and in retail, wholesale and banking, where larger employers are expected to intensify use of new technologies, involving cuts in every occupation, but expansion by small to medium size employers will mean growth will go on favouring low-skilled occupations – part-time sales staff, catering staff, butchers, bakers and lorry drivers, but also accounts, marketing staff and buyers as more 'professional' management increases.

Managers, says IMS, are seen as the key source of most organisations' future success, in all sectors and all sizes of organisation, in both private and public sector. Numerically, though, they are a small group, and numbers are not expected, according to IMS, to change overall. Small organisations expected to increase their managerial staff, but many larger commercial organisations expect to change organisational structure, reducing layers of managers and so cutting numbers, while public-sector organisations, eg the NHS, are turning their 'administrators' into managers with greater responsibility for decision making.

The role of the manager is changing, says IMS, in terms of both work content and the need for higher standards of performance. Both are said to need four kinds of skills – planning to cope with strategy (and anticipate and cater for changing consumer demand), commercial to allocate and 'prioritise' resources – human relations to get plans accepted, and administrative to implement it – and the last was most important only a few short years ago. Managers are now also expected to have keyboard, diagnostic and analytical skills and to be able to use on-line computer facilities, and analyse the data in their day-to-day work. Managers are involved in sales and marketing via value-added networks giving two-way links to retailers and wholesalers, and some firms are running down their sales forces.

The numbers of engineers, scientists and technologists is still not large, despite recent expansion, but all sectors expect to need (even) more especially in microelectronics and IT, either as technical specialists (eg electronics and software engineers), or as production engineers who can apply the technology to the development and integration of new manufacturing systems, architects using CAD techniques, chemists who can use computers to monitor and analyse processes. Multi-skilled professionals, who can work in teams, and have project management and commercial skills are increasingly needed, according to IMS – because of, eg the effect of the move to competitive tendering (from cost-plus pricing) in defence contracts. As shown elsewhere, people able to help develop and introduce IT financial management or networks are also wanted. Production and manufacturing engineers who can work in terms of 'systems' and use new technologies to boost productivity, improve reliability and increase production flexibility are another important group, confirms IMS. Only comparatively small numbers of biotechnology-related skills are needed says IMS, mainly in pharmaceuticals, food and drink industries. Technical staff are particularly crucial in electronics.

Amongst 'other' professions, employers expect to have more jobs for everyone from accountants to training officers, says IMS, although numbers are still small. Firms stress the need for HE-level education/training to enable professionals across a number of specialist disciplines as products and/or production methods or services become increasingly science/technology-based. The shortage of dp staff is highlighted, and IMS confirms the trends away from computing as a 'backroom' function' (see WORKING IN INFORMATION TECHNOLOGY/COMPUTING).

Accountants are wanted mainly to improve and extend IT-based financial management systems, and link branch networks – growing decentralisation of companies is, says IMS, generating demand for more management staff to have financial skills, with a financial specialist in each unit.

All firms want to improve the quality and effectiveness of marketing and professional sales staff.

Technicians and craftworkers are still seen as key for firms' future success too, according to IMS. Growth in actual numbers is expected to be, at best, relatively small, and the growing need for skills enhancement is stressed. Both technological factors and weakening job demarcations are steadily increasing the importance of multi-skilled – mechanical-, electrical- and hydraulic-based – craftworkers, confirms IMS, although change is uneven. One firm the Institute surveyed had integrated twelve production stages into three, while another still had 250 different job titles. The trend to multiskilling is, generally says IMS, enhancing the jobs of craftworkers and technicians. IMS has also found firms redesigning jobs so technicians can take on work formerly done by professional staff, to improve use of staff and counter staff shortages.

While numerically, the numbers of operatives and clerical/secretarial support staff is declining, technology and reorganisation may be increasing the import-ance of those left and upgrading their skills. Operatives are manning several – extremely expensive and often computer-driven – machines and dealing with simpler repair and maintenance jobs. Secretarial staff are taking on the work of co-ordinating within their divisions/units.

In the service sector, especially retailing and hotel/catering, firms are at last – according to IMS – recognising that fierce competition demands high-quality sales staff with good social skills and competence, and that 'quality enhance-ment' for these 'front line' people is vital. Part-time staff are now being treated – nurtured even – as a permanent resource. IMS is, though, uncertain whether this 'heightened awareness' of training needs will persist.

Sources UK Occupational and employment trends to 1990, by R Pearson and A Rajan (Butterworths 1986). MSC Labour Market *Quarterly Report. Technical change and employment*, by Roy Rothwell and Walter Zegveld (Frances Pinter 1979). *The manpower implications of micro-electronic technology*, a report by Jonathan Sleigh et al for the Department of Employment (HMSO 1979). *Technology, choice and the future of Work* (British Association for the Advancement of Science and the Intermediate Technology Development Group 1978). *Computer technology and Employment*, AUEW (TASS) (National Computing Centre 1979).

CHOOSING AND PRE-VOCATIONAL PREPARATION

It is somewhat ironic that it took mass unemployment to prove that school-leavers generally need better preparation for work. Paradoxically, it is poss-ible that many may have pre-vocational preparation for work which they may be able to get. 'Because the labour market is so highly competitive', said MSC's Youth Training Task Force, 'basic knowledge of the world of work, job search and other skills is essential', echoing Kevin Devine (once director of the Schools Council's defunct Careers Education and Guidance Project) whom we first quoted nearly fifteen years ago – 'All too often young people leave school ill-prepared for the demands which life will place upon them. Sadly the picture is usually one of ignorance of the world of work, total unawareness of real potential...' Moreover, it is still only the less able for whom this vocational preparation is now being provided. There is *still*, in 1987, no proper provision for those heading for A levels and higher education, who include tomorrow's professionals and managers and upon whom so much must apparently depend, and some even suggest that the most able do not even need it.

Advising and informing young people on their futures in a rapidly-changing and tough employment situation is increasingly difficult. Young people of all kinds of ability and aptitude face great uncertainty, and there is no way that careers advisers can promise them all reasonable, satisfying careers for life, however well they are prepared. This is so even for some of those who start with all the apparent advantages but is much worse for those who do not.

Young people have to be fully and properly prepared for this, for the uncertainty of the future, for all the consequences for them, personally, of a constantly-changing employment situation, and for the possibility that some of them could spend quite substantial parts of their lives without paid work. It is just as crucial to see that parents, who are still a major influence on their sons and daughters, and have understandable ambitions for them, are made aware of the real-world implications of the fact that many of the traditional patterns of career development that they have taken for granted are changing significantly and probably permanently.

By the time young people are in their fifth year at school they and their parents should understand the realities of the employment market as they relate to them personally. Careers education for all age groups should now include studies of economic, social, technological and political trends and policies as they affect employment, so that these young adults understand what they are likely to face in the future, be more ready to cope with it, and be prepared to take advantage of rapidly-changing opportunities. For it looks as though the employment opportunities for young people are about to go through yet another fairly dramatic change, and it will be only too easy to miss the chances coming up. The evidence is that there will be a growing and substantial divide in opportunities for those with higher-level skills and abilities, and those without them, and that the regional divide in career opportunities is getting worse.

Finding and negotiating the complex route from school into a reasonable future is a difficult process. Every young adult wants something different from and in their work, has different interests, and has different aptitudes and abilities to offer. Some people are ambitious – others are not; some are quite content to go through a lengthy training – others are not. Everyone can do something reasonably well; most people have their own unique package of abilities, aptitudes and skills, some or all of which will make the basis of a reasonable start in adult life. The problem is to decide which – not everyone wants to 'use' particular skills – or even a superb talent (such as music) – to gain an income. Being 'good' at science at school does not necessarily mean having to become a scientist. The abilities which make a good scientist – thinking logically, the ability to observe and deduce facts, imagination, curiosity, mathematical ability, and so on – are qualities that can be useful in many other occupations.

Deciding on individual personal priorities like these is just as important as ever – indeed perhaps even more so, because recruiters for jobs and training schemes, admissions tutors for courses prefer to choose the people who are well-motivated for the job, the training scheme or course, who can show their interest in and knowledge of the job or course, as well having as the right aptitudes and qualifications. With continuing competition for good jobs and for places in higher education – although this is easing now for some occupations and in some subjects – it is tempting to settle for whatever is available at the first opportunity, whether or not it makes the best use of abilities or aptitudes, or meets personal priorities or interests.

Yet whatever the employment situation, young people are still more likely to do well in a job or on a training scheme or course, and more likely to be chosen for the job, training scheme or course in the first place if it really interests them. Competition for work or educational opportunities is just one more factor – even though a major one – to be considered in deciding what route to follow, but it has to be treated in context. While more young people will probably have to make more compromises with their ambitions, it is still worth seeking out a job, training scheme, or course that is as interesting as possible for them. What is crucial is to know what the opportunities – and the alternatives – are, where they lead, what can improve chances of getting into a particular job or training scheme, or on to a course, whether persistence – repeated applications – is worthwhile, and what to do in the meantime.

It is probably no longer sensible to think or talk in terms of 'choosing *a* career' – if it ever was. Few of today's school-leavers can expect to find a single occupation to follow through for all of their working lives. Their 'careers' will almost certainly be made up of several different, even if related, kinds of work, periods of re-training, periods of temporary work and/or self-employment, and perhaps 'unemployment' too, and they need to be prepared for this, both in their thinking and in their educational and vocational preparation.

It is, of course, something of a myth that even in the more stable past most people stayed in a single occupation for all of their working lives. In fact, people have always changed the kind of work they do, often more than once in a working lifetime, as new opportunities have come up and old jobs died, and as they themselves have changed and developed. The difference now is that it will no longer be a matter of having the *choice* of doing something different, but of *having* to change, of being prepared for it, and ready to grasp new opportunities should they arise. Sensibly, teenagers (and their parents) will be as open-minded as they can about what they are going to do, and prepared to look beyond areas of work or study which are traditional for people with their particular backgrounds. If parents agree that industry/engineering needs more high-calibre people, for instance, then they will not encourage their boys and girls to think that the more traditional professions are 'better'.

Most people have the necessary potential, capabilities, interests, and even motivation to take them successfully into any of a number of different occupations – which means not being obsessive about one. Young people should now try to think in terms of a broad range of possible areas of work, or higher/ further education or training, as a first step after school, rather than latch onto a single, narrow fixed idea about a career, job or employer, or course. It is worth learning about 'families' or groups of work and training, to see the relationship between one area of work and another, and how it is possible to

acquire skills that help in transferring between occupations and areas of work.
Thinking and finding out about ideas for study and/or work has to start early –
especially as it is important to make sure essential and/or useful subjects are
studied – but *deciding* should be left as long as possible. Being flexible, and
prepared to change ideas or direction if necessary, having alternative plans and
ideas to follow up should be part of everyone's strategic planning.

Accident, chance, luck, and impulse will still inevitably play their part in
deciding on the next step on the education/training/careers path, but anyone
who wants to make the most of the available opportunities is going to give
more time to intelligent planning and preparation. For nearly forty years,
opportunities more or less presented themselves to the school-leaver and the
graduate. Opportunities were expanding and were largely limited only by
academic/educational achievement. Most young adults could assume they
would find reasonably satisfying work to match their interests and ambitions
without very much effort. Parents and young people alike assumed they would
have little difficulty and did not expect to have to work at it. Today everything
is different. The comparatively simple and straightforward educational and
career paths followed by young people in the 1950s, 1960s and even the 1970s
may have grown steadily steeper, the educational hurdles to be jumped higher,
but they were relatively easy to map and the routes through comprehensible
and stable.

In the 1980s, the paths have turned into an Alice-through-the-Looking-Glass
chessboard, with just as little predictability and a startling new habit of changing shape (although the educational hedges are still there and have to jumped).
To cope with this new world, young adults, with the help of their parents,
careers advisers and teachers, have to become expert decision-makers, to
develop a strategy for themselves, and learn how to chart their best possible
routes over changing ground. The skill is to make decisions for positive reasons
('because I want to do it') rather than negative ones ('there isn't any alternative'), to keep as many options open as possible, and to be flexible, to allow for
unforeseen change, and to be well-briefed on changes already happening (or
that have happened). All this makes training in personal decision making an
even more essential part of career education.

Evaluating each step and opportunity becomes more difficult as opportunities
grow fewer and competition more intense.

Should an academically-able sixteen year old with a reasonable batch of O
levels take the hard route to A levels with the apparent risks involved in
competing for a university place, or leave school and try for an *apparently*
'safe' but unexciting job in eg a bank or insurance company ?

Another sixteen-year-old may have to decide whether any of the locally-
available YTS schemes will give first training in a chosen skill and lead to
further training and a job, or whether it would be better to take a full-time
course at FE college or have an extra year at school.

By the fifth year at school, young people have to know enough about themselves, have access to the information which tells them which route will do
what for them, and be skilled enough at decision making to be able to assess,
with support, which is the best to choose.

Preparing for a different future, keeping options open and being flexible means it makes sense for young people to take as much advantage as they can of all available education – school, college, and university – and training. This is not just because there will be fewer opportunities for the least and unqualified – and rather more for those who have greater educational, and preferably vocational, preparation. A good educational background and sound basic training at whatever level should also make it easier to adapt to change as it comes. Every teenager should go on learning full-time for as long as they benefit from it and stay interested, keeping their studies as broadly-based as possible. With few exceptions, it is not good strategy to turn down educational opportunities, especially for an immediate job with no real long-term prospects and/or proper training.

Education-based learning does not suit all young people, however, and at some stage even the most academically-oriented must begin to acquire work-based skills. When and where this starts is obviously something to be decided individually. The Youth Training Scheme, designed to be the gateway to work-based training for all sixteen- (and probably seventeen-) year-old school-leavers, will hopefully result eventually in a wider range of different opportunities which can be more closely geared to individual needs. Again there are strong arguments for choosing initial training which is as broad as possible, preparing for a range of related areas of work, whether at craft, technician or graduate/professional level (and bearing in mind that the boundaries between these are blurring and the skill-content at each changing), so that it is easier both to change jobs and to add on new and additional or even somewhat different skills at a higher level. At present it is actually more difficult for able young people to gain work-based skills alongside their academic qualifications, especially where their courses have no direct vocational value, than for those not aiming for degrees (see DEGREES AND VOCATIONAL PREPARATION).

Acquiring extra, potentially useful skills is another way of becoming more employable and insuring against future change. For example, no teenager should ever pass up the opportunity to learn how computers work and how to use and/or program them. *Everyone* should learn how to keyboard (a view now endorsed by even the barristers' Bar Council). It is always worth trying to improve on mathematical and/or statistical skills. Even the most elementary training in business skills could be useful, and so is the ability to use one or more languages within the context of a chosen area of work. Everyone should learn to drive, and have a valid driving licence.

Work experience can be a crucial factor in finding permanent work. Difficult as it may be, everyone still in education should use every opportunity they can to gain experience of 'real' work situations. Ingenuity and imagination may be needed to find such experience. Failing paid temporary or part-time employ-ment, it should be 'simulated' via eg voluntary work, business games or their equivalent. Having, and keeping up, interests outside academic study and/or working life is also crucial. Employers and course admissions tutors like candidates to be 'rounded' personalities with a range of interests. Learning to run a club, organise some kind of activity for a group, producing a magazine or newspaper, being involved regularly in a spare-time activity can be a substitute for work experience. It also helps in developing the all-important social skills, learning to work closely with other people, and in finding out about personal interests. Spare-time interests can, in some cases, develop into a possible source of income – and there is likely to be more leisure time to be filled in future.

ALTERNATIVES TO, AND SELF, EMPLOYMENT

For forty years all the trends were towards more people gaining their incomes through employment with an organisation – commercial and industrial companies, local authorities, central government and so on. The push towards larger units for economy of scale made it increasingly difficult for small traders of all kinds to survive: the supermarket and large store crowded out the small local shop; in industries from electronics to textiles, in banking and publishing, and so on, the number of individual companies declined severely. Interest in traditional crafts declined, and the income to be made by providing services such as window-cleaning were not comparable with the pay provided by companies short of labour. Planning and re-development did not allow much space for small units. Even where the traditions of self-employment, or part-nership, survived – mainly in the professions, such as accountancy, law, architecture, general medical practice – the trend has been to larger units: few 'own practice' GPs remain, many working from health centres.

Even so, the tradition did not entirely die out. Surprisingly, perhaps, modern technology even brought some revival; for example, many computer program-mers work independently very successfully. New technology is likely, in future, to make it easier for people to work from home, and if this becomes generally socially acceptable, it may well change working relationships between individuals and employers quite considerably. At least one major company helps surplus staff to form 'spin-off' organisations, or to train for different work (eg scientists as teachers). Another has a pilot scheme which allows suitable staff to become independent, with the company as their first and initially at least, major customer. Job-sharing is another way of spreading available work, although it has not become a very common practice as yet.

Part-time working has grown considerably – 24% (nearly five million) of all jobs in 1986 against only 15% in 1971 – and is expected to go on expanding. Another 1.5 million people do temporary, 'contract', seasonal, and casual work, and this also is predicted to increase sharply by the end of the century. Firms want to operate in future with as small a 'core' of permanent employees as possible, and draw both expertise and physical labour from a large pool of part-time, contract, temporary staff as and when needed. Casual and volun-tary work are also useful ways of bridging between jobs, can lead to more permanent work, add to skills and experience, and at very least help keep up the habit of working.

Co-operatives are businesses set up by a group, or team, of people who each have an equal stake and equal (managerial) responsibility. After some rather spectacular failures, they are growing in numbers, although they still have major problems in finding finance. There are (1987) at least 900, possibly 1200-1400, co-operatives in the UK, with about 20,000 'members' (some also have non-member employees). Some (about 15%) are formed by groups of employees to take over firm in financial trouble, but most (67%) are brand-new co-operative businesses. The main areas for co-operatives are in building, entertainment, retail/catering, and printing, but others are in crafts, engineering (eg making central heating systems), manufacturing (eg clothing, garden products), community services (eg a village shop). While the failure rate for co-operatives is now only about 10% – better than the general run of new businesses – the managerial problems are said to be tougher than in a conventional business, and made more complicated by consensus decision-making.

Franchising is also expanding, and the franchise business is expected to double total turnover by 1990. An estimated 150,000 jobs have been created by some 440 franchises (1987), with an average of 45 franchised units each. Franchise companies sell licences to operate a branch of a business owned by that particular company. Many are in retailing/catering – pizza and fried chicken houses for example, but with a growing range of service franchises – eg print 'shops', mobile car servicing, parcel delivery, house insulation, drain cleaning and plumbing.

It can be very hard work indeed to bring in a reasonable income (the franchise owner takes either a royalty, or marks up the price of supplies). Although the services provided by the franchisor should help considerably, franchisees still need sound business and managerial skills, as in any other business, small or large.

The initial capital outlay can be very high (but banks will lend a substantial proportion for sound schemes). It is crucial to take sound advice (from eg a bank), on the viability of a particular franchise business before investing, to have the cash flow and profit projections given looked at by an expert, and ask questions (eg failure rates of franchisees, directors' business histories). The fee should cover training in both the practical skills and managing the business, and intensive back-up to start with. It is sensible to check out that the long-term technical support and supply of equipment and material is well organised, and talk to some existing franchise-holders. Any franchise consultant/broker dealt with should be a member of the trade association.

Self-employment high levels of unemployment, not surprisingly, have brought a revival of interest in what are now often called alternatives to employment. Some 11% (about 2.8 million people) of the workforce was self-employed in 1986, against only 8% in 1971. Organisations of all kinds, both companies and central and local government, are trying to reduce permanently the numbers they employ, so the alternatives are clearly going to be important for a long time to come. The government expects new jobs to be generated by new and by definition small, rather than older, businesses, and so is encouraging people to start up on their own with, eg enterprise allowances.

The conventional advice to people who want to work independently is that it is better to gain a skill or some kind of expertise, preferably through formal training, and then gain fairly extensive experience and build contacts, by working for an organisation which can give this, before even thinking of starting out alone. This is, of course, still essential for anyone who wants to practise as a solicitor, a GP, a chartered accountant. To do skilled electrical work, computer programming, hairdressing, nursing, chiropody, osteopathy, fashion design, or make musical instruments, for example, independently also needs fairly extensive training first.

But with high unemployment, people without such training or experience are also being encouraged to consider self-employment, from school-leavers and new graduates (under 1% of whom at present opt for it) through to skilled workers and managers made redundant or retiring early.

It is possible to build a business on relatively straightforward skills possibly built up from a long-standing hobby or interest – babysitting, delivery/despatch rider services, making/selling sandwiches – the main criteria for reasonable success are a gap in the market, business sense (and training), and very hard work. Self-employment is, though, still risky, for people of any age, training or experience. Some experience of employment, and/or a family background in self-employment or running almost any kind of business is still useful. Starting a business while still working part-time is a half-way house which provides at least some financial security.

Like any kind of work, going into business alone or with others takes particular qualities. Self-employed people have to be self-starters, to have initiative and drive. They should not need anyone to tell them what to do next, or to be supervised, so they need to be able to organise and plan their own time efficiently and effectively. They have to be prepared to work long, and very probably very irregular hours to build up the business.

It is relatively easy to think of ideas for a business, but the possible market has to be researched thoroughly to make sure there is a real gap to be filled, that a service or product will sell at a price that will bring in an income. Good advice, on finance and financial planning, detailed research and analysis, and careful preparation and planning can make a real difference between success and failure. Marketing and public relations advice can be expensive, but well worth having. Funding and enough money to live on while the business is being built up have to be arranged, and probably somewhere suitable from which to run the business. A (written) business plan is essential, both to see that nothing has been forgotten, but more crucially to gain any financial or other support.

Support and assistance A considerable number of schemes, agencies, etc have sprung up in the last few years to give support, information, training etc to help people of all ages, training, experience etc into business, either on their own or with others. A list of some of the most useful/helpful are given below, and it is possible to gain financial support, training and help with planning, preparing a business plan, suitable premises etc.

Finance: MSC's enterprise allowance scheme is the most straightforward form of financial support for people starting out on their own in a new business (other government schemes provide for eg expansion), and who have been unemployed (or given notice of redundancy) for eight weeks. This provides £40 weekly for a year for 100,000 people yearly (as of 1987), provided they have access to £1000 to put into their business. This can simply be an overdraft facility – and some banks also provide free banking and some counselling. The survival rate of people on the scheme is good – 86% of those who are still in business at the end of the year are still trading 15 months after start-up, and 61% are still going after three years,

Other support: some local authorities, some national schemes (eg the Prince of

Wales' Youth Business Trust), and a network of about 190 local/regional enterprise agencies (funded by local authorities and/or private sponsors), give various levels of support ranging from straightforward information, advice and counselling, help with preparing a business plan, through to actually providing workspaces and/or some funding. Some schemes are geared to particular groups, eg young people from Afro-Caribbean and Asian backgrounds. Some local authorities provide help in the form of rate relief etc.

Training: MSC puts on/supports a widening range of short and longer courses for people going into self employment, or starting new businesses. Many of these are put on at FE colleges, polytechnics and, for more 'ambitious' schemes (ie people wanting to employ 12 or more people) at universities. A special scheme for graduates is put on by Cranfield, Durham, Stirling and Warwick Universities.

Further information The British Franchise Association, Co-operative Advisory Group, Co-operative Development Agency, the Industrial Common Ownership Movement (ICOM), Council for Small Industries in Rural Areas (COSIRA), Crafts Council (for advice and help on all aspects of craft practice), Business in the Community, Small Firms Service (Freefone Enterprise), job centres for MSC schemes, local library or careers service for addresses of any local support schemes.

The Information Society

Information technology and computing   357
Library work and information science   388

In the late 20th century, information is power – economic power, political power and social power – for industrial and commercial businesses, for most other organisations, for countries and for individuals. Information, it follows, is valuable – and profits, even fortunes, are to be made from using and providing accurate, up-to-date, well-engineered and targeted information – as the City's 'big bang' shows. What is happening so publicly in the financial world is a probable forerunner for other sectors, and in other areas computer-organised information is making similarly revolutionary changes, even if they are not so high profile.

The sheer weight of information – knowledge – has increased explosively in the last hundred years. But to exploit what is known, the information has to be organised, managed, analysed. As the financial world shows, information technology does make possible 'fine tuning' of information – rapidly capturing, analysing, organising, and putting it on screen in a 'user-friendly' format so that fast and efficient decision-making can be based on it. Once such information is available to any group it becomes virtually essential to have it, or risk losing out – in finance, it has already rewritten the rules of competition. Staying ahead will mean developing and using even more sophisticated ways of exploiting information.

Sophisticated, accurate and up-to-date information is crucial to the candidate competing for a place at university. It is equally essential for the corporate treasurer of a multi-national company who has to know how much is in the firm's current accounts at any given moment, how much of it can be invested for how many days, and where it can be invested to make a maximum profit on what terms. Investors, equally, knowing the value of information on companies, now expect quoted companies to report results with increasing frequency – on the basis of their IT-based management accounting systems.

Any attempt to regenerate industry – via improved design, productivity, and marketing, innovation and new products for export etc – increases the importance of information. New technologies – biotechnology and information technology itself – make greater demands on information systems.

Information is now as important a resource as land, capital and labour – so the drive is to make information systems cheap, efficient and high quality. Systems providing factual information of all kinds, specialist and general, are growing, in numbers, coverage, sophistication. The market for business databases – such as Reuters' Monitor – was estimated to be worth £30 million a year in 1986, and to be growing by 50% annually.

INFORMATION TECHNOLOGY AND COMPUTING

Introduction   357
Information technology and computing – the employers   364
Working in information technology and computing   370

INTRODUCTION

Information technology has been officially defined as 'the use of computers, microelectronics, and telecommunications to help produce, store, obtain and send information in the form of pictures, words or numbers, more reliably, quickly and economically'. This describes the technology only in terms of its equipment and media, and does not take in its functional aspects. (It also leaves out one of the next leaps in the technology – the integration of voice and data transmission.) A better definition says

'information technology ... is the *engineering* of information – in other words, manipulating information, organising, evaluating and managing it – to achieve designed solutions' (Michael Harrison, Sheffield's former CEO). This makes it quite clear that information technology is not just a new form of telecommunications, broadcasting, or publishing, or even simply computing, but a completely new concept in information handling.

To qualify as IT takes three things, says Michael Harrison –
use of microelectronics as a technical vehicle;
raw data – 'feedstock' – processed to become useful information; and
a designed system within which the information is used.

The microelectronic 'technical vehicle' means systems which integrate the latest in telecommunication with computers and computer-controlled equipment of all kinds as well as other sophisticated information-handling components and microprocessor-based systems. The communications element increasingly includes satellites, lasers and fibre-optic (glass) cables. All these together will soon make it possible for voice, computer code, written text and pictures to be converted to the same digital systems used by computers, and so go down the same lines, at far greater speeds, with far greater reliability, less distortion, and (theoretically at least) more cheaply.

The 'designed system' may –
organise the information an engineer uses to design a new product or component, make the necessary calculations, display the result on a graphic display screen, go on to calculate the materials needed, to drive the machine tool, or provide the information to control the output of an automated production line or a robot system;
let a finance manager ask for and get the company's bank statements direct on a VDU screen on his/her desk via a local area network;
take the latest weather forecast to an oil tanker in mid Pacific via a satellite, so deck officers can calculate on computer-aided navigation systems (almost replacing compass and sextant), an optimum route to the next port;
let a retail chain's mini- and main-frame computers gather information continuously from the check-out micros in 1000 stores, to give fast feedback on cash flows, levels of sales, and automatic re-ordering;
give lawyers rapid access to cases and decisions held in a specialist data base

via desk-top terminals;
put the ground plan of, eg a supermarket or a kitchen on screen, and show the effects of adding or moving checkouts or fitting in kitchen units, cookers etc; link up a tour operator with travel agencies, so holidays can be booked directly, and the agency invoiced the same way;
give a small business computer keystroke access to the telex network, the latest Stock Exchange prices, a computer-service bureaux, and a view-data system, as well as to the office's other computers etc, and send and receive letters etc 'electronically'.

Information technology is not just an idea dreamed up by politicians to find a use for microelectronics. Information technology (potentially) affects every individual and every organisation. Information technology has the potential to provide the means to organise and transmit all the wealth of current knowledge and information so that it can be used productively.

For individuals to manage their lives, for managers to see that their organisation – whether it is a one-man or -woman business, a charity, a government department, or a world-wide manufacturing firm – is cost-effective depends on good decision-making.

Decision-making can't now depend just on hunches, guesswork or even untrained entrepreneurial flair. It has to be based on information so organised that it can be fully analysed, the variables assessed, the optimum paths calculated. The measurement of the variables, optimum paths, risks and so on – for both numerically-controlled (robot) machine tool and managers – have to be exact. All this is impossible without microelectronic systems. The information has be instantly available, and often constantly up-dated, which inevitably means using electronic media. Most major companies, for example, now give their top managers detailed financial reports monthly, and the City expects published results six monthly if not yearly – all impossible without IT systems.

The evidence is all there that information technology can give businesses a real competitive edge, and should now be playing a central part in strategy. The UK's leading holiday tour operator, for example, consolidated its market position by being the first to put a viewdata-based reservation system onto the travel agencies' counters. By putting a computer-based ordering (and invoicing) system into customers' offices a manufacturing company both improves sales and cuts running costs. Retailers can see what is selling and what is not from the information provided daily by electronic cash registers, and so 'fine tune' their ordering and stock control.

Report after report, however, suggests that UK business is being slow to exploit the latest in IT systems. The root cause seems to be that management is not geared to taking advantage of the systems available – and is reluctant to invest because of past disasters, some caused by poor systems, but more often by poor management. Most studies say it is not the level of investment which counts, but the way in which companies manage IT. IT can make good management better, increasing market share sharply, but often speeds the downhill slide of poorly-managed firms. The problems lie both with general managers who are not IT-literate enough, and with IT professionals who do not understand the business environment, and so cannot see the needs of the firm's 'mainstream' activity. To some extent, the problem is historical and reflects the way computers have been used – in support of administration, accounts etc – and so have never been central to the business, or a 'key' function. All the indications are that this is making it very difficult to get IT as closely 'integrated' into the business as is necessary now.

Of course IT systems have far wider applications, although the major employment opportunities are likely to be in the business sector for at least the foreseeable future. It is probable that lack of resources amongst other potential users is holding up some developments – libraries and education, for example.

Even so, by 1987, there were an estimated 3000 on-line databases world wide. At first these held information only as indexes or abstracts, but full text is growing – although numeric financial information data bases are now the most successful (over 300 available in London alone). Examples of non-financial systems include –

BLAISE, the British Library's (general) automated information service,
MEDLINE which covers medical literature,
INSPECT – for electronics, physics and computer science,
World Patent Index, and
Chemical Business Newsbase.

Just as books are 'produced' by publishers, firms – called 'hosts' – specialise in 'networking' data bases. One of the largest in the UK, Infoline, now 'hosts' over 50 data bases covering eg chemical business news, key business enterprises. But on-line systems holding information that does not change too often may be overtaken, for sheer convenience, quite soon by the computer's version of the compact disc, which can hold the equivalent of at least a full-scale encyclopedia.

Much that is written about information technology is in fact about computers and computing. Computers are still central to information systems – although this may well change (see below).

Computers are everywhere now. More and more people understand how to use the simpler machines and know something about how they work. Most people are now well aware that computers are not just number crunchers, but can process – store, sort, and analyse – huge quantities of information (data in computer jargon), of all kinds, at increasingly phenomenal speeds. For machines without (as yet) intelligence, which are not capable of original thought, imagination, initiative, reasoning or even plain common sense, computers can be incredibly useful, and every technological development increases their potential usefulness.

At present they are, though, still only as efficient – and useful – as the people who design, instruct, or program, them, and this has to be done with absolute logic and simplicity, in minute detail. Most computer errors are human in origin, and the most superb hardware is only so much junk without good programs. Computer hardware, the electronic systems which are the basis of computers, has developed with incredible speed, and continues to do so. Programming, the software side of the business, has lagged seriously behind – it can still take just as long to produce a program today as it did fifteen years ago – and this failure to develop better techniques for instructing computers is a real crisis, although developments such as the new so-called 'fourth-generation' languages (4GLs) are at last beginning to change this (see below). In 1970, the costs of the hardware and the software for a computer system were about equal. Today, because the cost of the hardware has fallen so greatly, software makes up at least 80% of the cost.

The microprocessor gives increasing flexibility, and the chance to use computer power in a growing, even infinite, number of ways. Computers come in every possible shape and form, and may not even be recognisable as such. A computer may not be a free-standing machine, because a microprocessor (effectively a computer less its input and output equipment), is small enough to go inside the equipment it controls – the calculator, the stitch selector on a sewing machine, and the digital watch all have microprocessors inside them, microprocessors 'dedicated' to doing just one job. The equipment people use in their work, like the surveyor's distance measuring equipment, can be microprocessor controlled. Computers can control machinery – which is then called 'robotic'. Small computers can be linked up to other equipment, via an interface box, eg a signal generator and a desk-top computer can form an automatic test system, which will collect the data, do all the complex calculations and display the results as graphs, histograms, and numerical tables.

Systems can be put together with increasing flexibility. Smaller 'local' computers can be 'dedicated' to do a single job in a factory more economically, for example controlling a fully-automated system for handling the 22,000 parts needed to build a Tornado aircraft. But at the same time, systems can be linked into a larger machine or a network of machines as needed – and using a network of small computers can be cheaper than having a single mainframe. The information held in the design-engineer's computer can go straight into the computer which controls the machine tool cutting the car body panels without any need for drawings. The computer at the supermarket check-out desk automatically tells the store room computer what is being sold – and the store room computer can order direct from the warehouse system when stocks of any item run low, and tell the accounts office machine what has been delivered (matching orders and deliveries more closely to stock turnover can save a store several thousands of pounds).

Computers both give access to enormous quantities of information in very sophisticated forms, and control gadgetry. In some applications it is surprising now to find they are *not* being used, where they can economically improve efficiency, do a better job, or provide a new service which would be impossible without them.

Applications range from the near bizarre – a merchant ship with computer-assisted metal sails which can cut fuel consumption by 40%, to the very large scale, such as new system for DHSS social-security operations using 70 large computers, 3000 micros and 30,000 terminals.

Computers drive the sophisticated simulators, used extensively in training pilots, ships' officers and oil-rig crews (because it is both cheaper and safer). Computers can help scientists design drugs or new materials, modelling and manipulating molecules in three dimensions easily on the screen instead of having to use ball-and-stick construction.

The latest generation of airliners have computerised cockpits.

The art treasures in the National Gallery are protected from harmful variations in temperature and humidity with microprocessor-controlled equipment which constantly monitors the atmosphere.

Britain's astronomers operate their telescopes 7000 miles away in Hawaii using computer links.

The civil engineer can take a hand-held computer on to the site and estimate progress by tapping in the key factors.

Images beamed down from satellites are computer processed.

Even describing computers in terms of their size and power is becoming difficult. The distinctions between micro, mini and mainframe have blurred. Microelectronics continues, seemingly endlessly, to drive up performance for computers of all size, and they are all getting steadily more powerful, more compact, and cheaper. While the market for 'home computers' has suffered a slump, some 224,000 business micros worth £630 million were sold in the UK in 1985, 24% up on the year before.

The computer has now come out of the special, air-conditioned and temperature-controlled room where it is ministered to by its own special acolytes, becoming as familiar a desk-top tool as a typewriter or a calculator, and needing not that much more expertise to use it.

High-powered, large systems (also becoming more compact all the time) are still in use, though. Suggestions that they might prove 'dinosaurs' have been proved wrong – indeed highly-sophisticated research-type 'super'computers are now getting cheap enough for medium-sized organisations to afford – and most organisations expect to go on using mainframes for many years yet. Their sophistication is crucial, though, in scientific research, on really complex problems which use large-scale modelling eg forecasting the weather, and in oil prospecting. For many organisations it is convenient to have a machine that can cope with a very large number of different jobs very rapidly, and which can be accessed through any number of terminals – which can be at different ends of the country from the computer itself. Airlines use them to cope with booking and reservations systems, flight operation and maintenance. PAYE is installing a mainframe with 20,000 access terminals, and big machines cope with unemployment and sickness benefit.

Information technology is still in its infancy. Much is promised, both of IT generally and computers in particular. Much of what is promised is spectacular – and the timescales for what will happen optimistically short. They ignore the massive technical problems that have to be solved, the difficulty of convincing all the 'players' that futuristic systems will work, will be cost-effective, will make a profit, and will not tip the competitive edge against them. The protracted negotiations between banks and shops on direct-debiting customers' accounts through 'electronic point of sale systems', the reluctance of retail banks to set up full-scale home banking systems, and the slow uptake for cable broadcasting franchises, show that there is rather more to revolutionary change than technology.

Increasingly, where information technology and computers go next depends not only on the skills and ingenuity of researchers, systems designers/engineers to devise new products, but rather more on the IT industry giving a satisfactory answer to users' now-insistent question, 'What's in it for me?' User-firms, according to several surveys, trimmed their IT budgets quite sharply in 1986, partly because they did not get a satisfactory answer. IT firms are also finding that too much 'hype' for futuristic technology is putting customers off. For example, the very idea of 'expert systems' – programs that can 'mimic' the skills of a human expert – is, apparently considered 'threatening' by the experts themselves, and firms do not want these programs if they do not fit in with business systems in use.

Even so, and with a strong dose of realism, it is certainly possible that information technology will bring more quite dramatic changes before the end of the century.

Less than five years ago the so-called 'fifth generation' computer seemed futuristic.

'Fifth generation' is planned to produce 'intelligent' computers which can 'use' information and not just process raw data into usable form. They are intended to hold almost infinite amounts of data, and sort out from it anything and everything bearing on a particular problem, organise it into a logical order, and draw conclusions, so they could be used in decision making, and be able to do (some) 'expert' tasks – eg diagnosing what is wrong with patients, given their symptoms. To do this it will have to be possible to communicate with computers in something like ordinary language, and to have some kind of intelligent dialogue with them.

But computer people are not waiting around for grandiose 'fifth generation'. They are looking for less demanding ways of making an income from what customers want now. With the result that some of the elements essential for such machines have already been developed. Ways of parallel processing (until now computers have always run sequentially) needed to make machines faster – aiming for 10,000 million operations per second (against today's fastest running at 1200 million) – are working now. Ways round the problem that 'fifth generation' will need to cram ever more onto semiconductors ('very large scale integration') – which is getting progressively more expensive and difficult as silicon chips near their theoretical limits – are being found.

And 'expert systems' have been developed as software to run on today's computers. Expert systems now in use or being developed are not at all 'futuristic' – one user defines them as any system which could replace a relevant expert to some extent – but tackle realistic tasks. They are proving particularly useful where the task takes high-level skills but is very boring to do – analysing pages of data to find out why a computer 'crashed', for example. Other working examples include systems that –

diagnose faults in a telephone exchange;

help marketing executives to produce econometric models of particular markets even though they don't know any statistics;

takes farmers through question-and-answer sessions on fungal wheat diseases, recommends a treatment (with costings), and estimates likely losses;

help City dealers assess companies for their take-over potential;

guide personnel managers through complex social-security legislation;

detect people making (illegal) multiple share applications.

Even so, developing expert systems has meant a major 'leap' in programming techniques. Expert systems are programs, but programs with some very special features. One is a 'knowledge' base, which is like a conventional computer data base, in that it is an organised store of information, but where a data base normally holds just straightforward facts or statements, a knowledge base also carries information, or sets of rules, on how to do a particular task. The second is a program module called an inference engine or system (because it applies the reasoning techniques of logical inference), which interacts with the knowledge base to tell the user what to do – or should happen – next. A very simple example is a knowledge base of 'if-then' rules, where the inference engine firstly searches for the rules which satisfy the 'if' and then triggers the appropriate 'then' corollary.

The software technology developed to build expert systems has some significant 'spin offs'. One is increasing 'user-friendliness'. But more importantly for the business, it is a major break-through for speeding programming generally and for coping with the huge problem of maintaining programmes developed in the past, and up-dating them. This is because these new software 'tools' describe the data the program will work on and the relationships between individual pieces of data, rather than writing instructions to tell the computer how to solve a problem, as now. This makes it possible for users both to build up applications, and to maintain them more easily for themselves.

At the same time, 'fourth-generation' languages or 4GLs (professional programming languages like BASIC and COBOL are third generation) are giving people who are not trained computer professionals a method of 'communicating' with their machines. Software applications 'packages' for eg word-processing and spread-sheeting are simple 4GLs which already let people who understand and use particular applications, but don't know much about computing, give the computer instructions for those applications. More powerful 4GL programming systems are now on the market – one user expects an 80% saving in programming time, and a 95% saving in running 'overheads'.

Taken together, software technology, expert systems and 4GLs, plus even more creative thinking amongst computer-language and software tool designers in the pipeline, have considerable implications for the future of careers in computing. Not least amongst them is that there will be less and less detailed 'conventional' programming to be done.

New research – into computers which work optically using lasers, rather than on electrical pulses (light is of course infinitely faster), and superconducting materials among them – could further change, fairly dramatically, what computers can do, if not tomorrow, at least in the working lifetime of those going into IT now.

But IT is not just about computers, but has to involve communications too. The next ten years should see major developments, although the problems are great and take considerable expertise to solve. Firms wanting to communicate between sites and within buildings must today have multiple networks – one each for telephones, fax, telex, computer-computer links etc. Using digital signals – the language of the computer – they can all be carried on a single network. While these new digital networks can use existing coaxial copper cable, they will be faster and better over optical-fibre cable and radiowave. On digital networks, data can be 'managed' – 'package switched' – to cut transmission times, and costs, even further. The possibilities, for flexibility and cost-benefit are such that experts suggest networks will become the most important part of systems, making computers peripheral to them.

Many companies already have significant private networks – at least 300 of the largest by the end of 1985 mostly in finance, energy, chemicals, and services. Most organisations using computers expect to have local area networks ('LANs') by the mid 1990s. Networks also generate 'value-added' business – 'hosts' giving access to data bases are effectively 'VANs', as are electronic mail systems.

See also COMPUTER SCIENCE

INFORMATION TECHNOLOGY AND COMPUTING: EMPLOYERS

Almost all employing organisations will sooner or later use information technology systems. At rock bottom, the basic 'packages' now widely available – word processors, spread sheets, and data bases – for all computers make it possible for every organisation to 'manage' their own internal information systems more efficiently and (cost) effectively. At the most sophisticated end of the scale, as one example,

an international motor manufacturer has already automated vehicle ordering, using a plain-language, menu-driven system on very cheap pcs which every dealer has – so the progress of orders can be checked, a model in the right colour located, and paid for, with no documents and fewer errors. Now the system is being further sophisticated so that customers will be able to see and check their orders on screen, and the firm will 'edit' the order before it leaves the saleroom. A single Euro-order bank is being created, so that the car-ordering system both tells stock control what parts will be needed, which in turn will set the scheduling of manufacturing plants across Europe, and automatically show where the finished cars are to go – so cutting the time it takes to supply a car. The system will also give marketing a fast and accurate picture of which models with what features are selling, where, to whom etc. The system will be very dependent on international telecommunications as well as computers – it is an information system.

The same company is trying to develop a financial database to give more effective support for decision making in the 1990s. They want to be able to call up on line the revenues generated by one model in one country, and compare them with the (variable) costs of production in another. This would involve having common product definitions, and single 'stores' of information on volumes, prices, costs, exchange rates etc. Again, telecommunications will be at the heart of the system. At the same time, the company is committed to reducing financial staff by 50%.

Employers of people with IT/computing skills divide (mainly) into –

USERS are estimated to employ some 80% of specialist IT/computer staff. Most organisations of any size are using computers as IT systems now in all sectors – the financial sector (banks, the City, insurance etc), the Civil Service and the Armed Forces, the transport industry, manufacturing companies of all kinds, the Health Service, the media (broadcasting, newspapers etc), local authorities, universities etc. But use of computers/IT systems is spreading fast through the professions – accountants, lawyers, general practitioners, architects, surveyors etc – and smaller businesses.

However, not all users employ specialist/IT computer staff. The extent to which they do so depends largely on size and range of both the organisation and their IT/computing systems, how much use they make of 'outside' specialist companies and staff, and how far IT responsibilities are being 'integrated' into other people's work. Most legal and surveying practices, for example, would go to outside specialists when installing or upgrading their systems, would expect to buy 'off-the-shelf' software, and train their own staff to use and operate the systems. In larger practices – especially the 'top' accountancy firms – use of IT/computing systems is expanding to the point where a partner may become a specialist IT manager, and some specialist staff employed.

But it is the larger firms and other organisations which employ the most specialist staff, often in semi-autonomous 'computer centres', 'data processing departments' or 'business services divisions'.

The data processing department's role is changing, and with it what staff do (see Working in IT below). Until now, the main job of data-processing departments has been to produce complete solutions to data-processing problems, and to deal with all data processing on a day-to-day basis. Within five years, say Price Waterhouse (*Information technology review* 1987-88), dp departments expect their main role to be producing 'core systems' – which 'capture' the basic information about what is going on, and do the unchanging day-to-day routines. But nearly as important, they say, will be 'designing and maintaining corporate IT standards' – especially when data, voice, pictures and the whole machinery of communication in organisations are integrated within computer-controlled systems.

In other words, the applications of information – which change with changing strategies, market conditions etc – will increasingly be implemented by the (end) users themselves, using 4GL (and database enquiry) languages (see above), working to a ground plan devised by, and with the support of what is likely to be by then an IT or business services division/department. Some larger firms have already set up internal 'computing information centres' offering advice, training, support and facilities, but with the basic aim of helping managers and other staff to become completely self-sufficient, to take over many of the tasks dp departments have always done for them.

Employment patterns will change as a result. Price Waterhouse question predictions that demand for IT specialists will fall slightly – because despite years of deskilling etc it hasn't happened yet (on their survey, the proportion of installations with 75% of their staff IT specialists rose by 7% to over 25% between 1981 and 1986). But their findings do bear out other surveys that the number of other in-house skilled data-processing staff will fall. Partly this is because firms expect to use outside contractors and consultants more. But it is also because firms overwhelmingly expect to shift systems development and implementation to 'end users' – staff in the departments actually using the information. In 1981, according to Price Waterhouse, this work was almost all done by dp staff. By 1986, over three-quarters of systems development was being done by end users in 31% of firms, and by 1989 they predict it will be 74% of firms.

Dp departments/divisions in larger organisations are being turned into semi-independent 'profit centres', working on 'contract' to other such separate units within the business, possibly competing with outside contractors for their work, and even working as an outside contractor for other firms in some instances. This forces dp departments to work to tighter budgets and schedules, perhaps with their own FINANCIAL MANAGERS, and means some dp staff effectively become consultants within their own employing organisation. This is amongst the factors making changes in dp management (see below).

Some larger user organisations (eg BRITISH TELECOM) also have major research facilities working on IT systems generally, and others may be doing advanced work on applications, eg a major chemical company has a unit developing expert systems for both in-company and customers' use.

The other 20% of IT/computer staff are divided between

MANUFACTURERS They are dominated by a number of very large, mostly international, companies, which develop, make and sell computers and systems of all shapes and sizes. Other manufacturers look for gaps in the market where, with a combination of 'innovation, modern technology and attention to customers' needs' they can make a profit. Some specialise in particular markets – eg retailing, manufacturing or financial services. In such a fast-moving business they may have to make fine judgements about how long to go on making products – one firm continues to make 'modems' which let computer data onto the traditional telephone system, while others are already investing huge sums in developing the 'chips' which will go into digital telephones to replace them. They also produce software (they took over half the 'packaged' market in 1985), particularly 'systems software', and may be involved in other parts of the service industry. Other firms produce small business and personal computers, and some make components, peripheral and ancillary equipment, networking systems etc.

The services that manufacturers provide for customers vary – the major firms not only sell computers, ancillary equipment, programs and programming services, but also provide systems design, back up, maintenance, staff training etc, although the trend is for maintenance etc to be done by service companies (below).

Much of the more fundamental research and development work on IT systems and computing is done in universities. Manufacturers, however, are also heavily involved, with massive investment into R&D and design on new systems, both hard- and software, and on more sophisticated production techniques, eg for silicon chips, both in their own labs and in collaboration with academics. They have even made some of the biggest breakthroughs – the first viable high-temperature superconductors were developed (in 1986) in a computer company's laboratory. Manufacturers, with universities etc, are working right out on the 'frontiers' of research in MATERIALS SCIENCE, PHYSICS, ELECTRONICS, and COMPUTER SCIENCE.

Actually making computers is in many ways not so very different from or more complicated than moulding and assembling any other equipment – mostly it is relatively simple light-engineering, with fewer and fewer components. The sophisticated, high-technology part of the operation is (mainly) in the production of chips and circuit boards, designing and preparing circuits, reducing them (by a factor of some 200), and printing them onto wafer-thin chips.

Producing the chips and 'printing' them are highly automated, since the lines – far finer than a human hair – making up the circuits must be drawn by an electron beam (itself computer-driven) on glass and then printed on the silicon wafers with light optics.

'Configuring' (working out what components are needed for a customer's system) and installing computers/IT systems employs mainly ENGINEERS, but systems are now designed to be set up by customers themselves wherever possible, and it is only the larger and more complex systems which need outside experts. While the technical requirement for special environments – air-conditioning etc – are falling all the time, full-scale IT systems – eg City dealing rooms – take up a considerable amount of space and need extra ducting etc for cables, but this is a problem for BUILDING SERVICES ENGINEERS, ARCHITECTS etc rather than computer manufacturers. Running in and testing larger systems, especially mainframes, can still be quite a lengthy business, and may need a team of systems experts and engineers.

Manufacturers also provide some maintenance and repair services, again employing ENGINEERS.

See also MANUFACTURING

SERVICE COMPANIES/ORGANISATIONS The UK software and services industry has grown by 20% annually for several years and by 1985 the market was worth an estimated £2000 million. The Computer Services Association has (1986) nearly 270 member companies, although estimates suggest well over 1000 in total – most medium-to-small, employing less than fifteen people each, often giving a specialist service to a particular group of users (eg law firms). Only about fifty are large enough to employ more than 150 people each. Service companies include software/systems houses and consultancies, computer bureaux, data preparation companies. Some companies provide only one of these services, but others are involved in more than one or give an all-through service. Some companies also offer maintenance services. All service companies are geared to constant change, to developing in parallel with what is happening in the IT business and to meeting – and anticipating if possible – demand from customers.

Software houses write, develop and implement programs. Programs come in two basic forms – those written specially for a customer, and 'off-the-shelf' 'packages' which can be used by any number of customers. Software houses provide both 'systems' and 'applications' software (see programming below), but a high proportion of systems programs are supplied by manufacturers. Specially written programs are extremely expensive, and US companies have a large share of the UK package market.

UK software houses therefore have to be very 'creative' to make a living. They 'customise' packages for clients, for example, so that programs match a firm's special needs or give a company a competitive 'edge' over other firms using the same package. Amongst other cost-cutting methods, they build 'prototype' programs which customers can try out – and then have customised, they have developed ways of building programs from sets of basic modules, so that modules can be put together to give clients a product mid-way between package and 'bespoke' programs.

A few of the larger software houses, though, specialise in advanced products, such as expert systems and the software tools needed to develop them, or in developing software which 'automates' programming for other software houses/dp departments to use, or in computer graphics. Some software houses specialise in products for particular sectors – systems for dealing room and accounting or insurance business for instance – but specialising can be risky, and so software houses often expand into other areas of business. For example, they may become –

Systems houses, providing a complete service for customers, starting with feasibility studies, designing the system and doing the programming, testing, running in, etc. Some, as part of this service, also buy the hardware for the customer. This may mean putting together a special package of components from different manufacturers as well as providing the software and training the staff (called a 'turnkey' service). Some select and recruit staff, and even manage computer units for customers.

Consultancies advise clients on any or all aspects of computing. They may provide a total service, simply suggest plans, write a 'specification' for the customer to give to a manufacturer, dealer or software house. They may simply write any necessary programs (many firms are so short staffed they rely heavily on 'contract' programmers), or design the complete system – hard- and software – systems and applications. Again, some specialise if they can find a 'niche' which will provide an income, but it is not always possible, so most consultants have to be able to do various kinds of work. Ideally, consultants should be completely independent, but it has been suggested that only a small proportion of the 2000 or so consultancies do not have some form of financial links with hard- and/or software companies.

Computer bureaux provide services for organisations which do not have their own computers, or who need extra capacity or computing power for short periods or particular projects. Bureaux may deal with payroll calculations, for example, inputting hours worked etc, and then calculating pay and deductions such as tax, national insurance, pension etc. Some customers have on-line terminals with direct access to a bureau's high(er)-powered equipment. Some major industrial and commercial companies offer bureaux services which use spare capacity on their own systems, eg a major car manufacturer sells time on its computer-aided design system.

The falling cost of computers, and the rising power of small machines and programs means demand for traditional bureaux services is falling, if slowly. Bureaux companies are moving, therefore, into other sectors of the business – supplying hardware, software products, and 'viewdata' and on-line databases among them.

Data preparation companies were essential when computer input was mainly via special punched cards and (later) paper and magnetic tape, and needed specially-trained staff to operate the machinery. The typewriter-style keyboard makes it simple for organisations to do their own data preparation on the spot, so few firms provide outside services – particularly heavy work loads are now mostly dealt with by taking on 'temp' keyboarders.

Dealers sell computers, software, ancillary equipment, computer supplies – printer ribbons, paper etc. Most either have outlets in locations suitable to the customers they aim to serve, or supply customers directly. The smallest, 'home' pcs are often sold now by electrical multiple stores. Some dealers provide smaller businesses with an over-the-counter consultancy service designed to help people with little or no experience of computers to choose the most suitable package of hard and software for them. If estimates are correct, the number of dealers has fallen sharply, to about 2000 in 1985.

Maintenance Manufacturers used to service all their own machines, and still service some 80%. Computers are increasingly reliable and soon many will be fault free, some can diagnose – and even correct – their own faults. However, with the growing numbers of smaller business machines in use, and as users install machines made by different manufacturers, it has become profitable to provide independent maintenance services, on contract or on request. Service companies also re-condition and re-sell second-hand machines, and provide a number of ancillary services.

INFORMATION PROVIDERS The information provided on many IT-based system is generated and organised within an organisation, for their own use – an example is the information which the engineer puts into the computer-aided design system, from which the system can generate parameters and show three-dimensional representations of projected designs on a graphic display screen. Information is also generated within an organisation to provide customers (or managers) with a new or improved service – an example is a bank providing customer companies with on-line access to their bank statements and instant analyses of their financial position. In both instances, there is no new source or provider of information – the engineer is using the same information, but manipulating it in a more efficient way; bankers are providing companies with a new service based on information which has always been available but not accessible. IT is here changing the nature of work being done by and in existing organisations.

But information is also provided by specialist organisations to sell to particular markets. Publishing in all forms – reference books, scientific and other journals, newspapers and magazines – has been the main way of delivering information until now. But a rising and significant number of people are now employed in generating, improving, managing and marketing information held on public- or limited-access data bases (as opposed to data bases for internal use) as well as or instead of in printed form. A high proportion of the work, though, is done by people who have been working in – or via – conventional publishing, such as financial writers, scientific abstractors and reference book editors, academics with the necessary subject knowledge, where the techniques of abstracting and editing are very similar. Most data bases 'package' information in such a way that it is presented on-screen in easy-to-understand and -use form. Marketing – which is usually closely linked to training users – is a quite different operation to selling books, though.

Data-base producers design services to be accessed directly by firms (and their staff), individual professionals – dealers, lawyers, etc – at their work place/ station, or by people at home. With some exceptions – eg ECCTIS (the government-supported data base on higher and further education courses and credit transfer) – services are market-led, and so data base companies are competing with each other to provide, eg business, and especially financial, information. Not all data bases are produced by the commercial companies 'selling' them – some, particularly in scientific areas, are produced by the professional bodies etc that published the material, as eg abstracts or indexes, before a data base was was possible. Most of the financial information services are produced by firms which published data on companies etc previously, although the most successful is a news agency. Data bases for home use have not been so successful.

'Hosts' or 'networks' do not generate or organise information themselves, but provide access to a number of databases, so the work is limited to developing and running computer systems, administration, marketing, and training, making the number of actual jobs generally quite small.

SELF-EMPLOYMENT has been common in the business for many years. Skilled and experienced programmers find it comparatively easy to make a living working from home. Some develop this into a 'small business' and become 'consultants', although they may also do some 'straight' freelance programming. Currently (1987) firms are employing quite large numbers of experienced people on a contract basis for particular projects, and partly to solve the problem of skill shortages. Support staff are also employed on a temporary basis.

WORKING IN INFORMATION TECHNOLOGY

The scope of information technology is so wide that there cannot be a single profession called 'information technologist', even though job advertisements often use the phrase. But more and more people do spend increasingly more of their working time handling information, increasingly using IT systems, which inevitably include one or more computers, without being formally employed in information technology – or computing – as such. Design engineers no less than financial managers work with information as their raw material, using IT systems to 'process' it. More people are, though, specifically involved in organising information, designing and making the equipment which becomes part of IT systems, and designing the systems.

IT systems – including computers – will be part of most people's lives from now on, and more and more people will use IT systems/computers as tools in their work, whatever they do. IT will go on changing the work that many people do, and the way they do it, just as computers have been for years now. More and more jobs will be transformed by information technology, as well as new jobs created and jobs lost.

This does not, though, mean everyone has to become a IT or computer expert – in fact much of the industry is now deliberately intent on making their systems as easy for anyone to use with as little training and IT/computer expertise as possible, with growing success. Estimates are that at most 300,000 people count as IT/computing staff, and some go as low as 200,000. To date at least, the work which is 'in' IT/computing has involved designing, making, making work and managing computers and computer-based systems for everyone else. As indicated earlier, though, users are starting to become more involved in developing systems for themselves, and this will in some ways extend the IT-expert 'community' further.

The jobs and type of work inevitably have to change as the technology and the business change, and this is now almost a continuous process. Work for computer 'professionals' – the experts – has commonly been divided between data processing, which includes 'software' development (with the majority of jobs) and the 'hardware' end – designing, manufacturing, installing and maintaining the physical equipment, including semiconductors ('chips'). The division between them has, though, been blurring for some time, especially amongst manufacturers and eg telecommunications firms, who increasingly want – for instance – people with training/experience in both software and engineering to work on systems design. And the trend to 'multi-skilling' is expected to continue – eg 'analyst programmer' is a job title recognising the fact that more programmers take on some (systems) analyst functions. In fact, most reports suggest demand can only increase for people with broader, more cross-disciplinary skills – all-rounders – and especially for people who combine computing skills with business/commercial 'literacy'.

And as IT spreads and more people become involved, the range of different kinds of work is growing, although it is easier to spot the work that is (already) declining – eg routine bulk data preparation – than to identify major new areas of employment. The job specifications, then, are changing all the time, and it would be optimistic to think that the *job titles* which have become accepted over the past twenty years will continue to remain the same. The basic *types* of work, however, are probably rather more stable, although there are no hard and fast rules.

The professional/technical functions

Computing has always been seen as a high-level 'technical' occupation, a 'backroom' job. While this is changing (see Managing in IT below), the main opportunities – at least to start with – are in these technical areas.

Collectively, this is a spectrum of work which stretches from the first ideas for a new, or improved, IT/computing system through to getting it up and running for a customer. The work involved ranges from very high level to fairly routine – although basic routine is slowly being automated away. It is usual to see each of the following areas of work as separate and distinct, but in practice the divisions between them are never that hard and fast – what people do invariably depends on the needs of the specific job. Many people combine systems analysis and programming in varying proportions, often as they gain the necessary skills and experience. Graduates may, for example, be recruited as trainee systems analysts, but spend a high proportion of their earliest years being programmers.

Work is frequently 'project' based, using teams of people with an appropriate 'mix' of different expertise and at varying levels of skills/experience. A team may well include eg systems analysts, designers, software engineers, and programmers – some of whom will be trainees of some kind. The work involved in a project is usually broken down as far as possible, so that individual members of the team work on a single problem, within an overall plan. Especially on more advanced projects, individuals within the team have a fair degree of independent responsibility for their own work and how they do it. Young staff, especially graduates, are encouraged, even expected, to show initiative, to get involved and contribute early, even while they are still technically trainees.

IT/COMPUTER SYSTEMS DEVELOPMENT AND DESIGN Designing the 'working' parts of IT/computer systems – the 'devices', the semiconductors, the circuitry and circuit boards – and the ancillary devices which link machines into networks. The boundary between designing the 'physical' hardware and the 'software' at this level is blurring, and increasingly firms want people who combine ELEC-TRONICS with COMPUTER SCIENCE (see COMPUTER ENGINEERING/INFORMATION TECHNOLOGY). At the development end this is often advanced research-type work and also involves physicists and chemists mainly dealing with materials. Most computer-based systems also have mechanical 'peripherals' – disk drives, printers, robot arms etc – and this usually involves MECHANICAL ENGINEERS.

SYSTEMS ANALYSTS/DESIGNERS work out the best way to organise an information system, investigating and analysing first the problem(s) that the system is expected to solve. While they may find that the solution is not an IT/computer-based system, in practice they would normally expect to recommend one, and it is more often a question of what IT/computer system and how it will work – the customer usually has to decide between an IT solution suggested by the analyst, doing the job some other way, or not doing it all.

Although there are still organisations buying computer-based systems for the first time, so that analysts have to plan for them from 'scratch', increasingly they spend more time redesigning systems, to do more tasks, to 'upgrade' the system to make it faster, to cope with larger volumes of work, to 'integrate' computer-based equipment into 'networks', to introduce 'distributed' systems, for example.

In small organisations this may be one job, but in many it is split between an analyst and a designer, or (on larger projects) between a team of systems people with varying expertise and varying levels of experience. All of the job or the design half of the systems 'function' is sometimes combined with programming (see below), depending on the organisation – the job specification analyst/programmer is in fact becoming quite common.

The systems analysis part of the job begins when an organisation decides to improve, for instance, the way in which their payrolls, costings, ordering procedures, stock control, schedules, are handled, to speed invoicing, to provide extra information on which to base management decisions, or make systems more efficient. Some organisations employ senior systems analysts just to monitor and investigate the efficiency and effectiveness of their systems, and to put through improvements and refinements as the technology advances.

The analyst first has to find out how the particular operation, or set of operations, is dealt with at present, what information goes into the system, what happens to it, what management and others get out of it, and how it relates to the business as a whole. Managers have to be persuaded to describe clearly what they want the new system to do.

The analyst may begin with a short feasibility study, and only go on to a longer analysis if this first step suggests that a new system make sense in economic and practical terms. Then the analyst goes through the existing system and reduces it all to logical charts. The analyst finds out why things are done in a particular way, what is essential and what is not, and looks for any problems – such as frequent snarl-ups and bottlenecks – in the system, and what would improve it. Much systems analysis is very similar to the first stage of an OR project or an O&M study (see MANAGEMENT SERVICES).

Once the analyst has a full picture of the existing system and the improvements wanted, he/she prepares a detailed report, showing what could be done, with what system, how to do what the customer wants, with what possible effects on the organisation itself. The analyst may suggest alternative plans and systems, depending on how much the customer wants, or can afford to spend, balanced against possible savings and the cost and availability of systems.

There may be a range of choices – having software specially written, which takes time and can be very expensive but gives a tailor-made system, 'off-the-shelf' software packages – which can be immediately available and cheaper but may not be exactly what is needed, but which can (now) be 'customised' at some extra cost. The analyst may suggest sophistications which a customer may decide are too expensive or complex.

Hotels, for instance, are offered as part of their computerised accounting and management processing systems, microprocessor-based room locks which automatically turn lights and heating on and off as guests go into and leave their rooms, and a telephone monitoring system and drinks dispenser linked to the computer, so that guests can make calls without going through the operator and get themselves a drink, with the cost of both recorded automatically.

When the customer has accepted the proposal, the design part of the job turns the outline scheme into a statement of requirements. It has to show what information goes in, in what form; define all the processes it goes through; and state what the output will be, and to whom, where and when it must go. All this is turned into a logical model of the information flow, to show what processes are needed to produce what the customer wants. Problems and conflicts have to be resolved, so the systems designer can write a full description of the system, with diagrams, the processing it involves and the equipment, staffing etc needed, in a form that the customer can understand, and finally approve.

The systems designer then produces a detailed specification of the system, often breaking it down into logical sections, lists the processes, the hardware and software, with flow-charts showing the steps in the processing and how they fit together, file layouts, program specifications, etc. Programs then have to be specified in detail – what they must do; what the inputs, processes and outputs are, and what files they will use. This stage is often done by senior programmers. Once the programs are written and tested individually, systems designers are involved in testing and implementing them as a linked system.

Systems analysts/designers are not, therefore, preparing designs for computer systems in isolation. The system has to be tailored to the particular needs of the customer, and so to do the job properly the analyst has to be, or become, expert in the way banks, retail stores, hotel chains, barristers, insurance companies, manufacturing industry, or stock controllers (for example), work and how best their particular problems can be solved in computing terms. Analysts have to be able to explain and discuss highly technical data in everyday language with managers, and other staff who may not really understand what is happening and may be hostile to change.

Systems analysts/designers are also involved in developing and designing software 'packages' – using their expertise, experience and understanding of business needs to design packages which will meet the needs of as many users as possible.

Systems analysts/designers work mainly for computer manufacturers or for systems/software houses and computer consultancies. Larger computer users have enough work to employ their own analysts/designers full-time, although for many users the work may include programming too. Analysts/designers working for computer manufacturers or systems houses are part technical experts, but often part sales man or woman too.

Producing expert systems involves a sophisticated form/extension of systems analysis, being called *'knowledge engineering'*. This is still, obviously, a very new area of work, but basically 'knowledge engineers' have to analyse and turn complex and unstructured information into sets of logical rules. There are two stage to the work. First, the knowledge engineer has to get someone with the relevant set of skills to explain as clearly as possible what is involved in doing the task for which the expert system is planned, formulating (with the expert) a set of rules from the information, and turning the rules into a 'paper model' or flow chart. The second part of the job involves mapping the rules onto the skeleton expert system.

SOFTWARE PROFESSIONALS All computer-based systems have to be told what to do, in 'programs' or so-called 'software' (which can be a misnomer). There are three main kinds of program –

First, the operating systems programs, which control the running of other programs, keep track of files, sort, locate records, edit and help debug new programs.

Second, compilers and interpreters, programs that translate high-level languages into machine code. (Other languages are used for scientific research work on analog machines, and more are being developed for other uses, eg 'declarative' languages for use in building expert systems.)

Third are the applications programs which tell computers how to do particular jobs – work out payrolls, do stock control, play chess or space invaders, teach physics or computer programming, calculate and print invoices from electricity readings, monitor a patient's heartbeat and temperature, organise and print letters, etc.

Programs are either 'loaded' separately into the computer, or they may be permanently written into the hardware/circuitry, and then called 'firmware' rather than software. This is now common for operating systems and compilers, but applications are usually only written in when a microprocessor is dedicated to doing a single job (eg change channels in a TV set).

PROGRAMMING has always been very time-consuming, difficult, and error-prone. Until some ten years ago, there was little reason to put any effort into improving programming techniques, because it was the hardware that was expensive. With far cheaper hardware, and a rapidly-growing range of possible applications, the programs needed grew more complex, and more expensive both absolutely and in comparison with the cost of the hardware. For at least seven years now, according to Price Waterhouse's survey, 'meeting (software development) project deadlines' has been the major IT problem – mentioned as such by around 50% of data processing managers.

Many solutions have been tried and have so far failed to produce a permanent answer (probably largely because the extra benefits users gain from each development – greater speed, more sophisticated applications etc – only make them want more, just as medical advances generate more demand for treatment). It is, clearly, a management problem (see below), but meantime the drive to boost productivity has led to technical developments which are currently changing the work and the jobs.

At one end of the scale, a major attempt is under way to give programming, or software development, a 'professional' methodology – tested procedures and rules to work to, sound routines etc – like architects, or engineers, to raise standards and improve productivity. The result is
software engineering Strictly-speaking this is the job of making software writing more disciplined, and developing better techniques and 'tools' – programs for programmers to use. In practice the actual work many software engineers do is the same as, or similar to that done by people called software designers or systems programmers elsewhere (see below) and the job titles are being used interchangeably.

At the other end of the scale, the development of higher-level languages (ie more like ordinary English) such as 4GLs (see Introduction above) and proper tools are both making 'conventional' applications programming more productive and increasingly pushing applications software development towards 'end users'.

Here commonly-accepted new job titles/specifications have not yet developed. But some of these new style 'software specialists' are already working for eg finance, rather than dp managers. They are generally people who understand what finance, marketing, or personnel managers want out of their IT systems but also have some computing background. They are trained to select, modify, and put into operation software packages to do specific tasks in individual departments, teach staff how to use them, monitor that they are working properly and cope with any problems. They need some of the skills of both systems analysts and programmers. They are not, though, programmers, in that they do not have to be able to write 'original' programs or routines in 3GLs like COBOL.

Software development, programming, is a rapidly-changing spectrum of activity ranging from very advanced and complex work on eg machine-software interfaces, developing software for real-time applications, for complex graphics, or networking – to allow old and new systems to communicate for instance – or expert systems, through to the fairly basic routines in what is currently called 'applications' programming. While programmers may work on their own, it is more often a team activity, possibly working with, or under, systems designers/analysts.

Programs have to be written in tight, logical, unambiguous, step-by-step instructions, to tell systems what to do. They may be written from a systems designer's specification, but systems and other experienced, senior programmers may do all, or some, of the design, breaking down specifications into programmable segments, or 'modules', which they may write themselves, or have a team of programmers to write them.

Until recently, all programs have had to be written in fairly complex, special computer languages which can then be translated into the codes used by the machine automatically. Writing in the low-level languages which are closest to the machine's codes is most accurate, but very difficult, and so 'high-level' languages such as BASIC and COBOL, using a kind of pidgin English have been used for most programming for some years. While most people can learn to program in these languages and make a simple computer do some tasks, a good professional programmer writes programs which use the machine's capacity and sophistication to the full, and in the most economical and 'user-friendly' way. More efficient programming techniques and 'tools', and (even) easier-to-use languages have been 'de-skilling' programming for some time, but the most recent developments look like actually cutting the need for low-level programming, largely by switching the work to end users as above, and to make 'programme maintenance' simpler, possibly turning it into a technician's job.

Programming is commonly divided into 'systems' – working at the hardware-software interface – and 'applications', at the software-user interface, but this doesn't prevent people moving between them, and there are areas of programming which don't 'fit' neatly into either. Developing applications for which the programming may be particularly original, difficult and sophisticated – on computer-aided design and manufacture systems, on expert systems, for example – is a blurred area which probably needs high-level skills, for example.

Systems programmers who may also be called software designers or engineers work on the more complex end of programming. This includes writing operating programs, compilers etc, which are needed to make systems work at all, and also to 'translate' applications programs. These – and some other programs eg to make a piece of equipment operate in 'real time' – may be 'written into' a system's circuitry – or into a device – when it is made and may have to be written in more difficult, 'low-level' assembler language. A significant amount of software development time is currently going into writing programs which allow different makes of computer to communicate with each other, and link into public networks. Much of the work then, is very advanced and can be equated with R&D in other sectors. Systems programmers/designers usually produce their own specifications.

Systems programmers may, then, work alongside the computer/electronic engineers who design equipment, and may themselves need an electronics, as well as a software background, and may be called software engineers. Systems programming/software engineering is far more skilled, taking greater brain power than more straightforward applications programming. Software designers/systems programmers work mostly for manufacturers, some for software houses, and some for users of very large and/or complex systems. CEGB, for example, have their own software design teams working on the latest systems to control and monitor power generation and the transmission network. While there are (currently at least) fewer actual jobs at this end of software work, it is the area where skill shortages are greatest.

Applications programmers write – mainly in 3GL at present but with increasing use of 4GL and 'tools' that make programming simpler and faster – the line-by-line instructions for programs which tell computers how to do a specific task. They usually have to estimate how long a job will take, must document their work, and have to 'de-bug' it. They may work alone, but more often they work in teams – which may include systems/analysts designers – on a specific project, on programs of a particular type, or for particular types of users.

Applications programmers write completely new programs, or sets of programs, working to specifications prepared by a systems analyst or designer (above), who may also be an experienced programmer. New programs may be for one user, or for a software package to be sold 'off-the-shelf', or it may be a program 'module' which can later be packaged together with other modules for a customer. However, much applications programmers' time is currently spent on program maintenance – 'mending', modifying, improving, up-dating and tidying up programs which have been in use for some time, particularly if they work for a user's dp department. Constant minor amendments, extra routines to cope with an unexpected problem or new task, etc can turn what started out as a neat-and-tidy program into a mare's nest – and the problem has been getting steadily worse.

The application programmer's job starts when the systems designer hands over a systems/program specification, which describes what the programs are to do, and their input and output. If it is a complete package or set of programs, the work is usually divided between a team of programmers; on a smaller job, one or two programmers may do it all.

Once the programmer understands the specification, the first step is to break down what the program must do first into separate components, and then into the step-by-step sequences which must be logical and interlocking, so that there is no ambiguity or missing step, and put these down on paper – or on screen – as a flow chart. The second stage is to convert each step into instructions in, usually, a 'high-level' language. Programmers can now work straight on to the machine, via keyboard and visual display screen, with all the 'debugging' and testing done continuously as the program is written. The machine has first to put the program through the 'compiler' to convert it to its own code system. This generally produces errors to be debugged, probably several times. Once it runs properly, the program must be tested exhaustively with samples of data to see what errors in logic there may be and to correct, and even improve it. One estimate suggested that an average programmer can write and test about 10-15 average instructions a day. Since even a simple program has about 300 lines, it can take 20-30 days to produce. But using new software tools, eg a 'program generator', can speed this as much as five-fold.

In a large software house or unit, programming may be broken down into stages, or levels of complexity, and trainees or junior programmers start with the coding sequences and simpler programs, program maintenance etc, moving on and up with experience and, if good enough, to more senior programming jobs. Senior programmers can do their own program specification and the borderline between systems design and programming gets blurred. It is possible to move on either into systems design, or systems analysis given an appropriate business background or experience in a large user organisation, less usually now systems programming, but there are no hard and fast rules.

Managing in IT

Ever since larger organisations began using computers on any scale, computing has been treated as a 'backroom', technical-support, rather than a 'line', function. In fact, until quite recently, the work done by computer installations was all in 'support' areas – just a more efficient way of dealing with payrolls, invoices and accounts and saving on overheads, rather than contributing positively to income and profits. Computing did not have a 'strategic' role in the organisation. The mystiques of computing, the special conditions needed by mainframes, helped to re-inforce the isolation of computer installations, and the computing staff. As a result few, if any, dp managers moved out/up into general, senior management.

This now has to change, since IT/computing systems are fast becoming central and crucial to the performance of most organisations. The problem is probably only contained because too many (general) senior managers are still not aware/convinced of this. Dp professionals have not been expected, or trained, to understand the needs of their business. Many (general or other departmental) managers are only slowly acquiring the computer literacy/awareness needed. Solving the problems of who is responsible for what, planning strategy, deciding between competing solutions is, as a result, difficult. One report estimates that as much as 20% of the £5000 million invested in IT in 1984 was wasted. Surveys suggest the situation might not improve until the older generations of both dp and general managers have departed. Some organisations expect to retire the 'traditionalists' early, and bring in people who are capable of managing IT properly on both sides.

Respondents to a 1987 survey were divided equally on the way IT should be organised in future. Half continued to believe IT should be managed centrally, half that it should be decentralised. However, since their views are generally in line with the way their firms are organised, and the trend is generally to decentralisation in separate profit centres, more decentralisation of IT can be expected. Senior/general managers, and managers in other departments, once aware of, for example, what 4GLs can do, are often keen to develop their own IT systems. But if this is done in an uncoordinated way, it only leads to problems later, eg when the time comes to install communications networks between departments and sites.

However, today's dp managers are well aware change has to come. Most are changing their titles to 'IT manager', and expect a further and major upward shift in status in the near future, according to Price Waterhouse. To whom a dp/IT manager reports and whether or not they have a seat on the board are indicators of status. By 1986, 80% of dp managers were reporting either to a board member or the chief executive (30% were not reporting directly to board level at all in 1982), and by 1991, 42% expect to be on the board themselves, and all the rest to report to a board member.

This has considerable implications for IT experts' career structures. While they are increasingly sharing responsibility for identifying and specifying their employers' IT needs with general and other managers/users, IT managers will have to be able to take a 'strategic view' of the business if they are to get the IT infrastructure right, and the systems will do the intended job. Their skills are crucial in the management of rapid change needed in most organisations.

They also have to manage IT departments which are under constant pressure, often understrength and not geared to the kind of changes they face. They can no longer simply respond to user-departments requests for systems, which often means they are attempting the impossible if the problems of failing to meet project deadlines are anything to go by. Instead they have to assess projects carefully, set realistic limits to what can be done with available resources, look for more effective ways of achieving what is needed – in other words positively 'manage' demand rather than throw inadequate resources at vanishing deadlines.

A dp/IT manager running a small department/unit, with a small staff. will deal personally with most functions, where the service exists. Within larger dp/IT departments/divisions, the growing range of managerial and administrative responsibilities may be divided, and in some areas a team of staff may be needed. Planning, tackling the thorny problems of future policy hard/software needs, responsibility for efficient services (despite staff shortages, machine and software failures, problems with input etc), dealing with recruitment, training etc are all part of the managerial job. Not least is managing people – expert people who expect to be treated well. The main specialist areas are –

Communications, or network, management – it is easy for an organisation to let everyone who already has some responsibility for one kind of communications – fax or telephone for instance – and even individual departments, develop new systems on a piecemeal basis. But the goal is to 'integrate' systems, so letting this happen risks major problems in future.

Telecommunications managers are, then, currently in great demand – and comparatively few people have the right technological background. Telecommunications managers are mainly at present dealing with the fast-growing use of networks, with traditional, non-IT staff (eg office administrators) still dealing with voice/telephone systems – but somewhere along the line the two have to come together. They have to be able to keep up with the fast-moving technology, to assess what is on offer and how important new products are, assess company needs, know what to buy, work out which bits and pieces will talk to each other, spot the problems, troubleshoot etc. Integrating data with fax, voice and graphics is likely to be increasingly important.

Computer operations management still the most common managerial work, which primarily involves keeping a mainframe installation – with or without a network of distributed terminals – working as efficiently as possible. It therefore involves seeing to staffing levels, working out scheduling, organising maintenance and repair to keep 'down-time' at a minimum, trouble-shooting etc. In a small unit, while managing computer operations may be a major part of the job, the manager also has to deal day-to-day with, eg programming, as well as planning, budgeting, advising general management etc. In a larger department computer operations managers will also have a team of shift managers/supervisors.

Computer operations managers will usually have a one or more (up to a largish team) of operators to keep the machine(s) working, often round the clock on a shift basis. Much of the work is routine loading and running – keyboarding instructions – monitoring that it is running properly (and that the air-conditioning etc is at the right levels), logging in up-dating material from departments, making back-up files, keeping records. Operators become skilled at detailed scheduling – when to run what to meet agreed deadlines – and also answer queries etc. They may run diagnostic routines when something goes wrong, and send for the appropriate expert – programmer, maintenance engineer etc.

Database management/administration databases bring together information which in the past would have been held on separate 'files'.

For example, the details on people with several insurance policies from one company may be duplicated on the files for each type of policy – so when they change address, the information has to be rekeyed for each file. A database brings separate files together, so that a policy holder's details need only be entered and revised once, yet can be accessed by staff dealing with any of their policies.

Database management ranges from planning ahead – monitoring what users want in future and how this is to be met, whether extra capacity is needed or whether the database can be 'weeded' for redundant information etc – to the day-to-day tasks of seeing that new and revised information is being loaded to schedule and accurately, organising staff, making sure that programs and equipment are maintained and up-dated, that users' problems are being solved, etc.

Information centre management/administration This is a comparatively new area of responsibility for dp/IT managers, existing as yet in only a proportion of organisations, and possibly developing in quite different ways. However the work is organised, it involves providing support to users within the organisa-tion. Increasingly this is aimed at helping users to 'manage' their own infor-mation needs. It can range from the internal equivalent of a full consultancy, through organising more independent use of mainframe facilities for a depart-ment (using their pcs as terminals), assessing software packages for use in departments, to providing expensive equipment which departments can share, eg graphics plotters, and training users on new software, equipment etc.

Systems/programming management A department of any size will have several project teams, of varying numbers from two or three people upwards, made up of systems analysts-designers, programmers. The traditional route up through a dp department is via project leader, who may be a systems analyst/designer and/or senior programmer, and from there to eg section leader. How much responsibility, and managerial work, team/section leaders carry varies from job to job. Most continue to do a considerable amount of 'technical' work, but they also supervise and co-ordinate the work of their teams, decide how to divide the work between the team etc. They may also have to cost the projects on which they are working, and deal with budgets. They may be involved in planning the work of the department, and in assessing new products etc.

Other IT/computing related work

This includes –

MAINTENANCE/SERVICING While computers themselves need less and less maintenance – electro-mechanical peripherals with moving parts (disk drives, printers etc) are still just as liable to break down – the increasing number of machines in use means there is just as much, if not more, maintenance work and servicing to be done. Straightforward physical maintenance gets easier all the time – components like chips and memory boards are simply replaced completely when they fail to work properly. Most machines now have programs which help to identify faults, but diagnosis – and whether they are in the electronics or the software – is still often the main problem for maintenance/service engineers.

The largest users and manufacturers employ their own technician engineers – who are increasingly trained to cope with both electronic and electro-mechanical systems. Depending on the size of the organisation or unit, they may specialise, or they may do any repairs, servicing, straightforward installation, cable configuration etc as needed. Many users, however, now have contracts with service companies and/or manufacturers. Large computers, like cars, must be regularly serviced to prevent break-downs if possible, but they can't be driven to the service centre, and so 'field engineers' go to each firm in their area when a check up is due. They also respond to requests for service when a machine or piece of equipment does go wrong.

Maintenance staff are often trained in-house by manufacturers, to work on simpler systems to begin with, moving on (with additional training), to more complex ones. Further promotion can be to trouble-shooting where the engineers doing routine work cannot solve a problem, supervisory work, and planning and organising new installations, etc.

SELLING COMPUTERS This ranges from the highly technical business of selling more sophisticated and expensive systems to commercial, industrial and other organisations, to the rather more straightforward jobs selling the smaller personal computers in high street shops. Selling pcs in the high-street shop is learnt, mostly on-the-job, in the same way as learning to sell other electronic goods, eg videos. General-purpose micros for smaller businesses are sold by specialist computer/systems shops, and here some experience both in computing and in running a business is normally needed.

Sales teams selling more sophisticated machines generally specialise in a particular kind of computer or system and/or selling to a particular market – insurance companies or banks, for example. These sales men and women need plenty of experience of the company's products, which is normally gained in sales support – answering simpler queries from potential customers, organising training for new users' staff, and so on. Some sales staff come through the programming route, and in some companies the line between systems analysis/ engineering and sales is very ill-defined. Promotion is to sales management and MARKETING, although it is possible to go over to data processing management.

TRAINING Manufacturers, software and systems houses, and larger users, employ their own training staff, and there is a growing number of independent training schools as well as opportunities to work in further and higher education. Training ranges from teaching the simplest keyboarding to YTS trainees through to giving seminars on the latest 'state-of-the-art' – eg in networking or expert systems – to already highly-qualified systems programmers. Training is usually a 'second career', for people who have the right aptitudes and extensive experience in the relevant area of computing. All firms are short of trainers.

Recruitment and entry

The IT/computing 'business' suffers from a severe and chronic shortage of skilled staff, although this may not be quite so bad as some reports suggest. The problem is not just about numbers, though. Rather more crucial is the shortage of high-calibre people with good potential – with demand particularly high from users, who are no longer attracting skilled staff from manufacturers. The shortages, however, may be to some extent self-generated. The main shortfall, according to a 1987 survey, was of an estimated 10,000 staff with *three to four years relevant experience*. This gives one clue to the problem – not enough organisations are training, but instead want to recruit people who are already both trained and experienced – software houses particularly. The problem is exacerbated by recruiters' belief, right or wrong, that 'academic' computing qualifications are not what they need. (This, in part, helps to explain why apparently well-qualified people cannot get a first post.)

Identifying the skills/experience needed is a complex business, made more complicated by constant change and by the difficulty of getting recruiters to be specific about their requirements.

Two themes predominate (at present), for all entrants at almost all levels, and for almost all 'functions' – high quality, and the ability, or potential, to apply IT to the organisation's business, and deliver practical and commercial IT solutions. Increasingly, employers are looking for people with broader, more cross-disciplinary skills/training, all-round abilities – 'adaptable, intelligent problem-solvers' according to COSIT. Demand for people with aptitude for (and skills/training in) analysis and design is still rising, but declining for more straightforward programming and most lower-level aptitude/skills. Interest in management potential should be increasing.

Research, development and design (including systems/software design/engineering/programming) need specific pre-entry qualifications. Here a specialist degree is probably most useful (see Qualifications and training below) although physics, maths and other sciences are also considered.

Maintenance/servicing and installation also need an appropriate technical background.

For all other specialist IT/computing work aptitude for the work and practical computing experience seem to be the two main criteria for gaining a foothold.

Despite the shortages of skilled people, there is considerable competition for the best opportunities, and it is essential to plan on up-to-date information, and to show motivation and determination to get in.

At present, most people start 'at the bottom' mainly in programming, or (main frame) computer operating (a useful way of gaining experience for all entrants). There are, though, no hard and fast rules and it is still possible to move into specialist computer work after starting in something else and gaining experience (especially if it includes using IT/computer systems) and training – MANAGEMENT SERVICES can give a useful basis. People with solid experience in an applications area can often move into systems analysis – it is in fact unusual to go straight from education into systems analysis/design (graduates recruited as trainee analysts/programmers generally spend a while just programming to begin with). However, recruitment patterns could be changing.

Programming takes the ability to think clearly and logically, to have good basic English, and to be able to understand what users need. Programmers have to be methodical, accurate, very painstaking, and able to concentrate for fairly long periods. To go on to more complex programming, into systems analysis/design needs also the ability to analyse complex situations and processes, reduce them to basic essentials and produce practical, sensible solutions in clear, easily-understood instructions. Systems analysis/design also needs people who can think themselves into the potential user's position, to see what they and their organisations do, and why, and what they want a computing system to do for them. They have to be able to explain technicalities in non-technical terms, know how to get people to explain their work, and be tactful. To go beyond this needs managerial potential, or very high-level technical skill.

Graduates are recruited, as elsewhere, for their intellectual training and potential, so a degree has advantages. The main – probably best – route in is via a formal training scheme, which usually means starting as a trainee (applications) programmer, but in most organisations with graduate-entry schemes, time spent actually programming is getting shorter all the time – firms want much more out of graduates. Degree subject is not important – some business awareness and/or 'hands-on' computing is useful but this can be gained via work experience/vacation jobs if not via the course. Employers are wary of people with computer-science degrees for this route in (see Qualifications and training below) and positively encourage arts/social science graduates to apply (preferring to train from scratch rather than take on science-based graduates with the wrong pre-conceived notions of computing). The ability to solve real-life problems, use information as the basis for decision-making, managerial potential, and the ability to think logically and clearly – to be able to break down a sequence of events into separate steps in the right order – and write English properly are all far more important than mathematics.

Alternative routes are via one of the qualifications or training schemes described below.

A-level entrants may be recruited as trainee programmers or computer operators, but for long-term career prospects it probably makes more sense to gain a higher qualification first. Without A-levels, it may be possible to start in computer operating, but a (good) computer-based YTS scheme is probably a worthwhile starting point.

Recruiting practices for computer staff tend to puzzle many entrants. One MSC survey gave some clues. For trainee programmers, for example, recruiters relied most heavily on interview. Second came the result of an aptitude test (but only half of all recruiters, contrary to what is often said, actually use them). Educational attainment comes third (ie at least A levels), and personal characteristics (including 'manner', appearance) fourth. Computing qualifications come fifth, result of a personality/interest measure sixth, previous computer training seventh – references and membership of a professional body come last.

Qualifications and training

Two problems have bedevilled IT/computing for years, and achieving permanent solutions seem to be as far away as ever. Firstly, far too few users and service companies train (manufacturers have a far better record), and this is improving only very slowly. Secondly, 'academic' courses/qualifications do not seem to meet the needs of many employers. To some extent this is because the industry does not say clearly enough what is needed, but partly it is due to the rapid change, which makes it difficult to keep course planning and syllabuses up to date.

While it is still possible to get into skilled computing work by a variety of routes, pre-entry qualifications can be useful. There are few firm rules or guidelines to follow, and no clearly-defined set of qualifications. But some courses are more suitable for some areas of work than others, and employers are becoming more discriminating. It is crucial, then, to analyse and assess very carefully what pre-entry courses have to offer – they vary greatly, and change frequently, so up-to-date information is essential.

For research, development and design (including systems programming and software engineering) with manufacturers and some systems/software houses. Intake is now largely graduate, and a specialist degree such as those listed under COMPUTER ENGINEERING/INFORMATION TECHNOLOGY, science-oriented COMPUTER SCIENCE (biased to or combined with ELECTRONICS, for hard/software design), is increasingly essential. MATHEMATICS or PHYSICS with a substantial computing content/option is an alternative. Most relevant courses need maths and physics A levels or the equivalent.

For other computing specialists a wider range of choice between routes is possible –

Graduate pre-entry courses Large users, and those computing service companies with graduate recruitment programmes, consider people with degrees in any subject – and seem happy to train them 'from scratch'. A degree course in science- or electronics-oriented computer science is not the best preparation because they do not normally cover the applications end. Courses do, though, vary greatly and more schemes now provide a basis for a business-oriented career. Essential elements include some business studies, computing which includes both theoretical and applications-biased practical project work (using appropriate languages such as COBOL), and preferably a year of industry- or commerce-based training. The drawback to these degrees is that it is probably difficult to get into the more complex 'systems programming' etc with them. One major new development is the IBM/Portsmouth Polytechnic degree 'course', which started in 1987. On this students are actually IBM trainees, and divide their time between 'real' work, the IBM training school, and Portsmouth Polytechnic, over three (twelve-month not academic) years.

More new/revised schemes can be expected, but examples of suitable courses include –

Universities – Birmingham: Aston (Management & computer science), Bradford (Computing & information systems science), City (Business computing systems), Norwich: E Anglia (Business information systems), Leeds (Data processing), Liverpool (Accounting or business studies & computing), Loughborough (Data processing), Manchester (Computing science & accounting), Salford (Information technology); polytechnics – Birmingham (Computing information systems), Huddersfield (Computing in business), Kingston (Business information technology), Manchester (Information technology in business), Middlesbrough: Teesside (Information technology), Preston: Lancs (Business information technology), Stoke-on-Trent: N Staffs (Information sciences), Sunderland (Business computing); colleges – Edinburgh: Napier (Computing & data processing), Hull: Humberside CHE (Business information systems), Shrivenham: RMCS (Command & control, communications & IT systems).

In addition, computer studies courses, especially sandwich-based courses, at most polytechnics and eg Brunel University, Manchester: UMIST.

Almost any subject will do, though. Firms still recruit people with degrees in eg classics because it often implies the right logical/linguistic attitudes. Business studies or economics are probably more useful. It is worth learning to program, have done some 'hands on' computing, and have some work experience. At some universities/polytechnics etc it is possible to take CGLI 424 (see below). While postgraduate training is not essential, it is possible to take special IT/computing conversion courses. SERC-funded MSc/diploma courses are on offer at well over 40 universities, polytechnics etc. Graduates who have been away from full-time education since leaving school are eligible for an MSC-sponsored course – which can be anything from a short introductory course to a full MSc – on the Job Retraining Scheme.

Other pre-entry awards/courses include –

BTEC awards – main schemes

Computer studies National courses (1986 guidelines) include introduction to programming, computer and information systems, quantitative methods, communication skills, a major option stream (from programming, small-business computer systems, microprocessor-based systems) with, for a certificate the option to study one of these (or operating) as a minor plus another option unit. For a diploma, either another major stream plus an option unit, or one option stream as a minor and two option units, or two minor streams. Entry requirements as for all BTEC Nationals††.

Computer studies Higher National courses (1985 guidelines) – polytechnics/colleges design their own individual programmes of study, within general guidelines. But at least 50% of HND, 75% of HNC courses are expected to cover the computer and its behaviour, methods for designing and implementing computer-based systems, and the environment of computer-based systems. Beyond this, courses can emphasise, eg business or industrial data processing, or computer systems maintenance. Entry requirements as for all BTEC Higher Nationals†† but if via GCE/GCSE to include a pass in maths.

Information technology Higher National courses (1986 guidelines) – polytechnics/colleges design their own individual programmes of study, within general guidelines. Schemes are to 'integrate' electronics, communications technology and computing – software and hardware – with a substantial element of practical work, as the basis for work in evaluating, analysing, developing and maintaining IT systems. Course design is to be based on three 'layers' – physical, logical and operational. Entry requirements as for Higher awards in computer studies.

Business information technology Higher National courses (1986 guidelines) – polytechnics/colleges design their own individual programmes of study, within general guidelines. Designed to train in promoting, facilitating and integrating IT-based systems within commerce, industry, and administration, understanding business information, the structure and processes for information management, and the practical use of information in running a business or in administration. Schemes must cover four broad study areas – problem identification and solution (including hard- and software), the business information technology environment, business operations, and business information technology applications. Entry requirements as for Higher awards in computer studies.

Computing can also be studied as part of BTEC schemes in eg business studies, and mathematics.

National Computer Centre (NCC) courses/awards: the Centre runs a number of courses itself, at all levels and in all skills. It also awards what has come to be the accepted basic qualification (a certificate) in system analysis (but this is normally taken by people with at least some experience). NCC's 'threshold' scheme for young people has been subsumed into YTS (below).

CGLI schemes (as of 1987): the most important of these are

Information technology (726) – a modular scheme being developed under the broad subject headings electronics/hardware, computer applications/related studies, programming and software, and at introductory, elementary, intermediate and advanced levels. Over 100 modules are planned, and these can be taken in various 'mixes', or be added to other qualifications.

Basic competence in information technology (424) – a practical/vocational scheme covering the (currently) three major business uses – wordprocessing, spread-sheeting, and assessing databases.

Other schemes are applications programming (417), computer programming and information processing (418), data processing for computer users (419), and inside information (444). No formal entry qualifications needed for any schemes.

Royal Society of Arts (RSA): Information technology is a modular scheme with cross-certification by RSA and SEG for GCSE. Keyboarding applications is also cross-certified but there is also a separate computer keyboarding skills test.

Professional qualifications are not (at least yet) pre-entry qualifications. Most people add them to other qualifications to help gain promotion etc. The main bodies are –

The British Computer Society (over 25,000 members) – full membership depends on completing the Society's two-part examinations (entry to part I is with five GCE/GCSE passes including one at A level, or the equivalent, plus a year's practical experience). A degree or HND exempts from one or both parts depending on computing content. Full members must be at least 24 with four years' practical experience, associate members at least 22 with at least three years' practical experience and part I of the exams. Courses for the exams are available at some 50 centres. BCS has applied for membership of the Engineering Council, and is piloting a professional development scheme.

The Institute of Data Processing Management: of the 5000 full members, about 44% are actually managers – the second largest group (about 23%) work in systems (8% are programming, and 6.6% work in operations). The four-part exams equate to BTEC National (first two) and Higher National (final two): entry requirements are at least four O-level-equivalent passes† but a range of exemptions are given for appropriate qualifications and/or experience. The Institute plans to add further exams to degree level. Full membership also requires at least eight years' appropriate experience.

Gaining training The main alternatives are –

An employer-based training scheme, preferably using a COSIT (Computing Services Industry Training Council) designed programme and/or BCS professional development scheme.

Youth Training Scheme: all trainees are supposed to learn basic computer 'literacy' and skills, but some schemes give more intensive specialist training. The NCC's data processing 'threshold' scheme is now (1987) a YTS scheme, combining work experience with college training for a BTEC National Certificate in computer studies for trainees who have four O-level-equivalent passes or can pass an aptitude test.

Information Technology Centres (ITeCs): as of 1986, 176 ITeCs were providing training under two-year YTS in electronics, computing and modern office skills to 7500 trainees. Schemes vary from centre to centre. The status of ITeCs has recently changed, and by 1988 they will be treated as ordinary managing agents. This means they will probably have to earn some of their income in other ways, so changes are underway. There are no formal entry qualifications for ITeC schemes, but trainees are expected to be able to show some practical evidence of motivation.

JTS and other local schemes: ask for details at the nearest job centre or careers office.

Private/commercial courses: these can be very expensive, and it should normally be possible to find appropriate training with an employer, at an HE/FE college or polytechnic, or on a government-sponsored scheme. If it is necessary to choose a commercial school, it is crucial to check that the course leads to a recognised qualification; that teachers are properly qualified and have the necessary equipment available for student use; and to ask for details of the kind of jobs gained by previous students. No school can claim to *guarantee* a job. A list of accredited schools is now published by the Information Technology Training Accreditation Council (ITTAC).

Further information from The National Computing Centre, the British Computer Society, the Computer Services Industry Training Council (COSIT), and ITTAC.

LIBRARY AND INFORMATION WORK

Librarians and information scientists have been the information-handling and -organising experts until now, and it is they who have been at the sharp end, coping with the explosion in information and knowledge of the last forty years which is one basis of the need for information technology.

For librarians and information scientists, the problem has, until recently, been one of growing masses of paper. Chemistry is frequently quoted as the most startling example. The half million articles covered in *Chemical Abstracts* in the *single* year 1976, was just half the output for the *five* years 1962 to 1967, which in turn equalled the *total* number of articles written by the pre-world war II generation of chemists. University libraries have been doubling their stock every sixteen years. Specialists find it increasingly difficult to keep up to date in their subjects without professional help. For everyone else, finding out means coping with growing complexity, the obscure language of the specialist, etc, as well.

New technology has been moving into the library for some years now. It began mostly with computer-based systems for cataloguing, recording library loans and other routine administrative work. Back issues of periodicals, newspapers, government papers, etc, have long been kept on microfile. Now most larger libraries use on-line computerised information services (see INFORMATION TECHNOLOGY above). These systems cut down long searches through reference books and journals. These mean that libraries do not have to keep so much material on paper, and result in a faster, better information service. Many libraries also use videotext systems such as Prestel. As a result, some libraries now call themselves 'multi-media resource centres'.

Libraries and information centres may look and be very different places by the 1990s. For the 500 years since print was invented, individual libraries have collected as much material as they considered they needed and could afford. Now the traditions of centuries are likely to be revolutionised as computer-based information systems develop and are more widely used. The image of a library as a place full of books, periodicals, and so on, is changing as information technology systems take over. Many libraries and information bureaux already have their own computers and terminal links into other systems. But these will not be just additional to the traditional bookstocks – they are beginning to replace them. Libraries have co-operated with each other over what each should stock to save unnecessary duplication for many years; the National Lending Library can supply books as needed within twenty-four hours, which means some libraries need not stock long runs of, eg journals which are not used very often. With computerised information systems, which can provide printouts of abstracts and even full articles on line, even fewer libraries will need to store long runs of journals or even some books.

While libraries and information bureaux will remain storehouses of books etc. for the foreseeable future, the national Library and Information Services

Council (LISC) expects strategy will have to change, from local holdings to shared and electronic access. LISC wants every library and its parent body to reassess the balance between maintaining comprehensive collections of their own, and using electronic 'gateways', planning for ready access to both printed sources, wherever it may be, and data available mainly on line. LISC wants a sharp improvement in present arrangements for co-operation, with planned interdependence on a national scale. This is likely to mean some kind of national information grid or network, with each subject speciality, locality, and region needing to justify exemption by reference to ease of access and special characteristics and circumstances. All this would have a great many implications for those working in libraries and information bureaux. LISC is currently (mid 1983) reviewing future manpower, education and training requirements, taking particular account of the impact of technological and other change.

Libraries and information centres

There are many different kinds of library, each providing a service for a different group of readers. They are, though, commonly grouped into three broad areas – public, academic, and 'special'.

PUBLIC LIBRARIES make up the largest sector still, and are the most familiar (even though only one person in three uses them). They are supported and controlled by the local authorities, and the organisation of public libraries and career structures within them are as LOCAL GOVERNMENT generally. These libraries have to be provided by law. Since 1976 the local authorities' financial position has made expansion almost impossible, and many authorities have cut budgets and services – book funds fell by 25% between 1979 and 1986, the total number of branch libraries is down 600 to 4300, and 'part-time' branches, open for a few hours a week in rural areas, down to 350 from 1000. The situation is unlikely to change in the foreseeable future.

Local authorities are still, though, the largest employers of qualified librarians, even though numbers are falling. No 'manpower census' has been taken recently, so figures are rather dated. Some 8300 professional librarians worked in 166 public library systems in 1981 (DES survey), over 47% of working librarians. (A National Audit Commission report suggested numbers were down to under 6900 in 1985-6 – a 12% fall on 1979-80 – just over 7900 Library Association members, under 44%, worked in public libraries in 1985 but this includes librarians not yet chartered.) Public libraries employ other professional and support staff – 16,200 people in 1981 (against over 17,700 in 1976).

Public libraries range from the large city-centre library offering a full range of lending and reference services, through smaller suburban libraries with less extensive facilities, to the country libraries which, in remoter areas, are 'on wheels', with specially-fitted vans taking the service to villages and outlying places. Public libraries mainly provide services for local people – books, records and video films to borrow; reference collections to answer questions on anything and everything from entertainment to employment, consumer affairs, social benefits, commercial and technical problems. Most public libraries have special services for children. Services offered, though, vary according to the area. The large city-centre library, for example, may provide a sophisticated information service for the business community, some with computerised on-line information services. Some libraries, again in inner city areas, provide services designed to give all kinds of support to disadvantaged and ethnic minority groups, and give back up help for people who are unemployed (for example).

Public libraries try to keep up a broadly-based, balanced collection of books across many subjects, but some also build collections in particular subjects – Shakespeare at Birmingham, for example, or music at Westminster – so that one library somewhere has specialist books if wanted. One library in a local authority may provide technical information services for local industry, perhaps in co-operation with a local polytechnic library.

Most public library systems are large, with a number of libraries of varying sizes spread throughout a borough or county. The structure is hierarchical, and staff work up from junior positions through, for example, the branch or reference library structures, from small children's library to group and borough children's librarian.

ACADEMIC LIBRARIES include the libraries of universities and university colleges, polytechnics, Scottish central institutions, and colleges of higher and further education of all kinds. This adds up to over 900 libraries employing, in 1981, just over 4000 professional staff (about 23% of all working professional librarians). Numbers had been increasing slowly for over ten years (3800 in 1972), but growth has ended and number are probably falling. (Just over 3300 members of the Library Association were working in academic libraries in 1985, but many academic librarians do not belong.) Academic libraries also employ support staff who are not professional librarians, though – over 4870 in 1981 against under 3300 in 1972. Academic libraries, too, are having to adapt services to sharply falling resources.

Universities have libraries ranging from the million or more book collections dating back to the middle ages at Oxford and Cambridge, through to the libraries started only in the 1960s by new universities, with rather smaller collections. U· iversity libraries are usually large enough to be split into large subject divisions, each staffed by teams of graduate librarians who specialise in the subject field (to the extent that some also teach), each division dealing with everything from their own book buying to special reader services. They have to cope with the very differing needs of university staff doing advanced research and the students who all have to read the same chapters of books and articles for an essay at the same time.

Polytechnic and FE college libraries are less sophisticated, and have to provide services for an even broader range of users including, for instance, people studying for professional or technician qualifications on a part-time basis.

All these academic libraries have to build collections in the subjects taught, and some are therefore specialised, such as the art schools where libraries have more slides than books. Most larger academic libraries now use on-line bibliographic and other information services. Use of non-book, including audiovisual, material is extensive everywhere.

School library services help pupils learn how to use libraries and books, provide material for study and project work, and a quiet place to study. Not every secondary school has a proper library or full-time librarian – some school libraries are run by teachers with some library training. Some schools have library services run centrally by the local education authority. Under 700 members of the Library Association were working in school libraries in 1985, but not all school librarians belong to the LA.

'SPECIAL' LIBRARIES (so called because they specialise) are the most diverse group. They include the five national libraries, the libraries and/or information bureaux of over 2000 industrial and commercial firms, of over 900 government departments, 150-plus public corporations, 200 learned societies and professional bodies, 130 research and research associations, and 130 'others'. Altogether, they are believed to employ (1981) over 5230 professional staff, up from 4500 in 1972. (Just over 3300 members of the Library Association worked in special libraries in 1985, but a high proportion do not join the LA.) As a proportion of all working professionals, special librarians now make up almost 30% of the total – against 27-28% in the 1970s. But the overall increase in jobs in special libraries may not be so great, because the numbers of non-professional people working in special libraries fell back in 1981 to below the 1972 figure of under 5000. A high proportion of special libraries (particularly the smaller ones) have in the past been staffed by unqualified people, but these figures suggest this has been changing.

National libraries, with some exceptions, serve mostly people doing academic or other research work. Most important is the British Library, a huge system (with a staff of over 1700), spread around the country. It now has two main divisions – humanities and social sciences, at present housed in the British Museum, and science, technology and industry with its 'document supply centre' (lending and photocopy service) in Yorkshire, and the reference library and information service at the Science Museum in South Kensington. Scotland and Wales have their own national libraries. Others are the Public Record Library, and the libraries of the Houses of Parliament, working for MPs and the Lords. Although many of these libraries, as well as those of the learned societies, are traditionally highly conservationist, conforming more closely than most others to the traditional image of the library as a quiet academic retreat, they are introducing electronic information retrieval for their users. Staff of these libraries are usually subject experts first, and the proportion of people with professional qualifications tends to be smaller than elsewhere.

Industrial and organisations in all sectors – oil and chemicals, drugs, electronics, coal, gas, steel, electricity, etc – have their libraries and/or information bureaux. Most of these libraries/information bureaux have been built around their companies' research and development programmes, and so have traditionally been heavily biased to particular areas of science and technology. They have to provide a steady flow of the latest technical and scientific information for the research staff, to keep them up to date on what is going on elsewhere in their particular field, give answers to highly technical questions, etc. Industrial, and commercial, firms also increasingly use up-to-date and sophisticated commercial information, including statistics and surveys, on potential new markets, government policies, the economy, industrial relations policy, and so on. Some companies have very large and sophisticated combined libraries and information services, while others are very much smaller and can be fairly basic. The most professional are using on-line computerised services etc quite extensively,

Most professional bodies, particularly the larger ones, from the British Medical Association, to the Institutes of Bankers, Personnel Management, and Mechanical Engineers, have libraries for their members which now form some of the most important collections in that particular field.

The 'Whitehall' group of libraries include those at the Foreign Office and the Treasury, which have historical collections. In the main, though, these, like those of the Home Office, the Department of Employment, and so on, are sophisticated working libraries for civil servants. Some, like the statistics and market intelligence library of the Department of Trade and Industry, can be used by the public.

The services provided by special libraries obviously vary greatly, from the large and very sophisticated, producing high-level abstracting and/or indexing services, providing access to a range of data bases etc, and maintaining a large collection of printed and other material, through to the fairly rudimentary.

WORKING AS A LIBRARIAN/INFORMATION SCIENTIST

There is no real difference between a qualified librarian and an information scientist. In practice, and wherever they are employed, they do broadly similar work – the difference is one of emphasis and degree rather than fundamental. Both are information providers, skilled at collecting, organising, and using whatever source material is needed. Information technology is likely to make the librarian more, rather than less, like an information scientist. But while librarians are making increasing use of computer-based systems, the main uses at present are still for 'housekeeping' – cataloguing material, keeping track of loans, etc – and on-line bibliographic searching. Financial constraints, as well as innate caution, are probably the main reasons for this.

At one end of the spectrum, librarians build broad, comprehensive collections for their readers, to meet as many of their possible needs as can be afforded, of books, newspapers, journals, maps, pamphlets, records, cassettes, micro and video film, tapes and so on. At the other end, the information scientist concentrates on acquiring up-to-date information needed by the staff of the organisation, and keeping them informed about it. This is most likely to mean working with journals, abstracts, published and unpublished reports (technical, scientific, government, marketing etc), patents and so on. It means a greater mass of paper rather than shelves of books – and probably increasing use of and reliance on, electronic data bases. In between, many people combine traditional librarians' work with more sophisticated information science in varying proportions. Qualified and chartered librarians run information bureaux, and scientists (often without formal information-science training) run the libraries of learned scientific societies.

The DES tried to quantify the number of posts which were mainly librarian, mainly information science and equally distributed in 1981. The results do not look entirely satisfactory, as the survey gave 99% of all public library posts as mainly librarian, and only 1% equally librarian and information science – suggesting rather that people working in libraries are extremely loyal to their professional association. In academic libraries, 86% of posts were mainly librarian, according to the survey, 12% half and half, and 2% mainly information science. In special libraries, 54% of posts were defined as mainly librarian, 19% half and half, and 28% mainly information science – over two-thirds of the posts in private industry involved at least half time on information science work.

Both librarians and information scientists have to acquire – mostly buy – books and other materials. This can be a complex business, both in finding out what is available and in matching budgets to purchases. There have to be policy guidelines, checks on what readers want (and sometimes why), on likely future needs, on how far to be selective on new books or journals in a specialist field, and what and whose judgements to use on what is worth acquiring.

Both librarians and information scientists must organise their material in some kind of order, so that particular items can be found easily, and related material is kept together. A library's books are usually somewhat easier to group in a meaningful subject order, easier and more straightforward to index, than is the more complex paperwork of all kinds that an information service stores, and where indexing may have to be much more detailed. Both libraries and information bureaux store and sort their catalogues and indexes using computers now. On-line information services are beginning to reduce the amount of indexing etc, that libraries/information bureaux have to do for themselves.

Both librarians and information scientists expect to help their readers find out almost anything they need or want to know, whether it is to look up a straightforward address or ferret out all the data available on an obscure chemical. The same questions may be asked of the staff of a city reference library and the information bureau of a chemical company, but the information scientists in the chemical company will spend more of their time searching through specialised scientific and technical literature mostly at an advanced level. The city librarians will never know what subject will come up next, or how simple or complex the question will be. On-line information services mean all staff now have to become expert in the best ways to exploit data bases and host networks, and the fastest ways to retrieve information from them.

Both librarians and information scientists aim to keep their readers informed. Librarians, though, are more likely to compile straightforward reading lists – on new holiday books, or on personal computers, for example. Information scientists, on the other hand, have to know in detail what research their readers are doing, often do much of the scientists' preliminary reading for them – eg 'scanning' a wide range of publications – prepare weekly 'current awareness' bulletins, and make summaries of papers in the scientific press, translate them if necessary, and sometimes help write technical reports.

In most larger libraries and information bureaux, professional staff specialise in the work they do. The different tasks include cataloguing and classifying, indexing, book purchase, reference work, work with children (which includes organising story readings and many other lively activities as well as more conventional library duties), advisory work with readers, running services for the housebound, or specialising in a subject area – music or medicine, for example. A small number teach in library/information science schools.

While professional librarians do switch from one kind of library to another, this can be quite difficult. They may also change the type of work they do, although in 'public' libraries it is common to stay on the 'lending' side (progressing through branch to central library, from smaller library system to a larger one, possibly up to senior and chief librarian) or in reference work (similar structure).

Most librarians/information scientists spend just as much of their time with people and on the telephone as with books, journals etc. These they use as tools to provide a service, and do not just look after them. A few places employ 'back room' librarians, living with and caring for historic collections, but for most library/information staff the job is mainly about helping people solve the problems of what to read or how to find out. Librarians/information scientists, though, cannot choose their own research topics. They are always doing just part of someone else's project (which can be frustrating). Working hours are irregular, as many libraries open in the evenings and on Saturdays.

Libraries try not to waste expensive professional staff on more routine work – for example, on lending-library counters or putting books away on shelves (although cuts in local authority expenditure threaten this). Most libraries employ assistants for this and for general administration.

Libraries take a lot of administrating. Just to get staff timetables right for a large library system is a major headache. Like all other managers, senior librarians have to cope with budgets, planning, deciding on priorities, and so on. All have ahead of them a period of major change and have to learn to manage this also. Librarians/information scientists aiming for the most senior positions, particularly in public libraries, have to accept that they will spend most of their time administrating and managing, and little in direct library/ information work. There are, however, many posts of intermediate responsibility which combine professional work with administration/management, and possibly a growing role in assessing and managing the information needs of organisations.

Prospects for professional staff are difficult to predict. There are problems for public-sector librarians, as local-authority expenditure is cut, and the same is true for academic librarians. Continued expansion in the number of jobs in special, and particularly industrial/commercial, libraries and information bureaux depends to some extent on how far staff become involved in the wider provision of expert information via new technology. Computerised systems – for recording loans and sending out reminders – are reducing demand for unqualified assistants.

Recruitment and entry A degree is required to become a professional librarian or information scientist. While some special libraries and information bureaux still recruit school-leavers, it is not generally possible to find professional work without a degree now.

The characteristics needed for professional library and information work depends to some extent on the type of work. Children's librarianship makes quite different demands to work with scientists and engineers, for example. The level of academic/intellectual achievement and depth of subject knowledge needed varies greatly. Broad rather than narrow, in-depth interests are most useful, except for a few very specialist posts. It is useful to have the kind of mind that must have an answer once a question has been asked, that has detective-like persistence, that likes to keep up with new ideas, can absorb and understand subjects and ideas easily, and is resourceful. It is essential to be logical, tidy-minded, and methodical. A good memory is helpful. Administrative abilities (especially staff management, handling committees and extracting resources, and making the best of budgets) are needed for more senior posts.

Being 'keen on books and/or reading' is not in itself a good enough basis for wanting to be a librarian, although an intelligent interest in books and reading is needed. Few libraries are places for people who want to retire from the world. In fact the reverse is more likely the case, and the reader is as important as the source material. Most librarians and information staff need the patience and ability to draw out of people what it is they really want to know, to be able to interpret vague and badly-expressed questions.

Library assistants are recruited directly by libraries of all kinds from amongst school-leavers. There are no formal entry requirements, but at least five O-level-equivalent passes are needed to gain a national qualification at this level.

Some YTS schemes are based on libraries, and can lead to work as an assistant.

Qualifications and training two routes to professional qualification –
One is via a first degree in librarianship and/or information science, which normally includes, or is combined with, one or more conventional academic subjects. The choice is wide, but most useful are science, technology, maths or statistics, and increasingly business studies, economics. Course titles vary, and the information science content is not always apparent from the name of the course. Courses are likely to be substantially revised over the next few years. Specialist degree courses are at present (for 1988 entry) available at –
Universities – Aberystwyth: UC with College of Librarianship, Belfast, Glasgow: Strathclyde, Loughborough; polytechnics: Birmingham, Brighton, Leeds, Liverpool, London: PNL, Manchester, Newcastle. Other colleges – Aberdeen: RGIT, London: Ealing CHE.

The alternative is to read for a degree in any subject or subjects – again, science, technology, business studies, maths, economics would be useful – and then to take a one-year postgraduate training course.

Professional bodies are –
The Library Association (1986 membership about 24,000) – corporate, 'chartered' membership is essential for all professional posts in the public-library system. It is increasingly required or at least preferred by academic and government libraries, and useful elsewhere. A period of supervised experience is required for chartered membership – this is shortest (a year) after a formal, approved training programme (in addition to an approved course), but can be two or six years.

The Library Association is working on ways of broadening its membership to include other professionals etc in the information field, and plans to make entry to membership more 'flexible'. The Association is also 'marketing' the professional skills of its members as crucial to 'managing' information generally.

The Institute of Information Scientists (membership c2000) requires an appropriate degree-level or postgraduate qualification for membership – which can be useful especially for jobs in industrial libraries, but is not compulsory.

Further information from the Library Association and the Institute of Information Scientists.

Commerce, Administration and Finance

Introduction   397
Administration and management   400
Finance (including accountancy, banking, insurance)   428
Marketing (including advertising, market research and public relations) 486
Purchasing and buying, selling and retailing   503

INTRODUCTION

Commerce is traditionally defined as the activity of buying, selling or exchanging goods, although in the 1980s 'services' are of growing importance both for the UK economy and for jobs.

Commercial activity is not limited to 'commercial' firms, but happens throughout industry too, because industry also buys, sells and exchanges as well as producing. Industry, or its commercial agents, must buy raw materials to manufacture products. Industrial firms also need to purchase machines, components, fuel and their employees' services. At the other end of the chain are the firms or other organisations which sell the raw materials. Machines are also sold (sometimes via agencies) and trade unions may be involved in the pricing or 'sale' of their members' skills and time. The transport to carry the materials and machines must also be 'bought' and 'sold', ie freight must be arranged, and in the process any import/export, customs, tax or currency regulations must be taken into account.

Once goods are made, they in their turn are sold by the firm, either to a wholesaler, or direct to a retailer or even a customer, sometimes to an agent. Wholesalers, retailers, and ultimately the user-customer, are part of the trading process.

Amongst other SERVICE INDUSTRIES financial institutions also trade, but in 'invisibles', effectively buying and selling money itself, and financial services. The City, the banks and the insurance companies also play a part in other commercial processes. Money and commodities are sold and bought in City markets (for example, the Stock Exchange, and the Metal Market). Financial institutions, which also include (for example) building societies, buy and sell investment and short- and long-term credit, and insurance firms sell cover against commercial risks.

The services of many other skills besides the central functions of buying and selling are crucial for commercial success. Expert financial management, including accountancy, is crucial. Advertising and marketing promote products and services, and market research attempts to analyse what customers want to buy and how it should be sold. Commerce also employs other experts, such as specialist business lawyers to cope with the increasing weight of British,

EEC and international commercial law, and public relations people to 'sell' the organisation itself. Firms must have people to administer and run them and their offices, to cope with legal requirements (company secretaries), deal with personnel, and to do the clerical and secretarial work. Firms need managers to plan, control, and make decisions.

Administration and management, though, are every bit as important in non-commercial organisations – such as the Health Service, charities and local government – as they are in commerce and industry. Today, all kinds of non-profit-making organisations increasingly employ modern business methods. The Civil Service, too, is aiming for greater efficiency and value for money, concentrating on improving managerial skills.

More aggressive selling methods, using sophisticated advertising and market-ing techniques, more positive public relations, more creative financial man-agement, and rapidly increasing use of information technology are all features of commercial life in the 1980s.

Coming to terms with, managing and exploiting efficiently and effectively all the bewildering variety of systems which come under the umbrella of infor-mation technology for the office is a major problem for most firms. They now know they cannot survive, let alone make a profit, without it. The investment for many, most notably City dealers on the new electronic markets, is enor-mous. Managers are having to learn how to get full value for money – to exploit information technology as a business tool to improve market position, and to make sure that IT strategies are closely tied to their business objectives – which means they have to decide, on the basis of sound information, just what those objectives are.

But exploiting information technology, it is now clear, at least until 'artificial intelligence' and full-scale 'expert systems' (see INFORMATION TECHNOLOGY) are a reality, depends heavily on people and their expertise. This is not just the skills needed to develop the systems. Exploiting IT in the office seems to demand a growing range of skills, skills which are often new and rather different. City firms – the new-style market makers, the merchant banks, etc – are at the lead edge of office and information systems, and demonstrate what is likely to come in other sectors.

They need, for example, people who have in-depth understanding of both the technology on offer and the business of the firm buying it. This is to see that systems they buy actually do the intended job and at the optimum 'state-of-art' level – which means technologically sophisticated enough to beat competition but not so far ahead that it is experimental and may be difficult to operate.

Exploiting the new IT systems seems to be taking new breeds too. City dealers – and their customers – are amongst the first to be working completely 'interactively' (even if the old-fashioned telephone still has to be attached to the ultra-modern work station). They have to make decisions, put those decisions through the system so that all their 'customers' can see them on screen, stand by the decision even when it is clearly not the best possible, and react almost instantly to customers' bids. The cunning ploys of the trading floor are no longer viable, or possible. Clear mindedness, the sharpest possible analytical skills, quick thinking have all, suddenly, become absolutely crucial.

Their customers, the investors, need people of similar calibre to take full advantage of these new systems. A great range of people, people whose work has nothing to do with computers as such, with jobs in sales, accounts, marketing, are having to come to terms with their micros or terminals, and the different forms of working they impose.

Internally, managers are also having to learn how to organise and manage all the new information they can now gather about their own operations. Firms of all kinds have to cope with the fast-falling barriers to competition – de-regulation of markets, professions etc. All kinds of traditional practices and relationships no longer apply and while firms may have new freedoms on where and with whom to deal, those freedoms mean both more careful decision taking (again needing better information), and more careful self-regulation. De-regulation of markets, and ending fixed commissions, monopolies and state support means firms need more sophisticated 'market technology' and cost information just to tell them how they are going to cover their costs, let alone compete effectively and make a profit. Once given the opportunity to maximise cash-in-hand and 'hedge' against the vagaries of exchange rates, through new money markets, companies are almost duty-bound (to their shareholders) to do so.

Firms now have to think 'globally' in terms of markets, investments, communications, and organisation (which can mean 'joint ventures' with firms from other countries), set up and maintain organisation systems which bring better co-ordination between divisions and branches, yet allow staff greater responsibility for their own performance.

The increasing 'globalisation' of business, particularly in the financial sector (so far), again based on information technology, is also changing working practices – especially since New York and Tokyo time zones have to be linked through London. But the most imaginative guesses at the future of the office include its eventual demise as a centre where large numbers of people work. It would take only just that much more sophisticated communication systems, and the impetus of sharply rising overheads (rents, rates, electricity etc), and transport costs, for more people to work from home.

Analysing what is happening to levels of employment in the mid- to late-1980s is extremely difficult, in view of all the changes. Recession undoubtedly meant lost jobs, at all levels, and in most commercial sectors. How many job losses were due to technological change is impossible to assess, although improving productivity and automation in the office does mean fewer jobs for people with few, or no, skills. But predictions of massive job losses from technological change have not happened, or at least not obviously, with the notable exception of routine commercial 'functions' in the NEWSPAPER INDUSTRY. The belief that information technology, linked to loosening the restrictions on competition, could actually produce jobs because more business would be possible, has been borne out in the City at least. But although the percentage increase in jobs has probably been considerable, the actual numbers involved have been nothing like enough to make up for losses elsewhere, and the expansion may still prove to be only short-term, and level off quite quickly.

See also THE FUTURE OF EMPLOYMENT under THE WORLD OF WORK.

Qualifications and training A comprehensive and structured pattern of education and training for the business world has never developed. Largely this has been due, in the past at least, to the fragmentation of the commercial world, but also because in many sectors and at many levels, employers have not thought it necessary. Oversight of preparation for so-called professional 'functions' has been left to professional bodies with, as a result (eg in accountancy) a confusing number of different qualifications to choose from. Degree-course studies in the various business disciplines are not co-ordinated, or subject to other than the narrowest oversight (in terms of exemptions from individual professional bodies' examinations), from any outside body. One result is that, despite the importance of financial management as a 'function' with far wider responsibilities than accounting, the only real formal route in is via a professional qualification in accountancy.

A number of organisations – most notably the Business and Technician Education Council, Pitmans, Chambers of Commerce etc, have been attempting to put in place a coherent set of qualifications at sub-degree level. YTS is now providing training, with certificate, for the youngest and least qualified to date.

Training, equally, is patchy, with some extremely good schemes in the largest and most professional firms and organisations, but very poor provision in and for the smaller firms, and organisations which to date have survived with untrained staff. Some in-house training schemes have been lost as firms find the routine work can be done with far fewer numbers.

Whether or not this is a satisfactory situation will now be up to the National Council for Vocational Qualification to decide.

See also ACADEMIC AND VOCATIONAL QUALIFICATIONS.

ADMINISTRATION AND MANAGEMENT

Introduction	400
Company secretaries and administrators	406
Management consultancy	409
Office, or administrative, management	412
Personnel management	415
Secretarial, office and clerical work	419

INTRODUCTION

All kinds of organisations have to be managed and administered, not just commercial and industrial firms. The National Health Service, charities, theatres, police forces, trade unions and local authorities, all need expert management and administration. The official American definition of a manager, also used by our National Economic Development Office, is 'a term applied to employees who direct supervisory personnel to attain operational goals of an organisation or department as established by management'.

This implies a distinction between management and administration. Technically, *administration* is supposed to be the function responsible for seeing that any organisation runs smoothly on a day-to-day basis, and for trouble shooting. *Management* then concentrates on decision making, planning, innovating, and preparing for change. In practice, of course, nearly every organisation has its own idea of what the terms mean, and applies them differently, and 'management' and 'administration' are often used interchangeably. The Civil Service has traditionally talked about 'administrators' when it probably meant management, but has recently begun to use more generally accepted terminology. Someone who runs the corner shop is as much a manager as the company director of a multi-million-pound industrial concern; so are the head of a school, the secretary of a trade union, and a chief constable.

MANAGEMENT is not really a career in its own right, rather a long-term career aim. It has always been open to anyone to try working their way up the ladder to take increasing responsibility for the work of others, and as a result doing less of whatever-it-is – selling, auditing, teaching, policing – oneself. (It has always been a problem that promotion takes people away from the kind of work they have chosen for themselves, although there are careers such as the law, medicine, and architecture, where promotion can mean higher level work in the chosen field and not administration or management.)

Managerial status is traditionally a reward for a relatively long period of service – stressing time-serving and promotion on an age and seniority basis, often without any real assessment of managerial potential or aptitude. For many people, and in many occupations and areas of employment, this traditional pattern continues, and the pace of change has been slow. But it is happening.

Continuously changing economic conditions, immense problems in financial management, knowing when and how to invest and innovate, rapid technological and scientific development and how to cope with it, very much tougher competition in world markets, are all amongst the factors making it more difficult to be profitable or even just cost-effective. Many companies and organisations find it tough just to stay alive.

One answer for all is expert, 'professional' managers who can understand and analyse what is happening in their business, who can look ahead, plot and plan efficiently for an uncertain future. As one commentator said, 'management has become one of the most intellectually-demanding jobs ... to cope with the multi-dimensional challenges of the late-1980s s/he needs 360-degree vision, the knack of anticipating the unexpected, the ability to make sense of an extraordinary amount of (often contradictory) information, and ... the ability to respond to rapid change by "unlearning" old ways of thinking and acting'.

They have all kinds of modern managerial methods and computer-based information systems which they must be expert enough to introduce and use. Managers, of all kinds of companies, now need to be people of the highest potential. They need skills which may well be different from those needed in 'primary' careers or functions, or for administration. Future managers cannot, anymore, be left just to learn what they can on an 'ad hoc' basis as part of their routine work and progress through the organisation. They must have planned training and experience to prepare them for management. In turn, organisations want to take advantage of these expensive skills rather earlier than is traditional – there is, in any case, less routine work to do (thanks to computers) – and highly educated trainees do not want to wait too long for promotion.

The prospective manager does not, however, avoid working his or her way up through an organisation (or series of organisations). Managers are still expected both to gain plenty of experience of how the organisation works and also to train and qualify in what is usually called a 'function'. The difference between management trainees and others is that the potential manager is moved at a faster pace, is normally given more varied experience, and additional, specialist training in management techniques.

The majority of potential managers start in one of the main 'functions', although there are some schemes designed to giving new entrants a chance to sample several functions before making a choice. In a specialist organisation like a bank or a retail store, this will be the main business of the firm (sometimes called 'line' management), in these examples, branch banking or selling. In manufacturing firms and some other organisations there is generally more choice, although the main route to management is most usually via the main interest of the firm – electronics specialists in the electronic industry, chemists and chemical engineers in the chemical industry, and so on. The main choice of functions is between production, research and development, management services, finance (which often means qualifying in accountancy), marketing/sales, general administration, and less usually (but probably increasingly), purchasing and supply, and personnel.

The signs are that, in all these functions, the emphasis on becoming a manager is increasing. Where people thought of themselves as accountants (say) first, and only second as financial managers, the trend now is to think of the management function first and the work, eg financial, second. One reason for this may be that organisations are developing (project) management teams, in which people in the various functions must work increasingly closely together, each contributing a particular expertise to more collective planning and decision making.

Managers prepare forward plans for the next year, the next five to ten years. They make the decisions on how to implement these plans, see that the resources needed (money, materials, equipment and people) are made available and organised efficiently, that time is organised and used effectively. To make sure the decision-making is soundly based, they must devise, plan and organise communication and information systems which monitor and keep managers fully informed of what is happening throughout the organisation.

Once potential managers have qualified in and gained reasonable experience of a function, and demonstrated the expected management potential (which usually means going through a fairly stiff weeding-out process), promotion may come fairly fast. This takes them through a series of increasingly demanding and responsible jobs, perhaps with experience of different types of work, as well as training in managerial skills, leading first to junior management.

Junior managers, typically, are responsible for a small group of people who are all usually doing the same work, or for a single production line (for instance). For the best, this level of responsibility can come eighteen months after qualifying professionally, although it will often take longer.

Middle managers take on wider responsibility, for a group of junior managers (and their staff), perhaps in regional sales management, as a branch manager, or in charge of a group of production lines. But of course the possible differences in levels of responsibility vary widely between different sectors of employment, but a first middle management position is possible in many sectors in five years.

Senior managers are responsible for entire departments, such as marketing, finance, production, personnel, purchasing.

General managers co-ordinate planning and policy making, with their departmental managers. They will have been promoted from the departments most important to the organisation.

Of course there are only top managerial positions for very few, and the majority of people originally recruited for management training find their upper limit somewhere in middle management. It is rarely straightforward or easy to reach senior managerial positions. Some organisations, like the major manufacturers of consumer goods, the clearing banks and the larger retail and supermarket chains, expect to keep their management trainees for life, and so usually give reasonably varied, planned career experience and regular promotion. In most industrial and commercial firms, though, while such prospects may be there, it is usual to have to use the drive, initiative and self-confidence demanded of management material to gain essential experience and promotion at the right times. It may be necessary to change firms to gain sufficiently broad experience and/or promotion.

It is a very demanding, competitive life. Managers, or rather potential managers, are expected to be ready to change jobs whenever asked, and often to move around the country or go overseas.

The proportion and number of managerial staff has increased steadily. Although the figures are not strictly comparable, recent (1986) estimates suggest about 2.4 million people are classed as managers (about 70% of them under the age of 50), against a 1966 Census figure of just under 1.5 million. Until recently technical/technological change seemed to increase the number of people involved in managerial processes, and companies also tend to confer 'management status' on an increasing proportion of employees whose work previously would not previously have been regarded as managerial in nature. An increasing number of employees see themselves as being of managerial status, whatever terms their employers may use.

However, all this may be changing once again, as a result of the effects of recession, tougher and changing trading conditions and the newest technology. Firms have cut, often drastically, the numbers of workers to be managed. Senior and departmental managers can also increasingly gain access to sophisticated information directly and rapidly from computer-based systems without any need to go through middle/junior managers. Firms are therefore thinning out the managerial communication lines, particularly in non-productive areas. It could mean even fewer chances of promotion in future, with more people moving out of the traditional companies, possibly into smaller firms, or businesses of their own.

Recruitment and entry Most firms, large, medium sized and even quite small, as well as other organisations, look quite deliberately for their next generation of middle managers and the senior managers of twenty years hence from amongst the most able young people available to them. For a growing proportion of firms and other organisations (including the Civil Service) these 'fast streams' are recruited from amongst graduates. Because so many of the best of the age group go on straight from school to university, many firms ceased recruiting managerial trainees at eighteen-plus (with A levels or their equivalent) some time ago, let alone at sixteen-plus (with O-level-equivalent passes at 16-plus†). The main exceptions are clearing banks, insurance companies, retailing generally, and areas of employment with a relatively large number of middle-management and administrative posts.

Anyone determined to go as far as possible in management as they are capable is clearly, therefore, going to start out with the highest possible educational qualifications. Except in areas like those quoted above, working up from lower entry levels – and this must now include all BTEC National awards as well as A-levels and 16-plus† passes – is generally getting more difficult all the time, although a BTEC Higher National award on top of A levels is bound to be an advantage. However, if the sharply declining numbers now coming out of the education system result in shortages of managerial trainees, some organisations may be forced to recruit again post-A level.

While firms and other organisations recruit their future senior managers, and even administrators, from amongst graduates, a degree, even a very good degree, is not enough. Graduate recruiters take academic ability for granted. Often they are not even concerned about the subject studied. Obviously in some sectors firms need a proportion of managerial recruits with particular degrees – electronics for the electronics industry, and so on. They also want their management trainees to be numerate. A subject which demonstrates this and some understanding of the 'real' world, eg in marketing, maths or statistics, economics, finance, or business studies is increasingly useful, but some graduate recruiters still prefer the Oxbridge-style intellectual rigour of history, classics, PPE etc, even for marketing consumer products.

But graduate recruiters are just as, if not more, concerned about personal qualities. They expect that most graduates will have learnt certain skills as part of their degree courses – to think logically and clearly, to analyse accurately, to be able to research facts, and to be able to assess what information is important in a given situation. They want them to be able to absorb, assess the importance and see the implications of, a great deal of very detailed and often highly-technical, statistical, information, and to learn how to forecast the consequences of known and possible future events.

For their future managers they are also looking for people with organising ability, who can work with anyone at any level and get the best out of them, create and keep up working relationships, and sum up people accurately. Ability to work as part of a team is, then, essential. 'Communicating' skills are paramount – the ability to explain and discuss clearly verbally, to write concise and clear reports and so on. Self-confidence, and the signs of a sound business sense are useful.

Qualifications and training Managerial training generally starts in a particular function – sales, marketing, purchasing, production, personnel, finance, company secretaryship and so on, according to the size and scope of the firm. In specialised areas such as banking, the specialised function itself may be the major route for managerial development. This generally involves gaining a professional qualification, in, eg accountancy, marketing, through part-time study. Engineers and scientists with appropriate degrees usually have to complete a period of practical training and experience before gaining their professional qualification, but this can be done largely 'on the job'.

Specific, planned management training is distinct from business education, which trains in functional, and administrative skills (although they are frequently confused and it is often almost impossible to tell them apart). It should come partly through this functional training, partly by in-company training, partly perhaps by more formal study at business school, on courses ranging from a day to a year or more.

Unfortunately, report after report – right up to April 1987 – shows that this is not happening. The failure to educate and train managers, first identified 25 years ago, is still as great as ever. As recently as 1982 (it has probably improved slightly since), only 7% were graduates, and only 2% had a business studies degree or the equivalent. Worse, only three in ten have had any kind of management training in their entire working lives. Since some of the largest firms spend up to 11% of labour costs on management training, and the average expenditure is only 1.8%, in large numbers of British firms managerial training clearly does not exist at all. One recent report suggested that this applies to over 50% of firms. This despite years of exhortation, pleading and a little financial encouragement from all kinds of experts and authorities.

Equally serious is the problem that no one seems to be able to agree what form management training should take. Indeed, the traditional view in Britain, that management is a job for 'gifted amateurs' to whom managing 'comes naturally' without any need for training, still lives – more than a third of firms surveyed recently said they saw no need for it (and 50% said they could not afford either the time or the money).

But even where the need for training is accepted, and amongst the trainers themselves, the form it should take is currently (1987) being fiercely debated. Criticism of the full-year, full-time MBA courses at university management schools has been growing for some years, with claims that they are too 'academic', and take managers away from the firm for too long. Certainly the figures show that even firms which otherwise have a good training record do not recruit people just because they are MBAs, or send staff on courses. The exceptions are management consultants, firms in the financial sector, and some financial managers, all of whom like an MBA to 'round off' professional training. Some firms prefer to send people to schools elsewhere, notably France's INSEAD.

Some business schools, particularly those in the private sector, most notably those at Henley, and Ashridge, as well as the Open University, are trying to 'sell' newer forms of management training. They include part-time MBA courses, MBA and modular forms of management training by 'distance learning', and (a major growth area), in-house 'packages' designed to give management training within the firm. Some indication that these may be the ways to persuade smaller firms to train is shown by figures from the Open (University)

Business School. In only three years, over 20% of the 2000 firms sponsoring managers on an OBS course had under 100 employees, 4% from firms with fewer than ten.
See also ACADEMIC AND VOCATIONAL QUALIFICATIONS, and BUSINESS AND MANAGEMENT STUDIES under ACADEMIC AND VOCATIONAL STUDIES etc.

ACCOUNTANCY
Considered by the profession to be a central management function, especially where the emphasis is on improving companies' financial performances and providing financial control and planning data. However, it is still fundamentally finance, so see FINANCE below.

COMPANY SECRETARIAL AND ADMINISTRATIVE WORK
The company secretary has a formal, legal role, but is normally also a senior, more general, administrator with much wider responsibilities. People qualified as company secretaries are employed in a very wide range of other kinds of organisations, including public bodies, not just companies.

Legally, company secretaries are the representatives of registered companies and the formal link between shareholders and management. They administer the Companies Acts within a company or group of companies. Company secretaries of public limited companies now normally have to hold a professional qualification, but this may be in, for instance, accountancy or law, and not necessarily in company secretaryship.

In all organisations 'the secretary' looks after the formal machinery, sees that legal requirements are met; that there is money to spend and income and expenditure are properly accounted for; that there is an efficient and accurate flow of information; and that there are the needed support services. The secretary is the link, in a company, between the shareholders and management, in other organisations between the people who control it (eg trustees, governors or elected committees) and the members. In organisations like professional institutions they may be the most senior member of the paid staff.

Secretaries are responsible for convening meetings – of the board of a company, a local authority committee, or the governing body of a college (for example), where policy is generally decided. They make up the agenda for such meetings, and see that the committee or board have all the legal, financial, statistical and technical information they need for their discussions, write papers for them on the implications of any suggested plans, in accurate but concise and easy-to-digest form. They take and draft the minutes of these meetings, and see that board or committee decisions are carried out. They maintain the register of members and other statutory books, and make any statutory returns. In companies, they also pay dividends and debenture interest, deal with capital issues. They are often involved with policy making, play a major role in the development of an organisation, and take part in board or committee discussions. A high proportion of company secretaries eventually join the board.

Being (company) secretary is often combined with another function. Some look after the financial affairs of the company or organisation (which usually means they are also qualified accountants). They may also manage pension

funds, or marketing. Some are also the office managers and link this with administrating management services, and also deal with, for instance, personnel and/or purchasing. It depends on the organisation and its size.

The Institute of Chartered Secretaries and Administrators (ICSA) lists a range of organisations in which chartered secretaries hold senior secretarial, administrative or financial appointments right up to and including top management and board level. ICSA qualifications are fully recognised for local government administrators. Other organisations include building societies, charities, the Civil Service, co-operative societies, docks and harbour boards, the National Health Service, nationalised industries, polytechnics and technical colleges, professional societies, research associations, stock exchanges, trade associations, the UKAEA, and universities. About half of all ICSA members work in private and public companies in all areas of industry and commerce, and only 20% of ICSA members actually are company secretaries.

Of new ICSA students registering in 1985-6, nearly 28% were working in local government, over 14% were working for 'service' companies, and over 10% for manufacturers (down from 17% from 1980-1). Nearly 11.5% were full-time students. Only small groups work in other sectors – just under 4% in electricity, 3% in banking, 3% for accountancy practices, 2.7% in insurance, 2.7% in other finance, 2.7% in teaching, 2.5% for the Civil Service.

Recruitment and entry Most people start out in secretarial-administrative work as trainee administrators within a firm or other organisation. The range of possible organisations is so wide that there can be no hard and fast rules about entry, although it probably is still possible to get onto a career ladder as a school-leaver with A levels.

Broadly, potential secretary-administrators ideally need to be organisation minded and good at organising, reasonably numerate, methodical, orderly, careful and meticulous, prepared to give great attention to detail, tactful, diplomatic and very discreet. They need to be good communicators both verbally and on paper, to be able to think and work logically, be able to analyse, summarise and write clear reports.

Qualifications and training Training arrangements vary between different kinds and size of organisation, and can range from formal schemes to very ad hoc arrangements. Much of the training tends to be on the job, combined with part-time study, for the examinations of the –

The Institute of Chartered Secretaries and Administrators, which has (1986) a total membership of over 44,750 plus about 21,300 registered students, and aims to provide a broadly-based, multi-purpose qualification in administration.

The Institute's entry requirements are –

Direct entry from school to ICSA exams requires three 16-plus† passes (O-level equivalent) level and two at A level (AS levels acceptable), to include English and a science at either level. Some 23% of students registering in 1985-6 did so with O/A-levels.

A BTEC National in appropriate subjects is an alternative (but only 7% of students registered with nationals in 1985-6). All BTEC Higher Nationals in business and finance or public administration fully exempt from the part 1 examinations – over 19% of students registering in 1985-6 had HNC/D as their highest qualification.

A degree (law, economics or business studies are considered particularly appropriate) also carries exemptions (depending on subject). Over 28% of 1985-6 new students were graduates. Over 47%, then, had gone through some form of higher education.

A further 6% of new entrants were already professionally qualified (in eg banking, law, accounting), and 7.6% counted as 'mature'.

The Institute's part I examination is on organisational behaviour, English (Scots or Irish) (business) law, economics, and quantitative studies. Part 2 introduces accounting, information systems, and office administration and management, plus further law or a (local) government option. The final examinations (parts 3 and 4) have three main divisions: company secretaryship, general and financial administration, and local government and public service administration. All streams include some financial accounting, law, economic policies and problems, office administration and information systems, personnel and management principles and policy. Other courses taken depend on the stream chosen.

Exemptions from part 2 and final papers for graduates and people with some other professional qualifications are on a subject-for-subject basis. ICSA gives substantial exemption, where justified, for BTEC Higher National awards, but on a course-by-course basis. In general, exemption from up to eight subjects is possible if courses follow joint BTEC-ICSA guidelines, but passes at merit grade or above are required. Exemptions are also possible with some college diploma and accountancy foundation courses.

Students taking all four parts will generally need about five years' part-time study (the most usual route), although the examinations can be completed in three years on a full-time basis, and there are a few sandwich courses. The final alone takes about three years' part-time study, but some polytechnics and other colleges offer one-year full-time courses for the final, especially suitable for those with substantial exemptions.

Relevant experience is also required for full membership, and ICSA is considering putting greater emphasis on properly-evaluated relevant experience, together with a new post-qualification education programme, as part of a wide-ranging review of future educational 'strategy'.

Further information from the Institute of Chartered Secretaries and Administrators.

LEGAL SERVICES

Many companies and other organisations employ both barristers and solicitors, and more are doing so, setting up their own legal departments to deal with the many aspects of the law which were of particular relevance to them. See also LEGAL SERVICES under PROFESSIONAL, SCIENTIFIC AND SOCIAL SERVICES.

MANAGEMENT CONSULTANCY

Management consultants give objective, professional, expert and sophisticated advice to all kinds and sizes of organisations. Management consultants deal with change, whether technological, organisational or behavioural, and the inevitable conflicts change causes. They pinpoint the need for change, and and provide the expertise needed to plan and implement changes.

Management consultants can provide greater, or different, expertise than is available within an organisation. Firms which slimmed down sharply during recession now 'contract out' more work instead of employing their own experts, increasing demand for consultants. Consultants make outside, and therefore more objective, appraisals, and may be able to see the broader picture and identify longer-term needs. They can also provide additional support when the load on management is temporarily increased. They make reports on an existing system or method, propose changes, or design completely new systems. Mostly they work for commercial and industrial firms, but government, local government and health services are now major customers as they search for value for money and greater efficiency, and museums and charities, and even religious organisations use them.

Services are constantly developing in range and technique to meet changing needs, in particular to the demand for more specialised services and to new technologies. The recent radical changes in financial services, and especially in the City, have created a major new market for consultancies.

Management Consultancies Association (MCA) members earn their UK fees mainly in the following fields –

Information technology (34.5% of fees) – ranging from developing IT strategies for organisations, through planning systems, integrating computing and telecommunications systems, giving advice on packaged software, to market research and product strategy for the IT industry, and developing management information systems (defining information needs, doing feasibility studies, systems analysis and design, providing the computer systems and software).

Finance and administration (nearly 28%) – for instance, planning and installing budgetary control systems, or planning the reorganisation of office administration.

Personnel management and training (over 26%) – advising on personnel policy and manpower planning, job evaluation and selection, finding people to fit particular posts.

Corporate strategy and organisation development (18.5%) – long-range planning, reorganising a company's structure, rationalising services or production, and making general appraisals.

Manufacturing management and technology (nearly 18%) – developing new strategies for manufacturing with the emphasis on new technology and its implications for the company as a whole, planning and installing advanced manufacturing systems, improving organisation and plant layout etc.

Marketing sales and distribution (over 10%) – for instance, organising and training a sales force for a new product, examining sales forecasting methods, surveying the potential market for a range of new financial services. Some consultancies have their own R&D labs – developing new manufacturing systems, assessing computer systems, for instance.

Economic and environmental studies (7%) – urban and regional development planning, cost-benefit and social-analysis studies. Examples are an environmental pollution study for Nigeria and drafting anti-pollution legislation, and reviewing a water and sewerage system in India.

Nearly 16% of MCA members' fees comes from overseas projects. Europe produced the largest proportion (49%), followed by the Middle East and North Africa (17%), the rest of Africa (15%), North America (7%), and the Far East (5%). Examples of assignments include a regional transport survey of the South Pacific followed by a strategic plan and an information database for the region's shipping and ports; formulating a programme of modernisation and restructuring for the Malaysian textile industry; making a tourism master-plan for a Greek island; looking for ways of improving communications in NW Ireland; advising a German department-store group on central buying structures and optimum distribution methods.

Every project is different. Each project involves a different 'mix' of specialists, depending on the nature of the project. How long they spend on it depends on its complexity and scope – it may be a few days, it may be months.

Management consultancy employs relatively small, but rising, numbers. But the total is still estimated at only 5000, under 2000 of them working for the top 25 firms.(The 'top twelve' employ between 80 and 650 professionals each.) The rest work for small firms (of under 50 employees) or are independent specialists working on their own or on short-term contracts for larger firms. A number of management consultancy firms are part of larger groups, a rising proportion of them accountancy rather than engineering based. One consultancy, with a UK staff of 600 professional consultants, is part of a world-wide group employing 34,000 professionals of all kinds, including 3000 consultants in all.

Well-managed consultancies prospered even in the difficult 1980s, benefiting from the problems caused by the harsh economic climate. Fee income of MCA members firms doubled in the UK alone between 1983 and 1985, and rose another 20% in 1986, to £200 million.

Recruitment and entry It is unusual to go directly into management consultancy from school or university, except for graduates with special skills. It is effectively a second career with most starting in their late twenties or early thirties. Management consultants want people who have had extensive industrial and/or commercial experience, preferably in 'line' management, and are well qualified, ideally with a very good first degree (preferably in a technology, computing, economics), topped with a professional qualification in eg accounting, and even a higher degree, such as an MBA. Language skills are increasingly important. One consultancy's staff is a third accountants, a fifth each economists and engineers, a tenth computer/telecommunication experts, and the rest marketing, personnel people. Although numbers recruited are not large, turnover of staff is fairly high and even in 1986, consultancies were saying that growth was slowing because firms were not finding the high-calibre staff needed.

Management consultants' staff must be able to work as part of a team, to absorb and assess new and often complex information, to analyse and think logically, to see what is important, and to understand organisational problems. Consultants criticise, assess and advise from the outside, inevitably creating tensions by the mere fact of their arrival, so they have to be able to work easily in new situations, to put clients' staff at their ease and work with them.

Qualifications and training Training is largely on-the-job, with an initial period of some months' induction, largely spent learning diagnostic skills, report writing etc. There are no formal examinations or qualifications and staff are eligible for IMC membership after six months.

Further information from the Management Consultants' Association, which is the organisation for management consultancy firms, and the Institute of Management Consultants, which is the professional body for individual consultants.

MANAGEMENT SERVICES

These are the modern analytical scientific and technological tools – operational research, organisation and methods, and work study, which serve not only management but production, research and development, and many other functions. See under PROFESSIONAL, SCIENTIFIC AND SOCIAL SERVICES.

OFFICE, OR ADMINISTRATIVE, MANAGEMENT

The, theoretically, relatively straightforward 'function' of keeping an office running smoothly is being made more complex by the huge increase in the amounts of information coming into all firms and organisations from the outside, the information being generated inside the organisation (more frequent and extensive reporting on a company's financial position, for instance), and information which must be sent out. All this information has to be organised efficiently, and systems and equipment, more often than not now computer based, developed to deal with it. As a result while many office managers still deal with the daily routines, record the decisions taken elsewhere in the organisation, see to practicalities like sharing out available office space, the job can have more positive aspects. The office is becoming rather more a centre for developing management information systems.

Despite the computers, the photocopiers and the dictating machines, not much attention has so far been given to improving office efficiency using technological methods. In the last twenty years or so, though, office costs have risen from about a fifth to nearer half of total overheads in manufacturing, and people absorb nearly 80% of those costs. Yet until quite recently office workers have had automated equipment equipment valued at only a tenth of that which the factory worker uses.

This is now changing. Nearly 90% of firms with £1 million turnover were using electronic typewriters, nearly 80% wordprocessors, 77% microcomputers, 77% mainframe, and 77% mini computers, by 1983. In 1985, 85% of firms with over 100 staff were using computers. Only the smallest are now reluctant. Forecasts suggest UK organisations will have three million computers installed by 1990, half for clerical/secretarial use, and half for more sophisticated executive functions.

Office managers may have to solve complex problems when it comes to new office equipment, balancing available resources against needs and comparing them with both what is available, and what might become available in the future – it is all too easy to wait to see what the next 'generation' of equipment has to offer. They have to advise senior management whether or not new systems could improve efficiency and reduce costs, at what capital expenditure, possibly working with an IT manager as organisations go over to integrated computing-telecommunications systems. Over 73% of large companies review their business systems every year, and over two-thirds make a major investment every year. Particularly in sectors using 'leading-edge' IT technology, as in the City, it is now impossible to plan more than three years ahead, because the technology is changing so fast.

Office managers are both organisers and decision makers. They have to decide, with advice (from eg, their O&M staff, consultants, etc), which new electronic dictation system will both best suit the way the company works, and is compatible with existing word-processing equipment and/or a more sophisticated distributed computer network system planned for the future; whether the volume of post warrants faster, microprocessor-based new machinery; what may be needed to enable machines to 'talk' to each other, and so on. One large building society office manager with 500 branches to equip has a staff of seventeen just to keep pace with developments in photocopiers, word processors, microfilm and telecommunications equipment, etc.

Office managers have also to cope with all the staffing implications of possible automation, working with PERSONNEL. Efficient office management also tries to see that office layouts improve staff morale and efficiency (by, for example, developing practical open-plan offices which retain the true advantages of smaller office units).

While, obviously, office managers become very knowledgeable about the work of the organisation in which they are employed, and the systems used have to be adapted to their organisation's needs, whether it be oil company, publishing house, trade union, government department or bank, the basic processes and services they provide are essentially the same. They range through sales invoicing and accounting, purchases, cash control, wages, stock control, departmental and cost accounting, to statistics, typing and correspondence, filing and indexing, photocopying and duplicating, and communications. They are obviously much involved in organising office staff (see below).

In some organisations the office manager does only this. In others he or she may be both office manager and, for example accountant, company secretary or, in smaller firms, managing director.

Recruitment and entry Not normally a 'first' job. Office managers are usually either promoted from senior office, eg supervisory, staff. Alternatively qualified accountants or company secretaries may do the job.

Qualifications and training Training is normally on-the-job.
The Institute of Administrative Management (membership about 9500 including some 3500 students) promotes training, and sets examinations for a Certificate and Diploma in administrative management. The former is the part 1 examination for the latter, but entitles the holder to associate membership. The Diploma is needed for full corporate membership. Entry to the Certificate/part 1 is via BTEC National awards, or relevant GCE/GCSE subjects

EXAMINATIONS

The London Chamber of Commerce
and Industry
Examinations Board
Marlowe House
Station Road, Sidcup, Kent DA15 7BJ
Telephone: 01-302 0261
Secretarial Examinations: 01-309 0440

SINGLE SUBJECT CERTIFICATES AND GROUP DIPLOMAS

Examinations in a wide range of Commercial Subjects at Elementary, Intermediate and Higher Stages.

SECRETARIAL

PRIVATE AND EXECUTIVE SECRETARY'S DIPLOMA
PRIVATE SECRETARY'S CERTIFICATE
SECRETARIAL STUDIES CERTIFICATE

SECRETARIAL AND ADMINISTRATION

FIRST CERTIFICATE IN OFFICE TECHNOLOGY
SECOND CERTIFICATE IN OFFICE TECHNOLOGY

SECRETARIAL LANGUAGES

SECRETARIAL LANGUAGE DIPLOMA
ADVANCED SECRETARIAL LANGUAGE CERTIFICATE
SECRETARIAL LANGUAGE CERTIFICATE

FOREIGN LANGUAGES FOR INDUSTRY AND COMMERCE/SPOKEN ENGLISH FOR INDUSTRY AND COMMERCE

Oral Examinations in English and Foreign Languages for the Student and the Businessman. Prices of Booklets etc. on application.

LCCI CENTENARY SCHOLARSHIPS

Scholarships (UK students £750 pa; overseas students £1,500 pa) are available to suitable applicants to assist them in business/commercial studies leading to a degree level at Colleges of Higher Education in Central London.

MBA SCHOLARSHIPS

Scholarships up to £1,250 to suitable applicants wishing to study for an MBA at a European or UK Business School.

CHARLES R. E. BELL SCHOLARSHIPS

Annual award up to £2,500 for suitable applicants wishing to pursue higher commercial studies in the UK or abroad.

For details of Centenary or Bell Scholarships apply to the Director at the above address.

including one passed at A level. A degree, the final professional examination of an appropriate professional body, BTEC Higher National awards or an equivalent exempt from part 1 and subject-for-subject exemptions are possible.

Each part of the examination has alternative syllabuses to give a qualification in administrative management itself or in organisation and methods. Both include business communication, office systems and mechanisation, and people and organisations in part 1, with an introduction to office organisation or organisation and methods. Part 2 continues similar subjects and adds management information and control and its applications in administration or organisation and methods. Tuition is available at colleges and polytechnics throughout the country; most students study at evening school or on day-release.

See also MANAGEMENT SERVICES.

Further information from the Institute of Administrative Management.

PERSONNEL MANAGEMENT

Personnel management specialises in making the most of the people – 'human resources' is the jargon phrase – working for an organisation. Organisations of all kinds, not just industrial firms – banks, the Health Service, local authorities, department stores, airlines, all employ personnel staff.

The development – and image – of personnel work has been hampered by its origins in industrial welfare work, by the early paternalistic attitudes of so many companies, and a reputation for merely being a way of keeping workers both quiescent and productive.

However, personnel management is now fairly well established as a fully-fledged management function, although it has still not developed its full executive potential in some organisations – a relatively few (although increasing) personnel directors are on the board of directors. In many companies personnel is still only an advisory function with little executive responsibility for decision- and policy-making. Some firms are now also 'contracting-out' some areas of personnel work, to eg management consultants, and this may bring some changes to the employment patterns of personnel staff.

There can be no doubt about the importance of really efficient and sophisticated personnel management, but personnel managers often have to fight quite hard to show that their expertise is needed as part of strategic planning, and is not just advisory or peripheral.

Not many employing organisations are increasing staff numbers any more – few can have had to cope with doubling numbers in three years as has the Stock Exchange. With the notable exception of the City, most have been contracting sharply, but complexity and pace of change for almost all organisations have, if anything, made expert personnel management still more, rather than less, important. Organisations need to recruit staff with up-to-date, often very different, skills; crucial skills and abilities are in short supply, and personnel may have to find ways to re-train existing staff to cope. Management wants more sophisticated information from personnel department for future planning etc. Reorganisation, automation in the factory, computerisation of the office involve personnel in assessing, re-training, re-grading, staff, and perhaps planning and pushing through redundancies. The legal framework of industrial relations has brought a different dimension to negotiations. Personnel must develop programmes for YTS trainees. Organisations are generally expected to be more responsible towards employees – although current cost-conscious policies have brought back some tougher attitudes.

The range of activities which make up personnel management is now extremely wide and varied. At its most advanced levels it involves both problem analysis and solving, to help implement properly and efficiently overall organisational policy changes, to improve efficiency, and make manpower planning a part of organisation's general strategic forecasting. This also involves complex statistical and other research studies of, for instance, trends in training, skill requirements and availability, job specifications (grading and appraisal) and pay policies.

On a more day-to-day level, the personnel management department must match recruitment to manpower needs, both in terms of the number of general trainees recruited at various levels of intake (school-leaver, graduate, and so on), and for specific posts. To do this it must liaise closely both with its own departments, to quantify their present and future needs and to make sure the right kinds of staff are recruited, and with the sources of staff such as careers offices, schools, university/polytechnic careers advisory services, recruitment agencies.

Personnel managers may also be responsible for day-to-day recruitment: carrying out detailed job analyses, preparing job specifications, dealing with advertisements for vacancies, the resulting applications, interviews and tests, and everything that goes to make up efficient selection. In some organisations, however, departments for whom staff are intended may also be involved in some or all of these processes; in others they may take full responsibility, and close consultation is necessary between personnel and departments.

Personnel management is, of course, closely involved with the whole field of employee-employer relationships – so-called 'industrial' relations. This normally means negotiating with employees' representatives (and, in more serious disputes, with outside union officials too) on salaries and pay, redundancies, hours, working conditions – in fact any area where company policy may be changing, and problems or disagreement arise. Radical restructuring and major upheavals in working practices may have to be negotiated. Industrial relations is a rapidly changing field, and personnel managers working in it have had to develop new expertise – on legislation, for example – to add to the growing range of highly specialist techniques and procedures which make up arbitration, conciliation, and consultation. Demand for industrial relations experts has risen quite sharply.

Education and training are generally the responsibility of personnel management. Organising education and training involves both setting up and running training schemes within the firm and arranging for employees at all levels to go on courses at educational institutions both on a short- and long-term basis, on day- or block-release, or on sandwich courses. Schemes may have to be designed for craft and technician trainees, sales staff, new graduates, and for management development. Personnel must deal with re-training, both for immediate and longer-term needs, as well as managing, eg YTS training.

Finally, personnel management also carries responsibility for all kinds of employee services. These include canteen, lunch and tea/coffee break facilities, industrial health and safety, sickness and pensions schemes, transport, which may also mean allocating company cars. In some firms, personnel organises day nurseries for staff children; some personnel departments also organise sports and other recreational facilities and activities.

Personnel departments also maintain extensive records, now mostly computerised.

The range of personnel work is so extensive that it is only in the smallest organisations that the personnel manager can cope with the entire field. In most, and especially those employing more than 1000, personnel work is likely to be divided between teams of specialists whose leaders will probably be titled according to the functions they carry out, for example, industrial relations manager, staff manager, education and training officer, recruitment officer, and so on, and it is possible each area of specialisation will become increasingly independent in the future.

Recruitment and entry Personnel work needs at least some maturity and experience, and so it has never been a career to start straight from school. Generally, entry is either via some other experience, normally in industry or commerce, or via a degree or BTEC Higher award. Graduates and others are accepted as trainees by some organisations, but it is possible to take a full-time course first.

Nearly 360 university graduates, plus at least 100 from polytechnics, went into personnel work in 1984 – with a further 100 or so from university alone going on to full-time study for professional qualifications (AGCAS figures). This continued the recruitment recovery, which 'bottomed out' at only 161 university graduates in 1981. Of the university graduates taking personnel posts in 1984, 31% went into retailing, 28% into manufacturing (down from 45% in 1977), 18% into commercial firms, 10% into local government, 8% into public utilities and transport, 1% into the Civil Service (down from 3% in 1975), and 3% 'other' organisations.

Personnel work can absorb a range of different backgrounds, qualifications and personalities. Collective bargaining takes one set of abilities, qualifications and experience, recruitment another, so it is difficult to be specific about the qualities needed. Most personnel staff spend more time in desk work – writing up reports and recommendations, making up statistics and records, writing letters etc – than is generally appreciated.

However, everyone in personnel has to be able to get on with other people, to communicate easily and well with everyone and anyone in an organisation, from top management to the shop floor. Much personnel work involves the patient creation or improvement of working relationships, so it takes a realistic, unemotional approach, the ability to stay calm and make cool judgements. Personnel managers must be able to listen and persuade, know how to discover the root causes of and resolve conflict, and have plenty of tact and patience. Anyone wanting to reach director level will need plenty of drive and persuasiveness, since personnel is not always accepted as a direct route to the upper echelons of management. Organising ability, and numeracy (to deal with statistics) are also useful.

Qualifications and training Training, for most people, is largely on-the-job, although personnel management is an option in many business studies degrees and courses for BTEC Higher awards, and it is possible to study for professional examinations full-time at about a dozen colleges up and down the country. While professional – IPM – qualifications are not mandatory, nor indeed essential, surveys show that some 98% of employers encourage graduate entrants to study for membership of the Institute, and over 60% give time off to do so.

Institute of Personnel Management (1986 membership over 27,500 against 1983's 22,000), entry qualifications and examinations are now in line with those of similar bodies, partly reflecting a real need for broader training and examinations as for other management functions (including economics, for example), partly to demonstrate more formally personnel management's claim to professional status. It is also clearly necessary to provide a sound educational and professional base from which personnel staff can try for senior managerial positions.

The Institute's professional education scheme includes a three-part examination. Stage 1 – 'introduction to personnel management', covers the main academic disciplines underlying the practice of personnel management, definitions and description of the function and its development and so on, and the major factors influencing it. Stage 2 studies in depth the three major elements making up personnel management, ie employee 'resourcing', employee deployment, and employee relations, and involves a course lasting two years on a part-time basis. Stage 3 deals with professional practice and must include a work-based project, and a course in research and presentation methods.

The examination (or exemption from it) must be passed for full membership of the Institute (some 70 colleges throughout the country provide courses). The minimum age for entry to student membership, and for entry to the examinations is 20, with three O-level equivalent and two A-level passes – but well over 50% of members are graduates. Students must also either have experience in management above supervisory level or be already engaged in personnel work or work closely associated with personnel management and have clearly demonstrated the ability to pass the examination and succeed in personnel management – membership application must be supported by a senior executive of the employing organisation and/or an IPM corporate member. Passing the examinations or an equivalent gives associateship membership, but full members must be 25 and have been carrying out executive and/or advisory duties in the personnel function for at least five years.

Students can choose their own method of study, but anyone studying wholly independently or through a correspondence course (at the International Correspondence School in London, or the Metropolitan College in St Albans) must attend a residential course organised by a college of further education, and must also have their project work assessed by such a college. Over 2000 people take IPM exams each year.

Only IPM-approved postgraduate courses fully exempt from the Institute's own examination (and even then candidates must take the Institute's own personnel management policies paper). They last twelve months full-time for social science graduates, 15 months for others, or three years' day-release, and are at –

Full-time, universities: Birmingham: Aston; Cranfield; Glasgow: Strathclyde; London: City, LSE; Warwick; polytechnics – Bristol; Kingston; Leeds, Leicester; London: Middx, NLP, PCL; Manchester; Middlesbrough: Teesside; Portsmouth; Sheffield; other colleges – Aberdeen: CC, RGIT; Doncaster MIHE; Edinburgh: Napier; Glasgow CT; Kirkcaldy CT; Newport: Gwent CHE; Slough CHE. (Also a few part-time courses.)

Other graduates may gain exemptions on a subject-for-subject basis; BTEC Higher National Diploma with appropriate core and option modules exempts from stage 1 of the Institute's examinations.

Further information from the Institute of Personnel Management.

SECRETARIAL, OFFICE AND CLERICAL WORK

An estimated four million people, a sixth of the workforce, are clerical workers – the junior staff, the clerks, the receptionists, telephonists, typists and secretaries who provide the support services for administration and management in organisations of all kinds and sizes. Obviously most work for organisations like industrial and commercial firms, the Civil Service, local government and health service, but university departments and their professors, legal and medical practices, theatrical agents and architects' offices all need office and secretarial staff.

Numbers of secretarial-clerical workers increased by 2.4% between 1971 and 1981, but then fell sharply between 1981 and 1983. The job losses were mainly amongst cashiers and customer-account staff, and the number of receptionists actually rose. Almost a quarter of school-leavers, it is estimated, have traditionally gone into office work of some kind.

Secretarial and office work is changing with office automation, the micros and the terminals to a remote mainframe machine (the end of the stand-alone word-processor appears to be in sight already). All the indications are that, after a slow start, the pace of automation in UK offices is speeding up, with most organisations now using electronic typewriters or word-processing packages on micros and pcs, and many office procedures now computer based.

For clerical staff, automation is the computer, or a terminal to it, which gives visual and keyboard access to, for example, customer accounts in insurance or mail order companies; booking systems in airlines and travel agencies; financial or other information systems and data bases. It is the compact telephone switchboard, cordless and plugless. It is the sophisticated photocopier. It is the telex and facsimile transmission machines. For some it is already 'electronic mail', with computer 'talking' to computer.

For secretarial/typing staff it is increasingly word-processing, whether they use a 'dedicated', stand-alone word-processor, a terminal to a mainframe, or (and increasingly) a business or personal computer with word processing software. With word-processing 'typists' no longer see the letters printed directly onto the paper. The machine both puts the keyboarded characters on to disk, and simultaneously throws them up on to a visual display screen instead. The document – letter, report etc – is only 'printed out' when the typist is satisfied it is correct – s/he can edit, correct, revise the text on the keyboard, and print it by simply pressing another key. Word-processing systems can be linked directly to the office telephone and computer system, and material can be directly stored there, and transmitted to other word-processors or terminals.

Like all expensive machinery, word-processing systems have to be used to maximum efficiency to pay for themselves. They bring with them electronic, often centralised dictation, via the telephone or into a machine. They often involve reorganisation of traditional working patterns and a lot of changes in the way even the smallest offices are run. For example, it becomes difficult to justify one secretary to one executive, if the secretary deals mainly with letters, when efficiency can be improved by 100%. The massive typing pool may be a less efficient way of organising typing than assigning a word-processing system and operator/typist to a group of executives.

Word-processing is not only more efficient, but also more versatile. For instance, information – text – can be gathered and merged from several different sources automatically. A page of typing can be 'laid out' automatically like the page of a book, with columns, charts, graphs etc, and can be indexed. Not only is there less repetitive work, but typists can take on a more varied range of tasks.

Automation in the office is likely to reduce, or at very least hold down, the number of jobs, especially for the unskilled, and for shorthand typists. It could increase demand for technical experts, administrative staff, and could create

some office jobs, simply because the machinery makes possible new activities for some people and organisations. For instance, with the newest, laser, printers and 'desk-top publishing' software, secretaries can produce reports etc themselves at a standard which to date has only been possible using conventional typesetting.

For young people going into secretarial or office jobs, the future will mean many, and frequent, changes, and many old assumptions will go. The route up for the poorly qualified school-leaver has already become much more restricted. Secretarial work may no longer be easy to return to after marriage and children. Above all, the new entrant must gain as much training and experience on new machinery as possible and try to stay abreast of technology thereafter.

Working in the office

The tasks involved in office and secretarial work have never been clearly defined, and in fact there are no proper job descriptions, and no accurate definition of – or distinction between – 'secretary', 'private' secretary, 'executive' secretary, 'personal' secretary or assistant, shorthand typist, audio typist, clerk. What work, responsibility etc is involved varies from employer to employer. Work which is treated as clerical in some organisations becomes secretarial in others. In some organisations the work is entirely desk-, or work-station-, based. In others, there may be plenty of contact with other people, variety of tasks, opportunities to move around. The degree and level of personal responsibility, scope for initiative, decision making etc, varies considerably, although these are usually fairly limited.

Size can dictate the nature of the job. In a small organisation a single secretary may be able to cope with all the different tasks done separately by many office or clerical workers in a larger one. In a small firm it is possible to gain all-round experience, while there is a greater chance of specialising in the larger one, and it may be necessary to move around to gain different kinds of experience.

While routine is still the hallmark of much office work, machinery and modern office equipment have removed the worst drudgery. The automatic vending machine relieves the office girl or boy of tea- and coffee-making; modern machinery speeds the task of photocopying and calculating; sophisticated mechanised, and increasingly computer-based 'filing' systems are less tiring to use and more efficient than heavy metal filing drawers. The post room has been mechanised, and is now acquiring automatic machinery. Even without word-processors, electronic typewriters, coupled with audio dictation, make life far easier for the secretary.

CLERICAL WORK is mostly assumed (there are few hard-and-fast definitions) to involve a considerable amount of record- and account-keeping (which shades off into financial work, book-keeping and accountancy: see FINANCE, below), filing, photocopying and dealing with letters and telephone calls.

Clerical workers can still begin as traditional office juniors, although there are far fewer of them now (and some will start as YTS trainees), learning how work is organised through a series of minor, the careers literature always stresses, but nevertheless crucial jobs which need little or no experience. They may collect, sort and distribute incoming mail, and collect and dispatch outgoing letters, learning about an organisation (what departments there are, what the organisation does, and who works where) at the same time. They may photocopy, do simple typing and filing, and generally help more senior staff, doing whatever jobs come up. In very large organisations, where something like the mail occupies an entire department and junior staff spend all their time on that one 'function', planned moves can help them to gain more rounded experience.

With experience, and training (in general office studies, in book-keeping, and/or in keyboarding/typing, for example: see below), young office staff are usually given a job of their own, dealing with one task or possible a series or group of related tasks. The work varies from organisation to organisation and from department to department. For example –

in sales departments each clerk deals with a group of accounts and sales records;

in personnel, clerks look after staff records, list applicants for interviews, sort out job applications, deal with letters;

'figure work', for instance calculating the cost of making parts in the factory from the production sheets from each machine and the operator's time records;

transport clerks in public services work out timetables, rates and charges, and chart and record the journeys; transport and haulage clerks keep vehicle and driver records, seeing that vehicles are tested, sending out new licences as required, organising insurance, making out accident reports, etc:

shipping and export clerks become highly expert in customs, currency and other export regulations and may need languages.

Examples like this can be quoted from a wide range of occupations and employers, such as banking, insurance, educational institutions (including schools), trade unions, local government and the Civil Service, TV and film companies or building contractors.

Some clerks become telephonists and/or receptionists, or counter staff, for example, in travel agencies, hospitals, local council offices, firms of all kinds. Here they deal all the time with the public.

Some clerks specialise in, for example, filing – to store all kinds of paper records such as letters and invoices, personnel data, technical reports, drawings and blueprints, technical information, photographs.

In industry, clerks can become progress-chasers, combining office work with visits to the factory floor. Progress-chasing is a kind of estimating, working out delivery dates for goods being made and finding out what needs to be done to meet them (for example, when capacity is available on the factory floor to produce the goods, what components and raw materials are needed and what needs to be ordered) and also involves some work on pricing a job. Work of this kind takes interest in, and some knowledge of, technical detail, but this can be learnt from experience and observation. Progress chasing, however, is one of the first jobs to go when a factory is fully automated.

Clerical work in more and more areas is being 'computerised', especially invoicing, making up pay, keeping records and accounts, calculating costs –

'figure work' of all kinds – address lists, even filing. Then the clerk becomes a business-machine, computer, or VDU operator – using micro- or mini-computer or mainframe terminals (keyboard or keyboard with visual display unit) to 'call up' (on VDU) 'input' and extract data as needed from the computer file, keeping accounts and records up to date, revising address lists, abstracting information like production costs, or a list of overdue accounts. The clerk answering the phone may also use a VDU screen, to find out what to tell customers about the latest position on their order, the exact amount owing, or what theatre seats are available, for instance.

Most modern office machines – photocopiers, calculators etc – are quick and easy for anyone to use, and rarely need clerks to be specially trained, or (except where the load is especially heavy), to spend all their time operating them. Teleprinters and telex machines generally require skilled operators. Both provide rapid, visual, typed communication links, the former as a series of fixed lines between a single set of subscribers (as with news agency services to various newspapers and others), the latter as a telephone-type service between individual subscribers. Both use typewriter-style keyboards on which the message is keyed, and it then appears on a length of continuous paper on the receiving machine. But facsimile 'fax' machines, which work like long-distance photocopiers, are increasingly efficient and easy to use, and do not need specially-trained operators. Some organisations have their own printing/reprographic departments where clerks may also be trained in eg micro-filming, which uses special cameras to record documents on film at a fraction of their original size.

Clerks have often learnt to type, and even been called clerk-typists. Today, everyone in the office has to be able to use a keyboard, to access the now-common computer-based systems.

SECRETARIAL WORK AND TYPING But while there is no clear distinction between a clerk and a typist, or between a typist and a secretary, at very least copy, shorthand and audio typists, and secretaries, should be trained to do particularly accurate work at extremely high speeds. Anyone who is a competent typist or secretary should be able to type at 50 words a minute (more on word processor), take shorthand at 90-100 words per minute, and/or transcribe directly from a dictating machine.

In some larger organisations, all the typists work together in one or more special sections, forming central and/or sectional typing services, typing for whoever has work to be done, whether it is a tape from a dictation machine or taking dictation, or documents to be retyped. The work is mostly allocated by a supervisor.

In other organisations, they may work in office alongside other staff, or in a room of their own. Copy typing lost the simplest of its tasks, straight document copying, to photocopiers some time ago. Copy typists – or more usually word processor operators – now mainly keyboard hand-written manuscripts, but also more complex documents such as invoices or other forms, and sheets of statistical data which may involve, for instance, taking figures from rough drafts.

Shorthand typists take dictation in one of the accepted shorthand languages, such as Pitman's, and transcribe it; much of the work is inevitably letters, reports and memos. However, this does not always take up all their time, and so shorthand typists may also do other work, some of which may be secretarial (see below). Typing/secretarial staff often do their own filing.

Audio typing is expected to supersede shorthand typing before very long. The audio method has grown steadily more popular with employers and typists, and is necessary to make word-processing really efficient. Here, the typist transcribes directly from the dictating machine on which the material to be typed has been recorded, eliminating the shorthand stage. The system not only saves typists' time in taking down the letters, but also makes it possible to arrange their work more efficiently, since anyone can type from a given tape, where shorthand typists can generally transcribe only their own shorthand. Sales and other staff away from the office can also dictate into these machines over the phone or other communication links. Audio typists generally need better English (including spelling) and grammar than copy and shorthand typists, since they work from a verbal, not written, draft.

Shorthand typists and other secretarial staff can go on to become personal, or private secretaries, but can also become office supervisor, and possibly office manager.

PERSONAL, OR PRIVATE, SECRETARIES, as the office is at present organised, must also be able to take dictation and type extremely well, but they generally have other work to do. In fact, it is difficult to define exactly the role of the secretary, since most employers and individual secretaries have their own, usually fairly firm, views on what it should be. Rather too often a secretary is treated as a personal typist.

Secretaries may work all the time for one, two, three or (but unusually) even more people, and rarely in 'pools'. They generally do rather more than dictation and typing – indeed all but confidential material may be done by someone more junior. A properly employed secretary is, or should be, an assistant, who organises the employer's personal office and tries to see that it runs as smoothly as possible, takes at least some responsibility for day-to-day affairs, relieving the employer of the more mundane and time-consuming minutiae of working life.

Mostly secretaries deal with correspondence, draft the simpler replies, see that appointments are made (and do not clash) and travel arrangements organised, keep the diary up to date, make sure that filing is dealt with. A secretary acts as a buffer, takes phone calls and messages, and generally tries to solve as many problems as possible without bothering the 'boss'. Good employers let experienced secretaries take straightforward decisions on their behalf (although too many do not delegate at all, however well qualified, mature and experienced the secretary may be).

SPECIALIST SECRETARIES Some secretaries specialise in the type of work they do. Demand for secretary linguists, fluent in at least one other language, appears to be increasing. Their work generally includes reading and translating letters and orders both into and from their other language(s); coping with telephone calls in the language(s) they know; interpreting when people from overseas visit and sometimes going with staff to other countries to interpret for them there; reading, translating, and summarising reports, memos, newspaper or other articles. Secretary-linguists work mostly for firms involved in importing and/or exporting either in the UK or overseas, multi-nationals, or inter- and supranational organisations.

Legal, farm, and medical secretaries specialise in working within one particular field, where secretaries have to understand and be able to use the specialised terminology and understand something of the nature of their employer's work – the legal framework, agricultural and EEC regulations, or Health Service organisation, for example. Legal secretaries work for legal practices, the courts, and in legal departments; in addition to the usual secretarial work they often prepare the more straightforward legal documents. Farm secretaries often work for agencies, and travel between farms, spending a day a week dealing with all the paperwork for the farmer. Medical secretaries work for general practices, private consultants, and in hospitals.

'PERSONAL ASSISTANTS', theoretically may have a fair amount of responsibility, to use their own initiative, delegating routine secretarial work such as typing etc to others. They may draft letters, reports, memos etc, collect and collate information, take minutes, greet and help entertain business contacts, organise meetings and conferences, have discussions with other PAs or customers, clients etc, and possibly supervise other staff. Genuine PA posts are normally only with very senior executives. Elsewhere there is no guarantee that the title means any more than secretary, or even shorthand typist.

Secretarial work as a route to other careers Many school-leavers and graduates, mainly women, believe that they can use secretarial training and work as a 'stepping stone' into more interesting work, especially in some of the more competitive areas. There are no hard and fast rules about this, except that it is usually much, much tougher than most anticipate, even where it is possible, and the competition is likely to be just as great. Initiative, drive, persistence, being ready and able to step in in an emergency, are all essential, but it still may not be easy to overcome the traditional attitudes that say anyone who can type is incapable of anything better.

In many organisations, especially industry and professional practices, there simply are no recognised routes through to management or professional work. This can be because set qualifications are needed. Legal secretaries, for example, however well qualified and experienced, cannot become lawyers without going through the full formal academic and vocational training required. Secretary-linguists in export/import, on the other hand, can and do frequently move on into sales and marketing.

Some industrial/commercial 'functions' are open to secretarial staff who are capable of the work, although it may be difficult to get through to more senior positions without formal qualifications. Personnel, sales/marketing, public relations are known to be possibilities. Just lately, though, the emerging shortages of skilled people for some junior or middle managerial positions have given experienced, 'computer literate' secretaries the chance they need to break through in other functional areas.

Publishing has generally adopted a policy of recruiting graduates first into secretarial work, to test motivation, aptitude and ability, although it is still easier to use this as a spring-board into the less-glamorous production, promotional/PR, and contract-administration sides, largely because the number of editorial openings is so small.

In broadcasting and films, the secretarial route is an accepted one, although the competition for production/creative jobs is just as intense as it is by the more formal routes in. Experienced secretaries who show initiative, practical and creative skills, compete for the formal training as production assistant some companies give, and in others work hard for a foot on the production ladder. Getting secretarial work in a non-production department – legal, personnel, engineering, publicity etc – may be necessary, to be on the spot when secretarial posts in drama, current affairs, news etc fall vacant.

Journalism, generally, is not easy to break into this way, although it may be possible on the magazine side.

Recruitment and entry Organisations of all kinds recruit clerical and secretarial staff direct from the education system, although most increasingly want trained, experienced and mature people, of whom there is a significant shortage. The trend is also to recruit more part-timers.

There simply are fewer and fewer jobs for the unqualified, although some organisations do still take on young people as clerical trainees, increasingly via, or following, YTS training schemes. Well over a quarter of all leavers, getting on for half of the girls, who found jobs after one-year YTS schemes went into administrative/clerical work.

Modern, more sophisticated, office equipment and competitive conditions probably do require better-educated workers. Just to learn how to use new machinery takes reasonable intelligence – although once learnt it can be rather boring to operate. Some organisations do take on people offering the best-available qualifications, even degrees, whether or not needed to cope with the job,

While formal educational qualifications may not be stipulated, in practice it makes sense to have the best possible general educational qualifications, and preferably as many appropriate skills as possible to stand the chance of a good career start.

For clerical-level work, the minimum should be at least three or four O-level-equivalent passes at 16-plus†, or CPVE with appropriate skills, either to include English, maths, and basic typing/keyboarding. A good YTS training and/or a BTEC First Certificate/Diploma may be useful.

For secretarial training, at least one or two A levels (in, for instance, geography, English, economics), or equivalent in AS levels, with a numerate background (eg maths at 16-plus†). The alternative is a BTEC National in business studies (entry as for all BTEC Nationals††). There is no real advantage to studying for an HND or degree just to become a secretary.

Office and secretarial staff are personal assistants to the people for whom they work, and it is a convention in some areas of employment that they should, therefore, conform to particular standards of appearance and behaviour. They are expected to be accurate, tidy-minded and meticulous, and a neat appearance is frequently thought, rightly or wrongly, to reflect this. Since much of the work still has to be learnt from experience, employers also prefer people who can demonstrate a willingness and ability to learn, so any additional qualifications are useful. A temperament that accepts a supporting position is helpful.

A secretary is expected to be able and prepared to follow instructions and yet be capable of showing initiative; to be a good organiser, and stay coolheaded and resourceful, particularly in a crisis; be loyal, tactful and discreet, able to protect an employer from trivia, and capable of adapting to the employer's (reasonable) needs. Secretaries are expected to be unfailingly polite and good communicators. Additional qualities, particularly intelligence, confidence and business sense, will be needed by anyone aiming for promotion.

Qualifications and training The advice is to gain as many business, secretarial skills as possible before trying for a job, which suggests a full-time course or training scheme. Very few organisations now give full-scale initial basic training, but 46% of leavers going into administrative/clerical work after one-year YTS schemes were given (further) training. It does not really matter how or where the essential skills are gained, but they now need to be as broadly-based, and as up to date, as possible. They should include understanding how the office works, how to process information, and organisational skills; word-processing as well as typing, audio-typing as well as shorthand. Additional skills, such as one or more languages, are always useful.

Around 3000 educational establishments offer secretarial training of some kind, including schools, and technical, commercial and further education colleges. Private colleges account for less than 5% of the total. In general, there is little to choose between a good further education college and a good private school, except cost, although the best intensive courses at private schools offer a time advantage. It is essential to check that students are taught on modern office equipment, and that the training is in current office practices.

The type and length of course will depend on the qualifications and intentions of the students, but it is probably better now to spend a year gaining a full spread of business/secretarial skills than simply to learn shorthand-typing in the shortest possible time. Most further education full-time courses last one or two years, depending on entry qualifications, and are generally 'integrated' courses covering the full range of office and secretarial skills backed by English, mathematics and other more general, if useful, subjects such as economics, finance, basic law, languages. Some include the 'basics' of a function – advertising, marketing, personnel management.

FE colleges also put on 'specialist' courses, for secretary-linguists (RSA/LCC and Institute of Linguists exams), legal secretaries (Association of Legal Secretaries exams), medical secretaries (Association of Medical Secretaries, Practice Administrators and Receptionists exams), and farm secretaries (BTEC agricultural- or business-based award, or college award). Most courses are post-O level or equivalent.

The variety of choice even within one college is often considerable, catering for all levels of qualifications and abilities from sixteen-plus school-leavers (normally now with at least some O level equivalent qualifications) through to 'crash' courses for graduates aiming to become personal assistants. The courses are rarely geared to one single, end-of-year examination (although a college diploma is usually awarded).

Students are generally entered for speed tests and particular Royal Society of Arts, London Chamber of Commerce or Pitman Institute examinations as and when they are ready, and as many of these are available at two or more stages, it is often up to the student how many are taken. All provide tests in typing, shorthand, shorthand-typing, audio typewriting, word processing, clerical duties, office practice and secretarial duties. The London Chamber of Commerce and the Royal Society of Arts award diplomas and certificates in more advanced private secretarial work.

Personal secretaries have to reach typing speeds of about 50 words a minute, and shorthand at up to 200 words a minute (although 100 words is acceptable). Audio typists are generally expected to type a 350-word tape in half an hour. Many colleges provide 16-plus† and A-level courses as part of a secretarial training if students need them. Languages are increasingly useful, particularly those used commercially in the EEC, and students should improve on their school-leaving skills if possible.

BTEC qualifications, which at the lowest levels cover office skills, and at all levels include option modules in eg typing, secretarial skills, business machine work, etc. are a useful alternative, and probably a more useful basis for promotion than straightforward secretarial training. See FURTHER EDUCATION AND VOCATIONAL TRAINING and BUSINESS STUDIES under ACADEMIC AND VOCATIONAL STUDIES.

Further information Examination syllabuses etc from the Business and Technician Education Council, the Royal Society of Arts, the London Chamber of Commerce, the Pitman Examination Institute, and the Associations mentioned above.

FINANCE

Background   428
Accountancy and financial management   432
Banking   448
Building societies   461
Insurance   463
Stock and other money/commodity markets and investment work   478

BACKGROUND

Efficient financial management is a major pre-occupation for everyone in the 1980s, from government which constantly tries to achieve an acceptable balance between what it must take in taxation and public expenditure, through to the rising numbers of families buying their own homes and therefore involved in the financial complexities of credit cards, mortgages, insurance, and for a growing number, share dealing too. Businesses, and indeed organisations of all kinds, have to manage their finances much more efficiently in today's economic conditions just to survive, let alone stay, or become more profitable (for commercial and industrial firms), or cost-effective (for organisations like local authorities, or charities). People and organisations alike are learning to use all the new and re-vamped financial services that are now being so aggressively sold to them.

All kinds of financial services, including banking, insurance, pension funds, the stock markets, commodity trading, accounting and financial management generally, have been expanding for many years, but the growth is now explosive. All companies must have their accounts kept and audited. Banking facilities, credit, insurance of risks, are essential to both organisations and individuals. Britain's financial related services earned nearly £7600 million overseas in 1985, more than double the 1981 figure. One commentator typified the role of finance in contemporary Britain by saying that, were Napoleon alive today, he would not have called us a nation of shopkeepers, but a nation of accountants. Financial institutions – pension funds, insurance companies, investment and unit trusts – are a major force in the securities, owning a high proportion of all company shares, and having considerable influence on all areas of the country's economic life.

Most forecasters agree that financial services will go on expanding for the foreseeable future, but that there will also be increasing competition and pressure on profitability. What have been, until recently, very separate, different and clearly defined financial institutions – banks, building societies, insurance companies – offering quite different financial services, have moved into each other's markets. Banks have been competing with building societies for mortgage business and for deposit accounts. Banks are competing with accountants to provide computer-based financial information services – and the banks have the advantage of being able to give companies direct, on-line access to their very latest financial position. But the banks themselves face greater competition too, from the building societies, from other, particularly foreign, banks, from retailing firms competing on credit facilities. The result may be that eventually consumers could find that they are being offered all types of financial services – banking, credit facilities, savings schemes, insurance, mortgages, shares and so on – by a single high-street finance office. For the consumer this is also likely to mean more 'self-service' using automatic electronic equipment like the already-familiar automatic cash dispensers, and home computers to check accounts, buy shares, etc.

The City has gone through a cataclysmic 'big bang', a phrase coined to describe the way the universe began, but describing only too graphically what it has been like for the participants, and only the start of a very different era for a traditionalist sector.

All financial institutions have been shedding traditional attitudes and have, especially, become aggressively marketing oriented. Their expenditure on advertising, for example, has been 'spectacular' for more than ten years now.

Financial organisations, and finance departments within companies and other organisations, were amongst the first to install large sophisticated 'mainframe' computers to record transactions and accounts – and without computers financial institutions would not have been able to expand so greatly. Current and future developments in finance also depend on even more sophisticated 'information-technology'. But these systems are extremely costly, and with greater competition and tighter profit margins, all organisations are rationalising hard and extracting the greatest possible savings – fewer branch offices and fewer staff – from them.

But financial institutions are still, and likely to remain, labour intensive, at least while services go on expanding and stay profitable. Over 2.23 million people (including almost 290,000 part-time) now (end 1986) work in banking, insurance, and financial and business services – and this excludes the very many people who work in, for instance, the finance departments of local government, industrial and commercial firms, and other organisations. Numbers employed have been rising steadily for over 25 years, with one or two relatively minor hiccups, and recruitment slowed somewhat during the recession. While financial institutions want to keep numbers down as far as possible, they say that expanding services should counterbalance the effects of new technology. Independent observers suggest much depends on the extent to which financial institutions adopt the more advanced technological options, and the speed with which they do so. This, in turn, depends on the competitive pressures, how far financial institutions consider they must reduce their level of staffing to improve profit margins, how far other sectors (eg retail stores) are prepared to co-operate in, for instance, direct debiting, and on how easily the public accepts more 'new technology'.

Working in finance
Finance is a very wide field of employment. It includes the broad areas of banking (which breaks down into different kinds of services, such as retail and merchant banking), the insurance sector, trade financing, building societies, the Stock Exchange, and other finance houses. It ranges from national policy-making, as in the Treasury (see CENTRAL GOVERNMENT), to the financial management of industrial and commercial companies, and other organisations including local government, educational institutions, trade unions.

Career choice parallels this. It is possible to be a financial expert in a financial organisation – an accountant in an accountancy practice or a banker in a bank for example. Alternatively, it is possible to be a financial expert in other kinds of organisation – a finance officer in local government or a management accountant, or treasurer, in a hotel company or an airline, a retail store or a TV company. Thirdly, it is possible to choose to work for a financial institution, but not to specialise in finance – most employ lawyers, computer staff, personnel managers, public relations experts, and so on. Large financial institutions also use a great deal of research, and therefore employ specialists such as economists and statisticians. Independent organisations also provide financial information, often now 'on-line' to terminals on customers' desks.

The financial world has a relatively large number of managers compared to other areas of employment – well over 12% of the total number of employees. In fact many institutions treat all, or most, employees interested in long-term careers as potential managers.

In the past, financial institutions have employed very large numbers of lower-grade clerical staff, many of them obviously directly involved in recording and calculating financial transactions (see SECRETARIAL, OFFICE AND CLERICAL WORK). In future, this may change. Although some experts disagree, computer-based systems could reduce the number of routine jobs (the counter argument says that even computers cannot put bank statements into envelopes). Most, though, see increasing demand for more skilled people.

The range of different kinds of financial institutions gives a choice between the very small and the very large, although generally the balance is moving towards larger organisations, largely because economies of scale still apply, and size is essential to compete in a wide range of financial services.

However, even the largest (like the retail banks) are mostly broken down into smaller, local units. The scope for the individualist small business to develop is not as great as in some other areas of employment, although some independent financial consultants and analysts make a reasonable income.

Larger financial institutions, particularly, tend to be fairly rigidly hierarchical organisations. Progress and promotion within them tend to be fairly formalised and there is less movement between institutions than in most other sectors of employment, so 'first choice' can be very important.

The traditional City (of London) is still the world's largest financial centre, and still dominates financial affairs in Britain. But in October 1986, when the Stock Exchange de-regulated and went all-electronic, many traditions vanished almost overnight. Personal contact was always considered essential, but the new computer-based dealing systems emptied the Stock-Exchange floor in weeks, with the markets now effectively on screen. And so while an estimated quarter of a million people still work in City offices, most having something to do with money or trade, physical closeness is no longer essential. Office space, and offices capable of taking the most modern IT systems, are. The 'City', then, is rapidly becoming a concept rather than a physical centre, with firms moving wherever buildings become available.

Some larger financial institutions, and some company 'head offices' have also moved out of London altogether. It is now usual to site bulk processing of accounts, etc, out of London, while keeping a small 'top' financial management team presence in the capital.

Recruitment and entry The traditional method of entry, straight from school, is still most common in the financial world, with exceptions like accountancy, where the balance has swung quite sharply to graduate entry. Banks, insurance companies and other larger institutions still take quite large numbers from those coming out with, preferably, two A levels, although the 16-plus intake (with four or more O-level-equivalent passes) is still quite large. Graduate intake, while still comparatively small, is rising. The larger institutions, at least, are taking fairly significant numbers of sixteen-year-olds on YTS schemes.

Instinct suggests that higher entry qualifications should mean better opportunities for promotion to senior management, but most large institutions deny this, and insist that entrants with A levels, at very least, stand just as good a chance if they show aptitude. A good general level of education, with reasonable numeracy and use of English, though, is essential.

Other aptitudes are those which generally only develop after experience, for instance problem solving in the context of complex financial situations. A logical and and analytical mind, capable of understanding legal and economic theory and practice, as well as the intelligence to learn enough of the technicalities of any business, are needed. Much financial work, especially at managerial level, is effectively decision-making, often dealing with large amounts of money, and in screen-based transactions, at speed. Although decisions are based on well-established criteria, an element of risk is always there, and the ability to judge risks and take decisions at the right moment is often a set of skills some people have and other do not. Attention to detail and painstaking care are important, but financial institutions are all now looking for people who will be capable of working in a highly competitive, heavily marketing-oriented environment.

Financial work often involves dealing with many different kinds of people, in negotiating, in communicating financial decisions, and in explaining complex financial matters, and this obviously requires the ability to develop good working relations, tact, the ability to explain clearly etc.

Qualifications and training Formal education for financial careers has developed only slowly. It is still common, indeed usual, to study for professional qualifications on a part-time basis, although there are exceptions. Most financial organisations have their own development and training schemes for all staff, usually supplemented by internal or 'association' courses, and these usually go up to management level. FE colleges put on part-time (usually evening) courses.

An accountancy qualification is claimed to be one of the best passports to careers in almost all areas of finance, and in some it is near essential. The emphasis on professional, and relatively narrow, qualifications in the separate financial specialisations – banking, insurance, actuarial work, etc is still strong – and the broadly-based, flexible BTEC National and Higher awards in business studies with a broad finance bias have not made any great inroads here. Given the predictions that institutions will be broadening the bases of their operations even further in future there is, though, an argument for acquiring such qualifications – a degree or BTEC award in finance – even so.

ACCOUNTANCY AND FINANCIAL MANAGEMENT

The work done by accountants has changed very considerably over the past thirty or so years. To begin with, they were only really responsible for seeing that the financial accounts of individuals or firms in business, or public bodies like local authorities, were recorded accurately and properly, under legislation passed to prevent fraud etc.

Accounts still have to be formally audited by law, but in fact under 20,000 chartered accountants hold practising certificates and can therefore audit accounts, and this is less than 25% of the membership of the English Institute of Chartered Accountants alone.

Effectively, the profession has been virtually transformed, taking on far wider, more positive and greater responsibility in the general field of financial management and advice. Although not every financial manager is, or has to be, a qualified accountant, a great many are. The increasing complexity of the business world, all the rapid changes which now affect the financial state of any organisation, the economic climate, inflation, and more intensive competition mean that firms and other organisations have to monitor their performance much more closely in financial terms, must plan their future operations more systematically, and need much more sophisticated advice on how to handle their finances – when and how to invest, where best to go for credit, and how to present the best case, and so on.

Accountants have taken on this role and developed it successfully, although they face increasing competition, from, for instance, financial banks, lawyers, management consultants.

Financial management, including management accounting, involves planning, budgeting, analysing and interpreting to control an organisation's financial affairs efficiently. Accountants design, develop, set up and manage modern and sophisticated financial and management accounting procedures and systems for their firms, or clients. They have to be able to report accurately on what has happened to a company financially, not just once a year – more frequent monitoring may be needed so profitability can be regularly analysed and measured, forecasts and plans made. This is done both for the company as a whole and for sectors of it and even individual products. Marketing managers, for instance, look for regular reports on products to check that objectives are being achieved, or if not why not. Obviously, such systems have to be computer based, and from the very start sophisticated financial management developed hand-in-hand with the technology, which accountants and accounting technicians must know how to use. Increasing use of mini- and microcomputers is having a further effect on the whole working environment of all accountants.

Accountancy, as a profession, has expanded enormously in the last thirty years, with its widening role – numbers have risen from 25,000 to well over 130,000. Despite constant predictions that demand for accountants must decline – and jobs were lost during the worst years of the recession although not so many as in some other professions – recruitment continues at a high level. The demand for high-level financial expertise is still considerable, especially in management accounting (much less in historical reporting), and employers want better-calibre people with good experience of the business world, even in 'line' management.

Jobs are moving, probably in line with the general movement of work, into areas not traditionally employing professional accountants, eg retailing and distribution, and even the Civil Service, although cutting overall numbers, is recruiting more accountants too.

Promotion prospects are getting tougher, though, at least in private practice, where there are unlikely to be enough senior positions and 'top' partnerships to satisfy the numbers of able people competing for them, since up to three-quarters of all professional accountants are now under 45. But in industry and commerce, the professionally-trained and -qualified accountant continues to dominate the financial functions, right up to director level. Accountants have had a fairly free run into general and top management until now, but other professionals, engineers – for example – are being encouraged to develop their management skills and play a greater part in running companies, and so accountants may have to compete harder for top jobs in the future.

Career planning is becoming critical. Young accountants' career paths can now be set within two or three years of qualifying (in minimum time for the best start). Employers increasingly want finance staff, including accountants, with expertise and experience tailored to their interests, or to a particular function, and so specialisation is growing.

Working in professional accountancy and financial management

Accountancy traditionally divides into three different types of work – public practice, industry and commerce, and public service. All organisations of any size employ accountants, and most have to use accountancy practices to advise them and/or audit their accounts. The intricacies of company law and taxation alone means that anyone in business must have an accountant, and all companies and public bodies must have their accounts independently audited. So the qualified accountant can work for organisations in broadcasting and television, the press, football clubs, retail stores, construction, the oil industry, in fact any and all areas of business and non-commercial organisations too.

Many accountants also move away and/or up from strictly accounting work, frequently soon after, sometimes even before, they qualify. A professional accountancy qualification is a passport into financial work which is not strictly accounting (eg treasury function), into more general financial and senior management, into consultancy (over 10% of members of the Institute of Chartered Accountants work as consultants or in consultancies, 5% of CIMA members), into Stock Exchange work (which has 5% of ICAEW members), into insurance and pension-broking, investment policy formation, operational research, systems analysis, tutoring etc.

Accountancy and financial management are mainly office- and desk-based work, but as much time is often spent talking to other people – listening, questioning, advising, discussing, reporting – as with a calculator or computer. But many accountants and financial managers spend quite a high proportion of their time away from their own offices and desks. In public practice, clients' offices may be far from base, and audit teams may have to work in whatever corner can be found for them. Accountants and financial managers in industry, commerce and public authorities spend a significant amount of time moving around their organisations. In larger organisations they are generally expected to change jobs and move around regularly. Hours can be long.

PUBLIC/PRIVATE PRACTICE ACCOUNTING employs most professional accountants, where most qualify via ICAEW (ICAS in Scotland) and the rest as ACCA (see Qualifications and training below).

Accountancy firms vary in size from the very small, with only one qualified principal, one or two trainees and a minimal staff of assistants ('technicians') and secretaries, to the very large, which may have more than a dozen offices in different centres, at home and overseas, have over 1000 trainees, a large number of young qualified staff, and managers to supervise the audit teams and head specialist departments, as well as the partners with financial shares in the firm. The largest firms have people working full-time on planning, marketing and technical development.

The profession is increasingly dominated by about a dozen multi-million pound 'firms', or rather partnerships (out of a total of about 13,500). Some 23 firms (1986) have between 50 and 270 partners and professional staff of between 500 and 3600, including eight with more than 200 partners and qualified staff of over 2400 each. All the 'top' practices have expanded considerably in the last few years. They are increasingly being run as businesses, going for growth, rather than as professional practices.

Current economic conditions also mean that accountancy practices must justify their services and costs, 'sell' themselves to customers, and keep costs down.

While audit is a secure business, since every firm must have auditors, there is little or no scope for bringing in more clients, except by luring them away from other practices. Widening services is the only way to increase business, and many practices, but particularly the larger firms, have greatly extended both their audit-related and wider financial services, only stopping short of actual market making and capital funding. Most larger firms expect their auditors to check and comment on their financial and internal control systems as well as on their balance sheet, and many go beyond this, to more general advice on financial problems. Even smaller practices are, in today's tough trading conditions, having to give their small business customers sophisticated advice on how to cope.

The largest accountancy practices have 'diversified' further, forming their own management consultancies – at least two major practices now earn less than 50% of income from audit – and a number operate internationally.

Preparing and auditing accounts, including accounts for tax authorities, is obviously, though, still the main work of most accountancy practices. This means a lot of routine checking of balance sheets and 'books' (increasingly kept as computer-based records even by small firms and one-person businesses), examining and verifying financial statements, and so on. Standard routines have cut the time this takes, and computer-based audit routines are now used more extensively. Nearly all practices now have their own computer systems. This leaves audit accountants more time to look at firms' accounting procedures, systems and controls, and suggest improvements, new reporting routines, etc.

In public practice, accountants audit for and advise a wide variety of organisations and individuals in many different lines of business. Smaller practices generally deal with smaller local organisations, and traders (who may, nevertheless, include clients of considerable variety, from local writers to farms, garages, stores and builders), while the larger firms usually also have major industrial and commercial companies on their books.

In medium-to-large firms, audit staff work in teams, mostly going out to clients' offices in different parts of the country, even abroad (so the job can be rather more peripatetic than in industry), to check on their operation, to see if their accounts give a 'true and fair' picture of the financial position of the organisation, on a given date. The size and make up of an audit team depends on the size and scope of the organisation being audited. It can be two, three or four people, it can be up to 50 or more. Audit teams generally consist mainly of staff in various stages of training, probably headed by a recently-qualified accountant.

In smaller practices, auditing for individuals and very small businesses in the locality is more usually done in the office by one person, and often involves putting together the accounts first, from a collection of bank statements, receipts, invoices etc.

Accountancy practices also act as executors and trustees, provide company secretarial and registration services, act as liquidators or receivers when companies become insolvent – a growth area during the recession. They make financial investigations of all kinds, for example, when a client is considering buying a business or changing a partnership, preparing and verifying financial statements when a company issues a prospectus offering shares to the public, and generally providing management information, statistical and similar services.

About half of all trainees are estimated to leave their practices within two years of qualifying, mostly to work in other practices, other financial services, into financial work in industry or commerce (below), other organisations – from broadcasting to charities – or into management consultancy. Some go on to be accountancy tutors, a few into financial journalism, Of those who stay, some continue to specialise in audit work, usually as a manager within a couple of years, some go into other divisions of the practice but most, especially in smaller firms, deal with the full range of the practice's services. About 8-10% become partners in the larger firms.

Accountancy practices are now allowed to advertise, and the larger practices have taken on MARKETING managers, some PUBLIC RELATIONS people too. Of course all practices employ office staff.

INDUSTRY AND COMMERCE, and most other organisations, employ trained financial staff, a high proportion of them qualified accountants. Financial staff – management accountants – are now crucial and integral members of an organisation's management team at all levels. While they may work in separate financial departments, they no longer do so at arm's length from the rest of the organisation, just recording what happened to it recently or administering financial transactions, but take part in all aspects of managerial decision making, strategic forward planning and forecasting. Financial managers provide information on which decision making and planning can be based, and performance measured and controlled; assess and evaluate financial information, plans and decisions; and actively look for ways to maximise profits and make the best use of available resources.

Central to all areas of financial management now are increasingly sophisticated computer-based systems, which provide and analyse more complex financial information far faster than has ever been possible. Financial managers can give senior management a more accurate, speedy service and can show the details in a way that is meaningful to them. Their advice is stronger because they can process more data, using more sophisticated 'models'. All financial staff have now to be familiar with, and capable of using, computerised systems, and recruiters also look for people able to help improve and further develop these.

Financial, or management, accounting can be divided up into several different types of work. At various stages in their training and subsequent careers, accountants and other finance staff may work in just one of these, and go on to specialise (and perhaps add extra qualifications), or they may move between them, or (in smaller organisations) combine them. Firms often have different ways of organising the functions – for instance, an accountant may be part of the project manager's team on a major construction contract, being responsible for all the records and controls to monitor and report on the project, reviewing its financial status, and providing information for capital budgeting.

But however the functions are divided, they have to maintain close liaison and information flows, and all financial functions are, in a sense, part of management accounting, since they all contribute the information on which it is based.

Financial accounting deals with the routines of keeping financial records. The main tasks are operating accounts – more often now computerised accounting systems, and doing internal audits, but also includes dealing with wages and salaries, paying accounts and sending out invoices, and coping with tax. Trainee accountants can expect to spend time carrying out the full range of basic accounting tasks, and go on to, for instance, interpreting accounts; later to supervising, controlling and organising expenditure and income, etc. It includes compiling regularly – monthly and yearly – management accounts as reports for directors.

Cost accounting deals with the complex business of working out what particular operations, jobs, products really cost to produce, taking into account all the relevant factors and not just labour and materials, but all the 'overheads' and less obvious costs too. It extends to budgeting and budgetary control, forecasting future needs and costs (for instance, looking ahead to rising or falling energy prices), monitoring expenditure to see that costs are not over-shooting, and providing reports etc for management accounting. It involves analysing and comparing costs, translating information from non-financial managers into financial terms, and explaining financial information for them. Cost accounting uses computer systems extensively, with much of the routine now 'automated' in most larger firms, which in the most sophisticated can input and extract the necessary information into/from integrated computer-aided design and manufacturing (CAD/CAM) systems.

Treasury management is the financial 'housekeeping' function, which has recently become much more critical to companies taking a much more positive and sophisticated line in managing their money. Tighter profit margins, high interest rates on borrowing and lending, fluctuations in currency exchange rates, and new ways of exploiting the money markets have all contributed to create what their Association is calling a 'new' profession.

Treasury managers see that receipts and credits are banked fast (four times, rather than twice a day can save a major corporation up to £75,000 a year); know exactly how much is in each bank account early enough in the day to invest the balance overnight and see that all idle funds are earning; avoid or minimise exchange losses on overseas contracts by, eg trading in financial 'options'; negotiate the best possible charges with bankers; negotiate the best possible terms for capital borrowing – which involves projecting the firm's needs well ahead and predicting movements in interest rates. Treasury managers work on the principle that time is money, so ensure that debts, and stocks (of eg components) are kept to a minimum, that terms of payment and discount rates are reviewed regularly, and that invoices go out fast once orders have been despatched.

Positive treasury management depends totally on efficient and rapid information, and this has to mean the latest in IT systems, and taking advantage of all the banks have to offer in real-time access to the very latest position on accounts. The largest firms with the most sophisticated and aggressive treasury managers even have their own dealing desks, monitoring share and currency prices on screen and trading direct with market makers. This is fast becoming the major role for large-company treasury staff.

Tax management is sometimes a separate function, sometimes part of treasury management. Tax managers specialise in optimising the firm's fiscal structure, to ensure the company pays as little as is legal. Increasingly they have to cope with taxation on an international scale, and with the very different tax laws of different countries – a 'world tax planner' data base can, in ten minutes, give managers ten alternative ways to repatriate the maximum amount of cash, some of them via several countries. They look at the tax implications of new plans, changes in company structures, in fact any major decision. They advise on the tax effect of performance goals, which includes pricing policies.

Management accounting collects, organises, collates and analyses information from all parts of the organisation, including all the financial departments. Particularly in larger organisations, this may be based on sophisticated, computer-based, systems designed to maintain detailed and up-to-date records of all the firm's expenditure via internal costing systems backed up by comparative information from elsewhere, so that it is possible to make regular critical analyses of past and present financial performance, with projections for the future.

Management accountants monitor all the many and varied costs involved in making a product or providing a service, from raw materials and labour through to transport, administrative costs, overheads on buildings, and so on. They record and analyse sales trends. By constantly monitoring performance and efficiency, they can spot and report on problems, for instance where performance isn't matching predictions (and why), provide figures on which to base future pricing policies, and suggest ways of making economies by analysing costs and the financial implications of different production methods, rationalising the number of factories, or finding a new source of components. They may also provide the information which helps (treasury) management to anticipate and ensure funds for expansion, and generally provide expert assessments of the possible effects of events outside the company, such as expansion or merger plans of competing companies, new company or other legislation, and changes in taxation.

Individual accountants, or finance staff, do specific jobs within these broad fields, and may move between them, particularly within large organisations, although many specialise in one aspect. They generally start with more mundane and routine tasks – keeping accounts, working on internal audits, costing and stock control, doing research like making price comparisons of different brands and types of a particular product. From there the work becomes progressively more responsible – designing a new financial reporting system for a factory to improve the accuracy of the information coming through, evaluating tenders in terms of their potential contribution to profits, or examining the financial consequences of the firm's changeover from being labour intensive to high investment in advanced technological production, or working as part of a team rationalising and reorganising a company's warehouse depots within a region, for example. Budget control – making regular cost reports for a factory, working out why one set of costs have suddenly risen and what to do about it – is another typical area of responsibility.

Other functions Finance departments, especially in larger organisations, will also have to prepare prospectuses for share issues. Finance departments may also be responsible for managing pension funds and long-term investments; investigate prospective investments, and do the preparatory work on the possibility of taking over another company. In some, usually smaller, organisations, the financial controller may carry out the legal responsibilities of the COMPANY SECRETARY.

Promotion can be to financial control – of a small unit at first, later perhaps to large units, regional centres, or the whole organisation – and 'top' strategic planning.

Recruitment and entry A qualification in accountancy is not absolutely essential. Especially in some functions – corporate treasury, for example – many find a City-dealing/banking background more helpful – and a broad-based business-cum-finance with IT qualification at degree/HND level is increasingly useful.

But an accountancy qualification is an undoubted advantage. Accountants who want to work in industry or commerce can qualify via any of the professional bodies (see Qualifications and training below), but can only train in industry, commerce etc for CIMA and ACCA (CIPFA also in public utilities). CIMA qualifications are specifically tailored to accounting as a management tool, but do not qualify in statutory audit work. Reports suggest that in future firms may prefer to recruit people who have trained in industry/commerce for CIMA or CACA qualifications rather than chartered accountants trained solely in public practice.

IN THE PUBLIC SECTOR, professional accountants are employed by local authorities, the Civil Service, and organisations such as the Health Service, water authorities, the British Council, the National Audit Office, and the Local Authorities' Audit Commission. As elsewhere, the emphasis in the 1980s is on effective and efficient financial management as well as on auditing.

Local government employs accountants in some numbers (5000 CIPFA members alone). The work itself may seem similar to that of accountants and financial managers in industry or commerce, but it is done within a very different framework – administrative, economic, and political – and with different aims. While 'value for money' is increasingly a major pre-occupation – and the willingness and capacity of ratepayers to provide the finance – the aim is not to maximise profit, but to provide services for the community. The resources are never enough to meet the potential demands made upon them, with central government expecting local authorities to work within tighter and tighter 'cash limits'. Even so, local government expenditure was about £35.3 million in 1985-6. Since every financial decision vitally affects both the economic and the social life of the community, local government too is demanding more and better financial management and information systems on which to make decisions.

While it is the elected members of the authority who are actually responsible for deciding what services to provide and what is needed to finance them – or how to allocate what they are permitted to spend with set cash limits – they must use the expertise of their financial officers to work out and implement their plans. Financial officers advise the authority, prepare annual budgets according to policy decided by the council, and show, for example, how economies can be made, how capital can be raised, what the different options for expenditure are. They have to analyse and interpret the complexities of government financial legislation and regulations, and work out the practical implications for their own authority.

The financial officers also set up and run financial control systems, administer revenue collection (of rates and rents), manage any loan debts and supervise capital loans, pension fund investments, mortgage accounts, and so on. They see that government grants arrive, and pay wages, bills, etc.

Again, most trainees start in audit work, and routine work on eg rate accounting, valuations, mortgage work. They move on to, eg problem solving and legal aspects (what to do when someone cannot pay their mortgage or rates), checking parts of the financial control system, or helping to develop new computer-based systems. They may work on separate assignments, for instance, estimates for a new sports centre, or showing the financial benefits of restoring property against rebuilding. They may specialise in work on one area of an authority's services, eg leisure and tourist facilities, dealing with subsidies, preparing financial accounts etc.

Promotion is to increasingly responsible work and/or to 'group' accountant as a team leader, and higher. Chief executives of local authorities are most often former finance officers.

Most local government finance officers start their careers in an authority, usually taking the examinations of the Chartered Institute of Public Finance and Accountancy, and it is not easy for anyone qualified on the basis of training and experience in other areas to get in without CIPFA examinations. However, reports suggest CIPFA-qualified accountants are now being recruited in some numbers by other organisations, especially public bodies, and by practices auditing and working with local authorities. Movement between authorities is also common.

See also LOCAL GOVERNMENT.

Central government, until recently employed relatively few professional accountants – 650 in 1982, but numbers are to be doubled, to 1300, by the early 1990s, and by 1986 were already over 800. The present (1987) government wants accountants who will 'play a vital part in the drive to improve financial and resource management', and to involve them fully in financial management and policy-making generally within government departments.

One of the main functions of the accountancy service just now is to develop, install and apply the measurement techniques of management accounting budgetary control, performance indicators, expenditure statements, memorandum trading accounts etc, to make people working in government more 'cost conscious' to achieve efficiency, effectiveness and economy.

Internal audit systems are also being developed in departments, not just to see that systems are working and are properly controlled, but also more widely to monitor operational efficiency and policy effectiveness.

Accountants are also used where government works with private firms – for instance, in pricing and negotiating government contracts and assessing appropriate rates of profit, making sure that potential contractors are financially viable.

They also help administer any government aid to industry, and see that legal requirements are met – by companies generally, by banks and insurance companies. In the department of energy they may work on oil and gas royalties, in industry on the impact of EEC financial legislation in the UK, etc.

Most accountants have in the past worked in the Ministry of Defence, but numbers are rising in other departments – Inland Revenue, Health and Social Security, Industry, Environment, Agriculture, HMSO. They generally move between departments more often than other civil servants. Promotion prospects are being improved.

The Civil Service at present employs mainly ICAEW- and CIMA-qualified accountants (under 9% are CIPFA, and comparatively few CACA) but expects to increase its CIMA intake most. Training is given in several departments (mainly CIMA and/or CIPFA depending on department preference, but not ICAEW).

See also CENTRAL GOVERNMENT.

Other public authorities employing accountants, both as accountants and financial managers, include –

The National Health Service: has always been a major employer of accountants and financial experts, but the drive to improve management, and to apply modern managerial and financial methods have brought financial staff closer to centre stage, and into general management. Accountants and finance staff work in district and regional health offices, and in individual hospitals. Finance teams have been involved in developing computer-based information systems used in generating budgets, controlling spending – the NHS budget is over £11,000 million a year – paying accounts, salaries etc, and providing information for management. NHS spending priorities and budgeting are highly-sensitive issues, and finance officers not only advise, monitor and control, but also have to take part in very difficult negotiations over what and how much to spend where.

NHS recruitment includes about 75 places a year to train future senior managers. Accountant training schemes – for CIPFA or CIMA qualifications – are organised mainly by regional authorities, although some districts also recruit direct. Both graduates and A-level entrants are taken on.

See also HEALTH SERVICES.

The National Audit Office (800 staff) gives independent information, advice and assurance to parliament on the expenditure, revenue and use of resources of the government, including international organisations to which the UK belongs (eg the UN). The staff, over 440 of whom are qualified accountants, deal with anything from military contracts to university grants, agricultural subsidies to atomic energy. They also 'audit' the financial aspects of organisations like the Church Commissioners.

The Audit Commission for Local Authorities (England and Wales) and the Commission for Local Authority Accounts (Scotland) audit local-authority accounts, mostly using their own staff, although outside firms do some. Training for both the above is for CIPFA qualifications.

Public utilities: electricity, gas, and water, fall between the public sector and industry. While only the gas industry has, at present, to produce profits for shareholders, services have to be made and kept cost-effective, and reconciling this with customer demand for efficiency and reasonable prices is difficult in today's economic conditions. These industries are also very capital-intensive, having to spend very large sums on new generating plant, sewage treatment schemes etc. All policy decisions and forward plans have to be made with information and advice from financial managers, who also work with, eg engineers on new projects, monitor expenditure, manage cash flows, supervise billing and accounts, work on revenue and capital accounting. See also WATER AUTHORITIES and the ENERGY INDUSTRY.

Recruitment and entry Most people start as trainees in public practice, larger industrial or commercial companies, local and other public authorities, including the Civil Service. The great majority of trainees start straight from the education system, although it is possible to go through the technician-level route (see below). Recruitment policies, especially amongst the largest practices, is changing, mostly to cope with City competition for top-flight graduates. Firms are taking fewer, more carefully-selected, new graduates, and offering (even) higher salaries, training packages (up to and including MBA) etc – filling the 'body' gap with computers and accounting technicians (see below).

Entry qualifications for professional accountants in England and Wales are standardised at a minimum of five GCE/GCSE passes including two at A level (and/or AS levels), the passes to include English language and mathematics. In Scotland, ICAS requires a degree (currently 90% of entrants), or SHND in accounting (5%), but will probably end SHND-entry soon. A degree is a strong advantage and the proportion of graduate entrants is rising, although unevenly between the professional bodies. By 1985, virtually 90% of the 6276 ICAEW students registering training contracts were graduates (under 1% had HNDs). CIPFA entry is over 61% graduate, CIMA about 30%, and CACA almost 27% (1986).

Competition for training places is extremely fierce, especially in the major public practices, and firms with good training records. A traineeship is not a guarantee of a long-term job on qualification, and most larger practices keep on only a relatively small proportion of their trainees. Choice of practice can influence accountants' careers – training in a small, country practice is unlikely to lead to work with, or for, large corporations, for instance.

ICAEW had 1723 authorised training offices (1335 firms) in 1985 (but only 200 or so firms take students in any one year). While over 50% of 1985-entry students found training in firms with over 100 partners, over 97% of them were graduates, as were 93% of the 14% of students in firms with between 21 and 100 partners. Firms with ten (or fewer) partners took just 28% of new students, but 68% of non-graduate entrants. ICAEW figures show a strong correlation between A-level grades, class of degree and pass rates for professional exams. A relatively high (but falling) percentage (AGCAS' latest figure for graduates with non-relevant degrees is 30%) cancel their training contracts, or have them terminated.

Degree subject is not crucial – over 70% of ICAEW entrants to the profession have degrees which are not apparently 'relevant'. Graduates with degrees in engineering, maths, law and Classics all do well in ICAEW exams, and graduates with 'relevant' degrees only do better if they have firsts or upper seconds. A degree in, eg engineering can be especially useful in industry, and for anyone wanting to get into consultancy work eventually. A good degree – preferably a 2.1 – is a strong advantage, particularly to get a good public-practice traineeship, and recruiters also look for good A-level and even 16-plus† grades as well.

School-leaver entry for good training places in both public practice and industry/commerce also demands high A-level and 16-plus† grades. A rising proportion of recruiters also want entrants who have already completed a foundation course (see below).

Numeracy is obviously essential, although high-level mathematical skills are not needed. It is more the ability to be able to 'make sense' of information in number form, to be able to 'think' numerically and be happy working with figures. Employers want people who are interested in the business and financial world. Accountants must also be able to work closely with others, to talk and listen to anyone with or for whom they may working. The information which accountants must collect comes from sources ranging from the factory floor, other professionals (eg engineers), and top managers, and they must be able to explain clearly, effectively and quickly what they want and understand what their informants are saying. They have to develop the ability to make reasonably shrewd judgements of people they work with or for. They may need considerable persuasive skills to, for instance, get colleagues to understand the need for and adopt new reporting procedures. At more senior levels, they may work as part of a management 'team' with production and marketing managers.

Computing training/experience at some stage is a must. Languages are increasingly valuable, especially to get into the international business of management consultancy.

Recruiters are increasingly looking for management potential from amongst their graduate entry – the qualities needed to take on responsibility for other staff within a relatively short period and learn to delegate, to be able to problem solve and know how to decide on priorities, to make decisions of increasing importance, to be able to think for oneself but know when to ask for advice. 'Social skills' are emphasised.

Qualifications and training All the careers literature stresses that training and qualifying in accountancy is a very tough, lengthy, and rather boring business, even for graduates. Trainees have to be prepared to work for long-term aims. A professional qualification is essential for public practice and public authorities, and major industrial and commercial employers ask for accountancy qualifications for many posts in their finance departments.

Training is largely on-the-job, with part-time study for professional qualifications, and all entrants, graduate or not, start with a period on the dullest work – learning book-keeping and audit routines, for example. Periods of study-leave are written in to ICAEW and ICAS training contracts, and CIPFA training is shorter with block (three years) than with day release (four years). It is clearly worthwhile trying for schemes which give study time and formal tuition – some practices and firms put on their own study sessions. Otherwise study has to be by evening or correspondence course. Even with time off to study, though, getting through the exams takes a lot of every entrant's spare time – often after a long day on an audit – for the first three to five years. Firms are taking an increasingly dim view (and terminating contracts) of students who do not pass them in the shortest possible time, and are selecting recruits whose academic 'profiles' indicate that they are more likely to do so (ICEAW now also sets time limits on resits). Graduate pass rates are on average around the 60% mark, non-graduate about 40%.

Entrants without a degree are normally required by all six major professional bodies to do a nine-month, full-time foundation course (at polytechnic or other FE college), which is usually taken before starting the four-year training period (although it is possible to do a preliminary period of training first), and some polytechnics expect students to have a provisional training place before accepting them.

Graduates normally have to do a three-year training. For both graduates and non-graduates, ICAEW and ICAS require formal training contracts; a period (at least three years) of approved relevant employment/experience is required for membership of other bodies. Graduates who do not have a 'relevant' degree must normally take a foundation or conversion course and exams, but need not do so full-time.

Professional bodies The profession has inherited six major accountancy bodies and several minor ones. The illogicality of this is generally recognised within the profession, but despite years of negotiation rationalisation seems as far away as ever. There is a growing consensus of opinion on eg education and training; the pattern of their examinations is similar, and all the professional bodies try to keep their examinations up-to-date on modern developments in accounting, and now IT. ICAEW and CIMA, for example, both introduced new syllabuses for students who began training in the autumn of 1986, CIMA particularly emphasising IT. Both ICAEW and ICAS are now making major reviews of their education and training, and CACA was reviewing its syllabus in 1986. However, each continues to bias its examinations and training requirements to particular aspects of accountancy work, and the restrictions can affect career options. Entrants to the profession must then make an informed choice of where to train linked to one particular set of professional exams. The major bodies are –

The three Institutes of Chartered Accountants, of England (1986 over 84,000 members plus over 21,000 students), of Scotland (nearly 12,000 members, but only about 60% work in Scotland, and nearly 1700 students), and of Ireland About 41% of all ICAEW members work (1986) in public practice as partners or employees (down from 49% in 1983), 40% in commerce and industry, 6% in other areas of finance, and 8% in the public sector or teaching etc. About half of all ICAS members work in commerce and industry. ICAEW and ICAS require entrants to serve a training contract with an authorised member of a public practice which means it is impossible to gain internal industrial/commercial experience during the training period.

The Chartered Association of Certified Accountants' 19,300 UK members (total over 29,000 plus some 71,000 registered students), work in public practice (37%), industry (26%), commerce (19%), and the public sector (13%). CACA entrants can train in, and move between, public practice and/or central/local government and industry/commerce.

The Chartered Institute of Management Accountants (CIMA) still has 51% of its 20,000 UK membership (25,000 total) in industry, with rising proportions in areas like services such as finance and retailing (15%), transport and distribution (7%), national and local government (5%), and consultancy (5%). Over half the 41,000 registered students are in the UK. CIMA entrants train mainly in industrial and commercial firms, and the qualification is best suited to those certain they want a future in the business world (CIMA expects trainees to gain 'real' working experience in departments other than finance, eg marketing), and who are not concerned about training for public practice.

The Chartered Institute of Public Finance and Accountancy (CIPFA) – 1986 membership 9750 plus 2500 students – is mainly for accountants in local government (52% of members), although its qualifications are used by other public authorities – the NHS (nearly 5%), government and governmental bodies (4.7%), the water industry (3.5%), 'other' public authorities (6.6%), with small numbers working in gas/electricity and audit firms. All entrants train in local authorities or other public bodies and this does rather restrict movement into other areas of accounting/financial work.

Degree courses 'Relevant' degrees may exempt from first-stage professional foundation/conversion examinations, and other graduates may be given subject-for-subject exemptions – this varies between the professional bodies. Relevant degree courses include those at –
Universities: Aberdeen, Aberystwyth, Bangor, Bath, Belfast, Birmingham: U & Aston, Bradford, Bristol, Canterbury: Kent, Cardiff UC and UWIST, City, Dundee, Edinburgh U and Heriot-Watt, Essex, Exeter, Glasgow U and Strathclyde, Hull, Lancaster, Leeds, London: LSE, Loughborough, Manchester/UMIST, Newcastle, Nottingham, Norwich: E Anglia, Sheffield, Southampton, Stirling, Ulster and Warwick; all polytechnics but not London: S Bank or Plymouth; colleges: Bournemouth: Dorset IHE, Dundee CT, Ealing CHE, Edinburgh: Napier, Glasgow CT.
Exemptions for BTEC HND is on a subject-for-subject basis only.

Related professional qualifications include those of –
The Institute of Administrative Accountants (1986 10,000 members and 1500 students) sets a four-stage examination (entry with four O-level-equivalent passes at 16-plus† including English and maths), recently up-dated and revised to include a local government/public sector stream, mainly for people working in company finance departments. BTEC National and Higher National awards including appropriate subjects exempt.

Institute of Taxation – 700-plus members plus 600 registered students in public practice, where they usually specialise in tax work or act as tax advisers, and central or local government, banks or commercial firms dealing with taxation. Most members are therefore also qualified accountants, bankers or lawyers. The qualifying examinations of any of a number of appropriate professional bodies exempt from the intermediate of the two stage examinations; full membership requires at least three years' specialised practical experience in taxation.

Association of Corporate Treasurers (formed 1979) – some 1000 members (1986) and nearly 300 students registered for exams introduced only in 1984. Entry to the two-part exams is at least five GCE/GCSE passes including two at A level, but most entrants already have a qualification in eg accountancy (which exempts from part 1), law, banking; subject-for-subject exemptions for some degrees and other professional qualifications. Full membership also requires at least two years' experience with responsibility for a wide range of treasury functions.

Further information from the Institute of Chartered Accountants in England and Wales (ICAEW), the Institute of Chartered Accountants in Scotland (ICAS), the Chartered Association of Certified Accountants (CACA), the Chartered Institute of Management Accountants (CIMA), the Chartered Institute of Public Finance and Accountancy (CIPFA).

Working as an accountancy technician

Accountancy technicians have not been a separately-defined group for long, and it still isn't a common job description, although many thousands do this kind of work – as cashiers, book-keepers, ledger and payroll clerks, accounting assistants, audit clerks, costing clerks, accounts supervisors and even more senior staff. The 'accountancy technician' label is designed to indicate competence and ability to take on responsible work.

Most qualified technicians work in the private sector, although estimates suggest nearly a third of AAT members work for local or public authorities. Accountancy practices, looking to cut their intake of increasingly-expensive graduates, are using computers more in areas such as audit. Since the work can be done by audit 'technicians', this is likely to mean more opportunities for them – and shortages are already showing up.

There is no hard-and-fast job specification for technicians – the work they do varies from organisation to organisation. It ranges from the more routine, but still technical, work – such as audit – within an accounting practice or office, through to quite considerable responsibility for staff and/or systems. In industry and commerce, there is nothing to prevent people with technician qualifications gaining promotion if they can handle the work, and undoubtedly some get into posts which might, elsewhere, be classed as professional.

Young accountancy technicians work as, for instance, audit clerks – checking records and bank reconciliations; they may be invoice clerks – checking invoices and arranging payments; they may prepare financial data to go into computer systems. They prepare accounts. They may work how much cash is needed in any one month to pay contractors for work which has been done on a particular project. They may check VAT and other official financial returns. They go on to more technical aspects of auditing, keeping financial records, costing and budgeting, and usually become supervisors in larger organisations, planning and monitoring the work of more junior staff.

Recruitment and entry At least four O-level-equivalent passes at 16-plus† (ie English language, a numerate subject, and two others of which only one can be a 'craft'), a BTEC First award with credit passes, or an equivalent. While most entrants register as students straight from school or FE (25% with O-levels or equivalent, 17% with A levels, 13% with BTEC National or equivalent), some 42% were 'mature' in 1986 – 1% were graduates.

Qualifications and training The six-year-old Association of Accounting Technicians now (1986) has a membership of over 11,700 (84% in the UK) plus some 22,900 students (62% in UK). It provides standard qualifications for people working as sub-professionals –
The regularly-revised membership examinations are in three stages, and cover basic numeracy, statistics, economics, accounting, communication, business administration and law, and information systems at preliminary/intermediate level. Finals are taken in practice work, industry and commerce, or public sector, in a combination of papers which may include financial accounting, cost accounting and budgeting, information systems analysis and design, auditing and taxation, organisation and financial control. A BTEC National in business studies with appropriate options exempts from the preliminary and intermediate.
Full membership also requires three years' practical experience. Senior accounting technician (SAT) status is gained with at least five years' experience at supervisory or managerial level. AAT members who have the aptitude are encouraged to study for full professional qualifications, and may gain some exemptions from the exams.
An AAT Certificate in Accounting has recently been introduced to give a business grounding for eg account clerks and book-keepers. The five-paper examination, which can be taken after one-year part-time, or four-six months full-time study, covers basic accounting, communication, business administration, numeracy and statistics, and computer applications. No formal academic qualifications are needed.

Further information From the Association of Accounting Technicians.
See also BUSINESS STUDIES under ACADEMIC AND VOCATIONAL STUDIES.

BANKING
One dictionary defines a bank as 'an institution for keeping, lending and exchanging ... money', but this hardly describes the range and variety of contemporary British banking. The banking system has been, and still is, going through a series of real revolutions, especially for anyone who thinks banking is synonymous with traditionalism. Banks have broken out of their conventional moulds. One bank chairman now prefers to talk about his 'financial service institution'.

Review after review charts the radical changes that have transformed banking over the past twenty-five years – and are continuing to do so. The staid, genteel image has been swept away. Banks, which used to play down the fact that they are commercial businesses which have to be profitable, have become increasingly competitive, using both aggressive marketing and promotion to sell themselves and their services (advertising went up 24% a year between 1980 and 1986), and the latest financial management methods (see also ACCOUNTANCY AND FINANCIAL MANAGEMENT).

Not only are banks moving into new areas of business, but distinguishing between the traditionally-very-different clearing, merchant and savings banks is becoming increasingly difficult. The difference today is between the banking *functions*, the type of services being offered, rather than between one *type* of bank and another, although every bank is trying to establish its own recognisable, individual image.

Much of the change has happened because other financial interests, notably building societies, began competing with clearing banks for traditional clearing-bank customers. In fighting back, the clearing banks not only introduced completely new services, but also went into their new competitors' business, eg mortgages. As competition has opened up further, with de-regulation the larger clearing banks have moved into areas such as merchant and investment banking, estate agency, insurance and the stock market, either developing their own divisions or (more often) buying into existing businesses, becoming banking and financial 'conglomerates'.

But technology is, of course, also instrumental in changing the face of banking, and many of the new services and other developments would have been impossible without it. Long users of highly-efficient huge main-frame accounting and transaction-processing systems, in the last ten years the banks have brought in the now-familiar cash machines, and the less-obvious 'back office' electronic clearing, inter-bank communication and information systems, both internal, with terminals for cashiers, and for services – computerised cash-management for companies. The latest, more sophisticated automated teller machines can be programmed to provide a widening range of services; systems can handle and rapidly process transactions in a 100 different currencies at airports, the first 'home banking' systems have started, and in 1988, the first nationwide electronic 'cashless shopping' – officially 'electronic funds transfer at point of sale' – system is expected.

More is in the pipeline. Branches will be further automated (with considerable implications for staffing), and huge sums are being spent on integrated data communications systems for the branch networks, to give at least thirty times the traffic volume of systems installed barely ten years ago, and to help, eg 'target' customers for marketing projects. Home banking may really take off when a palm-sized terminal, a 'bank in your pocket', can be plugged into a telephone socket for direct access to accounts – in fact almost all key developments now projected depend on direct communication between customers and bank data systems, via a terminal.

Some bankers think the massive investment has not saved costs or increased fees from services enough to be economic, but they may be the ones who let themselves be led by the technology, buying already-dated systems. The technology has, and is giving, banks major managerial problems. Making a success of the technology apparently demands a 'market-led' approach, tightly defining and controlling technological innovation to specific goals. Banks have, to some extent, suffered from being constantly in the lead technologically. Although efficient in their own terms, massive batch-processing systems are too inflexible for the newer, customer-oriented services. Banks are having to look to their younger managers for greater flexibility in thinking, and better awareness of technology and its possibilities and pitfalls.

The whole style of banking has been transformed, and with it many managerial roles and attitudes, and ways of organising work, with major implications for future careers. Bankers now have to combine the traditional virtues of stability, judgement etc, with modern managerial, especially marketing, and technological skills.

The banking system

The banking system is no longer split between different types of banks, but into different services. These are – retail banking, merchant and investment banking, central and regulatory banking (the Bank of England), and international banking.

RETAIL BANKING is the most familiar, the high-street branch banks and services for both the general public and business, large and small.

The 'banks' involved are the so-called 'big four' – Barclays, National Westminster, the Midland and Lloyds – plus Coutts' (owned by National Westminster), the three Scottish and two Northern Ireland banks, the Co-operative Bank, the Trustee Savings Bank (TSB), and the National Giro Bank. BUILDING SOCIETIES too, offer personal-account services in many ways similar to those of the traditional domestic banks. Standard Chartered is now also a 'clearing bank', as yet without a major stake in the high street; Citibank, the first foreign UK clearer, has barely a dozen branches so far.

Until now, 'domestic' banking services have been synonymous with a multiplicity of high-street branches. In theory, rapidly-developing automation, 'robot cashiers' which can provide cash, statements, information, perhaps even 'expert' advice, together with plastic-card payment for shopping etc, makes the traditional branch redundant. Automated teller machines can be installed almost anywhere. In practice, banks, recognising that personal customers matter most, have decided that 'human' contact between staff and customers is still important, and are now putting their automated machines etc inside the branch. But while the branches are unlikely to go altogether, there will be fewer, and they are changing considerably.

The branch system is being reshaped, both to 'target' customer services more accurately and to save some of the high costs involved in automation and marketing etc. Each bank has a slightly different policy, but the main themes are the same – separating personal from company services, and providing different levels and types of service at different branches, instead of every branch providing all services to their catchment area. Each bank's branch network might have some small, very streamlined 'robot' centres; some larger branches providing a range of services for personal customers and small businesses (eg local traders), and (because cash-dispensing etc is automated) designed to attract customers with informal, open-plan, carpeted areas with advisers/sales staff at ordinary desks; and the largest, area or 'key' offices, both providing sophisticated services for larger business customers and managing the other branches. TSB already has a full-automated branch, enabling customers to pay bills, and answering transaction queries.

The big clearers are steadily cutting their branch networks – the estimated net loss is now about 200 a year, giving only 10,440 in 1986 (against the 1976 peak of 13,200), and at least another 1000 seem likely to go by the mid-1990s. The TSB network was cut to 1625 by 1986, from the 1983 peak of 1650.

The number of full-time staff in the main clearers branches is now (1986) around 200,000 (from over 219,000 in 1980), but numbers working part-time are up, to well over 20,000. (The 1986 total for the biggest nine is nearly 300,000 including well over 30,000 part-time.) Employment rose by about 4% a year between 1960 and 1975, by 2.4% over 1975-80, but by 1984 was only 0.2%, with no prospect of any return to higher levels – although as wastage rates of people in their first year of employment fell from about 70% in 1971 to only 15% in 1981, the real increase may be higher. TSB staff has so far continued to increase – to about 24,000 full-time, and some 4500 part-time.

At least three of the main clearers expect to cut branch staffing by the end of the decade. But a 1985 study made for the clearing banks believes it likely that their staff numbers will stay roughly static to 1992, and even that they may find it difficult not to increase staffing, suggesting that any losses resulting from technological developments should be outweighed by expected growth in business. It does, though, accept that any major threat to profitability, or adverse changes in the competitive environment could easily change their projections. It says the prospect beyond the early 1990s is much more uncertain. Independent assessments suggest at best roughly unchanged numbers to 1990, but reductions of up to a third by the end of the century are possible. They point to the fact that staff costs rose by 16-22% in 1981 alone.

Cheque volumes, according to the clearers, look set to continue increasing at least into the 1990s – they now (1986) handle some five million a day, and every signature must still be scrutinised by a clerk. Some 63% of adults have current accounts (against under 40% in 1970) and an increase to 76% is projected for 1991.

'Cashless shopping' is expected to replace only some 10% of cheque volume in the short term. Automated teller machines (ATMs), while taking work from bank counters, encourage people to take cash out in smaller amounts, but more frequently, so increasing the work of up-dating accounts, and they produce more queries about balances. ATMs have, so far, increased the overall workload.

Credit card use – the banks had 19.5 million in circulation in 1986 – is also expected to rise rapidly, and further 'product diversification' is expected to increase business too. Amongst these will almost certainly be a whole new range of information-based services, and these should, in turn, improve marketing generally, so generating even more business. Retail banks expect, for instance, to provide instant insurance quotations or stock market prices at bank 'counters'.

Clearing banks have in the past monopolised the transfer of money – from one account to another, mostly as cheques via a 'central clearing house', but they also (and increasingly) do this directly through the bank giro and other direct debiting methods – and other financial firms are competing with them here. They handle foreign exchange and discount bills (for exports). They lend short- and fairly medium-term 'working' capital, making temporary 'bridging' loans for longer-term capital needs, both for individuals and firms.

The banks have moved into other services, including long-term lending – for instance mortgages (where by 1986 they had 25% of the market), funding new small (and even not-so-small) businesses, financing firms exporting capital goods, making medium- and long-term loans to industry, even keeping firms alive. Clearing banks give firms sophisticated financial information systems, based on systems which allow company treasurers direct, instant on-line access to the current state of all the company's bank balances. This, together with the need for banks to have much more sophisticated information themselves about what is happening to particular industrial sectors and firms, is paving the way for separate services to corporate and individual customers.

For personal customers, there are more and varied savings schemes, which is one way of fighting building societies for their depositors. Banks have long been involved in trustee and executor work (in which the bank administers wills, trusts etc), and in investment services. They have also greatly extended both these and other services; trustee work now helps organise family trusts, and with tax problems. Investment services extend both to financial planning in general and unit trust investment, and into services to companies, for instance, administering pension funds, international investment and organising employees' savings schemes.

CENTRAL BANKING: THE BANK OF ENGLAND is banker to the government and to the other banks. The Bank prints bank notes, manages government borrowing, regulates the money supply, registers government stock, and advises government on all aspects of fiscal policy and problems. In the fast-changing City and political environment, its work is continually changing too, and evolving, functions ended (with, for example, the end of exchange control), extended and redefined. The major task of supervising the rest of the banking system is developing into a wider role in supervision and (self) regulation for the whole financial system. Since 'big bang', the Bank's gilt-edged division has had its own securities dealing room; it manages the market in government debt and helps finance the government's longer-term borrowing. The money markets division deals with the discount houses to implement government short-term interest-rate policy.

Nearly 300 years old, and sited in Threadneedle Street since 1734 (the Bank also has seven provincial offices and a printing works), the Bank has (1986) a staff of almost 4050 (down from 4800 in 1976 but more than in the early 1980s). The Bank's size, organisation and structure changes – with increasing frequency – to reflect its current responsibilities, and job opportunities change with them. Policy and markets includes the divisions looking after gilt-edged, money markets, foreign exchange, international (advises on external policy), economics (which keeps its own model of the UK economy, making forecasts and economic analyses), and financial statistics; finance and industry is divided between industrial finance and financial supervision (of the securities and commodities markets). Banking supervision has expanded sharply (staff numbers were over 170 by 1986, from under 90 in 1983). Operations deals with banking, stock registrations and new issues, and printing (mainly bank-notes). Corporate services include personnel, accounting, computing, business systems etc.

MERCHANT/INVESTMENT BANKING Traditionalist they may seem, but merchant banks have always been entrepreneurial, living by their wits and seizing new opportunities as they came along, thriving on change – as recent City events have shown. They have long ceased to be merchants, and have been diversifying for some years out of their traditional business (although most still provide such services and keep up their prestigious international connections). This was originally mainly financing exports and international trade – through acceptance credits, for example; negotiating loans; and banking, loan business etc for governments and international institutions. Much of their business has always been in the currency markets, and they provide special services, such as bulk supplies of currency notes for travel agencies and other banks.

As bankers to companies rather than individuals (other than very wealthy ones), they have become experts in all aspects of corporate finance, especially in capital issues, the high-profile take-overs, mergers, and company 'flotations' (eg British Gas), as well as advising companies on their financial 'structures', and generally acting as financial intermediaries. They deal in bullion, organise medium- and long-term finance for major projects, trade in commodities, advise on shipping and insurance problems (some actually broking).

But managing large investment, especially pension, funds, for clients has more recently developed as a growing and major part of their business. With the opening up of the stock markets, merchant banks have taken big stakes in the market companies, and by so doing, become similar to American-style investment banks.

Merchant banking in the 1980s is highly competitive, with too many banks for the available business, and profit margins are slim. Banks are more competitive, and trying to be leaner, cutting costs where possible.

'Doyens' of the merchant banking world are the 16 members of the Accepting Houses Committee, most of them with long histories as merchant banks. They, and another thirty institutions, make up the Issuing Houses Association. The differences between the so-called 'accepting' and 'issuing' houses is now mainly historic. All the major clearing, and larger overseas banks now have merchant banking divisions or subsidiaries.

Merchant banking has, to date, opted for a traditionalist front, but aggressive competitive conditions, marketing, new merchant-banking interests without the historic backgrounds, and a more thrusting attitude are now bringing out their more 'swashbuckling' and risk-taking characteristics.

The older merchant banks were, and many still are, family business, run – managed – by members of the family and/or close associates. Changing conditions, and new merchant banking interests, are making rapid changes here, although it may still be difficult to break into the upper echelons of the oldest and most traditionalist accepting houses.

Merchant banking employs relatively small numbers. Figures are hard to get, especially at a time of rapid change. 'Career' staff probably total under 25,000, including about 5000 at management level. Even the largest employ no more than 1500-2000 staff, the smallest about 200, although some have grown sharply since 1985 – at least one increased staff by 60% in two years.

INTERNATIONAL BANKING Banks, both UK and those of other countries, have long operated overseas, providing traditional-style services both for individuals and companies – for the latter largely funding trade and development, and transmitting funds. Since the 1960s the international banking scene has been growing, with more sophisticated, comprehensive world-wide services mainly for business customers, and aggressive marketing inroads into foreign financial centres. The competition for business is intense, and developing new financial services is crucial to success. British and foreign banks have combined in completely international consortia.

Banks operating internationally still finance trade (as well as handling documentation and advising on trading conditions), and overseas investments. But with the more recent boom in loan business, they are increasingly getting involved in the new global securities markets, particularly currency trading, and in issuing the commercial 'paper' which firms are now preferring to loans.

Seven major UK banks have international operations, one still with over 1800 'branch' offices in around sixty countries, but another twenty, most either associates or subsidiaries of London clearing or Scottish banks, have been formed recently. While a high proportion of their staff are nationals of the countries concerned, they all recruit UK nationals.

The number of foreign banks with branches or offices in London has been rising for years – over 460 in 1986 (from 53 in 1950). Most (over 180) are European; 68 are US, 40 are Japanese, and 34 Arab. Only about half a dozen of the world's top 100 banks are not represented in London. The largest have bought into stock market firms or are building up their own securities trading departments, and use London as a base for trading international securities. Numbers employed are hard to estimate with all the recent developments, and individual banks vary in size from a handful running what is essentially only a 'listening post', up to one major US bank offering a full range of services, and over 2000 staff.

Working in banking

Most career opportunities are obviously in retail banking (including TSB), although the number of jobs in merchant banking is increasing. While individual banks may have diversified out of their traditional services, staff still normally specialise in one type of banking, since each is very different.

Banks of all kinds treat the majority of their long-term staff as 'bankers', and most managerial posts go to them. They also employ quite significant, and probably increasing, proportions of other professional staff – systems analysts and other computer experts, lawyers, economists, personnel managers, market researchers, marketing managers, public relations experts etc. Some of these are, however, wherever possible, 'home grown'. Studies suggest the hard distinctions between 'bankers' and 'specialists', particularly software designers, will blur, and managers will have to be as familiar with information technology as with traditional banking subjects. But specialisation in areas such as treasury management, leasing, money markets, and management services, dealing, plus staff management, is likely to become more important.

THE CLEARING BANKS (including TSB), start most of their career entrants, graduate or school-leaver, in a branch, and many spend all their working lives in them.

Traditionally, every career banker in the clearing banks is a 'generalist', but this is changing as banks separate the services they provide for larger companies from the rest of their customers. The new breeds of managers will specialise in either personal or corporate services, and at a fairly early point in their careers, the former marketing/sales-oriented, the latter more business analysts. But branch reorganisation is also changing the balances between different grades of staff in fairly complex ways, rather than reducing overall numbers.

Each branch has a considerable degree of independence, and the manager, at the top, is responsible for its profitability. Each branch has a range of staff (average per branch fifteen) at varying levels. All jobs in the branches cover a wide variety of tasks, and the 'mix' of tasks varies from bank to bank. Tasks have changed considerably over the past twenty-five years, and will go on so doing. While there is little evidence of wide deskilling, technology has cut the drudgery, and shifting skill requirements for individual tasks has become a near-continuous process. A continuing 'slow shift' away from junior clerical and technical/service functions is expected, towards more specialist, professional and managerial positions. Typically, though –

Lowliest are remittance clerks – who check and sort cheques and other credits for electronic reading – and terminal operators, who key in data to bring customers' accounts and other records up to date.

Next on the rung is dealing with standing orders, and cashiering. Foreign work – buying and selling currency, handling travellers' cheques, import-export documents, arranging trade finance, settling overseas accounts – follows.

At this stage many people gain some supervisory experience – being in day-to-day charge of terminal operators and remittance clerks. The top clerical grades are securities work – seeing that loans are properly covered, and being a manager's clerk, taking on some of the routine work.

Depending on the size of the bank, senior positions normally include a chief cashier and a branch accountant, loan officers, and assistant managers who may look after particular accounts, or are responsible for office management. The manager has to see that the branch is run efficiently. Management generally starts in a small branch, with progression to larger and more important places. In the TSBs, recent expansion means that many managers are still in their early thirties.

Most bank staff spend their days inside the bank, largely in desk work, but the manager and possibly other senior staff spend time out in the community, because they have to expand business and improve profitability.

The main route to promotion is still via the branch banks, although a rising proportion of graduates go into specialist divisions direct, and increasingly, the route up is likely to divide between personal and corporate banking fairly early. Despite any accelerated promotion (usual for graduates and possible for school-leaver entrants who show potential), progress through the branches, learning the day-to-day work of the bank in branches in different settings (rural, small town, suburban, industrial estate, shopping centre and so on), and in branches of different sizes, still takes time.

In the new corporate-finance offices, career staff will gain experience as, for example, 'account executives' who will diagnose company needs and design and deliver services such as leasing, investment management, treasury management, insurance, and export and expansion financing.

All these can be interspersed both with experience of 'special' (eg credit finance), and head office departments such as economic intelligence, financial control, marketing and personnel, and with training, mostly on banks' own schemes.

Promotion depends largely on entry qualifications and abilities. Graduates can expect, for instance, to reach assistant branch accountant in three to five years, and branch management (via branch accountant, assistant or sub-manager) by their 30s. Above that, the progression to larger and more important branches, area and general management is very restricted. In the 1970s, banks could talk about all 18-plus male entrants having the opportunity to reach managerial status in their early 30s (around 20% of all 'career' bank personnel are at present managers). However, this is unlikely to continue, even some graduates will probably not reach senior levels in future, and reports suggest the proportion of staff to whom the banks offer a real life-time career is likely to decline.

Career staff are still not expected to move between the clearing banks, and it is still not possible for staff to apply openly for some posts. The banks retain the right to send staff to jobs in different parts of the country, and all staff must be prepared to move.

As well as career staff, the clearing banks also employ large numbers of secretarial and office staff, computer staff (programmers, systems analysts, operators), and business machine operators.

BANK OF ENGLAND Only a small number are 'career' banking staff. Career patterns are flexible, and vary according to qualification, aptitude etc, but the work is increasingly 'technical' – and almost everyone can expect to use computers as necessary. As a national(ised) institution, the Bank is not a commercial organisation, and while it supports enterprise elsewhere, has no use for the marketing skills now crucial in other banks. While its managerial 'style' is more relaxed than it used to be, there is more formality and traditionalist structures than are now found elsewhere in banking.

After two or three years in one division (but in more than one job), career staff move around to gain broad experience, and taking increasing responsibility. Graduates, and many A-level entrants, can expect to reach senior positions. People with 'relevant' degrees, notably economics, but also mathematics, statistics etc can either go in the general career structure, or spend time doing specialist work (eg economic research/analysis, financial statistics, or operational research) and move into the main stream later on. Just over 9% of bank staff are specialists. They include data processing people, librarians, doctors and dentists.

A large percentage, some 46.5%, of staff are office/clerical (only 6.7% are secretarial). They operate computer systems, input data, process documents and check their accuracy, record and file information and answer queries, answer the telephone, take messages, and doing figure work, on eg interest rates, or collecting statistics.

MERCHANT BANKS (including merchant banking divisions of clearing banks): Merchant bankers have a comparatively small number of clients, but the accounts, and the sums involved, can be huge, so it is many ways the very opposite of retail banking.

In their early years career staff may move around between departments, to build up experience in a number of fields, graduates starting mainly in work involved in research, collecting information and analysis, A-level entrants in rather more routine clerical work. Career staff are specialising earlier now, though, in one area of the bank's business – banking, investment or funds management, corporate finance etc, or in a 'support' function, such as research or investment analysis. They may be part of a 'team' looking after the account of a single client, or providing information and advice on one area of investment, or actively looking for companies vulnerable to take over ('arbitrage'). Merchant banks expanding with City de-regulation are having to re-think their internal managerial 'styles', putting in place more formal organisational structures instead of the fairly loose 'entrepreneurial' frameworks that have been traditional, and this may change career patterns somewhat.

Much of the work is highly technical, and can be very intensive. Long hours may be necessary when putting together a 'bid' for a major company to a tight deadline. A first-time 'flotation' on the stock market can take up hundreds of hours of working time for the banker's team. Clients, and the Stock Exchange, expect very high standards, of research and investigation, accuracy in preparing prospectuses, etc.

Banks expect their career staff to show entrepreneurial 'flair', to be creative in developing new business, managing their clients' positively – suggesting how they should invest, diversify etc, and spotting new opportunities. Promotion is generally much faster than in retail banking.

OVERSEAS, INTERNATIONAL, BANKING Both UK banks with international divisions and overseas banks operating in the UK are changing in line with the whole financial sector, and the career opportunities vary from bank to bank, depending on size and range of services. Although some UK banks still run both domestic and corporate services overseas, branches in other countries mostly employ nationals.

Other UK, and some overseas banks concentrate on providing sophisticated and comprehensive services for international corporate customers. Here the career opportunities are very similar to those in merchant banking, including currency trading, but mostly with greater emphasis on funding international trade.

Overseas banks in the London may also try to exploit particular UK markets – recently, for example, they have been competing for mortgage business.

Opportunities to work abroad for British banks are fairly limited, although career staff in at least one bank can spend most of their working lives in other countries. Most UK banks send career staff on one- or two-year 'tours' in different countries, though, to gain experience. It is possible to get into the career structure of overseas banks operating in London, and then gain promotion overseas.

Recruitment and entry People going into career banking still come largely from the middle-ability range school-leavers, at sixteen-, but increasingly at eighteen-plus. Graduate entry, although still comparatively small, is significant and growing (about 27% of intake in 1986). All areas of banking are now looking for higher-calibre people.

But educational qualifications are not the only factor in selection. 'High standards of appearance and manners are just as important, as are integrity, initiative, pleasing personalities and sense of responsibility.' While the characteristics traditionally associated with banking are still crucial, banking now needs people prepared to be flexible, adaptable, and with the potential to develop marketing skills.

Clearing banks (including TSB) recruit the largest numbers. At present, entry to the 'career structure' of a clearing bank needs at least four O-level-equivalent passes at 16-plus† (including English and mathematics). Recruiting to the six main clearing banks is (1986) running at about 15,400 school-leavers (up from about 12,000 earlier in the 1980s). TSB recruitment is pro rata.

The ratio of people with just O-levels to those with O and A levels is now roughly 50:50 (TSBs 60:40), so even with YTS entry, recruitment at 16-plus is falling, and fewer are recruited with minimal qualifications.

The clearing banks also take about 2000 sixteen-year-olds mainly for two-year YTS schemes (numbers to some extent depend on matching locations where places are available to numbers of potential entrants). While the banks would prefer trainees to have 16-plus† passes in at least English and maths, they do waive their normal requirements, but expect them to pass a literacy and numeracy test. A proportion of these trainees may be offered permanent posts at the end of their training, but this is probably balanced by cuts in the direct 16-plus intake. TSB takes some 50 YTS trainees a year, and expects to keep most of them.

Clearing banks had been expected to recruit about 600 graduates annually between them (up about 100 since the early 1980s) for the next few years, but one alone has increased recruitment to 345 (145 for retail banking) for 1987. They all want people with good degrees. Except for those who go into specialist divisions, subject is immaterial. For specialist divisions a specific subject may be wanted – the international divisions say business studies, economics or languages are useful; trust divisions prefer those with degrees in law, business studies or economics. Again, banks recruit not just on academic ability, but are also looking for the right personal qualities, 'leadership, initiative, enthusiasm, the ability to adapt from theory to practice and ability to work as part of a team'. The clearing banks get between 20 and 80 applications for each graduate place. TSB has a small but full graduate recruitment programme (about 25-30 a year).

Bank of England recruitment has generally been falling for some time, and is difficult for the Bank to predict (in 1979 the sudden end to exchange controls forced the Bank to reduce planned intake by 200). 1986-7 intake was 54 graduates (including 50% 'economically literate' and 7 specialists), 67 with A levels, and 181 O level (in the 1970s the Bank was taking up to 175 at A level and up to 300 at O level, but fewer graduates). Numbers are likely to fall further – projections suggest 30-40 graduates (half economically literate), 25-40 at A level, and 100-150 at O-level equivalent, yearly.

The Bank also runs a two-year YTS scheme, taking about 30 trainees a year. The Bank keeps only about 30%, but almost all the rest get other jobs.

Merchant bank recruitment is normally not large, although 1986-7 may look different since banks have been recruiting extensively for their new securities operations. At least half their intake is already-trained professional lawyers, accountants etc, with experience elsewhere, and all banks are looking for greater expertise and higher qualifications. Estimates of annual graduate intake vary, from about 120 to well over 200. A good degree in accountancy, law, business studies, maths or computer science is probably most useful, but one bank says A grades at A level are more important than degree subject. Most recruitment is now for specific jobs, rather than to a graduate training 'pool'. Over 50% of intake is now from universities other than Oxbridge.

School-leaver intake, mainly with A-levels for long-terms careers, but with at least five O-level-equivalent passes at 16-plus†, is probably similar in numbers.

'Establishment' background is less important now, although the kind of self-confidence and confidence-creating this suggests is still needed (merchant-bank staff have to deal with clients' top management very early in their careers). Merchant bankers live by the quality of their decision-making, and have to make decisions and give advice which may affect the futures of multi-million pound businesses, and even governments. Entrepreneurial instincts, marketing/'abrasive' skills, and a sharp, profit-seeking mind are quoted characteristics. Physical and temperamental stamina to take the pace are also needed.

Qualifications and training Training throughout banking is still largely on-the-job and in-house. The clearing banks and the Bank of England operate their own, often highly-sophisticated internal schemes, programmed learning systems and training centres, but they and the merchant banks release staff to study elsewhere if necessary, eg for an MBA. Increasingly, staff studying for the first stages of professional qualifications get day-release.

Except in, eg specialist departments, for which specific skills or experience are needed, almost everyone aiming for a long-term career starts at the bottom, is taught each routine separately and then spends time practising it.

In clearing banks and TSBs, even graduates start with six to nine months learning quite basic clerical work in a high-street branch. After that, most graduates and some others are given accelerated training, with additional courses, on management development programmes.

In merchant banks, overseas banks, the Bank of England, training in systems also begins with routine work, learning the mechanics of finance and investment, and so on, gaining responsibility, but again normally with accelerated training, and higher-level work, for graduates. The first three years of any banking career should be seen as mainly training, very hard work and sometimes boring and frustrating. All young employees learn as junior members of a team, but at a pace set for each individual, depending largely on the level of entry/educational background and developing potential.

The banks give some training to other staff as well. Clearing bank YTS trainees are taught 'life and work' skills – how to use the phone, and accounting machines for a basic clerical-with-some-financial-content training, gaining a certificate from the Federation of Clearing Bank Employers, 'profiling' their achievements.

Professional qualifications While these are not compulsory, promotion past clerical grades in the retailing sector normally does now depend on gaining them. Merchant banking does not normally need a formal qualification, but some banks now encourage entrants to take IOB, ICSA, ACCA, or Stock Exchange exams.

The Institute of Bankers (UK membership 95,000 in 1986 plus 25,000 overseas), tries to keep pace in its examinations with the greater range of banking activity, and the breakdown of traditional boundaries between the various financial institutions. The aim is to see that junior employees have a thorough grounding in, for instance, investment, taxation, leasing and factoring, and are trained to advise both personal and corporate customers on a whole range of broad financial matters. Future managers also need increasing technical knowledge, and modern marketing and administrative skills. Bank employees' need for a qualification with wider acceptance amongst employers, necessary under modern conditions of increasing job mobility, even in banking, is taken into account. The Institute introduced a new educational/examination structure in 1986, for examination in and after 1987. This is not a 'licence to practise'-style qualification, but one on which a banking career can be built, and with internal bank training, gives an objective yardstick by which employees can show their level of skill.

Stage 1 is now either –

a one-year foundation course (entry requirement at least one A level and an O-level equivalent pass at 16-plus† in English language) covering English, economics, structure of accounts, basic law, and basic banking or investment. Candidates for the exam must have completed a course. Or

BTEC National in business studies, finance core plus accounting and elements of banking in both years. Or

a two- or three-year banking certificate course, a qualification in its own right, designed for senior supervisory staff, practical, job-related. The preliminary section covers business calculations and communications, and the business of banking; the final covers economics and the banks' role in the economy, basic accounting, the legal environment, supervisory skills, and banking operations (international, lending, customer services and marketing). No formal qualifications are needed.

Stage 2, for the Diploma and IOB membership, is taken in banking, international banking, or trustee work. Parts A and B are taken after a two-year study period, part C, two practical papers, after a further year. Graduates can gain subject-for-subject exemptions but for parts A and B only.

A stage-2 level credit card certificate can also be gained.

The financial studies diploma is an optional degree-level qualification, in advanced banking and financial and other management subjects, designed for people aiming at senior management. Entry is via a relevant degree, or professional qualification, or the stage 2 diploma. The main course lasts two years, but direct entrants must take a preliminary one-year course and exam covering the monetary system, international trade and bank services, and accountancy. To date, relatively few have taken the diploma.

Further information from the Banking Information Service, the Institute of Bankers, the Accepting Houses Committee, the Bank of England, and other individual banks.

BUILDING SOCIETIES

They traditionally operate a relatively simple two-way financial service. First, they make it possible for people to invest their savings with a reasonable rate of return, good security, and relatively easy access to their money when they want it. These funds are then used to make long-term loans to members (most of whom are already savers) to buy houses (and land) and/or to build.

While this will continue to be their 'mainstream' business, building societies have been widening and improving their services – with automated teller machines commonplace – to customers for some time, and effectively competing with banks for deposit and recently current accounts. Under new legislation, largely effective from January 1987, they are gaining new freedom, with considerable implications for employment, career prospects and the kind of work they offer.

Building societies can now offer a range of house-buying – from estate agency and surveying to conveyancing – and other financial services, including personal equity plans and pensions. They can hold and develop land for housing. They can, with approval, set up subsidiary companies (in eg banking, insurance broking, hire purchase), can make unsecured loans, and raise up to 20% of their funds from non-retail sources. But 90% of their commercial assets will still have to be in traditional mortgage loans.

As building societies, they will continue to be non-profit making and must invest any surplus funds in completely safe securities, but must use their funds as efficiently as possible. However, from 1988, they can, subject to complex rules and members' approval, become public limited companies.

It is early days to assess how far building societies will exploit this legislation. Early indications suggest they are being cautious, continuing their relatively conservative and traditional outlook and emphasis on reliability and respectability. Only a handful plan to 'demutualise' and offer full banking services to compete directly with banks, and most are being 'highly-selective' in the use of their new powers. Every society is planning a different 'package' of changes, but only the largest can afford to go for major expansion.

Some 75% of home ownership is financed by a rapidly-falling number of building societies, making them a key factor in the lives of over two-thirds of households who are owner-occupiers (and over 40 million people have accounts with them). They are also moving fast towards the point of representing the largest concentration of financial assets in the country, with total 1986 assets nearing £114,000 million between about 150 societies (down from 726 in 1960, and 2286 in 1900), although over 45% of funds are held by the three largest. Rationalisation – due to inflation, technology, competition, and now the new legislation – is likely to speed up, with predictions of only 50-60 societies, with five holding over 80% of assets, by the early 1990s.

Although the number of building societies is falling, the system as a whole was expanding until just recently. Between 1970 and end 1985, the number of branch offices rose from 2000 to over 6900, but fell to just over 6800 in 1986, although frequent predictions of more radical surgery have not (yet) happened.

Career prospects have obviously been improving, and employment growing. The overall number of staff (end 1985) has increased to nearly 65,700 (including several thousand part-time) from 1970's 24,600. The reasons for the mergers are likely to mean that societies will hold down staff numbers where possible, with help from technology, and rationalisation.

Working in building societies

This is largely an office- and desk-based career, with much fairly straightforward administration and routine, which societies computerise as far as is economic. Most staff work in the branches – where they deal extensively with customers, both over their accounts and when negotiating home loans. They can go on to more specialised work in savings or mortgages, or into the various departments of head office – eg mortgage accounts, investment accounts, finance, mortgage securities, accountant, audit, administration, mortgage advances, mortgage administration, mortgage control, marketing, management services etc.

Building societies also employ specialists, such as surveyors, accountants, computer personnel, and these posts tend to make greater demands on personnel than branch management, which is fairly tightly controlled centrally. The new opportunities for expansion may result in demand for other specialists, as well as giving building-society staff opportunities to go into new areas – societies traditionally 'home grow' their own experts. Societies also employ eg secretaries, computer operators, cashiers etc. The gap between career and other staff is widening, especially in the larger societies.

Promotion is generally through progressively more responsible work in the branch system and/or head office departments, on a similar pattern to the clearing banks, starting with clerical work and up to branch and more senior management via the various departments. Managerial opportunities – and training – are greater with the larger societies. Promotion usually involves moving, from branch to branch or head office, or to another society. The virtual end to growth in numbers of branches has recently resulted in a promotion bottleneck, but this, and problems faced by older staff in adapting to new services and systems has led some societies to introduce early retirement schemes, so prospects look fair for today's entrants.

Building-society management has been getting steadily more demanding, taking greater professionalism, as societies grew larger, with competition, and new technology. More home buyers at a time of high unemployment has lead to the need for, eg more careful arrears management.

The new legislation intensifies the problems of strategic planning; decisions on whether or not to expand out of traditional business will involve complex planning of organisational, managerial and staffing structures. Marketing strategies, still relatively new to building societies, will have to become more sophisticated, and ways found to deal with greater and (even) more intense competition and technology. Building societies work on very tight margins, and since they must, by law, maximise their investments, finance, especially functions such as corporate treasury, are also increasingly important.

Recruitment and entry Traditionally entrants have started straight from school, but in future the societies may have to 'buy in' particular experience and expertise, and widen/raise the ability range of new intake. Although it may be possible to get into a society with less that the stated minimal qualifications of four O-level-equivalent passes at 16-plus† (including English and mathematics), prospects are generally better with two A levels. CBSI figures also suggest graduate entry is already significant – of students registering for the first time in 1986 alone, over 33% (123) were graduates, 32% (119) had A levels, over 18% had gained BTEC Nationals, and 3% HND/C. At least four societies now (1986) have full graduate management trainee schemes, and a number of others recruit fairly regularly.

Building societies also take 'quite substantial numbers' each year onto YTS schemes.

Qualifications and training Training is largely still on-the-job, over three or four years, with some formal schemes and day-release for courses with larger societies, but most exam preparation still has to be by spare-time study. The Building Societies Institute also organises a range of residential training courses at all levels to complement society-provided. The CBSI and the Building Societies Association jointly sponsor training schemes. Some societies have accelerated training schemes for graduates, but reports suggest training for management is not yet matching the new demands being made on staff.

Professional qualification is via the Chartered Building Societies Institute (membership still small at just over 8000 in 1986, but growing). CBSI qualifications are not essential, but increasingly useful for promotion and career staff are expected to take CBSI, or other appropriate exams, eg ICSA, CIMA, ACCA.

Direct entry to the newly-revised and upgraded eight-paper membership exams requires four O-level-equivalent passes at 16-plus† and two A levels (graduates may be exempted from up to four papers on a subject-for-subject basis).

Students with 16-plus passes but no A levels can take either a BTEC National (preferably with specific modules in building society work), or the new CBSI certificate in building society practice (for which there are no formal entry requirements), or an equivalent.

Further information from the Chartered Building Societies Institute.

INSURANCE
The insurance business — working in insurance — specialist work: actuarial work — adjusting — agency inspecting — branch management — claims —

insurance broking — Lloyd's — pension management — risk or insurance management — surveying — underwriting — other work

The insurance business

Insurance deals in risks, but as a by-product, offers a means of saving for many. It is a multi-million-pound business built on the law of averages, so that if a great many people pay relatively small sums of money to protect themselves financially against some kind of loss which is only going to happen to some (and relatively few) of them, then those who do suffer can be compensated, from the funds collected.

It may sound simple, but at the scale on which insurance companies work, the business is very complex. Insurers also have to make a profit, and they have to make sound investments, so that they can cover their liabilities if claims are made. This takes considerable expertise, to decide on the exact degree of risk for each policy, and then to set fair premiums and conditions to meet it. They have a combination of long-established principles, guidelines and experience to work on, but it is still a form of gambling (using the law of averages) on a grand scale. Insurance cannot be too cautious, because if the premiums are too high or the conditions too strict, then people simply won't insure.

There is virtually no limit to the risks which can be insured against. It is possible to insure material possessions against the direct cash value of their loss, or to protect oneself or family against, for example, personal risks such as death or disablement. There are 'special' schemes such as these which enable parents to spread the cost of school fees. In general, however, there are eight generally accepted 'classes' of insurance: life (including industrial life assurance), property (including fire and theft), marine, aviation and transport, motor vehicle, personal accident and sickness, liability to third party (including employer's liability), pecuniary loss (including fidelity guarantee, credit and consequential loss insurance), and the fast-growing reinsurance of any of the above (in which the original insurers reduce their risk by taking out an insurance with another insurance company for part of the total risk).

Insurance has a very marked effect on the country's economy. The 840 or so insurance companies (including, for example, subsidiaries of major banks, and some 160 overseas companies), are the largest single group of investors, with some £171,000 million held in trust for policy-holders (1985). This is a major source of financing for industry and commerce of all kinds, and in fact supplies some half of long-term capital needs. However, the 400 member companies of the British Insurance Association account for 90% of the market, and the largest twenty take most of the business. Insurance also contributes to Britain's 'invisible' earnings overseas: £3.32 million in 1985, nearly 45% of total UK invisible earnings. Premium income was £11,200 million for general business and £14,800 million for life assurance, world-wide in 1985.

Life and general insurance differ greatly. Life is the only long-term insurance business, ie usually lasting ten years or more, and is the only form of business insuring against something that is inevitable – retirement or death. Other forms of insurance are taken out against risks which may not happen, and the premiums agreed at the start of the contract remain unchanged. Life insurance is generally, therefore, organised on rather different lines from more general activities.

New risks are being covered in non-life insurance all the time. Technology brings new kinds of cover: the British market first covered a satellite launching, of 'Early Bird', in 1965, including third-party risk against collision with other satellites. Insurers paid NASA to recover a satellite, and then re-sold it. Other 'modern' risks insured against include kidnapping, computer failure, North sea oil-rig disasters, and nuclear reactor leaks. The scale of modern construction – massive dams, and tower blocks involving the use of, eg tower cranes, produces further insurance headaches. All of these involve completely new kinds of problem-solving for insurance assessors. A substantial proportion of the non-life market is in fire insurance, and again the hazards of new materials (both building and furnishing) and modern construction methods have added to the insurance problems which still include contending with the difficulties of older buildings which lack proper fire protection. Over half of all business in the non-life sector is concentrated amongst just ten major companies.

While insurance business has expanded steadily for many years, it is not always so easy to make a profit. The industry has had some difficult years in the 1980s, and good results are needed just to maintain, let alone increase, employment. Numbers have fallen, and although they recovered to nearly 237,000 (including 15,000 part time) at end 1986, are still not back to the 275,000 of 1981. Mergers and increasing use of computer-based systems (for accounting, policy renewal, premium collection and records generally, claims applications) are also responsible. More office technology – with branches being linked up to head office – almost certainly means fewer lower-grade clerical and data processing jobs, but numbers of specialist and professional staff are expected to stay at roughly present levels for the immediate future.

Insurance is a very varied industry, employing a relatively high proportion of specialists. They may work in any one of the three broad divisions of the insurance market: the insurance companies, Lloyd's underwriters, and brokers.

Working in insurance
Companies vary considerably in size and scope. Some specialise in one kind of insurance (over a quarter in life, alone); others do business in several types, and are known as composite companies. Company men and women are said to work either inside (for example, actuaries and underwriters) or outside (for example, sales staff and surveyors). Claims officials, for instance, may work inside and outside, though.

The work of a large insurance firm is divided between its area branches and head office.

Branches are generally responsible for day-to-day business, which means finding and negotiating new contracts, calculating premiums and preparing policies, revising policies according to changing needs and conditions, and dealing with income, correspondence, and straightforward claims. The number of branches has been substantially reduced in recent years, following several mergers and the need to cut high staff costs; some have been replaced by small sub-branch offices but with only a handful of staff.

In head office, the division is between administration and underwriting departments. Head office deals with policy and guidelines for deciding on risks, premiums, etc in the specialist underwriting departments and claims. It also deals with investment management where company funds must be invested to give the highest yield consistent with security and with the fact that sufficient funds must always be available to meet claims and other company require-ments – total assets were over £134.1 million at end-84. Reserves must be properly and safely invested – involving highly trained investment analysts. Otherwise, administration involves the functions found in any commercial firm, such as the secretary's office, accountant, personnel, publicity.

Most insurance companies are highly automated and computerised (one of the industry's main problems is to cut the large percentage of premium income, about a third, which goes in expenses, and automation is one way of cutting expenditure, particularly on labour). Most have had large data-processing departments for many years, and are moving with new office technology to the extent that most people entering the industry now will routinely use computers and computer terminals.

The underwriting departments are generally divided according to types of insurance carried by the company and to the degree of specialisation – one company may have a single fire and accident department, another may separate them. In addition, separate departments deal with overseas insurance and supervise branch management.

While every branch or department is largely made up of specialist staff (see below), each also has a full complement of managerial and supervisory staff (mostly promoted from specialist insurance work).

General recruitment and entry Insurance companies recruit at a number of levels, both direct from the education system, and amongst mature and experi-enced people, depending on need.

Overall recruitment has been fairly static lately, after some years at low levels (resulting from technological change, tight economic conditions, and very low levels of staff turnover) and redundancies. Recruitment has, however, increased in, most notably, life assurance. CII claims that the increased versatility possible with new technology, increasing complexity and diversity of insurance offered, is widening the range of job opportunities.

No rigid entry qualifications, but for people planning a long-term career, most insurance companies prefer eighteen-year-olds with two A-level passes, or a BTEC National. One indicator of the ratio between differing qualifications is CII 1986 registrations – 35% A levels, 35% mature (over 25), 16% graduate, and 14% BTEC.

Figures are not available, but it is likely that recruitment of people with A-levels is still below the 3000 a year of the late 1970s. Companies do take some sixteen- and seventeen-year-olds with at least four O-level equivalent passes. Major companies have YTS schemes.

Graduate recruitment is rising steadily, and is probably at least 1000 a year, nearly half becoming trainee actuaries and most of the rest going into the thirty or largest companies, and the six largest brokers. Any degree subject is acceptable for general insurance work, although obviously some are more useful eg behavioural sciences, business studies, economics, languages, law or mathematics; engineering or some sciences for underwriting, surveying or claims inspection in specialist fields. While a relatively high proportion of insurance companies still recruit for specific posts and are therefore looking for particular disciplines, more companies are now seeing graduate recruits as potential managers. Competition for graduate traineeships is rising.

Most companies also recruit for clerical and other support work, such as computer operating.

As well as qualities needed for any business-related career, insurance takes intelligence to master technical information and problems, the ability to explain complex matters in simple language, and to develop a sense of judgement – of risks, situations, and people.

See also individual professions etc following.

Qualifications and training Training is largely on-the-job and in-house, and most people, graduates included, spend some time learning via routine work. All the major life and composite insurance groups have extensive training schemes, both administrative and technical, ranging from induction courses for school-leavers to specialist training for senior management. CII's 'College' provides comprehensive courses for the smaller companies unable to operate their own, including three-month and one-year full-time courses for associate-ship exams, and courses on more specialised aspects of insurance such as aviation underwriting. Training schemes and methods are improving, and some release for courses etc is usual.

Professional qualification Chartered Insurance Institute (1986 membership over 59,000) qualifications are now essential for promotion. Some 22,000 people sat for CII exams in 1985-6.

Direct entry to CII qualifying examinations needs at least two O-level equivalent passes at 16-plus† and two at A level (or the equivalent in A and/or AS levels). The subjects must include English and one of a stipulated range at A level, or three A levels in any subjects (Scottish requirements differ slightly).

Entrants without these qualifications may take the exams after either –
A BTEC National in business studies, or
CII's four-paper introductory exam (age at least 20, and at least four O-level-equivalent passes at 16-plus† in 'academic' subjects),
Associate membership examinations (taken only after at least four years' appropriate experience) take account of the specialist knowledge needed in the various sections of insurance. Associate membership is a general qualification, while fellowship papers allow students to qualify in one of: life, motor and liability, property, marine or aviation, pension, reinsurance. Some examinations require background knowledge in other areas: for example, the life branch requires sufficient anatomy and physiology for candidates to deal with underwriting problems. Graduates with appropriate degree subjects, people with other, related professional qualifications, or BTEC Higher awards may gain exemptions.

Other CII qualifications include –
Certificate of Proficiency: a basic qualification (six months part-time study and two exam papers) which anyone can take (no formal entry requirements), and optionally go on to professional exams without the usual age/

educational qualifications.
Life Assurance Salesmen's Certificate: based on a six-paper examination.
Entry qualifications as for associateship.
See also individual professions etc following.

The insurance specialists
The insurance world employs a very wide range of skills and training, and there
are a number of very clearly-defined specialist careers.

ACTUARIAL WORK Actuaries are the experts who minimise the financial risks in
the life assurance business. They do so mainly via complex statistical analysis.

Actuaries decide the terms on which life policies can be issued, surrendered or
changed (all of which must be kept constantly under review to keep pace with
changing conditions). They do so by (statistically) analysing the life expec-
tancy of different groups of people from known (but very complex) data drawn
from a wide range of sources and made up of constantly changing factors –
which affect how long people live (whether or not they smoke, or are overweight, or come from a particular area, for example), and how it changes with,
for instance, medical and social developments.

Second, they calculate the funds which must be built up to cover the long-term
liabilities. They also have to value their company's liabilities and assets in
relation to the policies issued regularly, and decide what bonus distributions to
make. This is more complex than it sounds – the number of policies at any one
time is likely to be immense, and the terms extremely varied as they will have
been issued at varying times and under varying conditions.

In each life assurance office, the actuary is legally responsible for certifying
that the life funds are solvent (ie that sufficient assets are held to meet
liabilities) to the Department of Trade. Few general managers of life offices
are *not* actuaries.

Actuaries are generally responsible for overall planning, and deciding on and
carrying out investment policy, since the expected investment return and the
nature and value of assets are also part of their calculations. They supervise the
underwriting of new policies and the design of types of contract especially in
the field of pension schemes, advise on legal and tax questions (because
actuarial calculations have to take account of these). Actuaries go on developing and refining actuarial techniques, including ways of using and improving
computer systems.

The actuarial profession is relatively small but highly influential, with some
2400 working in the UK (about 3600 world-wide) in 1985 – but has been
growing steadily (from under 800 in the UK in 1955) and is expected to go on
doing so. Demand for qualified actuaries continues to be high, and the
(English) Institute estimates it could increase by about 60% over the next ten
years.

Most actuaries still work in life assurance, or closely-related areas such as
employee-benefit work and pension fund management. A growing proportion
apply their skills to reducing other kinds of financial risks. They are no longer
narrow specialists just quantifying the uncertainties of life, but experts able to
assess the variables in all kinds of investments – at least 11% of the members

of the Society of Investment Analysts are actuaries, for example. Actuaries were reputedly in at the birth of operational research in world war II, but surprisingly few are in it now.

Under 60% of all English qualified/part qualified actuaries (1985) actually work in life assurance offices. The largest areas of growth have been in independent consulting practice (335 in 1985 against under 40 in 1955), and in pension consultancy (168 in 1985 against only one in 1955). About 90 work in industry and commerce, about 86 on the Stock Exchange (giving investment advice, in research and investment analysis), around 26 for the government (down from nearly 40 in 1955) and over 100 in other areas of employment – investment, insurance broking, merchant banking, academic work, computer development, for example.

In the CIVIL SERVICE, most actuaries work in the government actuary's department, a few in the DHSS, the Home Office, the Ministry of Defence, and the statistician's department.

The government actuary's department deals mainly with national insurance and similar benefits, but due to cost and political sensitivity, most importantly with state pensions. The department acts as an independent adviser to the government, for instance reviewing financing of national insurance and industrial injuries schemes and examining the financial effect of major changes in them. This often involves fundamental studies of population projections, morbidity and similar statistical and demographic work. It reports on the financial effect of uprating benefit levels, for example, and advises the Reserve Pension Scheme and the Occupational Pensions Boards. It also does the actuarial work on pensions schemes for government employees and nationalised industries and scrutinises actuarial certificates submitted by insurance companies. Actuaries in government service have to take account of political and social as well as financial considerations.

Recruitment and entry Most recruits start as trainees in life offices. Over 90% of entrants are graduates (most with first or second class honours), but the Institute deliberately keeps its entry requirements flexible: the minimum is five GCE/GCSE passes (including O-level-equivalent English) including two A levels – one a mathematical subject at grade A or B – two AS levels will probably be acceptable in place of the second A level. The percentage of A-level entrants is now 7-8% a year. The (Scottish) Faculty requires three H grades including maths at grade A and English, plus CSYS in two maths papers with grade A in one and at least grade B in a second.

A degree in mathematics is not essential or even the best choice, and in fact any degree subject, including a science, provided the graduate has A-level maths is acceptable. Two or all three of maths, economics, and statistics are recommended.

The number of entrants had been expected to settle at about 300 a year, but new registrations to the Institute reached 380 (550 including overseas), and 67 to the Faculty in 1985. (The Institute had 2750 registered students in 1986, the Faculty 322.)

Actuaries need mathematical flair rather than highly specialist knowledge, an interest in business as a career (but with a scientific basis), and the ability to communicate clearly and simply assessments based on highly complex technicalities to people outside the profession.

Qualifications and training Training for actuarial work is long and tough. The minimum is three or four years, even for a graduate, and it can take up to seven. Articled service is not required, but extensive practical experience is needed to pass the Institute of Actuaries' or the (Scottish) Faculty of Actuaries' exams. Most students therefore work in life assurance offices or under a consultant.

Exemptions, even for 'relevant' degrees, are not extensive. City U, Heriot-Watt U, London (LSE) first-degree courses in actuarial science give the maximum. Actuarial options at London (QMC) and Kent U also give some.

The Institute's ten-part examination covers probability, statistics, compound interest, life and other contingencies, investment principles and economic background, mortality and other investigations, institutional investment, life assurance, general insurance, and pension funds. Pass rates are low. Graduates can gain exemptions for up to five parts, on a subject-for-subject basis. One-year postgraduate diploma courses at City U and Heriot-Watt U exempt from most of the first six subjects. Tuition is given by the Actuarial Tuition Service.

ADJUSTING Adjusters are the industry's detectives. They are impartial and independent specialists, called in by a policy-holder, the broker, or the underwriter (or maybe all three) to assess and apportion legal and financial liability in a claim which may be very large, or where there is some disagreement on who should carry what proportion of the responsibility for the loss. Many claims are, of course, settled with comparative ease by the insurer's own claims officials (see below), and adjusters may not be needed. In marine insurance, however, losses are usually large and the issues involved generally complex. Some adjusters therefore specialise in marine work, and are called average adjusters. Those who deal with other kinds of loss are normally known as loss adjusters (they never, however, deal with life insurance claims).

The adjuster's importance lies in absolute impartiality, and they are therefore members of independent partnerships or firms, specialising solely in this, and advisory, work arising out of it. The adjuster may be involved in settling problems of, for example, disposing of a wrecked ship's cargo, repairs, towage. In reaching an adjustment the adjuster may help to compile a list of all the costs involved, and consults a wide range of other experts, including surveyors, lawyers, brokers and valuers, and the policy holder.

Adjusting is a very highly-skilled profession, needing extensive experience. It is also a very small profession, although numbers have been increasing. Fully qualified loss adjusters number (1986) about 700 in the UK (against only 500 in 1979), plus over 850 in training. Fully-qualified average adjusters number (1986) only 60. The growth in numbers has probably levelled off, and it is most unlikely that it will increase again at least for the next few years.

Recruitment and entry Most adjusters have already spent long periods working in the insurance field, mostly as claims officials, and already have professional qualifications in insurance, surveying, or accountancy, or a degree in, for instance, law. Although the formal minimum qualifications are GCE/GCSE O-level equivalent and A levels, the chance of an eighteen-year-old school-leaver being recruited as a trainee is extremely remote, although graduates are sometimes taken on.

Qualifications and training Professional qualifications are essential, and both professional bodies require entrants to train with recognised firms.

The Chartered Institute of Loss Adjusters requires entrants to pass a preliminary examination of nine subjects (based in CII's associate examination), an intermediate exam of two subjects, and a final of five subjects. Before attempting the final, candidates must normally have had five years' experience under supervision, Some qualifications (eg surveying) may cut this to three years, and give some exemptions.

The Association of Average Adjusters advises entrants to start by taking CII Associate exams. Before taking the Association's four-paper exam (to be passed at one sitting), students must complete five years' training with ACII, eight without.

AGENCY INSPECTING Inspectors are part supervisors, part specialists and part salesmen or women. They are a link between the people who deal with clients and the insurance company itself, and generally, therefore, work from a branch.

Insurance is 'sold' by a wide variety of different people, and about half is brought in by people who do not even work in insurance. They include solicitors, accountants, estate agents, people who sell cars, who arrange insurance for their clients or customers when they buy a house or car. The other half comes through insurance brokers (see below) or the full-time home service agents (below). Some companies also employ direct-selling representatives (below).

Agency inspectors supervise a group of agents, deal on a regular basis with a group of insurance brokers, and also seek to bring in new business. They deal, either directly or through brokers, with local clients whose insurance needs are more complex than the agent normally deals with, tailoring the form of cover to the client's needs. Agency inspectors have to know a great deal about the terms and conditions on which insurance is offered. They assess 'insurability' of any risk (which means having to understand the potential hazards of particular materials or processes, for example) often using an expert, such as a doctor on the medical viability of a client's life insurance or a surveyor on the soundness of a building. Inspectors know what types of insurance their areas will produce – for instance, in a residential area mainly life policies, but agricultural, industrial, or port areas will give a different mix – and monitor local values. Inspectors keep in touch with policy holders, deal with small claims, queries on accounts, and small surveys. They may also do some direct selling.

It is a job which needs extensive experience and technical knowledge. Most inspectors have normally worked for some time as branch clerks, and completed a professional qualification, and so usually become agents between the ages of 23 and 28, rarely before 21. Promotion is generally via branch management. In smaller branches the post of manager and senior inspector may be combined.

Recruitment, qualifications etc see general paragraphs above.

AGENCY WORK The home service agents represent the insurance world to many British households, on whom they call frequently. They mostly canvass for and arrange life insurance, explain policies and conditions, deal with problems and personally collect premiums regularly, but also bring in more general fire and accident insurance, and the newer, more sophisticated forms of life insurance. Home-service agents can be unofficial social workers in their areas and develop personal relationships with families.

Agents are usually recruited either after a period of grounding as a branch-office clerk or after gaining experience of this kind of work in another area of employment. They must, however, develop a comprehensive knowledge of insurance and related business matters.

A few insurance companies also employ direct-selling representatives, again mainly in life assurance, using sophisticated marketing skills more usual in other areas of selling. Such sales representatives often sell in the wider field called financial planning, making up insurance 'packages' providing for estate duty, taxation, and company insurance as well as more conventional life cover. Direct sales people usually have experience in another occupation.

Recruitment, qualifications etc see general paragraphs above.

BRANCH MANAGEMENT Branch managers are in charge of all the 'teams' working within the branch and any satellite sub-branches (the trend is to fewer branches), working through their supervisors. These include the agency inspectors, underwriters, claims staff, and administration. The branch manager must see that the branch meets cash flow projections. The manager may become involved in, for example, a large new contract, or a claim where the negotiations run into problems. The manager has to see that all sections are running smoothly, including staffing and training. Most branch managers have come through, eg agency inspection.

CLAIMS are handled by teams of officials and assessors, who work 'inside' the company, and inspectors who work 'outside', assessing and investigating.

With the value of single insured losses is rising steadily, this is very responsible work. It also takes great tact, as company reputation is dependent to some extent on the way in which claims are handled. Clients expect their insurance companies to settle claims fairly and efficiently, and since claims officials are the company's representative here, they must make decisions which are demonstrably reasonable, and cope with the personal distress which often goes with a claim.

In some companies, all claims are dealt with by one department in head office; in others, most are handled by claims departments attached to a branch office, or one claims department servicing a group of branches. Some companies use independent firms of loss adjusters (see above).

Claims inspectors investigate supposed insured losses and arrange settlement. Obviously the majority of claims are straightforward and need only straightforward checking, but a proportion give the inspector enough knotty problems to justify the claim of many that this is one of the most interesting aspects of insurance work – probably most demanding is settling claims under public liability policies which protect holders against legal liability to other people, so can involve hard bargaining before a settlement is reached. Some may have to be investigated more fully, and may involve asking for and assessing reports from legal, medical and technical experts.

Claims officials need extensive legal and technical knowledge and must be able to assess the reports of experts who may have to be called in on claims. It is, of course, the claims official who may be the first to detect the possibility of crime or fraud. However, these are rare and claims officials are expected to co-operate fully with the policy holder and give help where needed.

Recruitment, qualifications etc see general paragraphs above.

INSURANCE BROKING Brokers are independent professionals who advise on, arrange and negotiate individual policies or complete insurance packages for their clients looking for the best buy. The broker is therefore working for the customer. This may be an individual looking for the best deal for car insurance, through to large companies which have to insure factories in the Midlands, offices in London, machinery and computers, trucks and warehouses all over the country, raw materials and finished goods in factories and in transit, against personal liability, as well as employees. One group specialises in marine insurance, and are Lloyd's brokers.

Brokers must be able to give expert advice to clients on how to avoid expensive cover, and their knowledge of the insurance market must see that the initial plan takes into account the principles of insurability. Brokers must also have encyclopedic knowledge of all sections of the market, and know how individual insurance companies (and individual underwriters) work to get the best terms for the client. However, brokers are paid (with a percentage of the premium) by the underwriter and not by the client.

Insurance brokers provide a very large, and increasing, proportion of the insurance market's income. Their share of marine insurance business is at least 94% of the total (all business done at Lloyd's must be placed through approved brokers), 76% of commercial and personal accident insurance, 52% of private motor business, a fifth of household insurance, 80% of insured pensions, but virtually no industrial life, only 25% of ordinary life. Three-fifths of brokerage business is now done overseas, including the US, but with increasing penetration of the Middle East, South America and the Far East.

Licensed brokerage firms number about 5000, but the 3800 (employing 55,000) BIBA members account for well over 90% of business. The major 260 (employing some 20,000 people) are accredited to deal with Lloyd's underwriters (see below) and do most of the business. Firms range in size from the large London-based, employing up to 6000, through those in major provincial centres employing 20 to 30, to the very small private firms with a single principal. Some brokers accept any kind of business, others specialise in one or more of the main branches of insurance, particularly reinsurance, and others in overseas business. Brokers do not normally try to attract personal accounts, although they will usually handle them, if asked.

This is increasingly an international business, and is beginning to outgrow its more traditional, family-based attitudes.

Within the brokerage house are three main kinds of work –

Selling is done by 'account executives' who go out and get business. This is direct selling, mostly by personal contact and finding ways to offer a competitive insurance proposal – which often includes assessing possible risks, how to cover them and how to reduce risks (of fire or burglary for example), so that the insurance will cost less. All this usually needs the expertise of the technicians.

Second in the chain are the office 'technicians' who actually draw up the proposals for clients. Some may be 'standard' but often they involve insuring something unusual, or very expensive (and so the risk may have to be split between more two or more insurers), or involve a package.

Third, the brokers themselves, called 'placement' brokers, who go to underwriters with a proposal, to find the best quotation for covering the particular risk. They know which insurance companies or Lloyd's syndicates are most likely to accept a particular risk, must be ready to discuss the risk (and so understand the problems and be well briefed), negotiate terms and take split-second decisions based on extensive experience.

Recruitment and entry As general paragraphs above, but brokers have to be rather more 'entrepreneurial' than others in the industry. International business requires languages and brokers must understand the legal and financial systems of the countries they work with.

The largest firms take, on average, ten graduates a year, plus computer specialists, and about 50-60 school-leavers, mainly with A levels. Firms in the middle range (c600 employees), rarely take graduates, but still need about 50 school-leavers a year. Some 400 brokers take around 100 trainees a year between them under a BIBA-run YTS scheme. About 60% stay in broking, and 90% get jobs.

Qualifications and training Most larger brokerage houses provide training facilities, although some brokers begin their careers in insurance companies. The British Insurance Brokers Association (BIBA) supports training in brokerage firms with studentships and bursary schemes. Trainee brokers are normally expected to take CII examinations (see above).

LLOYD'S is not an insurance company, but an incorporated society of private insurers, an insurance market where individual underwriters do business for themselves, at their own risk, and in competition with each other. It is, traditionally, the centre for marine insurance and shipping intelligence, although marine insurance is now only 40% of business. Lloyd's has (1987) 32,000 'names' – underwriting members (over three times the 1970 figure) with an estimated total premium of £6000 million in 1985 (half in reinsurance, and 80% from overseas), formed into 370 groups or 'syndicates' varying in size from two or three to around one hundred.

Members are elected and must be able to underwrite insurance with unlimited liability, so they have to meet very tough financial standards – realisable assets of over £100,000. Each syndicate, which usually specialises in particular aspects of insurance (such as thoroughbred racehorses or legal liability risk), normally has a professional underwriter in 'the Room' (the traditional name for the huge hall where business is done) to act on its behalf (syndicate members may not be professional underwriters at all, but bankers, farmers, merchants, retired boxers, pop stars and tennis players).

Lloyd's underwriters Each syndicate is 'managed' by one of 240 underwriting agencies (down from 400 in 1985), employing an estimated 6-7000 between them. Each employs its own professional underwriters and a number of other underwriting staff who are usually training or gaining experience (eighty or more people altogether in the largest agencies), as well as other staff including accounts staff of sixty or more in the largest.

Lloyd's has no hard-and-fast rules on educational background for underwriting. Some only have a few O-level equivalent passes at 16-plus†, some A levels, but only a few are graduates so far. Intake is small. All learn their profession primarily by working their way up from junior clerk and learn underwriting by listening to seniors discussing risks. However, increasing numbers of Lloyd's underwriters are taking CII examinations, and professionalism is growing.

Lloyd's staff The Committee of Lloyd's provides a supporting and administrative service for the syndicates with some 2000 staff in 14 different departments. The larger departments are sited in Chatham, not London. The departments include –
policy-signing office employing over 700 people (from several professions and skills), who verify the accuracy of policies, sign them for the underwriters and provide accounting details of each transaction – the office processes several million items a year using computers – computing employs 400;
central technical insurance/claims office employs 300, training its own adjusters;
advisory department which specialises in rules and customs relating to certain types of business;
an agency department controls the network of about 1500 Lloyd's agents and sub-agents world-wide, who settle claims, carry out surveys and provide shipping information – it arranges arbitration following salvage of wrecked ships;
the aviation department has a staff of qualified aircraft surveyors who investigate accidents and supervise repairs, and also provides a world-wide information service;
other departments include average and recoveries, foreign legislation (which tries to see it recognises Lloyd's constitution, services arrangements made with foreign governments and advises underwriters), and intelligence (arranges reports on any subject of interest to underwriters and provides a shipping information service). The regulatory departments have expanded lately, and straight administration – which includes looking after the buildings – employs people with appropriate qualifications.

Recruitment, entry etc Intake is quite small, and mainly for Chatham. Some 50-60 school-leavers with O-level equivalents at 16-plus† or A levels, and about 15 graduates are currently recruited each year. 'Hundreds' apply for every vacancy.

PENSIONS MANAGEMENT developed following legislation which brought extensive growth of occupational pension schemes. Pension funds collectively have (1985) assets of £157.27 million, mostly held in securities, so managers are major investors. Schemes have to be designed, negotiated and the funds' 'portfolios' managed and invested. This is expert work, and employs actuaries, solicitors, accountants, pension consultants and brokers, investment managers (at least 2000) and corporate treasurers as well as administrators.

Qualifications and training is as in the general paragraphs above, but an alternative qualification is awarded by –
The Pensions Management Institute (formed 1976) sets examinations covering the operation, management and administration of pension funds. schemes etc. The nine papers are taken over a three-year study period. At least three years' relevant experience is also required for full membership. Entry qualifications are four O-level equivalent passes at 16-plus† and at least one A level, passes to include English language and mathematics, but qualifications are expected to alter over the next few years.

RISK OR INSURANCE MANAGEMENT Risk, or insurance, managers are employed mainly by large companies and organisations whose need for insurance cover is large enough to warrant having staff to keep it under continuous review, to see that the extent of the cover is in reasonable relation to the cost, that insurance is adapted and altered to changing needs, and that short-term risks are covered.

Risk managers watch out for new risks within the company, and suggest ways of controlling or avoiding them, eg by removing possible causes of fires or accidents. They therefore get involved in safety work and training. It is a relatively new function, and similar to the work of the insurance broker, only on the inside rather than as an outside adviser. Some brokers offer risk management consultancy.

Recruitment and entry normally via earlier and extensive experience in another other branch of insurance.

Qualifications and training see general paragraphs above.

SURVEYING, in the insurance world, is not the same as professional surveying described under LAND USE PROFESSIONS. Insurance surveyors act as fact-finders for underwriters, who rely heavily on their technical reports, mostly in fire and accident insurance. A fire surveyor reports on buildings to be insured, showing how it is built, what materials were used, what machinery there is inside, what work goes on, whether there are fire escapes or not, what fire prevention and hazards there are. Burglary surveyors examine premises to see what the security arrangements are or are needed, and the contents being insured. Liability surveyors report on precautions against possible hazards and avoidance of unnecessary risk.

Insurance surveyors not only report on anything which may affect the insurance contract, but also recommend improvements which could be made and may even advise on appropriate precautions before buildings go up.

Recruitment, entry, qualifications and training Surveyors are normally recruited from amongst 'inside' insurance staff who show aptitude, and have a 'technical' background (in eg engineering, science). They are trained inside the company and may be promoted to senior technical work or underwriting. Brokers' surveyors can combine broking with surveying.

UNDERWRITING Underwriters are experts in insurance itself. They decide whether a particular risk is insurable, and if so, on what terms and conditions to accept it. Premiums must be set in the light of some more generalised considerations – for example, they must provide a large enough aggregate to pay claims under the class of insurance concerned, cover their share of company overheads, contribute towards reserves and still leave a profit for the company. If premiums are too high or the terms too strict, the company loses business because people won't buy their policies, but if they are too low the company will lose money. Policies must also be worded very precisely, especially in terms of the liabilities to be accepted and any special conditions or terms.

In some areas of insurance, especially life, fairly standard premiums are charged according to the risk (as assessed by the actuary), but some parts of particular proposals, for instance a client's medical record, are looked into and assessed by an underwriter. Where risks are unique or unusual, an underwriter has to rely on experience and judgement, based on as much factual and often technical information (such as the surveyor's report) as possible and using records and analyses of related cases.

Underwriters also decide on and organise reinsurance with other companies or underwriters for high risks or very heavy liabilities, what proportion to reinsure, with whom and on what terms.

Underwriters usually specialise in one particular branch of insurance, because they need to develop considerable expertise in the field and understand all the technicalities involved. For example –

In life assurance, underwriters need substantial medical background knowledge, and must be able to assess, for example, what kinds of medical history are average or high-risk, what occupations and age groups are at risk to what hazards, and so on.

Marine underwriters (who may specialise in one aspect, such as hull, cargo or freight insurance) must know a great deal about ship construction and operation, the seas in which they operate and the cargoes they carry.

Motor insurance takes both knowledge of the vehicles themselves and extremely detailed knowledge of the accident potential and therefore the driving habits of all classes and types of driver.

Underwriters must also know about the legal implications of any class of insurance, be able to recognise and assess anything unusual about a proposal, and generally develop an 'underwriting flair' for detecting possible snags.

Company underwriters work along broad guidelines set by company underwriting policy (and sometimes companies will agree an even broader general policy between them) and have a great many statistics and actuarial reports to turn to. However, there are always new risks to be insured (safari park accidents for example), and technological and other developments mean that underwriters must continually make new assessments often based on their own personal knowledge of similar circumstances or parallel developments. Underwriters often travel, since so much insurance business is overseas.

Recruitment, entry, training etc see general paragraphs, and Lloyd's, above.

Other work

Most insurance firms are very large organisations, and have to employ large numbers of people in 'functions' other than those directly involved with insurance. They include –

COMPUTER STAFF The industry has always taken full advantage of computer technology, and constantly looks for ways of exploiting new developments, often doing much of the necessary adaptations to insurance needs itself. Companies are at present developing real-time management information systems. They employ computing staff in some numbers, in eg programming, systems design, with structured promotion, possibly into management.

INVESTMENT MANAGEMENT Efficient investment of premiums is crucial if companies are to meet their commitment – and the industry is the largest institutional investor on the Stock Exchange. Investment managers aim for the highest rate of return that does not jeopardise security, and gives the liquidity needed to meet claims. Large numbers of experts are employed.

ESTATE AND PROPERTY MANAGEMENT Most companies invest heavily in property, and this has to be efficiently managed, valued, bought and sold, redeveloped and improved. Most property managers are RICS-qualified.

PERSONNEL MANAGEMENT Insurance is labour intensive, and demands efficient recruitment and development management, has major training commitments, and has to plan for the future.

SUPPORT STAFF, including secretarial and clerical staff, work as –

Processing clerks give a back-up service to underwriters, doing routine work like keeping records up to date, taking information from proposal forms to be used in preparing policy documents, photocopying, collecting statistical information. This usually means learning to use a computer terminal.

Underwriting clerks help to prepare quotations for proposals (often using reference books and computer terminals) and send out forms.

Claims clerks check that policies on which claims are being made are up to date and paid up, checking records, often via a computer terminal.

Other clerical posts are in accounts, personnel, and with brokers.

Recruitment, entry etc see general paragraphs above.

Further information from the Chartered Insurance Institute Careers Advisory Office, the Institute of Actuaries, the British Insurance Brokers Association, the Faculty of Actuaries, the Chartered Institute of Loss Adjusters, the Association of Average Adjusters, Lloyd's Insurance Brokers' Association, the Corporation of Lloyd's, and individual insurance companies.

STOCK AND OTHER MONEY/COMMODITY MARKETS AND INVESTMENT WORK

Of all the recent revolutions in the financial sector, the transformation of the Stock Exchange has probably been the most radical. Long-established traditions have been overturned, and the City has secured its position as one of the three leading securities centres, sharing what is now virtually a single, global market with New York and Tokyo. London is looking to increase its share of worldwide financial business from 1986's 3-5% to around 10% by the early

1990s, which would mean an explosive growth rate, and would dominate UK economic development.

In October 1986, the Stock Exchange ended the system of fixed commissions charged by brokers, removed restrictions on outside (and foreign) ownership of member firms, and abolished the demarcation between 'jobbers' and 'brokers' (see below). Simultaneously with this 'de-regulation' and restructuring, the Stock Exchange introduced highly-sophisticated new computer-based dealing, and information, systems. SEAQ (Stock Exchange Automated Quotation) displays 'instant' share trading information – buying/selling prices, volume of trading etc – 'on screen' and records many deals within five minutes. Prices can be 'input' from anywhere in the British Isles. Anyone in the world with access to SEAQ's videotext information system can monitor, in 'real time', share quotations and dealings. SEAQ's success has been such that by the end of 1986, the traditional 'floor' of the Stock Exchange was deserted, with almost all trading 'on screen' and via the telephone. Trading techniques have changed dramatically as a result.

For all its sharp new image, the Stock Exchange (although London-based it operates country-wide), is still the same market where companies, and government, raise funds by selling shares to investors, and where shares are traded between investors, on prices set by supply and demand. The government also uses the Stock Exchange to 'sell' nationally-owned firms to investors.

Some £60,000 million goes through London's foreign exchange market daily, while the London money markets channel mainly short-term wholesale funds from lenders to borrowers.

Particularly since exchange control regulations ended in 1979, letting investors buy and sell shares in stocks and shares world-wide, the range of 'markets' being made, both on and outside the Stock Exchange, has grown explosively. The Stock Market itself started a new 'unlisted securities market' for medium-sized companies who do not qualify for full listing, and a 'third' market, for small companies has been opened. Via SEAQ, it is also possible to trade in stocks of foreign companies. With 'big bang', government 'gilt-edged' securities, were spun off into a separate market, with long-term sterling corporate bonds.

Trading in 'options' – paying for the right to buy or sell shares at a point in the future at a pre-fixed price – is a fast-developing way of investing with less risk without ever buying or selling a share. The five-year-old London International Financial Futures (LIFFE), which further exploits options and 'futures' trading, and the Eurobond (used to raise capital outside traditional markets) markets have been booming, and by-passing the traditional lending by banks. 'Commercial-paper' issues – companies lending directly to each other – accounted for over 85% of Euromarket lending in 1986; banks made 75% of loans as recently as 1980.

More developments are in the pipeline. The Stock Exchange, which computerised the settlement of trading deals a while ago, is planning to do away with share certificates altogether (several billion pieces of paper are currently transferred from sellers to buyers every fortnight) in 1989. SEAQ, which now (1987) only reports prices and trading on screen, so dealers must use the telephone to buy or sell, is to be upgraded to an all-electronic dealing system. Sharp-minded City firms, for the first time backed up by huge capital resources, will undoubtedly dream up new markets to 'make', more sophisticated 'paper lending', and services to offer.

The changes have brought major upheavals in the way the City is organised. The Stock Exchange itself has had to strengthen its self-regulatory function. A completely new Securities and Investments Board (SIB) has been set up to enforce codes of conduct and license investment businesses.

Stock Exchange firms have gone through a major reorganisation, and more shake-ups are likely. The new competition demands far greater capital resources than old-style trading, while major UK and foreign banks, investment houses and other firms wanted to become Stock Exchange members, but needed to buy in expertise. Almost all the old Stock Exchange members have therefore been taken over, mainly by other other financial institutions, mainly large, and very 'aggressive' international banks, but including eg an insurance broker. Even regional brokers have had to form larger groupings – one new financial services group formed by seven, started with 24 offices, 100,000 clients, and as official broker for 35 public companies, giving them an estimated £7 million in business.

All member firms can now be 'dual capacity', integrated broker/dealers if they wish, but in fact only 35 of the 244 member firms registered as equity 'market makers', buying and selling shares, 26 as gilts market makers. Nine firms specialise in money broking, and six are 'inter-dealer brokers', acting solely as sales intermediaries between gilts market makers.

The majority, then, are still like traditional stockbrokers, although they can buy shares on their own account and in some cases hold them for clients, but are now called 'agency brokers'. Market makers deal both with agency brokers and directly with institutional investors, can issue securities, and make markets work by buying and selling speculatively on their own accounts. Individual investors would normally deal with an agency broker, although all larger agency brokers also have institutional clients. While some of the larger market makers operate widely, many firms are choosing to offer specialised services. Smaller agency brokers mostly serve individual investors.

But the competition to stay in the market is expected to be phenomenal, with one of the largest market makers capitalised at over £2000 million (pre 'big bang' the total capital of all jobbers put together was about £100 million). Only two pre-'big bang' jobbers dealt in gilts, five did 90% of equity turnover. Most big investors, the pension funds etc, are cutting down on the number of firms they use, and all firms are having to fight to gain and hold onto clients. One major bank dropped out of gilts market making only months after 'big bang', and more casualties are expected. The resulting demands on dealers etc are obvious.

While only Stock Exchange firms may deal on the Stock Exchange itself, banks and other financial institutions form other markets, including LIFFE, the money markets, the Euro markets, and the foreign exchange market. Some markets include specialist firms, such as the foreign-exchange brokers, and the discount houses.

The eight 'traditional' discount houses are down in number from thirteen, and four are now owned by other, larger financial groups. They borrow surplus funds from the clearing banks 'on call' (giving the banks a source of interest for funds which be easily available for customers) and investing them in government Treasury bill, commercial bills of exchange, and short-dated government bonds. They too are diversifying into other financial business since it is expected their 'market' will be opened to other financial firms in 1988.

The City is also the base for the commodity markets, which are centres, markets or exchanges where member brokers of particular dealing rings trade in supplies of materials – metals, cocoa, coffee, sugar, rubber, vegetable oils, wood etc – traded internationally. The gold market handles bullion and other gold on offer. The markets play a major part in pricing these materials, and it is via them that producers sell and wholesalers, manufacturers and other customers buy their supplies. Prices change not only with supply and demand, but also with fluctuations in exchange rates. Investors also trade in commodities, using brokers to deal in 'forward' options, based on predictions of future trade and prices, without ever actually buying the commodity concerned. The goods often never even pass through the UK. Most markets have no more than 40 member firms, the gold market only five.

Commodity markets traditionally operate like the Stock Exchange. 'Trading' is via broker or dealer members of particular markets, on volatile, noisy open dealing floors, where traders shout prices at each other. Markets began switching to screen-based dealing systems even before the Stock Exchange. The London Commodities Exchange keeps prices up to date, like SEAQ, but also lets dealers 'call-up' prices on key-pads and then enter their bids and offers.

See also SHIPBROKING under TRANSPORT.

With the rapid growth and increasing complexity of financial markets, and availability of more sophisticated computer systems, a major growth area has been in market information, provided on screen and on line. While the Stock Exchange has its own official system, independent companies offer dealers and investors a widening range of services. These cover not only prices, but also analyses and predictions of price movements in graphs and charts, and news likely to affect the markets, and at least one offers full on-screen electronic trading. This major firm offers a display on 20,000 stocks from nearly 60 exchanges.

Working in the stock and other money/commodity markets and investment
Employers include – Stock Exchange and other market firms, the Stock Exchange, the dozen discount houses, investment and unit trusts investing on behalf of shareholders' or subscribers (over 150 management groups), finance houses specialising in credit finance, and investment departments of large firms, pension funds etc.

The largest city firms and investment banks – financial 'conglomerates' – may be members of one, two, or several markets, with a co-ordinated 'presence' in London, New York and Tokyo. Smaller firms specialise. The sums handled by any one firm may be huge, but although the number of jobs has undoubtedly jumped recently, numbers employed in any one Stock-Exchange firm, discount house or foreign-exchange broker is likely to be relatively small, several hundred at the most. The Stock Exchange itself more than doubled its staff, from 1000 to 2200 between 1979 and 1986. Investment/unit trusts and finance houses employ only between 500 and 1000 people each. Commodity houses (some doing both physical and futures trading, others specialising in futures) are also small, with (probably) no more than 150 employees each. About 400,000 people altogether work in this area.

Stock exchange firms, under the new rules, can choose for themselves how to organise their trading operations, and the way jobs are designed will vary from firm to firm.

Working for a City firm may no longer mean working in the City. Electronic trading can be done from anywhere. While firms are keeping their dealing operations in London, large integrated dealing rooms need a lot of space, so they are moving away from the traditional square mile. To save costs, the larger firms now also have out-of-town offices to house main-frame computers, and handle back-up administration, eg settlement and accounts. With London the time-link between New York and Tokyo, shift work is increasing, and much longer hours are becoming the norm.

Work in 'City' firms includes –

TRADERS/DEALERS large marketing-making firms employ up to 600 dealers/ traders in teams, each specialising in 'market making' in different kinds of securities (banks, oils, chemicals), or types of trading (options etc), although most have far fewer. In the main Stock Exchange equity market, almost all traders now work entirely on the phone in computerised dealing rooms, and only options trading, some trading on the LIFFE market, and commodity trading is face-to-face. Individual market makers use their experience and expert knowledge of the factors affecting share prices, and the way companies are performing, to make a profit on the difference between the price at which they sell and the price at which they buy – both of which they must now give clearly – and stick to – on SEAQ screens rather than verbally on the trading floor. Market makers have to do a lot of hard work on the securities being traded, what is likely to make the price of a security move, and who is likely to buy or sell them. The new trading conditions mean they must respond to what customers want, and work more closely with sales teams and research departments.

Dealers are also employed by agency brokers, and by banks and other financial institutions who also operate in the other financial markets. One large merchant bank alone now employs 350 where, again, they specialise, dealing in 'straight' foreign change for immediate use, forward currency, 'swaps' etc. Just before 'big bang', over a third of major institutional investment managers had their own in-house dealers, and numbers have probably increased since. Commodity traders work for commodity firms, each dealing with up to 30 or 40 different commodities, but generally they specialise in one type of commodity. Floor traders are backed up by more senior traders monitoring prices etc on VDUs, and phoning instructions to trading floors world-wide.

SALES STAFF (STOCK EXCHANGE): Market-making firms can now offer large investors a direct service, for which they do not charge a commission. But firms' market makers do not normally deal direct with investors. Most have built up teams of sales staff who act as the link between market maker and institutional investor, not only arranging deals as the investor asks for them, but also trying to sell the client 'special offers'. Some firms also have teams of specialist, or research, sales staff who look after particular sectors and 'market' new ideas to clients. Sales teams work closely with the market makers. A market-making firm may have as many sales staff as market makers.

AGENCY BROKERS (STOCK EXCHANGE): Firms not operating as market makers employ agency brokers in much the same way as pre 'big bang', although the environment has become much tougher. Most market-making firms are likely to continue to offer their clients agency-broking services. Brokers must trade for their clients at best possible prices, and so may not always trade with their own market makers. Agency brokers work for the investor, institutional (pension funds, insurance companies, etc), and individual. They buy and sell securities for their clients, using SEAQ screens to tell them what current prices are, and trying to better them. They also advise clients on what to buy and sell and when, and manage their investment 'portfolios' for them. Individual brokers usually look after a number of clients.

INVESTMENT ANALYSTS AND FUND MANAGERS work for any organisation which has large funds to manage, Stock Exchange firms, and other business providing advice and information on investment. Most so-called 'institutional' investors are in the financial sector – banks of all kinds, insurance companies, pension funds, investment and unit trusts, and so on. Many other large firms have investments large enough to warrant a professional department to look after them (some with over £2000 million a year to invest). A large Stock Exchange firm may have a 50-strong research team, which will also include professional ECONOMISTS, STATISTICIANS etc.

Brokers, banks, business information services, financial consultants, etc provide, or sell, expert information, analyse and advise on investment to their customers. Some 'manage' their clients' portfolios for them. Stock-Exchange market makers depend heavily on the back-up information provided by their investment analysts, usually being briefed by them before the dealing day starts.

Skilled investment means making money work and produce more money, regardless of how short or long a time it is available. Modern technology, and markets freed from many restrictions, make it much easier to make money on very short-term investment or lending. Some organisations, for instance banks and insurance companies, must keep a certain proportion of readily-available funds, and so invest a proportion for only short periods, whilst some may go into medium and very long-term projects. Investment staff must know exactly where to invest, and for how long, to produce a return. They need very thorough knowledge of the markets, and extremely good intelligence on what can be earned on different securities, markets etc.

Investment departments, whether handling funds, providing on screen or printed information services, or acting as advisers to those who do, store huge amounts of information, data about individual companies, about industries, about factors which may influence their growth or decline, etc. Analysts examine and question published figures, make their own investigations, break down, analyse and even re-calculate what they are given, and make their own projections of the future on a long- and short-term basis. They use an increasingly sophisticated range of computer-based information systems to keep them completely up to date on, for instance, exchange rates, company results, share prices. Analysts can move on to become fund managers, and this is the standard route.

COMMODITY RESEARCH, in individual commodity houses, is similar. Research departments gather information world wide, from producing and trading countries, from traders and agents, and analyse it. They prepare reports, compile regular bulletins, and give personal briefings to traders.

REGULATORY/COMPLIANCE OFFICERS Dismantling the old rules has not meant doing away with rules altogether, and events in several markets have proved the need for controls to protect investors, companies and City firms. The BANK OF ENGLAND has a major supervisory role, but the main emphasis is on self-regulation, through the Securities Investment Board (SIB), within a legal framework. SIB itself is delegating the task to 'Self-Regulatory Organisations' (SROs) which include, for example, the Stock Exchange itself, and both SIB and the SROs, as well as the Bank, will have a fair number of staff monitoring and checking regulations. The Stock Exchange also plans to have an investors' ombudsman. In addition, Stock Exchange and other firms subject to the new legislation, are appointing their own 'compliance officers', to make sure that practices within the firm fully protect the investor. One merchant bank alone has five directors now looking after compliance. This is, however, mainly work for people who already have extensive experience of financial services, banking, the Stock Exchange etc.

SYSTEMS EXPERTS The City and the markets are now totally committed not only to computers, but to the very latest in 'information technology' systems. In the run up to 'big bang' time was so short that many organisations were forced into 'bailey bridge' tactics, with many systems starting out as technological lash-ups. Systems now have to be properly developed and some virtually re-written altogether. At the same time, firms are forced by competition to keep up with technology as it develops, and most see advantages in using expert systems (see IT COMPUTING) as soon as they are developed. For all this City firms need a wide range of experts with skills in INFORMATION TECHNOLOGY, able to assess, develop and manage whole systems for the firm's business (which means understanding it), and in specific COMPUTING skills – in eg local area networking, linking up systems of all kinds, getting fast on-screen reaction times without overestimating capacity etc. Firms also use software houses with securities divisions to develop systems for them, and so employment opportunities have expanded amongst them also. But most organisations and firms also have in-house computer support services.

MANAGEMENT/ADMINISTRATION With so much expansion and development, all firms in the investment business have grown in size and complexity, and most are now developing more rigorous corporate management, and administrative, systems. These 'back office' functions (plus computer support) can involve as many as a third of all employees. They range from all the usual corporate FINANCIAL FUNCTIONS, but needing particularly strong and efficient settlement and accounting systems, and usually including corporate treasury and tax specialists, through to far more systematic and high-level PERSONNEL MANAGEMENT, training etc. Most large City firms now have to employ property specialists to manage and maintain buildings housing complex systems, and prepare for expansion.

Recruitment and entry No formal, or clearly-defined, routes into investment work. Entry is largely a matter of getting a first post, which often means starting in 'back-office' administration especially for non-graduates. Traditionally City firms recruited largely amongst school-leavers and people who already have relevant qualifications, often on personal introduction. Post 'big bang', all financial organisations and firms are looking more widely for young people able to cope with the new competitive climate and new technology. Generally they are looking for people with better educational qualifications, and broader backgrounds. Commodity houses, though, are still recruiting school leavers.

For market making, broking and sales, the right personality, a sharp and quick-thinking mind, and even an instinctive, innate aptitude for the job – a 'natural feeling' for prices and numbers – plus the physical and psychological stamina to cope, are still most important. Educational qualifications, therefore, are less crucial, but signs are that the complexities of the markets are beginning to give graduates with the right qualities more of an advantage. Languages are increasingly needed.

Investment analysis/management now largely recruits graduates, especially in economics, statistics, maths, with some need for specialists in eg surveying or land studies for property investment.

Qualifications and training Training is still largely in-house, and on the job, but beginning to get more formalised. Trainees start in, eg administration, accounting, investment analysis/research, and those with the right aptitudes move into market making, sales, and broking when they have learnt about the business, although some firms are recruiting more graduates directly for training in dealing etc now. For trading, it is still claimed that 'there is no known training except to do it'. More formal career planning is likely in future. The following training/qualification requirements must now be met.

The Stock Exchange, as an SRO, is responsible for authorising staff, and anyone working in investment business, eg dealing, arranging deals, managing or advising on investments, must be authorised. The first categories are individual SE members (separate from corporate membership), registered representatives, traders, options traders, inter-dealer brokers, money brokers, and directors. The Stock Exchange has two separate qualifying examinations –

The Securities Industry Diploma is designed to be taken by both people working for member organisations, from January 1987, but anyone wanting to be a member of the Stock Exchange must also take the Registered Representatives' exam below. Membership also requires age at least 21, and three years' training with a member firm, or firms, plus the Securities Industry exams in regulation and compliance, and two of: interpretation of financial statements, investment analysis, private client investment advice and management, institutional investment advice, financial futures and options, bond and fixed-interest markets, fund management. Exemptions are possible with relevant equivalent qualifications.

Registered personnel must be at least 18, have had previous relevant experience or worked for a member firm under direct supervision from a member for at least three months, and have passed the appropriate exam (all are multiple-choice and computer based). Registered representatives are any employees of member firms in contact with clients to get or solicit orders on behalf of the firm, anyone advising clients on securities and investment generally, and they may commit the firm in market dealings but not in traded options. Registered traders may commit their firm in market dealings and securities transactions including conventional options and investment products, but may not give investment advice or solicit orders. Anyone wanting to deal in registered options, to act as inter-dealer broker, or as a money broker must take the appropriate examination first.

City University and City Polytechnic run evening classes and Henley Distance Learning programmes in preparation for the three main exams. A number of private colleges also provide courses.

Investment analysts and managers normally qualify via the professional body in the field in which they work, eg Institute of Bankers, Chartered Insurance Institute, Stock Exchange (above), Institute of Actuaries (finance and investment certificate). However –

The Society of Investment Analysts (1986 membership nearly 2300 including 550 students) has full-scale two-stage examinations now. Companies are increasingly encouraging trainee analysts and fund managers to study for them. Minimum entry requirements are five O-level equivalent passes at 16-plus†, and age 18. Exemptions are described as 'generous', and at least 50% of candidates gain them from subjects like basic economics.

Other relevant qualifications include –

The Finance Houses Association runs a diploma examination complementary to the IOB scheme. Part 1 includes accountancy, law and elements of instalment credit; exemption is on a subject-for-subject basis for A levels or equivalent; full exemption is given for BTEC National, law and accountancy qualifications. Part 2 is divided between consumer and business credit (either can be taken for a certificate). Some 600 registered as FHA students in 1986. The Institute of Credit Management (c5000 members) has a two-stage examination, entry to which is with at least four O-level-equivalent passes at 16-plus†, including English and mathematics.

Further information from the Stock Exchange (Membership Department), the Society of Investment Analysts, the Federation of Commodity Associations, the London Commodity Exchange and other appropriate professional bodies.

MARKETING

Marketing (general)   487
Advertising   491
Market research   497

Public relations   500

MARKETING (GENERAL)

Industry and commerce today are supposed to be *marketing-* rather than *production*-oriented. Crudely put, this reverses the traditional attitude which says 'make it first and then sell it', and is based on a near-automatic demand for goods and services. It is reasonably easy to sell a product or service in a market where there is little or no competition, and for a long while few firms in the industrialised world had any problems in selling their goods. Now conditions are different – competition is world-wide and getting tougher all the time – and UK firms have to become 'marketing led'.

Marketing, then, is not just modern jargon for selling – although selling is a major part of the marketing process and the two are often confused. There is a great deal more to marketing than selling. Marketing is a strategy rather than a direct activity. Marketing has to see that a firm produces the goods or services which will make the most profit, and having decided on the most profitable goods and services, uses its expertise to see that the profit made is as high as possible. The Institute of Marketing used to define marketing as 'the management function which organises and directs all those business activities involved in converting consumer purchasing power into effective demand for a specific product of service to the final consumer or user so as to achieve the profit target or other objective set by a company', but has drastically simplified this, to: 'the management process responsible for identifying, anticipating and satisfying customer requirements profitably'.

A company's planning will include setting marketing objectives. As part of the planning, markets must be researched before any decision is made on what to produce, and so marketing has to find out as much as possible about potential markets. Marketing is used to find out what potential customers really want. Marketing looks to see if there is a gap in the market which a firm can fill, whether there is a market for a potential new product or service – and if so, tries to identify ('target') the people or organisations most likely to buy or use it.

One large company found that, of 600 ideas for new products, only 100 were serious candidates. Of these, only 57 reached the test marketing stage, only 40 were launched nationally, and only 30 were commercially successful.

Marketing is not, though, only concerned with new products. Marketing keeps checks to see if a product or service is still selling well, evaluates consumer response, and tries to find out why, if a product is losing customers. Markets change, and nowadays change faster than ever before, and it is marketing that must watch out for, and even keep ahead of, changing demands, so that the firm can respond quickly and flexibly.

Marketing, then, has to match what the firm can make, or the service they can give, as closely as is practicable with the customers' identified needs, work out and evaluate the possible profits. The price (and therefore the cost) of a product or service has to be pitched at the right level to give the best profit – higher cost and therefore lower sales volume, or vice versa perhaps – and to see that the product reaches sales outlets at the right time. Throughout a product's life, marketing has to go on trying to improve 'customer appeal' and profitability, look for ways to extend its life, see if there are ways of improving it or making manufacture cheaper and/or simpler and whether or not these are cost-effective. Sometimes marketing reviews the entire range of products or services.

Marketing therefore has to be closely involved with the firm's planning and entire strategy. Marketing has a complex and sometimes difficult role – it has to co-ordinate effort without actually being in direct control. What is often called the 'marketing mix' usually involves market research, product development and design, costing, production, packaging, sales promotion and market planning, distribution, advertising, merchandising and even after-sales servicing.

Ideally, a marketing manager would like to have the entire company marketing 'oriented', and may spend a lot of time trying to convince other managers of this – since all these activities are the responsibility of other departments with a firm, and even of other firms, like the retailers who sell the company's products to the customer. Marketing also has to create and maintain strong links between them, both within the company and outside it, so that the marketing effort on a product, group of products, or service is as far as possible a team activity.

But however important all these elements may be, the most crucial is the nature, quality and design of the product itself. Good marketing starts before a product is even designed.

Marketing strategies are different for consumer goods like soap powder and canned soups. products for industry such as machine tools or car parts, and services such as holiday packages, banking services, or insurance schemes. Within these broad groups, there may be quite different strategies for different types of product – for 'fast moving consumer goods' (like butter, tea, and washing up liquid) and consumer durables (TV and video sets, radios and washing machines).

In marketing consumer goods, the product is designed from the outset to attract a particular group of people, using information from market research to help define what it should be like, with product development, design and packaging adding their own distinctive 'styling' to the basic technical design, tailored to the purchasing patterns of the particular consumer group, and costed for that group's purchasing power. Distribution, sales promotion campaigns, promotional material, briefing retailers, are all usually treated as part of the marketing 'chain'.

Marketing may also have to see that there is efficient after-sales service for consumers.

Services, like insurance or holidays, are also designed to meet the needs of fairly tightly-defined groups of consumers. Service industries, like banking, have adopted modern marketing concepts, because they must now sell their services more widely. Part of the marketing role here is to 'educate' the consumer into wanting the service in the first place. Banks, for example, compete hard for the student market, because market research shows that customers once caught stay with their first bank. 'Package' deals, complete with smart 'styling' and offers, are designed each year for the young.

Industrial marketing sells goods and services to other companies or organisations. These may be 'one-off' products – a chemical plant, a dam, or a mainframe computer system – and the product is designed specifically for that customer. It may be finished goods, robot systems for car manufacturers, for example. It may be components – silicon chips for instance – from a production line or assembly room. Whichever, industrial marketing has to stay abreast of developments not only within the area in which it is selling, but also (for instance) the production methods of potential customers, to help predict future demands and open up new markets. Marketing has to see that the product meets exactly the customer's technical specifications, that delivery dates are kept, and problems solved quickly and efficiently. Industrial marketing advertises and promotes products somewhat differently from consumer-orientated marketing: promotion, for example, may involve demonstrating and displaying products at trade exhibitions.

The marketing 'function', then, varies from sector to sector (Institute of Marketing members are divided 50% industrial marketing, 37% consumer marketing and 13% marketing services).

Most firms have their own marketing departments, although some use independent consultancies, and some large advertising agencies offer marketing services. An organisation's marketing department is generally made up of a marketing director and a number of brand or market managers, each responsible for either for a range of similar products or for a particular market, which may be an area (usual in export marketing) or a particular group of customers. The shape and structure of marketing departments change frequently, especially as product ranges change more often.

Marketing managers must both try to improve the marketing of existing brands and develop new goods and services as these are introduced or the need for them identified. Within the overall strategy for the particular product or market, the manager must forecast income from its sales (deciding at the same time on the year's sales target and pricing policies, based on researching the market and its development). Generally s/he is responsible for the budget for the product or brand, and for deciding on the best 'mix' of marketing methods and resources to use. The brand manager then has to bring together and co-ordinate the various specialists needed to implement a marketing plan. This may mean organising particular parts of the plan with other departments, as well as deciding on, arranging contracts with, and supervising, an advertising agency and campaign for the product (for example).

Marketing managers spend a great deal of their time acquiring, assimilating and assessing information of all kinds. Most obviously this comes from market research, feedback from sales people, results of advertising audits etc. However, other reports come from within the company, for example the management accounting monitoring system, from production. Since much of the information comes in number form – market research surveys, sales figures, costings – analysis is often statistical, using computers.

Marketing managers must also pass on information to others, again in the form of reports and statistics – feedback from sales staff, for example, to product design about particular features of a product, or from servicing staff to production about a recurring problem.

New entrants begin as, for example, marketing assistants looking after, perhaps merchandising, the crucial but rather basic job of seeing that, for example, supermarkets put the product on the shelf in a prominent position (and don't leave it in a storeroom), and that special displays are put together and out in the store. Promotion to assistant brand manager, and brand manager can be fairly fast – 'front-line' marketing managers are generally young. It is one of the toughest and aggressive functions.

Progress upwards is via group brand management, marketing management and marketing directorship. Marketing is said to be one of the best routes into senior management, but marketing managers also move out, into consultancy, or starting their own businesses (using their skills to identify a profitable market gap).

Britain has lagged behind the rest of western world in developing marketing techniques, and as an identifiable career marketing has a history of not much more than thirty years.

Recruitment and entry It is unusual to start in marketing itself direct from school, but there are no hard-and-fast rules (and not all jobs advertised as 'marketing' are truly marketing jobs). Firms do recruit new graduates directly for marketing traineeships, but probably no more than about 500 a year. Degree subject is probably not too important for marketing consumer goods, although signs are that some business studies content or a postgraduate qualification could improve chances (competition for places is very fierce), but is no substitute for experience. For industrial marketing, a relevant engineering or science degree is needed. Fluent languages, and familiarity with the business life of the countries where they are spoken, are useful for export marketing.

More usually, though, employers want recruits for marketing with some form of business experience first, such as selling, sales administration, advertising, customer support, market research, although it could be, eg R&D. These are not formal routes into marketing, though, and marketing may take rather different characteristics.

Marketing demands the ability to communicate, both in writing and verbally, the ability to persuade, to explain, to sell ideas and to gain other people's co-operation. Marketing managers have to be intellectually capable of assessing complex information, and working out its implications for strategy. They have to be numerate enough to work with and be able to understand a mass of statistical material. They need self-confidence, It helps to be out-going and fairly thick-skinned, to be happy working inside largish organisations with formal structures, and to have plenty of physical stamina.

Qualifications and training It is possible to read for a degree, either in marketing or in business studies with a substantial marketing content, or a BTEC HND in business studies biased to marketing (see BUSINESS STUDIES under ACADEMIC AND VOCATIONAL STUDIES). Professional qualifications are still taken by only a minority of marketing people and are not compulsory, but they are increasingly useful and the number of new students (5400), and students completing diplomas (1712) shot up in 1985-6.

The Institute of Marketing (1986 membership nearly 21,000 against 8000 in 1960) provides the main professional qualification. Despite its title and stated aims (to unify and develop education and training in all the marketing services functions), the Communication, Advertising and Marketing Education Foundation (CAM) examinations have not replaced those of the Institute (which is, however, represented on the board) and in fact the CAM certificate and diploma schemes relate only to advertising and public relations (see below).

The Institute's minimum entry requirements are three O-level equivalent passes in 16-plus†, and two at A level, with passes in an English and mathematics. Entrants must be 18.

The two-year certificate course covers fundamental aspects of marketing and sales. An HNC/D in business studies with a marketing bias exempts.

The diploma course is biased to managerial activity and decision-making, and covers international aspects, marketing planning and controls, management organisation and communications, and marketing analysis and business.

Full membership also requires at least three years' practical experience in any of the specified functions in marketing, including at least one year in marketing management.

Over 100 further education colleges give tuition for IM certificate and diploma examinations. IM also provides a wide range of training packages.

Further information from the Institute of Marketing.

ADVERTISING

Advertising aims to attract attention, to create a particular and lasting image in the minds of consumers, and to persuade people to buy a particular product, to go on a particular holiday, to apply for a particular job, or not to smoke, for example. Most advertising is, by implication, also designed to inform, but some advertising is a great deal more informative than others – bus timetables, for instance.

Advertising started out by selling 'hard' products to consumers, and this still makes up a large part of the industry's income, although less than 36% expenditure on advertising now comes from manufacturers selling consumer goods. Some 20% of total expenditure goes on 'classifieds', over 17% comes from retailers, about 11% from firms advertising to each other (largely trade and technical), and about 4% from banks, insurance companies and other financial interests. About 3% is spent on advertising holidays, entertainments etc; government (largest single spender in 1986), charities and education, political parties, and so on, spend the rest.

Although, to most firms, advertising is a crucial part of the marketing 'mix' it is a relatively small part. Estimates say the cost of advertising makes up only about 10% of total marketing costs. But while it is only the tip of the marketing iceberg, it is a very visible, vocal and expensive one, spending a record £4400 million in 1985.

Advertising projects a glamorous, creative and entertaining image, giving the impression that it is all rather fun. It may be all gloss and froth on the outside, but underneath it is a very commercial, competitive, tough business where profits are taken as seriously as anywhere else. Proof of this lies in advertising's success in riding the recent recession. Company expenditure on advertising has actually been growing in real terms, with importers and UK companies in increasing competition, and some sectors have substantially increased their spending – car makers, for instance, by 500% over ten years. In the ten years to 1985, the industry had a 66% real growth rate. Only classified advertising really suffered.

Earlier efforts at becoming more businesslike, with better management and financial control, which are just as important as creative flair, have borne fruit.

Advertising people are by nature optimists, but their expectations for the rest of the 1980s are well supported. More and more organisations are now convinced they must advertise regardless of trade conditions, and the explosion in all the kinds of media in which they can advertise – colour magazines, TV channels, radio stations, newspapers – means more intense competition for advertising. Nevertheless, the industry is maintaining tight financial controls, and some agencies did cut staff in spite of increased billings.

Working in advertising
The choice of employers is between –
firms which actually do the advertising – the advertising agencies which sell their services to advertisers;
advertising departments of firms which do their own;
service organisations – medium- and smaller agencies 'contract out' work – creative work to independent art or film studios; media planning and buying, sometimes research; to account planning and other consultancies; to market research organisations; to promotions houses;
media firms which provide the advertising 'space' (newspaper and magazine publishers, television and other broadcasting organisations, etc);
companies which provide specialist services for advertising agencies or departments – market research firms, film units, and freelance artists and designers – where agencies or departments do not have their own;
marketing departments in larger companies, where buying advertising is a major job.

Advertising people have to produce a profit for their agency. They do this by creating original, imaginative lively 'campaigns' with maximum impact – even in bread-and-butter areas like job ads and selling cleaning services or tools for industry. The creativity has to be geared to persuading people to buy something, within a budget, to meet a tight marketing strategy and sales target, often with impossible schedules. Computers are being used to 'target' consumers and their views ever more exactly, to improve services.

Advertising people work in teams, with endless discussions and meetings, and much negotiation. Attitudes may be informal and relaxed, but the pressure is often intense, hours can be long, and the crises frequent. An agency's character usually strongly reflects the personal style and ideas of the directors. The first job of an agency is to project a strong image of its own, and staff may be chosen to fit a particular mould as well as for their talents.

Advertising agencies and departments
These provide most of the career opportunities.

It is a small, fast-changing industry, with some 260 major agencies employing about 14,000, and around 300 smaller ones with fewer than 3000 jobs between them (over 20,000 worked in advertising agencies in the mid 1960s). The 'top twenty' agencies employ between 125 and 550 staff each, others usually less than 100. Most agencies are still in London, but with growing numbers in other major towns.

For over two decades, the same agencies have stayed at the top, and most are still American owned. American dominance, though, is being increasingly and successfully challenged by a 'new wave' of British agencies – three are now in the 'top' ten and one has topped the billings chart for several years. Every year sees agencies closing or merging, and new ones opening. New agencies are rarely started by anyone new to advertising, though – extensive experience of running another agency is usually crucial. Agencies 'pride themselves on the high quality of their staff'.

Information on who works for the advertising departments of major manufacturing and other companies is not collected, but estimates suggest they employ fewer than 1000 people between them.

Agencies, and some advertising departments, plan, organise and run the 'campaigns' for particular products or organisations – agencies call their clients 'accounts'. Every campaign has to be carefully matched to the market for the product – so one manufacturer may use different agencies for different products because each agency has its own kind of market 'expertise'. The campaign has to be planned closely with MARKETING, or brand, managers, because it must linked into the 'brand image' which creates a common theme for packaging, displays, TV, newspaper and magazine advertisements.

Launching a new product takes one kind of campaign, concentrating on encouraging consumers to try it. Once a product is established, the formula may change to compete with other brands and keep up consumer interest. Advertising works through every available 'medium': newspapers, journals and magazines, TV and radio, posters, packaging, the cinema, shop displays, exhibitions, circulars and direct mailings. Agencies also produce all the myriad free- and cheap-offer coupons, promotional leaflets and so on, which do so much for sales, but an estimated 60 separate sales promotion agencies now do much of this.

In some organisations which have products or services to advertise, the advertising department may do all or some of the work of the agency, but in others the brand or advertising manager will contract-out most accounts, handling only small-scale work internally. S/he liaises closely with the agency to make sure that the advertising in the firm's name says the right things, at the right time to the right people, at the right cost, and monitors the success of the campaign with them.

The larger the agency the greater the range of accounts they handle and the more services they offer. Smaller ones tend to specialise in particular markets. Some agencies have their own marketing and market research units, and offer sophisticated services on eg product development, corporate image. Some employ their own writers and artists, others commission specialists from outside for particular campaigns.

Advertising agencies are highly individualist organisations, creating for themselves a very distinctive image, and 'selling' themselves on the basis of, eg strong creative, or marketing, expertise. Some are strongly hierarchical, others not. Broadly they use a common set of terms to describe the various functions, although how far those functions are carried out by one, or several, people, usually depends on the size of the agency.

ACCOUNT EXECUTIVES (who with their assistants, make up about a fifth of the staff of the major agencies) each look after a group of accounts (perhaps three or four), and are the links with the 'clients'.

The account executive must find out what the client is after, and as much as possible about the product(s). Under the account executive, a team then plans and designs a campaign, using all the available expertise, from market researchers to designers.

When, and if, the client agrees the resulting 'presentation' and budgets, the account executive must see that plans turn into reality, monitor progress and solve the inevitable problems.

Once the campaign is launched, s/he must keep track of its effectiveness.

Account executives must be able to weld all the different people working on an account into an effective team, understanding all their different jobs.

Account executives are leaders, organisers and negotiators, and need 'personality', drive, physical and mental stamina.

Account planners are a relatively new breed, not yet a separate 'function' in all agencies. Account planners provide consumer-oriented information input and analysis to campaigns. They use market, and other kinds of research to monitor consumer attitudes to clients', and their competitors', products; who buys what products and why; trends in what customers are thinking and wanting. For instance, they may spot rising concern about how healthy food products are.

CREATIVE STAFF are the copy- and script-writers, the artists and typographers.

Copywriters (at most 800 in the top 300 agencies), not only write the slogans, jingles and sharp headlines, but also the longer and more detailed sales brochures, the cheap-offer coupons, trade features and advertisements which are part of many campaigns. In some agencies copywriters may also write scripts for film and TV advertisements; in others the two roles are separate, because they take rather different skills.

Copywriters, it goes without saying, need a way with words, but it has to be a skill which persuades and doesn't only produce sharp prose (although one of today's most successful novelists was once a very sharp copywriter).

Art directors – every agency has one – look after the all-important visual images.

Some agencies employ their own artists, graphic designers, illustrators and typographers (there are some 2000 altogether in the top 300 agencies), or they may commission outside studios or freelance artists. IPA agencies employed 2860 creative people in 1978 (compared with a peak of 3950 in 1960 and a low of 2410 in 1975). See also CREATIVE WORK.

Television and film advertisements are generally made by independent film units, employing their own or freelance staff (including script-writers), but working under agency supervision (see also CREATIVE WORK).

THE MEDIA STAFF (about 1300 of them in the main agencies), are researchers, planners and buyers. They specialise in knowing how best to use television, radio, posters, newspapers, and magazines, depending on what is being advertised and to whom. They are expert at buying space and air or TV time at rates best suited to a particular client's product and budgets.

Media executives need business skills and must be expert in understanding and analysing complex statistics and pricing arrangements. All must become really skilled judges of the media.

The media department used to be just the place where orders were processed. Increasingly, campaigns are directed at specific groups and not at mass markets. Here a good media department can save large advertisers millions using people expert at negotiating with media owners.

PRINT PRODUCTION STAFF have to get the completed advertisements to the particular outlet in the right format, and must organise and supervise printing of posters, leaflets, showcards and so on (see also PRINTING under MANUFACTURING).

OTHER STAFF Some large agencies also have their own MARKET RESEARCH departments, and some also MARKETING departments. Most have information departments, but usually train their own staff to meet agency needs for information (eg desk surveys), rarely employing qualified librarians or information scientists. All employ 'service' staff, in finance, secretarial work (2000 in the main agencies), personnel (in the largest agencies only), and even computing.

Media advertising departments

They 'sell' space and air time to advertisers or agents. Publishers – of national and regional newspapers, magazines, trade and technical journals – carry about 65% of all advertising (down from 70% in the late 1970s). TV carries about 29%, posters and transport 4%, radio 2%, cinema under 1%. The largest media advertising departments are, therefore, in the major newspaper and magazine/journal groups. Independent TV companies have media sales staff of about fifty each.

Advertising revenue is crucial to the profitability of newspapers, magazines, and TV companies. Competition is fierce, and so considerable ingenuity and very sophisticated techniques are used to sell space. Sales staff may work on a single publication, or on a product or service, eg holidays, for a group of publications.

Recruitment and entry No accepted, straightforward route into advertising, and rarely easy to get started. Probably easier to start with an advertiser, a media firm selling advertising than to get into an agency, or even a marketing department, and to make the necessary contacts in agencies by working with them.

Competition for jobs and to be promoted has always been very intense. Agencies are reluctant to invest in untrained talent – clients now recruit many of the young graduates who might have once gone into the agencies. A special kind of flair, creative or organisational ability is needed to attract the attention of agencies, now interested only in the best of new talent. Advertising, though, needs a regular infusion of new talent and ideas 'to stand out in a noisy world', and is always looking for the right kind of creative or organisational ability, for people prepared to work very hard to tight schedules, within exact budgets, and who are ready to take advantage of any opportunities.

While academic qualifications are not important in themselves, a reasonable level of intelligence and good educational background are. Employers do therefore tend to choose graduates when recruiting the very few trainee account executives they take, which is at most four or five a year for even the largest agencies, an estimated 120 places, with most in the twenty largest. A degree is seen as evidence of a certain level of ability, although graduates are also expected to have the 'right' personal qualities. The subject(s) studied is therefore relatively unimportant, except for creative artists, who are normally expected to have a degree in art and design, although a relevant BTEC award may be acceptable. Some kind of relevant student activity or vacation work experience may help in getting a first post. Applicants have to sell themselves hard.

While a degree is not absolutely essential (one agency regularly interviews some of its own junior staff for trainee executive places), a Higher award in business studies (preferably with advertising and marketing options), two A levels (or the equivalent in A and AS levels) including eg English, economics, or art, are normally needed to get onto the career ladder.

Particular jobs within advertising require particular abilities, but in general, everyone needs the ability to persuade, some kind of creative talent, and business sense. Advertising also needs an intelligent and detailed interest in what motivates people, how they express their likes and dislikes, their buying habits, etc. It also takes the ability to work as part of a team, all of whose members tend to be fairly extrovert, self-confident people. Other qualities often quoted include imagination, ability to work under extreme pressures, and a mature approach.

Qualifications and training No industry-wide formal training schemes as such exist. Most training is on the job with part-time study, although some agencies give their new entrants a period of planned training with regular moves between different jobs and departments.

The Communication, Advertising and Marketing Education Foundation (CAM) certificate and diploma sets the only formal qualifications. CAM qualifications are not essential, and agencies vary in the weight they attach to them, some encouraging entrants at all levels to study for CAM exams. About 695 UK students registered for certificates, 136 directly for the diploma, in 1985. About 15% of students registering work for agencies, and about 8% each for advertisers and advertising services. However, the influential Institute of Practitioners in Advertising withdrew support from CAM in 1984, and is (further) developing its seven-stage training scheme (no formal qualification).

The full CAM scheme can be covered in three years part-time (at colleges in main centres or by correspondence course). New syllabuses are planned for September 1988. CAM is developing modern 'distance-learning' techniques. The two-year common certificate course, in communication studies, at present

(1986) covers advertising, public relations, media, research and behavioural studies, communication practice, business and economic environment (each can be taken separately).

Entry qualifications are three O-level equivalent passes at 16-plus† and two A levels (or A and/or AS equivalent), or a BTEC National; age at least 18.

The diploma is modular, so advertising people can choose three of the ten options to match their own professional needs – the options include international, industrial, and consumer advertising and marketing, advanced media studies, marketing strategy, management resources.

Direct entry to the diploma is possible with an appropriate degree, BTEC Higher award or professional qualification.

Other relevant qualifications and courses include –

BTEC HND in business studies with options in advertising and advertising design, and one college, at Watford, runs a full-time course for trainee copywriters.

Further information from the Communication, Advertising and Marketing Education Foundation, the Advertising Association, and the Institute of Practitioners in Advertising.

MARKET RESEARCH

Market research is used to test public opinion on anything and everything from a new drink to TV programmes and political policies. First and foremost, it is one of marketing's most essential tools, developed, constantly refined and used to pinpoint as exactly as possible the groups of consumers most likely to buy a particular product, and how that product should be designed, packaged, priced and advertised for maximum sales.

While marketing commercial products – and services – obviously provides most market research organisations with the largest part of their income, it is also used by a great many other organisations, to find out what the public thinks, or how they react, or would react to, for example, particular political policies or parties. Even more broadly, market-research techniques are used to find out basic facts and statistics for all kinds of other studies of people's behaviour, habits and attitudes.

Market research people also compare their company's or client's share of the market with that of any competitors, and make regular retail audits, which log the movement of goods in and out of the shops.

Market research organisations

There are two main kinds of market research organisation -

One is a department attached to another organisation, for example, large advertising agencies and manufacturers. Government, local authorities, and some other organisations have survey and/or research and intelligence units using market research techniques.

The other is the independent agency, which is generally quite small (most employ under 50 people, a few have only one or two staff, and a few over 200). Of just over 200 market-research agencies, the largest 30 account for 80% of annual commission (turnover for the industry was £204 million in 1985).

Market research agencies, while under pressure during the recession largely because firms launch fewer new products and services (and cuts in, for example, government expenditure too), suffered less than might be expected because clients have learnt that cutting market research budgets can be counter-productive. The food industry is market research's best customer, accounting for over a fifth of all business in 1981.

The broadest range of services come from the market research departments of large advertising agencies and the larger independent agencies, who generally provide many special survey services, and will take the nation's pulse on anything from censorship to motorway planning. Smaller agencies generally specialise, and there are a few specialist market audit companies. Market research departments within major firms generally concentrate on the company's own products, services and image generally, although they usually help in monitoring the effects of, for example, an advertising campaign designed by an outside agency.

Working in market research

The 1985 survey of Market Research Society members showed that 46% were then working for market research suppliers, mainly agencies/consultancies, but including 8% self-employed. Some 33% were working for marketing/manufacturing organisation – including 10% for service industries, 7% in each of food/drink and other consumer goods, 5% for industrial firms, and 4% for the media – and 3% for public sector employers. The 8% in 'other employment' included 4% in academic institutions.

Market research work consists almost entirely of obtaining, collating and analysing information, much of it statistical, and then turning the results into a report for the marketing department, or a client.

The information is collected via two kinds of surveys -

The first, desk surveys, gather information from published sources such as the press, trade and other specialist papers, research documents, government publications, statistical reports and so on.

Second, field surveys, mostly carried out by interviews and questionnaires using standard random- and quota-sampling techniques, but perhaps also involving panel and group discussions, some in-depth interviews, and even interviews on the telephone. Most field surveys are large-scale, 'quantitative', but some involve intensive psychological probing of a few consumers, and are 'qualitative'. Leading market researchers expect to use 'viewdata' to collect information from consumers in their homes in future, predicting a 'slow death' for the familiar face-to-face interviewing techniques.

Marketing also uses a considerable amount of research into consumer reaction to specific products via placement tests, pack testing and test marketing. The balance between the kind of surveys used for any one piece of research varies – looking into the potential market for a new industrial product (eg a machine tool) is likely to involve more desk research, for example, than researching possible demand for a better disposable nappy. The field surveys will differ between them too – the market for the machine tool will be fairly restricted, and so most potential customers can be contacted and interviewed directly; surveying the nappy market has to be done by careful sampling of a much larger group of people.

Surveys have to be designed scientifically, to ensure, for example, that the sample chosen accurately represents those who buy the product. Designing surveys is very exacting, and involves understanding thoroughly how people behave when they are asked questions, to eliminate any risk of bias and to find out what interviewees really think, rather than, for instance, what they think the interviewer wants to hear. At the other end, sophisticated statistical techniques and computer-based analyses are used to extract information from the raw results.

Surveys of this kind give manufacturers direct information on the type of people who buy, or are likely to buy, the company's products, how the company's share of the market compares with, and is related to, that of any competitors, and how it changes, for example in response to a new 'brand image'. Market research quantifies the existing state of any given market, potential changes in it, and forecasts of possible market trends.

RESEARCH EXECUTIVES supervise projects and, in agencies, are the 'link' with the client. The research executive plans and organises a project, briefs the people who organise the surveys and other research, supervises progress, and prepares and edits the final reports. Research assistants help to plan surveys and prepare questionnaires. They become market research executives. The normal route thereafter is via group leader generally into management, but it is possible to move into eg general marketing.

SPECIALIST STAFF, such as PSYCHOLOGISTS, MATHEMATICIANS and STATISTICIANS, ECONOMISTS and COMPUTER PERSONNEL, help prepare research projects and surveys, and supervise collating and analysing results. They can move into management functions in some organisations.

INTERVIEWING is generally a part-time occupation, done by people with good educational backgrounds, or by students, although some kinds of interview (for example, panel and group discussions) need trained psychologists.

Recruitment and entry Recruitment is generally on a trainee basis, usually as a research assistant. Although there are no hard-and-fast rules, market research is largely a graduate occupation. Recently, annual entry of university graduates has been under 100, against 148 in 1974 (no figures are available for polytechnic graduates). Well over half were social scientists, but a significant proportion were engineers and scientists. Specialists are also recruited for particular posts, as in computing services (see MANAGEMENT AND RESEARCH SERVICES).

Qualifications and training Training is still largely informal and on-the-job, although the Market Research Society and the Industrial Marketing Research Association jointly run a range of short courses including a basic training course for new entrants.

The Market Research Society started its own post-experience Diploma examinations in 1984. They cover behavioural aspects; statistics, sampling and analysis; market research techniques and applications, and a case-study paper. Candidates may study on a self-taught basis. It is stressed that all entrants should have a period of practical training under experienced supervision before they can be considered fully qualified. Some 73% of the Society's 5500 members (1986 – up from 3500 in 1982) are graduates, over 10% (25% under 24) have the MRS diploma.

Courses endorsed (1986) were (business studies unless otherwise shown) – First degrees at – Aberystwyth (agricultural economics), Glasgow: Strathclyde (home economics); at Birmingham, Coventry, Hatfield, London: City, PNL (appled social studies), Middx, Newcastle, Oxford, Portsmouth, Preston, Sheffield Polytechnics; Ealing CHE.

Postgraduate awards at – universities: City (MBA); polytechnics – Bristol, Kingston, Liverpool, Newcastle

HND in business studies with marketing research modules at – polytechnics: Birmingham, Coventry, Hatfield, Huddersfield, London: Thames, Newcastle; colleges: Hull: Humberside, London: Distributive Trades, Ealing, Luton.

Further information from the Market Research Society.

PUBLIC RELATIONS

Public relations complements advertising. Where advertising creates highly vocal and persuasive campaigns, actively promoting particular products or services, public relations is a rather more low-key, sustained activity. Public relations people (who may be called information or press officers) look after the general reputation of the organisation for which they work, although in large organisations some may deal only with a particular product or service.

All kinds of organisations employ public relations people – industrial and commercial firms, government departments, hotels, travel agencies, universities and polytechnics, trade unions, publishers, banks, charities. Use of public relations expertise is growing, although it is all-too often limited to reacting to events, particularly crises or problems, rather than exploiting it to shape opinion or influence what happens. But while many companies still fail to involve PR experts in crucial decision making, surveys show that by 1984, 69% of 'top' firms (90% of the 'top' fifty) were employing consultancies, against only 21% in 1979. The financial sector, particularly, is increasingly recognising the need for PR to cope with new competition.

Well-managed, professionally-run agencies, with proper financial controls, did not suffer much during the recession. Job losses were mainly amongst those working for industrial firms, but these have been compensated for by expansion amongst the agencies and, since 1984, business has been very good. Even so, PR remains a small profession, probably employing not many more than 10,000 people.

Working in public relations

Ideally, public relations staff should see that an accurate picture of what the organisation is and does gets over to both the general public and particular groups which matter to the organisation – their shareholders and customers, or the community in which a factory is sited, for example.

They must also see that people who need information about the organisation actually get it, and should also try to keep the organisation informed about what people outside are thinking about it.

Some public relations departments also look after internal communications, especially in companies which have factories and/or offices scattered about the country.

Obviously, public relations staff try to present their employers or clients in the best possible light, but the aim is, or should be, to explain the organisation's actions and decisions, not to conceal and excuse them, which is generally counter-productive. Public relations cannot substitute for good management.

The keynote of good public relations is a steady programme of positive publicity, deliberately designed to create and keep an informed public, who recognise the organisation and its products or services, have a favourable impression of it, and are likely to think of it first when they want that kind of product or service.

Public relations staff work through people like journalists, maintaining good contacts with them, sending out press releases and being available to answer questions.

The public relations office must counter, at source, any misleading information or rumours, and see that complaints are properly settled.

Public relations staff advise on (for example) the 'visual image' which stamps an organisation's personality onto notepaper, sales and publicity material, transport and store fronts, and packaging, so that it is instantly recognisable. In fact, public relations people expect to do anything that will help 'project' their organisation – preparing annual reports and careers literature, giving talks, organising promotional films and exhibitions, writing articles and speeches for managers, arranging press and other conferences, seeing that stands go into appropriate exhibitions, sponsoring events.

They may produce house journals and newsletters, both internally and for more general circulation.

They may be involved in 'lobbying' politicians.

In agencies or consultancies account managers may be responsible for more than one client; otherwise the work is more or less the same from organisation to organisation.

It is a very varied life, but tends to be hectic with long and often irregular hours (73% of IPR members say they work 40-60 hours a week, 11% over 60 hours). They spend much of their time in contact with other people, and the pressures can be considerable.

Public relations staff have to learn how to reach particular audiences through the mass media. This means knowing, in detail, how press, TV, and radio work, and how to make the best use of them. They have to understand all the technicalities of printing, photographic, film and exhibition work, to make maximum impact and use resources economically.

Public relations experts work either in organisations or advertising agencies with PR departments, or in public relations consultancies. A growing number are self employed.

The Institute of Public Relations 1985 survey suggests that about 39% of members now work for PR consultancies (of which there are over 400), against 25% in 1975; 13% work in manufacturing or construction, 8% in service industries, 4% for trade or professional bodies, 3% in each of finance and tourism, and 3% for corporate HQ/holding companies. Over 50% do work which is consumer-oriented, 44% corporate, 10% government, and 8% employee targeted.

Some 32% work for organisations with under ten employees, and 18% for organisations with more than 5000 (down from 23% in 1982). Even the largest consultancies probably employ no more than thirty people, while one major bank employs over 80.

Recruitment and entry Since so many of the qualities needed for PR are developed only with experience and maturity, it is almost impossible to start straight from school, and not common even from university/polytechnic, although some larger organisations take trainees. Generally, though, it is much more usual to gain experience of the communications field elsewhere first, most often in journalism, marketing, or advertising. Only 2% of IPR members are under 24, only 20% under 34; 51% are over 45. However, signs are that people with flair are now getting into PR earlier than has been traditional.

Whatever the route, and there is no fixed way in, wide experience is essential, of communications, and preferably also of an organisation's area of activity. Maturity is also needed. Academic qualifications are not, in themselves, crucial, but intelligence and a good educational background are, and a rising proportion of entrants have degrees.

Public relations needs the ability to get on well with anyone, to be persuasive, tactful, completely unflappable and able to stay calm and polite whatever the provocation. PR people must be able to explain almost anything to almost anybody clearly and simply. They need creativity, imagination, ingenuity, intuition and news sense linked to other journalistic skills, especially writing. They ought to be good organisers and planners. They have to be able to work under considerable pressure.

Qualifications and training No general formal training arrangements exist. Some companies have their own internal schemes – but only 28% of IPR members say they have a training budget. The IPR is once again running well-attended one-day workshops.

CAM (Communication, Advertising and Marketing Education Foundation) awards the only formal qualifications.

The one-year part-time CAM diploma (now held by about 12% of IPR's 2300-plus members), is an optional qualification, and doesn't necessarily improve career prospects. It is modular, so students can choose three (of ten) options to suit their own professional needs. The options include public relations for commercial concerns, public relations for non-commercial operations, PR strategy, and management resources.

Entry is via the common CAM certificate (see ADVERTISING, above), held by some 11% of IPR members, but a degree or HND/C in business or communication studies exempt from the certificate. IPR student membership is needed. The diploma is only awarded after a year's relevant experience. Two years' experience, plus the CAM diploma, is required for full IPR membership. Associate membership is open to anyone with other appropriate qualifications. Very few IPR members are currently studying for CAM awards, but IPR has 60 student members.

Courses are at some seven colleges including – Aberdeen CC, London: Distributive Trades C, Luton CHE. Correspondence courses also available.

A number of degree and diploma courses in communication studies include public relations. At postgraduate level, Cranfield's MBA programme now offers a major in public relations, and it is an option at London: Business School, City.

The London Chamber of Commerce also offers a certificate, for which a number of colleges put on courses.

Further information from the Institute of Public Relations and from CAM.

PURCHASING AND BUYING, SELLING AND RETAILING

Introduction	503
Buying, purchasing and supply	504
Direct marketing and mail order	507
Retailing and distribution	507
Selling	521
Technical service	525
Wholesale and warehousing	525

INTRODUCTION

Sales staff and buyers or purchasers are absolutely crucial to the viability of any industrial or commercial organisation, and without real efficiency in these areas the efforts of others in marketing and management are largely wasted. Industry and commerce must sell if the country is to have reasonable living standards, yet individual sellers are very poorly treated in Britain, out of what would appear to be very misplaced attitudes to 'trade'. This kind of work – with some 'trendy' exceptions – does not have an attractive image and is not thought of as 'professional'.

Professional buyers, purchasers and sales staff in industry and commerce today are expected to combine the skills of the behavioural scientist with those of the technologist. While formal training has been very slow to develop (although this is beginning to change), a reasonable educational background is needed to cope with both the technological changes affecting all products and the increasingly sophisticated selling strategies developed by marketing managers, which sales must put into effect in the field and to which buying and purchasing must develop equally sophisticated responses.

Maturity, both personal and in business judgement and experience, are hallmarks of the buyer, the purchaser and the salesman/woman. These are careers which generally develop out of a less specialised start in industry or commerce, although it is possible to start training straight from school.

People in purchasing and sales need drive and energy, numeracy, the ability to assimilate technical or other data quickly and easily, and later to communicate these again equally easily. They must be ready to travel extensively (but not necessarily abroad), often living in less-than-ideal conditions, and be able to make personal contacts easily. Above all, they must accept the true role of selling in the commercial world – any latent feeling that the market place is not 'respectable' automatically disqualifies.

BUYING, PURCHASING AND SUPPLY

Efficient, expert purchasing or buying is very much more important in the viability of almost all organisations than is often realised – only too frequently by the organisations themselves. It is reasonably obvious that the profits of shops and stores of all kinds depend heavily on the expertise of their buyers. But it is also true for manufacturing – where up to two-thirds of the cost of finished products may be in the materials and parts – every 1% saved on purchasing can increase gross profits by 5 or 6%. Industry not only buys parts and materials, though. It also has to buy increasingly-expensive new machinery, and almost all organisations are now investing in new technology, from new computer and automated systems, to business equipment, like word processors.

With high and some rising prices, for fuels, raw materials, and supplies of all kinds, the problems of purchasing or buying within tighter budgets, whether or not a profit has to be made, have increased tremendously for all organisations, although the scale of the problem is obviously greatest for the largest.

Every organisation, today, needs expert purchasers or buyers. From the government – the Ministry of Defence for instance – through the National Health Service buying drugs, sophisticated electronic machinery, millions of sheets etc every year, to manufacturing and other industries like construction (where it includes 'buying' sub-contractors), printing, insurance companies and banks.

Purchasing, buying, supplies – purchasing is the term industry uses, buying is the retailing word, while other organisations often use supplies and the Ministry of Defence 'procurement' – use common techniques and the demands of the job are similar. They are just as much part of the market place as selling and marketing, and need the same tough, expert commercial attitude.

Purchasing is probably at its most complicated in manufacturing industry, where products – like cars – are assembled from a great many different components, many made elsewhere. Purchasing officers may be involved right from the time when design engineers begin to specify the raw materials and the parts needed, starting to pinpoint possible suppliers and sorting out any problems on new designs with them, perhaps going back to the designers if their first specification won't work for any reason – perhaps cost.

A purchasing officer may consider over a dozen potential suppliers for a single item (looking at all their literature, samples, prices, asking for and assessing quotes etc) and any final contract will depend on achieving the best possible balance between technical specifications, the right delivery dates, and price. This can be multiplied several times when buying a component for cars, for instance. Obviously, the purchasing people take the specifications from the design engineers, the production manager, or even the office manager (for paper, etc), and the purchaser's job is to get the best possible commercial deal. They may 'buy forward' overseas to benefit from a change in exchange rates in their favour. They must know when and how to take advantage of capital allowances.

Purchasing must see that all the components for a particular product arrive at the right time. While components or raw materials arriving too late obviously hold up production, equally disastrous are purchases which arrive too early or in too large quantities – they tie up company money and valuable space and so affect overheads and therefore costings. Newspaper companies have the paper for tomorrow's editions delivered as late as possible. Keeping stock at the most cost-efficient levels is helped by computer-based stock control and manufacturing systems.

Purchasing officers have to know a great deal about potential suppliers – their ability to produce the product required and their overall reliability and stability – since continuity of supply can be a vital factor. Some purchasing officers specialise in buying one kind of component, material or product.

A purchasing department in a large firm, such as a brewery, can be responsible for a budget of over £200 million a year, and have a staff of nearly 40. The problems of supply can result in major companies buying shares in supplier companies. Purchasing staff monitor tariffs, prices and other criteria worldwide, and most raw materials have to come from abroad. Purchasing officers may also buy for overseas contract work, and this often means purchasing materials and goods suitable for use in quite different environmental conditions, for example, concrete for construction in the Middle East.

Purchasing officers or buyers may also buy services – in publishing the production manager is usually also a print buyer, and here the department has to stay abreast of new technology.

Buyers in retailing have to be expert forecasters. Retailing makes its entire profit and its reputation on the ability of its buyers to predict what will sell at a given point in time, and to acquire the products at the right time, and in the right quality and quantity. Buying too much or too many of a particular product not only means surplus stocks on the shelves and in store, but also leaves less shelf space for other lines which might have sold better. Too few or too little, and customers are lost again. Automatic stock control systems are, however, giving buyers faster, sharper analyses of what is selling best, and helping to cut down the basic routine in re-ordering.

Retail buying has achieved a popular reputation and status (often equal to the store manager's) so far, rather unfairly, denied to purchasing in other spheres.

Working in buying, purchasing and supply
The working day of a purchasing officer or buyer combines office-based work with a lot of time spent visiting suppliers. A great deal of time goes on negotiating, liaising inside the organisation with people for whom the purchasing/buying is being done, checking up and chasing suppliers. Detailed desk work includes dealing with the complexities of contracts – and understanding some contract law. Purchasing must keep up with technical changes in the firm's products, market and financial trends, monitoring contracts, watching for warning signals of problems or breaks in supply, and looking out for new price trends. Purchasing departments also contribute from all this to the information that management needs to plan and forecast. There can be a lot of pressure and regular crises to sort out. Buyers and purchasing officers travel a great deal, often overseas.

Purchasing officers and buyers have to become skilled negotiators and decision-makers, to develop sound business and financial sense, and learn to make objective judgements of people and companies. They need to learn to forecast trends and how to acquire and assess complex information. In some organisations they may need to learn about the technicalities of what they are buying, but not all purchasing officers agree on this. They have to liaise closely with colleagues within their own organisation and to create the right kind of personal relationship with suppliers' representatives. They need to be methodical and well-organised, especially if they are involved in stock control.

Recruitment and training It has been usual to go into purchasing in industry from a related 'function', for instance selling, and this is invariably the rule still in retailing. However, more and more organisations, particularly the larger manufacturing companies, now recruit trainee purchasers direct from school, university or polytechnic although time spent gaining experience elsewhere in an organisation is always an advantage.

Although recruiting organisations may not be too concerned about academic qualifications (apart from numeracy and English), it is easier to make a long-term career in purchasing or buying with a reasonable level of education, preferably at least to A level, or via a BTEC National award (the proportion of A-level entrants is still small though). An increasing number of graduates – about 25% of intake – are going into purchasing, especially where the work is technical and/or complex.

Qualifications and training Training is mostly organised by employers, mainly on-the-job, although a growing number of training courses make allowances for the wide variety of experience and qualifications with which trainees enter the field.

The Institute of Purchasing and Supply (1986 membership c16,000 – up 3000 from 1976 but down 1500 on 1983), is the professional body for all but those buyers working in retail and distribution.

IPS has been raising its own, and its members', status steadily over the past decade, and wants to become a 'first rank' professional body.

Although IPS sets foundation exams – including modern accounting methods, law in relation to purchasing, and general management principles and methods – but most students take a BTEC Higher National as the first stage of their professional qualifications.

The Institute's professional-stage exams includes specialist options, research and case studies. Full membership requires completion of the final examination and at least three years' experience in purchasing and supply, but the average study time from the lowest certificate through to finals is somewhere over six years (part-time), and during this most entrants complete the experience requirement. About 500 people a year complete their qualifications – about 40% are graduates, 30% have BTEC Higher awards, 10% another professional qualification, and 20% are 'other' mature entrants.

Minimum entry requirements are three O-level-equivalent passes at 16-plus† and two at A level (or equivalent A and/or AS levels), and including English language and a quantitative subject. However, of some 1000 new students a year, about a quarter are graduates, and only 5% have A levels only.

The Association of Supervisors in Purchasing and Supply (ASPS), administered by IPS, sets two-stage certificate exams in purchasing and stores. Entry requirements are at least four O-level equivalent passes at 16-plus†, two years' appropriate experience, or age 21.

For qualifications and training in retail buying see under RETAILING AND DISTRIBUTION, below.

Further information from the Institute of Purchasing and Supply.

DIRECT MARKETING AND MAIL ORDER
Selling direct to the consumer, via direct mail, mail order catalogue, TV or radio, magazine or newspaper, to produce a direct response or order, is one of the fastest-growing ways of selling, and is also one with the greatest potential. Practitioners identify several reasons for this: social – working women with less time to shop, too busy to cope with the problems of parking near a shopping centre, yet with more money to spend; economics – the increasing cost of taking the car to shop; and technological – the not-too-distant possibility of consumers using the telephone as a computer link to order goods straight from the TV screen.

Direct mail order, via catalogues and with a network of an estimated 4 million part-time agencies, at present makes up the largest proportion of direct marketing sales, although there are sizeable speciality firms and book and record clubs. Mail order trade grew dramatically over the 1970s, to take over 5% of of all retail sales by 1979, although it has tailed off somewhat since. About 40 firms employ over 50,000, but about 90% of business is done by four or five big companies, mostly based in the North of England.

These companies must keep operating costs to a minimum, and so took on computers early, with screen-based customer accounts, and standardised response letters etc. Even more crucial are sophisticated management techniques to provide good-quality, tested merchandise, at prices which must be accurately predicted to hold for the life of an expensive catalogue.

BUYING is therefore one of the key roles, and the firms employ large teams. Efficient WAREHOUSING, stock control and order assembly is equally crucial. Correspondence clerks look after agents, and VDU operators, in fairly large numbers, do the order-processing.

General administrators, as well as PERSONNEL, ADVERTISING (and promotion), ACCOUNTING, and COMPUTER PERSONNEL are also needed.

Training is largely in-house, although entrants are recommended to gain appropriate BTEC awards (see under RETAILING below).

RETAILING AND DISTRIBUTION
Background — retailing sectors — working in retailing (including retail management) — recruitment and entry — qualifications and training

Background
Retailing and distribution are the nerve ends of marketing, since it is here that strategies stand or fall, at the checkout. But while modern marketing methods contribute greatly to the so-called consumer revolution in retailing and distribution, other factors play a part. New tactics have constantly to be found to meet rising competition and costs in all areas, but especially on staff, premises,

rates. Customer demand, for more flexible opening hours, for greater choice, better design, style and quality, has to be met. Technology has been crucial too – supermarkets were hardly feasible until cheap and efficient pre-packaging was developed – and is still making changes.

Retailers have been slower than expected to use the latest computer and electronic technology, but it is happening, and falling prices for what have been very expensive retail systems should speed this. Laser-scanning checkouts are expected to be in use in most large supermarkets by 1990. These not only save time at the checkout, but also allow automatic stock control, re-ordering and invoicing, so costly store space can be saved while fast-selling lines are ordered in time to prevent running out of stock, and sales trends can be monitored and analysed daily. Sophisticated managerial methods and information systems quickly show through in company accounts – net profits for those without have risen at a much slower rate than costs. Even the family corner shop can have this kind of management information and calculate VAT, pay, stock-control, etc on relatively cheap micros.

Several 'electronic fund transfer' experiments, direct-debiting customers' accounts at the check-out-terminal are expected to be operating by 1990 too. 'Teleshopping' via interactive TV viewdata and/or home computers will also be more widespread by the early 1990s, though perhaps only popular with a minority.

Despite the trend to fewer, larger stores (which might be stemmed somewhat by 'gallerias') – the number of individual shops and stores has been falling steadily since the 1950s – well over 200,000 are still in business, and the range and variety is still large. They still include many 'traditional'-style large chain and department stores, multiples, smaller specialist shops – antique shops, booksellers, butchers, bakers, chemists. Supermarkets – and their edge-of-town big-brother superstores (400 in 1986 and more coming) and shopping centres – are an accepted part of life now.

But the retailing revolution which began with them and the 1960s boutiques has entered a new and much more aggressive phase, as younger, pace-setting retailers swallow up chains and department stores which have failed to target new markets or adapt to changing consumer demand.

While volume sales are buoyant and still rising – booming even – retail sales as a percentage of all consumer spending has fallen steadily to well under 40% in the mid-80s from 53% in 1950. Since much spending is credit financed, retailers know long-term problems loom. Further, shortages of prime sites, the drive for more customers in the high-spending social groups to grab a greater share of the market, high costs – of new technology, modernising and marketing, etc – which take greater financial resources, are all among the factors forcing a spate of take overs and major re-vamps amongst the survivors. About 75% of retailers redesigned their stores between 1983 and 1985.

Retailers, according to one analyst, can only succeed by closely identifying their customers, making sure they get the products they want and the stores are attractive to them. Even the most successful and largest chain store has been forced to rethink its winning formula – 'managing change' its chairman has said. Galleria – 'shops within shops', specialist 'satellite' stores, new product ranges and working more closely with suppliers to react faster to consumer demand, new store designs and promotions, credit-card schemes are amongst the ways managers are responding now to the impact of even greater competition. 'Image' is crucial to success. Targeting markets more closely – in clothes, food, 'high-tech' equipment, financial services, everything for the home – means some store groups are now running several different, 'parallel' retail operations, to get target-groups of customers to identify with them.

Increasing use is made of modern managerial methods – anticipating demand and regulating supply, determining optimum stock levels and mixes and controlling stock losses more accurately, reducing operating costs, looking endlessly for more economies in overheads – self service, fewer but larger stores, co-operative buying. Optimum use of staff – with a high and rising use of part-timers, especially 16- to 20-year-olds still in education – plays a major part.

Some sectors, eg butchers, shoe shops, fishmongers, bakers, have changed very little in their trading methods, with more than 90% of sales accounted for by one kind of product. In others, especially grocery, clothing, 'high-tech' electronics (and photography), DIY, furniture and other consumer goods for the home, and pharmacies, innovation is now near-continuous, and trading styles transformed. Completely new chains – of health food and video shops and record/cassette stores – have burst onto the high street. Computer dealers have come – and many have already gone.

Retailing still employs (1986) about 2.1 million people (including 740,000 part time), barely 10% of the working population, and down from 2.4 million and 11% in 1982.

While the great majority of businesses still specialise to some extent (see below), the 3300 or so mixed businesses account for over 14% of total turnover in retailing – and the largest fifty, with over 4500 outlets between them, for over 92% of business done in multiples.

The retailing sectors

The range and variety of goods sold by stores expands steadily both with technological innovations – for example, it is estimated that, since the development of man-made fibres, the number of different types of cloth has increased to 400 from the basic four made from natural fibres – and from greater opportunities to import. Expertise in type of product is often essential.

DEALING IN ANTIQUES AND ART, AND BOOKSELLING traditionally demand expert knowledge, both of the entire field and usually even a section of it. Both have a different kind of image from other areas of retailing. Yet selling works of art, antiques or books is still commerce, and traders have to make a profit. They need a business sense, must know what is profitable to buy and what price will make a profit, as well as management skills just as other retailers. Caring too much for antiques, paintings, books etc can be a positive disadvantage, since it can be a strong disincentive to sell.

As in other areas of retailing, shelf or shop space is valuable, and the accent is always on good turnover of stock.

In antique dealing, with an estimated 20,000 dealers, only 500 are accepted by the British Antique Dealers' Association, and the Fine Art Trade

Guild has only 1000 members. The field is divided between a fairly large number of medium- and small-sized dealers, and the large salerooms (dealing in both art and antiques). Interest in antiques and in hand-made objects generally has grown considerably, both for their intrinsic interest and as investments. Increased interest in antiques notwithstanding, the antique world can provide a living for very few, and it takes considerable dedication to make a career. It is a very close-knit world. Many businesses are run by families, or have been set up by friends with interests in common, and dealers frequently sell to, and via, each other, so personal contacts count for a great deal. Learning is mainly by experience, preferably under an established dealer, and may involve starting as a clerk or in packing.

The art world is even more specialised. Dealing in art can be similar to antique dealing, but galleries which exhibit and sell works of art (as opposed to the art galleries which are repositories, for which see CREATIVE WORK), are slightly different. Most specialise in the work of a group of artists, frequently with some thread (of period, or school, for example) linking their work. In the past the gallery-artist relationship could be very paternalistic, but galleries (and indeed even the artists) have become far more businesslike, backing their aesthetic judgement with very commercial contracts. Like antiques, art is now sold on an international scale, with London as one of the major centres. For a few, therefore, travel is possible.

However, neither galleries nor dealers employ very many people, and opportunities are limited. Luck or personal contact often play a part in getting a first post, but it makes sense to have in-depth knowledge of a particular subject as well as a broad background in art, normally via a first degree or similar course in history of art (although this is not necessarily accepted as a qualification). Some larger art dealers, particularly auction houses, now run regular training courses – a few last a year, but there are also shorter programmes. Training also involves gaining appropriate experience.

Booksellers face tremendous problems of rapidly-rising costs (premises, books, staff) with an explosive annual increase in the number of books published, which makes stock-buying increasingly hazardous. However, sales have been rising, quite sharply, lately, and larger firms have been controlling stock more tightly using computer-based systems.

Traditionally, bookselling was considered a rather erudite occupation, but modern conditions have forced the trade into a mould closer to the rest of retailing, with larger organisations, not necessarily only selling books. Many booksellers now rely on trade in things like stationery to maintain profitability, and use modern marketing methods. Specialist bookselling, of technical, business and scientific books, and for universities and other libraries, has expanded most. Some 4300 firms (with nearly 6000 bookshops) employ about 36,000 people.

Antiquarian bookselling is also highly specialised, and has close links with antique dealing, with one important exception: thanks to the relatively small size of the printing industry and censorship up to the industrial revolution, the titles and editions of most books published are known and catalogued. Of an estimated 1400 antiquarian booksellers in the UK, 400 belong to the Antiquarian Booksellers Association. Many do not have shops at all, but deal entirely by post or in person, and many travel the auctions and salerooms with antique and art dealers, often making a steady profit from the never-ending demand for individual titles from overseas university libraries.

The best booksellers provide highly personalised services for their customers. They help anyone not sure of what they want and trace individual books, both new and second-hand, for others. Bookselling suffers from a very out-of-date distribution system, despite computer-based ordering systems, compounded by the problem that booksellers cannot hope to stock even a reasonable percentage of books in print. It is not, therefore, easy to provide a good service for customers.

Opportunities for promotion are probably greatest in the larger organisations rather than in the bookshops with small staff. The level of subject expertise which most booksellers achieve is rarely as well rewarded in bookselling as it would be elsewhere. In larger organisations, of course, executive responsibility (as opposed to subject expertise) is generally more suitably rewarded.

Qualifications and training Assistants learn on the job, starting fairly menial tasks – keeping shelves clean and tidy, filling out order forms and keeping records. Most booksellers encourage their staff to read the trade press and stay abreast of publishing trends, and also to study for the Booksellers Association diploma in bookselling, designed to meet the needs of bookshops of all types and sizes. Candidates must gain certificates in all the examinations (the workbook, bookshop practice, bookshop bibliography, bibliography and classification, books and the mind of man, bookshop economics, a specialist subject or modern writing, and an oral) before the diploma is awarded (graduates in English literature may gain exemption from the specialist paper). No formal academic qualifications are needed, although most employers would expect new entrants to have a suitable educational background which should include at least some GCE O-level passes. School-leavers with A levels and some graduates are recruited by the larger, specialised bookshops, especially those serving universities. For management, a national qualification, eg BTEC, is suggested.

BUILDERS' MERCHANTS ETC, see under CONSTRUCTION.

BUTCHERS: the traditional sawdust-strewn shop is under threat, with only an estimated 15,000 shops remaining in 1986, down 10,000 in ten years. Specialist butchers now sell under 40% of carcass meat, their market eroded by supermarkets and freezer centres, and consumers eating less meat. The major chains have been rationalising and merging, and are looking hard for ways to widen their appeal.

Trained butchers, though, are still needed by traditional shops, larger multiples and supermarkets (where the work is mainly pre-packaging). Promotion is into shop management, inspection, or meat buying for large organisations – retailers, large hotels and caterers, and manufacturers producing cooked meat products, poultry producers etc.

Qualifications and training The national organisation is -
The Institute of Meat which promotes training and is also the industry's

examining body. The three-stage examinations are at affiliate, associate and full membership levels, the latter roughly equivalent to HND, and including marketing and managerial training, meat inspection as well as food microbiology, preservation and hygiene, food chemistry and nutrition, or meat factory and abattoir operation. The full scheme takes six years on a part-time basis, or four or five years combined part- and full-time. No academic qualifications are needed to take the affiliate exams, and exemptions are possible from some stages. The Institute has also introduced a modular skills testing scheme for apprentices, YTS trainees etc. In all, nearly 1500 students sat Institute exams in 1986

SELLING CARS AND OTHER VEHICLES is not the only function of the retail motor industry. It also does maintenance, testing and repair (for which see SERVICE INDUSTRIES), and sells tyres and other parts, and petroleum products.

Car sales staff work for dealers, and sell new and/or second-hand cars. Dealers selling new cars work closely with the manufacturer(s) with whom they have a dealership, often fitting in to nationally-designed marketing campaigns. Buying a car is the second largest purchase in many people's lives and so is a major event. Sales staff are expected to give them just as good service as they give anyone replacing their car annually. Sales staff have to be very convincing, and helpful. They may buy second-hand cars as well as selling them. To gain promotion, to sales manager and above, often means moving around. Competition for car sales is intense and showrooms have been closed, but manufacturers still franchise some 7000 dealers.

Recruitment/entry/training etc Most employers who can offer reasonable training and some prospects want a good standard of education shown by a good spread of O-level-equivalent passes at 16-plus†. Potential sales staff (generally recruited between the ages of 16 and 21) often start as apprentices and can take the CGLI first-year craft course to learn about the vehicles they will eventually sell. After the first year, a CGLI course in vehicle salesmanship, which some larger companies link to general training in administration, can be taken. Most manufacturers put on selling courses as well as on particular models.The industry is increasingly interested in recruiting trainee managers, with GCE A-level passes and even degrees. Larger firms provide the essential experience while entrants take the Motor Agents Association/Institute of the Motor Industry diploma in motor trade management, which can also be taken by anyone who has taken the CGLI schemes.

See also TRANSPORT under SERVICE INDUSTRIES.

CHEMISTS OR (COMMUNITY) PHARMACISTS Nearly 8000 chemists are in business, with some 12,000 outlets (1985), a steady rise from the 1980 low of just over 10,600. About 15% are owned by the major multiples (the largest with over 1000 branches). They employ (1986) about 110,000 people (over half part-time), of whom nearly 20,000 are qualified pharmacists and some are pharmacy technicians. Pharmacists may own their own shops, but more usually manage a pharmacy for someone else, or work for a multiple.

Although, on average, some 70% of independent pharmacies' turnover comes from dispensing drugs under contract to the NHS, most pharmacies also sell a wide range of other medical and related products, toiletries, cosmetics, and some a great many household and 'leisure' products. Pharmacists have, then, to combine a professional with a business role.

While drug companies now pre-package most drugs and other medical supplies, the pharmacist still has a major part to play. Interpreting, clarifying, recording and checking the 400 million prescriptions they process every year, is though still rather different from actually preparing and dispensing medicine, of which they now do little. Modern medicines, while more effective, are also more complex, potentially more dangerous, and more expensive. Pharmacists can expect to handle more complex forms of treatment, and with a rising proportion of older people, greater and more specialised advice and attention will be needed.

A recent report on pharmacy recommended a return to a greater use of the pharmacist's traditional advice giving, that pharmacists' skills should be more easily available to help the GP in prescribing, and that they should be more involved in helping patients to handle their medicines. It also proposed firmer guidelines on other commercial activities, a greater emphasis on the advisory aspects of a pharmacists' work in deciding how much they should get from the NHS, and more stress on professional standards.

Qualifications and training Pharmacists must qualify via a recognised degree course. See ACADEMIC AND VOCATIONAL STUDIES.

CLOTHING AND FOOTWEAR accounts, once again, for a rising proportion of consumer expenditure – 7% in 1985 (against about 6.2% in 1982 but 8.7% in 1967). In 1980, the number of clothing and related stores was estimated at 57,000 (against 81,000 in 1971) with stores specialising in women's clothes outnumbering men's by nearly two to one, and including an estimated 11,800 footwear stores. But employment has fallen sharply, and in 1986 was down to 242,500 (against some 290,000 in 1982), nearly half part time.

Ever since the 1960s fashion revolution this has been one of the most volatile retailing sectors, constantly changing in response to trends and coping with several trends and great variety of styles at once. But profits are hard to earn. Small shops, often specialising in quite a narrow range of the very latest 'designer' wear, greatly outnumber the multiples, and men's outfitters have joined, and are even ahead of, the trends. The retail trade has become accustomed to a much more fashion-conscious buying public, a buying public which is surer of what it wants, and less ready to buy just anything.

For the trade the skills it has always needed to make a success and profits are more important than ever. Crucial are the ability to predict trends, to see what will and will not sell, to find sources of supply at home and overseas, to keep costs down, and turnover up.

Qualifications and training see general section below.

CONFECTIONERS, NEWSAGENTS AND TOBACCONISTS The number of outlets has stayed roughly static at about 40,000 for several years (but it was about 60,000 in 1961). The half-dozen or so multiples (most combining newsagency with bookselling) are steadily expanding and increasing their share of the market, to around 40-50%, and the number of owner-manager shops is falling.

Between them they employ (1986) 132,500 people (down from 216,000 in 1982), well over half on a part-time basis.

Few independents can afford many full-time staff, so most openings are with multiples, where the size of operations gives considerable prospects for managers. The pace for owner-managers can be tough, but it is difficult not to make a fair profit at the moment (takings increased 25% in 1985), and 'prime site' shops sell well when their owners have had enough six-and-half twelve-hour days a week.

DIY AND HARDWARE STORES This £2000 million-market is dominated by seven firms, most of them multiple/supermarket chains, running some 3900 outlets, and independent hardware/ironmongers (about 7400 outlets) are having to fight for survival. All stores need staff who can help customers with advice as well as goods and service.

Qualifications and training The National Institute of Hardware puts on a range of correspondence and residential courses and seminars in retail management, skills and product knowledge courses. As a YTS managing agent (registering over 100 trainees a year), NIH provides a correspondence course and residential training.

ELECTRICAL CONSUMER DURABLES (radios, stereo systems, refrigerators, heaters and so on, accounting for some 5% of consumer expenditure) are an example of an area of specialised selling which needs extensive knowledge of the goods being sold. In the past it has been easy to gain this experience in the shop, but formal training is becoming necessary as goods increase in technological sophistication and customers require advice on both their suitability for particular purposes and/or the use and care of particular items, as well as efficient repair services.

Some 13,000 outlets employ 71,000 people. After-sales service is essential, and so many thousands of skilled service and installation technicians and craft workers are employed, although not necessarily at the point of sale. Some of the largest firms in distribution operate in this sector. Just one group employs 3000 service engineers, 900 installation engineers, 2000 accounting staff, and 350 branch managers.

Qualifications and training for service staff (see ELECTRICAL ENGINEERING) include BTEC awards and CGLI schemes. A national apprenticeship scheme is run by the Radio and Television Retailers' Association.

FINANCIAL SERVICES Retail banks and building societies have long had a presence in the high street, but have always managed to maintain a somewhat different 'image' from the rest of retailing, and have only lately begun to adopt sales-oriented marketing strategies. See FINANCE section.

FLORISTS not only sell flowers and plants, they also make up bouquets, wreaths, and decorative displays, both for individual customers, and many firms and other organisations with plant displays in offices, hotels, restaurants, at exhibitions etc. While most florists work for retail shops – specialist or multiple store – some work for independent contractors, and go out to create and maintain displays, window boxes etc.

Some people prefer to stay with display work, while others go on to become buyers, supervisors or managers, or start their own businesses.

Recruitment and entry While no formal qualifications are required, the Society of Floristry recommends 16-plus† passes (at least grade D) in some or all of English, maths, art, biology, business studies, a language, and a craft subject. At least four passes may be needed to study full-time. Most people start in a local florist, but some larger firms have traineeships, and the British Retail Florists Association runs YTS schemes in some towns. A 'Saturday job' in a florists while still at school can be useful.

Qualifications and training involves learning about plants and how to display and care for them. It also includes training in marketing, buying, financial and other retailing management techniques, and developing a business sense.

Most people learn while working, studying part-time for the examinations. It is, though, possible to study for them full-time over one or two years at a college of further education with periods of work experience in florists, or at a private school (but this can be very expensive). The main qualifications are - CGLI scheme 019 (three parts) or BTEC National (at Northop: Welsh Horticulture College only) or recognised private-school qualification can be followed by Society of Floristry diploma examinations, required for full membership of the Society.

FOOD SALES account for a falling proportion, of consumer expenditure – 14% in 1985 (including alcoholic drinks increases it to 21.4%). It is the area of retailing where rationalisation has been greatest, but recent take-overs have been by large firms wanting to expand. The industry's 48,200 firms employ 584,000 people, but over half of them part time (1986), in 100,000 outlets. Nearly 69% of turnover is accounted for by the 4400 multiples, but the eight largest account for nearly 50%. Specialist food stores still include, in addition to butchers (see above), greengroceries, bakers, fishmongers, dairies, and health-food stores, but their share of the market is down to barely 20%.

To maintain profitability and retain market share, the large multiples are having to be both aggressively efficient – in financial control, purchasing, stock control and turnover, and staffing – and innovative, in marketing – looking for new ways to attract customers, and diversifying out of food into household goods etc. Smaller chains and independents are having to turn into up-market, fine- or (eg) health-food stores.

Qualifications and training The Institute of Grocery Distribution has always tried to encourage training, and has now moved into technical services in business education. The BTEC National Certificate in distribution studies (below) is now offered by the Institute as a two-year 'open-learning' course with regional 'workshop' sessions. IGD also organises workshop-based schemes (mainly for A-level and graduate entrants) leading to examinations for a diploma in grocery distribution or marketing. IGD has developed a YTS distribution training package (trainees can also take a relevant BTEC First Certificate), a 'commodity-knowledge' programme, and a range of other open-learning schemes.

FRANCHISES A high proportion of franchise business are retail outlets – fast food, copy shops etc. See ALTERNATIVE EMPLOYMENT.

FURNITURE AND FURNISHING The sector furnishes homes, offices, hotels, ships, aeroplanes etc, and also leases, or sells to organisations which lease. The cost of furnishing is rising steadily, with fashions changing more often (furniture accounts for 4.2% of total consumer expenditure). Customers often need expert help in making choices, and staff have to be aware of the latest developments. Some areas of retail furnishing come close to ANTIQUE DEALING, especially in department and larger furniture stores.

Over 13,000 outlets employ some 70,000 people. Eight firms take over a third of the market; competition has grown, with multiples not traditionally selling furniture coming into the market, and prospects for young management trainees look reasonable.

Qualifications and training The National Association of Retail Furnishers works to improve the level of technical knowledge and efficiency in the trade. Their diploma course (two years part-time) covers all kinds of furnishing, history of furniture, interior decoration, selling and display (similar options can be taken for BTEC awards, below).

See also MANUFACTURING and, for furniture and interior design, ART AND DESIGN.

JEWELLERY is one of the few retailing sectors still closely linked to the craft, some traders (still) selling their own work, although most retailers' workshops deal only with repairs. The trade is still dominated by small independents, but the relatively small number of multiples take a high proportion of business. It is a sector which has been slow to modernise, but the multiples have recently started to adopt more aggressive marketing policies, other firms have come into the business, and others have merged.

Jewellery shops usually sell a range of products, silver and electro-plated ware, luxury leather goods, and clocks and watches – some deal in gems and 'precious' stones.

Qualifications and training Qualifications include –

The National Association of Goldsmiths is the trade association for retail jewellers and promotes educational schemes. Its diploma examination covers merchandise and materials, hallmarks, gemstones, horology, silverware, and salemanship at intermediate level and also gem materials, jewellery design, antique silver and shopkeeping for the final. It can be completed in two years on a part-time basis, either at a college of further education or by correspondence course (conducted by NAG).

The Gemmological Association's diploma is an alternative, but is more limited in scope and is mainly for craft work (covering elementary crystallography, physical and optical properties, apparatus and units of weight and measurement, gem materials and fashioning gemstones).

The British Horological Institute (1986 membership 3660) co-ordinates the craft as practised in manufacturing, retailing and by collectors. The certificate in technical horology is geared to equipping people technically to service clocks and watches, and is taken in three stages. Around 50 people took each stage of the exams in 1986. A new two-part diploma course in horological science starts in 1988.

Some craft training is still available, but retail jewellers prefer to start new entrants as junior sales staff, training on the job and taking appropriate qualifications. For promotion to buying or management, a national management certificate is recommended. See also ART AND DESIGN.

THE MUSIC TRADE includes shops which sell musical instruments (from guitars and the latest electronic equipment for pop groups, through to wind, string and percussion for orchestral players), and piano showrooms, which have recently increased sales. Records and cassettes are sold by several thousand retail outlets, in many instances alongside hi-fi equipment, although this is now as often sold in stores selling electrical and electronic equipment for home use. Many music outlets are part of multiples.

The music business generally needs a reasonable musical background, and a good knowledge of the products involved, preferably taking in all kinds of music. See also MUSIC and CRAFTS under CREATIVE WORK.

OPTICIANS Since 'deregulation' in 1984, anyone can sell spectacles, although only OPHTHALMIC OPTICIANS (or doctors) can prescribe them. Major chains still employ ophthalmic opticians and have most of their outlets managed by DISPENSING OPTICIANS. While sales have increased by over 5% since 1984, the number of outlets has risen by an estimated 12%, and the competition is considerable. The largest chain has nearly 450 outlets, and nearly 15% of the sight-testing market.

Qualifications and training for ophthalmic and dispensing opticians, see under HEALTH SERVICES.

OTHER EXAMPLES of specialist sectors of retailing include – sports equipment, garden centres, stationery and office machinery, and toys and games.

Working in retailing

Every shop and store is geared to one purpose, selling, so most people (except for office and display staff) who go into retailing spend some time selling, to gain experience of the point of the exercise, to learn about the stock and how to keep abreast of trends, how to handle money and cash registers, about stock and sales records and, above all, about good customer relations and the skills of selling.

Some people stay in selling and work their way up to supervisor, section, departmental, store, area, regional and more senior management. Others may, after a period of experience move either into buying (see also PURCHASING AND SUPPLY), into merchandising, personnel and training, or other areas of administration. Generally, people spend less and less time actually selling, with promotion fastest for those who show the greatest aptitudes.

The most obvious career prospects are in larger group and chain stores, although smaller independent shops do still offer a different kind of career and working life.

Large multiples, with well over 1000 stores will have as many managers, but six to twelve times as many departmental heads and a total sales staff of some 30,000 (but fewer than 40 regional managers). They can offer structured experience, career progression and promotion within a large, and somewhat hierarchical, organisation. Smaller stores may have less to offer in breadth of experience, training or promotion, but individual responsibility may come earlier, the work at any one time more varied, and the managerial structures less formal. To gain experience and/or promotion may mean changing jobs, but major multiples may have to move staff from branch to branch and from town to town to give them appropriate training and promotion.

MANAGERS, of departments or stores, are responsible for day-to-day operations, within the guidelines of company policy – usually transmitted by a stream of daily memos etc. Although major 'functions' like buying and some personnel management/recruitment may be centralised, the store or department manager still has considerable personal responsibility, and in a large store will have one or two assistants, plus office staff including someone to handle shop-floor staffing.

Managers must meet sales targets, using both established techniques and ingenuity to attract customers. They must prepare detailed reports on sales, progress, estimates and projections. They keep a check on their stocks, supervise sales staff and stockroom, see that goods are coming in as needed with no shortages, that the quality and quantity of goods is checked, that stock not 'moving' does not lock up shelf space, that price changes are made etc. The manager has to see that the store or department is properly staffed to meet the number of customers normally expected at any one time or day – neither too many, nor too few – recruit as needed (and know where to find staff), supervise them and arrange any training. Managers must watch local trading conditions, and report on what other stores are doing to head office. They report on aspects of buying policy too. Managers are responsible for security and keeping down stock losses. They organise and monitor displays and window-dressing, sales promotion and local advertising, service where this is needed, and cleaning and maintaining the shop premises. They have to be ready to solve all kinds of problems on the spot. Many managers are quite young, still in their 20s.

MERCHANDISING is a label given to several different jobs, but it is largely about seeing that stores are properly and fully stocked with the right 'mix' of products for what sells in the locality; watching and planning stock levels, and seeing that budgets are designed so as to minimise risks and maximise profits. Merchandisers monitor what is happening in individual stores of group, both visiting them and analysing computer records of stock levels and sales – which colours and what sizes have sold best and which have not, and where? Some merchandising teams layout and stock new or revamped stores and get them working profitably. It is usually part of the route up for management trainees.

SALES PROMOTION AND DISPLAY Very professional display and presentation – shop window and interior displays – are essential to modern marketing techniques for retailing. They use a wide range of sophisticated artistic and advertising techniques to attract customers both to the store itself and to particular items of merchandise. Larger stores employ their own teams of trained artists, window-dressers, sign- and even copywriters. Smaller ones may combine the work with other tasks or employ agencies or freelance staff to do this. In all cases they have to work closely with marketing staff, to know what to promote and how it should be promoted, and with departmental sales to ensure that the displays will fit in and their purpose be appreciated. See also ADVERTISING and ART AND DESIGN.

OTHER STAFF Some larger groups have technical departments, eg labs to test products, and so employ small teams of eg SCIENTISTS. Larger store groups employ relatively large numbers of administrative staff, including ACCOUNT-ANTS, PERSONNEL MANAGERS, MANAGEMENT SERVICES (including COMPUTER STAFF), and general administration (see also OFFICE WORK). Large groups also have their own property and maintenance divisions, employing eg SURVEYORS. All need supporting clerical staff. Service departments include transport and catering (see also SERVICE INDUSTRIES).

Recruitment and entry It is not, generally, difficult to get a start somewhere (except in very popular areas like antique dealing), but competition is increasing for the best opportunities for training and promotion.

Retailers readily admit that distribution 'does not yet present the image of a modern employer, and so is not able to attract and hold the best of workers. The human and organisational challenges, and the opportunity for early management, which are the industry's greatest assets as an employer, are largely unappreciated by many who would find most satisfaction in grasping such opportunities' (Management Training in the Distributive Trades). Since that was written, unemployment has soared, and retailing can be more selective, although it is unlikely that attitudes among the young have changed much.

Retailing is now recruiting fewer but better-qualified people for training as managers, and while this is mainly amongst school-leavers still, larger groups and stores expect to increase further their graduate recruitment (they have undoubtedly gained from cut-backs or oversupply elsewhere). Graduate (university only) recruitment has risen to around the 1500 mark (1985) from just 900 in 1979, and one large group alone takes several hundred, but reports have suggested that graduates are not staying. Over fifty major groups and stores are now (1986) known to recruit graduates regularly, and another thirty on an occasional basis.

Retailing needs entrants with some knowledge of modern managerial techniques, an understanding of the social and economic environment in which retailing operates, some knowledge of statistics and behavioural sciences, and ability to organise and operate modern communication systems in organisations which may have a large number of very widely scattered, quite small units.

With few exceptions, for example a degree in pharmacy is needed to become a retail/community pharmacist, educational qualifications are not the most important factor. However a good educational background is likely to improve prospects of promotion.

Retailers provide some 80,000 places a year on YTS schemes. However, 'delivery' is largely at local level, and schemes clearly vary from store to store.

Qualification and training Training arrangements within retailing, with some notable exceptions, have always been rather piecemeal and not particularly good. Some large groups have fairly large-scale in-house training schemes, but there has been very little increase in any form of release to study for national or professional qualifications. The traditional pattern in retailing was very ad hoc, with little in the way of formal qualification; any awards have been on a rather piecemeal basis, run by numerous different trade organisations.

Progress in getting viable voluntary arrangements to replace the disbanded statutory board was minimal up to 1986. As of early 1987, the situation looks rather brighter. The National Retail Training Council and the National Association of Colleges in Distributive Education and Training have together developed a new basic training 'framework'. The 'Retail Training Information Base' identifies some 48 'competences' – 22 foundation and 26 optional. The plan is, from September 1988, for modular accreditation of work-based assessment, with nationally-awarded qualifications. It is hoped that all trainees will be trained in the foundation competences and appropriate optional ones, in flexible, on- and/or off-the-job training.

Larger organisations, and stores selling goods which need a sound technical background and/or skills (eg butchers, electronic goods), have the best track records on training. A high proportion is in house, and in smaller stores, often fairly informal. Larger stores have their own training schools. Some retailers give day or other release to study for nationally-recognised qualifications, but it cannot be assumed – even some large chain stores expect to keep their best, including graduate, recruits for life, and so see no need for them to gain 'outside' qualifications, which they might need to change jobs. It may, then be a sensible precaution to study for a professional or distribution qualification on a spare-time basis. Training for management – theoretically possible for everyone with ambition, appropriate personal qualities and reasonable educational background – is largely by a combination of varied experience in the stores and training sessions. It should include direct selling experience in several different departments, and experience in departments not directly involved in sales, eg merchandising, finance, personnel. Graduates starting out in most large retail organisations are generally given accelerated training, with experience in junior supervisory posts within a very short period, and the possibility of a post as, eg assistant buyer or an equivalent function within two years of starting.

Only one degree course, at Manchester Polytechnic, specialises in retail management. The Business and Technician Education Council (BTEC), meanwhile, offers the main formal qualifications for retailing and distribution, but numbers taking these schemes are still relatively low.

BTEC Distributive studies schemes have been redesigned for the new 'framework' (see ACADEMIC AND VOCATIONAL QUALIFICATIONS) -
Higher National awards: courses share some core content (work organisations, external environment, operational techniques and procedures) with other business and finance schemes, adding units in the distributive industry, distribution and the market environment, and resource management and control in distribution, taking up eight of the twelve-unit certificate and 16-unit diploma course. The remaining option units are college based. Entry requirements are as for all BTEC Higher awards††.
National awards: courses share some core content (business-related skills,

people in organisations, finance and the organisation in its environment) with other business and finance schemes, adding two further core units on distribution. The remaining two option units (for the certificate), six for the diploma can be taken from a long list of options in commerce, general business, finance, secretarial, but including eg display, law relating to distribution, mail order, supervision principles and practice, buying principles, sales function and selling methods, storage and stock control. Entry requirements are as for all BTEC National awards††.

First Certificate/Diploma: the three core units cover eg customer/consumer, profit and profitability, people in distribution, the distributive industry and organisations, stock, marketing. The remaining two units (certificate), five (diploma) can be in business, finance, secretarial work etc, but specifically distribution units include commodity distribution, consumer legislation, display and merchandise presentation, food or hardware/DIY retailing, merchandising and sales promotion, product design and packaging, selling methods and customer relations. Entry requirements are as for all BTEC First awards††.

A Continuing Education Certificate in management studies (retailing) is also available.

SCOTVEC provides schemes/awards in distribution at National Certificate and Higher National level.

See also SERVICE INDUSTRIES.

Further information The National Retail Training Council.

SELLING (INCLUDING EXPORTING)

Selling, as opposed to retail sales, is the interface between manufacturer, wholesaler and retailer. It is complementary to marketing, which deals with overall strategy for which selling provides the tactical army, although when selling a single plant to an engineering giant the two may well seem the same. The salesman or woman, company representative, or sales engineer sells a company's product or services to their consumers who may themselves resell it, or use it.

While a large number of salesmen and women sell products to retailers, an equally large number sell products, parts and components to other industrial and commercial concerns, and yet others sell plant and equipment and other services. It is, therefore, not one but increasingly a range of careers, since the skills and processes involved in selling cosmetics to the high-street chemist are rather different from those needed to sell multi-million-pound chemical plant to a leading international company, or car components in Coventry. Sales staff frequently spend much of their working life within one of several broad areas, for instance, repeat consumer goods (food, stationery, cosmetics etc), consumer durables (home computers, television and video equipment, furniture, carpets), clothing, footwear, toys; industrial supplies (chemicals, bricks, components), capital equipment (office or factory), and services (print, business systems, financial services, packaging).

In principle, the more scientifically- or technologically-complex the products or services being sold, the more complex and lengthy the sales process.

Increasingly, the professional salesman or woman also oversees a contract, or installation of a new piece of equipment from start to finish, or is at least part of the team which does so in the case of large plant, equipment, main-frame computers etc. This can mean working on a single project for several years.

An estimated 200.000 people work in sales, of whom probably 20% can be classed as 'professional'. These are the men (and some women) selling computers, pharmaceuticals, chemical plant, machine tools, vehicles, office equipment, steel, engines, space, print, paper, fuel, consumer goods to retailers, and services (for instance, time-sharing computer facilities). In manufacturing industry and in plant manufacture, the sales staff are often called sales engineers (probably over 50,000 people), about a fifth of whom probably are graduates or have an equivalent technological background. In principle, anyone who sells must be expert in the particular field, so the more sophisticated, complex or technologically advanced the product, plant or service, the higher the qualifications the sales staff will need. Pharmaceuticals are mostly sold by those with degrees in pharmacy, pharmacology, life sciences, or even medical sciences, and the more sophisticated and complex computers and computing services by graduates or people with equivalent qualifications fully trained in the machines or services they are offering.

Whatever is sold, the sales force is a major point of contact between their own organisation and the customer, and the importance of this is recognised by reputable and responsible firms. Selling, in these terms, means rather more than gaining a signature on an agreement. Sales people have to build up a good working relationship with their clients. This often means that the sales staff must learn a great deal about the customer's business, and may be able to make constructive suggestions of new uses or possible modifications to the equipment or service they have sold. They must be able to assess what modifications or special needs the customer may have, and how best these may be met by their own company. The customers will want to know a great deal about the goods, equipment, or service they are buying; they may want advice on promotion of, for instance, certain consumer goods, or to tap the sales staffs' wider knowledge of current and future trends. In turn, a firm will expect its sales force to keep management informed of any market intelligence that reaches them, and to feed back customers' reactions on a wide range of issues.

Most sales staff, except perhaps those selling one-off or custom-built plant or equipment, or goods or services which have limited demand, each have their own clearly-defined geographical areas, the size of which will largely depend on the number of customers, or potential customers, the firm has in the region. Within their own areas, sales staff are generally able to organise their own working times and methods, so long as they produce satisfactory results. Selling is a very peripatetic career, whatever the size of the area: small, and the salesman or women responsible for it gets to know it very well, and becomes a member of the working community; larger, and there is greater variation and more frequent surprises.

Selling overseas, exporting, to be successful, needs even greater expertise, especially with current levels of competition. Export sales staff have to learn about the people to whom they are going to sell, to know and appreciate the effects of the environment in which they live and work, to understand and respect particular customers, and to be able to get on with people whose attitudes, thinking, etc are very different from their own. Exporters must know how their products can be exploited in particular regions, do research into what will and will not sell, be prepared to modify their products to meet local needs, and understand export/import procedures and regulations for the UK and country of destination. While technical skills are crucial, to be able to sell, and communicate well, in the relevant language, is about as important. A recent Newcastle Polytechnic survey showed a high proportion firms admitting they had lost export orders because their sales teams did not have the right languages. With so much to learn first, it is rare to start in export sales, except for graduates with appropriate degrees, business training and experience (see BUSINESS STUDIES under QUALIFICATIONS AND CAREERS).

Most people who go into sales start in sales administration. Although some major firms put people into 'the field' straight away, a spell inside a firm to learn the business, about products, accounting/invoicing and systems etc, is more common. For school-leavers, this may take a year or two, for graduates months.

Junior or trainee salesmen/women usually go on to more important field posts, in larger, or more densely populated (with customers, that is) areas; some may then go into export sales. Others may later become supervisors, with the possibility of promotion to area or regional sales manager, to sales manager and even director. Some people may spend time in training, or in sales administration at middle-management level, or in sales promotion, research or recruitment. At the lower levels, particularly, and in the less complex forms of selling, staff turnover is generally high, so promotion can come quite rapidly for those who do well in the field.

Hours are often long and irregular, with time away from home, travelling, and much waiting about. Reports have to be written, orders made out and sent in to the office, accounts recorded.

Recruitment and entry Although sales staff are trained, not born, selling does demand certain personal qualities. It takes physical and mental stamina, even toughness; it means being resilient, not easily offended, and adaptable; it needs drive, initiative, self-confidence, and persistence. Sales people have to be good at working with others, always ready to meet new people and prepared to get on with all types. Salesmen/women have to be able to live in the middle of a situation, between the problems and demands of an employer wanting to sell, but perhaps having difficulties meeting schedules, and the customer, anxious about the scale of investment involved. Sales people need to be able to keep up with what is new in their field, to stay abreast of technical change, to know what customers may want before they know it themselves. The ability to express, and sell, oneself well is essential. Appearance, dress and manner count.

Career prospects are best with a reasonable educational background – at least four passes at 16-plus, and a proportion with A levels. A BTEC National or Higher National, in business studies, or a technical subject, would be useful.

Exporting demands all these qualities and more – overseas buyers are generally said to respect tough negotiators, able to argue knowledgeably about the technical merits of their products, demonstrate real awareness of the customer's markets, and show persistence. It does not make sense to aim for exporting without a thorough understanding of the relevant part of the world plus complete business, technical, colloquial fluency in the appropriate language(s).

Qualifications and training Little formal training, and few widely-accepted qualifications have existed to date. Most training is in-house, but is becoming more intensive and high-level. Length depends on the age and educational background of the trainee, and the technical sophistication or otherwise of the product being sold, and can vary from a few weeks to a year or more.

Training mostly aims at improving existing abilities: guiding and formalising techniques for established sound working relationships, learning tact and how to avoid antagonising buyers and how to act in difficult situations, maintaining goodwill, learning facts and figures about the product and specific markets for it, learning how to arrange to see the right people (and how to find out who they are in the first place) and knowing how to judge the most convenient times, acquiring background business skills to be able to assess markets and companies for sales potential, and so on. Sales staff have to learn how to make rapid decisions, and how to negotiate terms, such as price, performance and delivery, and to make them realistic.

Attempts to establish national qualifications and college-based training in selling have so far not been successful, although it is hoped that BTEC programmes will eventually include appropriate modules. Some professional, and other representative, bodies have been making efforts to improve the situation. Most notably –

Institute of Marketing – Certificate of Sales Management: a two-year part-time course including not only selling and sales management, but also marketing, economics, business statistics and law, behavioural studies and management accounting. Successful completion gives associate membership of the Institute, and direct entry to the one-year diploma in marketing course, which can include a sales management option. Entry is with five O-level equivalent passes at 16-plus†, and either one A level or a year's work experience in sales – age at least 18 (over 21 entry on age plus experience basis).

Tuition (1986-7 start) at a large number of FE colleges, at some private colleges, and from four correspondence schools.

The Institute of Sales and Marketing Management, with CGLI, has developed two new (1987) schemes –

Operational salesmanship certificate, covering salesmanship, organisation for selling, communication, and marketing practice. No formal entry requirements, but candidates must take an approved course. With two years' experience in selling and marketing, gives associate membership of the Institute.

Sales management certificate, covers sales manager's role, business planning and control, forecasting, planning and organising, controlling the sales operation, business and company law, product development, and distribution channels. With five years' practical experience, and two years' in management, gives membership of the Institute.

Courses for both certificates are expected to be offered by FE colleges and other approved centres.

Institute of Export – part I of the Institute's profession exams is the foundation course in overseas trade (with the Institute of Freight Forwarders): covers marketing, law relating to overseas trade, international trade and payments, transportation and documentation – entry requirements are four O-level equivalent passes at 16-plus†. Part II, in export management, covers distribution, markets, selection, research and statistics, and relevant management principles.

BTEC HND in business studies: some polytechnics/colleges include export options. See also MARKETING.

Further information from the above organisations.

TECHNICAL SERVICE

The technical sales service gives assistance and advice to a firm's customers, both actual and potential. This is an extension to, and back-up for, sales, and is primarily intended to keep customers, who have probably purchased something very expensive – a major computer system, chemical plant, control system, business machinery etc. It is designed to see the customer gets the best use possible out of the purchase; makes sure problems are solved as quickly as possible, assesses the need for any modifications, trains customer's staff to use and maintain the new purchase. Technical service may also be responsible for finding additional uses for a new product, for testing it, and for verifying quality. Technical service staff often act as trouble-shooters, and so are always on call when problems happen.

Technical service teams are usually managed by experts, usually with appropriate degrees – in chemical engineering for plant manufacture, in chemistry for chemicals, in a physical or materials science for plastics, for example. See also SELLING, above.

WHOLESALING AND WAREHOUSING

This is a field of employment which is often linked with RETAILING, under the label of distribution, but is also closely connected to TRANSPORT, with warehousing especially, often a part of road haulage businesses.

Wholesaling and warehousing are becoming more highly sophisticated operations, and an essential part of the marketing chain. Modern systems are crucial, to help beat tight profit margins, rising costs and competition. New technology – computerised and automated warehouses give sophisticated stock control, and computer modelling is used to design the optimum distribution and warehousing system. Considerable expertise is needed to work out the optimum size and best location(s) for warehouses and/or depot chains, on the choice of freight methods, on delivery priorities etc.

Wholesalers provide a service sited (geographically and quantitatively) halfway between the manufacturer and the next customer in the chain, so that the manufacturer only has to deliver to a set number of points. The wholesaler operating for a particular area serves a specific range of people. Wholesalers often specialise in particular types of goods – food and other grocery products, electrical goods, hardware, gardening equipment, jewellery, clocks and watches, etc. Some manufacturers wholesale their own products, and may offer a wholesaling service to others. In some industries, for instance publishing, distribution is generally on a national basis and therefore a publisher's books are all warehoused together (although some regional distribution points have been set up).

The wholesaler acquires goods in bulk from manufacturers, breaks them down into smaller quantities, and re-sells them to customers, who may be retailers, contractors, other manufacturers, large organisations like local authorities, and industrial users. Stock may be made up of quite literally thousands of different products from hundreds of manufacturers. Wholesalers aim to provide a rapid delivery service, and also technical advice, the opportunity to inspect and compare similar products, and credit facilities for bulk purchases.

Wholesalers employ sales staff, both on trade counters and as representatives, buyers who maintain contact with manufacturers, accounts staff, a high proportion of managerial staff (who usually work their way up). Other jobs include storekeepers, order pickers (who must often be prepared to drive fork-lift trucks in the warehouses and stores), dispatch clerks, and van and lorry drivers.

Employment may be with manufacturers, with independent wholesalers in particular fields, with some retailers and retailer/manufacturers, and with transport firms in the freight business (see SERVICE INDUSTRIES).

Qualifications and training For administration/management, is similar to RETAILING, and the BTEC awards listed there can include option modules in wholesale distribution. See also TRANSPORT.

Creative, cultural and entertainment work

Introduction   527
Art, design, photography etc   529
Media careers   560
Museums, art galleries and archive work   596
Performing (including sport)   604
Recreation and leisure industries   635

INTRODUCTION

'Creativity' is a quality many young people want in their careers. It is often, though, rather loosely defined and thought of only in terms of a narrow range of rather overcrowded occupations and areas of employment. Certainly if creativity is defined only as working with words, ideas or visual images, the number of careers which fulfil these criteria (even partly) is extremely limited, effectively to the creative arts, and those areas of employment dependent on them (as publishing is on the people who write books or the theatre on dramatists, actors and producers).

It is then, perhaps, worthwhile to point out that a great many more careers other than those described in this chapter can be 'creative' in some way, and which might be just as satisfying.

The definition of creativity can be extended to include almost any work which takes imagination and inventiveness. These may, of course, be subject to commercial, cost-effective criteria, but this applies to most of the careers in this chapter also.

Scientists and engineers claim their work is creative, since scientific research is often aimed at creating new hypotheses and theories, and engineering design creates new products – after all one of the, arguably, greatest artists of all, Leonardo da Vinci, was also a scientist and an engineer, and clearly he saw himself as totally creative. The investment broker may well consider portfolio-building is creative, and plastic surgeons know they are. The builder no less than the architect has a hand in creating a house, and the management consultant who creates a new structure for a company may well feel creative satisfaction. Anyone can, in this way, inject a creative element into their career simply by choosing something with positive intent, rather than work which is simply custodial or outright destructive. It is, in fact, unusual to find careers literature emphasising anything else.

It is equally important to stress that in many of the areas generally considered 'purely' creative, creativity must in fact be related, and often subordinated, to the market place if it is to provide an income. Books, newspapers, magazines, commercial television and radio, plays, films, discs, and so on, are all expected to make a profit, and the writer, the producer, the musician, the actor, and the designer, are expected to play their part in this no less than the manager and administrator. Even non-commercial organisations, such as those supported by government grants, must balance their books and see that their income is properly and efficiently spent. Much of the introduction to COMMERCE, ADMINISTRATION AND FINANCE (above) therefore applies.

Even those writers and artists who see themselves as truly and perhaps 'purely' creative must have an income of some kind. They have then to decide whether to try to live on their creative talents and therefore be prepared to meet the demands of the market place, or whether to make an income from something else, so that they can fully preserve their independence and artistic freedom, which inevitably limits the time they can spend on their creative interests. Even to win any of the limited number of awards made to artists and writers means learning to 'promote' or sell one's own talents. To get an expert – an agent or a gallery – to do this means convincing the expert first that one has the talent to earn one's keep for them.

'Creative' and 'communicative' careers overlap extensively. Most artists and writers generally consider that their work has something to say, if not to society, then at least about society or a part of it, or about the human condition. Conversely, communication is, itself, a creative art. Creativity and communication are also closely involved with entertainment, and have been since the days of the mediaeval morality plays. Plays and television dramas are no less creative because they are also entertaining, and something which is entertaining may be as good a vehicle for persuasion and explanation as something which is more didactic, if not better, as writers of all periods have shown.

Entry to the careers conventionally described as 'creative', to the communication and entertainment industries, has always been extremely competitive. In some sectors, especially those badly affected by the recession – publishing of most kinds, and the theatre particularly – the opportunities have been cut very sharply indeed. Broadcasting – as communication and entertainment, and as part of the world of information technology – is perhaps an exception. Here there has been expansion, and this is continuing. The number of new jobs, though, is relatively small.

For most 'creative' careers talent is the first essential, but other qualities are needed too. Most of these careers demand a great deal of hard work, long and irregular hours; to succeed generally requires great determination and tenacity. Working for an organisation in this area (as opposed to being self-employed) usually means being able to work as part of a team, to know how to balance ideals against realism, to be able to argue a case, to be able to anticipate and appreciate what an audience wants. It usually also requires the ability to work to tight schedules and budgets, and to be able to manage resources.

An alternative way of entering the communications and entertainment industry is to qualify in a completely different area or profession first, and then to use the qualification as a stepping stone. Administrative qualifications, like ACCOUNTANCY, or professional skills, such as LIBRARIANSHIP, COMPUTING, and sometimes, but not always, SECRETARIAL SKILLS, are examples.

ART AND DESIGN (INCLUDING PHOTOGRAPHY)

Introduction   529
Design   536
Fine art   552
Photography   554
Related work   558

INTRODUCTION

'Art and design' is a blanket term used to describe a great many different 'careers'. They include painting and sculpting, and the many different areas of design – of books and newspapers, for exhibitions and plays, of clothes and fabrics, hotel interiors, even shoes and food mixers. 'Art and design' is used to describe the work of the most talented, producing the painting or sculpture of the century, and the work of the commercial studio assistant, pasting up a magazine layout, or producing airbrush drawings from technical sketches, with all manner of different abilities and skills in fine art and/or design in between.

Careers in art and design are most often described in terms of the way the subject is split up into courses in art schools, colleges, and polytechnics. This encourages students to decide (perhaps rather early) whether their interests are in 'fine art', graphic design, textiles and fashion, or three-dimensional design. In practice, careers do not fall into such rigid compartments – individual artists' and designers' careers do not have to stay within the strict bounds of their training, and it is quite common for them to change direction during the course of their working lives. The division between fine art and design or craft is not hard and fast: leading living painters began their working lives as professional designers, and many artists have become deeply involved in more practical design and crafts, often as a result of trying to make sure that their own work is accurately and properly reproduced.

It is very rare for any artist to survive, let alone make a reasonable living, solely on the income from their personal creative efforts. Some artists and designers have full-time jobs – teaching, or in a design studio – but a high proportion do not. Every artist and designer must decide how to divide their time between creative interests and earning a living. Some, of course, are quite happy to use their skills in a straightforward job in publishing (for example). Many choose to divide their time between two or even more different activities, and they may change what they do with their time more than once in their working lives. A high proportion work on a freelance and/or part-time basis, combining their own creative interests with work that will provide an income of some kind. What they do obviously varies with their skills, aptitudes and interests, but teaching is often a quite large ingredient of many artists' and designers' lives. Teaching, though, usually provides an artist with rather more than a pay cheque. Many artists and designers find that teaching in art school is a good way of exchanging and developing ideas and thoughts. Teaching also counteracts to some extent the isolation of the freelance artist. Artists and designers who teach generally find it genuinely interesting to work with students who are developing their talents, who are often enthusiastic and full of new ideas. Of course, no one should be teaching who does not find it enjoyable.

The only up-to-date figures there are on employment of art and design graduates come from the annual *First Destination of Polytechnic Students* (but see also BTEC figures under DESIGN below).

	1978	1985
total graduating	1900	2879
% of CNAA graduates in art/design	54%	64%
destination unknown	c500	859
believed unemployed Dec 31	182	336
teacher training	c180	97
research/further academic study	c150	119
temporary employment	c170	111
permanent UK employment	c600	1171
employers –		
commercial firms	c150	365
manufacturing industry	c140	190
education (including art schools)	40	58
entertainment/leisure organisations	c100	55
construction (incl architects)	11	51
local/public authorities	30	46
public utilities	4	17
civil service	18	14
type of work –		
artistic design	374	833
marketing/buying/selling	28	63
teaching/lecturing	20	57
non-specialist management/admin	18	18
creative/entertainment	34	18
health/social welfare	11	18
information/library	n/a	17

Recession did not help artists or designers, and it has become even harder to find suitable work in the UK, even for people with the kind of qualifications theoretically wanted by industrial and commercial firms. Reports show, however, that UK-trained designers are being recruited in some numbers by companies in other countries.

Recruitment and entry There is, of course, nothing to prevent anyone starting out as an artist or designer simply on the strength of their talent. Becoming a full-time, professional artist/designer obviously needs creative talent and originality which is considerably above average (as measured by art- and not secondary-school standards). It is one of those careers where it makes sense to be absolutely sure that there is no other possible choice, and to accept that the financial rewards may never be high, which means caring far more about the work than a steady income.

It is, however, probably now almost impossible to reach the standard of expertise demanded by those who *employ* artists and designers without training. Employers claim to give more weight to personality, work in a portfolio and relevant experience than to qualifications, whether in art or design or in general education, but this is not borne out in fact.

Employers say they want originality and creativity, the ability to turn these high-level skills to commercial or industrial use, basic art and design skills (particularly drawing ability), technical knowledge, and a professionally high standard of work and neat presentation. They want designers who can broaden their thinking beyond the design department and play a part in more general administration and decision-making, and who are prepared to cope with future development. They expect that designers will especially need greater scientific and technical knowledge as the new technologies affect the design process, particularly the techniques of computer-based design and the increased use of sophisticated reproduction, including photographic processes, litho and lithographic printing, greater use of films, television and other visual aids, new materials and colouring techniques. All of this is best gained at art school.

The choice is, therefore, between full-time art-school study (as below), or starting as a studio junior, learning mainly 'on the job'. It is not so difficult to find work as a junior, but it can be hard to find a job where the training is good enough to form the basis of a career. There just are far too few studios and trade houses which give their juniors formal training and/or time off for essential courses. Without release for study, it means evening classes and finding ways of gaining the necessary all-round experience. It is also much, much more difficult to gain promotion this way, except for the most talented and determined. It is also possible that, with the development of BTEC courses (see below), this route to a long-term career will become even more difficult.

Whatever entry route is chosen, every prospective artist, designer, or photographer must have a portfolio of their work. Without it, gaining entry to any course, being chosen for a full-time job, or for a particular project, is virtually impossible. A good portfolio is a work of art (or design) in its own right. It should be started as early as possible, added to regularly, and sometimes weeded. It must show as accurately as possible the artist's talent, originality, breadth of interests, technical skills, and understanding of the problems of some particular area or areas of art and/or design. It has to be kept up right through art school, and from job to job, since it is a passport to the next opportunity. The importance of a well-constructed portfolio cannot be overstressed.

Qualifications and training Although employers appear to play down the importance of qualifications, in fact it has been estimated that at least two-thirds of all artists or designers employed in industry and commerce have completed full-time courses. Generally, employers are most favourably impressed with artists' and designers' basic art and design skills and with their creativity and originality, slightly less so with their technical knowledge and its application. They are most critical of the relevance of their studies to commercial and industrial practice, and think training here could be improved.

Employers frequently know which art schools (including polytechnic schools), turn out the kind of designers, whether fully professional or assistant, who are likely to meet their particular needs. They are more likely to recruit from these than from others. Anyone who wants to push their career in a particular direction will, therefore, ask the appropriate questions of the college, employers and professional bodies.

Over 32,500 students were studying for recognised qualifications (CNAA degrees and BTEC awards) in art and design in 1985-6. Numbers have continued to rise so far, with only minor hiccups. The National Advisory Board (NAB) is attempting to put stricter controls on numbers, especially in fine art, and smaller schools are being encouraged to merge. Some colleges, or schools, of art (or art and design), are separate institutions, some are departments or schools within FE colleges, and 25 are part of polytechnics.

Most university courses are theoretical, historical and analytical, and only eleven provide any substantial element of studio training. See ACADEMIC AND VOCATIONAL STUDIES IN ART.

Education and training for artists presents some fundamental problems given that in the UK ability is generally assessed in academic examinations rather than by demonstrable creative ability. Some accept that artists should be able to gain formal, paper qualifications in their own discipline which are comparable with those in other fields, while others think that artists should not have to conform to academic standards designed for those studying subjects which are more easily examined formally, and fear that formal qualifications bring too academic an approach to teaching in art and design, too. The form, content, and structure of art and design courses are discussed endlessly – how art should be taught, what entry qualifications students should have, what the syllabus, if any, should include, and what form examinations should take. However, the battle for formal qualifications appears to be won, and there are levels of qualifications comparable with other sectors now. These are –

BA in art and design awarded by the Council for National Academic Awards: this is the accepted route for the most creative, original and intelligent, and gives a qualification equivalent to a degree in a more conventionally academic subject. Students study at a major school of art, which may be part of a polytechnic.

Although art and design were absorbed into the CNAA degree structure in 1974 (before that it was the Diploma in Art and Design), many courses still conform to the fairly rigid pattern of studies set down for the DipAD. This was designed to provide a liberal education in art with specialisation on one of four areas: fine art, graphic design, three-dimensional design, and textiles/fashion (for further areas of specialisation within these see individual paragraphs below), and most courses have kept to this pattern, although they need not.

There is variation, though. North Staffordshire Polytechnic integrated all its design studies some years ago into a flexible, multidisciplinary course which incorporates a wide range of main options (including typographic design, illustration, audio-visual design, photography, domestic products, printed surface pattern, industrial table- and hollow-ware, designer-craftsmen ceramics, designer-craftsmen glass, architectural and sculptural ceramics). A number of other schools have followed this – several Scottish schools included.

Several art schools have courses in specialist design areas which do not conform to the old DipAD pattern. For instance, in graphics, it is possible to specialise in scientific and technical aspects at Plymouth Polytechnic, science and technical illustration at Middlesex Polytechnic.

The media – film and TV, and photography – are now an established field of study, at (for example) the London College of Printing, and West Surrey College. Industrial design is now taught at eleven schools.

Some of these courses follow the recommendations of the 1970 Coldstream-Summerson Committee on art and design education, which suggested that 'at least some courses should be directed more specifically towards certain categories of industrial and professional design practice' with four-year sandwich-courses containing 'substantial specialised technological content which can best be studied in close association with the relevant industry or profession', and with less emphasis on fine art as a central component. Within chief studies, schools teach a widening range of 'supporting' studies, eg film, video and photography. In all, some 50 schools (1986) have CNAA degree courses in art and design. Some schools are likely to merge with others, or polytechnics.

Schools tend to defend the 'academic' approach still, arguing that the courses are intended primarily to develop students' personal creative skills. However, an increasing proportion do now include a grounding in the design problems of industry and commerce, and may include design management, marketing and similar elements of business and professional practice, aiming to improve the chances of commercial success both for those who will go into employment and those who want to run their own businesses. Links between art school and working designers ought to be close, with practising designers teaching regularly in the schools, and students spending time working in industry and/or other design organisations.

Entry to the BA course is via one of two routes –
The preferred route is via a one- or two-year full-time 'diagnostic' 'foundation' course, mainly designed to discover students' individual aptitudes and abilities, but also aimed at developing their interest and skill in art – introducing project-based working, independent thinking, methods, media and materials – and continuing their general education. Entry to a foundation course, at sixteen, seventeen or eighteen, requires five O-level-equivalent passes at 16-plus†, although some schools prefer one or two A levels, especially for a one-year course. Some schools have merged their foundation courses with BTEC National Diploma in design courses (so students who decide not to continue their studies can gain an award), others run the two in parallel.

Some schools accept students for a BA course directly from school with five GCE/GCSE passes including two at A level. In 1985-6, some 53.6% were admitted on the basis of GCE/SCE passes (including two A levels), but they may also have completed foundation courses; just under 30% on the basis of a foundation course only or 'other' qualifications, nearly 9% with a BTEC National (a sharp jump of 4% in a year, probably because more students are now taking BTEC Nationals instead of a foundation course), and a few with a BTEC HND/C.

BTEC awards: a high proportion of those not gaining places on BA courses have in the past taken supposedly lower-level 'vocational' courses instead. These developed on a very ad hoc basis, and the only guide to their usefulness was endorsement by professional organisations, most notably the the Society of Illustrated Artists and Designers (SIAD), giving them formal status (SIAD via a successful registration and assessment scheme, with a professional award for the best higher-level courses) or the value put on them by employers (some of whom preferred some vocational courses to the BA). These ranged from courses similar in depth of study and entry requirements to the BA, frequently providing training for the few senior designers needed by a small and localised industry, to a great many much-less demanding courses taken by studio assistants, generally in a narrower field – such as design for print, toy design, decorating and sign-writing.

A single set of clearly-defined, nationally-recognised qualifications was needed. The Business and Technician Education Council (BTEC) now has the responsibility for this, at all sub-degree levels, and potentially for all the possible specialisations. (The acronym DATEC for these awards is no longer being used.)

BTEC's concept of design is as 'an instrument of management, calling for a systematic design approach to all aspects of the operation of a business. It applies not just to products, packaging, presentation, but also to internal and external communications and the working environment generally. It is based on identifying the right things to do, and then fulfilling the need effectively.' While courses are expected to train in creative and manipulative skills and techniques, the emphasis is strongly on making design relevant to industry, on designing as a way of identifying and resolving problems. Courses are expected to run in close liaison with industry and professional practice, to be organised on a 'learning by doing' basis wherever practicable, to include business and professional practice, relevant new technology – computer literacy, CAD/CAM etc – has to be covered, and new initiatives and innovations encouraged. Where possible, European languages should be taught.

BTEC awards in design are, like awards in all subject areas, going through re-organisation under the new framework (see under ACADEMIC AND VOCATIONAL QUALIFICATIONS). Changes began in September 1987, but the main developments will not start until 1988. It is expected that core studies will increase emphasis on commercial awareness. Present guidelines, and probable changes, are as follows –

Design courses are at both National Certificate/Diploma, and Higher National Certificate/Diploma levels. New 'First' awards are likely to become generally available from 1988 (six pilots started in 1986).

National Certificate courses, under 1984 guidelines, emphasise specific development of practical skills and related knowledge. Creative awareness is developed mainly through the use of materials and processes. Since, under the new framework National Certificate courses can no longer be taken on a full-time basis, existing courses will either be converted to Diploma courses, be re-designed for local part-time students in relevant employment, become a First award course, or lead to a Certificate of Achievement.

Higher National Certificate courses, under 1984 guidelines, extend and consolidate National Certificate work, concentrating on developing procedures and operation to a high level, and interpreting and executing briefs to a high professional standard. Last entry to full-time HNC courses in design was September 1986. From 1987, existing HNC courses will be run as one-year courses leading to a Certificate of Achievement (if it fulfils a particular industrial need); run as a two-year scheme with the first year mainly or wholly in college and the second mainly in industry but with proper assessment of the work element; for mature students, run as a Continuing Education Certificate;

or converted to an HND.

Certificate and Higher National Certificate schemes are mainly linked to single specific subjects or in-depth specialisation and mostly designed to meet local industry needs and employment opportunities.

National, and Higher National, Diploma courses emphasise creative, analytical and interpretive design practice, based on broad development of practical and organisational skills and the acquisition of related knowledge. This involves developing the application of a total design strategy, evaluation of implications and applications of relevant technology (especially new developments), and production of creative design analyses, syntheses and solutions. They are more likely to involve broad subject categories, groups of subjects and/or contextually demanding specialisation. They are more likely to be identified with regional/national industry needs and employment opportunities.

Entry qualifications to each level of BTEC design awards are as for all BTEC awards††. However, considerable weight is given to portfolio work and an interview (to show evidence of students' ability to communicate effectively). These can substitute for one or more O-level-equivalent passes at 16-plus†.

Although running for only a few years, the numbers taking BTEC design awards have grown steadily. In 1985-6, over 13,300 students were registered for all awards. Over 9900 were registered for National awards, most – over 8400 – for diplomas. Over 3400 were registered for Higher National awards, all but 240 for diplomas.

BTEC multi-disciplinary courses While the majority of BTEC schemes are in specific areas of design (see following sections), and related technical areas (eg printing), nearly 70 colleges run National Diploma courses in general art and design (which can be taken instead of a foundation course), and 25 National Diploma courses in general vocational design. Although these schemes all have 'generic' titles (and some are diagnostic), the final diploma shows what units have been taken, and the student's exam results in each. The majority (78%) of students who completed these courses in 1985 went on to further study (69% on to HND courses, 19% on to CNAA degree courses in art and design). Of the 11% going into employment (only 1% were known to be unemployed), three quarters went into full-time employment, a fifth went 'freelance', and 6% into part-time work.

Other courses CGLI and the regional bodies continue to fill in gaps with a variety of courses. A number of courses carry school/college and professionally-endorsed awards.

Postgraduate study is normally essential for anyone aiming to become a 'top' designer in any field. So-called 'post-diploma' courses are intended to remedy the (academic) emphasis of the BA which results in so many students not knowing enough about industrial and commercial practices. A number of one- and two-year courses leading to higher diplomas or other qualifications are available at a number of major centres in, for example, industrial design (engineering), fashion, graphics, furniture production and design, interior design, and ceramics, as well as fine art. The highest qualifications come from the Royal College of Art (London), and have higher-degree status. School teaching now also requires a postgraduate qualification – the alternative is to take art as a major subject in a course for a teaching qualification (BEd) instead of going to art school.

Further information Directory of design courses in the UK, published biennially by the Design Council. The Society of Industrial Artists and Designers, the Department of Education and Science, the Council for National Academic Awards, Business and Technician Education Council, and individual schools and colleges of art.

ARCHITECTURE – While often called the 'mother of the arts', architecture as a career is equally about construction, land use etc. See ACADEMIC AND VOCATIONAL STUDIES IN LAND USE and LAND USE PROFESSIONS.

DESIGN
Introduction — graphic design — textile and fashion design — three-dimensional design
In the design field, artists and designers apply their creative talents and artistic skills to practical ends, whatever their chosen specialisation. They (usually) work to someone else's brief or instructions, and must normally work within set (and often tight) schedules, and within any stipulated technical, manufacturing, budgetary or other commercial limits. Whatever they design, whether it is a book, clothes, a vase, machine tools, or a stage set, the end product must do the job intended for it, meet consumer demand, and look as good as other constraints allow.

Demand for, and acceptance of professional standards of design have been growing steadily, stimulated by greater awareness of what professional design can do. Design is at present a very fast changing and developing field, and it is quite difficult to predict what might come next. Modern materials, like plastics, fibreglass and glues, have given designers greater freedom of form, than when they were restricted to metals. Smaller and fewer components for many products have a similar effect. Design techniques are changing, fast and often quite dramatically, with 'new technology' – computer-based, three-dimensional drawing with a light pen on a VDU is creating many new possibilities.
Designers generally work in either craft- or industrial/commercial design –
Craft design involves both designing and making things in traditional ways. For instance, type can still be set in metal and printed using a hand press that produces a limited number of prints, posters, or fine books, instead of working with computer-based typesetting in film and the web offset machine that runs off thousands of copies. Pottery and furniture can similarly be designed and produced by designer craftsmen and women.
Industrial and commercial designers usually have to accept constraints of some kind on their creativity and originality. Meeting schedules and deadlines means designers must usually work regardless of whether or not they actually feel creative. They normally work closely with the other people involved on a project, for instance MARKETING, DESIGN ENGINEERS, PRODUCTION, possibly as part of a team. The designer rarely originates the project, and may be brought in only when it is well underway. The designer may have to argue design principles with other people – who often have their own firmly-held ideas. A

great many firms still do not employ professional designers for their products, and the job specification, influence, and status of the designer differ from industry to industry, and from firm to firm.

Industrial and commercial designers can work full-time for employers who produce books, advertising campaigns, kettles, jewellery or signs. Alternatively, they work for, or as, design consultants, or on their own as freelance artists (illustrators, for example), or designers. Except, perhaps, for some areas of industrial design, competition for posts is considerable.

Designers are employed at several levels. The proportion of posts for professionally-trained and -qualified designers is relatively small, but there are a great many jobs for more average, competent, if not highly creative or original abilities. In some areas there may actually be shortages of these 'technician-level' skills, and for people who are quite happy to work as 'assistants'. They may, for example, turn designers' roughs into accurate working drawings and diagrams, adapt fabric designs for different colourways, extend repeat patterns, rework colours, do detailed layouts.

Recruitment and entry as Introduction above.

Qualifications and training Full-time training is normally essential for anyone who wants to be a professional designer, whatever field of design they choose. For technician-designers there is the alternative of combining on-the-job training with a part-time course.

The form and pattern of qualifications and training are as described in the Introduction above. Most degree students specialise in one field of design (see below). For anyone who is not sure which field they want to work in, courses are available which make it possible to defer choice of 'chief' study. Deferred choice is possible at –

Polytechnics – N Staffs, Sunderland; other colleges/schools – Aberdeen: RGIT, Bradford/Ilkley, Crewe/Alsager, Dundee CA, Glasgow SA.

Over 60% of students studying for a BA in art and design choose design specialisations.

Almost all BTEC schemes (except those mentioned in the Introduction above) provide training in specific areas of design.

Design is generally divided into three main areas. They are –

Graphic design
Now often called visual communications or communication design, is itself a modern name for a career which has developed quite considerably since the days when it was more usually known as commercial design.

Graphic designers work with print, pictures and patterns on flat surfaces. They decide how words and/or pictures should be 'laid out' on the printed pages of books, magazines and newspapers, posters, in advertisements, in sales brochures, on the wrapping of biscuit packets, on street signs, TV or video screen, or in repair manuals.

The aim of graphic design is to make all of these as readable and as understandable as possible, even when the text or instructions are complicated. At the same time, the designer must make the book or newspaper interesting and attractive to the reader for whom it is intended, to make them want to read it. The right design can be absolutely crucial for the success of an advertising campaign, so that it makes maximum impact. It can be very important for the sales of a book. In road safety, properly-designed road signs can make a great difference. New uses for the skills and techniques of the graphic designer are being found all the time.

The work is as much technical as creative. Graphic designers have to be really expert in understanding how to make 'visual communications' work, which means both the technicalities of what size of type to use in what circumstances, and the psychological methods of attracting an audience, making maximum impact, and getting a message across. They are skilled at designing a layout of words and illustrations or diagrams to 'integrate' them into a balanced and readable page. They know what typefaces or lettering to use to solve particular problems, how to use space and colour, to combine lines and shapes to create particular effects. They have to understand the possibilities and limitations of all the many different methods of printing and reproduction, and the cost.

Whatever the particular job may be, the graphic designer must create a design which is firmly based on the purpose of the book, the magazine, or poster, and must understand what it is trying to tell the reader, and who is supposed to read it. A book for a child will always look quite different from a technical manual, even though both may use attractive diagrams to explain, for example, how a computer works.

The designer must specify (to the printer) the different type faces and sizes, and show how words and diagrams or illustrations fit together, usually on 'layout' sheets. Much time may be spent on, for instance, calculating how many words will fit into a given space in a particular type face and size, on preparing the 'art work', on pasting up pages for the camera, or on producing transparent overlays. Computers are, however, now being used to do some of this, particularly in newspaper work. Routine work is mostly given to junior design staff, or junior professional staff still gaining experience. Some may be sent out to trade houses or studios. Unless there is a lot of work for an illustrator, drawings and other illustrations have to be 'commissioned' from a freelance artist.

The range of possible work for graphic designers is extensive. It is the most widely accepted of the design skills, with over half of all designers in industry and commerce working in graphics. The field is so wide, that most designers specialise, working for particular parts of the media – books or journals, or one kind of skill – illustrating or typography, for example. A high proportion, once established and after plenty of experience, work on a freelance basis or for design consultants.

The main areas of employment are –

Advertising, which employs some of the largest numbers (some 2000 in the major agencies), although agencies do also use outside studios, consultants and freelance artists quite extensively. Here graphic designers work as members of an art group, under an executive art director, all working closely with, for example, the account executives and copywriters. The art group is always involved in planning and selling a 'campaign' to a client. Within the group, individual designers mostly specialise, for instance, in poster work, preparing layouts and art work, designing shop displays or exhibitions, sales and other brochures (for instance, recruiting literature), or the 'graphics' for TV advertisements.

Sometimes an agency creates a complete 'brand image' for a client: stamping an instantly-recognisable 'label' on to every surface – sales material, packages, lorry sides, notepaper, and so on.

Packaging design is sometimes done by the advertising agency, sometimes by the manufacturer. Here there are often major technical factors to take into account, such as safety, or protection against damage; new methods are developed, like air sealing. Shape and size affect the design. Packaging design must take into account how strong the material needs to be. Instructions, perhaps with charts or tables (as on washing powder packs) may have to be incorporated into the design. Even so, the designer must create the kind of impact the marketing people want for the product.

Publishing Most larger publishers and printers have art departments staffed with graphic designers, but here most of the work is typographic (many graphic designers specialise in typography), with skills like illustrating or photography as back up. In a magazine publishers, designers may work permanently on one publication or several; in book publishing, designers may work on whatever comes up, or specialise, in eg children's books. Publishing and printing are very closely linked, sometimes even in the same firm, or through 'trade' houses which do both art and photographic work as well as typesetting.

Illustrating is not technically part of graphic design, but in fact many graphic designers learn illustrating, since the skills go so closely together. Graphic designers often have to specify what illustrations, or photographs, are needed, and brief the people who will do them. Most illustrators specialise, in drawings for children's books, in cartoon work, or fashion drawing, or illustrations of animals or plants, or greetings cards. One of the least competitive areas is technical, medical, and scientific illustration. People who specialise in illustrating a single subject area generally need to be well informed about it.

Other areas of employment include sign design, where the largest firms employ quite a large number of people in their studios. Animation, for film, TV and video cartoons, involves teams of artists working to produce the twenty four or five drawings needed for every second of film. Television, film and video companies use graphic designers to prepare titles and credits, and designing film strip and loops, wall charts, transparencies for educational use (schools and colleges), and for training units.

Recruitment and entry as section Introduction above.

Qualifications and training Form and structure as under Introduction above. Training is geared to developing creative abilities and teaching practical skills. Courses cover all the skills of the artist, such as drawing and illustrating, and techniques like typography, photography and printmaking. Students are usually taught to 'set' and print their own designs by hand, but must also learn about modern reproduction and printing processes (including the most modern computer-based processes and how they affect the designer), and the economics of production. Courses generally teach organisational skills, how to produce accurate specifications, to present ideas and work, to interpret a brief, write reports, and communicate easily and well with clients and, for example, printers.

Most courses train in a wide range of design skills – animation, publicity, computer graphics, photographic design, and on many courses it is possible to specialise in one or more areas, illustration or design. On some courses it is possible to spend a period gaining work experience in a design studio.

BA in art and design courses with graphic design specialisation at –
Ulster U; polytechnics – Birmingham, Brighton, Bristol, Coventry, Kingston, Leeds, Leicester, Liverpool, London: Middx, Manchester, Newcastle (media production), Nottingham: Trent (information graphics), Stafford: N Staffs (as option in Design BA), Preston: Lancs, Wolverhampton.
Colleges/schools of art – Aberdeen: RGIT, Bath, Bradford (in Arts/design), Bromley: Ravensbourne, Canterbury, Dundee, Exeter, Glasgow, Hull: Humberside, London: Camberwell, Harrow CHE, Inst (Central/St Martins, Chelsea), Printing C; Maidstone, Newport: Gwent CHE, Norwich.
Nearly 3700 students were reading for these degrees in 1985-6 (slightly down on earlier years but up on 1984-5).

BTEC National/Higher National schemes As of November 1986 –
Design (communications): National Diploma – Gloucester CA&T, Harrogate CA&T, Lowestoft CFE, Nottingham: S Notts CFE, Portsmouth CADFE, Southend CT, Watford C, Worthing: W Sussex CD; Higher National Diploma – Ashington: Northumberland TC, Bromley: Ravensbourne, Dewsbury/Batley T&AC, Ipswich: Suffolk CHFE, London: Ealing CHE, Middlesborough: Cleveland CA&D, Sheffield: Granville.
Design (graphic design): National Diploma – at nearly 80 colleges in most major centres; Higher National Diploma – Amersham CFEA&D, Blackpool CF&HE, Bournemouth/Poole CA&D, Colchester Inst, Derby CHE, Epsom SA&D, Gt Yarmouth CA&D, Lincoln CA, London: Barnet CFE, Croydon, E Ham, Richmond, Loughborough CA&D, Luton: Barnfield/Dunstable, Newcastle CA&T, Northampton: Nene, Plymouth CA&D, Redruth: Cornwall CF&HE, Rochester: Medway CD, Salford CT, Salisbury CA, Southampton IHE, Southend CT, Stourbridge CT&A, Swindon, Taunton CA&T, Watford C, York CA&T.
Design (illustration): National Diploma – Bournemouth/Poole CA&T, Bromley: Ravensbourne, Southampton IHE; Higher National Diploma: Blackpool/Fylde CF&HE, Cambridge CA&T.
Design (technical illustration): National Diploma – Birmingham: Bournville CA&C, Blackpool CFHE, Bournemouth/Poole CA&D, Doncaster MIHE, Leamington Spa: Mid Warwicks CFE, Northwich; Mid-Chesh CFE, Portsmouth CADFE, Redruth CFHE, Romford: Barking CT, Southampton IHE, Swansea: W Glam IHE, Wisbech CFE; Higher National Diploma – Birmingham: Bournville, Bournemouth/Poole CA&D, Redruth CFHE, Swansea: W Glam IHE, Sunderland P.
Design (typography): National Diploma – Blackburn CT&D, Watford C; Higher National Diploma – London: Printing.

Of those gaining Nationals in graphic design in 1985, 48% went on to further study (74% on to an HND, 7% on to a CNAA degree course, 15% something else), 43% into employment, and only 4% failed to find work. Of those finding employment, 87% went into full-time jobs, 10% went freelance straightaway, and 3% found part-time work. 89% found course-related work.

Of those gaining Higher Nationals in graphic design in 1985, 76% found employment, 8% went on to further study, and only 4% failed to find work. Of those finding employment, 84% found full-time jobs, 13% went freelance straightaway, and 3% found part-time work. Some 96% found course-related work, and 20% gained their jobs through work experience. Of those going on to further study, 21% were converting HNC to HND, 4% went on to CNAA art and design degree courses, 5% on to CNAA courses in other subjects, 1% gained university places, but 70% went on to do 'other' qualifications.

Postgraduate study at – polytechnics: Birmingham, Coventry: Lanchester (electronic graphics), Leicester, Manchester, colleges: London: Central, RCA, St Martins.

See also ADVERTISING, BROADCASTING, FILM WORK, MARKETING, PHOTOGRAPHY.

Textile and fashion design

These are frequently linked together, mainly because the fashion designer must know a great deal about fabrics, and the textile designer has to understand how fabrics are used. It is a very small area of employment, with not very many opportunities for designers.

'TEXTILE' DESIGN covers fabrics of all kinds and for many purposes – obviously for clothes, but also for curtains and furniture coverings, bed linens and towels, carpets and lace. Contemporary fabrics are made of many different fibres which are often mixed together, mainly cotton, synthetics of all kinds, and wool. 'Fabric' to the designer also means paper wall-coverings and wrappings, printed plastic sheeting and floor covering, because the design and printing processes are similar.

Because the design has to take into account the way fabrics are produced, textile designers usually specialise. Normally this is either in woven fabrics – including knitted cloth which is increasingly popular – or printed fabrics, and even in special types of woven or printed cloth. In woven fabric the design is woven in, and depends greatly on yarn quality and colour and the way the cloth is made: so the designer must know about and understand fully yarn-making, dyeing and weaving processes to get the best out of them. Designing printed fabrics is more like graphic design (above), and needs an in-depth understanding of printing processes.

Textile design in Britain today often means reproducing traditional patterns – pin-stripes for suits, shirt patterns, tweeds and paisleys, floral motifs, although there is scope for originality. The designer is strictly ruled by the market, and a cloth must be suitable for its likely uses – dress and curtain fabrics must hang properly, for example. Designs must be economic to produce, given the production process. There are always new fibre mixes, new and more advanced textile technologies (including forms of computer-controlled automation which can give the designer direct control of dyeing) to be taken into account.

Larger manufacturers have their own staff designers, and some independent commercial studios design textiles for other firms. However, there never were enough posts, although the UK TEXTILE INDUSTRY is recovering. There are opportunities overseas.

FASHION DESIGN is an extremely volatile area of employment. The chances of making a career or an income as a solo fashion designer are very small. There never have been more than a handful of designers, worldwide, who were successful enough to make a secure business, and even amongst these there have always been frequent, and heavy, financial losses. 'Name' fashion designers often have to rely on the sale of the name to, for example, cosmetic firms, or an exclusive contract with a major manufacturer.

There is no lack of talent or originality – the problem is the impossibility of making a profit without the support of customers no longer prepared to be dictated to on what they wear. Forecasting what will sell in today's clothes market is a very unpredictable business.

The majority of jobs for fashion designers are in wholesale garment firms and mass-production houses, where there is little scope for being original. Here, the company has to try to detect the styles and trends which will attract the maximum number of customers some months ahead. Everyone in the firm is usually involved, from the owner, whose ability to 'spot a trend' and get it out into the stores has probably kept the firm in business, through to the fabric buyers and the sales people who are in day-to-day contact with the retail-store buyers.

A firm's designers go from fashion show to fashion show, analysing and recording trends, and trying to identify the next 'gimmick'. They go back to their studios to put together what they have, and adapt the result to give it the firm's (or the retail-store customers') 'brand image' – taking into account the available fabrics within the given price range, and the demands of mass-production methods, all to a very strict budget and schedule.

Designers and their assistants generally make working drawings, cut sample garments and patterns using as little fabric as possible, keeping the number of operations needed to make the garment to a minimum, and calculating work schedules. At any stage design staff must be prepared to modify their designs if the costs are wrong or it is too complicated to make. All this demands technical skills, sound business sense, a good memory (sketching is not allowed at shows and toile samples are expensive), and the fashion sense to know what will sell.

Men have become much more fashion conscious, although the field is still more limited than designing women's clothes. Children also want trendy clothes much younger these days, creating perhaps a few more openings for designers here. There may also be more opportunities in the 'peripheral' areas: designing lingerie and corsetry, accessories, shoes, knitwear and sports clothes, and even hats.

Some designers have been successful in building small businesses over the last few years, often with support from schemes promoting self-employment, making up their own designs and selling them directly, via a small number of 'boutique'-style shops, or in markets. Sound business sense, as well as the ability to know what will sell at any one given moment, is essential.

Theatrical costume design, which can involve extensive historical research, offers very limited opportunities.

Recruitment and entry as section Introduction.

Qualifications and training Form and structure as under Introduction above.

BA in art and design: although termed textiles/fashion, in fact most courses give specialisation in textiles or fashion, and it is usual to specialise further within this. To improve career prospects, polytechnics and colleges are developing an increasing range of different options.

Fashion options – polytechnics: Birmingham; Bristol; Leicester (fashion/ fashion knitwear, contour fashion, footwear); Liverpool; London: Kingston, Middx, NELP (with marketing), PCL; Manchester; Newcastle (marketing option), Nottingham: Trent (fashion, knitwear), Preston: Lancs; schools/ colleges – Bromley: Ravensbourne, Gloucester CA&T, London: Harrow CHE, St Martin's.

Textile options – Ulster U; polytechnics: Brighton (fashion textiles design/ administration), Huddersfield, Leicester, Liverpool, London: Middx, Manchester, Nottingham: Trent; schools/colleges: Aberdeen: RGIT, Dundee, Farnham: W Surrey CA&D, Galashiels: Scottish Textiles C, Glasgow SA, London: Camberwell, Central, Loughborough CA&D, Winchester SA.

Embroidery options: Ulster U; polytechnics: Birmingham, Manchester; schools/colleges: London: Goldsmiths', Loughborough CA&D.

Carpet design: Wolverhampton Polytechnic/Kidderminster CFE.

Almost 2950 students were studying for degrees in textiles/fashion in 1985-6, still well up on the early 1980s.

BTEC awards National/Higher National Diplomas as at November 1986 –
Design (fashion): National Diploma – at over 40 colleges country wide; Higher National Diploma – Derby CHE, Epsom SA&D, London: Fashion C, Maidenhead: Berks CA&D, Rochester: Medway CD, Southampton IHE.
Design (fashion/surface pattern) Higher National Diploma – Dewsbury/ Batley T&AC.
Design (fashion/textiles) National Diploma – Canterbury CA&T, Rotherham CA&T, Salisbury CA&T, Southport CA&D; Higher National Diploma – Middlesbrough: Cleveland CA&D.
Design (footwear) – National Diploma/Higher National (Certificate) – London: Cordwainers.
Design (surface pattern) National Diploma – Barnsley CA&D, Dewsbury/ Batley T&AC, Leeds: J Kramer, Gt Yarmouth CA&D, Sheffield: Granville, Stockport CT.
Design (textiles) National Diploma – Bradford/Ilkley CC, Harrogate CA&D, Worthing: W Sussex CD; Higher National Diploma – Derby CHE, Huddersfield P, London: Chelsea, Taunton: Somerset CA&T.
Of those gaining Nationals in fashion/textiles in 1985, 54% went on to further study, 36% went into employment, with only 2% not finding jobs; for textiles/ surface patterns, the figures were 62% further study, 18% employment, and 8% unemployment. Of those going on to further study, 51% with Nationals in fashion/textiles, 75% in textiles/surface patterns went on to an HND, about 20% of both groups on to a CNAA art-and-design degree, 15% of the fashion/ textile group on to an HNC (none from textiles/surface patterns) and 14% from fashion/textile, 2% from textiles/surface pattern to 'other' qualifications.

Of those gaining employment 71% of the fashion/textile group gained full-time jobs, 27% went freelance, and 2% found part-time work (the figures for textiles/surface patterns are statistically insignificant). Some 96% of the fashion/textiles group found course-related jobs, 60% of the textiles/surface pattern group. 17% of the fashion/textiles group found employment through work experience.

Of those gaining Higher Nationals in 1985, 73% of the fashion/textiles group found employment, 31% of the textiles/surface pattern graduates. 8% of the fashion group went on to further study, 18% from textiles/surface patterns; 2% from fashion, 5% from surface patterns failed to find work. Of those finding employment, 98% of the fashion group found course-related work, 95% of the textile/surface pattern group, but the percentage finding work through work experience was fairly low (11–12%). Of those going on to further study, 25% of the fashion group, 7% from surface patterns, went on to university degrees; 13% from surface patterns, 6% from fashion/textiles went on to a CNAA art-and-design degree course. Most, though, went on to get 'other qualifications'.

Postgraduate study Fashion – polytechnics: Leicester, Nottingham: Trent; colleges: London: RCA, St Martin's. Textiles – polytechnics: Birmingham, Manchester, Nottingham: Trent; colleges: London: RCA, St Martin's.
See also MANUFACTURING and RETAILING AND DISTRIBUTION.

Three-dimensional design
This label groups together (largely for training purposes) the design of most solid objects (excluding clothes) and for some uses of buildings and space. It is unusual for the practising designer to work in more than one of these.

Qualifications and training: on most courses students specialise in one of the areas below. Some BTEC courses are broad-based three-dimensional design – National Diploma – Birmingham: Bournville SA&C, Carlisle: Cumbria CA&D, London: Barnet CFE, Kingsway-Princeton, Maidenhead: Berks CA&D, Middlesbrough: Cleveland CA&D, Nuneaton: N Warwicks CT&A, Portsmouth CA&D, Sheffield: Granville, Stafford CFE, Worthing: W Sussex CD, York CA&T.
Higher National Diploma – Ipswich: Suffolk CH&FE, London: Chelsea, Maidenhead: Berks CA&D, Preston: Lancs P, Sheffield: Granville/Poly.

CRAFT-BASED DESIGN covers ceramics, china, pottery, silver and jewellery, furniture, glass ware – all things which were once all made by skilled craftsmen using hand techniques – and techniques like bookbinding. Long ago, though, most of these industries turned to mass production methods, and today only a relatively small number of designer-craftsmen and women carry on the traditional methods in their own designs.

The choice for the designer in any one of these industries is to work full time for one manufacturer; to work either independently or with other designers in a design studio, working mainly for smaller manufacturers; or to be 'self-supporting' as designer craftsmen or -women. The number of posts for designers in any one of these industries is generally quite small. Life for the designer-craftsman/woman can be very precarious, and depends on identifying a market, possibly one too small for the mass-producers to satisfy. Mass- or designer-produced, most products sold in these areas are fairly traditional in design, but scope for originality exists.

Most of the items produced by these industries – such as beds and chairs, table and cupboards, mugs and cups, casseroles and jugs, wine glasses, vases – are intended to be used, and not just to look attractive. This is as true for the things made by the designer-craftsman/woman as by manufacturers: a teapot must pour properly and keep tea hot whether it is hand made or mass produced, and even something as apparently decorative as jewellery has to stand the surprising stresses of being worn. All designs, whether for objects to be hand made or mass produced, must take account of the materials to be used, the way they will be made, and the machinery involved. Designers must understand what properties their materials have, how they will be affected by the processes they go through, as clay and glaze are affected by the heat of the kiln, or the effect of a plane on wood; they have to know which particular materials are best for a specific job, and what stresses and strains they will be subjected to when they are used.

Craftsmen/women designers have to be their own technologists, production managers, and marketing experts, and can decide for themselves whether their designs should take account, for instance, of possible economies. In manufacturing, the designer must usually look for the cheapest way to make a product, and must also take account of what the firm's marketing department, technologist and production managers have to say about it.

Designers must produce exact working drawings, accurate in every detail (sectional ones too if there are parts, as in furniture), layouts, written directions and even models, to show how each is made and the product put together. Shape and material are the basis of the design usually, but there may be decoration (eg in pottery).

Recruitment and entry as Introduction, above. In some sectors, eg ceramics, some employers train on-the-job.

Qualifications and training Form and structure as section Introduction.

BA in art and design: three dimensional design with chief studies in –
Ceramics – Ulster U; polytechnics: Bristol, Leicester, London: Middx, Stafford: N Staffs, Wolverhampton; schools/colleges – Aberdeen: RGIT, Bath CHE, Bromley: Ravensbourne, Cardiff: S Glam IHE, Dundee, Farnham: W Surrey CA&D, Glasgow SA, London: Camberwell SA&C, Central, Loughborough CA&T.
Ceramics/glass – polytechnics: Birmingham, Sunderland; college: High Wycombe: Bucks CHE.
Design craftsmanship – Newcastle P.
Furniture – polytechnics: Birmingham, Kingston, Leeds, Leicester, London: Middx, Nottingham: Trent, Ulster; colleges – Bromley: Ravensbourne, High Wycombe: Bucks CHE, Loughborough CA&D.
Glass – Ulster U; polytechnic: Stafford: N Staffs; colleges: Farnham: W Surrey CA&D, Stourbridge CT&A.
Jewellery – colleges: Aberdeen: RGIT, London: Central SA&D.

Jewellery/ceramics – London: Middx P.

Jewellery/silversmithing – Ulster U; polytechnics: Birmingham, Sheffield; colleges – Dundee, Glasgow SA, Loughborough CA&D.

Metals – schools/colleges: Farnham: W Surrey CA&D.

Silver/metal – polytechnic: London: Middx; schools/colleges: High Wycombe: Bucks CHE, London: Camberwell SA&C.

Silversmithing: Leicester P.

Silversmithing/jewellery/allied crafts – London: City P.

Wood/metal/ceramics/plastics – polytechnic: Brighton; Bromley: Ravensbourne.

Wood/metal/ceramics – Manchester P.

Wood/metal/plastics – polytechnics: Bristol, Wolverhampton.

Nearly 3900 students were studying these subjects in 1985-6, almost 100 up on 1984-5.

BTEC National and Higher National Diplomas as at November 1986 –
Design (architectural stained glass) Higher National Diploma: Swansea: W Glam IHE.

Design (ceramics) National Diploma – Cinderford: RoyForDean C, Connah's Quay: NE Wales IHE, Harrogate CA&T, Lowestoft CFE, Nuneaton: N Warwicks CT&A, Rotherham CA&T, Swansea: W Glam IHE; Higher National Diploma – London: Croydon, Harrow CHE, Redruth: Cornwall CF&HE, Stafford CFE/N Staffs P, Swansea: W Glam IHE; Higher National Diploma – London: Croydon, Harrow CHE, Redruth: Cornwall CF&HE, Stafford: CHFE/Poly, Swansea: W Glam IHE.

Design (crafts) National Diploma – Banbury: N Oxon TC&SA, Connah's Quay: NE Wales IHE, Epsom SA&D, Maidstone: Medway CD, Northampton: Nene, Plymouth CA&D, Redruth: Cornwall CF&HE, Rochester: Medway CD, Southampton IHE, Thame: Rycotewood, York CA&T; Higher National Diploma – Birmingham P, Carlisle: Cumbria CA&D, Carmarthen CT&A, Chesterfield CT&A, Connah's Quay: NE Wales IHE, Derby CHE, Epsom SA&D, London: Chelsea, Rochester: Medway CD.

Design (jewellery) National Diploma – Connah's Quay: NE Wales IHE, Bradford/Ilkley CC, Epsom SA&D, Maidenhead: Berks CA&D.

Of those completing a 3-D National in 1985, 62% went on to further study, 28% went into employment, and only 2% were unemployed. Of those going on to further study, 68% went on to an HND course, 20% on to a CNAA art-and-design degree course, 5% on to an HNC, 2% on to a university degree, and 5% to gain an 'other' qualification. Of those going into employment, 78% found full-time jobs, 14% went freelance, and 8% took part-time work. 86% of those going into employment found course-related work.

Of those competing a 3-D Higher National in 1985, 77% went into employment, 6% on to further studies, and 7% had not found jobs. Of those finding work, 68% had full-time jobs, 27% went freelance, and 5% took part-time jobs. 89% of jobs were course-related, 14% finding them through work experience. Of those going on to further study, 29% went onto a CNAA art-and-design degree course, 24% onto a CNAA degree course in another subject, 10% gained university places, and 37% studied to get 'other' qualifications.

Postgraduate Ceramics – Cardiff: S Glam IHE, London: RCA, N Staffs P.

INDUSTRIAL DESIGN (ENGINEERING)/PRODUCT DESIGN This is a growing design specialisation, though still not as widely accepted as it should be.

In manufacturing industry, traditionally the engineer who designed the working parts of a carpet sweeper or a food mixer also designed its exterior and, without any art-based training, did so rather haphazardly, more or less according to the shape and size of the product's parts and the demands of the manufacturing process.

Rapid growth in consumer spending, and growing competition for sales led manufacturers to see the possibilities of designing products which not only look good and can be sold on appearance, but can also be more efficient, more convenient to use (for instance have better, even safer, grips and handles), easier to maintain and clean, and less likely to have protruding screws or jagged edges. These new developments in design, of course, have depended on technological developments – in manufacturing processes and in modern, more flexible (mainly synthetic) materials.

The problem now lies in integrating ENGINEERING DESIGN – which has to make a product which works – with the skills of the art-based designer. Some manufacturers and engineers want to graft these skills on to the engineer, while others accept that the art-trained designer has a place on the design team in industry. It varies from industry to industry and according to type of product. In the consumer goods sector – kitchen equipment, cameras, cars – the product designer is frequently on the design team. New technology, the computer, the word-processor, the visual display unit, tend to bring in the industrial designer. Products now controlled by small micro-chips inside them – radios, food-mixers – get smaller and have less components than their predecessors, and so are redesigned and restyled – by the industrial designer. On the other hand, where industrial equipment, machine tools, cranes, and earth movers, are being made, the industrial designer still has a long way to go to get established.

In any industry, the industrial designer ought to be part of the design team on a new project right from the start, making his/her own professional contribution to planning. Designing new products is a team effort – the design engineer is the technological expert, but the project has to take into account the marketing plan, the problems of materials and production. Safety, ergonomics, budgets and costs are all elements which can affect what the product will look like.

A single design will go through many stages, and much consultation, starting with rough sketches, through first drawings, modifications – one version of a component may be too costly, the next slightly larger so the shape of the product may have to be changed – redesigns, working drawings, possibly an accurate model, and finally exact prototypes for testing. The design has to take account of the characteristics of the chosen material – how it shapes, bends and stands up to stresses – and must please the customer in shape, style, finish and colour. Product design has to be integrated into the whole process which goes into bringing an item to the market, and should not be just a cosmetic afterthought.

Increasingly now, the product designer as well as the engineer will work with a computer which will hold all the technical information needed, and produce and adjust the designer's working 'drawings' in three dimensions, on the graphic design screen.

Industrial designers work on the staff of a manufacturing company, or for (or as) a design consultant, sometimes in partnership with design engineers. Industrial design may not have the glamour of advertising or publishing, but there are actually shortages of good product designers at all levels of ability and originality.

Recruitment and entry There are various ways into industrial design – it is possible to go through the engineering or the art and design route. Some manufacturers do take school-leavers for training, but for a career in professional design especially, formal full-time training is an advantage, although it should be combined with as much industrial experience as possible.

As well as the entry requirements given in the section Introduction above, industrial designers, even if they choose the art and design training route, will find a scientific background, including maths, useful. Strong interest in engineering and industry needed.

Qualifications and training normally via the art and design route – the structure and pattern of training is as in the section Introduction above. Courses obviously teach basic engineering and technology, but not so intensively as full engineering courses.

BA in art and design: industrial design options (all engineering unless otherwise shown) –
Polytechnics – Birmingham, Coventry (transportation), Leeds, Leicester, Manchester, Middlesborough: Teesside, Newcastle (design for industry), Sheffield; schools/colleges – Cardiff: S Glam IHE, Edinburgh: Napier (technology), London: Central.

Postgraduate qualifications (normally needed for 'top' professional posts) – polytechnics: Birmingham, Leicester, Manchester; schools/colleges: London: Central, RCA.

BTEC National and Higher National Diplomas as at November 1987 –
Design (industrial) National Diploma – Colchester Inst, Doncaster MIHE, Mansfield: W Notts CFE; Higher National Diploma – Colchester Inst.

For the engineering route, see QUALIFICATIONS AND CAREERS IN ENGINEERING.

INTERIOR, THEATRICAL, EXHIBITION AND RETAIL DESIGN have as much in common with architecture and planning as they do with art. The modern collective name for them is 'spatial' design. Architects and interior designers, particularly, generally work closely together.

Designers in many of these areas work in teams which include technical experts (lighting and electrical people for example) and craftsmen/women capable of turning sketches, detailed drawings and models into reality, although only too often the designer has to do some of the practical work.

Designers in these fields need to know a lot about, and be skilled in using colour, materials, texture, and style of decoration. They must be able to visualise spatially and keep ahead of new ideas. They must be able to communicate ideas both verbally and in sketches, and know how to get the most out of a tight budget.

Qualifications and training most professional designers specialise in one or other of these, but at 'technician' level it can be useful to have a more broadly-based qualification, eg

BTEC National and Higher National Diplomas as at end 1986 –
Design (mural) Higher National Diploma – London: Chelsea SA.
Design (spatial) National Diploma – Bournemouth/Poole CA&D, Hull: Humberside CHE, Leeds: J Kramer, Rochester: Medway CD; Higher National Diploma – Bournemouth/Poole CA&D, Dewsbury/Batley T&AC, Newcastle CA&T, Rochester: Medway CD.

INTERIOR DESIGN AND DECORATION are used not just to make the inside of a building attractive, but also to see that it is functional, practical and comfortable to live, work, stay, or play in, and is easy and cost-effective to run. The interior designer has to work closely with architects and BUILDING SERVICES ENGINEERS (who design systems – electrical, heating, air-conditioning etc), as well as the client. Architects are technically responsible only for the shell of a building. However, architects normally think in terms of designing a building as a whole, and some prefer to be their own interior designers, or to have an interior designer on their own staff/team.

Interior designers plan colour schemes and materials, for walls, floors and ceilings, furniture and fitments (such as built-in cupboards, bedheads, and bathroom suites), right down to the detail of light fittings and even door knobs and house plants. In both appearance and practicality, the design for a disco, or a fashion store, a hotel, a public house, a set of offices will be very different from each other. Choice of materials, for example, must take account of the kind of wear they must withstand as well as creating the right kind of image and atmosphere. Limits on cost, time, space etc must be met – and the space must be used efficiently. Safety may be an important factor.

Interior designers work mainly for commercial, and some industrial, organisations, less frequently on people's homes. Some very large organisations, eg brewers and hotel chains, which redesign their outlets quite frequently, and want to create an instantly-recognisable, nation-wide 'image', employ their own design teams. Most organisations, though, put the work out to tender: freelance designers or design consultancies submit sketches, ideas and estimates. Sometimes the work comes via an architect – and some interior designers work for architectural practices. A high proportion of the interior designer's work is not on new buildings at all, but on regular refurbishing of, for example, restaurants, stores, clubs or banks where there is heavy wear, and a restyled interior is part of the business of staying competitive.

Interior designers prepare the sketches and ideas for quotation. If the contract is won, they must then prepare detailed specifications and working drawings and get approval for them. They put out the contract for the actual work – the decorating, furniture, coverings etc – to tender, and then supervise it, and see schedules are kept and problems solved.

Interior design and interior decoration are difficult to separate. Some larger furnishing stores give customers a full design service, some may just advise or provide stock schemes, for colour and decoration, furnishings, carpets, etc. 'Home advisers' may help with layouts and sketch suggestions for customers, while store estimators also advise while measuring for curtains or coverings.

Demand for interior designers, never large, declined sharply in the early 1980s, although demand may have improved more recently, as stores etc have been redesigning to attract customers.

Recruitment and training as section Introduction above.

Qualifications and training Format and structure as section Introduction above.

BA in art and design three-dimensional design with interior design as chief study –
Polytechnics: Birmingham, Brighton, Leeds, Leicester, London: Kingston, Middx, PNL, Manchester, Middlesbrough: Teesside, Nottingham: Trent, Stafford: N Staffs; schools/colleges: Dundee, Glasgow SA, High Wycombe: Bucks CHE, Cardiff: S Glam IHE, London: Central.

Postgraduate courses (generally essential for 'top' posts): Leicester, London: Middx, Manchester Polytechnics.

BTEC Higher National and National Diplomas as at end 1986 –
Design (interior) National Diploma – Dewsbury/Batley T&AC, London: Furniture, Willesden, Torquay: S Devon CA&T, Trowbridge TC; Higher National Diploma – London: Furniture C.

THEATRICAL AND SET DESIGN covers not only the conventional stage, but also stages and sets for film and TV. Designers work to the director's overall plan for the production. This may be a realistic setting, a spectacular or abstract design for a musical, or a background for a current-affairs TV programme. The design must take account of the limitations of the theatre or the TV or film studio, the complexities of scene changing, and of filming sequences for film and TV. It may mean searching for locations which suit the script, and can in part be reproduced in the studio, although this is less necessary now as new-technology film equipment allows most films and TV plays to be shot on location. TV sets may have to take into account the technical requirements of camera crew and colour engineers, allow for film insets, back-projection, and so on. In theatre, film and TV, cost is an overwhelming factor for many productions.

Designers must work closely with the director, with technical staff (eg lighting experts) and costume designers, although some theatrical designers do both.

The number of openings for theatrical designers is very limited, and competition for them intense. Film and theatrical designers generally work on a freelance basis. The larger TV production companies have their own, but quite small, design teams.

Recruitment and entry as section Introduction above.

Qualifications and training form and structure as section Introduction above.

BA in art and design three-dimensional design with theatre design chief studies at –
Polytechnics – Birmingham, Nottingham: Trent; schools/colleges – London: Central, Wimbledon.

BTEC Higher National and National Diplomas as at end 1986 –
Design (theatre studies) National Diploma – Worthing: W Sussex CD; Higher National Diploma – Liverpool: M Fletcher TC, London: Central, Croydon, Fashion.

EXHIBITION AND RETAIL DISPLAY range from planning entire exhibition sites to designing individual stands. They merge with graphic design at this point, with either exhibition or graphic designers preparing display panels which are used both in exhibitions and in shop and other displays, and which do not need any construction work or complicated decoration.

Exhibition design work is done for trade or public exhibitions which bring together for a short while many different exhibitors – firms making/selling cars or office machinery, publishers, model train makers, all the firms involved in 'ideal' homes. A growing if still relatively small field of employment is in designing semi- or even permanent exhibitions, for museums and art galleries, for example.

General and trade exhibitions work to an overall plan and usually have a theme, designed to attract and interest a particular group of people, who may be in business, or are consumers, or hobbyists. The organiser's designers have to give the exhibition a design 'framework', to give it an instantly-recognisable 'image' both for the exhibition itself and its publicity and other material, while allowing individual exhibitors, who often have conflicting demands, to put their own images over on their stands. The design has to take account of the many practical problems in preparing plans and layouts – the right amount of space, with access, for exhibits, practical services, services for visitors (bars and lounges for adults, room to talk, ice cream and hot dogs for children), safety, and so on.

Stand design must fit into the theme of the exhibition, but must also meet the exhibitor's requirements, which may mean fitting the display into the theme of an existing marketing campaign, while suggesting particular ways of attracting attention for a product at the exhibition. The practical problems arc the same as affect the overall design, and what is usually a minute amount of space has to be used intelligently. Plans must be presented to the client in sketches and models, with specifications and costings, and once approved, the designer arranges and supervises the construction of the stand, decoration, any furniture, and the dispay itself. Tight time schedules and budgets are usual.

Most general and trade exhibitions are planned, organised and designed by firms specialising in the business, although some firms which exhibit frequently may have their own staff, or use an independent designer on contract. The best opportunities for employment are with contractors.

Exhibition design for museums, art galleries etc is similar, but the aesthetic and intellectual requirements are more demanding – settings must be historically or environmentally accurate, the lighting and placing of individual exhibits

more exacting, and they frequently require special care. Physical problems such as old or inadequate buildings must be coped with.
See also MUSEUM WORK.

Retail display work both window-dressing and interior displays, is increasingly sophisticated and developing as a design career, rather than as an offshoot of retail selling. While many stores still employ their own dressers, many now bring in specialist design teams from outside. Retail design is also often linked to advertising and marketing and may be planned as part of a co-ordinated effort.
See also RETAILING AND DISTRIBUTION.

Recruitment and entry as section Introduction above.

Qualifications and training as section Introduction above.

BA art and design three-dimensional design courses, with interior design chief studies generally include exhibition design; some graphic design courses also cover aspects of exhibition design.

BTEC Higher National and National Diplomas as at end 1986 –
Design (display) National Diploma – Ashton-under-Lyne CT, Bradford/Ilkley CC, Havering TC, Hereford CA&D, Leeds: J Kramer, Liverpool: M Fletcher TC, Sefton (H Baird) CT, London: Distributive Trades C, Hounslow, Southgate; Newcastle CA&T, Rochester: Medway CD, Plymouth CA&D, Sheffield: Granville, Southend TC, Trowbridge TC, Uxbridge TC, Watford: Cassio/Ware, Wisbech C.
Design (exhibition) National Diploma – Bradford/Ilkley CC, Hastings CFE, Northwich CFE, Plymouth CA&D; Higher National Diploma – Hull: Humberside CHE.
Design (retail/exhibition) National Diploma – Harrogate CA&T; Higher National Diploma – Salford CT.

FINE ART

This is the formal title traditionally given to painting, sculpture, engraving, or any artistic activity through which people try to work out very personal creative ideas.

There is little really sound information that careers literature can give such artists other than to be heavily pessimistic about their chances of finding any fulfilment other than the satisfaction of following what can only be described as a vocation. Although barely a handful of artists throughout the world in any one generation achieve any popular recognition or reasonable income, some third of all BA in art and design students opt for fine art. More fine art graduates eventually teach than any other art and design group, and a greater proportion of them have to find other work than any other group of art and design graduates. Only a small percentage find commercial or industrial work, and a high proportion go on to postgraduate courses.

This has nothing to do with talent. Whether or not artists can make an income from their art depends on their work attracting the kind of people who buy art, and also on the artist being able and willing to spend time going out to find them or to get a gallery to sell for them. It also depends on gaining acceptance and approval of influential people, such as gallery owners, dealers, critics, and even established artists.

An artist generally needs some ten years' hard work to become fully competent technically, and of that time six or seven years are spent at art school, including the BA in art and design course and some postgraduate training (which is doubly useful since it is also a preparation for teaching art). It is possible to prolong training, and therefore state or other support, with scholarships or exhibitions, or by winning competitions which carry such support for further study, possibly abroad. These competitions and awards are also seen as a measure of success for the young artist.

A great deal of drive, determination and single-mindedness are needed to be successful in selling work. Artists have a hard fight to get their work into worthwhile exhibitions so that it will be seen by influential people and potential clients. Artists whose work is likely to sell will probably have attracted some attention while still at art school, but it may still be hard work to gain a place first in mixed, group shows (put on by organisations like the Arts Council), and even harder to persuade a gallery or other exhibitor to put on a 'one-man' or '-woman' show. Some private galleries sometimes offer very promising young artists contracts against future earnings, allowing them to paint or sculpt full time. There are some grants, some industrial support (eg for sculptors prepared to work in modern materials). Some artists manage to live on commissions, for portraits or sculptures. The possible income from all sources is unlikely to be enough to live on. Most artists, then, have to find an income from eg teaching, illustrating, etc.

Qualifications and training it is generally sensible to go through the foundation course – BA in art and design – higher degree route.

BA in art and design specialising in fine art (painting and/or sculpture with supporting studies in eg film, photography, engraving, printmaking) at – Polytechnics – Birmingham, Brighton, Bristol, Coventry, Leicester, Liverpool, London: Kingston, Middx, NELP; Manchester, Newcastle, Nottingham: Trent, Portsmouth, Preston, Sheffield, Stafford: N Staffs, Sunderland, Wolverhampton; schools/colleges – Aberdeen: RGIT, Bath, Bromley: Ravensbourne, Canterbury, Cardiff: S Glam IHE, Dundee, Exeter, Falmouth, Farnham: W Surrey C, Glasgow SA, Gloucester CA&T, London: Camberwell, Inst (Central/St Martin's, Chelsea), Goldsmiths', Wimbledon; Newport: Gwent CHE, Humberside CHE, Loughborough CA&D, Maidstone, Norwich, Stourbridge CA&T, Winchester.
Just 5360 students were studying fine art for a CNAA degree in 1984-5, 10 down on the previous year, although first-year enrolments were up about 100.

Universities with studio-based courses – Aberystwyth (50%), Edinburgh, Lancaster, Leeds, London: UCL (Slade), Newcastle, Oxford (Ruskin), Reading.

Postgraduate (master's) degree/diploma courses in fine art at
Universities – London: RCA, UCL (Slade), Ulster; polytechnics – Birmingham, Manchester; schools/colleges – London: Chelsea, Goldsmiths'.
See also ACADEMIC AND VOCATIONAL STUDIES IN ART.

PHOTOGRAPHY

Frequently just as creative, just as demanding on artistic talent, aesthetic judgement and technical skill as the 'conventional' arts. May be more so, since as well as being as skilled in composition, perspective, use of colour, line, light and shade as any other artist, the professional photographer also has to be able to work at speed, and know which camera, lens, film, and so on will capture the best frame, often of a moving subject. The photographer has to be just as highly trained in techniques and know as much about cameras, lenses and lighting equipment, developing and processing film and the chemicals involved, improving negatives, making prints, and toning, mounting and finishing them, as an artist does about painting techniques, paints, etc.

Photographs are used in so many spheres (because, as one editor said, 'one slightly contrived picture is worth a thousand words'), that the choice of work is considerable, even allowing for the fierce competition for the most interesting jobs. It is quite common, even usual, for photographers to specialise, and given the technical demands of some areas of photography, may be necessary. Many photographers, though, will do whatever work is offered them, and in working life the boundaries between one kind of photography and another may not be quite so firm as they seem in some careers literature. Fashion photographers, for example, work for advertising agencies, for fashion houses, for the press, and on mail-order catalogues, which may provide their main income. Many firms expect a staff photographer to be able to do whatever work is needed, and only the most successful freelance can afford to turn away work. Many try different kinds of photographic work in the course of their working lives. Hard work, talent, training, preparation, and so on, count for most, but there can still be an element of luck – being in the right place at the right second, when something photogenic happens.

Most competitive areas of work are advertising, fashion, press and photojournalism.

ADVERTISING AND FASHION PHOTOGRAPHY Agencies and magazines are always looking for new talent, for a fresh approach to much-photographed subjects, a new style, an eye for a new trend, originality, and ingenuity. Fashion and advertising photographs have to be eye catching and look natural and instant, even if they are carefully posed, and must be exactly what the agency brief asks for. The work is very demanding on technical skills as well as needing artistic sense. Some photographers work full-time for agencies, or a studio specialising in advertising, but many work on a freelance basis. Much of the work is done in a studio, some on location. Pressures on photographers in a highly-pressurised business can be considerable.

See also ADVERTISING.

PRESS PHOTOGRAPHY Press photographers also work under pressure – to meet deadlines, to produce the most interesting shot when all of Fleet Street is trying to do the same, or to get an 'exclusive' photograph (news editors, if anything, care more about photographic scoops than journalistic ones and will always expect the photographer to turn in a better shot than rivals).

Press photographers can get into exciting, sometimes dangerous situations, but the work is more often uncomfortable and even boring, when days can be spent shuttling between press conferences, lunches, royal events, and banquets. All press photographers write their own captions, and some become photo-journalists, combining photographic and journalistic assignments – in-depth material, travel features, war assignments, for example.

Press photographers work for the staff of local or national papers, a press or photographic agency, or they freelance.

'SOCIETY' PHOTOGRAPHY Comparatively few photographers now make a living solely from posed portraits, or so-called 'society' work. Technically-superb, easy-to-use cameras on general sale, and the automatic photo-booth giving a rapid service for passport photographs, have eaten into the traditional work of the local, non-specialist photographers for whom this used to be bread-and-butter. There is work for fewer and fewer of them, and those that survive have to be increasingly good, and ingenious, to stay in business. There are still weddings, local functions, local dignitaries, banquets, dances, swimming galas, garden parties, shows of all kinds, to photograph, sometimes for local papers who do not have their own staff photographers, but it is difficult to make a profit. Some local photographers have shops dealing in photographic equipment as a part of their businesses, and may be closely involved with local societies.

INDUSTRIAL, SCIENTIFIC, MEDICAL, AND OTHER TECHNICAL PHOTOGRAPHY probably provide more opportunities, and there has been some growth here.

In industry, for example, the staff of a photographic unit may work for the public relations department (photographing new products, new machinery, or new plants), for research and development, and quality control. Public relations work may be more like advertising, and the best industrial photographers can produce shots of chemical plants or cranes which are as original and creative as any other.

In research and development, or quality control, the work is similar to photographic work in a university or research establishment. Here, special fluorescent ultra-violet and other techniques are used to photograph, for example, plant sections, crystals, fractures in metals and fibres under microscopes which can magnify many times the normal size to illustrate details which would be invisible otherwise. Scientific research also uses high-speed cine and time-lapse photography to examine processes and activities which happen either too fast or too slowly for the human eye to record the exact sequence of events. Photography is also used extensively in areas like astronomy, space research and meteorology.

Some areas of scientific photography are becoming very specialised –

Medical photography is one example where a wide range of both straightforward and highly advanced techniques and equipment are used to record the progress of a disease and/or treatment, to photograph slides of, for example, tissue cultures and sections, and under-skin photographs, and even to photograph inside the body. The work is exacting and highly technical – for example, colour accuracy is crucial, and depends on using exactly the right staining medium to prepare a tissue section, and/or on the use of the right film.

Forensic photography is another example of highly technical work. Here photographers must make very accurate records of the scene of a crime or of an accident; produce enlargements of evidence such as finger- or shoe-prints, tyre- and skid-marks or signs of forced entry, and use infra-red and ultra-violet photography to reveal microscopic detail – of cloth fibres or blood stains for example – or of evidence that has been been covered up.

Scotland Yard employs over 50 photographers, and one other large police force alone now employs a staff of over 60 in photographic work, making over 15,000 visits to scenes of crime a year.

Aerial and underwater photography are two other fields showing some growth.

Architectural photographers provide a recording service for architects, government and local departments and are also employed both by the architectural press and more generally in magazine work. Architects' records have to show stages of construction, general views and close-ups of architectural detail, and may also include interiors. Architectural work, however, is generally badly affected by recession in construction work.

Professional photographers work throughout industry and commerce, for the National Health Service, universities and other research and educational institutions, government and local government service, and the armed forces. Others work for photographic agencies, some general and some specialising in particular types of photography (eg aerial), or subject areas, eg sport. Many photographers work freelance.

PHOTOGRAPHIC TECHNICIANS Estimates suggest that at least 80% of people working in photography never use a camera professionally. Mostly these are the highly-trained technicians who process and retouch film, work in the printing industry on photographic copying of pictures as the first stage in the preparation of blocks, litho, photogravure and screen printing, and the more routine work involved in specialist document copying – of plans and drawings, reducing papers on to microfilms, etc.

Entry and recruitment Most professional photographers probably begin their careers as trainees, studying for professional examinations at the same time, but an increasing number start by taking full-time courses (below). Most prospective employers will want evidence of potential, and agencies, for example, frequently choose new staff from amongst young photographers from whom they have been buying individual photographs, or who have done one-off assignments for the firm efficiently. Some hospitals do take trainees without any formal training, but many prefer recruits to have at least some initial preparation. Press photographers are normally expected to complete a form of apprenticeship (below).

Photography takes creativity and originality, sharp observational skills, and an eye for form and perspective. Some scientific background and interest in the photographic possibilities of scientific and technical developments, and some mechanical/electrical skills is useful. Ingenuity, considerable tenacity and determination, and ability to get living subjects (human or animal) to co-operate are also helpful.

Qualifications and training Growth of properly-organised training in photography has been very haphazard, but the range of formal pre-entry courses in further and higher education has been expanding steadily for some time now.

The British Institute of Professional Photography (BIPP) estimates (1987) that about 1500 people complete courses every year. BIPP, which recognises courses but sets an exam only in medical photography, is making an MSC-supported study of training needs, which could result in a more coherent system eventually.

Degree courses (art and design courses may also include photography options) at (* courses recognised by BIPP) –
Photography/photographic studies – polytechnics: London: PCL (science); Nottingham: Trent*; colleges: Derbyshire CHE; Edinburgh: Napier; London: Printing*.
Multi-media courses with major photography content – polytechnics: London: Middx/Harrow CHE, PCL; colleges: Farnham: W Surrey CA&D*.
Just 974 students were studying photography, film and TV for a CNAA degree in 1985-6, three up on the year before.

BTEC Higher National and National Diplomas (courses may have options in or bias to particular aspects of photography) are at (* courses recognised by BIPP) –
Design (photography) National Diploma – Ashton under Lyme: Tameside CT; Birmingham: Bournemouth/Poole CA&D; Bournville CA&C; Crosskeys C; Dagenham: Barking CT*; Dewsbury/Batley T&AC; Harrogate CA&T; Hereford CA&D; Leeds: Kitson; London: Paddington C*; Luton: Barnfield*; Maidenhead: Berks CA&D*; Newcastle CA&T; Northwich: Mid-Ches CFE*; Plymouth CA&D*; Richmond C*; Sandwell CF&HE*; Sheffield: Granville*; Southport CA&T*; Swansea: W Glam IHE*; Ware C*; Watford C; Wigan CT; Higher National Diploma – Blackpool/Fylde CF&HE*[1] ; Bournemouth/Poole CA&D*[1] ; Gloucester CA&T*; Manchester P*; Newport: Gwent CHE; Plymouth CA&D; Salisbury CA*[1] ; Swansea: W Glam IHE*;
[1] Also courses for BIPP professional qualifying exam.

CGLI 744 General Photography (full-time) Ashton under Lyme: Tameside CT; Huntingdon TC*; Luton: Barnfield; Northwich: Mid-Ches CFE; Stafford CFE; also number of part-time courses.

CGLI 745 Applied/Scientific and Technical Photography (full-time) Maidenhead: Berks CA&D; Sheffield: Richmond C; also some part-time courses.

CGLI 750 Photography Assistants (full-time) Barking CT; Ewell: NE Surrey CA; Leicester: S Fields CFE; also some part-time courses.

Medical photography training schemes (on- and off-the-job) – Cardiff: UCH, Manchester: Royal Infirmary, West Midlands RHA.

Press photography: National Council for the Training of Journalists training schemes – normally six months' probation for aptitude assessment and three-year apprenticeship; includes eight-week course in each of first two years, with proficiency test at end of training period (entry at least five O level equivalent passes at 16-plus† including English language or English).
Pre-entry course (1-year full time): W Bromwich CC&T (entry: 2 A-level passes or equivalent).

Further information from the British Institute of Professional Photographers, and the National Joint Council for the Training of Journalists.

CAREERS RELATED TO ART AND DESIGN
Whether or not a career comes within the sphere of art and design often depends on historical factors.

Art galleries and museums
Those maintaining large collections of paintings, sculptures, and other works of art employ people with degrees in both art and design and art history in general museum work, to administer, care for, exploit, catalogue, them. The work is very similar to the keeper/curator work in MUSEUMS. The national art galleries are state-owned and have a career structure similar to the national museums. Other public and local galleries generally mount travelling exhibitions, so the work centres on organising these, associated publicity and catalogues, raising funds, organising lectures, etc. The number of posts in national or other public galleries is very small. Private galleries tend to recruit through personal contacts.

Art galleries also employ people with training in art and design in conserving all kinds of works of art, but restorers also generally need some scientific and technological background, have a good knowledge of art history, plus patience and an aptitude for painstaking and careful work.
See also MUSEUM AND GALLERY WORK.

Art journalism and writing about art
Writing about art, whether in books, newspapers or journals, requires considerable experience, generally of writing, combined with an in-depth knowledge of the art field, or part of it – although there are no hard-and-fast rules. Literary and picture research, for television companies, book and magazine publishers and freelance writers, can be a stepping-stone into writing, editing etc.

Art sales
The main and largest commercial galleries and sale rooms employ very small numbers of experts who have in-depth knowledge of a period of art history and/or a type of works, and a good grasp of the art market. They work mainly in valuing, and it is a commercially-oriented career. The main sale rooms put on 9-10 month training courses, but few students are taken on afterwards.
See also RETAILING.

Art teaching
Specialist art teachers are employed in secondary schools and schools and colleges of art, some of which are part of larger FE colleges or polytechnics. Teaching has, in the past, provided an income for practising artists, some of whom taught on a part-time basis. There are now generally fewer posts, and particularly fewer part-time posts.
A teaching qualification, gained either as a postgraduate qualification after a BA in art and design, or a BEd with art/design as a major subject of study, is

now needed to teach in schools. Most people recruited for art-school teaching have a qualification in art and design, but it is policy in many schools to bring in practising artists and designers on a part-time or visiting basis.
See also EDUCATION.

Art therapy

This is a way of helping people with emotional and psychological problems, teaching them, for example, painting or pottery. About 150 art therapists work mainly in hospitals with psychiatrists and occupational therapists, some in hospital schools with children, and the rest in ordinary or special schools with children who have special needs, child guidance clinics, prisons, borstals and community homes. Most posts are part-time, so therapists work for two or more institutions and travel between them, or for different bodies within an area.

The recommended route in is via a degree in art or design followed by a specialist postgraduate course: at eg Birmingham Polytechnic, London: Goldsmiths' College, and St Albans: Herts CA.

Model making

Models are used by most designers who work in three dimensions as well as by architects, planners, and design engineers, eg civil engineers. They have several uses. First, two-dimensional drawings on paper (or even on the screen of a computer-based design system) are never completely satisfactory. The designer wants to make sure designs that look right on paper will actually work in practice, and make any adjustments (if they will not cost too much). Secondly, models are the best way to show designs of (for example) a new car to marketing departments, a new building to clients, planning committees and public enquiries. Third, sophisticated models which can be taken apart help production managers to decide how to process the new product.

Film companies use models and model sets; museums and other exhibitions use models as settings and to show how some exhibits work. Other uses include, for instance, electronically-controlled working models 'sailing' on a water tank and used to train oil-tanker captains.

Some designers produce their own models. There are, though, specialist model-making firms; some model makers work on a freelance basis, or are employed by, for instance, larger architectural practices, museums, film companies and design consultants. Some firms make models for retail display.

Models can be extremely sophisticated – from full-scale 'mock-ups' to working models of cars, locomotives and ships. Model-making is mostly craft, but requires a great deal of dexterity, imagination, and technical skills which include fine carpentry, moulding and joining, and electronic engineering.

Qualifications and training Has been largely on the job, but it is now possible to take a –

BTEC Higher National or National Diploma in design (modelmaking): National – Dagenham: Barking CT; Higher National Diploma – Rochester: Medway CT.

See also, eg ACADEMIC AND VOCATIONAL STUDIES IN ART, ADVERTISING, ARCHITECTURE, CRAFT INDUSTRIES, DRAUGHTSMANSHIP.

MEDIA, FILM AND THEATRE

Introduction   560
Broadcasting and radio   563
Film and video making   574
Theatrical administration and production   577
Media agents   579
Newspaper publishing   580
Periodical publishing   582
Publishing books   584
Writing professionally   588

INTRODUCTION

'Media' describes what are, for the present at least, several separate industries using quite different technical methods – printing, broadcasting, and film – to put over ideas, information and entertainment, to large, mass audiences, through television, books, newspapers, magazines, and the cinema.

But technology, as part of the electronic and computer-based revolution in communications, is beginning to break down the divisions between the different media as they are today, to make quite major changes in the way ideas, information and entertainment are delivered.

Of course there is already a great deal of interchange between them. There is already as much film as live broadcasts on television. The 'book of the programme' is on the bookstall next morning, just as books have long been turned into a film or television series. Films can now be bought on video cassettes and shown on a television screen. Films and television can go on a video disc too, and technically it is possible to do the same for books, so they can all be projected on screen. Newspapers may one day 'arrive' on the breakfast table either via the screen or a facsimile machine (like a long-distance photocopier) as an alternative to breakfast television.

The television screen is also used to play games, and systems like Prestel, Ceefax and Oracle give printed rather than spoken information via the television set. By the 1990s it will be possible to call up television programmes or films from computer banks at any time, and not have to watch (or record) them when companies schedule them. Already 'television' programmes showing races are being beamed directly into betting shops, and not coming onto other sets at all.

Many people with home computers use their television sets as the visual display unit for their computer. Effectively, the television set/screen is becoming more and more all-purpose, is likely soon to be restyled as a 'video' screen and will eventually be used for everything from asking the computer 'library' to screen the latest novel, or for information on college courses in English, to ordering from the local supermarket or the mail order firm. Transmitting conventional programmes will be a very small part of what it will do.

It is difficult to predict what the full effect of all this will be on the media industries – publishing, printing, newspapers, television, and film companies – or to jobs and careers within them. There are too many uncertainties. Whether or not media industries will use all this technology depends to a large extent on consumer reaction, and on gearing the product correctly to the market. The more 'high-tech' possibilities – satellite and cable TV, screen-based shopping and banking – are not 'taking off' as fast as some predicted. Cost, and getting a return on investment on a time scale which can compete with all the new offerings of FINANCE seem to have halted projects already.

With the exception of the BBC, media companies are all commercial firms, in business to make a profit for their investors and shareholders, and so are no different in this to firms making and selling, say, soap-powder or pizzas. The same problems of competition for business, and hard trading conditions give the London-based publisher or newspaper owner problems very similar to those faced by the Midlands car manufacturer. New media products must pay their way, and the early problems met by Channel 4 and TV-am companies have raised questions on just how much media expansion the buying public wants. It is no use doubling the choice of entertainment available through the TV set if the viewing audience is all out of the house, running in marathons – which might make it more profitable to invest in making running shoes and 'Walkman'-style radios. Information systems delivered through the television set, like Prestel, have not so far been the popular success once hoped either, but for rather more complex reasons.

The only prediction it is possible to make, then, is that there will be change, and greater change than earlier technology – such as television itself – brought. If people do decide they will pay for even more choice of television programmes, for all the information and other services that, say, cable systems can bring, then there will further expansion in providing material for those extra channels. How far these will bring an increase in the total number of jobs is even more difficult to say. Television created new companies and new jobs, but caused job losses in newspaper and periodical publishing, and in the cinema. The newspaper industry has now adopted new technology, and created new papers and some jobs (but nothing like the numbers lost in production) as a result. All the existing media will have to adapt to further change, which means that people working within them will have to cope with change too.

This time, too, media industries will also have to cope with all the other effects of the 'converging' new technologies, as already discussed under INFORMATION TECHNOLOGY. For example, computer-based information and retrieval systems are already starting to erode some of the most profitable areas of publishing – lawyers can now have computer screens on their desks which give them instant access to up-to-date case law and precedent, so that legal reference books are becoming redundant. Only by becoming data-base companies can these publishers stay in business.

The business and commercial aspects of the media industries are often rather forgotten by people attracted to careers in them. Obviously the work is often creative, challenging, interesting, rewarding and satisfying, and can fully extend anyone's talents. The printed word is hallowed by time, giving it some kind of mystique based on centuries of philosophical discussion and political argument on the nature, liberty, privilege and power of the press, and by implication and extension, of broadcasting too.

All this makes it difficult to get people who want to work for the media to appreciate that these industries demand just as sound and practical managing and business sense as do supermarkets or hotels. If anything, the routine and pressures of the commercial world tend to be more obvious just because it can be difficult to reconcile creative demands with criteria on which a business must be operated to survive.

The media are, of course, glamorous. It is exciting to be at the apparent centre of events, to rub shoulders with public figures, to see a book into print, or a programme on to the screen. Press, publishers, and broadcasters can be influential, and do have a tradition of being the guardians of liberty and free speech. But it is still necessary to get over just how tough the business is to work in; that there is never enough time, money or resources to do a job full justice; that the strain of working continuously in the public gaze and the stress of producing high-quality papers, books or programmes every day of the week (when they may only be read or seen once), is considerable; that the hours are long and irregular – and that there is always someone ready to take on the job should the present occupant flag. Employers can, and often do, demand total dedication to the job, which means a reasonable private life is very difficult in many media posts.

Overall, the media are still expanding – but quite gently in job terms. Every part of the media was affected by recession and public expenditure cuts, with reduced sales and/or loss of advertising, and there have been redundancies, especially in publishing and in newspapers and magazines.

Working for the media There are four different kinds of work in media industries –

First are the people who write the books, the scripts, the plays, the news stories; the people who appear on screen, or are heard over the air. These are the actors and musicians, the journalists and disc-jockeys, the presenters and commentators, and other entertainers. Few of them, ie only some of the journalists, work full-time for one employer. Mostly they are employed for the length of a contract, to write a book or script, or to appear in a certain number of programmes, for whichever publishing or broadcasting company or theatrical or film management has work for them at the time.

Second are the policy makers, the editorial staff and, in broadcasting and the theatre, the people who make programmes, and put on plays. These are the producers and directors and their staff. Mostly these are permanent posts, and they form the career structures in the media, but some are also employed only on contract, and this is increasing as publishing tries to cut costs, and broadcasting companies aim to increase the number of 'independent' productions.

Third are the technical people who make publishing or broadcasting possible – the printers who produce books and newspapers; the radio and TV technicians, and the broadcasting engineers who see that programmes reach the listener and viewer.

Finally, efficient administration and management are just as important to media organisations of all kinds as to any other firm or organisation, and so all but the very smallest employ quite a few people to keep them operating as smoothly as possible. This means accountants, personnel managers, librarians, computer experts and operators, public relations staff, marketing staff, secretaries, telephonists, and so on. People have to take down news copy (in both newspapers and broadcasting) on the phone (but new technology is making inroads here), or operate machines which record and transcribe reporters' despatches.

Newspaper, periodical and some book publishers, and the independent television and radio companies, also employ quite large numbers of people to sell advertising, on which profitability is largely based.

Specialist jobs include looking after contributors' (authors, actors, script writers etc) contracts, and other rights (film rights to books, or the publishing rights to television programmes). Television companies also have quite large departments to negotiate the sale and purchase of films and programmes abroad. Some broadcasting companies publish their own books and the weekly programme and other magazines, so employing editors, journalists, production staff etc.

BROADCASTING

Until fairly recently, 'broadcasting' meant television and radio programmes made and 'transmitted' either by the British Broadcasting Corporation or companies licensed to do so by the Independent Broadcasting Authority. They are run as public services to 'disseminate information, education and entertainment'. The BBC gains most of its income from licence fees and the independent companies from advertising revenue, but both the BBC and the independent companies also sell their output, and exploit the book, record, and video possibilities as well. Broadcasting is a very expensive business – both in the capital equipment needed to transmit, record, etc, and because it is labour intensive.

Now there are so many new possibilities, mainly technological, for broadcasting, that it is almost impossible to be certain how it will develop in the future, except that it is more likely than not to go on expanding. The three main areas of development specifically in broadcasting are home video, national satellite transmission – due to start by 1990 – and cable, which is not proving as popular as hoped. The broadcasting network and the television set also carry 'videotext' information systems like Prestel, Ceefax and Oracle. Many people are already using their television sets as the visual display unit for their computers.

The main significance, especially for jobs, of these developments is that for the first time the UK broadcasting companies are losing their monopoly on programme making: with satellite transmission, home video, and video text it is possible for other organisations to by-pass the broadcasters, and compete for their audiences. Satellite transmission will beam directly into the country programmes from abroad. Cable makes possible many more channels, local and 'special' programmes for particular groups, and made by and/or for organisations other than the BBC and independent companies. The increasingly-popular home video (a third of households now have them) lets the viewer buy or rent programmes from completely outside sources. Videotext acts like a library. Both cable and videotext are potentially 'interactive', which means that for the first time the communication can be two-way – it is via these that people will be able to order directly from shops, or tap into their bank account. Videotext lets the viewer ask questions via the TV set, from a host of different information sources, which do not have to be the existing broadcasting companies. The boundaries between 'broadcasting' and other forms of mass communication are now breaking down, and broadcasting is becoming one of the main strands in INFORMATION TECHNOLOGY.

Technology has, of course, already extensively improved life for the programme makers, making possible more interesting programmes, giving the graphic designer and the vision mixer more scope for creativity and spectacular effects on screen, and has helped engineers make considerable improvements in quality. Light-weight 'electronic field production' cameras are replacing the old mammoths, making possible more authentic settings and flexible production, 'robot' cameras cope with simple situations, and 'electronic news-gathering' cameras with mobile transmission equipment give even more immediate coverage of news. In the studios, automated mixing desks allow producers to switch from item to item faster and more efficiently, and a day's output of pre-recorded material can be 'programmed' into the computers' schedule.

The employers

As of 1987, there are some twenty television programme-making companies, consisting of the BBC (with two channels), fifteen regional independent companies, ITN, the national 'breakfast' television company, TV-am, and Channel 4 and its Welsh equivalent. Channel 4 is slightly different from the other companies, in that it does not make many programmes itself, but commissions or takes most of its output from the other programme companies and from independent producers. IBA, which is purely supervisory/administrative, does not make programmes, but since it is responsible for transmission, a considerable proportion of its 1750 employees are engineers who manage and operate the network. By 1990, the first 'direct-broadcasting by satellite' – DBS – commercial contractor expects to be beaming programmes into UK homes. The number of independent producers will probably increase. They currently range from well-established and quite large companies making films, videos and TV programmes for a wide range of outlets through to very new and small units specialising in one type of programme.

Radio services are provided by the four BBC national channels and 32 local stations, and 44 independent stations (not as many as legislation allows, though). Local stations cover 90% of the country. The BBC also has external radio services.

No firm figures are available for the number of people with full-time jobs in broadcasting, but it cannot now be less than 45,000. The BBC employed, at peak (1986) almost 29,000 people (up from 25,000 in 1979). Independent TV companies range in size from Channel 4, with about 250 staff (1986) up to the largest with some 2500. ITN now has over 950 (up from 800 in 1983), TV-am 400. A local radio station employs up to 35 people (some more, most less), making another 1750 or so. The IBA employs about 1400, a mix of (mainly) administrators and engineers. Independent television and radio probably employ directly, therefore, some 16,000 people. Figures for independent producers are not known. None of these figures include the thousands of actors, musicians, script-writers, and so on who work for programme companies on a freelance basis.

Roughly, a third of the staff in the larger programme-producing companies are non-technical programme staff, and engineers and technicians account for another third. A sizeable proportion are administrators, security staff etc, although some service work, eg catering, cleaning, is now contracted out.

While services are expanding, and new jobs being created, all broadcasting agencies face escalating costs and funding problems. The licence fee does not allow the BBC to do all it would like. Independent local radio stations have problems in staying financially viable – 21 companies made losses in 1985-6. All organisations are having to tighten up on financial management, and are cost cutting, and this includes keeping tight reins on staffing. The BBC is cutting up to 4000 jobs, mainly in support services, engineering etc, but will also lose production jobs as and when more programming is put out to independent producers. Soundings suggest that most of the major independent programme companies expect to hold staff numbers steady for the foreseeable future. Any new jobs are likely to come from, for example, new services by existing organisations, amongst independent producers (but these can now only balance out losses in the programme companies), or entirely new services, such as DBS – cable TV seems unlikely to create very many for the immediate future. See also FILM AND VIDEO below.

Working in broadcasting
Although the BBC is so large, it is effectively managed as a series of semi-separate organisations. Radio and television are run separately, and local radio stations are semi-autonomous. Every programme-making company is organised differently, but broadly, the opportunities divide as follows –

Programme making
In television and national radio networks, programmes are made by teams of programme makers, each team brought together for a particular programme, or series, or semi-permanently for a long-running series, such as 'EastEnders'. At present, in the BBC and most of the independent companies, the teams are made up of a mix of permanent staff and people on fixed-length contracts. For Channel 4, programmes are commissioned (by the Channel's editors) from, and made by, mostly other ITV programme companies or 'independent producers', although other organisations may be involved, in close consultation with Channel 4 staff. BBC and other ITV programme companies are now committed to using independent producers in future (up to 25% of output). ITN produces Channel 4 news output. See FILM AND VIDEO below.

Programmes normally begin as ideas in one of the departments – drama, light entertainment, current affairs, sport, news services, features, music, children's, schools, further education, religious, and so on. Each department is 'managed' by a controller, and staffed by programme planners, producers/editors, and researchers. Depending on the type of programme, some departments also have permanent script-editors (often themselves writers); news services, for example, employ journalists, news editors and subs just like a newspaper, but also presenter-readers, although in some news services, eg ITN, news readers also work as reporters. Drama departments employ script readers. Some departments have presenters or presenters script writers on short- or longer-term contract.

A local radio station is organised rather differently. Typically, a station has a manager/programme organiser, a news editor, up to ten producers and up to

A local radio station is organised rather differently. Typically, a station has a manager/programme organiser, a news editor, up to ten producers and up to five station assistants who operate control panels, edit and play tapes, carry out simple microphone work, prepare and present some programmes, and do research. Promotion is usually from station assistant to producer, and most local radio producers are recruited from amongst station assistants. Local radio stations also employ journalists, and with engineering and administrative staff, the average is some 35 staff.

PROGRAMME PRODUCERS/EDITORS are the linch-pins of each programme or series – they get the programmes made, see them through from first ideas to transmission. They decide on the approach and format, organise the team needed to turn the ideas into reality, 'commission' the script, decide how and where the programme is to be made, how much will be recorded or filmed, how much will go out live, what 'performers' are needed, and put it all altogether. On current affairs or news programme they may have to organise several items to fit into the time 'slot' and may be working at very high speed and under great pressure. Documentaries and dramas may have a longer schedule but the pressure is unlikely to be any the less for that.

The number of people working on a programme varies considerably – a radio talk may need only a producer, a studio manager (see below), and the person giving the talk – and they will usually have done their own research and written their own script. At the other end of the scale, a television spectacular involves a huge team, including researchers, stage and perhaps film or directors, one or more presenters, script-writer(s), entertainers and actors, and a sizeable technical team (see below). A drama production will also need a director and a casting director. Researchers and technical teams are assigned from the permanent staff, but the producer normally has to find and take on the rest on contract.

Producers/editors usually have extensive experience of radio and/or television, but can come to the job through a variety of routes. In some departments – music, education for example – they are subject specialists with relevant qualifications.

RESEARCHERS, or ASSISTANT PRODUCERS, do the editorial donkey-work involved in preparing a programme or series. They do all the fact-finding for scripts, write clear and concise briefs on, for example, new programme ideas for editors and script-writers, and suggest question lines to interviewers based on their research. They go through the newspaper clips (from the library) for the background to a story, or do in-depth investigations for documentaries, prepare the questions for a quiz show, or look into the background for a play. They search out film clips or photographs (for television) or tape inserts (for radio) to illustrate parts of the script, find someone authoritative to make an instant comment on the news or a lively personality to take part in a quiz show. They may help find film locations, etc. Assistant producers may do some studio or film directing. Researchers have to be resourceful, to have initiative, be able to work on their own, and know where to go for what. Most work on contract to a particular department, such as drama, features, or current affairs. Few stay in this work permanently – they generally expect to use it as a stepping-stone to higher levels of programme making, normally producing, but others go on to presenting, interviewing-journalism, script writing. But they have to show extra initiative, for instance the ability to make realistic proposals for new programmes, be good at sorting out problems and trouble shooting, as well as being very efficient, to get there.

PRODUCTION ASSISTANTS (ITV)/PRODUCER'S ASSISTANTS (BBC) are more than just efficient personal secretaries (in the BBC the production assistant is a junior director). They are the producer's memory, and liaise between the producer and the rest of the programme production team. They have to keep track of script changes, make sure the producer's instructions are given to the right people and are followed, look after continuity, book studios and film crews as needed, see that people taking part in a programme arrive and are looked after, and time the programme. Very good assistants who are ambitious and have drive and determination can compete for promotion to eg research or floor management.

PROGRAMME CONTRIBUTORS, ACTORS AND ENTERTAINERS A high proportion of the most interesting work in broadcasting is done by people working on fixed contracts or on a freelance basis – they are not employed permanently or full-time by one programme company. This is especially so for script-writing, presenting, interviewing, narrating (mostly done by actors and actresses), compiling programmes, commentating and, of course, acting. Some producers work on a freelance basis and more are likely to do so in future. Contributors may combine reporting, interviewing, presenting, and script-writing. With actors and actresses, disc jockeys, and entertainers of all kinds, they work on contract, either for a single programme or a series, or sometimes for several years. For example, actors who are employed to read listeners' letters on the radio, or the presenters of a news magazine programme.

Anyone who contributes to programmes has to spend time preparing – actors and actresses have to rehearse, just as they do in the theatre. Programme presenters and interviewers must work on the script, talk to the researcher about someone they are going to interview, read the clips the researcher has found; disc jockeys must choose their records, and so on. Contributors may be commissioned by the programme's producer, or they may go to the programme company with their ideas first. Contributors usually have extensive contacts in the companies, and know what kind of programmes they will buy. They need a detailed knowledge of the technical demands of the media, which they have usually gained by working full-time somewhere in broadcasting previously, or as journalists, although there are some people who become successful broadcasters because they are able to put over their own specialist interest – eg astronomy. It is a fairly hazardous business, since even the most successful and talented cannot always predict the right trends, and may therefore fail to match up to the demands of the moment. See also PERFORMING, WRITING etc.

Studio/floor managers

Studio managers work in radio, floor managers in television. They co-ordinate – people, equipment etc – to see that everything is ready at the right time, and that the director's or producer's instructions are carried out.

In radio, studio managers have a creative/technical job to do. They interpret the producer's ideas for the programme and get the wanted effect technically – which involves setting up studios for recording or transmission, adjusting controls for sound balance, controlling and mixing on the studio panel, monitoring for quality, recording and editing on tape, setting up tapes and discs and running them at the right moment, and devising sound effects. Studio managers come in to radio as trainees, and generally expect to move on to production, or presenting-reporting.

Floor managers do similar work in television, but do not operate controls, and are rather more like theatrical stage managers. The floor manager (who has an assistant manager and often several assistants) has to keep order on the studio floor, see that sets are arranged properly, is the link between the producer (in the control box) and the people (actors, or interviewers and presenters, camera and sound crews) in the studio, seeing that they are in the right place, cueing them in, and relaying instructions from production to performers. They organise props, see that any still photographs are to hand, and look after the prompt book. It is a route into production and direction, and the main route for drama and light entertainment especially for the BBC. The BBC's production assistant is midway between floor management and production.

Technical operations and film crews
In both radio and television, technical staff work with some of the most sophisticated electronic equipment there is.

In television, the technical crew, which must work closely with programme production staff, is large. Controlled by a technical manager (who also designs the lighting etc), it consists of the camera team, vision operators and supervisors (who see that the pictures are right), the sound assistants and supervisors (who do the same for sound), with technical trainee assistants to set up and get equipment ready. Vision mixers change the pictures on the screen, through the mixing desk, from camera to camera, from camera to film insert and back, and set up effects, such as a split screen, under the producer's directions.

Radio needs fewer technicians (now called sound staff in the BBC) although the BBC has 600 in London alone. The audio assistants and supervisors look after, assemble and place equipment; record, dub and edit; look after sound effects, mixing and sound balancing. For outside broadcasts, staff rig equipment, test lines and operate mixing desks. Technical operators control the programmes, set up and play recorded items and inserts, music etc, and prepare and route programmes in control rooms, making sure the quality is right.

The BBC, because it has both TV and radio services, runs regional audio units, where technical staff work on both TV and radio production.

All television companies have their own film production services, since more and more television output is on film (or video), although most also contract some work out. These are staffed by film directors, cameramen and assistants (who load film, change lenses, set up cameras etc), sound recordists (and assistants), and film editors. See also FILM AND VIDEO.

Designers
Several kinds work in television –

TELEVISION DESIGN TEAMS including scenic artists, produce sets for programmes of all kinds – plays and serials, current affairs and interview programmes, rock music programmes and light entertainment shows – translating the producer's concept of the mood and atmosphere of a television programme. They produce sketches and working drawings, and select and arrange the furnishings and properties.

GRAPHIC DESIGNERS design and get produced television title sequences, credits, charts to show how people intend to vote, the weather, summaries of what people have said, the latest stock-market index, etc. Modern technology, mainly computer graphics, is giving designers more and more imaginative and creative techniques to work with, but technical skills are needed. Photographers and photographic technicians are also employed in graphics.

VISUAL EFFECTS DESIGNERS produce models and almost any devices or effects (including 'pyrotechnics') if needed to create visual 'illusions'.

COSTUME DESIGN AND WARDROBE are very similar to THEATRICAL WORK. Costume designers and assistants, dressmakers, dressers (who also look after costumers), wardrobe stock-keepers and operatives are all employed by television production companies.

TELEVISION MAKE UP is rather more specialised than in the theatre. Colour, tone, contours have to be exactly right for TV and film work, which will include close ups. Make up designers (and assistants) also create character and period make up and hairstyles, and senior staff are involved from the programme planning stage.
See also ART AND DESIGN.

Engineering
Engineers in the BBC, the Independent Broadcasting Authority, and independent programme companies, transmit radio and TV signals, and work on improving services. Both the BBC and IBA do advanced research on methods of transmission (working, for example, on digital-video techniques of signal processing, use of microprocessors, on standards for satellite transmissions, and on optical fibre), reducing faults, designing new and specialised equipment (eg slow-motion video-tape), but both the BBC and IBA are cutting down on research. Engineers design and develop new and expanded networks, transmitters and radio links. They manage, operate and maintain the existing networks and transmitters. Others do outside broadcast work, organising mobile power supplies and radio-link receivers and transmitters, or set up, test and maintain studio equipment. They look after internal communications. Technical assistants test, adjust and service broadcasting equipment.

The BBC's engineering departments employed nearly 6000 technical staff up to 1985, including over 2000 qualified engineers. But economies probably involve a loss of about 1000 jobs. Similar staff are employed by the IBA, which has also been considering cuts, and the independent television companies.

The monitoring service
This is operated by the BBC, and listens to broadcasting stations in all parts of the world, reporting to BBC newsrooms and programme departments, government departments and other customers (eg the press, public libraries, and academic institutions both in Britain and elsewhere). It is sometimes the only source of fast and comprehensive information on events overseas. Monitoring staff listen to news, commentaries and talks, and translate where necessary.

Administration
This is just as essential to broadcasting companies as to any other organisation. Both the BBC and the independent broadcasting companies employ ACCOUNTANTS and other finance officers, LIBRARIANS (BBC libraries employ 600 people in London), management service experts (250 in the BBC), including COMPUTING STAFF (programmers, systems analysts, operators) working on services for both programme making and administration, PERSONNEL MANAGERS, PUBLIC RELATIONS STAFF (or information officers), PURCHASING OFFICERS, and ARCHIVISTS, contracts and publications, SECRETARIAL AND CLERICAL STAFF.

Recruitment and entry
Different for different types of work, different companies. Competition for almost all jobs is considerable, although recruiters complain that the quality of applicants is often generally poor. In general, programme-making companies prefer to fill jobs internally from people already working for them, and if they have to go outside, always prefer people with relevant experience and a proven track record. Many people taken on start with short-term contracts which are only gradually lengthened – or terminated. Starting in, eg secretarial work, or filling in during holidays, is an accepted route in to work involved with programme making, but this takes exceptional patience, determination, being prepared to do all the boring jobs cheerfully, and showing great initiative and flair for the work.

The number of trainee posts is always very small. Companies can ask for a good educational background, but will always insist on practical evidence of interest in the work.

PROGRAMME MAKING AND RELATED TECHNICAL WORK Each programme company has its own recruitment policy. Generally they want people already trained and/or who have appropriate experience. Where competition is greatest – ie for jobs directly concerned with programme making or a known route into programme making (eg secretarial work) – this is rarely a problem. Alternatively they go for related previous training/experience in eg journalism, the theatre etc.

Some departments must have relevant previous training and experience, eg for music, science, education, and drama. Production posts in drama and light entertainment usually need experience in the professional theatre – initial recruitment is to floor assistant or assistant floor manager (posts often filled by people who have already done the job when someone has been ill or on holiday).

Nearly all senior posts above that are filled by internal promotion (by competition) or are advertised, but usually asking for directly-relevant experience.

Programme companies do, though, want to bring in new, and ideally young, talent. Few figures are available, but annual recruitment is probably only hundreds, across all TV and radio companies. The ITV companies recruited *altogether* (all functions) under 960 people in 1986, of whom only five were trainee journalists, one a researcher, two make up artists, and two graphic designers. Only 65 people were recruited straight from university, college, polytechnic, and only nine were school-leavers.

Remembering that the BBC is ten times the size of even the largest independent company, the scale of recruitment can be judged from BBC trainee schemes. These include, as at 1987 (they do change and now and again intake has been deferred) –

News trainees: the two-year journalist training scheme recruits no more than 12 people a year (in two intakes) for both TV and radio. After a solid 'induction' course, trainees go on three-month 'attachments' to different departments, regions etc. During the second year trainees apply and compete for any available permanent posts (usually on the level of newsroom sub editor), but are usually given short-term contracts until they get a post, which can take more than a year. Over 1000 usually apply; 250 have preliminary interviews, and about 60 are seen by a full board for a 45-minute interview, a two-hour news, and a voice, test. Degree-level education is wanted, but in-depth knowledge and interest in current affairs, proven journalistic experience and commitment to the job are probably more important. Successful candidates always include some who have already worked elsewhere in the media.

Production trainees: also two-year training schemes, starting once a year. For TV, up to 15 places train mainly for researcher or assistant producer jobs, on all kinds of programmes from 'Wogan' to 'Heart of the Matter', 'That's Life' and 'Tomorrow's World'. For radio, up to four train mainly producers, two in topical and feature programmes, one in light entertainment, and one in music. External services take up to three, and need an interest in international affairs and previous work experience. Good degrees and/or journalistic skills plus a very broad range of informed interests are all demanded.

Radio sound operations trainees: about 40 places a year to train (one-year basic plus further department-based training/work experience) for artistic and technical direction of programmes either for the domestic national or external services, possibly to specialise later (but not much chance of switching to TV). No actual educational qualifications are stipulated, but many successful candidates are graduates. Artistic 'flair' combined with technical aptitude (manual dexterity, numeracy, basic physics, use of microphones and tape recorders) are wanted, plus a wide general interest in arts and current affairs.

Other traineeships: make up assistants (A-level standard education plus artistic flair). For film crew (camera, recordist, editors, projectionists), audio assistants, and camera, recording, and sound operators, all need O-level equivalent passes in physics/electronics, maths, English, plus artistic flair, good hearing and/or colour vision, and be able to show practical evidence of 'keen and active' interest in both broadcasting and the specific job.

For all other programme-making/production jobs – in local radio (as programme assistants and producers or journalists); scenic, graphic, costume design (a relevant degree needed), secretarial work – appropriate training and/or experience is normally wanted.

Programme companies all look for people who will, first and foremost make good broadcasters, programme makers, technical staff. They are all expected to be imaginative, creative, able to take in new subjects and ideas easily, to keep up with current trends, and able to turn ideas into programmes. They need the ability to understand the technical demands of the medium in which they are working. They also need initiative, tact and persuasiveness, drive, and determination. They must be able to take on responsibility, work to budgets and schedules (which are both often very tight), at speed and under heavy pressure, in teams with other people, and be able to cope in a crisis.

While formal educational qualifications are rarely stipulated for programme making, in practice a very high proportion of entrants are graduates. With some exceptions, degree subject is not especially important, but for current affairs, news reporting etc, a subject like economics, or politics may be of more use than, say English or history.

Recruiters look for people who already have a realistic understanding of what working in the media is like and what is going to be demanded of them; who have taken the trouble to find out, for example, the difference between academic and programme research. Programme companies generally expect entrants to have taken any opportunity to gain appropriate experience, for example in good student journalism, campus TV or radio, on student programmes on local radio stations, or via voluntary work in hospital radio. Recruiters are looking for 'doers' who write, produce plays or papers, make films, organise events and people, rather than people who only watch, although they also expect candidates to be able to analyse radio and/or television output relevant to the traineeship.

Some work demands more – news trainees and trainee reporters obviously need the same potential as recruits to newspaper and periodical JOURNALISM. Anyone hoping to present or report has to have a trainable voice. Future studio managers, according to the BBC, 'need to be technically minded as well as having the artistic skills to appreciate producers' intentions and interpret the desired effect; a wide general interest in the arts and public affairs; considerable manual dexterity; and personal qualities which include confidence and tact, quick thinking, and calmness in an emergency; some experience in production techniques, stage management or knowledge of music is useful'. Local radio station assistants must also be interested in the local community.

Anyone who wants to get into programme making should take every opportunity to get involved in some kind of related activity before applying, eg student journalism or broadcasting, voluntary hospital radio, any kind of involvement with local or community radio. It is not usually possible to start full-time work in programme making under the age of 18 because it usually means shift work. However, some local radio and regional network TV companies take YTS trainees, and do give some trainees permanent jobs.

ENGINEERING Professional engineers are recruited mostly from amongst graduates in eg electrical, electronic, communications engineering or applied physics, or with BTEC Higher awards. However, the BBC also trains school-leavers (with O-level-equivalent passes in English, maths, physics) and has a scheme to 'convert' a small number of graduates in subjects other than engineering into engineers, on an intensive two-year training scheme. A few graduates with first or second class honours in appropriate subjects are also recruited as trainees for applied research, designing/developing equipment not obtainable commercially, and planning, installing and commissioning new and modernised studios and transmitters.

IBA intake of trainee broadcast engineers – with degrees or HNDs – fell to 15 in 1985-6, and the Authority expects only to recruit in alternate years for the immediate future. Independent companies also employ their own engineering staff, and a few take trainees.

Qualifications and training

Opportunities to train formally and/or gain suitable qualifications in preparation for programme making are very limited. Most training in broadcasting is on-the-job, with the programme companies. Programme companies do not seem to give any special weight to media studies degrees (see QUALIFICATIONS AND CAREERS), unless students have, at the same time, gained extensive practical experience of the right kind. Exceptions are a small number of mainly postgraduate courses in radio/TV journalism.

These are at – Cardiff UC, Falmouth: Cornwall CFE, Darlington CT, London: City U, Preston: Lancs P, Portsmouth: Highbury CT. (The National Broadcasting School has closed.)

Support is also given to courses at, for example, Bromley: Ravensbourne CA&T (technical and operational), Leeds P (engineering), the National Film School.

The BBC has always trained staff, and the 1980 Broadcasting Act built in requirements for training amongst independent companies. The IBA now has a training adviser. For both the BBC and independent companies most training is mainly in-house and on-the-job, although independent companies also contract out to colleges/schools which can provide the right training packages.

Training arrangements vary with the scheme, the post, and the company –

For programme-makers, BBC schemes range from six months for studio managers through to two years for news trainees (whose training must meet NCTJ requirements), assistant producers and general trainees. Training is both on- and off-the-job, which means trainees are observing and working on programmes very early. Training for people going into local radio or network independent television companies seems to last a year or two, although most entrants are actually contributing to station output in some way well before that. Some companies release a few staff for formal training – to Cardiff for a year's course, for example.

Engineers and technical staff are trained partly on-the-job and partly on formal courses. Both the BBC and IBA have their own engineering training centres, and graduate engineers and technicians and technical staff go on courses. IBA also has industrial training places for engineering students on sandwich-based courses. Most independent companies now have structured training schemes, many emphasising updating and use of new technology and equipment – making extensive use of manufacturers' courses.

Further information from the BBC, the IBA, and the Independent Television Companies Association.

FILM AND VIDEO MAKING

'Film making', to most people, means making full-scale feature films for the cinema. Today, few such films are made in the UK, and there is effectively no longer a British industry as such. Funding is very difficult to find in Britain. Astronomical costs and technological advances (in cameras, lighting equipment etc), which have made it possible for most films to be made on location, mean that the film industry no longer maintains large and expensive permanent film studios. The brief boom of the early 1980s has ended – Pinewood, the last fully-staffed UK studio, ceased providing much more than space in 1987, cutting staff to 170 from 800. (In 1984, the commercial film industry employed some 35,000 people in total.)

Film makers, in their own words, have become wandering gypsies – making films in 'natural' settings, wherever is best for the script and cheapest to work – which is only too often not Britain. The actors' and film unions can, therefore, no longer enforce agreements which ensured that work went to British actors and actresses, directors, film crews, etc.

Other kinds of film making, however, appear to be expanding. An increasing proportion of television output is on film or video, and most television programme-making companies employ their own film crews. Independent film makers have for some years been producing advertisements for television and cinema, and have a long tradition of making high-quality 'sponsored' industrial and other promotional films. Video is used for a steadily-widening range of purposes, from recruitment and training films to marketing and publicity. More and more large companies have their own units, or employ independents. Channel 4 commissions some 45% of its output – films and other programmes – from independent producers, and the other independent companies and the BBC are, in future, to use independent producers.

New outlets for original material on video are being suggested all the time. At present most video output for the home video market is copies of films etc made for cinema and television, but some original material is now being made. DBS and cable (will) also use independents.

It is, however, impossible to put any accurate figures to any of this, although the 'independent' producers associations now (1987) has 300 members (some of them subsidiaries of, eg television programme companies).

Working in the film industry

Relatively few people have full-time jobs in film making. The main permanent posts are in television programming-making companies, including the BBC. There is probably a growing number of full-time jobs making video-film for large organisations, eg for training, or in local education authorities. The majority of people, though, work on a freelance basis, recruited to a team to make a particular film.

FILM PRODUCERS, like their theatrical colleagues, are the entrepreneurs and managers of the industry, not the creative programme makers of television –

although there is nothing to prevent producers directing their own films, and some do. It is the producer who looks for a commercially-viable idea, novel or story for a feature film, and has it turned into a 'treatment' – with suggestions for the stars to appear in it – on which to raise the finance (from investors) to make the film. Or the producer may go to (for example) a Channel 4 commissioning editor with a synopsis for a programme (or series of programmes), or be commissioned by the television company, or another organisation (eg a training board), to make a film for them. When the finance is arranged, or the programme or film commissioned, the producer 'sets up' the production, probably deciding personally on the director, script writer, stars, lighting cameraman etc, and production manager. In a major film company, there will be staff to do the rest of the organisation and deal with practical day-to-day details.

FILM MAKERS A film is made by a team which has to work closely together. The script-writer works closely with the director throughout the production – the script is always being re-written, changed, refined. It is a technical as well as a creative document, and has to be broken down into scenes, and shots, for shooting.

The film director translates a script into visual reality on film. In feature and other independent film making the director is the creative driving force – welding actors and film craft together to achieve a personal interpretation of the original script. In television companies, the film director works rather more under the direction of the programme's producer/editor. In larger units, there may be one, two, or even three assistant directors, to cope with all the organisational and other problems, which may include, for example, directing a second unit taking background shots.

Before a film can be shot, the casting director has to find the actors and actresses for a feature film (for a documentary, only a narrator may be needed). The art director and staff have to design the sets and costumes. The production manager must see that locations, studios and so on are arranged and booked, and schedules worked out.

The lighting cameraman, or director of photography, works with the director to plan each shot to get the visual effects the director wants (some directors are their own lighting cameramen, or vice versa). The lighting cameraman gives directions to the electricians who organise the lighting and the camera crew.

Making a film involves a large number of other people, especially in feature films. The camera crew is made up of an operator (in television work the film cameraman may work more independently), with assistants to help with focusing, loading film, and moving the camera. The separate sound crew may be one or two people for television, usually three for features. Make up artists, hairdressers, and wardrobe staff prepare the actors and actresses. Someone has to look after continuity, keeping very detailed notes so that there are no inconsistencies. Technicians prepare the set or location.

Once the film is shot (and processed), it has to be edited and the sound track completed. Editing is just as creative a role as shooting the film in the first place: where and how it is cut and assembled, deciding which are the best shots to use, making the transitions from one shot to another, and creating the right effects is a highly skilled job. The editor works closely with the director (and often the producer too), at all stages.

Recruitment and entry Getting regular work in the film industry itself depends totally on gaining membership of the Association of Cine and Television Technicians. Proof of technical competence gives applicants priority consideration for membership, so the best route into the industry is via a course at one of the very few recognised film schools or an approved traineeships (below).

'First jobs' usually mean starting right at the bottom, even for those who have been to film school, as eg assistant cameraman, editor, or sound assistant, 'fetching and carrying'. If the small-scale side of film work is expanding, and shortages do develop, then it may become easier to find ways in – although most will probably still involve starting at the 'dogsbody' level.

For most first jobs, a reasonable educational background is needed (with O-level-equivalents at very least), and increasingly some understanding of electronics is useful (especially for video work, including editing). Practical experience of film making is essential.

Qualifications and training Opportunities to train are fairly limited.
Pre-entry courses include –
The National Film School: takes 25 yearly onto a three-year course – training is based on practical film making, aimed at developing artistic and technical control of the medium. Contemporary and past work in the cinema and TV (including economic aspects) and the media in relation to other arts and their changing role in society are also studied. No set educational requirements, but the School is not intended for beginners. Up to a half of students are normally graduates, and the balance is about half polytechnic/art-school graduates and half people with some professional experience (average age 25). All candidates must show ability in one or more of: writing, directing, producing or photography, and must have been practically involved to a reasonably high level. Most graduates find their first jobs in television.
Bristol University, Radio, film & television, Certificate, 1 year (postgraduate) – emphasis on technical and creative aspects.
Farnham: W Surrey CA&D, Photography, film, video & television, BA 3 years – a fully-professional and practical course (entry normally via an art-school foundation course).
London: Croydon SD&T, Intermedia, 1 year – intensive studies in film, television and animation.
London: RCA, Film & television, MA 3 years – covers all creative processes and techniques of film and colour television.
Other degree courses under ACADEMIC AND VOCATIONAL QUALIFICATIONS include film studies.

Training schemes –
BBC trainees are recruited as assistant film cameraman, film recordists and editors. After a year's practical training, which begins with a short full-time course, they can apply for promotion to full cameraman, editor or recordist, or try for other posts, as and when openings occur. Similar schemes in most independent companies (not Channel 4), but fewer numbers.
JOBFIT (Joint Board for Film Industry Training): set up by ACTT and two

major employers' associations in 1985. Two-year training is specifically for technical and production grades covered by ACTT (ie not producers, directors or writers) – art department assistant, assistant script-supervisor, assistant boom operator, clapper/loader, 2nd assistant editor, assistant sound recordist, 3rd assistant director – although there is nothing to prevent anyone who has gone through the scheme trying to work their way up. Up to 50 places a year. Trainees are attached to productions of all kinds of films, and this work experience/training is supplemented by short courses at recognised training centres. They gain experience of all the departments in year 1, and train in one in year 2. No formal entry requirements, but commitment and enthusiasm, communication skills, strong visual sense, all-round literacy and manual dexterity are stipulated. Training is for the freelance labour market, so resilience, willingness to travel, work long hours and live away from home are needed. Age at least 18.

Further information from the schools/organisations cited above, the Association of Cine and Television Technicians, and from employing organisations, eg the BBC.

THEATRICAL ADMINISTRATION AND PRODUCTION

Actors and actresses are only part of the team that put a play on the stage. Plays have to be organised, and theatres managed to make the entertainment possible.

Most theatres are owned by commercial companies, a few are nationally owned, some by trusts, and some by local authorities. Some, like the National Theatre or Stratford, have permanent companies, others are 'let' to producers for the length of time that a play runs, with a company (director, actors and actresses, stage manager etc), put together for that production. The owners employ administrators to look after the building itself, letting it out, etc.

THE PRODUCER/PRODUCER-MANAGER, in any theatrical production, play or musical, is impresario or presenter. Producer-managers have to combine the talents for putting together a production which is both artistically worthwhile and commercially viable, so that, while they are essentially organisers, they must have sound artistic and critical judgement and really good knowledge of the theatrical world.

The producer or producer-manager organises a production, and may have to finance it. In the commercial theatre, the producer is in business both to provide entertainment, to stage a creative work, and to make money personally and for the people who invest in the production. The producer of a subsidised, permanent company may not actually have to find investors for productions, but must work within a set budget based on known income.

Producers look for productions to stage in, say, London. They may bring over a New York success (or vice versa), but plays are also brought and sent to them, by the authors, and by their agents, by directors who want to direct a particular play, by an actor (or his agent) who wants to perform in a play he has found. A producer in the commercial theatre wants a commercial success, and has to be able to judge dramatic merit and entertainment value. In a permanent company, the producer works to an agreed policy on the plays to be staged – which may only be Shakespeare.

Getting a play into production in the commercial theatre is a balancing act which is not always successful. The producer has to find people to invest in the play, find a suitable theatre at a reasonable price, a director willing and able to direct the play, and perhaps a 'star' too. Investors may only be convinced by the whole package, yet director and star may only commit themselves when the money is 'up front'. Even permanent companies may have to wait for directors and actors to become available.

Commercial producers are as much business people and managers as theatrical. They must have a good financial background, and entrepreneurial instincts. There are very few of them, and they need initiative and contacts rather than formal training to get there. Some young producers are graduates, and may have worked in student and then professional theatre. Some producers have been actors or directors, others have worked up through a producer's office.

DIRECTORS are the orchestral conductors of the theatre. The director's personal interpretation of the play is stamped onto the particular production. The director must get highly-individualistic actors, actresses, possibly dancers and singers, as well as designers and technicians, to work together in a single team. Some directors have a completely free hand, others may have to work within constraints set by the producer – for example, to work with a particular playwright, or accept a particular star to ensure a commercial success. They generally decide on the cast together, at auditions.

The director studies and gets to know the play (which is rarely changed in the way a film script is re-written), and decides how to interpret and stage it. Sets, costumes, and so on are designed to support this. The director works hardest during rehearsals, working with the cast and technicians to make the play believable, to bring it to performance pitch. The director helps individual actors and actresses to interpret their parts effectively, to get their movements, the pauses and build up of tension right, and to find the 'rhythm' of the play.

Directing a stage production is very different from directing a film or television play, although some directors do all three. Some work, usually on a fixed-length contract, for a permanent company, some for the length of a production only.

Entry/training No set route into direction, but it does need plenty of experience in the theatre, and some kind of training. Some directors are graduates (a degree course in drama can be useful), some come to it through acting, or stage management. There are some trainee director posts. Some directors come to the theatre from broadcasting or film.

No accredited training/courses at present. Courses currently (1987) on offer include -
Bristol: Old Vic – not structured but classes and work for School's own directors (4 places a year);
Postgraduate courses at, eg universities – Hull, Leeds.

STAGE MANAGEMENT are directors' assistants, and the theatre's equivalent of the army's beach master. They have to see that everybody and everything is in the right place at the right time, that everyone involved in a production, from star down to scene shifter, knows what to do and when. They keep records of decisions as they are made, on everything from props to lighting, from costumes to sets, sound effects, even the moves actors and actresses are to make. They may sure that scenes and sets are made, props bought or made, that scene changes are realistically timed and sets are made, that lighting is organised, that curtains rise and fall on cue, and that the cast is ready when needed.

Stage management is a career in its own right, but many people use it as a stepping stone to, for example, directing. In larger companies there will be deputy as well as assistant stage managers (who may be the last people into the company, waiting to act).

Entry/training Stage managers need to be well-organised and very practical, able to deal with people from the most temperamental of stars to the scene changers, cope with emergencies, and be extremely resourceful. They have to care about the work they are doing, and not constantly pine for the (acting) job they cannot get.

Full-time courses at drama schools are broadly-based, training in a full range of skills needed in the theatre including, on most, the technical skills such as lighting, sound, photography, scenery construction etc. Courses are at (* NCDT accredited) –

Bristol: Old Vic*; Cardiff: Welsh Music/Drama; Glasgow: RSAMD*; London: Central Speech/Drama*, Guildhall*, LAMDA*, Mountview Theatre School*, RADA*; Loughton: East 15 Acting School. Length, and entry requirements vary (some are postgraduate).

STAGE AND COSTUME DESIGN: see ART AND DESIGN.

TECHNICIAN AND OTHER BACK-STAGE WORK Technicians work on the stage manager's team, operating lighting and other equipment. Many are qualified electricians, dealing nowadays with very sophisticated, computer-controlled equipment.

Stage carpenters make and paint scenery and sets, and stage hands move them around. All can go on to stage management.

Wardrobe staff hire, buy and make costumes and look after them for the length of the production.

Training Stage management courses cover most aspects of back stage work. A few pre-entry courses exist, –

Scene painting: London: Guildhall, RADA (incl carpentry, property making);

Wardrobe: Bristol: Old Vic;

MEDIA AGENTS

Because so many people in the media business work on contract or a freelance basis, because they are people whose skills are creative – as writers or performers – and not in business or marketing, they use agents, as their links with the firms and organisations that employ and use their services.

An agent works for the client, not the media company, to 'sell' their actors or actresses to producers, and writers to publishers or radio or television companies. An efficient agent does not only find a publisher, say, for an author's new manuscript. An agent stays closely in touch with the client's potential market, and finds out, for example, what plays are coming into production and when, and who will be the director. A literary agent talks regularly to publishers, and knows what their future plans are, or whether a projected television play series will have room for an author's new idea.

Agents negotiate the terms of contracts, and are expert at getting the best possible 'deal' – not only in terms of royalties (for authors), but also 'rights', repeat fees, and so on. They try to make sure that 'standard' contracts do not take away rights, that they are appropriate for the particular project, and that fees are keeping pace with those offered by other publishers, or companies.

Agents act as both buffers and links between the individual writers or performers and the companies they are at present working for. They ensure that their clients get publicity. They make sure their clients actually get paid.

Agents make their income by charging their clients a percentage of contracts successfully negotiated. A successful author or actor/actress is therefore more profitable than a new and unknown one, and it is to an agent's advantage to find work for clients. While agents must constantly look for new talent, they must also have a balance of established and potentially-successful clients, and clearly cannot afford to have too many people on their books who are not earning very much. New authors or actors are a form of investment. Getting on to the books of a successful agent is crucial for actors and actresses, and can be quite difficult. It is not so essential, although still useful, for a writer.

Literary agents need a blend of aesthetic judgement and skills. While the agent's interests are always with the client, they have to try to bridge the gap between the writer and the commercial realities of the market place. Agents may have to be at one and the same time wet-nurse, business and legal adviser, and devil's advocate: the relationship can be a close, if difficult, one.

Being a literary or theatrical agent is usually a second career, since to be of any use to clients, agents must have extensive experience and contacts, and will therefore usually have spent some time working in publishing, broadcasting, or the theatre. It is, though, possible to work up from the bottom, learning on-the-job, or to start as a secretary. There are not all that many jobs. Few agencies have more than 50 staff, and most only a dozen.

NEWSPAPER PUBLISHING

The newspaper industry in Britain today is going through a major revolution. While it is adjusting – somewhat painfully – to the hard economic realities of the 1980s and to new technologies, these same technologies and more competitive conditions have actually brought a number of new ventures, including several new newspapers.

Over 130 daily and Sunday papers are published (1987) in Britain. Only 23 are national, so-called 'Fleet Street' papers – but up from 16 just two years earlier – thirteen morning papers and ten Sundays. Some 1300 weekly papers are produced, including some 550 'major' regional or local papers. (The rest are specialised, business religious, community, sporting etc papers.) The number of 'free distribution' local papers (financed by advertising) has grown steadily, to about 850 in 1986.

Britain reads more papers than almost any other developed country – the 4.8 million circulation of the largest Sunday is near double that of the largest-selling US paper.

But the economics of the newspaper business are not easy to manage. One major difference between book and newspaper publishers is that the newspaper industry, because papers must be produced at such speed, mostly owns and operates its own presses, although some now 'contract out'. The costs are huge, even with the tightest financial management. Publishers have bitten the bullet of new technology, and almost all are now going over to computer-based setting and printing methods. Because this needs new plant and modern accommodation, the nationals are taking the opportunity to move out of their valuable Fleet-Street sites, mostly going to redeveloped docklands.

Newspaper editors are under continual pressure to sell more copies, not because extra sales will bring in more money, but because higher sales attract more advertising, and advertising produces up to 80% of a newspaper's income. The competition can be cut-throat, and dominate policy. 'Competition for both readership and advertising between different types of publication and between different publications of the same type is a dominant factor in the economics of most sections of the press. Methods used to attract readers include presentation and content of the newspaper, size, speed of production, and publicity, ranging from direct advertising to sponsoring competitions and exhibitions. Advertisers are attracted by ... the number and type of readers, the price of advertising space, services offered and publicity.' (The British Press).

Employment in the newspaper industry No accurate figures appear to exist at present. The training board was disbanded in 1982, and the dramatic changes and upheavals of 1985-7 must make earlier figures misleading. Major cost-cutting exercises and new technology have combined to slash – by 2-3000 out of 6-8000 in some cases – employment in older papers, but on the management/editorial side these have probably been balanced, if not outweighed, by new ventures. The number of jobs in production has most certainly been decimated, and will go on falling for the next few years at least. Twelve firms publish the national papers, and all but two probably still have well over 1000 employees each. The 267 members of the Newspaper Society, who publish a high proportion of local and regional papers, employ some 43,900 people.

Traditionally, only about a fifth of a newspaper's total staff were editorial, but as papers go over to computer-based production, this is rising sharply. Not generally because more journalists are employed per paper, but because far fewer production staff are needed.

Responsibility for the paper's content is the editor's, helped by deputy and assistant. Under the editor, senior editors look after different 'sections' of the paper – domestic and foreign news, city (finance), features, literary, sports, travel etc, with new ideas (sections on 'living', 'work', science etc) and ways to develop older sections – for women etc – always being tried. Art editors (running their own art departments) look after the photos and drawings. All the other editorial staff count as JOURNALISTS. The journalists are backed up by LIBRARIANS.

Managers and top newspaper executives are not usually ex-editors or journalists, but business people, although there is nothing to prevent a journalist or editor moving into management. They administer newspaper production, revenue and expenditure. Circulation, distribution and advertising are important departments in the industry. Newspapers have their own publicity people, and employ people in all the functions normally needed by any commercial organisation, from accountants to clerks and personnel.

Traditionally, up to half of a newspaper's staff were in production. No longer. Newspapers are rapidly going over to computer typesetting, which means journalists, and advertising people, 'input' their own copy into a computer terminal, from where it is 'set' (almost) automatically into film. Fewer and fewer 'compositors' – or more usually today keyboard operators – proof readers, etc are therefore employed. Even page make up can be done on screen by editorial staff. Modern, high-speed presses need fewer people to operate them, and papers are packaged by machine. Such jobs as remain, however, tend to be more technical and expert. See also PRINTING.

The three major news agencies are a crucial part of the newspaper industry. They collect news at home and overseas for subscribers (mostly newspapers and the broadcasting news services at home and abroad). One, Reuters, is now providing sophisticated business, stock market and other financial information services delivered on-screen to subscribers' offices in nearly 160 countries. Reuter's 5400 staff (1986) has nearly doubled in the 1980s, and includes nearly 900 journalists, most working overseas.

Other agencies collect and supply photographs to the press and publishers. The news and other press agencies employ large numbers of journalists and sub-editors at home and correspondents overseas, as well as managerial staff and computer, telex and teleprinter operators (see under SECRETARIAL, OFFICE AND CLERICAL WORK).

Recruitment and entry For editorial work and production, entry is normally via a union/employer-recognised training scheme.

Qualifications and training for the newspaper industry is by function rather than on a newspaper-by-newspaper basis. Training for journalists, for example, comes under a National Council (see below). Training arrangements are co-ordinated by the Newspaper Publishers Association (nationals), and the Newspaper Society (regionals).

PERIODICAL PUBLISHING

Some 7000 magazines, journals, periodicals etc are published in the UK. They are commonly divided into 'consumer', 'specialist', 'trade', and 'technical and professional', with an expanding range of 'alternative' publications, and a rather smaller (but no longer declining) group of several hundred 'house' magazines produced by employers mainly for their own employees, but some go out as part of companies' PR effort.

About a third of output is 'consumer' magazines and specialist publications. They include magazines for women, interior decorating and 'do-it-yourself' magazines; publications for particular leisure and sporting activities, such as gardening, angling, athletics, rock music, computers etc. Two deal with radio and TV programmes, several tell people what they can do and see in London. Several are 'political', some are scientific, some sociological, some funny or satirical. Some deal seriously with literature, international affairs, education, research etc.

The trade, technical, business and scientific press – some 500 publications on all – covers the very specialist interests of people working in particular industries, trades etc, keeping them up to date on new developments, technological and business, in – say – the chemical industry, or the grocery trade. Related are the many professional and quasi-professional journals in, for example, law, accountancy, medicine, nursing, librarianship.

Some journals appear weekly, others fortnightly, monthly, or quarterly basis. Some publishers or institutions produce only a single journal, others manage a 'stable' of periodicals, some in a single areas or type of publication, others in several. It is an increasingly volatile area of publishing, with new publications starting up to cater for a new or developing readership, while others which may have done well for a while, close down (eg in home computing), or merge with each other.

Working in periodical publishing But although there are a great many magazines, figures suggest only some 400 firms publish commercially, and at most 250 are of any size. Of these, only one has over 1000 employees (3000 in fact), four between 500 and 1000, with seven counting as major employers. A dozen commercial publishers have under fifteen staff. Total numbers are probably no more than 21,000 (but this is up from 16,300 in the mid-1970s).

Most commercially-run periodicals have their own editorial staff (one major science weekly has eleven editors), subs, and a smallish team of journalists, but on the smaller journals editors write and writers edit. About 25% of staff count as editorial. On technical publications, editors and journalists must have some subject expertise. On consumer magazines, more feature writers than reporters are generally needed. Most papers also have their own art editors and artists, photographers, production (including lay-out) staff. Many periodicals use colour and illustrations and for some, like fashion and house and garden magazines, appearance is everything.

Most periodicals expect to use a fair number of outside contributors. These may be full-time freelance journalists, but at least half the articles in a major science weekly are written by university teachers or staff of research labs, writing in their spare time. Some academic journals exist just to let scientists publish their research reports, so staff are solely editors. 'Alternative' publications are often put together by voluntary staff, and where people are employed, numbers are small.

Commercially-run journals, like newspapers, depend for their survival on advertising – and the popularity of particular leisure activities, or the job market for scientists or teachers. The advertising staff is therefore proportionately quite large. Few periodical publishers run their own presses.

After a period of slow decline, reports suggest that 'house' journals are becoming more popular again. These are produced by organisations either for in-house circulation (the majority), and/or to send out to people within the business, customers or prospective customers, shareholders, agents, schools and so on. Most people editing these journals do so on a part-time basis only, probably as one job among several in eg public relations, advertising or marketing.

Recruitment and entry to editorial work or journalism is less tightly controlled than in the newspaper business, but the number of trainee places is far fewer – only two major publishers have (graduate) training schemes.
Art department staff are normally expected to have a graphic design degree or technician qualification. It is possible to start in production as an assistant or junior, and train on-the-job, but experience is often wanted. The easiest route into the commercial side is advertising sales.

Qualifications and training Only four pre-entry courses, all but one (post)graduate, at Cardiff: UC, London: City U, Printing C (one graduate, one A-level entry).
While only two publishers have formal training schemes, the Periodical Training Trust does now have an industry-wide editorial training scheme for people already employed, and runs a range of courses on editorial work (including new technology), advertising sales, and circulation. See also NEWSPAPER INDUSTRY, above, and JOURNALISM, below.

Further information from the Periodical Publishers Association.

PUBLISHING BOOKS

Publishing, according to the Publishers Association, 'is a difficult trade, a compound of art, craft and business. The art is that indefinable but essential quality, "flair", the craft, the design and presentation of the author's work in the best possible form for the readers, and the business the source of finance. Publishers have to earn their living in a small, overcrowded and highly competitive market where one of the major forces, public taste, can change quite unpredictably at any moment. It is easy to lose money on books, and even the most experienced publishers do it. Sound commercial judgement is therefore essential. Lack of it in a publishing firm has always led to early insolvency.'

Publishing books is a commercial operation. Publishers are in business to make a profit from selling books, just as food manufacturers expect to make a profit from breakfast cereal. Publishers have books 'manufactured' (by printers) and distribute them (but through book shops or by mail order) just as do food firms. Making a profit from books is, though, probably more difficult than from breakfast foods. The market is small, and it is hard to find out ahead (through marketing), what will and will not sell. Books are amongst the first products to suffer when there is a recession. Book publishers do not control their own manufacturing plant, and suffer from an antiquated and inefficient distribution system which doesn't match today's trading conditions. Production and distribution costs are high.

It is not so much the ability to discover a literary success that is important in publishing, as the skill to find the books that will sell the most copies. High-level management skills (especially in FINANCE, MARKETING and in production, and 'human resources') are crucial, and the industry is using modern marketing methods to increase domestic sales.

Publishing is under great pressure, and has just been through some bad years, with many firms slimming, and merging. Publishers make most of their income from publishing factual books full of essential information. In the past, these have (mostly) gone to the education world, but sales here have been affected by public expenditure cuts and falling numbers of pupils and students; to lawyers, but data bases are eating into the legal market. While publishing is still maintaining substantial overseas sales, the proportion of income has fallen (1985) to under 38% (from over 40% in the late 1970s). Libraries have always been the largest customers, but their expenditure has been cut. Novels make up only one in eleven of all new books published. A third of turnover comes from paperback books, which is what the general reading public buys.

Although some 53,000 new titles were produced in 1985, publishing is a small industry. While 10,500 organisations produced at least one title in 1985, estimates (by the Book House Training Centre) suggest only about 3500 firms are full-time publishers. The 250 member-companies (500 imprints) of the Publishers Association produce two-thirds of the industry's 1985 £2300 million retail sales, and under 100 companies publish more than 100 titles each a year. Some 50% comes from the eight largest.

Employment in the industry is estimated (by BHTC) to be about 20,000 (against estimates of 13,800 for 1982 and 13,200 for 1978). The largest group employs 1500 in the UK, and BHTC suggests 500 is the average for the other top ten, with many small firms employing ten or less.

Large publishers produce several hundred titles a year in a wide variety of different subjects. Some quite large publishing houses specialise – in law, medicine, art, education, academic and technical books – but the trend is to multi-imprint large firms. Some small publishers, without the high overheads of larger firms, make a reasonable income by exploiting particular markets. 'Packagers' are a comparatively new feature of publishing. They do all the work in finding, creating and producing a book – usually one with a likely mass readership – but sell (in advance) the edition complete to a conventional publisher, who then puts it on their list.

Working in publishing There are three areas of work in publishing – editorial, production with design, and marketing, which combines sales, promotion and publicity. In the larger houses these are separate departments, and in the largest there may be several editorial departments, each with a specialised list, eg educational titles, reference books (eg dictionaries), novels, or art books. In the smallest firms, individual members of staff may combine several jobs. Publishers are, increasingly, putting out work, using packagers, and freelance for almost all functions, to save in-house costs.

Publishing policy comes from the top of the editorial tree. In the larger firms this means an editorial director or senior directors, and may be decided more by what the marketing people say will sell, or what is wanted by overseas customers, than by what the authors want to write – although lately publishers have been 'marketing' literary merit. Only 2% of unsolicited manuscripts are published. What to publish is often decided 'in committee' between editors, marketing staff, literary agents and professional writers, and may be a compromise between the original ideas of both sides. A few books, mostly large reference works like encyclopedias, are put together 'in house' by a team of editorial staff, but the great majority are written or edited by people working on contract or freelance. Publishers are now building their own computer data bases from which information can be 'sold' directly, or from which information can be extracted automatically for reference books, like dictionaries.

Editorial department(s) Probably no more than 10% of a publisher's staff, and increasingly outnumbered and outgunned by (marketing) managers, and some commissioning editors are more managers than editors. Some now spend more time in sales conferences than at their desks or with authors.

Commissioning editors each look after a 'list' of books and authors. The size of an editor's list varies with the publisher. Editors have books/authors assigned to them, but are also expected to produce profitable ideas and concrete proposals for books within the area of their 'list'. They must cost books, work out pricing and suggest (profitable) print runs. Editors also have to read widely and stay in touch with authors and editors. Many manuscripts must be read, perhaps by specialist 'outside' readers.

Copy editors (who may also be the commissioning editor, but less often now) spend most of their time in seeing a book through from first outline and manuscript to publication. Traditionally, all manuscripts are 'copy-edited'. This involves checking facts and references, spelling and punctuation. Sometimes the editor has to do some rewriting, or tactfully ask the author to do so. Then the typescript has to be tidied, and 'marked up' for the printer, in 'house style', and the shape, size, layout and typefaces agreed with the designer. Editors – or their assistants – get proofs read (or read) for printers' mistakes, control the author's urges to rewrite the book on proofs, see that manuscripts and proofs get to production on schedule, organise indexes etc. All this is painstaking, careful, detailed work, perhaps with another new novel to read at the end of a very long day. It is a desk job, but often with considerable pressure and some tensions. It isn't the leisurely, scholarly backwater it is often made out to be.

It is, also, changing. Growing numbers of writers are using word-processors, and want to deliver their books on computer disks, not manuscript – which complicates the traditional copy editing, since few publishers yet have processors, and those they have are often not compatible with the authors'. Manuscript, whether on paper or disk, from a wordprocessor is generally 'cleaner' than when typed or handwritten. Linked to publishers' drive for lower costs, all this is (slowly) cutting into the time spent editorially in-house on books.

The production department takes the manuscript from editorial, and turns it into a printed book.

Designers (who may be on the staff if the publisher is large or produces many illustrated books, or may be a freelance) specify what the book will look like, decide on the book 'jacket' or cover, and commission any illustrations. They work to a brief from the editor, and within set budgets.

Production decides on a firm to 'set' it into type (more often than not on film today), print and bind it to an agreed schedule and within a tight budget, and according to the designer's specifications.

Production takes careful planning and organisation. All the parts of a book, including illustrations, art work, and advertising, have to come together at the right moment. The paper must get to the printer just when needed, and the jacket must be printed as soon as the printer confirms the estimated thickness of the book, and so on. Production staff have to know a great deal about the print business, how to cost accurately, where to buy paper, what paper is best for a particular job, keep pace with very rapid technological changes in printing, and be able to assess their usefulness.

Production staff must work closely with editorial, with designers, and with printers and liaise between them, keeping them all to a tight and complicated schedule. They have to be very good organisers, and methodical, able to work under pressure.

Promotion and publicity staff have to gain attention for their books when some 50,000 other titles are also clamouring to be bought. Routines are set up for each book, to see that it goes into the right lists and catalogues, is advertised to the 'trade', that librarians are told about it, that it gets reviewed if possible, that publicity material is designed and printed for it. The book must be in all the right book fairs, exhibitions, and conferences. And because books often sell best through 'free' publicity, the publicity staff must use ingenuity and sophisticated marketing techniques to get their books on to radio and television, and into the press.

Distribution and sales Books are distributed through warehouses, but most publishers sell through teams of sales representatives (they may be employed full-time, or contracted), who visit bookshops, multiple stores, libraries, education authorities, schools etc. Sales staff provide the publisher with critical information from the market place. The actual number of sales reps is usually quite small, but with the sales manager and office staff may make up a third of a publishers' staff. Smaller publishers contract their distribution and sales to larger publishers or distributors.

Administration A significant proportion (probably at least 20%) of most larger publishers are administrative. Like all commercial firms, publishers employ FINANCIAL STAFF, PERSONNEL MANAGERS, SECRETARIES etc. But some aspects of publishing are more specialised, eg contracts, rights etc, and LEGAL WORK.

Recruitment and entry Vacancies are generally few, and competition for them great, with no structured entry route. Only a small number of larger houses have (very small) graduate recruitment schemes. It may be slightly easier to get in to marketing, sales or production than editorial, initially. A reasonable degree (but by itself not enough), evidence of wide interests and reading, and a demonstrable and very realistic understanding of publishing as a business are basic requirements. Some kind of previous experience, in bookselling, or sales and promotion generally, may help, or a pre-entry course (see below). People do get into editorial work by starting as secretaries, and it is possible to get into production by training in the print industry. Persistence, endless letter-writing, and extensive use of any contacts are all needed to gain a toehold. Book design and illustration – see GRAPHIC DESIGN.

Qualifications and training A number of courses have recently been added to the longer-established ones, but their record in getting students into publishing

should be checked (and for editorial work, cannot take the place of a degree) –
Publishing (with a bias to production) can be taken as part of a degree (or as a diploma) course at Oxford Polytechnic.
Other 'practical' courses at Edinburgh: Napier, Exeter CA&D, London: Printing, Watford C.
More 'academic' courses (postgraduate) at Leeds and Stirling U.

Training is otherwise, mainly on-the-job. The Book House Training Centre is the industry's voluntary training organisation, and runs a wide range of courses in all aspects of publishing (1200 people already in the industry attended one or more of their 70 courses in 1986). In-house training, at least in larger firms, seems to be improving.

All editors have to gain a wide and sound knowledge of all aspects of publishing as a business, plus modern production and printing techniques (including computer typesetting).

Further information The Book House Training Centre.

WRITING PROFESSIONALLY
Writing for a living — journalism — technical, scientific and other specialist writing

Writing for a living

There is a world of difference between being able to write, even to write extremely well, and being able to make a living from writing.

The central problem for writers is that publishers, newspapers, theatrical producers, in fact anyone who is likely to employ and pay them, are in business to make a profit. Most books, plays, poems etc, that authors really want to write never will sell enough copies, or attract large enough audiences, to make anyone any money. Yet for most authors there is very little point to their literary efforts if their books or poems are not published somewhere, or their plays are unseen.

Anyone with genuine literary or dramatic talent should eventually see their work produced if they persist (although it gets more difficult all the time). But the only way to write and survive is to begin, at least, by treating writing as a non-profit making activity, and to earn a living at something else. Writing is often improved by maturity (which does not necessarily equate with age, since many of the most creative writers have achieved this remarkably young) and as much experience of the real world as possible. It is also at least possible to write at any time and virtually anywhere.

For a lucky few, their talents may coincide with commercial success, which may bring them enough money to live on. Usually, though, this means getting several books into print first, and even then the largest part of the income generally comes from selling 'rights' to paperback publishers or film makers, or adapting the book for television, serialisation, and even royalties for foreign-language editions. Public lending rights (fees for library loans) have very marginally improved some writers' incomes but mainly go to the already well-established. Successful authors are often 'marketed' like any other commercial product, to 'maximise' the investment.

A small number of competitions, prizes etc help to create opportunities for younger/newer writers to see their work in print.

For many people, the only way to write for a living is to accept that they must write to a commission, from publishers, magazines, theatrical producers, broadcasting companies, or become a journalist or advertising copywriter. There is, of course, nothing wrong in writing for someone who is prepared to pay: Shakespeare and Dickens produced some great literature under extreme commercial pressure.

Most people who write for a living do not restrict themselves to one medium. They have also often been in full-time jobs which have given them contacts in the media world (although there are other ways). It is generally much easier to get a first book accepted if you already have a track record elsewhere, or a play put on if you have worked in the theatre or for a television company. Competition is enormous for all the writing outlets that pay fees (and some of the fees are pitifully small), such as magazine short stories; talks, plays, and short stories for radio; one-off plays (but television uses fewer original, 'one-off', plays today, preferring to put on series of plays with a single theme which have to be commissioned), scripts for serials and series on both radio and television. Film companies don't employ resident writers now, and the film scriptwriter freelances with the rest – and more of this goes to established novelists and dramatists. It is probably impossible to live on any one of these by itself, with the possible exception of regular script writing for long-running serials. Most writing for radio and television documentaries goes to established journalists, although it is possible to get into radio particularly by starting as an occasional contributor and having expert knowledge to offer (as well as writing skills).

To make a reasonable income from writing books and/or plays (and this applies particularly to TV drama), a good agent is essential. Agents are better able to negotiate contracts, with all the complexities of rights and royalties, than writers can, and because of their contacts in the media, keep writers informed of publishers' and broadcasting companies' future plans, and suggest 'their' authors for particular projects. Agents usually only take on writers they consider have some chance of success. They play little or no part in journalists' careers (unless, of course, they also write books or plays).

Most writers expect to spend a high proportion of their time doing research. Few novelists, even, can produce books without first delving deeply into the background of the book's subject material, whether it is a spy thriller, a story set in an earlier period, or even a novel about contemporary life. Alternatively, they must have extensive experience, which amounts to the same thing. Readers, today, expect books to be factually accurate and authentic, however imaginative they may be. People who write for television and radio documentaries, series, etc, can expect to have paid research assistance. Authors of even the most solidly factual reference book are expected to provide their own, and this can be very expensive.

Writing is both creative art and craft. Writing demands both creativity and craft skills, skills which must be learnt. Evidence suggests that the discipline of writing to a brief can be a valuable training. One of today's major novelists was first a successful advertising copywriter. Not everyone who has writing ability is necessarily capable of being successful in every form, though. While many young reporters and advertising copywriters may dream of writing a best selling novel, it could be that they are already making best use of their talents. For some dramatists the novel is an impossible form, while few poets write novels or plays. However, those who can are obviously at a great advantage: many journalists produce books of one kind or another, one recent poet laureate worked in publishing and wrote detective stories, and a public relations expert writes best-selling novels on the train to and from the office.

Learning one's craft, gaining experience and then recognition are the major problems facing the apprentice writer, whatever type of writing s/he chooses. Learning and experience go hand-in-hand in writing. Only journalists have formal training schemes (see below), and so for the majority it is mostly a matter of sitting at the feet of the experienced, either by working with or alongside an older writer, possibly as a research assistant, or metaphorically, by extensive critical reading. Most forms of writing involve learning special techniques, as for drama, for example, and of course the techniques differ between theatre, television, radio and film (most broadcasting companies produce booklets on writing for the media, covering technical points, and some also discuss writing dialogue). Most writers need a broad background of experience and this can be gained by working in almost any other job.

Writing is, in the last analysis, a lonely business. Even in a crowded newspaper office, reporters work alone on their copy. It is also very difficult. Few writers find it easy to write creatively (although those with the skills and techniques at their fingertips sometimes find it less agonising), and a great deal depends on self-discipline and the ability to concentrate.

Copy-writing
This is a skill used only in the advertising industry. See under COMMERCE etc.

Journalism
Journalists combine writing with news-gathering and interpretation.

Numbers appear, for the moment at least, to be rising, if at an 'unspectacular' rate. Combined NUJ and Institute of Journalists membership is (1986) nearly 36,000. Not everyone belongs, so the total is more likely to be over 40,000.

Journalists work on national and local newspapers, for news agencies, on periodicals, in radio and television, and on a freelance basis. The number of newspapers has been rising (each national employs up to 200), and broadcasting is also expanding. New technology affecting the rest of the industry's employees has not, so far, made any inroads into journalists' jobs. While the recent growth rate is unlikely to continue, the NUJ expects numbers to at least stay at their present level.

Working in journalism While the journalist's work obviously varies from newspaper to newspaper, and from magazine to magazine, all journalists are as much researchers as they are writers. They don't only write their own news or feature stories, but must find and research them first – but a great many stories hunt the journalist, who rejects most of them. Only a relatively small proportion of news comes from the unexpected, since most people who supply stories are aware that newspapers want advance warning to give good coverage to anything. The real 'scoop' is a very rare event. Every news desk and every journalist, gets vast shoals of paper every day, plus endless telephone calls on items that people want to get into the newspaper or magazine.

Much of what actually goes into local and even national papers is routine, and on 'anticipated' events, such as court cases, debates in parliament or the local council, weddings, royal occasions, company reports, or the month's unemployment figures. Much of the rest of the news is given to journalists through press releases, press conferences, and unofficial briefings, or can be anticipated, is planned (eg a commissioned public opinion poll), or is a running theme of the moment.

The journalist's job is to give the story an individual slant, to get a better 'quote' on the story than the next paper, to dig deeper behind the official line, or to find the crucial question to ask that will improve on the story. All of this often means doing a lot of background work first, and being able to think on one's feet. Obviously every journalist is also looking out all the time for a story that no other journalist has found, but this is fairly unusual. They do not very often come 'out of the blue', but from a journalist's well-nursed contacts, or because s/he has the hard-won expertise to see a story in an apparently trivial piece of information.

Journalists have to work fast, to meet deadlines that do not wait for events. Their stories must be checked, and they must be 'newsworthy'. They must put their stories together at speed, in crowded offices with a lot of phones all going at once, in a bar or at the back of a conference hall, in the street, or on a train. They must phone it in if necessary. Stories should be accurate, short, pointed, and interesting. Superb prose comes a long way behind these, but a journalist whose writing is lively, imaginative, sharp and very readable too has a strong advantage. Journalists move around for much of their time – going to press conferences, meetings, events, and so on, have to be on the telephone a great deal, and work long and irregular hours, under pressure.

Most journalists begin as general reporters, on local newspapers working under a news editor. The general reporter spends many days covering very routine, and often quite boring, assignments, and may go for some time with nothing out of the ordinary happening. However, they learn a very great deal through doing the basic stories: about sources of information, how to cope with people and with the less pleasant side of life, interviewing techniques (including how to listen), the use of simple, straightforward English and an economical style of writing, how to turn a basically ordinary story into an interesting piece of copy, how to write for a particular audience, and so on. They must also develop or acquire an instinct for news, an insatiable curiosity (especially about people and what motivates them), the ability to meet deadlines come what may, astuteness and endless adaptability.

Although traditionally reporters cover any story, and many still do, competition from television and radio means that many journalists are assigned to look after particular subjects – politics, finance, education, defence, local government, the environment, industry, farming, fashion, sport, travel, science, motoring. Mostly journalists specialise only on national papers, television and national radio, but on regional papers journalists combine general reporting with in-depth coverage of one area, for instance, education. Journalists who specialise do not just report on the latest news in their specialist subject, but deal with it in depth, commenting on events, pointing out trends, reporting on future developments, explaining causes and effects, etc. These journalists build close contacts in their subject areas, get to know and talk to experts on their own level, but must still write stories in non-technical language which the average newspaper reader can understand. Established specialist journalists have a more independent position than general reporters, and work directly under the editor.

With fast and fairly-efficient travel more or less world wide now, fewer foreign correspondents are based permanently abroad, and those that are cover larger areas. Even so, some still become established residents of one country, specialising in all types of news and comment on that country, but having to do whatever the editor wants, frequently at short notice. Other foreign specialists are based on the newspaper, or freelance, flying off to wherever a story breaks.

Some journalists specialise in writing in-depth articles or longer 'features', or interviewing, but with the growth of specialist journalism demand for feature writers as such is down, and most journalists get the chance to write 'in-depth' now. Some journalists combine reporting with photography, as photo-journalists (see PHOTOGRAPHY). Some work on the so-called gossip columns, others write humorous pieces, others become political columnists.

Leaders put over the newspaper's own views and policy on current affairs. Traditionally written (anonymously) by the editor, larger regional and national papers usually have small teams of specialist leader-writers.

Editing mostly means giving up reporting and writing, at least on daily papers, although some people do move between the two. Some do combine editing with some writing, particularly on weeklies.

Editing is desk and team work. A larger paper may have up to 25 sub-editors, agencies even more, all working as a team under a chief sub-editor, and senior editorial staff, the copy-tasters. They decide how important each story is as it comes in, and then pass them to the chief sub-editor, who decides what should go where on which page, how long it should be, etc.

The subs then 'work over' the copy to get it the right length; tighten up the language, grammar, style etc; check its accuracy and rewrite it if necessary; deal with running stories which may be coming in from different places, a bit at a time; write headlines which must be apt, concise, informative and perhaps amusing or ambiguous, but must always fit into the space allowed. This may have to be done all over again between editions if a story develops further, or is overtaken, or a major new story breaks somewhere in the world. Some subs specialise in particular subjects, eg sports, and also 'lay out' the pages. Subs work at very high speed and under considerable pressure. They need good memories and to be able to spot any links between apparently unconnected stories. Stamina and unflappability are crucial.

On large newspapers, or periodicals, editors are in charge of each section – home news, overseas news, features, sports, city pages. The news editor manages a team of reporters, decides which stories to cover, assigns reporters, and supervises progress. Features editors look out for ideas, commission articles from 'staff' and other journalists, and so on. Editorial decisions, on policy, on the 'balance' of the paper, on disagreements on which stories to print, or any major problems, are made at editorial conferences – throughout the day and night if need be. Editors are policy makers and organisers, and although this is a recognised promotion route, not all journalists want to take it because it may mean no actual writing or research at all. Top managers are rarely journalists.

On a large national paper there may also be a deputy and several assistant editors, and 'the' editor becomes more remote. Weekly papers have fewer editors. News agencies generally have at least three editors, one of whom is editor-on-chief, since the post must be manned round the clock.

A high proportion of journalists work for regional and local papers ('free' local papers don't employ many journalists) all their lives – but sometimes acting as a 'stringer' for a national paper, radio or TV. On national and specialist periodicals there may be a little more time to work on a story and more careful planning and thinking, but less immediacy. Life is different again in the news agencies.

The BBC is one of the largest employers of journalists for its radio and TV news services, with ITN close behind. On local radio stations, with news programmes throughout the day, life is probably even more hectic than on a daily paper. Like the BBC, the major independent TV contractors all have at least one 'current affairs' programme for which journalists work, normally on contract for a set number of programmes. See also BROADCASTING.

Some journalists work on a 'freelance' basis, but not usually as general report-ers. Most freelance journalists build up considerable expertise in a subject and so have a specialist knowledge to sell – perhaps in something that is too technical for papers to cover, or they have access to particular sources. Mostly freelance journalists have either worked as full-time journalists first, and so have the contacts to whom they can sell their output (or who will commission them), or they have been experts at something and find there is a market for their ability to explain what is going on in that field. Some people combine freelance journalism with technical writing (see below).

Recruitment and entry Entry to newspaper and news-broadcasting journalism is strictly controlled, although it is (just) possible to by-pass the official system. All entrants are supposed to go through a formal traineeship (indenture or apprenticeship) scheme with a provincial or local (ie not a national) news-paper, or with a broadcasting company. The aim is to pass the official NCTJ proficiency test, and gain membership of the National Union of Journalists, needed for a very high proportion of full-time posts.

Editors of training newspapers say they prefer to take people straight from school with five GCSE/GCE-equivalent passes including two suitable (eg English), A levels, at eighteen, or after a pre-entry course (see below) – anyone who has successfully completed the course is helped to find a trainee-ship. For some years there has been a shortfall of 'suitable' A-level candidates, and so graduate entry has been rising steadily, reaching 50% in 1986. The training council now advises any potential journalist who can to gain a degree. Evidence suggests that a degree in, eg politics, economics, a science, is more useful than, for example, English or history. The number of trainees varies from year to year, from around 400 to at most about 700, and there is probably an average of five applications for every vacancy, with many more for the more popular papers and the BBC news traineeships.

Periodicals take on about 400-500 new entrants a year (about double the number of ten years earlier). There is no formal scheme, but the larger publishers giving training. Periodicals probably take a higher proportion of graduates, especially professional, scientific and technological publications, than newspapers.

Journalism takes real curiosity, the ability to work up an interest in anything and everything, to absorb new subjects and ideas easily, to be good at simply finding out and always wanting to know, and a sense of what is important for the moment. Journalists need to be very observant and patient. They need the kind of scepticism that questions anything they are told. Potential journalists ought to show the ability to write clearly, crisply, concisely and simply, and should be able to work fast and very accurately. They need to be able to handle people of all types and from all backgrounds, be good at listening and putting people at their ease, but persuasive and persistent too. Journalism demands physical and emotional stamina, and the ability to cope with both moving around a lot and waiting through long and often boring events.

Editors also expect successful applicants to have shown determination and persistence in trying to get in. They also expect any applicant who has had the opportunity to gain relevant experience (in student journalism, for instance) to have done so, or to have done something in their spare time and/or holidays which demonstrates interest in the media, the ability to hold down any job, and to have had some kind of responsibility.

It is possible to by-pass the official entry scheme because anyone can become a (freelance) member of the National Union of Journalists by showing evidence of having worked and made an income as a journalist for two years. Many publications, including almost all the 'free' local papers, do not subscribe to the above national agreement, and recruit untrained school-leavers and graduates.

Qualifications and training Training for most journalists is still largely on-the-job, with a provincial or local newspaper.

School-leavers can take a one-year pre-entry course (230 places) at –
Cardiff: S Glam IHE, Darlington CT, Harlow C, Portsmouth: Highbury CT, Preston: Lancs P, Sheffield: Richmond C (selection is via an interview with a panel of journalists)

Graduates can take a one-year course at Cardiff: UC or S Glam IHE, London: City U or Printing C (these do not guarantee a training place but do exempt from the probationary period).

Formal trainee schemes last three years for non-graduates and two for graduates after a six-month probationary period. Most newspapers taking trainees have reasonably well organised systems of on-the-job training in basic journalistic skills, supplemented by eight-week block-release residential courses (one in each of the first two years) covering English usage, law for journalists, public administration, shorthand, practical journalism and current affairs. Because computer-based production systems mean that journalists will in future input their own copy and edit on VDU screens, most courses now include typing to a high level of accuracy. Graduates take an intensive version. The proficiency test carries cash benefits and is increasingly required for appointments and promotion. It is well worth while ensuring that the training provided by any employer is as stated, and it is questionable whether it is any use taking a first post which does not provide full and proper training.

Periodical publishers now generally give new entrants practical, on-the-job training. Some also give release from work to study for NCTJ courses at the London College of Printing, which also puts on a one-year pre-entry course in periodical journalism. Others give entrants a six-month trial-and-training period, mainly on the job but supplemented with NCTJ-approval external courses.

Further information from the National Union of Journalists, and National Council for the Training of Journalists.

Technical, scientific and other specialist writing
Probably expanding areas of employment, although it is hard to prove. The work ranges from writing, compiling and editing text- and reference books on specialist subjects through to preparing user, service and maintenance manuals and leaflets, abstracts and information bulletins. It can shade over into creative writing (eg biographical), into teaching (many textbooks are prepared by teachers and university staff), technical journalism, editing house journals, and information science.

Many people in this field work on a freelance basis once they have become established, others are employed by the technical press or by larger industrial and commercial companies. Publishers who produce a significant number of reference works, particularly encyclopedias and dictionaries, may also have professional editors on the staff, some with small teams of researchers and editorial assistants.

Recruitment and entry Generally a 'second' career. Most people normally gain relevant expertise and experience first, although graduates are recruited by some industrial firms on manual writing etc, and it is possible to go straight into technical journalism. Teachers, for instance, may have written eg textbooks in their spare time before switching to it full-time for an income.

Technical writing takes considerable expertise in a subject area, plus the ability to write clearly and concisely about the subject in a language which can be understood by those for whom it is intended, and which takes account of the needs of the particular public. While a user's manual must obviously explain to even the densest reader, it is no use writing at too elementary a level in an information bulletin on research designed for research scientists. For some technical work, particularly on illustrated textbooks and manuals, a good background knowledge of technical illustration and layout, notation etc is needed. Languages are increasingly useful.

Qualifications and training No formal training schemes.

ARCHIVE AND MUSEUM WORK

Introduction 596
Archive work 596
Museum work 598

INTRODUCTION

These careers are not necessarily directly creative, but they do preserve, care for and display the results of centuries of human creativity. For many years archives and museums were far more concerned with the 'preservation' to the near-exclusion of the promotion and display of the objects in their care, and so careers in this field inevitable suffered from this rather dusty image. Now, however, most museums see preservation as only one part of their role, and see positive presentation of their collections, as well as the development of services around them, as equally important and totally justifiable. Many museums have become places where the past is brought to life through creative displays and activities. These are, nevertheless, careers which demand fairly stiff academic qualifications. However, promotional and administrations skills are also needed. Staff must also have as great an interest in helping people who visit and use archives and museums as in collections themselves.

ARCHIVE WORK

Archives are stores, of the records of the past. In this context, the 'past' stretches from Anglo-Saxon times, right through Tudor and Victorian eras, to last year, and even this. Archives store any records which have historical interest or value, but which are no longer in day to day use.

Pre mid-19th century, records are mostly handwritten and printed documents, such as ledgers, loose papers, parchments, maps, plans and drawings. Material going into archives now may also be in the form of printed and typed papers, film, photographs, tape-recordings, and even computer tape or disks.

Archives range from large national collections to small local ones. National archives include the Public Record Office at Kew (there are equivalents in Scotland, Wales and Northern Ireland), where state and government papers (including court records) go back to, and include, the Domesday Book.

County, municipal and other local record offices house archives of their particular area, and may go back to the records of medieval manorial systems. All official administrative documents (for example, minutes of council meetings, court proceedings, market records, and planning papers), are automatically deposited there. They also acquire other material about the region, for instance poor law and parish relief records, records of local trusts and charities, family papers, maps, charts, and deeds, in fact anything which documents any aspect of the life of the community.

The churches also have their own repositories, at Canterbury, York, Westminster, and other diocesan centres. These hold all kinds of ecclesiastical records, ranging from sets of parish registers to original monastic documents going back beyond the 16th century. Older universities, the copyright and other larger libraries, some public institutions (eg the Bank of England founded in 1776), scientific societies (for instance, the Royal Society), keep archives on their own past.

A growing number of larger industrial and commercial companies now have their own archives, which document the history of the company, and employing professional archivists, often called record managers. Medical/health records also employ archivists. Some charities, local antiquarian societies are large and rich enough to employ archive staff.

Working as an archivist Archivists look after these collections. The work obviously varies from archive to archive, depending on the type of collection. They all look after the physical well-being of the records, to see that, for example, any parchment, frail paper and film is treated, handled and stored – which may have to be in special conditions – so they will not decay or get damaged. They also index and catalogue the records, so they can be found when wanted, and so that it is possible to find out what the collection houses on particular topics. For earlier documents, particularly, this means being able to decipher and read handwriting and scripts which are very different from those of today, sometimes to identify and date documents.

Archivists also help and advise anyone with a genuine reason for using the collections. They can be eminent scholars or young students, people who are trying to complete their family tree, or school pupils doing serious project work. They also answer specific questions, do research for other people, edit records for publications, produce documentary histories – for example, of industry in an area, or on the changing pattern of land holding and use on a particular manor house during the three centuries after Domesday. Archives can produce evidence, for example, for insurance companies trying to decide what caused subsidence on a housing estate (such as a long-forgotten mine), by producing records on previous use.

Archivists help to decide what should and should not be added to an archive collection, what is worth keeping and what is not, or whether material should be kept only on microfilm. They may go out to survey and assess material being offered to an archive.

It is a very academic-style career, mostly desk work with books and documents, but with some research, adding to an understanding of the past. It is a small profession – the Society of Archivists has (1986) membership of barely 1000 – but numbers are growing, if slowly, with the main growth in work for industrial/commercial firms (national and local-authority archives are vulnerable to expenditure cuts). However, over 55% of Society members still work for local government, 12.5% for national archives etc, and 10% for universities, with 7.5% working for health/medical and religious archives, and only 10% for industry/commerce (including 2.5% for oil firms). Because there are so few posts (the Society estimates 30-40 vacancies a year only) it may be difficult to find work in particular areas of the country and/or in particular types of archive.

Recruitment and entry An all-graduate profession. A good degree, normally in history plus a knowledge of Latin is most usual, although another subject (eg economic history, languages, or law) may be acceptable for archives storing mainly modern material. A professional qualification is also normally essential.

Archivists must have a very strong interest in history, particularly the kind of original source material stored in archives, and the very fine detail of daily life.

It means being very keen on academic work and study. Archivists need to be intelligent, careful, meticulous, and prepared to do detailed work, eg deciphering handwritten documents. Ability to judge and assess the importance of documents, enough practical ability and scientific sense to cope with the physical care of records are also needed.

Qualifications and training Training is normally via a postgraduate course at Aberystwyth, Bangor, Liverpool, London: UC Universities. Courses combine archive studies, practical training (eg physical properties of the materials from ancient parchment through to modern film, the conditions under which they must be stored to preserve them, what methods to use to prevent deterioration and how to repair them) with palaeography (the study of handwriting and scripts in the historical sense), which is one of the skills needed by archivists dealing with older documents.

Further information from the Society of Archivists.

MUSEUM WORK
Background — museum 'keeping' — conservation and repair — design — educational and schools services — other professional work — technical work — other work

Background
Britain has over 1700 museums and art galleries, with more being opened all the time. Recent additions include a national theatre museum, Liverpool's 'Tate of the North', and a museum of the moving image. The thirty or so historic national collections include the British Museum, the Victoria and Albert, and the Tate Gallery in London; collections in Edinburgh and Cardiff, and another twenty city and civic museums in places like York, Leeds, Leicester, Manchester, Aberdeen and Norwich. A growing number of smaller local collections include those which remember famous people, like the Bronte Museum in Yorkshire and Keats House in Hampstead. Many universities have major museums – the oldest and most famous are the Ashmolean in Oxford and the Fitzwilliam in Cambridge.

National and most civic museums have collections which spread widely over many artistic, archaeological, historic and other interests. Others specialise, like the Science, Natural History, Geological, and Maritime Museums in London, the York Railway Museum, the Welsh Folk Museum, and Durham University's Museum of Oriental Art. Smaller museums concentrate on toys, prams, windmills, or local industry. There are museums of war, for individual regiments, and for the Roman legions. Castles, ships and historic houses have been turned into museums.

Most museums today are more lively and imaginative places than they used to be. They put on permanent and 'special' exhibitions designed to bring alive for visitors part of the past, or an aspect of science, or another part of the world. They do this by re-creating scenes or themes, such as the Vikings or Pompeii, an Anglo-Saxon village, Vienna in the age of Schubert, or dinosaurs, with natural settings. This is in great contrast to the dusty, traditional room upon room full of glass cases packed with flints, coins, bronzes, weapons, Egyptian mummies etc, which were really the exotic store houses of 19th century travellers, overwhelming the casual visitor.

Museums are much more selective now. They still try to build collections which illustrate as many aspects as possible of particular periods, types of objects, or themes – but if only for practical reasons, even national museums have to set strict limits on what they collect now. Most new museums specialise, often collecting objects which may not seem museum material, such as a potato museum, an industrial hamlet (originally an iron works) in Sheffield, and a woodland museum of historic buildings saved from development schemes. New maritime museums seem extremely popular.

The public is generally much more interested in museums. The fascination of the past – fuelled by the media (especially TV), foreign holidays etc. Schools encourage families to use museums and galleries. Interest is not limited to the more glamorous exhibits of the distant past; museums and galleries of all kinds report a growth in attendances.

Museums, of course, face considerable problems in becoming more outward-going, and it is difficult for them – and their staff – to get the balance right between all the demands made on them. Few, like the Victoria and Albert, were actually started to foster public taste and improve aesthetic standards. Most were founded entirely as repositories and therefore were not built, organised or financed to act as educational or creative institutions. They have endless financial difficulties, and must cope in monumental buildings often ill-suited and difficult to adapt to modern ways of showing exhibits.

Yet they try to serve the widest possible public, experimenting with interesting and attractive displays and exhibitions. They must also collect and care for historic objects, not just for today, but for generations to come. Some collections, then, are clearly of the 20th century – the Beaulieu motor museum has Minis, Metros and Maestros as well as a 1926 Silver Cloud. Museums must still try to make their collections comprehensive enough to provide the material needed by research workers making detailed studies of the past, and things suitable for use by schools and children in project work.

Many national and larger regional museums provide full-scale educational services. They make space for lectures, film shows and holiday-time activities; put on concerts, sometimes using historic instruments; help researchers with information, pictures etc, for books, films, TV programmes.

Working in museums

The number of 'major' museums, about 100, does not change very much, and it is these which employ about 90% of trained professional museum staff. The largest national museums, government funded, are the major employer, but numbers are probably not much more than 5000 people, including about 3000 professional staff. Most of the rest come under local authorities, a minority are owned by universities and colleges, societies, hospitals, industrial and commercial firms, and a range of foundations. Only some 200 are large enough to employ more than a handful of professional people each. Very many small museums, existing without government aid, employ few people.

MUSEUM 'KEEPING' Professional museum staff are called 'keepers', or 'curators'. For them, museum work is a mixture of administration, work on the collections, exhibitions and exhibits, dealing with enquiries from the public, running services, and doing research. Although museum staff are still expected to be scholars, the emphasis is increasing on administrative efficiency. The imaginative approach to displaying collections also means they spend more time on the creative aspects of running a museum, for instance, exhibition design, preparing attractive, illustrated catalogues, etc.

The way the work is divided depends to a considerable extent on the size of the museum, and how specialised it is. A 'typical' national or large local museum is generally divided into departments each specialising in, for example, a historical period (Anglo-Saxon, or Tudor), or a group of like objects, such as computers or swords. Each department is generally staffed by a keeper, a number of assistant keepers, and possibly also research and museum assistants, all of whom are experts in a subject relevant to the collection they look after. The smallest museums, at the other end of the scale, may have just one, possibly retired, person to look after them. They may well live on the premises, and look after the building as well as the collection.

In larger museums, keepers generally have considerable responsibility for and freedom in they way they run their departments, within overall museum policy and a tight budget. The keeper supervises the collection and its care; plans and controls its development, looking for ways to improve it where possible, for example, watching out for items which fill in gaps and which the museum can afford; and takes policy decisions on, for example, better ways of exhibiting. Departments may put on special exhibitions, which usually means borrowing major items from other museums or private collectors, involving staff in extensive negotiations, or provide space for a major travelling exhibition. Keepers have to see that items are properly identified, classified and recorded in catalogues. They also supervise research in the department. Lectures and demonstrations, and and sometimes lecture tours, have to be organised.

Assistant keepers in large museums, keepers themselves in the smaller ones, do the detailed work. About half their time is spent on administrative work and looking after the collection. This ranges from dealing with letters to planning new layouts for exhibition rooms or deciding on new settings for particular objects, to supervising design, conservation and other staff (eg attendants, carpenters and joiners who make stands, model makers, and even taxidermists). Even keepers and assistant keepers expect to do the most routine work, like packing or mounting irreplaceable items, if they are the only people expert at the job.

Assistant keepers spend about a third of their time with people who come into the museum, write or phone for help, advice and information. They may bring in objects to be identified and/or dated, for example. Other people may want help with source material for their research; children may want help with school projects; a film or TV researcher may want detailed information for a period production.

Keepers and assistant keepers spend what time is left on research, books or articles for publication. Many senior museum staff are acknowledged experts in their own fields. In some museums, assistant keepers and research assistants (who are one step down from assistant keepers), are partly museum staff and partly archaeologists. At the National Maritime Museum, for example, one research assistant both excavates for medieval boats and does the post-excavation research and prepares gallery displays.

Museum assistants do the more routine work of the department, but may still have the opportunity to do some research.

Most museum staff learn to clean, repair and restore the objects they look after, and many also become expert in exhibition design. However, the larger museums employ specialist staff for this work.

Recruitment and entry Competition for almost all posts has always been considerable, and has been made worse by sharp reductions in recruitment, with posts left vacant. For the national museums, though, recruitment had recovered somewhat by 1985, with a total of 75 vacancies for all the four main curator grades, but with nearly 3600 applications for them. There never have been more than two or three vacancies a year for deputy keepers and keepers (grade A and B curators), and promotion to this level is relatively rare. In 1985, there were only three vacancies for conservation officers in national museums, only 15 applications. No recent figures for local and regional museums have been collected, but reports suggest they are very small.

Intellectual ability and other skills are need for museum work. Curators/keepers need a good honours degree (at least) and increasingly a second, higher degree too (the Museums Association says it is in the candidate's interest to gain the highest possible relevant academic qualification), in a subject which will make a good basis on which to build a detailed, expert subject knowledge of a museum's collection (or part of it), for example, anthropology, archaeology, art history, history, Classics, science – but not English or modern languages normally, although the ability to read and write fluently in one or two languages is an obvious advantage and essential for some posts. Scientific and technological/industrial museums usually want degrees in science, even engineering or a technology; art galleries/museums are likely to prefer a degree in art and/or design. The implication is that anyone thinking of a museum career has to decide on their area of interest when choosing a degree subject.

Administrative potential (as shown by, for example, being able to run a school or university society efficiently) is important. Museum work needs a kind of artistic sense which can appreciate objects both for what they are and for their significance in human history or the natural world. It also prefers people who have a strong interest in what museums are trying to do, not only in a subject, like railways – although enthusiastic, long-standing and detailed knowledge of something like this can be very useful. Museum staff have to be able to get on with people of all kinds, from the very scholarly to school-children, collectors, designers, packers and carpenters.

Work or voluntary experience, via a holiday job in a museum, working on an archaeological excavation, helping to restore old buildings, buses or industrial experience, for example, can help when applying for posts.

Qualifications and training While a qualification in museum work is obviously likely to help in gaining a post, the number of courses is small (see below).

Training for professional museum work is normally 'on-the-job', combining in-house training with study for the Museums Association diploma (the main professional qualification). Some museums have formal training schemes. Some two-year schemes, usually for graduates, are designed to give the necessary training and instruction for the Museums Association diploma (they are advertised in the Museums Bulletin as 'recognised by the Museums Association as a student post'). For other schemes, candidates should ask questions about the training offered (whether qualified staff are available, whether there is study leave, what collections there are, the nature of the library and so on).

It is theoretically possible for non-graduates to take the diploma and qualify for Museums Association membership, but the Association says that a degree is generally essential. There is no formal course of study, but registered students are expected to take a training curriculum in the museum where they work, supplemented by private study, with tutorial supervision for the final examination. Candidates must also go to at least two of the Association's residential courses. Direct entry to the diploma examination is via a degree relevant to one of: art, human history, natural science, science and technology. Candidates with non-relevant degrees, or non-graduates (with five GCE/GCSE equivalent passes including two at A level) must sit a qualifying examination (non-graduates must do two years' museum service first).

Other courses (both, plus 18 months' full-time museum service exempt from the main papers of the Museums Association diploma, although essay and practical examination still required) –

Leicester U: Museum studies, MA/MSc (2 years full-time, 3 part-time) or graduate certificate (1-year full-time, 2 part-time) – same syllabus for both, covering museum and collection management and museum services; both include practical experience. Priority given to candidates wanting to specialise in one of archaeology, geology, natural history, local history and folk life, or history of science, who have a relevant degree and show strong vocational interest in museum work (eg by doing temporary or vacation work in a museum).

Manchester U: Gallery and museum studies, diploma (1 year full-time) – emphasises art gallery work, concentrating on gallery administration and techniques and including a choice of special subjects within the decorative arts. In addition,

London, City U: Museum and gallery administration, MA (2 years part-time) – a post-experience course.

CONSERVATION Conservators clean, repair and generally look after anything collected by a museums. These may be the finds of archaeologists, sculptures, medieval textiles, early-industrial machines, animal remains, or geologically-significant rocks. Experts also work on ceramics, metalwork of all kinds, paintings (particularly oils), traditional crafts and folk items, textiles, furniture and woodwork, ethnography, watercolours and prints. They also advise on how to store objects to prevent them decaying (and to avoid the damage which large numbers of visitors can even inadvertently cause).

Conservation is scientific work. Conservators give scientific judgements on origins, dates, material composition, authentication and so on of objects and other works (such as paintings or sculptures). Some conservators specialise in particular types of objects, or in things made from one or more particular materials and they become extremely knowledgeable about them, but in some museums they may have to deal with anything that comes along.

Most conservators and repairers work in the conservation departments of larger museums, although there are some posts in smaller, specialist museums. Conservators also work for the eight area councils which provide local museums with more specialist services. A small number of commercial organisations specialise in restoration and repair of historic and other valuable objects.

Some museums have their own laboratories, and employ qualified SCIENTISTS and technicians to help conservators. They may, for instance, analyse the composition of 18th century paint, or textile fragments from an Egyptian tomb, so helping to work out how to preserve or restore them. Labs also do tests, for example, to date objects.

Taxidermists, who may also work for private firms, reconstruct animals, birds and fish using the creatures' own skin (and where appropriate, the skull also), to make them look as natural as possible. They prepare the hide, make a framework and give it form and substance with plaster of Paris or papier-mache; fit and sew the skin, and add eyes, whiskers, teeth, claws.

Recruitment and entry While it is still theoretically possible to start straight from school (with two A levels including chemistry), most major museums prefer a degree, normally in chemistry, physics or materials science or a related subject. Technical skills, ability to work with one's hands, patience and care (given the value and uniqueness of many objects) are all needed. Aesthetic judgement, and a good background knowledge of appropriate areas of art history and technology are very useful, as are appropriate (eg voluntary) experience and/or relevant expertise, possibly craft. School-leavers may be recruited as trainee technical assistants etc.

Qualifications and training Now essential. It is possible to train 'on-the-job' in some museums, combining this with study for the Museums Association diploma on the same basis as for keeper/curator staff, but a small number of courses give pre-entry training. They range from the general to the specialised, from degree or postgraduate level to craft. They include –
Degree courses
Archaeological conservation (BSc) at Cardiff: UC, and London: Institute of Archaeology. See also ARCHAEOLOGY for other science-based courses.
Postgraduate courses/qualifications
Archaeological conservation diploma (1 year) – Durham U.
Scientific methods in archaeology MA or diploma (1 year) – Bradford U.
Conservation of paintings or textiles diploma (3 years) – London: Courtauld Institute of Art.
BTEC schemes (technician level)
Architectural stained glass HND – Swansea: W Glam IHE.
Conservation crafts, National Diploma – Lincoln CA, London: Camberwell SA&C, CGL AS; HND – Bournemouth/Poole IHE, London: Camberwell SA&C, CGL AS.
Other qualifications/courses
Conservation diploma – London: Institute of Archaeology (3 years part-time)

– for people working in conservation but not getting any formal training.
Painting conservation – Gateshead TC.
Picture restoration diploma – Cambridge: Hamilton Kerr Inst (3 years)
Craft courses in eg repairing antiques, furniture, musical instruments, and in
book-binding/repairing, embroidery etc also useful

Taxidermy training is largely on-the-job in a museum or workshop, and can
take quite a long time, since very detailed knowledge has to be built up, and
the number of traineeships is very small. Taxidermists need manual dexterity,
artistic flair/ability, an eye for detail, colour and form, and craft skills.

Technicians and craft workers in museums can qualify via Museums Association certificates. These show that candidates have reached a recognised level
of technical knowledge and practical ability in one or more branches of
museum work. Entry qualifications are, for technicians, either a range of
GCE/GCSE-equivalent passes including A-levels, or appropriate CGLI
certificate.

DESIGN Larger museums have design departments, but employing perhaps, at
most, half a dozen qualified DESIGNERS. They (obviously) work on the design
of exhibitions and permanent displays, but GRAPHIC DESIGNERS are also
employed to produce catalogues and other publications, posters and publicity
material generally. Designers work under the direction of professional
museum staff.

Designers are usually expected to have a degree in art and design (some
courses have options in exhibition design) or, for design assistants/technicians
(display and studio), a BTEC award. See ART AND DESIGN.

Only the largest museums have their own PHOTOGRAPHERS. Others use freelances to record specimens, do site or scientific work, and provide photographs
for the public. A few MODEL-MAKERS are employed.

OTHER STAFF employed include –
Some museums have their own libraries, run by qualified LIBRARIANS not
museum staff.
The larger museums also have their own PUBLIC RELATIONS staff.
Growing numbers have commercial managers who help to improve museum
income with sales of, for example, posters, postcards, reproductions of
exhibits and books. They may also negotiate the sale of 'rights' to exploit some
of the museum's possessions.
Attendants and security staff – essential to the running of all larger museums
(they can gain their own Museums Association certificate).

Further information from the Museums Association, and from individual
museums.

PERFORMING (INCLUDING SPORT)

Introduction	605
Acting	606
Dancing	611
Light entertainment	613

Modelling   614
Music   616
Sport   624

INTRODUCTION

Acting, dancing, being a musician, singing, or being a professional sportsman or woman, demands very exceptional talent, trained to a very high level. Talent and training must be matched by the kind of personality which can go out and perform before an audience. In such intensely competitive fields, extreme dedication, being prepared to work hard and to fight for a place and hold on to it, the emotional and physical stamina which can cope with the stresses and the long and irregular hours, the knack of being in the right place at the right time, and then very often a great deal of luck too, are also essential factors.

The dedication and the hard work needed mean that for most people in these careers their whole lives are affected by the demands of their work, which for success has to come first at all times, regardless of how they feel. Personality factors must include the ability to press on against all odds – the kind of self-confidence which is not dented by rejection at audition after audition, or not winning, and can still go on to the next audition or competition, expecting to come first.

Qualifications and training When and how to begin serious training is a major problem for young people interested in any one of these (with the exception of acting), and by implication therefore their parents and teachers. It is generally accepted that training for performing careers where physical skills are involved should start in the very early teens, while the body or essential parts of it (the violinist's hands and fingers, for example) are still developing. Yet the odds against a successful career for those showing even the greatest talent at this age are enormous – and as students mature talent may fade, or they may not develop the right kind of personality, or they may simply not want to go into a career which makes such heavy demands or dictates such a restricted life style. It should always be remembered that music, dancing, sport, acting and so on make very satisfying spare time activities, and that some people with even the greatest talents are happier as amateurs, earning their living at something else.

The problem should not really affect people thinking of acting as a career, since there is no need, or even necessarily any advantage, in starting young. See ACTING below.

Starting training so very early, with the inevitable hours and hours of daily practice, almost inevitably reduces the chances of preparing for many other careers, because without great care it means curtailing general education too early. All this means planning very carefully and taking precautions. First, parents and pupils must have the very best possible advice, and independent assessment of a child's potential, which should be re-assessed regularly. Second, parents and teachers must watch very carefully that the student continues to enjoy, and is still interested in, the very time-consuming and hard work involved in reaching the standards needed, in spending so much of their free time on these activities, and always has (age-for-age) a reasonable understanding of what a professional career involves. Finally, and most crucially, the student's 'normal' academic and other education must be continued as broadly and to as high a level as possible. For pupils in the ability range, this ought to mean at least four O-level-equivalent passes at 16-plus†, and more if possible.

A few schools which have developed ways to see that talented children both have the specialist training they need and a good general education, but they are few and far between. Some state schools do this, but a high proportion are privately run, and finance has to be found. Some education authorities may be prepared to pay for a child to go to a reputable school in another area, although cuts in educational expenditure may affect this. Some local education authorities have schemes which give talented pupils specialist tuition out of school hours – on Saturdays and during the holidays, for example. Musicians are generally reasonably well catered for; acting, dancing and sport not so well. One group of parents have organised for themselves special holiday courses in dancing.

Any special scheme, private or state-supported, should be very carefully checked to see that it is suitable for the particular child – what is ideal for one child may not be the answer for another. Some commercial ballet, dance and theatrical schools claim to provide general teaching right through to GCE A level in addition to specialist training, but in practice, however good the general teaching, the child has to be highly motivated and positively encouraged by the school (and parents) to continue with general education in a non-academic atmosphere, and this does not always happen. Parents should, therefore, check very carefully on academic results as well as professional achievements.

ACTING

Actors and actresses are communicators and interpreters. They interpret (usually) someone else's creative writing. They have to achieve a difficult balance between getting over the script as faithfully as they can and becoming as far as possible the character that the dramatist created, yet adding to the part an original spark of their own. They must also work within the director's (or producer's) personal plan for that particular production, and absorb his/ her interpretation of the part too.

Obviously some plays ask more of the performers than others, but in general television and cinema have made audiences far more critical, demanding far higher standards, far more 'believable' and realistic performance, whether it is Shakespeare or a TV soap opera, from all actors and actresses. Today, actors and actresses also have to be very versatile, and be able to adapt to the very different technical demands of stage, film, television and radio. Very few in the profession can now afford to restrict their careers to stage or film. Being a 'specialist' actor or actress (eg 'Shakespearean') is virtually a thing of the past. Being 'typecast' is to risk very long periods of unemployment in a profession where some 80% are unemployed at any one time.

Prospects for young actors and actresses, however talented, however well trained, however tough and determined, go from very bad to much worse. The theatre has been declining for more than forty years and cinema for thirty, and both suffered very badly indeed from the economic recession. Even theatre for schools, and local authority support for theatres are affected by cuts in public expenditure. Few films are produced in Britain: films are made with money raised internationally, on an international basis, and in locations where costs are lowest, which means there is no protected film work for British actors and actresses. Television and radio drama can in no way make up for the quite enormous loss of work in the theatre and films, especially as TV and radio plays and series tend to have relatively small casts.

Overcrowding and chronic unemployment in the profession are not new. Equity, the acting union, has about 33,000 members (1987), about half of whom are actors and actresses (the rest are dancers, and other entertainers). Estimates of numbers of acting members unemployed at any one time vary, but are rarely less than 75%, with an average employment of 17 weeks a year for men, and 12 for women. This, of course, hides the fact that the most successful work most of the time – sometimes doing a film or TV production while also appearing in the theatre – and the least successful very rarely (perhaps only at Christmas). At best, and when the theatre is showing more life than during the recession, Equity has estimated there is only enough regular work (and therefore an income on which it is possible to live) for at most 6500 actors and actresses. Making television and film commercials cushions life for some, but not beginners. Educational and training films, 'voice over' commentary for radio and TV documentaries, readings (of serials and poetry) for radio, TV and radio quiz and panel shows are all quasi-dramatic ways of improving income – but again generally only for established actors and actresses who will automatically attract an audience by their presence on a show, or who have a recognisable voice for commentary etc.

Very few of the 300 or so theatres used professionally have full-time, resident companies. Only a very small proportion of actors and actresses have, then, long-term contracts. Most work only for the period of a production (it may be a one-off show or a longer season) and for many there are long gaps in between, when an income has to be found from other work (or money saved to live on), but work which will allow time to go to any auditions. Most actors and actresses are dependent on (and must pay a percentage of earnings to) theatrical agents to provide the link with theatrical managements or television or film companies, to get them engagements, to put their names forward for parts, to tell them when new productions are coming, and to help them plan and promote themselves. A good agent is important, but the best agents can pick and choose the actresses and actors they will have on their books – and they usually choose people already showing some success. Getting on to the books of a 'top' agent can be a major step in itself.

Efforts are made continuously to cut the size of the profession, but so far success seems to have been limited to slowing down the increase in numbers. Equity casting agreements with employers now mean that normally only members of Equity may be considered for parts in the London West End theatre, the major subsidised companies, major pantomimes and tours, feature films, independent television productions, TV commercials, BBC television and radio productions. (See Recruitment and entry below for engagements which can be offered to beginners, ie non-members of Equity.)

Most people starting out in the professions do so in the provinces, in 'theatre-in-education', children's or rep companies, 'small-scale' or fringe companies.

ROYAL ACADEMY OF DRAMATIC ART

62 Gower St. London WC1E 6ED

Patrons   HM The Queen
HM Queen Elizabeth The Queen Mother

President Sir John Gielgud   *Chairman* Sir Richard Attenborough
Principal Oliver Neville MA PhD   *Administrator* Richard O'Donoghue

The Academy, which receives Acting and Stage Management students from all over the world, is of international standing in the field of professional training.

For all information write to the Administrator-Registrar

Even for people with real potential and full training there can be ten years of such work. The main aim is to gain as much experience as possible in a wide variety of different kinds of work, in theatre, film and TV (even on a local network), and to learn the different techniques and problems of each thoroughly through practice. There are always difficult decisions to make, such as whether or not to turn down a certain small part on the vague promise of something better, or whether to risk the kind of type-casting associated with taking on a part in a long-running TV serial. However despondent, actors and actresses must always appear regularly in accepted theatrical haunts. Actors and actresses increasingly look for financing for themselves for both theatre and films.

It is a peripatetic life (even for the successful), with much of the early years spent in lodgings. Nowadays films and television plays are more often than not 'shot' on location rather than in studios, and radio plays produced outside London. Working conditions are rarely comfortable, and rehearsals take place in any available space, only too often draughty church halls or empty warehouses. The working hours and frequent travelling throw actors and actresses into each other's company a great deal, and make long-term personal relationships difficult, especially with anyone outside the profession.

Recruitment and entry Continuous efforts are made to limit entry to acting, but they are almost impossible to enforce completely. Equity now has casting agreements (see above) which make Equity membership virtually essential to become a full-time actor or actress. Provisional membership of Equity depends on a current Equity contract and full membership on having done at least 40 weeks work as a provisional member. The main way of doing this is via an engagement with an employer who has a casting agreement with Equity which allows them to employ non-members of Equity. The main categories for actors are – as performer or assistant stage manager in a repertory, theatre-in-education, commercial children's, or fringe company. Strict quotas are set for the number of non-Equity members any of these companies may take. It is also possible to work as a chorus singer or dancer, as an ASM in some other companies, as an opera singer or ballet dancer, as a director or assistant director, professional broadcaster, and to try for Equity membership on the basis of an appropriate contract for any of these. A contract for extra or walk-on work in TV, films, or commercials is not normally accepted as qualification for membership. Net increase in Equity membership was about 3000 over 1983-6, only 2000 between 1978 and 1983.

Proposals have been made to limit entry further by restricting entry to those who have been to certain approved schools, but so far these have not been implemented. Although actors/actresses who have not been through drama-school training do have very successful careers, they are exceptions, and surveys do show that graduates from the reputable drama schools do have the best chances of success. Directors say the level of technical training always shows at audition, and it can take ten years on stage to learn what the schools can teach in two or three.

Acting takes intelligence, imagination, sensitivity, and the ability to observe and listen to people accurately and analyse their behaviour. Actors and actresses need to be well co-ordinated physically and able to control their bodies well even before training. They need to be able to submerge their own identity, and to work under and learn from constantly-critical direction and teaching, to have a positive personality, and a good memory. Acting also demands self-confidence, determination, dedication, initiative, guile, and courage, all far above the average. Physical attractiveness is not necessary for acting, but can help in getting related work.

There are also arguments for not starting on stage training straight from school. Today's acting 'styles' depend on intelligence and maturity, on knowing a great deal about people of all kinds to bring intelligent observation and characterisation to parts. Regular experience in good amateur drama can also be useful. A significant number of today's most successful actors and actresses came into the profession comparatively late, and say they benefited from their experience of working in other jobs.

Qualifications and training The National Council for Drama Training (founded on the recommendation of the Gulbenkian Foundation's 1975 report, *Going on the Stage*), is responsible for accrediting courses. The Council is made up of equal numbers of members from British Actors Equity, the drama schools, and employers (including the BBC, IBA, the Council of Regional Theatres, and West End theatre management) and observers from local authorities, arts councils, MSC, the DES, and the Drama and Theatre Education Council. The Gulbenkian report also suggested that the major employers, such as TV companies, have a responsibility to contribute to training, and thought that the

NCDT should encourage closer links between them and established drama schools. Recommendations that all entrants to the profession complete approved training have not been implemented.

Acting courses (all except Q Margaret NCDT-accredited) are at –
Birmingham: SSTDA; Bristol: Old Vic[1] ; Cardiff: Music/Drama; Edinburgh: Q Margaret; Glasgow: RSAND; Guildford: S Acting/Dance[1] ; London: Art Educational Schools, Central Speech/Drama, Drama Centre, Guildhall, LAMDA, Mountview[1] , RADA, Webber[1] ; Loughton: East 15 Acting S[1] ; Manchester P; Sidcup: R Bruford.

[1] one-year postgraduate course as well as three-year schemes

Schools aim to give students complete control over voice and movement, to instill creativity and flexibility, and teach detailed acting craft skills. Each school has a different approach and theories, and its own 'method'. Most courses combine these in a syllabus which generally covers voice production, improvisation, play analysis, mime, sight reading, history of the theatre, practical training in fencing and stage fighting, movement and dance, music and singing, and the different techniques for film, radio and TV, costume and make-up. Courses include acting and rehearsal classes and frequent productions. Some schools also teach students stage management.

Intake to these courses is a maximum 45 a year, with ratios of applications to places as high as 25 to 1. Sample surveys by Equity (now rather old) have show that, out of a total of about 500 actor entrants each year, nearly 40% were trained at these drama schools, representing 80% of those going into subsidised and commercial regional theatre and children's theatre where the Equity quota system applies.

'Other' courses: a range of schools not members of the Conference of Drama also teach acting. They include some 'straight' acting schools, some schools of speech and drama, some teaching drama as an extension, or replacement, of work in training (school) teachers in drama. Eleven university drama departments teach some practical skills including acting. See also DRAMA under ACADEMIC QUALIFICATIONS AND CAREERS.

In the past, about 30% of new Equity members have studied at 'other' drama schools, 15% either at university or in a college of education, 5% have come from overseas, and 10% were graduates who did not go to drama school and entrants with no formal training. There are no recent figures.

Entry to drama school is generally by audition. Although academic qualifications are not the most important criteria, most schools now expect entrants to have a 'good' general educational background as shown by, for example, a reasonable number of O-level-equivalent passes at 16-plus†, and some ask for A levels as well. Schools look for potential rather than achievement at audition, for good movement and co-ordination, the ability to improvise, imagination, a trainable voice and good ear, for example. They are not likely to be impressed by a career, however apparently brilliant, in school drama or even as a child actor or actress.

See also THEATRICAL PRODUCTION, DRAMA (under QUALIFICATIONS AND CAREERS) and TEACHING (under EDUCATION).

Further information from the British Actors Equity Association and the National Council for Drama Training.

DANCING

Dancing is sometimes treated simply as entertainment, but some people see it as an art form. It uses the human body like a musical instrument, and it has to be tuned and played as finely as a violin.

There are two main careers for performers – ballet and modern stage dancing, and it is usual to specialise in one or the other (although the occasional ballet dancer does change to modern stage dancing). So many people learn dancing for pleasure, that teaching is also a possible career in its own right. Ballet makes the greatest demands on the dancer and on the dancer's body. A ballet dancer's life has to be totally dedicated to and disciplined by those demands. A ballet dancer may not ride a bicycle or a horse, because this develops the wrong muscles, for example. Professional-level training has to start extremely early (see Qualifications and training below), and before it is clear whether the child will in fact grow to the required height or shape. Progressively, more and more time of every single day, without exception, has to be spent in practice and exercise, to reach levels of physical fitness and agility greater than is needed by most Olympic athletes. Ballet dancers also have to be able to act, and to be able to interpret a role artistically.

Performing on stage is therefore only the tip of the iceberg for ballet dancers, who are generally employed full-time by a ballet company. Most of their days are spent in spartan practice rooms, and they must go on exercising even when technically on holiday or there are no performances. Probably no more than 250 ballet dancers have full-time jobs in Britain, and only a tiny proportion become principals or soloists. But UK-trained ballet dancers can find work abroad. An active performing career usually comes to an end by the age of 35 or 40 for women, possibly later for men.

Modern stage dancers work throughout the entertainment business – on stage, in musicals and pantomime, on television in light entertainment programmes, and in cabaret and clubs. Large film musicals are no longer commercially viable, and although there is probably more work than there used to be, it is generally for much smaller groups, although some large-scale stage musicals have been put on. Perhaps 1000 or so are in regular employment. Nowadays most stage dancers are contracted just for length of a production, but a few permanent troupes and some small groups still work together regularly. Again, more time is spent in auditions, and in rehearsing and building routines in draughty church halls than on the stage itself. The training, physical and artistic demands are not so great as for the ballet. Although early professional training is useful, it is possible to start rather later than for ballet, and the enthusiastic disco-dancer (for example), who has kept up with lessons may be able to start as late as eighteen. Competition for work is very intense. Again, the British-trained dancer can find work overseas, but it is sensible not to do so without experience in this country first, and Equity must be consulted before accepting any engagement abroad.

Almost all dancers, ballet and modern dance, though, have to find a second career normally by their mid-thirties. For a few, in either ballet or modern dancing, there is choreography, creating and composing dances. This needs years of experience, a good musical training and sense, imagination and creativity. Others teach – some from the beginning of their careers – in ordinary schools (full- or part-time), in private dancing classes or smaller dancing schools, and may specialise in teaching children, or adults, or in professional schools of dance and drama. Dancing is also widely taught in higher-education colleges, but usually by teachers who have come through the same kind of training, and have rarely been professional dancers. People who have the resources can start their own schools or classes. There is usually plenty of work for dance teachers, but the financial rewards are generally rather poor (some of the pay may be 'in kind', providing dancers with the facilities to practise etc) and this usually means having to supplement the school income with private lessons. It is possible to find teaching posts abroad. Teaching involves knowing a lot about ballet, classical, modern dance and ballroom dance techniques, being a reasonable organiser, able (and prepared) to direct student productions.

Recruitment and entry It is rare for dancers to be employed professionally without full training. Dancing can become a career only for a very small proportion of the many thousands of children for whom it is a dream. It has been estimated that even of those who are fully trained only one in ten become full-time professional dancers. Even an accident which would be a small problem to someone else – a damaged foot, for example – can end a promising career.

Before any child is allowed to start on the long and rigorous regime which is necessary for a career in dancing, parents should ensure that their potential is thoroughly and expertly assessed, preferably by an independent, leading teacher or dancer and not by a local school. This should include tests to predict growth rate, and medical checks to make sure there are, for example, no joint weaknesses. LEAs may use CDET testing before awarding places or grants.

A dancer's body has to be the correct shape, proportion and size. A strong back, well-formed feet (the bone structure is crucial), and good muscle co-ordination are essential. Neck and set of head are important for the ballet, and girls must stay slight and small boned. All dancers have to be naturally well poised and graceful, and not 'gawky'. Modern stage dancers can be, and often are, much taller than ballet dancers, and they should have long legs. Every dancer has to be very healthy indeed, and strong enough to stand up to the long hours of exhausting practice and exercise. Dancers need to be reasonably intelligent, to have a strong musical sense, of rhythm and timing, plus some acting potential, especially imagination and intuition. It is useful to be able to play the piano.

Qualifications and training Ballet students must start serious, near-professional level training by the age of eleven. Training is extremely demanding and must start when the body is still developing. Where possible this should be at a professional residential school where training is combined with a good general education, but the number of places is very limited. The alternative is to study part-time with a well-qualified teacher who prepares pupils for one of the officially-recognised grade examinations of, for example, the Royal Academy of Dancing (RAD), the Imperial Society of Teachers of Dancing (ISTD), the International Dance Teachers Association (IDTA), and the British Ballet

Organisation (BBO). The acceptability of any school or course should be checked with a relevant organisation.

Full-time training for ballet dancers at least must begin by the age of 16, and to have even the opportunity to dance for the Royal Ballet, this has to be at the Royal Ballet upper school. Not all Royal Ballet school students are chosen for the Royal Ballet, though. Many other companies recruit primarily from the Royal Ballet and Rambert Schools.

Modern stage dancers are generally advised to start full-time training also by 16. Many study ballet up to intermediate level, although there are no hard and fast rules. Many then complete the full ballet course, but they can do modern stage dancing. Most good ballet schools teach not only classical ballet and modern stage dancing, but also national and Greek dancing, mime and choreography, notation and musical appreciation.

It is possible to train part-time, but given the level of competition (there is no guarantee that even full-time training will ensure work), it is more sensible to gain as much training as possible.

A number of dance schools (post-16) have now been accredited by the Council for Dance Education and Training. They are –
Bedford: London College of Dance/Drama; Camberley: Elmhurst Ballet School; Chester: Hammond School; Crowbridge: Legat School; East Grinstead: Bush Davies School; Epsom: Laine Theatre Arts; London: Arts Educational Trust School, Brooking School of Ballet/General Education, Central Ballet School, Italia Conti Academy, Laban Centre (Goldsmiths' C), London Contemporary Dance School, London Studio Centre, Rambert Ballet School (W London IHE), Royal Academy of Dancing, Royal Ballet School, Stella Mann School, Urdang Academy; Manchester: Northern Ballet School; Sidcup: Doreen Bird College of Theatre Dance.

Colleges of higher education, some polytechnics, and even several universities offer a wide variety of courses. Some are linked with drama, movement studies, sports etc, and may have 'grown' out of courses designed to train teachers – and some still do. Although these do not train at all for ballet, or for the more down-to-earth requirements of the entertainments industry, some enterprising students and groups from the schools do find audiences for their creative work in dance. More usually, though, people from these courses go on to teach. See QUALIFICATIONS AND CAREERS for degree and related courses. To teach in schools, formal teaching qualifications are needed, see under EDUCATION.

Further information from the Council for Dance Education, the Scottish Council for Dance, the Dance Council for Wales, the Imperial Society of Teachers of Dancing, International Dance Teachers Association, and British Actors Equity Association.

LIGHT ENTERTAINMENT

This, the world of comedian/mimics and variety artists, singers etc, is a career which depends almost entirely on the ability to capture an audience, and on personality. While the majority of old-style variety playhouses are long gone, there is steady demand for such performers mainly from clubs and cabarets, and particularly the new-style night clubs of the industrial areas of Britain, cruise ships, holiday camps, and for the best, radio and television.

A career as a popular entertainer is never easy, and even the most successful can suffer long periods of semi-obscurity. It demands a high degree of intelligence and intuition about the business to be able to stay abreast of trends in public taste and not to go on with a particular act until it has been over-used. One problem faced by the modern entertainer is the insatiable demand for new acts and new scripts because so many people hear or see them on the media. Before radio and television entertainers could live for many years on the same act, but today they must constantly change their performances.

In the past, entertainers have generally come into the business via a family connection, but this is traditionally a field for the able amateur who has built up an act and gained audience approval on, eg a local pub circuit, to break into. Formal training, however, eg a drama course followed by a period with a repertory company is useful, and can improved entertainers' chances of success. Of course contacts, a good agent, and some luck come into it too.

Further information from the British Actors Equity Association.

MODELLING

Models are used in advertising, promotional and sales campaigns, for clothes, for holidays, cars, and domestic products, such as toothpaste and cosmetics. Modelling is used to create illusions and so uses 'show-business' techniques, which means it is often mixed up with the entertainment world.

There are two different types of modelling – live and photographic. It is difficult to combine the two, because they often require quite different physical characteristics, but they do overlap.

Most 'live' models work in the fashion business, either full-time for a fashion house, or on a full-time basis.

In the fashion house, designers 'create' clothes on the live model, cutting, pinning and draping the clothes as they go, which means long hours spent standing still. Models display the clothes to customers, who may be buyers for stores as well as better-off individuals, and show the clothes in regular, twice-yearly 'collections'. Freelance models work for fashion houses which do not employ their own, are taken on just for collections, work in fashion shows for larger stores, and also do promotional work – showing jewellery, and appearing at, for example, car shows and other exhibitions.

While the most popular photographic work is for the very glamorised fashion and other magazines, this provides work for only a very few, 'top' models. The 'bread-and-butter' work for most photographic models comes from mail order catalogues, holiday brochures, advertisements for toothpaste, cosmetics, and washing up powders. A few models find some work on filmed TV commercials, but generally these are done by actors and actresses with Equity cards. Good feet and hands can be used in advertisements for shoes, jewellery, stockings, etc.

Modelling really is a tough, physically demanding and exhausting life, except for the very few who get to the very top, and very hard work. Most models spend much of their time standing, or rushing from one engagement to another, or changing clothes as fast as they can, or repairing their make-up. Much of their time is spent in hot, over-crowded, airless, and generally uncomfortable places. None of which is good for their appearance, on which their livelihood depends. Even so they must appear cool and unruffled – no sweat, and no goose pimples – calm, even arrogant, all the time. The way the fashion business is organised generally has photographic models huddled in winter clothes under hot lights in a stuffy studio in summer, and freezing near-naked on winter beaches in swimwear. There is rarely time to enjoy exotic locations.

Men are generally employed mainly as photographic models, but may also do fashion-show work.

There is marginally more work for fashion than photographic models, at least at the top. Photographic models earn more, but have to pay more of their own expenses, clothes etc. Work lasts for as long as the model's face and figure looks young enough and fits in with the current trend. There is some modelling of clothes for older and larger people. Intelligent models use the time when they are working to make contacts for later on, for example, teaching in model school, fashion consultancy, or in public relations in fashion houses or stores, or selling. It is extremely rare and difficult to get into acting via modelling, except for those who clearly have acting ability and 'star' quality anyway, and even they must get Equity cards.

Recruitment and entry It is rare for agencies or other employers to take on untrained models.

To become a model, body and face must match the current 'image'. Height and other measurements are usually crucial too – they do change but 5 ft 6 ins is a generally-accepted minimum height for women and rather taller for men. An 'interesting' appearance rather than conventional 'beauty' is the ideal, but photographic modelling probably demands a good facial bone structure. Models need to be well co-ordinated, able to move well even before training. Models should usually have a flair for making any clothes they wear look good, and be able to adapt their appearances to different clothes, different fashions, and different conditions. They should have an interest in and ability to stay ahead of trends – in hair and make-up as well as clothes and accessories. Models need to be very healthy, and physically strong. They need intelligence and emotional stability to cope in a very tough business.

Reputable model schools will make a completely ruthless assessment of anyone's chances of gaining work as a model before accepting them – and do not accept for career training those who have no chance at all. If several reputable schools say that someone has no chance, it is sensible to accept their advice.

Qualifications and training Training is more or less essential for women. The smaller numbers of male models are generally allowed to look more 'natural', and so if their appearance is acceptable, can learn the few physical 'tricks' needed from eg photographers.

All but one school in Britain is commercially run, and costs are high. It is crucial to go to a good and reputable school, the best of which are linked to a reputable agency. Good schools introduce their successful students to agencies and possible employers, and generally tell students, during the course, if they are not going to be successful, normally refunding part of the fee.

The London College of Fashion and Clothing Technology course, for which entry is three O-level-equivalents at 16-plus†, lasts a year, is broader than most, including selling, business studies and fashion sketching as well as modelling techniques. At a reputable commercial school the four- to six-week courses generally cover, in addition to modelling itself, individual tuition in make-up, skin care, hair-styling, exercises, movement and mime, dress sense, and basic techniques of posing for the camera.

See also ARTS AND DESIGN, RETAILING and under INDUSTRY.

MUSIC
Music of some kind, serious classical, modern and avant-garde as well as 'rock' and 'pop', light music and jazz, is listened to by most people in Britain at some time and at some level. Most children can now learn to play a musical instrument at school, and rock/pop is still a major ingredient of teenage life.

Although music is still very popular, the economics of the music 'industry' change frequently. Musicians, as individuals or as members of orchestras or groups, depend for a living on a delicate balance between live performances and recording, with broadcasting too (or instead) for some. Musical skills, technical expertise and clever financing made London a major classical recording centre, and this is threatened. Now classical record divisions are relying more on old stock and going abroad to record because it is cheaper. While record sales have recovered, and cassette sales continue to rise, all kinds of 'new technology' from compact discs to digital audio tapes create many uncertainties for the future.

Orchestras are not threatened, but there are problems for musicians. The number of live performances of music continues to fall. Britain spends far less on serious music than other European countries, and rising costs are in any case cutting into the profitability of orchestras, and mergers have been suggested.

Working as a musician

Career opportunities for musicians never did expand with public interest in music grew. People may listen to more music than ever before, but it is played by fewer and fewer musicians. Radio, and technically high-quality, relatively cheap music systems have accustomed the listening public to hear the very best performers in the comfort of their own homes – and therefore the audience for all but world-class orchestras and performers has largely vanished. The disco revolution decimated the dance band, and hotels and restaurants have long abandoned their palm court and tea-dance orchestras, leaving mainly the club and pub circuits (many of which employ mainly semi-professionals), and much slimmer gig circuits for the rock groups. Now the computer-based synthesiser, which can simulate several instruments at once, is also replacing human musicians – largely at present in theatre orchestra pits (cutting numbers in half), and in 'session' work, providing backing for groups and solo artists in the recording studio.

The Musicians Union has some 40,000 members, but estimates suggest regular full-time employment for only a small proportion of them. Life for most professional musicians is very tough and insecure, whether they play serious/classical, pop/rock, jazz or any other kind of music, sing, or are composers or conductors. However talented and well trained, it may take some years to get established. Except for the full-time posts, it is usually necessary to take on all kinds of work to live – even otherwise 'serious' musicians will take on session work playing 'pop' music. It may mean extensive travelling, and rehearsals in difficult and uncomfortable conditions. Fame and fortune, to match the talent and hard work of the majority of professional musicians, happens to very few. Even the smallest accident to a pianist's or violinist's hands, or to teeth for a wind player, can mean the end of a career.

COMPOSING Under a dozen composers of serious music make enough money to live solely on their writing, and several hundred may be trying to do so. (The Composers Guild has about 500 members.) An unknown number, but it is not very many, make some kind of income from more popular music, although many groups write their own. The Performing Right Society, whose members write music of all kinds, has some 14,960 writer members (publishers also belong), but only 1712 are full members. To become a full member at present requires PRS earnings of £2000 in each of two out of any three consecutive years. Full members took 77% of royalties paid out in 1985, and only about 500 get £5000 or more in any one year. Most get less than £250.

Only a very small number of new 'serious' works are performed in any year, some of them commissioned. The real problem, though, for the composer is to persuade a publisher to print the work (with all the orchestral parts) so that it can go into the repertoire for all orchestras. Most established composers, except for the most eminent, make their living from writing film scores and music for television. Some also conduct.

CONDUCTING Full-time work for very few people indeed. Although young conductors are generally more acceptable to orchestras and audiences today, in serious music youth is still something of a disadvantage. Conducting a full orchestra demands a great deal of experience. A conductor has technical skills to learn, must know a great deal about all the instruments in the orchestra, and their capabilities. Orchestral music is extremely complex, and the conductor must know each work well. It takes maturity and in-depth knowledge to be able to interpret it properly. Plenty of experience of working with musicians and maturity is also needed to handle players, gain their confidence, and perhaps persuade them to perform works in particular ways. In a sense, an orchestra or choir is the conductor's instrument, and he or she must be able to persuade it to play for them as if it were one.

Aspiring conductors therefore generally find themselves spending years playing an instrument, teaching, singing, and at the same time working with any available amateur or semi-professional group, children's or youth orchestras while waiting to find an opportunity to work with a professional group or orchestra. There are also some posts in Britain and Europe for *repetiteurs* (rehearsal pianist) which is the traditional continental way for conductors to train. Since orchestras today have very heavy schedules, there are opportunities to stand in for a conductor at rehearsal or for the occasional concert (there are a few formal traineeships), or to take part in a festival – but it is still a long way to go to a contract. Some young conductors have started their own orchestras in the past.

INSTRUMENTAL PLAYING There is full-time work for, at most, 2000 instrumental players in the major British symphony, string and operatic orchestras, and this includes the 500 employed by the BBC. It also includes freelance musicians who fill in for full-time players, and about 200 who work for the London theatres (but of course the two groups may overlap). About 4000 musicians, in all (including both people who normally play serious music as well as those who play light and pop music), make some of their income from freelance session work. The only other full-time posts are in the regimental and other bands of the three armed forces, but mainly only for wind, pipe and percussion players. Few full-time bands now play popular music or for ballroom dancing.

Opportunities for work vary with the instrument. Prospects are probably best for string players, particularly violinists, since they form the largest section of most orchestras, and there has been a world-wide shortage of string players, particularly good ones, for some time. There is probably some demand for the more unusual and difficult instruments, like the bassoon. In between, there is intensive competition to play popular instruments, like the flute, where orchestras need only two or three each, and to gain an income as a concert pianist, for whom there is no place at all in any orchestra. Violin players, though, may have to work and wait for many years to move up to the front desks, while the flautist, once a member of an orchestra, can get solo work much sooner.

Orchestral life combines concerts, recording sessions, and regular rehearsals with quite a lot of travelling. Most orchestras are fully booked for long periods ahead – and they have to take on as much work as possible to make a reasonable living for their members, who have to pay for their instruments, dress clothes, and so on. Orchestral players work unusual hours, which can be long, but players can decide not to play for a particular concert – as long as they can find a good-enough replacement.

Many instrumental players want to become solo performers, but this demands much greater talent even than is needed to play in an orchestra. This is not just virtuoso-standard musical talent, but also the personality and stamina to match. Some players aim for a solo career from the moment they leave music school, while others go on playing with an orchestra while trying to establish themselves as soloists. Solo work involves far more and harder practice than is normally needed by orchestral players (most young soloists expect to study and practise for at least six hours a day), because the music is generally artistically, technically, and physically much more demanding, and a reasonable repertoire of solo parts has to be built up.

Over 200 attempt to make a living as pianists (including international stars). Only about six can fill a major concert hall. As an alternative to solo work, pianists are employed as accompanists for singers and choirs, and for rehearsals, but few posts are full-time. Concert and recital organ playing can support very few organists. Organ-playing is loosely linked with choir-training, since the majority of church organists are also choirmasters. Only cathedrals and largest other church centres have full-time organists; fewer and fewer can afford to pay their organists-cum-choirmasters more than minimal expenses. Crematoria employ organists on a sessional basis. Although interest in older keyboard instruments, such as the harpsichord, has grown it is difficult to make a living playing, so most musicians therefore play more than one such instrument.

Getting work, gaining experience, becoming known and established is the major problem for every instrumental player, orchestral or solo. This can take a long time and a great deal of luck. Orchestral places, for which players audition, are few and far between, and plenty of experience is normally asked for, so posts rarely go to people just out of music school. Most young musicians take whatever work is offered. Of six French-horn players graduating from music school in any one year, one may, through a chance contact, be given an evening's work, play very well, and find that s/he is in increasing demand, while the other five go on waiting for their first engagement. The traditional recital, for which the young musician pays and invites critics and impresarios to listen, is not now used so much, except by some hopeful soloists. For many soloists, though, and particularly pianists and violinists, much more depends now on competing in, and winning, international musical competitions. Music schools, concert promoters, and one or two trusts, try to make opportunities for young players to be heard, and some players now have professional agents. The chance to make a record is a major step forward. Occasionally, a group of instrumentalists manages to start an ensemble of their own while still at college, and to make a reasonable living from it afterwards, but it is rare, despite the increased number of ensembles in regular work.

Freelance musicians, young or older, have very varied working lives. They may fill in for a member of one orchestra (who may be sick, resting or have a conflicting solo engagement) one day, and play in a quartet another. Another day they may 'augment' another orchestra playing a very large-scale work. Versatility is needed to take advantage of 'session' playing – backing for records, television commercials, films, radio and TV plays, and documentaries. They may also play regularly with a group of friends from musical school in an ensemble which produces some income, and they may play in festivals where they have got to know the organisers. At the other end of the scale are summer shows, and a few musicians 'busk'. Many musicians also teach privately, and some take part in a wide range of musical activities for children, for instance running LEA holiday orchestras.

POP/ROCK MUSIC Making an income in pop/rock music depends not so much on conventional talent on an instrument or in singing, but on the ability to find and create a 'sound' and an image which will sell, and to stay ahead of what must be near-unpredictable trends, perhaps singing and playing alone, but more usually as part of a group.

It is a fast-changing business. Record companies make several thousand singles a year, trusting that a proportion will make an impact and a profit. Only a handful of groups make it to the top fifty, and only a handful survive more than three or four years, reforming with different names and different musicians to try to keep pace.

Most groups start in a small way, playing together as friends and then trying for local pub and club gigs. A new group can make a 'demo' tape, which is now often also needed to get on to the bigger gig circuits. Independent labels (of which there are now some 300 or more) will turn a tape into a disc if it has any commercial chance at all, paying percentages that only a Beatle ever commanded from the major record companies. The great majority of groups only ever manage to become semi-professional, and life on the gig circuits for groups trying to make the grade can be very uncomfortable. Increasing success brings increasing expenses, including the cost of a manager, public relations, technicians, equipment, and 'roadies'.

SINGING There are no figures to show how many singers can make a full-time career in opera, oratorio or concert work, but since there are only five opera companies in Britain, and fewer live performances of oratorio and other serious choral or solo concerts for voices every year, the number has to be very small. Operatic soloists, especially, sing internationally, contracted to sing for seasons or a number of performances all over Europe, in Britain, America and Australia, with recording sessions and sometimes concert tours in between. They have to be able to sing roles in several languages, and have a repertoire (mostly learnt in their own time) large enough to give them enough engagements to provide an income, yet not too heavy to keep in practice. Solo singers have especial problems of getting known and gaining experience, because their voices must be allowed to mature only slowly, and they may not sing the most powerful roles until they reach their thirties.

Singers also work for opera chorus (they rarely make the change from chorus to solo work), but otherwise the opportunity to sing professionally in a choir is very limited, except in a few cathedrals and very large churches. There is some session work, and still some light music for stage musicals, pantomime, radio and television, but this generally also involves some acting and dancing.

OTHER OPPORTUNITIES for people who are musically talented or have musical interests are not extensive.

Administration People with musical backgrounds and qualifications are employed in administering and managing concert halls, opera houses, musical festivals, orchestras etc. Some universities, polytechnics etc have their own directors of music to organise a full programme of concerts etc. See also ARTS ADMINISTRATION.

Broadcasting A high proportion of radio output is music, considerably less on television, where it is largely 'background'.
Pop/rock, light music output is generally handled by the programme production teams. Disc-jockeys are generally broadcasters with popular appeal first, but usually know a lot about pop music. Very few specialist posts need musical skills. The BBC's music division looks after all orchestral, chamber music, recital and operatic output. The division employs a small number of music producers who are responsible for programmes, assess standards of musical performance, keep in contact with artistes and orchestra, stay abreast of trends and developments in music-making from local to international level, and contribute generally to keeping up high standards. Performing ability is not needed, but producers must have good professional qualifications, some experience of organising and promoting music and of programme-building, sound musical and critical judgement, wide knowledge of repertory artists and so on, ability to plan, tact, and an imaginative approach to music broadcasting. One radio production traineeship annually is in classical music.
The BBC also employs three music presentation assistants in London to provide announcers with presentation material for music programmes. They must be able to write and have extensive knowledge of the musical repertory. There are a few staff accompanists.
Orchestral management staff assist with general routine and correspondence and although a professional music qualification is not essential, they do need to know how orchestras and chorus work and are made up, must be able read a score, know how to organise players for performance, have a wide knowledge of appropriate repertoire, and be able to work with young musicians.
Senior music librarians need a strong musical background.
See also BROADCASTING.

Journalism: music journalism expanded quite sharply with the pop/rock boom and the birth of specialist papers, but still supports probably at most 100 people. Only a handful of 'quality' newspapers and magazines employ 'serious' music critics. Both kinds require journalist skills combined with a solid musical background which should not be too narrow. See also JOURNALISM.

Library work Some public libraries, a few 'special' libraries (most notably the BBC's with a staff of 40), university and other college libraries where music is taught, employ music librarians to build and care for collections of books, scores, records, tape etc. While most such libraries of any importance employ only qualified librarians, a musical background, and preferably degree, is obviously useful. Most orchestras also employ someone to look after their scores. See also LIBRARY WORK.

Music therapy A few people work with adults and children suffering from emotional or mental stress/illness, or with some form of handicap. They use music, often teaching people to play an instrument, to relieve stress, or to help the handicapped develop musical skills and so self confidence etc, and possibly add other skills – eg co-ordination – too. Therapists work, usually on a session basis, for hospitals, schools, rehabilitation units, local groups etc.

Publishing Music publishers employ relatively small numbers of people with technical music skills, as editorial assistants, copyists, and arrangers. Book publishers do employ a very small number of people with music degrees if they publish books on music regularly. See also PUBLISHING.

Record business The business has been through a bad period, with major companies thinning their artistic repertoire and promotional staff drastically, and independents existing on the slimmest possible staff. On the technical side, recession made survival very difficult for the very many small studios.
Record company staff and the people who supply supporting services and contacts within the the music world are frequently trained musicians. The work includes negotiating with musicians, organising recordings, and arranging, to writing material for record sleeves, etc. Getting work tends to depend on making the right contacts.

Teaching of instrumental skills and techniques only, or more broadly-based in schools, universities, music colleges etc, has been suffering from cuts in educational expenditure. This is limiting opportunities in state-funded institutions quite severely. Some LEAs employ music organisers (some of whom double as inspectors), to co-ordinate musical activity in the schools and manage any special provision, eg youth orchestras and teaching for able pupils.
Competition for school and other full-time and even 'peripatetic' instrumental teaching is now considerable, although there may be some shortages of people to teach the less usual instruments. Teaching requires commitment and cannot be treated as a financial safety net. Full-time school teaching now requires a professional qualification.
Many musicians teach instruments privately. No teaching qualification is needed for instrumental teaching.
Universities, colleges of (higher) education, polytechnics, and music schools employ lecturers, and instrumental teachers, but the number of new posts is now very limited, and high academic and/or musical qualifications are needed. See also EDUCATION.

Recruitment and entry It is possible to find work as a musician, notably in pop/rock, without training first, but opportunities in an extremely competitive field are greatly improved for anyone who has gained technical skills. (Skilled musicians are recruited by all the Forces up to the age of 39 – standards of entry, especially for the senior regiments, are very high indeed but there is a training entry, see below.)

Exceptional talent for playing at least one, and normally two (or more), instruments, is essential. 'Perfect pitch', which means being able to identify notes and sounds accurately, is a major advantage, but can be learnt with hard work. Orchestral and ensemble players need faultless technique, must be able to read music efficiently, have a good sense of musical style, and enjoy playing (working) with others. Musicians need to have physical stamina and very good health – wind and brass players, for example, need strong lungs and teeth, and it takes real strength to play some instruments. Musicians have to be the kind of people who can get off a train or plane and go straight into a rehearsal or even a concert and play as well as ever.

With the level of competition, musicians need to have a certain amount of pushyness, initiative, and talent for being in the right place at the right time. It also helps to be rather more hard-headed about the music business than many musicians are now.

Qualifications and training Musical training ought to start extremely young, well before there is any sign of outstanding talent, or any suggestion of a potential career. No child should be forced to learn to play an instrument before they show an interest, however. It is generally best to start with an instrument rather simpler than a piano, and one that can be played in a group. A few children do show early virtuoso talent and are themselves keen to play seriously and in public, but for the majority talent should be allowed to develop as naturally as possible, without any pressure but with good teaching. A child still showing talent and enjoyment at nine or ten should start a second instrument, normally piano.

Serious work has to begin at eleven or soon after, but generally (and there will always be exceptions) and if possible this should be as part of, or alongside, normal secondary schooling (there are a few schools, including choir schools for boys, where children's musical talents are trained to professional level without affecting their academic work). Despite the cuts, most LEAs give (or pay for) instrumental teaching to advanced levels, have their own youth orchestras, organise Saturday music schools and holiday courses for their pupils who have musical ability and interest. It obviously means a great deal of extra work, but keeping up a good general education is extremely important. Careers in music are too uncertain, and no child should be committed to such a career any younger than is absolutely necessary.

The normal route from school into performing is via a specialist music school (preferably at eighteen with one or more A levels but possible at sixteen), although some very successful musicians have studied only privately with leading performers and/or teachers of their instruments. Gaining entry to a music school, competitive as it is, is no guarantee of a successful career. It is estimated that at most one in ten of those who graduate become full-time musicians. A place at musical school demands exceptional talent and achievement, and it is probably not even worth considering this with less than a distinction in Associated Boards examinations at grade VIII on one instrument, and grade VI on a second.

Few university or other degree courses give intensive enough instrumental training for a professional performing career – these courses are more academic/theoretical. For music courses at university and music school, see MUSIC under QUALIFICATIONS AND CAREERS.

An alternative way of training is via the Army, Marine and RAF music schools and military bands (the Navy recruits only trained musicians). They recruit 16-17-year-old boys (the Army also takes girls) with musical aptitude direct from school. They do not actually have to be able to play an instrument but it is an advantage. Entrants are given a thorough musical training as well as a general education for 18 months; anyone who shows exceptional promise is given advanced tuition on full-time courses and there are also three-year courses for potential bandmasters. Ex-military musicians are members of national orchestras.

Most intending professional musicians expect to go on studying after their first course at music school.

Instrumental players can go, for example, to the national orchestral centre (at London: Goldsmiths'), or to train for chamber orchestra work at Manchester: Northern College of Music. Some go to conservatoire abroad, and/or to study with particular musicians or teachers. For singers, voice training has to be spread over some ten years. The London Opera Centre provides training for postgraduate students who have already studied opera as part of a music training; singers normally spend one or two years at the Centre, which teaches operatic acting, roles movement, languages, make-up and fencing. The Royal Scottish Academy of Music has a similar course.

Music therapy training is available at – London: Guildhall, Roehampton IHE.

Pop/rock/jazz music training has barely existed, but a small number of courses have been reported recently, most notably at London: Goldsmiths'.

Further information from the British Actors Equity Association, the Choir Schools Association, the Incorporated Society of Musicians, the London Opera Centre, the Music Teachers' Association, the Musicians Union, and the Performing Right Society.

PROFESSIONAL SPORT

Sport is firmly part of the entertainments industry. Even the language of the entertainment industry is widely used in professional sport – top professional sports men and women are called 'stars'; the income, for a few, can be astronomic, and they have all the glamour and media-interest the entertainments industry expects.

Professional sports men and women are expected to entertain their audiences, to be 'personalities', as well as to play at ever higher standards, and so to ensure an income and a profit for all the huge sub-structure of interests which have developed around sport.

These interests range from the firms making and selling to the general public sports gear and equipment which is a replica of that used by the professional, through newspapers which sell more copies if their sports coverage is good, to the bookmakers. In some sports, eg boxing and snooker, players may be the earners for a management 'team'. Direct and indirect sponsorship of sport by business and commerce is also part and parcel of many sports (although the scale of investment fluctuates with the economic climate).

The effect of all this is an increasingly commercial attitude to sport itself, and of course greater demands on the players. Play may have to be geared to both crowd-attracting and winning, which are not always the same thing. Players live under enormous psychological pressures, both within their sport – since winning takes psychological as well as physical stamina and training – and from outside, the media and the fans. Conditions of employment are still not as good as they should be, and it is still only the smallest handful of men and women who make the kind of money that gets headlines.

The rate at which the more popular entertainment sports burn up players is increasing, and the success-rate of young entrants falling. The increasing demand for new talent (with no greater chances of success, however), only serves to strengthen the popular image of professional sport as a highly glamorous occupation, especially as the off-field activities of professional sports men and women are paraded across the newspapers and TV screens.

Nevertheless, the attractions of professional sport, with all the fun of doing something really interesting well, and being paid for it, and the added bonus of outdoor life, potential public acclaim, opportunities for travel, and the fact that professional sport can take people into new social leagues – boxing was traditionally the bright working boy's route up the social ladder – must be balanced against the disadvantages.

The competition, throughout sports careers and not just to get started, is always intense. There is always the pressure of someone else trying to beat you for your position in the game. Then, professional sports men and women don't always enjoy the social life the newspapers suggest – to achieve what is demanded of them most have to be totally dedicated to their sport and must stay in top condition. Even travelling can become unpleasant when it means going straight from one tournament to the next without any time to relax and enjoy the scenery. The physical conditions in which sports are played are not always comfortable, and players often have the pain and discomfort of minor injury to live with.

However, the main disadvantage is that careers in sport are almost all extremely short. All professional sports men and women must expect to find themselves a second career. If they are very lucky indeed they may be able to go on playing until they are 30 or 35, which leaves another 30 or 35 working years. A high proportion are forced to end their playing careers much earlier than that, and many barely get started at all. Partly this is a natural hazard: people are bound to lose form, or to suffer injuries which make it impossible to continue. However, with players being pushed into playing to far higher standards at ever younger ages, and into playing more often, the odds on players simply burning out, or suffering disabling injury, are inevitably increased.

For every ten people playing there are thirty or more who can no longer do so. There is only non-playing work – training, managing, coaching, umpiring, administering etc – within their sports for a very small proportion of retired players, and some sports can still find people to do some of this part time or on a voluntary basis. The other, rather obvious, areas of possible work, such as sports JOURNALISM, are also overcrowded, and demand skills which sportsmen and women do not necessarily have. Some professionals make use of the commercial and business contacts they may have made during their playing careers – with sponsoring firms or the sportswear business, for example. The problems they meet are those of anyone going into business without the appropriate training and/or experience in the techniques needed to make a profit (see COMMERCE etc), and again they may not have the necessary aptitudes. Investing money earned during a sporting career in order to turn it into an income for life is as hazardous as investment is generally.

Most worthwhile, interesting and reasonably paid work these days requires some kind of preparation and training, and this is just as true for work started in middle life as for any other. Training for a high proportion of careers just cannot be started as late as the thirties. The incomes paid to players (and their contracts) take little or no account of this problem, and it is made worse because few players manage to stay at peak income throughout their playing lives – which means that towards the end they may not have the financial resources to prepare for something new. Provision for players to prepare for second careers is still, generally, very inadequate.

Young sports men and women must, then, take this problem very seriously before starting out on the route to a professional career. It is no use just assuming that 'something will turn up'. The pressure can be extremely strong to begin professional-level training, with all the time and effort that this involves, in the early to mid teens, without worrying about the apparently distant future.

It is sensible to plan and prepare for every eventuality. This means, first, carrying on with as broadly-based a general education for as long as possible and to as high a level as possible. All prospective professional players of any sport have to continue their general education to sixteen anyway, and they should take as many sixteen-plus examinations as they can. The arguments are strong for going further along the education route (see below). Even if, after careful consideration, a young player decides to go into full-time training at sixteen-plus, they should by then have some idea of what alternative careers interest them, and be firm about spending time regularly on some kind of preparation for this. This can be a part-time course (there are, for example, professional footballers doing degree courses part-time at their local polytechnics), taken throughout the year, or some form of intensive study/training during the out-of-season period (if it exists).

Recruitment and entry There are generally two ways of becoming a professional sports man or woman. One is straight from school, normally via a kind of apprenticeship, the other is to become a top-level amateur first and then switch to a professional career. The prevailing school of thought considers that any sport ought to be started as early as possible, with professional-level training beginning in early or mid-teens at the very latest. It is, however, very difficult to reconcile this with the need to make certain every entrant has the educational background to ensure that s/he can begin a second career in the mid-30s.

This implies that the amateur route may well be in the long-term interests of many potential professionals. Most higher education institutions have unrivalled facilities, including training, for most sports, some specialise (eg Loughborough), and some (eg Stirling) have a few sports scholarships to offer.

First division footballers, for example, have taken degrees and did not begin their professional careers until after graduation. A degree in the area of sport and/or physical education can also provide the basis of an alternative career, eg in the recreation and leisure industries.

Some sports managers object to the educationalists' argument, because they think that the idea of safeguarding against the possibility of failure creates a negative attitude amongst young players which in turn could result in their not succeeding. Parents and pupils should, however, be properly informed of both sides of the argument, whatever decision they may make.

All potential professional sports men and women must obviously be absolutely physically fit, and be the right shape, size etc for the sport in question. Most players spend a high proportion of their time keeping their bodies in peak condition, with continuous and often very strenuous exercise and rigorous training routines which must be combined with a life of considerable self-discipline.

A very real aptitude and ability for the sport in question is also, equally obviously, an absolute necessity. Every sport requires different physical and mental skills, although some sportsmen do combine sports. Many organisations recruiting young sports men and women complain that today's comparatively good living conditions produce youngsters who lack the 'killer' instinct that many sports require to play the game in a particular way. A professional player, today, is usually also an intelligent player, capable of understanding and exploiting tactical and psychological techniques, which in turn makes a better educational background useful. Emphasis is increasingly on the ability to concentrate, determination and the ability to come back after a defeat, and on being able to cope with the psychological and emotional stresses of high level competition.

The sports
It is not possible to earn a living in all sports. The main opportunities are in –

ATHLETICS is dominated by the Olympics, for which amateur status is required, so there can be no professional careers as such. However, the demands of international competition mean that most top athletes must still spend most of their time training and competing, and find it difficult to earn a living. They therefore have to accept financial assistance wherever they can find it, and trusts are now set up to allow them to benefit from, eg sponsorship, advertising etc, without jeopardising their amateur status.

BILLIARDS AND SNOOKER have been played professionally for many years, but only in the last ten years, built on better organisation of tournaments, heavy television exposure, a sharp rise in players' skills, 'packaging and personalities', and sponsorships has it been able to support players in any number. The right to play in professional tournaments is strictly controlled by the World Professional Billiards and Snooker Association. Only 128 snooker players are allowed to compete. Based on a point-award system, players are put in rank order at the end of each season. The ten lowest-ranked have to compete against the eight amateurs with the most points and the world and English amateur champions for those ten professional places in the coming season. A high proportion of professional players make most of their incomes from exhibition matches and straightforward personal appearances, on top of any prize money. Some run their own clubs etc.

Most potential snooker players show ability in their early teens - and should be playing for a club, county or regional team, and winning regularly. Learning good technique early is crucial. The best younger players are now signed up by professional managers.

BOXING was declining steadily until the early 1980s, but has recovered recently, to some 500 licensed boxers and more tournaments. However, no more than 30-40 make a reasonable income from boxing.

Whatever constraints and medical checks are set, there is no avoiding the fact that professional boxers have to sustain, and inflict, considerable physical injury on each other.

Since boxers are only paid for actual fights, and not for the long periods in between them, many professionals have to earn 'extras' via exhibition bouts, or as sparring partners, for example.

Boxing is one of the most physically demanding of professional sports. While contests are the pinnacle towards which a boxer works, most of his time is spent following a particularly severe training programme, aimed at building up and maintaining physical stamina, endurance, and muscle, and developing and improving boxing skills and techniques. Training becomes really punishing in the weeks before a fight, when the boxer moves into a strict, training-camp regime away from home. But in between fights boxers have to stay very fit and control their weight, with exercise, gym-, ring- and road-work.

Most professional boxers are contracted to boxing managers (a few may be managed by relatives or friends), under arrangements approved by the British Boxing Board of Control. The manager arranges contests and negotiates terms for each fight. He provides gymnasium and training facilities, training and contest staff, and arranges publicity etc. In return the manager takes an agreed percentage of the boxer's earnings. Since few earn very much in their early years, it follows that the manager treats young boxers as an investment, getting the income to finance them from the earnings of those who are established (or from sponsors), for example.

All boxers, managers, trainers, promoters and anyone else connected with professional contests must have a British Boxing Board of Control licence. The BBBC mainly attempts to see that boxers are not permanently injured. Regulations stipulate that every boxer must have a medical before each contest, proposed contests are vetted to prevent boxers being wrongly matched or exploited, and boxers must have had appropriate training before any contest.

Boys cannot have professional licences until they are 17, and must also satisfy the Board that they have reached a minimum standard. Even then they may not fight in major contests until they are over 20. There are no formal apprenticeship or training schemes for professionals, and so boys traditionally follow the amateur route, becoming members of, training and fighting for, boxing clubs, taking part in amateur contests frequently up to Olympic level, since success as a professional can depend on this. Taken with the BBBC age restrictions, this used to mean that boys rarely turned professional under 20, but managers now take on boys at the pre-Olympic stage. A boy can wait for a manager to approach him, or approach any manager (but they may then have to pay their own training expenses, which are extremely heavy).

CRICKET, supported by sponsors, TV coverage, 'super-stars', and one-day competitions, keeps up its popularity. However, only 17 'first-class' counties compete for the championships and cups with, between them, fewer than 320 players on contract.

Most cricketers are in full employment only during the season from mid-April to mid-September, during which time they play 20 to 30 three-day matches, beginning on Wednesdays and Saturdays, one-day knock-out competitions, and a one-day league, played on Sunday. Test matches with overseas teams intervene for those selected to play for England, and most counties also play any tourists. Top players tour overseas for the other half of the year, but the rest must find something else to do during the autumn and winter. Some play or coach overseas, or play a winter sport, like football.

Cricketers can play for almost any county (only Yorkshire now recruits solely from within its own boundaries), but many still play for their 'home' county, all the same. Clubs can also have one or two overseas players on contract. There is no transfer system between the clubs, so players normally stay with one club throughout their playing careers. Most players can expect to get into the first XI by the age of 25 if they are going to be good enough, and many go on playing until around 40 or over, although others give up before then to get into a second career. Very few find employment with the game, as coaches, club officials, umpires or scorers.

Most umpires are former players, and they must qualify through the Test and County Cricket Board, showing evidence of being 'technically and temperamentally qualified to stand'.

Most potential first-class cricketers have been spotted by their county club during their schooldays and if they have not, the school is generally the first to inform them. Most boy cricketers with potential will have played for county schoolboy sides, in any case. Some boys play in local league cricket to gain attention. The chances of a boy who has not been spotted by the time he is ready to leave school are therefore very slim. County clubs see hundreds of boys at trials; only a very few are offered engagement and the failure rate amongst these is very high. Young players spend their first years playing for club and second-XI sides.

CYCLING has revived to some extent in Britain, but is still extremely popular in continental Europe. There are at most 50 British professional riders. Almost all began as amateurs and are members of sponsored teams (not necessarily by cycle manufacturers). It is difficult to make a living from cycling, but some British cyclists do find regular work on the continent.

DARTS has become a popular professional spectator sport, with about 20 people now earning a living from it, and about four or five classed as 'super stars'. Professionals now compete in half a dozen or more major national competitions, and in between travel the country taking on local amateur teams and giving exhibitions. The difference between a professional and the 5000 or so top amateurs is said to be showmanship, the ability to keep the psychological advantage, and knowing the fastest and easiest combination of shots to give a specific number of points.

FOOTBALL is probably the world's most popular participatory and spectator sport. It is supported by, and supports quite a large commercial industry giving real problems when the game loses popularity. Fewer and fewer people – about 18 million in 1985 against 40 million in 1950 – go to matches. The industry is being squeezed between rising costs and falling income, with failure to solve deep-seated problems going back over many years adding to the difficulties.

Although many thousands of clubs are affiliated to one of the three Football Associations (England, Wales and Scotland), only 130 employ professional footballers (92 clubs compete in the four English/Welsh league championship divisions and 38 in the three Scottish-league divisions). Between them they employ (1987) around 2000 footballers. Given the present problems, clubs could go out of business or merge, and the number of full-time players is likely to be cut further.

The more prominent and successful the club, the larger the number of footballers on its books. A club's success depends not only on its footballers and their manager and trainers. Skilful business management is also crucial: every club has a board of directors, generally made up of local businessmen and/or personalities who either can invest in the club themselves or have access to funds. Without this players may find (and have been) themselves sold to another club, not because their play is poor, but because the club has to realise the investment they represent.

The football season is now so long that, taking into account overseas tours played in the summer months, few footballers now have more than a six-week break, so do not have to find other work out of season. Modern pressures do, in fact, result in many players finding that the number of matches they must play, with mid-week and Sunday matches, is a considerable strain, injury rates are up, and younger footballers are gaining places in first teams possibly too early for their proper development. Only the exceptional player manages to survive in a first-division first XI throughout his playing career (which probably lasts an average of about eight years). Most are transferred from club to club, either upwards as their talents develop or downwards as they decline, with changes in income and status to match.

The Professional Footballers' Association works continuously to improve conditions for professional footballers. Players are employed on contract, the terms depending on the player's status, skill and bargaining ability, and the financial standing of the club itself. Contracts are for one or more years, with the club retaining an option on the player for a period after that. Players whose services are not retained by a club for any reason, or who wish to move, are placed on transfer; for those with future potential the club may ask for a fee appropriate to the player's standing and abilities, the player receiving 15% of this if the transfer is initiated by the club (none if it is at the players' own request). A good season generally produces bonuses.

Training and travelling take up a large part of a professional footballer's time. Training combines exercise routines with ball practice designed to improve dexterity, balance and skill in play. Football demands tight team work, so practice at this and strategy also forms part of a day's activity. Travelling, and therefore periods away from family and friends, means a great deal of idle time on trains and planes and in hotels. The close relationship between players in a club has its advantages but also produces strains and tensions which can affect team performance on the field; temperament in players is not, therefore, very popular with management or fellow footballers.

Only a few players are able to stay with professional football when they retire, as coaches, trainers, managers or club secretaries. The Professional Footballers' Assocation, which has about 2500 members, estimates that under 3% of its members find permanent careers in management when they stop playing. The Football Association organises a wide range of certificate courses in training, coaching, ground maintenance, club administration, care of injuries, and refereeing. The Professional Footballers' Association provides advice, information and counselling, and the Footballers' Further Educational and Vocational Training Society, financed jointly by the Football League and the PFA, also helps. The FA also has a scheme which helps match candidates to club vacancies.

Recruitment, entry, training Potential professional footballers are usually 'spotted' by talent scouts while they are still at school, and it is rare for them to miss talented boys, although there is nothing to prevent a boy writing to a club for a trial.

Despite the inevitable tensions between school and clubs, clubs are allowed to register 'associated schoolboys', under strict regulations, from 13 on, but only for coaching and training, and only with the consent of school and parents. Associated schoolboys may not play for the club, except against other schoolboys, until the season after their fifteenth birthday. Clubs have options on associated schoolboys' services when they leave school. Boys must tell the club when they are leaving school three months' before, and the club has to tell the boy within fourteen days whether or not they wish to sign him as a full-time apprentice. If not, the boy is free to sign for another club. If the club makes an offer which does not seem good enough, a boy may sign for another club, but that club must compensate the registering club. The Professional Footballers' Association suggests it is not in boys' best interests to sign as associated schoolboys, but to keep their independence until they are ready to leave school.

Apprenticeships have now been replaced by a YTS scheme, with clubs taking some 600 boys a year, not just for football training and formal coaching, but also all-round work experience, and day-release to study at a local college. Boys may be accepted as professional from 17 onwards. The PFA suggests it is still better to stay on at school, or go on to further or higher education. A growing number of boys are joining professional clubs after they have taken a post-school course, or have completed training in something else, and again the PFA recommends this.

Of those who join clubs at 16-plus, at least half are not offered contracts at 18, and a further 25% have left by the age of 21. It is therefore essential to prepare for an alternative career. Release to study is built in to the YTS contract, and anyone signing on with a club should have further time for study/training written in to their contract. Some professionals go as far as taking part-time degree courses at local polytechnics.

GOLF is the major leisure occupation of a great many people for whom it provides both exercise and a hobby. The constant effort to improve their playing takes help from professional coaches, although equipment manufacturers are also making the game easier by improving clubs and balls.

The Professional Golfers' Association has under 2000 members. Most work for private or municipal clubs, as club professionals, some as full-time golf coaches and teachers. Membership of the PGA European Tour, which manages the annual 30 major tournaments (for over £7 million in prize money), is restricted to the best 250 professionals (of those who want to compete, that is).

But estimates suggest only fifty or so players make a reasonable living out of tournaments. Since the travelling expenses alone are £500-£800 a week (the competitions are in fourteen different countries), this also depends on gaining sponsorships – which depend on winning.

While a large part of the club professional's day is spent on the course teaching or playing, as much or even more of their time is spent running the golf shop and repairing and maintaining golf equipment. The pro's income is therefore made up of a very small retainer paid by the club, and the rest from fees for teaching and repairs and from sales in the shop. Time off to play in tournaments has to be agreed with the club. Tournament play takes a very high level of ability indeed, with the right temperament, and golfers have to play well despite crowds and television cameras. Like other sports men and women, golfers must practise continually and stay at peak fitness.

Golf has one advantage over other sports, however, in that it is possible to go on being a professional, although probably not a tournament player, right through working life. While many tournament players turn to teaching after their playing days are over, this is now also becoming a young player's occupation, and a number of schools and centres employ, and train, full-time golf teachers.

Entry and training Separate for club and teaching work, and tournament playing.

For club professionals, the normal method of entry is as an assistant to, being employed and trained by, an established club professional. In return for a very low starting wage, assistants are taught workshop practice and helped to improve their game. They also have to help in the workshop and the shop, to clean equipment and do many chores. Training normally lasts about three years, and during that time the assistant gains increasing responsibility for teaching and playing in addition to other duties. All assistants register with the PGA and become provisional members after a trial year. Full membership normally requires three years in employment. The PGA runs an annual course for assistant professionals, emphasising the non-playing aspects of the work. Many young assistants of course hope to become leading tournament players, and working as an assistant does give plenty of time to practise. However, other entrants prefer to play as amateurs until they can show they have reached championship standard.

For tournament players, membership of the European Tour is only via an annual competition. The leading 200 qualify automatically. About 300 (from all countries) compete in a six-round tournament qualifying school (in Spain) for the other 50 places, and will usually have gone through a pre-qualifying school in England. Amateurs turning professional have to be officially two-handicap to attend the school, but realistically only one-handicap (or better) golfers stand any chance.

HORSE RACING is a largely spectator sport, with the main interest very often in betting on the results, rather than in the performance of horse and rider. Some 60 racecourses and 1000 trainers (employing about 6000 people) are licensed by the Jockey Club, and about 13,000 horses are in training.
Professional jockeys normally ride in either flat or national hunt (over jumps) races, although a few do both. There are about 125 flat race jockeys, and 470 national hunt. A jockey's time is divided between riding at race meetings, helping to training horses, and travelling from one race meeting to another or to a trainer's stables (and out of season many jockeys ride abroad). It is, then, a very strenuous life, for both male and female jockeys, with some danger of serious injury, especially for national hunt jockeys.
The Jockey Club licenses all riders. Jockeys may not own racehorses or bet, and Jockey Club rules against selling information or accepting money to ride in any way other than to win are strict.

Recruitment and entry The normal way to become a jockey is to be apprenticed to a trainer. Around 500 apprentices are in training in any one year, with about 60 boys and girls at most taken on annually. Entry is a matter of persuading a trainer of a boy or girl's potential as a jockey, or via the Racing School (below), or a YTS scheme. There is no guarantee that, at the end of the five- to seven-year period of indentures there is any certainty of qualifying as a jockey. An apprentice-jockey ceases to be an apprentice when he or she has ridden 75 winners or is 24, whichever is the earlier. Without 75 winners before the age of 24 a career as a jockey is most unlikely.
Flat-race jockeys have to be light, and must weigh no more than 8 stone, which normally means weighing no more than 7 stones for boys, 8 stones for girls, at 16. Despite this, a jockey must be physically strong, strong enough to control a very strong and high-spirited animal through all the vicissitudes of a race, to win, if possible. Ability to approach (without unsettling) and handle horses, and to ride, good hands and wrists should go without saying, and most top jockeys have a certain 'flair' for winning. National hunt jockeys need similar qualities, but they can be heavier. They must be able to race over jumps.

Training Most apprentices do a ten-week training courses at the British Racing School at Newmarket, where they are taught to handle racehorses and racing techniques, early on. Trainers who want to send apprentices they have already taken on get priority for places, but it is possible to apply direct. Experience in a stables is a useful advantage in gaining a place, possibly via a YTS scheme. Training is then with a trainer.
Only about 340 apprentices are licensed to ride (and usually not until they have been apprentices for at least two years). The failure rate is high, mostly because apprentices grow unexpectedly. However, apprentices who are good riders but too heavy for the flat can change to national hunt racing.
Apprentices work very hard. Work starts very early and ends late, with afternoons and one day a fortnight free. Apprentices are taught how to care for horses, to groom and exercise them, to care for and use riding tackle, and also,

of course, how to ride. Once an apprentice shows promise, he or she is entered for apprentices' races, of which there are about 100 every year. Apprentices go with horses to race meetings to care for them both in transit and at the meeting. Training during apprenticeship is thorough enough to see that apprentices who do not make the grade as jockeys can continue to work in racing or any other stables, working up to head lad, or even trainer (most jockeys also become trainers when they have to stop riding), but they are equally qualified to do other work connected with horses, for example in breeding or in hunting stables. It is also possible to become a race official.

See also WORK WITH ANIMALS, below.

Further information The National Trainers' Federation.

ICE SKATING A very few skaters manage to turn professional, mostly to work in the entertainment industry. Most of the country's some 40 rinks have instructors, although they are usually self-employed.

MOTOR-CYCLING probably supports fewer than 100 professionals in either branch (ie road and speedway) and most probably combine racing with manufacturing, dealing or cycle repair. Most start as amateurs, either scrambling or in grass-tracking (speedway on grass). Some speedway tracks give novices a chance to use their own machines, but competition for entry to the tracks' teams and training squads (who have coaching schemes) is fierce and requires contacts and/or proven ability on the grass track.

MOTOR RACING supports about 20 professional Formula One drivers of all nationalities (more compete in other formulas, or are semi-professional rally drivers), and they must compete on an international basis. It is a very expensive sport and unless the driver has an independent income, requires sponsorship or support of some kind from motor or component manufacturers, or other commercial interests. All professional drivers have to be licensed by the Royal Automobile Club, which requires evidence of ability. Most drivers began as amateurs and demonstrate their skills at race school, through rally driving and events, or by renting and racing a Formula One car.

RUGBY LEAGUE is, of course, played professionally in the North of England, but the 1500 players are not full-time professionals. They are paid a fee per match, although most also get a signing-on fee and some may qualify for benefits.

TENNIS, is an 'open' sport, with no distinction between amateur and professional status, so any player can compete for prize money. Only a very limited number of full-time professionals can make a living, and to stay in the game demands a punishing schedule of matches throughout the world, many played indoors and at very odd hours. British tennis players, with a few notable exceptions, have not done very well on the international circuits, but that is no reason why any talented youngster should not to attempt it.

To become a professional means starting to play seriously by the age of 7 or 8. Reaching international standard is, however, extremely hard work and requires expert tuition as well as the resources to live while training. Young players can try for first regional, then national training schemes in the UK, but these, and the key junior tournaments, are by invitation. There are also private training schemes. Training abroad, for example, in the US, may be necessary, and some young players gain scholarships to study and train there.

WRESTLING is primarily an amateur sport, but there is a professional circuit of 'all-in' wrestlers, most of whom began as amateurs and are prepared to combine a flair for showmanship with wrestling skills.

Further information from the Sport Council, and the governing bodies of individual sport (see Appendix).

RECREATION AND LEISURE INDUSTRIES

Introduction   635
Administering and managing for leisure and recreation   637
Arts administration   642
Coaching, instructing, leading and teaching   645
Gamekeepers and wardens   647
Ground maintenance   647
Work with animals   648

INTRODUCTION

A wide range of recreation and leisure activities and facilities are almost taken for granted, even though some of the major providers, dependent on public funding, cannot now spend at the levels of previous years. That recreation is 'one of the community's everyday needs', that people have more time for leisure activities (for whatever reason), and that the leisure industries can provide more jobs are not questioned. Evidence suggests people want to spend more time doing something active, less just sitting and, say, watching television. Many people are more interested in improving their health, with official encouragement. The 1000-plus health clubs are used by more than 500,000 people, spending about £50 million a year. But they want their healthy activities to be interesting, and something that can be done with friends and/or families. What interests them changes all the time and a rising proportion of older people will bring other changes too.

It is virtually impossible to define leisure and recreation. Any attempt to do so founders on what any one individual sees as recreational. While to one man or woman DIY or digging the garden may be a terrible chore, to another it is a welcome change of activity and a pleasurable way to spend time. People relax with books, music, films on video, at the theatre, watching sport, playing golf, going to a museum, walking a nature trail, taking photos, visiting a historic house or ancient monument, staying at a hotel for a weekend, camping, having a meal at a restaurant. Many of the other careers in this book, then, contribute to leisure and recreational services – the MEDIA, MUSEUMS, LIBRARIES, HOTELS AND CATERING, PROFESSIONAL SPORT, and TOURISM play their part in the leisure industries too.

Local authorities have, at least so far, made the largest capital investment in purpose-built facilities for recreation, especially for sport and other outdoor activities, and many are responsible too for so-called 'resource-based' activities, activities which need parks and other open spaces, sea and rivers etc. Despite financial restrictions, most expect to continue to find ways to expand

and improve their facilities and services – they collectively planned to spend £900 million in 1986-7. They mainly respond to what the community wants, but also see such expenditure as a way of attracting income – firms, tourists etc – to the area, particularly where job losses have been severe.

The private sector is the other major provider. The list of activities is a long one. It includes leisure and amusement parks, bowling alleys, casinos, 1200 bingo halls, zoos, country clubs, billiard halls, golf courses, horse riding, ice rinks, discotheques, squash courts, public houses, and a host more. Less than 700 large companies, though, are in the leisure and recreation business, and that includes firms seen largely as BREWERS, HOTEL CHAINS etc. A high proportion of private-sector leisure organisations are small companies, trusts and owner-proprietors, only some of them – an estimated 4000 – with managerial and other help. They include, for instance, the 250 owners of historic homes and gardens who open them to the public. Holiday organisations cater for the active and particularly children, with sports (including coaching 'schools' for eg tennis), pony-trekking, walking, canoeing etc. It is now also suggested that (more) farmers should provide sports and other recreational activities. All these organisations clearly see profits to be made from the leisure and recreation industry, but have to be constantly on the watch for changing public interest, effects of new technology etc.

Between local authorities and commercial firms come a range of other providers and provision. While great numbers of voluntary clubs, societies etc organise all kinds of activities, those which employ staff are concentrated mainly in sports like bowls, squash, golf, sailing. Universities, polytechnics and colleges of higher education all provide sports facilities, with staff to run them, and some have professionally-managed arts centres also. Most larger industrial and commercial firms provide sports and other recreational facilities for their staff. Other organisations either wholly, or partly, concerned with leisure and recreational activities include outdoor pursuits and adventure centres, the Youth Hostels Association, the FORESTRY and WATER industries, British Waterways Board (developing canals for leisure as well as commercial use and hiring out its own fleet of narrow boats), and many of the organisations whose primary interest is in CONSERVATION.

Finally, administration of recreation and leisure facilities also includes the quasi-independent bodies which channel government funds, attempt co-ordination, forward planning etc, and act as focal points for all kinds of pressure both upwards and outwards to improve, develop, and rationalise facilities etc. These include the three sports councils, the organisations listed under ARTS ADMINISTRATION below, and the governing bodies of individual sports and other leisure/recreational activities.

Sports facilities expanded rapidly during the 1970s, and development continues, if at a slower rate. By 1986, ten national sports centres, and on a local basis, about 800 multi-purpose sports and leisure centres and 1000 sports halls had been built – over fifty halls in 1985-6 alone. A number of national sports 'arenas' are now being planned involving government, local authorities and commercial developers. Local sports centres range from the very large and purpose-built such as Meadowbank in Edinburgh down to school sports facilities which can be used by the public. Centres include those at Crystal Palace in south London (a national athletics and swimming centre providing for a range of indoor sports), the Pickets Lock complex (planned eventually to stretch 23 miles from Ware in Hertfordshire to the Thames – over 10,000 acres – with five sports centres and facilities for almost every kind of land and water sport), the National Sailing Centre at Cowes in the Isle of Wight, the Holme Pierpoint National Water Sports Centre built from worked-out gravel pits near Nottingham (with a 2000-metre rowing and canoeing course, a new £2.2m 'white-water' canoe slalom course, water-ski-ing lagoon, facilities for power boating, angling and model boating), the National Sports Centre for Wales in Cardiff, and three mountaineering centres (one in Wales, one in Scotland and one in Northern Ireland).

Arts facilities, including the growing number of arts centres, are also part of the leisure and recreation scene. They range from the huge modern Barbican Centre in the City of London (which houses resident orchestras, theatrical companies, and a music/drama school), and the older South Bank complex, to adapted Victorian premises (formerly a teachers training college) in a small northern city. Most are local-authority owned and administered, and have developed from the tradition of municipal theatres, on which many such centres are based. In some local authorities the emphasis has been changing, from providing facilities where the public can only watch, see or listen to, professional performers, to creating conditions for the community itself to take part in a range of activities. Many authorities also put on programmes of popular and classical music, carnivals, events for public holidays, special programmes, and so on.

Commercial facilities for leisure, sports and the arts are not usually so large or multi-purpose, concentrating on specific activities – cinemas, bingo halls, skating rinks, golf courses, marinas, etc, although the number of country and 'theme' parks may be growing.

ADMINISTERING AND MANAGING FOR LEISURE AND RECREATION

Comprehensive leisure and recreational facilities of the kind which have been developing since the 1960s need professional administration and management. Resources have to be high standard, and such finance as is available used to maximum effect. Sports centres, etc, are costly to build and have increasingly expensive and sophisticated technical equipment. Some facilities have been under-used, suggesting poor planning and/or marketing. Running costs have been too high, and need more efficient and tighter control. Natural facilities – rocks for climbing, paths for walking, picnic sites etc in conservation areas – are easily damaged by wrong or over use, and must be as efficiently managed as more apparently-expensive centres. Ensuring the safety of participants and spectators also requires effective management.

Professional administration and management has been slow to develop though, with some resistance to more formal methods. This has been largely overcome, and all kinds of organisations are developing better management methods. The Sport Council is, for example, committed to improving the quality of recreation management. It is supporting development of a computer-based management information system, and monitoring usage, income, cost and energy efficiency of sports halls, having developed a design and construction package for high-standard 'off the peg' sports facilities.

The great variety in leisure/recreation providers (ie employers) and services makes a single, one-structure recreation-management function almost impossible, and people in it are still coming to terms with the resulting problems in hammering out a professional 'profile'. It has to be multi-structured, and multi-disciplinary. Recreation management in any one organisation may involve a single activity (eg swimming, golf, bird-watching), several activities in one area (eg sport), or activities across a range of different types of activity. Providing leisure activity may be the primary purpose of the organisation, it may be one of several which are equally important, or it may be subsidiary to the main activity of eg a water authority, and may then involve constant problems of reconciling conflicting interests as in, for instance, the national parks.

Recreation managers have to work within established organisational structures. Many live within the framework of LOCAL AUTHORITIES, working for the community; others work for firms – or themselves – where achieving a profit is the dominant purpose, yet others for organisations where conservation is the overriding aim, so leisure facilities have to be controlled and the public educated in their use.

Recreation managers, then, are not just people who see that the grass is cut, the pool water purified. They are not land agents or landscapers, although land management and advising on aspects of landscaping may be part of the job. Some local authorities include AMENITY HORTICULTURE within recreational management, and this can extend to, eg improving cemeteries. They have to cope with a great variety of tasks. Planning, finance, marketing and advertising, personnel management, negotiating, organising, leading may be involved. They may have to administer catering services and bars, shops, and coaching as well as the actual recreational facilities. Employers put great emphasis on skills common to any area of management – the ability to select and handle staff, financial skills – budgeting and accounting – and general business skills, including marketing and promotion, both for the public and private sector. Even the Sports Council talks of 'corporate' planning. Recreation managers are expected to understand and use modern management techniques – OR, O&M, 'critical path analysis', statistical research methods etc – just like managers in any other sector.

The Yates Report on recreation management training (1984) estimated (very roughly) some 8500 management posts in local authorities (out of over 90,000 employed by them in leisure/recreation), about 19,400 (including about 2300 part-time) in the private sector, and about 21,000 (including 6000 part-time) in voluntary organisations.

In local authorities, swimming pools, squash courts, parks and playing fields, climbing walls, ice rinks, even libraries and cemeteries, are administered by single, large recreation and leisure departments. They can have several hundred staff, organised as a single directorate, but divided by service, with recreation as one of several sections. Many people administering 'multi-disciplinary' recreation departments in local authorities probably still see themselves as librarians, entertainments officers or baths managers, although some are career administrators, and people are now coming up to the top who began their careers in broader sports/leisure centre administration.

The range of jobs in recreation/leisure is enormous, often with little in common between them. It is only really possible to give some general pointers. The main opportunities are in individual centres, or the relevant central department, which looks after overall planning, budgeting and policy, and may also manage some facilities and services, eg playing fields and bowling greens, or festivals.

Even the largest multi-purpose sports/leisure centre has a full-time, permanent staff of less than 100, probably a third of whom are administrators and a small number coaches (the rest include attendants, groundsmen, catering staff) – although more, including coaches, will be employed part-time. The general manager implements policy, deals with accounts and budgets and overall supervision. 'Middle managers' look after eg general administration (eg bookings, reception, sports shop), catering, or buildings and grounds. A team (three or four) assistant managers or recreation officers promote resources, monitor demand, supervise coaching, or may look after a group of activities/sports, planning programmes and events, liaising with promoters, local clubs etc, seeing that equipment is available and maintained etc. 'Recreation assistants' deal directly with the public, supervise activities (eg a swimming pool or squash courts), coping with problems and emergencies on the ground, etc.

In smaller centres, commercial units, university or polytechnic sports departments etc, fewer managers/administrators take on several functions, and this often means combining administration with, eg coaching.

Leisure/sports facilities are, by definition, used at time when people are not working, so staff running facilities have to expect 'unsocial' hours and shift work.

Voluntary organisations, especially if they organise national or other competitions, will have a small secretariat of administrators. Even one of the largest bodies, the Sports Council, employs only 280 people.

Recruitment and entry No single, straightforward route into leisure administration/management – given the wide variety of opportunities, probably not possible. Recruitment has, in the past, not normally been directly from the education system, and a high proportion of people are recruited on the basis of a training and/or specialist skills relevant to the organisation – PE teaching, swimming-pool administration, or horticulture for local authorities for instance, rather than business training. A background in professional sport, landscape architecture, hotel management, tourism, prison work or the armed forces, have been common.

The pattern of recruitment is changing, though, with more people taken on straight from school and higher/further education. Probably most professional leaders/managers will in future come from amongst people who have completed post-A-level higher/further education, but it is possible to start at the bottom at 16- or 18-plus (but with at least some O-level equivalent passes at 16-plus), to train on-the-job and gain relevant qualifications (see below). This would mean starting as, eg a 'leisure centre assistant', trainee gardener, LOCAL GOVERNMENT administrative trainee, or going through a relevant YTS scheme.

Some larger commercial firms and local authorities recruit graduates as trainee managers (starting in smaller units), whatever their degree subject/background. First jobs in smaller, poorer organisations are another way in. However, relevant training, and background (as a participant and/or eg unpaid experience running a club or society, as a play-group leader), is a great advantage, and for some posts, essential. A business/management qualification would also be useful.

Qualifications and training Major efforts, following several critical reports, are being made to develop comprehensive education and training for leisure/recreation management. The aim is to develop training and courses for a single, multidisciplinary leisure and recreation profession, with encouragement for proper training 'pathways' for management, and training for related specialist professions (eg PE, community education, tourism, hospitality management, arts, libraries, museums) should have a distinct element of general L&R training.

While training is still mainly for local authorities, education/training schemes are being developed for both private and voluntary sector managers.

Qualifications, some pre-entry, some of which can be taken while working, include (1987) –

Professional qualification Mainly now from:

The Institute of Leisure and Amenity Management (ILAM) formed 1983 by merging several older bodies whose members were mainly local government staff; 1986 membership c3000. ILAM has introduced a new two-stage qualification –

Certificate (part I) – covers management of leisure facilities, philosophy of leisure and recreation, general management/administration, plus a specialist module, eg sport and recreation, arts and entertainment, parks and amenity. Candidates are expected to complete a two-year part-time course, and have a qualification equivalent to five GCE/GCSE passes including two at A level.

Diploma (part II) – covers planning and provision for leisure, and management (finance, marketing, economics etc) for L&R, and includes a case study and extended management project. Also requires two years' part-time study. Candidates must have completed part I (exemptions may be allowed).

Arrangements for study are complex, and ILAM's latest booklet of guidance to students should be consulted. The Institute also puts on short courses, seminars, and training programmes.

The Institute of Baths and Recreation Management sets examinations at technician and supervisory level with two or three O levels required for entry.

BTEC awards BTEC has recently (1986) designed a new full-scale scheme for leisure studies at all levels.

Higher National awards (first intake 1987): the guidelines require core units on work organisations, the external environment, operational techniques and procedures, the need for leisure provision, planning and management of resources in the leisure industry, taking up 8 units (66% of a certificate course, 50% of a diploma), leaving the remainder for option units.

National awards (first intake 1986): the guidelines require a core element (at least 9 units) covering people in organisations, the organisation in its environment, finance, the leisure environment, marketing leisure services. For a certificate, students must take also two option units from – arts and entertainment, sports and physical recreation, tourism, countryside, cultural recreation, hospitality, parks and amenity horticulture. For a diploma, students take three or four options from this list, and make up their six options in business-related studies, eg display, supervision, advertising, statistics, law, buying, sales function and methods, storage and stock control, business law, information processing, languages, keyboarding, social services, industrial relations.

First awards (first intake 1987): include a core unit on working in leisure organisations' plus, for a certificate one, a diploma two, leisure-industry options (as National but not parks and amenity horticulture), and certificate one, diploma two, business-related options from, eg finance, information processing, sales, keyboarding, receptionist/telephonist duties, word processing, consumer legislation, display, merchandising, selling and customer relations. For a diploma, a work experience unit is also required.

Entry to courses for all three levels is as for all BTEC awards††.

CGLI recreation and leisure industries (scheme 481) – suitable for recreation assistants.

First-degree courses (as considered relevant within the profession)
Community studies with leisure/recreation BA: Bradford/Ilkley CC;
Environment studies[1] BA: Bangor: Normal C;
Human movement studies BA: Polytechnic – Leeds; colleges: Canterbury: ChCh[1], Cardiff: S Glam IHE. Derby CHE, London: Twickenham (St Mary's)[1], Ripon/York St J;
Human movement/recreation studies[1] BA: Leeds: Tr/AS;
Landscape management BSc: Reading U;
Leisure/recreation[1] BA: Warrington: N Ches;
Leisure studies (recreation & management) BA: Leeds P;
Outdoor recreation[1] BA: Bedford CHE;
PE/sports, science/recreation, management, BSc: Loughborough U; Reading: Bulmershe CHE;
Recreation BA: Dunfermline CPE;
Recreation & the community BA: Plymouth: Marjohn;
Rural environment studies BSc: London: Wye C;
Sports science/studies: Ulster U; polytechnics – Brighton, Liverpool, Newcastle/Sunderland, Nottingham: Trent, Sheffield; colleges – Bedford CHE, Bognor: W Sussex IHE, Crewe/Alsager CHE[1], London: Roehampton IHE[1], W London IHE[1];
Sport in the community BA: Glasgow: Jordanhill C;
Sport/recreation studies BA: N Staffs P;
[1] option within Combined studies degree.

Postgraduate/postexperience courses
Countryside management MSc/dipl/cert: Manchester P,
Environmental resource management (countryside recreation) MSc: Universities – Edinburgh, Salford;
Recreation/leisure management diplomas: Universities – Sheffield; poly-

technics[2] – Huddersfield, London: NLP, Middlesbrough: Teesside; colleges[2] – High Wycombe: Bucks CHE;
Recreation/leisure management MSc/MA: Universities – Loughborough, Sheffield, Ulster; polytechnic – London: NLP;
Recreation supervision NEBSS cert (f-t courses): Ashington TC, Luton CHE, Newark TC;
Recreational land management studies MSc: Reading U;
See also ARTS ADMINISTRATION, COACHING (for PE courses), HOTELS AND CATERING, and TRAVEL/TOURISM.
[2] part-time.

Further information from the Institute of Leisure and Amenity Management, BTEC, and the Sports Council.

ARTS ADMINISTRATION

This is a rather amorphous area of employment, never clearly defined, with no set career structure, and not simple to describe. It overlaps considerably with leisure/recreation administration/management, and some argue that they are indistinguishable. Arts administration is commonly taken to mean the non-performing, non-technical functions in any organisation which provides facilities to watch, or take part in, 'artistic' activities. In other words, the emphasis is on administration rather than the arts part of the title. Some sectors which might be considered 'arts', however, are administered and managed by people qualified in that field – MUSEUMS and LIBRARIES are two examples.

As in all other sectors, arts administration/management is a mix of the work needed to plan, finance, organise and run any organisation, with the specialist skills needed to solve the particular problems faced by organisations trying to provide facilities for performing, watching or taking part in arts-based activities. It is not, though, a single 'profession'. While arts administration, if interpreted fairly widely, can offer quite a few actual jobs, the number of longer-term career opportunities is never likely to be large. Vacancy lists and advertisements try to stretch the field almost beyond credibility – to media advertising, selling and administration of a musicians' benevolent fund, for example.

The main areas of employment, and employers are –

NATIONAL ORGANISATIONS These include –

The Arts Council, whose administrative staff supervise projects, investigate proposals for grants and supervise them, and do general promotional and liaison work. The Council is divided into seven departments – art, drama, music, regional/touring, finance, and administration/personnel, and most of the Council's 180-plus direct employees (1987) are specialists in one of these. The Arts Council now also administers London's South Bank complex and has transferred some work, eg exhibitions, there to give the South Bank over 260 full-time employees.

The British Council has specialist services in, for example, fine arts, drama, music and films, and tries to see that the best British drama, music, and visual arts is seen overseas. The Council can help British theatre, ballet and opera companies, orchestras and individuals to perform in other countries. In co-operation with local museums and art galleries, works of art, photographs etc are also sent for exhibition and on tour. Where there are bilateral cultural agreements between Britain and other countries, the Council is normally the British government's agent in carrying them out, and a small proportion of the Council's home staff work in this area. Overseas staff are expected to take an interest in the cultural life of the country in which they work, and to promote two-way cultural understanding (see also WORKING OVERSEAS and EDUCATION). The British Film Institute (BFI) helps to fund, and gives technical help to film makers, funds film and video workshops (with Channel 4), administers the National Film Theatre and the National Film Archive, has large information and education divisions, produces a number of publications (including a quarterly journal), promotes and helps to fund some 40 regional film theatres, and is helping to set up film and TV centres in several larger cities. Total BFI staff (1987) is 350.

The Office of Arts and Libraries plans and administers central government expenditure in this area. Total staff 50 (1986). See CIVIL SERVICE.

REGIONAL AND LOCAL ADMINISTERING ORGANISATIONS Mainly –

The fifteen regional arts associations funded by local authorities, the Arts Council, BFI, the Crafts Council and private funds. They support and promote the arts in their areas, by providing grants and subsidies, promoting particular events, putting out publicity material, helping to plan and co-ordinate activities, giving advice generally and supporting research. Their staff, some of whom specialise in eg drama, music, visual arts, community arts, or administer finance, range from only six up to about 20.

Local authorities: most of the larger authorities have some involvement in 'the arts' aside from their museums, libraries and art galleries. Some have their own theatres, many put on arts events such as concerts of all kinds, art exhibitions, and some provide arts centres etc. Mostly administration of these facilities and services is part of their LEISURE AND RECREATION MANAGEMENT structure.

INDIVIDUAL ARTS ORGANISATIONS The range of possible employers here is quite wide, although the numbers employed by them individually are mostly small, however large the centre or theatre. Smaller organisations may only be able to employ people on a part-time basis, or have to rely on volunteers –

Arts centres vary in what they do, where they are based (some are purpose-built, some are in converted premises, some are based on universities or schools), and in size. For most, numbers employed are very small, but Darlington's centre (for example) has a team of about a dozen, and many more run the Barbican. Centres designed for people to take part in a range of arts also employ professional staff to organise and support these activities.

The professional theatre administering and managing in the theatre may mean managing just a 'facility' including the building (which is often quite technically complex and may have eg catering facilities too), managing a building and a resident company, or managing just a theatrical company which does not have a permanent home. Managing a concert hall, or a cinema (still c1300 screens in the UK and cinema going on the increase) is in many ways similar to managing a theatre without a resident company.

Administrators control finance (including cashiers etc), organise the programme of events and/or bookings for the facility, liaise and work closely with the theatre's artistic director(s) or performing-company administrators, deal with publicity and marketing, and supervise services, stage management, maintenance etc.

Orchestral, ballet and opera administration every professional orchestra, ballet and opera company needs administrators, to organise finance, concerts or performances, arrange contracts, travel, look after players, the music, etc. But even a large national orchestra rarely employs more than ten people and that includes secretaries.

Community arts Community associations of all kinds, some specialising in arts, some organised by specific groups, eg a local Afro-Caribbean or Asian community wanting to organise their own arts activities, can afford to employ full-time administrators, organisers, co-ordinators, development workers etc. Some community workshops, many run as co-operatives, also employ administrators. One smallish-town arts workshop has a full-time staff of five, and 30 working part-time.

Festivals only the very largest maintain full-time administrators all year round. The main opportunities are on fixed contracts for the period of the festival itself with a run-up period.

Working in arts administration The work involved ranges from being responsible for allocating, distributing and accounting for many thousands, even millions of pounds, to collecting money at the box office or selling programmes in the auditorium. Some work involves subject expertise, especially where decisions have to be made on funding for specific arts, eg music, or events, such as art exhibitions, arranged. Some administrative posts overlap/shade over into EDUCATION – not necessarily teaching or instruction, but developing and running educational and 'outreach' programmes.

Since most arts organisations these days have to live within tight budgets, the number of administrative staff any one employs is usually kept as low as possible. Even in the largest organisation, then, managers and administrators will take on a range of different functions and tasks, and team co-operation is essential. A large theatre, though, must usually have a number of 'managers'/administrators, for eg front of house, box office (larger ones are now 'computerised'), etc.

Working in arts administration has many special aspects. Efficient FINANCIAL MANAGEMENT to make the best use of income is obviously essential. It may also extend to looking for alternative sources of finance, hunting and applying for grants etc. Finance may link closely to the growing need for expert MARKETING, not only to customers but, eg to potential sponsors, and in some organisations this is full-time work. PUBLICITY AND PUBLIC RELATIONS are also essential functions. Few organisations are large enough to have full-scale PERSONNEL MANAGEMENT departments, or even full-time personnel/staff managers, and so many managers must have this expertise. The box office manager of, for instance, a not particularly large arts complex (concert halls, theatre, galleries etc) may have box-office staff of up to 24, working in shifts over seven days. Staff turnover is inevitably high, and temporary staffing is often necessary.

Recruitment and entry no straightforward career structure, so no simple way in. Many posts take special expertise (and previous experience), not just for direct administration of arts funding or events, but also in, eg information and public relations for publicity, accounting for finance etc.

For any post which provides a start to a career, a degree in a suitable subject, which would normally have to be in art/history of art for any gallery/exhibition organising work, music for orchestra/concert organising administration etc, is probably esssential. A teaching qualification is also useful. Grafted onto that, all-round basic administrative skills – typing (including word-processing for all the mailing lists etc) and preferably full secretarial training, ability to keep books/use computer spread sheets etc.

The all-essential experience is probably best gained first by doing voluntary administration for eg a student society/club, a community or experimental arts (or dance, drama, music) group which cannot afford to pay. From there it should be relatively easy to get into either low-level jobs in larger organisations, or general administrating for a smaller, poorer ones. Initiative and being prepared to take on (almost) anything are both essential qualifications.

Qualifications and training Pre-entry training specifically for arts administration barely exists, and the Arts Council says relevant experience is always more important. Most of the available courses are mainly for people already in relevant work. They include –
Durham U (business school): Arts administration MSc (places for graduates wanting to prepare for a career).
Leicester P: Performing arts BA with arts administration option. Also in-service short courses.
London, City U: the established arts administration diploma course is being replaced with new diploma studies at postgraduate level from 1987-8. Also three part-time MA programmes (arts administration, arts management in education, and librarianship and arts administration), and a range of short courses.
See also ADMINISTERING AND MANAGING FOR LEISURE AND RECREATION above.

Further information from the Arts Council (Training Officer).

COACHING, INSTRUCTION, LEADING, TEACHING
These have offered only slender career prospects in the past, with the great majority of coaches working on a voluntary basis, but official promotion of sport for all, and expansion in the number of multi-purpose and specialist sports centres have led to a steady increase in the number of posts for trained and qualified coaches and instructors. Of course in the major professional sports, such as football, cricket, and golf, every club has always had full-time coaches (see PROFESSIONAL SPORT above), and in sports where there has always been a strong commercial interest, instructors are generally employed, particularly in skating (all ice rinks have paid instructors), in ski-ing in Scotland, and in horse riding, with an estimated 3000 schools (but only a tenth are approved by the British Horse Society).

National and regional sports centres (see above) now employ their own full-time instructors and coaches, some of whom work for the local education authority, and only train classes of school-children who have games lessons at the centres. Some centres employ part-time coaches for those who use the facilities in their leisure time. The larger multi-purpose sports centres may have a complement of between 15 and 20 full-time coaches, and 24 or more part-time staff. The 'mix' of coaches employed will obviously depend on the facilities offered by a centre, but it seems prospects are improving, especially for those able to instruct and coach in swimming, squash, tennis, golf, water sports of all kinds (but particularly sailing), table tennis, badminton, and the martial arts.

The Sports Council initiative 'Action Sport' programme is, with MSC support, going national. Directed towards target groups such as the unemployed, ethnic minorities, women, people of over 50, and the handicapped, it will employ over 1100 sports leaders by the end of 1988.

Instructors in outdoor activities, like climbing, canoeing, sub-aqua, ski-ing, and yachting, are also employed by Outward Bound schools and outdoor pursuits centres but in fairly small numbers. Commercial organisations selling outdoor sporting holiday also employ instructors and leaders.

Physical education teachers are, of course, normally employed in all schools.

Recruitment and entry will normally require training and qualifications appropriate to the sport(s) concerned, and to work in schools, a teaching qualification is normally required. Coaches and instructors are usually also expected to be extremely good at their sport (it is, of course, one way of financing a career as a sports competitor, particularly working part-time).

Qualifications and training Education and training for teachers, and coaches and instructors for some sports and employers, have been well established for some years. Efforts to improve training standards throughout sport are now being made, and a National Coaching Foundation established. The Foundation is developing a range of programmes, courses and packs, building databases and providing information. Every sport has its regulating body, and these set the appropriate training requirements and examinations for instructors and coaches.

Relevant courses include –

First-degree courses

Human movement studies: see ADMINISTERING AND MANAGING FOR LEISURE etc above.

Physical education BEd/teaching qual: universities – Exeter, Warwick; polytechnics – Brighton, Leeds, Liverpool, London: NLP, Sheffield, Sunderland, Wolverhampton; colleges – Bangor: Normal C, Bedford CHE, Bognor: W Sussex IHE, Canterbury: ChCh C, Cardiff: S Glam IHE, Carmarthen: Trinity C, Cheltenham: St P/St M, Chester, Crewe/Alsager, Derby CHE, Leeds: Tr/AS, Liverpool IHE, London: W London IHE, Newport: Gwent CHE, Northampton: Nene, Ormskirk: E Hill CHE, Plymouth: St M/St J, Reading: Bulmershe, Scarborough: N Riding, Winchester: K Alfred's, Worcester CHE, Wrexham: NE Wales IHE, York: Ripon/York St J;

Physical education BSc/BA: universities – Birmingham, Liverpool, Loughborough; colleges – Chester C, Leeds: Tr/AS, Liverpool IHE, Northampton: Nene, Ormskirk: E Hill CHE;

Sports science/studies: see ADMINISTERING AND MANAGING FOR LEISURE etc above.

Postgraduate courses
Physical education PGCE: universities – Birmingham, Exeter, Hull, Loughborough, Sheffield; polytechnics – Brighton, Leeds, Liverpool; colleges – Bedford CHE, Cardiff: S Glam IHE, London: W London IHE; Physical education & sports science MPhil/PhD: Loughborough U; Sports coaching studies diploma: Leeds P.

Further information: Sports Council, National Coaching Foundation.

GAMEKEEPERS/WARDENS
They work for game management firms as well as private landowners. Estimates suggest as many as 5000 are employed.

Shooting is increasingly popular, and is one of the most rapidly growing sports. Gamekeepers and their assistants rear game, whether it be grouse, pheasant, partridge, duck or, mainly in Scotland, deer, using the most sophisticated breeding methods; protect birds, deer etc from vermin and poachers (poaching is big business) and maintain covers. Some protect and manage salmon rivers and trout streams.

Many gamekeepers are developing wider responsibilities in countryside activities, especially where game management firms have related interests.

Entry/training etc Traditionally keepers are trained 'on-the-job', as assistants, but courses (with qualifications) are at Sparsholt: Hants Ag C, Thursoe TC.

GROUND MAINTENANCE/GROUNDSMANSHIP
Some 100,000 or so professional groundsmen (plus a further 50,000 or so casual workers), according to the Institute of Groundsmanship, care for over 300,000 acres of sports grounds provided by local authorities, professional and other sports clubs, universities and other educational institutions, and commercial/industrial firms.

Grounds staff make and maintain, for example, cricket squares, tennis courts, football and rugby pitches, golf courses and bowling greens. Sports grounds of all kinds are being used more and more intensively, and yet players and spectators alike demand pitches of peak perfection, and to achieve this ground staff have to combine traditional skills with modern scientific techniques, and know how best to use sophisticated machinery and horticultural products in doing so.

In large organisations the grounds staff may just look after the pitches, but in some they may also look after surrounding gardens, help organise events, or run pavilion facilities as well. Some posts provide work for husband-and-wife teams and housing is available.
See also HORTICULTURE.

Qualifications and training While most training is 'on-the-job', the Institute of Groundmanship sets a series of professional examinations, with a practical and a technical certificate and an intermediate and national diploma in the science and practice of turficulture and sports-ground management (no formal entry requirements).

Further information from the Institute of Groundsmanship.

WORK WITH ANIMALS

Opportunities for working with animals are not very great, and most involve a great deal of heavy and messy or dirty labour. The number of responsible posts is very small.

ANIMAL/VETERINARY NURSING

Animal nursing 'auxiliaries' work mainly for veterinary surgeons in town and country practices, animal hospitals etc. They work mostly with 'small animals' – pets – although the scope of possible work may get wider in future, the RCVS says.

Veterinary nurses care for animals recovering from operations or other treatment, collect and analyse specimens, help in the surgery, clean and sterilise instruments and other equipment, clear and clean up the surgery and accommodation for animals. They may be allowed to do some simple treatment, eg removing thorns etc. The RCVS has registered over 2000 veterinary nurses.

It is not possible to use veterinary nursing qualifications as a route to becoming a vet. Few practices are large enough to give nurses any promotion prospects.

Recruitment and entry is via a formal training and examination scheme (below), which must be with an approved centre. Competition for training places is considerable, and it is useful to have had a holiday job or done voluntary work in an animal hospital, which is also a way of being on the spot when training places come up.

Qualifications and training The veterinary nursing scheme is run by the Royal College of Veterinary Surgeons. To gain the qualification, trainees must enrol with the RCVS, and work full-time in an approved training centre (or centres) – veterinary practices not colleges – for at least two years. Practical training and tuition is provided 'on the job'. Trainees can gain the necessary theoretical background studying on their own, but two agricultural colleges run full-time courses (Berkshire and Staffordshire) and about a dozen part-time courses. The two-stage exams may be taken whenever the trainee is ready, but no one can be registered until the two years are up.

Minimum entry requirements are four O-level-equivalent passes at 16-plus† to include English language, and a physical or biological science or maths, and age at least 17. Many entrants have better qualifications than this, even including appropriate A-level passes.

Further information from the Royal College of Veterinary Surgeons, and the British Veterinary Nursing Association.

ANIMAL RESEARCH

ranges from work on breeding farm animals which will produce more or better meat, or wool, through to controlling diseases and pests which affect farm animals, formulating improved food stuffs, or working out the conditions under which animals will reach maturity most economically.

ZOOLOGISTS

study animals also. Animals are used extensively in many other areas of scientific research.

See QUALIFICATIONS AND CAREERS IN SCIENCE.

ANIMAL TECHNICIANS look after animals in laboratories or field research centres where they are used for research (scientific, veterinary or medical), or in schools, universities etc for teaching.

Animal technicians keep animals clean and fed, and maintain the conditions needed for the particular experiment. Diet, temperature, lighting etc may have to be strictly controlled. They generally observe the animals and keep records of their condition for the scientist doing the research. Sick animals may have to be cared for specially. At the end of the experiment they may have to kill an animal. They may also have to prepare animals for dissection by students.

Fully-qualified animal technicians may help with experiments, eg giving injections, or taking blood samples. Animals have to be cared for seven days a week.

Qualifications and training Training is largely on-the-job, with release to study for BTEC awards and membership of the Institute of Animal Technicians. It is theoretically possible to start without formal educational requirements, but more usual to have at least three or four O-level-equivalent passes at 16-plus† including English and a biological subject.

See also QUALIFICATIONS AND CAREERS IN SCIENCE.

ANIMAL WELFARE Quite a few organisations deal with animal welfare, but the number of full-time employees is relatively small.

The RSPCA, the largest, employs about 600 trained people including the uniformed inspectors and veterinary staff. Each of the 200 branches has its own inspector and the staff also includes eight travelling superintendents, about 40 senior inspectors, about 180 inspectors and about 30 special market inspectors.

A large part of inspectors' work is investigating allegations of cruelty, but the RSPCA tries to help any animal (and its owner) in difficulty, and the problems are many.

Training lasts six months at the Society's headquarters. No formal academic qualifications are required, but a reasonable standard of education is expected. A high proportion of entrants are mature people, many with a Service background.

The People's Dispensary for Sick Animals (PDSA), has some 58 treatment centres, and employs some 150 vets, and about 160 animal nursing auxiliaries. Blue Cross is similar but much smaller. They both operate similarly to veterinary practices.

See VETERINARY SCIENCE under QUALIFICATIONS AND CAREERS IN SCIENCE.

DOGS, CATS AND OTHER PETS Kennels, catteries and pet shops employ people to look after dogs, cats and other domestic pets.

Some kennels board and quarantine animals on a fairly large scale, some specialise in breeding and showing, or are racing (greyhounds only) or hunt kennels. The work is fairly hard, involving long and irregular hours, spent cleaning, feeding, exercising, training and grooming the animals, caring for litters, staying up late when puppies are born, travelling to and from shows or races. Most staff live in. Opportunities for promotion are few, since most kennels are owner-managed, but animal technician exams may help in finding more responsible posts.

In pet shops and parlours work generally involves grooming and clipping, although some may have a few animals to care for. Training is mainly on the job.

The Guide Dogs for the Blind Association employs about 560 staff, but most are administrative. The training centres employ about 70 kennel staff, about 63 guide-dog trainers, and about 63 guide-dog mobility instructors who train dogs and blind people to work together as a unit. Kennel staff are recruited at 17 with at least three CSE grade 2 equivalent passes at 16-plus†, trainee guide-dog trainers at 18 with at least five O-level equivalent passes at 16-plus†, and trainee mobility instructors at 21 with a similar educational background – but it is possible to move on from kennel work. Training is given – six months for dog trainers, at least 30 months for mobility instructors. The Association has a waiting list of suitable candidates, and a stiff selection procedure.

The ARMED FORCES and the POLICE all employ dogs, but handlers are usually chosen from people already in the service, and trained by them.

HORSE RIDING, RACING, HUNTING are popular leisure activities, and so provide a number of openings, in riding, instructing and in caring for the animals.
Many jobs are in racing – see PROFESSIONAL SPORT.

Hunt stables employ hunt 'servants', who work up from 'strapper' to second horseman, second horseman to second whipper-in, second whip to whip and then to 'carrying horn' as professional huntsman. Grooms are employed on a seasonal basis only. The best opportunities are with a well-established hunt with continuity of mastership and therefore security of employment (preferably under a professional huntsman rather than an amateur). Some private stables with hunters also employ grooms. Some allow grooms to hunt, ride in hunter trials, shows and similar events, as well as exercising. Most require some experience, because only one groom is usually needed.

Riding schools Only 300 or so of the estimated 3000 riding schools are approved by the British Horse Society (some so-called 'schools' are no more than hiring stables). A fair number of instructors are employed, but competition for jobs is considerable.

Qualified instructors teach ('school') both riders (children and adults) and horses. Hours are long, and usually include evenings and weekends, both for teaching and going to shows, gymkhanas etc. Qualified instructors with experience can become stable managers.

Some schools let their instructors ride in shows and other events, and may give a potential show rider or jumper facilities for training and practice and time off to attend events. It is, however, exceptionally difficult (and expensive) to become a successful show jumper even with the facilities of working in a stable or school.

Seasonal work includes –
Helping with pony trekking holidays (some 150 approved centres), for instructors, guides and grooms.
Work with polo and show horses: polo teams are usually stabled at centres where polo is played, although the employer of stable staff is generally the owner and not the centre. With only some 200 professional player/riders in

Britain (most come from the Argentine, bringing trained ponies), most of the available work is for grooms. Owners of show horses and jumpers employ both professional riders and staff to maintain the horses, and in both there is a considerable amount of exercising and training. Fewer professional riders are employed in jumping and the season is longer, so it is difficult to combine this with hunt work. A considerable amount of travel and 'living rough' is involved.

Bloodstock agencies Most stables breed horses, but the twelve bloodstock agencies, where horses are bred as a business, employ some 400 people. Most of the work involved is in selling, buying and leasing horses for stud, and in valuing, insurance and maintaining pedigrees, although the studs do employ people to look after the horses. Most of these jobs normally demand considerable experience of horses and of racing. A top stud can command a fee running into six figures, so stud, mare and foal can expect the most expert care and attention.

Transport agencies specialise in moving race and show horses, polo ponies and bloodstock mares and foals around the world. Horses travel by road, air and sea as far as Australia and Argentina. The work involves both caring for the horses and handling an enormous amount of paperwork.

Other opportunities It is possible to ride horses (and care for them) in the ARMED FORCES (mostly in ceremonials only), and the mounted POLICE. Both also employ VETERINARY SURGEON, farriers and saddlers.

Recruitment and entry is normally right at the bottom, but for reasonable career prospects should be in a well-run stables or school giving proper on-the-job training. Competition for jobs in the best stables and schools is stiff, but it is possible to start via a YTS scheme. Potential employers should always be checked with the British Horse Society list of approved riding establishments. Entrants should have a good general education (with at least four O-level-equivalent passes at 16-plus†) and preferably some kind of back-up qualification, in eg business studies, secretarial work, or farming.

Qualifications and training The main qualifications are set by –
The British Horse Society (BHS) runs exams at centres throughout the country for
Instructors: 3-stage qualification, the (final) certificate includes stable management as well as horsemanship and teaching. Entrants to the first, assistant instructor's exam must be $17\frac{1}{2}$ and. if under 19, have four O-level equivalent passes at 16-plus† including English.
Grooms: horse knowledge and care exams go through four stages to the stable manager's certificate.

The Association of British Riding Schools (ABRS): sets exams for assistant groom's certificate, and groom's diploma (prepares for stable management). No formal qualifications required.

A few colleges run courses for BHS exams, combined with general education, secretarial studies and/or home economics.

The National Pony Society sets two exams, the stud assistant's certificate, and the diploma in pony mastership and breeding.

BTEC and other national awards –
Horse management national certificate: 1-year course (post-O-level standard) at Budleigh Salterton: Bicton AgC, Moreton Morrell: Warwicks CAg, Witney: W Oxon TC (stud work);
Horse management advanced national certificate: 1-year post-national certificate or -experience specialising in equitation, teaching, remedial development: Moreton Morrell: Warwicks CAg;
Horse management BTEC national diploma: 3-year sandwich course (at least 4 O-level-equivalent passes at 16-plus† including two sciences): Moreton Morrell: Warwicks CAg, Witney: W Oxon TC.

YTS: an 'industry preferred-training pattern' has been produced. This includes horse management with practical experience. Trainees can take BHS groom exams up to level III, and the preliminary teaching test (if they have four O-level-equivalents), ABRS exams up to assistant groom, National Pony Society exams, and the national certificate.

See also HORSE RACING under PROFESSIONAL SPORT. and FARRIERY under AGRICULTURE.

Further information from the British Horse Society.

VETERINARY SCIENCE see ACADEMIC AND VOCATIONAL STUDIES IN SCIENCE.

ZOOS AND WILD-LIFE 'SAFARI' PARKS are the main opportunities to work with wild animals in Britain, although a few circuses and agencies providing trained animals for film and television (mostly advertising) also offer some work with them.

There are about 150 zoos, wild-life parks, bird gardens and aquaria, of which the Zoological Society of London is the largest and most important, although superb work is also being done in some provincial zoos and country wild-life parks. Steeply-rising costs, and some resulting fall in the number of visitors is causing zoos particularly severe financial problems.

Under 2500 have permanent jobs in 78 of the larger zoos. The London Zoo provides some indication of the kinds of careers and jobs available today. The Society's permanent staff is down to some 400 (against nearly 600 in 1972). Of these, less than half deal directly with 'animal management': about a quarter work on construction, maintenance, gardening, general and public services; 60 or so work in catering and the shops; 70 work in scientific departments and the library, and 25 in administration. But the Society, like other zoos and wildlife parks, employs a fair number of temporary helpers in the summer.

The four groups of employees are: professional, technicians, keepers, and administrative staff. Professional staff include curators who 'manage' particular animal groups, heads of research departments (eg nutrition, reproduction, and infectious diseases), six education officers (who lecture, demonstrate and help to run the young zoologists club) and editorial staff for the zoological record; there are occasional short-contract research studentships and fellowships. The Zoo has three vets. Technicians, including animal technicians, work in the labs. Keepers may become highly expert in caring for and breeding particular groups of animals, but everyone starts with 'mucking out'.

Provincial zoos are likely to employ staff in similar proportions, although they have even fewer posts for graduates. Wild-life parks both bring in staff who have trained initially in zoos, and also employ animal experts from other fields, for example, staff trained in safari work overseas or from circus families, on contract to provide and manage their animal exhibits.

Recruitment and entry the number of vacancies at any level is always small. For professional posts, a good honours degree in zoology or veterinary science is needed. Assistant education officers should have a teaching qualification. Library and senior administrative staff are also generally graduates with appropriate degrees.

For technician posts, competition is keen and candidates for junior posts should have at least four O-level-equivalent passes at 16-plus† in appropriate subjects. For intermediate posts at least two A-level science passes; and for senior posts HNC in applied biology or membership of the Institute of Medical Laboratory Sciences or Science Technology. Animal technicians do not need such high educational qualifications, although candidates should preferably have four O-level-equivalent passes at 16-plus† and some previous experience of laboratory animals. Hospital technicians should either be registered veterinary nurses by examination or have a suitable alternative qualification.

Keepers are recruited as 'helpers' from the age of 16 – with at least three O-level-equivalent passes including English, maths, and a science - most start in seasonal employment (from Whitsun until the late summer), and the best get any vacancies on the permanent staff.

Qualifications and training professional staff and senior technicians are recruited from amongst people who already have appropriate qualifications. Other technicians are encouraged/expected to complete professional qualifications. The Zoological Society has a training scheme run with Paddington College which entails passing examinations at two different levels; promotion is based on acquiring these qualifications, coupled with length of service, up to senior keeper grade (just over 20 posts). Some opportunities for short periods of training at overseas zoos.

Further information from the Federation of Zoological Gardens of Great Britain and Ireland.

Land- and Environment-related work

Introduction   654
Agriculture, fishing, forestry and horticulture   654
Conservation and the environment   675
Construction industry   683
Land use professions   697
Mining, prospecting and quarrying   721
Water industry   731

INTRODUCTION

Britain is a relatively small island, and its land resources limited. Agriculture, roads, housing, leisure, industry and commerce, nature itself, compete for space, and planners have to try to arbitrate between the competing interests. Making the environment produce an income inevitably produces conflicts between, for example, immediate profit and producing/extracting resources like food and coal or oil and the longer-term interests of conservation and preservation of landscapes and natural life. It means constant dilemmas in the working lives of many. Retrieving oil and gas from the North Sea has sacrificed some of the most unspoilt and beautiful coastline, and farmers have been constantly exhorted to produce more cheap food but are castigated for trying to do so at the expense of, for example, century-old trees and hedgerows.

Work in this sector is changing just as much as in other industries and areas of employment. The traditional skills used in growing crops, producing milk, or building houses or motorways are still needed. But technology of all kinds, the computer, scientific techniques, modern business methods, expert financial management, sophisticated marketing, efficient planning and decision-making techniques are as essential to the farmer and the builder as to the bank or the electronics firm. Higher levels of skills and expertise, better training, closer team work are needed to make a success of all enterprises. Technology, the drive for higher productivity, fewer and larger enterprises in both farming and construction, and economic competitive conditions also change the kinds of jobs – more managerial and technologically- and technically-skilled staff, fewer semi- and unskilled – combined with an overall decline in the total number of jobs.

The land and the environment can provide a wide range of different types of work, from the very scientific to the most practical, from the aesthetic to the commercial. By definition, working in these sectors frequently involves working out of doors, with all its obvious pleasures and disadvantages. In many jobs there is at least some element of practical work, and most deal with the physical and material, although some have a creative element too.

AGRICULTURE, FISHING, FORESTRY AND HORTICULTURE

Introduction   655
Agriculture   655

Fishing	664
Fish farming	666
Forestry	667
Horticulture	670

INTRODUCTION

Despite the steady take-over of land by homes, industry, roads, etc, over 80% of Britain's land area is still used productively – to grow food and flowers, wool and timber. These essential crop-producing industries have been and are still going through both a scientific/technological and a managerial/marketing revolution. As a result, long-established and traditional ways of working the land have changed. Crop growers have had to become technologically- and scientifically-minded and as astute managers as anyone running any kind of business. The men and women who work for them have had to become increasingly skilled too – and so are now technicians who can cope with very sophisticated machinery, and the scientific methods used to produce larger and more intensive yields of everything from lambs to peas, poultry to wheat, pot plants to pigs, rainbow trout to trees.

While the majority of jobs are on the land itself, in the very practical, hard work which, despite modern science and technology, is still farming, horticulture, gardening, forestry and fishing, there are related occupations. They include the advisory services (see below and also under CENTRAL GOVERNMENT), teaching (see EDUCATION), scientific research (see ACADEMIC AND VOCATIONAL STUDIES IN SCIENCE) and technology (see ACADEMIC AND VOCATIONAL STUDIES IN ENGINEERING). These generally require specialist training to degree level.

Agricultural production, though, now generally needs a rather better intellectual and educational background than has been traditional. The need to understand, operate and adapt to scientific and technological equipment and techniques, and to exploit modern marketing methods alone makes this necessary. Modern, sophisticated equipment has also considerably reduced much of the heavier, back-breaking drudgery of work on the land; animals, birds, and some crops are more often cared for under cover in clean, hygienic conditions. The weather, though, is still a major factor to cope with, and hours are still more often than not long and irregular.

AGRICULTURE

The industry — working in agriculture — entry and recruitment — qualifications and training

The industry

The agricultural industry has become a victim of its own efficiency and productivity. In Britain and Europe, at least, the industry is producing more food than can be sold. EEC quotas on output threaten profitability, and the industry is going through a real crisis.

Just over three-quarters of the country's total land area (about 24.4 million hectares) is currently given over to agriculture, with about 12 million hectares under crops and grass. Lately, the rate at which land has been taken over for other uses has fallen, but 1986 estimates suggested that up to a million hectares may have to come out of conventional production by 1996.

Fifty years ago, Britain's farms produced about a third of the food for 48 million people. By 1986, they were producing four-fifths of the food which can be grown in Britain for 56 million, and exporting some too. This was the result of investing heavily in science and technology – developing high-yield crops, sophisticated breeding techniques for both livestock and crop plants, feeding the soil, feeding animals better, improving seed germination and fertilisers, controlling pests and diseases, improving drainage and irrigation, and developing sophisticated machinery and intensive methods generally. But this has meant a huge and largely uncalculated increase in the use of resources.

This has also been achieved with a massive drop in the numbers of people working on the land – from about 800,000 in 1967 to 693,000 in 1985 (including farmers, partners and directors, regular full- and part-time employees and casual workers). Labour productivity rose by over 150% between 1961 and 1981, 69% between 1975 and 1985.

Modern farming methods have changed the face of the land, often dramatically, and there are now far fewer but much larger farms. Officially there are still (1986) some 240,000 'statistically significant' farming units in Britain. But estimates say 90% of output comes from the 50% employing at least one person full time, and 50% from the largest 12% – about 29,000 farms, employing the equivalent of about four people each. The trend towards fewer but larger units continues – the average size of full-time holdings is now (1985) about 125 hectares (against 114 hectares in 1978). Many farms are company-owned and -run, although with falling land values and profitability, investment funds are pulling out.

Farming is a business, and any profit farmers make depends increasingly on their business skills and efficiency, on a relentless drive to maximise performance. This depends as much on being able to ride the vagaries of the money markets and interest rates, to make the best use of fast-declining support systems as on more traditional farming skills. Farmers' incomes have been eroded by soaring costs – from fertilisers to the price of borrowing – at the same time as quotas have been imposed and subsidies effectively cut.

Farmers are increasingly using computers in managing their farms (an estimated 3000 had them by 1985), and employ management accountants, land agents etc to help them plan their finances and business generally. An arable farmer may, for example, have to decide whether it is efficient to lock up £1 million in harvesting and other machinery which may only be used for a few weeks each year, to be able to clear land quickly (so that another crop can be sown) with fewer workers. The benefits of economies of scale have had farmers co-operating – in building common grain stores so they can dry, store and ship their grain more cheaply and efficiently, for example. They have also moved 'down line' from just growing food into the middle-man business of getting produce to the right places and then selling it.

Farmers will, in future, have to be even more inventive, and fast thinking, to make a living. They can no longer simply increase output with intensive farming to improve profits, but must look for 'added value' products and services. 'Diversification' is the order of the day. Some are going into low chemical input, organic farming, to exploit the growing market for 'natural' foods. Some are turning to (even more) unusual 'crops' – the list of experiments includes deer, llamas and goats (for their fleece), willows (for cheap fuel), sunflowers (for oil), durum 'spaghetti' wheat, edible snails. They are being encouraged to grow more timber, to turn land over to recreational use, and provide more holiday accommodation.

What farmers produce depends on a increasingly complex balance between acreage, soil type and weather – and therefore locality – quotas, availability of markets, and which produce will bring in the best income. Officially, there are six different types of farming – arable, dairying, horticultural, livestock, pigs and poultry, and mixed – and although the trend has been to specialisation there may be all kinds of reasons now for one kind of farm to go into another type of farming. An arable farmer, for example, may fatten beef cattle on potatoes which are too small or badly damaged to sell. If the potatoes are being grown for a crisps manufacturer, they may be a type which needs irrigation, and once an irrigation system is installed, other crops may become viable, and so on. Rape, from which margarine is made, has been popular with farmers because it is easier to grow than sugar beet and can be harvested by the same combines as bring in cereals.

About three-fifths of full-time farms specialise in dairy farming and/or beef cattle and sheep. The West of England, with its higher rainfall, has better dairy pasture that the rest of the country. Dairy farming is the largest sector of the industry, but dual-purpose breeding, mainly of Freesians but also using Charolais and Limousin sires, means at least 66% of beef produced now comes from dairy cattle. Average yields in dairy herds rose by 42% between 1965 and 1985, but although dairy cows are bred for maximum milk output, at least half of a cow's yield depends on the stockman or woman's skill in caring for and feeding her. Any break in routine can upset production, and feeding has to be carefully balanced and regulated. Most dairy farms are highly mechanised, and most cows are milked in highly sophisticated and automated parlours, and even fed by machine. Dairy farming is very closely linked to milk marketing, processing and distribution, mostly via the Milk Marketing Board (see FOOD PRODUCTION under MANUFACTURING), which buys from some 76,000 registered producers in England and Wales.

Beef cattle and pigs are commonly weaned early and intensively fattened over shorter and shorter periods and as economically as possible, and to give the kind of meat consumers want, in indoor units which specialise in either breeding or fattening for market. Expert breeding – for the right kind of flesh and maximum numbers – accurate feeding, and meticulous care to keep them healthy (pigs particularly are disease prone) are crucial.

Sheep are the sole 'crop' of specialist upland farms. On lowland farms they are not often more than a minor part of the stock and the units smaller and intensive. Sheep can live in the open all the year round, so that as yet there are no permanent indoor units, the sheep generally roaming freely over what may be very rough country in the hills, or moved from pasture to pasture on lowland farms. To improve production, however, ewes either have lambs more often, or earlier, or are bred to have twins or triplets, which means lambing under cover and more work for shepherds.

Arable crops are grown mainly in eastern and central southern England and eastern Scotland. The crops grown (cereals and so on) need larger acreages than other forms of farming. The balance of crops grown has changed – oilseed rape output rose to 923,000 tonnes in 1984 against only 11,000 in 1970 (but fell in 1985) – for example, and farmers have increased grass production for winter feed instead of more traditional fodder crops. Whatever the crop, the annual cycle of ploughing, cultivating, sowing and harvesting is similar from farm to farm.

Poultry, for both meat and eggs, developed in less than 20 years from a sideline to an industry producing some 874,000 tonnes of meat in 1985 (1936-8 output was only 90,000). Chickens make up most poultry production, but turkeys, produced year round, and ducks make up a growing proportion. Laying birds, producing eggs for sale and for hatcheries, the hatcheries, and broiler fattening are all separate operations. Some poultry producers maintain laying birds, hatcheries and broiler production, but usually they specialise, broiler firms buying-in many thousands of chicks from egg producers, some also 'contracting out' broiler bird fattening to farmers who return them for killing, cleaning, plucking and packing. All operations are now highly automated, even industrialised, and bear little resemblance to traditional methods of poultry care. Over 95% of laying birds and broilers are handled intensively indoors, under deep-litter or battery systems. Laying birds live under artificial light to stimulate production. Feeding, watering and egg collection are mostly automated, but hygiene, ventilation and heating need great care, and cleaning has to be extremely efficient. Systems are constantly being improved and refined.

Working in agriculture

Fewer and fewer people gain their income from the land, and numbers are expected to go on falling. By the end of 1985, only 364,000 people were employed full-time (a further 252,000 were working part-time, seasonally or on a casual basis) – and first figures suggest a sharp fall for 1986. Some 291,000 people were farming in their own right, were partners or directors, but only 199,000 of them were farming full-time. Some 36,000 of the full-time workers were members of farmers' families, and 77,000 were wives/husbands of farmers. The number of salaried farm managers has stayed roughly static at 8000 since 1981.

FARMERS, TENANT-FARMERS, AND FARM MANAGERS are today expert in both farming techniques and business methods, and have to be skilled managers. They have to organise work on the farm and supervise staff, do their own purchasing – of feedstuffs and fertilisers which can cost several thousand pounds. They have to market their produce – which may range from the traditional methods of taking stock to market to agreeing major contracts with food processors and producers. They must assess and plan progress, decide on investment – in stock, equipment etc, negotiate with the bank, see that the farm is maintained properly, and so on. Paperwork – records, tax, applications for support, correspondence, orders – is as extensive as in any other business. Most farmers still also spend a high proportion of their time actually working on the land – only on the largest company-owned estates is farm management almost entirely administrative.

SUPERVISORY STAFF are employed on the largest farms and holdings. They may be in charge of, for instance, a number of poultry or pig units, or larger dairy herds where several stock men/women are employed.

SKILLED FARM WORKERS mostly specialise in the work they do, whether they work on a specialist or a mixed farm. But while there are fewer and fewer general farm workers, most people working on the farm expect to help out with almost anything when necessary – the pig stockman may take charge of the bailer at harvest time, or plough a field. Most farm workers are trained to drive or operate machinery, help with farm and equipment repairs, etc.

STOCKMEN AND WOMEN care for animals – dairy herds, beef cattle, pigs, poultry, or sheep – each in their own special units. They look after larger and larger units – 20,000 poultry, a flock of 1400 ewes, 2000 pigs, or 200 cows. Except for shepherds, whose lives are still very hardy, they work mostly indoors, under artificially-controlled, almost laboratory-like conditions, and mostly alone with only a large number of birds or animals for company (shepherds have their dogs). Feeding and watering is mostly automatic, but stock men and women must take great care to see that feeds are measured and mixed correctly, that all the equipment – feeding, ventilation and so on – is working properly, that bedding is changed, and must keep everything very clean, since hygiene is essential. Since most farm animals, especially under intensive conditions, are vulnerable to disease and do not react well to any break in routines, they have to be watched carefully for signs of trouble; dipped, injected, clipped, and inseminated at exactly the right times, and cared for when progeny arrive.

Stockmen and women are both midwives and nurses for sick animals. They must keep careful records, of weight increase and food intake, for instance, to monitor costs and efficiency, and dairy men and women must watch each cow's milk output. They must have animals ready for market when prices are best, and know just when to replace dairy cows – and have replacements available. Under intensive conditions, one electricity failure, one sick animal, can mean a major financial disaster if not caught in time, so stockmen and women carry considerable responsibility. Hours are long and irregular, since animals must be cared for round the clock, seven days a week (and cows milked).

ON ARABLE AND MIXED FARMS, the job is working the land – ploughing, fertilising, sewing, making hay and silage, harvesting wheat and barley, rape, potatoes, cabbage and cauliflower, beet and peas.

WORKING WITH MACHINERY is obviously now a large part of any farming career. On an arable farm, tractors plough, cultivate, drill seed, apply fertiliser, spray, and most have combine harvesters. Other kinds of machinery include hedge trimmers and ditch graders, and the highly specialised machines, eg pea-viners, for harvesting different kinds of crops. The rough-terrain fork-lift truck is a firm favourite. Fixed equipment ranges from large grain-drying and storage plant to complex computerised milking parlours and feed mixers. Most farm workers will use tractors and other machinery as part of their work, but larger farms may employ people mainly as tractor/harvester drivers, and the largest employ their own mechanics.

FARM SECRETARIES are important in the farm economy, to cope with the extensive records, books, orders, forms, correspondence, etc, efficiently. Most large farms employ full-time secretarial help, but many use peripatetic farm secretaries, who travel from farm to farm. Some secretaries are self-employed, some work for agencies.

AGRICULTURAL ADVISORY SERVICES The Agricultural Development Advisory Service (ADAS) is government-run. Following a recent review, changes are in the pipeline, with charges for some advisory and other services, use of computer-based systems to provide information and advice, greater concentration on the 'development' in its R&D, and more work on conservation and animal welfare work. ADAS advises and provides information on all aspects of farming and horticulture, including management, mechanisation as well as on crops, soils etc. The state veterinary service is part of ADAS. ADAS runs a number of experimental farms and horticultural stations, science/veterinary labs, and veterinary investigation centres.

ADAS staff, who are mostly graduates with degrees in appropriate subjects including veterinary science (see also ACADEMIC AND VOCATIONAL STUDIES IN SCIENCE), work either as advisory officers, or in labs, experimental farms etc. Not all are scientists – ADAS also employs agricultural economists, and other business specialists. About 6-7000 people work for ADAS – numbers are being reduced by about 200.

Large commercial organisations and manufacturers who supply the industry with seed, feedstuffs, equipment, and so on, also employ qualified advisory staff, but the service they provide is rather more limited.

AGRICULTURAL RESEARCH in universities and the public sector comes under, and is funded by, the Agricultural and Food Research Council (AFRC), although some publicly-owned units are to be sold. AFRC has recently been through a major reorganisation, with cuts in expenditure (more changes may be in the pipeline). It still spends, though, some £100 million a year on research – 10% in universities, the rest in its own eight 'institutes' (with some 39 units/stations between them). AFRC is now giving greater emphasis to research on food and biotechnology. In 1987-8, AFRC expects to spend 16% of its budget on crop production, over 14% on each of animal production and food science, 12.5% on crop protection, 12% on animal disease, 10% on plant breeding, 9% on soils and crop nutrition, over 6% on animal breeding, and 5% on animal nutrition.

Staffing, though, has been cut, from some 7000 in (in 1983) to just under 5100 (1986-7) – including nearly 2450 scientists – and is expected to fall further, to 4330 – including 2039 scientists – by 1989-90. Staff also include about 270 engineers and engineering technicians, some working on research programmes, and a small number of vets.

Agricultural research, whether in universities, AFRC research stations or industry (eg companies making veterinary products, agrochemicals, equipment), employs multidisciplinary teams of scientists. While agricultural scientists are needed, biologists (especially cell biologists, biochemists and microbiologists), chemists, food scientists and physicists are as important.

See also ACADEMIC AND VOCATIONAL STUDIES IN SCIENCE.

AGRICULTURAL CONTRACTORS provide services for farmers, generally on an occasional basis, especially at seasons when there is extra work or for work where the equipment may only be used for, eg harvesting, although some farmers now use contractors regularly for work such as hedging, ditching and drainage. Some 60% of farms employ contractors at some time.

Contractors employ managers and experienced workers, who have to be prepared to work in different places, often from day to day.

FARRIERS/BLACKSMITHS number about 1700 country-wide. Smaller farmers, who do not usually employ their own mechanics, use blacksmiths to do running repairs, eg straightening damaged ploughs, welding on machinery, joining broken chains, and most farriers do this as well as shoeing horses. In some areas, the numbers of riding schools, stables and racing stables make it possible to specialise in shoeing/farrier's work. Some trainers, one or two brewery firms, employ their own farriers.

Recruitment and entry opportunities, and routes in, vary –

Farmers Anyone wanting to be a farmer has first to acquire a farm. This is – at least at present – very difficult, with few farms or smallholdings to rent and so the chances of becoming a tenant-farmer – the traditional way to start – very slim. Of 7500 local-authority tenants in England and Wales only a dozen or so move on to their own land in any year. Local authorities let about 125 holdings a year. The Land Settlement Association (a co-operative) lets holdings on some ten estates and is run as a 'gateway on to the land' for promising young farmers, although only a quarter actually manage to buy their own land.

Two-thirds of all farms are owner-farmed. To buy and stock even the smallest farm (which is less and less viable economically) means having considerable capital. Inheriting is the only certain way now.

It does not make sense in today's conditions to try farming without gaining proper training (see below) and experience first.

Farm managers generally need an appropriate farming qualification, farming experience, and increasingly a management/business qualification as well. Although the number of managers' posts has not fallen lately, competition for vacancies is considerable. Managers are not usually taken on under the age of about 30.

Farm work While it is possible to find a job on a farm, for young people intending to make a career in farming the best route is via a training scheme and/or FE course (below). Two-year YTS is now the first phase of the recognised entry route.

A high proportion of entrants to farming have no formal educational qualifications, but some exam passes at 16-plus† at very least make promotion to responsible positions easier, and even better qualifications are now an increasing advantage.

Qualifications and training Profitable farming needs better-trained and highly skilled people who are able to adopt, adapt to, and make full use of new techniques and systems. Farmers are increasingly demanding high technical, supervisory and operator skills.

Training, and improving both its quality and quantity within the industry (especially in relation to changing technology) is mainly the responsiblity of the Agricultural Training Board, but its training programmes are run in close collaboration with the education service. The Board runs initial courses and the training scheme (below), crafts skills training for those already in the industry, and supervisory and management training courses emphasising decision making and work planning.

The (new) agricultural (and horticultural) training scheme is the main route for young people under 18 with school-leaving qualifications of up to O-level-equivalent passes at 16-plus†. It combines the old apprenticeship and craft skills training scheme.

It is designed to train young entrants in any of milk, beef, sheep, pig, poultry production, or as mechanised operators, tractor drivers/farm workshop operatives, farm mechanics. The three-year scheme combines comprehensive practical training on the farm or holding with day- or block-release to study at college leading to a recognised qualification (as below), and with national proficiency tests, and ATB apprentice certificate.

Entry to a traineeship (formal indentures are available still) is mainly via a Youth Training Scheme (one or two years depending on age). But YTS trainees do not have to commit themselves to a full traineeship unless or until they are ready to do so, and the same applies to employers.

The first two years of the full training scheme and the YTS preferred national scheme are the same (although individual schemes are organised locally with agricultural colleges as managing agents), so trainees who have completed a full two-year YTS scheme have to do only one further year. (On completion of the scheme, trainees can, after more practical experience, go on to further AHTS training in specialist skills, supervisory or management qualifications.) Each college arranges college-based training, and work experience/training with local farmers and other agricultural employers. There are no formal minimum entry requirements.

At the end of 1985, 5650 trainees were in the YTS scheme, with a total of 7831 apprentices/trainees in the industry. The Board would like to have more. About 75% of the 4650 completing their YTS year in 1984-5 stayed in the industry or went on to a related full-time course.

Agricultural qualifications include –

Agriculture and agricultural science degree courses: intended as preparation for scientific/advisory work and not to train farmers or farm managers, although intending farmers can and do take them. Anyone intending to farm or do related work should try to gain a year's practical experience before entry. See AGRICULTURAL SCIENCE under ACADEMIC AND VOCATIONAL STUDIES.

BTEC awards: new guidelines come into force for 1988 entry, in line with BTEC's new framework (see TECHNICIAN-LEVEL QUALIFICATIONS). Schemes have a strong scientific base to support the production technology areas. All schemes include crop and animal production, mechanisation, management and marketing, but specialisation is also possible.

Higher National Diploma: advanced three-year sandwich-based course, primarily preparing for practical farming at a senior level or for work in an industry related to agricultural or ancillary professions (specialised courses include arable or poultry husbandry, agricultural marketing and business administration). Entry requirements are five GCE/GCSE passes normally including a science subject at A level, and English with two maths/science at O-level equivalent; a BTEC national in an appropriate subject (specially-designed two-year HND schemes are planned for students who have a National Diploma in a similar subject area). About 700 students were registered for HND courses in 1985-6.

National Diploma: a three-year sandwich-based course, with a choice of either general agriculture or specialisation in eg, dairy technology, poultry husbandry, pig production, horse management. Entry requirements are four O-level equivalent passes at 16-plus† including English and two maths/science subjects O-level, plus at least twelve months' practical farming experience (which may be a YTS year). About 1200 students were registered for Nationals in 1985-6.

The National Examinations Board for Agriculture, Horticulture and Allied Industries (NEBAHAI) was set up at the end of 1985, to validate curricula and provide national qualifications for courses administered by examining bodies other than BTEC. The Board works within, and via, CGLI. It is acknowledged that there is some overlap between NEB and BTEC, but the aim is to establish co-ordinated and clearly understood structures of provision with adequate opportunities for transfer and progression. The following come within the scope of NEBAHAI.

National certificate in agriculture: a basic, practical one-year full-time course. Most students take general agriculture, but there are a few special courses eg biased to arable or upland farming or dairying, and one for farm secretaries. The certificate is designed for young entrants who have a good general education including English, maths and science, but no formal qualifications. At least twelve months' practical farming experience is also needed (which may be a YTS year). It is possible to go on to an advanced certificate course to train at managerial level in a specialist area, eg pig or dairy farming. A distinction or credit plus 70% in science-based elements of the National certificate exempt from year 1 of a BTEC National.

City and Guilds schemes provide a range of practical, craft qualifications for skilled workers which, although they can be studied for on a full-time basis, are normally taken as part of off-the-job training on a AITB training scheme.

Agriculture (scheme 018) phase I (no specific entry requirements) is general, and lasts a year on day release. Phase II, lasting two years on day release, can be general, or specialised with options in eg mechanised crop production (further divided by type of crop), farm and estate maintenance, machinery maintenance and repair, milk, pig, beef or poultry production (but mechanics train as engineering apprentices: see AGRICULTURAL ENGINEERING). Phase I and II are suitable for YTS/ATB preferred training schemes.

Agriculture (scheme 028) phase III and IV schemes are in specialist entrepreneurial management.

Farriers/blacksmiths Farriers are required (by law) to go through a four-year full time training with an approved training farrier, including residential training at Hereford Technical College school of farriery. Entrants spend a trial period of up to 12 weeks with a trainer, followed by written and practical exams with interview at Hereford. The diploma exam of the Worshipful

Company of Farriers must be passed to become a registered farrier.
See also ACADEMIC AND VOCATIONAL STUDIES IN DESIGN and ENGINEERING and MANUFACTURING.

Further information from the Agricultural Training Board, BTEC, CGLI, and the Registrar of Farriers.

FISHING

The industry has been declining steadily for many years, although recently more fish have been caught and sold and the industry is more optimistic for the future. The UK industry has been successively squeezed by, for instance, 200-mile territorial-water limits, fierce competition from other countries, EEC quotas and low quayside prices, as well as the need to conserve stocks. Landings have, though, recovered slightly – to 760,000 tonnes in 1985 – although still not anywhere near the million-plus tonnage of 1973.

But the country's fishing fleets are still contracting. Latest official figure (1985) for the deep-sea fleet was 217 vessels (against over 500 in 1974). Some 64% of the catch, though, is taken by some 6400 inshore vessels. Nearly 80% of landings came from the increasingly-profitable Scottish fleet, the big-company fleets have largely gone, replaced by family-owned purse-seiners and trawlers.

The latest, most efficient purse-seiners can catch at least twelve times more fish as the largest stern trawler, taking 400 tonnes of herring and mackerel in one haul, but it is still difficult to make them profitable, and their running costs are high. Deep-sea trawlers, including the 250-foot-plus 'factory' stern-fishing vessels, now sail only from Hull, Aberdeen and Whalsay in the Shetlands. They prepare and deep-freeze their catches at sea, fishing as far away as Newfoundland. Some middle-sized boats as well as smaller vessels still fish the northern North Sea and around the coast.

Working in the industry

By 1986 only 16,000 or so people were going to sea regularly, against 18,500 in 1973, and the number of part-time, mainly seasonal skippers and crews has fallen too, to only 5000. Numbers are expected to go on falling. Owners have economised by reducing crews, but the most modern ships, the purse-seiners, need a crew of only eleven against thirty for a factory trawler. Of course this also affects on-shore employment (for every fisherman at sea, there are between three and five people working on shore, in eg fish-processing, packing, ship-repairing).

Fishing combines sea-going with food production. Crews are, of course, primarily sailors and food producers second. They do not have to cultivate or care for the creatures they hunt.

Fishing is still very hard and dangerous, but the industry talks of greater comfort, sophisticated electronic equipment for navigation and locating fish, and efficient fishing gear, which turns deckhands into 'technicians'. But while actual fishing is under way, work is continuous and round-the-clock, with every hand working 18-hour shifts. On some ships much of the work is done on deck, in every kind of weather through to arctic conditions. Larger ships, however, process below deck, the catch is landed automatically, and only in 'shooting' the net and hauling it in again are crews exposed to the weather. On smaller vessels, which may still be very modern and have highly sophisticated gear both to handle the fish and to ward off ice, deckhands must sort and stow the fish once it is hauled in, and wash down decks. On the way to and from the fishing grounds tackle must be checked and repaired. Fishing fleets also employ cooks, engineering and radio operators (see WORKING AT SEA under TRANSPORT SERVICES).

Drifters land their catches daily, following the fish round the coast – hauling is a really stiff job, since nets can stretch some way, but otherwide the work is little different. Seine-net boats, which corral rather than drag in fish, mainly off the east coast, are small, with crews of only four, so they sail the ship and cook as well as fish. Here hauling-in is very skilled work – they fish for a fortnight at a time, and each crew is paid a share of the value of the catch.

Inshore fishing boats are generally small, trawling for white fish, sprats and herring in season, and using lines to catch cod, haddock, whiting etc. Shrimps are caught by trawling, lobsters and crabs in traps or pots; Cornish fishermen can catch squid.

Ashore, managers, administrative and clerical staff work for the owners, and for the processing industry (which includes frozen-food companies).

Recruitment and training Although numbers employed are still falling, the industry is recruiting. The preferred entry route for young entrants is via one of eleven area-based YTS schemes – 378 trainees were taken on in 1985-6. Most of those who do go into the industry have grown up in fishing ports, but there is nothing to prevent anyone from other parts of the country joining the fleets. All fishermen must be good seamen, able to do many different tasks, and to react in an emergency. Good health and stamina are obviously essential.

The industry recruits small numbers of school-leavers and graduates with appropriate qualifications for administrative/managerial work – including the main commercial 'functions' – in both fishing and fish-processing companies.

Qualifications and training Training is organised by the Sea Fish Industry Authority Training Council, mainly through 20 group training associations, although the Authority has a sophisticated training centre in Hull.

YTS schemes are run under a model programme/standards set by the Authority, and include 20 weeks off-the-job education which can lead to SCOTVEC or CGLI certificates.

Experienced deckhands can go on to full-time courses (at FE or nautical colleges at Aberdeen, Fleetwood, Fraserburgh, Glasgow, Kilkeel, London: Merchant Navy Coll, Lowestoft, Redruth, S Shields, Stornoway, Stromness, Ulster U) to qualify for Department of Transport certificates of competency as watchkeeping assistant, second hand (mate) and skipper, or in special skills (eg electronic navigation systems, radar observer, deck machinery and hydraulics, marine propulsion), with support from the Authority.

Two degree courses at – Hull: Humberside CHE and Plymouth Polytechnic, are designed for those planning managerial careers in the industry.

See also WORKING AT SEA under TRANSPORT SERVICES.

Further information Sea Fish Industry Authority/Training Council.

FISH FARMING

Some sea-creatures, eg oysters, have been 'farmed' under water for centuries, but as accessible stocks of naturally-bred fish decrease, fish cultivation is increasing. The technology is well advanced, and only the problem of getting the cost-price equation right holds back development. Even so, by 1986 this was a multi-million pound business.

Government-funded research has, for over 25 years, been trying to solve the problems of hatching and raising fish species from eggs under controlled conditions. They have been successful with sole and turbot, amongst others. A significant proportion of the white fish for the frozen-food market may well be cultivated on a kind of broiler-chicken basis in the foreseeable future, and the next decade could see a large-scale extension of fish cultivation, as techniques are developed to shorten the time needed to bring fish to maturity. Current government-supported research is helping to develop a viable shore-based industry to produce prime fish, to rear young fish from eggs, develop cages and heated water systems for rearing, and improve stock. Controlling and diagnosing disease in farmed fish has also attracted commercial interest.

To date, trout and salmon farming have been most successful (1985 output 12,000 and 7000 tonnes), with some shellfish and eel. The highly-successful and fast-expanding 30 or more Scottish salmon farms expect to triple output by the mid-1990s.

Although the number of fish farms is increasing steadily, most of the 500-plus farms still rear fish for stocking rivers and lakes for sport. The number of jobs is still fairly small, but numbers are increasing – Scottish salmon farmers alone employ some 700 people. Most farms are small, owner-run businesses, although a number of frozen-food manufacturers and other large organisations, particularly where heat and/or water is a by-product (eg electricity generation) or fish can be used to test artificial feeds, have farms.

The largest employers are the WATER AUTHORITIES, but government departments, the CEGB, the Freshwater Biological Association, the Sea Fish Industry Authority, and a number of trusts are others.

Many of the jobs in fisheries are effectively 'policing', and dealing with the public (ie anglers), as water bailiff. On intensive fish farms, the jobs include managing fish farms/hatcheries; caring for the fish, from hatchery through to harvesting, constantly monitoring them and their environmental conditions, checking for disease, giving regular and exact feeds, etc. As with any intensive farming, any accident, disease etc, can have catastrophic effects. Skilled marketing and commercial management are crucial functions. Most research jobs are in government, or research association, labs, a few with pharmaceutical and feed companies.

Fish farms are usually sited in remote areas, so weather, isolation etc are factors to take into account. Fish must be tended seven days a week, all year round, whatever the weather.

Recruitment and entry practical evidence of an interest in fisheries, a biological background, and experience are useful. YTS places are possible (via Hants CAg). To become a water bailiff an angling and/or police background may help. Hatchery managers, keepers, assistants need an educational background to A level, plus some relevant experience. Research needs a good, relevant first degree and postgraduate training.

Qualifications and training Few opportunities, but expanding.

The Institute of Fish Management runs correspondence courses for its certificate and diploma exams, which can be useful in helping to get work.

Fish farming/fishery management diploma (2-year course), and BTEC HND (3-year course) – at Sparsholt: Hants CAg.

Fish farming SCOTVEC National certificate (1-year course) – at Dumfries: Barony Ag C, Inverness TC.

Relevant postgraduate study at – Birmingham: Aston U, London: KQC, Stirling U.

Further information from the Institute of Fisheries Management.

FORESTRY

Britain grows proportionately fewer trees than almost any other country, and still (1986) imports 88% of timber used. The proportion of home-grown timber produced is increasing, though, and it is planned to double production by 2005. Woodland still (1986) covers only 2.23 million hectares, just over 9% of the total land area, but this is up from 8.5% in 1978 and it is hoped to increase it to over 10% by the year 2000, 14% by 2025. Productive forests cover 2.06 million hectares, about 40% at present owned and managed by the Forestry Commission (it was 50%), and the rest privately. Current annual expansion of productive areas is about 23,300 hectares by the Commission, and about the same (under Forestry Commission schemes) by private owners. This involves raising and planting up to 50 million trees a year.

The state-owned Forestry Commission establishes and manages the national forests, for which it continues to buy land, although it is also selling some of its holdings. The Commission produces and markets timber; provides recreational facilities; encourages private forestry and makes grants; does research and development work; and trains. In south Wales, the Commission restored a dozen derelict industrial/mining sites. The Commission divides the country into seven conservancies, each made up of a dozen districts, with offices close to the forests. Of some 249 national forests, over half are in Scotland.

For private owners, the Commission provides a technical advisory service, financial grants and schemes for planned management.

The Commission co-ordinates the country's forestry research through a forestry research co-ordination committee. The Commission itself works mainly on practical problems – eg methods of improving trees and sites to increase the volume of wood produced and improving some properties of wood for major future markets, new methods of propagating and growing broadleaved and coniferous trees (eg enclosing seedlings in plastic tubes), machinery development, and use of forest produce. Basic research is more limited and is mainly concentrated in soil physics, forest hydrology, tree genetics, physiology and biology of pests and diseases. The Commission has two research stations, one near Farnham (Surrey), the other near Edinburgh.

Working in forestry

Barely 18,000 people are estimated (1986) to work in forestry, against 20,700 in 1978 – and this includes office staff etc. Under 6000 work (1986) for the Forestry Commission (against 9000 in 1978). Despite steady expansion of the forests, mechanisation is keeping down the number of jobs.

Employers other than the Forestry Commission include private landowners (especially in Scotland), co-operative forestry societies, local authorities, and commercial firms, particularly contractors who provide tree-care services, and some timber merchants. Other agencies involved in forestry, such as the Ministry of Agriculture (which encourages shelterbed plantings), the Nature Conservancy Council and the Department of the Environment (see CONSERVATION AND ENVIRONMENT, below), do not employ forestry officers as such.

Within the Forestry Commission, aside from general care of woodlands, the work involves seed collection, preparing land for tree planting, raising and planting trees for afforestation and replanting, tree thinning, which involves marking and sometimes felling and transporting timber (some timber is sold still standing to the merchants who fell and remove it themselves), fire protection and road work – the Commission builds and maintains its own (extensive) roads. Some larger forest regions are now forest parks, for recreational use. The Commission provides and supervises facilities, such as picnic places, camping sites and information offices in the parks, and has made forest walks, trails, and drives and built holiday cabins. The work is highly mechanised, and some sophisticated machinery can be used even deep in the forests. A high proportion of forest staff work in such remote areas that the Forestry Commission provides not just houses but complete 'forest villages' (managed by Commission-employed estate officers).

In forestry work the main jobs are –
Forest workers: mainly manual work, or operating machines, in fencing, planting, draining, weeding, pruning, felling, nursery work. Workers can become forest craftsmen, and gain promotion to ranger or foreman.

Wildlife rangers: protect and conserve the forests and forest wildlife, control pests, create and keep up habitats for birds, animals etc, and act as guides for the public. It is a round-the-clock job.

Foresters: technical, on-site supervisors, planning, measuring and controlling work programmes, estimating costs, setting piecework rates, controlling and protecting forest property, etc. Mainly they look after planting, tree care and felling, but also liaise with other landowners and people using the forests. Some do more specialist work, eg wildlife conservation, research, training forest workers, work study etc.

Forest officers: district forest, or 'junior' managers do work similar to foresters at a more senior level, administer grants and felling licences, some going into recreation management, R&D, training etc. They may be promoted to district and senior forest officers – senior management. The 'top' managers are the conservators.

SCIENTISTS, with relevant qualifications are employed in research, with some forest officers etc.

MECHANICAL ENGINEERS are in charge of the Commission's £50 million of sophisticated mechanical equipment and vehicles. They select, inspect, and run workshops in the conservancies, and a few assess possible new equipment, deal with safety etc. CIVIL ENGINEERS look after all the Commission's civil engineering works, supervising and organising maintenance of roads and bridges, car parks, water supplies, tip reclamation etc, and a few are in R&D, planning etc. Clerks of works supervise construction, improvement and maintenance of houses, offices, farm and other buildings. LAND AGENTS manage the Commission's estate – buying, selling, letting land and buildings etc, looking after wayleaves, grazings, holdings, and managing some commercial operations, eg camping and caravan sites. The Commission also employs a few CARTOGRAPHIC DRAUGHTSMEN/WOMEN, and LANDSCAPE ARCHITECTS.

Other employers include the National Parks, the WATER AUTHORITIES, the ELECTRICITY BOARDS, forest contractors, some LOCAL AUTHORITIES, forest contractors, and large private owners (who may be investment funds etc).

Other work with trees Forestry, whether with the Commission or a private owner, is mainly aimed (ultimately) at producing timber and maintaining large-scale woodlands. 'Arboriculture' produces, plants and manages trees to make, and keep, the environment looking attractive, although arboriculturalists do help to manage woodlands of all kinds and forestry and arboriculture do overlap.

Tree specialists are employed in the commercial sector, and by LOCAL AUTHORITIES.

Producing trees – from seeds or vegetatively – is done mainly by nurseries, of which only some specialise in trees (see HORTICULTURE). Some nurseries, independent commercial teams, and local authorities supply and plant trees. Tree surgeons do remedial work, repair damage, trim and fell trees – they are mostly independent contractors, but some work for local authorities. Some large organisations, mainly local authorities, have enough trees in their care to employ professional tree specialists to manage them.

Recruitment and entry includes
Forestry: with falling numbers in the Commission, fewer vacancies, but numbers are holding up in the private sector. Most private owners would want people as well-qualified as the Forestry Commission –
Forest officers must have degrees (or higher degrees) in forestry or a closely-related subject with a substantial forestry content (see ACADEMIC AND VOCATIONAL STUDIES IN AGRICULTURAL SCIENCE), or corporate membership of the Institute of Chartered Foresters. Recruitment is via the Civil Service Commission (see CENTRAL GOVERNMENT).
Foresters must have a BTEC National Diploma or a degree in forestry, a SCOTVEC National (including supervisory and management level modules relevant to forestry), a Forestry Commission foresters certificate, corporate membership of the Institute of Foresters, or a CGLI stage III certificate in forestry plus a NEBSS or SCOTVEC supervisory certificate and two years' experience as a forestry supervisor.
Scientists will normally have a relevant degree, but some may be 'technically-qualified' experimentalists with relevant experience. Assistant scientific officers are recruited with at least four O-level-equivalent passes at 16-plus†. Engineers, clerks of works, land agents etc should have relevant qualifications and several years' practical experience.
Forest workers and wildlife rangers do not need any formal qualifications, but rangers must have some relevant previous experience (vacancies few and far

between). Recruitment is on a local basis.

An industry YTS scheme, supported by all major employers, is based on the colleges (below) as managing agents.

Other work with trees While it may be possible to start with, eg a nursery, or local-authority park department (see HORTICULTURE) possibly on a YTS scheme, some pre-entry training is useful.

Qualifications and entry For career posts, Commission staff must qualify before entry and most other potential employers will expect this too, which means taking the risk of there being a job several years hence. The main qualifications are –

Degrees in forestry: see ACADEMIC AND VOCATIONAL STUDIES IN AGRICULTURAL SCIENCE.

The Royal Forestry Society sets certificate and diploma examinations, but no formal courses available.

BTEC National/SCOTVEC Diploma in forestry (3-year sandwich courses) at –

Penrith: Cumbria CAgFor, Inverness TC. Entry with at least four O-level equivalent passes at 16-plus† passes, including two science subjects and one testing command of English, plus two years' practical experience of forestry.

BTEC National Diploma in arboriculture (3-year sandwich course) – Guildford: Merrist Wood Ag C. Entry with at least four O-level equivalent passes at 16-plus† passes, including two science subjects and one testing command of English, plus practical experience.

CGLI Forestry (scheme 012) four-part scheme (part IV equals BTEC National) at –

Grantham: Lincolns CAg&H (part I only), Guildford: Merrist Wood AgC, Penrith: Cumbria CAgFor. At least six months' relevant experience required.

SCOTVEC National Certificate at – Dumfries: Barony AgC, Inverness TC.

Forestry workers are generally given training on the job, and with the Forestry Commission can qualify (via the CGLI/SCOTVEC certificates) as forest craftsmen, with block-release study. Some contractors and large landowners also give on-the-job training, some with release to study for a certificate. The (two-year) YTS scheme includes ten months at college.

See also HORTICULTURE.

Further information from the Forestry Commission, the Forestry Training Council, the Royal Forestry Societies, the Arboricultural Association.

HORTICULTURE

Commercial horticulture — amenity horticulture — recruitment and entry — qualifications and training

The industry divides into two. 'Commercial' horticulture produces crops – ranging from lettuces to cut flowers – for a profit, in market gardens, nurseries and greenhouses. 'Amenity' horticulture is traditionally 'aesthetic', using plants to create an attractive environment, but it extends increasingly into the wider role of landscape management and providing outdoor recreational and leisure facilities. Horticulture is all too often equated with labouring on the land, or at best skilled craft-level 'gardening'. In fact, the main career prospects are in management which, while it requires a solid scientific/technical background, also takes expert business skills, the ability to handle people and especially, for the commercial sector, MARKETING.

Commercial horticulture

The sector accounts for about 10% of total agricultural output. Growers produce a wide range of crops – top and soft fruit, vegetables and salads, mushrooms, cut flowers, pot plants, bulbs, ornamental trees, shrubs, roses and herbaceous and bedding plants. The land under cultivation has fallen sharply lately – 226,000 hectares in 1985, including only 2230 hectares under glass (down by nearly half).

Different crops are grown in different parts of the country, according to soil and weather conditions, and holdings range in size from those growing, for example, large acres of bulbs or flowers in Lincolnshire, daffodils in the Scilly Isles through apple orchards in the South East and raspberries in Scotland, to smaller, intensive units specialising in tomatoes, cucumbers, etc. under glass. Field vegetables, though, are now grown widely throughout the country often, as are root crops in Eastern England, on a very large scale, using methods similar to arable farming.

Part of the industry caters for the country's very many gardeners. Nurseries specialise in producing seeds, or propagating and/or raising shrubs, roses, alpine plants, trees etc for amateur gardeners and for local authorities, landscape gardeners, firms and other organisations with parks, public gardens, town centres etc. Garden centres are an expanding part of this business.

Profitability is hard to maintain in the face of high fuel and fertiliser bills, intense competition from overseas growers, and changing consumer demand. Even to stay in business takes greater technical and marketing expertise every year. Like farmers, growers are trying to maintain and improve profitability with more scientific methods of propagating, growing and feeding crops, controlling pests and diseases. A small number of firms are already exploiting tissue culture and the cloning techniques of MOLECULAR BIOLOGY to produce plants.

Harvesting is mechanised – only flowering plants are now processed entirely by hand; heating and ventilating is automatically controlled in greenhouses, and watering is semi-automatically controlled. More crops are grown under plastic to extend the growing season, and each acre may now carry three or four crops a year (which means work in the fields also has to go on year-round). Improving profitability also means working closely with food processing firms, and some crops, like peas, are processed in the fields. Marketing perishable produce is very difficult, and producers try all kinds of methods – including co-operatives and allowing customers to pick their own fruit.

Working in commercial horticulture

Numbers employed are included in the figures for agriculture, given earlier.

GROWERS AND MANAGERS FOR MAJOR HORTICULTURAL PRODUCERS are today expert in both the scientific horticultural techniques and business methods, and have to be skilled managers and marketers. They organise work on the holding and supervise staff, do their own purchasing – of seeds, perhaps seedlings, and fertilisers which can cost several thousand pounds. They market their produce – which may range from sending crops to market in the traditional way, to agreeing major contracts with food processors and producers. They must assess and plan progress, decide on investment – in equipment etc, negotiate with the bank, see that the holding is maintained properly, and so on. Paperwork – records, tax, applications for support, correspondence, orders – is as extensive as in any other business.

SKILLED HORTICULTURAL WORKERS Each type of crop, from fruit grown on trees through to tomatoes, cucumbers, or pot plants, is generally grown on a specialist holding, and demands expert care and attention. Most skilled workers therefore specialise, both in particular types of crop – vegetables or greenhouse, for example – and on larger holdings, in particular stages of the operation. They may have to understand complex 'new' biological techniques.

People who are making a full-time career of horticulture need spend only a relatively short period doing routine work on the land – or in the greenhouse – itself. This is because high proportion of those working in commercial horticulture are part-time or seasonal workers, taken on as and when needed, particularly for setting cuttings or planting out, or harvesting, grading and packing, or when deliveries are being made to freezer or other food processing firms, or to garden centres. Once trainees have learnt the techniques of soil treatment and preparation, propagating, pricking out and potting on or planting out, or pruning and pollinating, for example, and have enough experience, they can be promoted quite quickly.

They may go on to technical work – deciding when to irrigate or apply fertilisers and setting up equipment, and/or supervisory work – in charge of a particular operation, like propagating or packaging, and responsible for the workers, keeping records, checking quality, etc.

RESEARCH AND DEVELOPMENT employs scientists – to develop the new propagating methods, new breeds of plants, more efficient fertilisers, better methods of controlling pests and diseases, etc. Engineers develop improved control and irrigation systems, harvesting equipment. Most research is done by specialist research stations, some larger and specialist firms and manufacturers. ADAS (see AGRICULTURE above) employs horticultural advisers. See also BIOLOGICAL SCIENCES.

OTHER OPPORTUNITIES Opportunities are not, though, all with the growers. Large customers, such as freezer and canning firms, employ experienced staff in inspecting crops, crop estimating, and organising crop processing.

Amenity horticulture

This is traditionally large-scale gardening, groundsmanship, etc. It is increasingly being treated as part of the RECREATION AND LEISURE INDUSTRY, as much of the work involves managing and caring for parks etc which are used recreationally.

Employers include local and national authorities managing parks, public gardens and other landscaped areas; landscaping contractors, the National Trust which maintains older larger gardens, and commercial firms who supply displays, window boxes etc, on contract. Some large private estates/gardens, particularly those belonging to historic houses, also employ professional gardeners.

About 80,000 people are believed to be employed in this sector, and although many more trees and shrubs are being planted and areas landscaped, cuts in public expenditure and high costs, combined with mechanisation, is keeping down the number of jobs.

Parks and gardens staff work closely with specialists such as landscape gardeners and designers. Professional gardeners are responsible for all stages in the care and planting out of flower beds, trees, shrubs, lawns etc – large authorities and contractors often have their own tree and plant nurseries. Promotion is to supervisory work.

More senior, managerial staff, deal with more than just the horticultural work. They may be involved in developing the use of grounds etc for recreation and managing facilities such as tennis courts, cafés, allotments, concert areas etc. They have to see that buildings, paths etc are maintained and cleaned, that rubbish is collected, and parks patrolled. But they may also be responsible for conservation, perhaps for making part of a formal park into a more natural habitat, or ensuring that developers do not destroy or damage woodland or specimen trees, for example.

See also ADMINISTERING AND MANAGING FOR LEISURE AND RECREATION.

Recruitment and entry can be at one of several levels –

Commercial growing Becoming a grower is possible, but it can be difficult and very expensive to acquire enough land and equip it to grow crops for which only a large acreage is economic, since very little land now available for rent. Some specialist markets – for herbs or a particular species of plants for gardeners – which need very little land, are possibilities. A few people are exploiting the new ways of propagating plants, which need little space (but quite sophisticated equipment). Proper training (see below) and experience is, though, needed.

Managers are increasingly recruited with appropriate higher qualifications, to degree or HND level, plus experience, although it is possible to gain promotion from skilled and supervisory work.

The formal (and probably best) entry route to the industry for school-leavers is via YTS and the Agricultural Training Board training scheme – see AGRICULTURE.

Amenity horticulture For anyone intending to make a career the best route is via a training scheme and/or FE course (below) – it is probable that most managers will in future have gained a post-A-level qualification. Even trainee gardeners are expected to have a range of exam passes at 16-plus†. YTS schemes are, though, available (see eg LOCAL GOVERNMENT).

Qualifications and training Both sectors of horticulture need better-trained and highly-skilled people who are able to adopt, adapt to, and make full use of new techniques and systems, at all levels from operator, through technical and supervisory, to managerial.

For commercial horticulture, training is the responsiblity of the Agricultural Training Board, with schemes as under AGRICULTURE. For amenity horticulture, the main opportunities for training are with local authority parks and gardens departments, for which the Local Government Training Board is responsible (see LOCAL GOVERNMENT), although some smaller schemes exist, eg the Royal Horticultural Society's Garden (Wisley), runs a two-year practical scheme (leading to CGLI part II), for which candidates with less than four passes at 16-plus† are given priority. See also ADMINISTERING AND MANAGING FOR LEISURE AND RECREATION.

The main qualifications are –
Horticulture degree courses: intended to prepare for scientific/advisory career and not to train growers or managers, although growers/managers increasingly take them. Anyone intending to go into the industry or do related work should gain a year's practical experience before entry.
See AGRICULTURAL SCIENCE under ACADEMIC AND VOCATIONAL STUDIES.

BTEC awards: two sets of schemes –
Horticulture: new guidelines come into force for 1988 entry, in line with BTEC's new framework (see TECHNICIAN-LEVEL QUALIFICATIONS). Two schemes at each level, both with a strong scientific base to support the production technology areas, both include management and marketing. Commercial horticulture also covers plant production and mechanisation. The second scheme is in landscape technology/management, amenity horticulture, landscape design and drawing office practice, applied design and landscape construction.
Higher National Diploma: advanced three-year sandwich-based course, primarily preparing for practical horticulture at a senior level or for work in a related industry. Entry requirements are five GCE/GCSE passes normally including a science subject at A level, and English with two maths/science at O-level equivalent; a BTEC national in an appropriate subject (specially-designed two-year HND schemes are planned for students who have a National Diploma in a similar subject area)..
National Diploma: a three-year sandwich-based course. Entry requirements are four O-level equivalent passes at 16-plus† including English and two maths/science subjects O-level, plus at least twelve months' practical experience (which may be a YTS year).
In leisure studies, schemes at Higher, National and First award levels include options in parks and amenity horticulture. See ADMINISTERING AND MANAGING FOR LEISURE AND RECREATION.

The National Examinations Board for Agriculture, Horticulture and Allied Industries (NEBAHAI) (see AGRICULTURE): The following come within the scope of NEBAHAI –
National certificate in horticulture: a basic, practical one-year full-time course. Choice between general, commercial, or amenity horticulture. The certificate is designed for young entrants who have a good general education including English, maths and science, but no formal qualifications. At least twelve months' practical experience is also needed (which may be a YTS year). It is possible to go on to an advanced certificate course to train at managerial level in a specialist area, eg crop production under glass. A distinction or credit plus 70% in science-based elements of the National certificate exempt from year 1 of a BTEC National.

City and Guilds schemes provide a range of practical, craft qualifications for skilled workers which, although they can be studied for on a full-time basis, are normally taken as part of off-the-job training on a AITB training scheme.

Horticulture (scheme 022) has two phases – phase I (no specific entry requirements) is general, and lasts a year on day release. Phase II, lasting two years on day release, can be taken in any of a range of specialised options eg decorative amenity horticulture, glasshouse and protective cropping, nursery stock production.

Phase III schemes are in specialist entrepreneurial management.

Royal Horticulture Society examinations are intended mainly for parks, gardens and other trainees working in amenity horticulture. See also GROUNDSMANSHIP.

Further information from the Agricultural Training Board, the Institute of Leisure and Amenity Management, the Local Government Training Board, and the Royal Horticultural Society's Garden.

CONSERVATION AND THE ENVIRONMENT

Introduction 675
Conservation 675
Environment 682

INTRODUCTION
The range of work directly involved in conservation, of both the natural environment and the heritage of the past, and studying, caring for and protecting the environment is relatively limited, although it is generally accepted that 'mankind and its advancing technology has violently disturbed the environment and compelled mankind itself to achieve some form of tolerance to crowded, ugly and noisy surroundings, dirty skies and polluted waters' (the National Environment Research Council). The links between organisations involved in conservation and those providing country-based leisure and recreation activities, are extensive, so see also ADMINISTERING AND MANAGING FOR LEISURE AND RECREATION.

CONSERVATION
Conservation aims at preserving as much as possible of the natural landscape which remains unspoilt, reclaiming derelict land, caring for and preserving the countryside as well as buildings and areas of historic interest, including churches, palaces, houses, monuments, and ancient town centres. Much of what is preserved in this way is used, positively, to provide recreation and leisure facilities (see preceding chapter), in AGRICULTURE and in FORESTRY.

Planning authorities are mainly directly responsible for deciding what should and should not be preserved, but most of the bodies described here are represented on planning bodies, and make a strong input to decision making.

Working in conservation
The main opportunities for work in the organisations described below are for people with appropriate qualifications, mainly SCIENTISTS, and people in the

LAND USE PROFESSIONS (especially surveying, land agency, but also architects, landscape architects etc). They may be managers, advisers (on conservation), field workers, and some do research. Management, marketing, market research, are as important to conservation as in other organisation. Most conservation organisations also look after resources themselves, and so employ wardens, rangers, gamekeepers, and other ground staff.

The employers These include –

THE COUNTRYSIDE COMMISSIONS (for England and Wales, and Scotland) are grant-aided bodies which aim to promote understanding of the countryside and countryside issues, give policy advice on conservation and recreational provision and technical advice on managing the countryside. They do research to establish facts on landscape shape and leisure patterns, and experimental work to develop and demonstrate new techniques in conservation or recreation management. They are responsible for designating areas of outstanding landscape, and distribute grants. They do not own or manage land other than for experimental purposes. They also prepare guides to national parks, footpaths and bridleways, publish and distribute educational material and help develop information centres. The Commission for England and Wales has about 90 staff – half are planners and researchers and the rest administrators.

THE FIELD STUDIES COUNCIL aims at 'environmental understanding for all'. It has ten field centres, and an oil pollution research unit. Nine centres run short residential courses (one day courses). Over 50% of students on courses are sixth formers studying relevant A-level subjects, but some courses are for teachers, some for university students, and some are general-interest.

Each centre has a warden who is also director of studies, a deputy warden, and up to three tutors – they do the bulk of the teaching, but are 'strongly encouraged' to do at least some research of their own. They are also encouraged to take part in the work of local bodies with interests in common with FSC, eg county naturalists' trusts. Each centre also has secretary, domestic bursar or housekeeper, and cook/caterer, as well as maintenance, cleaning and kitchen staff.

The oil pollution research unit has 12 research staff, secretary and bursar. A small HQ staff includes director, and research director.

Teaching staff must have an honours degree in an appropriate subject, and preferably a teaching qualification too.

GOVERNMENT DEPARTMENTS are involved in conservation. For example –
The Department of the Environment has overall, central control of land use, planning, and related areas. The department has sections dealing directly with countryside planning and management, and land-reclamation units. It has overall responsibility for the protection of the coastline against erosion. Protection schemes are actually carried out by local authorities, but departmental engineers do help them. Its direct involvement in conservation has been reduced, as administration of state-owned historic buildings and ancient monuments is now the responsibility of separate Historic Buildings and Monuments Commissions (below), but through the Property Services Agency it does still look after royal palaces and parks, and so employs specialist and

supervisory staff.

The Ministry of Agriculture, Fisheries and Food, clearly, is involved in conservation, and is responsible for eg the Royal Botanic Gardens.

See also CENTRAL GOVERNMENT.

HISTORIC BUILDINGS AND MONUMENTS COMMISSIONS (for England and Wales), now manage and maintain the 'ancient monuments' which used be looked after by the Department of Environment, and develop their commercial potential. The Commissions also make grants to other owners of historic buildings and ancient monuments, co-ordinate and finance rescue archaeology, and advise the government on listing buildings, scheduling monuments and taking them into care.

The English Commission —' English Heritage' – employs (1987) about 1300 people altogether.

Some 570 are administrative and professional. They include about 60 inspectors (all with appropriate qualifications in eg architecture, archaeology, surveying etc), who regularly check on the buildings and monuments in the Commission's care, look at buildings, sites etc whose owners have applied for grants, recommend conservation schemes and so on. The ancient monuments lab employs about a dozen scientists and half-a-dozen conservators; the central excavation unit 17 or so (qualified) archaeologists plus a back-up team which includes a graphics artist. A team of six or seven education officers organises a range of programmes and activities. A sales and marketing team of over 40 promotes English Heritage activities and monuments, which includes market research into what visitors want and setting up co-operative sales promotion schemes.

Other administrative/professional staff are involved in a wide range of activities such as dealing with applications for grants and scheduling, planning and administering improvement schemes, setting up management agreements with owners of sites, collecting information on other sources of grants, developing systems for local authorities to monitor listed buildings. Not all are qualified specialists – some area managers have worked their way up.

The Commission also employs its own team of 480 craft workers, and takes on 10-20 apprentices (scattered around the country) a year to train, some under the British Craft Training School, in specialised work, such as stonemasonry or as ironsmiths. The 150 or so custodians are mainly 'housekeepers' who have developed skills and 'sensitivity' in caring for monuments/buildings, but are also expected to 'market' their properties.

LOCAL AUTHORITIES bear much of the burden of conservation in practice.

The ten national parks, for example, are administered by local planning authorities, who look after the parks' landscapes and safeguard public access to them. They restore derelict sites, preserve and plant trees, provide parking, picnic and camping areas etc within the parks. National parks employ people with expertise in the full range of land-use, amenity horticulture/leisure-industry qualifications, plus wardens, rangers, and estate workers.

Local authorities also provide, equip and manage country parks of 25 acres or more where the use is mainly for leisure. They have some responsibility for seeing that derelict land is reclaimed, and work with English Heritage to preserve and maintain listed buildings etc. See also LOCAL GOVERNMENT.

THE NATIONAL TRUST acquires land and buildings of national and historic interest and improves and protects them. It owns, or controls, some 247,000 hectares of land and several hundred historic buildings, churches, country houses and gardens, 50 or so nature reserves and parks, and even entire villages and islands. It is the country's largest single private landowner. It is extensively involved in improving the environment – it restored, for example, 13 miles of derelict canal at Stratford-upon-Avon. A major project to is to save unspoilt stretches of the coast, of which the Trust now controls over 750 km.

The Trust, whose income is from voluntary contributions, legacies, grants and visitors' entry fees, employs some 1350 full-time staff. About 50 work at head office and the rest at other centres. Land agents number about 60, and some are cartographers. Most of the rest of the staff are 'aesthetic' experts who care for the historic buildings, foresters, gardeners etc, and administrative staff including lawyers and accountants. Appointments are very few and far between.

THE NATURAL ENVIRONMENT RESEARCH COUNCIL (NERC) encourages, plans and carries out research in the biological and physical sciences relating to the natural environment and its resources. The work is aimed at advancing understanding of the nature and processes of the environment, the relationship between people and their surroundings, and their impact on each other.

The main fields of research are, broadly –

the solid earth – its structure, physical properties and processes, minerals, bulk materials and fossil fuels (geology, geophysics and geochemistry);

the seas and inland waters – their characteristics and living and mineral resources (physical, chemical and biological oceanography, marine ecology, hydrology and freshwater ecology);

the terrestrial environment – structure, interactions and productivity of plant and animal populations and communities (terrestrial ecology and soil science);

the atmosphere – its structure and interactions; and

the antarctic environment – interdisciplinary studies of its physical and biological properties.

NERC now (1986) spends 40% of its research grant on geological sciences (against 51% in 1979-80), 17% on aquatic and atmospheric physical sciences, and 18% each on aquatic and 25% terrestrial life sciences (against 15% and 16% respectively in 1979-80).

NERC carries out research and training through its own and other grant-aided institutes, and by awards to universities and polytechnics, colleges etc. NERC is organised in three 'directorates' – earth sciences (mainly the British Geological Survey), marine sciences (Oceanographic Sciences and Marine Environmental Research Institutes, the UK and Scottish Marine Biological Associations, the mammal research and aquatic biochemistry units amongst others), and terrestrial and freshwater sciences (the Freshwater Biological Association, the Institutes of Hydrology, Terrestrial Ecology and Virology included), plus the British Antarctic Survey (BAS) which has five permanent stations there, and scientific services (computers, research vessels, radiocarbon dating, etc). NERC also runs a number of specialist services.

NERC research is very wide ranging indeed, and hard to summarise in a few lines –

The British Geological Survey prepares and constantly revises the geological database on the UK, collecting, interpreting and correlating available data, but about 70% of its research programme is work commissioned by government departments, eg surveying for mineral resources, environmental mapping, assessing the hydrocarbon potential on- and offshore. Funding on basic research has, though, been cut but some regional surveys have been maintained, and BGS is working on a computerised databank from which thematic maps can be generated interactively. BGS does work like making a report on the geological background to the Abbeystead methane explosion, produces maps to help developers on mining and ground stability, and also does work overseas – eg geotechnical studies in Cyprus, and looking at ways to improve groundwater yield in Africa and South Asia.

In marine sciences, the range of research includes – the effects of ocean turbulence, developing ways of collecting data using remote sensing by satellite, studying what happens in underwater sediments to make clearer the potential impact of effluent on it, the feeding habits of inshore fish, working out why farmed salmon get certain diseases, ways of conserving the Mediterranean monk fish, looking at South Georgia's elephant seals, and the effect of detergents on fish gills.

In atmospheric sciences, much of it done in the Antarctic, studies the global climate at one end of the scale and how water droplets and ice particles develop at the other, as well as problems like the greenhouse effect, acid rain, and nuclear winter.

In terrestrial and freshwater sciences, the main programmes include forest and woodland ecology, land resources and use, aquatic ecosystem management, human impact on the hydrological cycle, land surface water balance, environmental pollution, population and community ecology, virology. Recent research has included remote sensing and mapping of vegetation and rainfall in the Sahel, modelling the effects of acidification in surface water, examining antibiotic resistance in bacteria, studying shade tolerance of woody seedlings, and how nutrients are cycled from dying roots.

The British Antarctic Survey does work in all the above areas – studying the hard continent under the ice and mapping it, probing into the 100,000-year-old ice sheet and studying its history, making meteorological measurements and exploring the upper atmosphere, studying the food chain in the southern ocean and especially krill, birds and seals. Expenditure on Antarctic research has recently been doubled.

Working for NERC NERC permanent staff number (1986) about 2600 – down from 1979's 3100 but up on 1982's 2400. They include some 1410 scientists on permanent contract (1850 in 1979), but others are employed on short-term contract, especially to work in the Antarctic (about 50 a year). The staff of the various research institutes, units etc ranges from 780 (including 520 scientists) working for BGS, through 161 (90 scientists) for BAS, down to 15 (12 scientists) in the sea mammal research unit.

NERC research employs scientists from almost every discipline.

NERC employs nearly 200 people in scientific services – computing, radiocarbon dating, and research vessels (the crews number over 100), and about 190 HQ staff. BAS also employs builders, cooks, mechanics, and medical staff for the Antarctic stations.

Recruitment and entry depends entirely on individual vacancies, what research (especially now contract work) is currently under way. Competition is stiff, especially for short-term BAS contracts. Structure, grading and recruitment method is as for the Scientific Civil Service (see CENTRAL GOVERNMENT), although some posts may be filled by individual institutes.

Qualifications and training While NERC provides grants for postgraduate study, recruits to permanent/fixed-term contracts are normally expected to have an appropriate scientific qualification (structure and grading as for Scientific Civil Service – see CENTRAL GOVERNMENT).

THE NATURE CONSERVANCY COUNCIL advises the government on nature conservation and on how other policies may affect nature conservation, meaning the ecological consequences of changes in land use and other ways in which society has an impact on the countryside. The Council also maintains and manages the 214 national nature reserves, which now cover some 155,500 hectares, and it must also be consulted before work on any of 5000 sites of special interest. The Council also advises and gives help to anyone actively concerned with the natural environment. The Council commissions and supports relevant research, largely via the NERC.

The Council's staff, although still only about 750 (1987) has increased by some 200 since 1980. The 192 scientific staff manage the regions, as regional officers, assess and decide on acquisitions. The chief scientist and a small support team decide what research should be done, and negotiate and supervise the research contracts. Council scientists look for and monitor actual or possible ecological changes.

Assistant regional officers are the 'on-the-ground' representatives of the Council, travelling around their areas, talking to farmers, landowners, council officials and anyone else involved in land management. They keep up the schedules of sites of special scientific interest and represent the Council at public enquiries.

The (small) earth science division inspects, evaluates, and selects sites of geological importance, deals with conservation, gives advice, and liaises in the field.

The three small field-survey units and development officers co-ordinate and develop scientific surveys in each mainland country.

The Council's other staff include 150 working in the field, including wardens, about 350 administrative staff, and 55 other professionals including, for example, librarians, land agents and surveyors. A small maps section employs cartographic draughtsmen/women. The Council does not employ vets, and has no posts which involve caring for animals.

Reserve wardens patrol reserves and enforce by-laws, deal with general maintenance and conservation, advise and control the public, monitor what happens on the reserve, keep scientific and other records, write reports, supervise and organise voluntary wardens and other estate staff, service scientific research work, and liaise with local landowners and scientific staff.

Estate workers, who hedge, ditch, fell, reed-cut, operate and maintain machinery, and help with maintenance, frequently become wardens.

Recruitment and entry Competition for all posts is very stiff.
Assistant regional offices probably need an MSc in conservation/ecology in addition to a first degree in biology, geography, botany, zoology or geology. Reserve wardens are recruited by annual competitions. Candidate must be over 26 years of age, and be good, all-round naturalists (formal educational qualifications are not apparently required, although A-level biology is said to help), with skills in estate work and forestry, ability to drive and maintain vehicles, and experience in conservation, most often as a voluntary warden. Estate workers are recruited locally, but vacancies are fairly rare.

THE ROYAL SOCIETY FOR NATURE CONSERVATION, works mainly with 43 nature conservation trusts, but the Society does look after a number of special areas, and employs wardens and woodmen to care for them.

THE ROYAL SOCIETY FOR THE PROTECTION OF BIRDS has some 90 nature reserves, and employs wardens on all of them, assistants too on many. They look after the habitat (eg thinning scrub, cutting reeds, cleaning ditches and building hides). Hours are often long.
A-level standard education including biology or zoology and a good ornithological background are needed – many full-time posts go to people who have worked for the Society as voluntary and/or summer wardens.
The Society also employs surveyors in reserve management, and has posts in research (degree needed), conservation, protection (five law-enforcement officers), fund-raising, publicity, and general administration.

VOLUNTARY ORGANISATIONS are numerous, but have few full-time jobs to offer. The Civic Trust is one of the largest. It encourages high-quality architecture and planning, and tries to preserve buildings of aesthetic and historic interest, to protect the countryside, to eliminate and prevent ugliness, and to encourage public interest. It supports and assists local civic and amenity trusts and has initiated hundreds of schemes.
The Committee for Environmental Conservation is made up of representatives from amenity, wild-life, natural-resources, archaeology, architecture and outdoor-recreation organisations. It acts as a liaising organisation.
Other national societies, all completely dependent on voluntary support, include the Councils for the Protection of Rural England, Wales and Scotland; the British Trust for Conservation Volunteers; the British Trust for Ornithology; the Commons, Open Spaces and Footpaths Preservation Society; the Ramblers' Association; the Society for the Protection of Ancient Buildings; the Ancient Monuments Society; the Victorian Society. However, such full-time posts as these organisations can offer (and few of them even have full-time staff) are mainly for administrative/secretarial staff.

Recruitment, entry, training etc With such a diversity of work and employers, and the high level of competition for all the few posts, no clear route in exists, and there is no specific training. A relevant qualification, especially a (good) science degree or in a land-use profession, combined with plenty of voluntary, spare-time work in the chosen area of conservation probably gives the best chance.

See also ADMINISTERING AND MANAGING FOR LEISURE AND RECREATION, FOR-
ESTRY, (AMENITY) HORTICULTURE etc.

Further information from the organisations mentioned above.

ENVIRONMENTAL CONTROL

This can mean several different things –

It is used to describe control of the environment in buildings, ie heating,
ventilating and air-conditioning, for which see BUILDING SERVICES ENGINEERING
under ACADEMIC AND VOCATIONAL STUDIES IN ENGINEERING), for example.

This section brings together jobs which deal with protecting the environment
from pollution, and restoring and repairing the results of past pollution and
neglect.

Overall responsibility for improving environmental conditions, for ensuring
that decisions do not result in damage, for controlling organisations or individuals to prevent pollution, and for promoting measures to clean up the environment, lies with central and local government. Central government sets
guidelines, legislation and co-ordinates environmental control within the
framework of planning. Local government deals primarily with the detailed
aspects of environmental protection, for example, clean air, noise abatement,
and refuse disposal. However, some aspects of direct control come under
central government eg the Alkali Inspectorate of the Health and Safety
Executive, which enforces control of industrial emission of harmful substances
into the air.

Many of the posts which deal with control of environmental pollution are
largely administrative, and involve enforcing statutory control measures, such
as the Clean Air Acts. These are the responsibility of central government (see
CENTRAL GOVERNMENT), or local government (see LOCAL GOVERNMENT) mainly
environmental healthy departments. Backing-up the administrators are specialists such as the chemists of the public analyst's office.

Research into the environmental control and control of pollution provides
work for scientists. The Natural Environment Research Council (see above),
for example, supports research into areas such as river pollution, including
problems resulting from the flow of heated effluents from power stations, and
the artificial enrichment and deterioration of rivers; lakes and reservoirs from
excess fertilisers draining from farmlands. The Department of the Environment itself promotes research by, for example, the Water Pollution Research
Laboratory where, in addition to fundamental research into water-pollution
problems, specialised services are provided, such as technical information,
chemical analysis, and development of instrumentation. Others include the
Field Studies Council's oil pollution research unit, and work in these areas is
done in universities and polytechnics. Research requires the appropriate
scientific or engineering qualifications (see ACADEMIC AND VOCATIONAL STUD-
IES).

Seeing that industrial plant meets current legislation, and does not pollute the
environment with waste chemicals, gases or smoke has to be built into new
plant or equipment, which makes it part of the work of the DESIGN ENGINEER.

Seeing that plant operates properly, and does not accidentally pollute its surroundings, and upgrading existing plant, is part of the responsibility of the PRODUCTION ENGINEER. Some firms, though do now employ environmental control specialists, to see that company policy is kept in line with legislation and public pressure, costing it, turning public interest to commercial advantage, and in trying to save costs. For most firms, however, this is more likely to be just part of the work of the most suitable person. Other firms will call in specialists when needed, either consultants or the technical teams from equipment manufacturers. See also MANUFACTURING.

THE CONSTRUCTION INDUSTRY

The industry   683
How the industry works   687
Working in, and for, the industry   690
Recruitment and entry   694
Qualifications and training   695

THE INDUSTRY

The construction industry is an amalgam of what was traditionally two separate sectors – building, which conventionally means roofed structures, and civil engineering, which is the heavier end of construction, of roads, bridges, canals, docks, and so on. Nowadays the distinction is blurred, mainly because many large buildings, like office blocks, are built on civil engineering principles, using concrete or steel frames and foundations. Parts of the industry, particularly the large-scale end, make increasing use of advanced technology, highly-mechanised methods and industrialised techniques, but at the house-building end, which one commentator rather aptly described as a 'cottage' industry, it is still very much craft-based, although highly skilled, and being transformed by the use of, for example, timber frames.

Construction is a still-massive, but complex, troubled and difficult-to-run industry. The industry is very vulnerable to the economic climate – to the availability of finance, to interest rates and so on – so it is one of the first to be affected by changes in the economy, and usually suffers badly in recession. Harsh winters have an equally devastating effect.

The industry has great difficulty in achieving the even flow of output so necessary for maximum profitability. It is not easy to plan or manage efficiently. As a result, upturns in production tend to be unexpected, and frequently bring shortages, particularly of skilled people. It is hardly surprising that the construction industry holds the record for bankruptcies. Construction has not had a really good year since the 1973 oil crisis. According to the Construction Industry Training Board (CITB), the industry's workload improved in 1983 and 1984 after a disastrous decade, ebbing in 1985, and little better in 1986.

Any growth is in the private sector, in eg commercial building (for instance, expanded space for high-tech financial services), and repair and improvement, mainly of privately-owned housing. This has been however, mostly concentrated in the south and south-east. CITB projects (cautiously) that, if economic conditions remain relatively stable, and present policies (on public-expenditure mainly) continue, the workload could expand, but only quite modestly. This could be, says the Board, at a rate much less than the average 1981-5 annual output growth, perhaps an average of 1.5%. Recent trends – with any growth coming in private, especially commercial, development, and repair, maintenance and improvement, in the south/south east – are expected to continue. The industry looks to, eg new shopping centres, private housing, possibly a channel tunnel, and road building for more work, and is trying to 'market' new projects. Overseas contracts are more difficult to win, with increasing competition from other countries.

The industry has been modernising its business methods, developing more positive and sophisticated marketing – a major factor in house-building recovery. Long-established contract and organisational working methods, the rigid divisions and demarcations between architect, engineer and building contractor are being abandoned in favour of a range of possible contract arrangements to give greater efficiency, tighter control, and speed. Improving productivity is another priority.

CONSTRUCTION COMPANIES The construction industry consists (1985 figures) of some 50,800 firms large enough to come within scope of the CITB, ranging from the few giant internationals – with up to 40,000 employees, capable of building airports, complete harbours and dockyards, oil refineries, large housing estates etc – down to the very many, small 'jobbing' or specialist firms, employing fewer than 25 people each. Growing numbers are, though, self-employed, or in partnership – at least 33% of all construction workers in 1985, and it could be much higher.

The industry probably has at most 120 really large firms (ie with 600 or more employees each), about half of them true 'construction' firms, combining civil engineering with large-scale building, about a third general builders, and the rest specialist civil engineers.

CITB figures of firms 'in scope' give a 'profile' of the industry (size is based on amount of levy paid) –

Business	Total	% very large	% very small
General builders	20,533	19.4	19.9
Building/civil eng contractors	1436	51.9	16.8
Civil eng contractors	761	40.3	14.8

The rest of the industry is made up of firms specialising in one trade. They work mainly as sub-contractors for the larger contractors, sometimes directly for customers (does not include one/two-people businesses)

Electrical contractors	6695	12.2	46.4
Plumbing contractors	4115	7.7	56.9
Painters/decorators	3496	15.4	49.2
Joiners/carpenters	2565	9.4	58.4
Heating/ventilating	2187	21.6	31.6
Joinery manufacturers	1523	13.2	42.2
Roofing contractors	1217	23.3	29.3
Plastering contractors	1035	20.7	46.1
Plant hiring contractors	987	12.8	20.5
Scaffolders	518	24.3	27.4

Smaller groups (ie fewer than 500 firms in scope) include glazers (472), demolition contractors (268), reinforced concrete firms (66), asphalt and tar sprayers (179), flooring firms (211), constructional engineers (69), mastic asphalters (105), floor covering firms (98), suspended ceiling specialists (173), fencing firms (156), steeplejacks (51), felt roofers (201), wall and floor tilers (192), insulators (232), and shopfitters (366).

PUBLIC SECTOR BUILDING In describing employment in the construction industry, the part played by the public sector must not be forgotten. While capital expenditure has been drastically cut, LOCAL AUTHORITIES, THE HEALTH SERVICES, and CENTRAL GOVERNMENT (for example) are still major customers of construction – and so employ many staff to 'manage' contracts. They are also direct employers of possibly 25% of all construction workers.

The Property Services Agency (part of the Department of the Environment) is a major employer. PSA provides, manages, maintains and furnishes property used by the government at home and abroad. This includes defence establishments, embassies, offices, courts, prisons, research labs, national museums and galleries. PSA has new buildings designed (either by PSA staff or, and increasingly, by private consultants) and supervises construction (done by private contractors). PSA acquires, leases, sells, and allocates property as needed. Recent projects included a 'face lift' for Big Ben, the new Westminster conference centre, ammunition stores, and new labs for the Agriculture Ministry.

However, PSA has been steadily reducing staff since it was formed in 1972, but the reductions have been particularly sharp recently. Total numbers are now (1986) barely 25,400 – 35% down on 1979. The workload, though, has barely changed, and the reductions have been achieved by increased use of private contractors for maintenance and consultants for design, and by increases in productivity.

The proportion of professional and technical staff has increased – to over 34% of the staff. About 39% are industrial staff, and the other 26% administrative, clerical etc. The professional staff consists (1986) of some 417 architects, 436 civil engineers, 427 mechanical and electrical engineers, 382 quantity surveyors, 348 estate surveyors, 158 building surveyors, 15 landscape architects, and four land surveyors. Computer staff number several hundred.

Technical staff include 1960 in civil engineering/building surveying, 1887 in mechanical/electrical engineering, 285 in quantity surveying, 197 in estate surveying, 35 in land surveying. Nearly 40% of the 1310 drawing office staff (down from 1870 in 1982) work for architects, 22% in civil engineering, 31.5% in mechanical/electrical engineering, and 6% in estate surveying.

BUILDERS' MERCHANTS supply the industry with building materials of all kinds. To operate successfully, builders' merchants must understand the way in which both the construction industry and producers operate, they must keep up with new products and materials and new construction methods. They have to cope with the industry's periods of expansion and contraction, keeping producers informed of future demand and avoiding both shortages and overstocking in their own warehouses. Many builders' merchants now also cater for the general public, with the growth in 'do-it-yourself'.

Builders' merchants provide technical and cost information for building firms, deliver materials (often on schedules agreed in advance), and have showrooms for both the trade and public. Over 1000 builders' merchants operate more than 3000 yards up and down the country, but rationalisation means there are now only three nation-wide firms. As a form of retailer, the builders' merchant is increasingly using self-service and pre-packaging. Some firms specialise in 'heavy' goods (bricks, cement and so on) and others in 'light' (pipes, baths, taps, etc), but recession in building means merchants must sell as many items as possible, and more firms now combine both. There are some special firms, such as bulk cement-makers and suppliers, and the architectural ironmongers who specialise in the supply of door and window fittings, handles, knobs, locks, and so on.

Builders' merchants are like warehouses. Selling, to both the trade and the public, off the counter and for advance schedules, is obviously most important, but it has to be supported by efficient purchasing, stock control and warehousing, estimating and costing, financial management, computer programming, and in some firms even making and assembling components, and producing designs and technical drawings. Some firms make up fireplaces or assemble plumbing equipment, for example.

Efficient distribution is also crucial, and merchants have to maintain and operate fleets of lorries and vans, fork-lift trucks and earth-moving machinery, to shift goods in bulk in and out of the warehouse and yard.

RESEARCH AND DEVELOPMENT for the industry is done mainly by the Building Research Establishment, although it works primarily for the government. Much of its work is on building methods designed to cut heating costs, and the practical implications of changes in building regulations. It has a staff of several hundred.

How the industry works

A building, whether it is a house, an office block or a bridge, is not something that is bought new every day. For most organisations and individuals it happens only rarely, and is a very expensive business. Moreover, building projects are 'one-off' products – they are all different in some way and need different teams of experts to design and build them. Many of today's projects demand greater expertise, both in the technicalities of the building and in better understanding of the client's business. The customer, novice or experienced in buying buildings, has to find the best team for the particular job, which with today's high costs must be completed as economically, efficiently, and as fast as possible – and be safe.

A changing industry, fighting for work and profit, is having to change its working methods. The failure of some building systems and prefabrication processes alone has brought a major rethink of the selection and management processes, right back to the start of a project.

There is a traditional way of working. Each project begins with a company (industrial or commercial), local authority, government department or individual, appointing or commissioning a designer – architect for a building or complex of buildings, civil engineer for a bridge, dam or power station, chemical engineer for some kinds of industrial plant. The architect or engineer may put together a design team if the project is a complex one – an architect designing a tower block will need structural and building services engineers, a civil engineer designing a bridge may have architects on the team. The designer recommends a quantity surveyor to the customer. The quantity surveyor advises on, eg materials and systems (as well as itemising materials and work, and making up the 'bills of quantity' on which contractors tender). The designer has to get planning consent for the building, invite tenders from building or civil engineering contractors (based on the quantity surveyor's bill of quantities), advise the client which to accept, and then supervise the project on behalf of the owner. It is a hierarchical structure, with an architect or civil engineer in charge. The work proceeds in set stages, starting with a long period on design, preparation of specifications and bills of quantity, getting planning permission, and putting work out to tender, before any construction can start.

Some organisations are such large customers of the construction industry that they have always employed permanent staff to manage their construction work, building repair and maintenance, instead of commissioning. They include CENTRAL GOVERNMENT (via the Property Services Agency) and LOCAL GOVERNMENT (usually via the engineer's or work's department), the NATIONAL HEALTH SERVICE, the CEGB, the Civil Airports Authority. Here the responsible 'manager' is often a qualified engineer – who may be called a works superintendent or a clerk of works – or it may be surveyor. Clerks of works or their equivalent are also employed by other organisations with long-term and continuing maintenance and building programmes, for example, commercial and industrial firms and universities. For one-off projects or short-term development on a fairly large scale, the client (or the architect) may appoint a clerk of works for the duration of the contract.

Patterns of working have been changing for some years. Building nuclear power stations, or airports, are so specialised that engineers, construction firms, and other experts have put together permanent teams to bid for complete contracts, through from initial design to final delivery. Different methods of managing projects are now, however, being used more widely to give greater efficiency, better use of professional skills, and speed.

Management contracting, or project management, is increasingly used, particularly for large and complex projects, where the design has to build in construction methods and materials from the beginning, where changes are possible (eg in renovating an older building), and where speed is vital. A firm of management contractors may take on the entire project, putting together a specialist design team on which the demands of the client and the project are paramount (and not, say, the aesthetic aspirations alone of the architect). Each stage of the building can go to a specialist sub-contractor, still chosen by competitive tender, working under contract to the management contractor (whose construction companies agree not to bid). Clients may, though, choose to commission their own architects and employ a management contractor just to control the building work. Using management contractors means greater flexibility, an earlier start to building, and built-in systems for solving inevitable problems. Management contracting, however, changes quite radically the traditional roles of professionals involved in construction (see LAND USE PROFESSIONS).

Design-and-build, another new management system, works for smaller contracts. This has a full-time, on-site designer – usually an architect or a surveyor – effectively managing a building team of direct-labour craft/trade workers.

Management contracting, and variants of it, affect the building contractor – and brings contractors into projects earlier. While larger contractors, particularly, make increasing use of marketing experts and sales teams to help them gain contracts, they still have to put in a competitive tender.

Estimating staff, working with eg the planning engineer, buyers, plant specialists (advising on machinery needed), soil lab technician (providing data for planning foundations) etc, work out each operation, what it involves in time, materials and labour, and cost it, putting in a tender pitched low enough to gain the contract, high enough not to make a loss. If the contract is gained, the planning engineers/site planners and contract manager prepare a detailed plan (for which the latest analytical, graphical and computer-based systems are used), making as economical use as possible of materials, equipment and labour.

The contract manager plans, manages, monitors and controls actual building operations, usually handling several contracts at once. Site managers – on a large site there may be several, each with assistant managers in charge of sections – report to the contract manager. For very large contracts, however, a project manager may be in sole charge. Site managers are directly responsible for progress and day-to-day building work. They too are involved right from the planning stage, when methods and sequences of the operations are decided, through decisions on schedules, choice of plant, organising the site and site services (access, water, drainage, safety etc). They have to make sure other section managers and subcontractors are kept informed, that materials, equipment arrive on time, that the sequence of work is kept on time.

The buyers are crucial to profitability, since at least half the money tied up in a building contract is in materials. Their problems and responsibilities are similar to those met by PURCHASING AND BUYING officers in any industry. The buyers help prepare the initial tender, and they in turn put out to tender materials and work to be sub-contracted. They must find the specified materials, in the right quantities (with as little waste as possible), at the right time (too early and it is in the way and tying up capital, too late and expensive workers stand idle).

When construction begins, site managers recruit the skilled and semi-skilled workers needed, helped perhaps, by personnel staff. Some general and craft foremen and supervisors, craft- and tradesmen may be permanent employees. The builder's contracts surveyors constantly measure and value the work in progress, keep accurate records, make site surveys before the work starts, and agreeing ground levels. The surveyors check sub-contractors bills and prepare accounts for the client.

Larger firms have their headquarters, regional and even overseas offices; employees are then generally divided into office and site staff. Most professional staff spend much of their time on desk work, negotiating, etc, although surveyors and engineers have field and site responsibilities. On larger projects, a bewildering number and variety of people may be involved, working for several different firms, some of them independent consultants, some sub-contractors. Professionals, technicians, and skilled workers have to get on together, and understand the technical aspects of each other's work.

In addition to the professional and other construction jobs outlined above, a large construction company may also employ marketing staff, personnel and training officers, accountants and accounts staff, and clerical workers.

Except for staff whose work ties them to the office, work in the industry is extremely hard and physically demanding. On site it is an occupation for younger people, and a high proportion of even skilled workers look for indoor work as they grow older. Since every project only lasts so long (although it can be years), on-site work means moving around from place to place, and for everybody regular new projects make life somewhat different from work where there is greater continuity.

Working in, and for, the industry

While employment in construction continues to recover from the 1985 low of 979,000, it was still, at under 984,000 (including 64,000 part-time) in late 1986, below the million-plus of the late 1970s/early-1980s, and is never likely to get back to the early 1970's 2 million. Current indicators are that direct employment could stabilise, but employers are not likely to add significantly more permanent employees even if conditions improve sharply. This is because, according to CITB, short-term working and labour-only arrangements meet their current and anticipated market needs and the markets which favour such arrangements seem to be growing.

Public-sector employment in construction has continued to fall steadily, and was down to 253,000 in 1985, from 323,000 in 1980.

The self-employed are officially estimated (via tax certificates) at about 469,000 in 1985, up from 366,000 in 1980. However, CITB believes another 200,000 may also be self-employed. Even on the official figure alone, this is a 70% increase in the number of people working on their own, and a 30% increase in partnerships, since 1980. Self-employment, and small specialist sub-contractors, are expected to continue to be a key element in the labour and process markets.

Since 1980, the general decline in demand for unskilled workers has continued – employment amongst civil engineering workers and labourers fell by 30% between 1980 and 1985, but the number of specialist building trades was slightly up. Building workers and scaffolders are about a quarter and a fifth respectively down on 1980. The decline in numbers of mechanical and electrical engineering services workers was much less marked, and in electrical engineering actually rose again quite sharply in 1985.

Technical developments also affect demand for particular trades. For instance, use of timber-frame in house building changes the pattern of skills. With timber-frame building there are reportedly fewer trades to be co-ordinated, labour content is less and so there is less dependence on labour, trade supervision is reduced (and quality control is easier), and fewer wet trades are used. It cuts demand for bricklayers and associated wet trades, eg plasterers. Trades likely to benefit are non-manual occupations – because timber frame requires more detailing/design than traditional methods – foremen.

PROFESSIONAL AND MANAGERIAL STAFF The numbers of professional and managerial staff employed in the industry was about 77,000 in 1985, slightly down on 1981 and 1977, but proportionately up, to 11.6% of those employed in CITB firms in scope, from just under 8% in 1977. (Many of the 90,000 or so working principals must also qualify as managers.)

The majority (possibly as many as three quarters) of professional and managerial staff, whatever their original qualifications, not unexpectedly work for the relatively small number of larger combined building/civil engineering contractors (nearly a third), general building firms (nearly a third), and specialist civil engineering contractors (about 10%). A small number work for the few large heating and ventilating firms, and a similar proportion for a rather larger number of electrical contractors (many of these are engineers qualified in heating/ventilating, and electrical/electronic engineers respectively). Just a few work for plant hirers.

Combined numbers of professionals (separate from managers) has been increasing, if slowly – to 18,300 in 1985 against 16,800 in 1982.

Engineers, mostly civils and structurals, with some qualified in building services and electrical engineering, make up about half the professional staff employed in the industry itself. Well over half work for combined building and civil engineering contractors, and a further 25% or more for civil engineering firms. The proportion working for general building firms is smaller, but probably rising. While civil/structural engineers employed by construction firms may do whatever work for which they are qualified, construction firms do not usually do much designing themselves, and normally employ consultant engineers for this. Most engineers work in, for example, contract preparation, planning and management, and in site management in the construction industry itself. See also CIVIL AND STRUCTURAL ENGINEERING under ACADEMIC AND VOCATIONAL STUDIES IN ENGINEERING.

Civil engineers who work for local authorities effectively become municipal engineers and may have to deal not only with buildings, roads and bridges, but also waterways, coastlines, drainage, sewers, refuse- and sewage-disposal works, and water supplies. See also LOCAL GOVERNMENT.

Other engineers employed by the industry – largely for their specialist skills, include building services engineers. Mechanical engineers do research, design and produce much of the highly sophisticated machinery and equipment used in construction now, and in eg lift manufacture, heavy plant installation, power generation, hydraulic and compressed-air services. Electrical engineers work for both general and specialist contractors, on electrical distribution and protection, control systems, power generation generally etc. The Property Services Agency employs 427 mechanical and electrical engineers. See also ELECTRICAL and MECHANICAL ENGINEERING under ACADEMIC AND VOCATIONAL STUDIES IN ENGINEERING.

Building technologists work mainly for the larger general building firms or the combined contractors, some for organisations employing contractors, eg local authorities, but relatively few for purely civil engineering firms. The work building technologists do is only limited by their qualifications and experience (so they would be unlikely to do work which takes qualifications in civil engineering), and they work alongside other professionals in design, contracting, site management etc. The industry is said to want more qualified technologists, ultimately for management. See BUILDING TECHNOLOGY under ACADEMIC AND VOCATIONAL STUDIES IN ENGINEERING.

Surveyors are employed in quite large numbers in the industry. Around half work for combined building and civil engineering contractors, around a third for general building firms and a relatively small proportion for purely civil engineering contractors. Contractor's surveyors mostly measure work in progress and cost, although the work they do is changing. Only on very large-scale civil engineering projects do they do any land surveying as such (most people with qualifications in building or civil engineering learnt basic surveying, and on smaller projects general foremen or site engineers do the necessary survey work). See also under LAND USE PROFESSIONS.

Architects the industry employs very few, probably at most 1500, mainly working for general building firms or building and civil engineering contractors, although a number of smaller specialist (eg in renovation) firms have builders and architects in partnership. Under 420 work for the Property Services Agency. Other organisations with large-scale building operations, such as local authorities and the NHS, also employ architectural staff who work closely with other departments involved in construction. See also LAND USE PROFESSIONS.

Managerial staff in the industry totalled 58,700 in the CITB 1985 survey of firms in scope (against 56,000 in 1977). Between those dates numbers have fluctuated, with a high point of 59,400 in 1984.

Management in the industry, particularly of larger firms, is now more sophisticated and professional, using the modern techniques now employed in other industries. The type and number of managerial posts depend to a large extent on the size of the firm. In larger firms there are separate departments, and therefore managers, assistant managers, etc, for estimating and tendering, contract planning and management, site and project management, material and plant control and purchase, and drawing-office, and in some of the largest, design. An increasing number have marketing departments and managers. The largest companies also have managers who are not necessarily directly concerned with construction, eg personnel and finance. Managerial staff are also employed in the contracting organisations.

There is no single route into construction management. At the civil engineering end of the industry, many managers are qualified civil/structural engineers, but in building it is still just as common for managers to come up from supervisory and technician-level work as from the ranks of professionals. However, the proportion and number of technologically-trained people going straight into professional and junior managerial posts is probably increasing, and the industry is certainly looking for more people with relevant qualifications for management. Management development, on the scale of other areas of industry and commerce, though, is still not extensive as it needs to be, and the number of directly-employed trainees in the industry, at 900, has barely changed throughout the 1980s.

TECHNICIAN GRADES Technicians, draughtsmen/women, and foremen numbered some 60,500 in the CITB 1985 survey, against 77,300 in 1978. Numbers of technicians fell at one stage to 24,400 (from 32,600) but have since recovered to 25,300. Numbers of draughtsmen/women are down to 2800 from 4400, and foremen most, to 32,400 from 40,300.

Almost by definition most work for the larger firms, the combined building and civil engineering contractors, but an increasing number/proportion work for general building firms. A relatively high proportion of draughtsmen/women work for specialist constructional engineering firms, or for firms of heating and ventilating engineers, however.

Most foremen and supervisory staff work their way up from craft levels through trade foremen (with on-site responsibility for all craft workers, apprentices and labourers in their own trade). They will have had extensive experience in their own trades, must be able to solve problems and be good at explaining. General foremen have to know a fair amount about all the trades on the site as well as the one in which they were trained.

Draughtsmen/women prepare detailed working drawings and plans for everything from diagrams showing geological structures, plotting features of bridges or road routes, through to structural steelwork and concrete to drawings of individual installations, such as central heating, for sub-contractors.

The other main group of technicians work for surveyors and/or in surveying departments, particularly quantity surveying, where they do contract work – costings and compiling tenders, final accounts, etc. They may do land surveying, soil testing, manage plant and equipment on site, do site investigation, or manage traffic. Larger firms, especially in civil engineering, use technicians in laboratory work, in testing and specifying concrete mixes and so on. In some of these areas there is more scope in working for civil engineering consultants.

People get into technician-level work by a number of different routes, in the past mostly from craft work, but increasingly direct from school or FE college. Technician-level work is still a possible route into management, and professional qualification, although getting more difficult. Other aspects of the work, and the appropriate qualifications, are described in ARCHITECTURE and SURVEYING under LAND USE PROFESSIONS, in BUILDING TECHNOLOGY and in CIVIL ENGINEERING under ACADEMIC AND VOCATIONAL STUDIES IN ENGINEERING.

BUILDING CRAFTS AND TRADES Craft workers still form the backbone of the industry. In all, there were about 307,800 skilled and semi-skilled workers employed by firms in scope of CITB in 1985, against 327,000 in 1982. Most work for general building firms and building and civil engineering contractors, a relatively small proportion for purely civil engineering firms and the rest for specialist firms and sub-contractors. Local authorities, property companies, and some industrial and commercial firms employ craft workers to do maintenance work, and some building. Whether the work is on a massive housing estate, or repair and conversion for a small local jobbing builder, the work within each craft or trade is more or less the same.

The industry has some 19 or more recognised crafts and trades, of which about seven are counted as major crafts. They include (trainee numbers in brackets)

	1985	1982
carpenters/joiners	66,300 (12,600)	72,800 (13,600)
electricians	41,500 (17,400)	34,800 (11,600)
painters/decorators	28,800 (4100)	33,700 (5000)
bricklayers	27,900 (5600)	31,800 (6700)
plumbers/gas fitters	21,800 (5100)	21,100 (5900)
heating/ventilating eng	12,800 (2300)	12,700 (2700)
earth moving plant ops	12,200 (100)	13,800 (100)
plant mechanics	10,600 (1100)	12,100 (1600)
scaffolders	8400 (1000)	9400 (700)
plasterers	7200 (1200)	8100 (1300)
'other' mech eng plant ops	7200 (100)	8800 (100)
'other' mech eng service	4100 (400)	4500 (400)
roof slaters/tilers	3500 (1200)	3600 (900)
crane drivers	3400 (c50)	3400 (c50)
glaziers	2900 (500)	2700 (400)
roofing felt fixers	2500 (400)	2500 (400)
masons	2300 (400)	2400 (500)
floor/wall tilers	1000 (200)	1000 (200)
terrazzo workers	1000 (c50)	1000 (c50)

Fully-qualified craft workers are trained to work on their own, or as part of a small team. They are responsible for the quality of their own work, and for planning it. Craftsmen and women work to technical drawings or notes, must measure very accurately, and be able to work well with their hands.

Qualified craft workers may be promoted to foreman and supervisor, and from there can go on to management, although the route up is becoming tougher, especially in larger organisations. They may also become, eg sales representatives, building inspectors, craft instructors. Recently, many more have become self-employed, working part of their time directly for clients, part for building firms, as work is available.

Recruitment and entry
The industry recruits at all levels, and although recruitment has been quite low recently, to become and stay profitable, the industry has to increase the proportion of skilled managers and hence professionally-trained and graduate and technician staff.

Professional level engineers of all kinds, and architects, normally complete a full-time or sandwich-based degree or degree-equivalent course before entry. It is increasingly common for building technologists and surveyors to do the same, although they can also start out in the industry.

The industry took on nearly 3000 graduates in 1985, but this includes some 500 architects going into architectural practice as well as into the industry. The main groups were 680 civil engineers, 400 surveyors, 150-plus building technologists, 100-plus business/finance graduates, 80-plus chemical engineers, 50-plus planners, 50 designers, around 50 scientists, and a dozen or so geographers.

Of those completing HNDs in polytechnics in 1985, the industry took over 120 in building, nearly 50 in civil engineering, 16 in business studies, and 11 in surveying.

See ACADEMIC AND VOCATIONAL STUDIES IN ENGINEERING, LAND USE etc.

Technicians training in architectural work, building, or surveying, normally start either at sixteen/seventeen (with at least four O-level-equivalent passes at 16-plus†) or eighteen-plus (having studied two A-level subjects and passed in one) and train on the job with release to study for qualifications, see below, although they can opt for a full-time or sandwich-based course first.

Craft and trade skills The formal entry route is now normally via a preferred CITB (YTS) scheme (see below), although CITB figures suggest that two-thirds of all entrants still join the industry by other routes, including more traditional apprenticeships and/or FE courses.

Qualifications and training

The decline in direct employment and privately-sponsored training has meant, according to CITB, that the traditional – employer-led – training base is being eroded. Combined with a changed workload this has further eroded the capacity to train, says the Board, and give continuous work experience, as fewer sites have directly-employed operatives. Many of the advances made in improving the quantity, if not the quality, of training during the early 1970s may be at risk.

The Construction Industry Training Board deals with the development of training at all levels from managerial and supervisory levels through to craft and general work. While some of the Board's proposals have not always been generally acceptable, it claims to have achieved its primary objective of awakening the industry to the need for training at all levels.

Despite all the problems, some 62,400 trainees (ie under training for at least twelve months) were directly employed by the 51,000 firms in CITB's scope in 1985, against 65,800 in 1982. To improve and keep up training, CITB has constantly to develop new strategies to cope with the changing structure of the construction labour market, its training needs and the transformation in the training infrastructure.

While CITB supports training at all levels, and throughout the industry, running its own training centres etc, the Board's main effort goes into new-entrant training –

New-entrant training CITB is primary YTS managing agent for the whole construction industry, and this is the preferred route for new entrants, at operative, craft and technician level. A combined total of 19,000 places a year is currently (1986) available on two-year YTS schemes, including the electrical contracting industry scheme. However, to date CITB has not been able to fill all the available places – the shortfall was 1282 in 1984-5, and 1960 in 1985-6, with particular problems in the technician and clerical and administrative schemes. Yet 90% of YTS trainees who complete training (52 weeks up to 1986) find employment.

CITB estimates that, in addition to YTS entrants, another 18,000 are studying and/or training for craft/technician qualifications, 6000 adults are on first-year training in skill centres, another 20,000 on various government training, employment, work-experience schemes, and 4000 on informal on-the-job 'improverships'. Maintaining quality control and achieving standards in these circumstances is a major problem, and CITB has introduced (1986) achievement/skills testing, which is to become compulsory so that eventually craft status cannot be gained without passing the tests (and completing a pre-test training).

CITB two-year YTS schemes are entered via a selection test. Some schemes have specific entry requirements, eg –

civil engineering operatives scheme: at least four CSE-equivalent passes at 16-plus†;

the electricians' scheme: 'good' CSE-equivalent passes at 16-plus† in English, maths, and a science are probably needed to get through the CGLI exams;

the plant mechanic scheme: at least four CSE grade 1/2 equivalent passes at 16 plus including two of maths, sciences, engineering drawing, metalwork (but an equivalent test can be taken).

Technicians who want to study directly for BTEC National will need the appropriate four O-level-equivalent passes at 16-plus†.

Electrical contracting industry trainees go into employment from the start of their scheme. On other schemes the aim is to have trainees in employment by the end of the first year. Trainees may be registered under formal agreements, according to industry sector.

Schemes cover the basic training for all building/construction trades, skills, technician-level work, and clerical work. First-year off-the-job courses and YTS/ECI programmes in 1985-6 trained 10,700 building craft workers, 3325 installation electricians, 1900 in mechanical trades, 590 in specialist building trades, 500 in civil engineering skills, and 560 technicians. Schemes are tailored to the needs of the particular sector/skills, but all combine off-the-job training with work experience and training on the job. On most schemes, the first 13-24 weeks are at college or training centre. Successful trainees gain a YTS Certificate of Achievement and may also take appropriate CGLI or other qualifications.

In most skills/trades, trainees can continue on to a third year of skill training, and take further qualifications. Technicians continue into a third year of training, and some craft/mechanic/operative schemes allow trainees who have done well to go on to technician-level training.

Professional/graduate training The industry, mostly in the largest firms, mainly provides the all-round training and experience needed for professional qualification for, eg civil, mechanical and electrical engineers, surveyors etc. PSA has a large trainee office (with 335 trainees and students in 1986). CITB provides off-the-job training, for new graduate entrants and management etc, at its national centres.

Qualifications The industry recruits people with, and gives training for, a wide range of different qualifications. They include –

Graduate/professional-level degree and degree-equivalent qualifications mainly, see under ACADEMIC AND VOCATIONAL STUDIES IN ENGINEERING AND OTHER TECHNOLOGIES, LAND USE STUDIES etc.

Technician-level: at higher level, sub-degree (mainly BTEC/SCOTVEC) qualifications in appropriate subjects, see under ACADEMIC AND VOCATIONAL STUDIES IN ENGINEERING AND OTHER TECHNOLOGIES, LAND USE STUDIES etc. At the lower level, under the new framework (see TECHNICIAN-LEVEL QUALIFICATIONS), BTEC is 'integrating' preparation across the building and civil engineering fields (but see also LAND USE PROFESSIONS for surveying technician qualifications).

BTEC Nationals in building studies, civil engineering studies, and construction, share common guidelines, and a common core. The two-year, part-time certificate scheme requires 10 units, the two-year, full-time diploma scheme at least 16. All schemes include units on the built environment, construction science and technology, materials in construction, maths, and site surveying and levelling. For a national certificate, students then choose either building studies or civil engineering construction. For a national diploma, students continue a broad-based construction scheme, covering architectural and structural detailing, organisation and procedures, building and civil engineering construction, environmental science, and structural mechanics. This leaves one or two units for options for the certificate, at least three for the diploma.

Entry requirements are as for all BTEC Nationals†† but O-level-equivalent passes should include some relevant subjects.

BTEC First awards in construction: the certificate requires five units, all core studies, the diploma eight which can include two options. The core units are communication processes and techniques, introduction to the built environment, maths, science and, for the diploma, vocational assignments. Possible option units include construction applications, engineering fundamentals, instrumentation and process measurements. Entry requirements are as for all BTEC First awards††.

Craft/trade etc level While trainees will, in future, take CITB-designed skill tests, traditional craft certification, via CGLI, will continue. CGLI provides full schemes for all the building/construction crafts and trades (including some new schemes, eg in glazing), plus schemes for construction technicians, and in quantity surveying. Most schemes can be completed within three years, and the basic stages would normally be taken as part of a YTS scheme. Many schemes are designed jointly with employers' organisations, and joint certificates are awarded. A construction site supervision certificate is also available.

Further information from the Construction Industry Training Board Careers Advisory Service.

THE LAND USE PROFESSIONS

Introduction	698
Architecture	698
Cartography	702
Housing management	703
Landscape architecture	705
Planning	707
Surveying	710

INTRODUCTION

The roles of the professions involved in creating, improving, managing and maintaining an environment for people to live, work, and play in seemed to be clearly defined and firmly fixed. The architect is supposedly aloof from commercial/profit motive, concerned sole with style, taste, and aesthetics (in fact, though, they are educated in technical and administrative skills as well). Developing new kinds of structures has been left to the civil/structural engineer, and the now all-important costs to the surveyor. The modern property and construction business now uses professionals rather more interchangeably than the careers literature suggests, particularly in managing a project, in controlling and managing building, rebuilding and renovation. Clients decide for themselves whom to put in overall charge.

Competition is increasing between, especially, architects and surveyors, and today's sophisticated – and highly qualified – manager builder (see CONSTRUCTION above). As a result, the architectural code of practice has been revised to allow architects to have a direct interest in property development companies, manufacturing and contracting, but building may have become too complex – technologically and in every other way – and too commercialised for architects to keep their assumed automatic leadership of the building professions. Given, though, the modern problems of large-scale building – ensuring safety, giving maximum benefit for cost, reducing energy costs, designing buildings which use, and can be used for, modern technology – commentators think it is crucial that these professions move more closely together, and should all learn the same basic skills.

ARCHITECTURE

Architects design buildings of all kinds. They can be 'one-off' houses, but are more usually a number of homes for a new estate. They may be single office blocks or stores, or complete shopping centres and precincts, office complexes or city centres. They may be single factories or warehouses, or complete industrial estates. They may be hospitals or sports centres, schools or town halls, theatres or colleges. They also 'design' conversions, extensions and modernisations of older buildings, creating flats from family houses or historic warehouses, updating hotels, turning churches or mills into home, old factories into sets of small offices, workshops and studios, and large 1930s cinemas into complexes of smaller ones.

Design is not just a matter of sketching a three-dimensional drawing of a building or group of buildings so that they will look good aesthetically, fit into the surroundings, be interesting or startling, impress the critics, or project an impressive image for the owners. The design has to be practical in all sorts of ways. The architect has to produce a structurally-sound building (and so on larger projects will work closely with engineers skilled in working out how this is to be done). Practical also means not choosing materials for their appearance alone (and materials can dictate what can and cannot be done), but taking into account qualities such as strength and length of life, and also their cost.

Then the building should work for the people who are going to use it, which should mean much consultation, finding out about and taking into account the different ways in which people now live (smaller families with more leisure time and activities), and work (offices filled with computer-based equipment of all kinds need to be designed differently those with typewriters and large computers). Buildings being designed now must take greater account of energy saving. Costs and budgets are all important, and the final design is inevitably a compromise between frequently-conflicting demands of aesthetics and practicality, within the confines of a set, and often tight, budget.

The architect's job does not end when the drawings and plans are accepted by the customer. Traditionally (but this is changing, see INTRODUCTION above, and CONSTRUCTION), the architect then becomes a manager to see that paper drawings become a brick-and-concrete reality. The architect's office must gain planning permission, traditionally prepares and negotiates contracts with detailed working drawings, specifications and estimates. The architect may still be in charge when building starts, overseeing work on site, inspecting it as it progresses, giving instructions, discussing problems and certifying that payments can be made when agreed stages of construction are completed.

Opportunities for architects The profession expanded quite considerably in the boom building years of the 1960s and early 1970s, but for well over ten years now has suffered from decline and recession in the construction industry. Numbers have continued to increase, if more slowly, to 29,634 in 1986 (from 23,000 in 1971 and 26,600 in 1978) with between 900 and 1000 newly-qualified architects going on to the register each year.

A rising proportion (59%) of all employed architects work (1986) in one of the 2500 private practices – an increase on the figure for the 1970s probably caused mainly by the sharp fall in the proportion working for government. (More than half of those in private practice are 'principals'.) The proportion working for local government is down to under 23%, against nearly a third in the 1970s, and the proportion working for central government and national boards is down to barely 10% from some 15%. The proportion working 'elsewhere' in the private sector (for construction firms, property developers etc) has been increasing slightly, to just over 7% (from 5% in the 1970s). Under 500 work in architecture schools etc. Some architects are believed to be working on a freelance basis, taken on by practices or firms for particular projects. Some 5-6000 are estimated to be working overseas at any one time. Despite the problems, under 250 were registered as unemployed in 1986.

Private practices range in size from one or two principals working alone or with a few assistants, to very large offices with a staff of over 100. Some multi-professional building design groups are more than 500 strong, but architects may make up only a third of the staff, the rest being civil, structural and service engineers, quantity surveyors, and interior, graphic and product designers, with technicians etc. At least half a dozen government departments employ architects, but most (some 417 in 1986) work for the Property Service Agency (see CONSTRUCTION). Here too, multidisciplinary teams are increasingly common and they will be usual in construction and property firms.

While some architects do work on their own, it is more usual to be a member of a team, each team handling a particular project. The team may consist solely of architects or may be multi-disciplinary, depending on the project, and the

project and its complexity obviously determines the size of the team. The team will include qualified architects of varying experience, under a team leader, and may also include newly-graduated architects completing their training, as well as architectural technicians. Design work is generally split between members of the team, with the easier items going to the juniors who gain their experience this way. Most architects now expect to make use of computer-aided design systems.

This is a career which combines artistic design – which technology has given a whole new freedom, to clad a building entirely in glass or cover a vast area with a roof supported only on the perimeter, for example – with a hard practical technological input, and with management/administration of building operations. It combines office-based work, increasingly on VDU screen instead of drawing board, and at a desk (on reports, estimates, specifications etc) with climbing around in the mud and (apparent) chaos of building sites. It involves endless meetings and discussion with clients, other experts, planners, builders and so on.

Architectural assistants' (technicians) work varies, depending on where they work, but usually they take on many of the support duties short of actual designing. They collect, analyse and prepare technical information needed before design can start; prepare technical drawings for buildings; do the day-to-day work of administering contracts; liaise with customers' staff and with, for instance, surveyors; help with site inspections and take notes on site and other meetings; keep track of any problems when a building is completed, and keep the architects' office running smoothly. For senior assistants it can be a job with considerable responsibility.

Entry and recruitment divides between –
Professional architects cannot practise, and cannot therefore be considered for professional posts, until they have completed the statutory qualifications and training. Once qualified, most young architects go into employment, either in private practice or with an employer, since starting a practice requires financial resources and plenty of experience of the business as well as the professional side of architecture.
Prospective architects need to be numerate, and to combine creativity and imagination with the ability to absorb, understand and use very technical data. They need to be logically and analytically minded, to be able to plan buildings, and also to deal with the design and construction process. This takes administrative potential and some business skills.

Architectural assistants/technicians are generally recruited as trainees (see below).

Qualifications and training in –
Professional architecture see LAND USE STUDIES under ACADEMIC AND VOCATIONAL STUDIES.

Architectural technicians: the main qualifications are BTEC awards – National Certificate/Diploma, and Higher National Certificate/Diploma.
At National level, students follow the BUILDING scheme. At Higher National

level, some building schemes include special streams for architectural technicians. HND (or HNC with a supplementary year of study) is accepted for membership of the British Institute of Architectural Technicians.

Entry qualifications are as for all BTEC awards†† – at National level, the four O-level-equivalent passes† should include maths, a science and English.

Further information see LAND USE STUDIES under ACADEMIC AND VOCATIONAL STUDIES.

CARTOGRAPHY

This is 'the art, science and technology of making maps' of all types as well as plans, charts, sections, three-dimensional models and globes, 'with their study as scientific documents and works of art'. Map making has been made both easier and more innovative by modern technologies of all kinds. Map makers routinely use aerial surveys, seismic sensing methods, and satellite observation to give them better, more interesting and more accurate information. Computer-based techniques mean maps can be drawn automatically, and therefore more accurately, with better quality, and faster. Modern printing methods, also computer based, give the map maker greater freedom too, greater use of colour, infra-red and false colour, three-dimensional graphic techniques, etc.

This also means that maps can be much more sophisticated, and provide more and different information – in cartographic jargon, 'spatial variations and relationships'. Map makers can show the contours of the seabeds (crucial for the North Sea oil industry), or the results of, eg infra-red satellite photographs which map cities or mineral resources. Synoptic surveys of magnetic differences give aeromagnetic and gravity maps. Maps illustrate statistical variation in graphic form – patterns of unemployment, or population differences, or areas of industrial use, for example, or the distribution of particular animals. Photographs of moon and planets are turned into maps too.

Opportunities in cartography The profession is small. Estimates suggest not many more than 5000 posts in the UK for fully-qualified staff. It is a two-tier occupation –

Cartographers (they may also be called editors, map research officers, or civil hydrographic officers), research and then evaluate cartographic, geographic, photographic or statistical information for authenticity, accuracy, etc, and then 'edit' it in line with agreed specification.

Cartographic draughtsmen/women actually produce the map, chart or the equivalent in other forms. The work may still involve hand drawing, but increasingly the information is stored in computers programmed to produce the particular map required. They organise the graphic processing and map design, and produce final documents for printing.

Employers While the list of organisations employing cartographic staff is quite long, few employ more than a handful.

Government departments are the major employers of cartographic staff (nearly 3000 cartographic/recording draughtsmen/women alone). The largest is Ordnance Survey, but they also include Ministry of Defence units and departments, the Meteorological Office, the Department of the Environment (including PSA), the Ministry of Agriculture, and the Directorates of Military and Overseas Survey. NERC employs cartographers in BGS, the Institute of Oceanographic Sciences, and its information services. Other national-body employers include British Telecom, British Coal, British Gas, the CEGB, the Civil Aviation Authority, and the Forestry Commission.

Local authority architect and planning departments employ cartographers to produce maps, plans and other illustrative materials. Most university geography departments employ cartographic technicians, where they may experiment with and design and produce visual aids.

Commercial employers include about 25 map printers/publishers and cartographic companies; some dozen land, sea and air survey companies, some larger civil engineering contractors, oil and other exploration companies and a few service organisations (eg the AA and RAC).

Digital, computer-assisted cartography has opened up opportunities for cartographic staff to go into R&D, software engineering/programming, sales, machine operating etc. At least a dozen companies are employing qualified cartographic staff.

Recruitment and entry Competition stiff for the comparatively few vacancies (limits on public expenditure have cut job numbers).

Cartographers are normally expected to have a relevant degree and/or appropriate postgraduate training.

Cartographic draughtsmen/women traditionally trained on the job with release to study, but availability of pre-entry courses has cut the number of training places, so a relevant qualification now frequently wanted.
See also CENTRAL GOVERNMENT.

Qualifications and training At two levels –

Cartographers normally a relevant degree in eg geography or surveying plus postgraduate course.
Specialist first-degree courses at, eg Glasgow U (topographical science BSc), Newcastle U (surveying science BSc), Swansea UC (geography BA/BSc including options in topographic science/cartography); polytechnics – London: NELP (surveying and mapping sciences BSc), Oxford (modular BA/BSc in cartography and another subject).
Some cartographic training included in geography courses at: universities – Aberdeen, Edinburgh, Glasgow, Hull, Keele, Leeds, Leicester, London: UCL; polytechnic – Portsmouth.
Postgraduate qualifications: Glasgow U (diplomas in cartography, digital mapping and automated cartography), Swansea (diploma in cartography).

Cartographic draughtsmen/women normally via BTEC/SCOTVEC award in land use and surveying (see SURVEYING).

Further information from the British Cartographic Society.

HOUSING MANAGEMENT
Most professional housing managers work for local authorities, which between them still (1986) own about 27% of the country's housing stock, although quite

a few are employed by non-profit making housing associations and trusts, and by some property companies owning flats, or their managing agents.

A large local authority may have over 100,000 houses and/or individual flats to let, maintain and improve, and housing demands expert management. Housing departments have to advise the authority on housing policy under strict cash and political restrictions (although local authorities still spent £3500 million on housing in 1985-6) – eg monitoring and assessing need and how best to cope with it, preparing or revising any new-housing programme, deciding where and how to renew and renovate old property, consulting with architects and other authority staff in planning and designing new or renovated property, looking for ways to improve life on estates with major problems in high-stress urban areas, etc. Efficient management is essential both to meet the needs of the community and make best use of declining resources.

Housing departments may manage not only rented accommodation, but also authority-owned shops and community halls, and sheltered housing, and appoint and supervise wardens, caretakers and estate staff. They cope with all the practicalities of day-to-day running of housing – organising rent collection and dealing with arrears, interviewing people who need housing and helping the homeless, allocating and letting houses, visiting people to assess their housing needs or to see if property needs repairing (and organising the work), and finding ways to involve tenants in running estates or blocks of flats.

Most are involved in housing welfare and liaise with social services, many provide housing advisory services, and co-ordinate housing association activities. Many do some research. A proportion administer house purchase schemes, and grants.

A local authority housing department administering 70,000 or more properties (the average is about 15,000) may have a staff of around 650, of whom some 250 will be professional staff. In large authorities it is common to specialise, in eg housing advice or rent accounting (most authorities now use computers for this). Although the work is mainly office based, contact with tenants and the public is a major part of the work for everyone.

Housing associations are growing in number – over 2600 were registered by 1986 – and now own and manage some half-a-million homes. Many run 'sheltered housing', mainly for older people. They may own a group of a dozen almshouses, or over 10,000 homes, and house as many people – 23,000 in one case – as a district authority. The managerial responsibilities and opportunities are therefore similar.

Property companies, and property managing agents, usually employ people qualified in SURVEYING.

Recruitment and entry Most usually as an administrative trainee in a housing department/association, either with a degree or post-A level. See also LOCAL GOVERNMENT.

Qualifications and training no formal requirements for particular qualifications, and some housing managers qualify in eg accountancy or surveying. However,
The Institute of Housing, newly (1984) chartered, has a steadily-rising mem-

bership, of nearly 8100 (including 3500 students) in 1986. The Institute sets three-part membership examinations, taken by 2000-plus students yearly. Entry requirements five GCE/GCSE passes including two at A level (AS levels accepted in lieu of either), or age 25 plus five years' housing-related experience. Some local authorities release trainees to study for these, or they can be taken by correspondence course. It usually takes three years to qualify.

Alternatively –
First-degree courses in housing studies at Bristol, Nottingham: Trent, Sheffield Polytechnics;
Postgraduate diplomas in housing at universities – Edinburgh: Heriot-Watt, Glasgow, London: LSE, Stirling, Ulster; polytechnic – Sheffield.
BTEC awards: housing studies are an option within BTEC schemes in eg land use and surveying, business/public administration.

Further information from the Institute of Housing.

LANDSCAPE ARCHITECTURE

This has developed from the centuries-old skills of landscaping gardens and parklands into a broader discipline which designs environments – city centres, motorways, industrial estates, housing schemes. The intention is to integrate essential construction into the natural landscape to create a harmonious setting, or to bring nature into the built environment.

Landscape architects, or designers, then, try to create pleasant surroundings for people live, work, and play in. They turn the industrial scars of the past into parks and leisure areas, create attractive settings for new housing estates, shopping precincts, pedestrianised town centres and office developments, and tuck factory sites behind trees and green banks. They help to blend new roads into the existing landscape.

Landscape is rather more than arranging plants, trees and lawns to make a setting look attractive. It has to be very practical too. It is, for instance, no use creating a beautiful path which meanders through shrubs across a housing estate if it doubles the distance to the bus stop, and helps create hiding places for muggers. Other safety factors must also be taken into account – such as finding ways to prevent people crossing roads at dangerous places without using ugly barriers – cobblestone hillocks which are impossible to walk on do the job just as well.

The rules of perspective, balance of shape and colour, and so on, form the framework for creativity and imagination, but the 'art' of landscaping is, in fact, just as much a science and technology. The science is not only horticultural (landscape architects obviously have to take into account what plants will flourish where), but has to include geology and soil science, to understand how local ground and weather conditions may affect the reshaping of the land and the health of plants. Technology has to include materials and construction – what methods and materials can and should be used to achieve particular effects, and to stand up to particular levels of use. Landscape architects have to take into account the way people use their environment, to create surroundings in which the people using them will feel at ease, to allow for small children, to combat vandalism, etc. Of course schemes must fit into tight budgets, and be carefully costed, and this has to include the cost of maintenance (with complex problems to solve, eg whether initially expensive but long-lasting shrubs are better value than bedding plants which have to be changed with the seasons).

Landscape architects work closely with other experts – planners and architects, civil engineers and builders, gardeners – as well as customers. Ideally, the landscape architect starts work at the earliest stages of a project, alongside the planner and the architect. They can then suggest, perhaps, an adjustment to the line of a road or the positioning of a building to improve landscaping possibilities.

As well as preparing drawings, plans and detailed schedules, the landscape architect has to produce estimates, collect tenders, supervise the work as it is done, see that the right trees and shrubs are properly planted in the right places, and arrange long-term maintenance.

This is a small profession. Most people work for authorities, like the department of transport, local councils, new towns, but some do work for large contractors and property owners, design and architectural practices, and some are self employed.

It is also a relatively young profession, and may develop in various ways. Some people, for instance, work as landscape managers, caring long-term for an area and its landscaping, and may also administer grants to improve the environment. Here it may link with ADMINISTERING FOR LEISURE AND MANAGEMENT and/or CONSERVATION.

Appreciation of the changes and improvements landscape architects can make is growing. There should be scope for expansion, especially as landscaping is a natural area for job-creation, but public expenditure cuts do not help.

Landscape scientists do research and development work on improving methods for landscaping.

Recruitment and entry It is now usual to start by going through a full-time or sandwich-based course – or courses, rather than training on the job.

Landscape design needs strong creative design potential and imagination, linked to interest in and sensitivity to land, trees, and plants, in terms of their shapes and form. Entrants should also be interested in architecture, and in creating surroundings that people will enjoy. Designers have to be able to absorb and use scientific and technical (construction) data, with some drawing/ draughting ability. Designers have to be able to work on a team. Some business sense is useful. Minimum entry requirement is two A-level passes, normally including English, maths and/or a science, and history or geography or a language, at least at O-level-equivalent. There are obvious advantages to studying a 'relevant' subject at A level, eg geography, art, biology.

Qualifications and training Two/three main routes –
Landscape architecture/design first-degree courses: at universities – Edinburgh: Heriot-Watt, Newcastle, Sheffield; polytechnics – Leeds, London: Thames, Manchester; college – Gloucester CA&T;
First-degree courses in, eg agriculture, architecture, art/design, engineering, geography, geology, horticulture, planning, followed by a postgraduate

course (full- or part-time);
The Landscape Institute, which is the professional body (qualified membership over 1000), examinations. Approved degree and postgraduate courses
exempt from three of the four parts.

Further information from the Landscape Institute.

PLANNING
The main aim of planning, often called 'town and country' planning, is to
attempt to keep some kind of balance between all the conflicting and competing demands made on the land in a relatively small and fairly overcrowded
island. Space has to be found for homes, offices, factories, roads, schools,
hospitals, and reservoirs, yet land must be reserved for agriculture, and for
recreation and leisure. Coal must be mined but the English countryside must
be preserved. Someone has to live with the power station or the airport.
Planning has to try to protect the environment from over development and
physical damage, from projects which may spoil an area of natural beauty or
destroy an historic building, prevent social problems, and yet allow for a
reasonable level of new growth, and regeneration for decaying areas.

Planning can be controversial – at one extreme people often object to any
official interference, at the other are those who believe the planners usually
know best, with the majority generally accepting the need for planning in
principle, but often quarrelling with the effects of planning decisions in their
own neighbourhoods, especially when it brings, for example, a new motorway.
Policy on planning changes all the time, sometimes dramatically, sometimes
more quietly. At present there is a strong swing away from rigid and long-term
plans, to an attempt at broad 'strategies' which can allow for unforeseen and
unforeseeable social and economic changes and developments, and some
looser decision making. Strategic planning is being scaled down.

Planning is mostly done by local authorities (see LOCAL GOVERNMENT) – the
large county and district councils – with the Department of Environment as
adviser, co-ordinator and adjudicator in disputes and appeals, responsible for
national policy, and for deciding on national needs, eg road networks.

County planning offices work continuously on a so-called 'structure' plan for
the region. This sets out, in written form rather than as a map or plant, broad
policy guidelines, some of which are dictated by national plans (for, eg new
motorways) or by local needs, for instance to cope with a high level of empty
space. Structure plans set out the main priorities for conservation, redevelopment or improvement, examine levels of industrial and/or office development,
and show the possible consequences of major projects like power stations,
mines, reservoirs, and hospitals.

For example, new housing estates and industrial developments both involve
building new roads or improving old ones, and providing extra main services of
all kinds. Conversely, a new motorway may attract new businesses and land
und premises must be allocated for them. If new industrial development is
allowed, should there be space for extra housing too, or should the new firms
be expected to recruit from people already living in the locality? Authorities
can decide to have a period of consolidation if they have grown rapidly for a

while, but have to be sure they have allowed for more employers if the population is rising.

District council planners, who should work closely with county authorities on structure plans, and perhaps with neighbouring districts (on, for example, roads), turn the guidelines of the 'structure' into a detailed plan, pinpointing proposed conservation areas, earmarking places for redevelopment or improvement, showing where industry can be sited, and the exact routes of new roads.

In the now-abolished metropolitan county areas, structure and local plans are being replaced by new unitary development plans, prepared and adopted by the London borough and district planning authorities. They cover both general policies and detailed proposals for land use and development control.

District councils also process applications for planning permission, usually submitted by architects on behalf of planners, to build new offices, rebuild (for instance) a cinema, or extend existing factors or houses.

Working in planning The profession is not very large – the Royal Town Planning Institute has under 13,000 members. Most professional planners (obviously) work for county and district councils (which employ some 23,200 people altogether in planning), although a small number work for the Department of the Environment and a few for, eg property developers.

In county authorities planners work almost entirely on policy and strategy. In districts the work is more varied and detailed. Here planners may work on policy and strategy with county planners, but they may also work on the detailed local plan, or may guide planning applications through all the legal procedures, which includes making recommendations to the planning committee, and may include a public enquiry.

Work on structure and local plans involves a lot of detailed research before reports can be written or plans prepared or revised. Planners have to know a great deal about their county or district – anything and everything that could affect its physical development in the future. They collect data through the other departments of their own councils, through and from other organisations such as the Department of the Environment, local transport organisations, the area or district health authority, and the Chamber of Commerce, from library research, and through local surveys.

They must know, for example, whether the area's population is growing or declining in numbers; whether it is changing in any way, for instance, which local industries are not likely to recover fully when recession ends; whether more older people are retiring to the district or there are more young families. The former will need greater health provision and social services, the latter schools, and either would want different leisure facilities.

Planners watch local industry and commerce to see what is expanding or declining, and try to match future employment needs (as shown by their population studies) to the known plans of business. They investigate what may be causing any industries or commercial activities to decline, and want to know whether more people are travelling to work outside the area (and also changing the pattern of rush-hour travel). They ask questions about the use of, say, swimming pools or football pitches, to see if recreation provision is about right or needs changing. They try to decide whether anything could affect where and when people shop in the district, and whether therefore existing shopping centres are large enough, or have enough parking facilities.

In county planning departments, the information collected is fed into computers which put it all together to make a 'model' of the region, and how it will probably develop if the data is complete and accurate. The computer can be used to suggest several possible strategies, with the benefits and disadvantages of each, and to pinpoint unforeseen problems. But collecting and analysing information, and decision-making are complicated, and tend to be long drawn out. People and organisations, from local residents through to the Department of the Environment, must be consulted, planning committees have to deliberate, and objectors given the chance to have their views properly heard and considered, perhaps at a public enquiry. Planning must be done within the framework of planning law, and to a tight budget. Stitching new developments, new road schemes and even improvements into the fabric of the existing environment has to be done with care, and there are always many problems to solve.

Professional planning staff put up plans and recommendations to the council's planning committee, determine which analysis of the future to accept, carry out all the legal steps, act as negotiators, write reports, and see that detailed plans are prepared. They generally work in 'project' teams.

This is mainly an office-based job, but with much time spent in meetings and discussions, and in visits. Planners work closely with other experts – such as architects, economists, computer staff, statisticians, surveyors, sociologists – and other departments of the local authority (leisure and recreation, roads etc) to see that the right information is collected and that it is properly analysed. Promotion is to team leader, and senior managerial posts, but with under 500 planning authorities, the chances of a 'top' job are rather limited.

Planning assistants help to collect, collate and analyse planning information for the professional staff, and help present information, policies and ideas as effectively as possible. They organise surveys, compile statistical and other information from reports. They maintain the detailed records all planning departments must keep. This includes maps and plans, and making limited revisions to them, producing extracts from, and enlargements or reductions of maps for (say) simple site plans or diagrams, as well as photographic and written reports and records. They keep photographic and written records of listed buildings in the area. They record and check planning applications, deal with enquiries, prepare plans for committees and enquiries, and write more straightforward reports. They produce leaflets and set up exhibitions to help keep the public informed, and work up sketch layouts.

Entry and recruitment It is theoretically possible to get into a first planning post with a degree in a subject other than planning. But competition for posts – and scaled-down funding for postgraduate training – means that graduates in planning are now preferred and, with up to 1000 experienced planners losing their posts in metropolitan councils in 1986, has made even their chances slim for the immediate future.

Professional planners must be able to understand, absorb and assess all kinds of information, much of it highly technical and complex, and much in statistical form. They must be sympathetic to and understand the social and personal needs of the people who live and work in the area, and deal patiently with people facing the disruption of redevelopment, but with a sense of realism. They have to be observant, imaginative with a strong visual sense, but capable of detailed, patient research. They must be able to work as part of a team, be good at negotiating, and able to cope in difficult situations. They must be prepared to take responsibility for hard decisions, based on careful judgement. Administrative ability is useful.

Planning assistants are generally recruited as trainees from school or college with at least four O-level-equivalent passes at 16-plus† including English, maths and a science subject or eg geography.

Qualifications and training At two levels –
Professional planning it makes sense to study for a degree in planning. Planning takes in information from a wide range of different subjects – architecture, engineering, surveying, geology, geography, local government and planning law, demography, and social, including behavioural, sciences – studied in an integrated way. Planning courses are designed to train in technological and design skills, and demonstrate the legal, economic and social implications. Courses are at –
Universities – Belfast, Cardiff: UWIST, Dundee, Edinburgh: Heriot-Watt, Leeds, London: UCL, Manchester, Newcastle; polytechnics – Birmingham, Bristol, Coventry, Leeds, London: PCL, S Bank, Oxford; colleges – Chelmsford: Essex IHE.
While it is still possible to study first for a degree in a related subject (eg geography, architecture, civil engineering, estate management, economics, sociology, law, statistics, surveying), and go on to full-time postgraduate training, the grant support for postgraduate courses has been scaled down very sharply. It is possible to study part-time, but students should have a first post in a planning department. Courses are at present offered by (but check availability) –
Universities – Belfast, Cardiff: UWIST, Dundee, Edinburgh: Heriot-Watt, Glasgow, Glasgow: Strathclyde, Liverpool, London: UCL, Manchester, Newcastle, Sheffield; polytechnics – London: PCL, S Bank, Oxford; colleges – Aberdeen: RGIT.

For planning assistants BTEC award, either in surveying, cartography, and planning, or in town and country planning. Schemes start at National Certificate level, for entrants with O-level-equivalent passes at 16-plus† – there are no (full-time) Diploma courses.
Higher National awards: most courses (part-time) lead to certificates, at present only one full-time course, as an option in land use studies at Sheffield Polytechnic.
See also SURVEYING.

Further information Royal Town Planning Institute.

SURVEYING
Surveying is not a single profession, but a group of interlinked and overlapping

careers with broadly common interests – the land, the sea, and their resources. The resources range from minerals, such as coal and tin, deep inside the earth and under the sea bed, to the 'resources' people put on the land, such as buildings of all kinds and installations like harbours and mines. Surveyors map and measure, manage, value and sell, develop, maintain, and advise.

Surveying is commonly divided into a number of clearly-defined branches, but with sub-divisions within them. It is a changing and developing area of employment. The various titles used can be confusing – insurance surveying, for instance, is not generally included with the branches of surveying described here, but is usually treated as part of INSURANCE.

Confusion is often compounded because larger surveying practices may want to offer their clients as broad a range of services as possible, and may therefore employ surveyors from several different branches (and some may be qualified and/or experienced in more than one), depending on the character of the area (urban, rural, port, etc), the type of industry and/or commerce the area has, and so on. In the high street, the surveyor's practice may be known as 'the estate agent', or 'auctioneer', even though this may be only part of what the practice actually does, but an estate agency is not necessarily part of a surveyor's practice – it may now owned by, for example, a BANK, or an INSURANCE COMPANY. Some practices are 'multidisciplinary', employing surveyors, architects, engineers, etc.

Surveyors are also extensively employed by local authorities, by the Civil Service, by construction companies, and by firms, other organisations and individuals with interests in land, property, agriculture, mines, etc.

The profession is large and growing, with getting on for 70,000 qualified surveyors. Most surveyors specialise fairly early on, but people do change the type of work they do, especially on the basis of a broadly-based qualification. The differences, though, are considerable between the working lives of different types of surveyors – from the quantity surveyor who spends most time on desk work, to the land surveyor, who spends a high proportion of time out of doors, often in pioneering conditions. Most surveyors work with other people, but some, like quantity surveyors, work mostly with other experts – architects, engineers, builders – while others, like estate agents or agricultural surveyors, spend more time negotiating with, or advising, clients.

Surveyors today have highly competitive – even aggressive – instincts, and are steadily widening the range of work they do and the services they can offer (the profession has been described as 'volatile and arguably dynamic'). They take on, and compete for, work such as (building/construction) project management, budgetary control, property development, and giving expert advice in planning. Valuation and estate surveying are increasingly important when property is a major area of investment. Surveyors manage property interests for major pension funds, and are managing directors of some of the largest property developers. Surveyors now hold all the senior non-military managerial posts in Ordnance Survey.

Surveying, like most other professions, has been gaining and changing with new technology for some years, both out in the field and in the office. Now a major revolution is under way. The US NAVSTAR GPS (Navigation Satellite

Timing and Ranging Global Positioning System) will, by end 1988 or early 1989, have in place 18 satellites orbiting in six different orbital planes, so four will always be above receivers' horizons positioned anywhere in the world at any one time. The system can co-ordinate and height a point to millimetres in any weather conditions in a few hours (centimetres in a few minutes). The speed and accuracy the system makes possible, plus the fact that it can be operated whatever the weather, that no line is sight is needed, and the control point can be wherever needed – in places a surveyor cannot physically get at – will change field surveying and services dramatically in the next few years.

The main divisions of surveying
These are –

GENERAL PRACTICE SURVEYING, is still the largest division – RICS membership (including students) in general practice is (1986) some 44,000. It is itself divided into a number of sub-specialisations –

Estate agents negotiate the sale, purchase or lease/letting of any type of land or buildings, not only houses, but factories, farms, offices, etc as well. They provide support services, for example arranging and advising on mortgages, spelling out the legal position on letting, suggesting what the price or rent might be for a given property.

They may also manage property – flats, houses, office blocks – for the owners, although some property companies employ their own housing managers who are frequently qualified surveyors, as do the largest housing associations. (Local authorities also employ housing managers for their residential estates, but they are not usually qualified surveyors.)

Estate agents are often also auctioneers, and may be valuers. Auctioneers normally qualify also as valuers, so it is usual to be qualified in at least two of these three. A larger firm of estate agents may employ different people as property sales negotiators (dealing directly with sellers and buyers, and usually specialising in houses or industrial/commercial property), as valuers and as auctioneers. An estate agency practice managing property may also employ, for example, building surveyors (see below).

Estate agency is a tough, aggressive business, and has become more so in current competition, as the financial-services sector moves in. Negotiators suffer 'burn out' and so few stay at the front end past forty – and need to be well-prepared and -qualified for the equally difficult, but different, job of management if they are to survive in the business.

Traditionally it is a very fragmented sector with an estimated 11,000 firms working out of 14,800 offices in 1984 and up to then few big, country-wide networks – the largest had only 190 offices, 1600 staff, and handled under 2% of total sales. But by 1986, the five largest estate-agency groups were owned or controlled by financial institutions – a merchant bank, a retail bank, and three insurance companies – and it is expected the next five largest will be bought out by the end of 1987. Around 38,000 people are estimated to work in estate agency.

Auctioneers organise and run the sale by auction of property of all kinds – houses, industrial and commercial buildings, farms and other estates – land,

and the contents of houses, farms, and factories. In farming areas they also sell cattle, sheep, pigs, and machinery. Handling the sale is only part of an auctioneer's work – they have to know a lot about values, recommend reserve prices, have the items grouped into lots, and catalogued. Some firms specialise entirely in auctioneering, and even in selling particular types of property, while others combine auctioneering with estate agency or agricultural surveying (see below). The very few, mainly London, art sale rooms employ art experts who have grafted on auctioneering skills, rather than the other way round.

Valuers are also called valuation surveyors or even just surveyors. They have to decide just how much a property (which may be land, buildings, contents), is worth at the time of valuation – which may be when it is for sale, when a sale or purchase is contemplated, for the rating authority, or for insurance, accounting or death duties.

Valuers do not only look at the property itself and its condition, but also compare it with similar property in the area and at the potential for improvement or development. For houses, the neighbourhood is important – the amenities, such as shops, schools, parks and swimming pools; whether it is noisy; whether any local nuisance is bad enough to affect the value; whether public transport is close enough for convenience yet not close enough to be intrusive. Planned motorways or new housing estates may affect valuation, as may a conservation or development area. There is always an element of inspired guesswork – whether the area could become fashionable, for instance. Equally important factors have to be taken into account when valuing industrial sites or offices.

Some surveyors may specialise in valuing 'chattels', such as silver or paintings, but others may call in experts.

Valuers work for estate agents, in private practice, for commercial firms and property developers. They also work for local authorities, and for Inland Revenue's valuation office, which values property for tax and also makes rating assessments, acts for other government departments when they acquire or sell land and buildings, and for local authorities too when government money is involved.

Building surveyors look after the structural well-being of buildings of all kind, 'managing' maintenance and repair, and regular checks on their condition. They are also frequently take charge of improvements, renovation and extension of buildings, an expanding field of work as it becomes more economic and environmentally-acceptable to convert old buildings of all kinds for new uses. Here they frequently supervise the building work, having prepared plans, measured and specified the work to be done. It is building surveyors who make structural surveys for people (or their building societies) wanting to buy houses.

Some building surveyors are self-employed practitioners (or work for another surveyor who is), some work for large property owners (who are not only property companies as such, but also include firms like banks, hotel or chain stores, who have premises all over the country), for the government (in the Property Services Agency which looks after government and other state buildings), or for firms which manage property on behalf of the owners. For them, they set up and run maintenance programmes, which have to be properly costed, and also prepare plans for, specify and supervise work on conversions and improvements for them.

AGRICULTURAL SURVEYING AND LAND AGENCY Individual land agents traditionally managed large estates as employers of the owners (and over 500 still do). They care for the land itself, the buildings, woodlands, and estate roads; and deal with tenants, fishing and other game rights. In the past they also ran the 'home' (as opposed to tenant) farms. More large estates, including those owned by pension funds and other financial institutions, are now run by firms of land agents, who may also be agricultural surveyors.

While farms themselves may be run by people qualified in agriculture (and some agricultural surveyors start out in agriculture), land agents now deal mainly with the business management of farms, advising, for example, on ways of making a better income out of land – for example, by converting part to a country park or caravan site – on the design and development of farm buildings, and the management and development of commercial woodlands. They look after stocktaking valuations, and negotiate claims when there is a compulsory purchase. Agricultural surveyors/land agents are expected to help solve many of the current problems being faced by the AGRICULTURAL INDUSTRY.

About half the 2000 or more agricultural surveyors in private practice are livestock auctioneers, but many of the rest are also involved in estate agency, valuation and other auctioneering, but of country and farm properties, and agricultural machinery. Several hundred work for the Ministry of Agriculture's advisory services – on siting, layout, design and construction of farm buildings, drainage, land reclamation, as well as managing some government-run land, handling applications for grants, and advising planning authorities on the implications of proposals on agricultural land.

LAND AND HYDROGRAPHIC SURVEYING are two distinct specialisations, but both measure, plot and map.

Land surveyors measure and plot the earth's physical features to provide the data from which cartographers make maps, civil engineers lay out new roads or other major works, planners prepare a new development, and on which the boundaries of estates are settled.

Using ultra-modern equipment, such as aerial photography, satellite surveying and automatic measuring instruments (which use laser beams as light source and transfer measurements to computer memory at the press of a button), the problems of recording every change in the shape of the land, plotting exactly the route of a road or river, accurately locating buildings in relation to each other, checking the acreage of a wood, or measuring exactly the minute annual movements of the earth's crust, have been made somewhat easier, giving clients a better service. Distances, vegetation, and weather still mean surveyors need resourcefulness, determination and plenty of experience, though.

Land surveyors may be self-employed in private practice (or work for such a practice), work for consulting engineers, for large construction companies, aerial survey forms, and for the government's surveying departments –

Ordnance, and the Directorate of Overseas Surveyors. The Directorate sends experienced surveyors to work mainly in developing countries. In fact, about half of all land surveyors are generally working overseas at any one time – mapping the last few unsurveyed areas, mostly in the Middle East, Africa, the Caribbean and the Pacific.

Hydrographic surveyors 'map' the seas, rivers and other inland waterways, harbours and ports, producing charts which show, for instance, the varying depths of the seabed, hazards (like wrecks), tides and currents. Like land surveyors, they have modern, technological equipment, including infra-red, microwave and laser-ranging instruments to compute distances and, for instance, the exact position of an oil rig, and sonar, echo-sounders etc for underwater exploration.

North Sea oil and gas exploration, and super-tankers drawing twice as much water as they used to, have increased considerably the work of hydrographic surveyors. Much of the North Sea had not been surveyed at all, and where charts existed they were totally inadequate to plot accurately where, for example, the offshore boundaries are, to plan and route oil and gas pipelines, to build new terminals with the necessary channels for tankers, or locate production sites.

Most hydrographic surveyors are in the Royal Navy, since it is the British Admiralty charts produced by the Navy's hydrographic department which are used world wide, but there are some posts in the government's central survey branch and with the steady increase in exploration for underwater resources (not only oil and gas but, in future, other ores also), more opportunities in exploration and survey firms. Nevertheless, it is still a very small group – probably less than 200 in all.

MINING OR MINERAL SURVEYING Mining surveyors map deposits of mineable minerals, such as coal, metal ores, salt, and phosphates; building materials like sand, gravel, and aggregate, etc. They make detailed surveys of concession areas, and make and maintain plans of mine workings. The job includes responsibility for mine safety, stability problems stemming from mine operations, and for solving the environmental problems. Mine surveyors also value deposits, manage concessions, and advise on pricing policies and rates for leasing, deal with legal aspects.

In Britain, the major employer is British Coal, but there are also some posts in local council planning offices, water boards, and British Rail. Inland Revenue's valuation office employs a few in the valuation of surface and underground minerals, mineral-bearing land and damage from subsidence. The main opportunities to work in areas like metal mining are overseas, with some international firms recruiting surveyors in the UK.

QUANTITY SURVEYING Quantity surveyors are cost experts. Largely because they closely monitor soaring construction bills and so can make projects viable and profitable, it is the most rapidly-expanding division of surveying – 29,000 qualified RICS members and students, and rapidly developing too. 'The typical quantity surveyor is now a very powerful figure in the construction world', said the *Financial Times*; 'he has financial muscle and he is extending his role into the fields of contracting, civil and industrial engineering, services consultancy and project management and control.' Another commentator said, 'In today's competitive world, quantity surveyors are as commercial and as quick-footed as anyone in the property industry.'

All this is developing out of their traditional work of seeing that a building project is finished within budget and on time, looking after both overall and detailed cost control through pre-construction and construction. But the traditional working methods meant that, however good they were as cost managers, quantity surveyors could not always control other parts of the design/construction team – with buildings only too often late and way over budget. By becoming project managers (see CONSTRUCTION), working directly for the customer (and not just one of a team), and in control, quantity surveyors can provide realistic cost, time and quality targets and see they are kept. Quantity surveyors, brought into a project early enough, can evaluate the development, prepare several different costing options, and find one that is going to be cost effective. Because projects may be viable only if built fast, a skilled quantity surveyor can look into, compare and assess construction methods, to come up with the most efficient. 'Design-and-build' or package-deal contracts (see CONSTRUCTION), also give quantity surveyors a place as client or employer's representative. Quantity surveyors may make economic analyses of competing designs.

'Information technology' has made this possible. Much of the traditional – and very lengthy – nuts-and-bolts data collection, estimating, costing and tender documenting work of quantity surveying is now done by computer, faster, to give much more accurate information from the earliest days of a project. Information flows can be constantly and more accurately monitored and controlled. Old 'crisis management' methods and on-site problems can now be eliminated using such systems. Customers can also take a longer-term view of the real cost of buildings and their maintenance.

All this is relatively new, and only some – one estimate says 10% – quantity surveyors will be able, or want to, move into these new high-profile roles. And while project management teams may be quantity-surveyor led, they have to include other experts, eg construction managers and process engineers, who can fully understand what the design team is doing. Many, probably most, will continue to monitor costs on a more mundane level, responsible for advising designers on costings, controlling the computer-based process of turning finished design drawings and plans into a detailed breakdown of materials, labour and equipment and working out how much it will cost to build.

Quantity surveyors draw up building contracts, decide/advise on tendering methods. They monitor the budget throughout construction, checking and agreeing contractors' and suppliers' invoices, monthly, negotiating on pricing 'variations', and the final account.

Some 54% of the 19,000 qualified and practising quantity surveyors work (1987) in private practices, many of which are increasingly multidisciplinary, including architects, engineers etc as part of a team. Practices are employed by eg architects, contractors, property-owning clients etc for the length of a contract. About 18% work for construction companies, construction managers, and consultant civil engineers, 20% for government departments or local councils, and 7% for other commercial and industrial firms. In each case they do their costings etc, negotiating on their behalf with the 'other side'.

PLANNING AND DEVELOPMENT SURVEYING This is a relatively new area of surveying. These surveyors try to inject economic realism into planning, and aim to show what is possible in terms of given resources, and what the alternative uses of the resources might be. They may, for example, show how an extensive plan for a shopping precinct may be modified to allow funds for a sports centre elsewhere, or the difference in costs and advantages to renovating existing factories against a brand-new industrial site. They investigate to see that the investment decision is the right one – will a new shopping centre attract enough shoppers to justify the rents? Is there the demand for, and the groups to use, a new leisure centre?

Some development planners provide factual information for others to use and interpret. Some analyse and use it themselves as an equal member of the planning team in a district council, others work on strategic planning in counties. Some work for the Department of the Environment, advising on planning policies, acting as assessors in public enquiries. Some work for firms of planning consultants. Some go into general surveying practice, providing a service to clients in the development business – suggesting projects, advising on development proposals and planning procedures. Some work for property developers or construction companies, where they can become project managers on individual developments.

ARCHAEOLOGICAL SURVEYING A new, and still very small group. Archaeological surveyors use land surveying skills and cartography to make maps, plans and cross-sections of archaeological excavations and historic sites, normally working under a director of excavations or rescue archaeology. It involves learning about archaeological problems, methods, etc.

Surveying technicians

Some of the less demanding areas of professional surveyors' work is frequently done by 'technicians' – a term which refers to a level of qualification rather than a job specification. The dividing line between professional and technician is not hard and fast, though, and many technician-level posts are highly specialist and still carry considerable responsibility, although mostly they work under supervision from a professional surveyor (or architect, or engineer).

Technician-level careers range through all the branches of surveying. Examples of the work they do include –

In general practice the estate agent's negotiator is generally trained to technician level, and the valuer and estate manager will be similarly-qualified assistants.

In building surveying they may be the people who actually climb about the attics to look for dry rot. They may prepare the detailed plans and specifications for repairs or improvements, organise the work, and deal with the day-to-day business on tenders and contracts, checking accounts.

In a local council a building inspector is technician level, and so may be a site manager in construction.

In land surveying the 'technician' is generally an assistant, actually carrying out the measuring, and maintaining records.

In quantity surveying, assistants 'take off' the measurements and items from the architect's or engineer's specifications and drawings, and list them as materials, processes, and labour. They 'work up' (ie work out) the quantities, areas, and volumes measured in taking off, and describe them in standardised units. Much of this work is now computer-based. They are site measurers (of materials and labour used and the amount of work done).

Photogrammetric technicians prepare, under supervision, maps, photomaps, elevation drawings and digital data for a computer information store, by interpreting and measuring photographs. They have to give the information to the required scale, and put it into an appropriate format.

Recruitment and entry
Reports suggest a growing shortage of qualified surveyors. Entry divides between professional and technician, but routes through are possible still –

Professional Nearly 75% of all entrants are now graduates, and almost 68% have relevant/exempting degrees. The part-time route, with on-the-job training, remains open, but see professional bodies below.

Technician It is possible to start work as a trainee technician at sixteen-plus with at least four O-level-equivalent passes at 16-plus† (including maths and a science), but it is more usual to start at eighteen-plus having studied two subjects to A level and passed in one.

All surveyors (and their assistants) need numeracy, for measurement, valuation, and costing, but the level needed varies. Land surveyors are the most mathematical, but in all branches surveyors must be able to extract the story the figures tell, and explain it to others. Surveyors need to be accurate and exact, able to work to high tolerances, and have a practical approach to problems.
They have to
  be able to absorb and understand a lot of different kinds of information – finance and patterns of investment, land and property markets etc included;
  know a lot about the problems and practices of architects, planners, and engineers;
  understand building technology, the construction industry, and keep abreast of developments;
  may need to know a lot about agriculture or forestry;
  stay abreast of industrial and commercial change – and the new kinds of accommodation they need – and monitor social developments like where and how people want to live;
  have a sound business sense, and increasingly all kinds of managerial skills, in the public sector (to see that rate- or taxpayers get value for money), no less than in private practice or commercial employment – although the commercial pressures are obviously greater in the private sector;
  be able to get on with other people, work in teams, and co-operate closely with other professionals.

Qualifications and training
Divides between –
Professional level a broad-based training is useful. Four possible routes –
First-degree course, full-time, in a subject exempting from professional exams, ie

Building economics: Edinburgh: Heriot-Watt (with quantity surveying);
Building surveying: at universities – Reading, Salford; polytechnics – Leicester, Liverpool, London: S Bank, Thames; colleges – Glasgow CB;
Estate management: universities – Edinburgh: Heriot-Watt, Reading/Cirencester (rural), Ulster; polytechnics – Birmingham, Bristol (with valuation), Kingston, Liverpool (urban), London: PCL (urban), S Bank and Thames, Newcastle, Oxford, Pontypridd: Wales, Sheffield (urban);
Estate surveying (urban): Nottingham: Trent Polytechnic;
Land administration/management: university – Reading; polytechnics – Leicester, London: NELP, Portsmouth (urban);
Land economics: polytechnics – Leicester, Sheffield (urban); colleges – Paisley CT;
Land economy: universities – Aberdeen, Cambridge;
Minerals estate management/surveying: university – Leeds/Doncaster MIHE; polytechnic – Sheffield;
Quantity surveying: universities – Edinburgh: Heriot-Watt (with building economics), Reading, Salford (with construction economics), Ulster; polytechnics – Birmingham, Bristol, Kingston, Leeds, Liverpool, London: PCL, S Bank, and Thames, Newcastle, Nottingham: Trent, Pontypridd: Wales, Portsmouth; colleges – Aberdeen: RGIT, Dundee CT, Glasgow CT.
Surveying sciences: university – Newcastle; polytechnic – London: NELP (with mapping sciences).
Most fully exempt from professional examinations, but appropriate practical experience/training in approved employment is required for full membership.
Cognate full-time degree courses, in eg agriculture, building technology, forestry, mining, or planning.
Special entry schemes to professional bodies allow graduates to qualify via a two-part examination after at least eighteen months' appropriate training and experience in approved employment.
Part-time study: for a degree (at most of the above polytechnics and colleges), a BTEC Higher or other award exempting from RICS part 1, and/or for (final) professional qualifications, mainly at HE/FE colleges, or by correspondence course or other form of 'distance learning'.
Qualify first as a technician (below), and at age 30 (or over) take RICS direct membership exam.

Professional bodies: Despite some mergers, still a number –
Royal Institution of Chartered Surveyors – RICS (includes the Institute of Quantity Surveyors), is the main professional body with a membership (1987) of well over 75,000 including students.
RICS examinations are in three stages, but direct-entry part 1 exams are being withdrawn in 1988, so anyone choosing the part-time route to qualification will have to study for an exempting qualification (which may be a degree). Part II and finals are taken in one of nine divisions – building surveying, general practice, general practice (chattels option), hydrographic, land agency and agriculture, minerals, planning and development, or quantity surveying. All entrants, including graduates, must pass a test of professional competence, and must spend a set period in professional training and experience.
Minimum RICS entry requirements are five GCE/GCSE passes including two

at A level (and including English and maths), or the equivalent (eg BTEC diploma with five merit passes at level 3 and O-level-equivalent English).

Incorporated Society of Valuers and Auctioneers (ISVA) has 80% of its members in estate agency/auctioneering, but specialising in valuing etc of fine art and 'chattels', industrial plant/machinery etc (1986 membership 7500).

Exams are in three stages for entrants straight from school, with a special two-part scheme for graduates. Exams are taken in general practice, agricultural practice, fine arts/chattels, or plant/machinery. Appropriate degrees etc exempt. Full membership requires appropriate training and professional experience.

Mininum entry requirements are four O-level equivalent passes at 16-plus including English language and maths (or four, plus one at A level).

The Incorporated Association of Architects and Surveyors (1986 membership 2300 of whom about a tenth are architects) and the Construction Surveyors' Institute (1986 membership 3800) are introducing a joint syllabus for membership exams in 1987.

Entry requirements are as for RICS.

Faculty of Architects and Surveyors (FAS), membership (1986) c2000, with building surveyors the largest section, quantity surveyors second, architects the smallest group. Most are self-employed, in private practice, a few work in industry or commerce, a few are building managers. Exams are now set for younger students studying surveying subjects at technical college, where previously these were taken mainly by older people who have been in 'subordinate' posts.

Entry requirements are education to O-level-equivalent standard to include maths and English language, and other subjects appropriate to the branch of surveying.

National Association of Estate Agents (1986 4500 members) – for full professional membership entrants have to complete a correspondence or evening course to gain a certificate in residential agency (and have experience), and can go on to the NAEA diploma exam.

The Rating and Valuation Association has over 5500 members many of whom work in the public sector (about half in local authorities, 200 or more for Inland Revenue, nearly 200 for public authorities, and a few with valuation panels and rate officer services).

RVA's examinations (intermediate in two parts, and finals in two parts) can still be taken on a part-time basis. Degrees or examinations of appropriate professional bodies exempt.

Entry requirements are as RICS.

Chartered Institute of Building: surveyors working for construction firms frequently take CIOB examinations. See BUILDING TECHNOLOGY under ACADEMIC AND VOCATIONAL STUDIES IN ENGINEERING.

Technician level A number of BTEC awards are relevant, depending on area of work. All schemes are being revised according to the new framework (see TECHNICIAN-LEVEL QUALIFICATIONS) –

Higher National awards can be taken in AGRICULTURE, BUILDING STUDIES, CIVIL ENGINEERING (with relevant experience), or SURVEYING.

Entry requirements as for all BTEC Higher awards††.

National awards can be taken in AGRICULTURE, BUILDING STUDIES, CIVIL ENGIN-
EERING (with surveying experience), CONSTRUCTION (from September 1987), or
Land use/surveying: the guidelines for surveying stipulate core units on the
natural and built environment, cartographic practice, maths, surveying/car-
tographic technology, surveying practice, and a project. The 6-8 option units
for a diploma should include at least 4 of structured real or simulated work
experience. For a certificate, four option units can be taken.

Entry requirements are as for all BTEC Nationals††, with some passes in
related study areas. However, a 30-place YTS scheme based at Vauxhall
Building C (S London), and including National certificates, accepts trainees
on the basis of an interview.

As schemes are currently going through major re-organisation, it is not possible to list colleges providing courses.

The Society of Surveying Technician (SST) is the 'professional' body for
surveying technicians (although RICS and IAAS provide for associate membership for technicians especially those going on to complete professional
qualifications). Full SST membership is restricted to those who have completed the joint RICS/SST test of competence. Technicians with an appropriate BTEC HNC and two years' experience may become associates, but (as of
January 1987) they may not use AMSST designation.

Further information from the professional and other bodies cited above.

MINING, PROSPECTING AND QUARRYING

The raw materials which come from the ground, or from the sea bed, heat
homes, fuel cars and lorries and machinery, and build houses. They are turned
into metals and plastics, synthetic fibres, chemicals and fertilisers, jewellery
and mugs, glass and cement. The world uses more and more mineral ores,
chemical deposits, crude oil, sand, stone and salt every year – a growing
population ensures that, even without any new uses being found for these
materials, or any rise in standards of living. The underground reserves of some
raw materials – not only crude oil, but also aluminium and tin, silver and gold,
tungsten and zinc – are dwindling, fast. Not so long ago Britain could produce
most of the iron ore needed – today it is all imported. Today, the only long-
term reserves in the UK are of coal – Britain still mines some tin, and
industrial minerals, but offshore oils and gas will be used up quite quickly.

And so prospectors have to go further and further afield, into ever more
remote and inhospitable areas of the globe, and ever more difficult conditions.
The oil industry, for example, now works the North Sea and frozen Alaska.
Mining and oil companies have to go ever deeper, use more sophisticated ways
of finding reserves (such as surveys made by satellites), new methods to
extract, for instance, tar oil from sand, to refine poorer and poorer grades of
ore and develop new machinery to do it. Soon it will be worthwhile trying to
find and recover metal ores from under the sea, despite the huge technological
problems involved, as oil and gas are now brought up from under the sea bed,
first of all from the strange, manganese-rich 'nodules' which lie on the ocean
floor. New reserves will become increasingly difficult, and more expensive, to

develop – financially and in terms of the cost of the high amounts of energy needed, dealing with the environmental problems, etc.

The astronomical costs and the massive technological problems mean that only very large, multi-national, international or state-owned companies, or consortia (groups) of companies even, can afford to prospect for minerals or other reserves, and to spend the finance required to get them out of the ground. Many oil fields, many ore reserves, are known, but will not be exploited unless or until the price of the product reaches a level which makes mining or drilling for the oil or ore economic, and an economic price can include the cost of developing new technology to do it. The Athabasca tar sands in Canada were known for many years, but only the explosion in oil prices in 1973 made it worth developing machinery to squeeze the oil out. And so mines, wells, quarries, open and close with market trends.

Government control of some kind – whether government takes a stake in any company or the level of tax it sets – is another factor which companies take into account when deciding whether or not prospecting for and/or exploiting minerals etc, is worthwhile. Many mineable reserves on land are now located in 'third world' countries – putting the developed world at a disadvantage.

The industry
Is dominated by international companies. Seven major international oil companies (which have also diversified into mining, other areas of the energy business, chemicals etc), and about twenty mining companies, plus national organisations (eg the Soviet state oil enterprise, which is the largest, the Middle Eastern oil companies, and British Coal), dominate production of oil, coal and minerals world wide. In general, smaller companies provide mainly specialist services, such as geological/geophysical surveying.

In Britain, the industry consists largely of –

BRITISH COAL which mines, processes and sells all the coal extracted in Britain. Long-term prospects for coal are theoretically anyway, bright. Total reserves are estimated at 190,000 million tons, of which some 45,000 million are recoverable using only present technology, enough for at least 300 years, and 4600 million tonnes 'proved recoverable'. Coal will at some stage have to provide some replacement for crude oil (see also ENERGY PRODUCTION under MANUFACTURING).

In the short-term the problems have been well publicised. British Coal's markets were hit hard by recession and where demand for coal was predicted (in 1974) at 132 million tonnes by 1985, it is now unlikely to rise above 120 million tonnes for the immediate future – although 130 million is a longer-term possibility. 1986-7 output was just 108 million (against 220 million tonnes in 1956). Coal also faces the possible loss of up to half its largest market – electricity generation – currently (1985-6) 87.4 million tonnes, to nuclear power by the end of the century. Overseas, British Coal has to compete with open-cast Australian and third-world mines, where costs are only half those in Britain.

Investment in new and replacement capacity continues, but exhausted and uneconomic pits are being closed much faster – so by April 1986 just 133 collieries were operating (against 191 in 1983 and 958 in 1947). Large, modern, automated pits need much less labour.

British Coal, is still pushing hard for greater productivity, both by further closures and by introducing yet more sophisticated machinery, automation and computer control in the mines. It has shot up recently, to 3.58 tonnes per man-shift (against 3.08 in 1982).

Most underground tasks are now fully mechanised – giant machines drive 460 km of new roadways underground a year, and massive power cutters rip the coal face, at the same time loading the coal on to armoured flexible conveyors which keep up with the seam, each machine clearing over 8000 square metres of coal a week from seams 1 metre thick, power-operated steel roof supports advancing with the power loader – but the machinery is being further developed to give greater durability and power, and increased operational scope – by extending the length of faces, etc. Daily output at faces where the most modern equipment is used is more than twice that of older faces.

Increasing automation means developing better methods of machine guidance, sophisticated sensors (for eg natural radiation), coal-face 'surveyors' using low-intensity infra-red light for horizontal steering, and better methods of fault prediction using in-seam seismic techniques. Automatic coal clearance control installations monitor and control operations such as moving coal from the mine face, control pumps automatically by water-level changes, sample and analyse the air. Automatic guidance systems for coal-face shearers are being developed. In many mines, managers and officials have on-line day-to-day operational information and longer-term analysis of trends to highlight problems with equipment, face designs and operational organisation. Operations at coal preparation plants are also computer-assisted, showing trends such as plant availability, product quality, and tonnage rates.

British Coal also markets coal aggressively, particularly to industrial users. Modern coal-fired plant uses thermally highly-efficient fluidised bed combustion. It is also supporting a drive to sell fully-automated coal-burning space heating to consumers who cannot get gas.

British Coal spent £57 million on research in 1985-6, and has two main research stations. The mining research and development establishment works on mining methods and equipment, especially improving the performance and reliability of equipment and developing remote and automatic control systems. The coal research establishment works on coal use, is further developing fluidised bed combustion, and working on techniques for turning coal into petrol, diesel fuel and kerosene, and producing a substitute for natural gas. £15 million is being spent developing drilling techniques to extract gas from coal seams under the sea.

The scientific control service is done mainly by seven coalfield laboratories. They do the statutory analysis of eg mine air, dust and gases regularly, look after quality control, analyse coal seams and investigate local and national problems. The geological branch collects and assesses the geological information and coal-seam data used in planning new mining operations, and provides a general geological service.

British Coal subsidiaries include a coal products group, making smokeless fuels for the domestic market, coke for steel and foundries, and chemical products as by-products of coke making, and a mining engineering consultancy. The very large computer services unit operates as a wholly-owned subsidiary, Compower. Compower provides, designs and implements information systems on all aspects of coal operations – markets and customers, manpower/staff resources, purchasing and stores, and management accounting, etc – and also a technical service for engineering and scientists on surveying, ventilating, predicting coal qualities, machine use, workshop control etc. The company also operates a service bureau.

THE OIL AND GAS INDUSTRY 30 North Sea fields were producing up to 2.7 million barrels a day of crude oil in mid-1986. A further six are supposedly under development but only two are on schedule. Output is about at peak and is predicted to fall steadily from now on. The price of crude slumped dramatically in early 1986, making it uneconomic to develop fields at least for a while – and companies have slashed exploration budgets world-wide (few operate solely in Britain) by anything up to 40%. Plans have been abandoned, over 40 rigs stood idle in the North Sea in 1986, and the immediate future is very uncertain.

Before the price of crude fell, oil prospecting on mainland Britain was about to start in earnest. A dozen fields now produce crude, but 67% of output comes from just one, and most new discoveries are expected to be 'minuscule'.

OTHER MINING The most important non-ferrous metal mined is tin, but the fortunes of this small industry too are decided by prices and markets, and only two (of six) mines survived the 1985-6 failure of London's tin market. Britain is a major producer of eg clays, fuller's earth, salt, flurospar, gypsum, and anhydrite, but again they are very small industries.

QUARRIES produce a range of materials, such as sand, gravel, slate, chalk, clay, granite and limestone, which are used either in construction, or in manufacturing, eg ceramics. Some quarries also prepare materials for use, for example dressing or coating stone, making lime, or mixing aggregates for cement. Some quarrying firms produce and deliver ready-mix cement, others have extended into slag and crushed-concrete recovery. The industry is very capital-intensive now and very highly automated, and so has a small number of largish groups and some integration with civil engineering contractors (to give regular outlets).

The work of the industry
Whatever a company is bringing up from the ground, whether oil, ore, coal, sand, or gravel, there are three clear stages in the process. These are exploration and prospecting; mining, drilling or quarrying; and processing. Some companies carry out all three stages (and market the product too), but in prospecting particularly, it is now common for one set of specialist firms to do the geophysical survey work involved, and to interpret the data, another to develop and manage the mine or oil reserve. The emphasis on team work is strong, but the different stages employ different combinations of experts and skills.

EXPLORATION AND PROSPECTING – finding where the materials are in the ground or seabed, finding out how much there is there and of what quality, what problems there are in getting at it, how much it will cost to extract, and if it is economic to do so, given the quality of the material and the state of the market. Prospecting is a highly-sophisticated business, using the most advanced geophysical techniques and computers to collect, record and analyse the data.

When exploration was at its peak, just one international oil-logging company employed 300 geologists, but 1986 saw heavy redundancies and little recruitment. British Coal employs nearly 200 (plus four geophysicists) – the Coal Board prospects overseas as well as in the UK, helping to develop mines in other countries. Even major quarrying companies have their own small teams of geologists.

When recruiting, some survey companies train their own seismologists, taking on not only geologists and geophysicists, but also physics graduates, mathematicians and people qualified in computing. Most are trained on-the-job at, eg data processing centres, and then go on to field crews.

Prospecting also employs land and hydrographic SURVEYORS, who locate shot points and the levels between them, scout, and direct, and off-shore, do hydrographic surveys based on radio positioning systems and acoustic sensors. ELECTRONIC ENGINEERS and technicians do instrument work, computer maintenance, etc. MINING and drilling engineers and their teams do test drilling under the instructions of geologists. Mining engineers and minerals or petroleum engineers help assess potential mines or wells. CIVIL, ELECTRICAL and MECHANICAL ENGINEERS plan and cost the plant and equipment, allowing for, eg power and water supplies, construction, and roads to get to the site. A few CARTOGRAPHERS are needed.

MINING, DRILLING AND QUARRYING OPERATIONS If and when a mine, oil reserve or quarry is developed, geologists and mining or petroleum engineers work together initially, although the mining/petroleum engineer is usually in charge at this stage. Geologists work out where mining/drilling should begin, and how to produce the best grades of ore or oil with as little waste as possible. Mining engineers then plan mine development and oversee operations, so that the ore is recovered logically, economically, and safely, which means seeing that shafts are properly supported, ventilated, blasted and so on. Petroleum engineers decide whether wells are economic, and prepare the development plans.

Mining and drilling operations use very advanced technology. A North Sea oil rig is a major advance in naval architecture/civil/structural engineering technology. Half of all ore production comes from 150 giant, highly-automated mines, some 80% of them open cast. British Coal operates some of the most technologically-advanced equipment there is.

Mining operations are normally controlled by MINING ENGINEERS – all British Coal colliery and senior managers are mining engineers. Each of its nine areas has its own director. Deputy directors (mining) manage coal production within the areas, and are assisted by production managers and supporting specialist staff in, for example, mechanisation, planning, method study, ventilation, safety and tunnelling. All British Coal managers, right down to colliery level, have considerable independence, within certain targets and short-, medium- and long-term plans. They are responsible for efficiency and mine safety, and are in charge of a supporting staff of mining engineers including under-managers, electrical and mechanical engineers, mining surveyors etc, as well as underground and surface workers and office staff. They need considerable managerial as well as engineering skills.

Mechanical and electrical engineers design, construct, install, operate and maintain machinery both in the mines and elsewhere, dealing with very complex installations, including complex high-pressure hydraulic equipment. Colliery engineers, supervised by the area chief engineer and supporting staff, provide an engineering service within the area. Engineers also take charge of the large national workshops which overhaul, recondition and repair equipment. Mining companies also employ MINING SURVEYORS.

Oil production is controlled by petroleum engineers, who are the senior managers. Production or drilling engineers (including superintendents, production and workover/wireline supervisors), may divide their time between exploration and on-shore services – there are, on average 2.5 production engineers per rig. They control the wells and rigs, planning and budgeting drilling operations, appointing and supervising drilling and service contractors, looking after the engineering aspects of choosing new equipment and drilling systems.

Both mining and oil drilling operations need quite large supporting professional staff, usually made up of ELECTRICAL/ELECTRONIC ENGINEERS and MECHANICAL ENGINEERS, who design, construct, install and maintain machinery, from high-pressure hydraulic equipment, to electronic remote-control and monitoring gear, oil rig and platform equipment, pipelines, and associated machinery (eg turbines and rotary drills). They are supported by electrical/electronic, instrument and mechanical-engineering technicians.

Production also employs GEOLOGISTS – to help in planning and monitoring mine development through regular drilling and logging and assessing the cores which come up – to see which is the best area to develop next, and to advise on, for instance, safety.

All mines, quarries, and oil operations also need supervisory and technician staff, and skilled workers, from the colliery and quarry shot firers who supervise and carry out blasting, the mine deputies who supervise the work of a mining district, the overmen who are in charge of several districts, and the colliery under-managers, to the men who actually operate the modern mining and quarrying machinery.

On wells and drilling rigs the drilling superintendents and 'toolpushers', drillers and crewmen (including the derrickman, rig crewmen, roustabouts and crane operators) set up mobile rigs and permanent drilling platforms. Once a platform is in production, the production engineers would be supported by production operators and assistants, including workover/hoist crewmen, wireline operators and technical assistants, all shore-based.

Many mines and oil wells, particularly in more remote areas and certainly at sea, must also have their own support services, giving employment to cooks, stewards, clerks, storemen, radio operators, helicopter pilots and, for offshore operations, sailors to man supply vessels, and experts like divers.

PROCESSING ore, coal, or oil, once out of the mine, is the third operation. Here MINERAL TECHNOLOGISTS, extractive METALLURGISTS, and CHEMICAL ENGINEERS take over, using all kinds of methods to sort, separate, extract or purify the raw material. Separating useful raw materials from the soil, rock, sand, etc in which they are embedded becomes more of a technological/scientific problem as firms are forced to extract from the more difficult reserves such as Athabasca, where the sands themselves are mined and then processed to extract the oil. Chemical engineers are employed by oil refineries (see MANU-FACTURING), and eg British Coal's Coal Products Company, either in works management (in charge of a tar or coking plant), general management or in engineering services. An alternative is technical advice to management, evaluating, designing and improving processes.

Oil from wells is normally transported in crude or semi-refined form to refineries closer to the markets, where breaking it down into petrol, heating fuels, the chemicals from which plastics are made, and so on, is a chemical process, managed and designed by CHEMICAL ENGINEERS (see also ENERGY PRODUCTION under MANUFACTURING).

Quarrying firms also prepare their materials, dressing and coating stone, making lime, or mixing cements.

Processing can take plant and machinery every bit as sophisticated as that used in mining, quarrying or drilling itself, but much of it is highly automated. Most of the jobs involved are therefore technical, in quality control, in monitoring the processes and machinery, in laboratories where checks and some research and development are done.

Organisations like British Coal also want to improve the services they give to customers, and are experimenting with, for example, liquefying coal in the seam to pump it the surface, and converting coal into 'natural' gas, using chemical engineering methods.

MANAGEMENT skills, in an industry where the sheer scale of the operations, the size of the investments involved, and the level of technology needed, as well as the risks of all kinds, and the physical problems, have to be of the highest order. Most top managers are mining or petroleum engineers, but finance, marketing, purchasing etc, are also very important functions. Efficient planning, too, is crucial, and organisations like the British Coal, and the major internationals, have their own operational research units, very large-scale computer services, and legal departments, staffed by experts with appropriate qualifications.

Employment in the industry
The numbers employed have been falling steadily. Coal, oil and gas extraction plus processing employed only 213,000 at end 1986 (down from 344,000 in 1981), and numbers have fallen since. Ore and other mineral extraction employed a similar number at end 1986, down from over 300,000 in 1981.

The pattern of employment for qualified people within the industry is continuously changing. While many continue to work for prospecting and mining companies, more are likely work for companies which specialise in developing and managing mines for other organisations (for instance, the government of a developing country, or a semi-government agency), or for companies offering specialist services (eg survey work), or developing particular treatment processes. While the industry employs large numbers of appropriately-qualified engineers, scientists are also employed in research and development, scientific control etc. Most large firms also require a relatively large proportion of, eg operational research experts, computer personnel etc.

Promotion within the industry is generally from producing mine to consulting engineering or a mining finance house. Mining engineers work their way up from junior management within a mine through undermanagement and mine/colliery management. British Coal has a range of regional and national posts. In most mining/oil companies, head office employs experienced mining engineers in complex problem-solving and trouble-shooting, finding ways of improving performance, considering new projects, planning new mines, dealing with the financial and contractual aspects of developing new areas, and investigating and initiating technological development. All skilled miners may qualify for appointment as under-officials.

IN BRITAIN, though, the jobs and careers are at all levels, from the mine face, the quarry floor, and the oil rig, right up to top management.

British Coal is still probably the largest single employer, but of only 167,000 people in 1987 (against nearly 295,000 in 1977). The largest fall has been in the numbers of underground workers – down to 95,000 in 1987, from 240,000 in 1977 (and over 700,000 in 1947), and numbers are certain to go on falling.

The North-Sea oil industry was estimated to employ some 29,000 offshore, and a total of 150,000 in companies wholly related to the industry in mid-1986, which includes supply companies (eg rig manufacturers, other suppliers, the ship- and helicopter-service companies which maintain contacts with the rigs etc). Estimates suggest that at least 10% of all jobs may have been lost by the end of 1987.

Nearly half of those working directly for the industry are probably crewmen, production operators and their assistants, radio operators, divers, etc, maintenance technicians and craft workers, and several thousand are support staff like cooks, storemen etc. Geologists, petroleum and production engineers, mechanical and electrical/electronic engineers are also employed.

In quarrying, the number of jobs has been falling steadily for some years, and by 1986 was down to under 37,000 (from 64,400 in 1968). Ball and china clay, sand and gravel, and limestone and lime account for over half of all jobs.

The decline in numbers has been greatest amongst operatives (who include HGV drivers, shot firers and laboratory workers), but they still make up an estimated 50% or more of all workers. A relatively small proportion of craft workers (under 14%), mainly maintain plant and vehicles, with some bricklayers, carpenters, plumbers, etc.

Managers and supervisors make up most of the rest of those employed, with only very small numbers of sales/marketing people, scientists, technologists, and technicians.

The largest groups employ geologists, their own drilling crews, and mechanical and electrical engineers, both to work on the design and planning of new projects, and to manage and develop new vehicles and plant.

OVERSEAS, the number of permanent posts for UK nationals is shrinking all the time, as governments insist that more jobs and career posts go to their own nationals. This means that work overseas is now mostly limited to professional and other highly-skilled occupations for which local people have not yet been trained, and is likely to be short-term contract work, in planning and engineering design, prospecting and surveying, not in mine management or supervision. Virtually all work at technician level or below is now done by local people.

Anyone working for an international oil or mining company must expect to spend at least the first part of their working lives moving regularly from place to place. However, with the increasing use of computer-based exploration methods and more offshore operations, people like geologists will in future probably spend less time in the 'field', more at desks with computer terminals, engineers more time on the design and development of new equipment and processes, and then in office-based planning and management.

Even so, the early years in mining or the oil industry, even for professionals and graduates, will include time spent in the hottest and coldest, wettest and driest, and most uncomfortable and remote spots in the world, sometimes alone, and sometimes in some danger.

Recruitment and entry
Recruitment is likely to be low for the immediate future.

The modern mining, oil and quarrying industry needs progressively more brain and less brawn. Even the modern miner, although still working in very difficult conditions, no longer wields pick and shovel, but operates highly-sophisticated machinery, machinery which has to be expertly controlled and understood. All companies try constantly to cut the numbers they employ, and mechanisation and automation helps towards this, reducing all the time the number of jobs at the mine or quarry face (British Coal hopes to have no miners underground at all eventually), more than for professionals.

The mining and quarrying industry recruits British nationals as scientists and technologists, mainly GEOLOGISTS, GEOPHYSICISTS, MINING ENGINEERS, some METALLURGISTS, CIVIL, ELECTRICAL, AND MECHANICAL ENGINEERS, and SURVEYORS. Automating mines, putting mine information systems on-line, using computer-based systems in exploration, is all increasing demand for, eg ELECTRONIC/SYSTEMS ENGINEERS and COMPUTING experts.

British Coal's graduate recruitment (for mining operations, research, OR, coal products, etc) is now (1987) on a very reduced scale. Numbers peaked at 200 in 1975, and have since fallen steadily, to only 80 in 1987, and are unlikely to increase. A high proportion will have degrees in engineering, science, technology or mathematics, but for some posts (eg computer operations and administration), graduates with degrees in any subject are considered, and the fast-stream administrative assistant entry continues, but only eight people were recruited in 1986.

British Coal offers scholarships to school-leavers with appropriate educational qualifications and to those already working in the industry if they have relevant qualifications, to read for engineering degree courses at university or polytechnic, including mining engineering at North Staffordshire Polytechnic (see ACADEMIC AND VOCATIONAL STUDIES IN ENGINEERING).

British Coal also recruits student apprentices (in mining, mechanical and electrical engineering, and in coal preparation) for those with school-leaving qualifications which fall short of university entry (ie two subjects, normally mathematics and physics, studied to A level and one passed) but give entry to a BTEC Higher award course at a college near the student's home. Any recruitment for these, and administrative traineeships, in the 1980s is likely to be minimal.

Recruitment of young (under 18) trainee colliery workers is also at an all-time low – just 53 in 1986 (against over 3000 in 1982-3), although over 1000 'new adults' were taken on. School-leaver recruitment may rise again slightly, but to no more than 2-300. This low level of recruitment could make any expansion of output in the first decade of the next century very difficult. British Coal does not recruit young mine workers via YTS, because of the rigid statutory training requirements for young mine workers, but a small number of places give clerical and office training.

The oil industry For graduates, the main opportunities are with the major oil companies, but for oil exploration/production the main demand is for specific qualifications (as above). Few other graduate entrants find work directly in exploration/production but can work in the commercial functions such as marketing, finance, personnel etc.

Firms generally recruit for other work from people with relevant qualifications, training and/or experience. Some oil companies recruit school-leavers with four O-level-equivalent passes at 16-plus† including maths, a science and English for craft/technician training in instrument and electrical engineering, process work and maintenance. Most larger companies have technical-entry YTS schemes.

Qualifications and training

Varies between sectors –

British Coal trains extensively, under statutory regulations set for coal mining. Graduate engineers normally go through an engineering training scheme, designed to give the necessary practical experience required by the Mining Qualifications Board for statutory certificates. The scheme trains mainly for underground management, but also trains engineers who are going into coal preparation or workshop management. A special scheme for chemical engineers prepares for managerial and technical posts in the coal products division. Engineers and scientists going into other British Coal units do not have to follow a formal programme but twelve months' training is given for scientific services.

Student apprentices are given a common first year of practical training. Those who successfully complete the scheme are considered for management/technical careers via the engineering training scheme. See also MINING ENGINEERING under ACADEMIC AND VOCATIONAL STUDIES.

The Board's apprenticeship schemes for mining surveyors give co-ordinated practical training and technical education to gain the statutory mining surveyor's certificate via a BTEC Higher National award in mining surveying or RICS equivalent (see SURVEYING under LAND USE PROFESSIONS).

The junior administrative trainee scheme is designed to develop people at 18-plus for supervisory and management posts in staff, industrial relations, marketing, finance, purchasing and stores. Training is normally via day-release to study for a BTEC HNC in business studies or other appropriate qualifications.

Craft apprenticeship schemes include one in mining to train colliery officials in specialist and junior management (shot firers, deputies and overmen) and is an accelerated route, working up via the power-loading team, or in development and heading work, coal-face salvage operations etc, learning specialist skills, management and servicing, to gain the appropriate statutory qualifications in mining at the earliest age possible. The other, engineering craft scheme, trains fitters, electricians and other craftsmen for mines and workshops, and enables fully qualified craftsmen to seek promotion to supervisory posts. Both schemes include apprenticeship and opportunities for study at technical college.

Under 18s are trained to become underground workers under the mining training scheme. This emphasises practical skills, but with further engineering training, study on day-release at technical college, and the chance to transfer to a craft scheme.

The oil exploration/production industry, does not have any comprehensive industry-wide training schemes. Every company has its own training programme, which will vary with levels of demand for skills, which at present are low in exploration/production.

The industry has a drilling and production technology training centre (at Montrose in Scotland), which puts on a range of short courses (some for graduates), but most students are company sponsored (MSC also sponsors when skill shortages show up).

Divers must now legally have a valid certificate of competence and approved training. Three centres (at Falmouth, Fort William, and Fort Bowland, Plymouth) provide approved training. Students are mainly sponsored. Private students are accepted but courses are very expensive. Minimum age 18.

Specialist pre-entry courses include –

First-degree courses: see eg MINING AND MINERAL ENGINEERING, GEOLOGY under ACADEMIC AND VOCATIONAL STUDIES.

Postgraduate courses: quite a number have been developed over the expansion of the industry, but if the present (1986-7) problems of the industry persist, some may have to close down. The following were offering courses – Universities – Aberdeen, Bangor, Birmingham, Cranfield, Durham, Glasgow: Strathclyde, London: Imperial, UCL, Newcastle, Oxford, Plymouth, Reading; polytechnic – Newcastle; college – Aberdeen: RGIT.

In quarrying training has never developed to any great extent.

Doncaster MIHE provides BTEC Higher National courses in minerals processing and materials reclamation, minerals surveying, and quarrying.

THE WATER INDUSTRY

The water industry has gone through two major re-organisations in the last fifteen years, and may now go through a third. At present, ten regional water authorities manage water resources, distribution and supply in England and Wales (Scotland's are managed partly by regional/islands councils and a Central Scotland Water Development Board). Thirty water supply companies provide about 25% of supplies in England and Wales.

The water authorities are responsible for developing water resources; treating water and distributing it; controlling pollution, maintaining sewerage and treating sewage; managing rivers; dealing with land drainage, flood and sea defences; managing recreational facilities (fishing, sailing, etc); developing and improving fisheries. Thames has taken over some of the GLC's responsibilities and aims to develop the river's facilities with, eg water buses.

The industry aims to provide a continuous, universal and reliable high-standard service, which can literally be taken for granted. Everyone, including industry, depends on plenty of clean, fresh water, and effluent disposal. Maintaining a continuous supply of water, through frozen pipes in winter, and with drought in summer, is not always as simple as it sometimes seems.

England and Wales alone use about 29,000 megalitres of water, mainly for general use, but CEGB takes 7000 megalitres daily for power-station cooling. Industry uses less, mainly because output has fallen and because production has shifted away from industries which use a lot of water.

Making sure the system can meet demand is expensive. Capital expenditure on water supply, sewerage and sewage disposal totalled £1034 million in 1985-6, even though projections for demand have been revised downward. Thames Water hopes that its new fifty-mile distribution system will mean that far less water is lost in the pipeline. The huge Kielder dam and reservoir, the Thames flood barrier indicate the scale of development, and the management problems.

The Water Research Centre has three labs, and works on eg waste-water treatment, environmental protection (including water quality and pollution), and instrumentation, water mains and sewers. Staff spend about half their time out with the water authorities.

Working in the industry The regional authorities in England and Wales employed directly in the industry in 1986 under 51,000 (full-time equivalent), down from 62,300 in 1978. Numbers ranged from about 9000 working for the Thames Authority, down to about 1800 in Northumbria. Around 7000 people work for local authorities which provide public sewers, about 8000 for water companies. Under 10,000 people work in the industry in Scotland and Northern Ireland.

The industry has worked hard to improve efficiency managerial methods, and a high proportion of the professional/staff jobs are managerial and administrative (including finance/accounting, personnel etc).

'Technical' work involves directly managing plant which stores, distributes, and treats water and sewage. The water boards are making increasing use of computer-based control systems to, eg monitor water levels and flows and in quality control, and there is work developing these systems as well as for CIVIL, MECHANICAL, and ELECTRICAL ENGINEERS. Some scientists are employed in research, development, lab investigations etc.

Technicians work in laboratory and supervision, monitoring systems, in finance and administration, and engineering.

Craft and operative workers are employed in running pumping stations, and treatment plant, inspecting and maintaining equipment, looking after river and other channels, etc. Pipe-laying, construction work, etc, is most often done by contractors.

Recruitment and entry Recruitment is directly to one of the regional authorities or other organisations. At present, numbers recruited are very few, and only when there is a vacancy.

Professional and managerial staff amongst graduates, including a proportion with appropriate engineering/science degrees.

Technician-level work normally requires A levels and/or an appropriate BTEC award.

Qualifications and training Few specific national qualifications for the water industry – the engineering aspects are generally taught as part of CIVIL ENGINEERING.

Training is co-ordinated by the Water Industry Training Association, but carried out by individual authorities.

The Institution of Water and Environmental Management is being formed by the amalgamation (in July 1987) of the three existing professional bodies (the Institutions of Public Health Engineers and Water Engineers and Scientists, and the Institute of Water Pollution Control). Information on any qualifications etc was not available on going to press.

Further information from individual regional authorities (list from the Water Authority Association).

Central and Local Government, and the Armed Forces

Background   734
The Armed Forces   735
Central government   763
Local government   800
Politics   810

THE ARMED FORCES

The state, mainly via the Civil Service, local authorities, the health services, and the Armed Forces, is the country's largest employer, with over three million employees altogether, although numbers have been falling lately, both through cost exercises and by turning national organisations into commercial businesses. The public services employ the full spectrum of occupations, drawing people from a very wide range of educational and career backgrounds. They normally recruit at all levels, from school-leavers at 16- and 18-plus, from graduates, and from amongst trained and professional people.

By the very nature of state employment, a high proportion of people are administrators, but progressively larger numbers of entrants have high-level training before they join the service. Modern managerial methods and technology have come to the public service – Armed Forces, Civil Service, Health Service and local government alike – making substantial inroads into traditional attitudes and methods. While the public services can avoid the rule of the profit motive which dominates what industry and commerce do, they have, instead, to accept the equally tough financial controls which politicians may impose. They have to cope, then, with decisions which may conflict with what they see as the aims of their organisation, and even conflict with good management practice.

Equally, though, employees of public bodies have to be politically impartial and, whatever their own views, must accept and operate the policies of the government, or local government, of the day. In practice, of course, employees are at liberty to argue the case with politicians, and can sometimes bring considerable influence to bear. Public servants must also expect to be bound by formal rules of procedure, and to have great integrity. Treading the line between the formalities of bureaucracy and decision-making tempered with humanity creates some of the most difficult problems for public servants, both for those who must deal face-to-face with the public and for senior staff who have to turn political decisions into working regulations.

Change is as endemic to public-sector employers and employees as elsewhere. Some people who started out working for a state-owned organisation now find themselves in a quite-different, commercially-oriented environment, and so working to quite-different targets. Local government, and other re-organisations, make major changes in people's working lives. Computer-based systems are also having a major effect now, and will almost certainly cut the number of jobs in administering some state services.

For some people, public service, in the Armed Forces, the Civil Service or a local authority, is a career in itself. For others, it is merely a setting in which to be, for example, an architect or an economist, a surveyor or a scientist, often simply because the state is one of the major employers of particular specialists, for instance, museum staff. The advantage of a specialist qualification is that it makes it easier to move out of or back into public service, whereas the career public administrator needs some years' experience before he or she is considered valuable in other areas of employment. Nevertheless, it is a feature of the service that it is, in theory at least, possible to progress from the very lowest levels through to the most senior, and to gain appropriate qualifications en route. Direct entry into the equivalent of a management traineeship is traditional in the public service, and in some areas responsibility can come extremely quickly. While the pay may not be very good, employment is secure, and other benefits, eg holidays, can be comparatively generous.

THE ARMED FORCES

Introduction	735
The Army	739
The Royal Air Force	748
The Royal Marines	753
The Royal Navy	755

INTRODUCTION

Contemporary defence policy is based on a deliberate decision to have a relatively small, but highly skilled and trained, flexible military force which is capable of using to maximum efficiency the extremely sophisticated and complex equipment with which modern war, nuclear or not, is fought.

The sums spent on defence may seem huge – £18,783 million is projected for 1987-8 – but are, in fact, falling in real terms. The planned £19,000 million for 1989-90 is a 5% drop on 1986-7.

The technological demands made on the Forces and the cost- and productivity-consciousness needed to keep the budget down, mean defence has to use modern managerial methods in strenuous attempts to achieve maximum efficiency. 'Streamlining' is the watchword in defence, both nationally, and in NATO. It means near-continuous rationalisation in defence generally, as well as the armed forces.

Improving the 'management' of defence has, for some years, involved the Ministry of Defence in its own battle to re-structure for efficiency. The thrust is towards a single defence force rather than three semi-independent services, with greater central policy control and co-operation, and common central services. In the Forces themselves, senior officers increasingly work, and are trained, together. The battle is, however, taking a long time to win – MoD's engineers have only just (1987) been re-organised into a single service for all three forces, instead of being divided between them. Achieving 'good management practice', particularly in 'procurement' of defence equipment, use of resources such as land, is proving to be very difficult indeed.

The arguments on the balance between spending on nuclear systems and 'conventional' forces and weaponry continue. The cost of replacing 'Polaris' with 'Trident' is likely to keep down expenditure on conventional systems – and forces.

See also CENTRAL GOVERNMENT and MANUFACTURING.

The major role of Britain's armed forces for the rest of the 1980s and the 1990s, under present policies, still lies within NATO, although they continue to have some commitments elsewhere – including the Falklands.

Britain still provides the only European strategic nuclear force committed to NATO. All but a few ships and all Royal Marine units, wherever they are deployed, are earmarked for assignment to NATO in an emergency. The Army and Air Force units stationed in Germany are treated as components of NATO in Central Europe, backed up by combat units of both the Army and the Air Force in Britain – the UK mobile force. British forces also contribute units to the Allied Command Europe mobile force deployed to cover the northern and southern flanks of Europe. While the Navy has withdrawn its permanent fleets from the Mediterranean, it is still part of the NATO on-call Mediterranean force, and remains in the East Atlantic. The Air Force supplies appropriate support.

Outside NATO, Britain no longer has a strategic role, apart from roving nuclear submarines. Forces are now only permanently stationed in Gibraltar, Cyprus, the West Indies, Belize, and the Falklands. In the Far East are small units in Hong Kong and Brunei, with a small naval strength in the Indian ocean and Diego Garcia. Units of both the Navy and the Air Force continue regular visits to areas where Britain has defence responsibilities, however.

Apart from the 50,000 stationed in Germany, Hong Kong, etc, regular foreign postings are few. Instead, the Forces train and exercise regularly overseas – in the snows and ice of Norway, or the plains of Germany, for example.

The Forces, mainly the Army, also have to 'support' civilian authorities against armed dissidents, as in Northern Ireland. They have, then, to accept all kinds of anti-guerrilla/anti-terrorist-style activity as a normal part of their function. The Forces also consider they have a role to play in the community at large, at least as far as feasible, as in air-sea rescue, flood relief, building temporary bridges, etc. Maritime forces, both at sea and in the air, protect fisheries and the off-shore oil and gas installations.

THE ARMED FORCES
The Forces have changed very considerably since the end of the second world war, especially in terms of the expertise demanded of everyone, officers and ranks alike. However, many traditions remain, and anyone joining can expect to find themselves in an organisation which retains many traditional ceremonies, values and attitudes which are no longer so generally accepted in civilian life. By the very nature of the Forces, discipline remains central to efficiency, as do elaborate organisational structures and formal relationships

between the various ranks. It is still, also, a team business, with lives at stake if men and officers are not welded into an efficient 'machine'. It involves living almost all the time at close quarters with others, and living in communities mostly separated from civilian communities.

The authorities admit, though, that trained people are their major asset now. Within the inevitable restrictions imposed by budgets, the usual problems involved in managing – and providing living and leisure facilities for – large numbers, and the nature of the job the Forces have to do, a great deal is done to keep their people contented, on the theory that efficiency depends on it.

Many of the drearier routine tasks on which people in the ranks traditionally spent much time when not in combat, have been dropped altogether and others cut down, as the authorities try to see that boredom is reduced to a minimum. Nevertheless, life in the Forces is geared to intensive preparation for something which the entire world hopes and trusts will never happen, and this must inevitably bring a particular kind of strain and frustration to the life. Because of this, it is hardly surprising that some Army authorities have welcomed the action in Northern Ireland, and even the Falklands, as opportunities to sharpen capabilities and skills in 'real' situations. The Falklands allowed them to try out systems never tested in real life; to find out, inevitably with some tragic results, the power of modern weaponry and the weakness of some defensive systems.

Since the Forces now have to count very carefully the considerable investment they have put into their men, and women, from the ranks up, conditions of service have been improved. Standards of living are generally higher than they used to be; officer-training and selection has been sharpened and is geared to the kind of officer-rank relationships needed by combat and operational teams which must work so closely together. Life is, though, still tough. In addition to the still-strict discipline, work can be gruelling – with twelve-hour days, round-the-clock watches at sea, night exercises sometimes in appalling conditions, and very strenuous training. And war, with death and terrible injuries, does still happen. However, particularly for officers, the Forces offer good deals in terms of social status, educational opportunities, standards of living and even income.

Working in the Armed Forces Britain attempts to support its defence policy with as few people as possible. Until 1975, the Armed Forces numbered 370,000. Numbers fell to a low of 315,000 in 1979 (partly due to a shortfall in recruitment), rose briefly to nearly 334,000 in 1981, and have since fluctuated between 320,000 and 326,000. The projected figure for 1987 was 320,900. Overall recruitment was just over 34,700 in 1984-5, against a high of 50,600 in 1979-80 and a low of 21,650 in 1982-3 (largely because so few left). No official projections for future years have been published recently.

To make sure their needs are properly covered, the Armed Forces recruit at as many levels as possible, from amongst school-leavers at 16- and 18-plus, through to graduates and trained personnel. They are also increasing and improving the training and education for personnel at all levels, via both their own educational establishments and scholarship/cadetship schemes for entrants to study at universities, colleges etc.

Almost anyone recruited to the Forces must expect to become involved in combat if war happens, but the Forces aim to have teams of highly-trained specialists, and to some extent the combat men are now a separate breed from the men and women who provide the elaborate support services built up to aid them. For combat teams, the emphasis is on specialist training in one aspect of the art, or rather the science and technology, of warfare. Both officers and men become highly skilled as, for example, seamen, gunnery (which includes guided missiles) experts, or in tank warfare. The support services require engineers and mechanics, technicians and craftsmen/women, medical and dental officers, psychologists and nurses, educationalists, accountants, lawyers, purchasing and supply staff, etc.

Because many people who go into the Forces must have second careers, the Forces are trying, as far as possible, to integrate their own training with the national structure. Specialist officers take broad-based engineering degrees, and trades- and craftsmen are entered for CGLI and BTEC examinations (several training centres have their schemes validated by BTEC). Wherever possible, trades have trade-union recognition, so people can transfer to related civilian work.

Manpower planning, within the Forces, is very tricky. On the one hand, the Forces not unnaturally wish to keep personnel, on whom considerable time and money have been spent, for as long as possible. On the other, it is recognised that it is at times necessary to shed people; that some cannot be usefully employed throughout their working lives; and that not everyone wants to make the Forces a lifelong career. Being an infantryman, or a pilot, or a seaman, is a young man's job and it is not easy to tell how many of them will develop the right skills for 'management', or be suitable to move into other jobs. New technological equipment, new strategic methods demand different skills to the old.

To give themselves and the men and women they employ a reasonable degree of flexibility, therefore, a range of different-length engagements is offered. It is possible to stay in the Forces for as long as 34 years, but in practice most engagements range from three to 22 years, with intermediate terms of six and nine years.

There are special arrangements, too: for example it is recognised that it may be better to restrict length of engagement rather than expect members of the Forces to accept a ceiling on their promotion opportunities. Therefore, only those accepted for permanent, as opposed to special, regular commissions in the Army can try for possible promotion to major and above, and on a special regular commission it is possible to retire after 16 years instead of continuing on to age 55. Restrictions on changing the length of service under which the entrant signed have been eased, particularly for those recruited as boys under 18. However, it is still not possible to leave the services on terms comparable with those in general operation in civilian life, by simply giving notice.

As a general rule, the Forces expect men and women to stay long enough to give a reasonable return on the educational and training investment made in them. This generally means a minimum of three years, and four to seven years for those whose training was an extended one. Thereafter, whatever term of engagement was actually signed, it is possible in given circumstances to quit on

18 months' notice.

Those who sign on under age 18 may leave without cost, if they don't like the life, within the first six months of service. Once they are 18 they may revise the length of time they agreed to sign on at enlistment by reducing a six- or nine-year engagement, for example, to one of three years from their 18th birthday or from the end of their training, whichever is later.

The Forces recognise their responsibility to help people leaving the Forces transfer to the civilian world. This is obviously easier for those with training in skills widely used in civilian employment than for those who are trained as combat specialists and so must rely on less tangible assets, such as managerial skills, to get them into a new career, although the Forces do arrange specialist re-training. However, there is evidence to suggest that the problem is not simply one of acquiring the right skills for a new career. It may well be that the problems of adjusting not only to a new job in a strange setting, but also to a completely new way of life, are far more important, especially for those who enjoyed service life. The very qualities of life in the Forces – security, provision of basic needs, the structured society, and so on – are in direct contrast to the life of the average civilian today.

Recruitment and entry All entrants must be British subjects of European race or British subjects or British protected persons of non-European race who are resident in the UK. No boy or girl can be enlisted before completing the school term during which he or she reaches the school leaving age.

While the Forces encourage boys and girls to gain school-leaving qualifications (and for certain levels of entry these are mandatory), there is no formal bar to entry without them, although intelligence and aptitude tests are required at all levels. Pupils studying for recognised educational qualifications are encouraged to stay at school until they have taken the examination, provided they will not exceed the upper age limit for the particular type of entry. Such qualifications can usually be gained within the Forces anyway.

Young entrants are accepted for both commissioned and non-commissioned entry, although higher educational potential is needed to qualify for officer training.

In general, types of entry are classified by very specific age requirements linked to educational and/or skilled qualifications. Broadly speaking, the upper age limit is 29 or 30. Entrants over 25/26 must, in most cases, have qualifications which are of use to the particular arm of the Forces. Entrants must pass a medical and, for some types of entry, conform to particular physical measurements.

The Forces have their own version of YTS, called the 'short service scheme', lasting two years (since January 1987). Of the 5200 places, only 50 are available for women (to train as supply controllers, drivers, switchboard operators, postal and courier operators, kennel maids and grooms). Trainees can leave on fourteen days' notice. In mid-1984 (latest figures available), although over 4500 applied for places, only 2400 were accepted, leaving a 45% shortfall.

The Army
Introduction — officers — non-commissioned soldiers — Women's Royal Army Corps — Queen Alexandra's Royal Army Nursing Corps

The Army is traditionally the most-labour intensive of the three Forces and until relatively recently, less scientifically/technologically-orientated, compared to the Navy and Air Force. Now, says the Army 'the day of the simple soldier is past. These days almost everyone is an expert of some kind'.

In January 1986, 162,100 men (155,500) and women (6600) were serving in the Army, 2200 men over estimate. The estimate for January 1987 was 160,700 including the same number of women. The 17,100 officers (down only 300 on 1980), included 1000 women (up 100 since 1983).

Despite successive amalgamations and disbandments, the list of regiments and corps of the 1987 British Army still make impressive reading. Headed by the Household Cavalry (the Life Guards, and the 'Blues and Royals'), it continues with the Royal Horse Artillery, the five 'Guards' regiments (Grenadier, Coldstream, Scots, Irish and Welsh), the 17 regiments of the Royal Armoured Corps (which hides such historic titles as the four regiments of Dragoon Guards, the Hussars and Lancers as well as the younger Royal Tank Regiments), the Royal Regiment of Artillery, the Royal Engineers, the Royal Corps of Signals, the six regiments making up the Scottish Division (including the Black Watch, the four Highlanders and the Royal Scots), the three regiments of the Queen's Division, the King's seven, and the Prince of Wales's nine, plus two Light Division regiments. The Gurkha regiments have British officers.

Also part of the Army are the Parachute and Special Air Service Regiments, and the 17 'technical corps' – the Army Air, Transport, Medical, Ordnance, Electrical and Mechanical Engineers, Military Police, Pay, Veterinary, Small Arms School, Military Provost Staff. Dental, Pioneer, Intelligence, Physical Training, and Catering Corps.

Every regiment and corps has its own specific job to do, and so has specific requirements in terms of particular skills, in both officers and ranks. Officers and men in the armoured regiments, for example, mostly specialise in 'working' tanks, armoured cars, anti-tank weapons (which include guided missiles) and helicopters. The Royal Artillery employs mainly gunnery experts but also needs people trained in the use of radar and other electronic devices to locate air or ground targets and to guide homing weapons.

The Royal Engineers build bridges, roads and airfields, lift minefields and lay them, clear obstacles and carry out demolition, drill wells, build installations and supply power, all tasks requiring all kinds of qualified engineers and supporting trades and technical men. REME has to keep operational the Army's immense range of technical equipment, from tanks to guided weapons, radio and aircraft, and therefore recruits primarily trained mechanical, electrical, aeronautical and electronic engineers.

The Corps of Signals uses light aircraft, teleprinters, radio-relay and satellite communications in a highly sophisticated field system. A high proportion of men are, then, technically skilled in electronics. In the Air Corps, a few people get the opportunity to fly helicopters.

The Transport Corps operates vehicles ranging from quarter-tonners to 30-ton tank transporters and diesel locomotives, vessels from harbour launches to ocean-going tank-landing craft, light aircraft and hovercraft, and also had its own parachute squadron. All ranks are trained as both combatants and drivers, and the complex network of transport calls for highly sophisticated administration.

On the administrative side, the Pay Corps both recruits qualified accountants and trains its own. Chaplains, doctors, dentists, veterinary surgeons, educationalists and lawyers are recruited from amongst those already qualified.

All entrants, both commissioned and non-commissioned, may opt for a particular unit when signing on, and some regiments continue to recruit in the counties where they were first raised. But in general the Army aims to provide everyone with a wide-ranging introduction to all the opportunities open to them, depending on the type of entry, so that they can make an informed choice.

Choice of regiment or corps usually dictates what job most officers and soldiers get – especially in the 'combat' regiments.

OFFICERS (male), are expected to be managers and organisers just as soon as they finish their first, quite-short training period, and can then be put in charge of equipment worth up to £1 million. Even the most junior officers are expected to get their 'teams' of up to 30 men to top efficiency and keep them there, organising much of their training and instruction themselves, as well as making sure that food, welfare facilities, leisure activities etc are organised. While they have to learn a great deal about the systems they are deploying (and in technical corps like REME, must have engineering degrees), they are not technicians – skilled men in the ranks do the practical work. Officers, though, have to be able to operate equipment if need be – drive a tank, fire rockets etc.

The Army is (in 1987) lengthening and intensifying officer training. All entrants take an initial course (at Sandhurst Royal Military Academy), nongraduates taking a newly-lengthened 42-week 'standard military' course, graduates a 28-week 'standard graduate course'. All are commissioned as lieutenants on successfully completing it. After a 'special-to-arm' course with the regiment or corps (length depends on branch joined), all have their first period of regimental/corps duty. All Reg-C- and SRC-entry (see below) officers return to Sandhurst for a further 4-week, 'regular career' course 2-4 years later.

After the first two-year 'tour' of regimental duty, career officers are given varied experience of both regimental/corps and 'staff' – administrative and later, 'managerial' – work, both within their units and elsewhere. The Army claims no two tours are ever the same. A 'progressive qualification scheme' is designed to see that all career officers are trained for the next stage of responsibility – with signs that the Army is now 'streaming' for promotion with increasing emphasis on grooming graduates in a fast stream to the top.

Officers who are doing well can expect promotion to captain at 26 (but for a 'top' career should be by 29), and an early chance to do the first, intensive seventeen-week course (four at Sandhurst, three at RMCS Shrivenham, and nine at junior division staff college). This is followed by at least another two years with the regiment, as an adjutant or junior staff officer. Promotion to major can happen at 32-4, but means first passing a two-paper exam covering military, academic and current-affairs subjects. The best will go on the one-year staff-college course (with RN and RAF officers) at this point, preceded now by another 3-12 months at Shrivenham. Those who 'do well' can expect promotion to lieutenant-colonel in their thirties, and will spend most of their time on 'staff work' – management, policy making and working with the other Forces, police etc.

The range of posts – including specialist work – open to people not deemed suited, or who do not want to try for, 'top' command, is fairly extensive, however. The Army sees 'managing' catering services, the supplies work of the ordnance corps for example, as just as crucial to fighting efficiency as commanding front-line troops. A tank crew, however well trained, is useless without fuel, ammunition, and food.

Three main types of commission are available –
'Regular Commission' (Reg C): Only 'Reg C' officers, who serve up to the normal retiring age of 55, are eligible for promotion to major and above.
'Special Regular Commission' officers serve for sixteen years (from at least 21).
'Short Service Commission': initially for three years, but can be extended to a maximum of eight.

Recruitment and entry By 1986, intake was 50% graduate, and more complete degree courses after commissioning. Total recruitment in 1985 was 955, including 494 pre-cadets, 130 officer cadets, 76 university cadets, and 255 specialists, graduates and other entrants. 1987 intake was expected to be a total of 780 including 115 engineering and applied science graduates (for some corps these can be women).

The Army has about a dozen different ways to become an officer. All assume that recruits have, or are capable of gaining, at least five O-level equivalent passes at 16-plus†, or an equivalent qualification. For Reg C the five passes must include two at A level (or the equivalent in AS levels). Subjects should include English language, maths, and a science or a foreign language may be required.

Regular commission entry is, for direct entry without a degree, between the ages of 17½ and 22.

Special regular commission entry is divided between young and middle entry. Young entry has an upper age limit of 22, and provides an alternative entry for candidates who gain only two O-level-equivalent passes in A-level exams. Middle entry has a lower age limit of 22, and an upper limit of 26 for RAC, RA, RE, AAC, RMP and the infantry, up to 29 for other units, but no entry to Intelligence.

Short service commission entry is between 18 and 26 for RAC, RA, infantry, AAC, and RMP, up to 29 for the rest, but RPC will accept up to 30. No entry to Intelligence.

Graduate entry is to one of the above with, for Reg C a top age limit of 23 for Intelligence, 25 for most other units, but 29 for RE, Signals, RAPC, and 30 for REME. SRC and SSC upper limits are similar to those above.

Scholarships are available for 16-year-olds (upper limit 16½) so they can stay on at school to study for A levels. A special scheme is available for sixth formers taking A-level (or SCE H grade) in maths and sciences, and who already have O-level-equivalent passes in maths, physics, and at least three other subjects (including English and preferably chemistry).

Welbeck College, two-year A-level course in maths and physics: for young men aged 16-17$\frac{1}{2}$ with appropriate O-level equivalent passes. Mainly for commissions in one of the technical corps, but some go into RAC, RA, RCT, infantry. Most can go on to a degree course after commissioning.

Scholars, and Welbeck students who gain their A levels are exempt from the Regular-Commission Board and are effectively guaranteed a place at Sandhurst.

University cadetship/bursary: minimum age 17$\frac{1}{2}$, with a place to read for a degree (most subjects/courses acceptable) or already on a course. Cadets are commissioned as 2nd lieutenants and paid, with seniority antedated on completion of initial training, but cadets must serve for 5 years after graduating. Bursary holders stay civilians until they graduate, and must serve for at least three years.

Through the ranks About 5% of intake now (1987).

Type 'O' engagement: aged 17$\frac{1}{2}$-22 for Reg C or SRC (young entry) or up to 29 for SSC and SRC (middle entry), normally with O-level-equivalent passes in English and four other subjects. Free discharge if they fail to gain entry.

Serving soldiers on normal engagements can try for a commission up to at least age 45, but must be able to show they have reached the educational standard needed to do the RMAS course.

Doctors, dentists, teachers, engineers, clergy, accountants, bankers, secretaries, veterinary surgeons, caterers, solicitors/barristers and nurses are recruited to all three types of commission, with some restrictions. Medical and dental officers have the alternative of cadetship or pre-registration entry. For doctors, there is a university medical-cadet entry also. Professionally-qualified engineer-entrants must have appropriate experience.

NON-COMMISSIONED SOLDIERS A comparatively small modern army is heavily dependent on complex technological equipment, speed, flexibility, and intelligent use of resources. Its soldiers, as well as its officers, then, have to be more intelligent, more highly trained for the strategy to work. Most men have to be capable of working, and trained to use intelligently, that complex – and horrendously expensive – equipment. Many now learn to do more than one, often several, jobs – every member of a tank crew, for example, can do everyone else's job if necessary. This does not, though, obviate the need for strength and fitness, and if anything, the Army seems to be raising sharply the physical demands on its men, and 'roughing it' is still inevitable. But while it is common to think of the troops 'yomping', as they sometimes still must, even the infantry divisions are heavily mechanised and troops are moved by carrier rather than on foot wherever possible. Team work is the other ingredient of army life which is heavily stressed.

All soldiers are taught first and foremost to fight and handle weapons, as infantrymen, for example. But even infantrymen can also learn a second, 'follow-on trade', and the range of 'technical' jobs for which training is given is widening steadily. All can add to their skills, and also gain academic qualifications, such as GCSE and A levels, which may be needed for further training. The recruiting literature, however, puts less emphasis now than it used to on giving infantry and armoured-regiment combat soldiers 'second trades'.

Every regiment and corps employs different skills, so choice of trade can, of course, limit choice of unit. Almost all regiments and corps are mechanised, and so employ soldier-drivers, but only the Household Cavalry has mounted dutymen now (men in the Cavalry may spend one tour on horseback in ceremonial dress, and the next as drivers of 54-ton tanks). Some skills are unique to the Army – assault pioneer, gunner, parachutist, mortar man, bomb-disposal engineer. A wide range of trades would be useful in civilian life – radio technician, construction materials technician, data telegraphist, crane operator, recovery mechanic, building craftsman, chef, design draughtsman, electrician, operating-theatre technician, radiographer, fitter, and so on.

Technician and craft opportunities are mainly in the specialist corps –
REME trains electronics technicians (specialising in telecommunications, control equipment, or avionics), aircraft, and instrument technicians. Craft skills employed include vehicle mechanics and electricians, armourers and gun fitters, and metalsmiths.

The Royal Engineers employs, and trains, design technicians (specialising in construction materials, surveyor engineering, design draughtsman, or electrical and mechanical draughtsman), survey technicians (specialising in field or air survey, or survey cartography, photography or print), and electricians. Craft trades include bricklayer, concretor, carpenter, joiner, electricians, fitter, metalworkers, painter, decorator, plumber/pipefitter.

The Signals Corps also employs (and trains) electronics technicians (specialising in radio, radio relay, or terminal equipment). Telegraphy trades include radio and special telegraphists, and electronic warfare operators who have to be good at languages.

Other corps employ and train their own specialists. The Transport Corps trains its own marine engineers. RAPC accountants learn to use computers in handling pay, allowances and records, and RAOC supply controllers for stock control. The Medical Corps trains nurses, physiotherapists, radiographers and lab technicians. Chefs and cooks are trained by the Catering Corps.

In the 'front line' regiments, some of the jobs are just as technical and skilled – operating the Royal Artillery's computer-controlled missiles for example. The Artillery also employs surveyors, intelligence operators, and meteorologists.

Musicians are employed in some numbers (they also train as medical assistants). The Army currently (1987) has 15 staff bands and 54 regimental bands. Staff bands normally have 35-50 musicians each, regimental bands 21-25.

Promotion from the rank of private, via lance-corporal, corporal, sergeant, staff sergeant and warrant officer, depends on experience, educational and technical qualifications, and the ability to handle men. While there are minimum periods to be served in each rank in most cases, accelerated schemes exist and extensive use is made of incentives. The Army encourages non-commissioned soldiers to work towards a commission, although it is probably getting more difficult.

Accelerated schemes and continuous assessment of ability make it hard to generalise about promotion, but in general it is clear that those who qualify as technicians gain promotion faster than those in the other trade groups, with automatic rises to lance-corporal and corporal in two years after completing training, and promotion to sergeant after five. Time promotion, however, applies only up to the rank of sergeant; thereafter promotion is by selection to fill particular vacancies, except in certain supervisory appointments. Anyone who reaches junior NCO rank in certain trades is eligible for special training as a supervisory technician in, for example, the Royal Engineers, which has posts for clerks of works and military plant foremen, and in REME, which has supervisory artificers (who are encouraged to take HNC examinations).

Terms of service vary, and depend on age of entry and type of training. All entrants are offered a full 22-year career. The minimum period of service from age 18 or enlistment (whichever is later) is at present three years, but six or nine years if lengthy training is involved. After 18 months' ($4\frac{1}{2}$ or $7\frac{1}{2}$ years for longer service) service, any serviceman can give 12 months' notice.

On enlistment, recruits can commit themselves to serve for six or nine years and will be paid more. All junior entrants are required to sign on for six or nine years from eighteen, but can leave within their first six months, and at eighteen, can cut their service to three years.

Recruitment and entry 13,612 servicemen were recruited in 1985. Nearly half, just over 6500, were 'adults', just 4780 were juniors, 1312 were apprentices, and 1016 young soldiers (aged between 17 and $17\frac{1}{2}$).

Entry is either as a junior – under $17/17\frac{1}{2}$ – or adult.

While there is no discrimination between junior and adult entrants, the Army emphasises that entry as a junior carries considerable advantages, because the time qualification towards promotion begins earlier, and there is more time for educational and training opportunities to gain qualifications appropriate for selection to the limited number of more highly skilled posts or for a commission. Accelerated promotion schemes apply particularly to junior entrants, for whom there are special facilities, and transfer to pre-Sandhurst training is not uncommon.

Junior entry is via one of five routes: as an apprentice technician or arms and corps apprentice, junior musician or bandsman, junior leader, or junior soldier. The upper age limit is $17\frac{1}{2}$ for the first three groups and 17 for the latter two.

Technician apprentices should have, or be capable of gaining, O-level-equivalent passes in maths, English and physics or an engineering subject, and the potential to gain a BTEC National.

Craft apprentices should have, or be capable of gaining, at least grade D O-level-equivalent pass in the same subjects.

No formal requirements are set for the following, but aptitude tests are normally taken –

Junior leader entry is geared to preparing young soldiers for accelerated promotion to NCO and warrant officer and particular responsibilities in a number of regiments and corps, especially the front-line units, eg most tanks and armoured cars in the Royal Armoured Corps are commanded by NCOs most of whom started as junior leader.

Junior soldier entry is once again to specific regiments and corps, mainly front-line units, eg junior troopers for the Household Cavalry and for the Armoured Corps, junior gunners for the Royal Artillery, junior signalmen for the Signal Corps, and junior infantrymen in infantry regiments, which also recruit junior drummers and buglers (the Scottish and Irish regiments train junior pipers).

Junior musicians/bandsmen should normally have gained at least Associated Board grade V or equivalent, and are auditioned.

Adult entry is from 17, although those who enlist under $17\frac{1}{2}$ do so as young soldiers with the right of free discharge within their six months. Unskilled entry is possible up to the age of 25, with choice of training in up to 200 trades, depending on aptitude. Applicants aged 23-30 who have the equivalent of a BTEC National and have managerial/supervisory experience, are recruited for artificer training.

AFYTS entrants can apply for a full-term engagement.

Qualifications and training All new entrants start with a period of training, depending on entry, unit etc. Adult, normal entry starts with basic military training, then 'special-to-arm' training.

Apprentices and technicians are given both skilled and basic military training, as well as continuing their general education. Courses for technicians last up to three years and lead mainly to BTEC National awards initially. Apprentices who have not gained GCE/GCSE passes before entry are encouraged to do so while at college. Arms and corps apprentices do one- or two-year courses in craft trades (eg as electricians, plumbers, vehicle mechanics) leading to CGLI awards, or administrative skills (eg clerks).

Junior leaders are trained according to the division, regiment etc, but this lasts twelve months for all and concentrates on 'character development' and further general education. The Infantry Junior Leaders' Battalion trains potential senior NCOs for combat units; the Royal Artillery trains apprentice surveyors at the junior leaders' regiment; REME junior leaders are trained for clerical, storekeeping and regimental duty posts. Junior leaders are trained to become clerks, technical clerks, storemen or vehicle specialists for eventual promotion to eg quartermaster and Ordnance executive. Royal Army Pay Corps training can lead to CIMA qualifications and/or computer programming.

Junior leaders can still become tradesmen; for example, the Royal Engineers trains junior leaders in a wide range of trades, the Transport Corps trains every junior leader to drive and maintain two kinds of vehicle and then gives them the chance to become a specialist driver or to train in maritime transport and port operating or air despatching, and so on. Junior leaders for the Intelligence Corps, for example, are trained initially at RAC, RA or the Transport Corps, and then go to the intelligence centre for NCO training in, for example, photographic interpretation, interrogation, and languages.

Junior bandsmen are trained at either Bovington or Purbright, depending on regiment or corps, and usually go on to the Royal Military School of Music within four years of completing junior training.

Junior-soldier training is similar, but lasts only six, for some regiments ten, months.

Artificer entrants have 18 months' training, and are then promoted to staff sergeant.

ASYTS entrants are given specific training, as eg bandsmen, in building trades, as clerks, dental clerks, drivers, medical technicians, metalsmiths, petroleum operators, recovery mechanics, vehicle electricians, supply controllers or specialists, or storemen.

THE WOMEN'S ROYAL ARMY CORPS takes on whatever work the Army considers women can do, to allow men to be concentrated rather more in actual battle units. The range of work given to the WRAC is steadily expanding, and women now predominate in communications, administration and electronics.

Officers After intensive, 25-week training at Sandhurst, most WRAC officers generally start their Army careers in charge of up to 50 WRAC recruits or a platoon of servicewomen. Thereafter, tours appear to alternate between 'managing' within WRAC, eg in command of WRAC military policewomen in Northern Ireland, and staff appointments in other army units, garrisons, battalion HQ etc.

Alternatively, eight other corps/arms (Royal Engineers, Signals, Transport Corps, Ordnance, REME, Pay Corps, RAEC, and the Catering Corps) offer mainly suitably-qualified graduate WRAC officers permanent employment. The Royal Engineers, for example, takes professionally-qualified engineers and surveyors and WRAC officers for postal and courier communications.

Terms of service are similar to those for men, but with the option to leave on marriage. Promotion is normally at roughly the same stages as for men.

Recruitment and entry 116 entrants in 1985, 101 projected for 1986. Regular or short service commission, and graduate entry, on the same terms as, and with similar qualifications to, male entrants. Undergraduate bursaries are also now awarded on the same basis as for men. Entrants must be under 29.

NON-COMMISSIONED SERVICEWOMEN The number of possible openings for women seems to have stuck at around the twenty mark. These are – administrative assistant (includes eg stores, policing at the WRAC centre), analyst in the Intelligence Corps (can go on to special intelligence linguist), bandswoman, secretarial/clerical work (in offices throughout the Army), cook, data telegraphist (in Signals), driver (of cars, landrovers, 4-ton trucks etc), electronic technician (REME), kennelmaid, medical assistant, military accountant (Pay Corps), military policewoman, intelligence and security operator, physical training instructor, postal and courier operator, range assistant (Royal Artillery), mess stewardess, supply controller or specialist (Ordnance), switchboard operator, or terminal equipment technician (Signals).

Women serve on terms similar to men, can leave on marriage if they wish, but must leave to have children.

Recruitment and entry Only 700 women were recruited in 1985, against 945 in 1984. They are recruited between 17 and 33 years of age. For most openings no formal qualifications are needed, but some of the technical trades need O-level equivalent passes in mathematics and science.

QUEEN ALEXANDRA'S ROYAL ARMY NURSING CORPS (QARANC) combines a nursing career with Army life. Army hospitals treat civilian employees, families etc, so the range of work is not too different from an NHS hospital, although the patients are all likely to be younger. The Army has hospitals throughout the UK (six), in Germany (five), Cyprus, Hong Kong and Nepal.

QARANC employs RGNs, EN(G)s, ward stewardesses, dental clerks and hygienists, personnel officers and clerks. Officers are all RGNs.

Nursing officers serve on a short-service commission of 2-8 years. Length of service is at least four years from 18 for QARANC-trained RGN, three for others, but this may be extended (every two years) to a total of twelve years.

Recruitment and entry Qualified RGNs are recruited as nursing officers with a minimum age of 21. QARANC recruits with appropriate entry requirements (ie at least five O-level-equivalent passes at 16-plus† including English language, a science and two other academic subjects preferably including maths) to train as registered general nurses. Similar qualifications are needed for personnel officer and dental hygienist. No formal qualifications are needed to train as EN(G), or stewardess.

See also HEALTH AND MEDICAL SERVICES.

The Royal Air Force

Introduction — officers — non-commissioned airmen — Princess Mary's Royal Air Force Nursing Service

By comparison with the Army the Air Force is far smaller, with only some 93,400 men and women (5900) in 1986-7. It is also organisationally far less complex, with fewer units. It is an 'integrated' service, with women doing largely the same work as men, except that they can only fly as loadmasters.

The cost of keeping the RAF supplied with the latest generation of combat and other aircraft rises astronomically every year. Compromises, both between strategic needs and capital costs in terms of new aircraft, and on the use of the planes for practice, must constantly be found. Currently (1987) in the midst of a major modernisation programme, the RAF is replacing Lightnings and some Phantoms with seven squadrons of the multi-role combat Tornado strike/attack force, gets its first squadron of the air-defence variant of the Tornado in late 1987, and is to have 80 improved Harrier STVOL planes from 1988. New support helicopters are on order, and the tanker force is also being up-dated.

FLYING is the *raison d'être* of the RAF, and careers are firmly divided between flying and 'other', generally termed ground specialisations, all of them geared to support for aircrews. Except in such aircraft as the Nimrod, the day of very large aircrews is over, and most British combat planes now carry only pilot and navigator (the Nimrod has two pilots, an engineer, two navigators and six air electronics operators).

Contemporary combat planes are flying electronic laboratories and, with their phenomenally high speeds and altitudes, require men of considerable skill and aptitude to fly and navigate them. The RAF automatically assumes that all pilots and navigators should, therefore, be officers. Not every pilot or navigator, however, flies 'strike' planes. Other opportunities to fly include transport, maritime reconaissance, and helicopter operations.

Obviously aircrew officers do not spend their entire careers in flying duties, although in the early stages they are employed almost exclusively in the air. Subsequently, a great proportion of their time is spent in ground appointments, mostly related to flying operations and planning.

In peacetime, however, it is not uncommon for a pilot's 'flying week' to total as little as ten or 15 hours in the air. The close and detailed preparation for each sortie, though, can well take longer than the flight itself.

A great deal of time, even for trained crews, is spent in simulators and more hours in analysing the work done in the air – for example, fighter pilots develop tactics by studying the photographs of their own interception training flights, strike and attack men go over bombing and rocket exercises, and so on. In addition, most aircrews have 'secondary duties' which may be anything from divisional officer, looking after the welfare of airmen, to officer-in-charge of a sporting activity, and most flying officers must also take 24-hour spells as orderly officers, receiving and acting on messages.

GROUND CREWS While flying is obviously one of the major attractions of a career in the RAF, this does not mean that careers on the ground need be any less demanding. In many respects these may have more to offer. Aircrew are, of course, totally dependent on people like engineers and flight controllers. All three must, in fact, be welded into a tight and efficient unit if a combat team is to operate effectively.

Ground specialisations are aircraft and fighter control and photographic interpretation, engineering, supply, administration, catering, and ground defence, plus the educational and medical branches.

On aircraft and fighter control, the RAF likes to quote the old adage, 'the watcher sees most of the game', and applies this to 50-mile-a-minute supersonic aircraft approaching each other along computer-predicted flight paths, in support of its claim of key importance for the flight controller. Air-traffic control performs a function very similar to that of the civilian control tower (see also AIR TRANSPORT under SERVICE INDUSTRIES), but fighter controllers have an even more exacting role. Fighter control employs the most advanced long-range radar and radio, and computer-aided tactical planning to direct the airborne fighter aircraft and the ground-to-air missiles.

Fighter control keeps a 24-hour vigil all the year round at various permanent stations both in the UK and abroad, and even in mobile air control centres. Stations not only direct combat planes, but also, for example, keep track of satellites and spacecraft, using computer-plotted radar (for instance, at Fylingdales) to distinguish possible re-entry vehicles from space-junk, and in vectoring a combat plane on to a tanker for air-to-air refuelling.

Photographic interpretation is closely linked to control, and involves analysing air-reconaissance photographs to extract intelligence information.

RAF engineers do not only work on maintenance, although this is in itself very exacting, made so both by the highly sophisticated nature of the electronic and flight equipment in use today, and because all installations must be kept in constant operational readiness.

(Graduate) engineers also help to formulate the RAF's requirements in terms of new aircraft and defence and control systems, in shaping their development, translating them into a complete programme, and helping to introduce the end product into service. Engineer officers specialise, initially at least, in either aerosystems (the aircraft themselves, their weapons and air-to-ground communication systems) or communications/electronics (dealing with ground-based radio, including satellite, systems, radar and electronic systems for air defence, and command and control communications.

The RAF also has its own ground defence, the RAF Regiment, a highly-mobile force trained as infantry, gunners and parachutists all in one. It also supplies fire-control services to airfields.

The supply branch is responsible for moving aircraft personnel and equipment around the world, combining purchasing, forwarding and stock control with a kind of travel agency. It must be just as efficient at moving a complete aircraft as at ensuring the supply of parts required for maintenance, down to the smallest split-pin, and this can mean many millions of items to be made available on a world-wide basis.

The RAF also needs a considerable amount of straightforward administration, and has its own catering, medical and dental, legal and educational branches. Stations have a high degree of autonomy, handling their own accounts etc.

OFFICERS (men and women) are commissioned on a single list, but recruited for specific branches. The number of male officers was projected to rise to 14,800 in 1987 (but was 100 short of the projected 14,500 in 1986), with an increase of 100 in the number of women, to 900. Terms of engagement can vary slightly between branches.

The main branches are – general duties (flying); general duties (ground); air traffic and fighter control; engineer; administration (secretarial, education, physical education and catering), supply, photographic interpretation, and security (RAF regiment and Provost).

Permanent (PC) and short-service (SSC) commissions are available in most branches.

The maximum initial PC commitment is to age 38, or for 16 years from 21, whichever is later. A full career to 55 depends on promotion and/or availability of posts, and the competition. Graduates have 'built in' faster promotion through the junior ranks. They join as pilot officers, and with a 1st or 2nd class honours gain 21 months' seniority, with 3rd or ordinary/pass 15 months', and four-year courses qualify for an extra 12 months. Promotion to flying officer then, can come in six months, flight lieutenant within a year (for pilots or navigators) or two and a half years (for ground officers). Promotion from pilot to flying officer is normally after two years and from flying officer to first lieutenant after four years. Thereafter promotion to squadron leader (normally early 30s), wing commander (average age for aircrew 39), group captain, air commodore, air vice-marshal, air marshal, and air chief marshal is entirely on merit, with an examination before selection as squadron leader. All the most senior officers, however, come from general duties (flying).

Anyone not selected, or who does not wish to enter the career structure above squadron leader, can retire at 38, or follow a 'specialist' stream if they want to go on working within their professional speciality. All officers can choose to go back to civilian life at a 'marketable' age.

Short-service commissions can last three, six or eight years for ground officers, twelve (with the option to leave after eight) for aircrew.

The RAF divides officers' careers into 'tours of duty', each lasting 2–3 years, at the end of which officers move on to a new station. In many cases this means some kind of promotion or widening experience, and also a chance to serve overseas. Additional training often forms part of the third and/or fourth tour.

Recruitment and entry Recruitment was just over 500 men and 89 women in 1985, but numbers fluctuate from year to year.

Entry to most branches is at a minimum of 17$\frac{1}{2}$ for men and 18 for women, and a maximum of 39, 24 for aircrew (which means applying by $23\frac{1}{2}$ at the latest). Minimum entry qualifications are five O-level-equivalent passes at 16-plus† including English and maths, but the RAF prefers at least A levels, and 50% of entrants are now (1987) graduates. For some specialisations, eg engineering, education, medicine, a relevant degree is needed.

Graduate entry is also encouraged with cadetships and bursaries for students, and full sponsorship is available for sandwich courses in air transport engineering at City University, and electronic and electrical engineering at Salford University. Scholarships are available for A-level study.

Physical fitness is essential. Aircrew have to pass stiff aptitude tests. Competition for places is considerable.

Qualifications and training All start with an eighteen-week initial officer training course at Cranwell (men and women do the same course), and then go on to specialist training.

Aircrew officers are trained either as pilots or navigators, but for combat planes the emphasis is now all on welding the two-man crew into a single unit – the latest planes, especially the Tornado, are completely computer controlled, and the pilot cannot fly the plane without a highly-skilled navigator.

Student pilots with little flying experience get six weeks' basic training in Chipmunks. This is followed by 52 weeks, again at Cranwell, on Jet Provosts, but including some navigation. Fast-jet pilots then go for another 21 weeks to advanced flying school, practising with Hawks.

Navigator training has had to be sharply upgraded. Navigators now spend their first 60 weeks' training at Finningley Air Navigation School, also learning to fly Jet Provosts.

Fast-jet pilots and navigators then go on to the tactical weapons unit, where they are now trained closely together, although they also fly with pilot instructors, learning to use the weaponry, tactical formation flying, sortie planning etc. They finish off with five months at an operational conversion unit – for Tornados an international school at Cottesmore – where pilot and navigator are finally paired up.

Ground officers go on to specialist training, which varies in length. For instance –

Air traffic control officers do four months plus six–nine months' practical experience before certification. Fighter control officers train for six weeks.

Engineers start with an orientation course, and then 20-25 weeks' training in their specialist field. Further training is given later for work in eg R&D, procurement, and introducing new equipment.

Supply officers have four months basic training which includes computer familiarisation. Advanced training in eg movement (air and surface), fuels, explosives, data processing can lead on to higher qualifications in management and/or transportation studies.

NON-COMMISSIONED AIRMEN/WOMEN number (1986) 77,900 (including 5100 women), with a drop of about 200 men projected in 1987. They are, with the exception of air crew, employed entirely on the ground. Women are excluded from aircrew (but can be loadmasters), only four of 45 list 1 trades (three with apprentice-only entry and musician), and two of 33 list 2 trades (fireman and RAF Regiment gunner).

Air crew include –

Air engineers fly in the larger, multi-engined aircraft, not combat planes. They make the pre-flight checks, handle throttles during take-off, and monitor all the plane's systems (hydraulics, electrics etc), make fuel checks and redistributing fuel, cope with in-flight refuelling, diagnose and where possible solve any engineering problems.

Air electronics operators operate avionic equipment, eg communications, radar, underwater detection systems, used in locating, identifying and tracking ships and submarines, surveilling oil and gas rigs, and in search and rescue operations.

Air loadmasters despatch parachute troops and other air drops, supervise loading and check weight control/positioning for balance, supervise cabin service in passenger aircraft. Loadmasters also act as crewmen/women on support helicopters, do some servicing, and act as winchmen on search and rescue helicopters.

The range of ground trades includes –

In aircraft engineering, electrical technicians, mechanics (preparing and inspecting aircraft before take-off, fuelling and re-arming them), propulsion, and weapons technicians.

In electronics engineering, flight-systems, telecommunications, and air communications technicians, air radar specialists, and specialists who service the very sophisticated range of flight training simulators.

In general engineering, electrical technicians (looking after maintenance equipment, ground radar power supplies and vehicle electrical systems), ground-support equipment technicians, carpenters, and workshop technicians.

Airwatch teams include aerospace systems operators (guide pilots using radar), air photography processors, assistant photographic interpreters, and assistant air traffic controllers.

Security and safety – police (including dog handling, counter-intelligence and special investigations, maintain service discipline, prevent and detect crime), survival equipment fitters, gunners, and firemen.

Communications – aerial erectors, special telegraphists, voice radio operators, telecommunications operators, and telephonists.

Support – chefs and cooks, stewards, supply staff (locating equipment in stores on computers, packing, storing, handling and transport loading), drivers (of anything from high-power aircraft-towing vehicles, mobile cranes and refuellers, to jeeps and staff cars), administrative clerks.

The full range of PARA-MEDICAL/MEDICAL LAB PROFESSIONS are also employed.

Men serve on fixed engagements of six, eight (for aircrew and women loadmasters), nine or twelve years depending on trade, plus six years in the reserve. Women serve on nine-year 'notice' engagements, and so can leave full-time service on giving eighteen months' notice, although they must serve at least three years (from age 18 or end of training whichever is later). They must still do six years in the reserve, but liability for reserve service ends on pregnancy or 'acquisition of dependent children'.

Promotion depends partly on experience, training and qualifications.

Recruitment and entry The RAF recruited over 3800 men (including 672 under 17$\frac{1}{2}$, and 144 apprentices) and nearly 490 women in 1985.

For entry to most trades the minimum age limit is 16½ for men and 17 for women, with an upper limit for both of 40.

Educational qualifications are not needed for many trades. Four O-level-equivalent passes at 16-plus† (including maths and a physics-based science) are needed for technician apprenticeships (not open to women) in aircraft engineering (propulsion/airframe), and electronics engineering (air communication/radar) and (flight systems). Most other technician trades (open to women) need two O-level-equivalent passes at 16-plus† in maths and a physics-based science. For training in paramedical work, the school-leaving qualifications appropriate to the profession are required (it is also possible to join when qualified).

The RAF runs two-year YTS schemes.

Qualifications and training All entrants go through basic training, and then most go on to specialised trade training, in total anything from nine weeks to nearly three years. Further education/training is given as needed, with facilities and encouragement to qualify for promotion.

PRINCESS MARY'S ROYAL AIR FORCE NURSING SERVICE (PMRANS) operates on similar lines to QARANC (above). Nurses work in RAF hospitals and station medical centres, both at home and abroad. They provide nursing support when the sick and injured are flown to hospital etc.

All qualified nurses are officers, and all officers must be state registered nurses. They serve on two-, three- or four-year short-service commissions which may be extended to a total of eight years, or they may apply to transfer to a permanent commission after two years' service.

EN(G) nurses – men sign on initially for nine or twelve years, women for 'notice' engagement of nine years, but they can leave after four years (three if qualified on entry), or sign on for longer.

Recruitment and entry RGN nurses are recruited as officers, already qualified, aged between 22 and 35.

Student and pupil nurses are recruited on a similar basis to QARANC, and must have the appropriate educational qualifications. EN(G) training requires two O-level-equivalent passes including English language, at between 17 and 38. Qualified EN(G)s are recruited up to 40.

See also HEALTH AND MEDICAL SERVICES.

The Royal Marines
Introduction — officers — other ranks

Traditionally known as the Royal Navy's soldiers, the Marines are, in fact, actually part of the Royal Navy. Their contemporary role, however, is primarily as commandos and amphibious specialists, with considerably less emphasis on the detachments which serve in HM ships.

The Corps is relatively small, numbering (1986) 7600 officers and men, but with a projected increase of 200 for 1987.

The three commando units are each about 700 strong. Each unit has its own mortars and anti-tank weapons and is in many ways similar to the infantry. They are trained in mountain, Arctic, urban, jungle and desert warfare. They are mainly committed to protecting NATO's northern flanks, although they also serve in Northern Ireland.

As the amphibious specialists they are trained to make full-scale landings, as front-line assault troops even in major invasions. They use fast light craft as well as troop-carrying and heavy-duty tank and vehicle carriers. A 'special boats' squadron is made up of highly skilled frogmen, canoeists, parachutists who carry out reconaissance raids, 'clandestine operations', sabotage and demolition.

Marine detachments serving as shipborne infantrymen on board ship go wherever needed – to deal with emergencies, carry out search operations, help in disasters like hurricanes. Detachments serve as integral parts of ships' companies and their officers are encouraged to qualify for a bridge watchkeeping certificate.

Although part of the Navy, the Marines are a military corps. However, they pride themselves on their versatility, and on their extremely tough reputation – officers and men alike go through extremely gruelling physical training. Both officers and men change jobs every two years.

OFFICERS number (1986) only 600, but with a projected increase of 100 for 1987. Once trained (see below), they get a new posting every two or three years. All can specialise, for example, in signals and communications, or as helicopter pilots. They can become, eg troop officers in charge of new recruits, intelligence officer, motor-transport officer, mountain leader, landing-craft or special-boat officer. Administrative, 'staff', posts start around 26.

Most officers join on a 'full career' commission (see Navy below), but short-service commissions of four years, extendable to eight, are possible. Full career officers serve as lieutenants for seven years, and are then automatically promoted to captain, usually before the age of 30. It is possible to become a major at 35 and a lieutenant-colonel by the early 40s.

Recruitment and entry Just 65 recruited in 1985 (including 27 specialists, graduates etc, and three university cadets); 1987 intake was expected to include 15 graduates.

Entry to a 'full career' is between the ages of $17\frac{1}{2}$ and 22, with five GCE/GCSE passes including two at A level, but direct graduate entry has an upper age limit of 25. Scholarships with reserved places are available for boys with five O-level-equivalent passes to study for A levels, and cadetships for university/polytechnic students.

Short career entry is between ages $17\frac{1}{2}$ and 23, or 25 for graduates. Minimum entry requirements are five O-level-equivalent passes at 16-plus†.

Training is relatively long and very intensive. The first year is spent at the commando training centre at Lympstone. The second is practical with a commando unit in charge of a 30-man rifle troop. For full-career officers this is followed by a further year of academic studies at Dartmouth, plus a series of advanced and refresher courses at military and marine establishments. Staff training can start at 26.

OTHER RANKS 7000 men were serving in the Marines in 1986, with an increase of 100 projected for 1987.

The majority of marines serve in the general duties branch, where they can specialise in assault and weaponry (anti-tank gunner, assault engineer, heavy or platoon weapons, sniper), in equipment repair, crewing landing craft, as parachutist, swimmer-canoeist, in mountain and Arctic warfare (including cliff-climbing and ski-ing) or, less obviously, butcher, cinema operator, groom. The marines also have their own police with dog handlers for both police and other work, and after promotion it is possible to compete for jobs as drills or physical training instructor, and helicopter or light aircraft pilot or observer. The technical branch includes armourers, carpenter/joiners, drivers and motorcyclists, illustrators, metalsmiths, photographers, printers, radio technicians and vehicle mechanics. There are also jobs for clerks and signallers as well as buglers and cooks.

Marines can serve on a career engagement, for nine years (or 27 if under 18 on entry), or a notice engagement with the right to give 18 months' notice to leave after 18 months' service from 18 or the end of training. A notice engagement can be converted to a career engagement. Promotion is based on ability and length of service.

Recruitment and entry 741 recruits in 1985 including 319 juniors. Junior entrants (including musicians and buglers) is between 16 and $17^1/_2$, adult entry from $17^1/_2$ to 28. No formal educational requirements, but candidates are tested for reasoning, English language, numeracy and mechanical comprehension.

Training Initial commando and weapon training lasts 14 weeks, followed by more advanced training in, for example, use of weapons, minor tactics and seamanship. Marines are then assigned to a unit, but can continue with further training later.

The Royal Navy
Introduction — officers — ratings — Women's Royal Naval Service — Queen Alexandra's Royal Naval Nursing Service
Political and strategic policy dictates a Fleet with fewer and smaller ships, a Fleet with no battleships or full-scale aircraft carriers, and a sharply-reduced force of men and women. By 1987 (estimated) numbers were 59,100 – against 66,400 in 1981 and 82,500 in 1971.

As of 1987, the Navy has 16 nuclear-powered submarines, with four under construction/on order (another 13 are diesel-powered). Four are armed with Polaris missiles and are on constant standby, but have no real role outside full-scale nuclear war. Three anti-submarine through-deck cruisers act as command ships for anti-submarine forces, deploying Sea-King anti-submarine helicopters, missile systems, and jump-jet Sea Harriers. 'On the strength' also are fifteen guided-missile destroyers and 44 frigates (six under construction, another four on order). Primarily equipped for anti-submarine warfare, for which the destroyers carry specially-equipped helicopters and fitted with highly sophisticated missile and search systems, guns etc, they also patrol, and protect, eg fishing fleets.

Commando and assault ships with amphibious capability are equipped to carry Marines, other military forces and their equipment. The Royal Fleet Auxiliary Service, which supplies ships at sea, has 29 ships, large and small.

In all, the Navy has six different kinds of helicopter and a dozen kinds of missile ranging from Polaris down to Sea Skuas and Sub Harpoons. Support vessels include mine counter-measure and -sweeping surveying ships, and patrol vessels.

Modern warships, both large and small, surface and submarine, are built to highly-advanced technological specifications, and are armed, propelled, guided, and search with sophisticated, automated electronic equipment etc. Officers and ratings have to be skilled people to manage, operate maintain them. Warships at sea are self-contained communities and are manned by three groups –

Seaman officers and ratings, who are directly responsible for 'working' and 'fighting' ships and submarines.

Engineers and technicians, who specialise in marine, weapon, electrical, or air engineering; and

Domestic and supply services (cooks, 'writers', stores accountants etc).

Plus (on some ships) pilots and observers (all officers).

Not all naval craft are warships, however, and some officers and men man survey ships, minesweepers, etc.

The ships are supported by the shore establishments, mostly air stations or training bases, some of which have sophisticated communications stations. The Navy also uses specialist divers, and has its own instructors, medical and dental staff, lawyers, and chaplains.

OFFICERS (male), of whom there were 8800 in 1986 but with a projected increase of 100 for 1987 (against 10,000 in 1975), are recruited for specific categories.

Seaman officers 'work' and 'fight' their ships. They are trained in the ways and power of the sea, to handle and navigate ships and boats in all weather conditions, as well as in how to use them as weapons of war and make the most effective use of their armament, detection equipment and, if carried, aircraft. All seaman officers must qualify for bridge watch-keeping and ocean navigating certificates. Ships' commanding officers all come from amongst seaman officers.

Within seamanship, it is possible to specialise, for example, in submarines, aircraft control, aviation (flying), mine warfare and clearance diving, or hydrographic surveying. Officers who stay in general service can take a principal warfare officers' course which enables them to specialise in navigation, communications, and either above- or underwater aspects of naval warfare.

Engineer officers all have degrees in naval, mechanical, electrical or electromechanical engineering. They all specialise in one of –

weapon systems (surface ships) including the ship's sensors and weapon communication systems, eg sonar, radar, computers, satellite, gun, torpedo and missile;

weapon systems (submarine) as surface ships (but including Polaris if the submarine is equipped with them), plus control room watchkeeping;

marine engineering (surface ships) – controlling, monitoring, maintaining, repairing the hull and general structure, engines and machinery, generators and electrical distribution, air conditioning, ventilating, heating, fuel and water, refrigeration etc;

marine engineering (submarines) – as surface ships, but also nuclear reactors and specialised hull equipment;

air engineering (mechanical and electrical) – keeping naval aircraft fully operational and safe, 'managing' maintenance and repair of all systems, and aircraft flight-control radar and weapon systems electrical/electronic systems. May involve serving at sea or on an air station. Possible to learn to fly, and become a test pilot;

Supply and secretariat officers look after pay and cash, naval stores, catering, etc. The captain's secretary handles official correspondence, and deals with a range of administrative, welfare and personnel work on ship or shore establishment. A ship's supply officer feeds and pays the crew, is in charge of stores and spares – 40,000 items on a frigate – and usually has an 'operational' job as well, eg as flight-deck officer.

Instructor officers both go to sea, and work in training establishments, and the three Naval colleges ashore. At sea they do more than train and run classes – traditionally they are the ship's meteorologist and entertainments officer. Instructor officers are also involved in designing and developing fleet-training exercises, and analysing what happens afterwards, and in developing new tactical ideas, development and purchase of training facilities and equipment, manpower policy etc.

Only limited numbers of pilots and observers are needed, mainly for helicopters. Seaman officers may choose to fly, but the best opportunities are via short-service commission flying-duties direct entry.

Commissions are of two types –

Full-career, with the opportunity to serve until at least 50;

Short/medium, normally with options to leave after a specified time. Initial engagements are

eight years for seaman, supply and secretariat, with the option to leave after five;

engineers sign on for 16 years if not graduates, eight with the option to leave after five if they are;

pilots and observers (no full-career entry) can sign on for 16 years on entry or to age 38, whichever is later, but graduates can sign on for 12 and leave after eight years;

instructors (no full-career entry) can sign on for five or eight years, can leave after three or five, but can apply for transfer to pensionable commissions;

medical/dental officers sign on initially for five years, but can apply for pensionable commissions after two.

All officers change posts every two or three years. Even young officers in their 20s are given command of small craft, such as minesweepers or patrol vessels, with complete responsibility for their efficiency and up to 100 men. On a full-career commission promotion from mid-shipman (aged 17-26) to sub-lieutenant (between 19 and 26), lieutenant (between 22 and 34), and lieutenant commander (between 30 and 36), is automatic. Promotion to commander and above is by selection.

Recruitment and entry Just 422 were recruited in 1985 (including 136 specialists, graduates etc, and 63 university cadets). Direct graduate entry has risen to about 35% of the total, but as many of those who start without degrees go to Manadon etc, the final figure is around 55%. Direct graduate entry is currently (1987) projected at 250 a year.

Full-career naval-college entry is between 17 and 23 with five GCE/GCSE passes including two at A level (subjects to include maths and English, with maths and physics at A level for engineering). Scholarships to study for A levels are limited to seaman and engineering entrants. University cadetships awarded for all branches.

Short-service commissions naval-college entry at age 17-26 and five O-level-equivalent passes including English and maths for most. Engineers, however, still need at least A-level maths and physics or a BTEC equivalent.

Direct graduate entry to both full-career and short/medium service has an upper age-limit of 26. Instructors must have a degree or equivalent (professional) qualification, with an upper age limit of 34. Medical officers can join in their pre-registration year if under 33. Qualified medical entrants must be under 39, dentists under 32.

Training All naval officers go first to the Britannia Royal Naval College, Dartmouth, but the length and type of training varies according to entry, intended length of service, category and so on. Training begins with a basic three-month starting with 'action-centred' leadership training, but also 'sea-manship and naval knowledge'. Full-career officers not selected for degree courses stay at Dartmouth for a two-term academic course, studying the scientific principles of modern naval technology. Over half the Naval College entry officers gain degrees during training, though.

Flying-duty direct-entry officers go on to air-training for 16 months, while all the other entrants go on to practical training with the Fleet (followed two terms later by those staying at Dartmouth), varying from a term for engineering specialists who were qualified on entry, to a year for Naval College entry officers. Many entrants also have an initial nine weeks at sea during their Dartmouth course.

Thereafter training varies according to specialisation and type of commission. Full-career engineer officers who have not already graduated, for example, go to the Royal Naval Engineering College at Manadon, Portsmouth (some to Cambridge) to read for an engineering degree; seaman and secretariat/supply officers take a series of professional courses, mostly in the Portsmouth area, and so on.

RATINGS, of whom there were an estimated 47,000 at the start of 1987 (against 68,000 in 1971) are recruited to particular categories.

Seamen 'work' ships, attending to ropes and wires, anchors and cables, help in refuelling and restocking at sea, act as lookout, steer, lower and man boats, and also specialise in 1 of –

    electronic warfare, working equipment in the operations rooms to intercept 'enemy' transmissions;

    radar, working on warning radar, and plotting positions of ships' and air-crafts' positions;

    missile, controlling and operating ships' weapons systems;

    sonar, operating equipment to detect and hunt submarines, either in surface ships or submarines;

diver, mainly on mine disposal and clearance, but also experimental;

mine warfare, working in minesweepers and hunters;

survey recording, helping to collect navigational and oceanographic data for Admiralty charts, working on special computer-assisted survey ships;

tactical systems on submarines, involved in navigation, 'enemy' detection by radar and sonar, and computer-assisted plotting.

In the communications group, ratings specialise in one of –

tactical radio operating – working message-handling systems and communications procedures, in the tactical movement and working of ships;

general radio operating – all types of long and short range radio equipment and handling general signal traffic;

submarine radio operating – in conventional and nuclear submarines.

In the engineering branch, both mechanics and artificers specialise in similar areas, although the artificer is more highly skilled and therefore does more difficult work. The specialisations are –

marine engineering artificer – operating and mechanical maintenance of ships' propulsion machinery (steam, gas, turbine, diesel, nuclear powered) and associated plant; maintaining and repairing ships' structure, fitting, and boats, and power generation etc; associated electrical/electronic, including control, systems;

weapon engineering artificer (action data) – surveillance radar and displays computer and action information systems, computer peripherals, digital processing, sonars, software applications, radio navigation aids; or (communications and electronic warfare) – radio communication, cryptographic, satellite equipment, digital processing etc; or (weapon data) – weapon control and guidance, navigational aids, tracking radars etc; or (ordinance control) – gun mountings/turrets, rocket and missile launchers, torpedo systems, bomb lifts, explosives and ordnance;

air engineering artificer (mechanical) – airframe structures, engines, hydraulic and pneumatic systems, aircraft propulsion and transmission systems and other mechanical components; or (radio) – communications, navigation, sonar and radar systems of aircraft; or (weapons electrical) – power generation and distribution, flight control systems, flight instruments and weapons systems;

Mechanics work mainly on –

mechanical systems – boilers, turbines and so on, and auxiliary machinery, the ship's structure, fittings and boats;

electrical systems – propulsion machinery, semi-skilled electrical maintenance eg generators, switchgear, lighting, telephones;

weapons – either radio (radar, wireless and TV equipment, automatic plotting and data handling systems and sonars) or ordnance (navigation systems, internal communications, gun mountings, missile launchers, explosers and control of weapon and missile systems);

air engineering – mechanical (systems, airframe, hydraulic systems), radio (eg navigation, radar and sonar), weapons (electrical power supply and distribution, flight instruments, weapons and their control, release systems).

Mechanics work under artificers, but there is nothing to stop them becoming interchangeable with them eventually, or qualifying for accelerated promotion.

Naval airmen (Fleet Air Arm), actually 'ground crew', work on flight decks and airfields, in hangars and in aircraft control positions and towers, controlling aircraft movements. Training also includes fire-fighting and rescue techniques, and it is possible to specialise in this or become a heavy vehicle drivers. Some go on to flying duties.

Writers are the Navy's accountants and clerks, and although every ship's complement includes at least one, many work ashore. Stores accountants look after supplies aboard ship, while stewards and cooks also go to sea.

Medical technicians can become radiographers, physiotherapists or nurses, or specialise in nuclear health physics; medical assistants specialise in naval, commando or aero-medical work.

Ratings enter on 'open' engagements of 22 years from age 18 or date of entry (if later). They must actually serve at least four years from completion of training, and can give notice to do so 18 months before that. They may have to forfeit the right to give notice for an agreed period in return for any higher training. New entrants can usually leave within three to five months of joining. Entrants under $17\frac{1}{2}$ become junior ratings, with automatic advancement to ordinary rate at $17\frac{1}{2}$. According to category, and subject to tests, ordinary seamen are advanced to able rate after six to 15 months in the ordinary rate. Thereafter the average age of advancement to leading rate is 22 to 23, to petty officer 26 to 28, to chief petty officer (which is decided by seniority, recommendation and qualification) early to mid-30s. A fleet chief petty officer, the highest rating, is described as a manager and is expected to plan, allocate and control work, but is also expected to serve at least 27 years.

Ratings under 26 with five or more O-level-equivalent passes can apply for officer training for full- or short-career commissions. Another scheme offers appointment as special duties officer, for which selection is between 25 and 34, but GCE/GCSE passes including two at A level (or equivalent) are needed. Those selected are promoted to sub-lieutenant and can gain further promotion at least up to commander. About one in six artificer apprentices reach officer rank – they are automatically promoted to petty officer on completion of five years' service.

Recruitment and entry Just 2145 men were recruited in 1985 (including 952 juniors and 326 apprentices).

Ratings can join between 16 and 33 (but over 90% start before they are 20), and need only to pass a selection test (reasoning, English language, numeracy and mechanical comprehension). The exceptions are –

Communication technicians are recruited at between 18 and 27, with at least two O-level-equivalent passes, and pass selection and aptitude tests.

Artificer apprentices are recruited between 16 and 21, and must have O-level-equivalent passes at 16-plus† in physics or a physics-based science, maths and English language, or eg six level-1 passes in an appropriate BTEC scheme.

Direct entry artificers, at between $19\frac{1}{2}$ and 33, with an appropriate BTEC National or CGLI part II.

Medical technicians, at between 16 and 33, with qualifications appropriate to planned specialisation.

Training Except for artificer apprentices, all young entrants spend six weeks on an initial training programme (for seamen) or at a technical school. Length of training depends on category.

Apprentice artificers go straight on to a five-year training for the specialist categories. Training corresponds to a BTEC National Certificate in engineering (completed in the second year).

For other work at sea, see TRANSPORT under SERVICE INDUSTRIES, and FISHING under LAND- AND ENVIRONMENT-RELATED WORK.

THE WOMEN'S ROYAL NAVAL SERVICE is an integral part of the Royal Navy, with a complement of 3300 officers and ratings in 1985 (down to the 1971 level).

Although Wrens are still not employed on combat duties and may not serve at sea as crew members, some do now go to sea on a daily basis. Job opportunities have widened steadily, and Wrens are trained for (shore-based) operational and other duties on the same basis as men.

Officers, of whom there are (1987) just 400, combine specialist duties with eg being divisional officer in charge of a number of RN and/or WRNS ratings, acting as duty officer, or other staff/administrative work. Possible specialisations are:

In executive, administrative and operational branch – air traffic control, communications officers (in national and NATO shore centres), fleet analysis (assessing the results of weapons practice), photographic interpretation, personnel selection, computing/data processing, operations (mainly as staff officer in generational administration of a Fleet Air Arm squadron at a naval air station), public relations, staff work, training.

In engineering – air engineering in specialist jobs with the Fleet Air Arm.

In supply and secretariat – as for men, except they work only on shore stations.

As instructors – similar to men, except at sea, but may be trained as meteorological and oceanographic forecasters at naval air stations and then may go to sea on a temporary basis.

Officers are appointed initially on an eight-year short service commission, and can leave after five, or extend their service to sixteen (or possibly more) years. Promotion from third to second officer can be earned early (direct-entry officers have seniority ante-dated according to degree class etc) but is automatic after four years' service. Further promotion is by selection on merit, and means transferring to a longer commission.

Recruitment and entry only 23 direct entrants in 1985, but up from 13 in 1984. Three entry routes –
Direct entry: between $20\frac{1}{2}$ and $26\frac{1}{2}$ with, for non-graduates five O-level-equivalent passes including English language and maths. Fleet analysts need A-level maths. All direct entrants must, however, have an additional qualification. This may be a degree (air engineers and instructors must have degrees in relevant subjects), a year's secretarial training plus at least two years' responsible experience, an HND (or equivalent) qualification in hotel/cater-

ing or institutional management and two years' responsible professional experience, or a PE teaching qualification.

Cadet entry: between $18\frac{1}{2}$ and 25 with five GCE/GCSE passes including two at A level (or an equivalent). Cadets are trained as WRNS ratings and serve as such for the first 12-15 months. They are then considered for officer selection, but if not selected can either leave or apply to stay on as a rating.

Rating entry: is encouraged. As below but with five O-level-equivalent passes including English language or maths, and must be under 27.

Training Five-week basic training, two-month 'acquaint' period at a naval establishment, and officer training at Dartmouth, with specialist training as necessary.

Ratings Down to an estimated 2900 in January 1987. Like male ratings, women also specialise. In:

Operations – as weapons analysts; in radar interpretation, plotting and exercise evaluation; radio operating.

Supply and secretariat – as writers, stewards, store accountants.

General support – as telephonist, in education and training (dealing with audio-visual aids, working in libraries and display rooms, clerical support, possibly some teaching), quarters assistant (housekeeping).

Fleet Air Arm – as air engineering mechanic, meteorological observer.

Dental surgery assistants and hygienists.

Experienced ratings can transfer to 'regulator' (policing), family services, physical training, photography.

Ratings sign on for a nine-year notice engagement but can leave after three years from age 18 or end of training, giving 18 months' notice, or apply to sign on for further engagements. They may become able ratings after less than twelve months' service, acting leading wren after a further 18 months' and completing a qualifying exam, and leading wren after a year. Promotion in then to (acting) petty officer, chief and warrant officer, if recommended.

Recruitment and entry Only 169 ratings recruited in 1985.

Rating entry is between 17 and 28. Some specialisations need O-level-equivalent passes.

Cadet entry: see Officer recruitment above.

Training five-week basic training at Torpoint (Plymouth), thereafter according to specialisation (except for mechanics, three to twelve weeks for most jobs).

QUEEN ALEXANDRA'S ROYAL NAVAL NURSING SERVICE looks after Royal Naval, Marine and WRNS personnel, and families of those serving overseas, in three hospitals (one is in Gibraltar), and two dozen or so sick bays and other medical centres. QARNNS nurses do not serve at sea in peacetime, but nurse in hospital ships when there is a war.

Officers are all RGN-qualified ward or theatre sisters or more senior staff, although some clerical and quarters officers are also needed.

All nursing officers sign on initially for a five-year short service commission, but can either leave after three or extend to eight, or apply for a 16-year or full-career commission.

All nurses enrol on nine-year notice engagements with the right to leave after four years (on eighteen months notice), or to extend to fourteen years or longer. They can try for a commission.

Recruitment and entry Divides between –
Officers are recruited as fully-qualified RGN nurses (male or female) with at least two years' post-registration general experience, and age under 34.
Women are recruited to train as RGN nurses with at least five academic O-level-equivalent passes (four at one sitting) at 16-plus† including English language. EN(G) nurses are recruited already qualified.
See also HEALTH AND MEDICAL SERVICES.

Further information most easily from the local careers offices of the individual Armed Forces (addresses in the local telephone directory).

CENTRAL GOVERNMENT

Introduction 763
Government departments 764
Civil Service structure: general 777
Working in the Civil Service: administration group 779
Working in the Civil Service: specialist and other grades 784

INTRODUCTION

A civil servant is defined (in *The Central Government of Britain*) as a servant of the Crown (but not a holder of a political or judicial office) who is employed in a civil capacity and whose remuneration is found wholly and directly out of money voted by Parliament. Traditionally the title described only the 'non-industrial' members of the staffs of the various government departments in the UK or working overseas. However, no distinction is now made between industrial and non-industrial in terms of total numbers of central government employees. Further, some civil servants work for Crown bodies which are not technically government departments (eg the Manpower Services Commission and the Health and Safety Executive).

The formal definitions do not explain what civil servants do. Civil servants are the government's business managers, advisers, administrators, planners.

One part of the civil servant's role is to give ministers advice and information on which to base policy making; to look at the possible effects of a suggested change of government policy; how to deal with a particular problem, and to implement a new policy or legislation. They also give professional advice (eg legal). Civil servants must give their ministers totally impartial information and advice, and carry out instructions equally impartially, regardless of their own political views.

The larger part of the civil servant's work, though, is managing major public services, taking up some three-quarters of all departmental Civil Service time. This means collecting taxes of all kinds (personal, company, and VAT for example); paying sickness, unemployment and other benefits; inspecting schools and factories; dealing with customs and excise; administering the courts and prisons; giving advice to farmers, and services for industry and commerce; managing trading services, like National Savings, the Royal Mint, export credit guarantees, and passports.

About half of all 'non-industrial' civil servants are administrators of one kind or another, but the Civil Service has many other kinds of jobs –

Some are for experts and specialists who provide the information and analyses for government decision making, for instance the statisticians and economists.

Some are experts who monitor what happens with public-sector organisations, such as the school inspectorate.

Some are specialists who work out government policy, developing new equipment for defence, for example.

Some people work for the government just because it is the government that happens to finance and manage, for example the country's main museums and art galleries.

There is a certain conflict between the policy and managerial roles of the Civil Service, and this is one possible reason for the problems encountered in bringing 'modern' managerial methods into it. Nevertheless, strenuous efforts continue to make the Civil Service more efficient, streamlined, and cost-effective.

Despite sharply-falling numbers, the Civil Service is still the country's largest employer, of just under 2.5% of the working population. Just 594,465 civil servants were in post in April 1986, compared with a (post-world war II) peak of over 746,000 in 1977. Under present policies (spring 1987), it is planned to reduce numbers even further, to just under 588,400 by April 1988. The largest fall has been in 'industrial' staff, down to 96,000 in 1986, a ratio of 'non-industrial' to 'industrial' of over 5 to 1, against about 5 to 2 in 1981. Not all are lost jobs – the fall is partly due to transfer of functions to private ownership.

GOVERNMENT DEPARTMENTS

People joining the Civil Service are generally given the chance to say where, ie in what department, they would prefer to work. The choice is considerable, although obviously there is greater competition for some departments, particularly the more 'glamorous' ones (which also tend to be smaller). Most people stay for most of their careers within one department, although transfers are possible, eg for one partner of a marriage when the other is changing jobs and moving to another part of the country.

The Civil Service as a whole may be very large, but it is broken down into, mostly, much smaller units, many of them quite self-contained. Contrary to popular belief, only a relatively small proportion work in London, let alone Whitehall (under 15% work in central London). Dispersal of many departments means that over 81% of all civil servants work in offices outside the capital, mainly in twenty of the largest cities and towns. Largest numbers are in Newcastle (nearly 13,500), Edinburgh (12,400), Glasgow (10,000), Cardiff (9200).

Government departments are not static organisations. Changing policies and political decisions; widening, or contracting, scope of government activity in particular fields; changing conditions; constant attempts to rationalise, streamline, and improve efficiency; all have their effect. As a result change is fairly continuous, so that no description of the shape of departments is ever accurate for very long. Some departments have existed for over 200 years, some have been closed within a few years of being formed, others merged or reduced in size, and new ones created. For example, the Departments of Trade and Industry regularly change from one to two separate departments and back again (but usually retaining a 'common' services unit). Energy now seems to warrant permanent status, but Prices and Consumer Protection was abolished in 1979. The Civil Service Department's functions were divided between the Treasury and the Management and Personnel Office set up in 1981, which was itself expected to be phased out in 1987.

Until 1977-8, some departments grew steadily – Health and Social Security, Home Office, Inland Revenue, the Scottish and Welsh Offices – but even before 1979, numbers were being held down. Health and Social Security continued to expand until 1983, the Department of Employment until 1984, but since then almost all departments have shrunk further.

While the Civil Service itself has to remain politically impartial, the work departments do, as described here, clearly reflects a certain political 'tone'. The Civil Service Commission's precis of departmental work reflects the current political strategy –

THE MINISTRY OF AGRICULTURE, FISHERIES AND FOOD looks after government policy in these areas. It administers (with the Intervention Board for Agriculture Produce), EEC common agriculture and fisheries policy and various national support schemes. The Ministry provides technical advice (via ADAS) and does some applied research and development. It administers schemes to control and eradicate animal and plant diseases, and for help with investment in farm and horticultural business and land drainage. It 'sponsors' the food and drink industries and distributive trades. It looks after food supply and quality, compositional standards, hygiene and labelling, advertising, and has some responsibility for public health standards in manufacturing, preparing and distributing basic foods.

The Ministry has a total staff (1986) of about 11,200 (down from over 15,600 in 1976). About half work in central services, with about a third in the agricultural development and advisory service, and just under a third in the regional and divisional offices, with about 500 at Kew and Wakehurst Place, and some 900 in the Fisheries, Pest Infestation and Food Science Laboratories; the Ministry is also responsible for the Crofters Commission (staff 60), the Red Deer Commission (staff of eleven) and the Plant Variety Rights Office (staff of six). The Forestry Commission also comes under the Ministry.

The Intervention Board, in administering the Common Agricultural Policy, has a turnover of £2000 million a year. Its staff has risen to 750 (from 550 in 1980) but is to be cut to under 700 by 1988.

See also AGRICULTURE, HORTICULTURE AND FISHING under LAND- AND ENVIRONMENT-RELATED WORK.

THE CABINET OFFICE is made up of the secretariat, the central statistical office, and the new management and personnel office.

The cabinet secretariat helps to co-ordinate policy, serves ministers collectively, and administers Cabinet business – arranging meetings, preparing and circulating papers, and keeping records and minutes.

The central statistical office prepares and analyses the statistics used in economic policy and management including the national accounts, balance of payments, financial statistics and measures of production and output. It also produces a number of regular statistical publications.

The management and personnel office looks after the organisation, management and overall efficiency of the Civil Service, and policy on recruitment, training and other personnel matters. The Civil Service Commission is part of this office.

The Cabinet Office is small with (1986) about 1670 staff, of whom probably two-thirds work in management and personnel.

THE CENTRAL OFFICE OF INFORMATION provides specialist information and publicity services (using eg press, poster and TV advertising, exhibitions, booklets and pamphlets, films, photographs and displays) for government departments at home and overseas (including embassies). The department's main offices are in London, with ten smaller offices around the country.

About half the 878 staff (as of April 1986 – against 1400 in 1972) are media specialists, a fifth are clerical officers, nearly 5% executive officers, 2% higher executive, under 2% senior. Numbers, in 1986, were actually under the target of 920.

THE CHARITY COMMISSION keeps a central register and has the power to decide whether or not to accept an organisation as a charity. The Commissioners can investigate, and bring legal action to prevent abuses. The Official Custodian holds charities' investments, runs a common investment fund and sends out dividends. The Commission employs some 320 people.

THE CROWN ESTATE OFFICE sells, lets, administers and redevelops the Crown estates managed by the Queen's Commissioners (Scotland has a separate office). It employs only 100 people.

HM CUSTOMS AND EXCISE traditionally administers and collects indirect taxes, including VAT and taxes on tobacco, petrol, beer, wines and spirits. The department also sees that any duty and tax is paid on imported goods, collects duty on goods exported from 'bonded' warehouses. For tax collection, Customs and Excise is heavily computerised, and relies less and less on older 'physical' methods of checking and control.

Customs and Excise does not only collect taxes, though. Customs staff at sea and air ports, freight depots etc, see that import and export restrictions are observed (eg health and trade control), prevent smuggling, and control movements of passengers and crews of ships and aircraft.

Headquarters offices are in London and Southend, with nearly 900 local offices.

The 25,400 staff (end 1986 compared with 29,350 in 1977) are to be increased to over 26,000 by 1988. About a fifth are clerical officers, a third executive, a sixth higher executive, with 1000-plus senior executive officers, 300-plus principals, and 100-plus higher posts.

Under 1500 are actually customs and excise officers. Another 600 are specialist investigators. About 5000 of the staff work for the 'outdoor' service and about 3000 for the uniformed 'waterguard' branch (both groups are classed as executive officers). The rest work in revenue-collecting (the majority VAT), and are office-based, 'indoor' staff, who work either from area collection offices or at headquarters. Specialist training is given by the department.

THE MINISTRY OF DEFENCE has always been a massive department, the largest in the Civil Service, and in April 1986 still employed well over 28% (171,466) of Civil Service staff. But it is getting smaller both numerically (58,650 jobs have gone since 1979) and proportionately (it made up 39% of the Civil Service in 1973). The present target is further to reduce numbers to 168,000 by 1988. While the main fall has been in industrial staff (down to 75,000 from 1982's 116,100), the number of civilian engineers has almost halved since 1977, and is now down to some 13,000.

The Ministry helps to formulate, and implements, defence policy, and also controls, administers and supports the Armed Forces. The six main areas of work – policy, finance, personnel, resource management, project management and sales – are dealt with by six sub-departments, defence staff, manpower and budget, the three forces departments, and procurement.

Management is heavily emphasised in Ministry recruiting literature, not surprisingly since managing a defence budget of over £17,000 million has its own special problems. Computers – for management information systems, organisation and methods, and so on – are used extensively.

On policy, administrative civil servants and military personnel usually work together, the latter contributing military expertise, the former financial and political, to joint reports, assessments, advice to ministers. Ministry staff see that policy is carried out. Around 10,000 staff, including officers on secondment from the Forces, work in Whitehall.

Where possible, as in accounts and civilian personnel management, the three Forces are administered in single divisions. Detailed planning and administration of service personnel is done by the departments administering each of the Forces.

The Procurement Executive develops weapons and other equipment for the Forces, and looks after all aspects of purchase and supply. This includes administering the massive research and development budget, both commissioning work elsewhere and in its own dozen or so establishments (aircraft at Farnborough and signals and radar at Bracknell, for example). Central procurement establishes policy and deals with industry links, provides quality assurance oversight for all MoD contracts and work, and technical costing. Three systems 'controllerates' look after – 'project manage' – all aspects of defence systems and equipment procurement for air, land and sea systems.

Defence sales staff work alongside manufacturers on the export of British defence equipment.

Ministry staff work also in command and support services for the Armed Forces, including medical, education and training establishments.

The METEOROLOGICAL OFFICE is also part of the Ministry.

See also ACADEMIC AND VOCATIONAL STUDIES IN ENGINEERING and SCIENCE.

THE DEPARTMENT OF EDUCATION AND SCIENCE as of 1986, deals mainly with setting national policy and not with day-to-day administration of educational or scientific institutions. It works mainly by controlling the allocation of resources, by having the right to approve or veto the plans of the directly-responsible bodies, and by influencing the authorities in other ways – local authorities, voluntary bodies, the teaching profession – and via bodies like the University Grants Committee, which at present allocates government grants to individual universities, and the National Advisory Board, which at present advises ministers on higher education in the public sector (but the spring 1987 White Paper proposed major changes to the way higher and advanced further education are administered – see ACADEMIC AND VOCATIONAL QUALIFICATIONS).

It looks after the supply of teachers and their training and pay, school health and meals services, youth and adult services. It is taking more of a role in deciding on school curricula and examinations, The schools inspectorate comes under its wing, although it operates independently. It has service branches to produce and issue statistics and other information, and deal with financial and legal matters.

It also looks after science policy and supports scientific research via five research councils.

The DES employed some 2400 in 1986 (against some 2900 in 1976), mostly in central administration. Numbers had been projected to fall slightly, to just under 2400 by 1988. New policies may change this.

See also EDUCATION under PROFESSIONAL, SCIENTIFIC AND SOCIAL SERVICES.

THE EMPLOYMENT GROUP is made up of the Department itself, Manpower Services, the Health and Safety Commission and Executive, and the Advisory Conciliation and Arbitration Service. The total staff was almost 54,700 in 1986 (down from a peak of over 58,500 in 1982 but still up on 53,600 in 1979). Numbers are projected to fall by about 500 by 1988.

The Department of Employment itself looks anything involved with the 'efficient and socially responsible use of manpower'. This includes maintaining statistics, dealing with unemployment benefits, and manpower research. Staff are employed in the offices of industrial tribunals and in unemployment benefit offices (dealing with daily claims etc), as well as in preparing and implementing policies on employment, industrial relations, equal pay and race relations in employment etc. The Department also looks after small firms, tourism, and enterprise and deregulation.

The Department had a staff of about 30,500 in April 1986, still well up on the 21,000 of 1980. Obviously a high proportion of staff work in the 800 local offices around the country, or in the nine regional offices, but senior administrative staff work mainly in London, Runcorn or Watford.

The Manpower Services Commission develops and operates a comprehensive manpower policy, and on a more practical level, manages and organises employment and training services. It administers the high-street job centres, oversees arrangements for training and re-training via its own schemes and services for employers, and develops and manages schemes to help people into work.

Most of MSC's 21,000 staff (as of April 1986, compared with 25,400 in 1980), now work in Sheffield, or in the 1000-plus regional and local offices. Many staff travel extensively.

The Health and Safety Commission and Executive, is made up of a central executive, and the inspectorates (which used to be separate and are still fairly independent of each other) – Factory, Agriculture, Explosives, Mines and Quarries, and Nuclear Installations – plus the technical, scientific and medical group (which includes research and lab services etc), and the Employment Medical Advisory Service (see also HEALTH AND MEDICAL SERVICES). (The Air Pollution Inspectorate has transferred to the Department of Environment as part of a single Inspectorate of Pollution.)

Working through a network of twenty area offices, HSE inspectors visit and review working situations, monitoring and enforcing (where necessary and possible) standards via enforcement notices and prosecution, giving expert advice and guidance. They try to see that statutory requirements are met, to ensure that there are as few major and minor accidents as possible, that safety is built in and not an afterthought. They also work with designers, manufacturers, importers and suppliers of equipment, plant etc used in industry, commerce, or any area of employment, where safety is at stake. A substantial amount of research and lab work is done, and the Commission runs an information and advisory service. Senior staff work on policy development, and new legislation and safety measures – crucial as science and technology develop new processes and products.

The Commission should have (1986) about 3650 staff, rather fewer than the 4130 of 1981, but is in fact under strength. The Nuclear Inspectorate was short 18 of its 120 inspectors, for instance. The Factory Inspectorate numbers 850, the Mines and Quarries Inspectorate only 84. Most headquarters staff are moving to Merseyside.

THE DEPARTMENT OF ENERGY deals with overall policy for the different energy sources – coal, oil, gas, electricity, nuclear power and newer alternatives – and encourage efficient exploitation, supply and use. It works on the development of international energy policies. It looks after government relations with national energy suppliers, the UKAEA etc, and sponsors the nuclear construction industry. It also sponsors the oil industry, and looks after the national interests in the development of UK oil and gas resources. The off-shore supplies office helps develop an internationally competitive UK supplies and services industry, and deals with pricing, storage, and distribution as well as collecting oil royalties.

The energy efficiency office deals with overall strategy, and leads in monitoring, co-ordinating and developing efficient energy use, administering assistance, information and advice programmes. It has specialist divisions for economics and statistics, and finance, which helps the public-sector industries to produce long-term plans, and technology, sponsoring R&D in energy.

The Department has, as of April 1986, a staff of just over 1000, compared with over 1370 in 1976. Most staff work in London.

THE DEPARTMENTS OF THE ENVIRONMENT AND TRANSPORT cover the broad fields of local government and development, housing, planning, and construction, shipping, aviation and transport industries.

The DOE deals with local government reorganisation and finance, their powers and functions. Planning work includes regional strategies, land use and transportation studies, approving local authority traffic/transport plans, and dealing with planning appeals. It employs the special staff who audit most local-authority accounts.

On housing and construction, the DOE oversees general housing policy and sponsors construction projects, but is directly involved (mainly via the Property Services Agency for which see CONSTRUCTION) in building, maintaining etc public, including royal, buildings, and accommodation for the Armed Forces etc. Its responsibility for historic buildings has been 'devolved' to the Historic Buildings Commission (see CONSERVATION).

DTp plans and builds inter-urban roads via six road-construction units. It supervises public and private transport, including the nationalised transport industries, mainly now railways, but also regulates civil aviation. It deals with transport byelaws, licensing road haulage and bus services, and testing and licensing drivers and road vehicles. It deals with international transport policy, negotiations, and problems, and manages the coastguard service. The Department has its own research station.

See also TRANSPORT under SERVICE INDUSTRIES.

Both DOE and DTp have large central-London headquarters, but also an extensive network of regional offices, including the DTp's Swansea computer unit.

The combined staff of the two departments (they share common services) was just over 43,700 in 1986 (against nearly 82,600 in 1977), but with Environment staff minus the PSA numbering only 6500 and Transport 14,720 (although the 'target' was for 14,900). The fall in numbers has been mainly in the PSA, and otherwise has been achieved by 'hiving off' some functions (eg over 1000 went with the historic buildings), and research stations (to private owners), and by contracting out work, so not all the jobs have been lost, although some functions have been dropped altogether.

THE EXPORT CREDITS GUARANTEE DEPARTMENT insures exporters against the risks of not being paid by overseas customers (for whatever reason), and gives guarantees to banks so that exporters can finance their overseas business. It is, then, a business organisation, with staff handling credit insurance for over 10,000 policy holders exporting £15,000 million worth of goods a year.

Most staff spend their time assessing the risks of particular export markets and overseas buyers, underwriting business, handling claims, or providing support services (including business promotion). The rest work in the nine regional offices.

ECGD is supposed to have (1986) a staff of roughly 1800 – but it was actually 50 off target – about the same as in 1982 but down from nearly 2000 in 1979, with a projected fall of some 200 by 1988.

THE OFFICE OF FAIR TRADING watches over commercial activities in the UK, to protect the consumer and encourage competition, and divides its work accordingly. It reviews the effects of trading practices on consumers, and attempts to change unfair practices by legislation and voluntary agreement. It administers the Consumer Credit and Estate Agents Acts, registers restrictive trading agreements, monitors mergers and monopolies, and collects and organises relevant economic information.

The staff is small, only just over 300, and almost all work in London.

THE FOREIGN AND COMMONWEALTH OFFICE looks after British interests, interpreted increasingly widely, abroad. Its main job is to see that Britain and its government is properly represented on every relevant topic.

It is also the London headquarters of the Diplomatic Service.

The Diplomatic Service is the link between the British government and the governments of other countries, and international organisations. Diplomatic work stretches widely, from conventional political dealings and explaining British policies to representing Britain in, for example, the UN and NATO, on topics from outer space to the sea bed. It negotiates commercial treaties and financial agreements, helps exporting companies and promotes exports, administers remaining dependent territories, provides consular services for British subjects abroad, and issues visas.

In London, the FO gathers information and views from 208 overseas posts in 165 countries, as the basis of reports and analyses for ministers and their advisers. The departments are divided both regionally (ie gathering information on a wide range of subjects on the countries within the region) and functionally (dealing on a world-wide basis with particular subjects, such as defence). These 'political' departments are supported by research departments and legal advisers, professional economists and other specialist staff.

The FO also helps to formulate and implement aid and technical assistance to developing countries. This includes grants and interest-free loans, technical expertise and equipment, training, and support for research and advisory services.

Overseas, the FO runs 129 major embassies and high commissions, 61 consulates, ten permanent delegations (eg to the UN and NATO), and several trade offices etc. Large missions and embassies have several sections. In smaller missions, consulates or high commissions there may be fewer.

In an average-sized mission, the chancery looks after political matters, producing reports on political developments in the country and telling the country's government about British policy, as well as dealing with any negotiations. Chancery also co-ordinates the work of the entire mission.

The commercial and economic section's main job is to help British industry sell in the country, by collecting information about local industry and commerce, the economy, laws etc which affect exporters, and passing this on, as well as advising UK companies. It also negotiates any commercial/trade treaties and agreements. Up to a third of embassy staff do commercial work now.

The consular section provides a service both to British residents in the country and to visitors travelling on British passports. It issues passports and visas, and handles any formalities when British ships arrive in port. Consular work is done by about 12% of staff working overseas, and another 10% on immigration/visa work.

Information sections primarily promote a positive image for Britain, via the media, and any other available contacts. They also help the commercial section, trade and tourism in Britain. Some missions also have scientific sections.

All embassies and missions need efficient administration, and registries to look after correspondence, telegrams, files, diplomatic bags etc.

The Foreign Office has (1986) a total staff of about 9900, down from nearly 11,700 in 1980, and projected to fall to about 9600 in 1988. Of these, some 4616 are in the DIPLOMATIC SERVICE (see further on in this section), 1600 work for the Overseas Development Administration, and almost 1890 directly for the Foreign Office. The rest (presumably) work in communications, mainly for GCHQ (below).

See also WORKING OVERSEAS.

GOVERNMENT COMMUNICATIONS HEADQUARTERS is officially primarily a 'research' establishment, carrying out research, development and production work in 'communications' for the Foreign and Commonwealth Office, the Ministry of Defence and other government departments. Unofficially, of course, most people are aware that GCHQ is involved in information-gathering for security services.

The Foreign Office administered Joint Technical Language Service is housed with GCHQ. Foreign Office 'communications' staff can be estimated at about 1800, although outside sources suggest the numbers working for GCHQ and JTLS are considerably higher than this. GCHQ staff are now employed in special classes separated from the (Home) Civil Service – see Departmental groups below. Most work at the main centre in Cheltenham, some at UK outstations and overseas.

See also Communications under special and other grades below.

THE DEPARTMENT OF HEALTH AND SOCIAL SECURITY administers the National Health Service centrally. It administers and pays social security cash benefits, state pensions and allowances (to 'senior citizens', the disabled, the unemployed, the sick for example), child and supplementary benefits, and collects health contributions. It is responsible for child care, local-authority welfare services for people with problems resulting from age, ill-health, or who are in need. It looks after reception and re-establishment centres, and assesses the means of anyone who applies for legal aid.

Headquarters administrators advise on policy and legislation, work on changes to the benefit system etc. A high proportion of Department staff are employed directly in day-to-day management and organisation of regional and local offices.

The DHSS is very large, with a total staff of over 92,700 in April 1986, some 600 over target (due to the high level of benefit payments) but still well below the 97,400 of 1979. The projected number for 1988 is 87,500. A 20-year, major project to computerise benefit claims and payments could reduce staff by 20,000 by the late 1990s. Virtually 90% of DHSS staff are administrative; 67% are clerical, local and general executive staff, some 5% higher executive, 1.5% senior executive.

The Department has its headquarters offices in London, but some large central offices are in the North, twelve regional offices in the major cities, and a further 500 local offices deal directly with the public.

THE HOME OFFICE deals with law and order – criminal law and administration of justice. It controls and administers the police and prison services, treatment of offenders, probation and after-care services, and some courts. It deals with immigration and nationality, issues passports, looks after community relations and voluntary social services, and equal opportunities. It also deals with the use, control and licensing of explosives, firearms, drugs etc, and with public safety; controls betting and gaming; deals with addresses and petitions to the Queen, and ceremonial and formal business involved in awarding honours, has some responsibility for broadcasting, licensing theatres and cinemas, and is responsible for marriage, burials and cremations etc. A number of services (for example, police and fire services) are administered through local authorities, and the Home Office exercises control mainly through grant payments, inspections and the power to make regulations.

The Home Office itself is relatively small. Nearly 19,000 of the 37,500 people technically working for it are in the prison service (see PROTECTIVE SERVICES), and nearly 1600 in immigration. The number of central Home Office staff, at about 17,000 in 1986, is similar to 1981. Central staff include both administrators and a relatively large number of professional and scientific people, including legal advisers, and there are several Home Office research and training establishments. Administrative centres are in central and south London, but some offices are in eg Bootle, Liverpool, Glasgow.

INLAND REVENUE administers and collects direct taxes (mainly income, corporation, capital gains, and capital transfer tax), and advises Treasury ministers on policy issues, such as their effect on social and industrial policy, what happens when taxes are changed. It also values land and property for, eg taxation, rating.

Inland Revenue has a very large staff – 69,270 in April 1986, but despite the problems of collecting taxes, numbers have been reduced sharply, from a peak of over 85,000 in 1979. A further fall, to under 66,400 is projected for 1988. Most staff work in one of the 1000-plus offices, which can be quite large, spread throughout towns up and down the country, although headquarters are still in London.

Management is once again strongly stressed in the work of the department – looking after the organisation and staffing of all the offices. Computers are increasingly a major part of the operation, and a massive new centralised system, with some 20,000 access terminals, is being installed.

Tax is assessed and collected separately. The 750 local tax offices take in income tax returns and work out what is owed, applying PAYE codes. They are staffed by 14,000 tax officers (equivalent to administrative officer) and 11,000 higher-grade tax officers. The collection service employs some 3100 collectors and over 3600 assistant collectors. There are over 4600 tax inspectors. The 200 local valuation offices employ 2400 valuation clerks and 1200 professional staff.

See also Departmental groups below.

THE LAND REGISTRY records ownership of land, houses and other property. Some staff examine and record documents of title (with a plan of the property), others prepare and keep maps and plans up to date. The work ranges from straightforward copying to preparing complicated plans at various scales, but computers are being introduced.

The Registry has (1986) a staff of 7100 (up from 5600 in 1982), which is being increased to 7500 by 1988, as compulsory registration is extended and home ownership rises.

THE LORD CHANCELLOR'S DEPARTMENT administers all civil and criminal courts in England and Wales except magistrates' courts. A high proportion of the Department's work is on legal administration – court business, courts' jurisdiction, structure, workload, pay etc. The Lord Chancellor appoints magistrates, advises on judicial appointments. The Department deals with legislation, especially on property, family and commercial law, as well law reform, the Law Commission, and legal aid policy. The Lord Chancellor has general administrative responsibility for the Council of Tribunals (itself a supervisory body for administrative tribunals, the Lands Tribunal, amongst others, and provides judges advocate for courts-martial.

Under the Lord Chancellor's Office, the administrative work of the English and Welsh courts is managed through six circuit administrators, each looking after the business of the High Court, the Crown Court, and the County Courts within the circuit. Each circuit is divided into two or three areas, under a courts administrator.

Specialist departments of the Supreme Court which come under the Lord Chancellor include the Central Office of the Queen's Bench Division, which issues writs and mans courts, Chancery Chambers (dealing with matters of property, dissolution of partnerships, mortgages, accounts, copyright, revenue appeals etc), the Supreme Court taxing office (which adjudicates on disputes between solicitors and their clients), and the Court of Protection (which appoints receivers for people who have psychiatric problems).

The Official Solicitor's Department deals with personal problems, eg representing infants and anyone else incapable of dealing with their own affairs in court, acting as receiver if no one else is available, and looking after people committed for contempt of court. The Department of Bankruptcy and Companies Courts deals with individuals and coluntary and compulsory winding-up of companies.

The Public Trustee Office acts as executor for wills, administrator of estates, or as a trustee. The Public Trustee can manage funds of pension schemes, friendly societies, disaster appeals and individuals' funds.

The Department has (1986) a total staff of around 10,200, which is back to the 1979 peak, but now includes the 300 Public Trustee Office staff. Numbers are projected to fall again to about 10,000 by 1988. About half are administrators, but obviously a high proportion are legal staff. Work is mainly in London, but senior staff may work in circuit offices.

See also Lawyers under special and other grades below, and THE LEGAL SYSTEM.

THE NATIONAL SAVINGS DEPARTMENT administers the National Savings Bank, premium bonds and a wide variety of other savings securities, to all age and income groups.

It makes extensive use of computers, and so employs systems analysts, programmers etc, as well as a large administrative staff dealing with finance, advertising, planning and policy, relations with the Post Office and banks etc. Total staff was (1986) about 7800, against over 13,600 in 1976, and is projected to fall further, to 7400 by 1988. The main offices are in the north.

ORDNANCE SURVEY employs (1986) just under 3000 people (against 4700 in 1973) in officially mapping the country, producing a wide range of maps at various scales, and also providing specialist mapping services. It uses the most modern techniques for comprehensive surveying, drawing, printing and marketing, most of the actual mapping being done with the aid of aerial surveys.

The Survey employs mainly professional and technical staff in the actual surveying, drawing and printing, with administrative people to handle sales, promotion, advertising and so on. The professional and technical staff is made up mainly of surveyors, cartographic draughtsmen/women and reproduction craft workers.

See also LAND USE PROFESSIONS.

THE OFFICE OF POPULATION CENSUSES AND SURVEYS administers centrally the law on civil marriages and the registration of births, marriages and deaths, keeps central records, and controls the network of 2000 registrars and superintendent registrars. The central office provides copies of certificates, and an advisory service on the law on registration, marriage, legitimacy and adoption; it also prepares statistics of population, migration, fertility, births, marriages, deaths and diseases, and carries out regular population censuses. The Department's social survey division does survey research for other departments on social and economic problems.

About 70% of the 2140 staff (April 1986 – against nearly 2800 in 1975) do administrative work. Although it has headquarters in London, the main office, with its computers, is in Hampshire.

THE DEPARTMENT OF PUBLIC PROSECUTIONS is responsible for prosecutions in criminal law, and the new independent Crown Prosecution Service comes under the Director of Public Prosecutions. It also advises other departments, police forces and justice departments on criminal matters. Some staff instruct prosecuting counsel, others work in the registry, and others do casework, preparing briefs. Most staff are lawyers. As of April 1986, it had a staff of just under 300, but this is being increased rapidly as staff are recruited for the new Crown Prosecution Service, and is projected to reach 3750 by 1988.

See also Lawyers under special and other grades below, LEGAL SERVICES under PROFESSIONAL, SCIENTIFIC AND SOCIAL SERVICES, and THE POLICE under SERVICE INDUSTRIES.

THE PUBLIC RECORD OFFICE cares for documents amassed by law courts and departments of state since the Norman conquest, including the Domesday Book. Records to be kept are regularly transferred from departments, and Public Record Office staff help select records, others care for them.

The PRO has (1986) a staff of just about 400, and this is set to increase slightly by 1988. Three-quarters work at the modern offices at Kew, and most of the rest in central London.

See also ARCHIVE WORK.

RESEARCH COUNCILS, five of them – Agricultural, Medical, Natural Environment, Science and Engineering, and Economic and Social Studies – are the responsibility of the Department of Education and Science. The Councils themselves are primarily responsible for formulating research policy in their particular areas, for promoting and supporting research, and in some cases for implementing it. Technically, the Research Councils are not part of the Civil

Service, but terms of employment are similar. See under areas relevant to the work of the Councils.

THE SCOTTISH OFFICE has five main departments, dealing with agriculture and fisheries, development, economic planning, education, and home and health. Based in Edinburgh, these departments more or less parallel the major departments which operate for England and Wales. 'Scotland's minister' also deals with anything which affects Scotland generally, even if the Office does not have statutory responsibility for it – for example, unemployment in Scotland, and policy on eg steel. The Scottish Office has a staff of about 9900 (1986), down from a peak of over 10,900 in 1981.

Scotland also has other departments of its own – the Crown Office and Procurator Fiscal Service (1000 staff), the Scottish Courts Administration (900 staff), the Registers of Scotland (880 staff), the Scottish Record Office (125 staff), and the Lord Advocate's Department (22 staff).

THE STATIONERY OFFICE (HMSO), publishes and sells government publications, and is also the central purchasing organisation for the public service – for office supplies and machinery, printing and similar services. As a publisher, the Stationery Office claims to produce more titles each year than any other publishing organisation in the country. It runs its own 'book' shops, and although much more work goes to commercial printers, it still has its own print works.

About 41% (it was over 50%) of the 3400 staff (in April 1986, down from 7800 in 1971) are 'industrials', the rest administrative etc. The main offices are in Norwich, with regional offices and branches in other parts of the country.

THE DEPARTMENT OF TRADE AND INDUSTRY has alternated between being a single department and two separate departments. It has now (1987) been merged since 1982.

On trade, it looks after international policy, including UK interests in the EEC, and other international organisations. It promotes UK exports and gives help to exporters.

It deals with government general industrial policy, including general promotion of industrial interests and assistance. It handles government relations with all manufacturing and service industries except those dealt with by other departments, and regional policy and industrial assistance. It also covers policy on state-owned steel, shipbuilding, the Post Office, and British Technology.

It has overall responsibility for competition policy and consumer protection, including safety. It deals with policy on science and technology, research and development, standards and designs, and support for innovation, promoting information technology. It administers several government laboratories.

The Department has specialist divisions which administer company legislation, the insolvency service, and the Patent Office, and regulate the insurance business, and radio frequencies.

The Department has its own management services, solicitors, finance and resource management, and statistics divisions.

The Department staff is (1986) down to about 12,650 (against combined Trade/Industry numbers of nearly 18,000 in 1976), and is set to fall further, to under 12,300 by 1988. About half the staff work in London, others in branch and other offices elsewhere, including the Companies' Registration Office in Cardiff.

HM TREASURY helps ministers formulate and implement economic policy and control public expenditure. It is organised in six main sectors.

Public expenditure sector co-ordinates its planning and control, and is directly responsible for Treasury control of most major public-expenditure programmes.

Overseas finance deals with world economic development, international financial questions, relations between the UK and other countries including the EEC, and manages foreign exchange reserves and external debt.

The Chief Economic Adviser's office (staffed mainly by professional economists) deals with economic analysis and gives policy advice to ministers. The Treasury uses a computer-based 'model' of the economy to make short- and medium-term forecasts.

The domestic economy sector looks after monetary and fiscal policy, including taxation, banking and other financial institutions, and government lending.

The Treasury also looks after Civil Service pay, pensions etc, and the pay of judges, MPs and ministers. It manages the central computer and telecommunications agency, catering for the Civil Service, a computer centre, and rating for government departments.

The Treasury has a relatively small staff, of about 3400 people, but less than half deal with the main 'Treasury' functions. About half work in London.

THE WELSH OFFICE looks after many aspects of Welsh life, including agriculture and fisheries, financial help for industry, tourism, roads and transport, housing, education, language and culture, local government, water and sewerage, environmental protection, sport, land use, conservation, new towns, ancient monuments, the careers service, urban programme, health and personal services, and financial aspects of all these including rate support grant. It oversees economic affairs and regional planning too.

Based in Cardiff, it has (1986) a staff of some 2300, down from 2600 in 1979.

Civil Service structure: general

An organisation the size of the Civil Service needs a formal framework which decides grades, salaries, promotion and so on. In the past there was a great multiplicity of classes and grades which formed rigid barriers within the Service. Some progress in simplifying the structures, and breaking down unnecessary barriers has been made, largely stemming from the recommendations of the Fulton Committee – way back in the 1960s.

Fulton wanted the structure to be made more flexible, both to remove unnecessary barriers to the use of staff in posts for which they are best suited, regardless of original method of entry or first area of work, and to open up avenues of promotion for people with the right ability, again regardless of professional status or method of entry. This all as part of a plan to improve the managerial qualities of civil servants, for instance to run large projects and programmes, and manage large numbers of staff. Efforts in this direction are still going on.

Although the Civil Service did make some changes in response to Fulton, it is generally believed that they have not gone far enough. For example, the idea of a completely open system of grading has only been achieved at the top, when the intention was to give, for instance, scientists and other professional people other than administrative entrants, management experience in mid-career too.

A unified grading system down to and including under-secretary level has been in place since 1972, with all specialisms and disciplines in a common 'open' structure at the top of the Civil Service. But it consisted of a tiny proportion, under 700 people. Progress appeared to have come to a halt, but in 1984, three further grade levels, down to senior principal and equivalent, were added, and in January 1986, a seventh, to include principal and equivalent-level grades – 60 in all – and increasing by 11,800 the numbers in the open structure, so that by April 1986 it included over 18,100 people. The Civil Service appears to have fully recognised at last that, at levels where managerial skills are often more important than specialist expertise, the old class and grade barriers prevented the best people being chosen for the particular job. In particular, the new open structure should make it easier for scientists, engineers and other professionals to compete for 'top' posts.

A series of merged and somewhat simplified 'categories', subdivided by groups, with standardised grades, replaced most of the old maze of grades and classes some time ago, although it is still quite complex. There are three broad categories – general, science, and professional and technology. There are also 'categories' for legal and secretarial staff (for example).

Recruitment and entry As the country's largest employer, the Civil Service takes in very large numbers of people every year, even though recruitment has been heavily cut. Numbers have, however, picked up somewhat in the mid 1980s, to over 44,800 in 1986, from the low of 37,000 in 1983 – but this has to be compared with 68,300 in 1974.

The Civil Service still recruits at all levels, with full opportunities for training and promotion for everybody. At the same time, there are schemes designed to find and give accelerated promotion to people who are, in Civil Service terms, 'high fliers'.

Recruitment is still fairly firmly stratified –

School leavers with O level equivalents are recruited, mainly as administrative assistants (at least two O level equivalents), and administrative officers or equivalent (five O-level equivalents). Training schemes for leavers with three or four O-level equivalents (mostly including maths and a science), are offered for a range of posts, eg photography, as radio technicians, cartographic draughtsmen and women, assistants/technicians in surveying and engineering; apprenticeships in several areas of engineering and ship construction. This is also the lowest entry level for scientific assistants.

Up to this level recruitment is on a local basis, through advertisements or via careers offices, except for special departmental training schemes. Selection is normally by short interview, and there may be a short test.

School leavers with A levels are recruited, traditionally, to executive officer (with at least two A levels passed at one sitting), and this includes recruitment for eg Inland Revenue. There are also a number of special traineeships and sponsorships, in eg naval architecture, engineering, for people with two or three A levels including appropriate sciences, and in valuation.

Graduate entry has shot up recently. In 1986, the Civil Service recruited over 3900 new graduates (compared with 1900 in 1980). Of these, nearly 1470 (against nearly 900 in 1980) were recruited for posts which require a degree for entry – the 'fast' AT scheme, the tax inspectorate, the diplomatic service, surveying, engineering, science, and so on. Applications totalled 33,700 for these posts. The other 2467 (1300 in 1980) were mostly recruited as executive officers – over 6370 applied.

Training The Civil Service has a long track record of training for all its staff, through from high-flying graduate administrative trainees and diplomats to school leavers, frequently with the opportunity to gain formal qualifications. People who go into the Civil Service already qualified are encouraged and helped to gain further qualifications if needed for promotion. New graduates are given the practical experience and training they require to gain membership of professional bodies, and some departments are developing their own management training schemes,

Some departments, most notably the Ministry of Defence, offer sponsorships for degree courses, mainly in engineering, and technician-level training is given, again mainly by the MoD, but also the Property Services Agency, and GCHQ. The Civil Service is at present trying out a number of such schemes as a way of solving chronic recruitment problems in some areas, apparently with some success.

Working in the Civil Service

Civil Service careers still divide fairly easily into administrative and 'other', even though many of the 'others' are increasingly administrating –

Administration

By definition, a very large proportion of civil servants are administrators, working on policy and planning, managing, and implementing policy. The administration group consisted of some 220,000 people in 1986 (about 225,400 with the principals lost to 'open structure' grade 7 in 1986, and a few thousand lost to grades 4-6 in 1984) – which is not far off half of all 'non-industrial' civil servants.

The group's functions range from co-ordinating government machinery and managing departments at higher levels, to clerical duties in the departments in the lower grades. Members of the group may work in any one of over 60 departments, so that the type of work done varies considerably. There are now only seven grades in all within the group. The administration group is like a pyramid, with a broad base of clerical staff, narrowing towards the top. Theoretically, as it is a 'unified' structure it should be possible to work all the way from the bottom to the top, but in practice the higher people start, the higher they tend to go and the best graduate entrants get accelerated promotion.

Apart from occasional recruitment at principal level, entry from outside the Civil Service is normally limited to the first four grades below, their minimum qualifications corresponding to the levels at which students leave the educational system.

ADMINISTRATIVE ASSISTANTS (were called clerical assistants) are the 'junior clerks' of the Civil Service, doing work similar to their counterparts in any other organisation: dealing with incoming mail, keeping records, doing simple figure work (perhaps using a calculator), some straightforward letter-writing, and dealing with telephone calls, other enquiries from the public and so on. It is all fairly routine.

They number (1986) under 61,400 (compared with a peak of 76,100 in 1979), working in departments throughout the Civil Service – 10,000 in the DHSS, 8700 in Defence, 6400 in the Employment group for example – and in all parts of the country. Most are young, over 75% are under 30, and 30% under 20. Promotion is to administrative (clerical) officer.

Recruitment Entry is with at least two O-level-equivalent passes at 16-plus† (including English language). Departments occasionally recruit people without these qualifications, but they must take clerical tests. Recruitment is on a local basis, taking in over 19,700 in 1985, up from a low of barely 12,000 in 1983 and close to the levels of the 1970s. Over 60% are recruited between the ages of 18 and 24, 19% between 16 and 17.

ADMINISTRATIVE OFFICERS (were called clerical officers) are generally more closely involved in the function of the particular department, although most posts still involve routine desk work. They work alongside administrative (clerical) assistants, but usually have more responsibility. They handle incoming correspondence, write or draft letters, give the public advice, information and help across counters (eg in benefit offices), check accounts and keep statistics and other records.

They number (1986) almost 81,500 (compared with a peak of 97,400 in 1973), working across the country, in most departments – including 39,300 in the DHSS, 24,900 in the Employment group, 14,800 in Defence. A few are recruited for the Diplomatic Service, and some work overseas. Most usually gain promotion to executive officer.

Recruitment Direct entry is with at least five O-level-equivalent passes at 16-plus† to include English or English language. Departments do occasionally recruit people without these qualifications, but they must take clerical tests. Recruitment is on a local basis, taking in nearly 5900 in 1985, up from 4320 in 1983, but still well down on 11,500 in 1980. About 37% are recruited between 20 and 24, 25% between 18 and 19, and 17% between 25 and 29. Administrative (clerical) assistants may be promoted to administrative (clerical) officer on merit or by examination.

See also COMMERCE etc.

EXECUTIVE OFFICERS are the Civil Service equivalent of junior managers.

They may organise and supervise the day-to-day work of a branch or section made up of a number of administrative (clerical) officers and assistants within a department.

They may be an assistant to a senior civil servant, arranging meetings, collecting and collating information, and generally getting the spade work done on any policy development.

They may go out on the Department's work to factories, offices, or into people's homes, dealing with 'casework'.

They may deal with day-to-day administration such as finance, office records, communication systems, or personnel.

About a third are trained to do specialised work, eg in accountancy, or computing.

The Civil Service Commission cites as examples of executive officers' work –

being an inspector in the Department of Health and Social Security, supervising staff paying sickness, injury and maternity benefits;

dealing with applications for postgraduate training awards in the Science and Engineering Research Council;

giving advice in a job centre;

computer programming for the Ministry of Defence, in a branch looking after the personal records of Army officers;

examining in the Department of Trade's insolvency branch;

personnel work and general administration in a county court;

being a VAT field officer visiting firms (from small shop-keepers to large companies) to check their accounts.

Executive officers number, as of January 1986, over 44,850 (against 55,650 in 1982), working in all departments – 20,500 in the DHSS, 10,200 in the employment group, 5350 in Defence – right across the country.

All executive officers are given training for their jobs – for some it may be for work which is only done in the Civil Service (eg taxation work), but for others it may be in a skill useful elsewhere, eg computer programming.

All executive officers should become at least higher executive officers (after some four years), many will become senior executive officers, and may go higher.

Recruitment Direct entry to the executive officer grade is with at least five GCE/GCSE passes including two at A level. (The upper age limit has been raised to 50.)

Traditionally the entry point for sixth-form school-leavers, graduate entry to the grade increased steadily, from about 28% over 1972-5 to over 53% in 1981, but more recently (1985 and 1986) has stabilised at about 50%.

To make sure school-leavers have a fair chance of entry, a number of places are kept for people between $17\frac{1}{2}$ and $19\frac{1}{2}$ who expect to get the appropriate qualification during the year (anyone who already has the necessary O- and A-levels must apply via the 'standard' entry).

Recruitment statistics relate to both executive-officer entry and equivalent departmental (eg Inland Revenue) grades. For 1986, 5477 vacancies were reported, 29,600 people applied, and 4923 were appointed (another 800 were recommended for appointment). Included in these figures are the 2449 who tried for the 'school-leaver' only entry (down from 4500 in 1982), of whom 152 were successful. (The 1985 Civil Service statistics gives 1994 people recruited as administration group executive officers in 1985, up from 1335 in 1983, but against 8500 vacancies in 1974.) Over 55% of executive officers are recruited between the ages of 20 and 24, 17% between the ages of 25 and 29, and 8% between 18 and 19.

Promotion to executive officer is fairly common for administrative (clerical) officers, and a high proportion of executive posts are, in fact, filled from amongst them.

Executive officers who are under 28 and have been EOs for two years can apply for transfer to the AT scheme below. EOs can also 'jump' the AT grade and go straight on to HEO(D) – the aim is for 50% of fast-stream entry to come from internal sources. In 1986 76 candidates were considered but a 'disappointing' 17 appointed.

GCHQ (see Communications below) recruits separately, and some other departments have been doing so recently on an experimental basis. Executive recruitment is (1986-7) under review.

ADMINISTRATION TRAINEES spend only two years in the grade (normally), work only in the major departments, and are groomed and trained specifically for higher management/policy making posts – they are all expected to go to assistant secretary at very least – developing an expertise in getting to the root of complex problems quickly and devising solutions. Just 106 ATs were in the 'general' category administration group in January 1986 (but see also Inland Revenue below).

They usually do two different jobs during this time. The level/type of work they do is generally similar, although the subject matter obviously varies greatly.

Most spend some time providing 'secretarial' support for a working party or committee – arranging meetings, preparing and circulating papers for discussion, taking minutes, and seeing through any follow-up action.

Many work in the private office of a minister or senior civil servant, and ATs usually work closely with a principal who monitors their progress and help them learn the routines.

ATs are also given spells of intensive training at the Civil Service College.

ATs are normally promoted to higher executive officer after two years, or at 26, whichever is earlier. They are then given experience of a further range of jobs and can normally be expected to be promoted to principal in two or three years.

Recruitment Direct entry to the AT scheme requires a first or second class honours or postgraduate degree, and the criteria for selection are very high – vacancies are left unfilled rather than lower them. Candidates aged 26 or over are now appointed directly as HEO(D) (see next section).

The Civil Service Commission appears to aim for the 'most able', although its literature claims that an AT does not necessarily have to be outstanding academically. The Commission says it needs both conceptual thinkers and originators, and 'purely practical' people. Numeracy is increasingly important, Other qualities looked for include the capacity to work well with people, an interest in current affairs, the ability to explain complex problems/arguments clearly and concisely (orally and on paper), drive and determination, and the ability to work quickly and under pressure.

Nearly 3500 applied for AT/HEO(D) in 1986, for 88 vacancies – a substantial increase on the early 1980s. But only 78 were appointed. For the first time ever, candidates from Oxford and Cambridge made up a minority of those appointed – 46% (36 people) against 78% as recently as 1982. However, their chances of success are still far higher – 'Oxbridge' candidates made up slightly less than 15% of the total number of candidates.

Of the 78 appointed, 25 had gained firsts. Just 47 (60%) had read arts subjects, 20 (25.6%) social sciences, and 11 (slightly over 14%) science or technology. Arts graduates made up 57% of candidates, social scientists 26%, and scientists/technologists 16%.

Efforts continue to persuade more students with high administrative potential to apply for AT entry; to reassure candidates from universities other than Oxford and Cambridge, and non-arts students, that they are at no disadvantage; and to convince students that Civil-Service administration is interesting.

HIGHER AND SENIOR EXECUTIVE OFFICERS are the middle managers, but some also work on the first levels of policy and planning, and also do some of the more complex 'casework'.

As managers, they may start in charge of several sections doing similar work within a department – perhaps four or five units each made up of an executive with about four clerical staff under them. As they move up to senior executive officer, they may manage on a day-to-day basis several sections, and must see to everything, from making sure that office routines are running smoothly, and seeing that staff are used effectively and efficiently, seeing through changes, to coping with emergencies as, for instance, in a DHSS local office when a factory closes and the workers are made redundant.

Policy work for H and SEOs means less staff control, more time spent in, eg drafting documents, advising local offices on new policies and procedures, organising records and statistics, working on draft legislation, or dealing directly with complex 'casework'.

Ministers' private 'secretaries' (assistants) are usually HEOs. They keep ministers' diaries, brief them on anything they need to know, summarise long working papers for them, help draft speeches, travel everywhere with their ministers (and go to the House of Commons with them), act as liaison with the department.

HEOs can move up to senior executive within three years, and if they are in the small 'fast' higher executive (development) grade it is possible to go straight on to principal (below). But the number of posts (January 1986) at this level is smaller – nearly 24,400 HEOs (2400 up on 1982), only 235 HEO(D)s (60 down on 1982), and some 7700 SEOs (up 3500 on 1982).

Recruitment There is not normally any direct entry at this level, but candidates recruited for fast-stream entry who are aged 26 or over now go straight in at HEO(D). They must, however, go through the AT competition (see above).

PRINCIPALS AND ABOVE are top managers, and work on policy and plans. Principals may manage local offices. The Commission quotes as examples of principals' work, dealing with financing the coal industry, and looking after shipping relations with other countries. Permanent secretaries are the 'managing directors' of whole departments.

Principals, senior principals, and assistant secretaries have now joined under, deputy and permanent secretaries in the 'open' structure. Administration people have to compete with members of other groups for these top jobs.

With the huge increase in the size of the top 'open structure', statistical comparisons with earlier years become impossible. The 4270 principals in the 'general category' administration group in January 1985 (not very different in size from 1982) have vanished into an 'integrated' grade 7 of almost 11,800, which also includes people previously called economic advisers, principal information officers, librarians, statisticians, scientists and engineers. All, theoretically, can now compete on equal terms for more senior posts, although experience of broadly-based administration is still obviously going to count. Above grade 7, grade 6 (3377 people in 1986) is the old senior-principal level (probably about 600 of them from the old administration grade), grade 5 (nearly 2100 people) were assistant secretaries and equivalent. A small grade 4 numbers only 186 people. Under-secretaries, grade 3, number (1986) under 490 (522 in 1983), 134 deputy secretaries (one more than in 1983), and 30 permanent secretaries (also one up).

Recruitment While it is not common for people to start in the Civil Service at these levels, more people are being drawn in at levels including the most senior, especially where specific skills and experience are needed, and are not readily available within the Service. It still, though, appears to apply only to specialist grades/posts (below), rather than in the main career structure.

Specialist and other grades

The Civil Service employs a great many other people in specialist roles. Some groups are employed in many departments and so come into general categories. Some are employed only on work within a single department. In alphabetical order, the Civil Service has work for –

ACCOUNTANTS were not employed in any numbers in the Civil Service, but new attitudes to financial control have changed this. The accountancy 'functional specialism', set up in 1982, brought into being an expanded government accountancy service (GAS). The work of government accountants is described in ACCOUNTANCY AND FINANCIAL MANAGEMENT.

Recruitment etc see ACCOUNTANCY AND FINANCIAL MANAGEMENT for qualifications etc.
The Civil Service continues to have problems in recruiting accountants. In 1986, GAS wanted seven 'fast-stream' AT/HEO(D) accountants, 166 applied but only three were appointed. For 74 vacancies at SEO/HEO level, 467 applied, but only 41 were actually appointed with a further ten recommended for appointment.
Trainee accountants are also recruited, via separate as well as the normal EO competitions. In 1986, 75 were recruited via the normal entry, another 70 via a separate competition.

ACTUARIES work on, for instance, projections and analyses needed to guide policy on state benefits, particularly benefits. The Civil Service employs, however, under 30 of them.
Recruitment of qualified actuaries has been 'extremely difficult'. Only one applied (and was appointed) for the single senior post in 1986. While 84 applied for the other eight places, offers were made to 13 candidates before the four trainee places were filled.
See also ACTUARIAL WORK under INSURANCE.

ARCHITECTS in the Civil Service do design and work on the construction of buildings (eg prisons, defence establishments), mainly in the PSA. A high proportion of Civil Service architects, though, set standards and (eg) look for ways of improving efficiency in building programmes carried out by other organisations, eg the health authorities for hospitals, local education authorities for schools and colleges.

PSA has been (1986) having problems in attracting young, able architects. In 1986, they filled only 47% of vacancies for qualified architects, and only five of the ten places for post-diploma graduates (for whom a professional training programme is available).

See also ARCHITECTURE under LAND USE PROFESSIONS.

CARTOGRAPHIC AND RECORDING DRAUGHTSMEN/WOMEN work in a number of different departments, including the Department of the Environment, and in Ordnance Survey. They numbered just under 3000 in 1986.

See LAND USE PROFESSIONS, and ACADEMIC AND VOCATIONAL STUDIES IN ENGINEERING.

COMMUNICATIONS The Government Communications Headquarters (GCHQ) has its own careers structures, although the grades are similar to the rest of the Civil Service.

'Administration' staff may do work similar to that in other departments, although none involves regular contact with the public. In addition, though – Executive officers do a wide variety of analytical, research and intelligence reporting work with (possibly) a higher intellectual content than elsewhere. Some are employed full-time on computer work, in programming, handling large databases, information retrieval, administrative applications etc. Other work can involve use of languages.

Senior staff work in both administrative/managerial, planning, policy making and specialist functions. They may be involved in analysing and relating factual data and synthesising from the results to produce foreign and defence intelligence, in conference and committee work, and (increasingly) in managing the flow of work on computer systems and applications programming.

Communications Science and Technology (CST) is a new (1984) class unique to GCHQ, to which all scientists and engineers belong. It includes –

mathematicians – who work mainly on practical analysis 'of such complexity that a computer is needed', but some in longer-term theoretical work and mathematical consultancy;

computer scientists, systems designers and programmers – eg formal systems design and programming, and programming for specific applications, on a wide range of very advanced projects;

physicists and electronic scientists – mainly applied electronics R&D (eg developing communications systems and equipment, cypher machines, aerial design), but some basic research eg signal processing, speech generation and perception;

engineers – 'project' management of new systems including design, development, contract management, installation etc; trouble-shooting and problem solving; R&D etc. CST also employs the technician-support people who actually install, test, maintain communications/computer equipment, help with experimental work etc.

Radio officers mostly operate long-distance communications systems at one of a fairly large number of stations, in the UK and abroad. Promotion is work with more advanced systems, or eg with satellite or computer-related systems, or on developing new equipment.

Linguists are employed in both GCHQ itself and the Joint Technical Language Service (JTLS) which it houses. Mainly the work is translating, transcribing and research, which mostly involves using computer data bases, but 'many' linguistic specialists organise and direct language work and staff.

Recruitment All staff are recruited directly for GCHQ work, separately from other departments, and must pass a positive security vetting.

'Fast stream' administrative entry is the same as AT entry (above), but entrants are called Government Communications Trainees. 323 external and 19 internal candidates applied for four vacancies in 1986 – two of each group were appointed.

Executive-officer recruitment is as above.

CST officers are recruited as graduates, with appropriate BTEC awards, and as school leavers (with at least four O-level-equivalent passes at 16-plus† including English, maths, physics). For 100 senior, higher, and CSTO vacancies in 1986, 552 applied for CSTO level (21 appointed and another 17 accepted), 93 for Higher CSTO (one appointed and seven more accepted), and 52 for Senior CSTO (one appointed and two more accepted). About 630 applied for the 31 engineering posts, and 16 higher CSTOs – ten CSTOs were appointed.

Radio officers must have at least two years' operating experience, and should have either a maritime radio communications certificate, BTEC telecommunications national diploma, or a 1st or 2nd class certificate of competency in radio telegraphy.

Linguists: see below.

COMPUTING STAFF of all kinds are employed extensively throughout the Civil Service. The Civil Service is the largest user of computers in the UK. Both Inland Revenue and the DHSS are installing massive nation-wide systems.

Work ranges from systems analysis and programming to operating machines, and data preparation.

Programming etc is done mainly by people recruited as executive officers (who can return to or go into administrative work if they wish) and assistant scientific officers.

Clerical officers handle input and output, but one special group, data processors, operate computers.

No official figures for Civil Service computing staff. One 1986 estimate put the number of specialists at over 5000, to which can be added the 7000-plus operators (against 8600 in 1982).

Recruitment Data processors do not need any particular qualifications. Other people recruited for computing work need the same qualifications as other executive or assistant scientific officers. An aptitude test is normally set, but it is possible to join without any background in computing and be trained to a fairly high level – assistant scientific officers are expected to study for further qualifications and are given help for this.

As one indication of demand, in 1986 the Civil Service Commission set ADP aptitude tests for nearly 8000 people.

In 1986, the Civil Service offered existing staff 58 SEO ADP posts, and 230 at HEO level. From over 1100 applications, they found 41 SEOs and 115 HEOS. Two SEO vacancies were advertised, six applied and one was appointed, For the one HOE vacancy, three applied, but no one was appointed.

See also COMPUTING under INFORMATION TECHNOLOGY.

CUSTOMS AND EXCISE OFFICERS see Departments, above.

THE DIPLOMATIC SERVICE has its own grade structure, and is a self-contained service of the Crown, technically not part of the Home Civil Service.

Diplomats' work ranges from high-level negotiations on high-level affairs (including defence, energy, science policy), down to the everyday practicalities of looking after UK citizens abroad and promoting British exports. (See also Foreign Office above).

About 70% of the 4616 members of the diplomatic service are 'generalists', so-called career diplomatic staff, ranging from clerical people to ambassadors and permanent undersecretary. The other 30% are 'specialists' – legal advisers (22), research officers (57), secretaries (650) etc. Just over 55%, mostly 'generalists', are based overseas at any one time. Another 1900 members of the 'home' civil service work for the Foreign Office, and just over 100 of them work abroad. About 6800 people are engaged and employed locally overseas (1986 figures).

Diplomatic staff, says the FO, have to produce high-quality work in conditions that may be unpleasant or even dangerous. Responsibility for financial and personnel management, at home and overseas, is now assumed relatively early. 'Career' diplomatic staff of all grades spend about two thirds of their working lives overseas, in 'tours' of two to four years, interspersed with periods in London. Staff do not, normally, stay with one country or even one region, and may move each time to a quite-different continent. Part of their time in London, then, may have to be spent learning (yet another) language. The career structure more or less matches that of administration.

'Fast stream' graduates (like ATs) start at third or even second secretary level, working from the start on policy, including subjects such as financial relations or defence, as well as looking after political relations with individual countries. They go overseas after a year in London, usually moving up to first secretary, grade 5 (eg running the embassy chancery) in their late 20s, and virtually all go on to grade 4 counsellor. Ambassadors are all mainly fast-stream entrants.

Executive officers number about 1750, and are mainly junior and middle managers. Those starting at grade 9 do a wider range of work than administrative entrants, including consular, accounts and administration as well as some 'political', and often have to start in fairly routine jobs. They do not usually go abroad for three years. They make up the majority of commercial and information officers, and as they are promoted, most consuls and consuls-general. An above-average grade 9 officer would be promoted to grade 7E (second secretary) after about eight years. Normally all reach grade 5 (first secretary) and many reach grade 4 with an outside chance of going further.

Administrative (formerly clerical) officers (grade 10) – about 550 staff working at home and overseas – do general clerical work, mainly in registries where they do the (very complicated) filing and process paper work, encypher and decypher telegrams, deal with diplomatic bags etc. Some do accounts, visa and communications work. The first two or three years are spent in London, and no one works abroad until they are 20. Promotion to grade 9 is normally on merit after two or three overseas postings, ie eight or nine years after joining. On average, entrants at grade 10 can expect to reach grade 6, possibly as consul or head of information in a medium-sized embassy. Exceptional people may go to grade 5, with a chance of reaching grade 4.

About 24% of staff overseas are in European countries, 17% in Asia, 13% in Near and Middle East, and North African countries, 12% in North America and the Caribbean, 11% in the rest of Africa, 7% in the USSR and Eastern Europe, 7% in international organisations, 6% in Central and South America, and 3% in Australia etc. Everyone has to accept a very peripatetic life, with regular changes of country and job. However, career planning is expertly done (personnel is managed by diplomatic staff themselves, on London posting). Everyone is taught languages as and when needed and also gets training in, eg economics, marketing, information work.

Recruitment is along similar lines to the rest of the Civil Service.

Diplomatic staff need to be physically and mentally tough and highly adaptable, as well as intelligent and quick witted. Literacy, ability to communicate, numeracy and ability to master complex economic and technical issues are all wanted. Any degree subject is considered. Candidates are tested for aptitude to learn languages, but pre-entry language qualifications, although useful, are not insisted on. Those who do best in the aptitude tests, though, are most likely to be sent to countries whose language is difficult to learn, eg Japan, China, Russia.

Administrative level (grades 8/7D) candidates must have a first or second class honours degree (six 1986 entrants had higher degrees) and be under 32. Over 2000 people applied for 26 posts in October 1985/January 1986. Just 48% of intake in 1986 came from universities other than 'Oxbridge' (no polytechnics), and 42% went to state-maintained schools.

Executive level (grade 9) entry is with at least two A-levels, but 89% of 1986 intake was of graduates. Grade 10 officers can complete for accelerated promotion to grade 9 after a year's service. The upper age limit is 44. About 1900 applied for 24 posts in 1986. Some 75% of graduates recruited came from universities other than 'Oxbridge' (no polytechnics), and 65% went to state-maintained schools.

Administrative officer (grade 10) entry is with at least five O-level-equivalent passes at 16-plus† including English language, maths, and a foreign language – but many have A levels. Candidates must be over 17 and under 20. ·

ECONOMISTS number (1986) about 300 (against a peak of 400 in 1980). They are employed in a number of departments, eg Employment, Trade and Industry, Transport, DHSS, Treasury.

In 1986, four cadet economists, 30 economic assistants (400 applications) were recruited (52 combined vacancies), six senior economic assistants and 13 advisers (28 applications).

See also ECONOMICS under ACADEMIC AND VOCATIONAL STUDIES.

ENGINEERS from almost all branches – aeronautical, chemical, civil, communications, electrical and electronic, mechanical, and nuclear – work for the government. Most work as professional engineers with the 'professional and technology' group (see below), but some are recruited for research and development in the science group (also below). No figures are available on the total number of engineers employed.

By far the largest numbers – 13,000 in 1986 (down by 50% since 1976) including 2000 professional engineers – work for the Ministry of Defence. The MoD has recently (1986) 'integrated' its civilian engineers into a single defence engineering service (instead of dividing them between controllerates and the individual service departments). The MoD employs mainly mechanical, electrical, and electronic engineers, some aeronautical and chemical engineers, and naval architects. DES engineers work in one of (but may now move between) –

system controllerates – dealing with all aspects of defence systems and equipment procurement, divided between air, land and sea systems;

research and development establishments – doing either fundamental research or development and evaluation trials on new equipment – see also Science category/group below;

service support organisations – supporting front-line units in eg warship repair/refitting, maintenance and overhaul of armoured vehicles, servicing aircraft systems;

central procurement – establishing policy and relations with industry, overseeing quality control for all contracts and work, and providing technical costing service.

The Property Services Agency (Department of Employment) has a fairly sizeable staff of engineers (see CONSTRUCTION).

Other departments employing engineers include –

GCHQ (see above).

The Health and Safety Executive recruits engineers (most branches) for the inspectorates and R&D.

In the Energy Department, engineers are involved in policy work, check safety on eg North Sea oil rigs, estimate gas and oil reserves, meeting legal requirements on electricity supply, etc.

The Department of Health and Social Security employs engineers mainly on development, design of hospital and other Health Service buildings, facilities (eg operating theatres and intensive care units) and environmental control systems.

In the Department of Trade and Industry, engineers work in the Directorate of Radio Technology, for the National Weights and Measures Lab, provide technical advice to industry, on eg exporting technological equipment, R&D, and examining applications for sponsorship. They work on ways of improving efficiency and technology in industry, and service committees deciding the Department's R&D programmes.

The Department of Transport employs civil engineers on eg financial management of the national road programme, dealing with standards for road building, and (in the regions) directly preparing and managing road construction programmes. Highway engineers also manage plans for road construction through eg planning enquiries etc, and liaise with local authorities on transport policies. Electrical and electronic engineers develop and install traffic control, lighting and other systems. Mechanical engineers mainly inspect and monitor public service and goods vehicles, supervise MOT testing for cars, deal with safety and environmental aspects of road vehicle design and construction. Marine engineers work for the marine survey service.

The Home Office Directorate of Telecommunications employs mainly electronic engineers developing, designing, installing etc communication systems for the police, fire brigades, prisons etc. Mechanical and electrical engineers work on multi-disciplinary teams building prisons and services for them.

The Ministry of Agriculture employs civil engineers in the ADAS land and water service, advising on drainage, protecting land from flooding, developing harbours for fisheries. Agricultural engineers advise landowners and farmers on field engineering; structural, agricultural and building services engineers in advisory, development and technical support work on farm buildings and their environmental control etc.

Recruitment is for both individual vacancies, and on department schemes (as below). Engineers are recruited to the 'Professional and Technology' group. Professional engineers are recruited as Higher and Senior P&T officers. Both need an appropriate engineering degree, EC part 2 or equivalent (or higher) qualification, with at least five years' recognised study, professional training and experience. Senior officers should preferably be chartered, and have several years' professional experience as well.

New graduates who have not had professional experience are also recruited, and given the training needed for chartered status.

Ministry of Defence Engineering Service: DES recruits 140 graduate engineers annually, and from 1987 is recruiting 15 into a new 'fast stream' similar to the AT scheme (above). For this, candidates must have at least Class 2.1 honours degree in mechanical, electronic, or aeronautical engineering, or engineering science.

For school-leavers with two appropriate A levels (plus three O-level-equivalents), the MoD also offers 100 sponsorships a year for 1-3-1 sandwich degree courses. The PSA has a similar, but smaller, scheme.

Technician engineers are recruited with pass degrees or HND in appropriate subjects for the MoD, the PSA, GCHQ and some other departments. Technician apprentices are recruited by the MoD for four years' training in aeronautical, electrical, electronic, mechanical or metallurgical engineering, or ship construction (leading to a BTEC award), with the possibility of transferring to a degree course or CEI part 2. Technician apprentices need four O-level-equivalent passes at 16-plus† including maths, an appropriate science and English language.

For professional engineers, in 1986, the Civil Service had 157 vacancies for civil, structural and public health engineers, had 948 applications, and managed to fill about half the posts. Nearly 800 mechanical, electrical, electronic, chemical and production engineers and naval architects were needed (mainly for MoD and PSA), 2363 applied and about 320 appointed – shortages of electronic engineers and computer specialists were 'severe'.

For technician engineers, post both A-level and HND/pass degree, the Civil Service filled all 36 training places (17 in building/civil engineering and 20 in mechanical/electrical) in 1986. The pilot scheme started only in 1985, but already more departments are showing 'great interest' in this area of

recruitment.
See also ENGINEERING under ACADEMIC AND VOCATIONAL STUDIES.

FACTORY INSPECTORS are employed by the Factory Inspectorate of the Health and Safety Executive, of which it is the largest single division. Inspectors visit workplaces – ranging from hospitals and research labs to factories, building sites and fairgrounds – to identify health and safety problems. They give advice, and where necessary issues enforcement notices (over 4000 a year) for breaches of the law on health and safety, and often have to prosecute (1000 a year).
Inspectors start in one of the twenty area offices (as a trainee), with between 20 and 30 inspectors in each. They are divided into 6-10 industry groups, each responsible for a related set of industries, eg rubber, plastics and chemicals. In the first two years, trainees work in at least two groups, and then spend 3-5 years in one group, before moving on to another. Factory inspectors can also work in the Major Hazards Assessment Unit, and the Accident Prevention Advisory Unit, in policy making, and liaison with eg employers, unions, and the EEC.
The Factory Inspectorate numbers about 850. Promotion past the main grade (325 people) is by merit and competition.

Recruitment Entry is via either an honours degree (in any discipline but with the basis of an understanding of legal, technical and administrative matters) or at least three years' practical experience, preferably executive or managerial in production or similar work, plus a degree, HND or equivalent in a scientific or technological subject, with O-level-equivalent maths.
Just under 50 people were recruited in 1986 (for 57 vacancies, 1800 people applied).

IMMIGRATION SERVICE see Home Office under Departments, above.

INFORMATION OFFICERS are the equivalent of press and public relations officers elsewhere, promoting government policy, keeping the press and public informed on all aspects of government activity, and advising ministers and senior civil servants on public relations. All departments have information officers (99 work in the DTI, 90 in the MoD, 72 in the Employment departments for example). They can, and do, change departments more often than administrators.
Information officers numbered just over 1000 in 1986 (against nearly 1450 in 1978).

Recruitment Information officers are normally expected to have gained relevant experience, in eg public relations or journalism, elsewhere, although some people go into these posts from the administration grades.
In 1986, 116 information and assistant information officers were recruited (3175 applications for 153 vacancies), six senior information offices (154 applications), and one (of each) chief and principal information officers (16 applications for four posts).
See also PUBLIC RELATIONS under MARKETING etc.

INLAND REVENUE is a career on its own within the Civil Service, since specialist training is needed, but the jobs and the career structures are designed to run in parallel with administrative careers. The work is divided – between assessing what is owed in taxation, and collecting – and they are managed and run separately. Assessing is rather more technically demanding with more than four times as many posts as in collecting. There is also valuation work.

Inland Revenue has the same 'pyramid' structure as the administration group. Tax officers (equal to administrative/clerical officers) deal with individual tax payers personally (on the phone, through letters, and over the counter), each team of tax officers dealing with a particular group of tax payers. These may be the people working in one large firm, or in a particular district, or with a special group eg seamen or insurance brokers. Tax officers work from some 800 offices all over the country. Tax officers numbered just under 14,000 in 1986 (compared with 18,400 in 1979).

Assistant collectors (also equal to administrative/clerical officers) see tax demands are sent out (usually by computer), deal with letters or phone calls about payment, and also visit people personally. In 1986, this grade numbered just over 4600 (5900 in 1979).

Tax officers (higher grade) and collectors are junior managers. Higher tax officers, after two years' training (mixed with practical experience) are usually put in charge of a team of tax officers, to organise their work and deal themselves with the more difficult cases. Collectors, too, manage a group of assistants, deal with people who want time to pay, and with court cases – their training is also largely on-the-job and lasts some 18 months. In 1986 there were some 10,500 higher grade tax officers (up from 1982 but against over 12,000 in 1979), and about 3000 collectors.

Inspectors make tax assessments for businesses of all kinds, from the high-street shop to the multinational chemical company. To become a tax inspector takes three years' training (in book-keeping, accountancy, law and the expertise needed to check the credibility of taxpayers' accounts) combined with practical experience on the job. Trainees start on 'case' work very early, are expected to make their own decisions, and take responsibility for them. After exams have been passed, a year is spent in junior management, a year on more complex case work, with promotion to higher grade and responsibility for a tax district in six years. There are some 5500 inspectors (down from 6300 in 1982).

Recruitment Entry to the lower grades parallels those of the administration group.

Higher tax officers come up from tax-officer level or are recruited with five GCE/GCSE passes (including English), two at A level or a degree. Age at least 17½ and under 45.

Direct entry to inspection needs a 1st or 2nd class honours degree although it is also possible to come up from higher tax officer. Over 100 tax inspectors were needed in 1986, almost 5800 people applied, and about 140 were appointed.

LAWYERS, are employed throughout the Civil Service in some numbers – and if the way in which figures given in some official publications have been over-taken are any guide, have shot up since 1985. In fact over 3000 barristers, solicitors and advocates work (1986) for the government legal service, with some in almost all departments. With the start of the new Crown Prosecution Service alone, numbers are set to rise further.

The kind of work they do includes –

Legal work which is very similar to private practice. For instance, solicitors do the conveyancing when the government (via eg the Ministry of Agriculture) or a state-run organisation (eg the Forestry Commission) buys or sells property, buildings, offices, or land. They do commercial work – Export Credit Guarantee Department solicitors check contracts are legally watertight in the country to which the UK company is selling. Government barristers prosecute, for instance fraud under company legislation, and defend when individuals or organisations want to test the validity of a piece of legislation.

Administering the legal system in, eg the Lord Chancellor's Department, the Crown Prosecution Service, and the Scottish legal departments.

Advising on policy on issues ranging from methods of coping with crime to EEC law and human rights, and the legal aspects of a department's work and its legal responsibilities. For instance, in dealing with cases under mental health legislation.

Helping to draft new laws, in most departments, although the real specialists work in the very small Parliamentary Counsel office.

Working on issues which affect the legal relationship between people and the state.

The main employing departments are –

The Crown Prosecution Service, headed by the Director of Public Prosecutions. The DPP took over the conduct of almost all criminal proceedings instituted on behalf of the police forces (in England and Wales) in late 1986. Each of the 31 areas is headed by a chief prosecutor, and each area has a number of branch and sub-branch offices. Head office, and all the other offices employ teams of lawyers, with the emphasis on delegating as far as possible, although headquarters lawyers deal with some specialised types of casework. All cases are reviewed by crown prosecutors first to decide whether or not to take them to court. If the case proceeds, the crown prosecutor will normally conduct the prosecution case in the magistrate's court. If it is committed to a higher court, the crown prosecutor instructs counsel, and monitors progress. Fully staffed, the CPS is projected to need 1500 lawyers (plus over 2100 support staff), with over 200 recruited by the end of 1986.

Crown Office and Procurator Fiscal Service: in Scotland, the crown has always been responsible for all criminal prosecutions. Each of the 49 sheriff court districts has a procurator fiscal (plus legal staff), not only responsible for prosecutions but also able to direct police investigations.

Lord Chancellor's Office – only a small proportion of the 10,000 staff need legal qualifications (most are 'general' administrators).

Legal staff are (mainly) employed in the criminal appeal office (dealing directly with cases for the court), the Official Solicitor's department (effectively acting as solicitors or barristers for the people the Official Solicitor represents), the Law Commission (working on schemes for reforming the law including academic-style research, examining policy and formulating proposals), in the Public Trustee Office (as trust officers, consultants and managers), and at headquarters (mainly formulating policy, and dealing with all aspects of legislation on anything within the Lord Chancellor's responsibilities, monitoring and amending legal aid, and dealing with some aspects of international/EEC law).

Treasury Solicitor's Department – employs over 150 lawyers and some 200 legal-executive staff. The Department both works for the Treasury and provides the full range of legal services to departments etc which do not employ legal staff, or 'contract' some work to the Treasury Solicitor. Legal staff working conveyancing, litigation, or advisory work (on legislation etc).

Other departments employing significant numbers of lawyers include Agriculture and Fisheries, Customs and Excise, Employment (including MSC, the Health and Safety Executive), the DHSS (60-plus), the Foreign Office (22), Environment, the Home Office (including the Criminal Injuries Board), Inland Revenue, the Land Registry, Trade and Industry (which has a new serious fraud office whose 70 staff include lawyers), and the Scottish and Welsh Offices.

Recruitment all new entrants must normally be barristers who have already been called to the bar, or solicitors who have been admitted, or who have reasonable expectation of so doing within four months of the closing date for applications (in Scotland, they must be locally-qualified advocates or solicitors). Recent experience as a practising lawyer is generally necessary.

The Civil Service has been having severe problems in recruiting lawyers, for the (newly-structured) legal group in England and Wales, the new Crown Prosecution Service, and the Scottish Crown Office and Procurator Fiscal Service. Only the Scottish legal group managed to find the four legal officers it wanted. The legal group wanted 125 lawyers, had over 500 applications, but actually recruited only 78. The Crown Prosecution Service found only 210 of the 475 lawyers it needed last year alone, with the problems mainly in London. The Scottish Crown Office and Procurator Fiscal Service managed to fill only 15 of the 20 vacancies, despite 69 applications.

See also LAW under ACADEMIC AND VOCATIONAL QUALIFICATIONS, and LEGAL PROFESSION under PROFESSIONAL SERVICES.

LIBRARIANS work in most departments (eg 119 in the MoD, 55 in Environment, 45 in DTI, 23 in Employment) providing a library and information service for the staff, and sometimes for the public too. Librarians numbered just over 400 librarians in 1986, slightly up even on the 1970s. About 74 assistant librarians were recruited in 1986 (82 vacancies and 812 applied), and two librarians (30 applied).

See also LIBRARY WORK under INFORMATION TECHNOLOGY.

LINGUISTS, TRANSLATORS AND INTERPRETERS work in a number of departments, mainly in the (small) Joint Technical Language Service at GCHQ (Cheltenham) and GCHQ itself, and the Ministry of Defence. A few departments also employ translators, mainly of material from European languages into English. No separate statistics of how many, or where they work, are kept.

Recruitment a degree, or equivalent qualification, in at least one modern foreign language is usually needed. JTLC does not want French, and most posts would expect people to have more than one Western European language. Most posts, in fact, want people with Slavonic or oriental languages. The CCS reported 85 vacancies in 1986, had 790 applications, but filled only 62 posts. They partly succeeded in making good the 'serious shortfall' in Slavonic

and oriental languages by recruiting people competent in Western European languages with the right aptitudes, and retraining them.
See also TRANSLATING ETC.

MEDICAL OFFICERS are employed in areas like the prison medical service, the DHSS and occupational health. About 550 qualified medical people work (1986) full-time in the Civil Service (plus 25 part-time), down from 650 in 1981.

Recruitment is of fully-qualified people only, and experience is normally also needed. Demand has been falling for a year or two, with 90% of the 60 vacancies filled in 1986.

MUSEUM STAFF see under CREATIVE, COMMUNICATION (ETC) WORK.

PATENT EXAMINERS see under MANAGEMENT SERVICES.

PHOTOGRAPHERS The Civil Service employs (1986) about 460 photographers, nearly two-thirds of them in the Ministry of Defence, most of the rest in national museums and galleries. Assistant photographers do processing and help senior photographers. They are trained via a three-year day-release course.

Recruitment, as assistant photographer, on a local basis with three O-level-equivalent passes at 16-plus† in English, maths and a science.
See also PHOTOGRAPHY.

PRISON STAFF are technically Home Office employees. See PRISON SERVICE under PROTECTIVE SERVICES.

THE PROFESSIONAL AND TECHNOLOGY CATEGORY (and related grades) is made up of a wide range of different professionals and people with technician-level qualifications, from architects to civil, electrical and mechanical engineers, from nuclear inspectors to industrial chemists, from land and estate, quantity, and building surveyors to draughtsmen/women, the Ministry of Defence Engineering Service and the Royal Corps of Naval Constructors, port auxiliary and Royal Maritime Auxiliary Services, and graphics officers.

A high proportion of the category is employed by either the Ministry of Defence (engineers primarily) or the Department of the Environment (the land use professions/architects). Equally, only a small proportion are professionally qualified, with a relatively large number of draughtsmen and women and technical staff. The nature of the work varies widely between departments and for the different occupational groups – see individual groups, eg engineers, architects, surveyors etc.

In all, the category appears to have some 34,300 staff (1985), which is a sharpish fall from the 40,500 of 1979 even taking account of the loss of about 1300 posts to the 'open structure'. However, the category has been restructured, so figures may not be totally comparable.

Recruitment see individual groups, eg architects, engineers, etc.

Training Everyone in the category is encouraged to continue with their training courses to keep up-to-date and broaden their knowledge and skills both in their professional or technical discipline and in management.

Graduates are given the professional training and practical experience required for registration as a chartered engineer in some departments, and some departments train, or provide sponsorships and training for, school leavers (see under individual professional grades).
See also QUALIFICATIONS AND VOCATIONAL STUDIES IN ENGINEERING, and in LAND USE and ENVIRONMENT-RELATED WORK.

PSYCHOLOGISTS work for, eg the Prison Service, Manpower Services, and several departments, mainly the Ministry of Defence (studying operational and training performance, checking on motivation and morale, advising on personnel selection and allocation etc). Their numbers hover between 250 and 260. Most of the 45 vacancies (509 applied) were filled in 1986.

RESEARCH OFFICERS in the Civil Service are not normally scientists. They gather, analyse and evaluate information, much of it economic, geographic or sociological, studying the impact of government policies and providing the information on which to base future policy. They have to explain their findings to non-professionals.
They work in one of two main groups. The social science research group deals with patterns of behaviour among people in contemporary society, and uses people qualified in social sciences – sociology, social anthropology and criminology. The resource and planning research group studies government policy in relation to resource allocation and the environment, and its members are mostly qualified in geography, agricultural economics, economics, or economic geography.
Both groups prepare studies, reports and studies in multi-disciplinary teams. The number of research officers has been cut substantially, to just over 300 in 1986, against 460 in 1979.

Recruitment A first or second class honours, or postgraduate, degree in an appropriate subject is needed. No age limit, but most are recent graduates. Most of the 31 vacancies (389 applications) were filled in 1986.
See also Diplomatic Service, above.

SCIENTISTS are employed in quite large numbers still. Government scientists do and/or supervise fundamental and applied research, are involved in design and development (of eg navigational aids and weapons systems), work in advisory and inspection services, in working out how to measure things even more accurately and in setting standards of all kinds. They may be problem solving in the energy or agricultural fields (for example). Much of the work may be very similar to work they might have done in university or industry. About half are managers or administrators – directing research, or overseeing contracts placed outside the Civil Service.

The Service does not only employ professional scientists. As elsewhere, lab technicians are employed in practical and supporting roles, for example, in applying established scientific principles or supervising more routine scientific work.

Examples of scientific work include –
   looking for evidence in the Forensic Science Laboratories;
   measuring and analysing stresses in road bridges;

ensuring that chemicals and equipment produced by industry to clean up oil spills actually work;

investigating the use of meteor scatter as a medium for air-to-ground radio communication, and ironing out problems;

automating the analysis of the nutritional properties of different foods; investigating theoretical problems in the use of (mathematical) 'random walk' techniques to simulate atmospheric dispersion, and the way pollutants disperse in valleys, in the Meteorological Office.

The largest groups of scientists work in –

The Ministry of Defence employs some 7000 scientists in around twenty large and small research units – which include the METEOROLOGICAL OFFICE.

Examples of others are –

the three Admiralty Research Establishments – in one multi-disciplinary teams work on undersea systems, acoustic research for sensors, hydro-dynamics, analysis of complex mechanical structures, advanced signal and real-time data processing techniques, mathematical modelling of intricate systems, assessment of current and future equipment, and propulsion and control of torpedoes and underwater vehicles. The other does all the scientific research and systems studies for surface and above-surface equipment – defensive and communications equipment, command and control systems including the latest in computer developments, and also innovative navigation systems. The third does research to provide the basis for the design of future shops, submarines and weapons systems, and eg reducing the acoustic under-water 'signature' of ships.

Other labs do work on testing military aircraft and airborne systems, develop-ing warheads for nuclear weapons; R&D on chemical, including biological, defence systems; signals and radar (electronics – from fundamental research to developing devices, equipment and systems) materials quality assurance etc.

The Department of Trade and Industry employs mainly research scientists in the government chemist's lab, the National Physical Laboratory (which works mainly on accurate measurement), Warren Spring (mainly industrial and environmental research), and the National Engineering Lab (which employs multidisciplinary teams in mechanical engineering R&D, feasibility and design studies, testing, calibration etc).

The Departments of Environment and Transport employ scientists in the Building Research Establishment (with work on eg geotechnics, energy con-servation, fire prevention and detection, timber, soil testing), and the Trans-port and Road Research Laboratory.

GCHQ (see Communications above), and AGRICULTURE.

The majority of science group posts are now in the physical and mathematical sciences, and 'new technology' disciplines. People who work in the science category/group (who include those with qualifications in engineering) nor-mally start their careers in research and development, or related work, and many stay with it for most of their careers. There are, however, growing opportunities to move into administration and management, into areas such as project and contract management, and into policy advisory work. The recent extension of the 'open structure' (see above), should help career scientists compete for the most senior managerial posts in the Civil Service.

While most entrants to the science group are recruited on an 'established', pensionable, basis, it is possible to take 'period' appointments for specified terms, of up to five years; for example, research fellowships, tenable for three years, are offered to scientists of outstanding ability. Scientists are, of course, employed in a number of other specialist categories and groups, eg PATENT EXAMINING, and people with qualifications in science are encouraged to try for, eg administration.

Promotion is possible from the lowest grades, of assistant scientific officer, through to the top. It can, though, take quite a while to gain the qualifications needed to become a scientific officer on a part-time basis, and this inevitably affects promotion prospects. Most of those who start as scientific officers can, however, expect to reach higher or senior scientific level, and quite a significant proportion go further – to grade 7, for instance, between 28 and 33.

Total numbers in the science group have risen slightly recently, to over 15,600 in 1986, but are still down on the 17,000 of the late 1970s. Probably around 1000 scientists are in the top grades 1-6. The lowest, assistant scientific officer grade is now down to barely 2000 (it was over 4000 in 1973). Scientific officers now number about 2600 (it was 3200 in 1976), higher scientific officers 3300 (peak about 4460 in 1979), senior scientific officers 2900 (3800 in 1979), and principal scientific officers (now in open structure grade 7), probably about 2100 (over 2450 in 1980).

Recruitment Direct entry depends on qualifications, and age and is mainly at the lowest three grades –

Assistant scientific officers are recruited mostly from amongst school-leavers or anyone under the age of 26 with the appropriate academic qualifications. The minimum qualification is four O-level-equivalent passes including English language and a maths or science subject. Recruitment is normally locally by individual departments. Numbers recruited have been falling steadily, to just over 340 in 1985.

Scientific officer is the main recruiting grade. This needs a degree or equivalent, eg a BTEC Higher National, in a relevant scientific, engineering or mathematical subject. Some posts need a good honours degree, to undertake and direct others in research; others can take technically-qualified experimentalists able to manage groups of junior staff in relatively routine work or able to do experimental work themselves.

Higher and senior scientific officer grades provide entry levels for scientists or engineers of appropriate age and calibre who have completed specified periods of relevant postgraduate experience.

The CCS reported 927 vacancies for new graduates in 1986 (well up on most previous years), for which over 7750 applied. 470 were appointed as scientific officers, 137 as higher scientific officers, and 37 as senior scientific officers.

Direct recruitment to posts in the principal scientific officer and higher grades is made only when no internal candidate can fill the vacancy on transfer or promotion. Ten vacancies for principals were reported in 1986 (167 applied) and six were appointed.

See also ACADEMIC AND VOCATIONAL QUALIFICATIONS IN SCIENCE.

Training The science group gives considerable opportunities for additional education and training. Most assistant scientific officers study part-time on a day-release basis to gain minimum academic qualifications for the scientific officer grade, and some are given help to work for degrees on a sandwich basis. Outstanding assistant scientific officers are given bursaries to help them study full-time for degrees, or to complete first-degree work and then go on to postgraduate research. It is also often possible to gain higher degrees.

THE SECRETARIAL CATEGORY/GROUP is made up mainly of typists, many working in 'pools'. Numbers had fallen, but have recently recovered to almost 18,300 in 1986 (but including nearly 4400 part-timers), although nowhere near the 22,700 of 1979. Personal secretaries number nearly 4520 (against 4600 in 1979), and work mainly for the most senior civil servants, superintending staff just over 1700 (roughly the same as 1979).

Recruitment Typists are usually recruited locally, normally by individual departments on a temporary basis. Anyone who wants to become a permanent civil servant must reach certain minimum speeds (for example, shorthand typists must be able to do 100 wpm in shorthand and type at least 30 wpm, audio typists are expected to transcribe a 360-word tape in 30 minutes and type at 30 wpm). Nearly 2600 typists were recruited in 1985, over 50% aged between 16 and 24, but 40% were over 30.

Personal secretaries are recruited for direct entry mainly in the London area – the normal route is by promotion from typist. Candidates must be over the age of 18 and have three O-level-equivalent passes (including English language), and must be able to type at 30 wpm with a shorthand speed of 100 wpm or transcription rate of a 360-word tape in 20 minutes.

See also SECRETARIAL WORK under COMMERCE.

STATISTICIANS, working throughout the Civil Service, numbered about 430 in 1986 compared with well over 500 in 1978-80. This may be due to the chronic shortfall in recruitment. Some 74 vacancies were advertised in 1986, but only 40 filled (including seven 'cadet', ie trainee, statisticians).

See also MATHEMATICS AND STATISTICS under ACADEMIC AND VOCATIONAL STUDIES.

SURVEYORS (AND VALUERS) from all branches – building surveyors, valuers, estate surveyors and land agents, land and quantity surveyors – work in the Civil Service.

Most building and quantity surveyors work for the Property Services Agency, building surveyors also for Agriculture and the Scottish Office. Estate agents also work mainly for PSA.

Valuers work mainly for Inland Revenue (nearly 3580 of them in 1986 against 4800 in 1982). They value land and buildings, for taxes and rating, and when government and local authorities buy land, offices etc.

Land agents, managing estates, forests and country parks, work for the Ministry of Agriculture and the PSA.

Land and quantity surveyors also work mainly for PSA, but land surveyors are also employed by Ordnance Survey.

Recruitment Surveyors are recruited to the P&T group, as senior officers if already qualified and with at least two years' experience, or as graduate trainees having completed RICS finals or with an exempting degree.

Inland Revenue valuers are recruited either fully qualified, or as graduate trainees (qualifications as surveyors), or as 'cadets' for three-year training with at least two A-level passes at grade C or above (and gained at one sitting) and three O-level-equivalent passes (subjects to include English language and maths) – but all those recruited in 1986 were graduates.

The Civil Service wanted 429 surveyors in 1986, had 1955 applications, but recruited under 300. Over 90% of graduate vacancies (with training) were filled, but only 38% for qualified professionals. But worst was the problem faced by Inland Revenue – only 11% of the 80 vacancies for qualified valuers were filled, although all 36 places for cadet valuers were taken.

See also SURVEYING under LAND USE PROFESSIONS.

Further information from the Civil Service Commission. For details about work in specific departments, the Establishment Officer of the department concerned.

LOCAL GOVERNMENT

Introduction   800
Working in local authorities   802
Administration, legal and finance   804
The service departments   804
Recruitment and entry   807

INTRODUCTION

Local authorities provide services for their communities. Traditionally, this means the most practical and essential, like collecting rubbish, cleaning streets and looking after sewers. Over the years, though, they have taken on many other, and wide ranging, roles and responsibilities. The full list of these 'functions' covers (as of spring 1987) –

education – from schools at all levels to colleges and polytechnics;

planning – traditionally called town and country planning, which involves everything from making plans for the area, through controlling development, to checking regulations;

social services, and health education;

housing;

transport – from planning to managing, responsibility for managing services (buses, tubes, even airports) although many services are now operated by private companies, looking after highways and lighting;

police and fire services;

libraries, museums and the arts, which can include theatres, art galleries, and orchestras;

recreational facilities – like swimming pools and sports centres, parks and open spaces, and tourism;

environmental health – from collecting and getting rid of refuse, through street cleaning to food hygiene and controlling diseases, clean air regulations;

consumer protection;

markets, smallholdings and allotments;

cemetaries and crematoria;

licensing and registration – births, deaths, marriages, licensing hours.

The pattern of local government was radically simplified into a two-tier structure of county and district, and the number of authorities cut by about a third, in 1974. The six metropolitan counties created then were abolished in 1986. This means that in England and Wales there are now some 416 authorities (53 counties and 369 districts within 47 of them), plus London's 32 boroughs, and the City of London Corporation. Scotland's nine regions are divided into 53 districts, with both regional and district councils. Orkney, Shetland and the Western Isles have their own, almost all-purpose, authorities.

In England, there are two kinds of county and district. First, the 36 districts in the metropolitan counties, which look after the special needs of these heavily populated and urbanised areas. They range in terms of population from 164,000 to 1.1 million people. Second, the counties, which have populations ranging from 289,000 to over 1.45 million, and districts (between 75,000 and 150,000 people each). In Wales, counties range in size from 106,000 to 538,000 people, with 20,700 to 278,400 for districts. The largest English district is twice the size of the largest Welsh county, in terms of population. In Scotland, authorities range in size from a region with a population of 2.5 million down to a district with a rural population of under 10,000.

The London boroughs have populations ranging from 136,000 to 321,000. The City of London copes with only 8000 residents, but a day-time population of over 400,000.

Just as there are enormous variations in population between authorities, so of course their areas vary – from several hundred square miles, to the City of London's one. They vary in character, from those which are completely rural, through others with both dense inner-city centres as well as industrial estates, and residential suburbs, while others are entirely urban. It follows that every authority has a different mix of problems to manage and solve – cliff falls or inner city decay, potential flooding or collapsing sewers, poor housing to replace or massive unemployment to solve.

Counties and districts divide services between them. In general, larger counties tend to run services which benefit from economies of scale, such as education, social services, transport, structure planning, police and fire services. Districts run the more everyday services – street cleaning, housing, local planning, building regulations, cemeteries and crematoria, allotments. Museums, libraries, and recreational facilities, amongst other services, may be run by counties or districts. The London boroughs and district councils have taken over the responsibilities of the GLC and the metropolitan counties, although some services are run jointly, and London has a single (elected) education authority at present. Uniquely, the metropolitan police are the responsibility not of any London council, but of the Home Office. The division of responsibilities is not permanently fixed, and can and does change.

Local authorities can decide, within certain legal limits, on their own organisational and managerial structures. Although many changed their managerial structures in 1974, the traditional organisation of councils is strongly entrenched and it is difficult to bring councils into line with more modern organisational patterns. Traditionally, the full, elected council delegates day-to-day policy making for individual services to special committees – for education, housing, social services, and so on. Each committee has its own department of paid staff answerable to them, and not to any higher level of management within the council's staff. This means that individual services – housing, education etc – tend to be run in watertight compartments without much reference to what is going on in what may be a related service, and that individual departments have a high degree of autonomy. There can also be lack of cohesion and unity in running the authority.

Since 1974, most authorities have been looking for ways to improve their management methods, and in particular to try to introduce corporate management, in other words to create structures which allow councillors and senior, or chief, officers to watch over what is happening in the authority as a whole, across all the individual services. Typically, then, authorities have, for instance, added policy and resource committees to the functional ones. The very autonomous departmental structures have been replaced in many authorities by a series of directorates which co-ordinate the work of groups of related departments. This creates another management 'tier' – for example, libraries, museums, sports centres, entertainment, swimming pools, squash courts may now be the responsibility of a director for leisure and recreation. These directors form a top managerial team of officials led by a chief executive. As part of this modernisation, old titles like 'town clerk' have been dropped in favour of terms used in other organisations. However, the committee of elected members still inevitably has a major influence on what happens within a service, and therefore on the daily lives of the paid staff who work within it.

WORKING IN LOCAL AUTHORITIES
Even without the metropolitan counties, most local authorities are large organisations. However, tight financial control and some contracting of services to commercial firms have steadily reduced the numbers employed. As of September 1986, local authorities (in England, Wales and Scotland) had just over 1.72 million full-time employees, against nearly 1.98 million in 1979. They also employ nearly 987,150 people part time (1986), which is rather more than the 960,600 of 1979. The ratio of manual to 'white collar' jobs is about two to one.

Many local authorities have considerable responsibilities. One major county has an annual budget of some £600 million and over 50,000 full- and part-time employees. Even rural district councils with relatively small populations (but often spreading over a largish area) may have a budget of around £1 million.

Traditionally, local government is a lifelong career. Its unique conditions have led to professions or branches of professions set up especially for local government service – for example municipal engineering and accountancy – always with the accent on 'professionalism'. It has always been professionals who have filled the top posts. This exclusiveness has, to some extent, been slowly but steadily diluted, with increasing cross-fertilisation, mainly stemming from local government's need to bring in more and more professionals from outside the service, for example architects, and people with qualifications in the whole range of management services, such as organisation and methods, operational research, computer programming and systems analysis.

The work and career structures of local authority staff are changing in many ways. Larger and fewer authorities has obviously changed life in local government. These are a public-sector equivalent of very large businesses, spending a great deal of money; costs have risen very sharply, and greater expertise and efficiency are needed to control expenditure. While the number of posts at the top of the local government tree is comparatively small, the number of posts with intermediate responsibilty has probably increased, and the kind of responsibility they carry is considerable. Equally, these responsibilities require people of higher calibre and with even more systematic training, particularly for general management.

Local authorities need professional management and administrators and managers. Reforming structures and developing new systems are only one aspect of the problem. But well-developed skills and the right attitudes are equally important, says the Local Government Training Board, which can point to a range of imaginative developments in local government management. However, it is clear that local government intends still to train its own managerial staff rather than take in any large numbers of ready-trained people from elsewhere.

This suggests a new kind of career structure within local government, and increasing recruitment of, for example, graduates directly to careers in administration and management. While it is probable that more managerial posts will go to specially recruited graduate administrators, it is still more usual to go up through the ranks of one of the departments as a professional. Here, promotion begins with administering one service, may go on to managing several, and for a very few, there will be a chief officer or executive's job. Some professional careers in local government are more closely related to running the authority as an organisation, and not with just one of its services. It is still more usual for the chief executive and immediate deputy staff to come from these departments – it is still virtually unknown for a chief librarian or education officer to reach the top administrative post.

Local authorities employ people in a great many different jobs, and at most levels.

They are major employers of many professional staff, such as accountants, architects, computer/management services experts, engineers, lawyers, librarians, personnel managers, surveyors, some (relatively few) scientists, and (effectively) teachers. They are almost the only employers of, eg careers officers, consumer protection officers, environmental health officers, social workers, town planners. Mostly they work in a specialist area of local government (as below).

Technicians are employed mainly in engineering and construction, for planners and architects etc, with a comparatively small number of (scientific) lab technicians. Office 'technician-level' work includes accounting

Local authorities obviously employ, in all departments, secretarial and clerical staff, computer operators and data preparation staff, receptionists, telephonists etc.

About a million craft and manual workers are employed. The jobs include the building trades, gardening and groundsman, catering, maintaining vehicles and other equipment, road works, refuse collecting, traffic warden, driving, recreation and (swimming) baths attendants, caretaking and cleaning etc.

Administration, legal and finance

These are at the heart of local government, backed up by, for example, management services. Although local authorities may appear to be huge bureaucracies, in fact relatively few of their very large staffs are actually just administrators or managers.

THE CENTRAL ADMINISTRATION has general oversight of the authority's work and improving its organisation, but is also responsible for advice on policy formation, management services, committee and secretarial work for Council committees (such as making up agendas, taking minutes, drafting reports and so on), preparing and keeping up to date electoral rolls and arranging council elections, public relations and information services. Many local authorities also have centralised purchasing and supplies; some also purchase co-operatively. Staff administration (including training) is still the responsibility of central administration – not that many councils have fully-fledged personnel departments, although they do employ trained personnel officers.

While administration absorbs people from many backgrounds, in the past it has been common for senior staff to come from among legal and financial departments.

LEGAL DEPARTMENTS are important in all local authorities. All authorities have legal functions and responsibilities. They must be able to interpret government legislation where it affects them. Legal departments draft legislation, look after the authority's transactions which involve land and property, and of course deal with any legal proceedings.

Authorities' legal staff qualify via the usual routes (see LAW under ACADEMIC AND VOCATIONAL STUDIES).

FINANCIAL MANAGEMENT was traditionally done by what used to be called the treasurers' department, more often now 'finance'. Whatever the title, finance officers are responsible, under the finance committee, for controlling income (from government grants, from rates, from rents, interest, various entry fees and so on) and expenditure, raising loans, advising the Council on the financial implications of policy decisions, preparing budgets and financial forecasts, collecting rates, carrying out accounting procedures and generally ensuring that the authority gets value for money.

Most finance officers are, or become, qualified accountants, and gain qualifications designed especially for accountants working for public bodies. Ratings officers are also normally specially trained.

See also ACCOUNTANCY AND FINANCIAL MANAGEMENT under COMMERCE.

The service departments

Each looks after a particular 'function', service, or responsibility of the authority. Depending on the function, each department employs a range of professionally-qualified staff, sometimes technicians, some supporting administrative, clerical staff, and sometimes manual staff too. Land, buildings, and the related support services are a major concern of many local authorities –

PLANNING DEPARTMENTS carry out the local authority's legal responsibilities, and also prepare detailed schemes. Most professional planners work for local authorities, with the support of technical staff. Planning departments

employed about 22,850 full-time in late 1986 (against 24,000 in 1979). Part-time staff numbered nearly 800 (similar to 1979).
See also LAND-USE PROFESSIONS.

TRANSPORT DEPARTMENTS manage road systems, design and build roads. Some authorities also operate transport systems, but these are generally separately managed, and can now be operated by commercial companies. Transport departments employed about 23,700 people full-time, some 540 part-time, in 1986.
See TRANSPORT SERVICES under SERVICE INDUSTRIES.

ENGINEERS' DEPARTMENTS provide drainage systems, sewers, sewage treatment and disposal, land drainage and flood prevention, refuse collection or disposal, and street cleaning services. Some also supervise authority construction sites, using direct labour.
Engineer's departments employ qualified engineers (mostly civils and some mechanicals, most of whom become qualified municipal engineers whatever their original specialisation), surveyors and building inspectors.
See also ACADEMIC AND VOCATIONAL STUDIES IN ENGINEERING, and CONSTRUCTION and SURVEYING under LAND- AND ENVIRONMENT-RELATED WORK.

ARCHITECTS' DEPARTMENTS in local councils design and oversee the building of public buildings such as colleges, schools, community centres, libraries, youth and leisure centres.
Local-authority architects qualify in the usual way – see ARCHITECTURE under ACADEMIC AND VOCATIONAL STUDIES IN LAND USE.

Surveyors and valuers are also employed in all aspects of work concerned with the authority's land and building interests, including valuation, maintenance and management, although housing management itself is usually a separate department and a separate career.
See LAND-USE PROFESSIONS.

(Any major local authority projects involve all these departments, and the various professionals and experts work as members of a team or act as consultants, depending on the project, particularly on large-scale developments. Even building a sports centre involves co-operation between planners, valuers, architects, structural and municipal engineers, mechanical and electrical engineers, technicians, draughtsmen, landscape architects and heating and ventilating engineers, most of whom will be local government employees.)

ENVIRONMENTAL HEALTH DEPARTMENTS administer legislation and other government regulations designed to maintain and improve standards of health and hygiene.
Mostly this involves inspecting food shops, restaurants, slaughter and warehouses to see that food is being stored and handled properly and cleanly, that it is bacteria-free, and that staff, their clothing and equipment are frequently and properly cleaned. They have to check, for instance, for any kind of vermin. They also trace the source of any outbreak of food poisoning. They look into unhygienic housing conditions and approve schemes for improving them. They are responsible for disease-control at ports and airports, and administer all anti-pollution legislation (including noise as well as smoke, chemicals etc).

They see that working conditions in shops and offices are reasonable – sanitation, ventilation, lighting, hours of work for young people, opening and closing times, and so on.

More time is obviously spent out of the office than in, although obviously there is plenty of report writing etc. There are about 5500 posts for environmental health officers, but they may not always be filled.

Departments employ mainly environmental health officers – for whom there are some 5500 posts but they are not always filled – but also some other experts, such as chemists and public analysts, as well as support staff. In all some 23,160 work (late 1986) full-time in environmental health (against 24,000 in 1979).

Environmental health qualifications Officers qualify via either a diploma, following a three-year sandwich-based course, combined with working as a trainee officer in a local authority, or a four-year degree course. The professional body is the Institution of Environmental Health Officers. Minimum entry requirements are five GCE/GCSE passes including two at A level (subjects to include maths and two sciences, including one at A level).

CONSUMER PROTECTION DEPARTMENTS developed from weights and measures, and still take care of all kinds of trading standards. They make sure, for example, that cash registers of all kinds, petrol pumps and pub measures are all working accurately. They now also implement consumer protection legislation, investigating all kinds of complaints from customers, about sub-standard goods or services. Some authorities also run consumer advice centres. It is job which involves spending a lot of time out of the office, and often means trying to persuade traders to co-operate.

Local authorities employ about 1700 'trading standards' officers.

Trading standards qualification This is only via a diploma in trading standards, administered by the Local Government Training Board. Trainees, employed by local authorities, must complete a three-year course combining release for study with practical training. Trainees must have at least five GCE/GCSE passes including two at A level (subjects must include English, maths, and physics), but most authorities now also recruit graduates – and the exams do need academic ability. The professional body is the Institute of Trading Standards Administration.

The Diploma in Consumer Affairs is for other staff employed in consumer protection departments, and they are encouraged to take it. A two-year course is run by the NALGO Correspondence Institute, for exams set by the ITSA.

SOCIAL SERVICE DEPARTMENTS, which have some statutory duties, for children and under the mental health acts, are largely staffed by qualified social workers, as described under PROFESSIONAL, SCIENTIFIC AND SOCIAL SERVICES.

Social services employed, in all, over 172,100 people full-time in late 1986 (against 155,200 in 1979), with over 218,500 part-time (against 188,650 in 1979).

EDUCATIONAL SERVICES are a major responsibility of larger local authorities, primarily counties, which must provide full-scale education for children from the age of five through to 18-plus (and can do so from three or four), and further/higher education thereafter.

This involves everything from planning the services, which nowadays also means the problems of trying to contract the service, re-organising to cope with falling numbers of pupils and pre-vocational preparation for 16-19s, possibly designing and building new schools, through to day-to-day administration and inspection, together with supporting welfare (including school meals) and careers services.

LEAs are also responsible for teacher training in such polytechnics and other colleges as are maintained by the local authority itself.

People directly employed by the local authority are educational administrators and inspectors (many of whom will have had teaching experience first), welfare and careers officers, school librarians etc. Teachers come under a separate structure but are still counted amongst local authority employees.

In all, local authorities employed over 552,850 full-time teachers and lecturers as of late 1986 (against some 602,200 in 1979) with 123,630 part-time (against some 116,000 in 1979). Education employs a large number of support staff (in the school meals service, caretakers, cleaners etc), as well as administrators, specialists (as above), but again numbers have fallen, to under 204,900 full-time in late 1986 (239,000 in 1979) and nearly 507,700 part-time (against over 528,500 in 1979).

See also EDUCATION under PROFESSIONAL, SCIENTIFIC AND SOCIAL SERVICES.

LIBRARY, MUSEUM AND ARTS SERVICES may come administered as part of educational services, but some authorities group them with cultural or even recreational activities.

All county authorities are required to maintain free library systems, and the qualified librarians who run them generally specialise in 'public' library work – although their qualifications are largely the same as those of other librarians (see LIBRARIANSHIP AND INFORMATION WORK under INFORMATION TECHNOLOGY). Some authorities also have their own museum and art galleries – see MUSEUM WORK under CREATIVE CAREERS.

About 30,170 people were working full-time in libraries and museums in late 1986 (up from 28,800 in 1979), and just over 20,600 part-time (17,600 in 1979). Larger, urban authorities also run concert halls and some have theatres – see ARTS ADMINISTRATION.

RECREATIONAL AND LEISURE ACTIVITIES, ranging from games and sports facilities, swimming pools, country parks and adventure playgrounds through to arts festivals, is a major area of activity for most local authorities. They employ a range of specialist staff in designing, building, managing and maintaining open spaces and centres, and also in organising leisure activities, as eg recreation managers, sports officers.

Over 82,760 worked full-time in recreation, parks and baths in late 1986, (against 87,400 in September 1979), nearly 29,800 part-time (24,000 in 1979). See ADMINISTERING AND MANAGING FOR LEISURE AND RECREATION.

POLICE AND FIRE SERVICES are fully described under SERVICE INDUSTRIES

Recruitment and entry

Traditionally, people have started out in local-government service as school-leavers, and worked up, via part-time study for an appropriate professional qualification. Rising entry qualifications, especially for the professions, which apply to people working in local authorities as anywhere else, and less work for unqualified people generally has dramatically reduced opportunities to start from the very bottom.

Financial restrictions mean local authorities now have to keep a fairly tight rein on recruitment. The remaining local authorities have also been giving priority to absorbing staff from the abolished metropolitan authorities. However, they stress that the opportunities are still there.

Sixteen-plus entry: councils do still recruit some school-leavers at sixteen-plus, normally with four or five O-level-equivalent passes, for clerical posts, as computer/machine operators, data preparation staff, and for training as technicians.

Some sixteen/seventeen-olds may also be recruited for training in, eg gardening and other craft-level work in parks, playing fields etc, and in building trades. CSE grade 3 equivalent passes at 16-plus† are an advantage, but not essential.

YTS: local authorities run schemes, and may require sixteen/seventeen-year-olds to start in the above via YTS.

Eighteen-plus entry: with at least two A-levels, it is still usual to start training in, for instance, general administration, accountancy, computer programming, housing administration, environmental health or trading standards, leisure administration, and surveying. It is no longer possible to train from eighteen-plus for architecture, planning, librarianship, engineering, because they are effectively all-graduate entry careers. Authorities do, however, take people with one or more A levels to train as draughtsmen/women, architectural and planning assistants, engineering technicians, laboratory technicians etc.

Graduate entry: with the demise of the metropolitan authorities, there appear to be no formal graduate entry schemes. Graduates are mainly recruited for specific posts as and when vacancies occur. One county authority, for example, employing over 20,000 staff, recruits just two trainee accountants a year. When opportunities occur, they are mainly for 'functional' departmental training – eg in finance/accountancy, consumer protection, environmental health, housing, libraries, social work, with any degree. A degree in an appropriate subject is, though, needed for architecture, engineering (civil, electrical, mechanical), law, planning, surveying.

Professional entry: when these are appropriate, local authorities do recruit people who are already fully qualified, although in many instances this will be from amongst people who work in other local authorities, and therefore have relevant experience. This is probably essential in areas such as finance.

Qualifications and training Local government has long emphasised qualifications, not only for professionals, but also for clerical and administrative staff. Authorities make fairly extensive provision for entrants to be trained, by a variety of methods, either by in-service training and/or paid leave of absence to attend full-time, sandwich, or day-release courses, in professions employed by the authority.

Where necessary, ie if a suitable 'outside' qualification did not exist, the authorities have developed their own, via the Local Government Training Board, but few are now offered except in one or two specialist areas.

The Training Board has a wide-ranging role. Much of its work is geared to developing in-service training within authorities, which is closely linked to its advisory work. The Board is also responsible for identifying jobs and their training needs, making training recommendations, and helping to arrange courses.

BTEC now sets the main qualifications in public administration, which is closely linked with business studies schemes. This allows local-government employees in clerical and administrative work to study alongside people working in commerce, or training for administrative/clerical work in other organisations, and so gain broadly-based business qualifications which make it easier for them to change employers. Other relevant schemes include those in caring, leisure studies, and engineering and other construction skills.

BTEC First awards in business/finance etc, while not specifically designed for local-authority employees, do cover the skills etc needed, since many are common to both public and private sectors. Entry is as for all BTEC First awards††.

BTEC National awards in public administration are largely common with business and finance, and distribution. The required core includes two units in public administration, taken with business-related skills, people in organisations, and the organisation in its environment. Option units include housing studies, practical administration, library and information work, social services, social structure of modern Britain, although local government employees can also take options in, eg secretarial and keyboarding skills, finance, tourism etc. Entry is as for all BTEC National awards††.

BTEC Higher awards in public administration include some core studies in common with business etc. These are work organisations, the external environment, and operational techniques and procedures. The rest of the core studies cover public sector organisations, structures and processes, and resource management in the public sector. Option units are locally-designed. Entry is as for all BTEC Higher awards††.

Degree courses: a number of universities and polytechnics offer degree courses in public (and/or social) administration, which are policy-oriented. See ACADEMIC AND VOCATIONAL QUALIFICATIONS IN SOCIAL SCIENCES.

Professional qualifications: the main professional body is
The Institute of Chartered Company Secretaries and Administrators (ICSA). About 28% of ICSA members work in local government. ICSA's two-part examinations have a special stream in local government administration. Entrants with A levels or BTEC National take both parts; candidates with relevant degrees or HND can gain subject-for-subject exemptions. See ADMINISTRATIVE AND MANAGERIAL WORK.

The Institutes of Administrative Management, and Management Services, provide useful alternatives.

Further information from the Local Government Training Board, the relevant professional bodies, and individual local authorities.

POLITICS

For most people, politics is a voluntary interest, something quite separate from their daily work, and must stay so right up to and including membership of a local authority as an elected councillor. At this level it is rare to be able to earn a living from being a politician, although the leaders and people chairing the major committees of larger authorities are paid expenses which allow them to work full-time there. For some, like the Lord Mayor of London, it actually means having enough money to pay the expenses of a year in office.

MEMBERS OF PARLIAMENT AND MEMBERS OF THE EUROPEAN PARLIAMENT are the only people who can really be called 'career' politicians, in the sense that they are paid a salary to represent their constituents at Westminster or Strasbourg. At present there are seats for only 648 members in the UK Parliament and 81 for British members of the European Parliament. It is one of the most insecure of careers, since it can be ended so easily and abruptly by the whim of the electorate.

The prospective Member of Parliament, or candidate, has first to be adopted as such by a constituency party. To reach this point, the aspiring MP has to prove capability, political acumen, suitability, drive, and devotion to his or her party. Traditionally this is demonstrated by working hard and long within the (local) party, usually at constituency level. Most often this means serving as a councillor on a local council at some stage. However, younger MPs are increasingly coming straight into national politics via other political, or semi-political, activist organisations. Some constituencies even prefer candidates who have made a name for themselves already, even if this is in an area totally unrelated to politics, if this makes them immediately recognisable to local electors. Some constituencies have other preferences: for married candidates, for local or younger candidates, or mature candidates and so on. Of course it is means waiting until a candidacy falls vacant, and the competition for a 'safe' seat can be considerable. Constituency parties have a high degree of local autonomy in choosing their candidates, but the central party offices are becoming more interventionist. Central party offices offer constituencies lists of 'vetted' candidates, and may try to help some prospective candidates to gain experience of elections first in constituencies where they are unlikely to be elected.

All politicians have second, or perhaps they should be called first, careers, both to support them during the time before they achieve their ambition, and to fall back on in the event of a permanent or temporary decline in their political fortunes. While it is probable that MPs have come from almost every area of employment, some fit in with a political career better than others, these being careers which can be followed without working a full day or week, including, for example, the law and journalism.

While all Members are constitutionally entitled to choose for themselves how they will vote in Parliament, in practice they must also take into account the demands of the Parliamentary party and the views of their own constituency, which can on occasion cause conflict, especially when the Member develops a strong personal line on something. This is just one way in which an MP's career can be put at risk. While a local party can withdraw its support from its MP, it cannot remove him or her from Parliament except by waiting until the next General Election (unless the Member resigns by 'applying for the Chiltern Hundreds') and even then the Member may still stand as an independent candidate against the new official party nominee.

Most Members of Parliament spend weekdays (or at least Monday to Thursday) in London when the House is in session. At least one day a week is spent in the constituency, seeking to solve social and other problems for individual constituents. Members are also expected to be available to their constituents while at Westminster. This means a Member's day is a long one, since the House generally sits well into the evening, while the mornings may be taken up with correspondence and visitors, and a growing number of committee meetings too.

Most MPs have full lists of engagements outside their strictly Parliamentary work, with speeches, conferences, radio and television appearances. Since most MPs also expect to specialise in a particular subject (education, health, housing, and so on), this means a lot of background research and reading, so an MP's life can be extremely busy and full. It can also be very peripatetic, especially for the MP whose constituency is a long way from Westminster, and for the MEP.

Becoming a minister, a member of an opposition party's front-bench 'shadow' team, or chairing a 'backbenchers' committee, is obviously promotion, but this does not exempt any Member from losing his or her seat at the next election.

Members of the European Parliament are elected on the same party lines as British MPs, but they represent much larger constituencies. It is a relatively new career – the first MEPs were only elected in 1979 – and a high proportion of British MEPs are people who have already had a political career in national politics in Britain.

A FULL-TIME OFFICIAL IN A POLITICAL PARTY is the other main career in politics. In today's political parties this means becoming a either a regional or constituency political agent or working in the central office.

Constituency agents are the paid officials of the local branches of a party. They act as secretary to the constituency party, and are responsible for organising the local party so that it is ready and able to contest any election (and the agent is likely to be involved in local as well as national polls) with maximum efficiency. They organise their members, look after records and publicity, and also act as communication links, particularly with the candidate or MP, and try to ensure electoral rolls are kept up-to-date. Increasingly they have to be marketing experts, 'targeting' potential supporters, and use computer-based systems. To do the job, they are trained in the latest techniques, and are expected to have a really thorough knowledge of electoral law and practice.

No party can afford full-time agents in all constituencies these days, and regional offices handle much of the work, providing agents and organisers as and when needed. Numbers employed fluctuate, depending on how close a general and/or local election is, the state of party finances, etc.

Both the Labour and Conservative Parties have training schemes for agents. The Conservatives' is full-time, that for the Labour Party is by correspondence courses, leading via intermediate qualifications to a diploma in electoral law and party organisation for the Labour Party and the Agent's Certificate in the Conservative Party, with more advanced certificates for full-time officials. All appointments to posts in the Conservative Party are made at constituency level, while the Labour Party recruits both via a national agency service, where agents are appointed and employed directly by head officer, and at local level.

All agents generally have long voluntary experience within the particular party before becoming an agent, and it goes without saying that the job demands intense dedication to the party cause. Promotion, for the Labour and Conservative agent, is to larger, more key constituencies, and for some to posts at area and regional level, or to central office.

The Labour and Conservative central offices both have large permanent staffs, Liberal and SDP rather smaller ones.

Many of the jobs in central party offices are administrative and organisational, but there are also departments responsible for providing the background work on party policy, monitoring current developments, and gathering information, giving posts for specialist research staff. Central office staff also prepare material for speeches, service policy committees, deal with press and other publicity, do market research, prepare campaigns, fund raise, and provide information about the party and its policies, for politicians, press and general public. Central offices all use sophisticated computer systems, and employ staff to program and operate them. Much of the work on sophisticated 'marketing' and advertising/PR strategy is done either by professional agencies, or by professionals who are party supporters, though.

Staff may also be provided for the parliamentary party and MPs, working at Westminster, but some of these are unpaid researchers on study leave from colleges (but this gives useful experience for a later political career).

Organisational and administrative posts in both central office and area offices are generally filled from amongst party agents and women organisers. Most research posts need a good economic/social studies and political background, and particular areas of research may need additional qualifications.

Further information from the central, regional, or local offices of the appropriate political party.

Manufacturing and Production

Introduction   813
How industry works   819
Employment in manufacturing industry   824
Manufacturing sectors   832

INTRODUCTION

Britain's manufacturing industry still makes most of the things that are used every day, from pins to plates and pens to cars, for sale to the ordinary 'consumer'. It produces food, such as bread and baked beans, and drinks, such as beer, orange squash and instant coffee, and what are called consumer durables, eg furniture and bicycles. Industry makes products which other industries need to make other things, for instance the components for cars, bricks and cement for the construction industry, steel tubes, and raw plastics. Some of these are called 'capital' goods, expensive items like machine tools and cranes, aircraft and trucks, and main-frame computers, which mean heavy investment for the customer. Industry makes very ordinary things, like soap powder, in very large quantities; it makes 'one-off' products like generators; it makes things which it has made for centuries, like glass and leather goods, and new and often extraordinary things like silicon chips, lasers, optical fibres, space satellites and robots.

But British industry no longer makes a long list of products – typewriters, cameras, cutlery, mass-produced motor cycles, cheap shoes, many conventional toys ... This is a symptom of a long-term decline, a decline accentuated and accelerated by recession, at a time when world competition for trade in goods continues to intensify sharply. Although Britain was again the world's fourth largest exporter by 1985 (having briefly fallen to poor fifth), manufactured goods still make up about 50% of total exports, and just about two-thirds of all manufacturing output is still exported, since 1983 imports have exceeded exports, for the first time in 100 years. In mid 1986, although the volume of manufacturing exports was up about 13% on 1980, imports were up 51%.

Although productivity is improving, as measured by EEC economists, the annual average increase of 1.3% over 1983-6, while similar to the US, is still below the EEC average of 1.9% and well below Japan's, at 2.7%. Total output, although by 1986 estimated to be growing at 3% a year, and up 10% between 1983 and 1986, was still 3% below the 1979 level. Only 3% of companies started up in 1985 were in manufacturing. Investment is still 15% down on 1979 – Britain is the only country that appears to treat R&D as expendable, rather than as a necessary investment for long-term survival.

But as the Finniston Report showed, manufacturing is essential to Britain's prosperity. Growth in manufacturing industries is crucial, because 'the long-term growth of the economy depends on the value of domestic output of manufactured goods continuing to rise to meet a substantial share of domestic demand, both to meet those demands and to earn sufficient currency from sales abroad to pay for the imports of raw materials, food, fuel, manufactured products and services'. 'There is no prospect that growth from natural resources or from other sectors of the economy can generate wealth on the scale which can be provided by manufacturing industries. Past relative declines in UK competitiveness and output must therefore be stemmed and reversed...'

It is often suggested that service industries could replace the income lost by manufacturing – but to do so, services would have to increase their share of world markets almost fivefold. The UK share of the world invisibles market in fact fell from 12% in 1969 to 7.7% in 1984 – and a 1% increase in the export value of manufactured goods would take a 2% increase in exports of services to compensate.

Finniston, as many others have continued to do since, stressed that industry had to meet change with change, moving out of product areas in which earlier comparative technical and commercial advantages have been irrevocably lost, and suggesting that 'the strengths of advanced countries lie in inventing and exploiting new products and processes, incorporating high levels of human skill and knowledge, most often at the leading edge of technology, and in continual incremental improvements to current products and processes through reducing production costs ... The advanced countries must move up-market, continually seeking new ways to maintain their advantages by identifying, developing and accelerating the introduction of new technologies and potential growth products.'

Finniston concluded that 'prosperity depends on the production of high-quality, high value-added goods, utilising the best of current knowledge and technology. There is evidence that British manufacturers have not shared fully in the international trends among advanced nations to trade 'up market', and that room exists for greatly improving the efficiency of much of British production.' ... 'Changes in the world market for manufactured products are increasingly emphasising the need for companies to develop and maintain an advanced engineering capability to meet the challenges posed and to exploit the opportunities being presented.'

Since Finniston wrote, deep recession and lack of competitiveness forced manufacturing industry into drastic and dramatic retrenchment and rationalisation, making it far leaner and in some ways fitter to meet competition. Older and uneconomic plants have closed and much capacity in traditional sectors has been lost for good. Productivity levels have risen, but not nearly enough so far – one analysis suggests than, in 1986, output per hour in the US was 2.5 times greater than in the UK, in Japan nearly 80% higher, West Germany 84%, France 78%, and Italy 55%.

Manufacturing industry has still also to face the problems of investing and innovating, to fight for the needed share of world markets. Fears continue that the severity of the depression may have made industry too lean, that efficiency and profitability may have been undermined, and it may no longer be able to make some key products or components.

Some major producers think that, even with recovery, some markets, both at home and abroad, may never be regained, and that manufacturing may never go back to pre-1979 levels of output. Even with recovery, firms expect to have to go on living with very tough competitive conditions, and therefore with continuing cost-cutting and attempts to improve on efficiency.

THE CHANGING SHAPE OF MANUFACTURING

The shape of British manufacturing industry has probably changed permanently. Many traditional, 'heavy' industries are shadows of their former selves. Only firms already dominant in world markets for low-cost products, and which have already invested in up-to-date technology, can expect to survive – it is now too late to start trying to get into mass markets. The future has mainly to be with Finniston's high value-added industries and products where technology is critical to success, but analyses of export figures show the UK is still far too dependent on comparatively high-volume, low-cost products.

To produce wealth, companies must invest, research and development must produce new cost-effective (as well as, for example, environmentally-safe) products, more accurately identified by marketing and more carefully scrutinised by finance. But industry is still climbing back relatively slowly – and after a strong performance at the end of 1986, output flattened in the first quarter of 1987.

Manufacturing is changing in many other ways in response to rapidly changing conditions. It is, for instance, becoming even more multi-national. Increasingly companies think internationally, making the decisions where to manufacture on a complex range of factors which include availability and cost of raw materials and components, the right labour mix, accessibility to a particular market (and whether or not it is more profitable to manufacture within a trading area), and the level of overheads (which may be cut by eg development aid). One international computer firm manufactures in fourteen countries, and for the European markets makes VDU units in one country, disc drives in another, and keyboards in a third: chips and programs come from yet a fourth. Chemicals and cars are similarly produced on a European scale. The UK has to compete with other countries for its share of international companies' manufacturing capacity, the jobs that go with it, and a share of the profits and a say in what happens to them. Some industries – volume car production, steel, shipbuilding, petrochemicals, fertilisers – have 'migrated' to lower-cost countries on a massive scale. Such changes can also have 'knock-on' effects. For example, with a shift of volume car production to continental Europe, UK component manufacturers find it difficult to keep down prices to the remaining car firms, who are then forced to go abroad for cheap components, reducing business still further for British firms. On the brighter side, huge capital projects like airports, new steel works, petrochemical plants – and the electricity capacity that has to go with them – that these countries need built, give UK construction firms and their suppliers a chance to compete for the business.

Operating on an international scale does not now mean larger and larger single-plant operations. In chemicals, artificial fibres and steel, for example, simple economies of scale have not been as effective as managers believed in the 1960s, and no longer meet market needs. Large single-product plants have to operate at full capacity for a very high proportion of the time to be economic, and are inflexible – it is difficult to vary output to meet demand. Forcing large quantities of a standard product on to the market ignores the first principle of modern marketing – make only what the customer will buy. More often than not the customer wants variety. Process industries like these (and eg food) have been switching from single product production, with low profit margins to a widening range of high-value speciality products (such as liquid crystals for electronic displays), which are sold in smaller quantities.

The latest in manufacturing strategy, adopted from Japan and called 'just in time', takes this to extreme – manufacturing products only when orders come in. For this they must have very versatile process plant or productions lines with sophisticated control systems, which can make several different products and versions of the same product on a batch basis – or even continuously – as on the most modern car-production lines.

Modern conditions demand flexibility, which can mean some return to smaller plants nearer to sources of raw materials and/or markets. If automated batch-processing proves to be as efficient and cost-effective as large-scale continuous production lines or processes, it could become economic to go back to quite small plants and factories serving very local markets. Companies are, in any case, moving to greater decentralisation, giving local managers and staff greater responsibility, motivating them to do better.

Firms, large and small, have been forced – or have decided to – change completely the products they make (eg from mechanical to electronic components for telecommunications), with inevitable major upheavals. Firms are also looking hard at what they do and concentrating more on what they do best, shedding fringe activities taken on in the 1970s. Even 'vertical integration' – owning or part-owning supplier and customer firms, popular in the 1960s to force through rationalisations and greater efficiency, is being abandoned for tighter, more specialist operations.

The most recent official figures on the size of Britain's manufacturing industry date from 1983, and are rather obviously, given recessions and the rate of closures and redundancies, likely to look somewhat different for 1987. However, they give some clues. In 1983, manufacturing units numbered 102,445, against 118,700 three years earlier. Most units, nearly 76,740 (almost 75%), were very small, employing fewer than twenty people, but between them only 11% of total employment. Just under 24%, some 24,000 firms, employed between 20 and 499 people, over 42% of total employment. Only 1275 – 1.2% of firms – employ between 500 and 1499 people, 20% of total employment, with only 361 units, less than half of one percent of all firms, employed more than 1500 people each, but almost 27% of the total numbers employed still.

Engineering Industry Training Board (EITB) figures, representing approaching half of manufacturing industry, are more up to date, but give a similar picture. They show the number of firms in engineering rising to a peak of 25,230 in 1980, but falling to 22,069 in 1985. The number of engineering firms employing more than 5000 people also peaked in 1980, at 35, falling to 18 in 1985 – the number of people working for them also fell steeply from nearly 304,500 in 1978 to 143,519 in 1985. The number of firms employing between 1000 and 5000 fell from 474 in 1979 to 269 in 1985, and the numbers they employed from over 890,500 to only 494,200. The number of firms with under 25 employees went on rising, to almost 13,000, into 1981, but has fallen since then, to 11,700 in 1985 – they employed (at peak) 144,375 in 1981, but only 130,860 in 1985. However, the number of firms employing between 60 and 250 has increased recently, from a low of 3440 in 1983 to 3715 in 1985, and so did the numbers employed – from under 421,000 to over 452,300 in 1985.

Since 1982, there have been more engineering firms in London and the south east (3699 in 1985), the west midlands (3994) and the east and south (3628) than in the north east (2797) and north west (2498), according to EITB.

THE MANUFACTURING PROBLEM

Every manufacturing company is in business to make a profit, just as are shops, banks, hotels, public houses, accountancy and legal practices, and farmers. Manufacturing companies have to achieve their profits by selling products, either direct to the 'end-user', or to an intermediary, for more than it costs to make them, rather than by selling services on which banks, hotels, lawyers etc, expect to make their profit. They have, then, to invest money in creating a product to sell, on raw materials and/or component parts for their product, in the equipment need to make it, and in people to operate the equipment, all before they can sell a single car, washing-machine, computer, ship, machine tool, or coat – which is a cost most other commercial organisations do not have to carry.

Not so very long ago it was not too difficult to make an income, a profit, from manufacturing any reasonable product. Costs were rarely a problem in relation to the price at which a product would sell in sufficient numbers to be profitable. Raw materials and energy were cheap and plentiful. Britain's manufacturing industries had a head start on the rest of the world, and gained home and overseas market acceptance (more or less) for what firms decided to sell. Most British manufacturers could beat what competition there was with very little effort. Britain grew used to a very good standard of living on the proceeds.

The manufacturers' world has changed. At one end of their operations, costs rose steadily. The cost of raw materials, the cost of R&D, the cost of materials and parts, the cost of energy, the cost of labour, the cost of equipment, the cost of money itself, each individual cost increase caused most other costs to rise too, since suppliers have to meet the price rise in, eg, energy, labour, and money as well. At the other end, more firms, both in the UK and at first from other industrialised countries (more recently from developing countries too), have entered the markets traditionally dominated by established firms.

For many British manufacturing firms, a long industrial history became a real disadvantage at this point. Stability, high quality, reliability, established and well-tried products have been the hallmark of much of British industry for very many years. Many firms – managers and employees – had become, not unreasonably, set in their ways, and change did not seem to all of them to be, necessarily, a good thing. Older industries had – have – old and even not so-old (see PAPER MAKING) plant and equipment, costly to run in today's conditions, and have continued with traditional, comparatively expensive and slow, working methods. It is, of course, all relative. Industry's established, traditional ways were not wrong in themselves, and could have gone on being quite adequate if the world had not changed around it.

British manufacturing industry has no option but to accept change if it is to survive at all, let alone make profits and go on producing much of the country's income. It can seem, to managers and workers alike, a form of blackmail that forces firms to become so cost conscious that millions of jobs have had to go, with all the appalling social consequences. But the country has inherited a career as a trading nation, and has apparently no other way to maintain its standard of living. Adapting to different, ever sharper competitive conditions is part of the cost of this. With no government intervention to maintain employment in manufacturing, jobs will have to come from elsewhere, because it is probably not possible for manufacturing to produce an income for the country *and* create the number of jobs now needed.

In these conditions, each separate sector of industry, and every individual firm – which means the people owning and working for it – has to become much, much more expert at working out how to make an income and profits from manufacturing. Firms need to make sophisticated analyses of potential markets, to discover as exactly as possible what customers want of a particular product, and what new products they will buy. They must stay aware of what new technological developments can do to their business, both in their own products and manufacturing methods, and elsewhere (as, eg all-electronic telephone exchanges have forced firms making components for electro-mechanical ones to change completely the products they make).

Firms have to assess their competitors accurately, and decide if competing in a market is the best policy or whether an income is better made by, eg innovating and/or going for related products which will fill a gap in what the market wants. They have to develop a flexible, adaptable strategy for the company, a strategy which can respond to unexpected changes and new developments, and be changed radically if need be. They must work out the most efficient and effective methods of manufacturing, distributing and selling products which are better designed and just as reliable and efficient as they can be.

Most firms should be spending (more) on research and development, innovation and design, because this is the only way to compete. They should be increasing – and certainly not cutting – expenditure on training. Firms have to adopt new technologies wherever they can be shown to give an advantage in terms of product, production or administration, and to do so efficiently and effectively.

Being successful demands a much greater, and more sophisticated understanding of how success is achieved in the 1980s, developing and integrating strategies, and making sure these are carried through in decision making. It needs efficient and effective planning, constant, and tighter control and monitoring of all aspects of the business. Reliable delivery, product quality, design and volume flexibility, and price are all crucial. Financial control, and exploitation of all the new services FINANCE is offering, have to be more sophisticated and expert, especially in financing exports. Firms must have, therefore, fast and accurate information with which to do this – which is why INFORMATION TECHNOLOGY is just as crucial to the future of manufacturing as any other sector.

In the five years to end 1986, British industry has achieved much, helped by lower costs of raw materials and latterly energy, moderate inflation and buoyant consumer demand. But it has been done largely by 'crude cost cutting'. Signs are that they are still not working 'hard enough to redesign products and marketing strategies so that customers will want to buy for reasons other than competitive prices springing from a low-wage economy', and that 'the UK [could be] steadily falling behind in the technological skills that it needs to maintain a role among the leading manufacturing nations'. Firms now have to find 'more sophisticated ways of increasing productivity' (*Financial Times*).

All this has major implications for working in manufacturing. It is the people going into manufacturing now and in the future who have to carry through changes, and who must have the necessary expertise. Manufacturing may need fewer people, but from now on firms must have people of much higher calibre – technology may be important, but it is useless without top-flight people who can decide on the right strategy, and see it through, organise and manage it. This extends right through the firm, from the shop floor – which has to cope with machinery of increasing sophistication and frequent change – through all functions, to senior management. Raising output and sales, improving production, cutting costs, funding investment, development and production, keeping up quality without raising expenditure, industrial relations, and almost above all, extremely sophisticated marketing are all crucial. Industry needs people who take meticulous care, and not grand-sweep-of-hand managers.

The indications are that industry is having to raise sharply the skills and calibre of its work force, with training, re-training, and with a rising proportion of people with good results at 16-plus†, A-levels, and degrees. Industry's problem is that the right high-calibre people are not encouraged to see industry as a career with any real potential. Even during the recession, firms complained they could not find enough people with the all-round abilities that they needed, and recovery looks like being held back by managerial and other high-level skills shortages. One fear is that good people will write off manufacturing as a career because of recent performance, poor image etc, especially as sectors like FINANCE are now competing more strongly for the most able.

HOW INDUSTRY WORKS

A manufacturing firm is an organisation similar to any other company, with one major exception – it has to have the facility to make its product, the physical plant and equipment.

Making an income from manufacturing is a team effort, with all departments and parts of the company, however it is organised, working closely together, and communicating with each other efficiently, all the time. It demands a lot of intelligent thinking and expertise from a great many people; an enormous amount of information which is well organised and analysed; a great many skills which are cerebral as well as practical; and a great deal of efficient planning and careful decision making to which many people, not just the production manager and board of directors, contribute.

Microelectronics – and other new technologies – are crucial to the future of manufacturing. Automating production is obviously the major objective, but computer-based systems are just as important to the company generally as in any other sector (see INFORMATION TECHNOLOGY). Increasing automation, especially as it links departments closer together and integrates functions, will probably change the shape and structure of manufacturing companies in ways it is still hard to predict.

Automating, or further automating, production is the main way to improve efficiency in production and cut production costs. Manufacturing industry, unlike the City, has still not fully realised it cannot survive without computerisation. According to a 1986 survey, development is still patchy. Although the number of factories using microelectronics doubled between 1981 and 1986, under 25% of output was produced using microelectronically-controlled processes, and only 8% of products incorporated microelectronics in 1986.

Most firms want computers to help reduce design and manufacturing lead times and stock levels, and to improve the productivity of existing machinery. Over 50% of factories now use microelectronics in some form in production. They have been less enthusiastic about robotics and fully automated manufacturing, although where they have been installed, the results are generally good. Only one in 40 UK factories surveyed was using robots in 1986, and the total number installed at the beginning of 1986, at 3200, was smaller than the 1985 increase alone in West Germany. Japan has 22,000, the US 20,000 and West Germany 8800 in operation.

Industry urgently needs to get small-batch processing (used in 70% of manufacturing world-wide) as efficient as dedicated production lines, and automation here is crucial

But automation involves more than just putting microelectronic equipment separately into machinery and welding/painting/material-moving robots on the factory floor, giving designers and draughtsmen/women graphics screens, computerising stock control and materials handling, progress chasing, or scheduling. Automation can computerise production control in integrated systems from the start of design to delivery of the finished product, and the greatest savings can be made here. One conventional machine tool is in effective production only 6% of the theoretical maximum time available; a numerical controlled machine capable of making more than one part at a time is in use for 8% of the theoretical maximum time. Connecting the machines to stores and fully automating over three shifts gives 77%. Integrating design, production and testing of dies for pressing car-body panels reduces the time the three stages take by 30%.

Fully automated production takes a set of compatible computer systems, which can communicate with and interrogate each other, to integrate and directly control, eg the automated component store, the assembly line which is self routeing and can monitor its own performance, using microprocessor-controlled test cells to check the finished product, and management information systems to give second by second monitoring of production. Systems of this type already in use can assemble numerous different versions of a product (eg a car or a computer), but they are not fully automated yet.

Computer-aided design and manufacture are also already linked. The information the design team has stored in their computer is used by another to, eg design the tools needed to cut the material, and to program the machine tool which will fabricate the parts. All these and other systems can be linked together into what is called computer-integrated manufacturing systems (CIMS). CIMS effectively puts an order into the first computer, which generates the appropriate plans from the computerised drawing office, and tells robot trucks what raw materials to take from the store and deliver to flexible manufacture cells where teams of machine tools (serviced by robots) fabricate and finish parts. It goes on from there.

The fully automated, unmanned factory is a apparently a reality for the late 1980s – the first fully computer-integrated plants for the UK were being built in 1985. Most commentators think it will take most of British industry rather longer to accept it, and that they will go about it in stages. But since the rest of the world's manufacturers will use it, it is essential for UK firms too.

Production
Production is the core of any manufacturing company. The methods used by a company vary from sector to sector, from product to product.

Some products can be made in a series of linked processes, continuously (in eg chemicals, food), the machinery – more often called plant – has long been mechanised, then automated with 'wired' technology. Continuous processes are relatively straightforward to automate more fully. The plant may look like a tangle of pipes going in all directions, connecting huge containers in which chemicals are separated or mixed, crude oil 'cracked', foods like sugar treated, or limestone and clay turned into cement. Valves and pipes eject steam and vapour, and a plant can be smelly and noisy. Automation usually means there are relatively few people around, except those who monitor the dials and lights in central, ultra-modern control rooms, the process workers checking the plant, and occasional maintenance staff.

Other forms of continuous processing are different – the massive sets linked machinery and equipment oh which, for instance, sheet glass is made by 'floating' the liquid mixture on molten metal, or the half-mile sets of rollers through which a sludge is turned into paper.

Other items, eg cars, are produced and assembled on a series of continuously-moving mass production and assembly lines. Many lines are now automated, with fewer and fewer hands putting lids on bottles, welding or painting, or working on the car body, the cake or biscuit. 'Flexible' manufacturing systems enable firms to switch the lines to different versions of the same product, or even to a different product.

Yet other items and components are made on individual machines or at a bench. Here automation may be more difficult, although microelectronic control of individual machines and processes, and sophisticated, multi-purpose computer numerical control machines are a first step.

Many hundreds of parts and components, some large, some miniscule, may go to make up a single product, although for many products microelectronics means fewer and fewer parts and components (which in turn cuts costs because it reduces the number of operations and people needed). Metal parts start as strip, sheet, tube or pre-formed blanks, and are formed (forged, cast, stamped or pressed out, moulded or fabricated), machined (milled, turned, ground, planed, shaped and drilled) to tolerances of many-thousands of an inch to give keyways, rings, grooves, hollows etc, they may need to fit them into other parts, and smoothed to a fine finish, each part going through several processes. Plastics are extruded, moulded, trimmed, bonded etc.

Computer, 'numerical', control means that by simply changing the control tape – or increasingly, on instruction from a computer – a machine will do one of any number of different jobs, do them much faster and more exactly – with less waste. In integrated systems, the machine's instructions are generated when the product is designed, and put into action when orders go through the computer system.

Lasers are being used increasingly in the plant. To cut accurately not only metals, but plastics, and even pasta. To measure, weld, drill and in quality control.

In assembly, on a line, bench or floor, the various parts and components are brought together, possibly in sub-assemblies first, and then built into the finished product. Most finished products must be packaged in some way, ready for distribution. Packaging may be the final stage of a production line, or may be a separate operation, increasingly automated.

Quality control has to make sure that raw materials and components coming in are as ordered, in the right quantities and quality. All the way through production, checks, tests, and regular monitoring are made for quality and to see specifications are being met. At some stages, for some products, a simple visual check may be enough – and in some factories work done by robots is checked by computers using TV cameras without any need for human inspectors. For others, or at other stages, there may have to be more sophisticated checks – samples to be analysed chemically in labs, or welds or other joins under x-ray or by radiography or ultrasonics, for example. Finished products are usually fully tested to ensure that they are working properly. Automated – and highly sophisticated – testing and analytical equipment is increasingly used throughout industry.

Automation, though, is not the only method of reducing quality control costs. Firms are training workers to take greater responsibility for seeing that a job is done right the first time. Some are using 'quality circles' where all the employees in, eg a single department meet regularly to identify, analyse and try to solve common work problems.

Production is supported by several departments/functions, although what they do and how they are organised changes, with eg automation and computerisation, with new manufacturing strategy.

Before production can begin, detailed instructions, which may still be drawings, or programs, have to be prepared – or computer generated – for the factory to work from.

Production has to be planned and schedules made up. This ranges from WORK STUDY and designing what work will be done by whom, and how long it will take, through to producing factory layouts and production lines. Changing technology, developing batch production, mean taking account of continual changes, and newer manufacturing methods has production engineering constantly re-examining how best to produce and/or assemble components. Production engineers also design any special tools, jigs etc needed for production, and these are usually made in the company's own toolroom.

The raw materials, the components, the processes and labour that go into the product must all be costed, again increasingly using information generated by computer. PURCHASING has to buy materials, components, equipment, services.

Stores keep production supplied as needed with raw materials, components etc. The more complex the product, the more complex and crucial stores planning is – too many or too much of any part or material raises costs unnecessarily and can be as expensive as not having needed components at all. Computer control of stores both increases efficiency and can reduce costs by monitoring stocks and their movement more exactly.

Maintenance and repair workshops keep the factory's plant and machinery operating, both by regular, planned servicing, trying to avoid breakdowns, and dealing with breakdowns. Some, mostly more complex equipment, is serviced and repaired by the manufacturers or by independent service companies.

Transport and distribution departments get a company's product either to warehouses, or direct to the customers. Some manufacturers install and commission equipment on customer's premises, and may also maintain and service it for them on a long-term basis.

Research, development and design

Spending on research and development by industry has been falling sharply for some years, and went down steeply during the recession. Even by end 1986, UK industry's investment in R&D was some 3% below the OECD average of 20% of GDP. Finniston was concerned, 'The great majority of British companies are thus maintaining only a minimal level of innovative activity ... More worrying still, the situation has worsened, especially in those sectors which have lost world market shares and whose profits have been hardest squeezed.' British firms are regularly criticised for not giving design sufficient emphasis.

Research, development and design are usually closely linked, and may form a single team within a firm (although a significant proportion of industry's R&D effort is done in research associations supported by the industry, and/or university centres). While the final product may be the formal responsibility of the designer, it is usually largely a team effort.

Design, both product and production/process, is in most manufacturing industries an ENGINEERING function (see under ACADEMIC AND VOCATIONAL STUDIES), although in many industries design is a multi-disciplinary function with some art-based input. The exceptions, where product design is mainly art based, include CLOTHING, FOOTWEAR, TEXTILES (see also ART AND DESIGN).

Research and development in industry work mainly in support of design and production. There is usually much more development than research – a recent figure gives 71% of current R&D expenditure in industry on development, 21% on applied research, and just 3% on basic research. Companies have R&D departments for one purpose only – to help improve profits, and not to extend the frontiers of knowledge or provide facilities for researchers to follow up personal interests. Hence much of the work is very practical, and problem-solving rather than innovatory – for example, analysing faults, finding ways to iron out snags in a production process, finding and testing a more economic material for a product, trying to cut energy consumption in production processes, as well as improving existing products and the way they are made. Trying to make major technological and/or scientific leaps and exploit them is much less common, although in some industries, eg ELECTRONICS and PHARMACEUTICALS, the research needed may have to be very original. Firms generally take a very business-oriented approach to what R&D are doing. Decisions on whether or not to follow up a possible new discovery are being made much earlier in the research/development process. The scrutiny is more ruthless, with eg FINANCE and MARKETING brought in early on to see if there is a viable market for the new idea, and if so, in what form it might sell, what the costings are, and if the acceptable price will give a profit.

Commercial and other departments
Manufacturing firms, like all other organisations aiming to make an income from the market place, need top-flight general managers, to work out strategy, plan, take decisions, organise, set targets, co-ordinate, problem solve. Management needs the support of sophisticated and efficient MARKETING and SALES, FINANCE, MANAGEMENT SERVICES, and PERSONNEL (see COMMERCE, PROFESSIONAL SERVICES etc). Marketing, for example, has to establish that people do actually want a new product – it may not sell simply because it is revolutionary. It is no longer possible to rely simply on a product's technical characteristics, backed up by hard selling. Marketing and finance have to establish the right price for the product – and if it is pioneering, taking account of the fact that competitors will always be able to produce something similar more cheaply.

EMPLOYMENT IN MANUFACTURING INDUSTRY
Employment in manufacturing has been falling steadily for many years – it went, for example, from 10 million in 1968 to barely 7 million in 1979. By 1983, it had crashed to under 5.4 million, and in late 1986 was down to just 5.13 million – less than one in five of the work force.

Despite recovery, numbers are still falling, more slowly but still faster than many expected, and especially among unskilled shopfloor workers. As of spring 1987, no one is looking for any up turn in job numbers, and employers predict a further fall of some 77,000 by end 1987. Tough competitive conditions can only continue, and firms will therefore go on trying to save costs, including labour costs, wherever possible, by rationalising, automating, etc. The Finniston report said that 'the value of an industrial sector to national wealth creation need not correlate with its importance as an employer...' and that 'increased output and/or improved efficiency often rest on the introduction of more capital-intensive, and hence labour saving, processes'. In other words, the importance of manufacturing is in producing a high proportion of the national income – once the money comes in, jobs can be created with it elsewhere in the economy.

The pattern of employment within manufacturing is also changing. The move away from heavy industry, and increasing labour-saving automation is, as elsewhere, reducing steadily the number and proportion of traditional semi- and unskilled jobs. But all the changes have to be managed, and managed very efficiently. Sophisticated, automated modern production systems need higher-calibre people to design, manage, make, and operate them.

Manufacturing industry is, however, already short of many skills. Shortages of professional engineers, but especially electrical and electronic engineers are, according to all surveys, widespread. The City's 'big bang' made it hard for manufacturing to recruit data processing staff in 1986, and shortages of computer and management services staff continue. A significant proportion of firms in all sectors of manufacturing expect shortages of skilled people to limit output. Shortages are not only of 'high-tech' skills, however. Firms are having difficulty in recruiting welders, machinists – especially machine tool setter operators – and electrical/electronic and mechanical fitters. Industrial designers are needed for capital goods, mechanical engineering, metal products and motor-vehicle sectors. The south east and west midlands cannot find maintenance electricians. A common theme, says EITB, is the major problem of finding people with experience – and this is, of course, an obvious consequence of the failure to train during recession.

Accurate and up-to-date figures on employment in manufacturing industry are not easy to find, and the present rate of change is making a statistical picture of manufacturing even more difficult to draw. The Engineering Industry Training Board produces the most comprehensive and up-to-date statistics, covering nearly half of all those working in manufacturing.

Total numbers employed in engineering on the EITB register in 1985 were just over 1.986 million, against nearly 2.94 million in 1978. (Provisional figures for 1986 are even lower, at under 1.967 million.) In 1985, about 32% of employees worked for the 287 firms with 1000 or more employees (against over 40% for the 506 firms of similar size in 1978).

In 1985, employees on the EITB register divided into the following (1977 percentage in brackets) –

Managerial staff:	121,540	or	6.1%	(4.3%)
Scientists and technologists:	85,337	or	3.4%	(1.94%)
Technicians:	179,033	or	9.0%	(7.3%)
Administrative/professional:	132,459	or	6.7%	(4.8%)
Clerical/office staff:	202,467	or	10.2%	(11.6%)
Supervisors/foremen:	95,980	or	4.9%	(4.8%)
Craft workers:	352,096	or	17.7%	(18.5%)
All other:	817,298	or	41.1%	(46.5%)

Working in manufacturing

A manufacturing company has to be organised around the production of the goods it sells, around a coherent set of strategies – market, corporate, manufacturing, product – but it is the people who make up the company, and by the quality of their decision making, make it profitable. A successful manufacturing company operates as a closely-knit team, with all departments working together to a common aim, however different the actual work they do and the methods they use.

Finniston said, 'Manufacturing depends for success on balancing specialist contributions and their co-ordination to satisfy constantly-changing market demands. The response of many British companies to these demands is handicapped by lack of adequate engineering input to marketing and business planning ...' Finniston also said, 'Rapid changes in market needs and in the technology available for meeting them demand a flexible and rapid responsiveness from companies. Management must ensure that the contributions of engineers and managers in research, design, development and production functions are effectively integrated to provide that response and are directly related to the company's market strategy.' Finniston was concerned about the predominantly non-technical backgrounds – accountancy, marketing, etc without any engineering/technology background or experience – from which senior decision-takers are generally drawn in Britain even in manufacturing – although there are some signs that this is changing.

SENIOR MANAGERS may each be responsible for a whole sector or 'profit centre' of the business, including all types of departments from production to finance, if the firm is large enough to make a range of different products and/or manufacture in several places, or they may be in overall charge of a single 'function', eg finance, production, marketing, for the whole organisation. Together they plan, co-ordinate, monitor and assess the information coming in from the different departments, maintain tight control on the business as a whole, and make the necessary decisions. In smaller firms, senior managers may be responsible for several functions and/or production units. For some years now, it has been common for a rising proportion of senior managers to come from finance, or marketing, but in future more senior managers are expected to come from amongst the engineers and/or technologists who have come up through production, marketing, etc.
See also MANAGEMENT under COMMERCE.

PRODUCTION is generally managed by teams of professional engineers, technologists, scientists (the mix, and dominance of discipline depending on the industry). Under a production director, each factory or plant has its own factory or works manager, who has to meet the company's plan, the production targets to agreed schedules, costs, etc. The factory/works manager is a team leader, of middle and junior managers, the number depending on the size and complexity of the factory or plant. Between them, they have to produce work schedules and production plans; organise, plan and cost their 'resources' – people, machinery, components, tools, materials, etc; liaise with PURCHASING on items to be bought; control stock and have incoming items inspected; have tools and machinery designed and see they are available when needed; organise materials handling, process and production lines, assembly, finishing, etc; control progress, quality control, etc; ensure that finished products are inspected and checked.

Some professional work in production is technical/technological – figuring ways to improve manufacturing methods or changing them to meet new manufacturing and marketing strategy (including planning and preparing for the next stage of automation), reducing costs (by cutting use of energy, for example), and trouble-shooting (eg what to do about a thousand parts which have been been over-machined by a fraction of a millimetre), having parts re-designed, etc.

Much of the work, though, is managing people and resources, making sure that materials and components arrive as needed and that the right number of people are available to operate the machines; allocating work to people; seeing that the work goes through without hold-ups; seeing that testing and quality control is done properly; solving problems as they happen, dealing with labour relations, safety, etc. Inevitably, these jobs change with increasing automation – fewer people, but more system(computer)-generated information to monitor, control and manage, for instance.

Some of the detailed work involved is done by younger professional/graduate engineers, technologists or scientists (depending on the industry). Many of the tasks, though, such as design detail and draughting, costing, estimating, programming (eg numerically-controlled machine tools), scheduling, detailed production planning, supervising, some of the more sophisticated testing (of eg circuits, drugs, food), and maintenance (of, eg automated equipment), and working on instrumentation, is treated as technician-level work. Again, technology is changing these jobs. Computer-aided design, for example, means automatically-generated manufacturing drawings – or perhaps no drawings at all, but a programme to control a machine tool – and a task lost. But automating production lines and processes also makes work for technician-level skills – in production control, for example, monitoring the instrument panels and VDU screens, knowing when to adjust controls and settings, responding to the system's requests for information or decisions, and watching for problems and knowing how to react when they happen.

Operating the machinery and other equipment which actually forms the metal and plastic shapes, the parts and components which go to make a product, putting them together in sub-assemblies and assembly, finishing the product, and moving around the materials, parts, and products, are traditionally very labour-intensive. Depending on the machine and the task involved, and the level of training needed, the work may be seen as un-skilled, semi-skilled or skilled operative's work, or a craft skill.

Traditionally, each worker was trained in one task, or at most a fairly narrow range of closely-related tasks. Most tasks are manual, involving either a single task (or set of tasks) done repetitively, or directly controlling equipment or machinery to produce, for instance, a welded join, a mix of raw materials, a keyway on a part, a new tool head. Every job and skill traditionally had its own title and tight description, and the list can be long – assembler, cableformer, capstan lathe operator, coil winder, crane driver, driller, electroplater, grinder, guillotine operator, fitter (general, aero, auto, mechanical, pipe, tool, etc), fork-lift truck driver, machinist, maintenance electrician, metal plating operator, miller, paint sprayer, packer, power-press operator, presstool maker, setter operator, shaper operator, sheet-metal worker, tool maker, turner, welder, wiring operator, and so on. Promotion may be to viewer or checker, inspection, foreman and other supervisory posts.

The terminology of industry is changing, though, as 'multi-skilling' slowly becomes a reality. EITB breaks down the 352,100 craft workers employed (1985) in engineering into broader groups. The industry still employs nearly 44,100 toolmakers and toolroom fitters; 116,700 'other' production mechanical engineering craft workers, 25,200 electrical/electronic production craft workers, 56,000 mechanical and electrical/electronic maintenance craft workers, 36,200 metal fabrication craft workers, 23,000 skilled welders, and 5600 coach and vehicle-body building craft workers.

Automation both reduces the number of tasks, and changes the work done. The unmanned factory is a reality, and cannot be too far off. But before it arrives, each stage of automation cuts the number of people needed to produce the same number of items or do the same work. One German estimate suggested, for example, that the next generation of robots would halve the country's assembly workers, ie by some 500,000, on top of jobs already lost by automation in the previous ten years. BL produced 250,000 Metros at an automated Longbridge in 1983 with 9500 workers, against 145,800 cars on the unautomated line with 16,800 workers in 1978 – and the line has been further automated since.

The latest technology is changing the work, and combined with the pressure to improve productivity, is also breaking down the old divisions of labour. A numerically-controlled machine tool can do the work of several conventional machines, so the machinist has to understand several operations. But automated machine tools, robots, and other equipment *do* the work the machinist, or other craft worker or operator, used to do. The craft worker or operator working in an automated factory no longer spends all day repeating a task with their hands, but controls a machine, or production line or process plant. This may seem like 'de-skilling' work, and so it can be in terms of manual skills. But controlling and monitoring complex, fast-moving, computer-controlled equipment or plant needs people who can think, react and respond with their heads, and in industries which are already highly automated, eg cement making and some other process industries, the people monitoring the sophisticated control rooms are now called process technicians rather than operators.

Dividing work to be done into separate, watertight tasks is no longer the most efficient way of organising manufacturing in the factory or plant. Operating and monitoring one kind of automated machinery, one part of a continuous production or process plant is not so different from the same job elsewhere, and workers are being asked to be more flexible in what they do. In industry after industry, the old job titles are going. In chemicals, glass, cement, for example, it is now common to call everyone on the line a 'process' operator (or technician), who may be asked to control plant manually when systems fail, identify faults, and make routine adjustments.

But the new job descriptions are as varied as they are 'flexible', and are increasingly tailored to the changing and varied needs of individual industries, even individual firms. Examples are –

system-specialist craft worker – who can deal with the increasing integration of plant and central control systems;

machine-specialist craft worker who can deal with a type of machinery, and is already being trained both to operate and maintain it;

craft technicians – mainly electricians who are trained across the board (not just electronics, but pneumatics and hydraulics too) to diagnose faults in microprocessor-controlled plant.

Traditionally, mechanical equipment was maintained by a mechanical engineer, electrical by an electrician. Now that equipment, products etc, are controlled by electronics but still have moving parts, it is more convenient to have people who can deal with the whole system, both the mechanical and the electronic bits. In any case, the skill is often in deciding what is wrong and replacing a whole circuit board or part rather than repairing the part or doing any re-wiring.

'Multi-skilling' tends to favour people with basic training in electrical/electronic engineering, partly because this is sharper on diagnostics, partly because it is easier to add mechanical-based skills to electronic training than vice versa.

RESEARCH, DEVELOPMENT AND DESIGN in industry employ multidisciplinary teams, which again vary in mix of discipline with the industry and/or the product and process/production method.

Designers in most sectors of manufacturing industry are mainly engineers, but teams are increasingly multi-disciplinary. Microprocessor control, of both products and processes/production, for example, brings more electronics, systems, software engineers into design teams which were made up almost entirely of mechanical and electrical engineers. Where the product is intended for the consumer markets (cars, domestic appliances etc), art-trained industrial/product designers may be brought into the team too.

The exceptions are, for instance, in the CLOTHING AND TEXTILE, FOOTWEAR, FURNITURE INDUSTRIES, where product design is largely art-based work, although these industries still employ engineers in production/process design. Both product and production/process design employ technicians, as eg draughtsmen/women. Mostly the work is engineering based, but some firms also employ art-trained technicians.

See also ACADEMIC AND VOCATIONAL STUDIES IN ENGINEERING, and ART AND DESIGN.

Research and development employ teams of engineers, technologists, scientists (mainly chemists, physicists and materials scientists), and mathematicians, the mix depending on the sector of industry. In CHEMICALS, for example, there are generally more scientists than engineers (especially as chemical plant development and design is mostly done by independent CHEMICAL ENGINEERING firms and consultants), but in much of manufacturing engineers make up the largest proportions.

R&D staff do not have to spend their entire working lives in R&D, but can move out into, eg production, or marketing.

See also ACADEMIC AND VOCATIONAL STUDIES IN ENGINEERING, and IN SCIENCE.

COMMERCIAL FUNCTIONS, MARKETING and SALES, MANAGEMENT SERVICES, FINANCE, PERSONNEL, and PURCHASING are all fully described elsewhere.

Recruitment and entry

Manufacturing industry, like many other sectors, is looking for progressively more brain and experience and needs much less simple physical strength. As we have seen, making a profit from manufacturing is much more difficult in today's competitive conditions, and takes people with the abilities to cope. Industry is automating, or should be (if it does not, there will not be jobs), and automated manufacturing also, generally, demands/uses more intelligence and less manual skill – hands will control keyboards, light pens and instrument panels, replace easily-damaged computer boards, rather than wield hammers or even screwdrivers.

Finally, traditional, 'metal bashing' heavy industry which needed so much physical strength, is declining proportionately. More sophisticated, high-technology, 'light' engineering products – needing a far lighter touch where hands are involved at all – will be made in future, and even heavy industry – eg steel – can increasingly control its production from a control panel.

Graduate/professional entry Manufacturing industry in the mid-1980s is looking for graduates with relevant degrees (or equivalent qualifications), and as much appropriate work experience as possible, both for production and for functions such as marketing. Shortages, especially of electronic engineers, have already developed, as expected, and are likely to get worse. Manufacturing companies have problems in recruiting the best graduates in the face of competition from, eg, banks.

Manufacturing industry recruited just over 11,900 new university and polytechnic graduates in 1985. Well over 45% were engineers, technologists, surveyors, almost 33% scientists (including mathematicians and computer scientists), and about 8% had degrees in business/management studies, accounting etc.

School-leaver entry School- (and college-) leavers are recruited at 16-, 17-, and 18-plus, for long-term career prospects with at least some reasonable passes, in eg English, maths, a science, at 16-plus†, and for some traineeships, with at least one A-level pass (or eg BTEC/SCOTVEC equivalent).

Recruitment, as measured by EITB figures, is still falling, and shows no sign of improvement. Firms in scope of EITB recruit most craft and technician trainees on to a common, YTS, scheme. Estimated apprentice recruitment for 1986-7 was 9490, which is very little up on the all-time low of just over 9000 in 1984-5. (The peak was some 28,000 in 1967 and even in 1975-7 it was still 24-25,000.) This is not even enough to replace 'natural wastage', even allowing for falling demand in future with changing technology. Of the 9490, only 6750 had contracts of employment, the other 2740 being YTS trainees without contracts, many of whom may not go on to modular training, so the fall in numbers may be worse than at first appears.

One result is that the proportion of technician apprentices is now estimated to be one third of apprentice recruitment for the first time. However, says EITB, at an estimated 3290 in 1986-7, this is well short of the 5-6000 needed each year to replace natural losses.

Apprentice redundancies have been falling steadily, but look to have increased slightly again in 1986-7, against the low of 93 in 1985-6 (almost 3000 lost their jobs in the peak year of 1980-1 and another 2500 went in the two years after that).

Qualifications and training

Manufacturing industry now (1987) has few statutory training boards – Engineering, Clothing, Plastics Processing – with the majority of sectors now developing and organising training under voluntary arrangements. Both statutory and voluntary training organisations have major problems to solve in the face of tight resources and falling numbers, yet a clear need to persuade firms that training is crucial to their futures.

Industry generally is aiming for greater flexibility in training, at all levels. Induction training introduces entrants to relevant aspects of the industrial environment. However fast traditional craft skills vanish from the manufacturing process itself, all trainees, from graduates through technician to craft, are encouraged to learn practically how to process materials and turn them into simple items, as part of basic training which is generally designed to provide, at the appropriate level, a broad appreciation of processes and practices both in industry in general and in the work of the particular sector. Objective training is designed to develop expertise in a particular job. Provision for 'continuing formation' or training of people at all skill levels is seen as increasingly crucial, to cope mainly with changing technology.

Most graduate/professional-level entrants are given preliminary training which introduces the business of the firm, and how it operates. They are then generally given training appropriate to a 'function', although this is mostly combined with doing a 'real' job – in production for example, it may be as a factory-floor foreman/woman. Training is generally geared to preparing young graduates for an appropriate professional qualification. In engineering, EITB reports 5754 first-appointment professional engineers receiving training in 1984-5, still falling from the peak of almost 7400 in 1980-1.

Craft and technician entrants are increasingly being trained to set standards, rather than on time-serving apprenticeships. In engineering, most sixteen- and seventeen-year-old school leavers are expected to complete the common first-year training, as part of a YTS scheme, before going on to modular craft, technician or technician engineer training. This does not, however, necessarily shorten significantly the time needed (three to five years) to train them, although greater flexibility is being built in which does let people complete training in shorter periods, and trainees are awarded certificates of craftsmanship on completing the minimum of two modules. Training schemes have for some time been broken down into 'modules', now the 'modules' are being further split into 'segments' – EITB has identified and specified 254 segment skills to date (1986), and CGLI schemes are changing to 'engineering competency courses'.

EITB trainees at craft level continue to work for CGLI qualifications as well. CGLI schemes are being revised with increasing frequency.

Basic engineering competences scheme (201), highlighting transferable competences, and including practical work to ensure a systematic approach to the solution of engineering problems, became generally available in 1986-7.

Three new level 2 schemes, to follow on from 201, were piloted in 1986-7, with general availability in 1987-8 –

Engineering systems maintenance competences (214) – recognises that modern maintenance has become a multi-disciplined activity, and aims to provide the needed diagnostic and corrective competences – ic core processes, eg cutting and joining, maintenance management and organisation; sub-systems competences eg pneumatic/hydraulic, electrical/electronic; maintained systems eg machine-tool, or factory service. It is intended to replace scheme 205 part II.

Mechanical production occupational competences (228) – aimed at production machinists and fitters, has a unified structure.

Fabrication and welding occupational competences (229) – unified scheme restoring an element of trade-related studies (in eg welding, sheet metal and thin plate technology, thick plate and structural technology, pipework.

Technicians and technician-engineers can gain a joint EITB/BTEC certificate if they complete an appropriate BTEC national or higher national award as well as EITB-approved training. College-based full-time courses increasingly meet EITB's basic technician-training recommendations.

MANUFACTURING SECTORS

Introduction	832
Biotechnology	833
Ceramics, glass and other mineral products	835
Chemical industries	841
Defence industries	845
Electrical, electronic and information technology industries	846
Energy production	853
Food and drink manufacturing	862
Mechanical engineering (machine manufacture)	867
Metal manufacture	870
Packaging	876
Paper-making	877
Plastics processing	880
Printing	882
Shipbuilding	887
Textiles, clothing and related industries	889
Timber and furniture	900
Vehicle manufacture	904

INTRODUCTION

Manufacturing industry is divided into sectors. Industry changes and develops with increasing rapidity. For instance, defence and information technology are two of the newer major and identifiable sectors of manufacturing. A changing industrial classification means comparisons with earlier years are not always possible.

This chapter describes the opportunities that each industry can now offer to people coming out of the education system. It also attempts to show what has been and is happening to each industry, some of the problems they face, and in learning how to live in a world of intensive and intensifying international competition. This is very relevant to anyone going into industry, for these are the changes and problems that will affect them directly in their work for the foreseeable future – the pressures to improve productivity, to accept changes in working patterns and practices, to learn new methods and work with new technology, to live with changing products and markets. The changes and problems affect all employees, from the youngest entrants, now starting perhaps as YTS trainees on standard-led training schemes rather than time-serving apprenticeships, through to the graduates coming into firms where dramatic change, raising output, identifying markets and customers and what they need more precisely, being firm on product strategy are the facts of life which must be managed with great efficiency and sophistication.

There are problems in describing manufacturing industries in the 1980s. Industries have changed, often dramatically, since 1979 and the changes are not fully documented. Detailed information about individual industries, especially information which is relevant to work and training, used to be kept by the industrial training boards, but voluntary organisations on tight budgets cannot do this. The remaining boards continue to show what is happening to their industries. One other useful source of information is the reports of the National Economic Development Council.

BIOTECHNOLOGY

Although biotechnology is often described as 'an' industry, it is in fact more about applying techniques which can be used by a wide span of existing industries, such as pharmaceuticals, food, agriculture and agro-chemicals, plastics, engineering, fuel and energy, waste treatment. Biotechnology can give them not just new products and processes, but can potentially offer replacement processes wherever synthetics are now used, or may be needed to replace natural resources.

No longer a dream for the future, biotechnology is already a hard, commercial business, worth an estimated £35,000 million in sales in 1985, and one study suggests a growth rate of 7% a year, for the rest of the century. The largest companies, especially in chemicals/pharmaceuticals, food etc, are heavily involved. Health care, closely followed by products for agriculture and 'synthetic' food, is likely to dominate well into the 1990s. Later are likely to come, eg development of new ways of treating wastes – especially the highly toxic ones, and replacing energy-intensive chemical processes. Biotechnology began with small-scale plant, making high-value products, but firms are expected to try to shift to increasingly larger plants for lower-value products at high production rates.

Genetically-engineered insulin is already improving treatment of diabetes, and a human-growth hormone is available for children who lack it. Examples of other health-care products being developed, or on doctors' list of priorities are simple, cheap tests and genetic 'probes' to diagnose heredity diseases, viral, bacterial and parasitic infections; infection-free blood products; better vaccines for eg whooping cough and measles; a cheap substitute for breast milk that is better for babies than cow's milk; drugs 'engineered' so that, eg tumours can be targeted accurately, and normal cells not damaged.

Genetically-engineered pure antibodies treat 'scours' in baby calves. Genetic engineering linked to plant tissue culture is having a major effect on crops of all kinds, and vegetables, tomatoes, fruit as well as wheat will all soon be 'designed' to meet consumer taste, ease of harvesting, packaging, and transport etc.

Companies are developing products such as –

    ecology-conscious insecticides which do not kill bees because dosage rates are 20-100 times less than for conventional chemicals, and they are physically less volatile;

(bio)polymers or plastics which are biodegradable, non-allergic, etc. using microbes which, when fed on starch, sugars or gases excrete long-chain molecules;

non-woven fabrics 'grown' from microfungal hyphae to make better simulated leather, filter fabrics, and materials for medical use (eg wet-wipes), fabrics with better wet-strength, flexural rigidity, abrasion resistance and tensile/tear strength;

biological methods of pest control which cost 1% of chemicals now used in forests;

microbes that 'eat' metals, eg lead, from the surface of precious metal catalysts, so they do not have to be expensively re-cycled.

Biotechnology takes huge, and long-term investment, and until low-cost products can be made in bulk, it will not be a major money-spinner – or major job creator. The lead time between discovery and full production is lengthy, many good ideas will not be commercially viable, and companies have a tough time surviving. International oil and chemical companies have already suffered badly once, when they tried to develop markets for single-cell protein products. The cattle feed produced (from bacterium grown on carbon from methanol), is 75% protein (10% richer than fish meal and contaminant free), but much more expensive. Firms need an early success, a cash 'flywheel' to survive and protect them against the near-inevitable crises. Costs are too high, and it is still hard to find products which can compete with more conventional ones. Biotechnology, said one commentator, demands very good science, an earthy business approach (and the ability to pick commercially-viable products), and enthusiastic marketing.

Efficient, and cost-effective techniques, of eg 'harvesting', and deciding on the best growing mediums, are crucial – and of course full-scale production is very different to producing materials in the lab. Getting new products and processes from the lab to commercial production means going through 'scale-up' in the same way as in CHEMICAL ENGINEERING, but with some rather different but just as difficult problems to solve. Success in the biotechnology business depends on perfecting separating (from nutrient broth and bacterial cells) and purification processes – cleaning up products after fermentation. Firms which can develop this process technology are as, if not more, likely to be profitable as the 'high profile' cloners.

Some 2-300 firms are believed (1986) to be involved in biotechnology. They range from major petrochemical, pharmaceutical and food conglomerates through the many 'new biotechnology firms' which specialise in cloning etc, the largest of which employ (1986) around 200 people. Some 'companies' are based on universities, but funded mainly by industrial contracts. Some larger, eg chemical, firms have had people working in what is now called biotechnology for many years, and have sizeable research teams. One firm also has 20 technologists and a specially-designed pilot plant to solve the problems of 'scaling-up' processes, amongst which are ensuring sterile conditions (which means cutting down on crany-filled valves etc). Some firms are contract research companies only, some do their own research and then go on to manufacture, or firms buy research from a contract research company or fund university-based research. Some very small firms specialise in making the biochemical materials, eg peptides, which researchers need. Another 'spin-off' area is making the highly-sophisticated, computer-based and automated equipment used right the way through the biotechnology business from research to production.

Employment in biotechnology There are no accurate, up-to-date figures on how many people are working in biotechnology, especially as biotechnology work may also be done as part of R&D under other names, and products may be manufactured as part of, eg 'normal' pharmaceutical output. However, SERC estimated 1500 or more at professional level – engineers and scientists – in 1984, and numbers have certainly increased since. The main disciplines then employed were biochemistry, microbiology, and (bio)chemical engineering. A further 250 people with biotechnology skills are believed to be working abroad.

Some attempts at projecting demand have been made, but much depends on the rate of development and investment. SERC is attempting to see that needs can be met, particularly in process development. However, most firms expect to need only one or two new highly-qualified people a year, a few of the largest perhaps ten or so. Of course any new ventures will recruit, but one lab closed early in 1986, and the 300 redundant staff took up many of the next year's vacancies.

In such a high-tech area, scientists and engineers are employed not only in basic R&D and other lab-based projects, but also to work on eg technical feasibility studies, market assessments, and business development. In other words they need to be both technically skilled and able to help 'commercialise' biotechnology.

While many managers are scientists/engineers too, the financial demands of the business, and the problems of marketing should give some employment for other high-calibre people.

Qualifications and training see ACADEMIC AND VOCATIONAL STUDIES IN SCIENCE.

CERAMICS, GLASS AND OTHER MINERAL PRODUCTS

Based on the ancient, traditionally clay-based industry, modern ceramics and related products form the second largest group of factory-produced engineering materials (see also MATERIALS SCIENCE AND TECHNOLOGY under ACADEMIC AND VOCATIONAL STUDIES IN SCIENCE).

The new industrial classification divides these into three main groups – building materials and abrasives, ceramic and refractory goods, glass and glassware. About 192,000 people work (1986) in the sector, only slightly down on 1983, but well below 1968's 350,000.

The number of jobs has fallen partly because of recession and intense competition, and in some parts of the sector, with automation. Some sectors – eg building materials and flat glass – were relatively straightforward to automate, while others, particularly ceramics, have found it far more difficult. All, though, have adopted sophisticated electrical/electronic systems.

Most industries in the sector are traditionally craft-based, with operatives and craft workers making up well over two thirds of all employees. Where plant is fully mechanised or automated, the numbers employed have fallen sharply.

Automation and other modern technologies generally mean that some other jobs become more technical, but the proportion of technicians employed is still relatively small. The proportion of scientists and technologists is also small.

BUILDING MATERIALS AND ABRASIVES Manufacture of most building materials is now highly mechanised, and in some sectors, fully automated. Economy of scale is a major feature, with a few, very large, firms in each sector.

Brick making is dominated by five firms, producing over 70% of output. Tied to peaks and troughs in the construction industry, firms have both rationalised hard and marketed bricks and traditional products aggressively to compete with materials like concrete and sheet glass. High fixed costs, rigid capacity, and steadily declining sales make it very difficult for management to avoid heavy stock building in the bad years.

Modern, continuous process, factories have replaced a high proportion of traditional brickyards. From preparation of raw clay through to firing, these are operated by centralised, push-button controls. Bricks etc, move from process to process, and through processes, such as firing, on or by automated conveyors, on mechanised 'cars', or on fork-lift trucks, so eliminating most heavy manual work.

Cement and cement product manufacture, also a continuous and closely-controlled, highly-automated process, is dominated by three firms. The industry now (1986) produces an average 13.4 million tonnes a year with just over 5000 production workers, against 17.5 million with nearly 15,000 twenty years ago. Also tied to the state of the construction industry, the industry faces a growing threat from cheap imports.

Limestone, chalk and clay (or power station ash) is crushed, turned into slurry, screened and mixed, fired in kilns to form clinker, ground and mixed. The whole process is controlled from a single, central, control room, and different grades and mixes can be produced easily to meet customer specifications. Production and maintenance is increasingly team work, with less and less demarcation between jobs. As large companies, cement manufacturers need efficient managerial and administrative staff, if only in small numbers. The industry employs only small numbers of technicians, scientists and technologists.

A wide range of products are made from pre-cast concrete, from floor, walling and roof units for industrialised building, through to street and garden 'furniture' (such as street light standards) to pipes and tiles. The firms involved are closely linked in to quarrying and concrete making on one side, and the construction industry on the other, and some firms have interests in at least one of these. Some firms are subsidiaries of large contractors, and may erect and mix their own products, or assemble multi-storey car-parks, for example. Production work is in several stages – moulding, mixing, metal reinforcing, mould assembly and filling, stripping and finishing, etc. – but only metal reinforcing is a specialised job. Pipes and tiles are mostly machine made, but some fittings may be hand made by craft workers. Cast stone (generally a concrete filling faced with reconstructed stone or coloured concrete) is made in much the same way as cast concrete, although the stone maker is probably more skilled than the concrete mould maker. The industry also employs draughtsmen/women to design, eg moulds. Civil and structural engineers are employed in design and production.

The abrasives industry shapes natural abrasives into grindstones, grinds natural and synthetic abrasives, coats cloth and paper with abrasives, and makes abrasive bonded wheels.

About half-a-dozen firms produce most of the output in natural abrasives. The industry is completely mechanised, so production employs mainly semi-skilled machine operators. Qualified engineers and technologists manage production, and work on design of, eg, special machinery. Research and development employs technologists and, eg chemists to work on adhesives.

Employment in the industry Numbers are down to around 95,000, from about 120,000 in 1979.

Plant in the sector can be operated with minimal numbers of operators and craft workers, who mainly control, maintain and repair plant, drive fork-lift trucks etc, although the largest brick maker still stacks them for firing by hand. The opportunities for, eg skilled moulders to hand make bricks etc are now very limited. Comparatively small numbers of technicians work in process control, quality assessment, developing/improving products and manufacturing systems, with and under a few hundred scientists, technologists, and engineers, who also manage the plants.

Managerial and administrative staff include sales and marketing people, reflecting the industry's need to promote products more efficiently.

CERAMIC AND REFRACTORY GOODS The familiar 'domestic' porcelain and china – the tableware, vases and ornaments made in bone china and earthenware – make up some 60% of output. Two firms produce most of the tableware. Ceramic tiles, sinks, baths, and 'sanitary ware' are also made for the home. But the industry also produces less expected things. It makes electrical accessories such as fuses, switch bases and sockets, a wide range of giant insulators for use in power stations and on pylons etc, in the electricity distribution network, and ceramic burners for the newest gas-fired industrial furnaces (cutting fuel costs by two-thirds). It produces pre-formed ceramic cores for aircraft components, porous ceramics for filtering and aerating, laser guides, artificial hip joints, tips for plough shares, sensors for boiler controls, and refractory moulds for precision casting work.

Ceramics are, moreover, predicted to be one of the materials of the future – car firms plan to replace many engine parts at present made of metal with ceramics, and a new ceramic alloy, sialon, is being used for cutting and welding. Lately ceramics have proved to be the best bet for superconducting materials which can work at normal temperatures, putting them in the lead to replace (amongst other things) silicon microchips in computers.

The industry always suffers disastrously from recession, and the early 1980s were no exception, with the real disaster in tableware. The number of factories operating fell to under 140 in 1982 from 180 in 1979.

Although a difficult industry to mechanise let alone automate, investment in new technology is being made. The potter's wheel is a fairly rare sight, but hand production is still common. Some products, eg glazed tiles, are now made on production lines which are now being automated, but generally it is still only possible to mechanise/automate some stages. Clay preparation has been automated for some time, and automated glazing machines are now being introduced. Products with fairly simple shapes – cups, saucers and plates – can be made on semi-automatic machines, although they still need skilled operators (and cup handles have to be put on separately), and some decorating can be partly automated too. Sophisticated electronic control systems, however, have been installed with the new gas- and electricity-fired kilns.

Things with more complicated shapes, though, from basins and sanitaryware to china figures, still have to be cast in moulds by hand.

Employment in the industry About 52,000 were working in ceramic and refractory manufacture in 1986.

The industry is still heavily labour-intensive, most people working in production, most as operatives. Most production staff generally work in one of the four main processes – making, firing, glazing and decorating, and warehousing and despatch. The skill content of the work varies from process to process. Larger companies usually have their own design departments, where trained designers create new 'shapes' – for cups, plates, bathroom ware, etc. – and/or new patterns for new or standard shapes. The modeller carves a solid clay or plaster model of any new shapes, and from this makes a set of master moulds, or cases. These are used by mouldmakers to make working moulds (they can only be used some 70-80 times so new ones are always needed), and this is one of the few skilled crafts.

In production, the clay is prepared semi-automatically, but supervised by, eg a trained slipmaker. The slipmaker assesses the quality of the clay and liquid slip, and has to see that the quantities of raw materials are exactly right, and that they are blended and filtered properly. Making the shapes involves either operating a machine and finishing the shape, or casting more complex pieces, removing them from the moulds and finishing by smoothing and eg punching bolt holes in sanitary ware. Things like ceramic bullet-proof vests are formed by 1000-ton presses.

When the basic shapes have been dried and checked for defects, they are fired, glazed, fired again, decorated, and fired yet again. In firing, mechanised and automated, trucks and trolleys move shapes automatically through continuous ovens. Even so, loading and unloading the kilns and operating the kiln controls is skilled work for kiln attendants, who must know what physical and chemical changes are involved in firing and what temperatures and times are needed. They work in shifts because kilns cannot be shut down overnight.

Glazing is done by either dipping or spraying. Some decorations are added before glazing, others after. While some decorations are put on by machines, some tableware is still hand-decorated (with gold bands, for example) and figures etc, have to be hand-painted, which is skilled work.

The industry employs a significant number of technologists, scientists and technicians, in technical and ceramic development, laboratory work, and quality control. Much R&D goes into improving processes and lower firing temperatures. The increasing amount of plant and machinery means employing electrical and mechanical engineering craft workers and technicians, both for maintenance and in designing new equipment. The industry expects to employ more electronic and systems engineers, able to cope with modern control systems.

Pottery firms traditionally employ only a relatively small number of administrative staff, but they face the same complex business problems as the rest of industry, and so now need people with greater expertise to cope with them. MARKETING/SALES, PURCHASING raw materials, ACCOUNTING etc are all involved. Most supervisory staff are promoted from within their own departments, and may go on to become managers, although some form of technical or professional qualification is normally needed.

Recruitment and entry The industry has been forced to rationalise throughout the 1980s, and recruitment is expected to be low for the immediate future.

Professional/graduate level firms need CERAMIC TECHNOLOGISTS, ENGINEERS, SCIENTISTS but recruit in very small numbers, although the major firms try to maintain a regular intake for long-term management development. Recruitment is with appropriate degrees – or A levels – for technological and administrative functions, and it is still common to work up through the industry.

Designers are normally recruited with a degree in ART AND DESIGN.

School-leavers with, typically, at least four O-level-equivalent passes are recruited for training in, eg modelling, technician-level/laboratory assistant work (sciences needed), and design assistant/decorating (16-plus† in art and appropriate aptitude).

Recruitment for commercial posts would also be at this level.

Good CSE-equivalent passes in maths and craft subjects are needed for craft training, as electricians, mechanical fitters, mouldmakers, and (kiln) bricklayers. No formal qualifications are needed to train as a caster, machine operator, or kiln attendant, but manual dexterity is. The industry has a small YTS scheme.

Qualifications and training The Ceramic Industry Training Association co-ordinates and advises on training in the industry.

Specialist technologists are trained mainly by Leeds and Sheffield Universities, and North Staffordshire Polytechnic.

For technicians, the Polytechnic also runs courses leading to BTEC awards, and these can be taken on a part-time basis while working in the industry.

Training is otherwise largely on the job, with release for study where formal qualifications, eg CGLI certificates for craft workers, BTEC awards for technicians and commercial staff, are involved. Operatives are given training lasting from a week to six months or more as needed.

Further information from the Ceramic Industry Training Association.

GLASS MANUFACTURE Glass is both a very traditional and a very modern, technological material. It still has many traditional uses – in windows, as bottles, jars, vases and glasses to drink from. It is extensively used in industrial plant, as lenses, and for scientific and laboratory work. Glass has become a cabling material, as optical fibre, for faster and more efficient telecommunication and data transmission. Controlled release glass – which dissolves in any fluid at a pre-determined rate – will deliver eg drugs and insecticides over a long period.

Recession, and tough competition from overseas brought major problems to the industry, as declining demand from eg car makers for windscreens, and breweries, has been compounded by eg high energy costs (over 21% of all costs) and increasing competition from the plastics industry for the bottle/

container market – making containers for food and drink accounts for about a third of all glass sales. The window-replacement market has been in better shape – but the £7 million plant making high-energy coated glass (which lets the sun's heat come through but also reflects heat back from inside), created only forty jobs.

To produce glass, raw materials, in the right quantities for the particular product, are mixed and then melted in very high-temperature furnaces until they vitrify. Furnaces range from large, continuous, automated melting tanks to small clay pots. The viscous glass is formed by casting, pressing, blowing, drawing (into fibres, sheets or tubes), extruding, rolling or floating. After forming it is annealed in a special oven. All window and mirror glass is drawn flat using a very sophisticated, modern process which involves 'floating' the viscous glass on a bed of liquid metal. Most bottles are blown by complex automated or semi-automated machines, turning out over 200-a minute, and electric light bulb envelopes are also produced this way at over 1000 a minute. Even stemmed drinking glasses can be made by a combination of machine blowing and pressing and, eg oven-to-table ware, washing machine windows, and some scientific glasses are now also produced on automated machines. Machines also make ampoules for the pharmaceutical industry, safety glass, and vacuum ware. Glass fibre is spun or drawn.

Glass is still 'blown' and hand pressed in the traditional way by craft workers, but only to make fine and ornamental products, lead-crystal table ware, special pieces for scientific use, and things like aircraft runway lights.

Employment in the industry Some 47,000 people were working in glass manufacture in 1985 (a large proportion for four firms), against about 68,000 in 1978-9. Numbers fell by 11% between 1968 and 1978, 25% between 1979 and 1983, and about 8% between 1983 and 1985.

A high, but falling proportion of employees are operatives. Traditionally they included batch mixers, furnace men, machine operators and setters, optical grinders, some hand-forming operatives, and inspectors. In large-scale production, though, the divisions between the separate jobs are going, and workers who look after mixing raw materials, melting and forming the glass are all becoming 'glassmaking operatives' or 'glass process workers'.

Craftworkers include glassformers, engravers and decorators, as well as maintenance (mechanical and electrical craft workers), and construction workers (bricklayers, masons, joiners etc.).

The industry employs a small but rising proportion of technicians, and just a few hundred scientists (including chemists) and technologists (glass and fuel) in research and development laboratories which have made major breakthroughs in new products and processes. Mechanical, and electrical/electronic (including control/instrument) engineers are also employed, mainly in production and developing even more sophisticated new machinery.

Firms making containers, such as bottles and jars, drinking glasses, or fine glass ware, have their own design departments, staffed by industrial designers and artists. Even bulk-produced bottles have to be carefully designed and re-designed if a customer wants to make changes. Distinctive appearance is not the only factor – the bottle or jar must hold a particular quantity of a product economically and in a way that doesn't damage it, it must be easy to fill with the product (normally automatically) and be tailored to the manufacturer's particular production line, packaging and transport facilities, and so on. It must be economic to make.

Recruitment and entry The industry recruits in quite small numbers.

For professional-level functions and management training, the larger manufacturers recruit graduates (50 in 1987 for the largest up from 40 in 1984 despite a massive fall in overall numbers) over a wide range of disciplines, but especially in science and engineering, any disciplines for administrative functions. Only the largest firm offers a small number of sponsorships to read mainly engineering.

School-leavers are recruited at all levels with a minimum of CSE-equivalent passes at 16-plus† preferably in science/engineering based subjects for trade and craft apprenticeships, good CSE grades for commercial work, but starting at higher levels for people with O-level-equivalents and A levels, for training as eg technicians and technician engineers.

Glass Training is the industry's YTS managing agent, and is committed to over 200 places a year on two-year schemes, mainly with larger manufacturers.

Qualifications and training Training is largely industry-based, via the voluntary training organisation, Glass Training Ltd.

Glass technology can be studied only on a degree course at Sheffield University. MATERIALS SCIENCE/TECHNOLOGY is an alternative, particularly for research. A degree in engineering – general, mechanical/production, electrical/electronic/systems – is a useful preparation for production and management. The largest firms provide training for entrants, meeting the requirements of the appropriate professional body.

(Scientific) glass blowing, making, processing, and decoration at craft/technician level is taught by few colleges (Braintree CFE, Dudley CT, Hounslow BC), and skilled workers are largely trained on-the-job. The British Society of Scientific Glassblowers has developed basic training courses and syllabus, and MSC is supporting a small number of training places.

A BTEC National Certificate in process technology (glass) started in 1986, with some 60-plus funded places, mostly on 'distance-learning' schemes.

Engineering craft and other workers are trained along EITB guidelines.

Further information from the Glass Manufacturers' Federation, or Glass Training Ltd.

THE CHEMICAL INDUSTRY

Chemicals are manufacturing industry's fifth largest sector. Much of what is made goes to other firms to be turned into something else, for instance, the oil-based 'feedstock' chemicals such as ethylene, propylene and benzyne, are made into solvents, plastics and synthetic resins, synthetic fibres and detergents. The industry produces chemicals such as oxygen and sulphuric acid and oxides which also go into fertilisers, and paint. Pharmaceuticals is part of the chemicals sector, making antibiotics, vaccines, anaesthetics, and many other drugs and medicines. The industry also makes cosmetics, perfumes, detergents and soap, dyes and pigments, polishes and glues, explosives and fireworks, weedkillers, pesticides, and disinfectants. Chemical and pharmaceutical companies are closely involved in BIOTECHNOLOGY.

Chemicals were the success story of British industry from the end of world war II until the early 1970s. Competition on an international scale has always been intense, though, and was met by investing heavily in progressively larger, more efficient, but hugely expensive plant which has to be run at full capacity on a twenty-four-hour basis to be profitable. The rate of technological change, in plant, process and feedstock has been huge, making much of the industry very capital intensive. Research and development are crucial to success.

In the late 1970s, demand stubbornly refused to meet predictions, and by 1981 recession brought real crisis to chemicals. Growth stopped altogether. Home customer demand collapsed as the recession knocked out traditional markets like textiles and vehicles, and competitiveness was lost, particularly against US companies. Over-capacity has been acute in some products and some sectors and plant, both in the UK, and on a European- and world-wide basis, closed.

The UK industry, however, has fought back, some companies with fairly spectacular success (but at a heavy price in jobs), despite predictions of contraction. As with steel, shipbuilding and vehicles, chemicals have had to cope with the 'migration' of 'commodity' chemical production from developed to developing countries. Saudi Arabia now has (but jointly with international companies), seven petrochemical plants, on stream, and will have 5% of world ethylene production by 1990. Other newly-industrialising countries – Brazil, South Korea and Taiwan – are developing their own petrochemical industries. Canada has become a major producer/exporter, and Scandinavian companies are operating more in Europe.

Chemicals has long been an international industry. Most large companies plan their production and marketing strategies globally, and locate major plants where they can most easily satisfy demand within broad markets, such as Western Europe, or the US. Major chemical producers co-operate by operating networks of plants, each making an assortment of products supplied on a supra-national basis to, for example, the whole European market, so allowing maximum use of plant capacity. Firms have 'rationalised' by swapping plants, so that fewer companies make each major petrochemical, and letting companies get out of product areas where they are weakest. Those staying in the particular market have had to 'grow' even larger to stay competitive.

The European, including the UK, industry has had to change strategy. Marketing and finance have to analyse markets, costs, and profits much more exactly, and they are now much more closely involved in decisions on what to produce, where and in what quantities. The industry cannot now depend on simply building new, ever-larger, more advanced plant to churn out commodity chemicals provided by R&D – no new massive petrochemical plants are planned for the foreseeable future except to replace old with more cost-effective capacity. Chemical companies have also turned to high value-added, specialist products which can give a profit on much smaller quantities (which means developing automated batch processing systems). The UK's largest chemical company expects to increase sales of 'speciality' and other high value-added products (including drugs) from the 50% of 1986 to some 66% by the year 2000, and to expand in other areas, eg health, food, home/domestic products, all at the expense of bulk chemicals, which in 1986 accounted for 33% of sales. This also means changing marketing strategy, to a consumer-, rather than a product- or industry-oriented, approach.

Despite deep trouble in agrochemicals and fertilisers, caused by agricultural overproduction, and with the help of cheaper feedstocks, and a lower pound, 1987 was looking good for the UK chemical industry. Investment was expected to be up – by £400 million on 1986's £1300 million, and predicted to rise by a further 6%, to £4390 million over 1987-9, although on this figure the UK share of chemical investment is down.

The UK chemical industry consists of over 1000 companies. They range in size from the five major internationals whose interests stretch across several chemical groups – from oil refineries and petrochemical plants, through to drug, paint and other consumer products, to quite small specialist companies. Few companies, except perhaps in pharmaceuticals or industrial gases, specialise narrowly, although competitive conditions have now forced companies to look carefully at their product base and concentrate on product areas in which they have market strength, economies of scale, or specific expertise. One major company, for example, has pulled out of fertilisers, because it does not have access to the cheapest feedstocks, another from polyethylene production because it has fallen behind in the technological race.

Pharmaceuticals is one of the strongest sectors of UK industry, although growth is expected to be slower than in the past. The UK is the fourth largest exporting country, and the base for about 12% of the huge sums spent worldwide on research and development (and predicted to stay that way). The 150-plus pharmaceutical firms account for about 17% of chemical industry sales, and 9% of exports. The small number of large companies (including several multinationals), though, produce most of the output.

The pharmaceutical industry expects to find answers to many of the world's most-difficult-to-cure diseases in the next ten years, and to improve the way many others are treated. But it has to spend more resources on research and development (more on the latter than the former today) than most other industries (except aerospace and electronics). It is taking on more difficult problems, and researching deep into living cells to find reasons for, and so solutions to, disease. It involves a lot more basic research than other industries do these days (with molecular biology and biotechnology increasingly providing the breakthroughs). Computers, plotting even the most complex molecular structures and displaying them three-dimensionally on screen, are helping researchers to 'target' new drugs. Even so one new drug can involve manufacturing and testing over 10,000 different substances. It takes more time, is more expensive (£540 million in 1985, over a third up on 1970), and needs ever more sophisticated methods and equipment. Taking ten to twelve years to develop, the cost of a new drug is astronomical. Only a small proportion of new discoveries ever come to the market – the odds against are about 10,000 to 1 – testing, trials and so on, see to that, but profitability has also to be predicted, and these days marketing takes a close look at potential products much earlier.

Employment in chemicals overall numbers have been falling steeply since 1979, and were down to under 340,000 by 1986. (Numbers were almost static, with productivity keeping pace with output, at around 430,000 from the mid 1960s until then.) Some sectors have increased numbers though – pharmaceuticals, for example, to over 82,500 in 1986 from 74,000 in 1980. Ominously, the UK's leading chemical/pharmaceutical company now employs more than twice as many people overseas as in Britain, increasing its overall number of jobs by 3000, but cutting UK employment further by 1400 in 1985-6.

With research and development so crucial to many sectors of the industry, a relatively high proportion of employees work in R&D – the figure is as high as 17% (14,200 people) in sectors like pharmaceuticals, and at similar levels in eg agrochemicals and specialised organics.

The industry employs a high proportion of scientists for R&D – mainly CHEMISTS, increasingly BIOCHEMISTS and COMPUTER EXPERTS, smaller numbers of other BIOLOGISTS, AGRICULTURAL SCIENTISTS, PHYSICISTS, and MATHEMATICIANS, and for sectors like pharmaceuticals and agrochemicals, PHARMACOLOGISTS, PHARMACISTS and MEDICAL SCIENTISTS (see also ACADEMIC AND VOCATIONAL STUDIES IN SCIENCE). Research is largely project team work, the number and 'mix' of scientists depending on the project – all chemists, or chemists plus biochemists or other biologists – with junior scientists and/or technical officers, and assistant technicians/lab assistants, working under a senior project leader for anything from six months to several years, looking for potential new products, ways of improving existing ones, and new ways of delivering drugs.

Research teams generally have support from others, eg biology, for testing the effects of new compounds. Development, in technical departments, takes the research scientists' new compound and works out how to turn it into a product which can be produced economically, how it should be done, from what raw materials, etc. In other labs, scientists and technicians test new processes and try to iron out problems in existing ones on small scale versions of the full chemical plant. (Actual design and construction of chemical plant is done by CHEMICAL ENGINEERS working for specialist construction companies.)

Professional/graduate ENGINEERS and SCIENTISTS manage production units, run quality control laboratories etc. In large, continuous process plant, producing eg basic commodity chemicals, plastics, fertilisers in very large quantities, the plant is largely automated, running twenty-four hours a day, seven days a week.

Plants are staffed by small (3-4 people) shift teams, each looking after one largish section, under a senior controller, and shift supervisor. Plant operators, under a plant controller who monitors the control room instrument panel for the section, check what is happening in the plant itself, take readings, make adjustments, take samples for testing, clean out pipes, shut down faulty equipment etc, but are largely there to cope on the rare occasions when there is a serious breakdown.

In firms which make, eg medicines, inks, paints, cosmetics, a continuous production line takes raw material through a series of automated processes, but some production – eg drugs – still has to use single machines – 'cookers', tablet-makers, blenders, making items in stages – and electro-mechanical methods, operated by semi-skilled workers. Bottles are filled with tablets, tubs with face creams, cans with paint, and the bottles etc, put into packages on production lines, again increasingly automated, but still employing operators in some places, if only to monitor output.

Mechanical, electrical and instrument craft workers maintain and service plants. The routine work of testing whatever is being produced in the plant is done by scientific/laboratory technicians, under a professional/graduate scientist.

In management/administration, the industry is a large employer of COMPUTING staff, and people trained in MANAGEMENT SERVICES (OPERATIONAL RESEARCH, O&M etc), as well of qualified people in all the functions described under COMMERCE. In some sectors, eg pharmaceuticals, selling employs people with qualifications in appropriate subjects, eg life sciences, even medical sciences. Firms also employ scientists (eg pharmacists in the pharmaceutical industry), in advising on and dealing with statutory product regulations.

Recruitment and entry The industry recruits at all ability and age levels. Generally low levels of recruitment have probably pushed up the quoted minimum entry requirements.

Professional/managerial level the industry is a graduate recruiter in all disciplines, with some emphasis on scientists and engineers (mainly chemical, but also mechanical, electrical/control), computer scientists and mathematicians, but numbers recruited are not extensive. Even the largest UK-based multinational recruits only 200 graduates in total each year (and has 5000-plus applications). The number of sponsorships to read for appropriate degrees (mainly in engineering), is comparatively small, although this could change.

Laboratory and office staff for career training are recruited at both 16- and 18-plus with at least three or four O-level-equivalent passes or at least two A levels, respectively. Computer staff, eg for training in programming, normally need two A levels.

Craft apprentices (in instrument, mechanical, electrical, fabrication and building trades) normally need at least three or four CSE-equivalent passes at 16-plus†.

Process operators are recruited only at 18-plus. Otherwise operatives generally do not need any formal qualifications at present, although the increasing sophistication of process control systems may mean that before long the industry has to recruit process control staff at a higher level.

Qualifications and training Training is carried out by individual firms.

Professional engineers and scientists normally read for degrees in appropriate subjects prior to entry, but they and other graduate entrants are generally given appropriate training for any relevant professional qualification, eg in accountancy. See also the relevant section(s) under ACADEMIC AND VOCATIONAL STUDIES.

Other entrants are normally given training appropriate to the work. This may be mainly on the job, combined with release to study for eg appropriate CGLI craft, or BTEC awards.

Further information from the Chemical Industry Association (Training Information Officer), and the Association of the British Pharmaceutical Industry.

DEFENCE INDUSTRIES

The conventional classification of manufacturing industry does not recognise defence as a class in its own right. But Britain's continuing commitment to defence, even with reduced expenditure, provides a large income for firms in many sectors of manufacturing industry. Some 45% of the defence budget (over £18,000 million in 1986-7), goes on equipment, stores, etc (and 55% of government spending on R&D goes on defence). A high (but falling) proportion on procurement is spent in the UK – 80% wholly from UK suppliers, and another 15% from UK/foreign joint ventures (this could rise to 30-40% by the mid-90s). UK firms are also taking a rising share of world markets again – 9% in 1985 against 7% the year before – and estimates suggest defence equipment made up about 3% of visible exports in 1986-7.

ELECTRONICS (guided missiles, radio, radar etc) now gains most from defence, an estimated 36% of expenditure. In terms of type of equipment, AEROSPACE (eg for Tornados, Harriers and weaponry), takes 35%, SHIPBUILDING/REPAIRING and other naval equipment 31%, tanks, armoured carriers and other VEHICLES 18%. The rest goes on eg petroleum products, ordnance – ammunition etc. Contracts extend to CONSTRUCTION, TELECOMMUNICATIONS, and the FOOTWEAR and CLOTHING industries (and FOOD AND DRINK of course).

The Ministry of Defence estimated not long ago that defence-equipment expenditure supports over 200,000 jobs, and exports another 120,000. But some indicators suggest this may not continue. The Ministry's defence procurement staff are imposing new-style contracts which must make firms increasingly cost conscious and in any case the budget is tightening; jobs have been lost in the naval dockyards and ordnance factories newly turned over to commercial managements. Some commentators also suggest that firms' dependence on public money and the way in which contracts are awarded prevents companies developing products which will sell in more mass markets, which may in the long run lose rather than save jobs.

ELECTRICAL AND ELECTRONIC ENGINEERING

These industries make products which generate and exploit electrical current. The main differences between them are the strength of the current normally handled – in electrical circuits the flow of electrons is usually millions of times higher than in electronic circuits – and the fact that electronic products, systems, assemblies and so on, use devices which can alter or modify the rate of flow of electrons in parts of the circuits while electrical systems do not. Modern technology does, of course, mean that more and more electrical, or electro-mechanical products, like telephone exchanges and equipment, are becoming electronic, so products move from one sector to the other.

The industry consists of a very diverse range of companies. A few very large firms manufacture goods and equipment in both the electrical and electronic sectors, but most specialise in other or the other, and many specialise in a fairly narrow range of products.

ELECTRICAL ENGINEERING divides into several sectors –

One makes all the heavy gear needed to generate electricity, for example the generators themselves and the switch gear, another makes insulated wires and cables (being replaced in telecommunications systems by optical cables), and a third less-and-less telegraph and telephone equipment, now becoming all-electronic. This part of the industry is very dependent on a very small number of customers, at present mainly the CEGB in this country and, since electricity use has not grown as once expected, the industry itself is now very slim. One firm dominates machinery making, and no more than nine produce a third of total output. Four firms make half the wires and cables.

Another sector makes 'white' goods, domestic appliances for the home – washing machines, irons and kettles, cookers, dish washers, fridges and free-zers, sewing machines, vacuum cleaners – all 'stable' products which have basically changed very little for some years.

The industry has been slow to innovate, but a widening range of more sophisti-cated kitchen equipment is being marketed – food processors, microwave ovens, coffee makers, etc, and eg washing machines and cookers now have microelectronic controls, designs have been up-dated, and production lines automated. Innovation, new features to attract customers, and 'styling' of domestic products, it is suggested, are increasingly important. The working parts of, eg washing machines and refrigerators are more or less standardised, and it is on appearance, convenience, even colour and fashion, and very sophisticated marketing, that many domestic goods now sell. Most European markets are saturated, growing at less than 3% a year and dependent on replacement sales. For some, eg small appliances, the domestic market may even be shrinking. Competition is increasingly between a small number of international giants, and the UK now (1987) has only one full-range British appliance company of any size, although internationals from other countries manufacture here.

Electrical engineering firms also make the electrical equipment for cars and planes, eg lamps and batteries. Here the industry faces the same competitive pressures and problems as other vehicle component makers. See VEHICLE MANUFACTURE.

The wide variety of products made by the industry means that production methods are equally varied, from the huge machining, fabricating and assem-bly workshops where heavy power generating equipment, such as transfor-mers, is made, through bench assembly of, eg batteries, to the production lines for eg domestic appliances and fluorescent lights. Often there is a mix of methods, eg both bench and track assembly, for different stages of the same product. While some stages are still not easy to automate, the industry con-stantly looks for improved production methods and lower costs. Where auto-mation is possible, firms have been and are installing up-to-date machinery and equipment, for both manufacture, and packing. But production is being speeded in many ways, under pressure of competition. One washing machine plant, for example, has automated its assembly lines, cutting the number of workers needed by nearly half, and yet making it possible to make 14 different variants at once. New plastics moulding machines cut the number of machines needed from 20 to six, and the number of operators from three or four to one.

Employment in the industry The statistical breakdown of numbers employed has changed, and official figures are not now given separately for this sector. EITB figures suggest a total of just over 240,000 for firms in scope (the great majority) in 1986 (against nearly 253,400 in 1984) employed in about 1800 establishments. This is not too far off the 275-280,000 people given in official statistics for the early 1980s, and the indications are of not so very large a fall in numbers recently, but after a steep drop since the late 1970s.

Professional/graduate engineers are employed in substantial numbers, mainly in design and production (but R&D activity is rather less than in electronics). The majority are obviously electrical engineers, but with a significant proportion of mechanical and production/manufacturing engineers, and a rising proportion of electronics/systems engineers especially where advanced computer-controlled manufacturing equipment is being installed. The industry employs few scientists as such, and very few of them do scientific work.

A high proportion of managers in the industry are engineers. MARKETING is either to industrial customers, which usually needs a technological background, or to retailers and domestic consumers, whose preferences have to be closely targeted. The domestic-appliance sector employs industrial designers.

Technician-level staff make up a relatively high and rising proportion of employees, although the numbers are probably only half of those in electronics (below). In terms of first jobs, an EITB study in the early 1980s showed newly-qualified technicians going into testing and quality assurance (17%), customer-related jobs (15%), production, including planning (12%), draughtsmanship and laboratory/technical work (8% each), and development/design (6%), but for 13% there were no technician posts available.

Manufacturing electrical equipment and goods employs a wide range of semi-skilled and skilled operators, assemblers etc, and craft workers, not just electricians, but mechanical and metals trades too, although demarcation between crafts is being eroded.

Recruitment and entry Like other sectors of engineering, the industry is short of skilled people.
Graduate/professional level the industry's main requirement is for electrical engineers, but with a rising proportion of electronic/systems engineers. Other engineers, mechanical/production and electrical, mathematicians, and computer scientists are also recruited. Most major electrical engineering companies offer sponsorships for school-leavers mainly to study electrical engineering, but also electronic/systems engineering, mechanical engineering, computer science, mathematics. Firms also recruit graduates regardless of discipline for commercial functions.
School-leavers are recruited for craft and technician training mainly via EITB-based schemes, taking some 23% of all first-year engineering technician trainees.

Qualifications and training Training follows EITB guidelines.
Professional/graduate a first degree in electrical, electronic, systems engineering is the most obvious choice, although the industry does need smaller numbers with degrees in mechanical and production engineering, computer science, mathematics etc. Pure sciences are less useful. Most major companies give extensive training for graduate entrants, both in-company (generally following both EITB guidelines and the requirements of appropriate professional bodies) and on postgraduate courses where needed.
Technician- and craft-level training generally follows EITB guidelines.
See also ACADEMIC AND VOCATIONAL STUDIES IN ENGINEERING etc.

Further information from the Engineering Careers Information Service.

THE ELECTRONICS INDUSTRY is a large, complex, innovative, high-risk area of manufacturing. It makes a vast range of different products, some completely new, only made possible by electronics, and some electronic versions of things which used to be controlled/operated mechanically and/or electrically.

The industry, as presently defined, is divided into a number of sectors, but the products it makes are increasingly being linked together, to make up the technological basis for INFORMATION TECHNOLOGY.

One sector makes computers – main-frames for large-scale data processing and scientific work, computers for use in control and automation systems in industry, large and small business systems, and pcs for users of all types.

Office equipment is increasingly electronic, and computer/microprocessor-based, and the market has been taken over from traditional office-equipment makers by computer- and communications-based companies, exploiting their technological and product advantages, although many of them are overseas firms. Products include fast, high-volume photocopiers, microfilm readers/printers, and also 'point of sale' terminals – electronic cash-registers, and computerised ticketing equipment. The communications sector makes 'capital goods' – public network switching and transmission equipment – all undergoing a major microprocessor- and fibre-optic-based technological revolution – for public telecommunications businesses, mainly British Telecom. It also makes end-user, terminal/subscriber equipment such as PABXs, telephones, teleprinters etc. Although the liberalisation of telephone sales, and the boom in cellular radio-phones has given the industry new opportunities, it is taking time to get into these markets, and imports are high. Another expanding market is radio communications equipment, radar, radio and sonar navigational aids for ships and aircraft, thermal imaging systems, alarms and signalling equipment, and systems/equipment for public broadcasting. Sophisticated electronic medical equipment – ultrasound scanners and patient monitoring systems – is another significant part of the capital goods sector. Simulators, for training eg jet pilots and nuclear-plant engineers, and for use in research, are another growth area for electronics. Government, especially for defence, and large public bodies and companies are major customers.

Scientific and industrial instruments and systems make up about 40% of the sector. Only some 40% of products count as electronic at present, but it is impossible to separate electronic and other output and in any case the proportion of equipment which can be called electronic is increasing all the time, eg in optical instrumentation. The market for automatic testing equipment, made possible by the microprocessor, is alone reputedly growing at 10% a year. Products include industrial and process measuring and control instruments, optical instruments, testing equipment (including ultrasonics), and analytical instruments. The main market for electronic instruments is in industrial production and research, and especially for electronics (particularly integrated circuit testing), chemicals, power, petroleum, metal and food manufacturers. About half the market for analytical instruments is in the medical field. Major growth areas are measuring and control instruments for automated systems, in developing automated testing equipment and advanced analytical instruments for medical diagnosis, pollution control, energy conservation, etc.

Electronic components, made both for the electronics industry itself and other industries, is a £2200 million market (1985). Divided into 'active' (ie they have a power supply), and 'passive' (they don't), the former include diodes, opto-electronic devices (eg lasers), integrated circuits, transducers etc; the latter are resistors, capacitors, switches etc.

Electronic consumer goods – television sets, videos, radios, cassette players and high-fidelity audio equipment – are made in Britain, but mass production is mainly by overseas firms manufacturing here or importing.

Some two-thirds of tradeable output is accounted for by a few large firms, including subsidiaries of foreign-owned multinationals. They mostly make a broad spread of products. But much of the industry is fragmented, with resources (financial, technical, human) too thinly spread. Most firms have concentrated on the domestic market, and particularly the public sector, both too small to sustain a large enough volume of production, and few firms have tried to develop internationally competitive products designed for volume world markets. To compete, the industry has to develop strategies based on identifying world markets, designing, engineering and marketing products to reduce costs while keeping up quality and reliability, according to the Electronics EDC. The EDC wants the industry to concentrate resources on information technology systems and their applications (mainly to 'pull through' innovative products), high-volume production of IT products by building on viewdata/teletext, radio communications (as part of IT), exploiting technical and commercial strengths arising from defence contracts (MoD is the industry's biggest single customer), developing core technologies.

The industry spends more on R&D than other industries (with the possible exceptions of pharmaceuticals and aerospace), but this is still not enough to match major international competitors. Innovating has to be a way of life for electronics, but the industry is being encouraged to concentrate more on key technologies likely to have the most widespread applications. They include increasing circuit capacity in very large scale integration (VLSI) on silicon 'chips'; developing new kinds of memory, such as magnetic bubble devices; signal processing; developing microwave devices; and developing transmission systems using optoelectronic technology. Increasing emphasis is now on producing integrated systems to control anything from a simple, single machine through to a nation-wide communication and data transmission network.

Despite the sector's success, there are fears for the future. Some of the UK's overseas competitors have been even more successful. British companies' share of OECD trade in capital equipment has been falling for ten years, and will fall more sharply in future unless the industry changes strategy, becomes more marketing oriented, looks for growth products, especially more standard or modular products rather than 'specials', and markets where it has strengths and a viable and sustainable share of world trade can be gained, so increasing volume sales to support the necessary R&D and marketing costs.

Having survived the worst years of recession reasonably well, with output rising by nearly 70 points between 1981 and 1985, production then peaked, with a significant downturn which only showed some improvement towards the end of 1986. Although the long term growth rate is forecast to be much higher than that for engineering as a whole (at an annual average of 3.5% up to 1990), imports have been rising sharply and this has been projected to go on increasing, to three times the 1984 level, at least until 1993. Behind a range of specific problems – the collapse of the home computer market, uncertainties in telecommunications equipment, tightening defence budgets and MoD cost-cutting exercises among them – analysts are concerned about fundamental and long-term difficulties. These are said to range from the ability of UK firms to compete in world markets, to the clear shortages of skilled staff.

Production of electronic equipment of all kinds starts with making (fabricating) component parts, goes on through assembling the parts into components, and then assembling the components into complete products. (Integrated circuits, conventionally called components, are now, with all the functions packed onto them, more like sub-systems or -assemblies.) Some of the work is straightforward and some, eg producing semiconductors, is very high technology, done in conditions more like a scientific laboratory than a factory (the process is highly automated, since the 1/2000th-of-a-millimetre lines which make up the circuits can only be drawn by a computer-controlled electron beam on glass and then printed on the silicon wafers using light optics). Boards are also tested automatically. Other parts are stamped, pressed, moulded, etc from metal, plastic, etc, and these processes too can be automated. Some parts of the assembly can be automated, some done on either automatically or manually on production lines, and some by bench assembly. Electronic products which use integrated circuits have progressively fewer and fewer parts, and so get simpler to assemble all the time.

Employment in the industry has fallen, despite the success of some sectors, to under 400,000 in 1986, from 565,000 in 1970. Just to maintain present levels of employment the industry needs to grow at 15% a year, which is unlikely. Greatly simplified products, and increasing automation will continue to affect employment. Only one person is needed to produce a System X telephone exchange for every twenty-six involved in making electro-mechanical ones.

The balance of skills needed by the industry is changing, generally to a higher proportion of higher-level abilities, and needing people equipped with a range of skills which can be applied to different products and can adapt to new processes. However, simplifying production may, in some sectors (eg telecommunications equipment), mean more semi-skilled work at the expense of skilled craft workers. Skill shortages are critical. The industry generally also expects to need a more flexible work force.

Manufacturing electronic equipment employs a wide range of semi-skilled and skilled operators and craft workers, including electricians, tool makers and toolroom fitters, machine-tool setters and setter operators, wiremen, fitters and fitter assemblers, instrument makers and mechanics, sheet-metal workers, maintenance fitters, and other mechanics.

Technician-level staff make up a relatively high and rising proportion of employees, with numbers probably double those of electrical engineering (above). In terms of first jobs, in 1980-1 most young technicians started in development and design of new circuits, systems and products (27%), in testing and quality assurance (either prototypes or in production)(15%), as service engineers (14%), in production itself (including planning)(13%), and in lab or technical work (4%), with only 2% becoming draughtsmen/women.

Professional/graduate staff make up a third of some of the most high-tech companies. Engineers are employed in substantial numbers, and more are likely to be needed. They work in research and development, design, production (including quality assurance and testing), engineering planning, contract work and technical marketing. The majority are obviously electronic engineers, but the industry needs a wide range of microwave, systems, software and design engineers, as many as possible with training/experience on both the hard- and software sides. The industry also employs some mechanical, production/manufacturing and electrical engineers. People with qualifications in computing, eg systems analysts, designers and programmers work in, eg design and on software supplied by computer/systems manufacturers. Some scientists, particularly people qualified in physics and physical electronics, computer science, or mathematics work mainly in R&D.

A high proportion of managers in the industry are engineers. MARKETING/SALES may be to industrial or business customers, both usually requiring an appropriate technological background, or to the domestic consumer, whose preferences will have to be more closely identified in future.

Recruitment and entry The industry is looking for people of the right calibre and skills at all levels.

Graduate/professional level the industry's main requirement is for electronic engineers whose degree courses have given them a sound, fundamental training (preferably hybrid, covering both 'hard' electronics and the 'soft' computer side) as the basis for further specialist training. The industry needs innovators who can take the industry into new product areas, high-fliers who will make senior managers, and more practical people who will organise new designs through production, marketing, etc, plan and organise quality control, and so on. Other engineers, mechanical/production and electrical, scientists (mainly physicists), mathematicians, and computer scientists are also recruited. Most major electronics companies offer sponsorships for school-leavers mainly to study electronic engineering, with a few places eg mechanical engineering, computer science, physics, mathematics. Some firms also recruit graduates regardless of discipline for commercial functions.

School-leaver recruitment, is for technician- and craft-level training. The industry takes some 23% of all first-year engineering technician trainees.

Qualifications and training follow EITB guidelines.

Professional/graduate level a first degree in electronic/systems engineering, information technology etc (for main stream opportunities) or physical electronics (mainly to work on devices) is the most obvious choice, although the industry does need smaller numbers with degrees in other engineering subjects, computer science, physics, mathematics etc, and is supporting a number of specially-designed courses at eg Bath and Brunel Universities. While there is demand for people with more specialist qualifications, in eg control or instrument engineering, it probably makes sense to start with a more broadly-based degree, and specialise later. Shortages could be great enough for firms to be prepared to take any graduate with a degree in a reasonably appropriate subject, eg physics, combined electrical/electronic engineering, computer science, for training in a specialised aspect of electronics, production etc. Most major companies provide extensive training for graduate entrants, both in-company (generally following both EITB guidelines and the requirements of appropriate professional bodies) and on postgraduate courses where needed.

Technician- and craft-level training are as under EMPLOYMENT IN MANUFACTURING.

See also QUALIFICATIONS AND CAREERS IN ENGINEERING etc.

Further information from the Engineering Careers Information Service.

ENERGY PRODUCTION
Introduction — electricity supply — the gas industry — the oil industry
Modern, developed, economies, and their (comparatively) high standard of living, grew as a result of, and have been underpinned by, a cheap and plentiful supply of energy, for everything from industrial power through transport to domestic heating. Until the 1973 oil crisis, cheap and plentiful energy was virtually taken for granted.

It is now fifteen years since that first oil crisis, and the energy business is yet again in a state of change, as oil prices plunge, although probably only temporarily. Energy use has not risen as was expected in the 1960s, mainly due to the recession which oil price rises helped to cause, and partly due to some conservation and better energy management. Predicting the future of the energy business, whether use will rise or fall and what structural changes there will be between the various sources, appears to be impossible even for experts, not least because political and environmental issues, particularly post-Chernobyl, are major factors.

But just for developing countries to industrialise and modernise, world demand for energy is expected to triple by the end of century. Demand in the UK, though, is not likely to return to 1979 levels until 1997 with an estimated growth rate of less than 1% a year. While oil prices collapsed in 1986, long-term they have to go on rising more sharply, perhaps doubling in real terms by the year 2000. Oil's share of world energy consumption is now (1987) down to about 35% (against 50% in 1979), and is expected to be down to 16% by 2000. While oil will have to go on being the main transport fuel for some time (despite Brazil's 'green gas'), it will be used for electricity production and by industry less and less, so proven reserves are now (1987) predicted to last well over forty years.

In the UK, oil still accounts for 35% of energy consumption, coal 32%, natural gas 25%, nuclear energy 6.7%, and hydro-electric power under 1%. Conservation, and more expert energy management, are supposed to be the main 'sources' of energy for the next twenty years. In the UK, the government is attempting to persuade users to 'save' the 20% of consumption which it estimates is wasted annually.

Research into alternative, renewable sources – from wind, wave, sun, dung – of energy continue, although it seems less urgent than in the crisis years of the 1970s, and the enormous investment involved may just not give a good enough return. Developing commercially-viable alternative sources is still some way off, although by the year 2000, wind power could be supplying up to a tenth of Britain's electricity, and combined heat and power (heating buildings with gas-powered engines which also operate generators) up to 5%. Pilot schemes to convert waste into methane using genetically-engineered microbes will generate about 3.5mw of electricity from the mid 1990s. 'Passive' solar power could save about 1% of generating capacity. Wave energy is likely to be still in the experimental stage, but two tidal barrages could generate about 5% of electricity. Synthetics, and energy sources developed by BIOTECHNOLOGY, could begin to meet liquid/gaseous needs early in the next century, earlier if oil prices rise more steeply than predicted.

Since energy is such an essential commodity, long-term opportunities in these industries must continue. But the number of jobs is predicted to go on falling as the utilities push for greater productivity and efficiency, through more automation and sophisticated control and monitoring systems, etc. The greatest job losses are likely to be in manual, semi-skilled and craft work. While there is unlikely to be any real increase in the number of skilled and professional level jobs, the proportion will certainly be higher, and the demands made of managers etc, more exacting.

THE COAL INDUSTRY Coal is a major source of energy, but it is predominantly a MINING industry.

ELECTRICITY SUPPLY The industry generates, transmits, distributes, and sells energy as electricity. Currently producing electricity mainly by converting coal and oil, the industry expects to become a major 'primary' producer through nuclear power, with nuclear output predicted to rise from some 20% of output in 1986-7 to 42% by 2020. Hydro-electric, pumped storage, and 'renewables' could make up 5% by then.

It is quite difficult to make electricity supply efficient and therefore profitable. Because electricity cannot be stored easily, and because it takes so long to build power stations, matching capacity to fluctuating demand is a major problem, especially as forecasting demand as accurately as good planning requires has so far proved nearly impossible. It is not economically viable to have very expensive generating capacity lying idle just in case demand rises unexpectedly. The £400 million power plant in North Wales, generating electricity by sending water from one reservoir to another down some 570 metres through generators in the heart of a mountain, is the first attempt to 'store' electricity. It can put electricity into the grid in seconds, and so help even out the peaks of demand.

In the early 1960s, CEGB greatly overestimated future demand, and the result was surplus capacity. Although consumption has recovered, estimates of future demand have been steadily cut back, and is now expected to need capacity of only 66GW in 2020, against the 1986 capacity of about 58GW (down from a peak of 62.5GW in 1980-1). Smaller, older and less efficient stations have been taken out of commission, to leave (1986) about 80 power stations, against over 250 not so long ago, and there will be even fewer in the 1990s. In 1986, five were being built, four nuclear, one coal. The aim is to give greater flexibility in the primary fuels used, making it possible to switch from one to another, as availability and price changes dictate. CEGB has to decide which fuel or fuels are likely to most reliable in terms of supply, cost, and safety, at the point where new capacity is needed, which may be decades ahead. Oil consumption is down from a peak of 14.1 million tonnes in 1973, to the technical minimum of 5.1 million in 1985-6. Despite the strike, coal remains the major source of fuel, and likely to stay so for the foreseeable future – consumption is edging up again to the peak of 80 million tonnes.

CEGB searches constantly for ways to economise, using a computer-based mathematical model of a turbine and boiler to test modifications to plant operation and design, for example. Large modern plant can be shut down when demand is low, and the costs of this have been halved. New rail wagons and handling techniques are steadily cutting the cost of moving coal.

The state-owned industry is divided into three. The Electricity Council co-ordinates and makes policy for the entire industry, and manages central services such as finance, industrial relations, and scientific/technological, economic and market research. The Central Electricity Board, the CEGB, is the 'manufacturer', generating electricity in power stations, and supplying it 'in bulk' through the national grid transmission system to the twelve area boards in England and Wales. The CEGB has designed, builds and maintains power stations and the national grid, and does some research into technological problems, but delegates this, with day-to-day control of output, to five regional authorities. In Scotland, generation is divided between the South of Scotland Board, and the North of Scotland Hydro-Electric Board, whose title indicates the rather different nature of its operations.

The area boards distribute electricity via their own networks to individual customers, decide on their own 'marketing' policy, especially to industry, and have shops selling cookers, heaters, etc. The London Board differs somewhat from the others, but in general each board serves 3-4 million customers, and is further divided into district administrative units, districts varying in size from under 20 to more than 1000 square miles.

Employment in the industry About 131,500 people worked in electricity supply in 1986, against a peak of 228,500 in 1967 (it took four people to generate and sell a GWh of electricity in 1949, only 0.62 of one person in 1986).
  The CEGB employs (1986) some 48,000 against a peak of 66,000 in 1975);
  The Electricity Council employs only 1250, slightly down on earlier years;
  The twelve areas boards employ under 82,200, down from nearly 94,000 in 1981.
The number of jobs, particularly in generation, is expected to go on falling as the number of individual power stations is cut, and CEGB particularly is tailoring its organisational structure to this change. Despite maximum use of redeployment and natural wastage, there have been redundancies as power stations close.

Nearly 17% of people in the industry are engineers, scientists, or technicians, well over 52% industrial workers, 29.5% executive, clerical, accounts, and barely 1% managerial and higher executive.

Professional engineers, mainly electrical engineers, some mechanicals, mostly work in the power stations.

Under 400 people are needed to run a power station. Under a charge engineer, who controls the power station plant, professional engineers work on shift teams – as desk engineers in the control room, on plant operation (in charge of shutting down, taking off, or putting on plant as needed to meet demand, reporting faults, etc), or in charge of maintenance teams.

Electrical engineers also look after maintenance of transmission lines, cables and transforming stations.

Systems operation engineers staff the national, regional and district control centres, where they see that the right amount of electricity is being generated, that the system is not being overloaded, and that the most economical plant is in use, maintaining voltage and frequency etc. They have to keep track of what is happening to the weather, popular TV programmes, and anything else that helps them to predict sudden changes in demand.

Electrical engineers also work in 'utilisation', negotiating and planning supplies with larger customers, such as industrial firms or hospitals, and evaluating both the technical and economic aspects and problems. They also look for ways to improve electricity use, and for new uses in, eg industrial processes, where they may work with engineers designing new factory plant, or heating/ventilating systems for buildings.

Teams of electrical, mechanical and civil engineers plan, develop, and supervise construction of new power stations, generating equipment, and transmission. CEGB engineers design new system control facilities (using CAD systems). Back-up teams of technician engineers include draughtsmen and women.

In research and development, engineers and scientists (with technicians), work in interdisciplinary teams.

Mostly this is on generation problems and better generating methods, on improving efficiency, and reducing environmental pollution. CEGB research has developed improved burners and operational techniques which let power stations use cheaper, but difficult-to-burn high-viscosity oils, for example. A computer program has been developed to improve scheduling of generating plant to meet variable demand. A new method of calculation can specify more accurately an AGR power station's maximum gas temperature, allowing reactors to operate more closely to their design limit, and so increasing output of one reactor by 10MW.

The central research laboratories have five divisions – electrical engineering, engineering sciences, physics, chemistry and materials – with a staff of over 1000, at least a third of them scientists and engineers. CEGB's nuclear research centre has a staff of about 70 research officers, and the engineering labs employ about 400, half of them qualified scientists and engineers. Regional scientific departments attached to CEGB's operation regions do some research, and plant investigations.

In power station laboratories, scientists – especially chemists – for example, monitor water/steam composition for impurities, and check on the quality of oil and coal supplies. Laboratory staff in nuclear power stations, normally physicists, check on safety and must see nuclear waste is safely disposed of.

Computer-based techniques are crucial to the industry. For example, CEGB's computing and information systems department develops large-scale engineering programs, for eg, on-line monitoring and control systems for individual power stations and the national grid, model plants and control systems for training simulators, do critical path analyses etc. for network-based resource allocation, pipework design and installation, and cabling. Project teams design and implement both applications and systems software, and modern techniques are being developed to ease the problems of an evolving generating/supply system. Other computing centres do support work (mostly data processing/commercial applications but also management and decision-making tools) for eg, production, engineering, finance, planning, personnel and scientific services, and work for power stations and transmission districts.

Technician-level work, includes eg support work etc, for professional engineers in power stations and design; draughting; developing and operating distribution networks, supervising industrial and craft workers, negotiating and planning customer supplies, working on ways of using electricity in new industrial processes.

Craft workers are employed in power stations and transmission districts. Some work on the mechanical side – with boilers, turbines, pumps, valves and so on – and others do electrical work – on generators and transformers, switchgear, and so on. Electrical fitters install transformers and switchgear in substations, and linesmen add new overhead lines, inspect, check and renew lines where needed. For the area boards, electricians, fitters, meter mechanics and cable jointers work on the distribution system, and connect or repair supply systems for customers. Meter mechanics and testers clean, overhaul, repair, adjust and test several thousand meters a year.

Administrative staff include accountants and accounts staff (fewer now the system is computer based), personnel staff, legal staff, people to look after and negotiate wayleaves for the transmission systems and manage estates, customer relations staff, sales people (mainly for area board shops), secretarial and clerical staff.

Promotion to senior posts and management (CEGB had only 680 in 1986, the area boards 520, and the Council only 120) is as far as possible from within the industry. Most senior managers are engineers. Industrial and craft workers are promoted on merit and qualification, and can reach quite senior and responsible positions.

Recruitment and entry The industry recruits right across the 16- to 21-plus age-range, and at all levels of school/higher and further qualification. However, recruitment is being kept to a tightly-controlled minimum, with existing staff being redeployed and/or retrained wherever possible.

Professional/graduate level CEGB recruits mainly electrical engineers with the emphasis on power or heavy-current (but also some electronic engineers in, eg developing the industry's own integrated telephone and data communication networks), mechanical, and nuclear engineers. CEGB also recruits computer scientists, mathematicians, statisticians, and physicists, with some emphasis on recruiting for computer work. Total nation-wide recruitment of engineering graduates (including HNDs) was only 51 in 1985-6. For 1987, at least three boards were not recruiting at all, and the rest in only very small numbers.

Engineering-technician recruitment has been very low recently. In 1985-6, only eight people were recruited for training, nation-wide, all at A-level, BTEC/SCOTVEC National or equivalent. Two draughtsman/women and five cartographic draughting trainees were recruited, post A-level.

Administrative staff In 1985-6, the industry recruited 23 accountancy trainees (including 13 graduates), 57 administrative trainees (32 graduates), 70 EDP staff (22 graduates), 170 clerical trainees in 1985-6.

Craft apprenticeships a good general education is needed, but no formal entry requirements set. Only 565 apprentices were recruited nationwide in 1985-6. The industry also operates a YTS scheme, but trainees are unlikely to get permanent jobs in generating at least, although some may be taken on in distribution etc.

Qualifications and training The industry trains extensively at all levels, and training schemes are regularly reviewed and updated.

In 1986, CEGB had 65 technical trainees (against 718 in 1977) and 700 apprentices (against 1477 in 1981), the area boards 67 technical trainees (against 561 in 1977) and 1344 apprentices (2470 in 1977) between them.

For professional-level work within the industry, it is usual now to complete an appropriate degree course (see ACADEMIC AND VOCATIONAL STUDIES IN ENGINEERING and IN SCIENCE) prior to entry (just four students were given scholarships for degree courses in 1985-6). CEGB provides a two-year professional engineering training scheme for new entrants.

Administrative-level training is provided in accountancy, EDP work, etc.

Technician and craft apprentices and trainees are trained within the industry, under established schemes.

CEGB has a special training programme for nuclear station staff, using simulators. The Board also runs retraining programmes – in shortage areas such as telecommunications, electrical protection and computing – at its own training centres, on the job, and with some external courses.

Further information from the Electricity Council (Education and Training Officer). Specifically on generation and transmission from any CEGB regional office, and on distribution, from any local area board.

THE GAS INDUSTRY Gas became a re-vitalised source of energy with the discovery of natural gas in the North Sea in the mid-1960s, although by then the industry had already used a great deal of initiative to modernise itself. As of 1987, British Gas gets all its supplies from offshore gas fields. Thirty years ago it made all the gas used in this country, and thirty years hence it will have to do so again – British Gas is already looking elsewhere for supplies when the UK's own offshore reserves decline in the 1990s (present estimates suggest North Sea reserves will last 25-40 years).

Gas supplies (1986) two-fifths of all energy (other than for transport) used in Britain (nearly double the 1973 figure), and 56% of the domestic market, all produced/delivered by state-owned British Gas (in theory British Gas now has to compete not only with other fuels, but with any other gas producer from the North Sea who chooses to enter the market for larger industrial and commercial customers but no producer has yet wanted to sell direct).

Like other energy producers, gas suffered from recession (and conservation measures), although not nearly as badly as some other industries, staying highly profitable, meeting all its financial targets, and financing new investment from its own resources. Sales picked up again in 1982-3, and have continued to rise to record levels, of 18,845 million therms in 1985-6 – against 5200 million in 1969-70, and 12,900 million in 1974-5 – on course for about 19,000 million therms in 1987-8, with half the increase coming from domestic sales, although industrial sales fell slightly in 1985-6.

Continuing expansion means huge investment – £3400 million over the five years 1983-8 (at 1982 prices). The Corporation is still searching and drilling for gas offshore, and the biggest single current development is the major Morecambe Bay field. The main transmission system round the country is being continuously extended, and compression stations and storage facilities added. Over 2000 miles of mains and 485,000 services a year are relaid mainly with less-leaky plastic pipes, using special, highly-efficient trenching equipment (developed by British Gas) including earth-boring moles.

British Gas has a central organisation to manage exploration, production and transmission, and research and development, and co-ordinate finance, engineering, marketing and personnel. The twelve regions operate semi-independently, dealing with day-to-day operations of, eg supplying gas, servicing, invoicing.

Employment in the industry British Gas achieved its massive increase in output and sales with a steadily declining work force (although numbers did increase over 1977-81), of just 89,700 in 1985-6. The main fall came as manufacturing plant was closed (137,000 were employed in 1949), but tight economic conditions has forced a further decline. Numbers employed overall will probably continue to fall.

Largest region is the north west, with about 11,100 employees, followed by North Thames (9200) and south eastern (9100), and smallest is Wales with under 4350.

The profile of the industry's workforce in the 1980s is quite different from earlier years –

The ratio of staff to manual grades was about 61: 39 in 1985-6, against 45: 78 in 1963-4.

In 1985-6 –

Customer services employed the largest numbers, some 26,000, 63% of them manual grades, against over 30,000 in 1976-7 (proportions similar).

Transmission and distribution employed 20,400 (still up from 16,700 in 1973-4 although falling from the 1980-2 peak of almost 25,000), over 58% of them manual workers.

Administration and general services accounted for just over 21,400 (down from a peak of 24,500 over 1980-2 but still up on 1973-4's 19,700), over 75% of them staff grades.

Customer accounting, using advanced computer systems, employed some 9000, all staff grades, against a peak of 12,400 in 1974-5.

Marketing and sales employed 8900 (against 11,700 in 1973 4), again mootly staff.

General engineering and production are down to 3400 (against 7600 in 1973-4), with only 600 manual workers in 1985-6 against 3700 in 1973-4.

Professional/graduate engineers – chemical, civil, mechanical, fuel, gas, electrical, electronic, communication and instrumentation – mostly work in (regional) distribution. They deal with planning, design, and supervision of construction, operation and maintenance of the thousands of miles of high-pressure pipelines, the coastal reception terminals, compressor stations, storage facilities etc.

They forecast and plan the overall engineering programme, work on developing new techniques, communications and instrumentation systems, including computer-controlled telemetry, and in quality assurance, safety etc.

Engineers run the technical consultancy service which designs and installs air-conditioning plant, tailor-made central heating systems, and large-scale heating systems for industry, as well as advising on energy conservation.

Headquarters engineers design, construct, commission and maintain all engineering plant and pipeline for the national transmission system and bringing gas ashore, and on gas storage (as liquid, or in salt caverns or exhausted offshore fields).

Some 850 engineers and scientists (physicists, chemists, mathematicians and computer scientists) work in research and development (total staff up lately, to about 1900) in one of five research stations, or the on-line inspection centre, with an annual budget of £70 million.

They work in small teams, mainly on specific and very practical problems. British Gas develops its own sophisticated on-line inspection equipment for pipes, including magnetic and electric wave inspection vehicles. A development centre is working on process plant to make gas from coal on a commercial scale now. The engineering research station works on improving pipeline materials, finding new ways of detecting gas, and repairing and controlling leaks. Microelectronic equipment is developed to control and measure gas pressures and flows more accurately and effectively, and to hunt out buried cables and pipes. Computer programs are developed for, eg complex network analysis and optimisation of compressor usage.

Another centre works on improving and developing ways of using gas, and gas appliances, especially on high-efficiency systems using eg heat pumps, and microelectronic control systems. Some more basic work at the central lab is divided between studying chemical, metallurgical and biological aspects of operations from exploration through to distribution; providing scientific analytical services; developing engineering software eg modelling systems such as production fields; basic work on combustion, chemical kinetics, catalysis etc.

Craft workers are employed on the gas pipelines, on installing and servicing equipment which controls gas pressure and flow. Some are service engineers, installing and repairing central heating systems, cookers, boilers, water heaters in homes and offices, and industrial plant.

In administration, British Gas employs a full range of professional and clerical/secretarial etc. support staff, in eg finance/accountancy, the relatively large marketing and sales force, management services (using O&M and OR to achieve optimum use of resources), planning, purchasing and supplies, personnel, public relations and legal departments.

Promotion is from within British Gas as far as possible.

Recruitment and entry British Gas recruits across the 16- to 21-plus age range, and at various levels of qualification.

Professional/graduate, British Gas both recruits new graduates, mainly for specific posts/traineeships, and sponsors students going on to degree courses (around 60 a year mainly in engineering and technology). Engineers are recruited for a wide range of functions, computer scientists and mathematicians/statisticians (a numerate subject is normally needed for management services), as well as graduates in any discipline for the administrative functions. Graduate intake was up again to about 150 by 1986-7 (against some 200 a year in the late 1970s) – engineers, for management services, including computer services (reflecting the importance of getting the sums, planning and projections etc, right), for marketing, sales and customer service.

O-level-equivalent and/or A levels People are mainly recruited for commercial functions, in quite small numbers.

Craft apprentices for training as service engineers and distribution craftworkers, are recruited with good CSE-equivalent passes at 16-plus† in English, mathematics and a science or practical subject, at 16 or 17.

British Gas has its own 'Youth Programme' which operates on 'similar lines' to YTS, but it remains a one-year scheme with, in 1985-6, British Gas providing 700 places.

Qualifications and training The industry trains at all levels.

Professional/graduate functions most entrants have appropriate degrees (see ACADEMIC AND VOCATIONAL STUDIES IN ENGINEERING etc) before entry, although British Gas sponsors some students. Entrants are given training appropriate to the function, and where necessary, are expected to study for professional qualifications (eg in accounting).

Apprenticeship training lasts three or four years including release to study for an appropriate CGLI certificate.

Further information from British Gas plc – graduate and scholarship from the personnel division, other from local offices (personnel department).

THE OIL INDUSTRY The industry only partly comes under energy supply, even though some 90% of refinery output (75.273 million tons in 1985), is converted into fuel of one kind or another (the rest is turned into raw material, feedstock, for the petrochemical industry, into lubricating oils, bitumen, etc).

Oil companies built their profitability on involvement in all aspects of oil production, right from exploration and crude oil production (see MINING etc) through to refining and transportation, marketing, research, and petrochemical production (see CHEMICAL INDUSTRY).

The future of the oil industry, and oil as a basis for fuels and energy, is full of uncertainties. While supplies for Britain are secure for the life-span of the North Sea fields (see MINING etc), oil output world-wide will before long decline, and use of oil will probably have to be progressively concentrated in premium uses like road transport where economic replacement fuels are more difficult to find. On present estimates, though, the oil industry will survive well into the next century. Europe-wide, the refining industry has been suffering severe overcapacity for some time (80 refineries were closed over 1975-85). The UK's thirteen refineries (down nine on 1973) have been working at only

80% of capacity lately, even though this is only 65% of 1973 capacity. The recent (1986) slump in oil prices has made the problems worse.

Employment in the industry Oil refining is a highly-automated process. A typical refinery employs no more than 750 people, although distribution, marketing etc, even excluding exploration and crude production, employ many more.

Oil refining is basically a CHEMICAL ENGINEERING process, and the same types of technologies and qualified people are employed in, for example, process design and supervision, technological control and development, laboratory and pilot-plant research, construction project work and maintenance, instrument engineering, and engineering research. Chemists, chemical and mechanical engineers, instrument engineers, some electrical engineers, physicists and metallurgists/materials scientists, and supporting technicians and operators, work in testing and quality control, plant control (and automated systems), development and processing, maintenance, instrumentation and safety.

Marketing and distributing petroleum products is a very complex operation, and can be extremely competitive. Oil companies employ graduates, including engineers and scientists, in administration, distribution, marketing, personnel, planning and technical services, economic forecasting and market research.

Further information from the Institute of Petroleum.

FOOD AND DRINK MANUFACTURING
One of the largest manufacturing industries, it makes a wide range of products – bread and biscuits, chocolates and other sweets, sausages and pies, milk and milk products, canned, frozen and dried fruit and vegetables, soups, sugars and jams, orange squash and beer, savoury snacks and potato crisps.

The industry is highly rationalised and streamlined. Production is mostly concentrated in a few large 'conglomerate' companies, many of whom diversified out of fairly narrow, craft-based specialities – bread, sausages, flour, fish, chocolates. About 80% of beer comes from just six brewery firms; two biscuit firms account for some 60% of branded products, and they also make around half of all snack foods (crisps and nuts); two companies produce 70% of soft drinks; two make most of the wholesaled bread, one makes half of all canned soups (and 40% of baked beans), and six have some 80% of frozen food output. However, the industry also has over 5000 small firms, including about sixty local or regional, and 100 small independent breweries.

For years the industry has been squeezed between rising produce prices and operating costs on one hand, and increasingly aggressive supermarkets, locked in a discount war with each other. People actually eat less every year. Food manufacturers are having to fight harder for sales.

In a static market, manufacturers' success depends more and more on clever marketing, on being able to spot a trend in food sales, and react to it faster than competitors, as well as constantly improving productivity and efficiency. Retailers, with their stock control linked to the electronic cash register are now 'product' managing more efficiently. They can detect slow-moving lines rapidly, and so de-list them even faster, but manufacturers at least get better and more sophisticated market information. Consumers are less and less interested in a 'standard' product and want increasing variety.

The food industry has responded sharply to consumer demand for 'healthy' high-fibre, low-salt, sugar- and fat-free and better-quality, as well as more 'convenience', foods. Signs are (1986) that families who can afford to are actually spending more on food again – after a decade of falling expenditure – with less being spent on red meats, white bread, dairy products, fats etc. More than 300 new 'frozen-food' products were launched in 1986, including nearly 100 ready meals. But the population is no longer rising – so the market is about static – and UK consumers are generally getting as much to eat as they need, so significant overall growth in demand is unlikely.

Diversification, for food and drink firms, also means 'vertical integration', to increase efficiency as well as profits. Larger brewers, for example, are just as much pub operators and even hoteliers and caterers, as beer makers. Canning and frozen food firms invest heavily in, for instance, harvesting machinery for their producers, and employ people to help improve growers' productivity. All stages of milk production, from the farm right through to customer deliveries, are closely integrated, with the co-operative Milk Marketing Board not only acting as wholesaler and processor, but also manufacturing dairy products (butter, cheese etc) too on a large scale (the Board also runs an artificial insemination service, owning 1000 bulls, and runs a computer-based farm management service).

International trade in manufactured food is, traditionally, not very large, but is increasing, although given, eg transport costs, food and drink companies more usually set up – or buy into firms – close to local markets overseas than try to export, and some have bought European and US companies. UK food exports of manufactured foods and soft drinks have been rising, especially to Europe, and imports falling, but performance is still not good compared to that of the French, Dutch and West Germans, and even a small increase in imports of some items threatens UK manufacturers' profitability.

The food and drink industry is a highly competitive, technologically-based industry. Scientific techniques have always had a part in producing food and drink – beer and bread, for example. Scientific and technological develop-ments have been extensively exploited – from large-scale processing and preservation, especially of frozen and other convenience foods, through to modern packaging materials, although ideas for new products which will attract customers are as important now.

The industry uses all the latest production methods, including automated production lines, for economies of scale. It took 126 hours to produce a tonne of biscuits in 1959. By 1982, this was down to 25 hours, and the most advanced plant can now do it in two. The limits of large-scale production have, though, probably been reached. The major bread makers have plant which is only cost-effective if it is working at over 80% of capacity – and 'standard' loaf consumption is still falling. However, food manufacturers can go over – if they can find the necessary investment – to new technology which will give them batch production lines even more efficient than existing continuous lines, with 'intelligent' robots etc which can be re-programmed rapidly to allow frequent line change-overs and let them produce several different kinds of bread (for example) on one line. New computer systems give ever more accurate weighing (a legal requirement) and packaging equipment, and sensors monitor, eg temperature, humidity, speed, colour, on the production line. New technology also allows firms effectively to automate the remaining 'inefficient' aspects of existing lines, eg in final decoration and packing.

Cost saving, using technology where possible, is also a major preoccupation. Pies can be filled more economically using modern hydraulic delivery systems. Brewers use 20% less energy for beer making in 1986 than they did in 1978, and have automated keg and bottle washing, racking, and handling plant.

The largest firms are also investing in BIOTECHNOLOGY, eg producing mycoprotein from plant starch as a fibrous edible fungus which can be used to make palatable imitations of eg chicken, veal etc.

Employment in the industry Numbers employed fell to a low of under 540,000 in 1986. The trend continues downwards as automation and other technological changes cut the need for people. In some sectors, though, automation has already cut staff levels in production to a near-irreducible minimum – brewing has been static at about 50-55,000 for a while (but down from 71,000 in 1971). The problems caused by eg EEC milk quotas, have also meant some redundancies, especially amongst dairy firms (1000 alone in the Milk Marketing Board subsidiary over 1985-6). Only a near-impossible growth in demand for food and drink, including improved market shares for UK firms can offset the impact of technology on numbers employed.

Already highly-automated (it is one of the largest microelectronics users in production), manufacturing and processing food and drink products, employs fewer and fewer people. A rising proportion of work in production (including packaging) is in process control, and in quality control and inspection – in an industry where not only consistently high quality and 'freshness' but also absolute hygiene and cleanliness are essential. Many processes, even in the most modern continuous-process plant, are complex and need very accurate measurement and control of operation (cheesemaking is one such). Many processes involve meticulously sterilising both the product (or raw/intermediate material) and the equipment, which has to be thoroughly cleaned regularly.

Plant or process workers, under process-plant supervisors, look after and control the production lines/process plant, increasingly mainly watching for problems, checking that instruments are reading correctly and adjusting controls where necessary. Fewer and fewer people actually have their hands on the food or drink as it is mixed, flavoured, shaped, cooked, decorated and packaged or bottled.

Technicians and other control staff carry out the frequent quality tests and checks – of moisture and salt content in butter for instance – to make sure raw materials meet requirements, and to see items are bacteria free, for example – and provide the controls and figures needed by both operatives and management.

What goes into the food and drink, and how products are mixed and made, is largely controlled by FOOD SCIENTISTS AND TECHNOLOGISTS. Some industries have, though, traditionally have their own specialists – for example, beer-making is controlled by qualified technical brewers who ensure consistency and quality of the product however the raw materials, such as hops and barley, may vary from batch to batch, and 'trouble shoot' when process operators have problems they cannot solve.

Not every firm is fully automated, or is likely to be, and many smaller firms cater for people who want their food and drink produced in more traditional ways. A growing number of independent and small brewers make 'real ale'. While traditional 'corner shop' bakeries still fight for survival, in-store and fresh-baked-bread stores are doing well. Some dairy firms still make, eg butter, cheese, yoghurt in traditional ways. Opportunities still exist, therefore, to become craft-based bakers, brewers, butter- and cheesemakers, etc.

Production employs engineers. Designing, developing and implementing new high-technology process plant has extended the range of disciplines needed, and further increased the numbers of chemical/process engineers, systems designers, electronic engineers with systems design/instrumentation, in addition to the mechanical and electrical engineers traditionally employed. Maintenance teams look after the machinery and equipment.

Experimental and control laboratories, and kitchens, back production. Here new products, from health foods and exotic-looking ice-cream deserts to chocolate bars and soups, are developed. FOOD SCIENTISTS AND TECHNOLOGISTS, CHEMISTS, MICROBIOLOGISTS, DIETITIANS, some AGRICULTURAL SCIENTISTS etc (supported by LABORATORY TECHNICIANS), find ways of exploiting new ideas from agriculture, horticulture and fishing, from ingenious meat products made from year-round turkey production to uses for rainbow trout and salmon, coming out of fish farms in large quantities and so no longer a luxury food.

They take account of feedback (via marketing) of new consumer preferences, in creating or modifying products which are, for example, more 'natural' or have greater fibre content.

They devise, with marketing, new snacks and easy-to-serve meals that will attract busy, working mothers and children always keen on something different.

They work on more economic production methods, or try to get consistencies that are more easily handled by automated machinery, or find ways of making packaging easier and cheaper (for example, to use plastic bottles for beer a coating had to be devised to prevent oxygen seeping in).

Food researchers do some work on, eg nutritional values, supervise and devise new tests for quality and other control systems, and work with the agricultural and horticultural industry in improving output, developing new crops, or crops which are better geared to what the consumer wants and/or to modern processing methods. They may do research which is primarily agricultural, eg cocoa manufacturers are funding research into new cocoa varieties and diseases which threaten crops.

A few larger firms have more advanced experimental units, working on the possibilities of exploiting BIOTECHNOLOGY in making new or replacement/ cheaper food products. Brewers are already genetically 'engineering' their yeasts, however, 'constructing' industrial strains to improve fermenting efficiency, give better control over flavour, for example.

PURCHASING, for the food/drink industry is a skilled business. Fresh produce, meat, and other raw materials have to be bought, in the right quantities, at the cheapest possible price consistent with quality etc from farmers, growers, producers, often world wide. The quantities involved may be very large. Buyers must plan, and watch out for problems, eg alternative sources if poor harvests look possible. Food manufacturers often negotiate contracts well ahead and supervise production closely. They also have to buy all the materials and bottles, film, cartons, foil, cans, and jars, labels etc, used in packaging food.

MARKETING, including merchandising, planning and scheduling distribution, and sales, particularly where it involves highly-competitive selling to major supermarkets and chains, is crucial to profitability in food manufacture. Large food manufacturers have highly sophisticated marketing departments.

DISTRIBUTION/TRANSPORT take increasingly sophisticated management in. Food and drink is bulky, and products like beer, frozen food etc., need special handling. Organisations like the Milk Marketing Board, with all the problems of collecting vast quantities of milk daily from thousands of farmers by over 1000 tankers have highly-sophisticated transport departments. Firms look to computer-based systems to give better scheduling, route-planning etc. Drivers, etc, are obviously employed in some numbers. In some sectors drivers are also sales staff, with their own retail outlets to service on a regular basis. See also TRANSPORT.

Recruitment and entry Long-term, career opportunities in the industry are largely restricted to (reasonably) well-qualified school-leavers, graduates and technologists, and people already professionally qualified, with not many opportunities for unskilled people or school-leavers with few qualifications. The industry has, so far (1987), not suffered from skill shortages, and appears to be able to recruit the people it needs.

Professional-level functions, in both research, product and process development, production control, plant engineering, ingredients technology, and in production supervision/management, purchasing, marketing (including market research), and management services, the industry recruits in quite small numbers, but across a broad spectrum of disciplines, including FOOD SCIENTISTS AND TECHNOLOGISTS; SCIENTISTS including CHEMISTS, BIOCHEMISTS and MICRO-BIOLOGISTS (some for conversion into eg BREWING SCIENTISTS), and some AGRICULTURAL and VETERINARY SCIENTISTS; ENGINEERS (CHEMICAL/PROCESSING, CONTROL, SYSTEMS, INSTRUMENT, ELECTRICAL AND ELECTRONIC, and MECHANICAL). Scientists (mainly BIOCHEMISTS etc) are recruited to train as technical brewers. COMPUTER SCIENTISTS, ECONOMICS, STATISTICIANS are recruited in small numbers etc. For administrative work, graduates with degrees in any subjects are recruited.

Technician-level, for training, generally at least a reasonable number of O-level-equivalent passes at 16-plus including some sciences, but many entrants probably have A levels.

Craft-level trainees are recruited mainly for training in engineering skills. YTS schemes are organised by a number of companies.

Qualifications and training Training is fragmented between sectors, with each sector having its own voluntary organisation. Training is provided mainly by the larger groups and firms.

Professional level most people gain appropriate degrees pre entry (see above and ACADEMIC AND VOCATIONAL STUDIES IN ENGINEERING AND TECHNOLOGY, and in SCIENCE). Particularly relevant are FOOD SCIENCE/TECHNOLOGY, and BREWING (the Institute of Brewing provides a professional qualification for graduates and post-A level entrants).

Few sponsorships are available, although some firms give scientists postgraduate training in eg brewing, meat science, dairy science or technology. It is possible for science graduates to take postgraduate 'conversion' courses to qualify in food science, technology, engineering etc.

Technician level emphasis increasingly on science-based technician training, at the expense of traditional craft skills. Training is mainly on the job with release to study for, eg BTEC awards in FOOD TECHNOLOGY, or in SCIENCES or the new process-industry scheme – both can be oriented to the food industry.

Craft-level While it is still just about possible to train in eg breadmaking and flour confectionery, flour milling, meat trades, and dairy work, firms mainly train now in engineering crafts, on EITB-designed schemes with release to study for CGLI certificates.

Further information from the Food Manufacturers' Council for Industrial Training, the Institute of Brewing.

INSTRUMENT MANUFACTURE

Instruments are the precision tools used in scientific laboratories, the measuring and control systems used in industry, the surgeon's tools, watches and clocks of all kinds, and photographic equipment. The industry's products are almost all ideal candidates for electronic, microprocessor control, especially industrial control systems, automatic testing equipment, and medical instruments (for monitoring patients in intensive care, for example), and most new watches and clocks are digitally controlled. As a result, at least 40% of products now count as electronic, and the sector is rapidly on its way to joining the capital equipment sector of ELECTRONICS.

MECHANICAL ENGINEERING (MACHINE MANUFACTURE)

This is manufacturing's largest sector, second largest in output and still the largest group of employers, making a vast range of non-electrical machinery. Much of what it makes is very traditional – cranes and pile drivers, steam-raising boilers, industrial pumps and compressors, nuts and bolts ('industrial fasteners'), pumps, ball bearings, chains, agricultural machinery, textile machinery, paper-making machines, machinery for packaging and bottling, and metal-cutting machine tools.

However, more and more is very modern, eg crop harvesters and automated revolving milking parlours, big earth moving equipment, escalators, air-conditioning plant, and office equipment. The industry is now developing and making a growing range of computer-based, microelectronically-controlled machinery — numerically controlled machine tools, automated conveyor systems and production lines (for, eg the auto industry) and 'flexible manufacturing systems', robots, sophisticated coal-cutting and face-loading machinery, machinery for under-ocean mining, for example.

Because so much of the equipment the industry makes is bought by other industries (an estimated two-thirds of all orders count as capital expenditure), mechanical engineering suffers greatly from recession, and from the fact that demand for its products is never evenly spread, but comes all together when other industries see better times ahead. It is also highly dependent on exports which still make up 40% of total sales – more in some sectors, eg 65-66% for both agricultural and textile machinery. With problems in British mining, the mining machinery firms have had to boost exports from the traditional 50% to 80% to survive.

The 1980s' recession resulted in near disaster for some sectors. Most, though, have fought back – through 'prudent' financing (negotiating good progress payments from customers), high-quality production, a clear product strategy based on specialisation, and alert management. Recovery started for most sectors in 1984 – although the special problems of agriculture continued to affect agricultural machinery – and the industry as a whole increased output by 6% in 1985. Growth was slower in 1986, and the outlook is for a continued slow improvement, perhaps by 1.5% a year up to 1990. Some sectors still suffer from over-capacity, however, and the oil-price slump did not help, since eg rig-building has virtually stopped and other oil-producing countries are the industry's main customers.

Not all the machinery produced by the industry is dramatically affected by technological change, but for many sectors a second or third technological revolution is upon them. For example, the market for individual machine tools is being cut dramatically by integrated and automated systems for whole processes and even factories (as now used in eg volume car production) which incorporate all the individual machine tools which can both do a number of different operations and can be re-programmed and re-tooled automatically. Traditional machine-tool manufacturers found it difficult to survive the earlier technological wave of computer numerically controlled (CNC) machine tools. Over half the cost of such fully flexible manufacturing systems (FMS) goes on computer-related products and systems, in which traditional machine tool manufacturers have little expertise. The shape of the industry supplying factories with equipment is therefore likely to change over the rest of the 1980s, especially as leading electronic firms have moved into the field (see ELECTRONICS).

Although R&D investment is relatively low, expenditure has had to increase, largely because firms now have to invest in new, technologically-sophisticated products and production methods, just to survive. In machine tools, for example, the industry's research association, MITRA, has increased its income.

The wide variety of products made by the industry means that production methods are equally varied, from machining, fabricating and assembly workshops where eg factory machinery, is made, through bench assembly of, eg components, to the fully-automated production lines for eg nuts and bolts. Often there is a mix of methods, eg both bench and track assembly, for different stages of the same product. While many stages cannot be automated very easily, the industry constantly looks for improved production methods and lower costs. Where automation is possible, firms have been and are installing up-to-date machinery and equipment, for both manufacture and packing. But production is also being speeded in many other ways too, under pressure of competition.

Employment in the industry has been falling steadily for many years, and by late 1986 was down to under 720,000, against 1.25 million in 1968.

The industry traditionally employs a relatively large proportion of skilled craft workers in all the mechanical engineering trades – fabrication and sheet-metal workers, millers, grinders, turners, platers, welders, machine-tool setters, tool-makers, fitters, electricians, and maintenance engineers. There is apparently no up-to-date information on how far these traditional divisions are breaking down in mechanical engineering.

A rising proportion of people have technician-level qualifications. In machinery manufacture, of the technicians going into their first jobs in 1980-1, 33% became draughtsmen/women, 14% went into servicing and other customer or supplier related work, 10% went into production (including planning, scheduling, estimating), 6% into central service jobs, 5% into test and quality assurance, and 4% into each of laboratory or technical work and development/design. For 16% no technician jobs were available. The breakdown is slightly different for 'other' mechanical engineering – 25% became draughtsmen/women, 16% went into test and quality assurance work, 16% into production planning and 12% into other production work, 7% into central service type jobs, and only 2% into each of development/design and laboratory/technical work. There were no posts for only 6%.

Most of the professionals, who work mainly in production and other managerial functions, are engineers, mostly mechanicals, some electrical, with a rising proportion of electronic/systems (especially where microelectronic controls are being incorporated in products or used in production), and some MATERIALS SCIENTISTS/METALLURGISTS. There is a limited amount of research and development work, often done by industry-funded research associations (that for machine tools employs 70 people). Few scientists are employed.

Recruitment and entry Recruitment inevitably fell during the recession, and is probably still quite low.

Professional/graduate level the main requirement is for mechanical and manufacturing/production engineers, probably a rising proportion of electronic/systems engineers, and some electrical engineers. Major firms offer sponsorships to study mainly mechanical/production or electrical/electronic engineering, occasionally metallurgy/materials science.

Technician/craft entry technician trainees should normally have at least four O-level-equivalent passes at 16-plus† (normally including mathematics and physics), craft at least CSE-equivalent passes in maths and a science. Entry may be to EITB YTS scheme.

Training and qualifications generally follows EITB guidelines, and although largely industry-based, includes release for study. About a third of first-year craft/technician training is college based.

Professional/graduate a degree course in mechanical, manufacturing or production engineering is the most obvious choice, but electrical or electronic/

systems engineering are also useful. Post-entry training is given by most major manufacturers, along EITB guidelines and designed to meet the requirements of the appropriate professional body.

Craft workers and technicians follow EITB training schemes, which lead also to CGLI craft and BTEC technician qualifications.

See also ACADEMIC AND VOCATIONAL STUDIES IN ENGINEERING.

Further information from the Engineering Careers Information Service, and trade associations, eg the Machine Tool Trades Association.

METAL MANUFACTURING

The industry both produces crude metals from mineral ores, and manufactures semi-finished and finished products, ranging from iron castings through to plates, wire rods and bars, light steel sections and hot rolled bars, bright steel bars, hot and cold rolled strip, sheets, tubes and pipes, and special products such as high-speed tool and magnetic steels.

The industry is largely dominated by iron- and steelmaking, and manufacture of iron and steel products. The rest of the industry is very small by comparison. It includes aluminium and aluminium-alloy production. Aluminium is produced on a world-wide basis by six firms, all trying to find locations for their plant where they can have cheap energy – reducing alumina to aluminium takes vast quantities of power – and as close as possible to bauxite reserves. Energy is expensive in Britain, the early 1980s were traumatic, two firms merging – leaving only two – and smelting capacity cut back hard. However, output has now risen and profitability improved.

The industry also produces copper, brass and other copper alloys, and 'other' base metals. They include smelting and refining lead, zinc, magnesium and titanium, and manufacturing their alloys as well as finished products from them.

The industry now depends almost entirely on imported ores, although a few are still mined in Britain. Remaining domestic ores, though, are too low grade for iron and steel production to compete with imports, which at present come mainly from Canada and Sweden. One effect of this is that metal production is now largely concentrated near major deep-water terminals.

THE STEEL INDUSTRY has been in deep trouble throughout the industrialised world, with considerable overcapacity and stagnant demand. Installing their own steel production is an industrial priority for many developing nations, and countries like Brazil, Venezuela, Argentina, India, South Korea, Morocco and Yugoslavia now have new, modern, efficient steel-making plant. Many of these countries have their own ore and coal, less costly energy and labour, and so can produce steel much more cheaply. Steel is very vulnerable to economic conditions, and markets are concentrated in surprisingly few industries – vehicles, construction and civil engineering, industrial plant makers, can and metal-box makers, wire makers, shipbuilding, and consumer durables. These are all industries which have suffered badly from recession and have therefore cut their steel purchases affecting both British Steel and the private sector.

As for so many other basic industries, steel has to concentrate on smaller scale, high-value added products, drive up productivity and be ruthlessly cost efficient, inevitably at the expense of jobs.

BSC management has transformed the business, making a £38 million profit in 1985-6, although it has fallen to fourth (from third) largest producer in the world. Capacity has been slashed by some 10 million tonnes since 1976, to under 14 million tonnes (although production is still below 13 million). Reducing costs and making better use of expensive energy, manpower and materials are a major priority. After extensive closures, BSC's integrated steel making is concentrated in only five big centres – Port Talbot and Llanwern in South Wales, Ravenscraig in Scotland, and Redcar (Teesside) and Scunthorpe in the North – and at least one may still be at risk.

British Steel does not only make 'raw' steel. Steel is produced in many different shapes and forms – as 'billets', in strip, slabs, sections, plates, tubes, rods, wire, etc. Steel is galvanised and coated electrically. It is turned into finished products like pipes, girders, castings, jointed rings, springs, and parts of offshore oil-rigs.

BSC is now run as a set of separate product-based businesses. The general steels group combines sections and commercial steels, special steels, and plate-making. Strip products divides into strip mill products, tinplate, electrical steels and narrow strip. Stainless also includes two companies making track components and tyres for the world's railway systems. Tubes is further divided into three businesses – seamless, welded, and stockholding, with its own management systems and consultancy, and technical centres.

BSC has rationalised and reorganised extensively, where possible forming joint companies with private sector steelmakers to improve viability. Non-mainstream activities, like chemicals, pipe couplings and fittings, have been sold. However, investment continues – £28,000 million in the ten years to 1986, including £187 million spent on modernising Port Talbot's strip steel plant. Continuous casting is being steadily extended; computer control is being installed at more and more plant, and so on.

Under present (1987) government policies, as much steel business, particularly of rolled and finished steel products, as possible is to be returned to private ownership as soon as conditions permit. Privately-owned steel companies have been suffering from the recession too, and there has been near-constant re-organisation and rationalisation of interests, involving both privately-owned companies and BSC. Few small manufacturers of special steels (used to make mainly special industrial tools and components which can resist corrosion etc) are left. The shape of the industry will, therefore, go on changing. Privately-owned companies vary enormously in size (although none has capacity of more than half-a-million tonnes), and in character. They range from vertically-integrated groups which both manufacture steel and steel products and are involved in other activities, to smaller companies, some all-through steel makers, others specialising in, eg high-quality steel or particular finished products. Private firms make finished products for the engineering industry, alloys and stainless steels, high-speed steel tools and magnetic steel, etc.

Employment in the industry has fallen sharply, to about 140,000 in 1986. British Steel alone has cut numbers dramatically, to 54,000 (1987), from 255,300 in 1972 and 152,000 in 1979, and further streamlining is possible.

Production employs well over 85% of BSC's work force. BSC has changed working practices for everyone from the shop floor to the senior manager's office, cutting right across traditional demarcation lines. On the shop floor, steelworkers do more maintenance and repair of their own machinery, craft workers both operate and maintain machinery. Leading hands do supervisory work, foremen can pick up tools to speed a job. Productivity is up 50% on 1980.

Production work ranges from smelting iron ore into metallic iron, converting iron into steel, and shaping the steel into the forms consumer industries want. Production workers look after coke ovens and blast furnaces, man steelmaking furnaces, and operate rolling mills and forges which produce steel bars, wires, sheet etc. They work in teams under a team leader. Foremen are in charge of operations in each part of a plant, for example, in a steel melting shop they supervise charging raw materials, sampling the steel, and teeming liquid steel (most new graduates recruited as production trainees start work as shift foremen).

Managers at all levels of the mill control production, and look after all aspects, including packaging, warehousing, shipping, and pollution control. They must run production lines smoothly and economically, planning, supervising and meeting output and other performance targets. Steel is produced in large quantities at very high speed, which takes high levels of man management, the skill to trouble shoot and solve problems fast.

Metallurgical and technical services work closely with production. Here staff deal with quality control and assurance. Every stage of every process is crucial in making iron and steels which will perform as demanded by the customer, and customers' new robot and automated processing lines must have steel products with physical and metallurgical characteristics which are even more exacting than for older systems. And so content, temperature, timing etc, whether iron making in blast furnaces, or steel making with oxygen-blowing techniques or in electric arc furnaces, have to be controlled exactly and monitored carefully. Specifications for steels must be precise, quality is tested regularly, chemical composition may have to be checked, and there are always problems to be solved. Metallurgical services do specialised investigations into works engineering and customer problems. Graduate/professional staff, mainly metallurgists and materials scientists, with some physicists, chemists, chemical engineers and mathematicians, as well as technicians, are employed.

Engineering, including maintenance, fault diagnosis and safety, employs about a quarter of the work force. Most are craft workers, looking after plant and machinery which is both highly sophisticated and in near-continuous use. Some crafts are special to the steel or metal industry, eg mill turning and grinding, caring for the rollers which shape the steel. The industry also employs pattern-makers, moulders and core makers. Other craft workers include bricklayers who line furnaces, fitters and turners who work on machinery, boilermakers, machinists and welders; carpenters and joiners, electricians, plumbers and pipe fitters. They are backed up by semi-skilled workers, eg riggers, and labourers.

Works (professional/qualified) engineers (mainly mechanical, electrical, and electronic), see that all plant and equipment – including power supplies, instrumentation and control systems – work at maximum efficiency. They inspect, maintain and improve the availability and reliability of machinery; look after quality control, and see that raw materials, energy etc are used economically, mainly in the earlier stages of their careers. They may begin as, eg shift electrical engineer and be promoted to look after first a line, then a whole complex. They may then go on to, eg join a team of process control and automation specialists; work in design and development, improving existing plant, introducing new processes or equipment, etc; project engineering, commissioning and running in new plant. Any major new capital projects are formulated by multidisciplinary development engineering teams, which include finance, sales and marketing experts too.

The Corporation has MANAGEMENT SERVICE centres for all groups. Systems and programming teams either serve local works, working in production and especially computer-based planning and control systems, or are information systems teams, working at corporate level, developing and implementing business systems in finance, supplies, personnel and engineering. Systems developed by these teams are run on internal computer bureaux serving all locations via BSC's own telecommunications network. Management services employs people with degrees in all kinds of subjects (but with some emphasis on computer science and business studies).

Research and development has been cut back, and laboratories rationalised, although expenditure was still a massive £19 million in 1985-6. Although some basic work is done, practical problem-solving and developing and commissioning new processes predominates. Research is concentrated in three main areas – chemical and metallurgy, all aspects of engineering (from electronics to heavy plant performance and design), and cast-iron and non-ferrous pipe technology.

Examples of recent research include cutting coke consumption by injecting pulverised coal and coal/water slurry into the blast furnace; extending the range of tubular products for use in deep oil and gas wells and in adverse geological conditions; a combined microwave and optical scanning technique to surface inspect continuously-cast billets; and more advanced computer-assisted steelmaking techniques. Metal fatigue and fracture, corrosion, welding, and machining are also major areas of interest. Fundamental work includes eg structure-properties relationships.

Lab complexes, with massive pilot plant etc, are located near the main manufacturing centres. Three corporate labs deal with process and engineering research (ironmaking and plant engineering, continuous casting and rolling, and process development), products (includes fundamental studies on structure-property relations but mainly develops carbon, alloy and stainless steels for engineering, power generating and oil/gas industries), and one specialising in manufacture and use of flat-rolled steel products. A technical support lab for both BSC and private sector electronic arc furnace steelworks. The tinplate R&D department helps provide a competitive edge for PACKAGING firms fighting off competition from alternative materials.

R&D employs people with degrees in, mainly, engineering, electronics, control systems, metallurgy, materials science, pure sciences, maths and computer science.

Some commercial functions also take special expertise. For example,

PURCHASING Half of BSC's sales revenue goes on raw materials – which involves visiting and negotiating with overseas ore producers – capital equipment – even single projects may cost millions. Uses computerised computerised purchasing, stock control etc.

MARKETING for BSC is an increasingly sophisticated operation, fighting for contracts and customers world wide – exports, at £900 million a year are 27% of sales – marketing and sales teams now work for particular businesses within BSC, so selling particular products.

FINANCIAL CONTROL and economic planning obviously have a major role to play in maintaining and improving BSC's position.

PERSONNEL staff have to cope with all the problems of a dramatically changing industry and the function is expected to fill a key role in trying to make steel profitable – they deal with industrial relations; staff selection, career development, and organisation structure; education and training; and safety and health.

The Corporation says that promotion, through to management, is open to all from the production operative and apprentice to the trainee graduate, although a rising proportion of mid-ranking engineers are graduates, and it would now be very difficult to reach senior management without a degree. Even research scientists can gain experience in supervisory work, and people can change function, from eg R&D, metallurgy or engineering into production, or finance into sales, etc.

Recruitment and entry Despite the massive redundancies of the last few years, the steel industry in general, and BSC in particular, still need to recruit people for the future. BSC, in any case, is decentralised, so plant closures in one area have had little effect on staffing in another. Staffing levels are, however, being cut all through the Corporation. BSC, particularly, is trying to up-grade the quality of intake at all levels.

Graduate level the Corporation is currently (1987) recruiting at about 200-250 a year. About 60% of intake is engineers and metallurgists, with a significant proportion of people with computing skills. For management services there is some emphasis on graduates in mathematics/computing, economics, and business studies. Otherwise, BSC recruits graduates from any discipline. Recruitment by other employers is currently very low.

School-leavers are recruited by local plants and divisions, and so entry requirements and numbers vary. BSC recruits mainly via YTS at this level, but numbers are decided locally.

Qualifications and training Training is largely based on individual firms. BSC emphasises that there have been no cuts in its multi-million-pound training programme, essential to ensure efficient use of costly and complex steelmaking equipment. BSC wants to improve further the quality and effectiveness of training by raising standards.

All entrants are given training as appropriate to their first post, and thereafter as needed. Training may include both short and longer courses, and is geared to the requirements of relevant external, eg professional, bodies.

Further information from employers, including the British Steel Corporation.

THE FOUNDRY INDUSTRY mainly makes metal castings used by many other industries – eg, ships' propellers, engine blocks, turbine casings, crankshafts, metal chains – as well as some 'consumer' products, for instance church bells and taps. Pattern shops supply the rest of the industry. The industry is fairly capital intensive, needing both space and expensive plant. In decline for years, recent recession hit the industry extremely hard indeed. It has also had major problems in staying competitive in export markets, with overseas firms making inroads into UK markets. The number of companies is down sharply, with iron- and steel-founding capacity slashed particularly hard.

All sectors – iron, steel, aluminium, copper, and zinc – have gone through massive rationalisation schemes, and many have got out of casting and forging completely. In steel castings, for example, 22% of capacity was shut down in 1983, and the number of foundries cut to about 50 (from 70). Yet in 1985, most were still working at only half capacity, and estimates suggested that just twelve, fully equipped with the latest technology, would be a more viable number. EITB figures gave a total for all five sectors of just over 1000 establishments in 1985 (against 1418 in 1978).

Much of the industry is already highly automated and even more sophisticated systems, including robots, are available if firms can afford them. Standard moulding boxes move through the plant from mould preparation through pouring to final shakeout, by automated conveyors. Moulding sands are selected, mixed, weighed and delivered automatically too. New, more efficient, methods – one using an inexpensive polystyrene pattern – give high-strength, high-integrity castings with better surface finishes, needing less cleaning/smoothing off. Smaller foundries still use traditional hand methods for one-off jobbing, and large/unusually-shaped castings must still be floor moulded.

Employment in the industry Numbers employed have been falling steadily for years. EITB figures give under 59,500 for 1986 against 123,000 in 1978 and 149,000 in 1970.

Operatives make up nearly 60% of the work force, including dressers and finishers, followed by machine moulders, coremakers and shell process operators, metal melting and heat treatment operators, diecasters, investment casting and plaster cast operators, and plate moulders and loose moulders.

Craft workers are about a sixth of all employees. They include moulders and coremakers (but many of the traditional skills have been taken over by new techniques), pattern- and modelmakers, and a very small number of die and toolmakers.

Foundry technicians still form only a small, but rising, proportion of the work force – around 3%. Most work in engineering, including draughtsmen/women and estimators. Process technicians work out how to handle a new job, and put the technique through tests. Others work in the foundry and patternshop, eg in inspection (which may involve x-raying or ultrasonic testing). Metallurgical technicians analyse metal samples from casting to check quality. The rest work in eg labs making chemical, or spectrographic tests of metals.

Very few (300 or so) scientists and technologists work in the industry, and they are concentrated in a few large establishments. They may be in charge of production or work in research and development (but budgets have been heavily cut). The industry has its own research organisation.

Managers and supervisors make up a rising proportion of the work force – over a fifth – but administrative, professional and sales staffs are small.

Recruitment and entry Numbers recruited are (obviously) small.

Graduate/professional very small numbers, mainly graduates in METALLURGY/ MATERIALS SCIENCE, ENGINEERING (eg ELECTRONIC/CONTROL AND COMPUTING, MECHANICAL and PRODUCTION) for production and eventual management, and occasionally SCIENCES for research. Larger companies recruit other graduates (eg ECONOMICS, BUSINESS STUDIES, MATHEMATICS, LANGUAGES) for non-technical functions.

School-leavers recruitment largely as for the rest of the engineering industry.

Qualifications and training Training should follow EITB guidelines. Numbers trained have fallen sharply.

Professional/graduate degree or BTEC Higher awards normally gained pre-entry. No specific degree courses, but many metallurgy courses include foundry studies.

Technician/craft training EITB schemes, plus release for CGLI (foundry craft studies for moulders and coremakers, and pattern making, but being changed to engineering competency courses) and BTEC awards (in cast metals technology).

Further information from the Engineering Careers Information Service, and the Institute of British Foundrymen.

PACKAGING

The market for packaging is worth getting on for £6000 million a year. Although it is talked of as an 'industry' in its own right, and some major firms specialise, making packaging in a range of different materials, many firms which compete for their share of this are also part of as many as twenty-five different industries, depending on the materials and/or processes they use in making their product. The main materials are, of course, paper, board, cellulose film, thermoplastics, glass, tinplate, aluminium and aluminium foil, laminates and wood. They are turned into cans, drums, tubes, bottles and jars, containers, cartons, pallets, packets, aerosols, bags and sacks.

The packaging business is affected greatly by the state of the industries which use it – recession hits it hard. All manufacturers are constantly on the alert for cheaper, lighter, yet more efficient and more attractive packaging for their products. Packaging has to preserve and protect products, be simple to stack and handle, and simple to open. Yet despite the inroads made by plastics into areas traditionally using, eg paper and glass, no one material dominates the market, and the trend to more flexible types of container using more than one material continues. For all kinds of business – eg self service and take-away foods – the industry has developed a wide range of imaginative packaging processes, such as shrink, and skin-and-blister, wrapping, and goes on developing new technology – like 'controlled-atmosphere' packs for food. It has learnt to print efficiently in rainbow colours on metal, foil and plastic, as well as paper and board. It is automating steadily.

Employment in packaging A wide range of firms make packaging, including a number of very large national and multinational companies, and a great many medium and smaller firms. Some of the largest firms develop and make packaging and handling machinery and other equipment for themselves and other firms. It is also possible to work in packaging in eg major manufacturers who must constantly monitor, and develop and improve where possible, the methods they use in packaging their products.

Both packaging firms and major manufacturers employ people for a wide range of functions related to packaging. These include research and development, packaging design, design and development of production systems (where the employers also include machinery manufacturers), production of packaging equipment and packaging products (including eg quality control), marketing, technical sales and services, buying (eg materials, print, machinery).

Recruitment and entry Firms recruit at all levels for all types of skills.
Graduate/professional traditionally mainly in engineering (mechanical, production, electrical/electronic), but some demand now for people with specialist packaging training. Scientists, especially chemists and materials scientists, for testing, control and R&D, which also employs people who know about the products being packaged, eg food technologists. Firms with their own design departments recruit small numbers of product and graphic designers. The largest firms take graduates in most disciplines for commercial functions.
School-leaver entry mainly for technician and commercial training, with at least four O-level-equivalent passes at 16-plus†.

Qualifications and training Training is mainly industry based, but some specialist courses are available. These include –
Printing and packaging technology BSc: Watford CT;
BTEC HND printing with options in packaging technology – Nottingham: Trent Polytechnic, Watford CT;
BTEC HND design with packaging options – Sheffield: Polytechnic/Granville C.
Part-time courses at a small number of colleges, mainly for people already working in the industry, and Institute of Packaging/National Extension College correspondence course.

Further information from the Institute of Packaging.

PAPER MAKING

Britain has only a small industry which has to fight hard just to survive. With too few forests to support bulk raw-material production, almost all the wood needed for lower-grade papers and the grasses for better-quality ones have to be imported. After nearly twenty very tough years, the industry has come out of the recent recession 'battered but still alive'. Restructured and reshaped, studies suggest it is even on course to expand, with capacity – at 4.47 million tonnes, up 16% on the low of 1978. Exports, though, take well over 50% of home sales.

The industry consists of some 80 major paper makers, but is dominated by about seven large firms. It is a vertically-integrated industry, not only producing the 'raw' paper and board, but also converting them into packaging products, building board, wallpaper, stationery, tissues, office copier paper, and many other paper goods. It is a high-investment business. A single paper-making 'machine' costs many millions of pounds – one of the latest mills, with just one, 180,000 tonne-capacity machine, cost £135 million to build in 1985. The industry's current recovery is founded on managers able to pinpoint the opportunities and how they can be exploited, backed by heavy investment.

The industry has recovered by concentrating resources in products where UK firms can compete with producers from countries with plentiful supplies of wood and cheaper energy. This means goods which can be made from waste paper or for which home-grown timbers are right; high-quality papers; products which are difficult to transport, eg tissues, or take a mix of pulps and can profitably be made in non-integrated mills. Although production of newsprint in the UK is rising again, production is largely concentrated in two mills, both owned by overseas firms.

Firms already use highly sophisticated technological equipment and techniques but are investing heavily in computer equipment for even more sophisticated control of, eg paper quality, cutting and wrapping equipment which can handle three times as much paper, and generally modernising and refining production. Cost cutting and increased efficiency means paper makers can begin to compete with overseas firms in the middle range of papers. Paper-making firms are also trying to raise sales by improving services to customers – eg making the better quality papers faster running printing presses prefer. New thermodynamically-efficient methods can slash energy costs, and biotechnology, far from competing for wood pulp as was feared, has come up with a new pulp-making processing which could mean cutting the cost of mills by half.

While there are paper mills all over the country, the major centres are in the south east, the north west, the south east and Scotland. Since it takes nearly 40,000 gallons of water to make a tonne of paper, all mills are sited away from industrial centres, close to plentiful water supplies. The industry also has pulp mills near the major forests in the Scottish highlands, Cumberland etc, and Wales (see also FORESTRY).

Some paper mills are very large indeed, covering many acres, the largest capable of making a range of products, although they are specialising more and more. A number of small mills, usually producing specialised, often high quality paper, for eg bank notes are still in business.

The basic principles of paper making have not changed since it was invented, and continuous-process machinery invented over 150 years ago. This has become steadily more sophisticated. Raw materials are 'cooked' into sludgy pulp, which then goes in one end of the machinery, over a wire grid, draining off most of the water, through many massive steam-heated drying rollers to emerge at the other end, up to 90 metres away, as huge rolls of paper or board. Highly automated, and able to detect and adjust minute variations in eg moisture or sizing, these multi-million-pound plants still demand careful attention.

Employment in the industry Numbers employed have been recovering, to over 140,000 in 1986, but still well down on over 230,000 in 1971.

Most people employed in a mill are process workers, variously called reeler-men, dryermen, beatermen and machinemen. Some work in stock prep-aration, eg grading waste, operating pulping equipment. Promotion is to supervision (eg machine superintendent) and possibly management (eg finish-ing or production manager). Producing paper products involves operating machinery such as corrugators, or which prepare and print carton blanks, or print wall-paper.

Engineers are only a small proportion of the work force, and most of these are craft workers, responsible largely for maintenance, although machinery manufacturers' support services have been extended recently, and so more service engineers work for them. The industry needs comparatively few tech-nicians (including draughtsmen/women), and professional engineers (mainly mechanicals) who are usually the mills' chief engineers. Engineering staff also plan and install new plant and equipment.

Scientists and technologists (excluding engineers), with technical and other support staff, make up a very small proportion of the work force, with only a few hundred professional scientists and technologists, and a roughly equal number of technicians, mainly lab assistants. Some scientists and scientific technicians in the industry work in quality and other control – they monitor paper thickness, for instance, with radio-active equipment.

With steeply-rising costs, R&D was cut back sharply in the 1970s. The empha-sis now is on feasibility studies and very practical development work based on research carried out, increasingly co-operatively, in- and outside the com-panies. The industry's own research association employs about 200 scientists and technologists, working on materials, energy use, manufacturing technol-ogy, and machinery development.

Traditionally, promotion is from within the industry. The proportion of administrative staff is quite high, and FINANCE, MARKETING and SALES, PURCHAS-ING, PERSONNEL etc, people have to expect to work in a very competitive environment.

Recruitment and entry This is mainly at
Graduate/professional level the largest companies recruit no more than 20-30 new graduates a year. The industry's needs are mainly for a very small number of paper scientists/technologists, some engineers (mechanical, electrical/elec-tronic, and chemical) and other scientists – mainly chemists, physicists, materials scientists. Larger companies recruit small numbers of graduates for commercial functions.
School-leavers a proportion of trainee engineering technicians and craft-workers are recruited with CSE-/O-level equivalent passes. No formal qualifi-cations are needed to train in process work, although larger firms recruit some school leavers with a reasonable number of CSE- and/or O-level equivalent passes for, eg production training.
The industry has some dozen YTS schemes, taking no more than 240 school leavers altogether (1986).

Qualifications and training The British Paper and Board Industry Federation and the British Fibreboard Packaging Association are the industry's voluntary training bodies.
Professional/technical only one technological degree course, in paper science

Professional/technical only one technological degree course, in paper science at Manchester: UMIST.

Higher-technician and technician qualifications (SCOTVEC) available only in Scotland – Aberdeen: RGIT, Glasgow CB&P.

Craft/other skills Some larger firms have formal training schemes for younger entrants, but few process workers in the industry actually gain formal qualifications. New entrants join the 'minimal-skilled' labour pool, from which crews are chosen for the various departments, and they gain their training/experience mainly on the job, taking some years to reach top grades (but these are not necessarily transferable skills).

PPITB-developed self-instruction packages counteract the shortage of college training places (only Blackburn CT&D, and Bury CFE provide courses leading to CGLI 500 in paper and board making).

The industry copes with its need for higher-level, technician-style skills by re-training skilled process workers via an Open-Tech scheme, rather than increase school-leaver training at this level.

Engineering entrants (craft and technician) are trained under EITB schemes and may be given release to study for appropriate CGLI and BTEC awards.

Further information from the British Paper and Board Industry Federation.

PLASTICS PROCESSING

The industry takes its raw materials – from a huge range of different raw plastics and plastic-based 'composites' – from the CHEMICAL INDUSTRY and turns them into an ever-widening range of both finished products and parts/ components for other goods. Finished products range from consumer products – kitchen utensils, cling film and floor coverings – to industrial equipment – milk bottle and bread crates, pipes and guttering, for instance. Components and parts range from car bumpers to telephone casings. The industry's customers cover the whole spectrum of manufacturing and service industries, with main sales to firms in motor vehicles, domestic electrical appliances, telecommunications, buildings and toys.

It is a young and volatile industry, with new firms starting up, others going out of business, and many mergers. Usually too much capacity is chasing too few orders. Major industrial customers can decide to set up their own moulding capacity easily, causing serious loss of business.

It has been relatively easy to start up in plastics processing, for which the needed technical expertise is easily accessible – materials suppliers give needed information on compounds, temperatures, feed rates etc – and second-hand machinery has been cheap. However, the industry is automating, and the cost of robots can be up in six figures, which is making it harder to get started.

The industry uses a wide range of production processes, mostly based on heating the raw granules or powder that have come from the makers. Moulding is the most usual, and injection moulding – forcing the hot material through a small hole into a shaped mould – the most common. Compression moulding brings the mould down onto the hot plastic. In blow moulding a split mould is clamped round a pipe of plastic, and compressed air is forced in, expanding the plastic to fit the mould. Pipes – both for blow moulding and for finished products – rods, and 'profiles' (eg curtain rails) are extruded, or formed by forcing hot plastic through a nozzle or 'die'. Plastic film (eg wrapping) is made by first extruding a pipe, and then stretching it using compressed air. All processes are mechanised, and increasingly automated.

Plastic sheet can be 'formed' using a vacuum mould; it can be used to line or coat other materials, eg paper sacks, or laminated onto board or wood. It can be mixed and reinforced with glass or carbon fibre before it is moulded.

Employment in the industry Total numbers employed were barely 99,300, against over 150,000 in 1980. Only 1886 firms registered with the Training Board in 1985-6 (against over 2100 in 1980). Over 70% of firms (1325) were very small, with under 50 employees each. Only three firms had between 1000 and 2000 employees, and only 17 between 500 and 1000.

Operatives/process workers make up over 54% of the work force. They set up and start the machines, check they are running correctly, load and unload them, and may have to trim and smooth the finished shape. Some products have to be further shaped or specially finished. A process operator may control one machine, or several automated machines, although some need more than one operator. Machines take time to heat up, so are generally run round the clock, which means shift work. Promotion is to, eg instructing, inspection and, with training, to supervisory and managerial work.

Craft workers are mainly engineers, toolmaking, maintaining and repairing machinery. Numbers (under 7% of the work force) are fairly small.

Technicians set, or program, the more sophisticated machines; do lab work like analysing raw materials or testing strength and quality of products; work on developing new products or new uses for new plastics (although they are more likely to work for the plastic manufacturers than the processors); help plan production, and design ways of making products or moulds. Some become technical salesmen/women or work in technical services. Numbers employed, at barely 3000 in 1985-6, are small though.

Supervisory staff are often recruited internally, from amongst process and craft workers, technicians etc. Numbers were just under 7000 industry wide in 1985-6.

Scientists and technologists are employed in very small numbers – under 750 of them in 1985-6, mostly for the larger firms. They work in research and development, particularly on uses for advanced plastics and problem-solving, on specifications, engineering design, quality control etc. Many go on to management.

Recruitment and entry Key staff have traditionally been recruited from amongst experienced people trained in engineering or chemicals, or they have been 'home grown', but larger firms increasingly look for new graduates or high-calibre school leavers.

Professional/graduate the industry recruits a small number of polymer and materials scientists/technologists, chemists, physicists, and engineers.

School-leavers demand is probably higher with at least four/five O-level-equivalent passes at 16-plus† for technician-level training, or with CSE grade 3 equivalent passes at 16-plus† for craft, or lab-based technician training. Some indications of shortages of both craft and technician entrants.

YTS: a 300-place scheme for craft, technician, processing and clerical trainees is managed by the Training Board.

Qualifications and training Training is largely industry based, under the Plastics Processing Industry Training Board. PPITB has recently introduced a new 'standards of performance' scheme, has a new training centre which provides a range of courses and services, and has developed a range of 'Open Tech' distance learning packages.

Professional/graduate normally on a pre-entry degree or BTEC Higher National course, and can go on to professional membership of the Plastics and Rubber Institute.

Technician and craft training is via YTS schemes, craft apprenticeships for CGLI awards, and for technicians, via PPITB-sponsored training for BTEC or SCOTVEC awards.

Further information from the Plastics Industry Education Service, Plastics Processing Industry Training Board, and the Plastics and Rubber Institute.

THE PRINTING INDUSTRY

Printing 'produces' books, local and national newspapers, periodicals and magazines of all kinds, greetings cards, brochures and pamphlets, posters, banknotes, stamps, cheque books, office and computer stationery, packaging, wallpaper, airline tickets, forms, credit cards, etc. Only in the newspaper industry, and less often there too, are the printers part of the same organisation as the people who provide the raw materials – the manuscript, or 'copy', for books, periods etc, the art work for posters.

The printing industry, or large parts of it, is fighting its way through a major technological revolution, based on new film and photographic techniques, on electronics and the computer and microprocessor. Setting type in 'hot metal' letters and printing on a letter press machine from the raised surface of the type, processes which have not basically changed (despite mechanisation) since Caxton, are now rapidly on their way to becoming a thing of the past, except in some specialised work.

Most type is now 'set' on film, and printed by very fast offset litho machines. Working on the fact that oil and water do not mix, the film setting is made into a plate on which the type is flat, but greasy, the 'white' areas damp, so that in printing the ink sticks only to the greasy letters. It is faster, cleaner, less cumbersome and generally more efficient than the old 'hot metal' methods.

Film and litho paved the way first for the simpler 'numerically controlled' typesetting, using a keyboard to punch paper tape which drives the film setter, and then for full computer-based setting. Here the keyboard operator works at a computer terminal, complete with VDU, just as does the airline clerk or the accountant's assistant, 'inputing' the copy, together with coded instructions on what type etc is to be used, and how the page is to be laid out, straight into the computer. The 'compositor' can read and check the copy on the screen, move it around, correct and edit it. Once the copy is right, the computer 'drives' the typesetter, producing either complete pages already 'laid out', or film in columns to be cut up and laid out by hand (but the latest scanning equipment makes it possible to prepare automatically even the most complex layouts impossible or difficult to do on earlier machines). After printing, copy can be stored on discs so that any publication can be revised on a VDU screen in a fraction of the time needed for conventional 'resetting'. Increasingly, the originators of the text – the author, the journalist, the advertising staff – 'input' their own copy, either direct into the computer, or onto disk from where it can be 'converted' automatically to drive the computer-based setting machine.

Other electronic machines make printing plates automatically, and other skilled jobs, eg controlling the inks in the fast printing presses, are now being done by computer-controlled systems.

New technology is forcing the industry to operate in an increasingly international market – film and tape can be shipped from country to country where hot metal could not, for example, and in future direct, computer-to-computer links will make it possible to set and print where it is most economic for the customer. The industry also foresees loss of business from new electronic information media – they expect some of their best customers, eg mail order catalogues, holiday and travel brochures – to reach consumers via TV and other interactive systems. Photocopying, 'instant-print' shops, and 'desk-top' computer-based systems which make it easy for firms to do their own printing are creating more competition. Longer term, though, the industry expects demand for printed matter to increase rather than decline as a result of new technology, as it did when, for example, television reached virtually every home.

The home market for print, though, declined rapidly during the recession, and all sectors of the industry suffered badly as competition from overseas printers intensified. Recovery has so far (1986) managed to produce an annual growth rate of 1% – printing firms who say things are better-than-normal currently outweigh those who think they are worse-than-normal, although in late 1986, 72% of print firms were working at below capacity.

No figures are now collected to show the shape and size of the industry. The BPIF estimates that there are (1987) about 5500 major printing establishments (excluding newspapers), against training-board figures of 5942 in 1982, and 7535 in 1975. The number of firms is far fewer, since many are owned by a small number of large groups. Most major firms in the industry call themselves 'general' printers, and probably some 90% of them are very small, with under 50 employees, only around twenty have more than 500 staff each. Although more and more firms specialise, few print only books, only manufactured stationery, or packaging. Some firms carry out just one part of the print process, eg typesetting (including a growing number of firms computer type-setting), block-making and engraving, or binding.

Employment in the industry has been falling for some years. By 1987, BPIF estimated that numbers (excluding newspapers) were down to 140-160,000, from 211,000 in 1983 and 315,000 in 1975. The industry EDC, which projected that productivity would rise through the 1980s by at least 5% per year, says that even if demand for print were to increase by 2.5%, the loss of jobs would still be substantial.

On top of this, the EDC says that word processors and electronic copy assembly systems are likely to affect dramatically the manpower profile within the print industries beyond the pattern which has been seen so far with other new technology. They are also likely to change the structure of the printing process insofar as much of the work done by printers, says the EDC, may in future be done by customers, authors etc, before the work reaches the printing plant. EDC cannot yet quantify the effects of this on employment.

And so new technology is giving the industry problems, in that jobs are changing drastically. The effect is most dramatic on national newspapers, where more and more journalists are now directly inputing their own copy, as they already do on local papers. For the present, 'keyboarding' in the rest of the print industry is mostly still with people trained to do just that – although growing numbers of authors and editors are writing straight into computers too, so cutting out the intermediary keyboarder.

All the jobs remaining in printing are becoming more 'technical', as all the machinery becomes more sophisticated, faster, and electronically-controlled. Changes and problems are endemic to the industry – not least the cost of staying with the technology – but until books and newspapers all come through computers and facsimile machines directly into the reader's home, office or classroom, print workers will have jobs, if fewer of them.

The traditional print skills are, though, progressively giving way to the new ones, with an increasing proportion of skills at technician level, to cope with the more complex machinery and processes, and for office and supervisory work.

Composing is now keyboarding, increasingly inputing copy directly into the computer rather than on to magnetic or paper tape – it may be newspaper copy, novels, train timetables, examination papers. Fewer craft workers now operate machines casting hot-metal type – more and more the job is running the very fast (over 100,000 letters an hour) film-setting machines which work electronically, 'photographing' each character on to bromide paper. The finished film goes into an automatic processor which 'develops' it on to paper.

Proof readers still have to check that the typesetting is accurate, although again the higher levels of efficiency generally possible on keyboard and VDU is cutting the amount of reading needed. For most jobs, proof readers check the galleys or film-setting proofs when they are run off, but on some systems they first check the keyboarding is accurate on print-out from the computer.

Camera operators photograph, or scan electronically, illustrations etc for film setting. Retouchers make sure the film is 'clean' by 'painting out' blemishes and evening out tone. For hot-metal setting, illustrations have to be engraved, but this too is now mostly a machine job.

Hot-metal setting meant that acres of heavy type had to be laid out and locked together in pages ('imposition'). Film is put together and laid out into pages on plastic foil, using an illuminated table, by a make-up compositor, but this too is now being done on screen by sub-editors, and the machine generates film already laid out. For litho printing, the platemaker produces a thin metal printing plate photographically. Machine 'managers', whether litho or letterpress, position and fix the type (film or metal) on to the machines' rollers;

load them with paper, ink and, for offset, water; set the controls; make sure they print evenly and properly ('packing' the cylinders where necessary), that the ink runs smoothly, and so on, and then watching to see that nothing goes wrong. 'Setting up' the machine and 'making-ready' is one of the more technical jobs in printing, particularly where colour printing may mean the pages have to be printed up to four times – and the colours must all match on the page.

Finishing (putting the printed sheets through machines to cut, trim, fold, drill, and stitch into book form) and, bookbinding are also now mostly skilled machine operating and setting.

Some office jobs in printing are linked closely to the craft/technician skills. While some people start on the office side, others come through craft and technician training (because office work needs technical knowledge) into clerical work, estimating and costing, as production clerks. They can work up, perhaps through sales, perhaps through production control, overseeing the production of a number of books or magazines, and then on to production and works management.

It is still quite common to work up from the bottom to management in printing, from both craft- and technician-level, with clear routes upwards through supervisory work, departmental management or the office. The new flexible training agreements should keep these routes open.

Some print firms also employ their own GRAPHIC DESIGNERS AND TYPOGRA-PHERS, some technical/copy writers, advertising sales staff etc.

Recruitment and entry Recruitment, as of late 1986, was still at very low levels. Although small and medium-sized firms have almost all stopped cutting employment, over 60% thought the trend to fewer numbers would continue, if at a lower rate. BPIF is trying to encourage firms to recruit more graduates and A-level leavers.

Graduate entry Graduates are recruited only in small numbers, some with specialist printing qualifications (see below), but people with degrees in virtually any subject may be recruited for a wide range of functions, including production, marketing, finance, personnel.

School-leavers with at least four O-level-equivalent passes (including English, mathematics and a science) are recruited for administrative training (as eg order or cost clerk, estimator, in production planning, processing or quality control). People with A levels, or equivalent, are recruited as management trainees, starting in 'functions' such as sales.

For craft-level training, at least CSE-grade-2-equivalent passes in English, mathematics, technical drawing and a science-based subject, with aptitudes suitable for skill training, eg spelling etc for keyboarding, good colour vision and mechanical aptitude for machine printing, are required. All crafts still need the traditional aptitudes for dexterity and precision, an eye for line and design in print etc. Film and modern electronic equipment take skilled handling.

The new BPIF/NGA/SOGAT agreements require companies' managements and chapels to agree annual manpower plans.

YTS: a BPIF/NGA scheme qualifies for YTS grants, with 750 places for production operative training. BPIF says this is a 'major boost to recruitment at a time when parts of the industry are suffering from skill shortages and colleges cannot afford to buy high-tech printing machinery'.

Qualifications and training The rate of technological and other change in the industry means that all entrants need better and more sophisticated preparation and training. Training in the industry is strongly supported and encouraged by the British Printing Industries Federation which is the main training organisation, and the unions. Independent reports have described the industry's modernised craft training schemes as a model for other industries. The flexibility of the new training skills agreements is allowing firms to provide retraining for the existing workforce, and newly-recruited adults, on an 'unprecedented scale'

Degree level, the industry supports only one technological course –
Printing and packaging technology, at Watford CT (a 4-year, sandwich-based scheme emphasises basic sciences and engineering in the first two years, specialising in printing or packaging in the final two years; entry is with A-level passes including mathematics or a science subject, or eg a BTEC National in appropriate subjects.

BPIF operates a full-scale management development programme, of courses, conferences, and correspondence courses. CGLI offer a printing production management certificate.

Professional level qualifications include –
BTEC/SCOTVEC Higher National awards (full-time/sandwich for a diploma, part-time for a certificate) in printing are the main external qualifications. Courses cover eg design for production, materials, production methods, printing processes, and business/management studies, and can be biased to technology or administration. Entry is as for all BTEC Higher awards††, if with GCE/GCSE passes to include maths and a science. Courses are at –
Leeds: Kitson C (HNC), Manchester P (HND), Nottingham: Trent P (HND), Watford C (sandwich-based HND).
SCOTVEC equivalent at: Edinburgh: Napier, Glasgow CB&P.
BTEC HND Business studies with printing industry/administration specialism at London: Printing College.

BPIF also sets certificate exams (and provides courses) for office staff in, eg general technical knowledge, costing, estimating, printing office procedure.

Technician level mainly –
BTEC National schemes prepare entrants to work in a number of different print areas. Core courses cover printing principles, materials, design for printing, physical sciences, and mathematics. Option units allow choices of, eg estimating, costing, print-office administration, job planning, departmental supervision, production control, instructing, machine maintenance, troubleshooting, technical sales, R&D, materials testing, quality control, machine management, and machine, process and equipment development and evaluation. Normal entry requirements are as for all BTEC Nationals††, with O-level-equivalent passes at 16-plus† to include maths and a science. Courses are at –
Diploma: Exeter CA&D, Liverpool CCFE, London: Printing C, Southampton CHE, Watford C; Certificate: Bristol: Brunel TC, Cambridge CA&T,

Colchester Inst, Guildford CCT, Leeds: Kitson College, Leicester: S Fields CFE, Liverpool CCFE, Manchester Fielden Park CFE/P, Nottingham: S Notts CFE.

SCOTVEC equivalent awards, at Edinburgh: Napier, Glasgow CB&P.

Craft level Under new training agreements entrants will no longer serve a set apprenticeship. Instead, they are given a comprehensive, unit-based training and further education programme leading to full qualification, but with the length of training based on individual ability/need and achieving an agreed standard – able entrants are completing training in two years.

All young entrants go through an induction period, have a broad-based training in the basic skills of a primary occupation, and undergo further training designed to give 'experienced worker' standard in a particular job title. No period of time is set. All trainees under the age of 18 are given release for further education, to study for the –

CGLI printing scheme (523) – a modular scheme made up of 900 hours' study over two years, but students have to complete a further 15 60-hour modules during this time. Skilled-worker status is awarded when the objectives in the specified training modules have been successfully achieved.

Over 900 new entrants under 18 were enrolled for CGLI 523 in 1985-6, a 30% increase on the year before.

Other CGLI schemes include printing machine operatives (501), flexographic printing (509), screen process printing (517), bookbinding (521).

See also ART AND DESIGN for graphic design work and training.

Further information from the British Printing Industries Federation.

SHIPBUILDING

The headlines tell most of the story – 'battle to keep shipbuilding afloat', 'yards get close to the rocks', 'crunchtime looms for yards', are some of the most recent. Part of the UK's industrial tradition, shipbuilding is, across most of the world, in the deepest possible trouble. The surplus in world shipbuilding capacity was still (end 1986) some 40%, even though European capacity has been cut by 60% since 1975 – leaving EEC countries holding only 18% of world markets – and Japanese by nearly 30%. As in other 'traditional' industries, the advantages are with low-cost developing countries, in this instance, South Korea. The gap between European costs and world prices is some 40%.

Most forecasters agree that the market should improve in the early 1990s, when shipowners will have to begin replacing about half the present world fleet. At present they have far too many ships, so orders are only 25% of the early 1970s level. The problem for Europe in general, and the UK industry in particular, is how to survive in the meantime. In the first half of 1986, UK yards won only 1.6% of new orders, world-wide, against 2.7% in 1985, and 50% in 1956. Work could well dry up completely by the end of 1987.

An accurate picture of the UK shipbuilding industry in 1986-7 is extremely difficult to draw. As yards fight to stay alive and get slimmer all the time, the industry has also been reorganised, with the six yards which specialised in building warships privatised. This left state-owned British Shipbuilders with most of what remained of merchant ship- and marine-engineering-building

(Northern Ireland has its own state-owned yard), although some defence yards may diversify. At the other end of the scale are the (small) boat and yacht builders.

BS is fighting to keep about 200,000 dwt capacity (1985 contracts filled barely 10% of that) against the industry's million tonnes of twenty years earlier. Despite the problems, BS is investing in reorganisation and advanced technology – £30 million on computer-aided design, production and engineering – and aims to compete in selected areas of the market when trade recovers, for instance ferries, dredgers, and North-Sea support vessels. It has (1987) only half-a-dozen yards now.

The whole industry has to modernise in every way, to improve management, marketing, design, production methods, etc, and many traditional methods have to go. Ships are still built individually, and indeed are increasingly 'customised'. Computers can be used – for example, to produce a specification from the customers' requirements (eg speed, cargo capacity, draught and weight), to plan production more efficiently, to calculate the size and shape of each part, to guide flame-cutters – or lasers – burning out shapes in steel plate, and some welding. Modular construction systems, using standard sections which can be pre-assembled, is being developed.

Employment in the industry Continuous closures, modernisation and rationalisation have brought a massive fall in numbers, to well under 90,000 in 1986 from some 168,000 in 1979. British Shipbuilders alone has cut its workforce to about 8500 from 86,000 in 1977, and is expected to cut it further. One of the newly-privatised yards, building nuclear submarines, had (1986) 12,500 employees. Many more redundancies are probable unless order books fill.

Whatever the future shape of the industry, and however far it is modernised, it will still need a high proportion of manual and skilled craft workers. The traditional narrow skill bases, however, are changing, to increase productivity. BS has been working towards 'system-' rather than 'craft-'based skills, but the traditional groupings – of metalworking, outfitting, engineering crafts, and woodworking still exist.

Boat-building employs rather more woodworking and outfitting trades and fewer metalworkers, and there is also a significant proportion of jobs for glass-reinforced plastic laminators.

Technicians will be increasingly important in the industry in the future. While many will continue to work in the traditional areas of draughting, estimating, and planning, a growing proportion will work in the increasingly complex production control and supervision.

Traditionally the industry employs relatively small numbers of professional engineers, and technologists, and these are mainly mechanical and production engineers, marine engineers, some electrical engineers, and metallurgists, and some naval architects. Most engineers and technologists work in production, planning and management, and in design. Only a few work in research and development.

The industry's research stations have been 'privatised' – the British Ship Research Association (BSRA) has merged with the National Maritime Institute to form British Maritime Technology. They now employ over 350 engineers (eg naval architects, marine and production engineers), computer scientists, mathematicians and a few physicists, metallurgists etc (the industry itself employs few scientists). BMT works on projects ranging from safety of ro-ro ferries through to 'tomorrow's ship'.

Recruitment and entry British Shipbuilders probably expresses the views of the whole industry, in that it is 'currently seeking young men and women of the education and calibre necessary to carry change forward into the 1990s'.
Graduate/professional level mainly engineers (naval architecture, and marine, mechanical, electrical, electronic, systems, production), but also computer scientists, mathematicians, some physicists. Occasional vacancies for people with particular qualifications to do research for BMT.
Craft-/technician-level levels of recruitment are difficult to predict. A rising proportion of any vacancies are likely to be for technician-level (with at least four O-level-equivalent passes††) rather than craft training.

Qualifications and training company based.
Graduate/professional level training as needed for professional status, and to get experience in as many different parts of the industry as possible.
See also ACADEMIC AND VOCATIONAL STUDIES IN NAVAL ARCHITECTURE etc.

Craft apprentices and technician trainees are similarly given fully integrated training, leading to CGLI and BTEC awards.

Further information from employers.

TEXTILE, CLOTHING AND RELATED INDUSTRIES
Clothing — footwear — leather and leather goods — textiles
This closely-linked group of industries historically used natural resources – cotton, wool, leather, etc – to make a great variety of products ranging from clothes and shoes, rope, twine and net, through carpets and other furnishings, to lace and furs.

These traditional industries have been suffering just because they have long histories, and because they failed to invest. The relative buoyancy of the late 1960s and early 1970s, mainly based on cheap synthetic figures, masked the growing problems, but they were badly placed to take advantage of new developments. Textiles/clothing, particularly, is one of the first industries to be set up in developing countries where costs are low, and the UK cannot compete in basic products because there is no technological advantage.

For a while it looked as though much of the industry would go under, but over the last year or so, most sectors have made dramatic progress. 'Technology is replacing manpower and brain power, enabling the industry to become increasingly efficient and better able to produce high-quality products at speeds thought unobtainable ten years ago. But to stay competitive, these industries have to follow the lead of other countries, with 'a combination of (further) heavy investment, computerisation, robotics and redundancies'. (*Financial Times*). It is now possible to automate some production completely. On this basis, the industry is now competing hard on fashion, quality and design.

Despite decline, this is still a significant group of industries, fourth largest in the UK. The market for their products at home and overseas is worth thousands of millions of pounds and, for the time being at least, employs around half a million people in total. Although unlikely to remain so labour intensive for very long, paradoxically the viability of the industries' recovery is threatened by skill shortages. High-quality products, produced using highly-sophisticated machinery needs a highly-skilled workforce through from shop floor to top management.

The industry divides along very traditional lines. Modern technology, and the changing shape of the industry, makes old classifications very dated, to the extent that 'textiles' is often used when both (traditional) clothing and textiles are being discussed. However, the industries still have employers, and training, bodies in line with the traditional divisions, and the facts and figures come from them. Rationalising the industries into larger groupings has often meant 'vertical' integration – of textile with clothing firms mainly – but today large groups believe in decentralising as far as possible, so textile and clothing divisions and factories still keep the characteristics of their own sectors. The knitting (and lace) industry does not, though, fit neatly into either, since so often it makes up the fabric at the same time as it turns them into end products like sweaters and shirts. Knitting as a process is increasingly popular in the industry – it produces an attractive fabric, has a cost advantage, is ideally suited to synthetic fibres, and is easier to automate – so more and more clothing is knitted. The knitting sector, however, is not traditionally part of the clothing industry, and is still treated as part of textiles.

THE CLOTHING INDUSTRY is large, complex and fragmented, with a comparatively large number of very small firms, despite steady rationalisation and mergers which have been under way for some years now. It includes the *haute couture* houses, wholesale manufacturers, and the rapidly-falling number of 'bespoke' (made-to-measure) tailors. It is traditionally divided between, at one end, firms which are very design- and fashion-conscious, making good-quality, high-value garments in relatively small quantities, and at the other, those supplying volume markets with larger production runs, although this is changing as wholesale manufacturers try to take advantage of the 'designer' trend, and have to switch to shorter runs of more varied up-to-the-minute fashion goods. Firms generally specialise – making some form of men's, women's or children's outerwear (suits, coats, raincoats, anoraks), sportswear, baby clothes, dresses, skirts, blouses, shirts, ties, uniforms, underwear/nightwear, etc.

The industry is fighting back hard against intense world competition, and is showing clear signs of recovery from recession, with production over 9 points up on 1980, although still well below the level of 1975. Export sales, however, are still barely half of imports, which take 50-60% of home markets. The future of the industry depends, according to the industry EDC, on firms' taking advantage of their closeness to UK and European markets; becoming much more flexible and responding quickly to changing fashion and demands, and doing more to lead and influence market patterns – upgrading their marketing, improving use of designers, and concentrating more on specialist or high-value added merchandise, or market outlets. They have to improve on productivity and their competitiveness – with heavy investment in new technology and methods, and a major training programme. UK retailers are pushing for an efficient home industry which can get the latest fashion idea to them far faster than firms the other side of the world, making clothes which project a sharp, recognisable 'designer' image for the individual retailer.

The industry now has 3409 firms within scope of the training board (1985-6 figures), against over 5100 in 1979. Most firms, 2966 (87%) of them, are small, employing under 100 people each, 60% have under 25. Only 19 have more than 500 employees each (but four up on 1982). Many firms are owner-managed, but the trend towards larger groups is expected to continue, and the number of firms with more than 300 employees has risen to 80.

Comparatively slow to accept new technology, the industry is now investing substantially, with considerable effects on productivity – one firm can now produce 3000 suits a week with 370 people against 4-500 a week with 300 people only a few years ago. New, faster equipment is being installed at all stages from materials handling, preparation and cutting through to garment construction, sewing, finishing and pressing – the industry even has robots, to pick single piles of garment parts from a stack, and place them exactly where needed, for example. Garments are handled mechanically as they pass from stage to stage; cutters have had fast, electrically-operated shears and machine band knives for some time, but laser cutters are now a reality; bulk quantities can be die cut; sewing machines are electronically controlled. Computers, from customer's measurements, automatically prepare 'lays' for cutting, and pattern cutting can be automated too. Computerised stock control, costing, and ticket printing systems are also helping to improve efficiency.

Employment in the industry Numbers have been falling steeply for many years and are now (1986) down to under 161,500 (from 290,000 in 1979 and 552,000 in 1951), but 'ppear to have more or less stabilised. As much as a third of the industry's labour force works on a part-time basis, and homeworkers are employed extensively, particularly for finishing and pressing.

Just over 25% of all employees work for companies with fewer than 50 employees (but this is down slightly on 1982), 40% for firms with fewer than 100 staff each (down from 45%).

The falling number of firms has affected all sectors, but employment has actually risen in some, although levels fluctuate. The main sectors, with number of firms and employees, are (1986, with 1982 figures in brackets) –

dresses, lingerie, babywear:	1250 (1900)	54,326 (66,342)
tailored men's and boy's clothes:	537 (700)	29,467 (39,103)
overalls, men's shirts and underwear:	457 (500)	28,082 (31,275)
women's and girls' coats, suits etc:	347 (350)	19,288 (16,610)
furs:	249 (330)	2244 (4000)
waterproof clothing:	107 (140)	8000 (7420)
hats, caps etc:	89 (100)	3362 (2980)
gloves:	54 (80)	1690 (2330)

Semi-skilled work The great majority of people in the industry work on the shop floor in wholesale manufacturing. Most – about 70% – are semi-skilled (sewing) machinists. They may work on complete garments, but more usually on one part of it, or they operate the special machines which eg overlock or embroider. Most machinists become skilled in five or six different machining jobs. Sample machinists help designers, do trials for specifications and quotations etc. Pressing is the other main semi-skilled work.

Promotion may be to garment examining, supervising etc.

Skilled work The numbers are rather smaller, although the proportion is probably rising. The work includes –

pattern technicians, or design pattern cutters – who turn designers' drawings into production-line patterns;

lay planners – who are generally experienced cutters and work out in detail the most economical method of placing patterns on the cloth, but the job is being 'computerised', and then involves loading the information into the machine, making calculations and working out the lay on VDU screen;

pattern-makers;

cutters – using traditional knives, dies, and computerised, including laser, cutters;

the people who do the marking or fixing – putting together all the different pieces for a garment and marking the stitch lines; and

hand sewers.

Promotion is to supervisory work, organising a section or department, including quality control and training.

In bespoke tailoring and dressmaking there is more emphasis on hand work, although automation is being introduced here too wherever possible. The cutter both drafts the pattern on to the cloth and measures the customer, and may supervise the sewing, which is done partly by machine, partly by hand. Most workshops, except in the multiple retailers still making-to-measure, are small, with close teamwork. Some experienced bespoke cutters and tailors go into manufacturing, as eg pattern cutters or cutting room managers.

Engineering The growing sophistication of the machinery means the industry needs increasing numbers of mechanics (up 36% over 1981-5), technicians and engineers to design/develop, install, maintain and service them. Some machines also have to be adapted to do different jobs. Some clothing firms employ their own maintenance staff, especially for the large numbers of sewing machines, while other, more sophisticated, machinery may be serviced by the manufacturers, for whom maintenance staff then work.

Design Not all firms have their own professional designers, although the numbers employed are increasingly sharply – by 43% between 1981 and 1985. See ART AND DESIGN.

Managerial/administrative work An estimated one in ten employees are managers. While there are clearly defined functions to fill, with so many smaller firms one person may do more than one, and the areas of responsibility are rarely clear cut.

Production managers are still mainly promoted from the shop floor and supervisory work, but some, mostly larger, firms now take on production assistants specially to train as managers.

Commercial functions – FINANCE, MARKETING/SALES – are increasingly important for the industry. In PURCHASING/SUPPLY firms have support and back-up from textile companies and fibre makers with whom they work closely. It is a skilled job to know what materials will be in fashion some time ahead, and which will be suitable – including quality and cost – for the designs.

Young executives are generally given experience of several functions.

Promotion is largely from within the industry, and it is still common for people to work their way up. Business acumen, entrepreneurial flair and ambition are still frequently more highly rated by existing managers than formal qualifications. EDC reports suggest, though, that firms need to develop more sophisticated managerial skills, and the industry seems to be recognising this.

Recruitment and entry While numbers employed may have fallen, the industry – with aggressive PR help from the training board – urgently needs to recruit people of the calibre essential to run a modernising industry fighting for market share. The shortages are not restricted to high-level skills – 30% of all firms reported problems in recruiting machinists in 1985-6.

Graduate/professional level the Clothing EDC and ITB are both encouraging recruitment of people for future top-grade management. They suggest the industry needs at least 500 new junior executives a year (including A-level entrants as well as graduates), for production management and technology, design and design management (see ART AND DESIGN, marketing and sales management particularly. Specialist qualifications are not essential, but are supported with grants, sponsorships etc (see below).

School-leaver level Trainee engineering technicians now need four O-level equivalent passes at 16-plus† ideally including maths, a science, and English. For other work, formal qualifications are not essential, but the firms offering career prospects do prefer people with a good general education including some exam passes at 16-plus†.

YTS: while the industry's first plans to take on at least 10,000 young people a year proved over-ambitious, numbers recruited have been rising steadily, reaching over 5000 (in 550 firms) in 1985-6, and CAPITB aims to increase the number of annual starts to 6000-plus.

Qualifications and training The level and quality of training is being steadily improved with the support of the Clothing Industry Training Board (CAPITB), and the Clothing Institute. While most training is on-the-job and within the industry, for everyone from semi-skilled through to management trainees, CAPITB is promoting and supporting pre-entry courses and qualifications.

Graduate/professional qualifications Mainly –
Bradford University – Industrial technology & management (BTech 4-year sandwich) with clothing option (CAPITB supports with scholarships);
Manchester UMIST/Polytechnic – Clothing engineering (BSc 4-year sandwich);
Manchester Polytechnic – Clothing studies (BA 4-year sandwich): biased to production management.
Clothing technology, postgraduate diploma (1-year full-time) at Leeds University, Manchester Polytechnic: conversion course for graduates in other subjects.
Clothing and Footwear Institute exams – 4-year sandwich courses at Belfast CT, Galashiels: Textile C, Manchester P, Middlesbrough: Teesside P.
BTEC/SCOTVEC Higher National awards: Belfast CT (HNC), Galashiels: Textiles C, Leeds: J Kramer (HNC/D), Liverpool: M Fletcher (HNC/D), London: Fashion (HNC/D), Manchester P (HND), Rochdale TC (HNC), Rochester: Medway CD (HND). Entry as for all BTEC/SCOTVEC Higher awards††.

Technician qualifications Mainly –
BTEC/SCOTVEC National awards in clothing, at –
Leeds: J Kramer C (f-t/p-t), Leek CFE&SA, Liverpool: Mabel Fletcher TC (f-t/p-t), London: Fashion C (f-t/p-t), Southgate TC (f-t/p-t), Manchester P (f-t), Oxford CFE (f-t/p-t), Rochester: Medway CD (f-t).
BTEC/SCOTVEC National Certificate for clothing machine technicians (3-year block release), at –
Glasgow: Bamullach, Leeds: J Kramer, London: Fashion, Manchester: Hollings.

Craft training via 4-year on-the-job training combined with study for
CGLI clothing craft (scheme 460) in either wholesale garment or handcraft tailoring.

Other Most shop-floor employees, ie sewing machinists, pressers etc are trained mainly on-the-job, some with preliminary training in (larger) firms' own training schools.

Further information from the Clothing & Allied Products Industry Training Board and the Clothing and Footwear Institute.

THE FOOTWEAR INDUSTRY still makes most shoes, boots etc from leather, and has to stitch them in the traditional way – the synthetic that lets feet 'breathe' has still not been discovered.

The footwear industry is also trying to fight back again intense foreign competition – and in 1986 had succeeded in cutting penetration back to 56%, from the 60% peak of the previous two years. To do this means staying out of products like trainers, and concentrating on making shoes in the latest fashion, however quickly it changes, beating importers who cannot possibly get their products into the market fast enough. Firms have to be able to make a wide variety of well-styled shoes, in short runs. This means having innovative designers, and flexible, up-to-date manufacturing equipment.

Shoe making, though, is very difficult to automate, and is still at the stage of putting electronics into individual machines rather than setting up automated lines. Computerised, numerically-controlled stitching machines mean one operator can do the work done by four on traditional equipment, and computer-controlled conveyor belts speed the leather shapes round the machinists. A robot has been developed to check that 'uppers' are properly glued to soles, and another can pick and place leather. Computer-aided design is being developed, but it needs highly sophisticated software to get over the problem of converting a three-dimensional design on a last into a two-dimensional pattern. CAD/CAM systems could automate last and mould making, but cutting the leather still needs human skills.

The number of firms has been falling for some years, and is probably down to around the 300 mark. Although many of the smaller, family businesses have been forced out by the competition, few are very large, and most are both manufacturers and retailers. Most specialise in one kind of product – women's or children's shoes, or boots, for instance.

Employment in the industry Numbers employed have been falling since 1970, to barely 47,000 in 1986 (against some 88,000 in 1973), even though the industry remains labour intensive.

Most people working in the industry are semi-skilled operatives, who then move up into more skilled trades, and into supervisory work. Shoemaking is a skilled craft. The pattern cutter drafts out the separate pieces which will make up the pattern for the shoe. From this is produced a sample, and then the pattern makers produce grade patterns for the various sizes. As many as 30 pieces may be needed for a single shoe. Many of the processes, such as clicking or cutting the uppers, are skilled work, even though shoes may be cut with a hydraulic press rather than by hand. Preparing the pieces for stitching may involve as many as 40 or 50 separate operations. Soles and other 'bottom components' are generally made by specialist firms, but joined to uppers by the shoe manufacturer.

However, the increasingly sophisticated production processes mean some aspects of production are now treated as technician-level work. The industry also employs technologists and technicians in research and development, as well as production control.

Most firms employ their own designers, who have to work closely with production. See ART AND DESIGN.

Expert management, marketing, finance etc, are as crucial to shoemakers as any other industry.

Recruitment and entry Traditionally, the industry recruits people for work as semi-skilled operatives, but there are now more schemes for young people with good school-leaving qualifications to train as technicians. Firms also recruit some school-leavers with A levels and graduates for management training in both production and commercial functions.

Qualifications and training The industry has always trained extensively, especially at operative/craft, and now also at technician, level. On-the-job training is combined with release to study for national awards.
Professional examinations are set by the Clothing and Footwear Institute.
Advanced courses in, eg footwear design, footwear technology, and production management are at – London: Cordwainers' TC, and in manufacturing technology at – Leicester: S Fields C.
BTEC HNC courses – at
Accrington/Rossendale C (p-t), London: Cordwainers' C (f-t);
BTEC National courses – Accrington/Rossendale C(p-t), Kendal: W Cumbria C (p-t), Leicester: S Fields CFE (f-t), London: Cordwainers C(f-t), Wellingborough C (p-t).
CGLI footwear manufacture (scheme 454) – courses at above colleges.

Further information from the Clothing and Footwear Institute, and the British Footwear Manufacturers Federation.

LEATHER AND LEATHER GOODS MANUFACTURE Some firms specialise in preparing leather, some in making leather goods, some do both.

Leather manufacturers tan and dress the hides and skins, and prepare them as heavy, light and fancy leathers for boots and shoes, gloves and handbags, clothing and upholstery, saddlery and industrial use. Leather is produced from animal skins and hides, using different manufacturing agents depending on the kind of leather being produced. A chemically-based industry, the processes are based on chemical interactions, which include tanning agents, dyes, fat liquors and finishes, on the skins. Recession hit the industry hard. Observers now believe it has stabilised, but with under 50 tanneries country-wide.
The industry uses as much automatic and semi-automatic machinery as possible. However, the processes have to be constantly adjusted to allow for variations in the quality of the skins and/or the requirements of a particular product, making full automation very difficult. The industry has also to cope efficiently with, ie tightly control, its effluent problem.
Leather goods include luggage and bags of all kinds, saddles, fancy goods etc. The industry keeps the same name although a large number of its products are made of synthetic materials, often made to simulate leather, rather than leather itself. The industry divides between a small number of large firms making a range of products using very modern machinery and production methods, and a very large number of quite small firms who specialise in particular products, eg saddlery and harnesses, and quality leather goods, using traditional craft methods still.

Employment in the industry About 23,000 people were working (1986) in these industries, against some 35,000 in 1979.

The leather industry employs a relatively high proportion of scientific, technological and technician-level staff, not only in production and control, but also in the commercial functions, particularly buying and selling, with a fairly high proportion of executives holding appropriate qualifications. Research posts are few, though.

The leather goods industry still employs quite large numbers of craft workers, particularly for products like saddles which are still hand made. Even a simple saddle takes the equivalent of three working days to make. Other skilled work includes designing fancy goods, bridle and other hand stitching. In mass production, goods are usually produced by bench assembly, which includes a considerable amount of machining and machine-sewing. Engineers, technicians, tool and jig makers are also employed.

Recruitment and entry For junior executive/technological/scientific work, the industry recruits a small number of trainees annually, and usually sends them to study full-time (see below).

Technician-level entry is with at least four O-level-equivalent passes at 16-plus†. Leather-goods designers need similar qualifications. Apprentice saddlemakers etc should have at least CSE-grade 2/3 equivalent passes at 16-plus.

Qualifications and training Training is largely industry based, with release for study.
Technological/scientific training is generally via a degree, for leather manufacture, normally in CHEMISTRY, CHEMICAL ENGINEERING, or other SCIENCE-based subjects.
Leather technology is now taught mainly at Northampton: Nene C, for BTEC HND, BTEC National, a College certificate, CGLI craft (scheme 457), and operative (scheme 456) awards.
Leather design and production – f-t courses at London: Cordwainers' TC.
For saddlery, training on the job lasts some five years. Training in other leather goods manufacture is also on the job (with release to study for CGLI scheme 470) but takes rather less time.

Further information from the National Leathersellers Centre (Nene College), and the British Leather Goods Manufacturers Association.

TEXTILE MANUFACTURE turns raw cotton, wool, and synthetic fibres first into yarns, and then into fabrics. It produces fabrics for woven cloth, knitted goods, carpets, lace, and the growing industrial-fabric 'non wovens' market. It has changed from a labour-intensive, craft industry, into a capital-intensive (its machinery is now very expensive), highly automated one in a very short space of time. Some textiles are still producted traditionally, however, by eg the 400 mill workers and 600 weavers of the Harris tweed industry on the Outer Hebrides. Thirty-five firms still make traditional lace, but on increasingly high-tech machinery.

The industry is fighting rising imports – taking 44% of the home market in 1985 – and a massive trade deficit. Although all commentators talk of an impressive turnaround in 1985-6, 1985 production was still below the 1980 level, which it just touched again late in 1986. Exports, although increasing steadily in value – to almost £2000 million in 1985 – are still 40% down on imports. The industry has had its confidence badly dented, and as one report said, 'About the only permanent truth to emerge [from the many in-depth studies of the industry] is that conclusions... tend to be over-optimistic and are often overturned shortly afterwards by unforeseen events.'

The industry is tackling its problems by becoming more marketing oriented, especially in the richer markets of Europe, Scandinavia, the US, Japan and the Middle East. It is being forced to be more design and fashion conscious. It is investing in new technology still further, innovating, and spending more on R&D. It is, however, totally dependent on shrewd management and manufacturing decision making – going into making fabrics etc for more than the traditional single (summer or winter) season, to help even out the peaks and troughs, for example.

The textile 'industry' is still, in fact, several industries, even though the largest groups extend both out to synthetic-fibre production (technically part of the CHEMICAL INDUSTRY), and out into clothing manufacture, and across the sectors too. Wool, worsted and knitting are still distinguishable from the Lancashire, cotton-based, sector, for technological and technical as well as historical reasons. Until the early seventies, the industry was still made up of a great many small, specialised operations – spinning, weaving, knitting, dyeing, finishing etc. The industry went through a tough period of rationalisation which, particularly in the Lancashire sector, resulted in a small number of vertically-integrated mega-groups, and the recent spate of takeovers has merged three of these. One company, itself one of the two main synthetic fibre makers, now makes up the 'backbone' of the whole UK spinning sector, with 28 mills. Central control, however, is no longer in vogue, and the emphasis is on local profit centres and management motivation – one of the larger groups, with a total workforce of 9000, has just sixteen people, including secretaries, at head office. But at the other end of the industry, over 80% of companies in the knitting (and lace) industry are still small, family-type businesses, with under 100 employees each.

The technological changes are little short of revolutionary. Reports which one day insist robots cannot possibly handle cloth are confounded the next. But innovation is not confined to automation. In weaving, for example, the 'weft' is no longer taken between the 'warp' by shuttles, but can be guided by jets of air or water. 'Friction', instead of traditional 'rotary' spinning doubles the rate at which machines can produce yarns. Modern machinery can produce textiles and knitted fabrics in much more sophisticated and interesting patterns, faster.

The industry has several research centres, some serving specific sectors. Recently they have been restructured on far more commercial lines, and do far less fundamental research. They include –

The Shirley Institute: R&D, test and analytical services on all kinds of textile products, processes and equipment, but also does related work in bio-technological, forensic areas.

HATRA (Hosiery & Allied Trades Research Association) concentrates on all aspects of knitted-garment making, and other applications for knitted processes, eg upholstery, industrial textiles etc.

Wira Technology Group (was the Wool Industries Research Association): deals with textile products, instrumentation, technology, testing, carpet technology, cleaning/maintenance, research and services.

Employment in the industry has plummeted to well under 280,000 in 1986, from some 600,000 in 1970. Largest sector is knitting with over 80,000, followed by woollen and worsted (41,000), and cotton etc (38,000). Increased productivity is likely to bring employment down still further, but the speed of the fall is dependent on levels of investment, and on how strongly the industry manages to combat imports and increase exports.

'Process' workers, controlling an ever larger number of highly-sophisticated, automated machines, still make up a high proportion of people employed, although it is falling. Knitting operatives, for instance, increasingly control eight, twelve, or banks of up to 40 high-precision machines. They keep them supplied with fibre or yarn, adjusting them, watching for faults, etc, whatever the process, from spinning through to weaving or knitting. While lace making is still skilled work, the complex machines controlled by pattern cards, are now also being replaced by computer-controlled looms, operated via VDU screens and keyboards. The draughtsmen/women and designers are still crucial though.

Technicians The industry has a rising proportion of jobs for technicians. Technicians work in product and process development. They may be in charge of particular production sectors. They also work in quality control. In yarn and fibre production, they check machines to see that they are set and running properly, service and maintain them, install and adjust new machines, supervise machine operators. In bleaching, dyeing, finishing etc, they work out the recipes for chemicals or colours for different fabrics, work out machine settings (temperature, speed, pressure, timing), supervise dye mixing, and test to see that the fabric has been properly treated, for flame resistance, for example. Technicians and mechanics keep the sophisticated electronic, computer-controlled machinery operating smoothly.

Designers are employed in increasing numbers, although still mainly by the larger, and specialist (eg lace) companies. See ART AND DESIGN

Textile technologists work as production managers/controllers (which includes quality control), general managers, or technical officers/advisers, in research and development (working on, eg new machinery, computer control methods, especially in dyeing and colouring, improving fibre characteristics, such as strength and durability, etc), and in marketing.

Recruitment and entry Although the industry is never likely to recruit in huge numbers again, it is clearly looking for its share of higher-calibre people at all levels. Recruitment is fragmented between sectors, and tends to be locally based.

Professional/technologist level, the industry recruits graduates with appropriate degrees (see below), but may take small numbers of, eg chemists, mechanical/production engineers, electronic/systems engineers, and people with business-related degrees, especially for sales and marketing.

Technician-level entry normally requires at least four O-level-equivalent passes at 16-plus†, including mathematics and a science subject, with increasing recruitment at eighteen-plus with at least one A level.

Craft-level no formal qualifications stated, but needs a 'good' educational background, preferably with some CSE-equivalent passes.

YTS: at least one sector of the industry, wool textiles, is introducing a two-year scheme.

Qualifications and training Training is mainly industry based, with the support of voluntary training bodies, which are fragmented between the sectors, and are devolved to the main centres of the industry.

Professional/graduate level Technologists normally qualify pre entry. A number of degree courses are designed specially for the industry (but only a few the largest companies have been sponsoring students for textile-related or engineering courses), ie –

Carpet/related textile design: Kidderminster CFE/Wolverhampton Polytechnic;

Textile chemistry: Leeds University;

Textile/clothing studies: Galashiels: Scottish Textile College;

Textile design: see ART AND DESIGN;

Textile economics/management: Manchester: UMIST;

Textile/knitwear technology: Leicester Polytechnic;

Textile marketing: Huddersfield Polytechnic;

Textile studies (options in engineering, clothing, management): Leeds University;

Textile technology: Huddersfield Polytechnic (p-t), Manchester: UMIST (chemistry or materials/processing).

The professional body is the Textile Institute.

Technician-level training, on-the-job with release for college study, leads to BTEC awards, at National and Higher National levels, in science-based general, or specialised schemes eg on coloration.

Examples of training schemes include the Wool Textile career structure scheme (1986-7 intake 70), with formal programmes (leading to BTEC awards), including supervisory training, for combing, worsted-yarn production, weaving, woollen carding and spinning production, technical dyeing and quality control, colour matching and warp preparation.

See also ART AND DESIGN

Craft workers also train on-the-job, and may study by release for CGLI qualifications in textile techniques (scheme 414), textile organisation and control (scheme 430), dyeing of textiles (scheme 431).

Further information from the British Textile Employers' Association, and the sector training organisations, eg the Confederation of British Wool Textiles (training department), and the Knitting & Lace Industries Training Resources Agency.

TIMBER AND FURNITURE INDUSTRIES

Wood is still a staple material for many industries, such as paper making, furniture making, and construction. Although more modern alternatives may be longer lasting and less liable to decay, wood is still popular for many uses and it is often only cost which is the problem. Britain imports over 90% of timber and wood products used.

THE TIMBER TRADE is now a national rather than a locally-based industry, after extensive restructuring – larger and stronger groups are nationally, or regionally, based. Timber and other wood materials are imported on huge bulk carriers, and so have to be discharged at specially-built timber terminals. Some importing companies are now involved also in manufacturing end-products, mainly components for the building industry, such as wood flooring, sawn fencing, veneers, plywood and chipboard, wooden doors and window frames, greenhouses and sheds.

Timber agents (of whom there several hundred) represent overseas suppliers in this country, and use their expert knowledge and marketing intelligence to sell the shipper's output to importers. They also help both shipper and importer to make arrangements for delivery, which includes arranging insurance, documentation, chartering and financing. Importers buy timber from overseas suppliers either via agents or directly. They normally sell to merchants or direct to wood-using customers or through their own merchanting outlets, but sometimes to each other. They carry stocks of a wide range of wood materials of varying species and in numerous grades and dimensions. Most companies therefore have sizeable yards, and have their own sawmills, drying kilns, chemical treatment plants and fabricating shops.

Merchants buy from importers, not only handling the raw wood, but also stocking a wide range of wood products. Merchants may be multi-purpose building merchants, but they may serve a wide range of customers, and may operate sawmills and wood treatment plant too. Modern machinery, especially powered equipment (increasingly computer controlled), new glues and stapling equipment, have revolutionised timber preparation.

Employment in the industry About 40,000 were working in the timber industry in 1986, against some 99,000 in 1973.

A high proportion of people in the industry are machine operators, drivers, wharf and yard operators. Skilled work includes wood machining, maintenance (including sharpening and generally caring for industrial saws) and fitting, preservation and kiln work. Promotion can be to, eg sales, supervisory and yard management. Commercial staff – in sales, buying, and general management – all have to be skilled in timber technology.

Recruitment and entry Junior executive staff are expected to have at least four O-level-equivalent passes. A small but growing proportion are recruited with higher qualifications, including appropriate degrees (see below) – senior positions are usually filled by internal promotion.

Timber agents are not normally recruited direct from school/college – most are recruited from people already working in the trade, and are fully experienced and qualified.

Operative entrants do not need any formal entry qualifications, but a reasonable educational background is wanted to start training as eg wood machinist or mechanic/fitter.

YTS: a two-year scheme (managed by the TTTA) is open to all 16- and 17-year-olds (see below).

Anyone wanting to make a career in the industry is advised by the TTTA to look for vacancies in companies who are members of the Association.

Qualifications and training The industry now has a voluntary training organisation, the Timber Trade Training Association (TTTA). TTTA has developed a modular training course structure for the industry. It includes –

YTS scheme which, in the second year, gives specialisation in mill and yard work (but no one can use dangerous machinery until they are 18), distribution, sales, or clerical work, combining in-company training with open/distance learning and short residential courses. Certification is by the Institute of Wood Science.

Basic timber trade course: a flexible, five-module package for all, other than YTS, entrants, including graduates.

Career development: a series of sales, practical/technical (eg timber drying, import procedure, milling), and management modules, which can be taken as and when needed.

Institute of Wood Science: a new two-year course starting in 1987-8, for which the only entry requirement is a credit pass in the timber product knowledge module as part of a YTS scheme or basic timber trade course.

Specialist/professional-level qualifications –
Bangor, University College: Wood science (BSc)
High Wycombe: Buckinghamshire CHE: Timber technology (BSc).

Further information from the Timber Trade Training Association.

FURNITURE is no longer made only of wood, but the industry still keeps close links with the timber trade.

The industry is only slowly recovering from recession, although production has been rising steadily since 1983. Partly this is due to soaring imports (up to 20% of sales), partly to the industry's inability to meet the quality, volume and delivery demands of the sharp, new-style retailers. It was also slow to move into growth areas like fitted kitchen and bedroom furniture.

The industry now has less than 900, mainly small family, firms, with fewer than fifteen workers, and only a very few (half-a-dozen or so) large manufacturers. Several hundred, including some larger firms, have gone out of business in the last five years. In addition there are a great many small craft workshops, making furniture entirely by hand, but these are mainly owner-run businesses and employ only one or two people, if any at all.

Almost all firms specialise in making a particular type of furniture, and for particular markets – the home, the office, school etc. Self-assembly furniture is an increasingly important area. Few firms make more than a fairly narrow range of products. Also part of the industry are the 30 or so piano makers.

The industry is still mainly craft-based, although sophisticated wood-working machinery is used in most firms, even the smallest, and few now entirely hand make their products. Generally the larger firms with big modern factories use most machinery – and a few are automating – while the smaller workshop is likely to use machinery for the preparatory work and hand tools in finishing.

Employment in the industry An estimated 60,000 people were employed in 1986, against 90,000 in 1979.

Craft skills Most production processes are craft skills.

Sawyers cut the wood into suitable sizes and shapes.

Machinists shape the wood into the various parts, and usually operate a number of different machines – to saw, plane, mortise, route, drill, turn, etc. They have to be able to follow drawings and be extremely accurate.

Veneering involves covering the exterior of the furniture with very thin sheets of attractive wood, or (for eg kitchens) a plastic surface. The most suitable wood has to be chosen for the particular piece of furniture and the design. Line, colour and grain must be carefully matched and the veneer put together to look as natural as possible, or to a prepared pattern. Expensive veneer has to be cut economically.

Cabinet makers fit and assemble the furniture. They do not just bond the parts together, but must make sure they fit together properly, that doors hang correctly on a cupboard, that drawers slide easily and fit their frames, that legs are even. In large firms, cabinet makers may work on just one or two stages of construction, while in smaller workshops they may assemble the entire piece. Some craft workers specialise in making, eg chairs.

Polishers and finishers mostly use large high-speed industrial sprays or electrostatic spray guns now, but there are still some opportunities for hand staining and finishing.

Upholstered furniture is made in stages. Skilled framemakers build the basic frame. Cutters produce pieces for the covers, which are then sewn. Upholsterers cover the frames with filling materials (nowadays mostly foam plastic), and then fit on the covers.

Promotion can be to

Technician-level work in the industry includes draughtsmanship, tool room and machine shop work, making prototypes, method study, production and quality control, charge hand and supervisory work.

Design see ART AND DESIGN.

Management/administration including MARKETING/SALES, PURCHASING, FINANCE etc. Management generally needs a technical as well as a business background.

Recruitment and entry The industry recruits a small number of qualified people for production/management (see below). Direct school-leaver entry for technician-level training is with four O-level-equivalent passes, but it is still common to take the craft route, for which no formal qualifications are needed. The British Furniture Manufacturers' Training Division runs a Youth Employment Scheme.

Qualifications and training Training is largely industry-based, although it is possible to train full-time in college prior to entry, especially for those mainly interested in more traditional craft skills.

Possible qualifications include –

Furniture production BSc – High Wycombe: Buckinghamshire CHE.

BTEC Furniture studies HND and ND at – Burnley CA&T (ND), Leeds: J Kramer (ND), London: Furniture C (HND/ND), Nottingham: Basford Hall (ND).

See also ART AND DESIGN for furniture design courses.

The British Furniture Manufacturers' youth employment scheme covers the first two (of three) years' craft-level training on-the-job and can be supplemented by release to study for CGLI qualifications in furniture craft studies (scheme 555), which allows specialisation in a particular craft.

Further information from the British Furniture Manufacturers' Training Division.

THE VEHICLE SECTOR

The industry makes cars, tractors, buses, aeroplanes, hovercraft, space craft etc. Powered vehicles have not been around for so very long, yet their manufacture is crucial to the economy, and has an importance and influence in manufacturing out of all proportion to its age. The car industry, for example, is one of steel's largest customers.

The industry as a whole has been moving for many years towards greater and greater concentrations of production and control, mainly to give greater economies of scale, but also to make the necessary investment a viable proposition. The number of separate companies producing vehicles and their components at national, European and international level has fallen sharply over the years as a result of mergers and closures.

THE AEROSPACE INDUSTRY makes not only civil and military planes and engines and avionic equipment and systems etc for them, but also guided weapons and missiles, hovercraft, and space gadgetry. The cost of plane-making and of the crucial research and development, on which expenditure is probably higher than in any other industry, has been soaring for years. The large-scale plane-makers have been meeting the problems with cross-national co-operative ventures – eg the European airbus, and the multi-combat Tornado plane – but lately smaller countries have been trying to develop aerospace businesses as a 'spearhead' technology giving access to huge markets, increasing the competition still further. The Air Force, for example, is buying a super-efficient trainer jet designed in Brazil, although it will be built at Short Brothers in Northern Ireland.

Companies and consortia compete intensively on an international basis for a total world market estimated to be worth over $1300,000 million over the next dozen years. This breaks down into some $800,000 million on military aircraft and guided missiles, $300,000 million on commercial aircraft (on top of current orders of over $30,000 million), and $200,000 million on space hardware (mainly communications satellites). Most analysts expect the market to grow even larger in the next century. Despite some problems – cuts in defence budgets, hiccups in space programmes, rising costs and tightening revenues for airlines – the long-term outlook for the aerospace industry is bright. Airlines have no option but to replace their ageing fleets with newer jets that are more efficient and economic to fly.

Despite government plans to trim defence expenditure, and the phenomenal cost of the newly-arrived Tornados, European, including British, aerospace firms are working together on several major new ventures, including a new fighter. On the commercial side, planemakers are now both continuing to develop improved versions of 1980s planes, and working on complete new generations of airliners, across the full range from 'jumbo' jet through to 100-seat or less, including so-called commuter and regional jet and turbo-prop planes. All are designed to cut operating costs, improve payload performance, and extend the distances planes can fly. All will incorporate very advanced technology – and bring down fuel consumption by some 40% (just 1% off saves an airline several million dollars a year). New planes have re-designed engines, make extensive use of advanced lightweight materials, more refined aerodynamics, less weight (so less power is needed to get them off the ground), and sophisticated fuel management systems, from accurate electronic control of engine settings to on-board computers which can calculate the most economical route from moment to moment, eg avoiding cross winds where possible. On-board computers and electronic cockpit control and coloured cathode ray tube displays instead of vast arrays of instrument dials for the crew, make planes easier and safer to fly. Manufacturers now also have to build, as economically as possible, less noisy and less atmospherically-polluting planes.

To fill order books and factories, aircraft manufacturers constantly try to talk customers and governments into new projects – and governments into funding their immensely-expensive development. Aircraft manufacturers depend greatly on being able to raise huge sums for investment, and can never be absolutely certain of sales, so there's always an element of insecurity.

The UK aerospace industry, despite considerable rationalisation over the past few years, is still the world's third largest, with a 1986 turnover of over £8000 million, of which 60% came from exports – and exports exceeded imports by an estimated £2000 million. Orders at the end of the year were £20,000 million and rising, with prospects for a high workload until the end of the century. EITB had 257 aerospace establishments in scope in 1985, against 269 in 1982.

Britain's aerospace industry makes a wide range of aircraft from crop-sprayer to wide-bodied jet, from jet trainer to fighter plane. British Aerospace is the industry's main linch pin, developing a wide range of civil aircraft. BAe is putting considerable effort into one of the most rapidly-developing sectors, the so-called 'regional' (seating 50-100) and 'commuter' (seating up to 50) markets, for which it has a new 146 four-engined short-range jet, and has developed the new Advanced Turboprop. BAe also has two smaller planes – the 19-seat twin-engined jetstream 31 turbo-prop which can be used as a commuter or an executive aircraft, and the 125 business jet. BAe has a 20% stake in the European Airbus Industrie consortium which is competing hard with US firms in the long-haul jet market, and with European Airbus is to develop a new generation of short-to-medium and long-range planes. On the military side, BAe builds part of the Tornado multi-role combat plane, Harriers, and Hawk trainers. The British and European industry expect to get a go-ahead by the end of 1987 to build over 1000 of the new European fighter. BAe is also working on the HOTOL re-usable space vehicle/aeroplane for the 21st century.

Short Brothers makes 330 and 360 turbo-props for the short-haul market too, and is working on new plans for more commuter planes with a Canadian partner. Westlands, the helicopter makers, continues to suffer, with the rest of the industry, from falling demand for helicopters both for civil – in eg oil and gas support services – and military use, and is having to slim down considerably; Westland also makes hovercraft. Britain also has several light one- and two-engine aircraft makers, and one company looks as though it has at last fully revived the airship, with orders from the US Navy.

Space is supposedly a major source of income now for the UK industry, but where recession failed to damage it, the spate of launch failures and technological problems has, hopefully only temporarily, stalled the business. BAe

Dynamics and one other, electronics, company manufacture spacecraft and satellites. BAe is leading contractor for the L-SAT 1 (and expects to build up to 40), is building military satellites, an £117.6 million contract for three 'Inmarsat' satellites for ship/oil rig-to-shore communications. BAe expects to help build a European manned space platform. BAe also makes military missile systems.

Britain's major aeroengine company, one of the world's 'big three', has a fierce fight on for its share of the estimated £175,000 million market. Again the development costs force engine manufacturers into collaborative programmes, eg Tornado's RB-199, and the EJ-200 for the new fighter – huge technological advances are needed to meet the required performance. New engines for civil planes can now cost £1000 million to develop, and for military planes the figure is even higher.

Employment in the industry Numbers employed in aerospace equipment are (1986) around 162,000 (nearly 40% of them working for BAe), against 198,000 in 1979 and 312,000 in 1952. BAe alone shed 11,500 jobs between 1981 and 1986, and Westland is still shedding jobs. Future employment depends on orders, the level of government funding, and few defence cuts.

Aircraft, aircraft engines, satellites, etc, have to be built individually. Parts of planes, eg wings or noses or frames, may be built in different locations, even different countries, and then transported to yet another factory for final assembly (as BAe builds airbus wings for the French to put on to the plane).

While production is difficult to automate fully, manufacturers employ the most technologically-advanced techniques and machinery, including robots – often specially developed by the companies themselves – feasible. Computer-based systems are used wherever possible, from computer-aided design and manufacture (CAD/CAM), through to systems for handling – storing and retrieving – the 22,000 different parts needed to build, for instance, a Tornado, and the latest in flexible manufacturing systems and numerically-controlled machines. Parts made in composite materials, which start out as powder/granules, can be formed and bonded using mass production techniques, so there will be less and less 'metal bashing' and welding/riveting etc in the future.

But building planes is still a skilled business, and even using the most modern and sophisticated equipment available, still employs comparatively large numbers of people, trained to use sophisticated, modern machines and techniques.

The proportion of highly-skilled people employed, at both professional/graduate and technician level, is inevitably high, across the full spectrum of 'functions', and not just in R&D. Developing, designing, building and marketing/selling end products as complex, costly and technologically sophisticated as high-performance aircraft and space equipment takes multi-disciplinary teams of experts of all kinds, and aeronautical engineers are only part of them.

The electronics and computer-based equipment going into commercial planes, for example, is now at least a third of the total cost, considerably higher for military and space craft, and while some aeronautical engineers are trained specialists in these 'avionic' systems, developing and designing them also involves, eg electronic and control engineers, and computer scientists. Similarly, redesigning, developing and manufacturing aircraft structures, using the latest in composite materials, also employs mechanical engineers, plus just a few civil engineers and materials scientists.

(Engineering) designers may work on structures, or on electronic and avionic systems. But they may also be involved in developing computer-aided design systems and methods, in developing and designing data base and information retrieval and transmission systems for CAD/CAM systems, or in design support – dealing with design standards and procedures. Designers may have to solve particular problems, produce prototype models, design lab tests, analyse data, write reports.

Production management is a complex business of co-ordinating both manufacture and assembly of specific aircraft, and each area of manufacturing – wing skin panels for example – 'project' and 'product centre' management.

Aircraft manufacturers mostly also design and develop their own (advanced) manufacturing technology and systems both for making many of the components and parts, and for assembly. This can involve, for example, developing the new processes needed when metals are replaced by plastic or carbon fibre composites. Efficient production depends heavily on work/method study, which has to live with continual changes, preparing optimum factory layouts and production flow lines, deciding on work packages and monitoring output. Production engineering works out how to produce and/or assemble components, designs (and has made) tools etc, and plans manufacturing sequences and processes.

Quality assurance in plane making has to meet legal standards and control throughout all phases of manufacture, assembly and testing, starting with the materials and parts made by other companies as well as the machines used in manufacturing, through to the point of delivery. Monitoring for defects throughout manufacturing, and preventing them happening again, is part of the function. Test programmes and equipment have to be designed and produced.

Production employs mainly aeronautical, mechanical/production, and electrical/electronic engineers, some scientists (eg physics graduates in production of opto-electronic sensing devices), and some manufacturers involve people with business qualifications too.

Research and development may be in avionic systems and electronics (as above), or structures and materials – eg evaluating airframe fatigue, investing and evaluating new and existing materials and manufacturing systems for them, predicting and controlling total aircraft mass and inertia, and aerodynamics – finding the optimum aircraft geometry to meet all the conflicting demands on an aircraft, eg aeroelastic tailoring the aerodynamic surfaces to give the most load/deflection characteristics for overall aerodynamic and flight control system performance.

Research can come close to some very fundamental work, on eg laminar (continuous smooth) flow of air over plane wings, new alloys for engine components, super-efficient engine fans, and multi bladed propellers. All research involves sophisticated state-of-the-art computing. While R&D still involves extensive testing, in eg wind tunnels, computer simulation methods are now helping to cut the time and cost.

Again, research involves multi-disciplinary teams, of engineers (aero, mechanical, electrical/electronic), computer scientists, some scientists (mainly physicists), some (applied) mathematicians.

Accurate, up-to-date figures are hard to come by. But of technicians going into their first jobs in 1980-1, 26% went into central-service type work (eg technical writing, software preparation, and work study), 19% joined development/design teams, 14% went into production planning, 12% became draughtsmen/women, 11% went into test and quality assurance work, and 9% became service engineers.

Commercial functions and support services deal, almost with routine, with huge sums and long time scales. They all have a significant technical/technological content which makes an engineering/science background as useful as commercial training. Pre-planning market research, attempting to predict needs decades ahead, takes considerable experience of the aircraft business, civil or military. Sales engineers monitor and analyse the airline business, traffic and revenue predictions, prepare sales material, visit airlines and take part in sales presentations – the battle for an airline's business, and can have a dramatic effect on the success of an aircraft and so company profits, is fierce and very sophisticated. Negotiating contracts is a highly technical business with significant legal content. Finance has to evaluate and control projects with multi-million cash-flows which can last twenty years or more. Reliable and competitive estimating on design, development and manufacturing costs can make a considerable difference to the commercial viability of a plane, as can purchasing. All commercial functions make extensive use of computer systems to provide and manage data quickly and accurately, and companies do their own development work on these.

Recruitment and entry In a highly-sophisticated business, the small number of firms are always looking for very high-calibre people at all levels, although the numbers are never very large.

Graduate/professional BAe, for example, expected to recruit about 520 graduates in 1987, from whom they plan to develop managers for the next century. About 80% of the intake is for engineering and scientific work, the rest in commercial, financial and other business administration. The main demand, then, is for graduate engineers – aeronautical obviously, but also mechanical and production, electrical and electronic/control, computer, etc, as some materials scientists/metallurgists, and some scientists, particularly computing, physics and mathematics. People with technological backgrounds are recruited for marketing, sales, purchasing etc. as well as for production, R&D, and design.

School-leaver with at least four O-level-equivalent passes including mathematics and physics or another appropriate science, for technician training. Appropriate passes at 16-plus† are also preferred for craft-level training.

Qualifications and training High-level training is crucial to the industry – which comes within the scope of the Engineering Industry Training Board.

Professional/graduate Most people gain their degrees before entry, although larger companies offer a small number of sponsorships to read for appropriate degrees (mainly engineering but does not have to be aeronautical), which can include business studies (see ACADEMIC AND VOCATIONAL STUDIES). In an international business, languages are useful in all functions.

Technician/craft largely in-company, on-the-job and in training centres, with release to study for appropriate BTEC and CGLI awards.

Further information from the Society of British Aerospace Companies.

THE MOTOR INDUSTRY makes not only cars, but also commercial vehicles of all kinds (goods vehicles, buses and coaches etc), taxis, tractors, trailers and caravans, and the engines, components and accessories for them.

Manufacturing cars, trucks and vans takes a great deal of money. This is not just for research and development, although more more is now being spent on R&D and design than in the 1970s, since innovation is one of the ways of fighting the intense competition. Much of the investment is needed for today's highly sophisticated plant and equipment, and to buy components (which make up 60% of a car's cost), to produce large numbers of cars and trucks as fast and as economically as possible. Economies of scale, then, are still crucial – despite new technology. And so the majority of car makers these days are international companies, manufacturing in several countries, or have close links – in a 'vast web' of joint ventures – with companies in other countries. Car manufacturers fight each other across the world for a viable share of the global, and as well as regional and local, markets.

After several years of crisis and near-crisis conditions particularly in the British industry, late 1986 saw European car producers recovering strongly, and this continued into the spring of 1987. For years the talk had been of severe excess capacity, but the turn-around has been such that firms have actually been increasing the number of cars they can produce, on top of the extra capacity the sharply-improved productivity has given them. Lower energy prices, lower interest rates, and less aggressive competition from multinationals, on top of internal changes, made recovery possible. Even so, 'reconstruction' of the industry continues, with more mergers and buy-outs expected.

Although there are still some forty volume car/commercial vehicle producers world wide, just a dozen multi-nationals account for over 78% of production. The British industry is down to four volume car makers, only one entirely British, but with a fifth, Japanese, company, now (1987) building up volume output, just two volume commercial vehicle makers, and two 'luxury' car makers. According to EITB, the industry still has (1985) some 1000 separate 'establishments'. By early 1987, the UK industry was doing better than for many years, with imports falling as productivity improvements lead the multi-nationals to build more cars for the UK market in UK plants. With imports under 50% in 1986 for the first time in seven years, the industry expected to gain 60% of the home market in 1987, around 1.14 million cars, against 829,000 in 1986, and to sell 250,000 overseas. The industry is cautiously talking about expansion, and planned investment is (1987) high.

Dramatic cost cutting, rapidly-rising productivity, and more frequent, innovative, sharply-styled and engineered new models are central to maintaining recovery, meeting competition, and expanding. While there is less incentive to improve fuel economy, manufacturers are still seeking to design lighter, more efficient engines (which will soon use ceramic materials) and batteries, more exact aerodynamic shapes to make cars more economical. While there is no shortage of bright new technological ideas for cars, manufacturers have to be sure they are what the customer wants – 'speaking' cars that lecture drivers and constantly-flashing electronic dashboards have proved not entirely popular. On top of constantly-variable transmission systems, all-wheel drive, anti-lock braking, and electronic instead of electrical circuitry (20% of cost by 2000, double the 1987 figure), safety and a comfortable quiet ride are the basis of many current and future developments. Electronic control of suspension and steering, using sensors and computers, and sonar or radar-based anti-collision systems are all being developed.

The industry is already extensively automated and computer controlled, with some areas of production already 90% automated, and manufacture fully controlled by computers within prospect. Flexible manufacture, with lines capable of building several different models, and even completely 'customised' short runs (eg for a hire fleet), is in operation. On some lines, programmable controllers, linked to central minicomputers, deliver the right parts for a given model to the right assembly point at the right time, also saving on stock holdings. Major manufacturer use robots, which can change their own tool sets, wherever possible – in die-casting, welding, paint-spraying etc, machining, machine loading, palletising, and moving parts and sub-assemblies.

Robot sensors can check for, eg body leaks on the final assembly line, and on the most advanced lines do all the quality control. Production is increasingly integrated, although some sub-assemblies are still produced by component manufacturers. The industry is one of the largest users of machine tools, and the many parts still have to be shaped, by pressing, forging and casting, and machined, although firms look constantly for ways of making parts in eg aluminium and plastic, both for lightness and because manufacture is easier. But rising productivity and cost cutting depend as much on better management and manufacturing strategy – cutting down on inventories and parts in stores, improving quality control and saving on materials and waste, etc.

Employment in the industry has continued to fall sharply, to under 239,000 in 1986, against a peak of 514,000 in 1969 (it fluctuated between 440,000 and 470,000 in the 1970s). Numbers are expected to go on falling, regardless of any recovery in production, since further rationalisation and automation is likely to counterbalance any increase in output.

Production still uses well over 70% of car firm employees, despite sharply rising productivity – automated production at Jaguar is boosting production from 42,000 in 1986 to 60,000 by 1989 with no increase at all projected in the 10,500 workforce.

Most people working in production are semi-skilled, but with craft workers in, eg maintenance, electrical work, and some tool setting. Automation has cut jobs in body plants and paint shops most (by well over half in the newest plants). Assembly and trim are still labour-intensive, but just ensuring that work is done right the first time has also cut out a great many jobs in inspection and rectifying throughout production. Qualified engineers, normally mechanical/production, manage production units, supported by supervisory staff/technicians.

For its size, the industry employs a fairly small proportion of technicians. Of those going into their first jobs in 1980-1, some 28% became draughtsmen/women, 21% went into production (including planning), 9% went into each of development/design and laboratory/technical work, 7% became service engineers, and 5% went into test and quality assurance work. For 10% there were no technician posts available.

Engineering functions The industry traditionally employs a relatively small proportion of qualified engineers, mainly in production. In addition to production and quality control, the industry employs engineers in a range of functions needed to translate designs into production – process engineers to decide on the necessary operations and specifying new machinery; tool engineers to specify, design etc special tools, gauges, fixtures for new models; industrial engineers to establish work standards and work out capacity; layout engineers to plan the factory; materials engineers to devise and implement systems to improve and standardise storage and flow of materials and components, etc.

Though there has certainly been an increase in R&D and design recently, much of this is done on a multi-national basis, so the actual numbers involved in the UK are quite small. Research, development and design is multi-disciplinary team work, mainly for engineers, some scientists, and supporting technicians (eg in the 'drawing office', testing). Manufacturing problems engineers must solve are mostly very practical – it took, for example, eighteen patient months to work out how to stop thermal expansion in polyester bumpers so that they could go through paint ovens on the body shell.

Design is an engineering activity. Even the car's appearance, or styling, is today integrated into the engineering design, the work of designers with engineering training, and has to achieve a tricky synthesis between technical efficiency – the aerodynamic answers from thousands of hours in a wind tunnel or their equivalent in a computer model, for instance – and market appeal as identified by marketing. Design teams do, though, include eg interior designers. Use of CAD-CAM – computer-aided design and manufacture – techniques is now widespread in the industry. Initial design ideas are translated into computerised complete body surface models, and computer models simulate loads, stresses etc to confirm structural strength and safety. Finite element analysis, using idealised computer representations of the body structure, is used to find the best weight/strength ratio and on, eg steering and suspension systems. Computer simulation can be used to make initial tests of virtually every operating aspect, including crashes and their detailed effects, although sophisticated scale and full-size (clay) models and prototypes are still built. Cars have to be designed now so that they can be built by robots, and once the design is finalised, detailed specifications are retrieved automatically to design the press tools and dies needed to produce the very many panels that make up a modern car.

Commercial functions MARKETING and product planning – finding out what the mass-market customer will buy in several years' time and analysing competing firms' plans go together in the automobile industry, and so marketing managers are often qualified engineers. Sales teams liaise with dealers, or work on sales to, eg hire-car fleets or firms which buy cars in large numbers for employees. Customer services, mainly employing engineers, set standards for dealer facilities, develop marketing programmes on service facilities etc.

With components such a major element in a car's cost, the scale of orders is huge, and PURCHASING is a crucial function in ensuring secure, economically-priced supplies of parts which meet new technological specifications. A car manufacturer's purchasing department may still deal with more than 500 suppliers, although they have reduced the number of contracts.

In FINANCIAL MANAGEMENT sophisticated budgetary and inventory and other financial control systems are used.

Major manufacturers using sophisticated computer-based systems – for eg product development, sales, finance, and parts – have their own large computer divisions (one such employs some 1000 people). Having developed sophisticated software, eg in simulating and designing advanced factory systems for their own plant, some are marketing and selling these, as well as services, outside the industry. See COMPUTING.

Promotion is largely from within, for people with extensive experience of the industry. A high proportion of today's top managers started as engineering apprentices (ie aiming for professional qualifications) in the industry.

Recruitment and entry The combined effects of recession and labour-saving investment cut recruitment sharply, and overall will not go back to earlier levels, although there were signs of some improvement in 1987.

Graduate/professional level Firms are now recruiting in some numbers, eg the larger manufacturers are now (1986) taking 100-150 a year, and a smaller one about 30 a year. The main requirement is for mechanical/production (including automobile), manufacturing and electrical/electronic engineers, computer-aided engineering, computer/systems scientists, with occasional requirement for aeronautical engineers. Up to half of all vacancies may, however, be in non-technical functions, and are open to graduates in any discipline.

School-leavers are recruited for craft- and technician-level training in comparatively small numbers. Larger motor manufacturers have EITB-based YTS schemes, with several hundred places.

Qualifications and training Training is based mainly on individual firms, and largely follows Engineering Industry Training Board guidelines.

Professional/graduate level normally pre-entry via a degree or close equivalent in eg MECHANICAL/PRODUCTION (MANUFACTURING) or COMPUTER-AIDED ENGINEERING, ELECTRICAL, ELECTRONIC, COMPUTING/SYSTEMS. Some manufacturers offer sponsorships for engineers. See ACADEMIC AND VOCATIONAL STUDIES IN ENGINEERING.

Firms provide training for professional engineering qualifications, and the larger ones have developed postgraduate training schemes with universities to cover eg car electronics, mathematical modelling, aerodynamics.

Craft workers and technicians are trained under EITB schemes. They may also study for national qualifications, ie CGLI, or BTEC awards.

Further information from the Society of Motor Manufacturers and Traders.

Professional, Scientific and Social Services

Introduction	913
Education	915
Health and medical services	950
The legal system	1019
Management services	1030
Religious organisations and services	1039
Social work	1048
Translating and interpreting, working with languages	1061

INTRODUCTION

The term 'profession' is nowadays used very loosely to describe a steadily widening range of occupations. The tight descriptions once used to define the professions are now rarely applied. Even the idea of service, to society and the community in general, and to the individual and the disadvantaged in particular, which used to be considered a major characteristic, is seldom raised.

Lewis and Maude (in *Professional People*, published by Phoenix House, 1982) argue that the true basis of professional life is in fact an essentially ethical relationship, a contract between practitioner and client (or patient, or patron). Since the standards are, or have been, set generally by and for those in private practice, even where private practice is declining or does not exist, this confidential relationship between individual practitioners and whoever employs them, marks many, if not most, true professions.

But when it comes to actually deciding whether a particular occupation or service, is, or is not, in practice a profession, the problems of definition become almost insoluble. To accept the Carr-Saunders definition, 'any body of persons using a common technique who form an association the purpose of which is to test competence in the technique by means of examination', would now mean including over 75% of the occupations in this book in one chapter. It seems, therefore, simplest to accept the definitions of the Standard Industrial Classification, with the addition of social services, excluding those professions which seem to fit better elsewhere.

These latter should, then, be considered in the setting of this chapter as well as within the chapters in which they are fully described. They include ACCOUNT-ANCY AND FINANCIAL MANAGEMENT, ACTING, ACTUARIAL WORK, ADVERTISING, ARCHITECTURE, ARCHIVE WORK, ARMED FORCES, ART AND DESIGN, AVIATION, BANKING, CIVIL SERVICE, ECONOMICS, ENGINEERING, ESTATE/PROPERTY MANAGE-MENT AND AGENCY, JOURNALISM, LANDSCAPE ARCHITECTURE, MANAGEMENT, MUSEUM WORK, MUSIC, PUBLIC RELATIONS, SURVEYING, UNDERWRITING, VETERIN-ARY WORK, WRITING.

Almost by definition, the idea of a profession suggests stability, security, a clearly-identifiable occupation – and little fear of fundamental change or risk of unemployment. Competition between professions, even between members of one profession, the very idea of working for a profit or commercial interest, have all been greatly played down as not in keeping with high standards or the 'image' of the professions. Many professional bodies have traditionally had strict rules which members have to follow, and many have not, in the past, even allowed them to advertise.

Along with most occupations, most professions are now going through, or facing, considerable changes. For most, stability, security, and an unchanging job specification are vanishing rapidly. It is, indeed, something of a myth that the professions have not had to cope with change in the past. For instance, in the 1960s, accountants began to change their profession quite radically when they took computers on board, and developed significant new skills as a result.

Changes now under way, and coming, are rather more drastic and wide ranging. Twin challenges face the professions –

The first is technological. 'Information technology', computer-based systems are affecting them just as greatly as all other occupations. Access to information and ways of organising and analysing it, which have been the critical basis and monopoly of so many professions, is opening up and making users less and less dependent on professional interpreters with each succeeding technological generation. 'Expert systems', essentially computer programs which can emulate professional skills (see COMPUTING), are now a reality, and will be in widespread use before the end of the century. The effects can only be dramatic. Already information technology has made possible hugely increased competition for services which were traditionally provided exclusively by one set of institutions, notably in FINANCE.

Second, competition is now officially and deliberately promoted, both in and between professions, and from outside the professions. The professions, as well as other occupations, are being forced to 'de-regulate'. Since one of the effects of professional rules has been to create monopolies, this is creating some major upheavals. Long-established demarcations between professions, and accepted professional rules, are being challenged and overthrown. Solicitors have lost their monopoly on conveyancing, opticians on supplying spectacles, and patent work is being opened up. All the financial professions are going through a major shake-up. Multi-disciplinary partnerships, a mix of accountants, solicitors, surveyors, estate agents etc, are now possible. Architects, surveyors and building managers are competing for project control, traditionally an architect's role (see CONSTRUCTION). This could be the first stage in some very far reaching changes.

Widening entry to occupations could create a third problem for the professions. The ways in which entry to the professions are limited by the professions themselves to some extent act as a barrier to competition, and can also make 'progression' impossibly difficult – nurses and other paramedicals cannot, for example, gain any exemption from any part of the training to be a doctor. Most professions set some fairly stiff academic requirements which, intentionally or not, create difficult barriers for, eg people who are 'late developers', who do not go through the conventional educational routes to a qualification, or who want to change occupation. The National Council for Vocational Qualifications is now (1987) seeking to 'articulate' higher levels of professional qualifications within the NVQ framework (see ACADEMIC AND VOCATIONAL QUALIFICATIONS). If NCVQ is to establish routes through to qualification in the full range of occupations, including the more traditionalist professions, for everyone capable of acquiring the necessary 'competences', then changes will have to be made to some of the more restrictive entry practices too. See also the first chapter on ACADEMIC AND VOCATIONAL QUALIFICATIONS.

Professions have other crises to face, which in the 1980s are the result of rapid change, different perceptions of what is wanted from them, complex issues on how restricted resources can be stretched to meet public demand. Here technology is barely involved, and competition not at all. The political dimension and fierce media attention add to the problems. For different reasons, morale is at present (1987) low in professions such as teaching, social work, and nursing, to the extent that recruitment is affected and qualified staff are leaving in worrying numbers. This is not a situation for professions crucial to people's well-being to be in, as the numbers of qualified (for entry) school-leavers fall, and other sectors of employment are intensifying the competition to attract them.

EDUCATION

Background	915
Schools and school-teaching	917
Further and higher education	932
Other teaching opportunities	938
Other work in education	940

BACKGROUND

Education is a major industry, and a large employer. It includes not only the schools – primary and secondary, maintained, independent, and in future more 'direct grant' – but also universities, polytechnics, colleges of higher education, further education and technical colleges, and specialist schools and colleges (teaching eg handicapped students, ARCHITECTURE, ART, DANCING, DRAMA, HOME ECONOMICS and MUSIC). It still employs over 1.5 million people, a high proportion of whom teach, plus administrators (in eg local education authorities), other professions (LIBRARIANS, CAREERS OFFICERS, EDUCATIONAL and CHILD PSYCHOLOGISTS, MEDICAL STAFF), LABORATORY TECHNICIANS, INSTITUTIONAL MANAGERS and domestic staff.

Other organisations have their own educational facilities (but they are usually restricted in scale and normally have a fairly narrow educational aim), for example the educational/training facilities of the larger employers (eg the BANKS, CIVIL SERVICE, BRITISH TELECOM), managing agents for MSC training schemes, training centres run by professional and other bodies, and other major organisations. The ARMED FORCES each have their own education corps. Many other organisations provide education/training for specific purposes, from learning to swim or play golf to private business schools.

The education 'industry' supports parts of a number of other other sectors, for example, educational PUBLISHING, JOURNALISM, BROADCASTING, and professional bodies.

THE EDUCATION SYSTEM

For years a steadily expanding (and improving) state-provided educational system has been virtually taken for granted in the UK, with compulsory schooling for all between the ages of five and 16, and expanding opportunities for those under five and over 16. From the start of the co-ordinated national education system in 1902 to the mid-1970s, education was a growth industry. For example, state expenditure on education rose by 154% between 1946 and 1970, to a peak of 6.3% of GNP in 1975 (against 4.5% in 1965-6).

Expansion ended effectively about 1975, with the sharp fall in the birth rate, economic problems, and later changing government policy. Although the actual amount spent has continued to rise – to about £17.5 million in 1986-7 – this is down 2% in real terms since the mid-70s, and the share of GNP spent on education is down to about 4.25%.

Education, expanding or contracting, is always changing, often radically, with all kinds of political, social and economic forces exerting pressure – for expansion, for reform of one kind or another, for improved standards or greater vocational input – and this is never likely to stop. Indeed, political 'initiatives' in the education sector have, in the mid-1980s, become almost endemic, and are now (1987) apparently to change the present system totally, with unforeseeable results especially for those who must teach or administer in education. Argument and debate about education is endless – what it should be and do, how it should be done, how far it should be 'relevant' to the needs of employers, etc.

By the mid-1970s, secondary schools were (largely) reorganised into the comprehensive system, linked to the virtual end of the selective eleven-plus examination; the school-leaving age was raised twice, to sixteen; more subjects were taught; more pupils took and passed more examinations; teachers became more innovative and experimental with what to teach and how to teach it, using a developing range of new teaching aids.

Expansion and innovation were not limited to the schools. Some 17 universities and university-level institutions were created, as well as the Open University, thirty completely new-style polytechnics were set up, and the further education system was reorganised. Here, too, innovation and experiment became the vogue.

From the late 1970s to the mid-1980s, the climate was rather different. Expenditure on education fell in real terms. The whole education system had to come to terms with both less state financial support and fewer pupils/students. Overall, the result has been fewer opportunities and jobs, and despite some relaxation on the limits on public funding, the education system is still widely considered to be under-resourced.

Change has not ended, however. Indeed, education has become a focal point of radical political 'initiative', with new 16-plus exams, standards and plans for a national curriculum; with new types of schools (the proposed 'city technology colleges'); with greater involvement of parents and local businesses in school management; plans to devolve more financial and managerial control to the school from the LEA with the option of becoming an independent 'trust'; and on the whole way the teaching profession is organised.

At the same time, local education authorities are still coping with the effects of falling numbers, with the changes in provision for 16-to-19-year-olds, with developing schemes such as TVEI to make learning more work-oriented, etc.

Change and innovation in education have always happened against a background of debate and controversy. Education involves, through parents, a large proportion of the electorate, as well as prospective employers. Consumers generally hold quite strong views on the form education should take and how young people should be taught, so that those working within the educational system are directly affected by political decisions. Traditionally, direct central-government intervention in what happens inside educational institutions has supposedly been minimal, but now everyone working in the educational field has to live not only with the indirect, but also centrally-directed change, and under much greater scrutiny and debate on educational issues and methods.

SCHOOLS AND SCHOOL TEACHING

The total number of schools in the UK is now (1986) under 36,000 (down nearly 3000 in ten years even with the 100% increase in nursery schools). Over 92% are state schools. Even the number of nursery schools has dropped slightly from the peak of 1260 in 1983-4. The number of primary schools is down to under 25,000, secondary schools to below 5200, and special schools to about 1900. 'Independent' schools number under 2600 (down 1100 in ten years). About nine million children and young adults are (1986) at state schools, about 700,000 at independent schools. Numbers in primary schools 'bottomed out' at about 4.1 million in 1985, and are now slowly rising again, so more teachers will be needed. Numbers in secondary schools will go on falling until 1991.

Schools are communities, hopefully caring communities where, ideally, children can develop their full potential, whether they find learning easy or difficult; whether their abilities are conventionally academic, creative, practical, or a mixture of any of these; whether they are keen to learn or need motivating, and regardless of background. In practice, of course, these aims are extremely difficult, perhaps impossible, to achieve for all children. Identifying and developing the teaching methods which will do all this has still a long way to go and is anything but straightforward; schools have to cope with conflicting demands, from for example, the public examination system and the employment market; resources may be inadequate; the problems are many and varied.

Schools are traditionally run quite differently to most other organisations. State schools are at present (1987) formally controlled by local (education) authorities (LEAs) and they are at present the teachers' employers. (Independent schools are managed by trusts or governors.) In practice head teachers have a great deal of independence and personal responsibility. Recent legislation has, however, given governing bodies of LEA schools, with larger numbers of parents and business representatives, greater say in how they are run. It is now planned to give head teachers and governors an even greater managerial role by letting them control their own budgets, as agreed with the LEA, and by the 1990s schools are to be allowed to 'opt out' of LEA control altogether, becoming independent trusts directly under the Department of Education and Science. From 1988-9, a number of 'city technology colleges', with some funding and input from industry and commerce, will directly employ their own teachers.

The individual teacher is traditionally master or mistress in his or her own classroom, and can decide how and, to some extent (ie as limited by, for example, examination syllabuses), even what to teach. This will change if, as currently (1987) planned, a national curriculum is introduced. Nevertheless, schools are still run by a kind of consensus. The head has to gain the agreement of the teaching staff for particular policies, plans or changes, and will have to consult governors more in future too. In practice, the head mostly attracts, and has appointed, teachers who broadly agree with the school's approach and head teachers, as well as (subject) department heads in the larger schools, have their own strategies for gaining staff co-operation. Running a school is increasingly a team business.

SCHOOL TEACHING

This is still first and foremost a 'scholarly' and academic occupation, whatever the type of school. But it also involves communicating, making relationships, working with and getting on with people (of all ages), and also organising, both people and resources. 'Management' is set to become an increasing part of senior teachers' work.

Schools try to achieve a balance between educating the whole child, helping them to develop their potential, teaching them how to learn, to find out and think for themselves, and passing on subject knowledge, teaching them specific skills, helping them to pass examinations, and are increasingly expected to prepare them for employment.

At peak, in 1979, there were over 578,000 teachers in all kinds of schools. By 1986, this was down to under 540,000, of whom under 490,000 were working in maintained schools, 49,600 in independent schools (where numbers have continued to increase, if slowly, from the 44,700 of ten years earlier) and some 19,400 in 'special' schools for handicapped children in both maintained and independent sectors (also up from 12,500 in 1972). Numbers are set to fall further. Pupil/teacher ratios, overall, have continued to improve steadily: the average size of primary classes is (1986) about 22 against 27 in 1971, and of secondary classes under 16 against 17.8.

Jobs are still being shed, mainly by early retirement (10,000 a year 1983-5) and 'natural wastage', but with a few compulsory redundancies, although teachers are having to accept moves to other schools. But the balance between numbers qualifying and available jobs for new graduates seems to have improved. In October 1985, 85% of new graduates had found teaching posts in the UK, against only 71% in 1982. Only 6% were still unemployed and looking for a teaching job in 1985, against 16% in 1982. Particularly in sciences, growing shortages are projected if more graduates do not go on to train.

Working as a teacher
The time teachers spend in the classroom is only part of their working day, week, and year. While it might seem that teachers' working days are short by comparison with most other jobs – and the (proposed) new contract appears to endorse this by stipulating the equivalent of only a 39-week year – in fact the teaching day and term are only too often the proverbial tip of the iceberg. The new contract says clearly a teacher will work 'such additional hours as may be necessary...', and they always have.

Not only must teachers mark pupils' work done in school and at home (even five minutes per pupil per week means several evenings' work), but today's teaching methods demand far more pre-lesson preparation than traditional 'talk-and talk', and teachers must prepare for new and different exam syllabuses. Modern methods also require some practicality, ingenuity and creativity. Many teachers make all kinds of teaching aids for themselves. For many teachers computers are also an important teaching tool which must also be prepared – with programmes and projects.

Teachers are also expected to spend time on extra-curricular activities, often after school hours, ranging from sports, drama and music, through fund-raising, home-school links and parent-teachers' associations, to school journeys, country courses and community social work. Teachers must also spend time keeping up with new developments, and should go on regular courses. This can all add up to a working year no shorter than the national average.

Teaching is, for most people, a very demanding job, mentally, emotionally and physically. Contemporary demands on the education system; more demanding teaching methods; children and young people who are more independent minded, less passive and less amenable to traditional discipline. All combine to ask much more of today's teacher.

Promotion in secondary schools is mainly via the subject route, with senior teachers going on to more academically-demanding teaching, for instance for GCE A levels, and then on to departmental head – head teachers usually come through this way at least in maintained schools. Alternatively, it is possible to move up via the pastoral system, to head of year or house, or head of upper or lower school – in boarding schools especially, this is more often a route to a headship in independent schools. To gain promotion, in state and/or independent schools (teachers are not in any way restricted either except by choice or availability of posts), it is often necessary to change schools. The number of senior teaching posts is finite, and falling, particularly in state schools. Intermediate posts in large schools give scope for considerable responsibility. Smaller, and independent, schools, have fewer posts of middle responsibility. Some move out of teaching into, eg EDUCATIONAL ADMINISTRA-TION, or the INSPECTORATE, as a form of promotion.

Although school teaching is generally considered as a single profession, it is now almost essential to decide whom, what and where to teach before training. Different qualifications, and different personal characteristics too, are needed to teach, for example, a lively single group of seven-year-olds all day, than physics to a succession of different classes of teenagers of different ages and abilities.

PRESCHOOL AND NURSERY TEACHING While the legal age at which children start school is still the traditional five, it is today generally recognised that children under that age can benefit from a stimulating environment of 'creative play', organised by trained staff. Some provision is also made for children with special needs, eg if they live with one parent, or are handicapped in some way. However, funds are difficult to find, and provision for the under-fives is consequently very uneven.

Teaching the under fives is either in state nursery schools or classes in primary schools, or in private play and part-time 'nurseries'. About 768,000 under fives go to nursery classes in primary schools, about 96,000 to the 1250 separate nursery schools employing 2600 teachers throughout the UK. They are sup-posed to be helped by one or two trained nursery 'nurse' assistants. Nursery classes, of about 20 children, are not 'taught' in the conventional sense. Free play, which is physically and creatively stimulating, is mixed with activities which help children to learn simple skills like painting, printing, making masks, acting, story telling, singing and making music generally. They work with sand, water, climbing equipment, 'wendy' houses, pets, etc.

The very many private and very few council nursery groups (about 16,000 of the former, 125 of the latter) give three to four year olds similar opportunities of a few hours' 'structured' play. About two-thirds of these, however, are run by play-leaders or nursery nurses and only about a third by qualified teachers. See also NURSERY AND CHILDREN'S NURSING.

PRIMARY (STATE) AND PREPARATORY (INDEPENDENT) SCHOOL TEACHING Five- to eleven-year-olds (sometimes five- to thirteen-year-olds) are taught in primary schools in the maintained sector. Independent preparatory schools traditionally teach from seven or eight through to thirteen, but many now take younger children, certainly down to five, in 'kindergartens'.

Maintained primary schools normally 'stand alone', separate from secondary schools. They are all day schools, usually small, and mixed, all but 3% with under 400 children each, and 90% under 300. The 'average' school has about 250 children, six full-time teachers, one or two part-time, and a head. At peak (1975) primary schools numbered over 27,000 with over 240,000 teachers and over 5.9 million pupils. By 1985 the number of schools was down to under 25,000, the number of teachers down to 205,000, with only 4.5 million pupils. 'Prep' schools have not lost quite so many pupils, but parents are sending children to them later (after some time at a maintained school), and so expansion has slowed sharply.

Independent preparatory schools range from the junior departments of public schools, through to cathedral choir schools. Some, apparently quite separate, in fact prepare children for entry to specific public schools. Over 600 schools are members of appropriate associations and can therefore be considered 'efficient'. Some are boarding schools (40% for boys, 10% for girls); a growing number are co-educational, but many more still teach boys rather than girls.

In primary school, teachers normally have a single class throughout the day, for the whole academic year, teaching the same children all the time, whatever and however they are being taught – whether an 'integrated' project-centred curriculum, or subjects like reading, writing, maths, painting, music, games, basic science, separately. Primary teachers are rarely full subject specialists, but the government wants greater emphasis on basic skills and subjects, including science. Primary teachers are, then, being encouraged to take responsibility for one aspect of the curriculum (such as science, maths, or music), to act as consultants to fellow teachers on that aspect and, where appropriate, to teach it to classes other than their own.

Primary teachers try to build a close relationship with their pupils, and get to know them as well as they can. Children are taught to be part of a community, and helped with their physical development and use of language, as well as maths etc. Classes, on average, have about 22 children, mostly all of the same age and with all kinds of different abilities and aptitudes. Some schools, though, use different methods, for example 'team' teaching, which involves two or three teachers working together with a rather larger group of children. The infant school introduces purposeful activities and basic skills, often still through self-chosen occupations and not formal lessons. In these earlier years, then, days may not be 'structured', and teachers can organise the time in different ways. But older children do have more formal lessons with a combination of 'active' project-centred methods and more formal teaching.

Teaching in independent 'prep' schools may be similar to maintained primaries, especially for younger children. However, all but the most 'progressive' independent schools are in business to get pupils through common entrance exams for public school, at thirteen, and so formal subject teaching starts by eight or soon after, with English, maths, and French lessons from nine, sciences and Latin (now optional) from ten. Days and classes have to be more 'structured', and people able to teach specific subjects as well as generalists are needed.

Surveys show that most primary teachers work an average of forty or more hours a week, including at least three hours each weekend, and spend only a quarter of their 'break' time actually relaxing. Teachers in maintained primary schools normally have no homework to mark or exams to prepare for – although it is now planned to introduce formal testing at seven and eleven – it is obviously quite different teaching at eight-plus in prep school. But they all have a great deal of preparation to do for class work, research projects, dig out books and materials, arrange outings, organise plays and concerts, look over children's work and keep a check on their progress, write reports, and cope with emergencies and problems. In boarding prep schools, teachers also have to spend time with the children in the evenings and at weekends, organising and helping with hobbies and other activities; many boarding-school teachers have to live in.

SECONDARY SCHOOL TEACHING Most maintained secondary schools teach pupils from eleven through to sixteen and a proportion on to seventeen and eighteen, although this varies. For example, some education authorities teach nine- to thirteen-year-olds in 'middle' schools, and some the sixteen- to eighteen/nineteen-age group separately in sixth-form colleges. Independent schools generally teach from thirteen, sometimes eleven, and a higher proportion of pupils tend to stay on at school until they are eighteen.

Maintained secondary schools are now mostly 'comprehensive', teaching all the young people, of whatever ability, who live in the school's catchment area. All are day schools, many are co-educational but some are single sex. They are not all the same – they vary just as much as other types of school – if only because each LEA plans and organises its schools differently from others, and because the head has considerable personal responsibility. (If government plans go through, state schools will become more diversified.) They vary greatly in size, but only 200 or so have 1500 or more pupils, under 30% have more than 1000 pupils, and quite a few have under 300.

The number of maintained secondary schools has been falling for many years, first as smaller schools merged to form comprehensives, and then as pupil numbers fell. By 1985, numbers were down to well under 5300, against over 6600 twenty years earlier. They teach (1986) under 4.2 million pupils, against a peak of over 4.6 million in 1980. Numbers will go on falling until 1991. Numbers of secondary teachers peaked in 1980 at 281,600, and had fallen to 267,700 by 1985. Pupil numbers in independent schools have stabilised lately, and staff numbers are still rising.

Independent schools are generally a great deal smaller than maintained secondary schools. Few have more than 800 pupils. A high proportion are still single-sex, although many boys' schools now take girls into their upper forms. Quite a few are boarding schools, although day schools are expanding most. Just under 800 independent schools, including about 120 former direct-grant schools, are recognised as efficient. Each independent school chooses for itself the kind of children it will teach. Many are highly selective academically, although some do teach children from a wide range of different abilities, and some 'progressive' independent schools have liberal teaching policies, put less emphasis on public exams, have fewer rules etc.

Secondary schools teach a wide range of subjects, which vary with the school. Maintained comprehensive schools theoretically cover the widest range, although tight funding and staff shortages have forced schools to reduce the choice. Both maintained and independent schools teach what is now called a 'common core' – English, maths, sciences, geography, history, French, and some form of religious studies – and in future the government wants to formalise with legislation a national curriculum for state-funded schools (although CTCs will be allowed to vary this). Many schools teach social sciences, like economics and sociology. A fully comprehensive school will teach all abilities from remedial right up to GCE A level in all of these. An independent school with a high academic reputation will teach only at the highest levels, ie to GCSE/GCE standard and much of the emphasis will be on working for public examinations, which are often taken earlier than in maintained schools. Some comprehensives and most of the major independent schools also teach subjects like Latin, languages other than French and German. Maintained and some independent schools also teach commercial subjects, technical skills, etc. The 'Technical and Vocational Initiative' (TVEI) gives opportunities to teach vocational-related subjects. Subjects like music and drama are on the curriculum of most schools, but the extent to which they are taught seriously varies considerably.

Most teachers at secondary level usually specialise in teaching one subject, but an increasing number teach a second. In contrast to primary school, each teacher takes different groups of children in the same subject, throughout the school year. Classes may stay together for all their school work, or they may break up into ability groups for different subjects. Independent schools tend to set or stream more tightly than maintained schools, and test progress more frequently. In larger schools teaching is organised in departments, each with their own team of teachers and a 'head of department'. Teachers may both specialise in a subject, and also teach just part of the age range. A maths teacher in one large school may teach eleven- and twelve-year-olds in all-ability groups, or specialise in teaching for GCSE and/or A-level. Another department, even in the same school, may 'band' or 'set' pupils into ability groups from the first year.

What the teacher teaches, and how, can be a complicated mix of what the teacher personally wants to teach and his or her own chosen methods, the school (or head's) policy, the subject department's practice and plans and, as pupils move up the school, the demands of the public examination system. The influence of any of these elements varies considerably from school to school – in a school where English, history and geography are taught as an 'integrated' subject in the junior years, for example, anyone teaching any of these subjects has to fit into the team. All schools teach a range of sports and games. Other specialist skills are needed for particular types of teaching, eg remedial work and, with an increasing 'vocational' element in teaching, practical subjects are needed too.

Secondary school teachers must both prepare their lessons and teaching material, organise classroom and other displays, and set, mark and check pupils' work, out of class time, although they may have some 'free' periods in which to do some of this. Exams and other tests have to be prepared, supervised and marked; reports on individual pupils must be written. For GCSE and some other exams, course work has to be assessed. At most schools, staff meetings are regular events too.

Superimposed on the teaching structure is a 'pastoral' framework, designed to make sure every pupil has the right kind of support. Every teacher is generally also a form, or class, teacher, but may not actually teach them. Looking after the class includes basics like seeing who is away and why, and supervising their progress and behaviour, looking out for problems, acting as mediator when problems crop up, and being both disciplinarian and counsellor. At various stages, form teachers must see pupils make decisions on what they will study in the next phase of their schooling, and perhaps what public exams they will take. This has to be discussed with pupil, parents and other staff. A form teacher is everyone's point of contact for all the pupils in the class, from head to parent, from English teacher to careers officer. For pupils, a form teacher is someone to go to with problems, and to get practical help and advice. The form teacher is usually supported by 'house' and/or 'year' heads or tutors, who may have a lighter teaching load to allow them to deal with the many and varied problems their group of forms throw up.

As well as teaching and looking after up to twenty pupils, most teachers also help organise other activities such as drama groups, chess clubs, musical activities, sports fixtures, camping and climbing expeditions, and holidays abroad. In independent boarding schools, teachers spend time with pupils on out-of-school activities, and teaching times may be different.

SIXTH-FORM AND TERTIARY COLLEGES Traditionally, a mark of a school with a strong academic record has been a sixth form capable of getting pupils through A-level exams and into university. Teaching intelligent and well-motivated sixth formers is a form of bonus, or promotion for many teachers. Today, the traditional sixth form may not be the best or most cost-effective way to provide for the post-sixteen age group. Educationally, falling numbers make it difficult for some schools to teach a wide enough range of subjects. School-leavers need better qualifications, more of the academically less able want to stay on to improve their opportunities, and their educational needs are often quite different from the traditional, high-flying sixth former. Sixteen- to eighteen-year-olds want to study in an environment which treats them more as young adults rather than as school-children.

Local authorities are developing colleges which specialise in teaching this age group, combining subjects and courses from school and FE, as well as teaching newly-developed schemes, eg CPVE, especially designed for the age group. This is creating new kinds of teaching posts, working solely with students who are young adults, and teaching either academic subjects to a high level or more vocationally-oriented studies.

SPECIAL AND OTHER SCHOOL TEACHING The other main area of teaching is in special schools for children with some form of handicap, physical or otherwise, and for children who have 'special educational needs'. Estimates say some 20% of all children have special needs at some point during their school years, but that at most 2% are so handicapped that completely special provision has to be made for them. A small proportion of children have in the past gone to schools with appropriate facilities and especially trained teachers. National policy is now to 'integrate' as many handicapped children as possible into the 'ordinary' school system, despite reservations from some parents and educationalists.

Some special schools will certainly remain. Numbers have been falling, slowly though – from a 1980 peak of over 2000 maintained schools and nearly 147,000 pupils to under 1950 schools and 132,400 pupils in 1985 – partly because there are fewer children in total, and fewer children with severe handicaps, and partly because integration has already started. Numbers of teachers have fallen too, but only by 100, to 19,400 in 1985.

More handicapped children will, in future, then be taught in ordinary schools, either alongside children without such problems, or in special units within ordinary schools, or a mixture of both.

More handicapped children will be taught by the school's ordinary staff. But the schools will also still need teachers trained to cope with children's special needs and learning difficulties, whether physically handicapped, mentally or emotionally disabled, are badly disturbed, or just going through a difficult period for some reason. Teaching patterns will have to change though – for example, demand is likely to increase for teachers with special expertise to train other teachers, to be advisers, and to be 'peripatetic'.

Recruitment and entry Local education authorities, and reputable independent schools, recruit only properly qualified teachers (see Qualifications and training below). The government attempts to match output of qualified teachers to demand. Intake (England and Wales) is now being increased –

For primary teachers:	to 9850 (1987)	10,400 (1988)	10,950 (1989)
For secondary teachers:	to 9450 (1987)	9650 (1988)	9850 (1989)

Intake has recently fallen short of target, by 5% in 1985. Within the figures for secondary teachers the shortage of maths, physics and some craft teachers is severe, and intake for maths training was 35% short of target in 1985.

A genuine, and strong, interest in teaching for its own sake is essential. Teaching is not now a 'safety net' career or something to do while waiting for something more interesting. The emphasis is on having a scholarly/academic mind, with real enthusiasm for a subject. Anyone planning to be a teacher must really like and get on with children and young people generally, and not be irritated or annoyed by their behaviour. Prospective teachers need to be good at building working relationships, and must be able to work with children of all backgrounds and abilities within a chosen age range – not only those who are well-motivated and clearly intelligent in the conventional sense, but also with children whether creative or clumsy, who are keen or bore easily.

The best teachers try to do all they can to help all pupils to develop their potential, and not be negative about pupils' failures, or let them feel their school years are a waste of time. It takes skill to attract and hold pupils' interest, and not bore or underestimate them. Teachers have to be able to explain clearly, concisely, coherently and simply, without (for example) sarcasm or talking down to anyone. They need to be adaptable, patient, and unflappable. They need organising ability, physical and emotional stamina, and usually plenty of energy, enthusiasm and adaptability. A sense of humour helps, being shy or easily upset does not. It is also useful to have a hobby, outdoor or other interest to share with pupils.

Qualifications and training Teachers must now have a degree, and a teaching qualification (the two can be combined), with at least O-level-equivalent passes† in English and mathematics. Practising teachers now take part in selecting students, and that selection, in terms of suitability for teaching, has been made 'more rigorous'. Candidates are encouraged to spend time in industry or commerce, and gain experience of the classroom before initial teacher training.

Newly-qualified teachers' certificates now specifically draw attention to the age-range and subjects for which their course of study was intended, and for primary courses indicate any relevant specialism. This does not formally limit any teacher to teach only this age range or subject(s), but is intended to see that teachers are more closely matched to the needs of individual schools.

The pattern of education and training for prospective teachers has gone through several quite radical changes over the last fifteen years. The main aim is to produce a better educated (and graduate), teaching force, via a more flexible, open-ended pattern of courses without losing any emphasis on the development of professional skills, and bringing the post-school education of teachers closer to that of other graduate professionals. Unfortunately, redesigning education and training for teachers has had to be carried out against the background of successive, and severe, reductions in the numbers being trained. This has involved traumatic college and departmental closures and reorganisations. The choice of course can therefore be quite complicated.

The effect of changes, to date, generally means that most teachers will, in future, not only have a degree, but an honours degree, and will have studied for four years. Colleges are expected to be tough on students whose classroom performance is 'suspect' even though their academic work is satisfactory, and transfer them to another course. All newly-qualified teachers also have to complete a further, 'probationary' year in school.

The main routes to qualification are –
First, via a course leading to a BEd degree, which combines, and often partly integrates, studies of one or more academic subjects (normally those which students want to teach) with professional educational studies and practical training. Theoretically, it is possible either to try for honours and study therefore for four years, or to study for only three years and gain a BEd without honours. In practice very few three-year courses remain. Most BEd courses are taught in polytechnics and colleges of (higher) education, few at universities. Although the number of courses is down sharply, the choice is still considerable. BEd courses are tailored to the needs of particular age groups, and must include at least two full years' course time devoted to subject studies at degree level. For the primary years a wide area of the curriculum, whereas for secondary teaching the two years has to be spent studying one or two subjects from the secondary curriculum – these could be special subjects for instance, physical education, home economics or craft, design and technology. Initial training for primary teachers must now include a sufficient, and substantial, element devoted to language and mathematics development.

The main alternative is to read for a conventional degree in one or two academic subjects (again preferably ones which will be useful in a teaching post), normally at university or polytechnic, and then to follow it with a one-year postgraduate certificate course to qualify as a teacher.

Some universities and polytechnics also have courses which 'integrate' the study of one or two academic subjects in the normal way (and alongside other students studying those subjects), and professional training, in a four-year course, for a conventional BA or BSc with a Certificate in Education.

Either of these is the more usual route (followed by nine out of ten of all new secondary teachers) for anyone planning to be a specialist teacher of one or more academic subjects, such as maths, sciences, English, history, at secondary school (including post sixteen), although there are BEd courses for secondary teachers. Equally, though, it is possible to train to teach in primary or junior/middle school via a postgraduate course after a conventional academic degree. However, in future, first-degree subject is expected to be suitable for the type of training. For instance, business studies is unlikely to be acceptable as a basis for primary school teaching.

Those sure of their choice of teaching as a career, and of the group and/or subject(s) they wish to teach can go straight onto a course designed for this. Alternatively, either via the conventional degree course plus PGCE, or a BEd course which starts with subject studies in parallel with BA or BSc students (so allowing a complete change of mind often up to the end of the second year), it is possible to defer choice of teaching as a career and/or of the group to teach, for up to three years. A conventional subject degree obviously provides a broader base for other careers if there is a shortage of teaching posts.

Educational institutions with courses leading to qualified teacher status (excluding PGCE) must be validated by the DES. The required criteria include – appropriate subject content; adequate training in teaching methods of the chosen main subject(s); language and maths for primary teachers; training closely linked with practical experience in school and involving active participation of experienced practising school teachers. A reasonable percentage of staff must have been successful teachers in school, and their school experience should be recent, substantial and relevant.

Courses leading to qualified teacher status (excluding PGCE) as at May 1987 are at –
Universities

Bath:	Applied physics, Chemistry, Computer software technology, Engineering (aeronautical, chemical/bioprocess, mechanical or systems), Materials science, Mathematical sciences, Maths, Maths/computing, Physics with geophysics or physical electronics, or Statistics concurrently with education for qualified status.
Brunel:	Design and technology with education
Cambridge:	Tripos subject with education (BA & teaching cert); Homerton only – Art, Biological sciences, Chemistry, Drama, English, Geography, History, Maths, Music, Physics or Religious studies and education (BEd).

Cardiff (UC):	Home economics or Textiles/design (BEd).
Durham:	Education with subsidiary subjects for primary teaching (BEd).
Exeter:	Educational studies and art[1] , Biology/science, Chemistry/science, English/drama[1] , French[1] , Humanities[1] , Maths, Music[1] , PE (secondary only), Physics/science, or Science (BEd) ([1] primary only).
Hull:	Biology, Chemistry, Geography, Maths, Physics, or Psychology with education (BSc/CertinEd).
Liverpool:	Maths and education (BSc/CertinEd);
London:	Goldsmiths' – Primary, or Craft, design and technology secondary (BEd).
Loughborough:	Design and technology with education (BA/CertinEd).
Warwick:	Art, Biology, Drama, English, Geography, History, Maths, Music, PE, or Religious education (BA with qual teacher status).

Polytechnics (all BEd)

Birmingham:	Primary (infant or junior) – creative arts, environmental studies, or humanities.
Brighton:	Primary (infant or junior) – two from language, literacy and literature; science and technology; PE; environmental studies; visual or performance arts; or Secondary – PE and a minor study.
Bristol:	Primary, Secondary, or Severe learning difficulties, and art, biological science, business studies, CDT, English, geography, history, or maths.
Hatfield:	Primary (infant or junior) and subject studies in eg humanities, social studies, environmental studies.
Leeds:	Primary – two (two years), one contd (two years) from art/design, English/drama, geography, history, maths, music, PE, science/technology; or Secondary – CDT, Home economics, or PE.
Liverpool:	Secondary – CDT, Home economics, or PE/dance/outdoor education.
London, Kingston:	Nursery/first or junior/middle – English/drama, music, time and place and society, or science of the environment.
London, Middx:	Primary – either one of art, computer education with maths or science, dance, English, music, or two of geography, history, religious studies; Secondary – CDT or Home economics.
London, NLP:	Primary (incl multicultural and special) – English, Jewish studies, maths, PE, science, or social studies.
London, S Bank:	Secondary – Home economics.
London, Thames:	Primary – 2 of art/craft/design, geography, history, language and literature with drama, maths, music, PE, religious studies, science; Secondary – CDT, movement studies, or Youth and community studies (community education).

Manchester:	Primary – art, drama, English, general subject studies, geography, history, language or maths in education, mathematics, music, PE, religious education, science; Secondary – Home economics or Maths.
Newcastle:	Primary – environmental and social studies, expressive arts, language and literature, maths, science/technology; Secondary – Home economics.
Nottingham, Trent:	Primary – main subject in humanities or science; Secondary – CDT, or Science (maths, physics, chemistry, biology).
Oxford:	Nursery/first or junior/middle – subject from main degree programme.
Sheffield:	Primary – English, environmental studies, home economics, maths, or science and technology; Secondary – CDT, home economics, or PE.
Sunderland:	Primary/Middle – choices from social, environmental, creative, or movement and health studies; Secondary – Business studies.
Wolverhampton:	Primary – art/design, CDT, English, geography, history, maths, music, PE, religious studies, or science; Secondary – business education, CDT, or maths.

Colleges/institutes of (higher) education (all BEd)

Ambleside, Ch Mason:	Early/primary or primary/middle – arts, English, maths/science, outdoor and environmental education, or social studies.
Bangor, Normal:	Primary – art/design and technology, communication, drama, environmental studies, humanities, maths, music with movement and literature, physical and adventure education, science, or (Welsh) linguistic, literary and cultural heritage.
Bath:	Primary – combinations from art, childhood, creative studies, English, environment biology, geography, health studies and child development, history, home and community, music, numerical methods, religious studies, sociology; Secondary – Fashion/textiles or Home economics.
Bedford:	Primary – the arts, humanities, language and literature, mathematics, or science; Secondary – Dance or PE.
B'ham, Newman/W'hill:	Primary – art/design, biological science, English, geography, history, math, PE, or theology; Secondary – Community and youth studies or Severe learning difficulties.
Bradford/Ilkley:	Primary – creative arts, environmental studies, history, language and literature, mathematical studies, social and religious studies; Secondary – Home economics.
Canterbury, ChCh:	Primary (3-8/5-8/7-12) – art, English, geography, history, maths, movement studies, music, religious studies, or science.
Cardiff, S Glam:	Primary – one from English, geography, maths,

PE, Welsh, and one from drama, history, music, religious education, science; Secondary – Drama or Music.

Carmarthen, Trin: First, first/junior, junior/middle – major field from art/design/craft, English, geography, history, maths, music, PE, religious studies, science and environment, Welsh, Welsh/drama.

Chelmsford, Essex: Primary – art, language and literature, maths, or science.

Cheltenham, St P/Mary: Primary (5-8/7-11) – art/design, biological science, English, expressive arts, geography, history, maths, religious studies; Secondary – Maths, PE, or Religious studies.

Chester: Primary – art, biology, computer studies, drama, English, geography, history, maths, music, PE, religious studies.

Chichester, W Sussex: Primary – art, dance, English, geography, history, maths, music, science; Secondary – Maths or PE.

Crewe/Alsager: Primary – biology, dance, drama, English, environmental studies, French, geography, history, maths, modern studies, music, PE, physical science, religious studies, special education, visual arts, writing; Secondary – biology, business education, design and technology, environmental studies, maths, physical science, or youth and community studies.

Derbyshire: Primary (3-8/7-12) – art, biology, English (incl drama), geography, history, maths, music, PE, religious studies.

Exmouth, Rolle: Primary/middle – art/design, drama in education, English literature, geography, history, maths, music, science.

Lanc, S Martin's: Primary – art, biology, English, geography, history, maths, music, religious studies: Secondary – community and youth studies (with English, geography, maths, or religious studies).

Leeds, Tr/All Saints: Primary – English, French, geography, history, maths, psychology, sociology, theology; Secondary – Business studies, Home economics, Maths, or Theology.

Lincoln, Bp Gr: Primary – art, drama, English, geography, history, music, or religious studies.

Liverpool: Infant/junior – art, biological or computer studies, divinity, English, environmental studies, French, geography, history, maths, music, PE, or psychology.

London, Roehampt: Primary – art, biology, chemistry, dance, drama, English, environmental studies, French, geography, history, maths, music, religious studies, social biology, sports studies.

London, St Mary's: Junior – biology, chemistry, classical studies, drama, English, geography, maths, movement studies, physics, religious studies, sociology; Secondary – Biology, Chemistry, Maths, Physics, or Religious studies.

London, WLIHE:	Primary (3-8/7-12) – environmental studies or humanities; Secondary – PE.
Newport, Gwent:	Primary – creative arts, environmental studies, expressive arts, humanities, maths, or science/technology.
Northampton, Nene:	Primary – art, early childhood studies, environmental and social studies, language and literature, maths, movement, music, science.
Ormskirk, E Hill:	Primary (3-8/7-12) – art/craft/design, English, maths, music, PE, science and technology, social studies.
Oxford, W'minster:	Junior/middle – creative arts, English, French, geography, history, maths, religious studies, or science in environment.
Plymouth, Marjons:	Primary – English, geography, history, maths, PE, religious studies, or science; Secondary – CDT, Maths, or PE.
Reading, Bulmershe:	Primary – art, geography, history, literature and drama, maths, music, PE, science.
Scarboro', N Riding:	Primary (3-11) – art/design, biology, drama, English, geography, maths, music, PE, sociology, or religious studies.
Southampton, LSU:	Primary (3-5/5-8/7-12) – art/design, biological sciences, English, French, geography, history, maths, or theology.
Swansea, W Glam:	Primary – humanities, literature and media studies, or maths and science; Secondary – Business studies or Computer studies and maths.
Wakefield, Br Hall:	Primary (3-9/5-11/8-13) – English, environment studies, music, or visual arts.
Winchester, K Alf:	Primary – art, biological sciences, drama, English, geography, history, human movement studies, maths, music, or religious studies; Secondary – design and technology.
Worcester:	Primary (4-8/7-11) main subject – art/design, biological science, English, geography, history, maths, music, PE; Secondary – Biological science, Home economics, or Maths.
Wrexham, NE Wales:	Primary (3-7/8-12) – art, English, geography, history, maths, PE, religious studies, science; Secondary – Business studies.
York, Ripon/Yk St J:	Primary (5-8/7-12) – art, biology, chemistry, design and technology, English, French, geography, history, maths, music, PE, rural science, theology; Secondary – design and technology, maths, or theology.

'Mature entry' courses in shortages subjects are also available, and it is possible to take a shortened course after, eg an HND.

The training, as opposed to the assessment, aspect of the probationary year has been strengthened with more effective help and support, and during this time student teachers are not expected to carry more than 75% of the 'normal' teaching load.

In-service training is generally available, enabling teachers to add to their expertise, to help them cope with change (eg for new exams or new courses), to train and qualify them for posts of special responsibility, in, eg counselling, curriculum development, special education of all kinds, teaching English to foreign students, educational administration, or developing audio-visual aids and educational technology.

Further information from the Department of Education and Science, the Scottish Department of Education; local education authorities.

FURTHER AND HIGHER EDUCATION
Education after school is normally divided between further and higher education, although the boundary between them is not rigid. In fact they overlap considerably. Some colleges and even polytechnics straddle the two, and may teach in both areas. This is largely because there are several possible definitions: for some people, the division is between level of teaching, to others it depends on who controls the teaching institutions, and so institutions like polytechnics which teach at HE level are in fact part of the FE sector. Further education is often, then, divided into advanced and non-advanced.

The further education sector
This includes colleges of further education, colleges of technology, technical colleges, community colleges, and so on. A few colleges specialise – in building or agriculture, for example – but most provide a spread of courses. They (mostly) come under the local education authority, providing almost any kind of course or off-the-job training, full- or part-time, needed and for which there is sufficient demand in the area, for people ranging from sixteen-year-olds through to mature managers.

No two colleges teach exactly the same subjects. In some areas, colleges teach both 'advanced' (ie HND, degree level and above) and 'non-advanced' (craft, technician etc), in others the two may be split between higher and lower level colleges. The possible range of studies is from the most practical to the most academic. A typical large college may have up to ten departments, of engineering, construction, science, business and office studies, and distributive studies, general education etc. Courses can range from GCSE and A levels, CPVE and other pre-vocational studies, day- or block-release (from work) courses for trainee electricians or garage mechanics, bank staff preparing for professional qualifications, and young office workers taking BTEC schemes. They may put on full-time 'foundation' courses for articled accountancy clerks, train computer programmers and systems analysts, or help people to gain professional qualifications in building or chemistry. They put on short and evening courses to teach people how, for instance, to use word processors or learn languages. While most courses are for younger people trying to gain their main qualification they will also have to cope in future with more people needing to re-train and up-grade their qualifications.

Unlike at school or university, only a proportion of students study at college full time, from September to June. Each college has a constantly-changing student population, although teaching goes on from early morning to mid evening. Some students come in only one or two days a week, but may stay on into the evening. Some arrive once or twice a year for six-week bursts of study.

There are some 700 FE colleges. They vary greatly in size, and full-time staff may also vary in numbers from 25 to 300. Further education colleges are often loose federations of fairly independent units (which may even be in different places) specialising in a particular set of skills. The teaching staff are generally specialists and professionals in their field, often with extensive experience in practising (rather than teaching) their profession, and their attachment is normally to their profession and department, rather than to the college. Some may be trained school-teachers, in FE to teach 16- to 18-year-olds. Some may be qualified electronic engineers, now teaching young technicians. Former accountants may teach commercial students, and so on. Most of the teaching is necessarily directly skill training and down-to-earth, with few frills. A high proportion of FE staff obviously teach technological, scientific, and business-based subjects, but there are some posts for people teaching subjects like history, English, languages etc. Just as much hard thinking, discussion and effort goes into finding improved ways of teaching as anywhere else.

A large department of, for instance, engineering or construction, might have about 50 full-time lecturers, a dozen senior lecturers, two principal lecturers, and a head of department. Most work up to 40 hours a week, but the actual teaching time is not usually more than 20-22 hours for lecturers, 13-16 for senior lecturers. However, the hours may include evening work. There is always a great deal of preparation, and administration. Courses must be revised frequently to meet changing industrial and commercial demand, and teaching staff have to spend some time talking to colleagues in industry and commerce – finding out what needs to be taught, selling their services, discussing apprentices or trainees and their training in detail with their firms. They must develop new programmes, eg for two-year YTS schemes, CPVE, or engineering craft 'competences'. Some FE staff are also involved in developing new ways, including 'distance learning' methods, for people to add to their qualifications – at technician and supervisory level for example – and to re-train.

Some 93,000 people (1985) teach full-time in further education in England and Wales, including the polytechnics. Prospects, and promotion, are generally linked to whatever is taught. Demand has fallen sharply for people to teach traditional metal-working skills, for example, while YTS, CPVE etc have increased the need for more people able to give more general vocational preparation, teach basic business skills etc.

Recruitment and entry Teaching in FE is usually a second career. While a few new graduates may be recruited, it is more usual to have spent some time working in industry or commerce, having already gained the right educational/ academic and professional qualifications. For instance, to teach electronics will normally require an appropriate degree, a professional engineering quali-fication, and extensive industrial experience. There is, however, as yet no requirement for a teaching qualification.

Qualifications and training Over 45% of all teachers in FE are now graduates. A teaching qualification is not required, but is obviously useful: at least 45% of

FE teachers have some form of professional qualification. It is intended that before long a much higher proportion of those teaching in further education should have initial training, as well as special support in the early years on the same basis as for the schools, and more later in-service training, but this, of course, depends on finance being available.

Training for FE teaching (PGCE only) is available at –
University education depts – Cardiff UC, Keele, Leicester, Manchester; polytechnics – Huddersfield, Wolverhampton; colleges – Bolton IHE, London: Garnett, Swansea: W Glam, Wrexham: NE Wales IHE.

The higher education sector

This is made up of universities, polytechnics, colleges/institutes of education and higher education, and a few other educational establishments which teach at the higher academic levels and (possibly) do research. However, although there are these basic similarities between the different kinds of institutions in the higher education sector, they are in many ways quite different, and the academic work within them – often rather more than teaching – can vary greatly too.

EMPLOYING INSTITUTIONS include 43 universities (two split up into a number of near-autonomous university colleges), one postgraduate institution, one 'polyversity', 30 polytechnics in England and Wales, 14 central institutions in Scotland, and some 60 colleges or institutions of (higher) education. The higher education sector, after a twenty-year expansion, followed by a period of relative stand-still, has been – and still is – going through some major upheavals. Sharply-reduced resources have lead to considerable rationalisation. While no major institutions have closed (as of 1987), two (in Northern Ireland) have merged, as have a number of London University colleges (the two Cardiff colleges also look set to amalgamate). See HIGHER EDUCATION under ACADEMIC AND VOCATIONAL QUALIFICATIONS.

Universities, both ancient and modern, are dedicated to serious scholarship, to pursuing knowledge for its own sake. 'Knowledge at the highest level is the domain of the universities; their function is to preserve it, hand it on, and expand it,' wrote one academic. However, they are now being persuaded to take on somewhat more practical roles, ranging from educating and training graduate engineers along lines preferred by industry, through to problem-solving, industry-oriented research.

They still teach, though, only students studying for first or higher degrees or other postgraduate qualifications, most of whom study on a full-time basis, although part-time study is growing slowly. Slightly less than half of all university students study science-based subjects (including engineering, technology, medicine), a quarter social and business studies, and just over a fifth languages, English, history, philosophy, music, drama etc. However, universities differ considerably from each other, and some are more science- and technology oriented, some emphasise arts and social sciences. All universities are much larger than any school, with over 2000 students and at least 200 academic staff, and some are very large places to work in. Manchester, for instance, has over 15,000 students and some 2300 academic staff.

Polytechnics were intended, when set up in the late 1960s (from then existing FE colleges), to provide teaching at a level similar to the universities, although at a less intensive level perhaps, and with a more 'vocational' slant. Although nearly three-quarters of students studying either full-time or on a sandwich basis are now (1986-7) aiming for degrees (most of the rest are trying for higher-technician qualifications), under 40% (38.6%) study science (19.6%) or engineering- and technology-based subjects. Just under 30% study business and social studies, 9.7% 'other' professional and vocational subjects (including ancillary health), 8% study art and design, music, drama etc, nearly 8% subjects like languages, English, and history, and 6.5% are teachers in training. Most have a fairly high proportion of part-time students. Again, all have more than 2000 students each, and again Manchester is the largest, with over 9600 full-time and sandwich-based students, and nearly 5000 part-time students, and an academic staff of about 1000.

Colleges of higher education are different again. Most developed from colleges which specialised in training teachers, and merged with other such colleges and/or with further education colleges, during the 1970s, and at the same time expanded their range of teaching (only a few 'monotechnic' colleges of education remain). Most still educate and train teachers, but they now combine this with teaching at degree level in mostly 'liberal arts' (English, history, religious studies, drama, etc), environmental studies, and social sciences, professional training (eg social work, the para-medical field), although those which merged with further education colleges may also teach other professional and business studies, art and design, and some (but not that much) science and technology. Colleges range in size from under 500 to several thousand students, although only a proportion of students at the largest will be on advanced – degree and similar – courses.

Academic staff in higher education do not only teach. They also, and equally usually in university (but to a lesser extent in polytechnic and college), do research. In university at least, the two traditionally go together, and time allows for both.

A survey once (1972) showed that the average university lecturer works, on average, 50.5 hours a week. This includes 18.5 hours on undergraduates – actual teaching time, writing and marking examinations, preparing lectures and seminars, and other 'contact time' with students. The 'average' lecturer spent 12 hours on personal research in an 'average' week, 9.5 hours on administration and personal reading, 5.5 hours supervising and teaching graduate students, 5 hours on committee work, and 5.5 hours doing work elsewhere (eg lecturing, being an external examiner for another university or a polytechnic, going to conferences). The balance probably changes during a career, with more time on research and active teaching in the earlier years, and more on administration, committee work etc for older and more senior staff. No comparable study has been done on polytechnic or other college staff, but they probably spend rather more time teaching their full-time students, and some may have to teach in the evenings as well.

Lecturers do not only work in term time (which can be only eight weeks and not more than ten). Term time is normally spent mainly to teaching, and so most research is done in vacations, especially where this is a geological survey in the Antarctic or an anthropological field expedition to a Pacific Island.

University teaching, particularly, tends to stress intellectual training, and stimulating 'intellectual curiosity'. Academics train their students in analytical and logical skills, teach them to think clearly, to present ideas and facts in the best order, to be able to decide what information is important and what is not in any given situation, to be able to analyse and criticise, to assess and weigh evidence, to be objective, and argue logically. They teach academic 'method': how to find out, how to observe accurately, how to extract information from books, reports and journals, and the rules of scholastic argument. They do not try to teach everything about a single subject: they start by teaching fundamental principles, and then concentrate on intellectual training via the basics of the subject, and sometimes (eg in subjects like English) the parts of the subject that interest the teachers personally.

Degree teaching combines formal lectures for large classes of 25-100, with 'small group' teaching in seminars (for 6-12 students) and tutorials (for one or two). Staff also supervise students in both undergraduate final-year project work and graduate research or study. 'Small group' teaching can be very demanding. Scientists teach experimental work in labs; engineers experimental and design work; mathematicians take 'examples' classes. Creative subjects like art and design (mostly in polytechnics and art schools) are taught differently again.

Academic staff in most universities, polytechnics, and colleges, are based on their departments, so they spend most of their time with people teaching the same subject (at Oxford and Cambridge many are college based). Academic staff in higher education expect students to learn to organise their own work and their own time, and don't usually tell them what they should be doing when, so the staff stay more in the background than in schools. Most lecturers, though, act as personal tutors to a group of students, giving them any support, on academic or personal problems, they may need. In some universities, and many polytechnics and colleges, students may build their courses by taking 'units' from several different departments, and so some academic staff are course co-ordinators, helping to see that students make sensible choices.

Research in university, at least, is carried out on the principle that any new knowledge is better than none, and better than ignorance. In theory, no restrictions are set on the avenues of knowledge that an academic may explore, so long as it meets certain scholarly criteria. Research may be abstract or theoretical; it may be very practical; it may start as 'pure' and disinterested research and end up with practical applications.

There are very few places other than universities where research can be done entirely for its own sake, especially in subjects like history, literature, or philosophy. The philosopher, the German specialist, and the historian need only their brains, their interests, and access to the right libraries. Engineers, scientists, and even social scientists (surveys cost a lot), need financial support for their work. The Science and Engineering Research Council alone spent over £300 million on research in 1986-7, but it made possible only a small proportion of the research projects that scientists and engineers wanted to do. Both universities and polytechnics have turned to industry, and therefore to more applied work, for funds. Polytechnic research is mostly on a smaller scale than in university.

Academic researchers work to strict rules. The problem being researched has to be defined exactly, facts must be carefully collected, and observations made with great objectivity. Research workers may set up possible explanations, or 'hypotheses' – for why unemployment continues to rise, or how the continents came to be formed, or why the industrial revolution happened when it did. They then test these theories – through experiments, or against other evidence (see also eg subjects under ACADEMIC AND VOCATIONAL STUDIES). Research can involve working in a laboratory, in a library, at a desk, out in the 'field' (or city), depending on the subject.

Research also means 'presenting' and publishing results: as a paper in the appropriate journal, at the relevant conference, or in a book. There are rules about this too. Academics do not work in isolation. Argument and discussion (often quite acrimonious), and dissecting each other's work in print is an integral part of the system of setting up – and knocking down or modifying – hypotheses. It can be a highly competitive business, and what promotion prospects there are may depend on the 'right' research track record, on the quality of original and even imaginative thinking (and rather less on teaching skills). The successful researcher knows which problems to choose to research – problems to which the answer matters and which can be solved, either using existing techniques or where techniques for which the basic technology already exists and are practical propositions.

Not all academics go on researching throughout their working lives. Some think it is a young man/woman's game, and some give up full-time research when they have clearly reached their promotion ceiling. They may then give more time to, for instance, student counselling, being a warden of a residential hall, external examining, popularising their subject through books or the media, or being a consultant to other organisations, eg in industry.

There are four 'grades' of university teacher (polytechnic and college promotion ladders are as further education). About 59% of staff are on the lowest grade, lecturer; the next two grades, senior lecturer and reader, make up about 26% of the total, and professors about 13%. Most of the rest are full-time research staff, employed mostly on short-term contracts, and financed from research grants. Promotion prospects are obviously rather poor at present, especially as the mean age of university staff is only 43.

The number of full-time academic staff in universities peaked at just over 43,000 in 1980-1, fell to 42,100 in 1983-4, but rose again to 42,500 in 1984-5 (but the numbers state financed continued to fall, the increase being paid for by eg outside research contracts). About 1,600 posts will go through 'natural wastage', and the rest will be shed through early retirement and (mostly) voluntary redundancies. Polytechnic and CHE staff numbers are not given separately from other FE (above), but there are probably around 20,000 staff in polytechnics, and about 11,000 in CHEs.

Recruitment and entry In general, opportunities to start a career in any sector of higher education are not good at present. However, studies for the SERC show that in some subjects, especially engineering/technology, severe shortages could show up, for a complex range of reasons. Generally, for academic posts, extremely high academic qualifications, and research, teaching and/or other appropriate experience are needed. This applies equally to any new posts which may result from financial 'pump-priming' of disciplines like information technology or biotechnology, as to any 'normal' recruitment there may be. To help overcome the problem of an ageing teaching/research force, some 'new blood' posts have been funded.

Academics are recruited mainly on their academic, scholarly, intellectual capabilities. This is generally based on the evidence of a very good initial degree (ie a first, or at least an upper second), plus a higher degree (so it is rare to get a first real job before 24). The degree(s) have to be in the right subject. Departments usually want to recruit someone whose research and teaching interests, and recent experience, 'fit in' with what the department is doing, and/or fill in a gap. This, of course, reduces the number of opportunities still further, since (for example), a biochemistry graduate (however good) may only be qualified for a small proportion of biochemistry vacancies in any one year. Engineering departments are being asked to increase the proportion of their courses devoted to industrial and design studies, and may reserve posts for staff who have the needed expertise. In education, lecturers are now expected to have had several years' teaching experience, as well as evidence of further study and possibly research too. Where relevant working experience is wanted, departments are unlikely to recruit anyone under 28.

Qualifications and training Apart from the academic qualifications and any experience as above, little formal training in teaching is given (a higher degree is designed to train in research). Any training for university and polytechnic teachers is normally given by the employing institution.

OTHER TEACHING OPPORTUNITIES
These include teaching in the Armed Forces and penal institutions.

THE ARMED FORCES All three have extensive educational and training services, despite recent reviews and economies. If anything, the Forces are increasing the length of training (eg for young army officers), and raising standards to cope with the technology of modern warfare.

Teaching in the Forces is in a wide range of subjects and at all levels, but is mainly designed to teach both officers and soldiers, sailors, airmen/women the military, technical, and managerial ('staff') skills needed. The work ranges from straightforward classroom teaching, often leading to exams for external awards (eg GCSE/GCE, CGLI, BTEC, CNAA degrees), through lab and workshop training, to training in military skills. There is a strong emphasis on adventure- and 'outward-bound'-type training for everyone, and even people teaching class subjects may take their students camping, sailing, climbing, canoeing, orienteering, etc, and may also supervise, eg rifle practice.

Much teaching is very practical with a strong emphasis on vocational skills, training at craft and technician level – in eg mechanical and electrical engineering, electronics, aircraft maintenance, repairing tanks, guns and sophisticated weapons guidance systems, for example. All young entrants are given training at technical/apprentice schools and centres, on courses lasting up to three years. Later they may go back to have their skills up-graded, or go on to something new.

Some junior entrants are also taught basic school subjects – eg English, science, maths (as at the Army's Welbeck College). To be eligible for promotion soldiers, sailors, airmen/women have to gain an education promotion certificate, and may need formal teaching. While the schools which teach the children of servicemen/women overseas mostly employ civilian teachers, supervision etc is done by education/instructor officers.

Officers, equally, have lengthy initial training which combines classroom teaching with learning and practising specific military skills. While an increasing proportion of officer entrants already have degrees, the Forces still train a proportion of their own professional/graduate engineers and some scientists to degree level, and at postgraduate level too.

All officers get additional managerial/staff training, some add further technological skills, and they may have to be taught eg, languages, computing etc. All officers go to staff college at set points in their careers, and promotion above certain ranks depends on passing stiff exams covering academic and current affairs as well as military subjects, and then doing a year at staff college where officers from all three Forces study managerial and strategic subjects together.

Education (RAF/Army)/instructor (Navy) officers may work, then, in one of the Forces' very many education/training colleges, schools, centres, etc, ranging from Dartmouth, Manadon, Shrivenham, Camberley, Cranwell through to apprentice schools. Or they may work at a base or naval establishment, with a regiment, on a ship providing teaching/training on the spot.

They, obviously, start their careers in work for which their previous education/qualifications are relevant, but can change the type of teaching they do, and may even go on to other work. As Forces' officers first and 'teachers' second, they are expected to be military minded, capable of fighting, and most do work additional to their education/training duties in any case. It is traditional for them to do some welfare, advisory work. In the Navy, instructors are traditionally trained in meteorology, oceanography, survey work. At sea their operational duties often include weather forecasting, and they are often entertainment officers. Marine instructors are trained as commandos and become operational members of a commando unit. Helping to plan and analyse the results of training exercises is a natural area of promotion for education/training officers, and more senior, managerial postings are possible.

Recruitment and entry On the same basis as other officer entrants to each of the three forces – see ARMED FORCES. The main requirement is for graduates in engineering, other technological subjects, or sciences, but with a small intake of arts/BEd graduates.

Qualifications and training Education/instructor officers are given initial training on the same basis as other officer entrants. On full-service commissions, they may go on to further technical training, postgraduate courses etc, and can take exams/staff courses/training for promotion to senior ranks. See also ARMED FORCES.

CUSTODIAL INSTITUTIONS Education, and training, is provided in community homes run by local authorities for young people under care orders, detention centres and prisons. With young people, the work is obviously similar to teaching in the schools, while for older people it gets closer to further and adult educational work, with some emphasis at both levels on remedial teaching.

Most children and young people in care go to local schools, but residential teaching is provided for a proportion by the local education authority. Only a very small proportion of the staff working in community homes are teachers or instructors. They are expected to work as members of a team with other care staff, and the teaching needed depends on the needs of pupils living in the homes at any one time.

At detention centres, younger offenders have at least fifteen hours' education a week, and at both junior and senior centres an hour of physical training a day. A detention centre with 240 young inmates may have an education officer, three full-time teachers and 30 or more who come in to teach in the evenings.

In adult prisons, education services are staffed by local education authorities. Every prison has an education officer and a team of teachers. Education is compulsory for anyone under school-leaving age, and part-time for anyone aged between 16 and 21. Again, there is a high proportion of remedial and trade training, with considerable emphasis on teaching reading. Only about 10% of the prison population actually takes public examinations (although of those who do, some 70% pass), but the range covers everything from CGLI craft examinations through O and A levels to degrees (some 100 students in eleven prisons study in the Open University). Teaching conditions are rarely ideal, and must fit in with prison routine. Resources are tight, and shortages of prison officers mean prisoners do not always get to classes.

TEACHING CREATIVE AND VOCATIONAL SUBJECTS ART, MUSIC, DRAMA, BALLET, ACCOUNTANCY, LAW, LIBRARIANSHIP and the craft subjects are generally taught post-school by people who have trained in and practised their profession or skill first (but to teach art, music, drama, dance etc in school a full teaching qualification is required). They are taught in state-maintained schools and colleges, but some are also, or alternatively, taught in private colleges and schools, and some by correspondence colleges (see under individual subjects).

OTHER WORK IN EDUCATION
Administration — careers advisory work — educational research — health and welfare services — inspectors and advisers — librarians and information scientists — support services — training officers, advisers and instructors — other
The rest of the million or so people working in education run what are generally called 'support' services.

Administration
Professional educational administrators are employed by local education authorities, and by larger educational institutions such as university and poly-technics. Civil servants in the Department of Education and Science are also involved in educational administration. There are also countless smaller organisations and administrative bodies, national and other central organisa-tions like the Council for National Academic Awards (CNAA), the Univer-sities Central Council on Admissions (UCCA), the new Polytechnic Central Admissions System (PCAS), the National Advisory Body for Local Authority Higher Education (NAB), and the University Grants Committee (whose staff

are seconded Civil Servants) – although the government is planning to replace these last two. Permanent staff are needed in organisations like the Committee of Vice-Chancellors and Principals (of universities) and the Committee of Directors of Polytechnics. Teachers' professional unions also have relatively large staffs.

LOCAL AUTHORITIES Education is at present one of their major responsibilities, absorbing a large proportion of their resources and employing a large number of people. In one Midlands town with a population of about 335,000, the director of education administers two nursery, 138 primary, 22 secondary, and 13 'special' schools, one hospital school, a child-guidance centre, a polytechnic (the college of education merged with the local university), four further education colleges, a drama and a music college, 26 adult education centres, a careers service with centre, training centres for young people, and assorted youth and community centres.

The decision-making, planning and problem-solving for education services is now so great that a rising number of LEAs make the (elected) chairman/woman of the education committee a full-time employee. For the full-time officials in the education department, this is a career which means working within the framework of LOCAL GOVERNMENT, with all the associated committee work, etc.

For clerical/administrative staff the work involves the day-to-day routines of running the schools, colleges and so on – keeping records, organising supplies and equipment for schools and colleges, paying teachers and other staff, advertising posts. 'Middle managers' may be in charge of one type of school (eg primary), or age group (eg 16-19), or all the schools and colleges in one area of the authority, or they may be in charge of any building programmes, or overseeing allocation of children between schools.

At the most senior levels (chief education officer or director of education), the work is forward planning and budgeting, organising and re-organising as, for example, the number of pupils drops, new training facilities are needed for unemployed young people. They liaise and consult with eg other departments within the authority, with central government, with the inspectorate.

Recruitment and entry Some professional administrators join education departments as school-leavers, but now more usually as graduate trainees (see LOCAL GOVERNMENT). For a high proportion of more senior posts, though, this is a second career, requiring a teaching qualification and extensive teaching experience first.

THE DEPARTMENT OF EDUCATION AND SCIENCE is not at present (this could change under 1987 government plans) directly involved in running schools or appointing teachers, setting detailed curricula etc. DES staff deal with education on a national scale, with future policy and forward planning, setting minimum standards (for which it has its own assessment units), and controlling building programmes, teacher training and supply, and the standards of qualification. They administer salary scales and teachers' superannuation, research and other funds under the control of the Secretary of State, and settle disputes, between parent and LEA, or between LEA and school managers. DES staff

are mostly career civil servants, with a few specialists.
See also CIVIL SERVICE.

INDIVIDUAL EDUCATIONAL INSTITUTIONS Some, mostly the largest and/or residential, employ full-time, career administrators.

Mainly these are universities, polytechnics, and other colleges in the higher education sector. Universities are run by committees of academic staff (with representatives of other staff and students), and the administrators provide the information on which these committees can make decisions, and then carry out the decisions, 'managing' the institution on a day-to-day basis. They produce budgets and look after the finances. They maintain records, organise examinations, run complex admissions systems, produce student prospectuses and provide public relations, and generally see that the academic life of the institution runs as smoothly as possible.

Most universities and polytechnics are like small towns with a great many buildings, complicated engineering plant, boilers, sewers, lifts, labs, telephone systems, student residences, grounds and even streets to be maintained and cleaned. All this, and the large number of people – students and staff – means that running such an institution is a complex business. University and polytechnic administration is nowadays a career in its own right, with most career administrators starting as graduates in junior posts. However, the present financial retrenchment means that there are now few opportunities, and staff are being made redundant or taking early retirement.

Schools are traditionally administered by teachers themselves, with help and support from LEA staff. Although many schools now have secretarial staff, only the largest state and independent schools (where they may be called 'bursars') have full-time administrators who are not qualified/practising teachers. This may change if government plans to let schools manage more of their own budgets, and/or cease to be controlled by LEAs, go through.

Careers advisory and information work

Separate services are provided for young people and adults. For young people, they are generally run by education authorities, for adults directly by Manpower Services and the Department of Employment, although there is some overlap between them. Government policy on the service is the responsibility of the Department of Employment, and MSC publishes careers literature for young people.

Wherever careers advisers work, and whichever age-group they deal with, the job is similar. They give people help in coming to decisions about work, training, and any extra education they may need. They help to assess as realistically as possible their abilities, interests and potential, and provide the information – about occupations, employment generally, courses, etc – on which an informed decision can be based. They may also provide an employment service to help people find jobs, and employers to find the recruits they need.

Careers work for the under-eighteens is divided between the school and the careers service.

IN SCHOOLS, careers work in schools is generally an additional responsibility for a subject teacher, whose teaching 'load' is (ideally) reduced. It is rarely a full-time post and rarely has the status or is given the resources it needs (see CHOOSING AND PRE-VOCATIONAL PREPARATION). Some 60% of schools, according to the National Association of Careers Guidance Teachers, have the equivalent of less than one full-time careers teacher. Much careers advice is still given informally – by form teachers, for example, particularly at the point when decisions are taken about subjects to be studied for school-leaving examinations, and by subject teachers, keen for their best pupils to go on to university perhaps.

What careers teachers do varies from school to school. Some may simply provide information, others may also be involved in extensive programmes to prepare pupils for life and work. They advise, and talk to, pupils about their plans. Careers work can mean a great deal of organisation – of information which also has to be collected, exhibitions, visits; imaginative teaching on preparing, planning and deciding about the future, and on the world of work; counselling individual pupils; working with eg the careers service.

LOCAL-AUTHORITY CAREERS SERVICES Most careers advisers work as careers officers for local education authorities, within a service which is run separately from the schools and colleges. They work both from their own offices, and within the schools, where the help they give has to be dovetailed into the way careers education and guidance is organised by the school, and colleges (one or two authorities also integrate polytechnic careers advisers into the LEA service). Again the work varies according to the needs and organisation of the local education authority, but there is increasing emphasis on educational and vocational guidance for young people. Working with individual schools and colleges involves knowing how each is organised and its curriculum, developing a working relationship with the staff and planning with them a careers programme for the school, as well as getting to know the pupils.

Careers officers spend much of their time interviewing and advising individuals, giving talks, providing up-to-date information, and giving careers teachers technical back-up. Helping young people find jobs, or increasingly places on (YTS) training schemes, is a major part of their work, and so careers officers also spend some of their time with employers. Although they should be able to provide information and contacts for jobs or training/courses anywhere in the country, they try to get to know the local situation very well indeed. They have close contacts with individual employers, with whom they will probably keep up a fairly continuous two-way flow of information and discussion on changing educational and employment patterns, at all levels and for all kinds of work.

With youth unemployment still (1987) so high, the careers officer has to keep up to date on local schemes to help the young unemployed, and may even be involved in designing them, as well as advising school-leavers which schemes to try for, and helping trainees get into full-time employment.

Some careers officers specialise – in working with particular age groups, or ability ranges, or special groups (eg handicapped teenagers).

Careers officers also supervise and organise administrative and clerical work in the office – see that any vacancies are recorded, processed and followed up; that the careers library is kept up-to-date, ensure the appointments system is running smoothly, and that arrangements are made for visits, careers conventions etc, and that statistics are recorded.

Promotion within the service is to supervising an area or district, and from there to principal careers officer for an LEA, or to the inspectorate, or other advisory work. Some go on to work for central organisations like the Careers and Occupational Information Centre (part of the Manpower Services Commission), which produces government-published careers literature, runs a monthly magazine, distributes careers literature.

The service has expanded, if rather slowly given the work it has to do. In late 1986, the service was LEA-funded for 3120 careers-officer posts (against 2210 in 1975), plus 540 paid for by government (since 1975) to cope with the problems of unemployed young people. The 1986 shortfall was 150, with only 70 of a funded 100 trainees in post. The service also employs 3040 support staff, including 'employment assistants'.

HIGHER-EDUCATION CAREERS SERVICES Only one group of educational institutions employ their own careers staff. These are the universities and some polytechnics and other colleges (the LEA careers service is used by the rest). University careers services began as appointments boards and simply brought graduates and potential employers together. Now they have developed a professional expertise similar to that of the LEA services, except that, in a sense, they have to operate as a sensitive and sophisticated marketing department for their university or polytechnic, and they are both 'selling' a particular product, and preparing those products, the graduates, for an employment market which can be very demanding, and changes continuously, often in unexpected ways.

The services run by individual institutions are supported by a small but highly professional Central Services Unit, which co-ordinates effort, organises the publication of careers booklets for graduates, and issues vacancy lists. The majority of university and polytechnic careers advisers are graduates, mostly with experience in other areas of employment. Training is fairly ad hoc.

Recruitment and entry A degree, or an equivalent qualification, is normally needed, although people aged 25 and over and with some five years' relevant experience may be considered.

Careers teaching has no formal entry system. The work is generally taken on by a teacher already employed in the school as an additional duty. It is therefore necessary to become a qualified teacher first (see TEACHING).

LEA careers officers (and other careers advisers) come from a variety of backgrounds, and although it is possible to begin training immediately after graduating, a high proportion have had experience in another occupation first – as teachers, or personnel officers, for example. Many careers officers specialise, and so a specialised background may be relevant for a particular area of careers work.

Careers work combines counselling with gathering and passing on information. It needs a strong interest in young people, and in helping them to make the most of their abilities or to solve career problems. A great deal of time is spent in talking to people, particularly young people, from all kinds of background and of all types of ability and interest, and advisers have to be able to establish a relationship with them, and gain their confidence. It means developing sensitivity and shrewdness to gain the necessary insights into people's make-up and motivations to be able to advise them properly.

While many careers officers begin their working lives as teachers, it is not a 'didactic' career. Careers officers must also be interested in the world of work, and in gathering a great deal of very complex information on occupations, educational requirements, etc. They must also develop good working relationships with employers and be able to persuade them of the importance of, for example, education and training for young people.

Assessing young people and occupations and matching one to the other takes some maturity, so careers officers need a great deal of tact and persuasiveness, in coping with the conflicting views of schools, parents and the pupils themselves, in dealing with entrenched attitudes and opinions, in explaining the far-reaching effects on the careers and jobs of technological and social change, and solving difficult problems.

Qualifications and training New LEA careers officers must gain the diploma in careers guidance (awarded by the Local Government Training Board) within a 'reasonable period' after appointment, if not on appointment. The diploma is in two parts. Part 1 involves a one-year full-time or a two-year part-time course, part 2 a period of on-the-job training and development in an LEA careers service. The courses are vocationally slanted and very intensive, covering principles and practice of careers guidance, study of employment and training, and education (including further education). About 400 places are available annually, and about 200 people are grant-aided or seconded.

Full-time courses at – Kent Careers Service Training College (Swanley); polytechnics: Birmingham, Bristol, Huddersfield, London: NELP and South Bank, Manchester, Newcastle, Nottingham: Trent, Wales; colleges: Edinburgh: Napier, Paisley; universities: Reading and Strathclyde.

Part-time – Edinburgh: Napier, London: NELP, Torquay: S Devon TC.

For careers teachers, very little formal training exists. In 1986 only 4% of careers teachers had taken a one-year, full-time training course, and 41% had less than five days' training. There are no pre-entry courses.

Educational broadcasting, publishing etc

Both the BBC and independent companies devote a substantial proportion of daytime and late-evening output to education, both conventional schools programmes and adult education (including radiovision, which matches radio broadcasts to slides and film which can be projected in the classroom). The BBC also relays Open University programmes. Radio and television also put out a variety of other educational programmes, both vocational and non-vocational, for adults. The BBC and IBA companies employ several hundred each in educational broadcasting.

Most universities, polytechnics and other colleges also have their own closed-circuit television systems which can be used in a variety of ways for both live and recorded lectures, demonstrations and so on. These systems all employ both technically-trained people (see MEDIA WORK) and teachers to script, present and direct the educational programmes. Preparing 'software' for other audio-visual aids (programmed learning machines, language laboratories, for example) within manufacturing takes professional expertise, but is often done under supervision of research staff from universities etc.

Few educationalists find full-time careers in educational PUBLISHING in general. Most of the people employed are professional publishers rather than teachers. Professional teachers do, however, find second or spare-time careers writing textbooks, and preparing other types of educational material.

Educational research and curriculum development

Research is supported by the DES, directly through its own research programmes and indirectly through other bodies (eg the Economic and Social Research Council), by local education authorities, by charitable organisations, by universities and by teachers' organisations.

Most research is done in universities, mainly in departments, schools and institutes of education, to a lesser extent in departments of sociology, psychology, etc. Some educational research is also done by polytechnic schools of education and other colleges which train teachers.

Outside the universities, the main research organisation is the autonomous National Foundation for Educational Research, whose programme covers most aspects of primary, secondary, and further education. It also provides test, statistical and information services. Some research is carried out by the Schools Examination and Curriculum Councils.

Health and welfare services

In education, these include the school health service, which provides medical and dental examinations and some treatment services, and is now part of the National Health Service (see MEDICAL SERVICES).

Child guidance centres and clinics are provided by local education authorities, by the NHS and by some voluntary organisations. Intended to treat disturbed children, whether they have learning difficulties or emotional or behavioural problems, the clinics are staffed by teams of qualified educational psychologists and psychiatric social workers under the clinical supervision of a medically-qualified psychiatrist.

Educational psychologists, who try to diagnose the causes of disturbance and to treat them, are also employed in the school psychological service. Some large schools have full-time educational psychologists (who may be called counsellors) on their staff and they may organise programmes of remedial teaching and therapy within the school, often with the help of trained voluntary social workers. However, fewer than 800 educational psychologists are employed by local authorities. There is unlikely to be any increase in the immediate future.

See also PSYCHOLOGY and SOCIAL SERVICES.

Local education authorities also employ teams of welfare officers, who used to be called school attendance officers. Although they do some other work, they are still mainly responsible for enforcing compulsory school attendance.

Universities and polytechnics are now mostly large enough to need full-scale health services on the campus, for students and staff. A university or polytechnic with 3000 or more students can easily support what is, effectively, a National Health practice, although the kind of medicine practised differs from that of the usual general practice, since students and the staff have different medical problems – accidents (especially from sports activities), preventive medicine (eg for students going on expeditions), and psychiatric services, are generally more important than in the family general practice. Campus health services are staffed by full- and part-time state registered nurses, and some have a full-time medical practitioner. The traditional support given to students by the personal tutor in university is now supplemented by full-time professional counsellors, employed by the university and/or the student union. Practical welfare problems, like where to live, are generally dealt with by lay staff.

Inspectors of schools and advisers
They work for both central and local government.

HM Inspectors observe, report and advise, most specialising in a subject or area in which they have trained and have extensive expertise and experience. Senior staff and some other inspectors look after particular subjects or areas (eg careers advice or multi-racial education) on a national basis, or liaise with other educational bodies. While their main role is to inspect schools of all kinds, colleges etc, they also prepare detailed reports on 'matters for discussion', such as mathematics in the sixth form, girls and science, the curriculum, and gifted children. They also prepare educational literature, organise courses for teachers, liaise between the DES and local education authorities, and generally give advice and assistance in the school.

While they work from the DES, they are independent of the department and ministers. The number of inspectors has been increased recently, to 516 in England and Wales in 1985.

The education authorities have their own inspectorates and advisers, who also specialise in a subject or part of the curriculum. They help teachers in a particular group of schools develop their work, they look into parents' complaints, organise in-service training for teachers. There are probably some 3500 posts in all.

Some LEAs have resource centres for teachers – examples are music centres (which may also run the authority's extra-curricular music activities), history, and teaching aids. There are at least 400 posts in these for administrators-cum-advisers, although some are partly run by inspectors. There are sometimes also short-term posts in areas such as curriculum development, project co-ordination, advising in particular topics.

Recruitment and entry Inspectors (and other advisers) are generally recruited from amongst experienced teachers and other academics, normally between the ages of 35 and 45. Since most inspectors specialise, extensive knowledge of the field and its educational requirements are essential – for example, inspectors working in commercial and technical education are normally expected to have held a responsible position in industry or commerce as well as extensive teaching experience. An inspector in a particular field may have considerable influence on the development of his or her subject.

Librarians and information scientists
They are employed extensively throughout the education system, not only in universities and polytechnics, but also in other colleges of further and higher education, and in schools, particularly larger comprehensive schools.

Librarians are also employed in careers offices, in both LEAs and universities and polytechnics.
See LIBRARY AND INFORMATION WORK.

Training officers, advisers and instructors
They work for any organisation which trains its own staff (such as industrial and commercial companies), for training boards and voluntary training organisations, and for national and local training agencies. A growing number of commercial organisations provide training for other companies or organisations, individuals, often specialising in, eg computer or language training.

Training officers do not, normally, do the training themselves (although some may train instructors). They are managers. Their job is to identify training needs; plan, formulate and implement training policy; organise and administer schemes, monitor and assess their effectiveness.

Schemes may range from training young people starting work straight from school, through induction courses for graduate trainees, to development programmes for managers. Increasingly they involve training for change (which means identifying the changing needs in the first place), and newer schemes, such as MSC's Youth Training Scheme, and the related Information Technology Centres (ITECs).

Company schemes may be run internally, or they may send people to, for example, FE colleges, and therefore negotiate the courses they will follow there. They may be within a single large firm or other organisation, for a 'group' training scheme (for a number of employers in an area), or on an industry-wide basis. Organisations employing training staff include not only industrial firms, but also banks, retailers, local government, for example. In industrial and commercial firms, particularly, education and training are usually a function of PERSONNEL MANAGEMENT.

Training advisers, who advise training officers and their management, are the theoreticians of training. They work for, for example, an industrial training board, a voluntary training organisation, the Manpower Service Commission.

The Manpower Services Commission employs (1986) over 8500 people whose work is concerned in some way with training, and this is projected to rise to nearly 9500 by 1990, under the 1986 Corporate Plan. MSC's 6000-strong training division is responsible for YTS, adult training schemes, and 'Open Tech', and controls LEA expenditure on a proportion of work-related non-advanced further education. On YTS, for example, staff of the Training Standards Advisory Service (which employs professionals from industry and education as well as MSC staff) has recently been carrying out in-depth inspections of individual schemes throughout the country, and other Commission staff have been working with the (voluntary) industry training organisations to produce illustrative/model, industry-preferred schemes. Another 3000 MSC staff run the Skills Training Agency, now operated as a semi-independent training business, providing training in some 60 skill centres and via a mobile service.

While the need for training, even for a steadily increasing level of training is generally recognised in theory (see ACADEMIC AND VOCATIONAL QUALIFICATIONS), in practice it is proving an uphill task to get many sectors of industry and commerce to put it into practice, largely because it is so very expensive to do. It is government policy to encourage training, but the present (1987) government believes that training should be taken on by organisations voluntarily.

Estimates of the number of training officers vary, with a top figure of about 25,000 altogether (the TSD once suggested a figure of 10,000 in industry and commerce).

Instructors are employed throughout commerce and industry, by training boards, the TSD and so on. They do not form any kind of coherent group. They may be experienced craft workers, and teach the most elementary and practical skills to apprentices on the factory floor. They may work in skill centres, training experienced people in new skills, for instance operating numerically (computer) controlled machine tools. They may be former computer programmers teaching computer programming. At the other end of the scale, large accountancy practices may employ their own instructors for trainees.

Recruitment and entry Training and instruction is normally a second career, which usually comes after training, qualification and experience in another area of work. For training officers and advisers this is normally a profession, such as personnel management, engineering, teaching. For instructors it is more likely to be a specific set of skills, ranging from a craft in its most modern form, through technician-level work to more advanced skills like computer programming and systems analysis. For professional people, training may be a stage of career development; for instructors it is often a form of promotion, often as an alternative to some kind of supervisory post.

Qualifications and training Training for training is mainly by short courses and/or internal to the organisation.

The Institute of Training and Development awards a diploma in training management for which at least 200 hours formal study time, including 30 hours of full-time attendance, are required. There is also an Institute certificate in training and development for which study at an approved centre is stipulated. Candidates for membership of the Institute must (normally) have a degree, BTEC/SCOTVEC Higher National or equivalent; have successfully completed a course and the examination for the diploma (or an equivalent qualification); and have worked in training for an aggregate of at least five years or three years continuously. This means that full membership is not likely to be possible before 24.

Diploma courses, at: university – Manchester; polytechnics – Huddersfield, London: NELP, Wolverhampton; colleges – Derbyshire, London: SW London, Luton, Stockton-Billington, Wigan.

Certificate courses, at: polytechnics – Huddersfield, Liverpool, London: NLP, Portsmouth, Wolverhampton; colleges – Ipswich: Suffolk CH&FE, Slough, Stockton-Billington, Wallsend: N Tyneside, Wigan, Wrexham: NE Wales IHE; other – BACIE Training Services, Coventry Management Training Centre, Lancastrian Management Centre (Borwick), Manchester – Fielden House Productivity Centre.

Further information The Institute of Training and Development.

Other work
Other people working in the educational system include laboratory and work-shop technicians, a small number of media resources staff, school meals staff and caretakers.

Further information from the Department of Education and Science; the Scottish Education Department; local education authorities; Local Government Training Board; the Institute of Careers Officers, the National Association of Careers and Guidance Teachers, and the Institution of Training Officers. See also ACADEMIC AND VOCATIONAL STUDIES

HEALTH AND MEDICAL SERVICES

Introduction   950
Health services and their organisation   954
The medical and dental professions   957
Professions supporting and supplementary to medicine   967
Other health care   999
Scientific and technical services   1002
Managing and supporting the health services   1012

INTRODUCTION
The art of contemporary Western medicine, to paraphrase the British Medical Association, is the application of scientific principles to the solution of human problems.

Caring for the nation's health is very expensive – not only financially, but also in terms of other resources and the numbers of people employed. About a million people work for the National Health Service, far fewer in the private sector. Demand for health services has been growing ever since the NHS was formed in 1948, and with it the number of people employed. It is very difficult to reduce the number of health workers without adversely affecting the service. Mechanisation and automation can have only a marginal effect in primary care, although they are used in support services like cleaning and catering. Machines can help to keep accurate, second-by-second checks on patients' conditions; computers are being programmed to start the process of asking patients questions about their symptoms; computers can make record-keeping more efficient. However, robots cannot (yet) replace surgeons, nurses, or physiotherapists.

Only really major advances in treating a range of illnesses, or repairing damage caused by accidents or, and rather more likely, in preventing either in the first place – as has happened by making seat belts in cars compulsory – and so reducing the number of patients, can cut the numbers needed to staff the health services. However, although this ought to mean that careers and jobs in the health sector are protected in ways not possible in other spheres, in practice problems of financing means that the service cannot employ as many people as it would like. Doctors within the Health Service are overworked whilst others are unemployed.

Jobs and careers within the health services change and develop all the time. Many of the changes are a direct result of scientific and technological developments and improvements in diagnosis and treatment. Their effect is to bring much greater specialisation into many jobs, and to make the work more technical. Science and technology have tended to dominate developments for some years, but recently the pendulum has been swinging somewhat in the direction of 'humanising' health services, treating patients as whole people and not just their symptoms and illnesses, in isolation from the rest of the person and his/her environment. More thought is being given to the psychological effects of illness; the social problems caused by illness are being 'treated' too – it is accepted that families should be involved, and supported where necessary. Letting mothers stay with their children in hospital, and relaxing rigid visiting hours so patients can stay more closely in touch with their 'normal' world are just two examples.

New diagnostic techniques and methods of treatment, and new attitudes to caring for patients, are only two factors which are increasing the level of expert knowledge needed throughout the health services. This expertise is now so extensive that it cannot possibly now all be held or controlled by doctors. This is one reason why the tradition that the doctor takes all the decisions (on the basis that he or she knows most/best whatever the patients' problems) is beginning to break down. Most health workers, doctors among them, now accept that treating patients is team work involving a number of experts – which and how many depends not only on what is wrong with the patient, but on factors like their home circumstances as well. For instance, the decision on whether or not to send a patient home from hospital at a certain point may depend on the care available in the community, and generally a social worker will assess this. The health services now use phrases like 'multi-disciplinary care team', and 'primary care team' – involving general practitioners, district nurses, social workers.

Doctors are not unnaturally somewhat reluctant to give up their long-held and exclusive rights to make the decisions about patients. Obviously they must still be the decision makers where their clinical judgement is the major factor. Surgeons, for instance, despite the growing team of experts that surround them, must decide what should be done, even though they may have to listen rather more to other experts than they used to. But in other circumstances other professionals, for instance occupational therapists, physiotherapists, and nurses, have been developing new expertise. They now have greatly improved training, are generally better educated altogether (often to the same school-leaving standard as the doctor), and expect this to be acknowledged with greater responsibility where their expertise is most crucial to the patient. Doctors now generally accept that when they refer a patient to an occupational or physiotherapist they give only the general aims of the treatment, and leave the detail to the expert. Some para-medical experts want to go further – for example, the physiotherapist may expect to be able to make decisions on whether or not treatment is actually worthwhile. Where older people are concerned and the problem may be mainly to do with nursing care, occupational and physiotherapy, nurses may consider that they could well take more of the decisions about individual patients than they have in the past, and that they, rather than the doctor, could actually 'lead' the care team in these instances.

The Royal Commission on the Health Service (1979) raised these problems – 'The role of health workers is subject to many kinds of change, particularly those brought about by developments in techniques in health care'. The Regional Medical Officers told the Royal Commission, 'The character of health care is constantly changing, sometimes rapidly and extensively, more often quietly and imperceptably, and this condition in turn gives rise to a continuous although unstructured process in which tasks and functions are redistributed between professions'. The Commission also commented '... roles are not always clearly defined, and the levels of training required may not be clear...'.

The Commission talked about relations between professions: 'Uncertainties over role, the drive for professionalism, developments in the approach to treating patients, and the difficulty of giving guidance on how health professionals should work together in the treatment of patients can all be observed in the evidence we have received about what is referred to as the "multi-disciplinary clinical team" (MDCT). By this is meant a group of colleagues [with] a common involvement in the care and treatment of a particular patient. The staff in question may be doctor, nurse, social worker, and members of other disciplines, depending on what is wrong with the patient. The relations between members of the MDCT are unlikely to be formalised. The same questions arise whether one is talking of care in hospital or the community... Most heat is generated over which member of the MDCT is to be regarded as its leader. The BMA told us, "No doctor fails to recognise the necessity of co-operation with the nursing profession and with other medical workers and the benefit which can derive from their experience. But this does not mean that the doctor should in any way hand over his (*sic*) control of the clinical decisions concerning the treatment of his patients to anyone else or to a group or team ..."'

But the Royal College of Nursing told the Commission, 'In the MDCTs the leadership role should be determined by the situation in some circumstances, eg geriatrics, the nurse may reasonably assume the leadership role in continuing care situations, this currently happens and should be formally recognised'. The Report commented, 'In the past the doctor's long and broad training, and his higher pay and status, made him pre-eminent amongst his non-medical colleagues. Many factors have come together to change this, among them changes in social attitudes and the increasingly sophisticated nature of the training undertaken by the other professions. Whereas formerly the doctor probably took most decisions affecting the patient on his own, he may now look to the nurse, speech therapist or dietitian for advice on particular aspects of treatment or care. Non-medical members of the MDCT will be experts in their own right, and... there will be aspects of care where the doctor is not necessarily the best person to judge the patient's interests...'

The Commission thought it extremely important that 'flexibility of role' be exploited and built on, and that training arrangements should be flexible too, to counterbalance the trend to ever more, and narrow, specialisation and to make it easier to cope with change. It pointed out that the Dentists and Medical Acts do not try to define medicine (or dentistry) or to confine its practice to those on the medical register. The Commission pointed out that this would have created severe problems for the present-day nurse or physiotherapist undertaking procedures which the doctor of yesterday would certainly have kept to him- or herself.

Work within the health services, then, will go on changing, with tasks and 'functions' being redistributed between the many separate professions, and the professions themselves may well change too. Suggestions have, for instance, been made that nurses and doctors should start with the same initial period of study, and that all should learn nursing care and have a period of clerkship before deciding whether or not to become a doctor. This would make it possible to have doctors and nurses with varying levels of expertise, and greater flexibility in their employment.

Experiments go on all the time. For example, in some general practices qualified (SRN) nurses have been trained, on an 'apprenticeship' basis, to become what is called a 'nurse practitioner'. They have learnt to take case histories and basic diagnostic techniques and so can deal with some patients instead of the GP, but under supervision. They do not prescribe, have learnt which problems must be passed on to a doctor, and must discuss any referrals they want to make with the supervising GP. The idea is not so much to ease the GP's case load, although this is obviously useful, but to give patients the choice of someone they may feel is more approachable and easier to talk to about some symptoms or problems than a GP.

In the past, except for the medical profession itself, the main concern has been to increase staff to meet steadily rising demand. On manpower planning, the Royal Commission recommended a more positive approach, and saw an urgent need for more adequate data. As well as improved statistical information, the Commission wanted to see more work on numbers and roles, experiments with different mixes of staff in different contexts, and the development of inter-professional training. So far, none of this has happened. The Commission said that unless 'matters of this kind are studied deliberately, changes in function to meet changing circumstances may occur haphazardly and become established before they can be evaluated'. Up to 1981, numbers employed by the NHS continued to rise steadily (by 30% over the decade), but in the 1980s numbers have levelled off and may even have fallen slightly.

WORKING IN HEALTH CARE then, increasingly means working more and more closely with other health workers, as part of a team. It is work which combines a concern for people who have health problems with a high scientific and technical content – there are more and more machines, more and more technical equipment, more scientific tests, more computers. Most of the work combines doing, observing, and talking, but paperwork generally (except for administrators) comes second, although obviously records are crucial.

It is a way of life which can swing from extreme to extreme, from the humdrum to the harrowing, from the ultra-clean to conditions of appalling mess, from periods of tedium and waiting to days or hours of continuous rush and great stress. The hours are inevitably long and irregular, and have not improved very much lately. For most there is shift work. Not everyone cares directly for patients, but those who do have to deal sympathetically, patiently and reassuringly with both patients and relatives, and must accept that patients are now less willing to accept paternalistic and authoritarian attitudes in health workers, and want to be be treated as intelligent people.

All health workers must have the same aims and the same standards. Everyone has to take the same care, and cleanliness and sterile conditions are as important for the laundry worker as for the surgeon 'scrubbing up'. Although everyone tries to maintain sterile conditions, accidents and operations, and the unavoidable symptoms of some illnesses do mean much unpleasant mess.

Caring for patients directly involves situations ranging from the relief of seeing a new baby howl or a child recovering from a serious illness, and joking with patients to help their morale, to coping through long nights with patients made bad-tempered by pain or continuous discomfort, and the inevitable reality of incurable illness and death.

Staff who are in closest day-to-day touch with patients, which generally means nurses and physiotherapists rather than doctors, often find themselves being counsellors, listening to and helping to ease problems such as loneliness and anxiety. Patients may also tell them about factors which may help to solve medical problems, and they in return can explain the mysteries of modern medicine and therefore clear up unnecessary fear, or perhaps just stop for a welcome chat which by itself may ease tensions.

Recruitment and entry Most professional health workers must train and qualify before they are recruited. Direct entry is only to lower level occupations, and to traineeships.

All careers in the medical and health spheres are extremely demanding, on mind, body and emotion. Concern and compassion for suffering has to be combined with the ability to learn to understand and use scientific and technological equipment, tools and techniques. Professionals in the health service have to learn keen and careful observation, to make skilled analyses of situations and sound judgements; they need emotional and physical stamina, and the ability to remain calm and reassuring in crises. They have to accept responsibility for patients' lives.

Qualifications and training Most health professions have their qualifications (and so effectively their training also), laid down by law, and by law every professional must be 'state registered' before they can practise. Generally, training standards (and therefore educational requirements too), have been rising, and now involve three or more years' full-time study. Stated minimum entry requirements for courses may not always be enough and so it is important to check the actual requirement with the schools. Patterns of training have been changing too – more degree courses for para-medicals and some schools have become part of polytechnics and other colleges, so that training is less isolated.

HEALTH SERVICES AND THEIR ORGANISATION
The NHS — the private health sector — occupational health services
Health care is split between –

The National Health Service
The (state run) NHS looks after most of the nation's health and medical needs. Spending £18,700 million (in 1986-7), and the country's largest single employer, with over a million people working for it, this is a massive organisation. Not surprisingly, its size, importance (to almost everyone at some time in their lives), and cost mean it is extremely difficult to make the NHS both

efficient and effective. Demand for more and better services, which keep pace with increasingly-expensive medical and technological advances, grows and grows, and the problems of an ageing population almost cancel out elsewhere improvements in health care.

Despite the criticisms and the problems, the NHS provides a service which compares reasonably on most criteria with those of other countries. However, the managerial and organisational problems have been endemic for all of its 40 years, with regular attempts to solve them. The massive 1974 reorganisation brought together into one structure the previously separate general practitioner services (medical, dental, ophthalmic and pharmaceutical), the hospital and specialist services (including blood transfusion, scientific and radiography units), and the services formerly run by local authorities (eg medical social work, school health services, ambulances, family planning, health visiting, maternity and child health care services).

In 1982, streamlining brought in a two-tier, region-and-district administrative structure. At the apex of the structure is a full-time management board, currently headed by the health services minister, and reporting to a supervisory board. This controls, plans and monitors the working of the service as a whole.

The 14 regional health authorities are responsible for regional strategy, producing regular five-year plans as well as annually-drawn-up and -revised operational programmes, and agree priorities with the management board. The emphasis is on improving management (see MANAGING AND ADMINISTERING THE HEALTH SERVICE below), management systems, hopefully making lines of management more direct, simplifying procedures, speeding up decisions and reducing administrative costs, while improving patient services. Regions administer building programmes and the facilities for teaching and research. The 192 district health authorities are the main operational bodies, organising and administering health services within their boundaries. Each district has a population of 120,000-300,000, and typically up to twenty hospitals, with about 300 hospital doctors and 2800 nurses, 200-plus GPs, 110 dentists and 300 community nurses amongst its 8000 employees.

The balance of resources is heavily weighted to the hospitals (1890 in England alone in 1984 down from almost 2300 in 1969 with some 334,500 beds), still absorbing nearly 70% of total spending. Some 480,000 people work in hospitals, under 137,000 in community care, which includes not only GPs but also health visitors, district nurses, social workers and home helps. The 1979 Royal Commission could not reach a firm judgement on whether the balance between community and hospital care is right, but thought that the emphasis should be on the development of community services. In the community services, the main feature has been the steady development of group practices and health centres, bringing together general practitioners, dentists, etc under one roof, with other members of the community services such as health visitors, home nurses, attached to each. A government review in 1986 suggested a number of changes in community services.

The private health sector
This consists mainly of registered private hospitals, nursing homes and clinics.

Some private practices are staffed by medical and dental practitioners and other professionals qualified to work in the NHS, but choosing to work outside it, and by practitioners not normally employed by the NHS, such as osteopaths and chiropractors. Professional people working for the NHS can also practise privately at the same time. Many private hospitals belong to health insurance companies, and are run by professional managers.

The private sector is still small-scale in relation to the NHS, and growth has slowed sharply since the early 1980s. Most of the 1400 or so private hospitals and nursing homes care permanently for older people, and some look after the mentally ill. Just over 200 hospitals provide some 10,000-plus beds for short-term, 'acute' surgical/medical care, a third of them added since 1979. Hospitals are still being built, and too many beds are chasing too many patients.

More private hospitals are now providing 'high-tech' surgical treatment, and have radiotherapy and advanced diagnostic facilities, sharing some of them with the NHS. Hospitals and centres provide a range of other services, including health screening and diagnostic testing, and are trying out outpatient, psychiatric and alcohol abuse care. There has been little growth in private general practice, with very few which take only private practice, and only a small number of individual doctors practising only privately.

Occupational health services
They look after people at work.
The Employment Medical Advisory Service gives a broad, nation-wide service of advice on all medical aspects of employment problems, to employers, employees, trade unions, family doctors, doctors working for firms, and so on. The service also has some legal responsibilities – to carry out medical examinations which may be required by law. The service should have a staff of some 110 medical advisers, plus ancillary staff. It is based on the main industrial centres.

The larger employers, particularly industrial firms, have their own medical services for employees over and above those legally required (the regulations have recently been tightened up). Here doctors and nurses provide a service which gives emergency and rapid medical treatment for anyone taken ill at work, or hurt in an accident. They arrange regular checks for people at risk, for example in labs where radioactive materials or dangerous chemicals are used. They may also deal with minor illness and accidents, may give immunisation or vaccination, for instance against a particular form of flu so that staff do not have to take time off work. The medical service may also deal with other preventive measures, especially on safety. Most organisations employ local GPs on a sessional basis, but services are now being offered on a contract basis by some private companies. Only the largest firms have full-time medical staff. Many, however, employ full-time nurses.

The ARMED FORCES each have their own extensive medical services which specialise in the occupational hazards of the Army, the Navy and the Air Force, with their own hospitals. They treat soldiers, sailors and airmen as war casualties and dealing with the peacetime effects too – even training and simulating war can result in some extremely serious accidents. The Forces' medical services do a fair amount of research and development work into treatment for wounds caused by modern weapons. As the Falklands war showed, they have made considerable advances in, for example, treating burns, and the Navy has made extensive studies of the physiological and other problems of diving and other underwater work. The Forces also provide a general-practitioner service for both serving men and women and their immediate families. They employ qualified doctors, nursing staff, and technicians.

Universities, polytechnics, colleges with resident students, and some boarding schools, also have to provide medical services. University and polytechnic health services combine occupational health services – for staff – with a general-practitioner-style service tailored to the needs of students, whose age generally makes them healthier than the patients in the conventional practice, but they are prone to, for instance, accidents on the sports field or in the lab, to stress and psychological problems linked to their studies. In addition to a medical centre or room for on-the-spot treatment, some have small sick bays. Again, few employ full-time doctors or dentists, using local GPs on a sessional basis, but they do usually have a small team of nurses working full- and/or part-time. See also EDUCATION.

Medical staff in the Prison Service both care for inmates' physical and mental health, and also help in any rehabilitation, by diagnosing and treating where possible any physical, mental or psychological problems. Every prison has its own hospital accommodation, although where necessary outside medical services are used. The service carries out its own research into ways of treating and otherwise aiding offenders. Medical staff have to be at least 28, and postgraduate experience and/or training in psychiatry is useful.
See also PRISON SERVICES.

Other organisations employing medical, and para-medical, professions and supporting health staff include the POLICE, Missionary Medical Services (see RELIGIOUS SERVICES), and the MERCHANT NAVY (see TRANSPORT SERVICES).

THE MEDICAL AND DENTAL PROFESSIONS
Introduction — medicine — dentistry
Although they still make up less than 10% of all NHS employees, and probably even fewer in other health sectors, doctors and dentists are the key personnel in health service provision (numbers have, however, been rising steadily – in England alone from 66,800 in 1975 to over 82,100 in 1984. As the Royal Commission points out, most people expect that a doctor will diagnose what is wrong with them and prescribe the treatment, they initiate most health service expenditure, and play a major part in both financial and general management.

World-wide, there is a shortage of medically- and dentally-qualified staff, although provision is uneven. The greatest shortages are in underdeveloped areas which find it difficult to afford qualified doctors, and there is a danger of too many doctors in some developed areas such as continental Europe.

The medical profession
Medicine is not just one career. While it is common to think only of becoming 'a' doctor, there are, in fact, many different kinds of doctors. Certainly, most doctors spend most of their time doing what is generally considered to be a

doctor's job – diagnosing (trying to discover what a patient's health problem is) and treating illness. However, they may also (for example) do research, look for ways to prevent disease, become medical advisers, or indeed not practise as doctors at all (see ACADEMIC AND VOCATIONAL STUDIES). Doctors also have a wide choice of different specialisations and settings in which to practice medicine.

As the 1979 Royal Commission pointed out, the role of the doctor is not defined, and varies according to individual inclinations and circumstance. The doctor's role has also changed in response to developments in medicine, and as a result of changes in attitudes and aspiration, not only amongst doctors themselves, but in changing aspirations and roles amongst health workers as well, and in the demands of the public. The Commission noted that few detailed studies have been made of medical work in the UK, and suggested this is an important area for future research.

Authorities are in total disagreement, it would appear, on how many doctors will be needed in the future. The last two official predictions were based on very inaccurate estimates of, for instance, the birth rate. The Royal Commission suggested that current output of the medical schools was about right, and that there was unlikely to be any medical unemployment up to the end of the century – but did say, quite sharply, that 'doctors will not have the choice of speciality and place of practice they have at present...'. There has, however, been some unemployment, despite the fact that there is a shortage of some specialities and many doctors work very long hours, and (further) cuts in medical-school output have been suggested.

Working as a doctor The main choice is still between becoming a family doctor in general practice, or working in the hospital service. Of about 95,000 registered qualified practitioners in the UK, about three in ten are GPs, and four in ten are hospital doctors and consultants. While the number of hospital doctors has more than doubled in the past 30 years, at an average growth rate of over 3% per annum, the number of GPs has increased by only 36% at an average rate of under 2% a year. Now, though, about equal numbers go into general practice and into hospital work.

Younger doctors have, in the past, been able to spend a few years in the hospital service, and then switched to general practice, possibly with a part-time hospital appointment. The compulsory training year for GPs means this is not so easy now. It has always been more difficult to transfer from general practice to hospital service. Hospital work and general practice are, of course, very different. The doctor in general practice needs a broadly-based knowledge of medicine and must expect to deal with the more common ailments of the community (but still be able to detect the less usual), while the hospital doctor or surgeon goes on to specialise in depth in one aspect of medicine or surgery, and treats mainly patients with more serious conditions.

About one in ten of all doctors teach in medical school and/or do research full time. Even fewer work in the community medicine, in occupational medical service, or are members of the Armed Forces, Civil Service, prison service, etc.

Hospital doctors usually specialise in a fairly narrow branch of medicine or surgery and, according to the Royal Commission, the specialities are likely to become narrower with advances in scientific knowledge and technology.

The Commission reported that numbers of general physicians and general surgeons have been declining as new specialist skills develop in particular areas – heart surgery, for example, is a relatively new speciality. Change in the range of specialities (of which there are currently nearly 50, six of them introduced in the last fifteen years) is almost continuous within the hospital service. Some diseases have been virtually eliminated, reducing the need for doctors who specialise in treating them, while other areas have become more important – treating the victims of road accidents is now a major specialisation, for instance, simply because there are more serious road accidents.

However, the decline in demand in some areas of medicine does not always result in fewer specialists. The fall in the birth rate theoretically should have reduced the number of obstetricians, but in fact it has been counterbalanced by having virtually all babies born in hospital. Medical advance means more lives are saved, so there is more demand for specialists able to deal with the problems of those who survive with some form of handicap, from babies with spina bifida to the very old. Some diseases are on the increase simply because people live longer and more stressful lives, which means more cancer and more people with heart conditions.

The Royal Commission also thought that increasing specialisation, and the rigidity in staff roles which tends to go with it, was likely to lead to higher staffing levels, as were patient expectations and influences. But cutting NHS expenditure has kept down the number of additional posts.

Other developments could bring more changes. For example, doctors in the acute specialities, the Commission suggested, may see their role as being predominantly physically orientated and dependent on the findings of bio-medical research and development in technology. In other specialities, eg those dealing with the people whose behaviour is disturbed, the emphasis will be on developing better relationships between doctor and patient.

Young doctors planning to make a career within the hospital service have to choose their specialisation by the time they qualify. Since it is policy to treat as many people as possible at home, by choosing hospital work any doctor is choosing to work with the most seriously ill, with people who need surgery, or groups where hospitalisation is believed to mean a better service, for instance delivering babies. Medical students can use the clinical years at medical school to gain insight into the work of the various specialities; many medical schools now let students to choose between a series of 'elective' studies of the various specialities. Not all specialities involve directly treating patients: radiologists and anaesthetists, for example, administer services for other doctors and surgeons, only coming into contact with patients at certain points in their treatment.

The Royal Commission urged that students should be encouraged to work in the specialities where more staff are needed. The evidence is that the main shortage specialities are mental illness and handicap, geriatrics, radiology, anaesthetics, and the pathological specialities. Large percentage increases in the number of consultants in geriatric posts since 1966 hides the fact that there were still only some 452 of them in 1985, and only 277 specialising in mental handicap.

Although most hospital staff specialise, in England 4244 or 11.8% (in 1985 against 13% in 1974) still work in general medicine. Anaesthetists – 3960 or 11% of the total (slightly up on 1974) – make up the next largest group. General surgeons are still a large group, but a declining proportion – 3390 of them but only 9.5% of the total (against 11.8% in 1974). Obstetrics and gynaecology is still also a large group, over 2570 but barely 7% of the total (against over 8% in 1974).

Numbers working in mental illness, handicap and related areas have risen, to almost 4100 in 1985, and the proportion too, has gone up to over 11% (against under 10% in 1974).

Within the specialist surgeries, the largest groups are traumatic and orthopaedic (nearly 1950 doctors or 5% of the total in 1985, a smaller proportion than in 1974) and accident and emergency (1470 doctors in 1985 or over 4% of the total, also up on 1974). Smaller specialities are eg paediatric, plastic, cardio-thoracic (only 330 jobs), and neuro-surgery. There are almost 2000 radiologists and radiotherapists (5.3% of the total, up slightly on 1974).

Largest of the medical specialities is still paediatrics (children's medicine) with almost 2000 staff in 1985 (about 5.5% of the total, slightly up on 1974). But fastest growing is now geriatrics with 1600 staff (4.5% of total, against only 3.6% in 1984). Ophthalmology has just 1000 staff (2.8% of the total, 2.4% in 1974). Other medical specialities – rheumatology and rehabilitation, infectious diseases, chest diseases, dermatology (skin), cardiology, genito-urinary – have far smaller numbers each. Under 900 work in ear, nose and throat medicine/surgery. Only 320 specialise in neurology.

Doctors specialising in 'scientific' aspects of medicine form quite small groups, and in fact the number and proportion of general pathologists has fallen, to under 160 in all. Numbers of chemical pathologists, haematologists, histopathologists, medical microbiologists, immuno-pathologists, and clinical pharmacologists have all risen. These specialists administer and work in medical laboratories and are almost entirely backroom men and women.

For newly-qualified doctors, already twenty-four, there is still a long way to go, and much hard work, to reach a senior position in a speciality. The young doctor joins a team of doctors, traditionally called a 'firm', within his or her chosen speciality, for several more years of training. The firm is led by a consultant, a fully-qualified and experienced specialist, who takes responsibility for diagnosing what is wrong with and treating patients referred to the hospital by a GP. The consultant physician or surgeon holds out-patient clinics, visits and examines patients on the wards, and decides on treatment, and in surgical fields, may operate. However, most consultants delegate much of the day-to-day work with and for patients to the members of the team, most of whom are still training, learning mainly on-the-job under supervision from the doctor in the next grade up. They normally also try out – pioneer – new methods of diagnosis, testing, treatment and/or surgery, and write up, give and publish papers on these, or write up observations on unusual cases, all of which is essential for promotion.

The newly-qualified doctor spends about three years as a house officer, a job which involves admitting new patients, taking their case histories, making the first examination, organising and in some cases carrying out tests, recording findings, perhaps starting on treatment, and then keeping up-to-the-minute checks on patients' conditions, reporting all the time to the firm's registrar. House officers usually live in the hospital and must often work long hours in the day-to-day care of very ill patients.

After the house posts, hospital doctors work their way up through a series of, usually (but changes are planned), two-year short-term contracts (which means everyone except the consultants change jobs and move from hospital to hospital quite often), first as registrar, then as senior registrar. Each step up usually involves taking increasing responsibility for patients' treatment or for more difficult surgery, but these are still junior, training posts. It is also usually necessary to pass further, highly specialised, tough, examinations. For some specialities it can also be useful to spend a period gaining lab experience. The total time spent as a registrar depends on both the popularity of the speciality – competition in some fields is intense – and the expertise needed: it can be short as four years or as long as ten, but on average anyone who is going to become a consultant does so by the age of 37 or 38, and rarely after the age of 40. Becoming a consultant involves a combination of hard work, ability, and some luck, and it is crucial to gain the best and widest possible experience and training: younger doctors compete to train under the best consultants in their field.

The ratio of junior staff to consultants in the hospital service is (1985) about 3 to 1 (against 2.7 to 1 in 1974). Career prospects for some junior hospital doctors are not good. It has been policy to increase the number of consultants faster than junior grades for ten years now, and the DHSS has agreed that the number of hospital consultancies should be doubled over 15 years, but so far the reverse has happened.

The 1979 Royal Commission suggested a revised hospital career structure, but conflict of interest between senior and junior doctors has made agreement on how to change the system 'difficult'. There are just too many doctors in the training grades below senior registrar for the present number of consultant posts: most senior registrars can be sure of a consultancy in due course, although the wait can be a long one, given that many consultants spend over 30 years in the grade; for example there are about 850 registrars and senior registrars in general medicine but less than 30 consultants will retire each year for the immediate future. The number of registrars and SHOs together out-number consultants. Hospital doctors also complain that they do not gain true clinical responsibility (which they often carry in all but name) early enough, and that the training aspects of the lower grades are neglected at the expense of using registrars simply as 'pairs of medical hands' to maintain the service.

Consultants work increasingly closely together, and surgeons, in particular, are especially dependent on teams of specialists. Some consultants work full-time in the Health Service, but about half work part time, combining Health Service work with private practice and/or clinical teaching in medical school. The hours consultants work are rarely shorter than those of junior doctors. A full-time consultant is on duty for some 49 hours a week, on a part-time basis

43, not counting emergencies which happen out of hours, being on call, time spent keeping abreast of new developments, teaching, or doing administrative or committee work.

General practitioners look after the day-to-day health problems of a 'list' of people (maximum 3500 each, average 2030 and falling), who have 'chosen', and been accepted by, them as their GPs. Although there are no rigid catchment areas for doctors' practices, normally most of their patients live within reasonable reach of the surgery, and so the kind of practice may vary with the locality. Since GPs mostly live close to their surgeries, this often means being a member of the same relatively small community, at least in rural areas. Some practices may be mostly residential estates, perhaps with a high proportion of young families, which means plenty of work with children and their mothers; it may be in a country or seaside town with a high and rising proportion of older people; it may be an industrial centre which means that working conditions may be particularly hard on people's chests or feet; in rural areas, farm workers, living in isolated spots, may predominate.

GPs treat 90% of all illness, physical and mental, and so expect to meet and treat almost any kind of ailment the community can produce. In most practices, GPs spend most of their time treating a wide range of different illnesses, most of them very ordinary, such as childhood ailments, influenza, stomach upsets, traumas and small accidents, the daily problems of ageing and anxiety. Normally they will see only a few people with very serious conditions, although they must always be on the watch for the unsuspected, for the threatening coronary, for example. There may be unusual symptoms to diagnose, patients with chronic or recurring disease to care for, and only too often, patients who are fatally ill.

A general practitioner tries to find out what is wrong with a patient quickly, and to catch all illnesses in their early stages if possible. They care completely for most of their patients, from deciphering the first symptoms through to final outcome, whatever it may be – full recovery, the problems of long term care, or helping relatives through a patient's death. Modern drugs and the use of vaccines (for example), have cut the length of time people (and particularly children) actually spend being ill, but as people live longer there are more diseases of old age to be treated, more patients who have conditions caused by, for instance, smoking, and more stress and anxiety problems to deal with.

The general practitioner is not under any close supervision. No one tells GPs what they should or should not do, or how to do their work – although they must keep to certain professional standards, and may be disciplined by the General Medical Council if they don't. GPs work 'on contract' to the National Health Service, and are not direct employees, so they have considerable independence – they have even been described as a 'kind of small businessman' (or woman) – although the local NHS family practitioner committee does have some powers over them. But it is entirely up to the GP to decide how to treat each patient, and if and when to call in a consultant or send the patient to hospital. GPs are encouraged to treat the 'whole' patient, not just the present illness or symptoms, taking into account also the more general effects on patients and their families. The Royal College of Practitioners has explicitly proposed a comprehensive approach to the physical, psychological and social aspects of patients' illness. Not every GP, though, accepts that it is part of the job to help solve non-medical family crises.

General practitioners can and do practise on their own, but in England as of 1984 only 11% of almost 26,000, did so (against over 4130 out of 20,200 in 1969), and so more and more GPs work as part of a team. The size of 'group' practices is also increasing. The numbers of doctors in partnerships has risen steadily –

	2 doctors	3 doctors	4 doctors	5 doctors	6 doctors
1969	4828	4875	2876	1290	898
1984	3866	5103	4288	3490	3967

Group practices make possible more regular working times, better emergency and night-service arrangements, better chances to take time off for further training, and generally improved working conditions. It may be possible to specialise: many group practices run their own ante-natal and maternity clinics, and some GPs specialise in mental illness. Many practices now share purpose-built accommodation provided by the NHS as local health centres, which may also house, for example, dentists, chiropodists, opticians, district nurses and health visitors, family planning, and medical social services. This makes it easier to develop 'primary care' teams, where nurses, for example, can take over, eg dressings and injections.

A GP's day is based on morning and early evening surgeries, which can take up to four or five hours, increasingly seeing patients on an appointment system rather than first-come, first-served. Home visits, checking on lab or consultants' reports, signing prescriptions (and passport forms), writing letters, discussing cases with colleagues, and so on, are fitted round surgeries. Some GPs run special clinics, some work part-time in hospitals, or for a local university or college, or a firm's health service. Some find time to do so research or report writing. Of course patients are never ill to order, so that working days can be long and difficult. However, most group practices now have rotas for evening/night and weekend duty, so GPs can have more 'normal' working hours/lives – even though they are still personally responsible for 24-hour care for the patients on their lists.

Most young doctors join a practice as an assistant, 'with a view' to being made a partner, although now that doctors going into general practice are required to do a year's traineeship this is taking the place of time spent as an assistant. Once settled into a practice, GPs tend to stay put – life is relatively uncompetitive, since promotion to senior partner normally comes naturally with age. Most practices have room for doctors who want to work only part time.

It is possible to start a new practice (literally 'put up a plate' on a door or gate and wait for patients to arrive) rather than join an existing one, although plenty of experience is needed first. But this is only allowed in areas which the NHS consider are 'under-doctored' – and they tend to be predictably unpopular places. Most doctors work for the NHS, some also practise privately, but less than 400 have only private practices.

All newly-qualified doctors planning to become general practitioners must now spend a year as a trainee, under the tutorship of an established general practitioner.

Community medicine divides into two different kinds of work.

Community medicine staff, who include regional medical officers, district community physicians and other specialists in community medicine, are 'doctors who try to measure and predict the health care needs of the populations, who plan and administer services to meets those needs, and who teach and research in this field'.

Community medicine is a relatively new speciality. The main functions are medical administration, environmental health and preventative medicine in the community, and epidemiology. This means they help plan health care for each region and district, as well as tracking down the reasons for particular epidemics, and dealing with the problems and consequences of trying to find people who may be carrying a dangerous disease (eg typhoid), investigate outbreaks of food-poisoning, or work on the manifold problems of 'new' diseases, like AIDS. They deal with all environmental health problems, with preventing disease where possible, and with health education. They do research into the patterns of illness in different areas, trying to discover why (for example), more people suffer from heart disease in one place than in another, and so help the NHS to plan the distribution of resources, what should be given priority, and whether or not prevention is feasible. Some community physicians do research in these areas in university rather than the NHS. Over 800 qualified medical staff work in this branch of community medicine in the NHS. At least until recently there was a shortage of quality recruits for the service.

Clinical medical staff in community health service run the school health service, giving children in state schools regular health checks, mother-and-baby clinics, family planning services, immunisation programmes, and so on. Over 5300 doctors are employed, but most work part-time – they may be women doctors working part time or combine community health work with other part-time doctoring – and quite a few doctors do occasional sessions. The Royal Commission suggests that they have been somewhat isolated from the GP and hospital service, and should be properly integrated into whatever pattern of child health services ultimately emerges.

Linked to community medicine is the national Public Health Laboratory Service which has a country-wide network of ten regional and 54 area bacteriological and virological laboratories which do research and help with the diagnosis, prevention and control of epidemic diseases, study the way in which microbial diseases are spread, and look for new methods of controlling them. It is usual to enter the service as a newly qualified medical graduate after two house appointments, since the postgraduate training lasts five years. See also CENTRAL GOVERNMENT.

Research and teaching Some 8500 people with medical qualifications do not practise as doctors at all, but work in medical schools (which are generally part of universities) as teachers (although they may combine this with some clinical work) and do research too, or may be involved entirely in research, in a university department or other research unit. As already discussed (in MEDICAL SCIENCE under ACADEMIC AND VOCATIONAL STUDIES IN SCIENCE), medical qualifications are on a par with other scientific degrees as a basis for a career in teaching and research, and qualified medical people are recruited for fundamental general or clinical research, where often they work as members of a team which also include other scientists. Some make a life-long career in research and teaching, others spend only part of their working lives in this. Postgraduate training, under MRC fellowships and scholarships, in medical research methods and clinical trial techniques, is available.

Other opportunities Doctors also work in OCCUPATIONAL MEDICAL SERVICES, the ARMED FORCES, the PRISON SERVICES.

Recruitment and entry No doctor may practise in the UK without going through a long and formal education and training. For entry requirements and courses see MEDICAL SCIENCES under ACADEMIC AND VOCATIONAL STUDIES IN SCIENCE.
Prospective doctors need to be highly intelligent, and scientifically minded, just to get into medical school and through the course. They must also be able to work hard, often for long and irregular hours, and this means having physical stamina, energy, and really good physical health. Being a doctor involves carrying considerable responsibility and being very conscientious. It needs the ability to concentrate, to be resourceful, patient, and good at listening. Doctors must be able to deal sympathetically with people of all kinds, and be able to get them to talk about themselves. Doctors need a practical, hard-headed and realistic, but not emotional, concern for people and their health problems. Doctors should not be easily upset by the unpleasant symptoms of disease or accident; they need to be psychologically and emotionally stable, and must be able to live with the more brutal facts of life and death.

Qualifications and training Degree courses in medicine are described in the paragraphs on MEDICAL SCIENCES under ACADEMIC AND VOCATIONAL STUDIES IN SCIENCE.
Training does not, however, stop on graduation day, despite the five or six years already spent studying and training. New graduates in medicine are 'provisionally registered' once they have completed their final examinations, and are considered qualified doctors, but full registration requires satisfactory completion of a pre-registration year, involving two six-month appointments as house officer (houseman) at specially approved hospitals. Each six-month appointment must be spent in a different branch, ie in two from medicine, surgery and obstetrics.
Hospital doctors then go through a further series of training grades, and must usually also study for postgraduate qualifications if they want to be promoted. All doctors going into general practice must also spend two further years working and training in hospital departments, followed by a year as a trainee under an experienced GP.

Dentistry
Most dentists today spend more time treating the results of gum disease and bacterial attack on teeth, stressing continuous care and conservation, or at least they should be, because the two main dental 'diseases' are preventable. Less time has to be spent on treating emergencies like sudden toothache, or extracting teeth, but dentists still see their main role as repairing the effects of dental disease – which means drilling and filling, scaling, putting crowns and caps on damaged teeth – rather than preventing it.

Dentists also design and fit (but have made by technicians), replacement teeth, from bridgework to full dentures. Some dentists, but mainly those who work in hospitals or as specialists, also treat children's teeth which are growing in the wrong directions (orthodontics). Others help to mend jaw fractures and are members of the teams (including plastic surgeons), which deal with all kinds of facial injury, mostly in general hospitals and accident repair units.

Dentistry has gained greatly from modern technology, with its highly sophisticated equipment – the ultra-high-speed air turbines for drilling, cutting and slicing; modern materials for filling and coating; laboratory equipment for making prostheses, plus modern anaesthetics and improved radiological techniques. A recently-developed vaccine could prevent dental decay altogether.

Dental 'fitness' in adults, and even more in children, has improved dramatically over the last 25 years, with levels of decay down by as much as 50%. In theory, there is still a shortage of dentists, despite the fact there are now twice as many dentists as there were 30 years ago, which could mean the breakdown of the service if everyone who needed and is entitled to treatment actually asked for it. However, in practice, the combined effects of rapidly-improving dental health (and this could be improved more sharply and quickly if preventive measures were to be speeded up) and rising charges for dental treatment has actually cut demand, so fewer are now being trained.

Registered dentists number (1986) about 24,600. Under 16,500 dentists now (1986) work as general practitioners (against 18,000 five years earlier). They have total independence, working on a form of contract to the NHS and, if they wish, also treating patients privately (90% do so, but only a 'few hundred' treat only privately). Dentists don't have set lists of patients: they give each patient who comes to them a course of treatment, and the patient can then choose to go to another dentist the next time, although in fact many stay with the same one. Dentists can decide for themselves where to practise, what hours to work, and what treatment to give.

Although some dentists employ assistants, in fact it is so easy to set up in practice (agencies provide loans against future earnings to allow them to do so) that there are very few assistants (77 in England in 1985). Some dentists have set up in practice in health centres, and a scheme encourages dentists to work in areas of social deprivation. Some areas are very short of dentists.

About 1100 dentists work for the hospital service in England, some combining this with part-time general practice. Some work in community clinics. They include some 400 consultants. Most hospital dental staff specialise – over half in oral surgery, some 250 in orthodontics, and over 220 in restorative dentistry, doing more difficult repair and replacement work. Some 750 do more general dental work in hospital, largely running emergency services, but most do only a few sessions a week. There are some opportunities for research (eg into the causes and cure of dental decay, the causes and repair of malformation), and some full-time teaching posts.

The community health service employs the full-time equivalent of about 1500 dentists. They inspect and treat the teeth of children, mothers-to-be and mothers with children under a year old. Mostly the work is general, but the service does employ two part-time consultant orthodontists.

The ARMED FORCES have some 400 dentists on short service and permanent commissions, and they are eligible for cadetships. Dental surgeons in the Forces both specialise in treating and repairing the kind of oral and facial damage which happens in modern warfare, and also provide a general service for members of the Forces and their families.

Recruitment and entry All dentists have to qualify through a long period of study and training at dental school before they can practise. See DENTISTRY under ACADEMIC AND VOCATIONAL STUDIES IN SCIENCE.

Prospective dentists need to be intelligent and scientifically minded enough to be able to gain entry to dental school and get through a difficult course. Dental schools tend to put academic ability well above the generally-quoted need for manual dexterity (they claim this can be taught), but clearly anyone considering dentistry is going to like working with their hands and inside the mouth, using fine instruments. Dentists have to treat their patients as whole people, not just as mouths or inanimate objects. Dentists have to recognise that many people find dental treatment intolerable, and so must be able to put them at their ease as far as possible, and try to gain their co-operation.

Although dentists normally have DENTAL TECHNICIANS to do most of the day-to-day technical work, they must be interested in the technical aspects. Dentists also need some aesthetic skill to be able to re-create the foundation of bone and teeth which give each face its own character. Dentists need good health, physical stamina and good eyesight.

Qualifications and training Dentists are trained via degree courses in university dental schools, as under DENTISTRY in ACADEMIC AND VOCATIONAL STUDIES IN SCIENCE. In future, it is possible that dentists will be required to complete pre-registration training year also.

Further information from the British Medical Association, and the British Dental Association.

PROFESSIONS SUPPORTING AND SUPPLEMENTARY TO MEDICINE AND DENTISTRY

Introduction — chiropodists — dental hygienists — dental surgery assistants — dental technicians — dental therapists — health visitors — nursing — occupational therapists — opticians — orthoptists — orthotists and prosthetists — photographers — physiotherapists — radiographers — speech therapists

Introduction

'Supporting' and 'supplementary' professions these may be, but as the 1979 Royal Commission noted, potential demand for their services is very large indeed and they are crucial to the health needs of very many people. Numbers of professional and technical staff in the NHS rose by 55% between 1971 and 1981 alone.

The expertise of each profession is increasing, whether they treat specific parts of the body (opticians for eyes, chiropodists for feet), or specialise in particular diagnostic or remedial techniques. Highly-skilled as they are, the work involved does, for many, have its own satisfactions. However, it is generally recognised that at their present levels of expertise and skills, these professionals are not yet gaining the independent responsibility to match, and promotion and careers structures are still rather limited. Partly this is because decision-making and clinical management has always been in the hands of the medical and dental professions, but it is also because (for example) training has in the past been too narrow.

The professions themselves are keenly aware of this, and hope for more senior posts at both clinical and administrative levels. The nursing profession is, in fact, having some success in achieving senior status in administrative roles, but so far lacks similar opportunities in clinical work. Members of all these professions are frequently included in multidisciplinary clinical teams, but the medical profession can be reluctant to allow other medical workers to take responsibility.

While each profession has its own, traditional, area of specialisation, they do share a common role. Because they all spend so much time in close contact with individual patients – talking to them as they treat them – they are most naturally the people to whom the patient turns for information or advice, or to talk about a problem, anxiety, or straight loneliness. By simply accepting that many patients need just to talk, or by helping to solve problems, or by discovering, just because they tend to be rather more 'approachable' than some doctors, a crucial new factor about a patient's condition, these professionals can contribute even more than is apparent from their formal skills to patients' recovery. It is, however, an aspect of the work which tends to be forgotten, especially when describing the work of para-medicals to young people.

Recruitment and entry The para-medical professions which have, to date, largely been staffed by women, appear to face some severe recruitment problems. They have, in the past, absorbed a high proportion of qualified female school-leavers. The decline in their numbers between now and the mid-1990s, plus the increasing competition from other occupations for them, is already a serious problem.

Except for dental support staff, the NHS does not recruit into these professions without prior full training and state registration.

For all these occupations, a combination of intelligence and personal qualities is needed. The academic achievement needed to start out in these careers has been rising steadily, and with some exceptions is generally now roughly equivalent to that needed to gain two or three GCE A-level passes with reasonable grades, and for some, the ability to go on to a degree course. For most of these professions, entrants also need to be scientifically minded. Partly this is because the amount of theory, and scientific and medical background, taught on the training courses is being increased all the time, which takes a higher-level educational background to cope. Partly it is because the work itself demands a greater understanding of relevant sciences, of medicine, and of the psychological background to dealing with patients, and to be able to cope intelligently with the increasingly-sophisticated equipment and machinery which they must use. For a variety of reasons, EEC regulations relating to parity of qualifications are also increasing the pressure for higher qualifications.

Personal qualities, though, are still extremely important. Almost all the people in these professions spend most of their working days with patients, who will come from all kinds of backgrounds. Many of them will be upset, worried, and tense. To help them successfully means being the kind of person who makes friends easily with anyone, who can put people with problems at their ease, gain and give them confidence, listen and chat to them easily, explain what is going on clearly and simply, reassure, and get them to accept what may be painful or unpleasant tests or treatment. It is no use being put off by patients whose reactions to stress, illness, pain, depression and so on are extreme. While they must obviously find it easy to be sympathetic and understanding, they must also be realistic and practically-minded, and help patients, and their relatives, to accept the inevitable however bad. They may have to be firm and even tough to put patients back on the road to independence. Tact, patience, perseverance, and the ability to stay calm in any situation are all essential qualities. Paramedicals need to be responsible, reliable and conscientious, level-headed, and sensible. A sense of humour helps.

Finally, these are all professions which make considerable physical and emotional demands. It is essential to be really healthy, to have plenty of energy and physical (and emotional) stamina, and be able to take long hours and time spent 'on one's feet'.

Qualifications and training Full-time, three-year training courses are required for entry to most of these professions.

At present, entrants to these professions are mostly trained separately. Courses are broadening, and more basic biological, physical, medical and behavioural/social sciences useful in the medical world if these professionals are to develop wider and greater responsibilities, are being taught. However, they still tend to concentrate largely on the skills needed for the particular profession, and often in isolation not only from other future para-medicals, but also from young people studying for other qualifications and different careers.

While it seems most unlikely that 'generic' training will develop across the range of these fairly diverse professions, most developments in education and training are in the direction of broader-based studies, and more links with the 'main-stream' education system and other professions. The new pilot schemes in nursing (see NURSING below), for example, include several which bring a polytechnic or CHE into training for nursing. Ulster University is now training nurses, occupational therapists, physiotherapists and speech therapists in one faculty (even if nurses are on a different campus from the rest).

The so-called remedial professions (occupational therapy, physiotherapy, and remedial gymnastics), do, however, appear to be moving (if slowly) towards more common training. Physiotherapy and remedial gymnastics have effectively merged altogether. People in the professions have been generally in favour of proposals for broader, more generic initial courses covering a wide range of clinical practice, possibly with specialisation delayed, possibly with introductory para-medical courses which would allow them to delay their choice of profession without lengthening the basic course. Suggestions have also included common teaching programmes, particularly for an expanded academic content (which, in addition to basic subjects eg anatomy and biology, could include comprehensive coverage of the types of problems met and services needed in the community, and of the roles of the professions in community care).

A small number of degree courses increase the academic content of training for a proportion of those coming into these professions. Now the Welsh College of Medicine is planning to start the first 'integrated' generic health sciences degree course (for 1988 entry) with specialisation in physiotherapy, occupational therapy, diagnostic or therapeutic radiography, orthoptics, or medical photography.

It is also possible to add to training after qualifying – for example, via a part-time degree course (at the Polytechnic of Central London) for people already qualified and working in one of the remedial professions. For nurses, there are a range of postgraduate courses ranging from an advanced diploma to research studentships, as well as the second qualifications in eg district nursing.

Chiropodists

They care for and treat feet. Many of the problems they deal with are caused by neglect, by fashionable but wrongly-shaped shoes for example. They are, however, primarily trained to diagnose and treat the more serious conditions and diseases, and not just minor discomforts or superficial problems. This gives them considerable clinical responsibility, and they only call in a doctor for the most serious problems, for example, when surgery may be needed.

Chiropodists care for people's feet when they have had surgery or after an accident, and help to get them back into the best possible condition. They try to correct the effects of any bone or muscular weakness. They deal with the day-to-day foot problems caused by other diseases (eg heart conditions and diabetes), the effects of ageing, the pressures of, for example, standing all day – or pregnancy – on the feet, as well as common problems with corns and nails. They treat sprains, rheumatism, and some skin lesions.

Where possible they try to keep healthy feet healthy, to prevent minor problems getting worse, and to teach people how to look after their feet, to walk and stand properly, and wear shoes which help in avoiding problems. They prescribe special shoes or adaptations for patients who need them. They make plaster casts, and can adapt shoes or make appliances themselves where necessary. Chiropodists inevitably work more with older people (especially in community clinics where the elderly take up 78% of their time), and they may be treated at home. Although a significant number of children are treated, they take up only 18% of chiropodists' time. In hospitals, chiropody is available only as a specialist service for patients already receiving some other form of treatment, and much of the work is post-operative care.

State-registered chiropodists numbered (late 1986) 5933 (an increase of over 400 since 1983), but many work part-time. Many are self-employed, over half working mainly in private practice or commercially-run clinics, with some employed by firms to treat employees. However, an increasing number work for the NHS. The Society of Chiropodists gives a (1986) figure of 2878 full-time equivalents (against under 1500 in 1974) working mostly in community health clinics but also in hospitals – involving 3500 chiropodists altogether, with an estimated 2000 working full-time, the rest part-time (on a three-hour 'sessional' basis). Demand for treatment rises steadily, and NHS staffing levels are generally considered inadequate – a recent survey showed 49% of clinics/ departments with vacancies and 65% claiming to be understaffed, 30% severely. About half of all clinics/departments expect staffing levels to be increased in the next ten years.

Most chiropodists in private practice expect to work fairly long and/or irregular hours (including evenings), since many patients are themselves working during the day. Chiropodists do visit some patients at home, but normally they see patients in a surgery, which can be in their own homes, although increasingly chiropodists have offices in the same buildings as, for example, dentists, or in community health clinics which house general medical practices. Nevertheless, they still work alone most of the time, and do their own administrative work.

The Royal Commission suggested that there is a need for an auxiliary grade of foot hygienist to take over simpler tasks from the chiropodist.

Recruitment and entry Normally entry is via a recognised training course and state registration. While it is possible to set up privately to treat feet without gaining officially-recognised qualifications, unrecognised courses do not give essential training and without state registration it is not possible to work for the NHS.

Chiropodists need the same kind of intelligence and personal qualities as other paramedicals (see INTRODUCTION above). Treating feet and using special tools also needs the ability to work easily with the hands, to have a sure and steady touch, and not be clumsy, with good eyesight.

Qualifications and training All recognised training courses are full-time and last three years, and are deliberately designed to train chiropodists not only to diagnose and treat a wide range of foot disorders, but also to be able to detect conditions that need medical help. Half the time is spent on practical work (including appliance making), and half on scientific/medical studies of the structure and function of the human foot, and their relation to the rest of the body, foot abnormalities, and diagnosis and treatment, and so on, involving anatomy, physiology, bacteriology and pathology, chemistry, physics and biology, as they relate to chiropody. State registration and membership of the Society of Chiropodists (1986 – almost 5300 members) depend on successfully passing the final exams.

Approved training schools (with over 440 places a year) are –
Polytechnics – Brighton (at Eastbourne); Huddersfield; colleges – Belfast CT; Birmingham: Matthew Boulton TC; Cardiff: S Glam IHE; Durham: New C; Edinburgh: School of Chiropody; Glasgow: School of Chiropody; London: Chelsea School of Chiropody, London School; Northampton: Nene; Plymouth CFE; Salford CT (Northern College of Chiropody).

Entry requirements have risen steadily. While the minimum is GCSE/GCE (or equivalent) passes in at least five subjects, including normally two at A level (subjects to include English language and a science subject or mathematics) schools can and do ask for more. Some want a third A level or reasonable grades, and at least one two science A levels, including chemistry. About 5% of entrants are graduates, and the Society reports that more and more members are adding degrees to their initial qualification.

Further information from the Society of Chiropodists.

Dental hygienists

They clean and scale teeth, put on preventive preparations (eg fluoride), do any preparation needed for mouth surgery and care for patients afterwards, but do not give any other kinds of treatment or fillings. They look after both adults and children and must work under the supervision of a dental surgeon.

Hygienists work for general practitioners, in clinics and in hospitals (100-plus in England), and in the ARMED FORCES. Hygienists number (1986) some 2100 (against 464 in 1972), but not all are currently working as hygienists.

Recruitment and entry normally via an approved training course.

Hygienists need intelligence and personal qualities similar to those of other paramedicals (see INTRODUCTION above), as well as the dentist's dexterity, carefulness etc.

Qualifications and training Full-time training lasts about a year, starting with pre-clinical studies of anatomy, histology, physiology, bacteriology and pathology and tooth morphology, followed by practical clinical training.

Training courses (200 places) are all at dental hospitals – Birmingham, Bristol, Cardiff, Dundee, Edinburgh, Glasgow, Leeds, Liverpool, London (Eastman, Guy's, King's, and UCL), Manchester, Newcastle, Sheffield. The Royal Army Dental Corps also trains hygienists.

Entry requirements are at least five O-level-equivalent passes at 16-plus† including English, and one of chemistry, biology or human biology. Some schools ask for one or more subjects to be studied at A level, although not necessarily passed. The minimum entry age is 17, but most schools want students to be older (the average age of entry is 21), and to have had some previous experience as, for instance, a dental surgery assistant (preference is given to people with the National Certificate, or an equivalent).

Further information from the British Dental Hygienists' Association.

Dental surgery assistants

Surgery assistants do whatever the dental surgeon they work for asks of them. In some, usually smaller, practices the assistant both helps at the chairside and has to be receptionist-cum-secretary as well. In larger practices or in a dental hospital, the assistant may only do chairside work. Chairside assistants look after the patient before and after treatment, both putting them at their ease first and helping them to recover from, eg an anaesthetic, afterwards. They look after the instruments and other equipment, keeping them clean and sterilised. They help to mix materials for fillings and taking mouth impressions, and tidy up after each patient; they see that patients' records are kept up to date. They may also process x-ray films.

There are believed to be over 20,000 dental surgery assistants, of whom just over 3000 full-time equivalents (1984, against under 2560 in 1974) work directly for the NHS, in dental and other hospitals – more work in community health clinics.

Recruitment and entry Some dentists prefer to train their own assistants, and probably many start this way direct from school. It is possible though to train on a full-time course first, and this is normally needed to work in dental hospital or community health clinic.

Trainees are normally expected to have had a good general education to GCSE standard, and schools and practices will normally want at least two O-level equivalent passes, normally including English. It is possible to start at 16, but some schools and practices prefer 17- or 18-year-olds. Assistants are generally expected to be neat and tidy, and be sympathetic, tactful and caring in dealing with patients facing treatment. The technical side of the work needs meticulous care and attention to detail, and some manual dexterity.

Qualifications and training Most assistants train on-the-job with a dental surgeon in general practice, at the same time studying for National Certificate exams in part-time day or evening classes.

Full-time training facilities are increasing. It is possible either to do a one-year full-time course at an FE college, and follow this with another year of part-time study for the National Certificate (two years' practical experience are needed for this) or to do a more practical one- or two-year course at a dental hospital. Studies include practical surgery work, and associated theory, eg anatomy and physiology, dental and surgical instruments and their use, x-ray developing, oral hygiene, mixing dental fillings, bacteriology and sterilisation, plus some coverage of receptionist's work, including clerical work and typing.

Full-time college courses – Belfast, Bracknell, Chichester, Coventry, Durham, Edinburgh (Telford), London (Hendon, Tottenham, West Ham), Lytham St Anne's, Nottingham, Portsmouth (Highbury), Sheffield (Richmond), Southampton (Eastleigh), Stoke on Trent (Cauldon), Weymouth, Worthing.

Full-time dental hospital courses – Belfast, Birmingham, Bristol, Cardiff, Dundee, Edinburgh, Glasgow, Leeds, Liverpool, London (Eastman, Guy's, King's, London, UCL), Manchester, Newcastle, Sheffield.

Training for dental surgery assistants is also given by the ARMED FORCES.

Further information (including up-to-date details on courses) from the Examining Board for Dental Surgery Assistants, and the Association of British Dental Surgery Assistants.

Dental technicians

They make and repair dentures, gold or other plates, bridges and inlays, 'caps' and crowns for individual teeth, splints and braces for straightening teeth or post-surgical treatment. They work with a very wide range of materials, from precious metals, through steel, chrome, cobalt and porcelain, to the very latest in plastics and using an equally wide range of metal- and plastic-working techniques, including spot-welding, electro-plating and deposition, moulding, curing. It is not just a technical or craft job, since the technician plays a considerable part in making the patient's mouth comfortable and keeping their appearance as natural (and attractive) as possible. This means no two jobs are the same, and replacements for lost teeth do not come off a production line, but have to be crafted for each individual, normally using a cast.

Dental surgeons in general practice all used to employ their own technicians, but today they use commercial laboratories, which can afford to employ a wider range of staff, can buy the latest (and usually very expensive), increasingly-sophisticated equipment, and do the work more economically. Some practices have set up joint labs, and some technicians have formed their own groups. Some technicians work for clinics and in hospitals. Technicians today often specialise – in orthodontic work, in making dentures or crowns and bridges, or making appliances for patients who have had operations, or accidents, which have affected their teeth and jaws, for instance, wiring for a broken jaw. Larger laboratories obviously provide the main opportunities for promotion.

There are some 4000 dental technicians in all, of whom just over 650 full-time equivalents work directly for the NHS in England, in hospitals, and some work in clinics.

Recruitment and entry is still via either an apprenticeship, or a full-time course (see below), although at a date still to be decided the part-time route is to be phased out. Entry requirements vary with the route chosen, but the minimum is three CSE- or two O-level-equivalent passes at 16-plus† (for an apprenticeship), and some labs may want the minimum requirement for the BTEC award, namely four O-level-equivalent passes, including physics and chemistry.

Technicians need to be scientifically and technically minded, to be skilled with their hands, and able to do fine work.

Qualifications and training via either –
an apprenticeship (with a commercial lab or in private practice) lasting five years for 16-year-olds but may be shortened to three for older entrants. This is combined with release to study for the CGLI certificate. Or –
a training scheme, lasting four years and leading to a BTEC or SCOTVEC diploma in dental technology. Students combine on-the-job training in a hospital, dental school or community dental clinic, with course work at college, either on a day-release or sandwich basis. After passing the diploma exams, students must complete a further year of full-time practical training.
Courses for BTEC or SCOTVEC diplomas are at –
Birmingham: Matthew Bolton; Cardiff: S Glam IHE; Leeds: Kitson; Liverpool: North East TC; Manchester: Polytechnic; Nottingham: Peoples CFE; Sheffield: Richmond; Southampton CFE; Weybridge: Brooklands.
Dental-hospital-based training is at all dental schools.
It is also possible to train as a member of the ARMED FORCES.
After initial training it is possible to go on to more advanced studies in a specialist area of technicians work.

Further information from the National Joint Council for the Craft of Dental Technicians.

Dental therapy
This offers limited opportunities to work mainly with children under twelve. Dental therapists do simple forms of treatment, eg simple fillings, extracting first teeth, cleaning, scaling and polishing, after the patient has been examined by a dental surgeon and under written instruction. They also go to schools and give talks on looking after teeth.

Introduced experimentally in 1960, dental therapy has never really gained acceptance. Only some 240 full-time equivalents (of some 700 who have been trained) work for the NHS, mainly in community health services, some in hospitals (dental therapists may not work in general practice).

Recruitment, training etc One course (entry eight a year), at the London Hospital dental school survives.

Entry qualifications are at least four O-level-equivalent passes at 16-plus† with English language, biology and mathematics preferred. Age at least 17.

Further information London Hospital dental school.

Health visitors

They go out into the community, helping generally to solve family problems but specialising in child health. The formal definition of the health visitor's work gives five main areas – preventing mental, physical and emotional ill health or alleviating the consequences; detecting ill health early, and surveilling high-risk groups; recognising and identifying need and mobilising appropriate resources where necessary; health teaching, and providing care where needed (including support during periods of stress and advice and guidance in cases of illness as well as in the care and management of children). Health visitors are links between patient and hospital, between mother and post-natal clinic, between a teenager and a drug-dependency unit. Health visitors listen, talk, counsel, watch out for health problems, and try to find out what – if anything – is wrong. They give support to mothers with new babies and help with any problems through the early years. Health visitors help families to adjust, to the shock of a handicapped baby, to the loss of a parent. They try to encourage families to try to anticipate or prevent problems, for instance getting the elderly to have regular health checks.

Formally, they are part of the community health service, which employs the equivalent of well over 9000 full-time health visitors in England (in 1984 against under 6500 in 1974), with about 1000 students in training.

Recruitment and entry All health visitors have to be registered nurses, and also have approved midwifery or other obstetric qualifications. They must also (then) qualify as health visitors.

Health visitors need the same intelligence and personal qualities as other paramedicals (see INTRODUCTION above). They also need considerable maturity, as well as a solid grounding in nursing.

Qualifications and training Two possible routes –

First via state registered nurse and then a post-registration one-year course in health visiting, or

Via an 'integrated' degree or nurse/health visitor course starting at 18, so gaining all the appropriate qualifications together – but the entry requirements are at least five GCE/GCSE passes including two at A level. Such 'integrated' degree courses for health visitors are at –

Manchester University/Crumpsall Hospital: 4-year Bachelor of Nursing;

Southampton University/St Thomas' Hospital, London: 5-year BSc(SocSc) specialising in sociology and social administration;

London: NELP: Sociology with professional studies.

Post-registration courses are available at a number of colleges of further education and universities.

Courses are designed to train in observation, in developing relationships, in teaching both individuals and groups, and in organisation and planning; to sharpen students' capacity to see early deviation from the normal, to provide practice in working out a programme of help for the individual where needed, to show the student how to choose the most appropriate method of health education in given circumstance, and to introduce the principles of learning and teaching.

Further information see NURSING, below.

Nursing

'It is difficult to overestimate the importance of nursing services in the NHS' wrote the Royal Commission on the Health Service. 'Nurses', they continued, 'are the most numerous and most costly group of health workers, but more important is the close relationship they have with patients.' The Report concluded that, 'The role of the nurse is varied and is being further extended and expanded by, for example, research into the caring function of the nurse, and development of specialisation'.

Expanding on this, the Report said 'Within nursing there are many levels of skill and different roles. Nursing in the NHS may involve providing unskilled but devoted care which might otherwise be given by relatives and friends. It is carried out by nursing assistants and auxiliaries, with the minimum of in-service training, under the supervision of trained nurses, and it forms a substantial part of the care given to patients. Skilled professional nursing care is provided by trained nurses or those in training....'

'Nursing is an immensely varied profession. In hospitals, nurses work in acute, long-stay, children's, psychiatric, maternity and other specialised units. But growing numbers work outside hospitals – as health visitors, district nurses, midwives, community psychiatric nurses, and nurses working in clinics and in general practice as part of a "primary health" team. Nurses also work in administration in the NHS and health departments, in education and research, the Armed Forces, voluntary organisations, occupational health (company, school or university health centres) and international agencies.' Nurses also work for private hospitals, and agencies – which includes nursing people in their own homes; some care for children.

Most nurses, though, are still hospital nurses, caring for patients in the wards, the intensive care units, the casualty and accident departments. They care for them round-the-clock, hour in, hour out.

The NHS alone needs to employ the equivalent of some 480,000 nurses (up 40,000 since 1979) – nearly 400,000 in England alone. Eight out of ten work in hospitals, about 9% in the community health services (as health visitors, district nurses, school nurses etc), 6% as midwives, and the rest in administration, blood transfusion services etc. About 45% of the NHS nursing force is unqualified, fairly equally divided between nurse pupils and students, auxiliaries and assistants.

The profession has been going through a difficult period. It has suffered major structural changes following the recommendations of various reports, and has been affected by management changes. Nurses themselves are putting their professional role under the microscope, and are surer of the positive contribution they have to make to patient care, and of their own ability to determine this. They are consequently even more critical of the career structures which mean that promotion is limited to administrative positions and gives them no clinical ladders to climb.

As well as the traditional areas of nursing specialisation, nurses take on other 'extended' roles – in renal dialysis, care of spinal injuries, and special-care baby units, for example. Advances in medical science often need parallel advances in nursing care, and nurses working closely with doctors are pioneering new roles – in keeping very small babies alive, in heart-transplant units etc.

Modern nursing practice means caring for the whole patient, not just a condition, and building a working relationship between patient and nurse without any of the traditional 'nannying' overtones. Nurses now have more responsibility for treating and caring for patients, as discussed earlier. The profession believes the role of the nurse should be extended, enabling them to undertake tasks traditionally the province of the medical staff, for instance in some long-stay care areas, they could take the lead. Nurses should be enabled and encouraged to prescribe nursing care programmes, including the mobilisation of other services such as physiotherapy and occupational therapy. It is increasingly recognised that the major health need of groups such as the chronic and long-term sick, and the elderly, is for nursing care. Nor should the tasks of other groups as a matter of course be given to nurses simply because they are always there, and staff shortages, whether of domestic or other professional staff, should not be an excuse for persistent misuse of nurses.

Nurses do not, however, want to lose their role as the medical team's closest link with the patient, and will keep the bedpan and bedmaking routine to this end, even though it makes it more difficult to achieve the new kind of relationship they have been trying to create with the medical profession.

But new roles for nurses – acting as consultant in nursing practice, developing new ideas and teaching – have emerged in only a few places. The management role leaves little time for clinical involvement, because training has emphasised management, because the medical profession has traditionally consulted the ward sister and has not been prepared to change, and because there is a real difficulty in grades above ward sister acting as consultants and advisers if they do not take responsibility for the care of individual patients.

The profession has recently been assessing the future of nursing, mainly as part of 'Project 2000', which puts forward a radical new plan for training (see below). Project 2000 proposes that nursing should become more positively health-, instead of (as now) illness-oriented, promoting healthy living and teaching people self care.

Working as a nurse Nurses have a widening choice of different jobs and places to work, although the great majority are still hospital based.

In medical/surgical hospitals wards and departments are run on tight routines, staffed and managed by nurses. Nurses are in contact with their patients round the clock, observing, monitoring – reassuring, comforting and listening if they can. The wards are staffed mainly by auxiliaries and assistants, by nursing pupils and students, by enrolled nurses, with a relatively small number of qualified, registered nurses, ward and charge nurses.

In general hospitals, the ward may have a mixed group of medical or surgical patients, or all the patients may have bone and joint problems, or they may all be mothers and new-born babies, children, old people, or neurological cases. Caring for patients is now described as an integrated 'nursing process', which includes planning, monitoring, assessing for each patient individually, as well as doing the necessary tasks. Each nurse takes total care of, and 'manages' the needs of a group of patients – how many depending on how sick they are – instead of just doing set tasks – eg taking temperatures etc – or responding to any patient on the ward.

The nurse's working day is not an easy one. For some it is not even a 'day', but a night, since there must be shifts. The more practical, 'domestic', and less skilled routines, of waking and washing patients, giving out meals, bedpans and bedmaking are usually done by students, juniors and auxiliaries, or EN(G)s, as may be some of the simpler medical routines like taking temperatures and pulses. But this does not mean these routines are not important: they are, both for the patients' comfort and improvement, and also because through these apparently ordinary, daily contacts, young nurses learn to observe their patients, to watch out for danger signs, to reassure and comfort patients who are in pain or distress, listen to problems, and ease any tensions.

Even trained nurses do their share of routine, as part of the job of keeping a watch on patients. They, though, also do the expert work, which ranges from planning the skilled nursing care needed for each patient individually, to measuring and administering drugs and injections, dealing with dressings and post-operative care, monitoring the complex machinery, drips and drainage to which patients may be attached, and watching for sudden crises, assessing the significance of changes, either coping themselves or calling for medical help.

Trained nurses are also the ward managers and organisers, who see that work is done within the tight routines (designed to see that as little goes wrong as possible), who check and re-check everything because patients' lives and health are at stake. They must create an atmosphere in which it is possible for the patient to recover without anxiety. They are the point of contact with doctors, to whom they report on patients' progress. They not only look after their patients, but also cope as sympathetically as possible with anxious relatives (including mothers who come into hospital with their children), and supervise, teach and support junior staff. The organisation of the ward, of each patient's day (for instance, ensuring they have drugs at the correct times, go to physiotherapy or surgery and are got ready for this, or see social workers), and of meals and ward supplies; checking cleaning; keeping patients' records up-to-date, is all a demanding administrative job for staff nurses, charge nurses and ward sisters, on top of direct patient care.

Life on the wards is changing all the time, with all the new medical ideas and modern technologies. Advances in treatment mean that most patients get better faster than they used to, are out of bed sooner, go home earlier. More of the people on the ward are more acutely ill, then, than used to be. Many time-consuming and dirtier routines have, however, been cut down, by new medical and surgical techniques, and by disposable equipment and materials.

Modern electronics, modern drug therapies, life-support systems, new surgical techniques like neuro- and microsurgery (so severed nerves and muscles can now be joined), more implants and transplants, new diagnostic techniques (such as the tiny electronic eye which can inspect more and more of the body from the inside), and modern treatments like kidney dialysis, make the nurses' job steadily more technical. Nurses themselves are also involved into improving methods of nursing care, and doing research on the way individual patients react to illness.

Psychiatric, mental health/handicap nursing There are considerable differences between nursing people with physical illnesses or traumas, and those who have psychiatric problems or are permanently mentally handicapped. In psychiatric hospitals and residential homes for the mentally handicapped, routine is less tight, and nurses become more closely involved, first in helping to discover why patients have suffered a breakdown and trying to understand their problems and background, and then in helping to solve the problem. As members of the treatment team (in which all staff work even more closely together than in general hospitals), with psychiatrists, doctors, psychologists, and occupational therapists, they contribute equally to the diagnosis of and treatment plans for their patients. Where patients are permanently handicapped, nurses try to help them lead as active and normal a life as possible. While the psychiatrists and other therapists see psychiatric and handicapped patients only at intervals, nurses are with the patients all the time. They develop a close relationship with them, take part in all kinds of activities with them (games, shopping expeditions, outings), teach them new skills, or just listen and talk to them.

Psychiatric and mental health/handicap nursing is, however, changing. Fewer and fewer patients are now spending long periods in hospital. Instead, they are being encouraged, and helped, to live as normal lives as possible, either in their own homes or in small residences which are as home like as possible. Nurses will, therefore, increasingly work in the community, visiting people at home, seeing them in a 'surgery', and/or caring for some in sheltered accommodation or day hospitals. Some community psychiatric nurses are still NHS/hospital-based, some health authorities have already set up their own community mental health units, and in some areas the service is run from the local authority social service department.

Promotion The profession still has a tight hierarchical structure. Within the hospital, promotion past ward sister has been into purely administrative posts, such as nursing sister/charge nurse (in charge of up to six wards, a theatre unit, or intensive care unit), or senior nursing officer (formerly matron). It was, and still is, very difficult to gain promotion and still have direct involvement in caring for and treating patients. Clinical responsibility stops with the ward sister who reports to the consultant on patients and to the nursing officer only on ward administration. It was intended that senior posts would give responsibility for 'patient care of a high order, for seeing that the requirements for nurse education are met and that the unit is efficiently managed'; that nursing officers' functions, for example, would include keeping abreast of clinical developments, advising unit nursing staff on nursing practice and helping to solve problems in patient care. Attempts are being made to transfer to senior nurses some responsibilities traditionally held by doctors, eg deciding on the kind of care needed by older people or long-term sick, but progress is slow.

Apart, therefore, from administrative posts – which give responsibility for all nursing services within a region, particular sectors, districts, or hospital (over 3000 posts) – moving away from the ward is mainly still sideways.

Within the hospital, the opportunities to specialise include theatre work, the intensive care unit, outpatients, children, or special kinds of nursing – orthopaedics or midwifery (there are full-time equivalent posts for over 17,000 midwives in hospitals), for example. Nurses can also choose to become tutors and/or teach in nursing schools (after training) – some 6500 full-time equivalent posts.

Nurses can also move out of hospitals, into –

The community health service, either as a home or district nurse, or HEALTH VISITOR.
Nurses in the community have a considerable degree of independence, but this can mean some isolation too. Here again, the role of the nurse is being extended, to running some kinds of clinics, taking blood, making 'first assessment' visits instead of a doctor, and being trained in the use of more sophisticated equipment and drugs for patients at home. Proposals are being discussed to extend this further, to include the right to prescribe eg dressings, and some forms of treatment, to be able to control drug treatments for eg the terminally ill.

Home, or district, nurses provide skilled support for families who are caring for patients at home. They give injections, change dressings or administer any special treatment; provide support for people on kidney dialysis at home; help give baths, and generally give support and advice. They liaise between the family and the GP or hospital, or with other services if needed.

In all, some 54,000 nurses (including health visitors and midwives) work in the community. There are full-time equivalent posts for over 14,500 home nurses (1984, against under 11,000 in 1974).

The number of midwives employed in the community has been increasing through the early 1980s to well over 3800 in 1984, having dropped to under 3000 in 1980 (it was 4200 in 1974).

OCCUPATIONAL HEALTH SERVICES: these are the centres that firms run for their staff, universities, schools have for their staff and students. Few of these have full-time medical staff, so the nurse carries the day-to-day responsibility, dealing with any emergencies, minor accidents, or ailments; giving injections; changing dressings; perhaps running a sick bay; keeping medical records; dealing with health education.

The ARMED FORCES, each of which has its own nursing service.

Recruitment and entry Nursing absorbs some 25% of the qualified age group. The profession is already (1986-7) suffering from a shortage of new recruits, and fears this will get much worse as numbers of eighteen-year-olds fall (to keep the same proportion nearly 50% of those qualified would have to be recruited by then). The situation is made more acute by the increasing numbers leaving the NHS – 25,000 a year in England alone by the end of 1986. To replace them, and to allow for those who do not complete training, 28,000 new entrants a year are needed just in England. In fact, numbers recruited for RGN and equivalent training have already fallen sharply, from 30,000 in 1981-2, to under 25,000 in 1986. At the end of 1986, the English nursing schools had a shortfall of 15-20%, the equivalent of 1000-1500 empty places over a year.

There are a number of routes in, but all nurses have to gain (state) registration, and to go through approved training (as below).

Entry requirements depend on the level of entry and the route, see Qualifications and training below.

Nursing requires considerable personal commitment. It is not an easy career. Personal qualities are most important, but intelligence is needed too (both as described in the INTRODUCTION above). Nurses are probably in constant contact with unpleasant physical conditions, severe suffering, and death, more than other paramedicals, and young entrants need to be aware of this.

Qualifications and training Qualifications, and training, for nurses are going through a very lengthy period of change – it is now almost twenty years since the Briggs Committee started the process, eight since the Royal Commission endorsed Briggs – and the profession estimates it will take another ten years to complete the process.

The process of change started in 1983. The UK Central Council for Nursing (called UKCC), and four national boards replaced the old statutory bodies. They are specifically required to 'improve standards of training and professional conduct for nurses, midwives and health visitors'.

A new professional register was the first step taken by UKCC (it contains 1.25 million qualified nurses, midwives, health visitors). The titles and designations are now –

Part 1   Registered General Nurse: RGN (was SRN/RGN)
Part 2   Enrolled Nurse (General): EN(G)(was SEN)
Part 3   Registered Mental Nurse: RMN
Part 4   Enrolled Nurse (Mental): EN(M) (was SEN(M))
Part 5   Registered Nurse for the Mentally Handicapped: RNMH (was RNMS/RNMD)
Part 6   Enrolled Nurse (Mental Handicap): EN(MH)(was SEN(MS))
Part 7   Enrolled Nurse – Scotland, N Ireland: EN (was NE (Scotland/Ireland)
Part 8   Registered Sick Children's Nurses: RSCN
Part 9   Registered Fever Nurse (no more registrations)
Part 10 Registered Midwives: RM (was SCM)
Part 11 Registered Health Visitors: RHV

But the Council believes that there should be a clear separation between the award of a qualification (which is the national boards' responsibility), and registration (UKCC's responsibility). It also believes that designations used by people should derive from their professional qualifications rather than from their registration. However, until the four national boards can decide on the terminology they propose to associate with qualifications, designations will continue to derive from registration.

Registered nurses are termed 'first-level' nurses, and enrolled nurses 'second-level' nurses. Although these terms were originally intended to be just for rule purposes, in fact they are frequently used in careers literature and need to be recognised.

UKCC put forward the profession's plans for reforming training for nurses in a document, called 'Project 2000' (1986), which looks forward to the next century. Two main themes are a stress on health, and positively promoting it (so nursing is no longer just concerned with people when they are ill), and on extending 'primary' care into the community. UKCC suggest that future goals should be to make services local, accessible and appropriate, to encourage further the move towards supporting people in their own homes and in the community, redressing the balance so that health care is not so centred on high-tech hospitals. UKCC sees an even greater trend towards shorter stays in hospitals, rapid turnover, more day cases, five-day wards, and investigation units. The strategy for training, then, they say should be to make initial preparation more community oriented, breaking with the hospitals as the basis for so much training, with new thinking on placements and practical experience, to be developed over the whole range of care settings.

The strategy also suggests initial training must be designed to cope with uncertainty, ie make nurses flexible, with the confidence and readiness to deal with change, to have problem-solving skills, and to be able to think 'creatively'. They must also be better informed, on eg planning processes, information systems, and able to debate policy, to evaluate their own practice and argue for necessary services.

UKCC wants to end the system of once-for-all, 'encyclopedic' training, cut off from other sectors and closely tied to practical work. First-level nurses, says UKCC, should in future be competent to make nursing assessments of patients' needs; to plan, implement and review nursing care; to teach, and advise on the promotion of health, and to recognise situations which adversely affect health. The emphasis should be on team work, on managing the care of groups of patients, and organising appropriate support. But while nurses should assess need, providing, monitoring and evaluating care, combining thinking with analytical skills, they will still give care, and not just supervise.

UKCC proposes a broadly-based 'common foundation' programme, lasting two full academic years. This would be health, not illness, based, teaching self care, promoting 'independent living', and covering social and behavioural sciences – 'normal' living, reactions to stress, coping and support etc – as well as nursing theory and practice. Part of the time would be spent in a range of placements, not just hospitals and community health services, but also work places, residential homes etc, and with other care groups.

The final year would give the necessary training for the main areas of nursing (adult, mental, handicap, children's, midwifery), again with placements in both hospitals and in the community. Health visitors, occupational health, school, district, community psychiatric nurses, clinical specialists, and 'team leaders' (managers and teachers) would be trained, more or less as now, after full registration.

UKCC wants nursing training to be more closely linked to 'mainstream' higher education (see below), and for students to become 'supernumeraries', and no longer employees of the NHS. It is also suggesting that enrolled-nurse status should be ended, possibly to be replaced by a new grade, of 'aide'.

While 'Project 2000' is a clear indication of the direction in which nursing training can be expected to go, the proposals have attracted some expected criticisms, especially on the length of eg midwifery training, and on ending EN status. Possibly the major hurdle is the additional cost. As of spring 1987, health ministers had not given any official reaction to the plan, and no change is anticipated in the immediate future.

For the time being, then, the basic form of training remains the same, although individual schools are moving in the some of the directions suggested above, including rather more community-based training, innovative teaching methods, 'modular' schemes, and some study (instead of working) days on the wards. The English Board has a number of 'pilot schemes', running over the five years 1985-90, to assess new ideas in nursing training.

First-level training (mainstream route) continues to be via a three-year period of training, combining theory with practice. In England and Wales, most training courses lead to specific qualifications in general, mental or mental handicap nursing, although at some schools it is possible to combine general with mental or mental handicap nursing in a slightly extended (up to four years) course, and all general courses include some training/experience of mental/mental handicap nursing, obstetrics etc. Children's nursing is normally taken with, or after, a general nursing course, and lengthens the training by eight months.

Scotland has already changed to 'generic' training for the first half of the course, with specialisation in the second half.

RGN training (in England and Wales) covers nursing, the individual, and the nature and cause of illness with its prevention and cure – social, biological and psychological sciences are integrated into all three sections. All aspects of nursing are dealt with comprehensively. While keeping a very strong practical element, courses do include a substantial proportion of classroom time on theoretical and scientific studies. All courses include some training in community, mental-handicap and mental, maternity, and children's nursing, and care and welfare of the elderly.

RMN training divides into nursing, organisational and management skills, professional skills and the knowledge base with experience in a wide range of different types of care and psychiatric problems.

RNMH training covers nature and causes of mental handicap, development of individuals in and outside the family, and the process of learning, plus practical experience with a range of people with different handicaps, and in social, adult educational, occupational and recreational training.

Training is at a nursing school (of which there are over 200) attached to a hospital, although student and pupil nurses are employees of the Health Service, and make up about 20% of the nursing staff. Bringing training up to EEC requirements, or in any way extending classroom hours, tends to give problems in finding extra study time. The training is tough, and quite a few people don't complete it – about 65% of those who start training in England and Wales actually reach the register.

While the basic syllabus is common to all schools, the way it is taught, and the range of experience varies from the school to school, so it is important to read the prospectus. In particular, the English Board has agreed six innovatory 'pilot' schemes. Some schemes include studies at an HE institution. 'Pilots' are at – Birmingham: Q Elizabeth (with Birmingham University), S Birmingham (with Birmingham Polytechnic), Lincoln: N Lincs (with Bp Grosseteste C), Sunderland (with Newcastle Polytechnic), Poole: Dorset, Yeovil: Somerset.

Minimum entry requirements are five O-level-equivalent passes at 16-plus†. Under an agreed point system, at least five points in at least three different subjects, the requirement can be made up of a range of exam passes. An O-level-equivalent pass (including CSE grade 1) equals one point, an A-level pass 2.5 points. Individual schools may ask for specific subjects (most often English and maths or a science), some may want all five passes at one sitting, and a few want one, or two, A levels. It makes sense to take the most appropriate subjects – eg sciences, sociology, economics, languages.

The UKCC sets an educational (entry) test for people who do not have any of the named qualifications, but it is for schools to decide whether or not they will accept students on the evidence of this (under 3% of those accepted have taken the test).

While the formal lower limit is 17½, in practice most people do not start training before 18. Entry to courses in England is now via the Nurses' Central Clearing House.

First-level training degree route Nursing is not likely to become a fully graduate profession, but graduate entry is expected to rise to some 5% of the total (it is currently about 1%).

There are two kinds of degree course. Most integrate nursing studies with theoretical/academic studies and lead to degrees in nursing. The second type grafts training for state registration on to a conventional degree course, normally in life or social sciences, although one or two of these do include some integrating courses. There are obvious advantages to the integrated degrees, although it is quite difficult to combine the roles of undergraduate and student nurse.

Full nursing degrees are offered by –

Universities – Cardiff: College of Medicine, Glasgow, Guildford: Surrey, Hull, London: KQC, Manchester, Southampton, Ulster; polytechnics – Bristol, Leeds, London: S Bank, Sheffield; colleges – Dundee, Edinburgh: Q Margaret, Glasgow.

SRN grafted on to a degree in another subject is available at –

Universities – Brunel, City, Edinburgh, Liverpool, London: QMC, Southampton.

Entry requirements are as for any degree course, but usually with specific subjects required at A level (eg a biological subject).

Training courses specially designed for graduates in subjects other than nursing (and shortened to 110-137 weeks) are available at – Cardiff: S Glam; Edinburgh: S Lothian C; Glasgow: Northern C; London: Charing Cross, Guy's, St George's, St Mary's; Nottingham.

Second-level training This is a restricted form of qualification, also in general or psychiatric nursing. The training is completely practical, lasts only two years, and there are no exams at all.
Educational entry qualifications – theoretically none except for evidence of a good all-round education, but many schools ask for at least two O-level-equivalent passes.
Uncertainty about the future of EN training has lead to a sharp fall in entry – down to 5000 in 1986 (from 12,000 in 1982).

Pre-entry training Since training cannot start before the age of 17½, and more usually 18, there are good arguments for staying on at school to add more O levels or one or two A levels, or to take a special pre-nursing course at school or at a college of further education. Alternatively, a job with people, and/or voluntary work (especially in hospital or the community), is useful preparation. A YTS entry route is being considered.

Post-registration After registration and some experience, there is an increasingly wide range of further training possibilities for nurses. They can go on to train as district or occupational nurses or health visitors, take advanced nursing diplomas or specialist clinical nursing courses, read for a degree or higher degree, train to teach or do research, or take courses for nursing management.

Further information from the English National Board Careers Advisory Centre, or the other National Boards.

Occupational therapists
They help patients to get back to active life after an illness or an accident, or help them to adapt to any disability resulting from either. They try also to keep long-stay patients in hospital in touch with 'normal' life, and stop them becoming institutionalised. They work with patients in psychiatric hospitals, building up relationships with them, trying to get them to learn new skills and to join in everyday activities with others. They work with older people, helping them to keep their joints flexible and mobile, their circulation moving, and their minds alert.
Occupational therapists help people to settle back into their homes after they have been in hospital, and as part of their work may organise any necessary adaptations. These can range from simple handrails beside steps to installing a lift, or having a ground-floor bathroom built. By giving people practical, independent skills again, occupational therapists help them to regain their self-confidence, to feel that they can be useful, and plan for the future.
There is probably no limit to the kinds of activity occupational therapists try in treating their patients. Once it was mainly crafts, but today they use mainly the practical, familiar tasks of ordinary life, and attempt to find activities that may help individuals or groups over a difficult problem. The modern occupational unit uses foot- and hand-powered lathes and drills, engineering machinery, forging and welding equipment, carpenters' tools and printing presses, and typewriters. It has a kitchen adapted for all kinds of disability and usually a laundry as well. All these make possible activities which can strengthen muscles, improve co-ordination, help people to re-learn or practise their old

skills, find ways to do things with fingers deformed by arthritis, weakened muscles, or a stiffened limb. Occupational therapists design ingenious gadgets to help patients hold pens or spoons, to dress or wash themselves. They make special splints for bent fingers, and get patients in the workshops to make or adapt equipment.

In homes for the elderly, occupational therapists may, for example, start a knitting circle, to keep fingers working and, by chatting and listening to the knitters, keep their minds active too. They may also organise gardening or picnics for patients who can get around, run drama groups, dance and art classes, and craft work. They find things to do for patients confined to bed.

Occupational therapists also work with handicapped children. They look for ways for them to 'explore' the world as naturally as other children, eg special sandpits, water trays, and air-filled mattresses. They use toys which can be handled easily, and use them to teach the children as many ordinary activities as they can.

Most occupational therapists work in hospitals. There they may treat a frequently-changing population of patients with all kinds of different problems, or work with long-stay patients (eg the physically handicapped). Some areas of work, particularly with, for instance, children with congenital handicaps, are very specialised and need special training, but otherwise occupational therapists can change the type of patient and kind of work they do. A growing number work for local authorities, in day centres or residential homes, or planning and arranging home adaptations for disabled people. There are also some advisory and some teaching jobs.

In most units, occupational therapists spend most of their time with patients, gaining their confidence, trying to find out what their problems are and what activities might best help to solve them, and that they will most enjoy doing. No two patients react to illness or disability in the same way, and the emphasis in occupational therapy is now on making the right response to individual patients.

The occupational therapist's job is to assess what their patients might be able to do, plan and work out a programme of activity for them, perhaps trying to find something that will help solve both the physical and the psychological difficulties, but within the available resources, often limited by cost, and therefore needing ingenuity and imagination. They may have to be very skilled, to persuade, for instance, frightened or withdrawn patients to join in, and they cannot always be successful.

Occupational therapists plan and organise, write reports and attend case conferences, supervise patients – assistants and technicians in workshops do most of the actual teaching and help the patients when they need it – and liaise with other specialists, such as physiotherapists to see, for example, that a patient is getting all the help needed.

There is, theoretically, a chronic shortage of occupational therapists. For many years there has been a shortfall, but quite a few registered therapists do not practise, some cannot work because they lack child-care facilities. The NHS employs (1984) over 3600 full-time equivalents (over 5550 people) in England – against under 1600 in 1974 – and another 1000 or so work for local authority social services.

It is also possible to work as an occupational therapist helper (the NHS employed over 3500 full-time equivalents in 1984) or technician.

Recruitment and entry Occupational therapists are recruited only after full-time training.

Occupational therapists need the same level of intelligence and personal qualities as other paramedicals (see the INTRODUCTION to this section). Resourcefulness, ingenuity and imagination, with some practical skills are also useful. Occupational therapists have to learn to be good managers and negotiators, and to work closely with fellow professionals and assistants.

Qualifications and training A number of routes are opening up –

The conventional route is via a three-year full-time course at a recognised school, and leads to the diploma of the College of Occupational Therapists (part of the British Association of Occupational Therapists). National examinations have been phased out, and replaced with college set, externally moderated exams. Courses still cover subjects such as anatomy, physiology, psychology, sociology, psychiatry, medicine and surgery, and orthopaedics, plus the techniques and skills used in occupational therapy, organisation and management of occupational therapy departments or units, and providing aids and appliances for patients. About a third of the time is spent gaining practical experience. The schools (over half of them now attached to hospitals or other educational institutions) are –

Polytechnic – Newcastle; colleges – Edinburgh: Q Margaret, London: WLIHE, Ripon/York St John, Salford CT; occupational therapy schools – Aberdeen, Derby, Exeter, Glasgow, Liverpool, Northampton, Oxford, Wolverhampton.

Minimum entry requirements are five GCE/GCSE passes including two at A level, which should include 'suitable' subjects – each school has its own requirements but English, a science subject (biology is most useful) and/or mathematics are most usual, Minimum age 18. Some schools also set entrance examinations (they are heavily oversubscribed and there is normally a waiting list for entry). Entry requirements are currently (1987) under review.

Degree courses are now available at – Universities: Cardiff: College of Medicine, Ulster.

Shorter courses for graduates (in relevant disciplines) are being developed, but the policy has not yet (1987) been fully implemented, although at Canterbury: Christ Church it is now possible to go on to a degree after completing the diploma, making a five-year course in all.

A small number of colleges provide in-service training courses for helpers.

Further information from the British Association of Occupational Therapists.

Opticians and orthoptists

These are two of the three professions who look after eyes and sight. There is some overlap in the work done by the various specialists. Medically-qualified ophthalmologists diagnose and treat eye diseases and damage, and/or specialise in eye surgery. They work normally in hospitals and eye clinics and may, as part of any treatment, prescribe spectacles for patients. Their careers are along the same lines as other professionals in MEDICINE.

Opticians

They have a two-tier profession – ophthalmic and dispensing. Ophthalmic opticians (who now call themselves optometrists) are trained to do all aspects of the work, ranging from testing, through prescribing to dispensing spectacles. Dispensing opticians are mostly restricted to supplying and fitting spectacles, as prescribed by an ophthalmic optician or an ophthalmologist, although they may also supply other aids, such as artificial eyes, and some are trained to fit contact lenses. While ophthalmic opticians may have more technically-demanding work, dispensing opticians do just as well in gaining promotion to executive and managerial posts.

Ophthalmic opticians examine and test eyes, look for and measure the kinds of defects which produce (for example) short or long sight, any kind of inability to see properly. They then decide what kind of lenses will help the patient to see most clearly. They can also do orthoptic work (below). Ophthalmic opticians use sophisticated instruments to measure accurately the errors in refraction which cause blurred vision, and also examine thoroughly the interior of patients' eyes to make sure there is no disease, or evidence of side effects of other diseases which can affect the eyes. Ophthalmic opticians refer any disease to doctors, but 'treat' or correct defects in vision themselves.

Many ophthalmic opticians do their own 'dispensing', ie have made the lenses, help the 'patient' decide between different kinds of frames, work out with them the frames which fit best and look well, and check that the lenses – which are made by technicians either working for the optician or for a lens-making firm – are accurate.

This is the part of the work done by dispensing opticians, who are not qualified to examine or test eyes, or decide on the lenses needed. They must work to prescriptions supplied by ophthalmologists or ophthalmic opticians. They may fit contact lenses, if trained to do so, but any after-care has to be done by the ophthalmic optician. They also supply and fit aids specially designed for older people to use for reading, and deal with optical instruments of all kinds – such as the equipment used by ophthalmologists and ophthalmic opticians, labs, and so on.

The technical side of this work is changing considerably. The lengthy and time consuming business of measuring exactly visual refraction errors will be cut to seconds with microprocessor-based automatic refractors which will also print out the measurements automatically. A computer-based system is being developed to test the accuracy of new lenses automatically, and three-dimensional holography will make it much easier to measure the cornea more accurately for contact lenses. Laser-based equipment is also possible.

Most opticians, ophthalmic and dispensing – as of 1986 there are nearly 6500 of the former, over 3150 of the latter – work in private practices, either as employees or, when they have had experience, setting up in business alone or with partners. Only a small proportion of spectacles are now provided by the NHS, but opticians seem not to have suffered from any 'new' competition. A significant proportion of their gross profits come from selling optical instruments (eg microscopes), sunglasses etc. There is an increasing trend to fewer, larger, practices – the UK's largest group (470 shops and 2700 employees) controls over 15% of the spectacle market.

A few opticians work in eye hospitals and departments, but numbers are down, to 108 ophthalmic and 14 dispensing full-time equivalents in 1981.

They may also work for commercial firms making lenses, frames and instruments, either in management or, mostly for ophthalmic opticians, in research and development on (for instance) improvements to lenses or developing new optical instruments.

There are a few teaching jobs – those in university (for ophthalmic opticians only) also give the opportunity to do research.

Recruitment and entry Ophthalmic opticians must train full-time before they can start work, but some dispensing opticians are recruited as trainees and can qualify via part-time study.

Opticians of both types need to be scientifically minded, and to have the kind of mathematical understanding which can cope with complex and intricate measurements. This means a reasonable level of academic ability, higher for ophthalmic than dispensing opticians. All opticians need to be able to work with their hands. They need to be meticulous, accurate and patient. They must get on easily with clients, be able to help them relax, and cope with their anxieties. Owning or managing a practice requires organising, administrative and selling skills.

Qualifications and training different for ophthalmic and dispensing opticians. *Ophthalmic opticians* are trained on full-time degree courses (there are also exams to be taken for registration with the General Optical Council, but most degrees exempt from these). See OPHTHALMIC OPTICS under ACADEMIC AND VOCATIONAL STUDIES IN SCIENCE.

Dispensing opticians can at present train either full- or part-time. The full-time route involves a two-year course followed by a year's practical experience. Part-time involves three years' practical, on-the-job training combined with day-release or evening study, and it is also possible to study by correspondence course. The qualifications are awarded by the Association of British Dispensing Opticians.

Courses approved by the General Optical Council are at – Bradford/Ilkley CC, Glasgow CT, London: City/E London CFE.

Entry requirements are at least five O-level-equivalent passes, to include English, mathematics or physics and a third science-based subject (eg general science, biology, human anatomy, chemistry or zoology).

Dispensing opticians can go on to take specialist courses and examinations (set by the Association) in eg contact lens fitting.

Further information from the professional bodies quoted above. See also OPHTHALMIC OPTICS under ACADEMIC AND VOCATIONAL STUDIES IN SCIENCE.

Orthoptists

They mostly work as aides to medically-qualified ophthalmologists, although the work may also be done by OPHTHALMIC OPTICIANS if they qualify to do so. Many eye problems, for example squints or 'lazy' eyes, are caused by difficulties in co-ordinating eye movements, or because eye muscles do not work properly. Orthoptists do the detailed testing needed (which means using very complex equipment), to find out what the causes really are, and to make sure that there is not a more serious problem (some ophthalmologists also delegate other diagnosis and non-surgical treatment to them). The ophthalmologist may decide to operate – in which case the orthoptist measures the exact angles, and does tests before and after the operation – or prescribe spectacles. More often, though, the ophthalmologist tries more than one approach. This generally involves the orthoptist in trying to correct the defect using exercises to 're-educate' the eye muscles, including teaching the patient exercises to do at home.

Some other consultants also use orthoptists, for instance to test handicapped children, in neurological diagnosis, and to screen children in schools. Most patients are children.

The NHS employs under 450 full-time equivalent orthoptists. Most work in ophthalmic hospitals, or hospitals with ophthalmic departments, a few in the school health service, and a few with ophthalmic surgeons in private practice (orthoptists may only treat patients referred by a medically-qualified practitioner). It is possible to work on a part-time, sessional basis, and so combine hospital with private practice or work in other clinics.

Recruitment and entry Orthoptists are only recruited once trained and state registered. Orthoptists need the same kind of qualities as opticians, plus teaching skills.

Qualifications and training The full-time training takes 33 months in all. The course starts with a three-month introductory study of general anatomy and physiology, and normal child development; the main part of the course covers the eye, the use of diagnostic and measuring equipment, and treatment of eye abnormalities.

All schools providing recognised training courses are in ophthalmic hospitals or hospitals with major ophthalmic departments; they are –
Birmingham and Midland Eye, Cheltenham General, Chester Royal, Coventry and Warwickshire, Glasgow Eye Infirmary, London (Moorfields), Manchester Royal Eye, Reading: Royal Berkshire, and Sheffield: Hallamshire.
At Cardiff: College of Medicine, orthoptics will be integrated into the new Health sciences BSc from 1988 entry.
Minimum entry requirements are five GCE/GCSE passes including at least two at A level. The subjects must include English language, mathematics and at least one science subject, but some schools have additional requirements, eg biology or zoology.

Further information from the British Orthoptic Council.

Orthotists and prosthetists

Orthotists fit and supply surgical appliances such as cervical collars, surgical footwear, plaster casts, leg supports, finger splints etc. Most orthotists work for the manufacturers who are contracted to supply the particular appliance for the Health Service. And so while the orthotist does not actually work for the NHS, a large part of his or her time is spent in NHS hospitals and clinics, working closely with medical and other professional staff. The specialist decides on the appliance needed, and mostly these must be made specially to fit the individual. The orthotist measures the patient, or takes a cast, and writes out the specification for the technician who will make the appliance. The orthotist tries the appliance on the patient, checking that it fits, is comfortable, is doing the job needed etc, shows the patient how it works, how to get it on and off, how to adjust it etc. They may have to help the patient come to terms with the appliance, and will check at intervals to see it is still comfortable etc. Qualified orthotists number about 500.

Prosthetists measure and fit amputees for artificial limbs, mostly legs, for patients of all ages, shapes and sizes etc. Even if the limb fits, and works properly when first made, they usually have to be checked, adjusted and repaired frequently, and eventually wear out – children grow out of them – and have to be replaced. Like orthotists, prosthetists are employed the firms making limbs on contract to the DHSS, but at present they work from DHSS artificial limb and appliance centres throughout the country. The limb service and these centres are currently (1987) being re-organised, so where – and for whom – they work may change, but the job itself will remain essential, and essentially the same. If, as hoped, the service is improved, demand for prosthetists will probably increase (at present they number about 200).

Recruitment and entry Because training includes a large 'practical' element, entrants have to be taken on as a trainee by an approved organisation (eight orthotic firms and two hospitals, four limb companies). Minimum entry requirements are as needed for entry to a BTEC Higher course, ie at least four GCE/GCSE passes with at least one at A level (subjects to include English and sciences/technological subjects) or an equivalent, eg a BTEC National.
Orthotists and prosthetists have to be intelligent enough to understand both the medical/anatomical basis of what they are doing and the (rising) technological basis of the appliances they provide. They have to be practical and accurate, and be prepared to take time and care. They must work sympathetically and helpfully with people whose quality of life depends to some extent on their efforts.

Qualifications and training Both orthotists and prosthetists must go through statutorily-required training, which is organised by the Orthotic and Prosthetic Training and Educational Council (OPTEC).
For both, the scheme lasts four years.
In England this starts with a three-month induction period with an employer, followed by alternating periods of practical training and academic study over three years, studying at Paddington College for BTEC Higher National Diploma in orthotics and/or prosthetics, ending with a further 'intern' year of in-company training during which students must produce a 'substantial' project and pass the OPTEC final training exams. Orthotists do all their practical training with their firms, while prosthetists spend all but the final year at the Roehampton London School of Prosthetics gaining clinical experience. To qualify in both orthotics and prosthetics students must gain appropriate practical training.
In Scotland, students are taken on as trainees by health boards, and study for three years at Glasgow CT/Strathclyde University National Training Centre, for a SCOTVEC Higher National Diploma in prosthetics and orthotics.

Further information from the Orthotic and Prosthetic Training and Educational Council.

Photographers

They are employed by a number of hospitals, although the photographic department itself may be very small. The NHS employs some 350-360 full-time equivalent medical photographers. For a description of the work of the photographer, including medical photography, see PHOTOGRAPHY, under CREATIVE WORK.

Physiotherapists

They work on the physical damage resulting from injury (a motor cycle or football accident) or disease (a stroke or virus), trying to restore or improve function. They try to prevent the effects of disease or injury from getting worse, help some people to get over operations (eg hip joint replacement), and gain confidence again, and teach others how to live with any permanent damage.

They use a wide range of scientifically-designed exercises, some 'manipulation' (of arms, legs and bodies), and games and other recreational activities, and also (increasingly) use heat treatment and electrotherapy. They work with people whose fractured legs have been in plaster and/or traction, to get their muscles strong and supple again; they exercise bed-bound patients; they do all they can to help disabled children become as physically active as possible, trying to prevent their growing bodies becoming deformed. They teach patients how, for example, to walk on crutches, how to get from a wheelchair to a bed or bath and back again. They run exercise classes for the many people with back problems. They try to ease the worst effects of arthritis.

Physiotherapists decide what kind of appliances patients need, from wheelchairs to leg supports. They are also involved in assessing a patient's level of, perhaps permanent, physical disability, and work with the OCCUPATIONAL THERAPIST and SOCIAL WORKER in helping them back to as much normality as possible. Some physiotherapists specialise in, for example, orthopaedics (diseases and injuries of bones and joints), rheumatology, working with children or old people, or with people suffering from diseases which affect the nervous system.

Most work in the Health Service – some 8150 full-time equivalent physiotherapists in 1984 against barely 5000 in 1974. Most work in hospitals, and most of their days are spent in hospital gymnasia and exercise rooms, on the wards with bedridden patients and patients just learning to walk again, and in some hospitals, in heated hydrotherapy pools, where patients are exercised in water. Physiotherapists have also acquired along the way the job of keeping patients' chests clear after operations and helping to avoid thrombosis, and so are also often members of the intensive care team.

A small number of physiotherapists work for the community health service, particularly in rural areas where it may be easier for the physiotherapist to visit some patients at home, although most work for day clinics. Some physiotherapists work full-time in residential homes, maternity clinics and schools, although they may travel around, doing three-hour 'sessions' in different centres.

Professional sports clubs mostly employ their own physiotherapists, as do some large firms, to help employees recover from injuries at work, and teach them how to avoid back injuries by lifting and carrying correctly, for example. Some university and polytechnic health services have a physiotherapist on the staff too.

The work is fairly strenuous, since most of the day is spent in some form of physical activity. Physiotherapists do not only teach people how to exercise, they also physically help to exercise limbs and so on, when muscles are weak or nerves damaged. They have to support, lift and move people around, for instance from wheelchair to exercise bed, when they are often 'dead' weight. Many of the techniques they use are based on theories which require them to be fairly tough on many of their patients, and they have to be firm as well as sympathetic if they are to help patients gain independence again.

While most physiotherapists work a 'normal' nine-to-five, five-day, week, in most hospitals physiotherapists have to be 'on call' some evenings and week-ends, and they may have to work out of normal hours if needed to help with seriously-ill patients.

Physiotherapists are steadily gaining more responsibility for planning patients' treatment, although they can still only treat patients when they have been referred to them by medically-qualified people. The career structure, however, does not give them any real managerial opportunities, and there are not nearly enough senior or responsible posts for the rising proportion of well-educated and intelligent people in the job. As a result, physiotherapists tend to move from post to post regularly, to gain variety.

An estimated 3000 qualified physiotherapists work in private practice.

Generally, there is a shortage of physiotherapists, and although Health Service expenditure cuts may be leaving some posts vacant, as of 1987 there are no problems in finding a post. The Chartered Society of Physiotherapy has (1986) an active membership of over 20,000.

Physiotherapy departments also employ helpers who are trained on the job. About 1700 full-time equivalent helpers work in the NHS.

Recruitment and entry Physiotherapists are recruited by the NHS only after training and state registration.

Potential physiotherapists need the same level of intelligence and personal qualities as other paramedicals (see the INTRODUCTION to this section). Physical fitness is emphasised. They should enjoy spending most of their time in physical, sports-type activities.

Qualifications and training Training for both groups lasts three years full-time and must be taken at a training school approved for state registration.

The recognised qualification is membership of the Chartered Society of Physiotherapy, but there is now also a small but growing number of degree courses which last four years (with clinical training). The membership courses last three, and cover anatomy, physiology, psychology, pathology, and the theory and practice of massage, movement and electrotherapy; degree courses extend the academic/theoretical, scientific content considerably. The Society has been actively considering all-graduate entry, but it has not happened yet.

Degree courses: Cardiff: College of Medicine, Ulster U; London: NELP (with London Hospital); Glasgow: Queen's C.

Other polytechnic courses: Coventry, Newcastle, Sheffield, Teesside, Wolverhampton.

Other college courses: Edinburgh: Q Margaret, London: N London School for Visually Handicapped, Salford CT.

Other ChSocP approved courses/schools (mostly hospital-based): Bath, Birmingham (Queen Elizabeth Medical Centre, Royal Orthopaedic), Bradford, Bristol (Royal), Cambridge (Addenbrooke's), Leeds (Gen Infirmary), Liverpool (Royal), London (Guy's, King's, Middx, Prince of Wales's, St Mary's, St Thomas's, W Middx), Manchester (Royal Infirmary, Withington), Nottingham, Oswestry.

The RAF-based Joint Services School also accepts civilian students.

Minimum entry requirements are five GCE/GCSE passes including two at A level; the subjects should include English language or literature, two sciences and two other academic subjects, and physics, chemistry and physical education should have been studied. Some schools, however, ask for higher qualifications, and 90% of entrants in fact have three A levels; it is rare for students who offer the bare minimum to be accepted. Normal minimum entry age is 18 years. Competition for the 900 places a year is very high, and early application (via the Society's clearing house) is advised because although the official closing date is in June (prior to an autumn start), in fact in at least one year recently the number of applications received (over 3000) was so high that no more were accepted after March.

Further information from the Chartered Society of Physiotherapy.

Radiographers

They specialise in either diagnostic work (taking 'x-rays') or in giving radiation treatment. They work under medically-qualified radiologists. They usually have considerable responsibility and independence, although the radiologist decides what treatment should be given, and/or interprets what the x-ray films show.

Most radiographers work for the National Health Service, which employs (1984) nearly 8000 full-time equivalents in England alone, a significant proportion of whom work part-time. Membership of the (qualifying) Society of Radiographers – most of whose members work for the NHS – is (1986) heading for 11,600.

All types of radiation are dangerous, and radiographers have to protect themselves and their patients from over exposure, although all diagnostic and radiotherapy departments have to be properly equipped and monitored to prevent any accidents.

There is usually a shortage of radiographers, especially for diagnostic work. There are senior and superintendent posts for radiographers, but no promotion or responsibility beyond that, except for teaching. UK qualifications are recognised overseas, but it may be necessary to learn a language to work in particular countries.

DIAGNOSTIC RADIOGRAPHY The majority of radiographers (about 85%), do diagnostic work. In most hospitals this is done in central diagnostic departments (although mobile equipment is used where patients cannot be moved). Here the familiar x-ray films are taken to show where and how bones are broken, spines or skulls damaged, or how far they have mended; to show the state of teeth or lungs, or how and where to continue a surgical operation. For stomach or other soft tissue x-rays the patient takes (or is injected with) something opaque to x-rays. Diagnostic departments are also responsible for operating the newer machines which explore the body internally, for example ultrasonic scanning, imaging, gamma photography (to check on progress in bone-fracture repairs).

Doctors who want x-ray films or scans of their patients simply tell the radiographers what it is they want to see. The radiographer works out the technicalities – for example, which machine to use (there are, for example, special units for skull x-rays); the angle at which the patient should sit, stand, or lie; how many different frames to take; whether or not the machine should be adjusted, and how; what film and exposure to use. X-ray machines become more technologically sophisticated all the time, and although they have more automatic controls, the radiographer has to understand how they work to get the best results. The radiography must also take great care of the patient, and may have to find ways to take x-rays so that they do not cause pain, or make any injury worse.

In more complex work – on casualties where speed must be combined with care for the seriously injured, for example – the radiologist works as a member of a team which will include the medically qualified radiologist, and when screening techniques are used, as assistant to the radiologist.

Diagnostic departments keep patients only as long as it is necessary to take the film or scan, but radiographers must nevertheless reassure them and try to ease any anxiety or stress. In some departments, or out of normal working hours, the radiographer may have to develop the x-rays as well, although in most hospitals they have dark-room technicians to do this.

THERAPEUTIC RADIOGRAPHERS directly administer radiotherapy to patients with malignant and non-malignant conditions. Treatment of all forms of cancer is changing rapidly and continuously, and results are improving. New treatments link radio- and chemo- (drug) therapy, and the doctors administering these programmes (which have to measure dosages so exactly that computers must be used to work them out) have to work together very closely, and the radiographer with them, in a team, and so works less independently than the diagnostic radiographer.

The radiographer has to see that the sophisticated, and very delicate machinery, with its battery of instruments and controls, is accurately angled, and the patient positioned for the radiation to home in on one small area. The radiographer operates and monitors the controls and, although these have to be outside the actual treatment room (for safety), must watch the patient (through a glass panel), and reassure them over a microphone. The radiographer may also have to prepare the patient, and help treat any side-effects. The radiographer also helps the radiotherapist to administer treatment with radium and other radioactive isotopes, and makes devices to apply them.

Patients who are given radiotherapy usually have a course of treatment, and so over weeks or months the radiographer must help to keep up their confidence and create and keep a friendly relationship under very difficult circumstances. The radiographer must also keep accurate records of the treatment, and can never afford to make a single mistake, because radiation treatment cannot be reversed.

Recruitment and entry Radiographers are recruited only when trained and state registered.

Radiographers need the same level of intelligence and personal qualities as other paramedicals (see the INTRODUCTION to this section). They must be meticulous, accurate, and careful people.

Qualifications and training Training for both diagnostic and therapeutic radiographers lasts three years.

There are various ways of training –

At a hospital training school, or on a group scheme where students from a number of hospitals are given collective theoretical training (sometimes with a local technical college) and gain their practical experience in hospitals within the group. Training is available in most areas, but there are more places for diagnostic than for therapeutic radiographers. The first part of the Society of Radiographers' Diploma examinations, required for state registration, is common to both branches, and covers physics, hospital practice, patient care, anatomy and physiology. Part 2 in diagnostic radiography covers equipment, radiographic photography and technique: for therapeutic radiography, the subjects are radiotherapy physics and equipment, and radiotherapy technique.

Training centres are –

Hospitals/infirmaries: Aberdeen (Royal), Bath (Royal United), Belfast (Royal Victoria), Birmingham (General), Bradford (Royal), Bristol (Royal), Cambridge (Addenbrooke's), Cardiff (Velindre), Carlisle (Cumberland), Coventry (Coventry and Warwickshire), Derby (Derbyshire Royal), Dundee (Royal), Glasgow (Royal Beatson and Western), Guildford (St Luke's), Ipswich, Lancaster (Lancaster Moor), Leeds (General, and regional radiotherapy centre), Leicester (Royal), Lincoln (St George's), London (C Middx, Greenwich Memorial, Guy's, Hammersmith, King's, London, Middx/UCL, RFH, Royal Marsden, Royal Northern, St Bartholomew's, St George's, St Thomas's), Luton (Luton & Dunstable), Manchester (Christie), Norwich (Norfolk & Norwich), Pontypridd (E Glamorgan), Portsmouth (St Mary's General), Shrewsbury (Royal), Southend (General), Stoke-on-Trent (City General), Wolverhampton (New Cross).

Group schemes: Birmingham (W Mercia School), Leeds (E Leeds), Liverpool (Merseyside), London (Joint Services School at Queen Elizabeth Military Hospital, Woolwich), Manchester (Salford CT), Middlesbrough (Cleveland), Newcastle (Royal Victoria), Northampton (General), Nottingham (Queen's Medical Centre), Oxford (John Radcliffe), Sheffield (N Trent Schools), Southampton, Swansea (Morriston), Worcester (Royal), Wrexham (War Memorial).

Other schools: Bromley, Canterbury, Edinburgh, Exeter, Gloucester, Hull, Newport (Gwent), Nottingham (Hogarth), Plymouth, Truro.

Minimum entry requirements are at least seven GCE/GCSE passes including five different subjects at O-level-equivalent and at least two at A level (but these may be in the same subjects passed at 16-plus†) either both at grade D, or at least four points (ie at least DD or CE). Subjects must include English, maths or physics, a science subject, one academic arts subject.

Degree course: Cardiff: College of Medicine – Health sciences BSc (from 1988) to include specialisation in radiography (diagnostic or therapeutic).

Further information from the Society of Radiographers.

Social workers

They are not now employed by the National Health Service. Medical social workers, who help patients with personal and social problems resulting from illness or disablement, are employed by local authorities, although individual social workers may be based in hospitals. See SOCIAL WORK, below.

Speech therapists

They assess and treat speech defects, mostly in children but also in adults. Speech defect is more than just talking badly – putting that right is a job for schools. Speech therapists deal with the kind of problems which result from, for example, a cleft palate or loss of larynx (removed possibly because of a growth), or brain damage after a stroke or an accident. The problem may be emotional and/or psychological, and cause someone to stammer, or it may be the result of a congenital disease. They may also treat children or adults who find talking, reading and writing difficult because their language skills have not developed 'normally'. Their aim is help people to communicate as effectively as possible.

At present, speech therapists work mainly with children, and most work in NHS clinics. Few speech therapists work in hospital full-time, most dividing their time between the community service clinic and the hospital. Some work in special schools or units for the mentally and physically handicapped. A small proportion work with deeply-deaf patients, for whom speaking clearly is a major problem. There is a great deal of work to be done with adults, but services are expanding only very slowly. Under 2500 full-time equivalent therapists work for the Health Service. The College of Speech Therapists has (1986) just over 4600 qualified members (plus nearly 800 student members), of whom some 90% work for the NHS, the rest for charities or in education, or they work privately). There is generally a considerable shortage of speech therapists, although posts may be left unfilled for financial reasons.

Speech therapists are trained to assess and evaluate problems, and not only to correct them. A speech therapist begins by trying to establish the cause of the defect (if it is not already obvious or has not been diagnosed by someone else), before assessing and evaluating the case, and deciding what to recommend. No two patients are ever the same, however similar the symptoms may be, so each has to be assessed and their treatment planned individually. Assessing and evaluating involves finding out a great deal about the patient, with time spent observing and talking to them, getting to know them, perhaps talking to parents and teachers as well as other therapists, and possibly having tests done

– for deafness, for instance. They may decide speech therapy as such is not the best way to treat a problem, and recommend, for example, some form of counselling or psychotherapy.

Mostly speech therapists work on a one-to-one basis, but they also organise play groups, so children can learn to talk naturally to each other, and may have group sessions for some patients. They may see patients once or twice a week, or more often if the treatment is intensive. Much of the treatment involves ear-training and breath control, 'structured' language programmes, remedial voice work and exercises, practice in relaxation, conversation practice. Where problems have psychological and/or emotional causes, treatment is designed to help solve these as well as to control the symptoms. Where possible, therapists treat children through play, to gain their confidence and interest, and to create a relaxed atmosphere. Speech therapists also counsel parents and train them to help with the child's treatment, and work closely with schools and anyone else involved in a case.

Although most speech therapists work alone, they do come in contact with other people besides their patients, and where cases have complex causes, they may work as part of a team. Speech therapists attend case conferences, keep case notes and prepare reports for hospitals, schools, GPs, etc.

Recruitment and entry Speech therapists are recruited by the NHS only when trained and state registered.

Speech therapists need the same level of intelligence and personal qualities as other paramedics (see the INTRODUCTION to this section). Good hearing, with the ability to analyse sound accurately (a musician's 'ear'), and clear, accurate speech are essential, and a real interest in sound and language very useful.

Qualifications and training Entry to the profession at 18-plus is only via officially-approved degree courses (diploma courses are being continued by two London schools, but they are mainly for mature entrants). Not all degree courses that look appropriate are in fact approved speech therapy qualifications, so it is important to check. It is also possible to qualify via a postgraduate training course after a degree in another subject.

Degree courses approved as of March 1987 are –

Universities – City (Clinical communication studies); London: UCL (Speech sciences); Manchester (Speech pathology & therapy); Newcastle (Speech/Speech & psychology), Reading (Linguistics & language pathology); Sheffield (Speech BMedSci), Ulster (Speech therapy).

Polytechnics – Birmingham (Speech & language pathology & therapeutics); Leeds (Clinical language science); Leicester (Speech pathology & therapy); London: PCL with Central School of Speech & Drama (Speech therapy); Manchester (Speech pathology & therapy).

Colleges – Cardiff: S Glam IHE (Speech therapy); Edinburgh: Q Margaret (Speech pathology & therapy); Glasgow: Jordanhill (Speech pathology & therapeutics BEd); Glasgow: Queen's (Speech pathology & therapy).

Syllabuses and entry qualifications are set by each school individually, but at least two appropriate A levels are needed, to include a science.

Further information from the College of Speech Therapists.

OTHER HEALTH CARE
The natural, complementary therapies — psychotherapy
A wide range of treatments are available outside of conventional medicine.
They divide into two –

The natural, complementary therapies

'Complementary' or 'alternative' forms of treatment and therapy mostly see
health, disease and treatment in terms of the 'whole' person, and are in many
ways a reaction against the very scientific and technological approach of
conventional medicine today. Anyone who is not a member of the established
medical or other para-medical professions can have problems in practising
these therapies, often because they are misunderstood, and because the
increasingly scientific trend of the medical sciences has led the profession to
discount forms of treatment which are not based on proven scientific methods.
Outside Britain and Western Europe, older methods of treating illness have
continued to develop, and over the past few years. Interest in these therapies is
estimated to be growing by about 15% a year.

Since these occupations are not officially recognised, the chances of employment, except in private practice, are very limited, at least at present, and
because they have not gained state registration, treatment cannot be provided
under the National Health Service. The Institute of Complementary Medicine
estimates that by the 1970s, some 2000 people were qualified in natural
therapies, although the numbers remain very small in each.

The Institute of Complementary Medicine (formed 1981) is attempting to
bring together the numerous therapies (it estimates some 20 are in general use
and another ten not so commonly used), and (amongst other aims) to establish
standards of training. ICM has set up an independent co-ordinating body able
to assess and define standards in any of the therapies, and has begun an
assessment of professional training standards. This is the first 'outside' body
providing moderation of standards and examinations. ICM is hoping to establish a school for the natural therapies in the not too distant future.

ICM says that to make a career in the natural therapies, it is essential to make
sure the professional training is right, and that they can become members of a
reputable association which has a strict code of ethics and furthers the professional development of its members. ICM suggests training should be college
based, rather than by apprenticeship. This will usually mean a course lasting
three or four years, and ICM specifically warns against short courses lasting
only two or three weekends. The course should cover basics such as anatomy,
physiology and differential diagnosis; thorough training in the particular skill
or system of treatment including practical demonstration and supervised practice as well as classroom teaching; general studies ranging from ethics, relationships with patients and colleagues, business management etc. ICM
considers that reputable courses will ask entrants for at least two A levels,
preferably in sciences.

ICM suggests that professional therapists will, in future, look to practise in a
specially-designed clinic or health centre (even a 'health farm'), and seems to
be implying that treating people in the sitting room is not a good idea. Sharing
accommodation with other therapists makes it possible to employ recep-

tionists and secretarial staff, and ensures legal requirements etc are met. It is certainly likely to attract more patients.

ICM has identified thirty therapies, but suggests there are basically four types – structural (eg osteopathy, chiropractic), nutrition (eg macrobiotics, naturopathy), psychological (see below), physical, emotional and spiritual development (eg acupuncture, homeopathy, herbal medicine).

The main career opportunities appear to be in –

ACUPUNCTURE is widely practised in China and other parts of the Far East as part of established medical practice. Acupuncture tries to treat a wide range of conditions, but particularly 'functional' disorders, and to anaesthetise, by penetrating the skin very accurately at predetermined points (acupuncture theory states) to correct imbalances in the dual energy flows which acupuncturists believe are within the body, and which are considered to cause the disorder in the first place. The practice of acupuncture is at least 3000 years old, but it is still developing. For instance, electro-acupuncture helps practitioners locate the acupoints on the skin.

An estimated 5000 acupuncturists practise in Europe. It is used officially in some hospitals in France and Germany and can be provided under their national health schemes. In Britain, two associations have about 200 members each, the two others about 50 and 30.

The Acupuncture Association aims to persuade the government to legislate for adequate training and registration, but in the meantime sets its own standards. The Association, with the Acupuncture Research Association, runs a training college, but trains only postgraduates. All entrants must already have a degree or other recognised qualification in medicine, naturopathy, osteopathy, physiotherapy, nursing, or homeopathy, and they must first have completed appropriate full-time training in one of these. The first-year diploma course involves some 140 hours' attendance at the college plus 400 hours of directed individual study; a further years' study leads to a licentiate, and a thesis prepared over another year's study leads to a bachelorship; the doctorate requires a further two years' work in the preparation of another thesis.

HOMOEOPATHIC MEDICINE, in which small quantities of substances are used to stimulate the body to produce its own defence to disease, is despite its rather unorthodox nature, practised by qualified doctors and is available under the NHS.

NATUROPATHY is based on the belief that the living body, in health, is a self-regulating, self-maintaining organism and, provided internal and external environments are favourable, broadly speaking, a self-repairing organism. Natural therapeutics are therefore primarily aimed at correcting body chemistry by such methods as fasting and eliminative routines (partial fasts, restricted diets, hydrotherapy, and so on). It is closely linked to osteopathy (see below) and most naturopaths are also osteopaths, although the reverse is not necessarily true.

The British Naturopathic and Osteopathic Association, which is the most generally accepted representative body in the field, has some 200 members, all of whom work in full-time practice as naturopaths. Full-time training (lasting four years) in naturopathy and osteopathy is given by the British College of Naturopathy and Osteopathy. Entrants must have studied to GCE A-level standard, including A-level chemistry and physics, and/or biology or zoology with chemistry and O-level-equivalent physics; O-level-equivalent English is also required.

OSTEOPATHY is mainly a manipulative therapy, aimed at correcting disorders of muscles and joints, and in relieving pain and disability from a wide variety of conditions, based on the theory that the body is a vital organism whose structure and function are co-ordinate, and that disease is a perversion of either. The value of manipulative therapy is increasingly accepted by established medical authorities, but they disagree on how it should be applied, how long is needed to acquire the skills and, above all, the range of conditions in which it can be of value. As a result, relations between osteopaths and qualified medical practitioners vary considerably, some remaining hostile whilst others refer patients to osteopaths. Osteopathy is only available under the NHS if the osteopath is also a qualified medical practitioner or physiotherapist. It is, however, increasingly accepted by patients.

The three osteopathic bodies have approaching 800 members, with some 550 belonging to one body. The British School is increasing numbers quite considerably (there is a shortage of qualified osteopaths). The General Council and Register of Osteopaths is a voluntary body, but confines registration to those who have completed an approved training course.

Recognised schools are the British School of Osteopathy and the London College of Osteopathy (which takes only registered medical practitioners). BSO requires at least five GCE passes including two at A level (over half, in fact, have three or more A levels), with preference to A-level passes in chemistry and either biology or zoology. Qualified physiotherapists are exempted from the basic science course and anyone who has studied medicine can be exempted from others. The four-year, full-time course, taking about 80 students a year, begins with basic science and practical anatomy, with extensive practical training in the school's clinic during the clinical years of study.

Osteopathy has always been part of the nature-cure practitioner's work, and it can also be studied as part of the training in naturopathy.

Further information from the Institute of Complementary Medicine, the Acupuncture Association, the General Council and Register of Osteopaths, the British Naturopathic and Osteopathic Association, and from the schools.

Psychotherapy and analysis

Psychotherapists and analysts generally work by trying to gain their patients' trust to help them put into words, 'talk through', their thoughts, feelings and problems, which the therapist/analyst then helps them to explore, examine in depth, and understand – which usually takes some years. With children particularly, therapists may use forms of play, and get them to express their problems through, for instance, drawings. The exact form of the therapy used varies according to the 'school of thought' that the therapist/analyst accepts, if any, which may be analytic, or may be behavioural. Psychotherapy and analysis are often used interchangeably, but analysis is always on a one-to-one basis (psychotherapists sometimes work with groups), and is more 'in-depth', ie the analyst generally works on the assumption that the problems lie deep in the patient's unconscious, and often that they stem from prenatal and early experiences.

Almost all analysts, and many psychotherapists, treat their 'clients' privately, either on a self-employed basis or working for a private clinic. Psychotherapists may work in other clinics, student health centres, marriage guidance etc. Qualified child psychotherapists are employed to treat and assess children and young people mainly in local-authority clinics but also in special schools and hospitals, where they work in teams with eg PSYCHOLOGISTS, SOCIAL WORKERS etc. Numbers employed are small, though – under 60 full-time equivalents (most psychotherapists combine sessions in clinics with private work) – and have fallen since 1980.

Recruitment, training etc Therapists do not need to have studied psychology, but in practice many do. Few people go into psychotherapy before they have had reasonable experience in other relevant work, such as teaching, social work, medicine or other hospital work, and a degree, preferably relevant to the work, is considered essential by reputable training organisations. For child psychotherapy, professional experience of working with children may also be required.

Training depends on the 'school' or type of therapy chosen – while it is possible to practise privately without formal training it is not recommended. Training, especially for those preparing to be analysts/therapists under the Freudian or Jungian systems, is intensive, long and expensive, largely because the trainee is expected to go through a full personal analysis (three times a week), to conduct full analyses (for as long as they take) under training, attend lectures/seminars, write reports on their training cases (and other papers), and on some schemes, gain experience of working with disturbed people in eg a psychiatric hospital. Training usually takes at least three years, therefore, and on some training schemes students may not start formal training until they have completed a probationary period (6-12 months) under personal analysis, and their analyst/therapist has given a favourable opinion on the student's suitability.

Training in child psychotherapy recognised by the Association of Child Psychotherapists (needed for NHS/local authority posts), is via one of three schemes, and lasts four years. The British Association of Psychotherapists scheme (Freudian only), requires personal analysis, weekly visits to observe a baby and mother at home (discussed in regular seminars), and intensive treatment of three patients of different ages plus work with their parents.

Further information from the Association of Child Psychotherapists, the British Association of Psychotherapists, British Psycho-Analytical Society.

SCIENTISTS AND TECHNICIANS IN THE HEALTH SERVICES
Introduction — scientists — medical laboratory scientific officers — technicians

Introduction
Science and technology have been helping the health services make gigantic

strides in diagnosis and testing, patient monitoring, surgery and treatment ever since the NHS was formed, 40 years ago. Heart pacemakers, life-support systems, radiation therapy, artificial hips, kidney dialysis and scanning machines, are only a few examples of sophisticated developments now taken for granted.

No less important are the vastly-improved backroom lab equipment and other machines – for recording, measuring, sampling and analysing – which have improved substantially the techniques for analysing blood, tissues etc, and therefore accurate diagnosis of all kinds of conditions. New developments appear all the time – ultrasonic scanning (of the brain, for example), and most of the lab equipment is now almost completely automated.

The equipment, the machines and the scientific techniques are not necessarily actually developed in NHS labs, although they do take some part in fundamental research and development work, especially trials. University departments and research centres, firms which manufacture medical and surgical equipment, and chemical and pharmaceutical companies are also involved.

However, the wide range of the science-based techniques and equipment in use mean the Health Service has to employ a comparatively large scientific staff, as well as a large number of technicians. The figures spell out the effect of science and technology. The number of professional and technical staff (excluding doctors and dentists) working in the NHS rose by 300% between 1949 and 1975, and by 55% in the decade 1971-81.

NHS labs, and other science-based diagnostic/treatment services employ multi-disciplinary teams of scientific staff, with some units also employing technicians. While labs need people with varying levels of skills, ranging from PhDs through to young staff (trainees) with just A levels, automation and other technological advances have cut the most low-level and routine tasks considerably. Together with some strong 'marketing' by the professional body, this has given almost everyone working in the science-based NHS labs the status of 'scientist', if they are professionally qualified, but not necessarily graduates – although they may still be colloquially called 'technicians' within the hospital. Differentiating between the work of one kind of NHS scientist and another has become quite difficult as a result. The NHS grading distinguishes between 'scientific' staff, ie biologists, biochemists, physicists etc, and 'medical laboratory scientific officers' (MLSOs), so it seems safest to describe the work under these headings. Biologists, biochemists, and chemists (particularly) may, and do, though, go for MLSO posts, probably because there are more of them than there are within their own disciplines.

Scientists working within their own disciplines probably do some of the most specialist work, and have more opportunities to do research, and the younger and least-qualified MLSOs the most routine. In addition to the work of the lab or department, staff have to monitor equipment, and often work on developing new equipment and techniques, as well as trying to improve on present methods. They may also work with doctors on clinical trials of new equipment, materials, machines, prostheses, and drugs.

Scientific and related services in the NHS grew in a very haphazard way. For many years, scientists in particular disciplines were recruited to work alongside individual medical staff for specific jobs, as and when needed, to provide expertise doctors did not have. Labs grew and expanded in individual hospitals as and when the hospital saw a need and could finance development. Attempts to rationalise and integrate services have been going on for twenty years, without very much success. Medical physics and pharmaceutical services are now mostly organised on a regional or district basis, and many medical labs are now attached to the larger district hospitals, providing a single service both for smaller local hospitals and to the family doctors. In future, laboratory services are likely to be organised regionally, many smaller labs have been merged, and so some scientific staff now work in teams of up to 100. Managerial changes in the NHS have changed the way labs are organised and managed – many have MLSOs, or other scientists, managing and organising the data-producing service, although clinical responsibility stays with medically-qualified consultants.

In large hospitals laboratories may be divided into sections: haematology, dealing with blood analysis; clinical chemistry, biochemistry, chemical pathology, where body fluids, tissue and excreta are analysed; medical microbiology and bacteriology, where bacteria and viruses are isolated and identified; and histopathology, where tissue samples taken during surgery or a post-mortem are preserved and studied.

'Professional' scientists

They now number some 3500 (1984 figure) full-time equivalent professional scientists working in the NHS, against under 2000 in 1974. The work they do is largely at the same levels as any other professional scientists, trained to graduate and even higher degree level, working elsewhere, although graduates are also recruited as medical laboratory 'officers' too (see below). In the NHS, most scientists are doing work which is directly related to the discipline of their academic studies, although there are some working in multidisciplinary teams.

The main groups are –

AUDIOLOGICAL SCIENTISTS Traditionally most of the work involved in measuring hearing has been done by technicians (see below). This is unlikely to change very much. However, more sophisticated techniques for difficult cases means some posts for qualified scientists, who deal mainly with the tougher problems involved in assessing and measuring hearing loss and speech defects, using electronics to make more efficient instruments to test more accurately (eg a device for a cot which can help detect whether a small baby is responding to sound), and developing new forms of hearing aids. The number of jobs is small – probably no more than fifty in the NHS and a similar number doing research etc, in universities and research units.

Audiological scientists are largely recruited from people with a relevant science degree (eg biology, physics, physiology, psychology), topped by a postgraduate degree in audiology, and a one-year in-service training course for a certificate in audiological competence.

CLINICAL BIOCHEMISTS as a group working within the NHS, has grown fast – to some 1750 full-time equivalents by 1984, against barely 700 in 1974. Several hundred others do clinically-related research, mainly in universities.

In the NHS, mainly in hospitals, clinical biochemists work in teams alongside medically-qualified pathologists (and MLSOs) in laboratories analysing blood samples, making microscopic sections of skin and tissue, and examining them for signs of disease, using highly complex chromatographic, spectrophotometric, radioactive and other techniques. The routine laboratory work is highly automated and is done mainly by MLSOs. Biochemists are the supervisors, who check the accuracy of results, make expert assessments of test results, look for ways of improving methods (such as computer-based and automated systems) and efficiency. They may do some tests themselves, especially where the problems are unusual or particularly critical, or in an emergency. They report non-routine tests, or unexpected results to routine tests, to the clinician responsible. They take part in case conferences and discussion of particular forms of diagnosis and treatment or cases with clinical staff where needed. Biochemists may also do some research, for instance on the biochemical causes of particular diseases, and if they work in teaching hospitals, may teach clinical biochemistry to student doctors, dentists and nurses.

Training is normally in-service, but with study leave for short courses. On this basis it takes about five years to work for Master of Clinical Biochemistry examinations, set jointly by the Royal Institute of Chemistry, the Royal College of Physicians and the Association of Clinical Biochemists. Alternatively, postgraduate degrees can be taken at about half-a-dozen universities. A number of first degree courses include some specialisation in clinical biochemistry.

BIOLOGISTS, mainly MICROBIOLOGISTS but with a few ZOOLOGISTS and PHYSIOLOGISTS, number about 500 at present. Few work in hospitals – most work for the Public Health Laboratory Service and the blood transfusion service. They screen and test for bacteria, viruses and so on, and combine this with research into the spread and control of microbial diseases.

DIETITIANS Over 800 full-time equivalent dietitians work for the NHS, largely in the hospitals, where they plan and advise on diets. In some hospitals they may be employed as catering officers. For a fuller description of dietetics see under ACADEMIC AND VOCATIONAL STUDIES IN SCIENCE.

GENETICISTS are employed in NHS medical genetics advisory services (each region has one), but work only in the labs (for counselling a medical qualification is needed). The work in the labs is mainly, for geneticists, identifying chromosomes using tissue culture (the labs also do enzyme analyses but more usually employ biochemists and/or microbiologists for this). Some research into genetic aspects of medicine is done, but most posts are only short-term.

MEDICAL PHYSICISTS About 750 full-time equivalent physicists work for the NHS (against some 700 in 1974). Most district hospitals have medical physics departments providing a wide range of services.

They deal with clinical use of radiation. Here they work in treatment planning – to see that required doses are kept as far as possible to the part of the body being treated, and also supervise safety and protection for both patients and staff.

They must be involved in planning and designing any department where radioactive materials are to be used, and they must monitor the control on hazards. They work with both doctors and engineers – on development and use – of the growing range of equipment and techniques using radiation, in both radiotherapy and diagnosis, in developing the uses of ultrasonics, nmr imaging, computerised 'whole-body' tomography etc, and on the physics and electronics end of new machinery to monitor patients' condition, or on the various ways in which radioactive material is used to provide information on bone, stomach conditions. Using the increasing amounts of data being collected from patients from these newer systems, physicists work on improving both them and the use being made of them.

Physicists also work in audiology, above.

Physicists also work closely with BIOMEDICAL ENGINEERS on the growing range of implants and other electronically-operated prosthetic aids.

Medical physicists work in respiratory physiology (eg on the properties of bronchial secretions), urology, and pathology.

They also teach at all levels – lecturing, for instance, on radiation hazards – and can do research, particularly in medical schools.

While it is possible to find a post in medical physics on graduating, the NHS prefers higher degrees and/or relevant industrial experience. Some physicists now start as technicians but transfer to a professional post can be difficult.

PHARMACISTS working in the Health Service (rather than general retail practice, industry or the academic world), mostly deal with the supply and quality of drugs and other medical preparations used in the hospital, and compound and dispense them for both in- and out-patients.

They also, though, work with the medical and dental staff to see that medicines are used safely, effectively and economically, and are consulted by them on pharmaceutical problems – for example, drug interactions, whether or not there are contra-indications to using a drug in particular circumstances, and whether or not there may be side effects, and if so what can be done to alleviate them. Pharmacists order drugs and other medicines for the whole hospital, and may also be involved in buying medical and surgical instruments and other equipment.

Most get the opportunity to do some research, often with other researchers – developing new treatments, investigating pharmaceutical problems, working on clinical trials of new drugs, and so on. In teaching hospitals senior pharmacists lecture to both medical undergraduates and other student trainees.

The NHS employs nearly 3000 pharmacists in England alone, and is having some difficulty in recruiting.

For other areas of work for graduate pharmacists, and education and training, see PHARMACOLOGY AND PHARMACY under ACADEMIC AND VOCATIONAL STUDIES IN SCIENCE.

PSYCHOLOGISTS The Health Service in England alone employs (1984) some 1400 full-time equivalents (against around 600 in 1974).
See PSYCHOLOGY under ACADEMIC AND VOCATIONAL STUDIES IN SCIENCE.

STATISTICIANS Estimates suggest rather more than 100 working in the health field, in the Public Laboratory Service, for regional health authorities and government departments (mainly the DHSS, with some in the Office of Population Censuses and Surveys), for the Medical Research Council, and major teaching hospitals.

They work on, for instance, medical investigations, for example statistical analyses of drug trials; the relation between social conditions and ill health; the incidence of particular diseases in particular parts of the country, as the basis for a better understanding of the spread and control of disease, or discovering the causes of some conditions. They may do surveys, eg a detailed study of the use of hospital outpatient departments. Statisticians are also used in administrative work on, eg manpower forecasts, budgeting, planning problems, statistical analysis of patient waiting times, or trends in births and deaths. In medical schools they also teach and do personal research. Highly sophisticated techniques, including computer analysis and modelling, are used, and graduate statisticians are usually involved in developing these.

See also STATISTICS and COMPUTER SCIENCE under ACADEMIC AND VOCATIONAL STUDIES IN SCIENCE.

OTHER GROUPS The NHS also employs professional ENGINEERS, and COMPUTER SCIENTISTS, but in quite small numbers.

Recruitment and entry directly into specific vacancies in the NHS or organisations like the Medical Research Council, with the appropriate qualifications.

Qualifications and training normally via a conventional first degree in the science concerned, ie physics, biochemistry, biology, electronics, maths, statistics, computer science, followed by postgraduate training. Some degree courses in these subjects include options in the medical applications. Higher degrees specialising in medical applications are available in most sciences, and on-the-job training linked to some form of release to study for appropriate qualifications may be provided.

See also ACADEMIC AND VOCATIONAL STUDIES IN SCIENCE.

Medical laboratory scientific officers

They make up the largest group of scientific staff – numbers rose by 440% between 1949 and 1977, and by 1984 there were some 19,000 full-time equivalents.

Mostly they work in hospital-based services.

Most staff the pathology (clinical chemistry) departments. They are the familiar 'technicians' who take blood samples on the wards and in out-patients, and the 'back-room' scientists – who do the actual examining, testing and analysing samples of blood and urine, etc, sent in both by GPs and from hospital wards and clinics, and the scraps of tissue, spinal fluid and other samples surgeons send for analysis during and after operations to find out what is wrong with a patient, to monitor the progress of treatment, or to try to isolate bacteria or viruses. For a few, in some hospitals, promotion can be to supervisory work, and even lab management.

While much of the routine testing has been automated away, and graduates (degree and HND/C) recruited, most of the work is still very practical and may not always 'stretch' highly-qualified people. On the other hand, promotional prospects are probably generally better with a higher-level qualification.

The techniques and equipment are mostly very similar to those used in any scientific laboratory (see SCIENTIFIC LABORATORY WORK under ACADEMIC AND VOCATIONAL STUDIES IN SCIENCE), but adapted to or specially developed for medical work. It is fairly common in larger labs for qualified MLSOs to specialise in eg –

clinical chemistry – analysing blood and other specimens to diagnose disease or identify toxic substances, monitor body metabolism etc;

blood transfusion – identifying blood groups, checking on compatability, and preparing blood products for use;

haematology – doing blood-cell counts in eg leukaemia, anaemia, investigating clotting defects;

histopathology – preparing and studying tissue samples from patients, or for post mortems;

medical microbiology – culturing organisms taken from patients, food, water etc, and identifying them;

immunology – work related to allergic reactions, infectious diseases, organ transplants, immune deficiencies etc.

Automation may have reduced the routine substantially, but diagnostic tests and other investigations have to be given priority, and be done with great care and accuracy yet as fast as possible, especially when there is an emergency, or a surgeon needs information while operating. The work ranges from fairly basic but absolutely crucial work of booking in specimens, loading tests into machines, and recording results, through operating some very complex computer-based equipment and carrying out more difficult non-routine tests to some more advanced scientific work which may include being involved in any research.

Labs are largely under the clinical direction of, eg medically-qualified pathologists. However, principal/senior MLSOs may be the actual laboratory 'managers', with 'line' responsibility for organising the data-producing service itself within agreed budgets, in charge of other MLSOs and other lab staff. Promotion, though, is generally into administrative rather than more advanced scientific work, and cannot give any clinical responsibility. Experience of two or three areas of MLSO work is normally needed.

MLSOs may also work in, for example, the 'special' services. These include –

The Public Health Laboratory Service, where they run the emergency service, which tries to find causes of epidemics – often in a great hurry – and also continuously monitors and controls potential sources of disease, which may be water-, air-, or food-borne.

The blood transfusion service, where they analyse blood to decide its exact group, do a range of other tests on blood cells and sera, prepare plasma and blood for transfusion, and test donors' fitness to give blood.

Clinically-related research in Medical Research Council units and in university, government and industrial labs also employs some MLSOs.

Other employers include pharmaceutical firms, veterinary services, forensic labs, private diagnostic lab services, government departments, universities, and the Armed Forces.

Recruitment and entry The minimum is four O-level-equivalent passes including two science/maths subjects and one testing use of English, or a relevant

BTEC National, and it is still possible to gain entry at this level, especially if individual labs are short of recruits. Career prospects might be better with four GCE/GCSE passes including either A-level chemistry and another science/maths, or A-level biology and another (non-biological) science plus chemistry studied to A level. Until 1986, the proportion with relevant BTEC HND/Cs or degrees rose steadily, and was up to about 50%, but the NHS is now having to compete with other recruiters for graduates, so opportunities for people with lower-level qualifications may be improving again.

The work takes people with a range of scientific skills (see SCIENCES under ACADEMIC AND VOCATIONAL STUDIES), although some MLSOs do come into contact with patients, for example taking blood samples. This means that they have to be able to put patients at their ease, deal with their worries, etc.

Qualifications and training The NHS trains, and gives release to study for professional examinations, essential for state registration, upgrading to the basic MLSO grade, and further promotion. All MLSOs are trained on the job, and so courses are normally closely linked to training in the laboratory. The Medical Laboratory Technicians' (State Registration) Board keeps a register of approved laboratories which includes most large hospitals, public health authorities, blood transfusion centres, and some industrial and research laboratories. On-the-job instruction is generally linked to lectures and individual tuition from senior staff.

The qualification route depends on level of entry –

O-level starters would normally take BTEC National in (appropriate) sciences, either for a Diploma (full-time pre-entry) or a Certificate (part-time on release from work with training).

A-level starters would normally take BTEC Higher in medical laboratory sciences, again either for Diploma (full-time pre-entry) or a Certificate (part-time on release from work with training), or the SCOTVEC equivalent.

Graduates, with a degree in (preferably) biochemistry, chemistry, microbiology, animal physiology/zoology, and people with BTEC/SCOTVEC Higher awards can become student members of the Institute of Medical Laboratory Sciences (1986 membership 17,100 including 900 students), and can apply for state registration (and associate membership of the Institute) after a year's professional experience. For promotion, it is usually necessary to take the 'special' examinations (with the alternative of a thesis), for IMLS fellowship, for which a further year's experience/study is needed.

IMLS also sets exams for a diploma in medical laboratory management.

Further information from the Institute of Medical Laboratory Sciences.

Technicians

The NHS, and other firms/organisations in the medical field, have technician-level work for a number of groups. There is no coherent, 'technician' grade or career structure. Each group specialises in a particular type of work, and as each group works for professional/medically-qualified seniors, and also in small numbers in any one hospital, there are few senior posts.

MEDICAL PHYSICS DEPARTMENTS employ 2000-plus full-time equivalents (1984) against only 125 in 1957. About half work in hospitals, and half in research departments and medical schools.

Some work under physicists on radiation therapy: technicians prepare and carry out tests which use isotopes; prepare sterile radiopharmaceuticals; help to design, construct, set up and operate the equipment used in radiotherapy; do checks to see that staff have not been over exposed to radiation; check and monitor leak-detection systems, and generally make sure that radiation exposure is kept to a minimum and proper protective measures used.

Others work with the wide range of electronic equipment now used in hospitals for measuring and counting, monitoring, testing and so on. They may work on design, development and manufacture, check and maintain it.

Medical physics departments also use a wide range of mechanical and optical instruments and other equipment. Technicians produce, adapt and maintain and often operate very complex equipment built to a high degree of precision.

OPERATING DEPARTMENT ASSISTANTS (some 3000) help to keep theatres running smoothly and relieve medical and nursing staff of some routine tasks. They help the anaesthetist (checking they have the right patient, checking the anaesthetic equipment is working, preparing the trolley, getting the patient into the theatre, monitoring equipment), check the patients' notes and x-rays are available and correct, see that equipment and materials are there and ready, prepare plasters, move lights and equipment. They help clean up and check stores and equipment between operating sessions.

PHARMACY TECHNICIANS help pharmacists dispense medicines, check stock and generally do all the less demanding work. The NHS employs at least 3000. See PHARMACY under ACADEMIC AND VOCATIONAL STUDIES IN SCIENCE.

PHYSIOLOGICAL MEASUREMENT TECHNICIANS is a newish collective name for three groups of specialised occupations, and mostly they continue to specialise in audiology, cardiology or neurophysiology (EEG). They all set up, operate and maintain a wide range of electrical, electronic and other equipment used to measure particular factors about patients, and sometimes to treat them.

Audiology technicians do the tests used to assess hearing, mostly using highly complex and advanced equipment like speech audiometers and psycho-acoustic apparatus, of adults, children and even the very young. Some audiology technicians fit and issue hearing aids, make specially-moulded ear inserts for them, and train patients to use them. They make any adjustments and do some repairs. Audiology technicians work with the patients as well as on equipment, and need the personal qualities to do this. There are some 900 full-time equivalent audiology technicians (1984) working for the Health Service (against under 500 in 1974), mainly in hospitals but some in community clinics.

Cardiology technicians set up and operate the increasingly-sophisticated equipment used in diagnosing and treating heart conditions. They sterilise and prepare apparatus for cardiac tests and examinations; attach electrodes to the patient; operate and monitor equipment used to measure and record, for example, a patient's heart rhythm; monitor heart readings during surgical operations. They do respiratory function tests, record heart sounds photographically, analyse the level of oxygen in the blood and measure its circulation, help monitor patients' conditions after surgery, and look after monitoring and recording equipment in cardiac units.

Cardiographers do routine electro-cardiology and minor maintenance. Cardiology technicians and cardiographers work with patients as well as machines. The NHS has (1984) over 1000 full-time equivalent cardiology technicians and some 500 cardiographers (against around 600 and 250 respectively in 1974), mainly in hospitals.

Neurophysiology or EEG technicians set up and operate equipment which records the brain's electrical activity and also measure, for instance, heart and breathing rates as they affect, or are affected by, brain activity. They have to know which technique to use, where to place electrodes, what level of stimuli to give, see patients have any necessary drugs, operate the equipment, and generally look after patients during the recordings. They work in surgical units, under neurologists, or in psychiatric hospitals. About 350 full-time equivalent neurophysiology technicians (1984) work for the Health Service (against just over 200 in 1974).

OTHER TECHNICIAN GROUPS employed by the NHS include animal technicians (but there are less than 50); artificial kidney assistants (about 150); dark-room technicians (well over 1200) who work mainly in radiography departments; electronics technicians (under 200); and post-mortem room technicians (about 500).

Recruitment and entry The NHS does not have a single entry to technician work – recruitment and entry levels vary from group to group.

Medical physics technicians usually need at least two relevant science A levels (or an equivalent).

For other groups of technicians, lower qualifications are generally acceptable, but without the school-leaving qualifications (ie at least four O-level-equivalent passes at 16-plus†) needed to take the appropriate qualifications (see below), promotion is difficult.

The work needs the same kinds of abilities as scientific laboratory work (see SCIENCES under ACADEMIC AND VOCATIONAL STUDIES), but some groups of technicians do come into contact with patients, for example operating equipment which measures hearing, the heart, or brain activity. This means that they have to be able to put patients at their ease, deal with their worries, etc.

Qualifications and training vary from group to group, but promotion within the NHS depends on passing appropriate examinations. All technicians are trained on the job, and so courses are normally closely linked to training. On-the-job instruction is generally linked to lectures and individual tuition from senior staff.

Technicians in these groups study for BTEC awards which are variants on the medical laboratory schemes. For example, the BTEC Certificate in sciences can be taken with elective physics and physiological measurement, and the HNC in medical laboratory sciences has special options in physiological measurement and radiation technology. Entry requirements to BTEC Certificate and Higher Certificate are the same as for medical lab technicians.

Operating department assistants study for CGLI scheme 752, usually on block release.

See also DENTAL TECHNICIANS (above).

Introduction — general management and administration (including medical records) — support and auxiliary services (including ambulance services, catering, domestic services, laundry, works: architects, engineers and surveyors)

Introduction

Managing an organisation as large and complex as the Health Service is a difficult and highly-skilled business and so far, it has proved hard just to get the organisational structure right. There are special problems in providing health care to everyone in the country, in inner cities as well as remote rural areas, to the very ill and those with minor ailments, for people who are sick for a short period and for those with long-term problems, for the very young and very old.

Management of the NHS has, until quite recently, been handled rather differently than in most other organisations. The uppermost tier of management is (still) outside the NHS altogether – in the hands of health ministers and the DHSS. Political factors also have to be taken into account. Inside the NHS, management was a collective responsibility, shared mostly between the professional medical staff – mainly doctors, but also nurses and other groups – and professional administrators, with other groups, such as representatives of local communities and health-service unions, also involved. The problems are further complicated by the numbers of so many different professional groups, with varying degrees of autonomy, each with long-established and complex lines of responsibility, both within their own professional groups and to others as, for instance, the ward sister is responsible to each consultant for the day-to-day care of the consultant's patients, but to the nursing officers for the administration of the ward.

In 1984, the decision was made to 'strengthen', and introduce 'more dynamic' management into the health authorities. In the last three years, management structures as used in other organisations have been replacing the distinctive NHS collective style. The main career effect has been the appointment of 'general managers' who carry greater personal responsibility and are accountable for seeing that decisions are made, actions taken, to make the organisation more efficient and effective with the available resources.

Management and administration

Hospitals were traditionally 'managed' by medical staff – 'superintendents'. They then employed administrative staff simply as assistants, but the job expanded and developed as they took over functions from the medical staff. However, they did not gain the kind of responsibility that managers in other organisations have. The growth of the service meant the administrative problems grew also, but given the background, and on the evidence of continuing major difficulties, the authority and skills of the managers and administrators did not develop as fast as perhaps were needed. Although hospital administrators have been developing their skills ever since the Health Service was formed, the difficulties of running an integrated, regionalised organisation without full responsibility were very different and came at a time when costs were rising sharply as resources became harder to find.

Up to the early 1980s, the problems were dealt with by increasing numbers, by 275% between 1949 and 1977 (against 240% for medical staff), and by 54% between 1971 and 1981, and by 1984 was well over 110,000 in England alone. Some of the increase was attributed to the 1974 re-organisation which, it is generally agreed, created too many layers of administration – numbers were expected to level off as the 1982 re-organisation took effect, but did not. However, as the 1979 Royal Commission pointed out, more administrative staff were needed, because doctors and other professionals had to be relieved of clerical and secretarial paperwork, because communications needed improving, and because the Health Service must have people with modern managerial expertise, in eg management services, personnel (including industrial relations).

Health service administration has constantly to take account of the fact that any decision, large or small, may affect patients' health. Health service planning, within tightening government-set budgetary limits, and given the costs involved (of labour, of scientific and technological equipment particularly) always presents considerable problems. Public demand for better health care is growing faster than the available resources.

Despite the special factors, Health Service management and administration has always had a great deal in common with the MANAGEMENT of other large-scale commercial, industrial, and state organisations, and the latest developments (see below) are a deliberate attempt to bring in the most up-to-date 'commercial'-style managerial methods.

The NHS employs some 25,000 administrators, over a third of them 'senior' administrators.

GENERAL MANAGERS They take charge of operations in each of the regions, districts, hospitals and other units. At regional and district level, and hospital general managers, are planners, co-ordinators, setting objectives, working to achieve set targets, within agreed budgets – and the top 800 or so managers are now on 'rolling' three-year contracts and their pay is performance related. District general managers are responsible for planning, implementing and controlling the full range of health-care services across the area.

Within the district, most 'unit' general managers are responsible for several hospitals, although a few large hospitals have their own managers. Some manage a particular service or group of services, including community care for eg people with mental handicaps.

The work is extremely diverse, ranging from planning major changes (eg turning surgical wards into long-stay accommodation for old people), seeing through practical changes to improve services/budgeting (eg going over to cook-chill methods so meals can be prepared ahead more cheaply), negotiating (sorting out problems between theatre staff and porters or trying to improve the admissions system), trouble shooting (industrial relations, dissatisfied patients, dealing with the consequences of breakdowns), interviewing new staff, discussing budgets and preparing financial reports, etc.

Some administrators specialise, in a 'function', but with promotion routes through each to more general management. For example –

FINANCE posts range from, for instance, salaries and wages officer for a single hospital, through management accounting in a district (which may involve, for example, developing and operating a 'functional' budgeting system, estimating annual allocations, monitoring expenditure against budget and analysing in detail any variance with monthly and yearly statements), and district finance officer, or regional management accountant, who provides and assesses costing data across the region as just one part of the exercise of allocating resources, to regional treasurer.

Most professional finance staff are, or become, qualified public-sector ACCOUNTANTS.

PERSONNEL MANAGEMENT The NHS is putting greater stress on professional personnel management, especially in recruitment and training for management.

PURCHASING AND SUPPLY The NHS buys in great quantities. It buys high-cost capital equipment like high-technology kidney dialysis machines, whole-body scanners and radiotherapy cyclotron units, as well as the never-ending daily supplies of bedpans and surgical dressings, face masks and surgical gloves, syringes and thermometers, sheets and pillow-cases, prescription pads, etc, etc, etc. Purchasing officers also buy supplies for the people who maintain the hospital buildings, and replacement parts for the very many machines hospitals have (many of which cannot be allowed to break down). Firms supplying the Health Service, or NHS staff themselves, develop or ask for new equipment, better designs of existing equipment, or suggest that something can usefully be made disposable, or more cheaply. All the possibilities have to be studied with the professional staff concerned, for practicality and cost effectiveness – will a new type of bedpan really cut out cross-infection, take less time and effort to sterilise, be easier for patients to use, and therefore justify and partly save the extra price?

Like PURCHASING AND SUPPLY officers in all organisations, the NHS staff have to be expert at all the techniques which bring down costs, such as whether or not to buy in bulk to hold down prices, against the cost and problems of storage. Over 600 people specialise in managing central sterile supply departments with their 4000 or so staff. The NHS also employs well over 4000 storekeepers.

Some posts, though, are unique to the Health Service, for instance –

The dental estimates board and prescription pricing authority need (1984) nearly 4000 full-time equivalent staff (it was less than 3200 in 1974) to run them.

MEDICAL RECORDS (sometimes called 'patient services'), is another. Medical records officers organise and supervise the system and the staff who give patients appointments, for admission to hospital or for an out-patient clinic; maintain waiting lists; actually admit patients; book transport or ambulances; keep patients' records, and see that case notes and items like x-rays are added and logged; record, maintain, and analyse statistics; organise the medical secretarial service.

At district level, the medical records officer also supervises systems for the family health services. MROs set up and manage computer-based systems to handle, for example, appointments, waiting lists, registrations, scheduling, and statistics – but there are still problems in putting patients' actual records onto computer files because they must be kept confidential.

Accurate information systems in the Health Service are crucial, and there are also senior posts for health intelligence or information officers. They keep numerical and statistical records and analyse and report on them, and are involved in statistical aspects of areas like who gets what diseases. In some areas, the MROs also help with medical research work.

SECRETARIAL STAFF The NHS also employs the full-time equivalent of some 15,000 SECRETARIES, over 53,000 CLERICAL WORKERS, around 15,000 typists and machine operators, and some 2500 telephonists. They work in hospitals, in administration and for general practitioners. It is possible to specialise in medical secretarial work.

Recruitment and entry The NHS recruits for administrative work at all levels from school-leavers with at least four O-level-equivalent passes (it may be possible to start in clerical work with fewer), although long-term career prospects are probably rather better with (two) A levels or a degree.

The vast majority of administrative staff start in the lower grades, and then apply for promotion when they have appropriate experience and/or qualifications. The exceptions are –

General management training scheme: designed as a 'fast-stream' entry for the next generation of most senior general managers, with about 50 places yearly. Entry is with a first degree or a suitable professional qualification, but NHS staff who are over 21, have been in the NHS for at least a year, and have either two A levels or the intermediate exam for a suitable professional qualification (ie they can be pharmacists, nurses, physiotherapists, doctors etc), are eligible.

Finance training scheme: special entry for graduates.

Qualifications and training The NHS trains extensively at all levels of administration.

General management training: trainees are normally employed by a region. The formal scheme lasts 21 months, including 12 months' practical working experience in a junior management post, followed by a more senior post. Formal courses are helped throughout training, with opportunities to study management at different levels in the NHS and other organisations. GMT trainees are expected to study for a relevant (see below) professional qualification during training, and promotion is conditional on gaining it.

Finance: staff are generally trained and qualify as accountants, via CIPFA, or accounting technicians depending on basic qualifications. See ACCOUNTANCY AND FINANCIAL MANAGEMENT.

Other general administrative staff: release and help normally given to qualify. for school-leavers starting with BTEC National (16-plus† entry) or Higher National (A-level entry) awards in public administration. Purchasing and supply, and personnel staff are expected to gain appropriate professional qualifications (see COMMERCE etc) for promotion.

Professional qualifications: the main qualifying body is –

The Institute of Health Services Management (1986 membership c3200 plus c2800 students). Most members work in the NHS, only 2-3% in the private health sector. The main qualifications available are –

Associateship examination (for full membership) – a three-part exam (four papers each) at degree standard, normally taken over three years. Minimum entry requirements are at least five GCE/GCSE passes with two at A level (or an equivalent, subjects to include English and a maths-based subject. In practice, some 60% of those registering to take the exams are now graduates.

Certificate in health services management – designed for health-services staff who already have a relevant professional qualification in, eg nursing, medicine, scientific work, ambulance work.

Certificate in health service administrative practice – designed mainly for young administrative and clerical staff, and is awarded to anyone gaining a BTEC Higher award in public administration with health service option modules. Exempts from some part 1 Associateship papers.

Other relevant qualifications include –

The Association of Health Care Information and Records Officers – sets exams for a certificate (O-level-equivalent passes at 16-plus† in English and maths) and a diploma (five O-level-equivalent passes at 16-plus†) – which is normally needed for promotion.

Further information from the professional bodies quoted above, and from the personnel department of any regional health authority.

Support and auxiliary services

Over 200,000 people provide essential support and auxiliary services for the NHS.

Each service has its own specialist managers and other staff. The services are controlled and co-ordinated by district managers who, in each case, supervise the service throughout the district; advise senior managers on future developments; liaise with supplies on purchasing, eg food and kitchen equipment; look for ways of improving and economising on the service on a district and hospital basis, perhaps by, for example, concentrating laundry services in one hospital in the district, by 'contracting out' some or all of the service, or by more standardisation of items being used. They also monitor budgets, and look after staffing and training within their service.

AMBULANCE SERVICES must get sick and injured patients to hospital as fast as possible and at the same time try to see that their condition does not deteriorate. They are now also being trained in rather more than straightforward first aid – they can use emergency treatment equipment where needed, and this may be extended in future. Ambulance staff have to know how to move and care for patients, ranging from the victim of a stroke or road accident, to the elderly patient going for day treatment, without causing pain or further damage. They have to calm relatives, control crowds, and drive very well.

But emergency work takes up barely 10% of their time. They also take patients to and from out-patient and other clinics, to physio- or occupational therapy.

Promotion is to work in the office, allocating work, and manning the radio controls. Health authorities employ some 20,000 ambulance staff (including maintenance staff).

Recruitment, training etc A full, current, clean driving licence is the main requirement, although some authorities recruit 16-17-year-old cadets – the normal age range is otherwise 21-35. A first-aid certificate is useful. Specific academic qualifications are not usually asked for, but a reasonable educational background (to O-level equivalent) and intelligence to understand emergency-care techniques are needed. Training in patient care, first-aid etc, and driving (for a special licence) is given (it takes up to a year).

Further information from area chief ambulance officers.

CATERING SERVICES provide meals for both patients and staff in hospitals, and in NHS offices' staff canteens, in numbers ranging from 250 to 3000. Some 30,000 people (full-time equivalent 1984), work in catering, but numbers have been falling since 1976. Centralised kitchens, advanced preparation of meals, 'contracting' out and economies have continued to cut staff numbers.

Most of the catering is fairly straightforward, although obviously special diets must be provided for some patients and a careful watch has to be kept on the nutritional value of meals. It is the sheer numbers (several thousand meals at a time), timing and problems of getting hot meals to wards, and so on that create the headaches.

The hospital catering officer is responsible for the entire department and organises and controls the work, under the district catering manager, planning menus (with the dietitian), seeing that supplies are delivered, supervising food preparation and cooking, advising wards on servicing meals, and managing staff dining-rooms. In large hospitals there is normally a deputy catering officer; assistant catering officers and catering supervisors are the grades below this. Skilled workers are also employed – kitchen superintendents; head, assistant head and assistant cooks and dining-room supervisors, and in some hospitals, experienced butchers and bakers.

DOMESTIC SERVICES have to see that every part of every hospital is kept as scrupulously clean, and therefore germ-free, as possible, and uses the most advanced cleaning equipment available. Over 65,000 people (full-time equivalent 1984) are employed, plus about 10,000 ward orderlies. Fewer hospitals, increasing efficiency, and some contracting out have all reduced numbers since the peak year of 1979.

Under the district domestic managers, services within each hospital are managed by a domestic superintendent, who is responsible for the care, maintenance and cleaning of the inside of the hospital, its furniture and fittings, for services to the wards, reception areas and clinics, and for intensive care units, theatres and maternity wards. The hospital is generally split into smaller units, each managed by an assistant. The senior housekeeper normally looks after the domestic services of about 120 beds, while a domestic supervisor sees to day-to-day cleaning of an area of the hospital.

'HELPERS', support professional staff in a number of hospital departments. They are trained to do specific routines.

On the wards, they are NURSING auxiliaries and assistants, who help patients bath, dress, eat, etc.

In OCCUPATIONAL THERAPY departments (where nearly 4000 work) they help patients to learn to do things again, under instruction from the therapist. PHYSIOTHERAPY helpers (of whom there are some 2000) meet patients and help them to change (if necessary) or with some forms of treatment (eg applying ice packs), check equipment, and help keep the department neat and tidy.

LAUNDRY SERVICES deal with some 20 million items a week, and have to maintain a constant supply of sheets, towels, blankets, staff jackets and overalls, all of which must be sterilised and are likely to be more difficult to clean than the normal laundry's throughput. Amalgamating laundry services for part or all of a district; increasing use of disposable materials; installing more modern, labour saving equipment, and contracting out have steadily reduced the numbers of people needed to handle NHS laundry, to less than 9000 people (full-time equivalent) in 1984 (against well over 10,000 in 1974) with some 700 managers, (skilled) staff to care for and repair linen, and clerks etc.

WORKS STAFF design, build, manage and maintain NHS buildings – hospitals, offices, laundries, training and recreational centres, and so on. New and rebuilt hospitals incorporate the latest in automation, mechanical-handling, communication, sterilisation and labour-saving equipment, with energy-saving environmental control systems. The NHS employs some 28,000 full-time equivalent staff, most of whom work full-time (1984), against some 24,000 in 1974.

Amongst the staff are the 2200 or so regionally-based ARCHITECTS, ENGINEERS (BUILDING SERVICES, CIVIL, MECHANICAL, ELECTRICAL), and SURVEYORS (BUILDING AND QUANTITY). Works staff also include just under 1000 building officers, the equivalent of clerks of works. Maintenance employs about 7000 technician engineers (who supervise the operation and maintenance of mechanical and electrical plant, mainly central heating, air-conditioning and ventilating and electrical systems), electricians (well over 4000), plumbers (some 1500), and operatives (over 8000) who mend windows, maintain heating, lighting and air conditioning plant, etc.

OTHER SUPPORT AND AUXILIARY STAFF include some 24,000 porters (who take patients from wards to operating theatre or physiotherapy department, and back again, and take supplies to departments), drivers (well over 3000 of them), and stokers (in steadily declining numbers, down to under 700 from over 2500 in 1974).

Recruitment and entry managers (catering, domestic service, laundry etc), professionals (eg architects), and skilled staff (eg cooks), are normally recruited from amongst people who have completed appropriate professional qualifications (eg degrees or higher diplomas in INSTITUTIONAL MANAGEMENT, ARCHITECTURE, ENGINEERING) or, for skilled workers, CGLI qualifications in eg cooking. However, the NHS does recruit people to train as managers or in some skills.

For long-term career prospects, it is generally necessary to meet the educational entry requirements for the profession or skill in question. The NHS now usually asks for two or three O-level-equivalent passes for jobs like 'helping'. Experience, for work like cleaning and in the kitchen, is useful.

The NHS provides several thousand YTS places, mostly in areas such as catering.

Qualifications and training Induction training is given to entrants with appropriate qualifications. Anyone joining in the basic grades of support and other services is given on-the-job training, and those who prove suitable may be given full-time or day-release to study for appropriate exams. Some groups (eg medical secretaries, and ambulance staff) have their own organisations which award special qualifications. See also the relevant sections on individual professions, skills etc.

Further information from the Department of Health and Social Security.

THE LEGAL SYSTEM

Introduction   1019
Legal profession   1020
Other opportunities for qualified lawyers   1025
Legal executives, clerks, and conveyancing   1028

INTRODUCTION

The legal system administers and enforces the 'law of the land' – as laid down by Parliament in legislation, in the unwritten common law and law of equity, and in EEC law which applies to Britain. The law is the country's rule book, which tries to set limits on the way people, organisations, and even the state should behave, and sets up systems which decide what should happen when the rules are broken or there is any disagreement.

Society is, however, extremely complex, and the activities and possible situations for which rules must be set are many and varied. Since the law and the legal system must mirror society, they are also very complex – like society the law and the legal system have grown haphazardly over many centuries. The law has many problems in trying to make rules to take into account any conceivable situation, and to keep a balance between the traditional and the modern.

The courts administer the law. Each branch of the law has its own courts (but some courts deal with more than one branch). The two main types of court in England and Wales deal with civil and criminal law – the other branches are service, administrative, Admiralty and ecclesiastical law, each with its own courts. Courts have other definitions – some are 'courts of record' (ie 'courts of which the acts and judicial proceedings prove themselves anywhere else and have power to fine and imprison for contempt of their authority') and some are not; some are lower courts, others higher.

Criminal law and the criminal courts deal with offences against the community or which contravene an individual citizen's rights. Civil law and the civil courts deal with disputes between individuals which affect only the disputing parties (changes have recently been proposed which would rationalise and simplify the civil courts).

The 700 magistrates' courts in England and Wales form the lowest levels of both the civil and criminal courts, dealing with more minor cases or deciding whether or not a case should go on to a higher court. The 300 or so county courts are the main civil courts but they try lesser cases.

The supreme court is divided into three. First, the high court which tries the most important cases in one of three divisions – Queen's bench, chancery and family – each with quite different procedures based on complex rules and custom. Second, the crown court (which replaced the centuries-old assizes and quarter sessions) is a single court with some 90 different centres, dealing with criminal cases, and administratively divided into six 'circuits'. Third, the court of appeal also has civil and criminal divisions. The supreme court of appeal is the House of Lords.

The legal system in Scotland is rather different. The sheriff courts exercise both civil and criminal jurisdiction. The high court of the justiciary is the supreme criminal court, and the court of session the supreme civil court. The two lower criminal courts are the burgh or police courts and the county courts.

Anyone coming into contact with the law, whatever the reason, normally finds it impossible to cope without expert help and guidance. This they get from the people who make a profession out of translating the law to lay men and women, and dealing with the legal processes on their behalf. The law also has to be administered, by legal experts such as judges who form the courts, and made by people, the government lawyers and, again, the judges. Lawyers now also decide on who should be prosecuted, in the new crown prosecution service.

THE LEGAL PROFESSION

Although it is called a single legal profession, it is in fact two quite separate careers – as barrister or solicitor. They have to work very closely together, and their work even overlaps in some places, but the division of the legal profession into two quite distinct branches has a very long tradition. There is constant talk of 'fusion' between them, and some cautious moves in that direction, but they are still separate at the moment. A committee is currently (1986-7) considering the future of the profession.

The solicitor is the general practitioner, the barrister is the second opinion, the expert who also does most of the legal surgery in court – solicitors may undertake 'minor' surgery in some courts (their rights have been extended recently), or may choose to become an expert, in for example, company or contract law.

The main formal difference between barrister and solicitor is that the former may only be briefed or consulted by a solicitor, on behalf of the client.

The work of barristers, solicitors and judges has a common basis, though. They must all 'think as lawyers', and be able to use all the complex sources of the law expertly and intelligently. The law is not rigidly fixed. Much legal time goes on deciding what the law on any point at issue actually is. Even the law passed by Parliament can be, and is, interpreted differently by different judges, and the way they interpret the law overrides whatever Parliament thought it said. Much common law is not set down by Parliament at all, but has been built up by judges themselves over many years, through case-by-case decisions. This is where 'test' cases come in, when the law as it stands is not clear enough, or a new, unexpected situation arises. Judges work on 'precedent', and theoretically only make new rules where none exist already. In practice, though, it is all too easy to get conflicting decisions, which have to be pronounced on in appeal courts, and even the House of Lords.

Facts are central to the lawyer's work, and a great deal of all legal time is spent on facts. The law only exists in relation to facts, to what actually happened. Whatever they are dealing with, lawyers first dig out the facts, all the facts (however apparently unimportant, trivial, or irrelevant), check and recheck them for accuracy, analyse them and decide which are relevant to the case, examine them for inconsistencies and mistakes, and then put them into logical and understandable order. If any facts are in dispute, it is a jury which must decide on the basis of the evidence presented (by both sides) what the facts really are, and verdicts are given on proven facts.

All lawyers also spend much of their working lives with documents. They search for the relevant law through the many pages of legal reference books – although this is now changing as case law, statutes, statutory instruments and legal texts (containing opinions) are being put into computerised legal reference systems, and can be recalled in seconds. Lawyers still have to deal with the documents of the case they are working on, though.

The law applies to people and their personal situations. Most solicitors and many barristers also spend as much of their time talking to, listening to, and arguing with people as they do in court or at their desks reading or drafting.

Lawyers have to adapt to change. They are, after all, in business, and in business to make an income. The legal service they give widens steadily as the law moves into new areas – into consumer protection and industrial relations, for example. More people are buying their own homes, and contract and company law grows steadily more complex. Science and technology bring legal problems in the train of new inventions – personal protection from computer data files, copyright difficulties with video tapes and the many forms of electronic data transmission, or deciding on the responsibility for genetic damage to babies. The EEC has both produced legal problems for UK lawyers, and means some of them must take greater account of the law of continental countries.

The computer-based files and indexes in lawyers' offices will result in other changes, as will any revision of legal aid. Lawyers find themselves in competition with other professionals – solicitors have already lost much of their tradition taxation work to accountants, and their monopoly of conveyancing. The decline in matrimonial work as divorce becomes steadily easier caused the Bar some problems. The trend to negotiate 'out of court' settlements is also reducing some legal incomes, and the ability to attract large-company business is increasingly important.

Barristers (advocates in Scotland)
They are legal specialists, the expert advisers who work only for, or through, solicitors. They appear in court on behalf of solicitors' clients when 'briefed' to do so, but more of their time is spent in giving expert advice than is generally realised.

When solicitors consult barristers on a point of law, the barrister (or his/her pupil) may have to search through many years of legal cases to find court decisions with a bearing on the case, compare them, analyse what they mean in relation to the present case, and then give the solicitor a carefully considered, usually written, reply. This may involve much detailed research, much legal analysis of fact and precedent, and much unravelling of legal intricacies. The barrister may also be asked for an opinion on the likelihood of winning or losing a case on the basis of his/her experience and knowledge of the courts.

If a case does go to court, the solicitor gives the barrister he or she thinks most suitable a 'brief', or instructions, to act on the client's behalf in court. The solicitor does much of the preparation of the case for court, but when a barrister gets down to the documents, he or she must do an enormous amount of hard work, and get to know the case in all its complexity, and the client too. Barristers have to understand, learn and speak knowledgeably about the most technical matters, and be able to cross examine, for example, the most expert witness on, eg very complex aspects of nuclear physics where someone is claiming damages from a radiation leak.

Most barristers specialise. Their main choice is between the much larger common law, and chancery. If they choose common law, they do not usually deal with all branches, because there is too much to learn, but most barristers working at the common law bar do deal with a range of cases – crime, divorce, family and unspecialised civil work – although some chambers specialise entirely in eg crime, particularly in London. Out of London most practices are general. Individual barristers may specialise in more complex aspects, eg libel and slander, or patent and copyright work. Barristers specialising in eg commercial law or chancery may spend up to 20% of their time abroad.

The very small chancery bar operates only from Lincoln's Inn in London. Here barristers specialise in company law, trust, property and conveyancing, tax cases or estate administration.

How much time a barrister spends on research and drafting 'opinions', how much time advising, how much time in court and preparing cases, depends on which part of the law he or she chooses. Generally, much more time is spent in court in common law practices, very little in chancery – which is generally much more 'academic' and intellectually demanding, a backroom job drafting agreements as well as writing opinions. Even in common law, only barristers specialising in criminal law spend a high proportion of their time in court, or preparing for it.

Appearing in court takes not only the ability to 'put over' a case, but also to explain even the driest and most abstract evidence on (for example) obscure contract law, clearly and logically, so that inexpert judge and jury can understand it. Three quarters of a barrister's success in court is usually based on the very painstaking preparation and the rest on practical experience. Barristers are experts on the laws of evidence, the rules of court procedure, the techniques of cross examination, and making legal submissions, and can 'manipulate' them to great advantage.

The Bar is a small profession, with at present (1987) some 5500 practising – over 8000 have been 'called' – barristers in England and Wales (but it was only 2400 in 1970), at least 70% of them in London. It is a profession still ruled by centuries-old traditions and procedures. Young barristers, once through their pupillage, must find a 'seat' in barristers' chambers (offices), mostly sited near the senior courts in any town or city. They may not set up practice anywhere on their own. Although barristers share chambers and the services of clerks, they are not partners – each is self-employed. Even when they find chambers there is no guaranteed income: they are dependent on the other barristers in the chambers, or the barristers' clerks, passing on work – they may 'devil' (do work on an opinion for part of the fee), or appear in magistrates' or other lower courts for another barrister's client in easier 'minor' cases, until solicitors begin to notice them and send work along, which can take time. In their early days young barristers take on 'minor' cases (between landlord and tenant, hire purchase, road traffic and matrimonial disputes); in the crown court experience is gained in prosecuting or defending or making pleas in mitigation in a wide variety of criminal cases.

Once established at the bar, at least 15 years experience are needed before a barrister can apply (to the Lord Chancellor) for a 'patent' as a Queen's Counsel – called 'taking silk' (QC's wear silk gowns in court while 'juniors', who can be much older than the 'silk', wear 'stuff' gowns). Although it is necessary to take silk to become, for instance, a high court judge, there are financial penalities, because QCs cannot appear in court without a junior, automatically restricting them to more important cases (because both must be paid) and they lose other income, for example writing the statement of the case ('formulation of pleadings') which is always done by a 'junior'. Some barristers therefore stay 'juniors' throughout their career at the Bar.

Solicitors

They are general legal advisers for anyone who needs their help with their affairs or problems, from the proverbial man or woman in the street through the small business to the major company. Mostly these will involve the law in some way, but once solicitor and client have established a working relationship, clients often use their solicitors' experience and trained objectivity as a source of general advice, counselling, and so on.

But even the strictly legal work solicitors do is quite extensive. Some of it can be quite routine, some is more demanding. A large proportion of many solicitors' income is from conveyancing property (houses, flats, offices, farms, factories) from seller to buyer, which means they (or more accurately their articled and other clerks who do most of the routine), make sure there is no problem with the title to the property, or that (for example) it is not likely to be bought or demolished by the local authority in five years' time, and draft the contract of sale, and so on.

Solicitors draft wills, and act as executors and administrators to see that the terms of the will are carried out. They advise landlords on arrangements with tenants, and draft the lease or agreement, or advise tenants on their legal rights. They tell clients whether or not they may get compensation for faulty goods, or damages for injury in a road accident, or in an accident and work, and make claims on clients' behalf. They deal with divorce cases, especially where children's futures must be settled, property divided, and any mainten ance agreed. They act for local businesses, collect debts through the courts, prepare partnership agreements, set up companies, and deal with contracts and agreements of all kinds.

Anyone faced with criminal charges, whether it is a road offence, burglary or even murder, must go to a solicitor if they are to be defended in court.

Solicitors try to keep their clients out of court. They may ask for counsel's opinion just to show a client how risky, difficult, and expensive going to court may be. It is not, technically, a solicitor's role to tell a client whether or not to take action: the solicitor defines the client's position in legal terms, and explains the legal consequences of any action the client may, or may not, take. All the same, many clients will expect their solicitor to advise them.

When solicitors go to a barrister for advice, they choose someone who specialises in the particular area of the law, or who is known for defending a particular kind of case in court. Most solicitors have a working relationship with particular barristers, but may look out for a bright young barrister, who will be cheaper, for simpler cases. Whether it is a 'case for opinion' or an actual brief, it is the solicitor who must put together the relevant facts, make sure the main documents are in order, and summarise the rest. The solicitor is responsible (again, it is the clerks who normally do the work), for finding and interviewing witnesses, and collecting all the information needed by the barrister. During the case, the solicitor is the go-between between the client and counsel, and also 'wet-nurses' the client if necessary.

Outside the legal field, solicitors often advise clients on anything from whether or not it is a good time to move house, or what to do about a disagreement with an employer, to pension schemes, investment or business strategy generally. Solicitors must, though, always think of the possible legal consequences, immediate and long-term, of whatever their clients may want to do, and be prepared to advise on them.

Solicitors therefore spend quite a high proportion of their time talking to people – clients, other lawyers, officials – either in the office or on the telephone. They also have to write many letters, many of them in formal and legal terms, to clients, to other solicitors or other people against whom a client may have a claim, and to barristers. They draft a great many documents, and issue writs. They can conduct their own cases in magistrate and county courts, and usually go into other courts with counsel.

There are a great many more solicitors than barristers: about 46,500 at present (1987), with numbers rising steadily. Solicitors' practices vary greatly in type and size. There is nothing to prevent solicitors setting up in practice on their own, but most go into partnership eventually (starting as assistants/employees in other practices). Rural practices are generally quite small, with at most five or six partners and a staff of up to 50-60, but some large London firms, for example, have 150 practising solicitors and a total staff of over 400. In small towns, in rural areas, practices generally accept any kind of work that clients bring in, although only a proportion of practices will deal with commercial work, while others specialise more in conveyancing, or road cases.

In larger centres, and especially in London, firms - and individual solicitors - increasingly specialise, and there has been talk of dividing the profession into commercial and litigation solicitors. In the City there are large firms most of whose 'clients' are companies, and they may specialise in forming and re-forming companies, issuing stocks, drafting contracts, and so on. Other firms specialise in trust work, or in working for trusts, companies or families with large property holdings and who must have continuous access to legal assistance, on estate duties, taxation, conveyancing. Some firms specialise in work for publishers, or writers and entertainers. In most practices of any size, individual partners and their assistants specialise – in litigation work, for example. Younger solicitors may have to move from firm to firm to gain experience, or for a chance to become a partner.

Other careers for qualified lawyers
Although the great majority of qualified barristers and solicitors spend most of their working lives in private practice, there are alternatives –

ACADEMIC LAW Law is taught in some 40 universities and polytechnics. The academic lawyer is usually a rather different breed from the practising barrister or solicitor, and it is rare to combine the two. Academic lawyers usually combine teaching students with research and analytical and speculative writing about the law. They tend to live on a more theoretical and idealistic (about the law) plane than practitioners, although some do specialise in applications of the law.

Law schools expanded quite considerably during the 1970s, to meet demand for more places as the profession moved towards all-graduate entry. The number of posts was increased substantially then, but this has now stopped. See also EDUCATION

THE CIVIL SERVICE employs (1987) some 3000 barristers/advocates and solicitors, tripling numbers in the last few years. See CIVIL SERVICE.

COMMUNITY LEGAL SERVICES Law centres numbered over 55 in 1985, but over half were under threat of closure – funding is always a problem (it may come from the department of the environment, a local authority, or the lord chancellor's department). They vary in their policies, but generally provide a free legal service in areas under-served by solicitors' practices (and therefore by definition poorer places). Many give advice and assistance also on the blurred edges of the law: many cases deal with consumer problems, problems with landlords, employment and social-security difficulties, youngsters who have clashed with the police, and queries on, for instance, a gas bill. Most law centres are run as workers co-operatives, and all 'employees', including qualified barristers, solicitors and social workers, take turns at being, for instance, the receptionist, and take home the same pay.

THE COURTS All high-court judges, and recorders, were originally barristers (some continue to practise after appointment, to eg a crown court circuit, and so may be part time), and have usually been QCs. Solicitors are eligible for the lower courts. Most judges work in one type of court and at present each court or division has a separate judiciary. The judiciary numbers about 800, including the ten law lords, 23 appeal judges, 79 high court judges, 388 circuit judges, 45 masters and registrars of the supreme court. Nearly 1000 recorders and assistant recorders sit on a part-time basis in the crown and county courts.

Judges need appropriate experience – for example, to qualify to be a lord justice of appeal or lord chief justice, master of the rolls or president of the family division it is necessary either to be a high court judge or to have had at least 15 years' experience at the Bar. A high court or circuit judge must have been a barrister for at least ten years or a recorder for at least five, while recorders need the same length of service as a barrister or solicitor. However, there is no set pattern of promotion, and vacancies in the superior courts are filled more often from the Bar than from judges in the lower courts.

The supreme court is administered by law officers, called masters and registrars. The eight masters of the Queen's bench division, for example, exercise the authority of judges in chambers, issue directions on points of practice, assess damages in certain cases, and supervise the court's central office, where the clerical work is done, the masters acting in turn as 'practice master'. The eight masters of the chancery division make interlocutory orders and take accounts under the direction of judges, and are assisted by registrars. The family division has eleven registrars who, for instance, exercise the authority and jurisdiction of the court in divorce, wardship of minors and so on. Qualifications for these post vary, but they usually go to experienced barristers and solicitors. The supreme court and the county courts are administered by a unified court service under the Lord Chancellor's department (see CIVIL SERVICE). The senior officer for each circuit is the circuit administrator, with court administrators for each sub-areas. They arrange the business of the courts and see that the right number of judges and recorders are there when needed.

Bodies like the Criminal Injuries Board and the tribunals usually have chairmen/women and at least some other members with legal qualifications and experience.

In Scotland, each sheriff court district has a sheriff-principal and a number of sheriffs who act as judges. The lords justice general and clerk, and the 18 lords commissioner of justiciary (who are also judges of the civil court of session) are the judges in the high court. Burgh or police court judges are town councillors (although stipendiary magistrates sit in Scotland).

Other posts for which both barristers and solicitors qualify include the 60 (1986) 'stipendiary' magistrates who staff the busiest London and other inner-city magistrates' courts: they must have seven years' legal experience.

Justices' clerks All other magistrates' courts are staffed by unpaid 'justices of the peace' who don't need legal qualifications, but have the support of a justices' clerk, who is a qualified barrister or solicitor with at least five years' experience. There are about 310 of them; two-thirds work full time for the courts, the rest part time as justices' clerks, part time as solicitors. Justices' clerks advise magistrates on points of law, see that proper procedure is followed, arrange court lists, and see that administrative work (eg preparing summonses and warrants, collecting fines, dealing with drink licences) is done. Their offices employ between two and fifty assistants, who may be completing articles or are otherwise training.

INDUSTRY AND COMMERCE the largest firms usually have their own legal departments staffed by qualified barristers and/or solicitors. These firms need instant, 'on-the-spot', legal services, and lawyers who are closely involved in the company's affairs, understand the background and therefore do not need special briefing. The amount of UK and EEC legislation affecting companies has increased sharply lately – contract law has been heavily affected by the EEC, and they have to cope with current, and complex, legislation on, for instance, employment protection, sex and race discrimination, consumer protection and credit, health and safety, banking registration, food and drugs.

Lawyers in business firms spend most of their time on advisory work, and on contracts. Barristers employed by a company may not also practise at the Bar. They have to balance their trained caution against the firm's need for fast and firm decisiveness. The number of lawyers employed in industry and commerce has been rising steadily, and they probably number several thousand, but few companies recruit young solicitors or barristers to serve articles or pupillage, most preferring experienced people.

Lawyers can and are promoted to management and/or become, eg company secretary.

LOCAL GOVERNMENT Most of the services that local authorities provide for their communities are the result of government legislation which either 'delegates' services to local authorities (for instance education, planning and housing, refuse collecting and library services) or expects them to see that other people do what the law says, on environmental health or consumer protection, for example. Complex laws dictate how much money local authorities can spend, and how they must account for it, and rate payers can challenge expenditure in the courts. Local authorities can write their own by-laws. Local authorities must also work within the common law – on landlord and tenant, on contracts, and on employment protection or race or sex discrimination, for instance. Most laws which affect local government are complex, and are frequently amended.

Local-authority lawyers must see that the council always acts within the law and translate the effects of new legislation for council members, so there is a great deal of advisory work. There is also plenty of court work – recovering rates, enforcing laws, defending a council against claims. Solicitors do all their council's conveyancing – on sales and purchases of land, leases (for eg shops), licences, and mortgages. Lawyers also advise on and help to draft minutes, council resolutions, orders, notices, and so on, making sure there are no legal loopholes.

Local authorities employ several thousand lawyers, mostly solicitors, and a high proportion of senior administrative posts (eg chief executive) go to them. It is usual to serve solicitors' articles with a local authority.
See also LOCAL GOVERNMENT

Recruitment and entry
All entrants to the Bar, and over 90% of new solicitors are now graduates. They must complete the required training before they can practise. There is no guarantee that fully-qualified barristers or solicitors will be kept on by the chambers or practice where they have trained.

For barristers, it has in the past been difficult to find a place in chambers for pupillage. The General Council of the Bar wants to ensure that 200-300 places are available, and students funded. An increased number of studentships, grants and awards are now available. A working party is looking at ways of improving the pupillage system, especially centralising arrangements, advertising vacancies, securing minimum standards of supervision.

All lawyers need to be reasonably intelligent (law exams are tough, and take memory and endurance), logical and very clear thinking. They need the kind of mind that can be trained to think analytically and factually, to be able find facts and extract what is important from a mass of data. They must be able to absorb and understand all kinds of information easily (and equally to forget it again when the case is over). They have to be precise and accurate with words.

Most lawyers should be good at interviewing and 'handling' people (in an office or in court), in getting the necessary information from them, at assessing them and what they are saying, and able to make reasonable guesses at what is below the surface. High court barristers must be self-confident and have the skills needed to perform well in court.

Qualifications and training
See LAW under ACADEMIC AND VOCATIONAL STUDIES IN SOCIAL SCIENCE.

LEGALLY-RELATED WORK
Barristers and solicitors are the experts of the legal world, and depend on a large army of 'support' staff, many of whom also have considerable expertise. Legal executives and barristers' clerks, together with the courts' staff, actually make the cumbersome machinery of the law work. They are both administrators and experts in the day-to-day mechanics of the law. Contact between solicitors' offices and between solicitors and barristers is mostly via the clerks, who form a tight network of their own, and sort out many problems unofficially.

The policy of increasing competition for professional work is also increasing the range of quasi-legal work.

Barristers' clerks
They 'manage' the set of chambers and the barristers who work from them, and the success of the chambers can depend on them. The clerk not only sees that the chambers run smoothly, and so is effectively the office manager, but also (mostly) decides which 'briefs' to accept, which of the barristers should have which brief (and in this way can help to get a young barrister started), and negotiates (with solicitors) the fees to be paid, taking a percentage of them. The clerk is an influential member of chambers, has a say in the choice of barristers to join the chambers, and frequently earns more than the barristers. Juniors run errands, make tea, carry robes and books, as they learn.

Competition for posts – there are a few hundred only – is considerable. There is no shortened route to becoming a barrister for barristers' clerks.

Recruitment, training etc mainly as school-leavers with a good educational background, for training mainly on-the-job.

Conveyancing
All conveyancing – essentially the legal processes involved in transferring buildings and/or land from one owner to another and dealing with the financial transactions – was the sole responsibility of solicitors until 1987.

Under new legislation, it is now possible for anyone to become a conveyancer, although a licence is required. It is not yet possible to say what opportunities for employment this will create outside solicitors' offices, although it is suggested that eg estate agents, building societies, banks (especially those providing mortgages), legal advice centres, may employ conveyancers. It might also be possible to provide an independent service, but for the first three years conveyancers will not normally be allowed to set up as 'sole principals' or in partnership with anyone else who is newly licensed.

Qualifications and training Anyone wishing to become a conveyancer must meet the requirements of the Council for Licensed Conveyancers.

The Council requires at least four O-level-equivalent passes at 16-plus† (or one or two A levels plus three or two O-level-equivalents or a BTEC National) including English. Candidates are vetted to see if they are 'fit and proper persons'. The Council sets two-part exams, plus an accounts paper – and all the papers in one part must be taken together. LLB degrees, CPE or ILE part 1 will normally exempt from part 1.

Candidates must also complete two years' practical training, at least one after passing the exams, ie full-time employment in conveyancing, supervised by a solicitor or licensed conveyancer entitled to practise as a sole principal.

Further information from the Council for Licensed Conveyancers.

Court work

Every court has to be staffed, in the largest court houses, where up to fifteen courts may be held at one time, the administration may employ up to 200 people.

The senior staff who advise magistrates (justices and court clerks) are mostly qualified barristers and solicitors, or are partly qualified, but all the Courts employ office administrators and clerical/secretarial staff. They get all the papers on each case ready for the court, and clear the paper work after a decision has been made, answer queries from the public, deal with fines (some courts have special accounts staff) etc.

Recruitment and entry junior staff are generally expected to have an O-level-equivalent pass in English, although most have considerably more. Some posts need experience or qualifications, in eg accounts, computing, office administration.

Further information from the Home Office (C2 Division).

Legal executives

They do most of the administrative and practical work in a solicitor's office (in private practice, local government and the Civil Service). Although the work varies from firm to firm, experienced legal executives can gain considerable responsibility. This is especially so for the great mass of practical, detailed, technical and routine work – conveyancing, probate for wills, and getting a case into court. The legal executive, more often than not, actually issues writs, gets statements of claim drafted, gathers together the material needed for an affidavit, collects documents, takes out summonses, checks titles to deeds, etc.

In all but the smallest practice or office, legal executives (of whom there are well over 5000) usually specialise – in probate work, litigation, conveyancing, costing, and may be more expert practically than the solicitor. 'Muniments' clerks look after the clients' files, which include not only the records of past work but also, for instance, wills. They may 'manage' the office or department of junior and secretarial staff, and deal with accounts etc. Legal executives can go on to serve articles and become a solicitor.

Recruitment and entry as a school-leaver.

Qualifications and training see LAW under ACADEMIC AND VOCATIONAL STUDIES IN SOCIAL SCIENCES.

Further information from the Institute of Legal Executives.

MANAGEMENT SERVICES

Introduction	1030
Operational research	1031
Patent agents and officers	1033
Work study, organisation and methods	1037

INTRODUCTION

The methods and techniques available for both decision-making (in commerce, industry and public service) and research (in disciplines as widely spread as archaeology and sociology as well as the sciences and technology) have been getting increasingly exact, and numerically-based, for many years now. In particular, scientific methods of observation and analysis, quantification of data, mathematical and statistical analysis, and mathematical model-making, are now used by more and more organisations, not only by academics and research workers.

The use of scientific and mathematical tools and techniques would, of course, have been impossible without the massive advances in computers and computer technology. These in turn, made possible the development of more techniques designed to improve decision-making, such as operational research, organisation and methods, and work study.

In many occupations this means that both training and work content have become much more mathematically orientated – as shown by the fact that numeracy is now almost universally demanded for entry to most careers.

While work in these fields obviously demands a reasonable degree of numeracy and the ability to work with, and an interest in, figures, it does not necessarily require graduate-level training in mathematics. Just as crucial are logical thinking, linguistic abilities, and an interest in problem-solving.

The demands, and therefore the satisfactions of these careers, are mostly intellectual, although they also need people who are exact and meticulous.

While the careers described below are those which are most closely involved with scientifically based management and research services, they are not the only ones. MATHEMATICS AND STATISTICS (under ACADEMIC AND VOCATIONAL STUDIES IN SCIENCE) are obvious examples. ACCOUNTANCY AND FINANCIAL MANAGEMENT apply techniques like these.

COMPUTER SERVICES

It now seems a long time since computers were only research tools. The second 'generation' machines were tools for both research and management. They have now become all-purpose tools, and are being integrated rapidly into more extensive systems. See INFORMATION TECHNOLOGY

OPERATIONAL RESEARCH

Uses scientific principles to define and solve the more complex and difficult organisational, policy, and technical problems met in industry and commerce, local and central government, transport organisations, health and education service, defence, etc.

Most of the problems dealt with by operational research experts are by definition difficult because the 'system' involved is a complicated one. Any problems or any attempt to make changes will therefore inevitably bring more problems and disruption. The 'system' itself is probably extremely difficult to describe and analyse in the first place. A problem is given to OR experts to solve just because so many factors have to be taken into account, and because some of the factors may involve chance, risk, and uncertainties, all of which must be treated as variables, variables which can interact with each other to give a great many different possible outcomes. It may be very difficult to identify all the factors involved. There may be a great many different possible solutions to a single problem, and it may be very difficult to decide which is the 'best' in any given circumstances. 'Best' itself may depend on a great many variables, and objectives themselves may change when the possible solutions are identified. OR experts often find that the problem they are working on is a symptom of another problem.

Operational research may, of course, be used to set up a new system from scratch, or it may be used, for example, just to assess and measure the effectiveness of an existing system, or to look forward to try to estimate future developments.

The OR expert – it may be one person, or it may be a team of people – has first to decide what the problem is and define the objective. To do this, the team has next to understand how the system involved works, what factors make it operate and what creates problems. They collect all the information they can about the system and watch and listen to the people who operate it. They use the data they have collected to build a mathematical model (expressing the factors involved in numerical terms so that they can be analysed mathematically), which then has to be tested against the real situation to see if it is accurate, and adjust it if necessary. They then analyse the data and use the model to produce all the possible solutions, and to simulate them, given the stated objectives. Frequently computers are used to do all this. Everything has to be checked and re-checked. The possible solutions are assessed in relation to the objectives, and a report written analysing the whole exercise.

Operational research is not a particularly new set of techniques (it goes back to before world war I). Its use in world war II – when it was first used as a way of consulting more than one kind of specialist – by creating teams from different disciplines, and success in, for example, analysing why air and sea forces were not sinking German U boats and then producing a more successful plan, gave it firmer standing. Experts returning to peace-time employment tried their techniques on non-military problems. Today, most organisations of any size have their own OR groups or use independent consultants. Some 10,000 or so people either work as OR experts or do something similar, the OR Society estimates.

OR at its most sophisticated today is used extensively by, for instance, the oil industry. Oil companies have to decide how to plan their long- and medium term futures, given that oil reserves are known to be finite, but that it is not clear how long they will last, given changing patterns of demand. Linked to this is the increasing unpredictability of oil price structures, which makes it difficult for oil companies to plan, for example, their investment policies (in new oil fields, for example), and their own pricing arrangements. Oil companies import, and bring into the UK from the North Sea, around 100 different types of crude oil, by ship and by pipeline. Each type has to be delivered to the appropriate refinery, which at any one time may be making up to 100 basic products. These must be further treated and blended to produce 200 finished products, which must be what the market is currently demanding and not waste a single drop of crude, so that it is often necessary to change the proportions of both basic and finished products made. The refined and blended oils, petrols, feedstock for chemicals and plastics, etc, must be distributed to plants and depots all over the UK and Europe, going by ship, rail, pipeline, and road.

Oil-company OR experts must build and keep up to date with new factors and changes a model of the whole oil industry, the company, and the production system. This they monitor to see that it constantly operates as efficiently (ie profitably and economically) as possible. The system may have to be examined because, for example, more crude is coming into the country by pipeline from the North Sea, and so less is arriving by tanker. Is the whole tanker fleet still needed, then? Analysis shows that it might be, because more refined petrol or chemical feedstock may be going to European plants. Are the refineries still in the right place if, in five years time, double the present proportion of crude comes from the North Sea, or half? Which depots and filling stations are still economic, and what is the optimum number of deliveries of how much petrol per month? And so on...

Operational research staff in electricity boards study the Radio and TV Times in working out how best to meet peak demands for electricity economically, which means having as little very expensive generating capacity on 'stand by', given that the entire nation switches on the kettle when 'match of the day' ends; what effect does breakfast TV have on demand for electricity at 6.30, 7.30 and 8.30 am? Simpler, perhaps, is trying to find the most efficient way of getting newspapers from printer to newsagents in different parts of the country. Many OR exercises deal with planning – for companies and government – with stock control, with scheduling, with financial forecasting or manpower planning, with shift planning (e.g. for airline pilots or train drivers), optimum ship sizes for given routes and cargoes, and re-routing bus services.

Working in OR can be very varied. It is not as heavily mathematical as is often thought. Time is spent out of the office, observing, and finding out; time is spent discussing, working on solutions, preparing and writing reports, putting forward and explaining suggestions. It is usual to change jobs fairly regularly. Prospects seem to be reasonable, and promotion into general management not unusual.

Recruitment and entry possible to start as a trainee, or to train before looking for a job. It is common to go into OR after experience in another occupation. Most entrants have degrees (good honours generally), in mathematics or statistics, but engineering, economics, business studies, computer science, physics or psychology are as useful, provided A levels include maths, a science, or statistics.

Operational research does take numeracy, to about A-level equivalent. People considering OR as a career also need to be well-organised, capable of thinking logically, with analytical minds, interested in complex problem solving – and 'creative intelligence'. OR experts need to be happy to work as part of what can be a very closely-knit team. They have to be good communicators, able to explain complex matters simply and clearly, and to write well-argued and clearly-presented reports.

Qualifications and training There are a some first degree courses, in eg maths, or business studies, which include studies in operational research. Some, larger OR units have good training programmes which may be linked to postgraduate study (for a higher degree or postgraduate diploma) at a university.

Further information from the Operational Research Society.

PATENT WORK
Introduction — patent agents — patent examiners — patent officers

Introduction
The patent system gives a legal, twenty-year monopoly on the use of a new invention, so that the patent owner gains some financial return on a new process or product, but in return the patent has to be published.

Rapid technological advance, intensifying world competition to be first in the field, and the difficulty of meeting everyone's needs in legislation makes the patent system hard to operate and produces great tensions, understandable when profits may be at stake. Patents are expensive; a simple, collapsible home work bench cost £500,000 in world patents and court actions in only six years. The system is inevitably complex and time consuming – it can take four-and-a-half years before a patent is granted, largely because of the time needed to print specifications. Early publication of a patent means many firms and inventors think they are giving competitors time to make the few design changes necessary to get around a patent. In electronics, innovation is now so fast, and new developments spread so quickly that many manufacturers have given up patenting.

Traditionally, patents were (and mostly still are), granted on a national, country-by-country basis, and every invention has, in the past, required a separate patent for each country, which means multiple applications, different specifications, and language problems. The system is slowly being internationalised. Both an international Patent Co-operation Treaty (signed 1970) and a European Patent Convention (signed 1973), finally became fully operative in June 1978. These make it possible to obtain patent coverage for as many countries as sign the Convention and/or Treaty via a single application (and therefore a single search) and a single patent grant – the patentee decides how many countries to cover with one application, but it is (at present) an alternative system, existing side-by-side with national procedures. An EEC patent convention does allow for a single patent, valid for all EEC countries, but still has not been implemented. The European convention set up a European patent office in Munich, with other offices now in Berlin and near The Hague.

Obviously, these changes will have long-term effects on patent work. What they will be is not entirely clear – the situation has been described as 'fluid'. British patent agents have also been losing work from abroad, because overseas patentees who used to come to them can now go straight to Munich for their English language patent – 50% of applications to Munich are English language.

Patent agents

They are the experts who prepare and write the very detailed descriptions, called specifications, which form the basis of all applications for patents, registered designs and trademarks, and which must be submitted to show that an invention is completely new. Inventors can, of course, make their own applications, but the advantages of using a professional expert means few do.

Specifications are legal documents but the content is scientific and technological. They must be drafted in legal terms, but must be clear, concise and exact, leaving no loopholes or ambiguities describing the invention in a way that gives the maximum possible protection. They must stand up to testing in court if necessary. In addition to drawing up the specifications, patent agents must also negotiate with and answer any objections to claims by the Patent Office examiners (below) and possibly re-draft the specification.

British patent agents organise and supervise patent applications for as many countries as the client wants. They make direct application to the British, and if qualified to do so, the European Office too. For other countries they work through local patent agents, who in turn ask British agents to make application for them here. The local agent, whether British or foreign, has to revise specifications to meet local patent law, and translate them. British patent agents have to learn a great deal about patent law and procedures in a widening range of countries, since there is increasing emphasis on patenting on an international scale. Most patent agents specialise to some extent, usually in a broad subject area like mechanical engineering or chemical processes.

Patent agents must make searches through patent records, advise clients on the chances of getting a patent, and whether it is worthwhile, and on the validity and risk of infringement of other people's patents. They advise on the terms of licensing agreements and are involved when patents are contested or there is an alleged infringement.

The work is mostly office and desk based, but a proportion of all patent agents' time is spent discussing and negotiating, both the clients and technical staff, and with officials. They may have to brief lawyers, and appear in court as expert witnesses. Young patent agents spend a high proportion of their time on patent searches.

It is a small profession: numbers rose fast during the 1970s (from some 700 in 1973), slowed quite sharply in the early 1980s so that new entrants barely kept pace with retirements, with under 1250 fully-qualified agents in 1986.

Almost 60% are self-employed or work for other patent agents. Private practices number about 168, exactly half of them 'sole practitioners', 44 employ between two and four agents, 20 five to nine, 15 ten to fourteen, and only five more than fifteen.

Just over 40% work for 111 organisations with their own patent departments, such as companies investing heavily in R&D of new products and processes. Forty employ only one patent agent, 46 employ between two and four, 16 between five and nine, five between ten and fourteen, and only four 15 or more.

Most patent agents work in London, or other industrial centres, but some London firms have moved out into the home counties and the south coast towns. There are probably increasing opportunities to work abroad, especially in Europe.

The profession is facing a slightly uncertain future. Recession, and some years of declining investment in new inventions in Britain, combined with factors like some loss of work from overseas as firms go straight to Munich office (above), mean that growth of a still-small profession (which will never be large) has slowed. The Office of Fair Trading produced a report on the profession (in September 1986) recommending changes to increase competition, and wants patents agents to be able to work in 'mixed' professional practices. Some of the legal protection patent agents currently enjoy may also be lifted, again to permit greater competition.

Recruitment and entry Entry is to a 'technical assistant' post in a private practice, an industrial organisation or government department. Recruitment of trainees picked up in 1985, to 49, after five years when it hovered between 24 and 36 (down from an average of 40 in the 1970s).

Normal entry is via a degree (usually first- or second class honours) in science, engineering or a technological subject – the Institute suggests that a broadly-based and not too specialised course is most suitable – and it is now virtually impossible to start with the official minimum of five GCE/GCSE passes with physics and chemistry A levels. Languages are increasingly useful. Not all trainees are recruited straight from university or polytechnic; some work, for example, in research and development for a while first.

Patent agents need a keen practical interest, and curiosity, in technological and scientific developments. They should have the kind of intelligence which 'catches on' easily, and can take in new and sometimes very advanced ideas in science and technology. They have to be capable of learning to write legally-watertight prose, which means being able to think clearly, analytically and critically, reason logically, and be able to use the English language. They have to be able to negotiate and argue. Tidy-mindedness, accuracy, and precision are needed.

Qualifications and training Patent agents have to be state registered (at present). They qualify via examinations set by the (British) Chartered Institute of

Patent Agents, while training on-the-job – but there is no published syllabus to work to. Final exams cannot be taken without three years' experience of patent work (graduates can take the intermediate after a year's experience), but no training guidelines are set. Technical assistants have to spent quite a large part of their spare time studying – some help is given by an informal group of CIPE members.

To practise at the European Patent Office, patent agents must also take the exams of the European Institute of Patent Agents, for which the entry requirement is a degree and four years' experience; the exam includes questions in French or German.

Patent examiners

The Patent Office has, to date, been a government department. It is now to become a non-departmental, non-Crown public body, under independent management. Although this means staff will no longer be civil servants, no significant change in the nature of the work, career prospects etc is expected as a direct result. However, the declining number of applications to the UK Office implies that either the Office will get smaller and/or that it will have to develop additional services.

The London Office employs about 300 examiners (down from 550 in 1976-7), out of a total of 1150 employees (1600 in 1972).

They examine patent applications to assess whether or not they are novel enough to justify awarding a patent. They search through earlier specifications and other published papers, prepare reports, interview patent agents (or the applicants), and if there is a dispute of any kind, they act for the Patent Office. Examiners also write and index the shortened version of the specification for publication.

This is also mainly an office-based career, combining desk work with discussion and negotiation. Patent examiners usually specialise in one subject area, working in one of 26 specialist groups.

UK-trained patent examiners can work for the European Patent Office. Britain has held a number of key posts, eg the vice-president responsible for for examination and opposition, the principal legal-division directors, and the secretary to the president are all British, as are a number of the higher-grade administrative officers, a senior programmer and a formalities officer, and four Britons are on the personnel directorate. About 100 British Nationals are employed by the European Office, out of 1800 in total – half of them working in The Hague office.

Recruitment and entry the Patent Office was not expecting to recruit any examiners in 1986-7, although it hoped to recruit in 1988 (but no more than ten people at most). The European Patent Office is keen to recruit some 15 British graduates a year.

Entry requirements are good honours (ie first- or second-class) degrees in engineering, physics or mathematics, and/or membership of a major professional institution in an appropriate field. Mathematics graduates should also have studied physics or a technology. A language (French or German) is useful for the British Patent Office, essential for the European Office, which prefers a second too.

Training is in-house.

Patent officers

They work for the Ministry of Defence and deal with patent work arising from the research, development and manufacturing activities carried out by, or on behalf of, government departments in the scientific, technological and engineering fields – they are, in effect, government patent agents. This includes arranging patent protection for Crown rights in new inventions and developments, assessing and settling claims for compensation for Crown use of patents, designs, processes and other types of industrial 'property', and general advisory work with government departments on the use of inventions. The staff of the patents directorate must keep totally up-to-date on government and related research and development and regularly visit research establishments. Numbers of patent officers are very small.

Recruitment, entry and training as Patent agent above.
See also CENTRAL GOVERNMENT

Further information from the Chartered Institute of Patent Agents, the Patent Office, the European Patent Office, and the Civil Service Commission.

WORK STUDY, AND ORGANISATION AND METHODS

These are closely related and overlapping techniques used to ensure that working methods are as efficient as they can be, and that employees are being used as effectively as possible. Work study originated in the factory, organisation and methods in the office, but they use more or less they same principles and methods, so they joined forces to become a single profession.

This is an advisory (rather than a 'line') 'function'. Work study/O & M staff advise management how to achieve set targets with as few resources (manpower, materials and capital equipment) as possible, and how to best co-ordinate their use. The techniques are not only used in industry and commerce, but also in, for instance, farming, the Armed Forces, and the public services.

There are two main aspects to modern work study/O & M, and work study officers are usually expected to be able to do both.

Method study examines and analyses critically and closely the way particular jobs, or series of related jobs, such as assembling a car, cleaning a hospital, delivering mail, organising a filing system, estimating or ordering, sales forecasting, keeping statistical records, or running internal communications, are being done. Its techniques are then used to see if there are any ways to improve the existing method or system, both for greater efficiency and if possible to make the work easier – perhaps using robots on an assembly line or micro computers for word-processing. They may have to plan changes to a system, eg when a food manufacturer decides to make several versions of a breakfast cereal instead of just one in bulk, and so has to batch produce.

To do this, the job or system is broken down into all its stages, and the stages laid out on paper in the form of a flow chart, so that it becomes possible to see where there is a better route through the stages, whether one or more can be eliminated, or whether some tasks should be split, to make them easier to do. A method study expert will look to see if there is any equipment which will speed the process, reduce manpower and so costs, and perhaps make the work easier to do. Method study may be used to solve a problem, such as a bottleneck in a production line, or in supplies. It may be used to try to improve efficiency, or in planning and designing a new system. Since many new office and industrial systems involve computers, this will usually mean working closely with computer experts, normally SYSTEMS ANALYSTS.

Work measurement, the other half of the function, does what it says. Work measurement experts measure the time it takes someone to do a job, or part of a job. Again, the job must be analysed, by breaking it down into all the individual actions, and then timing and observing these actions over and over again, using a number of different people, to find a mean time for the operation. Work measurement is used to provide standards against which output can be measured, and is usually the basis for pay calculations and costing, but is also used in evaluating working methods.

There are four broad working grades. At the most junior level, the observer is generally sufficiently trained to be able to make measurements of most straightforward activities for method study. The main working grade is that of engineer or officer, normally able to do any work measurement or method study project, while senior positions include senior or section, team leader, and manager or consultant, who organise and co-ordinate mixed teams of management specialists. Experienced work study practitioners are expected to able to detect a need for a change in the system, decide on the form it should take, organise and collect the necessary information, analyse it, and help to carry out the new procedures.

The work is painstaking, with days spent in careful observing and timing. It is part desk work, part time spent in other departments, or even different parts of the country for a multi-site company or a management consultant. Most large organisations have their own work study units.

The work is technological, mathematical and psychological, involving at various times accounting, communications, computers, costing, economics, ergonomics, industrial relations, layout and designing, management and organisation, network analysis, OR, payment and incentives, production planning, psychology, quality control, social science, statistics, systems analysis and value analysis. Demand for work study experts is steady. There are plenty of opportunities for promotion, and for career development in eg production or personnel management, data processing, and eventually general management. Some go into MANAGEMENT CONSULTANCY.

Recruitment and entry it is not usual to start training in work study/O & M without some experience in industry or commerce, usually in mid-twenties, and even graduates are advised to spend a year or two working in an industrial or commercial environment first.

Although people start work in work study with a variety of educational backgrounds, for the best long-term prospects above-average intelligence is needed, and it is worth extending academic studies as far as possible, to at least BTEC Higher award standard, and a degree is increasingly useful.

Work study takes maturity and tact, with the ability to work with people – who may feel threatened by work study processes. A reasonable level of numeracy is needed, as is the ability to think logically and analytically, to be methodical, and have organisational skills.

Qualifications and training Training is normally and mostly on-the-job, with part-time study for professional qualifications.

The Institute of Management Sciences (1986 membership c13,000) now asks for a BTEC National (or the equivalent) for entry to the certificate examinations, for which the course lasts a year part-time. There is no longer any direct entry to diploma examinations. Subject-for-subject exemptions are possible with a wide range of other qualifications.

CGLI also offers a certificate in work study, mainly for people working in a technical field: it is a part 3 technician-level award and can count towards a full technological certificate. The Institute of Administrative Management also sets examinations which are useful for O&M staff.

Further information from the Institute of Management Services.

RELIGIOUS ORGANISATIONS AND SERVICES

Introduction   1039
The Christian Churches   1039
Christian missionary work overseas   1047
Jewry   1047

INTRODUCTION

Religious organisations in Britain today are mostly Christian, despite increasing interest in other religions, and with the exception of the Jewish, Muslim and other faiths practised by ethnic groups living in Britain.

Careers within all religious organisations, whatever the faith, demand a vocation, a conviction, based on a firm belief in the faith in question, that the entrant is called to carry out the will of the deity. Acceptance of such a calling generally implies being prepared to devote one's entire life to the service of God, to members of the religious organisation, and also the disadvantaged. It implies a rejection of materialistic values, and being ready to go without many material comforts. In most instances the training is long and fairly arduous, as well as intellectually and emotionally demanding.

THE CHRISTIAN CHURCHES

General — Baptist Union — Catholic Church — Church of England — Church of Scotland — Methodist Church — Salvation Army — United Reformed Church

For the most part, the Churches are looking for people with a calling to the ministry, or priesthood.

All the Churches have serious philosophical and practical problems in defining their role in the modern world. It is easy for ministers to be seen as dedicated social workers or teachers, or merely as reminders of a bygone age. Entrants to the contemporary ministry work for their beliefs in a world only too often indifferent to religion of any kind. The purpose of the Christian ministry – to bring the people to God and God to the people – is immutable, but the methods of the ministry change; for instance, the priest can no longer expect people to go to church automatically, but must go out into the parish to them.

The majority of ministers or priests are attached to a community church (the parish for Anglicans and Catholics), conducting corporate worship, preaching, teaching, and doing pastoral work within the church's 'parish'. The pattern of ministry changes in response to changing society, and in all churches the clergy have the freedom to search for and implement new pastoral ideas and approaches, geared to the present day and contemporary conditions, to be creative in their approach to the ministry and to help, where necessary, to 'push pastoral methods over into the second half of the 20th century'.

While the traditional organisation of the local church remains generally the same, with an incumbent assisted by one or more assistant curates (who may be priests or deacons), some churches try different approaches, eg the team ministry, where a group of priests work as equals, sharing responsibility for effective pastoral care and service in a specific area or community, often in an industrial setting. Despite their commitment to the propagation of the faith, clergy are also expected to help build a better world, and to make such criticisms as may be necessary.

But increasingly the churches are going out to meet people in other ways, through chaplaincies and other special pastoral ministries.

In EDUCATION, for example, all university and most polytechnics have teams of chaplains, normally including one from each of the major churches and faiths. Other colleges, Church-aided educational establishments and public schools employ chaplains.

Most chaplaincies now concentrate on pastoral care for the community and on conducting services etc. To combine this with teaching (as was traditional) now requires a degree and a teaching qualification.

All three ARMED FORCES have chaplains from the major churches. They usually enter on short-service commissions initially but can (with permission), stay in on a permanent commission, and may be promoted. The service chaplain cares for any community to which he may be sent. Often this will be very like a parish, as the families of service personnel under his care may live on or close to the station, but like other officers, a chaplain rarely spends longer than three years on the same station. Chaplains in the Forces normally enter fairly young, but have usually had three to five years' experience in a local church first.

The PRISON SERVICE employs chaplains. The accent is supposed to be on rehabilitation, and chaplains work with other prison staff here, although they also conduct services and provide conventional pastoral care for the prison community. Full-time chaplains are normally appointed for seven years, although this can be extended to twelve. For the first year, priests normally serve as assistant chaplain. Entrants to the Prison Service should usually be mature men with several years' parish experience. Most prison chaplains are, however, part-time, working from churches in the area.

The HEALTH SERVICE employs some 200 full-time chaplains. Other hospitals have part-time chaplains, usually working in the local parish.

BROADCASTING companies have a few chaplains on the staff to work on religious programmes.

Since clerical life is a vocation more than a career, it seems inappropriate to discuss promotion, but nevertheless, not all clerics spend their lives in the service of a local church or in other special ministries (see below). Of course, in the non-hierarchical churches (the so-called free churches and the Church of Scotland) there is no other role to be filled – the moderator of the assembly of the Church of Scotland, for example, is elected annually.

Within the hierarchical churches certain ministries are filled by those who are considered to have the appropriate qualities for leadership. In the Church of England and the Catholic Church the hierarchical structure of parish, deanery, archdeaconry, diocese, archdiocese or province remains. The cathedrals of both Churches also have their own clergy, who generally hold senior status. In the Catholic Church the hierarchy goes higher, to cardinal and pope; however, the papal seat has not been occupied by a priest from the British Isles for several centuries. The proportion of priests who are promoted to senior positions within either church is clearly quite small.

Both the Catholic Church and the Church of England have religious orders for men who do not want to be parish priests (or priests at all), and for women. There are several different kinds of orders, for instance contemplative orders, in which the religious spend the larger proportion of their time in prayer and contemplation; others devote most of their collective energies to active work, such as training ordinands, doing missionary or community work, teaching or nursing, or caring for children. Religious take solemn vows of poverty, chastity and obedience, after a period of novitiate or training, and prayer, which usually lasts between three and nine years after entry to the order. The life, which is lived in a closed or semi-open community, is often one of extreme self-sacrifice, although some orders have relaxed the more stringent rules and modernised their dress.

Recruitment and entry Traditionally, the churches take candidates for the ministry from amongst (university) graduates, or school-leavers. However, this has been changing, both because the number of suitable candidates coming forward has fallen, and because the churches have seen a need for clerics who come from a wider background and from among those who have had some experience of living as an ordinary member of society. For entry to both the ministry and religious orders, vocation and personal qualities are the most crucial qualifications.

Qualifications and training see RELIGIOUS STUDIES AND THEOLOGY, under ACADEMIC AND VOCATIONAL STUDIES IN ARTS, and individual churches below.

Further information see individual churches listed below.

The Baptist Union of Great Britain and Ireland
This is an association of some 2000 churches, with a total membership of about 170,000.
Full-time service in the ministry is open to both men and women (most colleges now have women training for the ministry). Women may also be deaconesses, serving with a minister in a parish, and working mainly with women, children, teenagers or the elderly, but may become leaders of a local church.

Entry All candidates for the ministry must first be recommended by the applicant's own church. The applicant is next interviewed by the general superintendent of the area and then by the ministerial committee of the appropriate county association. The final step is a college interview and probably an entrance examination. During this process, prospective entrants are expected to take every opportunity to practise preaching and leading congregations in worship.

Candidates are normally expected to have the intellectual ability shown by five O-level-equivalent passes and two A levels. However, candidates may be accepted without, if they have 'marked compensating strength of personality and character'.

Deaconesses must be at least 21; there are no educational entrance requirements, but candidates are recommended to gain O-level-equivalent passes in at least English and religious knowledge.

Training normally via a four- or five-year full-time residential course at a Baptist theological college (but for married entrants or anyone who cannot attend a college in-service training is possible).

Seven colleges, either affiliated to a university and so preparing those qualified for that university's theological degree or a diploma, or degrees awarded by the CNAA: Bangor: N Wales, Bristol, Cardiff: S Wales, Glasgow: Scottish, London: Spurgeon's, Manchester: Northern, Oxford: Regent's Park.

Further information from the Baptist Union of Great Britain and Ireland.

The Catholic Church

The Church in Britain has about 4.27 million members spread through some 3000 parishes. Despite its traditional international hierarchical structure, the Church selects its priests on a diocesan basis in the British Isles (the 29 dioceses are divided between seven provinces in Britain; there are nine dioceses in Northern Ireland some of which cross into the Irish Republic).

The Church has, at present, some 5000 parish priests, and a further 2500 in religious orders. Over 12,000 nuns are members of some 1500 convents.

Entry A candidate for the priesthood is normally expected to have discussed his vocation with a priest, preferably one known to him. He is then put in touch with the diocesan director of vocations, since the first stage is to gain the acceptance of a bishop. Training does not normally begin before 18.

The Church prefers candidates to show the sincerity of their vocation by working for whatever educational qualifications they can; for example, if a student can qualify for university, then he would be expected to work for this. However, the Church does not consider such qualifications essential, and treats personal qualities, experience or professional status as more than compensating for lack of GCE/GCSE qualifications in appropriate cases.

Training Catholic seminaries are going through a period of transition and change. The rising number of mature candidates for the priesthood, and of candidates capable of reading for a degree or similar qualification, has led to some changes, while the demands of the modern priesthood have brought revisions in the syllabus of the training courses. For example, the normal seminary course is six or seven years, but for mature candidates courses have been adapted and last only four years. In all seminaries the emphasis is on pastorally-orientated courses.

There are five colleges in the UK, three on the continent which accept English-speaking students, and five in Ireland. The courses differ to some extent from college to college.

In England and Wales, the seminaries are –

For junior students – Nottingham: Tollerton Hall (St Hugh's); Skelmersdale: Upholland (St Joseph's); for senior students – Durham; St Cuthbert's (Ushaw); London: Allen Hall; Sutton Coldfield: St Mary's (Oscott College); Womersh: St John's; late vocations – Osterley: Campion House.

Overseas – Rome: Venerable English College, Pontifical Beda College (which specialises in training men who have already qualified or worked in something else); Spain: English College in Valladolid.

Further information from the Commission for Priestly Formation.

The Church of England
This is the established church, has some 1.8 million confirmed members, in about 13,400 parishes. The Church has about 10,400 priests and is at present ordaining about 400 men each year.

Entry The Church has a centralised selection procedure, but expects candidates to discuss their vocation first with, eg a priest, and then the diocesan director of ordinands, who will decide if and when the candidates should be sponsored for a three-day selection conference. All candidates for the ministry must attend a selection conference arranged for the diocesan bishops by the Advisory Council for the Church's Ministry (ACCM). The selection board consists of four selectors and an ACCM secretary, the selectors being a representative group of clergy and lay men and women drawn from each diocese and each candidate is individually and informally interviewed by each selector; talks and discussions are also designed to help candidates consider, with the selectors, where their vocations lie.

Although the Church traditionally expects clergy to read for a degree, and therefore to qualify educationally for university entrance, there is less insistence on this, and entry is possible for those who do not conform to it.

The normal entry requirement for candidates under 25 is as for university entry (ie five O-level-equivalent passes including English language, and at least two at A level) or the equivalent (eg a BTEC Higher award with O level or equivalent in English language or a completed recognised professional qualification). Over 25, no academic standard is set in terms of particular qualifications, and each candidate is considered and assessed individually.

Training Graduates aged up to 29, if they have a theology degree, normally do a two-year course at a theological college. If not, they must study at theological college for three years.

Non-graduate candidates under 25 do either the Aston training scheme (below) and a three-year full-time course at a theological college, or a 4 year degree and ordination training. Non-graduates aged 25-29 normally do a three-year full-time theological course, but some may do the Aston scheme first. Over 30, the training course is normally two years' full-time, or three

years' part-time; some candidates may also have to do the Aston scheme.
First-degree courses in theology are described in RELIGIOUS STUDIES AND THEOL-
OGY under ACADEMIC AND VOCATIONAL STUDIES IN ARTS.

The Aston training scheme is a non-residential, pre-theological-college education. It is intended for candidates who have not had the chance to develop their
potential to the point where they can reasonably be expected to begin direct
theological study, but who have shown evidence of this potential since leaving
school, and for candidates whose education and experience has trained them
in ways of study and thought which make theological thinking difficult without
preliminary training. Candidates following the scheme stay in full-time
employment, under the care and direction of a tutor chosen by the course
principal in consultation with the diocese. The academic work is based on the
Open University degree programme under an OU tutor; four residential
weekends and a two-week summer school are an integral part of the course.
All ordinands must pass the General Ministerial Examination, or an approved
equivalent, or be exempted from it (degrees in theology usually exempt from
some papers). The GME is shortened for older candidates, and there is an
alternative essay scheme for those over 30.

Most theological colleges are linked in some way to a university (some are an
integral part), and their awards are generally those of the university. Most
have a strong link with one of the 'movements' within the Church (evangelical
or anglo-catholic, for example), and the academic and religious environment
differs quite considerably from one to the other.

Colleges with full-time courses are –
Birmingham, Queen's: the first fully ecumenical college;
Bristol, Trinity: evangelical tradition; degrees CNAA validated;
Cambridge Federation (Ridley Hall, Westcott House, Methodist Wesley
House and United Reformed Westminster): possible to read for Cambridge
degree; strong practical emphasis;
Chichester: catholic tradition; Southampton University BTh;
Cuddesdon (Oxford), Ripon: broadly catholic tradition; Oxford University
awards;
Durham, St John's/Cranmer Hall: evangelical tradition; constituent college of
University;
Edinburgh: Scottish episcopal, Edinburgh BD;
Hawarden, St Deiniol's: for men over 30 only;
Lincoln: wide range of churchmanship; Nottingham University awards;
Llandaff (Cardiff) St Michael's: part of Cardiff University College;
London, Oak Hill: evangelical tradition; degree CNAA validated;
Mirfield, College of the Resurrection: closely linked to religious order, pre-
dominantly graduates, Leeds University awards;
Nottingham, St John's: evangelical, with a strong missionary tradition; Not-
tingham University awards;
Oxford, St Stephen's House: catholic outlook, mainly graduates; Oxford
University awards;
Salisbury and Wells: Southampton University awards;
Part-time schemes at 14 centres and colleges.

Further information from the Advisory Council for the Church's Ministry.

The Church of Scotland

The Church has an adult membership estimated at over a million. All ministers of the Church are of equal status, and every church is governed by the local kirk session. Men and women are accepted as candidates for the ministry.

The Church also employs some 1200 people in its eventide homes, homes for children and young people, and handicapped people, rehabilitation work. Young men and women are also employed as field workers, in parishes, hospitals, prisons, in isolated communities etc.

Entry Anyone seeking recognition as a candidate must be accepted by the Committee on Education for the Ministry, and must be nominated by his or her presbytery. Candidates under 23 must have the SCE passes needed for admission to university in Scotland. Mature candidates are expected to have two H-grade passes, including English, and one further subject at O grade.

Training for the ministry normally takes not less than six years' full-time study. Candidates may take either the regular or the alternative course; there is also a special course for mature students.

The regular course consists of a first degree, which may be in any subject, followed by at least three years' study for a BD or LTh at a university.

The alternative consists of four years' study leading to a BD as a first degree at a university, followed by a further two years' study.

The mature students course consists of either a two-year pre-divinity course and three years' study for LTh, or a one year predivinity course and a four-year course for a BD.

Further information from the Church of Scotland Department of Education.

The Methodist Church

The Church is based on a 1932 union of most separate Methodist churches (there are still a number of independent Methodists, and some in the Wesleyan Reform Union), has some 500,000 full adult members.

Entry Candidates have to be fully-accredited local preachers, and must have passed the local preachers' exam in the old and new testament, Christian doctrine and worship and preaching at grade A, B or C. O-level-equivalent passes in English language and three other subjects are needed. Candidates must be nominated by the members of the circuit meeting. After nomination, the candidate must pass two three-hour written examinations (one on the Bible and the other a general paper), conduct trial services (with sermons), and be interviewed by various committees, plus a psychologist.

Training The Methodist Church has four residential theological colleges, where courses normally last three years full-time for those under 30, two for those over 30. Training requirements are decided for candidates individually, but those qualified to do so normally read for a degree in theology. Including the course, candidates under 29 are 'on probation' for five years, over 30 for four. Between one and three years must be spent on a circuit appointment under a superintendent, academic studies are continued, further training continued, and tests given.

Further information from the Methodist Church Division of Ministries.

The Salvation Army
The Army has some 100,000 active members in Britain, working from more than 1000 centres of worship (the total community strength is estimated at about 350,000). They also run centres which give help to people in need.
Both men and women are accepted for training for full-time service as officers in the Salvation Army, and as accredited ministers of the gospel.

Entry Age normally between 18 and 35 (in special cases up to 40), to have been recommended by local Salvation Army officials, and to have completed a preliminary examination and a pre-residential correspondence course. The Army does not set any formal educational entry qualifications, but expects an average secondary education, supplemented by diligent personal effort.

Training takes two years full-time, at the International Training College in London. Graduates normally take a further two-year correspondence course thereafter.

Further information from Salvation Army International Headquarters.

The United Reformed Church
The Church was formed in 1972 from a merger between the Congregational Church and the Presbyterian Church of England, and now has 1941 churches and some 144,000 members. The Church accepts both men and women for the ministry.

Entry Candidates must be recommended by the local church and the minister, and have the approval of the district council. Selection is by a national assessment conference followed by a provincial synod ministerial committee. Educational entry requirements vary from college to college.

Training is at one of seven colleges –
Birmingham, Queen's: ecumenical, see Church of England (above).
Cambridge, Westminster and Cheshunt: share accommodation; entrants must be graduates or have a professional qualification, but mature entrants are accepted with at least two A-level passes; three-year ordination course.
London, New: accepts graduates, students qualified to read for London BD (for which College prepares them) and those with at least five O-level-equivalent passes (to take London academic diploma in theology); an entrance examination includes elementary Greek; normal ordination course lasts four years.
Manchester, Congregational College: course depends on entry qualifications, ie
with a degree – three-year course for a BD;
with university entry qualifications – six-year course for BA and BD;
with at least five O-level-equivalent passes – five-year course leading to certificates in Biblical knowledge and theology;
all candidates take an entrance examination on the Bible, Free Church history and general knowledge.
Oxford, Mansfield College: normal ordination course requires two degrees, the second in theology and the first in another subject, involving six years' study, but direct entry to theology degree for graduates from elsewhere.

Swansea, Memorial College: candidates with appropriate qualifications may read for University of Wales BD, which is a first degree, or for theology diploma (six O-level-equivalent passes needed). All candidates must take entry exam which includes elementary Greek.

Also provision for college-based, but non-residential, study.

Further information from the United Reformed Church Ministerial Training Committee.

CHRISTIAN MISSIONARY WORK OVERSEAS

This is still seen as crucial by the churches. However, the churches in the areas which were missionary territories now have their own programmes and projects, leaders and workers. They do, however, frequently ask Christians from other countries, and particularly from Britain, to join them in full-time service. Contemporary missionaries, then, go only where they have been invited, and accept the direction of the Church in that country.

Priests, for example, frequently volunteer for between three and five years abroad. The Overseas Council of the Church of Scotland sends its own missionaries overseas for a minimum term of three years. Work overseas is more and more an ecumenical activity, supported by the British Council of Churches, the Catholic Church and the Conference of British Missionary Societies.

In general, direct service through a church is not only for clergy but also for professionals of all kinds, particularly teachers, doctors, nurses, welfare workers, booksellers, agriculturists, personnel officers, accountants, etc. The Churches also encourage their lay members who are fully committed to the faith, to carry that faith overseas into the secular world, as teachers, in government service, the professions, commerce and industry.

See also WORKING OVERSEAS.

Further information from Christian Overseas Information Service.

JEWRY

The Jewish community in Britain totals some 400,000 people, including both Sephardi (who come from Spain and Portugal) and Ashkenazi (from Germany and Eastern Europe). There are two main religious schools of thought: the Orthodox, to which about 80% of practising Jews belong, and the Reform, or Liberal Jewish Movement. There are about 450 congregations. The Chief Rabbi is head of the Ashkenazi group within Orthodox Jewry, the Haham is head of the Sephardi group.

Training for intending rabbis is basically similar, however, for both schools and groups. It involves a period of intensive study which lasts, on average, six to eight years, although it can be longer. Part of the time is spent at a secular college and part at a recognised institution of higher Jewish learning.

Orthodox training is mainly via a three-year degree course at Jews' College (London) – with GCE/GCSE passes – followed by a further three to five years' intensive study of rabbinics, or possibly a three or four year course at, for instance, the Gateshead Talmudical College (entry is via an examination testing knowledge of rabbinics in Hebrew).

Reform/liberal training is via any degree followed by a five-year rabbinical training course at London: Leo Baeck College.
Some (also) go to Israel to study.

Further information from the London Board of Jewish Religious Education and the Leo Baeck College.

SOCIAL WORK

The social worker   1048
Areas of social work   1051
Recruitment and entry   1058
Qualifications and training   1058

THE SOCIAL WORKER

There are many definitions of social work ranging from the most palliative to the most positive, the latter shading over into radical political activism, and it is probable that no two social workers would have exactly the same aims.

Social work is put regularly under a microscope and the need for paid workers questioned, but in evidence to the Barclay Committee, few suggested that it is either possible or desirable to do without them. Reportedly, much of the evidence pointed to widespread respect for them from, for example, their clients and other professionals who work with them, such as doctors.

Most social workers would probably agree that they are problem solvers for the community. That they are there to help individuals – children, teenagers, adults – families, even whole communities as well as other groups, with problems which have become too great for them to cope with on their own. Beyond this, there is much disagreement. Disagreement on what 'problems' social workers should deal with: should they, for instance, try to help anyone who is socially 'inadequate' in any way, or should there be some limit, and if so what is it, and anyway, how do you define a 'problem'?

There is disagreement, too, on how far social workers should go in trying to 'solve' social problems. Should this be done regardless of how much it might 'cost' – in money, time, emotional stress, people, or any other resources, and how far should social workers help people to adjust to their situation – to mental or physical handicap, to ill health, bad housing, unemployment, or simple bad luck. Are social workers entitled to try to influence or change political decisions which they may consider have caused problems in the first place?

Recently, some of the dilemmas faced by social workers have been shown up in sharp focus. Creating support, and decision-making systems which can prevent damage to children without breaking up families unnecessarily has proved far more difficult than might seem.

Social work is still a relatively young profession, barely as old as the century. It developed from the charitable, voluntary pioneering research of the late 19th and early 20th centuries, when the damage caused to many people by the post-industrial revolution economic and social system was first recognised. Even then, and right up to the 1970s, the generic title 'social work' had little meaning, and there was no such person as a 'social worker'. Social work was a series of fragmented specialisations, with various bodies and authorities sponsoring specific services, and independent agencies dealing with specific types of problem and particular groups of 'clients'.

Everyone specialised – there were child care officers, welfare officers, mental health officers, medical social workers (once almoners), welfare officers for the deaf, mental handicap officers, and so on. As more social problems were recognised, or ways of approaching problems suggested, so people were trained to deal with that specific area, and the conflicting and overlapping responsibilities grew more and more difficult to cope with. Co-operation was difficult. Each group had its own professional organisation; each group was trained separately on very specialised courses.

It meant that 'clients' were all too often treated as a set of problems rather than as real people. A family with more than one problem member – a delinquent child, a physically handicapped father, a mentally-confused grandmother, and an exhausted mother, could be dealt with by several different people, as a series of unrelated problems treated in water-tight compartments, which could mean solutions proposed for one person might conflict with the needs of others in the family.

The end of fragmentation came with the Seebohm Report (1968), which recommended unified social services. By the mid-1970s most of the social services were 'integrated' and 'turned round' to put people, not their problems, first, as the focal point of the service. Which means a problem family would be helped by only one social worker, who sees the family's problems as a whole, is in a position to consider whether (for instance) the child's difficulties are a reflection of problems in the rest of the family, and can try to find solutions which will help everyone in the family as much as possible.

Most social workers, therefore, are now trained 'generically' – although probation officers (for example) have remained as a separate group. Seebohm was not, however, the last word on social work. Social work is still developing and changing, learning what it can and cannot do, how best to help, and how best to organise the help.

In practice, although trained to take on any job, or to tackle any problem, many social workers can and do choose the kind of people they would prefer to work with, or decide not to deal with particular kinds of problems. In choosing their first job, for instance in a hospital, they automatically decide to specialise to some extent. The difference is that they are not restricted in their choices, and they have a broader view of people's problems than before Seebohm. In fact, concern is increasing that the completely generalist approach is not satisfactory, because it looks as though some problems do need specialist handling. Within the broadly-based social services, then, some social workers do take on special responsibilities for, for example, children at risk, and there may well be increasing return to a greater degree of specialisation.

Ideally, social workers have two aims. First, they try to help the 'client' get over the immediate crisis or problem which has brought them to the social services in the first place: rescue. Second, the long-term aim is to look for ways to help clients to learn how to manage their lives better, to avoid crises, to gain or regain self-confidence, to make decisions, to be more independent, and so on. A social worker will try to work on and strengthen a client's own abilities to cope with their own lives and problems. Social workers do not tell their clients what they should, or should not, do; they aim to get them to understand their own difficulties, so that they can work out for themselves what to do. For instance, they will not tell a girl whether or not to keep her baby. Instead, they will try to help her see what the problems are and what may happen whichever course of action she takes. Social workers will support her, and give any practical help, whether or not they agree with her decision. The aim is always to see an end to the client's need of help from the social services, while avoiding quick solutions.

Where they can, social workers try to prevent crises, to identify problems and deal with them before they can become acute, for example, knowing which families are at risk and giving them support to prevent, for instance, the need to take children into care.

However, although social workers must aim high, and do the very best they can for all their clients, they must also be realists, and accept that there are limits to what they can do; that in many cases they may be only partly successful in their aims. They have to accept that people's problems do not fit into neat categories and that there are rarely any easy answers to them. They have to work with people for whom it is just too late to learn to cope; for many the realistic answers are often unacceptable, and some even find it too difficult to accept social workers' help. People may have been apathetic, or accepted an unsatisfactory life for too long to change. Social workers also have to make many difficult decisions and know they will inevitably make mistakes – classically on whether or not to take a child at risk into care.

Often there is little anyone can do about the central problem in someone's life. The social worker is then left to find ways of helping a client to, for example, live with a physical disability (but with adaptations and aid), come to terms with fatal illness, or make the best of poor housing or long-term unemployment. On the other hand, for many just a sympathetic ear may in itself be enough.

Social workers' ability to help may be limited by lack of resources, such as people, time, and money. This means that rescue, or crisis management, tends to dominate and will go on doing so while finances are so heavily restricted. Prevention, and attempts to make positive improvements in social conditions, have to take second place.

Social work is neither woolly-minded humanitarianism, nor official interference – nor is the social worker a universal aunt. Social work has a strict, some would say scientific, methodology, which both researchers and practising social workers are always trying to improve and refine. They try, for example, to define the process of prevention, and to find ways not to lose the therapeutic value that a degree of conflict and learning to manage a crisis have for people in difficulties. Some social workers also consider they have a duty to act as a bridge between the disadvantaged and society, and to educate the appropriate authorities and the public on the human problems and social needs of their clients.

Social workers generally deal with clients on an individual, one-to-one, person-to-person, 'casework' basis, although family-based casework is also used a great deal in some areas. Social workers treat the crises which bring people to the social services as the tip of an iceberg of likely problems. They set out to build firm, long-term relationships with their clients, individually or as families, to help them understand their problems, to make it possible for social worker and client(s) to work together to improve their whole situation longer term.

In crisis situations, the social worker must often first negotiate with another authority – preventing an electricity board cutting off the supply from a family with a new baby, for example. Then, patiently and carefully, using all their training in interviewing, listening, the social worker must discover how the crisis occurred. Practical help may be possible, such as checking that a family is receiving all the state benefits to which it is entitled. The social worker may be able to help the family organise their budget better – and get the family to discuss the priorities for the money that does come in, suggest cheaper recipes, help them look into cheaper forms of heating, and so on.

In helping their clients, social workers use a range of psychological and other techniques, their knowledge of how people behave, and their experience of similar situations. They give them positive encouragement, advice if wanted, sometimes being firm, but staying detached and not getting emotionally involved – or disapproving.

Some clients are helped through group work, but it is less usual. Here the social worker can bring together people who have related problems – young mothers living in local high-rise flats, or people who feel isolated and lonely. They bring together 'helpers', like foster parents, again to discuss and 'talk through', the problems they all have, together, in regular sessions, on the principle that some people find easier, and more helpful, to talk about their problems with people who are going through the same or similar difficulties. Community work (see below) is a form of group work, since it deals with groups of people where they live.

AREAS OF SOCIAL WORK
The employers — community social services — hospital social services — probation service — residential social work — non-professional social work

The employers
The great majority of social workers are employed by –

Local authorities, which have large, multi-purpose social services departments, which provide a comprehensive service to virtually anyone living in the area who needs the kind of help they can offer. A high proportion of social work time goes to coping with children, young people and families under stress, but they expect to deal with problems posted by the elderly, the homeless, or people who are physically and mentally handicapped. Most of these services are organised on an area, community, basis and are oriented to the family. Other sub-divisions of a social services department run residential and day-case facilities of various kinds (for the handicapped, or the elderly); another provides home helps, another 'meals on wheels'. Within central administration may be staff responsible for certain services, eg OCCUPATIONAL THERAPISTS who deal with home adaptations for the handicapped.

Local authorities also organise social work services in hospitals, and manage child guidance clinics. Local authorities also have specific legal responsibilities which are delegated to social services – under the Mental Health Acts, and the Children and Young Persons Act, for example. They also supervise adoptions and work with the juvenile courts. Some local authority social service departments have people to do research, and someone has to administer training.

Local authority social service departments in England alone employ, between them, some 295,500 people (1984), of whom about 31,000 are professional social workers, and about 110,000 work in residential homes – the rest are administrative and clerical staff (about 22,000), home helps (about 97,000 but most work part-time), and day-nursery staff (over 10,600).

Social services within each authority are centrally managed – there are about 4500 senior directing, managing, professional and advisory posts – but most services are run on an area basis. There are some 5000 senior social workers (including team leaders) running day-to-day services, with over 17,000 trained social workers. Promotion to senior posts in a social service department is now generally from amongst people who have come up through the area or other (eg medical social work) teams and have plenty of experience, although some senior staff and directors are sometimes outside appointees. Promotion is largely at present into administrative/managerial work, with little opportunity to stay in field work.

Voluntary, independent agencies range from some which are quite small and based on a single locality, to some which are very large, national bodies. Most were first formed for very specific purposes and to deal with the needs of fairly narrow groups, but have now mostly developed into more broadly-based services. Examples include a society which was at first concerned only with unmarried mothers but has now expanded to provide help for all one parent families, and societies founded to look after orphans which now work with all disadvantaged children. Other agencies provide services for the disabled and handicapped, both generally and for specific groups – the deaf, the blind, or people with multiple sclerosis, for example. The inspectors who work for the National Society for the Prevention of Cruelty to Children are social workers. Social workers cope with problems in a way similar to the local-authority social services, sometimes supplement what the social services can do – especially where resources like residential homes are concerned.

Community social services
Each local-authority area social-service office is a semi-independent unit, responsible for case work within the area or neighbourhood, but working within policy and budgets set by the social-services committee, and implemented by the authority's director of social services. Social workers within each area office work in teams, each social worker having a 'case load' of between 20 and 40 'clients', who may be individuals or families, or both. Most social workers in the team will cope with most problems, but there may be some specialists, eg a psychiatric social worker.

A high proportion of a social worker's time is spent with clients, and a high proportion is spent out of the office visiting people. This may mean a daily check to see that someone who is living alone and is physically handicapped or elderly is all right, or going to see the mother of a child supposedly in care who has absconded from a community home, or seeing a GP to talk about the problems of someone coming home from hospital. It may mean talking to the home-help supervisor to see if a home help is available, or looking for a place in a residential home.

Many clients, though, visit their social workers in the office. They may be young parents who are desperate for better housing, a young girl who is pregnant and needs support, or a mother worried about a truanting son.

A considerable amount of time is spent telephoning – finding out about the availability of aids or home helps or residential places, talking to other social workers, to disabled resettlement officers about jobs for ex-psychiatric patients, to doctors, to the police, to hospital staff.

Every social worker has to spent part of the week being 'duty' officer, dealing with emergency calls and crises. Since it is a round-the-clock service, seven days a week, every social worker also has to be on call some nights and some weekends too.

Every area office has regular 'case' conferences, and there is generally also a regular weekly area team meeting to discuss problems, and allocate new cases. There are endless letters to write and answer, and reports to be written. It can never be a nine-to-five job, in fact hours are often long and irregular. The work is physically and psychologically tough and strenuous most of the time.

Hospital social services
In the hospital social service, most social workers still specialise, working either with patients who are physically ill, or with psychiatric patients and the mentally handicapped. Pre-reorganisation they were called medical and psychiatric social workers, and still are in many places.

Medical social workers aim to see that patients have as few worries as possible, help them (and their families) to adapt to any consequences of their illness, and help to solve any practical problems, such as making sure that children are being looked after while their mother is in hospital. They may also look into any social/personal causes of or contributions to illness; they will explain the illness and what the treatment is or means to patients and their relatives. They may explain the long-term treatments of diseases like diabetes, or the after-effects of a duodenal ulcer or a heart condition. They help with problems over jobs and money. They give information on statutory benefits, addresses of helpful organisations and help with counselling. They help patients accept forms of treatment which may be, for instance, frightening, such as radiotherapy, and patients and their families to come to terms with a fatal illness, or an amputation or other permanent disability. They start the process of organising any home adaptations, wheelchairs or other appliances, working with local social workers or occupational therapists.

Medical social workers are usually attached to specific departments or specialists, eg radiotherapy, general surgery, or paediatrics. Their jobs are more on a nine-to-five basis that in community social work, and they spend more of their time in their own office seeing patients and relatives there, although they obviously make many ward visits. They spend quite a significant part of their time in case conferences, and have to liaise with, for example, community social workers, occupational and physiotherapists, and chaplains.

Psychiatric social workers do similar work, mainly in psychiatric hospitals or wards, but increasingly in the community service. Obviously they cope with the social consequences of emotional and psychological breakdown: patients in hospitals have problems – over their jobs, money, their families and home backgrounds. They may not need physical adaptations to their homes, but they may need considerable help in settling back into the community, especially if they have been in hospital for any length of time.

It is now policy to return psychiatric patients home as quickly as possible, and so social workers may also have to arrange support for them with their local community office. In psychiatric hospitals, social workers often contribute to patients' diagnosis and treatment – they may, for example, try to discover if there are any social problems that may have contributed to a patient's break-down, perhaps interviewing relatives, and at the same time helping them to understand the patient's problems. They may run group-therapy style sessions for some patients.

Community case workers also expect to cope with the social consequences of any illness physical or psychological, and more and more work with people who have been in hospital is being done in local offices. Although hospital social workers are local authority employees, once the patient goes home, the continuing social care is taken over by the local 'fieldwork' team which, because of the statutory requirements of the Mental Health Acts, usually includes trained psychiatric social workers. Here they try to see that people with psychiatric problems or who are in some way subnormal, have the support they need to live their lives as independently as possible.

Some psychiatric social workers work for child-guidance clinics, alongside therapists on the social problems of disturbances in children, particularly within the family.

The probation service

The service concentrates mainly on people who have broken the law, and so is separately organised from most other state-supported social services (it comes under the Home Office).

The 6000-plus probation officers mainly supervise offenders under probation orders made by the courts, which allow them to stay at home instead of going to prison. This normally means a not-so-serious offence, a first offender (young people are now supervised by the local authority), and anyone a court thinks might benefit from such an order.

They also supervise people released from prison on parole, and organise activities for people sentenced to do community service, for instance, doing household repairs for older or handicapped people.

Probation officers advise magistrates, making 'social enquiry' reports when asked by the court. This involves looking into an offender's background and circumstances, talking to him or her and to the family, and anyone else who may be able to contribute. Courts take these reports into account before deciding on a sentence.

They also provide an 'after-care' service for people newly released from prison; they try to help them find somewhere to live, that they have clothes, and help them look for a job, and so on. All prison welfare officers in the PRISON SERVICE are seconded probation officers, so that probation, prison welfare and after-care are now a single integrated service.

Probation officers also act as a kind of marriage counsellor. Formally they are expected to try to reconcile couples when a wife or husband asks for a court separation, but they do try to help informally too. They write reports when there are 'care and custody' proceedings involving children.

Most probation officers work from local area officers. Like community social workers they each have their own 'case load' which can be up to 50 clients, who may be on probation, on parole, and so on. Clients are required to report regularly to the office, although most probation officers visit their homes sometimes, if only to get to know more about the client's background. Probation officers usually work along the same or similar 'casework' lines as community social workers.

They do not act as a kind of prison officer or just try to keep their clients out of more trouble. They look for any emotional, psychological or social causes for the kind of anti-social behaviour which has brought their client into conflict with the law, and try to sort out any other personal, emotional, social, educational or work problems, even anything that is physically wrong. They have to cope with clients' hostility and resentment, and being treated as a symbol of antagonistic 'authority'. It is often difficult to build the essential relationship, to gain trust, and to get probationers or parolees to accept help. Probation officers have to accept that there is not always much they can do for some people, and inevitably some will find themselves in court again.

Probably no more than half a probation officer's 'day' is spent behind a desk in the office. Since a probation officer must be available whenever a criminal court sits, most probation officers spend at least one day a week in court. The office also has to be staffed continuously in case of emergencies. Otherwise, probation officers often work on a 'flexi-time' basis because many clients can only get in after work. Probation officers also have to make visits, go to a full complement of meetings, liaise with other social workers and other agencies (eg on hostel places, jobs, social security etc), write reports, and keep records. See also PRISON SERVICE and LEGAL WORK.

Residential social work

This involves working, and often but not necessarily living, in a home or hostel. These may be for children, who may be 'in care' because they are disturbed or have been in some kind of trouble, or because their parents are ill, or have lost their home. There are homes for the physically or mentally handicapped, and for the elderly. Some homes are quite large, but the trend is for them to become much smaller, to be no larger than a large family. Generally, policy is to return as many people as possible to live in the community, even if it has to be with some form of supervision or support, in 'sheltered' housing. Nevertheless, increasing numbers – over 111,000 people (83,800 as full-time equivalents) – work in local authority homes in England alone (1984), and this leaves out the very many homes run by voluntary bodies (Barnardos, the Cheshire homes, etc).

This isn't necessarily social work in the same way as family or personal case work. In some homes – for the very old, and the disabled – the work is also part NURSING, part INSTITUTIONAL MANAGEMENT, and can be part TEACHING.

A home, for children perhaps, is often 'managed' by a married couple, one of whom has a social work and/or educational background and the other qualified in nursing or institutional management, and together they form a superintendent-matron management team.

There are still fewer fully-trained social workers in these homes than elsewhere. The social work content is strongest in homes caring for children under court 'care' orders, who are in some way disturbed, in homes and hostels for the mentally handicapped. However, even the warden of a hostel for homeless people may have to spend time trying to cure some of the social inadequacy of the people who stay there. In some homes the level of social work cum psychiatric skills needed might be quite high.

Much of the work in the homes is the strictly practical business of organising day-to-day life – meals, getting people out of bed and back in again, seeing they have baths and haircuts, dental treatment or exercise, that children go to school, and some adults to work. It also involves encouraging people to keep up some kind of activity, taking them out and about if possible, organising entertainments, or just talking. Poor residential care can do as much damage as the original situation, and 'institutionalisation' has to be avoided, which needs skilled staff.

In even a medium-sized home, housing perhaps 30 or 40 people, the staff will consist not only of wardens and care staff, but also several care assistants, cooks, domestics, and so on. Occupational and other therapists, teachers, psychologists and so on may visit. The hours are inevitably long, and most people are more 'tied to the job' than in other occupations.

Community, youth, and youth-and-community work

This is part social work, and part education. It has been a developing area, and in many places the most radical in approach and effect. There is a great deal of overlap and lack of definition, and differs in concept and practical implementation from authority to authority, since local needs, real or perceived, vary so greatly.

The work evolved on the one hand from providing leisure activities for young people, mostly in inner-urban areas, and on the other from the work of organisations such as the traditional settlement association and rural community councils. Youth workers may be employed by education authorities or voluntary organisations; community, or youth-and-community workers by social services.

Youth workers still organise and administrate traditional-style clubs for young people living in a particular area. Clubs used to be based on fairly formal leisure (and sports) interests, but today are more likely to be 'social centres' with discos and coffee bars, informal activities often geared to the latest fashion, and catering for younger and younger children. Many young people visit and shop or decorate for old people, get involved in conservation, help in hospitals, adapt and repair accommodation for homeless people, etc. The youth worker frequently leads these activities. Youth workers also run adventure playgrounds.

In some areas the job has widened. The 'youth-and-community' worker goes out into the community, and tries to make contact with young people who might not normally think of joining a club.

In other areas, the youth club may be part of a community centre, set up to cope with needs of groups other than young people. These may be mothers with young children living in gardenless (and perhaps high-rise) flats who need a play group, lunch club meetings for senior citizens, sports for handicapped young people, all of which the community worker may help to organise as part of his or her role in trying to solve local group problems and difficulties – such as helping Asian wives to learn English.

A newly-appointed youth and/or community worker may, for instance, find him- or herself with a building, which may be expensive and purpose-built or a large house due for demolition in a few years' time, and the freedom to plan and put into operation something completely new. Or there may already be a fully established programme. Community, and youth, workers always have to keep in close touch with local needs, which can so quickly and easily change – with high unemployment for instance – and they have to be ready to persuade their local authority or management committee to do something different – a voluntary training scheme for unemployed school-leavers, for example. They also train and encourage part-time voluntary help, work with members of clubs and groups to plan and develop activities for themselves. Youth and community workers 'lead from behind'. They arrange events, like sports fixtures. They have administrative work to do, such as accounts, and seeing that buildings are cleaned and maintained. Much of their time may be devoted to apparently routine things like driving the snooker or darts team to a match in the minibus, or mending the record player.

Like other social workers, youth and community workers try to build relationships with, and gain the trust of, the groups they are working with. Working day-by-day in the community, the community/youth worker gets to know families and individuals in the groups well, and is in a position to understand their problems, and to see crises coming. The community/youth worker is on-the-spot, to talk information to people as a counsellor when they need and ask for it, through the daily contacts over a cup of coffee or tea, during a drive to a match, while mending gear. The community/youth worker can help people through difficult patches, know when they have problems, listen to their worries, channel energies into non-destructive activities, be supportive and encouraging. Some youth and community workers are completely 'detached', and work on a roving commission with young people in the coffee bars, discos, pubs and on the streets.

Some social workers specialise, eg in liaising with local ethnic groups.

This is a very varied job, sometimes rather isolated from other professional social workers, and with very irregular hours, including working evenings and weekends.

Semi- and non-professional social work

A relatively small proportion of staff working in social services are qualified social workers. Within the social services there are a range of other posts. For example –

Social work or welfare assistants are general aides to teams of professionally qualified social workers, doing a range of tasks which do not demand the skills and training of the professional. It is normally treated as a job in its own right, rather than as a stepping stone to professional training. Some 4000 people work (1984) as social work, or welfare, assistants in social service departments in England alone. In addition, there are posts for home help organisers (2600 of them in England alone).

Welfare officers are employed by a wide range of organisations, ranging from voluntary agencies, through to universities and polytechnics. These officers provide information, help, and sometimes services, eg finding accommodation for students.

Residential homes employ quite large numbers of care assistants – over 42,500 of them in local-authority residental homes in England alone (1984). They do many of the practical, day-to-day tasks of caring for residents.

Recruitment and entry

Social-work agencies can recruit social workers without formal qualification (one in five of field workers, and 85% of people with 24-hour responsibility in children's homes are still unqualified), but formal qualifications are more often than not required for community work, and with tight finance (and therefore recruitment) agencies are likely to choose qualified people. In any case, career prospects probably depend on them.

Social work of any kind is extremely demanding physically, emotionally and intellectually. Maturity is essential, with a realistic view of what life is like for so many people, and a stable personality. It needs a genuine interest in making life easier for others, but it takes the ability to stay reasonably objective, not to be easily hurt by rejection, not to be paternalistic, not to be someone who always 'knows best', or who is over-protective. The work requires endless patience, the ability to listen and encourage people to talk, to hear what is not said as well as what is. Social workers must be able to get on with people from all kinds of backgrounds, with all kinds of problems.

Florence Mitchell in *The Social Worker* wrote: 'People in trouble look for certain characteristics in the person from whom they seek help. They hope to find someone who will treat them seriously without being critical or shocked; who will respect their feelings and their confidence; who will assure them that help will be given without robbing them of their independence, and who will give them a feeling of security and worth. It goes without saying that workers must have a real concern for people, warmth, integrity, tolerance, imagination and a sense of humour.' It is not a career for those who are rigid in their outlook or views.

Qualifications and training

Whatever the formal position, the complex problems of social work are easier to cope with after training, however suitable a candidate's personal qualities. It is, though, getting harder to gain training – numbers being trained by local authorities have fallen, to 19.5% of those on social-work courses in 1986 (from

42% in 1980), and total numbers qualifying have also fallen, to under 3200 in 1986 against 3440 in 2982.

The Central Council for Education and Training in Social Work (CCETSW) which oversees social work training, is committed to a revised form of training, which it is hoped to introduce in the academic year 1991-2, although government approval is needed, mainly to ensure the necessary financing. The main changes will be that the two main qualifications (below) will be merged in a single Qualifying Diploma in Social Work (QDSW); the period of study will be lengthened to three years (from two); and both the academic and practical training will be strengthened. It will be possible to start education/training at eighteen, but the QDSW will not be awarded before the age of 22.

CCETSW also plans to integrate into a new Certificate in Social Care (CSC) the Preliminary Certificate in Social Care, and the in-service courses. This award is to be for the large numbers who have little or no training or qualifications at present. It is planned to be both a qualification in its own right, and although most holders are not likely to seek training in (professional) social work, it will provide a route for entry to qualifying training for those who do, and built-in flexibility will make it a progression route to other related professions. (CCETSW is working with the NHS and local government training boards to try to set up an 'industry lead body' for the social care sector.)

For now, however, CCETSW-approved training remains as follows –

The pattern of training is complex, with various different courses for different entrants. CCETSW does not set its own examinations or syllabuses, but approves courses run by individual educational institutions, and awards the nationally-recognised certificate.

All training courses are now broadly based, preparing students to practise in a variety of services, in public and private agencies. Courses vary, though, in the extent to which they train for residential or day services. Some give extra attention to special aspects of social work, eg probation and after care, community work, work with ethnic groups.

Which course depends mainly on academic qualifications and age; the older the entrant, effectively the less academic qualifications matter. No one can start training for professional qualifications before the age of 20, and in practice 21- and even 23-plus is more usual. Whatever route is chosen, some experience of social work (paid or voluntary), or in related work, is normally needed.

Certificate of Qualification in Social Work Fieldwork courses for this are designed for either graduates or non-graduates, with a further distinction between graduates whose degree subject is 'relevant' and those where it is not. Courses are widely offered at universities, polytechnics and some other colleges.

The graduate route (which of course requires two or three A-level passes) gives three choices –

1. A degree combining study of 'relevant' social science(s) with the CQSW course (they must include social administration and practical experience in a social work agency) in a single four-year course;

2. A degree in a 'relevant' social science lasting three years (but course titles

may be misleading and do not indicate whether or not the course is approved for this by CCETSW, so check), followed by a separate one-year (or 15-month) course for CQSW;

3. A degree in any subject (lasting at least three years) followed by a separate two-year course for CQSW. Alternatively, a one-year postgraduate course in social administration followed by a one-year professional course.

People without degrees (and who do not want to study for one), take a two-year, full-time course. The entry qualifications are at least five O-level-equivalent passes at 16-plus† for those aged 20-25 (but for some courses two A levels are also needed). Over 25 it is usually only necessary to be able to show evidence of ability to benefit from the course. Relevant experience is generally required.

While fieldwork courses are now more and more broadly based, they vary in the extent to which they emphasise particular aspects of social work, and it is important to ensure that individual courses provide the kind of content needed for a career in a particular area.

Some courses are specially designed for particular groups, eg –

two-year courses for people over the age of 35 who are sponsored by employers;

one-year courses for students over 27 going into the probation and after-care service (they are supervised and continue to study during the first year of employment);

a special training scheme for long-serving unqualified social workers which includes day-release study followed by a full-time one-year course;

married, non-graduate, women can take a three-year course tailored to the needs of those with a family;

non-graduates with a diploma in social service can take a one-year course for professional qualification.

Post-qualifying training/qualifications for some areas of work, additional (assessed) training may be needed, eg to carry out statutory duties under the Mental Health Acts. It is also possible to take advanced courses in some specialisation.

Certificate in Social Service (CSS): for non-professional posts in the social services, 'generic' courses lead to this qualification. The courses are designed by individual institutions but must be approved by the CCETSW. They last two or three years normally.

Each consists of three units of study – a common unit on the development of services to meet the needs of individuals, families and groups and the contribution made by students' own jobs. A standard unit relating to a group of clients, eg 'children and adolescents', adults, the elderly, communities, with opportunities to develop personal interests within these groupings; and a special option related to a defined set of tasks, eg management of day or residential groups. Schemes include appropriate units for staff who are managers, senior staff and instructors in day services; organisers of home helps or volunteers; specialist workers with the handicapped; social work assistants; staff working in residential homes of all types; care staff in residential special schools.

Students must be employees, or exceptionally volunteers, in agencies approved by the CCETSW to take part in CSS training, including social work departments, LEAs, probation and after-care services and voluntary organisations; be in an appropriate staff group and be supported for training by the employing agency; normally be aged 18 or over; be able to show capacity to complete the course, and if under 21, have five O-level-equivalent passes and/or relevant experience.

Preliminary Certificate in Social Care for 16-to 18-year-olds. The courses last two years, and involve half-time in a social work setting, and half-time on general education, normally including the chance to gain GCSE and possibly A levels. There are no educational requirements for the course, but many students do have some passes at 16-plus, and some courses may set their own entry requirements. Although the course does not act as a qualification in its own right, it is obviously an advantage to have completed the certificate - of those who gained the PCSC in 1984, only 1% were (still) unemployed a year later.

Further information from the Central Council for Education and Training in Social Work or the Home Office Probation Service Division.

TRANSLATING AND INTERPRETING
Introduction   1061
Interpreting   1062
Translating   1064
Teaching languages   1066
Working with languages   1066

INTRODUCTION
Language skills on their own do not, and cannot, make a 'career'. To make them marketable, it is normally necessary to graft on to them (or graft language skills on to) another set of skills and/or knowledge to be of practical use to any employer. This can mean being a qualified lawyer who is fluent in, for example, French both as a colloquial and a legal language and has a detailed knowledge of French law; or a scientist or technologist who is fluent in, for instance, German as a technical language and can translate eg technical material (for eg PATENT WORK) or computer programs; or having business or secretarial training and being able to work in at least one language as well. See WORKING WITH LANGUAGES below.

Secondly, for the very small number of openings for which language skills are the most important qualification it is rarely possible to reach the level of fluency and skill needed just by taking a course. For these posts, it is essential to be able to 'use' the main language (and more than one is usually needed) with the same fluency, freedom, ease and understanding that would be normal in the 'mother' tongue of someone who is both intelligent and well educated. This takes long years of practice (for most people from childhood), and a great deal of time spent living and preferably working in a country where the language is generally spoken. GCE/GCSE levels in languages, even a degree, however good the result, are never enough.

There are only two occupations for which languages are the most important skills, namely interpreting and translating. Both demand exceptional skill with languages and a strong background knowledge of a broad subject field, such as science or technology.

The number of posts in interpreting and translating is extremely limited, and is likely to remain so, since the increase in demand for interpreters and translators resulting from extra work created by the EEC (for example) has been quite small. Competition both for such full-time posts as exist and in the freelance field is therefore extremely intense, and the level of linguistic competence demanded, normally in at least two languages, is very high.

Interpreting and translating take quite different skills and abilities, even personalities – yet it is often only possible to make a living by working as both translator and interpreter.

INTERPRETING

A full-time career is only possible in conference interpreting, and then for only very few people – probably barely 2000 world-wide – although numbers creep up year by year. The Association Internationale des Interprètes de Conférence has some 1500 members world-wide (including 400 in Britain), and admits only 50-60 members each year (on the basis of proven competence to practise professionally and having practised as an interpreter for at least 200 days).

In Britain, most interpreters work on a freelance basis, and have to do some translating as well to live. Outside conference interpreting, only a dozen or so organisations in Britain are known to employ full-time interpreters, and then only in ones and twos. Other organisations, like transport firms, usually have people on the staff in other 'functions', whose language skills are good enough to cope with situations or problems when and as they happen. If not, the firm can always hire a freelance interpreter.

Interpreters are employed for all international 'set piece' occasions, such as disarmament conferences, UN debates, foreign ministers' conferences, state occasions, and banquets, when foreign delegations or visitors are present. There are many less glamorous events too – international conferences, seminars, working sessions between experts on, for instance, methods to improve third-world agriculture or irrigation, in the medical field, or economic co-operation.

Interpreters don't make mechanical, word-by-word translations of speeches or discussions. They attempt to get over the real sense of what is being said, to use expressions and phrases that will sound right to people listening in the language of the translation, to make it as alive and spontaneous as the original. They use one of two methods. In simultaneous interpreting, the speech is translated as it is given, normally by interpreters sitting in soundproof glass boxes, who hear the speech through earphones and transmit the translations to their audience through a radio or telephone link. The alternative method is consecutive interpreting, when the speech is delivered in full first in the original language, and interpreters give the translation afterwards. Simultaneous is obviously better for the audience, but is much harder for the interpreters.

Conference interpreting is generally limited to a relatively small number of languages – English, French, Spanish, Russian, Chinese, Arabic at international level, and the languages of the member countries of the EEC in Europe. There is comparatively little demand for interpreters trained in non-European languages in the West, although demand for people trained in other major Asian languages like Japanese is increasing. Interpreters normally translate *into* their mother tongue, only into a second language if they are exceptionally good.

The only full-time jobs for conference interpreters are with international organisations. The average intake at the UN in New York is normally between three and five a year (the total establishment is only 120, of whom about 30 are British). The EEC employs a 'large' number of staff. NATO's standardisation of military equipment centre rarely has more than five interpreters on the staff, like the FAO in Rome, while OECD has about 20. In all, the total number in full-time work is about 500. There is no real career structure, and therefore no promotion, in interpreting, except for some dozen semi-administrative posts for those who head the interpreters' divisions of international organisations.

Freelance interpreters have a greater variety of work, more travel, but much less security. Most have second occupations to fall back on – which may be translating and/or teaching languages, or something quite different. In season, there is work for interpreter-guides, but they have to know enough about a tourist centre like London, Edinburgh or Stratford, to be accredited and accepted by travel agencies and tour operators.

It is, of course, possible to make an income from translating, and interpret as a side line.

Recruitment and entry Competition for the estimated 50-60 posts per year is intensive. An estimated 25,000 students are at interpreters' schools in Europe alone, and for some the success rate, as measured in terms of posts, is said to be one in every 200 students.

For private-sector conference work membership of the AIIC is virtually essential – especially as it only takes people who have already worked as an interpreter for at least 200 days. To do this probably means working at something else to gain an income, and make the necessary contacts, for some time.

An interpreter needs to be able to translate two languages both ways, or two or more languages into one or two other languages. Also essential are the ability to talk clearly and fluently in one's own language; complete and 'colloquial' and/or technical mastery of (preferably) two other languages, and the languages must be those in demand for conference work. Wide and varied knowledge of as many subject areas as possible is needed: a degree is useful here, but it need not be in languages – law, economics, politics, international affairs, a science, or a technological subject are all useful. Interpreters need also to be able to think analytically, to think and react, and so interpret, very quickly indeed, and be adaptable – to different speakers, subjects, and situations. Interpreters must be able to concentrate for relatively long periods, take in ideas easily (and do not need telling anything twice), have a good memory, and sharp intelligence. Physical stamina is needed, and it helps to be completely unflappable.

Qualifications and training There is no single route.

A degree is useful – and some language courses do train in interpreting (and usually also translating) skills, and students also study a useful subject (or subjects) in depth – see LANGUAGES under ACADEMIC AND VOCATIONAL STUDIES IN ARTS.

Other ways of gaining the necessary skills include, for example –

Bath University: one-year postgraduate diploma specially geared to preparing candidates for the entry tests of the international organisations;

Bradford University: postgraduate diploma/degree course in interpreting and translating;

London, PCL: two-term, diploma course in conference interpretation techniques (AIIC recognised);

Salford University: range of postgraduate courses in interpreting alone, or with translating.

The Institute of Linguists sets professional examinations. Continental Europe has a large number of interpreters' schools, but their success rate is very variable and expert advice should be sought before applying to any of them.

This combines language expertise with the ability to write clearly and well. A translation should read as smoothly as though it were written originally in the language of the translation, make complete sense, and not be 'awkward' in any way.

There is, though, a considerable difference between translating scientific, technical, business, and legal material, and the literary side of translating. In scientific and business work complete accuracy is needed, to get over exactly what the original says, using the correct technical terms and phrases, in language the reader will expect and understand. In literary translation, there is a creative element, and the translation should somehow get over the style and 'flavour' of the original. The best literary translations have an originality all of their own, while not departing from the author's original intentions.

While there is more work for translators than for interpreters, it is mainly scientific, technical, business, legal, and so on, with very little demand for literary translators working into English, translating novels, biographies, or academic studies.

Translators work in a slightly wider range of languages than do interpreters, but demand for non-European languages, with the exception of Arabic, Chinese and Japanese, is still quite small, although it could be increasing. Professional translators rarely, unless they are really bilingual, translate out of their mother tongues.

Most translators who have full-time posts work for international organisations, for example, the United Nations and its agencies, and the EEC, for the larger government departments and the joint technical languages service at GCHQ at Cheltenham (see CENTRAL GOVERNMENT), for major firms – especially those operating internationally and/or who are major exporters to the non-English-speaking world, research organisations, and the larger translating agencies. The number of translators employed in any one organisation is generally small and few teams number more than a dozen. Translators who work full time, while mainly employed for scientific and technical work – translating from, for instance, journals, research papers, patent documents – are usually expected to deal with any other paperwork, such as letters, reports, sometimes contracts, instructions on packaging, and maintenance manuals.

Many translators, though, work on a freelance basis, working mainly for and through agencies, who have on their books people who can translate anything from a particular language. They do not, however, guarantee a regular income. Most people who translate on a freelance basis do other work as well, for instance some interpreting and/or teaching.

Few make a full-time living out of literary translation, and as a possible career it is comparable with trying to make an income out of creative writing. Many literary translators do so as part of an academic career in university teaching/research, or they make part of their income from other forms of writing. A few work for publishers, either on contract for particular works or authors, or even on the staff, but most produce their translations on a royalty basis, as do other writers. Unlike technical translators, who are always trying to improve their indexes of translations so that they do not produce new translations unnecessarily, literary translators quite often try to improve on earlier translators, or to present the original writer in a new light via a new translation. In contemporary literature, writer and translator may achieve a fairly close relationship.

Translating is mainly desk and library work, and tends to be more isolated than interpreting, involving more time and thought. Theoretically the pace should be slower than interpreting, with time allowed to 'polish' prose, but in practice most clients want their translation quickly.

Recruitment and entry There are probably more openings than for interpreting, but not that many. There is also (probably) a shortage of people able to combine a strong subject background in the scientific and technological field, with the linguistic expertise to translate well. Freelance work usually needs some years of experience and some well-established contacts.

Qualifications needed include technical mastery of at least two, and preferably more, languages, to a level far greater than is needed to pass an A level or even a degree. This has to be linked to 'in-depth' knowledge of a subject area, most usefully science, technology or in the business field, to at least degree level. A 'traditional' modern language degree which combines study of the language with literary studies will not normally do, even with a year abroad. Translators need to be intelligent, quick to grasp a point, adaptable, accurate, and intuitive. Ability to write clearly, simply and understandably.

Qualifications and training A limited number of degree courses provide the necessary type and level of language training (see LANGUAGES under ACADEMIC AND VOCATIONAL STUDIES IN ARTS). A degree in a subject useful to potential employers is probably of more value, for example in science, technology or business studies, especially if it also includes one or more languages geared to day to day use in translating.

In addition to the courses listed under INTERPRETING above, Kent and Surrey Universities, and PCL (London) train in translating. Polytechnics, FE colleges etc also put on courses, some leading to Institute of Linguists qualifications.

TEACHING LANGUAGES

Good language teachers are in short supply. However, although languages are taught in almost all secondary schools, the range of languages taught is quite narrow (the main demand is for French and some German). Financial restrictions have, until recently, kept down recruitment, but the government has lately announced policy moves to improve language teaching in schools.

In universities, most academics make scholarly studies of one language and the literature of the people who speak it, and teach within the same area. 'Practical' language teaching has tended to come second, except where courses are biased to teaching interpreting/translating skills, but the entrepreneurial thrust of government policy has been changing this. The government has recently agreed to inject extra funds into teaching in less common languages with the stress on training for business and diplomacy, and some new posts have been funded by industry to improve graduates' linguistic skills. Most languages are taught somewhere in higher education, but the number of jobs teaching non-European languages is very small.

Most intending teachers and academics read for a degree in modern languages, normally studying at least two.

See also EDUCATION.

Private teaching, mainly in commercial schools, provides employment for some, but the opportunities are generally better overseas, teaching English. There are training courses for this.

OTHER OPPORTUNITIES TO WORK WITH LANGUAGES

The usefulness of languages, as a second set of skills grafted onto other qualifications, is increasing, and major efforts are being made to persuade British firms to see that they need to work in the languages of their customers. The EEC, EEC regulations, centralised European bodies (eg the Patent Office), more trade between Britain and continental Europe (up to 46.2% of total exports from 32.6% since 1975) and less with Australasia/South Africa (down to 5.7% from 10.8%) have all been increasing demand for people who can use European languages fluently and efficiently. Now increasing 'globalisation' of business – as in the financial markets – is boosting the demand, and widening the range of languages needed, especially Arabic, Japanese, probably Chinese, and the less common Asian languages too. Exports to some Far East and Middle Eastern countries have rocketed.

Organisations, firms, do not want people who are language experts first. They want people who are, where possible, complete 'hybrids', who are trained professionals in a 'function' like marketing, law, accountancy, and who can *also* speak and write at least one language fluently and have in-depth, practical knowledge of their field (accountancy, law, marketing, purchasing, insurance, trade finance etc) in the country or countries concerned.

In industry, commerce, buyers, salesmen and women, and others dealing with non-English-speaking countries regularly are increasingly recruited from amongst those who are already proficient in the relevant languages, although it is possible to start in the 'function' and then acquire the languages.

In some sectors of industry and commerce specific languages are important – Swedish, for example, for those who import timber or paper. Particular developments may increase demand for foreign-language speakers – the development of aircraft co-operatively between firms from several countries needs managers and production people capable of conversing idiomatically and able to use technical language.

Sales and development engineers, particularly in chemical plant manufacture and indeed in any field where plant and equipment is sold on an international basis, may need languages – German, Russian, Chinese, Arabic – since plant may take a long time to sell and even longer to construct.

Any commercial or industrial company with strong links abroad is likely to give preference to specialists or other professional staff who are able to converse fluently and have some skill with technical vocabulary. Travel and transport firms – airlines, travel agents, freight forwarders, hotels expect many of their staff to learn to speak other languages as a matter of course.

In LAW, universities and polytechnics are now training people in English and French, German, Spanish law, as well as teaching them to use the language colloquially and in legal situations. They spend time at European universities, and graduate able to practise in Britain and another country or useful to firms with a considerable amount of commercial and legal (including contract) work in Europe.

In ACCOUNTANCY a similar range of opportunities is expanding.

Bilingual, secretary-linguists are in demand with more and more firms, both British and overseas, and there are posts in, eg the European Community, and in the Diplomatic Service. They want high-level, 'normal' secretarial skills, plus one or more languages in which the secretary can read and translate correspondence, deal with phone calls in them, look after visitors, write some letters, type in other languages at more or less full speed, and use the different keyboards easily. See also SECRETARIAL AND CLERICAL WORK under COMMERCE.

The Diplomatic Service recruits people first and foremost who will make good diplomats, but also looks for those able to learn languages easily. Although French, and to some extent English, are widely used in the diplomatic community, diplomats generally expect to learn the language of the country where they have been posted. Since postings rarely last more than three or four years (usually interspersed with periods in London), most diplomats have to learn several languages during their working lives.
See also CENTRAL GOVERNMENT.

In BROADCASTING, the BBC's monitoring services employs small teams of people listening to broadcasts from overseas stations, round-the-clock, seven days a week, noting and translating important material and making transcriptions for the news service. The BBC's external services also employ people who speak and write another language fluently, both in programme preparation and presentation, but the total number of posts is very small.

Other occupations where languages are useful include JOURNALISM, LIBRARIANSHIP AND INFORMATION SCIENCE, and PATENT WORK.

Recruitment and entry Unlikely to be on the basis of language skills, although these may be useful, if not essential, for a growing range of posts. First and foremost, though, selection will be on suitability, and possibly qualifications, for the particular function or sector of employment.

Qualifications and training While a growing number of teaching institutions in both private and public sector are providing linguistic training for people already working, it probably makes sense for more people to gain the necessary skills pre-entry.

First-degree courses are now widely available in a variety of different forms, combining a range of business studies with one, two or more languages, most usually at present European.

BTEC Higher National awards in business studies can also include language options, and this may be extended to schemes in other subjects if demand can be proved.

See BUSINESS STUDIES under ACADEMIC AND VOCATIONAL STUDIES.

Secretary-linguist training – with at least A levels, but also for language graduates, leading to eg Royal Society of Arts certificates and diplomas, is available at a number of colleges and half-a-dozen polytechnics.

Some institutions specialise in practical language teaching at several levels – Kent University, for instance, has a diploma in vocational techniques for career linguists which includes applications in industry or international organisations.

London: PCL – has a long tradition of teaching over 30 languages, in various 'packages'.

Leeds, London: S Bank, Sheffield Polytechnics have language-for-business teaching facilities. Eight new language-export centres are being (1987) set up, around the country, bringing together local university-polytechnic-college (and some firms) expertise in a network of 'consortia'.

Institute of Linguists examinations, in many languages, and at levels from beginner through to degree-equivalent, and with a vocational bias, can be studied for at some polytechnics and many FE colleges.

See also LANGUAGES and REGIONAL STUDIES under ACADEMIC AND VOCATIONAL STUDIES IN ARTS.

Further information from the Institute of Linguists, and the Institute of Translating and Interpreting.

The Service Industries

Introduction   1069
Communications systems/services   1070
Hotels and catering, and institutional management   1081
Personal and domestic service   1095
Protective services   1101
Tourist industry   1116
Transport and travel   1117

INTRODUCTION

These industries do not deal in commodities, visible as in manufacturing industry and commerce, or invisible as in banking or insurance. Instead, they cater for the personal needs of the community – food and accommodation for people travelling, transport, the services which protect and deal with emergencies – fire, police etc – and personal care. Obviously, the distinctions between these and other services are very fine and rather arbitrary – many sectors included under commerce, particularly RETAILING, even BANKING and INSURANCE, might well qualify for this chapter, while many of the sectors included here, particularly HOTELS AND CATERING, would qualify for COMMERCE, since their services are sold on a commercial basis. Equally PROFESSIONAL AND SOCIAL SERVICES should at least be considered in this context, although they are rarely so included. The Standard Industrial Classification also classes ENTERTAINMENT (cinemas, theatres, radio, etc) and SPORT as 'services'.

However, most of the services described in this section are generally seen to serve the individual and the community directly. They are, indeed, mostly traditional industries, since the services they provide have, in one form or another, been in use since the earliest days of civilisation, and essential to its development. Any differences are of method (modern forms of transport and communications, for instance), rather than of change in the purpose of the service. For a century or more, most of these services have developed in sophistication, but economic conditions, especially, affect how much they are used, which is a major element in creating, or losing, jobs. The considerable interaction with other sectors also affects job levels. The initial decline in domestic service as a consequence of world war I led to the development of sophisticated domestic appliances and the further decline of domestic work was influenced by this as well as by social conditions, for example. Domestic 'public' transport has been declining steadily since the car was invented.

These industries are traditionally very labour-intensive. Numbers employed declined during the 1970s, and recession did not improve the job situation. Now many sectors are expanding again, and the number of jobs is increasing, although a significant proportion are only on a part-time basis. Technology appears, so far, to have had little direct effect — one way or the other — on employment, or indeed – except in communications – on the work itself with one or two exceptions (eg lighthousekeepers are a doomed species). These industries are largely craft-based, but a few, such as telecommunications, depend entirely on technology, and technology brings changes to transport.

While the economic situation may have improved somewhat, trading conditions are still tough, making a profit – or being cost effective – is just as difficult as in other sectors, and these are among the factors forcing improvements in standards of management. Financing development is also forcing economies of scale, with fewer, but larger, groups in sectors such as hotels and catering. Most sectors throughout the personal services have been short of well-qualified and well-motivated staff in the past, and with expansion, and competition from sectors like FINANCE, the problems of recruitment are recurring.

COMMUNICATIONS SYSTEMS/SERVICES

Background   1070
Postal services   1072
Telecommunications   1075

BACKGROUND

Tomorrow's world, a world dependent on rapidly-transmitted and up-to-date information – the information society – effectively arrived with the biggest possible bang when the Stock Exchange went over to an electronic dealing system in October 1986. Without the sophisticated, high-technology communication systems 'Big Bang' would have been impossible.

Communications provide the practical systems by which information is transmitted, as distinct from the systems which provide the information – traditionally, the letter carrier as distinct from the letter writer. For centuries information transmission was a slow business, and it is really only in the last hundred years that faster systems have been developed. Yet now it is feasible, quite literally, to move information with the speed of light, from one side of the globe to the other in fractions of a second.

Understanding modern communications systems is complicated by the breakdown of boundaries between technologies, which are meshing and merging in ways that were inconceivable only a few years ago. The systems used for telecommunications and broadcasting (radio and television), are converging, and both are using, involving and linking up with computer-based systems. The modern telephone 'switchboard', for example, is effectively a computer, capable not only of making telephone connections, but also of receiving, storing and distributing data. World-wide, totally integrated, computerised communications (including broadcasting) and information networks are a reality – computers can be plugged directly into the public telephone network, and exchange data with anywhere in the world. Offices can be linked up, for conferencing, sales staff can transmit orders from hand-held computers down line to the office mainframe, and working from home for many more office workers gets closer.

Television screens carry 'teletext' – viewdata systems like Prestel, Oracle and Ceefax. Networks, like Euronet, allow data terminals in EEC countries access to data bases storing scientific, technical, medical, legal and business information. 'Interactive', two-way systems, allowing customers to order directly and instantaneously what they see on the screen, to 'call up' their bank statement, are being tried out. Electricity and gas meters can be 'read' remotely. Documents can be sent from one place to another via a sophisticated form of photocopier – 'fax' – eventually letters and newspapers could arrive on the breakfast table via a low-cost version of this rather than through the letter box, although the 'electronic mail box' which transmits messages from VDU to VDU is a real competitor.

Although the microprocessor is crucial to developing modern communication systems, other technologies are just as important. Communications satellites hovering in space carry radio and television signals, telephone and telex, and straight data. Getting on for 100 communications satellites are now in geostationary orbit, and some estimates suggest the number may triple by 1990, if launching problems can be solved. They take at least 50% of international telephone traffic.

Satellites are flexible and versatile, and the uses for them grow daily. Using satellites to transit pages to printing plants in cities that are far apart, American newspapers can provide true national dailies for the first time; a UK paper prints in Germany and the US, and a Japanese paper in Europe, using the same system. Special systems allow remote sensing (as well as existing visible and infra-red) of features on the earth's surface, for instance, detailed measurements of wave heights in the North Sea for oil rigs. Satellites give vastly improved radio-telephone links between ships, aircraft and their land bases, and astronomers can remotely control telescopes across the world via satellites. Firms can have their own dish aerials and use special business satellite systems to carry data rapidly across continents and seas, and similar systems, 'direct broadcasting' satellites, will beam yet more programmes, and information into homes.

Revolutionising the communications business also depends on optical fibre. A 'cable' of very pure glass as thin as human hair can transmit impulses of light instead of sound waves, using light-emitting diodes or laser beams, and is therefore very much faster than conventional copper, and even satellite. A single fibre with a core only one-tenth of a millimetre in diameter can carry 8000 telephone conversations simultaneously. Optical fibre is immune from electrical interference, needs less boosting and therefore fewer repeaters, and is very hard to tap. It can also carry voice, picture and other data along the same cabling. The possibilities will be endless once optical fibre cable is linked to the digital telephone systems now being installed.

Not surprisingly, commercial interests are no longer content to leave the communications business to the public utilities which have operated them for so long, despite the fact that this fast-moving sector carries such huge costs and is a very high-risk area. They undoubtedly see a mushrooming business, and vast new markets in transmitting and processing computer data, in electronic mails and banking, for instance, in providing local microwave links. The success of paging systems and radio phones has proved the case, demand outstripping all predictions, and estimates say that by 2000 some 80% of adults will have their own cordless phones and one in six of all vehicles.

Modern, high-technology communication systems, though, do not need very large numbers of people to operate them. All-electronic communication systems need little maintenance. The main opportunities are for the relatively small proportion of very highly skilled managers, capable of sophisticated decision making, flexible and responsive to what is a very volatile business, and for eg marketing experts.

A high proportion of the work involved in developing and introducing communication systems, initially, is done by manufacturers. Many longer-term career prospects are probably in developing new systems and software for the lengthening list of ways in which computers and communication systems can be meshed and linked – from 'electronic mail boxes to 'VANS' (or value added networks). Installing the necessary (cabling) links is, like installing systems for North Sea gas, a one-off operation, so the job opportunities here are fairly short term.

POSTAL SERVICES

It is, perhaps, ironic that the Post Office, relying heavily on traditional methods and with comparatively little very-advanced technology, has gained considerably from the information explosion, for example, from the ability of computers to generate tightly-targeted mass mailings, as well as from events such as the sales of shares in nationally-owned organisations like British Gas, which have posted literally millions of 'prospectuses'.

Although still state owned, the Post Office has lost some of its monopolies – for express mail, and to charities which can now deliver Christmas cards, for example – and has to compete increasingly fiercely with other ways of communicating, from telephone through to computer-to-computer 'electronic' mail boxes. The costs of keeping up nationwide mail- and counter-networks are high and difficult to bring down, and so the Post Office has to sustain a high volume of business, and even try to push it up. The Post Office says its marketing has to be as 'innovative and dynamic' – aggressive some might say – as in any other commercial organisation. In an unavoidably labour-intensive business, managing people well runs marketing a close second.

The Post Office is being run as a commercial business, working to a corporate plan, a business strategy, and targets – on profit, performance, cash limits, investment etc. It has recently been reorganised into three separate businesses – letters, parcels, and counters – aimed at making them more flexible, and so they can each develop their own specialist skills. The Post Office also runs the National Giro Bank.

The letters business has recovered sharply from over ten poor years, with deliveries reaching a record of almost 11,200 million deliveries in 1985-6, giving a growth rate of nearly 19% for the four years ending in 1985-6. Rationalisation, modernisation and mechanisation have cut the number of sorting offices, leaving the business with four 'territorial' and 64 district offices across the country, with deliveries going out from a network of local sorting offices. Some 80 offices are now fully mechanised.

The parcels business handled over 194 million items in 1985-6, up nearly 24% since 1977-8, although profits are still tight. It also runs a courier delivery service, Datapost, and uses bar-code technology to confirm to customers that packages have been delivered. Streamlined, the parcels service is run from a dozen district offices and a network of 'parcel concentration offices', but with local collection and delivery still handled by the letters business – but on contract to parcels. Again, mechanised equipment is used to sort and move parcels.

The counter business – the network of over 1500 main and 19,700 sub-post offices is run from 32 district and four 'territorial' offices. Over half the work done by counters is on an agency basis, mainly for government departments, eg the DHSS, and this is likely to drop sharply as ways are found to handle the work more cheaply, and from competition from banks and new technology. The post offices have to compete to keep business, and look for new business. Although rationalising, the Post Office is committed to keeping 95% of the network. But heavy savings are needed to finance the current programme of modernisation, which includes new 'Post shops' selling stationery etc as well as running the usual counter services (26 open by 1985-6), cash dispensers, and linking the offices in a computer network. A public 'fax' network is based on main post offices.

Letters and parcels share a sales, marketing, organisation.

A new, £4 million R&D centre is working eg on faster code-sort equipment, machines which can read typed or printed addresses electronically, new franking machines, codemark printing, advanced training systems. A headquarters information technology department develops computing systems for the whole business, working eg on the network for the counter business.

Working in the postal services The Post Office needs large numbers of people. However far sorting and handling mails and parcels in the offices is mechanised and automated, men and women will still have to collect mail from boxes and local offices, and deliver them to their destinations. After 'bottoming out' at 170,100 in 1978, numbers have been fluctuating between 175,000 and 181,000, and in 1986 were over 179,700, including nearly 12,700 part-time staff. If the Post Office achieves its target of a 5% annual increase in mails through into the 1990s, numbers could rise by 28,000 by 1991, but the proportion of part-time jobs will increase.

Mails operations, obviously, employ the largest numbers – almost 139,200 in 1986 (they have fluctuated between 135,000 and 140,300 over the 1980s). Productivity, though, is up 20% since 1979-80, so much more mail is handled by roughly the same number of people.

Letters and parcels each have their own staff now, each running what is in effect a DISTRIBUTION business. Operations are run by managers and 'executive' staff from territorial headquarters and district offices. Operations managers, and their staff, have day-to-day responsibility for the service in their district, with supervisors in charge of the local sorting offices and eg coding desk operations in the mechanised offices. Both businesses have their own headquarters and district FINANCE staff, and the function has been strengthened, since both the businesses and the districts have to work within budget, and 'pay' for the services etc they get from central departments and other businesses. Both businesses also handle their own PERSONNEL WORK, which includes training.

Both businesses have their own teams of inspectors, who travel round, checking the networks, seeing what can be done about problem areas and working on possible improvements. A high proportion of the staff of both businesses are postal workers, actually handling the letters and parcels, or operating the equipment that sorts and codes it.

The national sales department deals with marketing and local sales for both letters and parcels. The managers of the six sales districts look after some 200 sales representatives who work from 36 sales areas. Each area has an office manager who, with a support team, prepares and monitors contracts, arranges sales conferences etc. Sales staff deal mainly with firms and other organisations making bulk mailings, or sending out goods etc, negotiating sales and making sure detailed arrangements are made with the operations and finance staff.

Transport is vital to the mail services. Mainly this means 28,000 vans and trucks etc, which need 2700-plus people working from 300 workshops to keep them running, and the fleet has to be very efficiently managed (over 3000 are employed altogether). The sorting office rail coaches are managed by British Rail, and all the aircraft currently used are chartered, but the Post Office does look after its own 6.5 mile London underground railway.

The counter business is a form of both RETAILING and BANKING. Traditionally dealing mainly with stamps and money transactions, some are now more like shops, selling goods as well as services. The 1500 main post offices, district offices and headquarters offices employ (1986) over 34,500 people, and managers are also responsible for dealing with the 19,800 people who run sub-post offices on an agency basis.

The counter business is planned and run by managers and other administrative staff working from territorial and district offices, with their own FINANCE, PERSONNEL, MARKETING, and CUSTOMER SERVICES departments. The majority of those employed, however, are the 22,000 postal officers who actually staff the post offices, mainly doing counter work.

In addition to central policy-planning and co-ordinating finance, personnel, (company) secretary's/legal offices, public relations, estates office (looking after buildings, land etc), supply, a number of services are centrally-run –

The engineering department designs and develops all kinds of letter- and parcel-handling equipment, which increasingly uses computer-based control systems, electronic mail systems etc. It oversees installation and maintenance of equipment, and liaises with the operational managers. Over 4200 engineers work in multidisciplinary teams – electrical, electronic, mechanical, automotive engineers, computer and applied scientists – and are expected to be skilled as technologists and managers. Some 200 engineers, mathematicians and chemists work specifically in R&D.

Information technology also employs multidisciplinary teams in developing computing systems.

The philatelic bureau deals with stamp design, mailing out 'covers', etc, but employed barely 200 people.

Also employed are eg CATERING staff (the Post Office has over 200 staff restaurants), SECRETARIAL/CLERICAL STAFF.

Promotion is from within wherever possible, and is mainly by competition. Even from the basic grades it is possible to get through to junior management (for postal officers) or supervisory work (for postmen and women), and for some, management. Promotion is now more likely to be within the 'business' in which entrants start, although movement between them is not ruled out.

Recruitment and entry The Post Office recruits at several levels, and created some 2700 jobs in 1985-6.

Graduate entry Some graduates are recruited for their specific skills, in eg ENGINEERING (ELECTRICAL/ELECTRONIC and MECHANICAL), SURVEYING, COMPUTER SCIENCE, but graduates in any subject (with some preference for eg ACCOUNTANCY, BUSINESS STUDIES, ECONOMICS, MATHS/STATISTICS) are recruited for a wide range of functions (and their managerial potential). Numbers recruited each year are comparatively small.

School-leavers are recruited as postal officers mainly for counter, but also some administrative, jobs (no set formal qualifications but some O-level-equivalent passes an advantage and a test set) or postal assistants for mainly clerical work (no formal qualifications but a test must be passed).

Postmen and women do not need any formal educational qualifications, but must pass an aptitude test. The minimum age of entry is 18, but postal cadets are recruited at 16 or 17 (via YTS), normally to transfer to postman/woman at 18.

YTS – about 1500 places a year, either for the postal cadet scheme (above) or in sub-post offices where they learn both post office transactions and retailing skills.

Qualifications and training Full training is given to all new entrants, for some at special training schools. Where appropriate this is for external qualifications. Some 100 accountants are now being trained to strengthen finance, and graduate engineers are expected to become fully chartered, for example. Further training, up to and including management, is given.

Further information from the Post Office.

TELECOMMUNICATIONS

While straightforward telephone systems are still the mainstay of the telecommunications business, 'telecommunications' increasingly means much wider communication systems, as a result of the technological advances already described. 'Telecommunications' now means data transmission networks of all kinds, radiophone and paging systems, telex and 'viewdata' systems which allow subscribers to 'call up' information on a screen. Telecommunications also carry vision and sound circuits for broadcasting.

Until 1981, telecommunications and postal services were both run by the Post Office. They were then divided into two separate businesses. Since then, British Telecom's monopoly has been loosened – both directly, allowing one other firm to compete with British Telecom directly in 'basic conveyance' telecommunications – which may be further opened up in 1989, and for many others in equipment supply and peripherals like radio phones and local microwave networks. BT has itself become a public company, and the industry has a new regulatory body – the Office of Telecommunications (Oftel).

BRITISH TELECOM is still, however, the main UK supplier of telecommunication services, and is likely to remain so for at least the immediate future. Although BT is regulated in areas which will face least competition – eg domestic rentals and local calls – it still has a dominant market position.

With competition and privatisation, BT is a rapidly-changing business, looking for and introducing new products and services, tailoring tariffs to markets and to beat competition. British Telecom interprets telecommunications very widely indeed, and in fact sees itself now as an increasingly international 'information-technology' business. It provides a full range of modern communications services, also selling eg computer-based office systems, networks and equipment. It has 22 million telephone subscribers (over 80% of households have them), and 111,000 use telex services. The viewdata system, 'Prestel', now seems almost commonplace in comparison with the products BT is aggressively marketing.

Business services is a major area of competition for BT, and it is developing a range of networking systems, 'KiloStream', 'MultiStream' etc, mostly geared to moving data from place to place at high speed, and letting terminals which work at different speeds communicate with each other. One of the latest, though, 'VideoStream' is a videoconferencing service. With electronic terminals, telex customers can interconnect, via Packet SwitchStream into other services, such as teletext, electronic mail (British Telecom runs its own system) etc. 'SatStream' gives private satellite links via firms' own dish aerials to Europe and North America, and is now being used to print Japan's leading daily paper in London. BT provides a world-wide direct-dial satellite service for ships, and in-flight calls for aircraft. BT distributes live coverage of horse and greyhound racing to high-street betting shops over Europe's largest private satellite TV service.

The LinkLine services range from free calls from customers to advertisers – and a charity – to financial information. BT has moved into 'mobile' services in a big way, running a radiopaging service which has (1987) 370,000 customers, and the cellular radio mobile telephone network 'Cellnet' (owned jointly with Securicor) had signed on 31,000 customers in barely two years. Mobile payphones go on to inter-city trains in 1987.

The programme to install the £2000 million fully-digital trunk network has been speeded up and should be completed by 1988 (instead of 1992) by which time 40% of traffic will be on optical-fibre cable, boosted by some small dish-aerial systems, and the new technology is now moving into the local network – over 200,000km of fibre are in place. A stored-programme control 'System X' exchange is being installed every day, and all 6600 electro-mechanical exchanges will have been replaced by the early 1990s. Over a million private circuits are now in use.

BT is closely involved in developing and administering international systems, from satellites to the seven cross-Atlantic cables (optical fibre is being used for the eighth).

BT aims to spend 2% of income on research and development – £158 million in 1986-7 (down from £188 million in 1982-3) – and has one of the most advanced research centres of its kind in Europe. About 60% is spent directly on improving network performance and developing new terminals and customer services. The other 40% goes on more longer-term work, often in collaboration with equipment manufacturers in the ELECTRICAL AND ELECTRONIC INDUSTRY and UNIVERSITIES, and in major advanced collaborative programmes in the UK and Europe.

Current R&D ranges from the practical business of designing and developing telephones out to futuristic studies in areas like artificial intelligence – reasoning computers – where work is being expanded and includes developing 'expert systems' (see COMPUTING). The research labs monitor new technologies, explore ways they can be used in BT services, and help develop standard specifications for them. The labs have developed 'photovideotext' so colour photographic images can be displayed in a 'normal' videotext frame. BTRL works on computer-aided design, on speech recognition, synthesis and coding, on radio, satellite and mobile communications, on optical communications, on submarine optical systems, and develops much of its own systems software.

British Telecom is a huge operation, with assets worth £9000 million, and a 1986-7 turnover of over £9400 million. The labour force has been trimmed, but is still (1987) 234,400 (against nearly 246,000 in 1983).

British Telecom now operates as a fully commercial organisation. It is structured into several separate divisions –

UK communications plans, provides, operates and maintains the entire UK network, local and long distance. It looks after exchanges, lines, transmissions systems and switching centres. It deals with customers ranging from multinational companies using highly-sophisticated equipment through to the family with more straightforward needs.

It also designs and develops network services and products for business, and looks after the specialist needs of the largest 500 companies – who produce nearly a third of BT's revenue – providing long-distance inland private networks, including private circuits, packaged-switched data networks, and telex networks. It includes a systems/software house (see COMPUTING) specialising in custom-built computer systems, networked office automation, data communications networking and network management. It has its own marketing division.

It employs most of BT's labour force – currently (1987) almost 200,000, but likely to be cut by about 5-6000 a year from now on, as digital exchanges replace the old electro-mechanical systems, particularly in maintenance, switchboard operating, and administration, but with a few more managers. Cuts of the order of 20% are planned for some regions.

BT International plans, provides, markets and runs the country's international and maritime telecommunications and aeronautical services. It deals with international telephone, telex and telemessage services, direct circuits with other parts of the world, data transmission and specialist business communications services. It manages services for ships and aircraft, oil and gas production platforms etc. BTI employs over 9500.

Engineering and procurement, employing some 7000 people, divides into two. Technology Executive looks after R&D, technology applications etc, employing 3000 people (including 1700 engineers and scientists and 700 technicians) mainly at labs in East Anglia, but also in software centres in Belfast and London, and commercial test labs in London. Procurement Executive employs 4000 people who 'purchase' equipment from suppliers – and this involves both working with firms developing products and systems for BT and looking after quality control.

BT Enterprises has three major divisions. Value Added Systems and Services handles Prestel, yellow pages, new information services, cabletext magazines, TV shopping, telemarketing and direct telephone marketing services, Mobile Communications covers services such as radiopaging and mobile phones, including the Cellnet company. Applied Technology is a systems and software house which markets, develops and provides purpose-designed computer-based information systems. Numbers employed are rising, reaching over 4400 in 1987.

International Products is divided into units, each responsible for a market sector, marketing or distribution. Products include telephones, PABX 'switchboards', and computer equipment. Its banking information system is in use in every financial centre in the world. It employs over 4400.

Overseas Division runs overseas telecommunications operations, and has a consultancy service which provides experts for projects anywhere in the world. Numbers employed are only 2600.

BT has only a small headquarters staff, of under 1300, and a common services staff of under 1600.

BT has a design, development and manufacturing company, with two factories, employing 2300 making and repairing all types of telecommunications equipment. BT has bought other companies to develop quickly in areas like making and supplying PABX 'switchboards'.

Working in British Telecom BT is now in business to make a profit, and as it is no longer a complete monopoly, is having to learn to compete in tough, volatile markets. This, together with the fast-moving technology, is having a major effect on everyone working for BT, from top management through to the most junior employee. The changes are not only structural – staff now have to be commercially minded, profit- and marketing-oriented, and cost conscious. Sales, of services and products, have to go on rising with progressively fewer staff. Schedules are tighter.

Almost all BT employees now work for one of the divisions (above) which are run as independent 'profit centres', almost as separate businesses, and sometimes even compete with each other.

In what is now a hugely diverse operation, it is virtually impossible to describe all the available jobs. Work in areas such as FINANCE, MARKETING, PURCHASING, PERSONNEL etc, is now very similar to that in any other large-scale, capital-intensive, business. The business has, though, some special employment features, especially in –

UK Communications is a unique operation, running the traditional long-distance and local telephone network. It is currently divided into some 30 districts (down from 60 and to be cut to about 15 by 1991). Each has its own team(s) of managers, engineers (professional and technician), marketing, accounts, sales, computing, administrative and clerical staff, telephonists etc. Each district has to be marketing oriented, geared to meeting the needs of the locality, such as the specific requirements of firms in the area, and looking for ways to improve customer services profitably. Each district has its management services unit.

UK Communications managers are also responsible for planning and forecasting, provision of services, staffing, service efficiency etc.

'Telecommunication officers' do much of the day-to-day work of the districts. Mainly they work in one of two areas. In planning, they help to forecast the volume of 'traffic' both short- and long-term, using computer-aided and statistical methods to study population trends, commercial and industrial developments etc. In customer service they monitor reliability and quality, deal with customers' problems and complaints, queries on bills etc. Telecommunications, commercial, and sales support officers can gain promotion to junior management dealing with letters and committee papers, supervising clerical staff, helping with policy formulation, or general administration. All A-level entrants, including trainee programmers and systems analysts, as well as graduates, are treated as future managers, and graduates' first posts may be as eg exchange managers, or a liaison officer.

Engineers and scientists mostly start in research and development – where a significant number of projects are involved with planning and developing new computer-based systems including software. Other areas of work include planning, designing, developing and organising systems, services, and computing. Engineers supervise, plan and organise commissioning, installation and maintenance of the physical lines, exchanges etc in the districts, working with teams of technicians etc. Other graduates may begin work on projects such as improving customer services using information technology, evaluating new computer hardware, consultancy and database support work, developing a new electronic mail system, etc.

BT's technician-officer engineering work force still (1987) numbers some 110,000, although it is expected to shrink further over the next ten years. The work includes fitting and maintaining customers' equipment, installing and maintaining exchanges and transmission systems, servicing complex equipment used in satellite communications, supervising other technicians, working on future planning. They are expected to take on some programming and data processing in future. Some technicians work in BT's factories. A significant proportion of executive engineers and above began their careers in BT as engineering apprentices.

BT is still one of the largest employers of drawing-office staff, although increasingly using computer-aided design. Drawing offices deal with equipment design and maintenance (which includes recording all equipment), and it is possible to specialise in eg work on aerials and other satellite-tracking equipment, cableships, radio stations and research projects.

Some 3400 technicians and mechanics etc maintain BT's 60,000 vehicles at over 300 transport workshops. BT also crews three cable ships.

Telephonists are employed on local exchanges, and in the international system, French speakers are needed. All telephonists are eligible for promotion to supervisor.

Recruitment and entry Although BT is reducing staffing levels as far and as fast as possible (by a net 9800 over 1985-7), staff are recruited as needed – 13,000 in total in 1985. Recent recruitment has included bringing in experienced financial and marketing executives, and BT is increasingly in the market for top-flight systems experts.

BT's CATERING service runs nearly 400 staff restaurants, employing over 3200 staff (48% part-time).

British Telecom continues to recruit at several levels.

Graduates are recruited for specific posts (but are mostly earmarked for management) throughout the organisation. A high proportion of current (1987) vacancies are, though, still for engineers (electrical, electronic, communications, mechanical) and scientists (physicists, chemists, mathematicians, computer scientists) to work, at least initially, in research and development (mainly at the Martlesham Heath labs in Suffolk). Engineers and some scientists are recruited for work on switching and transmission, customer equipment, and computing. Graduates from a wide range of disciplines are taken on in planning, finance and accounting, marketing and sales, and procurement, with some opportunities in personnel.

For school-leavers with A levels/H grades –

Sponsorships are available for candidates who gain a place at one of – Birmingham: Aston U (electronic systems engineering MEng), Newcastle U (microelectronics and software engineering MEng), York U (electronic systems engineering MEng). BT gives training, with project work, in the vacations.

Direct recruitment is as trainee programmer/analyst or junior management (both two A levels plus three O-level-equivalent passes), telecom officer (four GCE/GCSE passes including two at A level, subjects to include maths and physics/chemistry-based science), commercial/sales support officer (four GCE/GCSE passes including one at A level). English language (at least O-level-equivalent) is needed for all four.

For school leavers with passes at 16-plus† –

Trainee technician apprenticeships/factory technician, for 16-18-year-olds preferably with at least O-level-equivalent passes in maths and a relevant technical or scientific subject.

Clerical officer (five O-level equivalent passes including English language) or assistant (two O-level equivalent passes). (Typists and word-processor operators are only recruited when trained.)

Junior drawing office assistant (O-level equivalent maths and English language).

No formal qualifications are needed for general assistants (eg messenger, handywork, lift attendant, doorkeeper), telephonist (must speak clearly, have good hearing, be able to spell and write neatly), catering (trainee cook, assistant, clerk, storekeeper), apprentice mechanic (training includes driving).

Qualifications and training Training is mainly internal, although staff are sent on courses, eg MSc in telecommunications engineering. All staff are encouraged to study for relevant qualifications. BT has its own management and engineering colleges, and a computer school. It uses its own 'Prestel' viewdata system extensively for training.

Initial training for technicians (including those going into the factories) and mechanics lasts three years, with periods at a regional engineering centre, technical college studies for BTEC awards in engineering, and supervised field training on operational equipment. Opportunities are available for more advanced training, with some awards for technicians to take degrees leading to professional qualifications.

Further information from British Telecom.

OTHER EMPLOYERS Competition in UK telecommunications is being opened up in stages, and so far only one other organisation has been licensed as a 'basic conveyor', with the networks actually to transmit voice, data etc physically round the country. After 1989, new competitors are to be allowed to set up networks, to 'buy' circuits from BT and Mercury, and resell capacity to other users.

Mercury is, meantime, the only other basic carrier. It has (1987) built an 800-mile fibre-optic cable network (using British Rail's wayleaves), connecting over a dozen major centres from London and Bristol in the south to Leeds in the north, and centred on Birmingham, and another for the City of London. 'Switched' services for larger business customers started in 1986, and by the end of 1986 30% of City firms were using some Mercury services. Mercury is aiming for 5% of the telecommunications business by 1990, mainly from amongst business customers, lines between firms' different centres etc, but the company is also planning a service for domestic users. By 1986, Mercury had 1300 employees, a high proportion of them working on systems – the sales staff is comparatively small.

In the cellular telephone business, one company is competing with BT/Securicor's Cellnet.

Other opportunities to work in telecommunications are with organisations and firms able to run their own, and this is an expanding area. Examples of firms/organisations with their own (tele)communications systems include the Civil Aviation Authority's AIR TRAFFIC CONTROL system, and the RAILWAYS (British Rail).

HOTELS AND CATERING, AND INSTITUTIONAL MANAGEMENT

The industry	1081
Working in the industry	1084
Administration and management	1085
Craft and supervisory work	1088
Recruitment and entry	1091
Qualifications and training	1092

THE INDUSTRY

This is a very large industry made up of a very wide range of organisations, companies and institutions, with one thing in common – they provide food, drink and/or accommodation, either for the public generally, or for specific groups of people, such as patients in hospital. They divide fairly neatly into two groups. One is profit-making and commercial – hotels, motels, public houses, restaurants and cafes, holiday camps, catering facilities for trains, airlines and motorway service stations. The other is called 'institutional' and is (theoretically) non-profit-making – it includes universities, polytechnics, colleges and schools, hospitals, firms' staff restaurants and canteens, members' clubs, the Army, Navy and Air Force.

After a decade (to around 1976), when the commercial sector grew sharply, and the institutional sector – especially universities, polytechnics etc – expanded too, recession and financial curbs on eg higher education hit both sectors hard. The commercial sector is recovering and expanding – after a brief dip in 1986 – but the institutional sector has still to live with tight budgets.

The industry is very competitive. Costs have risen sharply, and it is unavoidably labour-intensive, which is also expensive. It is difficult to cut staff numbers without damaging services. There have also been outright job losses (in the school meals service, and where firms have closed down). But social changes which have brought more 'adventurous' eating habits, more women working with less time to cook and more money to spend, young people wanting fast food, and strenuous marketing have helped recovery. The institutional sector has to find ingenious ways to provide the necessary service within budget and 'selling' extra services.

All sectors constantly look for new areas of business and for ways of improving managerial methods and reducing costs. Conferences and exhibitions, for instance, not only mean hotels can 'sell' their space, but also bring in people who will usually spend money on food and drink. Universities 'sell' conference facilities in the vacations to make their rooms profitable while students are away. All this implies highly sophisticated modern management methods, particularly in finance and marketing, and hoteliers are going out and selling their services hard.

Technology, too, plays a part, especially on the commercial side – in the 'practical' work of catering etc, it cannot do so much. Technology does, though, make possible meals mass-produced in large central, or contractors', 'production' kitchens, to be frozen or chilled for delivery to restaurants or canteens, airlines and hotel chains for heating in micro-wave ovens. The computer industry offers hotels sophisticated integrated systems for day-to-day running and management – if they can afford them. These look after everything, from reservations and accounts, through issuing room 'keys' (which are in fact plastic cards unlocking a microprocessor-controlled lock), to systems which log guests' use of the telephone and drinks consumed in their rooms. The door 'key' will, amongst other things, automatically turn lights on and off and heating up and down as a guest enters or leaves a room, so saving expensive energy.

Cutting costs in other ways – by using 'convenience' foods and centralising cooking, 'throw-away' products, self-service and vending, and by making rooms easier to clean and maintain – does cut the numbers employed. Staff costs account for 30% of turnover in the industry, so managing with just one or two fewer people makes a difference.

Statistics on the industry have always been very sketchy. The Hotel and Catering Training Board has made some studies.

HCTB surveys suggested (1985) some 190,100 different establishments. owned by about 117,750 businesses, with employees in the commercial sector (earlier estimates put the number of 'family' businesses run without outside help at up to 90,000). Total numbers employed were put at 2.374 million in 1986 – up from 2.25 million in 1981 (but with a small dip in 1982). HCTB expect numbers to rise further, to 2.524 million by 1988.

HCTB has some 2575 employers in scope, employing over 564,000 people.

This is still a very labour-intensive industry which is, more than most, heavily dependent on part-time employees. Only 45% of those working in the 'main activity' sector (hotels, restaurants, contract catering etc) work full-time. In organisations for which catering etc is a 'subsidiary' activity (education, health, travel firms, the Forces, industrial/office catering etc) it is only 38%. Excluding LEAs and the NHS, over 70% of establishments have been estimated to have nine or fewer than nine employees (the largest group, 33% of all employers, between five and nine employees), and under 1% have 100 or more. Over 70% of employees therefore work for less than a third of the total number of firms.

The commercial sector has a small number of large hotel and catering groups at one end, and a very large group, probably more than nine-tenths, of smaller hotels and restaurants. Most 'units', or individual restaurants and hotels, are small, even those belonging to the largest groups. Institutional 'units' may be larger – a university, for example, may house and feed several thousand students and staff.

HOTELS AND GUEST HOUSES HCTB estimates suggest some 31,100, owned by about 14,500 businesses. Most have under 25 rooms and cater for the great majority of people who want accommodation as cheaply as possible. Even the largest groups tend to have a large number of small units – the largest group in the country has some 150 hotels with an average of only 150 beds apiece. A major problem faced by the industry is to get visitors to spend more time in areas other than traditional 'tourist' centres – London, Edinburgh and Stratford-upon-Avon, since most hotels are still sited in coastal areas. Hotels, guesthouses and other tourist accommodation employ some 375,000 people, about 59% working full-time. About half of all hotels have 50 or more employees, only 10% under nine. In guest houses the position is reversed – 66% have nine or less employees, and only 7% over 50.

CATERING interlocks with hotels, in that the majority of larger hotels also have public restaurants. HCTB estimates suggest there are some 56,600 restaurants and cafes employing outside help. The majority of independent restaurants and cafes are mostly small and specialised, with relatively few at the luxury end. American-style 'fast food' outlets serving anything from chicken-and-chips through hamburgers to pizzas dominate the 'popular' market, with many small restaurants serving national food – Chinese, Greek, Indian and so on. 'Take-away' is a feature of all these. Around 252,000 people work here, 58% of them full-time. Under a third of restaurants have between 20 and 49 employees; 54% of cafes have under nine, only 6% over 50.

CATERING CONTRACTORS of which HCTB estimates there are some 8000, traditionally include firms which provide anything from banquets and buffets for hunt and Oxbridge college balls through to a meal delivered to the door. More modern-style contractors are larger organisations selling meals in bulk to airlines, hotel chains, and so on. They range, therefore, from relatively large organisations to one-man/woman businesses. Some 121,000 work in contract catering, about 52% full-time.

PUBLIC HOUSES Nearly two-thirds of the total turnover of the catering trades comes from the sale of alcoholic drinks. Some 60,800 public houses employ (1986) around 114,000 people. Most public houses are now owned by a falling number of BREWERY groups. Public houses are marketing themselves elegantly but hard with a 'friendly' image, bold paint work, a wider range of drinks, food and pub games, catering for customers from as many backgrounds as possible.

Another 156,000 work in some 33,600 night- and other licensed clubs – but only 20% of them have full-time jobs.

INSTITUTIONAL RESIDENTIAL AND CATERING ORGANISATIONS (including industrial and office canteens), include some 36,000 educational institutions (universities, colleges, private schools), and 3000 'other' institutions (hostels, residential homes etc), 47,000 local authority establishments (eg school meals services, residential homes), and 11,500 hospitals and other health service units. About 14,000 firms do their own catering. In all, this sector employs over a million people, including 302,000 in catering for schools and other educational institutions, 214,000 in recreational and cultural service catering, 191,000 in hospitals etc, 124,000 in canteens.

These organisations cater for fairly stable groups of customers – the staff and patients of a large hospital, staff and students in a university or polytechnic. They are now run as commercially as possible, trying to maintain services while keeping down costs. At one end, the rather austere image of the 'canteen' has been replaced by something rather closer to the popular restaurant, but college and university 'hall' catering has moved down market.

TRANSPORT CATERING SERVICES provide refreshments and meals on train, plane and ship, and also at stations, airports, etc – about 1000 'units' in all. Here staff have to be expert in working in confined and unstable conditions, and cater at unusual times. On some train services, and at sea, accommodation is also provided. In this sector, particularly airlines and railways, pre-packaged meals and contract catering are now increasingly the norm. Standards of both catering and accommodation are generally highest in what is left of the sea travel industry, and in the very small luxury-class air travel sector. Numbers employed are about 24,000.

WORKING IN THE INDUSTRY

The success of any catering or hotel operation depends almost entirely on its staff. The industry makes any profit out of providing a personal service, to customers who generally expect high standards of food and accommodation. The recruiting literature emphasises that this is a career for 'people who like people'. To be successful and profitable, the industry needs to attract recruits of as high quality as other industries, not only in 'line' management of hotels and restaurants, and not only only chefs, but also financial controllers, marketing and service staff.

The industry's track record as an employer is not generally very good, although some employers are trying to improve career structures and working conditions. Even those working within the industry tend to be somewhat disparaging about it and to lack self-confidence. Staff turnover is high – 42% of operatives, 21% of craft and semi-skilled workers, 14% of supervisors, and 8% of managers leave the industry every year.

There is apparently a built-in resistance to this kind of work amongst young people in this country, and the industry is to some extent reliant on staff from other countries (best estimates suggest 12%-14% of employees are foreign, as against about 7% for all industries – in London the figure is much higher) where hotels and catering as businesses have rather better images.

It can be a very stressful occupation, with long and irregular hours, and all the problems of keeping customers happy, day-in and day-out. Life is obviously going to be better in organisations – hotel chains, large restaurant groups, universities – where the facilities are usually modern, comfortable, and well-designed, where sophisticated management techniques (especially in personnel management) are employed, and recommended training practices followed.

'Despite obvious employment disadvantages, the hotel and catering industry, offers much to employees that other industries do not; for example, many employees do not appear dissatisfied with their renumeration, few complain of boredom... and the opportunities... for variety of work, personal expression and for the development of individual skills compare favourably with other kinds of manual work. Moreover, at managerial level the autonomy of individual establishments offers comparatively high rewards for most young men and women and the opportunity of independent command at a relatively early stage in life.' (NEDC Report) NEDC wanted more scope for staff to improve their performance and status and regular reliable pay, reflecting skill at the job rather than a facility with tip-getting techniques. The industry can point to some improvements, and emphasises the challenge involved, the opportunities for responsibility and promotion, and also the demands and satisfactions involved in providing an efficient service.

There isn't any formal career structure in the industry and, except at craft level, job descriptions aren't standard. People move regularly, cross from the commercial sector to institutional management and back again, largely to gain experience – career progression is largely by changing employers rather than moving up within a single organisation.

Careers divide into two – managerial and craft. It is still common to move up from craft to management, and there is a difficult-to-define area of supervisory work between them.

Administration and management

Managerial careers within the industry are steadily coming into line with management in other areas of commerce, especially in the larger hotel and catering groups, if with their own special slant.

The Training Board describes the special skills needed as an understanding of and an interest in food and drink and/or accommodation services based on sound technical training and experience, with an awareness of technological developments and their applications, an ability to establish good relationships not only with staff and colleagues but also with customers of all kinds, and to create an appropriate atmosphere; social skills; an ability to deal with practical problems and crises quickly and effectively; an ability to manage properties; and creative abilities in marketing and a readiness to innovate.

Good managers are particularly concerned about improving staff relations, and managerial support for front-of-house and service staff in their relations with the customers, ending the traditional gulf between management and staff which was largely the cause of high staff turnover and over-subservience to the customer.

Modern management also needs increasingly good financial control, forward planning and efficient marketing. For instance, the more competitive hotels now use market research to find out more about their customers, who they are, their ages, hobbies, buying habits, how they booked. They then attempt to match service more closely to customers – or perhaps look for a more profitable group of customers. Management in catering, institutions, hotels and so on is just as much concerned with coping with change, and efficient planning, decision-making, organising, staff supervision, and problem solving as in other industries. In addition to 'line' management then – of the hotel or restaurant – a growing number of posts are in finance, marketing, public relations, personnel and training.

HCTB estimated, in 1985, that about 404,100 people, about 18% of the workforce, are working proprietors (175,000) or managers. Mostly they work in the 'main activity' sectors – under 28,000 work for organisations for whom catering etc is a 'subsidiary' activity.

GENERAL HOTEL MANAGERS run individual hotels. This can mean being the working proprietor of a small hotel with a staff of up to fifteen, doing all the managerial jobs, from supervising the kitchen (and even cooking in crises), the housekeeper, and the front office, to doing the stock control, the financial paper work, and 'marketing' and personnel too.

At the other end of the spectrum, it can mean being the manager of a large hotel, perhaps as part of a chain, with several hundred bedrooms. Here the staff will be much larger – up to 1000 perhaps – and depending on its size, there may be a single assistant manager, or a number of 'middle managers', each with their own area of responsibility – food and drink, finance, accommodation, personnel and training, perhaps marketing, and so on. If the hotel is large enough, there may be assistant 'middle managers', who may be trainees, and supervisory managers in charge of specific departments – the chef, the housekeeper, head porter, and so on.

The larger the hotel, the less involved is the manager in day-to-day routine, and more responsibility is carried by the middle managers. Here the general manager is primarily a co-ordinator, planner and trouble-shooter, making decisions on, for instance, maintenance and repairs, discussing designs for redecorating, new marketing plans, checking sales returns and preparing forecasts, reporting to head office. In the smaller hotel the manager may have to do more some of the day-to-day work of supervision too.

HCTB suggests some 59,400 people were managers, or owner/managers of hotels in 1985.

CATERING AND RESTAURANT MANAGERS Here the work is very similar, whether the manager is in charge of a polytechnic's student meals service, a 'top' restaurant, a fast-food franchise, or meals for a hotel's guests. There are some differences of course. In institutional and industrial catering, the manager knows how many people he or she is feeding and when – university students, hospital patients and staff – who all need balanced and varied meals at set times, and so menu planning is a major function. Restaurant managers, on the other hand, usually work to set menus (once they know what local customers will buy), but have all the planning problems of never being quite sure how many customers to expect, and when.

Some catering managers, of airlines or school-meals services for example, may not be directly in charge of food preparation at all. Their job may consist of planning the service, arranging contracts for meals prepared in bulk kitchens by contractors (eg 450 identical chicken salads for a jumbo jet), and seeing that it all happens. In the contracting companies, their opposite numbers are in charge of food preparation, and their job is to see that the meals are prepared efficiently, and delivered on time to the right place in the right quantities, and control quality.

Catering and restaurant managers are expected to give value for money and customer satisfaction within tight budgets and, where the operation is a commercial one, have to meet profit targets. Even where planning and ordering are done centrally, managers are normally given a fairly free hand to 'manage'. They are usually quite closely involved with day-to-day problems. Efficient catering managers have to be personnel officers, and be good at choosing and supervising catering and service staff, and scheduling work. They have to be good at finance, able to budget, forecast, keep books and records, know how to keep stocks at the right levels, control portion size, and minimise waste. They need at least some culinary skills – to be able to plan menus, control quality. They need marketing and promotional skills, and know how to create the right atmosphere and deal appropriately with customers. They need to understand and take advantage of any new technology.

Industrial and institutional catering managers have to see that menus are varied, balanced and the standard is consistent, but are not quite so concerned about the refinements of service so important in a good restaurant. The level of expertise demanded of the restaurant or catering manager obviously depends to a large extent on the size of the restaurant and the quality of service it aims to offer. HCTB estimated that in 1985, there were 128,000 restaurant managers and manager/owners.

INSTITUTIONAL MANAGERS look after the 'domestic' organisation of places like hospitals; colleges, boarding schools and universities (where they are usually called bursars); residential homes for old people, children or the handicapped; day centres, and so on.

At one end of the scale, this may be as demanding a job with responsibilities similar to, and with many of the problems of, hotel management, at the other –

and for people in junior management – it may be closer to HOUSEKEEPING. It may involve not just the general management of a home or student hall – overseeing everything from maintenance to cleaning – but also include responsibility for the catering (as above) as well.

Institutional managers may have to provide domestic services for an ever-changing population, as in a hospital or conference centre; the population may be semi-permanent, like students, or permanent, for instance elderly people. The manager may have little to do with the 'residents', as in hospitals, or part of their work may involve day-to-day contact with them, as in old people's homes.

PUBLIC HOUSE, 'LICENSED' MANAGEMENT Managing a public house is a seven-days-a-week, all-the-year-round job, closely tied to set (and long) hours, and usually means living on the premises, as manager or tenant of a 'tied' (to a brewery) 'house', or managing or owning a so-called 'free' house. It is often seen as a career for married couples, and is more than just a job, rather a way of life.

Although the publican is popularly seen as a 'host', serving drinks, the work is just as much managerial/administrative. Breweries expect their licensees to meet sales targets, to find ways of improving sales and profitability using proven as well as new (and imaginative) ways to attract custom (food and games, music, for example), to control cash and stock efficiently, and to manage staff (recruit, train and organise) well.

The licensee must have the right social skills and outgoing personality needed for life behind a bar, and be able to understand the licensing laws and to keep stock records and books, stay abreast of popular trends in drinking and pub games and entertainment, and know how to keep the local clientele happy.

Related jobs include managing bars and cellars in larger hotels, clubs, and so on. Some barmen, particularly in large establishments and hotels, may have a degree of independence in running their own bars. There are also openings in the 'off-licence' retail trade.

HCTB estimated that in 1985 123,400 people were working as pub or club/bar managers or manager/owners.

Craft and supervisory work

The industry employs very large numbers of craft skills, and has a quite high proportion of supervisory staff too. It is common to start at the bottom of the ladder, train in a craft, and move on to supervisory work. Many aim eventually to start their own restaurants.

COOKING AND FOOD PROCESSING The traditional, highly-sophisticated and indi-vidualistic skills of French *haute cuisine* are still taught and practised in leading hotels and restaurants, but demand for them is declining and in the industry generally simpler, if still fairly technically demanding techniques are more generally used, with increasing use of quickly-learned methods like frying chicken portions or making hamburgers. Most modern, large-scale kitchens have the latest in high-speed 'micro' ovens, and use convenience and pre-packaged foods.

The choice of work for the fully-trained chef/cook ranges from the kitchens of a large hotel, where there may be a strict hierarchy of chefs, each with their own special area of work (cold larder, soups, vegetables, pastry, patisserie, meat, poultry), each with assistants and trainees, to the small specialist restaurant where two or three share all the cooking. Many trained cooks work in staff canteens, hospitals, universities, schools, and so on, or for catering contractors. Some work on a 'freelance' basis, for directors' dining rooms, for banquets and parties, or preparing business lunches.

In some kitchens the chef may do his/her own planning, budgeting, buying, and food ordering, in some it may be done by, or with, a food and 'beverage' manager or the general manager (who may also be the working proprietor). Some food may be prepared in advance, but food also has to be cooked when ordered, sometimes in front of the customer. In some kitchens, courses or whole meals may be prepared and frozen or chilled. In some kitchens, for instance in hospitals, cooks may be involved in preparing special diets. At the most senior levels, the chef's job can be increasingly supervisory.

Cooking is, at its best, a highly developed creative art and skill, with satisfactions of its own. Despite increasing mechanisation, including the latest in food preparation and dish-washing equipment, life in the kitchen is still physically hard, often unavoidably uncomfortable (hot, steamy and often noisy), with a great deal of standing, lifting, difficult hours and periods of great rush, when it takes a lot to stay calm and produce good food.

The HCTB 1984 survey gave some 728,800 people as working in food preparation – chefs/cooks (some 102,100 in the commercial sector alone), kitchen assistants, counter hands and kitchen porters. (In 1977 HCTB surveys found over 170,000 professional and trained chefs and cooks, of whom 34,000 were working in hotels, 43,600 for local authorities, 25,200 in restaurants, 38,400 in industrial catering, 6700 in cafes, and 1700 in guest houses.)

FOOD SERVICE This is the modern term for waiting. The major career opportunities (as opposed to short-term jobs) are still in the larger hotels and more expensive restaurants, especially those which still practise *haute cuisine* cooking or provide 'silver' or table service. Waiters and waitresses are the main 'point of contact' with the customer, and must always be welcoming and patient, take the orders (and get them right), serve food efficiently, cleanly and unobtrusively, sometimes cook at the table, and follow the formal rules of the kitchen. They often have to help keep the restaurant clean, hoovering etc, as well as laying tables etc.

Wine waiters and waitresses must be well versed in their 'mystique' – which wine should accompany what food, and how to serve and store them properly. All waiters and waitresses must be able to work with, meet and get to know people of all kinds. Promotion is to head waiter/waitress, and higher supervisory positions.

The work is physically hard. Waiters and waitresses must be able to meet all kinds of situations and stay calm, however tired they may be. Social skills, a neat and tidy appearance, physical stamina, a pleasant personality and a good memory are considered essential.

The HCTB survey gave 301,500 waiters/waitresses and barmen and women in 1984, about 107,200 working in the commercial sector.

FRONT OFFICE AND RECEPTION This is the industry term for the people who welcome guests into hotels and larger restaurants, who make the bookings, allocate rooms, do the billing, keep account of the 'extras' (such as room service and drinks) and prepare the accounts. In small hotels all this may be handled by one receptionist, but in most, and especially in the larger ones, there is an entire team, under a reception manager.

Reception staff keep detailed records of rooms and guests, tell the house staff who is arriving (or leaving) when, and about special problems. The front office itself may have a cashier and a receptionist, or a receptionist-cum-cashier. A clerk may look after reservations.

The cashier's office is where bills are paid, traveller's cheques and currency changed, and valuables cared for. In small hotels the front office and the manager normally deal with accounts, but in larger hotels there is often a separate control manager or accountant with a sizeable staff who deal with accounts, wages and insurance, and so on. Larger hotels have computerised systems to keep most of the records, and these can also show which rooms are occupied and which vacant, supply 'keys', keep track of room service and telephone calls, and so on.

Receptionists and cashiers spend a lot of time with customers. The job also involves being able to keep records, telephone work, running around, and so on. HCTB gave 27,300 receptionists working in the commercial sector in 1985 (another 1000 or so work in the services sector).

HOUSEKEEPERS They look after the domestic work in hotels, hospitals, residental homes, student halls. They actually organise and supervise cleaning and general care of bedrooms, bathrooms, corridors, lounges and other 'public rooms' and offices; they see that linen and curtains are changed, bedding and furnishings cleaned and mended as needed. In large places the housekeeper will have several assistants (a 1000-bed hospital needs five assistant managers, 20 supervisors and 300 domestics), in smaller ones the housekeeper may work alone, but each is in charge of cleaning staff, maids, housemaids, linen staff, and may have, for instance, people to do any sewing. Special problems include avoiding cross infections in hospital cleaning. The housekeeper must keep an eye open for problems, and report quickly where maintenance or repairs are needed. The housekeeper works closely with the front office and reception staff, and there is a trend for the function to become part of the work of the front office. It is a 'backroom' job, with little contact with residents except in emergencies.

TOASTMASTERS There are only some 20 toastmasters, who announce toasts at royal and state banquets, civic and government occasions. Training is given privately to two pupils annually by the Guild of Professional Toastmasters.

UNIFORMED STAFF They are the porters, night porters, door keepers, lift operators, cloakroom attendants and page 'boys'. Mostly they work for hotels and larger restaurants. The hall porter and staff look after guests' personal comfort. Senior porters and door keepers count as 'front-of-house' staff, greeting guests, showing them to reception, calling porters, taking messages, suggesting places to see, how to get from one place to another, sending for cars, booking tickets. Night porters may serve refreshments and act as night security. There is a considerable amount of fetching and carrying for junior staff. Hall porters and their staff are traditionally expected to be able to anticipate guests' needs and solve unexpected problems. Discretion and experience are needed.

OTHER STAFF Hotels are often large, and hotel chains may have a number of buildings to look after. Most employ their own maintenance staff, and the large ones property/building managers, surveyors, etc.

Recruitment and entry
The industry takes only 13% of new entrants straight from the education system – 3% (22,000 people) from relevant courses, and 10% (69,000) straight from school. Some 24% are (married) women returning to work, and the rest (63%) 'other' adults.

People aiming to make a long-term career in the industry, particularly in management, increasingly start with full-time or sandwich-based training, or via a formal training scheme with a large organisation, eg the NHS Hotel Services. However, it is still quite common to start at the bottom with training in one of the 'craft' skills, but it should be linked to some form of release to study for formal qualifications.

Theoretically, it is possible to gain entry to the industry with minimal academic qualifications, but in practice, for openings with career prospects a good educational background is essential now, and the best prospects are probably with a hotel/catering qualification (below), although HCTB want to see more people coming up through the industry. The industry has constant problems in attracting people to start right at the bottom.

Management training schemes with the larger hotel groups is increasingly 'structured', and competition for places is considerable (recruiters emphasise that degree/BTEC graduates are expected to have worked in the industry in their vacations). While a pre-entry degree or BTEC Higher is a major advantages, it is possible to get to the top without, although it takes rather longer.

Where the entrant starts depends largely on educational background, although obviously there is nothing to prevent someone with A levels starting with craft training in cooking if they want to.

For the 'craft' skills only a 'good educational' background is needed.

For entry to training schemes giving direct routes to management, see Qualifications and training below.

Graduate training schemes recruit only people with a degree or Higher BTEC award in hotel, catering, institutional management, or graduates in other subjects who have completed a postgraduate course.

At all levels, firms prefer trainees who have already worked in the industry, in basic jobs, such as kitchen, reception, bar and food serving. For some jobs (eg licensed trade, receptionists' work), entrants must be at least 18.

HCTB is managing agent for an industry wide YTS scheme, filling nearly 6000 places a year. Other schemes, based on individual firms etc, bring the total to 8000. The HCTB has MSC approval to double these numbers, but has problems finding people to take up places.

The industry needs people with a real interest in making a success of the kind of personal service from which the industry makes profits, in the people who are its customers, in making them feel they have had value for their money. Everyone in the industry has to work closely with other people, whether customers or other staff. Everyone needs to be able to work under pressure and stress, to have physical stamina. Appearance and dress, for anyone who comes into contact with customers, is emphasised, and may have to be very traditional in some companies. Anyone aiming for a career which will involve supervisory or managerial responsibility needs to be intelligent enough to understand modern business methods; to be reasonably numerate to deal with budgeting, stock control, accounts etc; to be able to organise.

Crafts like cooking need practical ability and creativity, practical numeracy (to measure ingredients), and some simple scientific background (to understand cooking processes).

Qualifications and training
The Hotel and Catering Training Board co-ordinates training in the industry. The Board estimates that 94% of the workforce has no formal catering qualifications, but suggests the figure does not accurately reflect skill levels, and is trying to give employees more chances to gain certification (see 'Craft-level training' below).

Traditionally, education and training for long-term careers in the industry have generally been via a combination of full-time or sandwich based courses in colleges, polytechnics and universities, and on-the-job training – some large organisations and groups have their own catering colleges. There are also some private schools. Up to now, numbers completing pre-entry courses to give better career prospects have been rising steadily, but HCTB is now trying to open up promotion routes for people who go into the industry without relevant qualifications, most of whom start at the bottom. It intends to link practical, industry-based training with the various education-based schemes so that the two are compatible – and industry-based qualifications can be counted towards educational qualifications, and vice versa.

Competition for places in progressive groups giving well-organised training and properly planned career development is considerable. Some students go abroad, especially to Europe, to gain experience.

Management/supervisory-level It is possible to start at one of several levels.
First-degree courses –
Catering at: university – Ulster; polytechnics – Oxford, Sheffield; colleges – Bournemouth: Dorset IHE, Edinburgh: Napier C, Glasgow: Queen's.
Food/accommodation management at: Leeds P.
Hospitality management at: Norwich CCF&HE.
Hotel/catering management/administration at: universities – Glasgow: Strathclyde, Guildford: Surrey; polytechnics – Brighton, Huddersfield, London: Middx, Manchester, Portsmouth; colleges – Aberdeen: RGIT.
Hotel/tourism management at: Ulster U.
Institutional management at: universities – Cardiff: UC; polytechnics – London: NLP.
Competition for places on the university courses is extremely stiff, and high entry grades are needed.

Postgraduate diploma courses (giving entry for graduates in other subjects) at: polytechnics – Manchester, Plymouth/Devon TC.

BTEC awards are now at three levels –

BTEC Higher awards (diploma full-time/sandwich, certificate part-time) are designed for future managers. Entry requirement is as for all BTEC Higher awards††, with some restrictions on subjects via A-levels.

BTEC National awards (diploma full-time/sandwich, certificate part-time) cover core units in applied science, hotel and catering administration, the industry, people at work, purchasing, costing and finance, accommodation and front office operations, food preparation, food and drink service, with option units from, eg food and drink operations, accommodation services, food production, front office operations, financial control, marketing, tourism, languages, small business enterprise, vegetarian catering, information technology. Entry requirements are as for all BTEC Nationals††. After appropriate experience trainees can aim for supervisory posts (in eg housekeeping) or go on to a higher qualification.

BTEC First award (diploma full-time, certificate part-time) includes core units introducing hotel and catering, food preparation and service, and 'the clean environment', plus core themes (people, money, change, technology), and common work-related and personal skills, with option units in eg food preparation, food and drink service, cleaning operations, front office operations, hotel and catering costing and control, nutrition, and catering for eg the elderly, vegetarians, fast-food outlets. Entry requirements are as for all BTEC First awards††. Courses start in September 1987.

The professional body is the Hotel, Catering and Institutional Management Association (HCIMA) – 1986 membership 23,000. Both BTEC Higher awards and degrees (above) exempt from HCIMA examinations, but full membership takes two years' appropriate experience after completing formal training. HCIMA sets its own two-stage examinations also, and some colleges provide courses for these. Part A is broad-based, dealing with all sectors of the industry, and is studied on a part-time or block-release basis over two years while working in the industry; entry requirements are as the BTEC diploma. Part B includes management-biased studies and options – the course can be taken full-time (one year after at least twelve months' appropriate experience), on a sandwich basis (two years), or part-time (over three years) while working in the industry.

Supervisory-level: people who come up through the craft route can take a part-time (usually day-release) course leading to a NEBSS certificate in supervisory studies. Normal age of entry is over 21, and a suitable CGLI award (or equivalent) and relevant experience are needed.

Licensed trade management Training is restricted at present to over-eighteens (no one under that age can work in a bar on licensed premises). But professional standards are rising (according to HCTB).

The British Institute of Innkeeping (formed 1981 – 1986 membership 4000), supported by the industry, is providing training packages, and setting a range of examinations. These include –

A certificate of induction – designed for new tenants, and covering the basics.

Brewery companies providing training for tenants can operate the test under licence from the BII.

Qualifying examination – two-part exam for associate membership for tenants with two years' management experience (10-day training course).

BII membership is open to tenants with five years' management experience who have successfully completed either the two-part membership exam or the exam for the business management certificate which is based on an 'open learning' programme.

The Brewers' Society (through its Licensed Trade Training and Education Committee) has a licensed house course (10 weeks part-time) and a licensed trade catering course (13-26 weeks part-time) which are taught at a number of technical colleges. The Society also puts on short residential courses at its own training centre.

HCTB puts on a number of short (3-5 day) courses.

CGLI awards a 'specific skills' scheme for bar service staff.

Craft level It is possible to start training either on the job, or with a full-time course. While there are strong arguments for at least some full-time study for long-term prospects, HCTB is making major efforts to improve the availability of training and certification within the industry. A range of different training, course and qualification 'packages' is now available, and it is essential to check that recruiting employers are providing training and certification to HCTB standards.

Full-time courses all lead to CGLI awards –

The one-year, full-time general catering scheme (CGLI 705) for school-leavers is generally followed by a two-stage specialist scheme (or one of these can be started direct from school) in cookery, service, accommodation service (housekeeping), or hotel reception. The basic stage takes one year with block-release study, two with day-release, and it is possible to go on to more specialist schemes – for cooks, advanced pastry work for example, alcoholic beverages for trainee wine waiters/waitresses.

Joint HCTB/CGLI certificates are awarded to people who have trained in an HCTB approved establishment under a registered trainer.

There are no formal entry requirements for these CGLI schemes. For cooks some passes at 16-plus† are suggested. Receptionists should have a reasonable level of English and maths. Languages are an advantage.

CGLI also has a number of specific skill schemes (with certificates) – for eg call order cooks, room attendants, food and counter service assistants, and bar service staff. Training for these should take 6-8 weeks and is mainly on the job. The tests are mainly practical. There are no entry requirements.

HCTB's 'Caterbase' is designed to give trainees and other staff the chance to gain nationally-recognised occupational qualifications based on 'normal activities' in the workplace. The qualification is modular. Each module is independent and is a qualification in its own right, but they can be built up to recognise a range of practical skills. Assessment is by immediate supervisors in the workplace.

Some colleges design their own schemes (in catering crafts, for chefs, or receptionists) awarding their own certificates. There are also some privately-run courses (but not all so-called 'cordon bleu' courses train for professional work).

Further information from the Hotel and Catering Training Board Careers Information Service; the Hotel, Catering and Institutional Management Association, the Brewers Society, and the British Institute of Innkeeping.

PERSONAL AND DOMESTIC SERVICE

Introduction	1095
Beauty care, culture or therapy	1095
Hairdressing	1097
Laundries and dry cleaners	1099

INTRODUCTION

Two world wars, social changes, and cheap and efficient domestic appliances, combined to bring to an end full time, living-in domestic service over, historically speaking, a very short period – under fifty years. The laundry and the hairdresser, the beauty parlour and the dry cleaner, the window-cleaner and the daily help took over. After world war II, the trend accelerated. Washing machines and laundrettes absorbed much of the work of the laundry, and the window-cleaner became something of a rarity. Not every occupation has suffered, however. Demand for trained children's nurses (nannies) has not fallen, for example, because the steadily-increasing number of mothers who want to go on with their professional careers have made up for the fall in the number of families which employed nannies for more traditional reasons. And child-care cannot be automated. Hairdressing has survived, using sophisticated techniques to make it essential for the trend conscious, and so has largely resisted efforts to create a 'do-it-yourself' market.

However, many people see these services as luxuries, and take advantage of them only if they can afford them. The degree, therefore, to which they can provide jobs/careers must depend on the extent to which the service is seen by its clientele as essential – hairdressing, for example, has a solid hold on many women right across the age and social spectra, and increasingly also on men.

High unemployment has undoubtedly led more people to try to make an income in this area. It is relatively easy to offer many of these services. The incomes of a high proportion of the people likely to use these services were comparatively unaffected, and are now rising for significant numbers.

Personal qualities are at a premium in these occupations, especially the right sort of temperament, interest in people, patience and physical stamina. Academic qualifications are not so important, although a reasonable educational background is needed for some fields, and is an advantage in others.

BEAUTY CARE, CULTURE OR THERAPY

Beauty therapists provide (non-medical) 'treatment' designed to improve the client's general condition and looks. They try to improve skin condition, to teach people how to use make-up. They help to make or keep muscles firm and supple, to correct figure faults, and reduce weight, using massage, exercise, diets, electrical treatment, and other reducing techniques, remove unwanted hair, clean the skin properly and remove blemishes, and only finally apply cosmetics and cosmetic treatments.

Some people specialise in particular aspects of beauty care, for example, manicure or electrolysis (removing unwanted hair). Some may work in consultancy, in advisory work on the use of cosmetics, but of a particular brand, or as make-up artists for film or television companies.

Beauticians work in the specialist salons of the cosmetic manufacturers or independent firms. Many are employed in HAIRDRESSING salons, in hotels, large department stores, in cruise liners, and in residential health clinics. It is also possible to work from home, either with a room set aside for beauty treatment, or by providing a service to people in their own homes.

Recruitment and entry Manufacturers and some salons recruit people for training. The alternative is a full-time training course (see below).

As well as the qualities referred to earlier for anyone entering personal service careers, beauticians are normally expected to be well-groomed, attractive, neat and with a friendly personality. Under the age of 25 it is usual to have two to four O-level-equivalent passes, including English and a science subject, but schools can ask for up to two A levels. Salons prefer girls to be reasonably mature, and so it is not normally possible to begin training before 17 or 18.

Qualifications and training There is no single, recognised method of training. The choice is between the schools run mostly by the cosmetic manufacturers, private beauty schools, and FE colleges.

The cost of training at a private school is likely to be high, and considerable

care must be taken in choosing a school, by checking with, eg local careers officers, which are the most reputable. The schools generally award their own diplomas, but it is also possible to take examinations leading to various certificates and diplomas, ie

BTEC awards – National Diploma and Higher National Diploma science-based beauty therapy schemes at a small number of companies.

The Confederation of Beauty Therapy: awards diplomas for beauticians, body therapists, and electrolysists – requires 300 hours' training for practical exam and written paper. Entry with at least three O-level-equivalent passes to include English and preferably biology or another science. Candidates must be at least $17^1/_2$.

International Health and Beauty Council: awards a number of diplomas and certificates in/for eg aesthetics, beauty specialist or consultant, epilation, cosmetic make-up, health and beauty therapy, electrology, body massage, manicure, beauty receptionist, sauna treatment, theatrical and media make-up. Entry requirements vary between two and four O-level-equivalent passes.

Further information from the Confederation of Beauty Therapy, and the International Health and Beauty Council.

HAIRDRESSING

A great many women go to the hairdressers fairly regularly, and younger men have become much more fashion-conscious about their hair – 'styling' has taken over from straightforward 'barbering'. Even so, this is a 'fiercely competitive' business, according to the British Association of Professional Hairdressing Employers. Turnover is estimated at £1,100 million a year, from 28,000 salons (down from 33,000 in 1983) employing over 130,000 people. While the industry is still largely made up of owner-managers working from one or two salons, 'multiples' are growing – whilst owning only 19% of salons they employ 35% of the industry's staff. The largest 30 or so run salons overseas, put on hair fashion shows, and have their own, international training schools.

Hairdressers cater for a very wide range of people, from older women who prefer traditional styles through to the more natural and livelier styles of the younger generation, for which hairdressers have had to develop new and greater expertise, particularly in cutting, upon which so much depends in modern styling. The qualified hairdresser has to be able to cut, set, colour, and permanent-wave hair, and dress (but not make) wigs. Hairdressing involves both art and craft – the art of creating a hair style for a client which is both in fashion and suits her (or his) appearance, and the craft of knowing how to produce the best result, and the materials and techniques to use. Most hairdressers learn to deal with the practical side of running a salon.

Most qualified hairdressers work in medium-sized, high-street salons, but there are opportunities in larger salons in town centres, in beauty salons, in department-store salons, in residential beauty and health clinics, in hotels and clubs, at sea on passenger liners, etc. Some provide a home service – for people who cannot get to a salon, or who want their hair done just before they go to an event. It is possible to work abroad, especially in European resorts popular with English-speaking tourists.

go to an event. It is possible to work abroad, especially in European resorts popular with English-speaking tourists.

Film and television work offers a very limited number of openings for skilled hairdressers, and they must usually also know how to set hair in historical styles, and have make up training.

While many young men and women want to own their own salons eventually, the trend is to larger firms running 'chains', and the investment involved is substantial. Hairdressing is a business like any other, and so owner-managers, or managers for multiples need management training, an ability to handle staff and to to organise.

Recruitment and entry Entry is via one of, a three-year apprenticeship, a BAPHE-run YTS scheme (2000 places in 400 salons), a JTS scheme, or a full-time course at an FE college, or private school (but it may be difficult to gain nationally-recognised qualifications).

A 'good' educational background, with some passes, including a science, at 16-plus† is probably needed to get a place in a good salon or on a full-time course. The normal entry age is between 16 and 18.

Hairdressers need artistic and creative ability, manual dexterity, and should be friendly people, who enjoy working with customers. Conventional employers generally expect entrants to be well groomed, to look neat and be tidy, but some popular styles clash with this – and hairdressers promoting them like their staff to 'advertise' the newest styles – so it is a matter of judging what a particular employer may want. Adaptability, and the kind of intelligence which can keep pace with fashion changes, are a considerable advantage. Business skills are also useful.

Physical stamina is essential – most salons are very busy places, with long hours of standing, and usually at least some evening work. Salons will not normally accept entrants with major skin problems.

Qualifications and training The industry has (spring 1987) just agreed a new national training scheme, which is planned to be fully established as the only means of entry by 1990. This 'nationally-preferred scheme' will expect trainees to complete 41 different practical modules (eg cutting hair, identifying scalp diseases), but there will be no final exams. The foundation certificate is a joint Hairdressing Training Board/CGLI award. Certificates of achievement will record passes in individual modules, which are free standing. No periods of study, or time limits on completing the modules, are set.

Traditionally, hairdressers are trained under an apprenticeship system, – now partly replaced by YTS – but it is equally possible to take a full-time course at a college of further education.

Apprenticeships last some three years, under a master hairdresser. Choice of salon is crucial. It is important to know what training is given, and what arrangements are made for release to study for CGLI 300 at college. Entry via BAPHE's two-year YTS scheme may well be an advantage, since the training is laid down nationally, including 20 weeks' off-the-job at college or an in-company school. YTS students who gain their certificate of competence can go on to complete the final year of the standard apprenticeship. Training should now be as the 'nationally-preferred' scheme (above) administered by the recently-formed (1986) Hairdressing Training Board.

FE college courses normally lasts two years full-time, but students are generally expected to gain a year's experience as well (short-term, intensive courses at commercial hairdressing schools are not recommended by the professional bodies). The single, standard examination, is the two-stage CGLI 300 in ladies' or mens' hairdressing examination.

The National Diploma in Hairdressing is a joint award from the Guild of Hairdressers (1500 members) and the National Hairdressers' Federation. The practical test and two-hour exam papers can be taken by anyone who has completed 85% of a recognised training course, or is already certified by the Hairdressing Training Board.

Further information from the Hairdressing Training Board, the National Hairdressers' Federation and the Guild of Hairdressers.

LAUNDRIES AND DRY CLEANERS

The industry has been suffering from substantial inroads into business since the end of world war II, particularly competition from self-service launderettes and the washing machine, steadily developing in technical sophistication ever since its invention. Easy-to-wash materials, have cut use of laundries etc still further. Increasing automation too has helped to cut the number of people working in laundries. Numbers employed are no longer published separately, but in 1983, it was under 40,000, against 126,000 in the late 1960s, and in dry-cleaning to under 19,000, down from 45,000.

The industry is dominated by the larger firms whose laundering and cleaning operations are done in large factories, with collection and delivery increasing via retail outlets – few firms operate door-step deliveries. However, although the number of small, independent firms is still falling, at least in urban areas there is some return to the local 'valeting', on-the-premises cleaning and pressing, made possible by modern, compact cleaning machinery.

A high proportion of the people working in the industry are semi-skilled. The most skilled tasks in the laundering and cleaning processes themselves are in, for example, hand-pressing, care of specialist materials or garments (eg leather) and removal of difficult stains. It is here that there has been the greatest fall in employment. There are, however, career opportunities, even if the actual number of openings is relatively small, in laundry and dry-cleaning technology and engineering, and in supervisory and managerial work.

Engineers and technologists develop new equipment and techniques, both to improve the service offered and to cope with new materials. Efficient management is crucial in an industry constantly fighting to maintain its position.

Training etc The industry's needs for senior staff are met by –

Derbyshire CHE with a BTEC Higher National Diploma in textile care, a two-year sandwich course for management trainees. The course covers applied science, engineering, textiles, statistics, computing, work study, management, and cleaning technology, textile control, marketing, distribution and transport etc. It gives licentiate membership of the Textile Institute and the Guild of Cleaners and Launderers national diploma.

Entry qualifications are at least four GCE/GCSE passes including one at A level, with subjects include maths, a physical science, and one testing use of English, or an equivalent.

Further information from the Association of British Laundry, Cleaning and Rental Services.

NURSERY AND CHILDREN'S NURSES

These are not 'nurses' in the accepted sense of the word, in that they look after children who are not (normally anyway) sick. Mostly they work with children under the age of seven.

The falling birth rate has been counterbalanced by the rising number of women with professional careers to keep up demand for people prepared to look after young children – usually in the pre-school age group – in the family, at home. This modern version of the 'nanny' role is rather different from the traditional one. Nannies (for want of a better title) do not nowadays work just for wealthier families. Rather more of the opportunities are with families where both parents are professional people, out at work all day. Here the nanny cares for under-fives during the parents' working day, and younger school-children after school and during the holidays. Such nannies have a more 'normal' working week, with free week-ends and evenings, but they are mostly on their own with the children for long periods. Some families share nannies, and some nannies organise local playgroups. Some nannies work for agencies, as 'temps'.

Nursery and children's nurses also work in nursery classes and infant 'play schools' run by local education authorities (see EDUCATION), day and residential nurseries run by local authority social service departments, privately-run nursery schools and playgroups, and hospitals (see also HEALTH SERVICES). A few work on cruise-liners, in hotels and holiday camps in resorts in Britain and abroad, as children's 'hostesses'. Opportunities in local-authority classes and nurseries have been severely reduced by cuts in public expenditure – there are now under 600 local authority day nurseries.

In all these, a children's nurse usually looks after a small group of babies, or young children (the rules for local-authority nurseries say four or five children to each 'nurse'). The staff organise play activities for them, read them stories, take them out, as well as coping with feeding, washing, toileting and so on. The work varies somewhat between different organisations. In nursery schools, for instance, nurses work under a trained infant teacher. In local-authority nurseries, both matrons and nurses are usually qualified nursery nurses. Local-authority nursery places now provide only for babies and under-fours in 'special need', for example the children of single parents, handicapped children and children with difficult home backgrounds, so the work is especially demanding. In hospitals, nursery nurses can look after new-born babies, or help to amuse sick children. In both the home and the nursery, children's nurses are generally expected to cope with routine chores. Most nursery nurses work very hard.

Apart from promotion to matron in local-authority nurseries, there is little or no real career structure in working with children. It is easy to gain variety by changing posts – families tend to keep nannies for much shorter periods now –

and there are reasonable opportunities to work abroad for qualified people with plenty of experience.

Recruitment and entry It is always possible to find work looking after children without qualifications and to learn on-the-job, but it is sensible to take a training course as early as possible.

Theoretically, no formal educational entry qualifications are set. In practice, the competition for training places means colleges are able to ask for several O-level-equivalent passes, and some even one A level (private colleges routinely ask for three O-level-equivalent passes), and in any case the course syllabus would be hard to study for anyone not able to gain O levels.

Personal qualities do, however, count most. Obviously interest in young children is important. To develop their full potential and be emotionally stable, young children need to be cared for by people who are themselves emotionally stable and patient, imaginative (to cope with the 'creative play'), reasonably intelligent, and happy to spend their time talking to young children. People working in families need to be able to get on with parents as well as children.

Qualifications and training Training is on a two-year, full-time course at either one of about 150 further education colleges (about 5000 places a year) or at one of three private colleges. All students at present take the Nursery Nurses Examinations Board's certificate examination (English and Welsh or Scottish), and the private colleges also award their own. The NNEB syllabus, currently (1987) being revised, covers private family work as well as training for nurseries. Three fifths of the course is 'academic' (and goes into areas like 'role and role conflict' as well as constructive play, safety, nutrition, emotional and intellectual development), and the rest practical, in nurseries and now, in families. Training can start at sixteen.

Most girls from private colleges still become nannies. About 40-50% of those trained in FE colleges go to work for families, about 15% are recruited by LEAs, around 10% for health authorities, and well under 10% for social services.

Further information from the Nursery Nurses Examination Board.

PROTECTIVE SERVICES

Introduction   1101
The fire services   1102
The police   1105
The prison service   1113
Private security operations   1115

INTRODUCTION

Here the purpose is to provide the community with services to protect it against hazards ranging from fire to theft, and to help people involved when such events happen. Partly this is enforcing the law and keeping order. Most of these services are provided by the state, through the fire, police and prison services, as a legal responsibility, but private, commercial security organisations have been expanding.

Traditionally, these services have much in common, with each other and with the ARMED FORCES, in that they have similar, semi-military organisational patterns, with very formal hierarchical structures and traditional discipline, and uniforms are worn. However, within the formal framework, these organisations are developing modern management methods, making use of new technology, and (sometimes) taking into account the results of research in the behavioural and clinical sciences, so that some simplistic attitudes, seeing the world in terms of black and white, have changed.

Until job opportunities declined so sharply, these services did not attract many young people, who grew up to see the police as rather remote men and women, most often in a speeding car or van. Those who do consider them are often motivated by the security, and by the idea of a life of activity, variety, even excitement and risk. They are often seen as a substitute for a life in the Forces, either after leaving them, or as a home-based alternative, while many choose the prison or fire service because they do not qualify for the police.

A high proportion of people do not start straight from school. The average age of entry is in the mid-20s, many having tried several other occupations before entry, including military service – although the influence of this is declining sharply amongst younger entrants. Although these services, and in particular the police, are trying to raise the educational standards for entry, many still start with craft or related skills. Promotion is better with post-school education and training.

People working in these services see them as giving security, and as being worthwhile, since they help the community. The pension rights, the comradeship, and reasonable promotion prospects are attractive, and the work is often interesting and varied. However, there is shiftwork and relatively long hours, discipline, the periods of boredom and tedium, routine chores, and such close ties to the job that, even when officially off duty, officers have to be ready to deal with an emergency. In all these careers too, the element of danger and risk may be exciting for the younger man or woman, but can become worrying when they marry and have family responsibilities.

THE FIRE SERVICES

Coping with fire-fighting and prevention is mainly the responsibility of local authorities, under the supervision of the Home and Scottish Offices. In all, there are some 64 fire authorities in the UK, mainly at county level. However, these are not the only fire-fighting organisations – others include the Ministry of Defence for the Army and the Air Force, the British Airport Authority's fire services, and some major firms, eg oil companies, have their own.

The only legal responsibility on the fire services is to fight fires, from the smallest domestic blaze in an over-heated frying pan, to major outbreaks in large factories (and obviously there are more of the former than of the latter). However, fire authorities must also see that there is a comprehensive system of fire prevention and control in, for example, places of entertainment, public resorts and some kinds of residential accommodation, as well as under the Factories and Offices, Shops and Railway Premises Acts. Fire services also provide advisory services on fire prevention and spread, and escape methods.

Fire authorities can also use their fire brigades and equipment for emergencies other than fire-fighting, and of course they do. They deal with the tanker that crashes and pours an unnamed but toxic chemical across the high street; they cut and lift apart crashed trains or cars, deal with the consequences of floods, extract children from between railings, get cats down from trees, and cope when old buildings collapse and cranes topple over. Although they don't usually charge for these services (except where the fire brigade may want to deter an adventurer from constantly repeating a mistake), the fire brigade can also be employed on a commercial basis, in emptying and filling swimming pools, water tanks and lakes, for instance.

The statistics are impressive. The number of fire and special service calls fluctuate between about 290,000 and over 500,000 a year. The fire authorities control about 1800 fire stations (including two on the river in London), operating about 5000 fire-fighting appliances (including pumps, turntable ladders, water and emergency tenders, and hose-laying lorries).

The expertise demanded of the fire services increases steadily. Office and residential tower blocks, massive chemical plants, juggernaut tanker lorries, and modern materials (which produce toxic fumes on burning), present more and more new problems to be solved even as the number of hazards caused by lack of fire precautions in older buildings is slowly reduced. The whole of the country has been surveyed for fire risk, right down to the street and individual type of building. Each district is classified by degree of risk, and the services geared accordingly – high-risk areas include congested docks and concentrated heavy industry, while risks in non-forested rural areas are treated as relatively low. The services make increasing use of modern technology, from a computer-based information retrieval system on dangerous compounds to infra-red thermal cameras (to see through smoke) in remote monitoring and directing fire-fighting operations.

Working for the fire services
About 40,000 people work for the country's fire services full-time (end-1985), and a further 21,000 part-time or as volunteers. Most full-time staff and virtually all part-timers are 'operational' firemen (with just 22 women on the engines). Over 1500 men but mostly women now, run control and watch rooms. Large cities and urban areas are now mostly served by full-time forces, but some 60% of county fire brigades are still staffed by part-time firemen, some of whom are paid a retainer and a fee per incident attended, and some are volunteers. The size of individual services varies from 7000 full-time staff in Greater London to 30 full-time and 257 part-time in Powys in Wales.

Almost all those working in the fire service are trained, operational fire-fighters – the number of purely administrative posts for fire service personnel is strictly limited to the senior officer levels, with most general administrative and clerical work done by local authority staff. There are, however, a number of specialist posts at officer level, in fire prevention, training, communications, transport, water supplies, and so on. Since every area faces different problems and hazards, practice varies from locality to locality, but in general the size of the staff of each station varies according to the number of appliances; the rule of thumb is that each appliance needs five personnel to crew it, but some 25 are needed to operate a pump at all times.

All calls for assistance come through to a control room, in the larger services a central control at brigade headquarters. While the message is being taken down, maps and detailed street indexes are consulted, and the charts which show which appliances are where, so particular stations can be alerted at the touch of a button. Even before a message is fully received, the appliance is manned with its engine running, ready to leave within a minute. Radio contact with the appliance gives the crew continuous information. After the fire, detailed reports must be prepared. More and more brigades use computer-based control and information systems.

In between fire and other emergency calls, on-duty crews have other duties both inside and outside the station – inside they maintain the appliances, man the watch-room, keep the station clean, and carry out drills and exercises. They also have lectures and demonstrations, to maintain and improve fire-drill efficiency. Some station duties are carried out by a relatively small number (only 1500 country-wide) of firewomen and men, who work mainly in the increasingly sophisticated control or watch-room. Outside the station, firemen spend time trying to improve fire prevention, visiting shops, offices, factories, cinemas, even homes, to recommend and advise, and giving lectures on fire precautions. At night, crews sleep between emergency calls, but on both day and night shifts an emergency call means an automatic reaction, to stop whatever they may be doing – eating, sleeping or station duties – and reach the appliance as fast as possible, so that the pattern of firefighters' working lives is totally unpredictable.

There are also a small number of jobs in fire prevention and control – mainly these are in the Joint Fire Research Organisation which is supported by central and local government, and a Home Office unit which specialises in studying operational problems. There are also some opportunities in providing packaged and programmed learning material.

All firefighters have equal opportunities for promotion based on ability, not academic background on entry. All have to work their way up from junior firefighter and firefighter, through leading firefighter to officer, although for those with the right aptitudes it is possible to reach station officer by the mid-20s. Up to leading firefighter promotion is by examination, thereafter by interview and selection.

Recruitment and entry Recruitment has been rising steadily over the 1980s, to reach 1635 in 1985 (against just under 1000 in 1981) – and wastage rates are fairly low.

Although most people join the fire service in their 20s, it is possible to start at eighteen (junior entry for sixteen- and seventeen-year-olds has ended, at least for the time being), with a normal upper limit of 30, but ex-regular servicemen/women may be accepted up to the age of 34. There is no direct officer recruitment.

Formal academic qualifications are not set in England and Wales, although the level of competition is now such that passes at 16-plus† in at least English, maths and a science are probably needed. In Scotland two SCE O-grades are required, preferably in English and mathematics or a science. All recruits must be extremely fit physically, must be not less than 5 feet six inches in height, with unexpanded chest measurement of 36 inches and chest expansion of 2 inches, and the ability to carry a man weighing 12 stone 100 yards in a minute.

This test is a stiff hurdle for many women, and the service has been having problems persuading them to apply.

Qualifications and training Firefighters are given thorough and extensive training. Every new recruit spends up to 16 weeks at training school (at one of 17, most based on larger fire authorities). The courses combine lectures on everything from building construction through to first aid and fire-station work, with practical exercises in fire-fighting and emergencies, often in conditions which very realistically simulate the real thing. Drivers are specially trained, and must gain an HGV licence.

Firefighters go on studying and training throughout their careers, and promotion largely depends on completing the appropriate practical, and some written, examinations. Many firefighters study for membership of the Institution of Fire Engineers, although the examinations are not compulsory. Officers are given additional training in residential courses at the fire service college.

Further information from the Home Office Fire Department, the Scottish Home and Health Department, individual fire brigades, the British Airports Authority, or the Ministry of Defence.

THE POLICE

The police, according to a particularly succinct definition, are responsible for saving people from the worst they can do to themselves and to each other. Their position and powers are balanced delicately on typically traditional British theories of the relations between the state and the police on the one hand, and the police and the courts on the other, whilst emphasising that the police are not an arm of the state and have never been 'recognised, either in law or by tradition, as a force distinct from the general body of citizens'.

A police officer, the official definition says, is not an employee or agent of either the local police authority or the central government, but is 'an independent holder of public office and exercises his [*sic*] powers as a constable, whether conferred by statute or by common law, by virtue of his office; he is an agent of the law of the land...' Although all police officers can exercise their powers as constables anywhere in the country, therefore, as members of a disciplined body they are subject to the orders of superior officers. Constables may not take any active part in politics, to maintain impartiality, but they do not lose any of their constitutional rights as citizens – they can vote in elections and so on.

The police protect people and property, prevent and detect crime and look for the culprits, enforce laws of all kinds, control 'traffic' (people, cars, buses etc) in the street and other public places, deal with all kinds of emergencies and generally provide 'assistance', advice, and information. There are ordinary, everyday problems of the local community to solve, crowds of all kinds to control, and crises – from 'terrorist' bombs and gas explosions through to missing children – to deal with. Deterrence – simply being around on the streets, in crowds, at events – is a major part of the job, as is a lot of patient backroom work, both planning and detecting. The police acquired both extra powers and extra rules – mainly giving suspects further rights – in 1985, and must now keep to tighter codes of practice.

It is an enormous job, and a difficult one, demanding hard decisions and exceptional tact, because maintaining 'law and order', and combating crime can so easily mean acting in ways which people see as infringing traditional personal freedoms. The police can never hope to prevent or detect 100% of all law breaking, so it is an endless balancing act and a hard battle to keep up, let alone improve, police effectiveness in a rapidly-changing society, and be the fair and impartial police force the public expects. The 'rule of law' is only possible with the total support of the public for what the police do, and the police always have to be sensitive to public opinion. The problems get worse when 'the public' has conflicting opinions.

The police have been under intense public scrutiny for some time now. Policing raises increasingly complex problems, to which it is correspondingly hard to find answers. Questions are raised on the way the police respond – to strikes, to inner-city disturbances – on their use of firearms, about their professionalism, the policing system generally, and the way police forces are organised. Many thousands of words have been written for and against community policing and relations with ethnic groups, on the accountability of the police to the community, on complaints procedures, on whether or not the police force has to introduce modern management methods, on police training, and so on. Lord Scarman analysed the principles of policing and how it should be carried out, back in 1981, but events have to some extent overtaken his report. The police, like everyone else, are having to learn to cope with a world of change, to be flexible, and have to be better trained, and educated, to cope.

The 52 separate police forces divide the country between them, most covering relatively large areas (to give economies of scale). They range in size from London's Metropolitan Police of over 26,000 to mainly rural forces with under 1000 officers. Each is independent, policing a county, or two or more 'joint' local authority areas. Mostly they are 'maintained' by a police authority which is a kind of local authority committee, but in London the Home Secretary is responsible for the Metropolitan Police. The Home and Scottish Offices nationally oversee police services generally, but they have no day-to-day involvement. They set guidelines and make suggestions, approve the appointment of chief constables, make regulations on conditions of service, provide common services (below) and do research, develop a planning/programming/budgeting system for the forces and for medium- and long-term planning of police resources.

But although each force is still completely autonomous and indeed often has a distinctive character of its own, co-operation between them has necessarily been increasing for many years. A major example is the regional crime squads, made up of teams of experienced detectives from several forces, which investigate major crimes which usually mean enquiries in more than one police area. They are supported by a network of regional criminal intelligence offices.

Some services are organised nationally, and centralisation of services is also increasing. The criminal investigation department (CID), helps, on request, any other police force in criminal investigations. Special branch deals with 'offences against state security, terrorist and subversive organisations, protection duties, and enquiries about aliens'. The fraud squad is run jointly by the Metropolitan Police and the City of London Police, and the National Central Bureau handles Interpol business for Britain. The Home Office's police department houses units like the scientific research and development branch, criminal records and the police national computer unit, the fingerprint bureau, telecommunications, and the forensic science labs. Forces report all recordable offices to a national identification bureau.

Science and technology plays a major or increasing part, wherever feasible. Local forces are linked via terminals directly to the national computer with its complete file on vehicle registrations, and index to the fingerprint file. Computers are now being tried out in processing and analysing all the information collected on serious crimes, like murders. Police officers' personal radios are linked to increasingly sophisticated control systems in police headquarters. Forensic services are equipped with the latest automated equipment for scientific analysis, and molecular biology has just made a major new breakthrough, to give completely foolproof 'genetic fingerprinting'.

Working in the police
Between them, the regular police authorities employ (1986) getting on for 135,000 police (including nearly 12,000 policewomen), some 4800 traffic wardens, and another 40,000 'civilians'. Numbers have been rising since 1979. Graduates now make up 4.45% of the police in England, Wales, and Northern Ireland.

While there are a great many different jobs in the police force, most people spend a large part of their early years out of doors, on their feet, in all weathers, and/or behind the wheel of a car. More time may be spent in desk and office work as promotion comes, but for most police officers it is a very active life, with long and difficult hours. There is a lot of routine, report writing, and time spent in court, which means giving evidence. Almost all police work involves contact with people of all kinds. Police officers have to learn to accept that, even when off duty, many people will be wary of them.

Over 75% of all police men and women are constables. Most spend their working hours trying to see that ordinary, everyday life goes on as normally as possible in a particular area.

On the beat After initial training (see below), all police officers spend at least two years as probationer uniformed constables attached to a local station, and going out alone on the streets within a very short time, effectively learning on-the-job.

Most constables work as part of a 'unit' looking after an area, which may be a housing estate, a residential suburb, or a shopping centre. A typical unit beat is made up of two police officers, who work as in a team with a back-up detective constable and a panda-car patrol team, all in touch with each other and with their station, via the radio. The unit has to know the area as well as possible, to know what usually happens and when, the regular pattern of activity in the neighbourhood, to know what is suspicious and what is not, to spot the unusual and out-of-the-ordinary. Where police forces use 'community' policing, constables are expected to become as closely involved as possible with the local people, to join in local activities and events, to help solve local problems which have little to do with policing (eg helping to raise money for a play area), and work with younger people.

Beat constables are briefed daily, and are then given particular jobs to do. They have stolen cars to watch out for, and enquiries to make, such as seeing a witness for more information or showing someone stolen property that has been recovered.

At the end of these two years, constables can theoretically try for other jobs within their force, although in practice, since changing jobs depends on vacancies, it may be much longer. Most policemen and women stay on the beat for several more years (and even longer), and do other work in or from the local station.

Station work Up to a dozen constables may be on a station shift at one time. Some go out on patrol (on foot, in a 'panda', or perhaps as a team in a van), some work on the enquiry desk, dealing with people who come in or telephone – to report a crime or ask for help or information. One or more officers operate the radio links with their patrol constables, cars and force headquarters.

The collator looks after the station's information centre, with its walls covered in local maps and photographs, its card or computer-based indexes of all kinds of information, reference books, and computer terminals. The collator has to keep track of all reported crimes and incidents, missing cars, dogs, and children, and helps to build up evidence from information coming in all the time.

One or more police officers may specialise in liaison work with local schools.

The tutor-constable, an experienced officer, is in charge of day-to-day on-the-job training of probationers.

Rural policing Some experienced constables choose to become country policemen or women. They may look after a large area (and therefore have to use a car), which may include several villages, a length or two of major road, several large farms and estates. Rural police have their own police house with an office. They work mainly alone, under long-range supervision, and with rather more direct responsibility than the city constable. Many of them put down roots and stay with a district for some time. To be successful, the police officer has to build a close relationship with the local community.

Patrol cars Constables can go from the beat to work on the 'panda' cars, patrolling the area also covered on foot by two resident constables, although some forces are now reducing the number of car patrols. Cars patrol, or can be sent out to incidents or to help a constable. Like the beat constable, the panda driver also makes calls and enquiries, looks out for anything suspicious or unusual, and sorts out accidents. From panda patrols, constables can go on to the larger area patrol cars with their driver-observer team, and work with both divisional headquarters as well as the local station.

Criminal investigation is another area of 'promotion' for uniformed constables. Detective constables often start, though, back out with unit beat teams (above). Here much of the work is patient, routine questioning, interviewing, collating, painstakingly collecting detailed evidence, trying to build a case from a mass of unrelated facts, and trying to find all the pieces in a complex jigsaw. Many cases are undramatic, straightforward thefts and minor crimes. Many forms have to be filled in and reports written.

Every detective works on a number of things at once. The work is all very time-consuming. Scene-of-crime work involves collecting evidence, interviewing witnesses and potential suspects and analysing the results, working with the forensic experts. They may work in criminal records. CID officers also deal with local crime prevention, ranging from advising a large company on a complete electronic system for a factory to persuading local housewives to lock all their windows when they go out.

Although every force has its own CID, they vary in size from 2000 in London to about 100 in a small provincial force. From local CID, experienced detectives can go on to work in headquarters, or in a regional crime squad, or into a special unit. In regional crime squads (employing 1110 in all) there are an increasing range of specialised duties, for example, intelligence officer, who deals with and organises the information coming into the squad, and selects 'target criminals'.

Traffic departments employ quite large numbers. The work ranges from office-based planning to actually driving police cars. Traffic departments plan and operate the more complex traffic control systems, administer intelligence units which analyse traffic and accident information and identify and try to cure problems. They work closely with local authorities and government departments in planning or changing traffic schemes. They also operate the car and motorcycle traffic patrols which sort out traffic snarl-ups, cope with emergencies and accidents, stop dangerous drivers, breathalyse drinking drivers, and look out for dangerous, defective and unlicensed vehicles.

Smaller units (for which competition is always keen), include –
the river patrols;
underwater search units (whose members are always trained 'frogmen');
the mounted police – in 18 forces with 442 horses between them, working mainly in crowd control at football matches, race meetings and demonstrations;
mountain rescue teams;
teaming up with a dog (over 2000 are 'employed'), to look for missing children, track and trap suspects or escaped prisoners, do general search duties and patrolling, or specialise in hunting for, eg drugs, explosives, or buried bodies.

Promotion Every police force has a strictly hierarchical structure – and the chief constables, who administer them (there is no central command), have been described as akin to feudal barons, often moulding their forces in a very personal way. All senior positions, right up to chief constable, are filled from within the ranks of the police themselves, but except for the most senior posts there is not that much movement between forces – although numbers have been increasing a little (to 344 in 1985 mostly from London to a provincial force).

Promotion is strictly on suitability and 'merit', on being the kind of police officer the interviewing board decides it needs for the particular job. There is no automatic promotion on age or length of service. Before promotion to sergeant or inspector, qualifying exams must be passed, but this does not guarantee promotion – over 9% of constables, and 39% of sergeants had qualified in 1985, and in 18 forces, over 50% of sergeants were qualified.

Although there are some technical, 'backroom' jobs for more senior officers, the police emphasise that promotion is in terms of 'man' management, in being responsible for running a team of more junior officers, deploying them and equipment –

a uniformed sergeant leads a team of constables;

an inspector in a sub-division is in charge of one or more sections, consisting of 10-15 constables and sergeants, responsible for seeing they work together as a unit (but detective sergeants may work alone on some cases);

a sub-divisional detective inspector is in charge of a team of detectives, but perhaps dealing directly with investigations where enquiries are particularly difficult or lengthy;

a control room inspector is in charge of a shift of the constables dealing with emergency calls, and ensures that the right response is made.

All inspectors deal with day-to-day administration. Most senior officers are also given experience of specialist duties outside the main route of their career development – they may be seconded to the Police Research Services at the Home Office, or to the Inspectorate of Constabulary (33 posts), for example. The five training centres employ 291 personnel, including 33 at the Bramshill staff college.

Promotion is now noticeably faster for people with good educational qualifications, slower for the rest. There is at least one special scheme for some 60 younger officers, at least a third of them usually graduates (see training below) who show the potential to rise about inspector, and have passed the sergeants' exams at the first attempt. They spend a year working as a sergeant and are then guaranteed promotion to inspector.

Although there are only posts at sergeant and above for about one in five of all police men and women, it is possible to become a sergeant in three years, an inspector in less than five. In practice, only 177 sergeants are (1985) under 26 (17 of them women). One inspector is only 25, but the number aged 26-30 is up sharply, to 134 (including eleven women), and one (male) chief inspector is only 30. The youngest superintendent is 34, and six chief superintendents are 38. The youngest assistant chief and deputy chief constables are also 38, and the youngest chief constable 44.

Women police officers have been 'integrated' into the force, with the same powers and responsibilities as men, since 1976. While duties such as searching prisoners may still be done by police officers of the same sex as the prisoner, many duties traditionally reserved for women officers (eg dealing with women and children in any kind of trouble) are now done by the best-qualified officer, regardless of sex, and vice versa. Women now theoretically compete for promotion on equal terms with men. In 1985, there were 132 women inspectors, and 87 in higher ranks, which is still well down on 1976. Just two women are in ranks above chief superintendent, as assistant chief constables. Under

2% of women therefore hold the rank of inspector or above, against over 10% of men.

Civilians in the police forces are being increased in numbers (nearly 44,000 in 1985 against only 18,000 15 years earlier). The range of work they do is being extended to release police officers for operational duties. For example, some now work on station reception desks.

Many work in administration (pay, records, finance and so on), catering and cleaning.

Some are specialists. For instance,

The forensic science service employs (1987) 480 SCIENTISTS (mostly chemists and biologists). They help solve all kinds of crimes, examining and analysing a wide range of materials which might give a clue to the identity of the culprit, eliminate the innocent, or establish a major factor about the crime itself – the laboratory work involved is mainly chemical and biological. Other work includes investigating documents and inks, comparing, for instance, hairs and fibres, identifying blood groups from dried stains, and so on. Much of this is being automated. The laboratories are almost entirely regionally based at present (London has its own) but organisation and management are under review. The Aldermaston central laboratories do research in eg toxicology, biology and serology, and house the service's information centre which has a computer-based literature retrieval system.

The scientific research and development branch mainly studies ways in which modern technology can be used to improve police efficiency. Major projects include applying real-time computers to problems of, for instance, command and resource control and allocation, retrieving intelligence information, and fingerprint comparison. The branch uses a wide range of statistical and mathematical model-building techniques, Small teams of scientists (under 50 in all) eg mathematicians, physicists, chemists, psychologists and engineers, work closely with police officers. Much of the work is contracted out.

Other specialist work includes fingerprinting and PHOTOGRAPHY.

Traffic wardens are employed by all police forces, and now number nearly 5000 country wide. They mainly patrol the streets to see that parking and other restrictions are not being broken, and if they are, tell the drivers what they should (or should not) be doing and/or issue parking 'tickets'. They also monitor schemes – such as one-way systems, controlled parking zones, and yellow lines – to see if they are improving or impeding traffic flow. They watch out for stolen cars, check road-tax licences, and note licence numbers of cars etc which are clearly not safe to be on the roads. They sometimes do point duty if jams build up or traffic lights are out of action, supervise car pounds, and may control crossings when children are going in or out of a nearby school.

Recruitment and entry

Recruitment rose again in 1985, to nearly 5600, but is still down on the 9400 of 1979. But at the end of the year there were still 1782 vacancies.

Entry to the police is normally between the ages of 18½ and 30, although older entrants are sometimes accepted. About half of all new entrants are now 19-20, but the forces do have some preference for older recruits (eg 23-24) because they are usually more mature. It is possible to start as a cadet between 16 and 18, but cadet entry is being cut to 10% of intake, and so numbers have fallen sharply, to 356 in 1985 (against nearly 4000 in 1972).

Theoretically there are still no formal educational entry requirements, but candidates with fewer than four O-level-equivalent passes have to take an entry test of the same standard. In practice, the vast majority of entrants now have four or more O level-equivalent passes. The Metropolitan Police have a 'new' cadet-entry scheme (300 places a year) recruiting at 17-17½ but with delayed entry to sit A levels, for people with at least five 'good' O-level-equivalent passes at 16-plus†.

A steady 64% of recruits in fact now have the equivalent of five O-level passes or above, and some 12% now have degrees.

About 25 graduates are recruited under a special entry scheme, and normally qualify for the 'fast training' course (below). Other graduates (492 in 1985) join via the 'normal' route, but can apply for the special entry scheme during their first year if they have not been considered for it previously. It is possible to be reconsidered for the special course on passing promotion exams for sergeant for those then still under 30.

The minimum height for policemen is, in most forces, 5 feet 8 inches (in one or two, for example the City of London, it is more), and for women 5 feet 4 inches. Most forces accept entrants who wear glasses or contact lenses, if their sight meets certain minimum standards. Good health and physical stamina are needed to work long and unusual hours, and to stay on one's feet for long periods.

Personal qualities are also very important. It isn't possible to get in on educational and physical qualifications alone, and the rejection rate on personal characteristics and motivation is high. The police say they want people intelligent enough to be able to sum up situations quickly and efficiently, and who can make the 'right' decisions. They want well-balanced personalities, plenty of self-control, tact and level-headedness. Police recruits need to be objective and observant, to be able to keep their opinions to themselves, cope with people easily and firmly (a sense of humour helps) in all kinds of situations. They must be able to work in a team.

Qualifications and training All recruits start with an intensive, full-time training course (14 weeks generally, 20 for London) – cadets in the Met get a 46-week training. The next two years are spent as a probationer, training on-the-job, under experienced officers (most stations now have tutor constables) returning to college to take the first exams. After that there may be additional training courses for specific jobs or groups. Anyone going into CID work, for example, has to go to a detective school, to study criminal law and methods of detective investigation.

The amount of training given is being increased steadily, with what are described as a 'carousel' of short courses for police officers of all ranks. The normal route to promotion as sergeant and inspector is via extremely stiff examinations: although the pass rate has improved lately, the proportion of those passing sergeant's exams was 14.9% in 1985, and for inspector's exams, 40%.

A 'special' (and very tough) one-year course (at Bramshill Staff College) is put on for 60 young officers (25 of whom are specially-selected graduate entrants) considered suitable for promotion to inspector or above. Those selected are promoted to sergeant (they must have passed the exams at the first attempt). Increasingly sophisticated courses (using, for instance, computer simulations) are given each year for those being promoted to intermediate, junior and senior command, all emphasising high-level administration.

See also CENTRAL GOVERNMENT and LEGAL SERVICES.

Further information from the Police Recruiting Department of the Home Office, the Police Division of the Scottish Home and Health Department, or the headquarters of any individual force (see telephone directory).

THE PRISON SERVICE

Prison staff have a job with two purposes, which can easily come into conflict. They have to see that people committed to prison by the court stay there, but the Service also plans to develop 'constructive methods of treatment and training designed to lead to the prisoner's rehabilitation and reform'. Long-term, the aim is to concentrate increasingly on the latter, whilst using sophisticated technical systems to replace the security of the prison staff, but this is an ideal unlikely to be achieved for a long time.

Conditions within the prisons are widely agreed to be, in many instances, almost intolerable, both for prisoners and staff. Even staff accommodation is cramped and facilities poor. This is largely due to massive overcrowding, and to old and out-dated buildings. Conditions are unlikely to improve substantially in the immediate future – despite the considerable building programme now under way – unless the number of people held in prison is reduced (and it topped 50,000 for the first time in 1987).

Currently there are just over 80 prisons with another dozen being or to be built, some secure, some 'open', plus over 30 detention centres for 'young offenders', and fifteen remand centres.

Working in the prison service Prison officers' main work is looking after a group of prisoners on a day-to-day basis. They supervise them at work, in their cells, exercising, and at 'recreation'. An officer is also in charge of prisoners' training and rehabilitation, and is expected to help them sort out practical and other problems, make reports on any illness, on their conduct, and pass on to senior staff any special requests, or difficulties, and see that any problems, including psychiatric crises, have professional attention. Some officers are trained to help the prisoners they look after through group and other forms of counselling. They also have to deal with disruptive behaviour.

Prison officers are also in charge of receiving new prisoners. They run classification units which decide which prisons new inmates should go to; supervise workshops, visits by relatives and friends, and training. They escort prisoners to and from courts, and guard gates and doors.

The job is obviously easier in open prisons, sited in attractive countryside, and with prisoners who are fairly well adjusted and able to work. In some of the older, more crowded city prisons, where work and training programmes cannot always be implemented in full, the problems are greater, but it isn't an easy job in any institution.

Prison officers are promoted through a series of supervisory grades, which for some can lead to management, as assistant governor (although there is also direct entry at this level).

Assistant governors generally have administrative, managerial responsibility for part of a prison/borstal. They manage both staff and resources, supervise inmates' progress, treatment, training and so on. They plan and organise work and training schedules, arrange for counselling, psychiatric treatment, educational programmes, entertainments and leisure activities. They look after the prisoners' records, deal with parole requests, discipline, and other routines and procedures.

Further promotion is to governor. The prison service emphasises that running a prison is a managerial job, and expects governors to use modern managerial techniques, to have clear priorities, and to have an efficient and effective organisation. A large part of the job is managing a large and varied staff, doing difficult work.

It is possible to go on to work in regional management or administration, to take on a training post. A few people work for the prisons inspectorate.

The prison service also employs some specialists, most notably PSYCHOLOGISTS, but also some DOCTORS and NURSES for hospitals. PROBATION OFFICERS staff prison welfare offices. There are also jobs for caterers, and instructors for trades and other skills, and in physical education.

Over 27,700 people work in the prison service (up from 24,250 in 1983). Most, over 18,400 are prison officers, 596 are governors, 5700 are non-industrial and 3000 are industrial staff.

Recruitment and entry There are no set educational entry requirements for prison officers. Selection is by interview, with a short written test, many of whom join after time spent in the armed forces or in industry. Entry age is between 21 and 42 for men, 49 for women. Men must be over 5 feet 6 inches, women 5 feet 3 inches. Good health is needed. Competition for posts is now considerable, and there is a waiting list for entry. About 900 men and 135 women were recruited in 1985.

Direct recruitment as an assistant governor needs a degree or equivalent qualification and/or experience in eg social work. The minimum age is 21, but anyone recruited to be an assistant governor under the age of 24 has to spend a year working as a prison officer first. Twenty-eight trainees were recruited in 1985, including three who were prison officers.

Prison staff should, ideally, be well-balanced, stable people. They should be able to understand the need for, and carry out, both the custodial and social-work aspects of the job. They need to be level-headed, extremely patient, and self-controlled. They should have a realistic attitude to the underlying causes which result in people going to prison, and to be able to develop an understanding of any psychological and/or social problems and help to solve them. A basically friendly nature with a sense of humour might make the job easier.

Qualifications and training All entrants are given a month's induction training, followed by a nine-week course at a (new) training school. Training has been reviewed, and 'greatly increased' emphasis put on developing relevant, especially inter-personal, skills. Training for governors is spread over two years, after a short introductory course at the staff college.

Further information from the Prison Department of the Home Office or the Director of Prison and Borstal Services (in Scotland).

PRIVATE SECURITY OPERATIONS
This is a growth industry, expanding by about 25% annually, and employing possibly 200,000 people (the two largest firms have 40,000 people between them). The industry is made up of a small number of large companies, offering highly sophisticated, nation-wide services, and rather more small units, usually working on a local basis. Some firms specialise – in protecting precious metals, for instance, or in providing security equipment. Large-scale security now takes full advantage of all that modern technology can offer, guarding property with radios, electronic detection devices, closed-circuit television, and so on, often to give advanced warning of fire or flood as much as of a break-in.

The industry's mainstay is still protecting cash in transit, using armoured vans, but many other services are provided, including delivery services for valuable packages and documents, advice and quotations on security systems, protection against industrial espionage, protection for people vulnerable to attack or kidnapping, and store detective services. Security services are used mainly by, eg industrial and commercial firms which regularly handle anything valuable enough to warrant the cost of protecting it.

Working in security Careers in security organisations do not have any formal structure, nor is there really any factual information on the people employed.

Security companies, like all commercial firms, must have really efficient MANAGEMENT. This is a business which has to be ready to change or develop the services it offers and to spot the changes coming. As less and less cash is moved around physically, for example, security firms will find less business in this. There are also posts in day-to-day administration, finance, personnel etc.
Most people in the industry work as guards, drivers, or patrolmen, although there are some couriers, and a declining number of dog handlers. Technicians and engineers install and service alarm systems and all the other electronic and technological devices, as well as looking after the vans, cars and motor cycles.

Private investigators, a few, probably no more than 500, make a reasonable living. Few will find work with worthwhile agencies without some prior background training, normally in POLICE or related work, the law (usually as a LEGAL EXECUTIVE), the ARMED FORCES or industry, normally in MANAGEMENT SERVICES.
The work, according to one association, involves research, research and yet more research, plus checking research, some surveillance and very, very little glamour indeed. A highly developed instinctive sense is crucial in order to achieve a reputation. It is advisable to begin with a very reputable agency before even considering freelance work.

Store detectives are mostly employed by larger retailers, although some shops use contract staff from security firms.

Recruitment and entry Companies prefer, where possible, to recruit experienced people, especially those with the kinds of skills acquired in the police or Armed Forces. Recruits to a security firm are expected to have completely 'clean' records and the right kind of character. A successful career in the police or Forces is supposedly a good indicator of these.

Qualifications and training None formal. Larger companies now offer a reasonable level of training, particularly on legal responsibilities, the police, and relations with the community, and with the kind of equipment being used, as well as in emergency procedures.

The International Professional Security Association (which includes the Institute of Industrial Security) puts on a number of short and correspondence courses, some leading to membership of the Institute. Guidelines on employer-based training for store detectives have been prepared by IPSA, the Association for the Prevention of Theft in Shops, and the British Retailers Association.

Further information from the British Security Industry Association, and the International Professional Security Association.

THE TOURIST INDUSTRY

It is only comparatively recently that 'tourism' has been promoted as a single industry, or area of employment. Most of the sectors which are included under the 'umbrella' of tourism are, in fact, industries or activities in their own right, gaining only part of their income from 'tourists'.

Tourist boards and other promoters

The British and four national tourist boards, the network of regional organisations (twelve in England, three in Wales) and many LOCAL AUTHORITIES (for instance), promote holidays in this country, to both British holiday-makers and people in/from other countries. Some local authorities have special departments to develop their area's tourist potential almost from scratch to help solve local employment problems.

They use modern marketing methods – 'promotional' campaigns, advertising, and brochures to attract visitors, and at the same time try to have facilities (such as hotels and transport), improved, perhaps also organising new activities in an area. They may also provide information centres. Boards have funds to help encourage firms to fill in gaps in services, and help develop new ideas to attract visitors.

The tourist and local authorities involved, employ people in MARKETING, PUBLIC RELATIONS/PROMOTION, FINANCE, development work, and information centre staff (an estimated 2500 people are employed but mainly seasonally and/or part-time) etc.

Recruitment and entry A high proportion of staff will probably have experience (and qualifications) from elsewhere in the tourist, or LEISURE/RECREATION INDUSTRY, and/or in eg MARKETING, PUBLIC RELATIONS. Information-centre, and administrative staff may be recruited with a reasonable educational background, of at least three/four O-level-equivalent passes.

Qualifications and training Mainly pre-entry in one of the above areas, and for senior staff, preferably a relevant degree or postgraduate qualification.
CGLI and the English Tourist Board offer a certificate of tourist information centre competence.

Further information from regional tourist boards or local authorities.

Tourist guides
They take visitors, tourists, around towns, show them the 'sights', or a historic building, and tell them interesting facts about the place. They may take groups on short- or long-distance coach trips, take smaller parties out by car or mini-bus, or specialise in an area or building which can be covered on foot. Some guides specialise in tours for special groups, eg younger people, or in eg historic gardens, or cathedrals.

Most tourist guides are self-employed, although some tour operators and other organisations hire guides full-time for the tourist 'season'. Some work for organisations owning historic or other places on the tourist 'map'. Demand for guides fluctuates with the number of tourists, which often depends on currency changes, or other political/economic events, and so is unpredictable. It is not easy to get work between November and March/April, which means either earning enough in the summer to cover the winter months, or having a second, winter occupation.

Recruitment and entry is very competitive, and means building contacts, and proving reliable, interesting and helpful to tourists. It may be useful to gain experience first with a tour operator. It is essential to have in-depth, detailed knowledge of several area(s) and/or subjects, and also a good, clear speaking voice, to be relaxed about speaking in public, to be imaginative and humorous, be patient, and good at shepherding groups of people without upsetting them. Fluent language(s), especially the less usual ones (eg Arabic, Chinese, Japanese), are an advantage.

Qualifications and training The London Tourist Board gives a six-month training for a 'blue badge' which allows holders to work in London. Entry requirements are age at least 23, ability to pass a test on current affairs, history and the greater London area, previous experience of public speaking or a language. Similar training schemes are being developed elsewhere.

Further information London Visitor and Convention Bureau, or regional tourist office.
See also eg CONSERVATION, HOTELS AND CATERING, LEISURE AND RECREATION, MUSEUM WORK, TRANSPORT AND TRAVEL

TRANSPORT AND TRAVEL INDUSTRIES
Background   1118
Working in transport   1119
Civil aviation   1120
Railways   1131
Road transport   1138
Sea and inland waterways   1146

Travel business and freightforwarding 1155

Transport systems which give people the freedom to move about at will and for goods to be sent freely throughout the world are a central feature of modern life. Efficient transport is crucial to economic growth, and travel and tourism are major earners for the country. While life today would be unimaginable – and probably unsupportable – without the forms of transport we now have, tomorrow's COMMUNICATION SYSTEMS could cut demand because they make possible teleconferences and meetings and may let many more people work at home. This could even become necessary if an economic replacement for oil as fuel is not found comparatively soon.

The transport industry is large and complex. Achieving efficient passenger-transport systems which benefit as many people as possible as cheaply as possible has proved hard. Attempts to plan and develop integrated, co-operative transport, never too successful except in a few cases, have now been abandoned. De-regulation, and increasing competition between commercially-owned bodies, are being tried, with fewer state-owned organisations and less involvement for local authorities. Most transport operations now work hard to make a profit from the services they provide. Competition is both between sectors, and between operators in the separate sectors – air transport ended long-distance sea transport for passengers, while road transport systems take business from rail. All passenger services are competing with the car as well as each other.

Transport systems are not, then, easy to manage. They are also costly – even if fuel prices are (temporarily) down. Transport systems are mostly labour intensive, also expensive, and they use very expensive hardware – aircraft, ships, railway rolling stock, freightliners, even buses – which have to be planned for and ordered well in advance of need.

Most national and international transport firms have widely distributed 'bases', and even local transport organisations have to 'manage' systems which are widely scattered and on the move most of the time. Just keeping track of them, and staying in touch is a major problem – although again modern communication systems are making this easier. Many transport systems run seven days a week, all year round, and some round the clock too.

The problems, then, range from the need for high-level strategic forward planning at one extreme, to solving the myriad day-to-day problems of moving people and things around at the other. Operating transport systems in today's economic and competitive conditions takes increasing managerial, marketing and financial expertise, and greater technological skills. Transport fleets and systems have to be managed and operated with increasing efficiency and great control. For instance, many transport fleets now have computer programs which can analyse routes to give the best routes for speed and economic fuel consumption.

Transport organisation come in two different types –

First, are the organisations which specialise mainly in providing a transport service (although some have also diversified into other, related sectors, for instance, hotels). They range in size from major national and international companies down to the one-person operation.

Second, are the organisations in other sectors which have their own transport, mainly road, systems which they need to do their own business – examples are the POST OFFICE with its fleet of vans (and even aircraft) to carry mail, BRITISH TELECOM which needs vans and trucks mainly for its engineers, and BREWING, OIL AND CHEMICAL companies who must move their own products from producing plant to warehouse and/or retailer.

The transport industry is also generally taken to include the ports where ships dock, airports, and so on. The transport industry uses a range of services, from fuel suppliers, through to specialist freight/air forwarders.

All transport operations, whether by independent carriers like the railways, or in transport sections of manufacturing or other companies, involve a similar series of operations. Goods, or people, have to be 'loaded' onto the 'vehicle' being used to transport them (which means having somewhere to do this); they are then transported as efficiently, directly, cheaply, and safely as is cost-effective to their destination, where they are off-loaded.

Transport services by definition involve 'managing' a fleet of vehicles – deciding which planes, buses or trucks to buy, possibly having special vehicles designed and developed, maintaining and repairing them, planning their replacement, fuelling them (which includes buying the fuel and seeing it is safely stored), etc.

Transport services operate round-the-clock, and involve both complex planning and scheduling and large numbers of people. Most transport services meet regular problems which must be solved rapidly and efficiently – vehicle breakdowns, traffic 'jams', accidents, bad weather, people and things in the wrong places, and the like. For longer-distance passenger services catering and sleeping accommodation may have to be provided.

Working in transport

Under a million people now (1987) work in the transport industry, down from a peak of well over a million in 1979. While recession had a major effect, the industry has also been restructuring and attempting to cut staffing levels permanently, with some help from automation and other new technology.

The Chartered Institute of Transport identifies a number of functions common to all transport operations. These are planning, policy and financial control, operations and management, physical distribution management, technology, research and education, and social and environmental aspects.

SPECIFIC AREAS OF WORK are –

Management and administration directly managing and administering a fleet or facility (eg an airport, port, railway station, bus or freight depot) on a day-to-day basis. Specific specialist jobs include scheduling/timetabling. The work includes commercial 'functions' common to all businesses – such as FINANCE, MARKETING, PERSONNEL – but dealing with the particular needs of a transport firm.

Engineering designing and developing systems and vehicles, maintenance and repair at all levels, from managerial through technician to craft etc.

Operating transport systems as driver, pilot, ship's officer/sailor etc.

Supporting work includes, eg AIR TRAFFIC CONTROL, MARINE PILOTAGE.

Related work transport and traffic planning etc in LOCAL AUTHORITIES and the

CIVIL SERVICE, where they have direct responsibility for traffic. TRAVEL AGENCY, TOUR OPERATING, FREIGHT FORWARDING.

Recruitment and entry normally directly into a transport operation, for training in a specific function – in administration (clerk or management trainee), engineering, or working on the transport system itself.

Entry is possible from a variety of different educational backgrounds, but CIT and RTITB believe it crucial that the industry recruits a rising number of people with a 'high standard of general and vocational education and practical experience'.

Qualifications and training Depends to some extent on sector and function, but is mainly on the job and part-time, with comparatively few opportunities for pre-entry qualification.

Professional qualifications Professional bodies for the industry have been slow to develop on any scale, and 'professional' qualifications are helpful, but not essential, for managers.

The Chartered Institute of Transport, founded early in the century, has (1986) a membership of c20,000, some 50% of them based overseas.

Full membership needs an approved relevant degree, or completion of the Institute's three-stage qualifying exams. These are broadly based (and now include management and marketing) but provide for some specialisation in a branch of transport. Minimum qualification for entry to these is at least five O-level-equivalent passes at 16-plus† (including English language and maths).

The Institute of Transport Administration, founded 1944, has a membership (1986) of 5000 – 74% of them work in road transport (as owner-operators or fleet managers). The Institute sets a three-stage (graduate and associate membership parts 1 and 2) examination, but is considering changes to 'harmonise' with related bodies.

Degree courses include –
Universities – Birmingham: Aston (transport management), Cardiff: UWIST (international transport), Loughborough (transport management and planning), Ulster (transport technology); polytechnics – Huddersfield (transport and distribution), London: City (business studies: physical distribution and transport option), Plymouth (transport)
Postgraduate/postexperience courses are at, eg universities – Birmingham, Bradford, Cranfield, Glasgow: Strathclyde, Leeds, London: Imperial, Loughborough, Newcastle, Salford, Sheffield, Southampton; polytechnics – London: PCL; other – Berkhamsted: Ashridge Management C.

BTEC Higher awards BTEC Higher awards can be taken with a bias towards transport administration at a number of polytechnics and other colleges. Most give at least some exemptions from CIT exams.
See also ACADEMIC AND VOCATIONAL STUDIES.

CIVIL AVIATION
The airline industry — working in airlines — working in airports
The world airline industry came out of recession in 1983, making a profit again in 1984 and 1985 too, only to hit some turbulence in 1986 after the Libyan

bombing and Chernobyl. Capacity is still growing faster than traffic, although world air traffic rose 5% in 1986 to 938 million scheduled passengers, and further growth of 5-7% a year into the 1990s is predicted. This is, however, still nowhere near the idyllic early 1970s, when traffic soared by 10% year after year, giving airlines the revenues needed to finance new fleets. They all face real problems in replacing their ageing craft in the next ten years. Pressures to bring down fares and rising costs (eg insurance) are outweighing any gains from falling fuel prices, which are in any case not coming down everywhere, and where they are it is probably only short-term.

This is, then, a complex and difficult business to manage, with very high – and rising – fixed capital and running costs, and problems in predicting traffic levels far enough ahead to have the right numbers and types of planes, ground facilities, and staff, available. Competition is intensifying, with airlines merging to create 'mega-carriers'. They now have no option but to be heavily marketing oriented – customers will no longer take poor service. Governments and hijackers both create political crises. Safety is a major, and costly, factor.

Passengers make up the bulk of air traffic, although air freight business is growing.

The airline business is made up of the airlines themselves, the supervisory Civil Aviation Authority, the airports, and other support services. No industry-wide employment figures have been published recently, but in the main airline business numbers are probably no more than 75,000.

The airlines

The UK's major carrier, British Airways, is the world's sixth largest, accounting for 76% of all UK scheduled services, five smaller lines, all carrying passengers on domestic and international routes and some freight, five charter companies, and two all-freight lines. Over 40 other firms have air transport licences, and a great many other firms run smaller flying operations, including over 100 air-taxi firms, crop sprayers, charter companies (who work for eg the POST OFFICE), air survey companies, and helicopter services (run mainly by two firms) for eg the North Sea oil and gas rigs. Some organisations have their own, fairly small, flying operations, eg the POLICE and search and rescue services.

British airlines' total available tonne-kilometres rose to 13,408 million in 1985. The number of passengers entering and leaving Britain by air has been rising again, to nearly 53 million (against under 39 million in 1978), with almost 71 million people altogether passing through the country's airports. Freight traffic accounts for nearly 19% of exports and 16.5% of imports, by value, largely of goods that are valuable but not too heavy (eg diamonds) or which have to be moved quickly, for instance perishable tropical fruit, mail, and racehorses.

British Airways is one of the world's largest carriers, and the major UK employer. Newly privatised, the company has made a 'remarkable' turnround since 1981, in the quality of service and management, and in financial performance. Although it has trimmed its route network, it still covers 323,700 miles of unduplicated route, to 145 places in 72 countries (down from 180 destinations in 80 countries). BA has a fleet of 159 planes (down from a peak of 190), including seven Concordes, and 31 helicopters (operating in the Scillies at one end of the country, and from Aberdeen at the other), and is buying new airliners worth £2500 million.

As part of its recovery programme BA slashed the labour force to under 36,000 (from 59,400 in 1975), although numbers have risen again to around 40,000 in 1986. The second-largest line employs about 8000 people, and smaller lines employ far fewer, at most only a few thousand each and the smallest only hundreds.

Working in airlines etc
Airline staff can be divided between aircrew and ground staff. Considerably more people are employed on the the ground than in the air.

FLYING is possible for only a small proportion of people in the civil aviation business, probably well under 20% of the total, including flight engineers and cabin crew.

Everyone who flies, from senior pilot to the youngest stewardess, has to work irregular hours, although the number of hours they can spend in the air is strictly controlled. On long-haul routes they usually have enforced 'stop-over' rest periods abroad, although it can only be a single night with no time for sight-seeing etc. They may have to go through several time zones on one flight. On short-haul routes they may be on four (or more) consecutive flights without even leaving the plane, and be home again most nights.

Pilots – 12,000 people hold (1986) commercial licences – and British Airways employs 2000 of them.

In the airlines, most planes are flown by just a 'captain' and co-pilot – only older, long-range planes need a third person in the cabin (a flight engineer or third pilot), and specialist navigators are a defunct species. The pilots spend less and less of their time flying planes 'manually'. Mostly they monitor the increasingly-sophisticated computer-controlled automatic systems with their greatly-improved control panels (as in the Boeing 757), and navigating. Normally, even over the sea pilots are expected to follow routes precalculated by computers (for safety, tight schedules, fuel economy, a smooth ride etc), and obey changes given by flight control. Decision-making is most demanding during bad weather when quick thinking may be needed, and the sophisticated all-weather landing systems which let the most modern planes land in almost all conditions, take considerable expertise.

Flying is team work, although crews rarely fly together regularly, and is by the book (manual) and computer. Every procedure is reduced to tightly written and rehearsed drills. Flight crew use the latest computer-based systems from the moment they come on duty. The flight plan which calculates the fuel needed for a particular aircraft is fully automated, taking input from the reservation computer (for the payload) and from a meteorological computer, which gives information on expected winds and temperatures. In starting the engine and going through the take-off routine (for instance) pilot and co-pilot go through long question-and-answer checks of all the controls and instruments involved.

Flight crew are busiest at the beginning and end of each flight. For the rest of the time, they spend a lot of time checking and monitoring – fuel, speed, estimated time of arrival etc. During the flight, they must keep in touch with air traffic controllers, with the navigating radio beacons, with weather ships, and airline headquarters. Throughout the flight, pilots must be ready to react fast to any warnings or unusual readings, however rarely anything may really be wrong. They have to cope with unexpected weather changes and turbulence, be prepared for delays above and at airports, and always be ready for the unexpected. Boredom can be a real factor on long-haul flights.

Every airline has its own system, and the larger the airline the greater the range of opportunities, although promotion may come faster in a smaller airline. In British Airways, newly-appointed second officers, once trained, start on short-haul routes as co-pilot. The chance to transfer to long-range aircraft (still as co-pilot) does not come for at least five years. On present agreements etc, promotion to probationary captain is unlikely to come until mid career – retirement is normally by 55 – and means going back to short-haul routes and planes. Airline pilots can try for senior managerial positions on the ground.

Other opportunities to work as a pilot are in the air-taxi and charter business, flying helicopters, or smaller 'executive' jets. They take people to business meetings or sports events, carry mail or urgent cargoes, schedule-fly helicopters to and from North-Sea oil rigs, or fly reporters around. There is some aerial survey work and photography, and crop spraying. Some experienced pilots work as instructors.

Smaller planes have increasingly complex systems too – navigational aids and auto-pilots – but there is still more 'manual' flying than in an airliner.

All the indications are that small firms have been expanding recently. The best chances of employment (but only with a commercial licence first), are with smaller independent operators and in charter work. It means starting at the very bottom of the ladder usually.

Recruitment and entry Intake of trainees was at near zero for over ten years (to 1987), with the only routes in via the Forces or training privately. Ex-RAF/RN pilots are now increasingly going to work for foreign airlines. In 1986, the airlines suddenly discovered they faced severe shortages of pilots in the 1990s – BA estimates it alone will need 1200 new pilots by 2000. Now British Airways is taking on about 100 trainees a year for the foreseeable future, and may also have to recruit experienced pilots from elsewhere. Other airlines may pay 50% of basic-training fees to suitable candidates prepared to pay the rest (see training below).

Entry requirements (BA) are at least five O-level-equivalent passes (including English language, maths and a science) and two A-levels (or the equivalent). Candidates have to be extremely fit (and get through a stiff CAA medical), be between 5 feet 4 inches and 6 feet 4 inches in height (and not overweight), and have good eyesight (but spectacles accepted) and hearing. Stringent aptitude tests are set – BA does not expect more than one in ten of those interviewed to pass them. Pilots are expected to be intelligent, alert, and quick-thinking with fast reactions. They have to be able to accept information presented in unfamiliar ways, co-ordinate, make sensible decisions quickly, and lead and motivate others effectively. They have to be stable people (personality profile tests are taken). At least some flying experience – eg club or ATC – is likely to help.

Qualifications and training All commercial pilots have to gain the Civil Aviation Authority's commercial pilot's licence and instrument rating, and to have trained for this at a CAA-approved school or college. Training is now available via BA, with the alternative of doing so privately (possibly with some sponsorship).

British Airways' new training scheme (starting in 1988) begins with a 69-week basic training, which is to be at a new flying college being set up under contract by British Aerospace at Prestwick. In addition to the basic licence, trainees are expected to gain the airline transport pilot's licence. BA expects to recruit those who pass as trainee pilots, but does not guarantee it. A further period of training is needed to fly the airline's own planes – a 'type rating' conversion course – which continues theory, flight simulator and practical flying. Throughout their flying careers, pilots are expected to go on gaining qualifications, and must take further 'type rating' courses whenever they switch to a different 'make' of plane.

Basic training is also available at two other CAA-approved colleges, but costs (1986) at least £45,000 for the twelve-month course, and does not include 'type rating' training, for which it is necessary to be taken on by an airline. These are Airwork Services at Perth (taking 50-60 students a year), or the Oxford Air Training School based at Oxford (Kidlington) and Carlisle Airports (taking about 250 students a year). Entry requirements are as above.

It is also still possible to start with a private pilot's licence, and build up the required 700 hours' flying time (possibly as an assistant flying instructor), then take the CAA tests. However, the sophistication of modern airliners makes it doubtful if airlines will accept this – it probably means not getting any time in airliner simulators – as a qualifying route for their pilots.

Flight engineers are needed only on the largest, and older, long-haul planes – and within twenty years will be 'obsolete'. They check on the plane's condition before a flight, for instance making sure that reported defects have been repaired, that tyres are not worn or damaged, that all panels etc have been shut properly. During the flight, they watch the instruments which monitor fuel, electrical, hydraulic, and mechanical systems. They keep records, diagnose problems, keep check on the plane's trim as fuel is used up, look after air-conditioning, pressuration etc.

Recruitment and entry Flight engineers are not recruited direct from school. Normal entry age is 23-25, although airlines may take on well-qualified people up to about 40. This is because airlines want them to have had extensive direct experience of maintaining advanced modern aircraft first. The formal entry requirements are four O-level-equivalent passes preferably including passes in English and maths, and successful completion of training in aeronautical engineering (to eg BTEC National standard), or an appropriate equivalent, with adequate experience in maintaining advanced aircraft.

Qualifications and training normally airline based, including maintenance familiarisation, to gain part 1 of the CAA's flight engineer's licence (type endorsement), part 2 and radio telephony endorsement, with flight operation and flying training.

Cabin crew the stewards and stewardesses, look after passengers' safety and comfort while they are in the aircraft. They check stores, see that blankets, cushions and so on are available, welcome passengers on board and make them comfortable, look after children travelling alone, answer questions, and try to calm people who are worried by flying, taking particular care of travellers with problems. They sell duty-free goods, serve drinks and meals etc, and make announcements. The work is physically, and sometimes emotionally, demanding. There is always a lot to do and little time to relax. Cabin crew have to work in very confined space (and a big jet may have a cabin crew of up to fourteen), in close contact with a lot of people.

Promotion, after about three years, can be to chief steward/stewardess, and on large jets, to 'cabin service' officer, responsible for what is at present treated as one of the major ways of winning the battle to attract passengers. However, a high proportion of staff are recruited on temporary contracts, for the summer season only. The industry is estimated to employ about 9000 aircabin crew in all, most by the larger airlines.

Recruitment and entry Cabin crew are expected to have a good educational background, to at least O-level-equivalent standard, with reasonable, conversational fluency in at least one European language. The lower age limit is 20, the upper 30 – catering, nursing or any other experience of work with people is 'highly desirable'. Personality counts a great deal. Airlines no longer look for 'debby' stewardesses – while some may want the 'Dallas' look to attract business customers, more generally they want cabin crew to make passengers feel 'at home', which means the 'girl next door' type. Cabin crew have to be friendly and out-going, good at being reassuring and organising people tactfully. They must be able to stay calm and organised whatever happens. They should have common sense. It doesn't help to be clumsy or awkward. Many airlines have height and weight restrictions. Good health and eyesight, plenty of stamina and energy are essential, as is the ability to swim. Some airlines recruit 'support' cabin crew, doing the same work as stewards and stewardesses, but on a part-time basis and with no promotion.

Qualifications and training Basic training usually takes six weeks, and includes 'personal grooming', language and cultural differences.

ON THE GROUND, a number of services are needed to keep planes flying and passengers and freight processed smoothly. Airlines employ a wide range of skilled and other people, most of them working at or near airports, and mostly working on a shift basis, to cover all the hours when planes are landing and taking off, and to ensure that the planes are maintained, repaired, loaded etc.

Engineering divisions of airlines do three things –
First, they (or an independent servicing contractor), maintain, service and overhaul planes, replace parts or whole engines, strip a plane down, and modernise systems. The technological sophistication of commercial airliners, with their many millions of parts and (for instance) sophisticated 'avionic' and electronic systems and on-board computers, make this a very exacting job. There are a great many different systems, a great many moving parts. All the instruments and electrical installations, hydraulics and pneumatics, fuselage, wings, control surfaces and undercarriage, as well as the engine, have to be carefully checked and tested, often by equipment every bit as sophisticated as the plane itself, each on a separate schedule. Fault-finding is equally complex.

All planes have pre-departure checks, and if they are on the ground for any length of time, a short maintenance or non-urgent repair which has been waiting for a suitable moment, gets done.

This is round-the-clock shift work. Every part of every job, even tightening nuts and bolts, has to be double checked, inspected and certified. With such complex systems, maintenance engineers generally specialise, for instance on avionics (landing aids, auto-pilots, navigation systems etc).

Second, aircraft manufacturers do not design and build hugely expensive planes without consulting their customers, the airlines. An airline's (professional) engineers are generally in on the ground floor on the next generation of airliners, first discussing the planes they want and then detailed specification, new equipment or improved engine and aerodynamic design (to use less fuel, for example). Airline engineers may decide they want some 'custom-built' modifications to the production model, and work out the specification. Airlines' professional engineers may do some R&D alongside the manufacturer, for instance in improving engine performance.

Finally, airline engineers also search for ways to reduce servicing costs, improve reliability, look into problems, and develop eg improved engine-control monitoring systems, and try to improve workshop turnround times.

Airline engineering divisions (and specialist maintenance companies) of any size employ engineers with a range of skills – BA alone employs over 7000. They include craft workers (sheet metal work, avionics, engine/mainframe, carpentry, painting etc), and technicians, who can possibly (the chances get fewer every year) become flight engineers (see above) or go into the technical offices dealing with production planning and control, quality control, or developing aircraft systems and installations. Graduate engineers can normally expect to become managers.

Most airlines also have fairly sizeable fleets of vans, lorries, fork-lift trucks, tankers etc, and these have to be driven and maintained. BA has 4000 vehicles and employs over 800 staff to operate and maintain them.

Recruitment and entry Airlines generally recruit across the range of educational qualifications for engineers, mostly for apprenticeships.

A small number of undergraduate apprenticeships, mainly for City University's air transport engineering degree, are available, mostly for those considered likely to make senior engineering management.

Technician apprenticeships – four O-level-equivalent passes including maths, physics, English language and (preferably) a technical subject needed; evidence of practical ability/interest: age 16-18.

Craft apprenticeships may also be available – entry requirements are CSE (grades 1-3)-equivalent passes at 16-plus† in maths, physics or general science, English language and a technical subject.

Qualifications and training Larger airlines train their own engineers.

BA gives sponsored students support industrial training during their degree courses.

Technician and craft training is given in appropriate skills, leading to, eg BTEC/CGLI awards and EITB skill standards. A few FE and private colleges have pre-entry courses.

Airline flight operations deal with the very complex business of moving many thousands of people around the world on as few planes as possible. It involves having the right types and size of plane in the right place at the right times, in a fully-operational condition, and with crews (who have had their legal rest times), ready to fly them. It is an enormous planning operation – although computers make it easier. Passenger and freight schedules have to be produced many months ahead, and flight operations have to work out as accurately as they can the number of flights that can be filled, or at least flow economically, at different times of the year, using available aircraft as profitably as possible. However, schedules often have to be changed – when an aircraft breaks down, when weather conditions (now rarely) make flying impossible, or aircraft have to be diverted.

Day-to-day direction and control of aircraft movement means close team work between flight operations, generally managed by qualified aircraft captains, maintenance and crew control. It takes experts and computers to work out flight schedules, crew itineraries, and maintenance programmes.

Flight planners – using computers – select the most economic routes, and optimum operating heights for each flight, depending on weather conditions, time of day and hazards – eg defence exercises. They may calculate the fuel needed, take-off and landing weights – although these are often now computer generated – for aircrew and load control. They have to see that aircrews have their flight plans – which include weather forecasts, pay-load information, and any special instructions from air traffic control.

Operations staff/assistants monitor aircraft movements using eg telex, send, receive and log other 'movement' messages (eg diversions and re-routings), keep logs of air-to-ground messages, compile weight and balance data – but increasingly being computerised – print out flight information and keep control of operations sheets, brief crews, deal with loading diagrams, update weather reports, and maintain daily records.

Airline airport services are generally run by a station manager and a traffic superintendent.

Airline ground staff – called 'passenger service agents' by BA – look after, 'handle', passengers, answer flight and general enquiries, deal with computerised check-in procedures, help passengers who need it through control points, check boarding passes, prepare cargo documents for customs, check that everything and everyone is on the plane.

'Ramp agents' (BA) load and unload passenger baggage, freight and mail, clean aircraft inside and out (and sometimes de-ice them), sort luggage in the baggage hall, help in the departure hall, take disabled passengers to and from planes, take meals to the aircraft, etc.

Airline commercial management depends on and employs the same functions as any other commercial organisation, including FINANCE, MARKETING, PERSONNEL, MANAGEMENT SERVICES, PUBLIC RELATIONS etc. Senior managers are responsible for strategy, route planning and developing eg charter work. Most managers – the industry is estimated to have at most 4000 mainly in technical, operational or eg marketing. Promotion to management is mainly from within. All the usual jobs have to be done – with the addition of reservations sales staff who make flight reservations. Larger airlines are mostly fully computerised, so there is demand for people with appropriate COMPUTING expertise, and operators etc, and SECRETARIES/TYPISTS mostly use word processors.

Recruitment and entry is at a number of levels.

Graduates (in any discipline) are recruited in small numbers for management training (mainly BA), and as computer programmers. BA takes on a few people with postgraduate qualifications in OPERATIONAL RESEARCH.

For most commercial posts, airlines want at least O-level-standard education including English and maths. Because shift work is often involved the minimum age is 18 and 20 is more usual. It helps to live within commuting distance of an airport. Staff whose work involves contact with the public are expected to have a warm, friendly manner, be smart, talk clearly and preferably have a second language, and have experience of similar work. Secretarial and clerical/typing staff are only recruited fully trained, and normally with previous experience.

Further information from individual airlines.

Air traffic control and services

The Civil Aviation Authority runs air traffic services (below) but also licenses pilots and other personnel (including maintenance engineers), planes, airlines, and routes, deals with safety in the air, and airworthiness regulations. It is responsible for airport development, and generally 'regulates' and supervises the industry. Through the licensing system it has considerable effect on the industry.

The main area of employment, however, is in

AIR TRAFFIC CONTROL Air traffic over Britain and some of the surrounding sea areas is controlled by the National Air Traffic Services (NATS), run jointly by the Civil Aviation Authority and the Ministry of Defence. They operate an intricate network of country-wide communications including radar equipment, computer-assisted control, navigational aids, and so on, keeping aircraft movements over Britain under continuous surveillance.

Controllers have to keep air traffic moving without snarl-ups or accidents through what is almost impossibly crowded air space. They are in charge, and pilots must obey them. The electronic equipment they use to do this has visual radar displays showing aircraft positions, track, height and number; radar and landing systems which can pierce fog and bring an aircraft down 'blind'; computers which analyse facts and figures at speed – all of which helps to make the work more manageable (although the systems now need updating to cope), but never easy. Planes get faster and larger, the amount of traffic is increasing steadily, and one controller may have to handle up to 100 aircraft an hour. Even with the electronic assistance, air traffic control still depends on control tower and pilot talking to each other.

Pilot and controller have to work in three dimensions, and so air space has to be divided into manageable territories, both horizontally and vertically.

One group of controllers operates the 'en route' services which keep all aircraft (commercial, military, private), in transit along the imaginary airways, separated from each other (1000 feet up and down, five nautical miles horizontally), even if one is a slow light aircraft and the other an Air Force fighter jet. Each controller watches a 'cube' of airways, and passes the planes on from one centre to the next, or to the approach controllers.

Approach controllers fit incoming planes into the other traffic coming into the airport, 'sequencing them down' (perhaps through a waiting 'stack' of planes), and filtering planes taking off up into the airways. Aerodrome controllers guide in-bound planes on the last stages of landing, give them clearance, course and heights, direct them to unloading areas, and make sure the runways are kept clear.

Air traffic control is a very difficult job, which gets harder when the airways are busy. A traffic controller must watch a display screen covered in complex and changing patterns and figures, take in new information all the time, and listen and talk to pilots (whose English may not be perfect), all at once. Also at the same time, he or she must make very fast decisions and react rapidly to new situations, such as changing weather conditions or emergencies.

Controllers work from the two control centres and about twenty airports (some employ their own). They can gain promotion eg to management and planning.

NATS employs (1986) about 2660 people in air traffic control – down from 3000 in 1983, and numbers – mainly of assistants – are to be further reduced (with more sophisticated systems NATS says), possibly to under 2300.

Air traffic control radar, computers, air-to-ground communication systems and visual display units must all work at maximum efficiency, since it is extremely difficult for controllers to work without them. NATS therefore employs its own engineers, both technicians for day-to-day maintenance, and graduate/professional for field management, development and installation.

Recruitment and entry The CAA expects to recruit about 45 air traffic control officer cadets a year at least until 1990 (about 1000 apply). It has stopped recruiting assistants.

CAA cadet entry is with five GCE/GCSE passes including two at A level (one must be in maths, geography or a science), although alternatives are acceptable. The age limits are 18-24. A high level of physical fitness is needed, and eyesight (normal colour vision) and hearing have to be very good. Ability to concentrate, to retain essential facts, to make decisions and act firmly, and stay totally calm whatever happens are all essential.

Employing airports each have their own requirements – some take only trained and experienced controllers, but some recruit trainees (the minimum entry requirement is likely to be five O-level-equivalent passes including English, maths, science).

NATS now recruits only qualified engineers, with at least a BTEC Higher award in telecommunications (or equivalent), age at least 20, and some relevant experience.

Qualifications and training CAA air traffic control training lasts two years, starting at the air traffic control college (Bournemouth), and interspersed with practical work at control centres and airports, plus 15 hours' 'introduction to flying'. Specialist training in eg programming, management etc is available for experienced officers.

Some employing airports train on-the-job, and/or at the air traffic control college or with a training company. A CAA licence is required.

Telecommunications engineers are given training to keep them up to date, and may be released to study part-time for additional qualifications.

OTHER WORK The rest of CAA's responsibilities employ people who are normally already qualified on recruitment, in eg ACCOUNTANCY, ECONOMICS, LAW, ENGINEERING, SCIENCE, and some posts require previous experience in the industry, eg in accident investigation. Excluding NATS, CAA employs (1986) some 4000 people.

Further information from the Civil Aviation Authority.

The airports

Airports are very much more complex places than, say, railway stations, and need very expert management. More people go through them, more services are housed there – for passengers, for the airlines, for air traffic control, immigration, freight handling, catering, car parking etc.

Although the country has some 200 working airports, the largest 30 or so deal with most of the traffic, and provide most work.

BAA plc (formerly the British Airports Authority), owns and manages seven airports, including the two largest – Heathrow and Gatwick – as well as Stansted, Glasgow, Edinburgh, Prestwick and Aberdeen. They handle about 75% of passengers and 85% of freight. The Civil Aviation Authority controls eight, and twenty or so – including Manchester, the third largest, are managed by local authorities. A private, 'STOL' (short take off and landing) airport is being built in London's dockland.

WORKING IN AIRPORTS Several thousand people work in a large airport, but only a small proportion are airport administrators or other employees. However, Stansted, where some 1700 (including airline and other staff) work now (1987), is expanding – numbers should go up to 3000 in the early 1990s, and possibly 10-12,000 not long after. BAA, the largest airport 'manager', has only some 7000 people working for it altogether, and some are headquarters staff, with only 400 managerial and professional staff working in the airports.

An airport is like a small town, with the airport managers providing the accommodation for airline service staff and air traffic control (as above), immigration authorities, freight-handling companies, caterers, banks, shop concessionaires, and so on. Services like security are provided by specialist firms on contract.

Airports are administered and managed by staff employed by BAA, the CAA, or a local authority. Although the teams running them may be small, the job is a major one, which ranges from having the land and buildings available to cope with the level of traffic through developing and installing highly-sophisticated systems for planes, passengers and freight, to ensuring the airport runs efficiently and economically.

BAA is now a commercially-owned organisation, and is likely to change quite considerably in the next few years. It is suggested it may, for example, extend its operations into developing and managing airports in other countries, and as a land and property developer. Each of its airports is to be run as a subsidiary company, so most BAA employees are employed to work at one airport only. Currently it also has a small headquarters staff (about 400) whose work includes forecasting future demand for air travel, planning short- and long-term airport development, deciding on and commissioning sophisticated electronic and communication systems like the automatic train which connects two terminal buildings at Gatwick. Property and commercial management involves dealing with both tenants in the airport and contractors, from the airlines themselves to the shops and banks in terminal buildings.

Airport managers have to make enough space available for customs and immigration; provide for huge quantities of volatile fuel to be stored safely ready for use; provide fire and other safety and security services; build and operate baggage and cargo handling facilities.

On the airports themselves, terminals are administered by terminal officers with teams of traffic officers.

They may be in charge of, for instance, the 'aprons', help to organise arrivals and departures, allocate aircraft to stands, log their arrival and departure, and how long they stay.

Traffic duty officers have to see that passengers and their baggage are in the right places at the right time, that baggage is moving properly on conveyors, that lifts and escalators are working etc.

Professional engineers plan, design, and supervise construction, maintenance etc of eg terminals, runways, transport systems; design and manage installation and maintenance etc of computer-based communications, information and other electronic systems, automated equipment for eg baggage handling etc.

Some engineering, maintenance staff work full-time in the airports, clearing runways, maintaining landing aids, repairing conveyors, escalators etc.

Every airport has its own FIRE SERVICE specially trained to deal with aircraft emergencies, but with routine work like de-frosting runways.

Information desks have to be staffed, and flight arrival and departure indicators kept up to date, people paged. Nurses and children's nurses are also employed.

Recruitment and entry Most airport staff are recruited from amongst people either with relevant qualifications, eg in ACCOUNTING, ENGINEERING, SURVEYING etc, or with some previous experience. A few may be recruited at clerical-level with GCE/GCSE passes, and there is a small graduate-entry management training intake (BAA only).

Further information from BAA, the Civil Aviation Authority, and local-authority airports.

RAILWAYS

Railways in Britain have been fighting decline ever since the private car and road haulage became popular, and have gone through frequent rationalisations. Despite this, wholly state-owned British Rail – it is the only transport system to be run by a single organisation – still has (1986) nearly 10,500 miles of standard-gauge routes (cut by over 8000 miles since 1961). It suffers heavily in competition with the convenience of 'door-to-door' road travel, and has severe financial problems – the railways are very vulnerable to economic conditions, and capital investment – in electrification, modernising stations, replacing rolling stock etc – is enormously expensive. However, the government is committed to maintaining a railway system now even though financial support was cut by 25% between 1983 and 1987 alone.

To compete and survive, British Rail has rationalised heavily, and restructured. It has switched from being production led to being driven by business needs – customers. The most recent re-organisation is aimed at adapting the regional and area structure to make front-line managers – those in day-to-day contact with customers – responsible for performance, and carried through the change to management by business sectors. In 1985-6 and 1986-7, BR made small surpluses, and has started on the largest investment programme for 25 years, currently (1986-7) spending over £400 million a year mainly on electrification and new trains. If the Channel Tunnel goes ahead, BR plans to spend £400 million on trains, stations, track improvements etc.

Despite the cut-backs and the problems, British Rail is still a very large organisation, with a 1985-6 turnover of £3145 million. It is divided into five main business sectors – the three passenger services – InterCity, Provincial Services, and Network SouthEast, plus Parcels, and Railfreight.

BR does a substantial amount of R&D, all geared to maximising a transport system using a steel wheel running on a steel rail, to exploit technical know-how to improve the railways' cost effectiveness, improve safety. Research ranges from day-to-day scientific support for railway operations, through to identifying and developing technology for future guided ground transport systems. Among current projects are developing new forms of train control and signalling, improving track design and construction, and developing computer-aided techniques.

Although businesses have been sold, BR still has a number of subsidiaries – 'Travellers Fare' provides retailing facilities and catering both on trains and at stations. It is a commercial business, which recently spent £5 million on upgrading buffets etc, is developing new marketing ideas for catering, and is starting up eg station pubs as joint ventures with brewers.

Freightliners is the world's largest road/rail container transport operator. See ROAD TRANSPORT below.

BR Property Board is still the country's largest landowner with 180,000 acres, but over 85% is used by the rail operations. Even so, it is a major developer – 27 schemes were completed in 1985-6 and 18 started, jointly with private developers. Income from letting was nearly £70 million, and from sales over £81 million.

BR Engineering (BREL) is being developed as an independent and free-standing company, and now has to compete with the private sector for nearly all contracts for BR vehicles – which makes achieving profitability difficult, at least in the short term. BREL has been restructured into two business groups – one dealing with new build and heavy overhaul, and the other doing light repairs and maintenance for BR. Three yards have closed, but eight sites remain.

Transmark is BR's consultancy subsibidary, which markets railway expertise world-wide – working on 125 projects, in 33 countries, and earning nearly £4 million in 1985-6.

BR has its own advertising company, and its own police force, dealing with everything from suspected bombs, and theft, through to troublemaking passengers.

Working in British Rail

British Rail has slashed its staffing levels, to barely 167,000 (1986-7) against 244,000 in 1976), and on current plans this is to be cut still further, to 154,000 by 1991-2 (mainly amongst administrative and support staff). With the 1984-5 6000 cut in administrative staff numbers, the ratio of administrative/managerial to 'manual/skilled' workers is back to 26: 74. Numbers actually running the railways were (1986-7) about 143,000 and are planned to fall to 133,000 in 1990-1.

THE RAIL BUSINESS Railways run round-the-clock, seven days a week, and so most people directly involved, including managers, must do shift work. The commercial nature of the work, pulling in and keeping customers, is emphasised. It is not only the train drivers etc who have to be mobile – BR expects its managerial and professional staff to move about the country to gain broad experience of the system.

Managerial/administrative staff Managers work either for one of the five businesses, or in operations – 'line' management of their common production line, the rail system. Although managers work at any one time in one of these, they do not have to stay in the same business throughout their careers, and are encouraged to move between them.

Operations covers all aspects of running trains – timetables, signalling, managing stations and station/depot staff, train crews, locomotives and rolling stock, and supervising actual services. Operating managers are the supervisors, station and depot managers, operating and movement managers, area and divisional managers who must keep the trains running on schedule, and supervise every aspect of the service. Junior managers may, as part of their jobs, have to bid for and negotiate freight contracts.

BR quotes as 'first jobs' –

traffic assistant supervising 50 staff on a 30-mile section of main line, including seeing that eight signal-boxes, a passenger station, and five rural freight depots ran smoothly, dealing with as many problems as possible on the spot;

area carriage cleansing supervisor at Euston, followed by managing a major cleaning and maintenance depot;

station supervisor in Newcastle, followed by managing and planning movement of coal from mines to power stations in Northumberland, a spell developing microcomputing for operations and (after eight years), provincial manager for Anglia local services.

British Rail also employs people in the full range of usual business 'functions'. For example –

MARKETING staff work mainly for one of the five businesses. They start, for instance, in sales and customer service management at local level, although some posts are available in market research at headquarters. In the freight businesses, staff may, for example, try to solve an industrial customer's bulk transport problem more cheaply and conveniently than road transport. There are senior marketing management posts in all the rail businesses.

FINANCIAL MANAGEMENT AND CONTROL areas of work include planning business strategies, analysing investment opportunities, budgetary control, financial accounting, cash management and auditing. Accountants are employed in the business sectors' management teams, planning and implementing new marketing strategies and policies. Qualified staff can either specialise in any branch of accountancy or develop careers ranging over the whole field of accounting disciplines, and it is possible to switch into general management.

PERSONNEL MANAGEMENT Personnel work at local or area level concentrates on effective management of administrative staff and systems, and providing professional expertise for 'line' managers. First appointments are usually in a personnel management team of an area manager or engineer, followed by a post as an area personnel manager, followed by more senior posts in areas with up to 2000 staff. From areas promotion is to regional and board HQ posts where most work is in employer relations, with some opportunities to specialise in training and personnel development, research on future policy.

PURCHASING AND SUPPLY BR spends some £1250 million a year on materials, goods, services and capital contracts, ranging from locomotives costing up to £1 million each down to paper clips, as well as computers, stone ballast in unbelievable quantities, food, electricity, machine tools etc. BR quotes as a career progression –

personal assistant to the director of supply;

a civil engineering commodity group buyer;

managing the computerised system which controls ordering of uniform and protective clothing for all 130,000 staff;

studying inventory management options;

supplies officer purchasing fuels, chemicals, cleaners and paints used throughout BR;

MANAGEMENT SERVICES BR is a major computer user, operating eight large mainframes, hundreds of micros, and thousands of terminals, linked by a sophisticated telecommunications network. Data collection, enquiry and reporting aspects of systems is distributed to the point of use, and users are involved in design, implementation and operation of their systems. Computers are used in train scheduling and planning, control and deployment of rolling stock on a real-time basis, seat and sleeper berth reservations, as well as for the business functions. Computer staff develop more sophisticated computing tools and techniques, data dictionaries and graphics packages to aid design, databases and high-level languages to help in implementation etc.

Computer staff start as programmers in a management-grade post at one of four computing centres, progressing normally through systems analysis and design to project management, and/or through operating systems, micro-computers, telecommunications, to computing operations management.

BR also has an OPERATIONAL RESEARCH division, working in small teams, or individually, on a wide range of projects – ranging from strategic to tactical – for the rail businesses.

Engineers join, initially, one of three functional groups (below), and usually start at local or area level, but are expected to become effective managers as well as being technically highly competent. Over 1300 chartered engineers are in management posts, and experienced engineering managers can move into general management at area and above, into management of one of the five businesses where engineering experience is needed in planning and implementing strategies. The three functional groups are –

Traction units, rail vehicles, plant and power supply (mechanical, electrical, electronic or production engineers) – at area level engineers manage maintenance facilities and provide technical support. Budgetary control, staff planning, welfare, changing practices, and problem solving are all involved. Board and regional staff plan, install and maintain equipment. At the technical centre, engineers specify and procure new vehicle designs, develop and set maintenance and performance standards for the vehicle fleet. First posts are normally as technical assistant or junior manager at a maintenance depot, technical support office at regional or board HQ, or technical assistant in design/development.

Control systems, communications and data-transmission networks (electronic, electrical, control, communications, computer engineers, computer scientists) – divides in two. Signals engineers look after design, manufacture and maintenance of railway control systems (signals) both bringing in the latest technology and maintaining/adapting electro-mechanical or interlocking equipment. Telecommunications engineers design, install, and maintain BR's automatic telephone network, the on-line computer and message-switching network (using a track-side transmission systems now using optical fibre cable), automated platform indicators and public address systems. First appointment as a senior technical officer is usually in design, followed by project work, and area engineering management.

Track, buildings and structures (civil engineers) – mainly deals with maintenance and renewal of track, bridges, tunnels, and buildings. Work has to be planned and carried out to keep service disruption to a minimum. A first job can be in, eg bridge maintenance for an area, supervising bridge reconstruction and raising for electrification, followed by responsibility for 160 track miles of permanent way maintenance, with a team of two supervisors, seven assistant supervisors and 110 men in 11 gangs.

Research and development employs 900 engineers, scientists and technicians. In all engineering and building works, BR employs its own QUANTITY SURVEYORS (over 150 of them). They work in regionally-based teams, with responsibility for projects at 'an early stage' after training, and can work in both architectural and civil engineering sides of construction.

Technicians and craft workers BR employs technicians in all the engineering functions, but mainly in installing, maintaining and servicing electronic and electrical signal and communications equipment. Craft workers are employed on train and track equipment maintenance and repair. Permanent way, signal and telecommunications staff number (1986) over 24,700 still, and 18,000 are employed in workshops.

'Traffic' staff include (1986) the 20,350 drivers (they work either on main/ branch lines or in shunting) and other footplate staff (down from 23,000 in 1983), 10,704 guards and other train staff (down from 11,700), 6780 signalling staff and crossing keepers (down from 8200). Some 10,260 work in stations, yards and depots (down from 22,000) – railmen and women carry luggage, answer queries, deal with eg doors, load and unload parcels etc when trains arrive, keep stations clean and tidy, paint platform edges etc. A further 940 work on carriage and wagon examination (down from 1700).

BR ENGINEERING (BREL) BREL has to compete with other firms for both BR business and orders world-wide, and this is a tough market. Despite a gross income of £471.4 million in 1985-6, and orders from as far away as China, BREL is 'rationalising' hard to become competitive. It has to extend its product range – BREL engineers have designed new prototype trains for London Underground, and is to start making 'light rapid transit' vehicles – and this takes investment. Total employment was cut by over 2500 in 1985-6 alone, to 22,800, including 4000 professional/managerial etc (from 35,000 in 1980), and BREL wants a further reduction of up to 5000 by 1989-90.

BREL employs mainly engineers (electrical, mechanical, production) – professional and technician, with skilled craft workers by far the largest group. Design teams have been enlarged to enable BREL to compete in new markets. Specialist MARKETING, PERSONNEL, ACCOUNTING and COMPUTING teams are being strengthened.

'OTHER' BR BUSINESSES BR's other companies are, by comparison, very small, with comparatively few opportunities –

BR's Property Board, although it looks after a massive estate spread all over the country, employs (1985-6) only 924 people. They mainly work in one of seven regional offices, and most are qualified, or trainee, SURVEYORS. The work involves property valuation, rating, building and maintenance, planning, property management and valuation, and negotiating sales, purchases, leases, wayleaves and easements. BR quotes as a first job (after training), dealing with railway arches in South London.

Travellers Fare employs (1985-6) over 5300 people (including some 940 managers, professional staff etc) in all CATERING functions. Junior managers usually start assistant 'unit' managers – in a bistro or hamburger restaurant – and career progression is said to be most rapid for people who get results and will work anywhere. Other jobs quoted include managing all station vending machines, project manager for computerised cash register field trials, station catering manager.

Transmark, the consultancy firm, actually employs only 90 people, but other BR staff – especially engineers – may be seconded to particular projects for which they have the expertise and experience.

Freightliner – see ROAD TRANSPORT.

Recruitment and entry Despite the steady cuts in staffing, rapid turnover and a high retirement rate over the next years means BR expects to recruit about 7000 people a year to fill essential vacancies.

Graduates are recruited for operations management (any subject), marketing (any subject but eg business studies, marketing preferred), engineering (all main disciplines), financial management/control (any subject), computing (subjects showing numerate and linguistic abilities preferred), R&D (2.1 or higher degree in engineering, engineering science, physics, chemistry, maths or metallurgy), personnel (any subject but may give preference to relevant degree/pg diploma), purchasing (any subject but one exempting from IP&S exams an advantage), OR (maths, statistics, economics, science, engineering, or pg OR qualification), estate management and surveying (any exempting from RICS exams), catering management (any subject).

Transport police are recruited at 19-plus with a small graduate intake.

School-leavers are recruited at both 16- and 18-plus –

A-level entrants are recruited mainly for training in accountancy (two A levels at grade C or above, plus five O-level-equivalent passes, or equivalent eg BTEC National, subjects to include English and maths) and for engineering via sponsorships (requires a place on any suitable course, grades A or B in A level maths and physics, and age under 21).

O-level (and equivalent) entrants are recruited as trainee engineering (civil, electrical and mechanical) technicians (subjects to include English, maths, physics), signal and telecommunication technicians (no subjects specified), and craft apprentices (no subjects specified). Upper age limit 18.

Traction trainees, junior railmen/women, junior track staff, clerks (mainly for booking offices) and catering staff are recruited at 16-plus, no specific qualifications wanted.

BR's two-year YTS scheme has up to 900 places a year. 54% of trainees stay with BR, and some 17% gain jobs elsewhere.

Qualifications and training BR trains extensively, reviews training regularly, and plans to double the number of managers going on training courses each year, as well as extending on-the-job training for all employees.

Graduate entrants are all given training, varying in length from scheme to scheme, and what is needed to gain appropriate professional qualifications (which BR requires). Operations managers have 15 months' training (including three months' attachment to an area or business management team), marketing takes about 8 months, engineering 24 months, R&D up to two years, accountancy 24-30 months (for CACA, CIMA or CIPFA), personnel 6-10 months, purchasing up to 18 months, computer programming about 24 months, surveying 24 months, catering up to 6 months.

A-level accountancy entrants train for 42 months for CACA, CIMA or CIPFA qualifications.

Sponsored engineering students are given two years' training (plus vacation jobs) on a 1-3-1, 2-1-1-1 or thin sandwich basis.

Engineering technician training lasts up to four years, and normally includes release to study for appropriate BTEC awards. Other technical trainees work for either CGLI or BTEC awards, according to aptitude.

Craft apprenticeships last up to four years, and are based in EITB modular training schemes, linked to release for CGLI awards in mechanical and electrical engineering.

Traction trainees learn almost entirely on-the-job, with an initial training period of about eight weeks. The first job in the driving cab is as assistant driver, first on a relief basis, then as a regular secondman/woman. At a later stage they get several months' training on a particular type of locomotive, plus further short training courses to widen the driver's (motorman/woman's) skills in controlling various types of trains.

Further information from British Rail – either the management recruitment officer, or via local area managers.

ROAD TRANSPORT

Road transport rapidly became the most popular way of travelling and transporting goods, and has a major impact on all aspects of life out of all proportion to its age. By 1985, 21.2 million vehicles were licensed to go on the roads (up nearly 3 million in only four years), of which the vast majority (almost 86%) are cars or light vans – 82% of passenger mileage is by car and taxi, only 8% by bus and coach.

Road transport is a very fragmented 'industry'. The road system is provided by the government, so unlike the railways the industry does not have amongst its costs expensive building and maintenance of any 'permanent way'. It is possible to start up in road transport rather more cheaply than other forms of transport, and the 'one-person' business is fairly common.

Road transport divides into two main sectors –

PASSENGER TRANSPORT – buses, coaches, taxis – is one. Bus and coach services suffer from the same, severe, problems as the railways, in that they have to compete with the greater convenience of cars. But they also have to contend with the fact that the more cars there are on the roads, the more difficult it is to run efficient and cost-effective services which bring in customers. Fewer passengers means higher unit costs and so higher fares, and the total effect is a downward spiral of provision.

It is at present (1987) impossible to give any kind of realistic view of the passenger-transport industry. In October 1986, the industry started on the biggest shake up for some 50 years, with almost complete de-regulation. For the first time since 1930, anyone who wants to operate a bus service – whether it is one bus on one (short or long) route or a fleet serving many – can do so, just by buying the vehicles, satisfying safety regulations and hiring drivers with PSV licences (London has only partly been deregulated, though). Prior to de-regulation, some 120,000 passenger vehicles (including taxis), were licensed.

Local authorities no longer license bus operators in their area; their own transport companies must now operate at 'arm's length' from the authority (and other owners can compete on their routes), and the National Bus Company (which operated some 14,500 buses and coaches through some 60 subsidiary companies) is in process of being broken up. Local authorities can subsidise routes which have not attracted operators, though, giving the subsidy to the lowest tender.

Some 15,000 services were registered under the 1985 Transport Act – but only 200 new operators registered, with competition on only 3% of routes (but Glasgow found itself with 190 operators against only 20 pre-deregulation). Some routes have lost many, even all, of their buses – and about 30% of routes may have to be subsidised. Prior to deregulation, seven local-authority passenger transport executives ran 9000 buses, other local authorities had a total of 5300, and some 5700 privately-owned firms ran over 30,000 vehicles, but most had fewer than five each, and only a small proportion operated scheduled local bus services. In the months since de-regulation, competition has been very fierce.

It will be some time before a clear picture of the re-shaped industry emerges – indeed it will take some time for it to 'shake down' – and future employment prospects become clear. The pattern of employers is clearly changing, with fewer large operators – the government has insisted on National Bus breaking up some subsidiaries into even smaller units to increase competition. London Regional Transport is probably now one of the largest (it operates some 5000 buses) even though it has sub-contracted some routes – and more medium-sized and smaller units. It is clear (from figures produced by manufacturers) that 'mini-bus' services are increasing at the expense of the traditional buses. The Post Office's 'post buses' (120 of them) are now a crucial part of the rural passenger-transport network.

Taxi and car-hire services provide a more personal service, but as of 1987, taxi firms and drivers can provide shared-ride services at separate fares. They can also run regular local services, and can tender in competition with bus operators for services being subsidised by local authorities (but only 50 had registered by the end of 1986).

Taxis 'ply for hire' on the streets, must legally accept any fare, and generally do the shorter journeys. Figures suggest some 39,000 licensed taxis, including some 13,500 in London.

Hire cars, and 'mini taxis' may be booked for an immediate journey or in advance. The work is generally more varied – journeys to more distant stations or airports, for weddings or funerals.

Both taxis and hire cars are run by firms which own fleets of cars and/or taxis, and employ drivers full- or part-time. Many, though, operate a kind of 'franchise' system – traditionally this is a 'journeyman' (or woman) system, where the driver in effect hires the cab or car from the owner, paying the owner an agreed proportion of the takings. Many taxi-drivers, and quite a few car drivers now, are self-employed, although they may 'work' for a firm, or belong to a co-operative, which provides a booking and in-car radio link.

Car hire is an expanding business, with over 160 firms (according to an RTITB survey), but employment has fallen sharply, to under 5000 people. Only six firms have more than 100 employees each and employ 77% of those working in the industry – 106 firms have no more than five employees.

ROAD HAULAGE is the other sector – ranging from huge container trucks traversing Europe, the Middle East and sometimes Africa, down to the local delivery van. This further subdivides. The largest group consists of firms which are purely road haulage operators, carrying other people's goods etc from one place to another. The other is made up of industrial, commercial and other organisations which prefer to operate their own vehicle fleets (although quite a few firms have their fleets run by a specialist contractor). Firms which operate, or have operated for them, their own fleets range from manufacturers (of bread, flour, electrical goods), through petrol and chemical companies with their tanker fleets, to the Milk Marketing Board collecting daily from farmers, the Post Office (delivery vans mainly) and British Telecom (installation and maintenance vehicles).

Road haulage has expanded almost continuously since world war II, and now (1986) carries over 86% of goods traffic. However, the actual number of goods vehicles licensed has not risen very much – largely because the size and capacity of vehicles has increased steadily, so about 71% of the traffic is now carried in vehicles of over 28 tonnes. International road haulage has grown fast – some 23 million tonnes a year are carried in and out of the UK, with France the main destination.

Road haulage suffered very badly during the recession – largely, say commentators, because modern marketing and selling techniques have been ignored, and managerial competence and efficiency vary so widely – properly managed firms survived and did reasonably well.

The Road Transport Industry Training Board (RTITB) 1985-6 figures showed some of the effects of recession. The total number of firms had fallen to 6924 (against 8285 in 1978), and the total number of employees was down to 145,500 (from over 196,600 in 1979) although this was 1000 or so up on 1984-5. In more detail (1984-5 figures) –

Sector	Employers		Employees	
	1978	1984	1978	1984
General/contract	4447	4292	94,426	79,018
Tippers	1615	1173	13,934	9895
Furniture removers	656	806	10,960	8994
Parcel carriers	223	138	32,476	26,370
Heavy/abnormal load	190	180	5459	3429
Tankers	157	137	7871	6915

In terms of size, the industry is still very pyramid-shaped. Some 53% of firms have no more than five employees each – and employ only 7% of the total workforce – and another 16% between six and ten, 6% of total employment. Only 42 firms had 251 or more employees, but they accounted for 40% of those employed in the industry, 95 had 101-250, employing 11% of the total workforce.

Largest of the haulage groups is the National Freight Consortium, owned by its 25,000 workforce. One of the few groups to operate nation-wide, it has some 18,000 vehicles and extensive warehousing and cold storage, with its own maintenance capacity. BR's Freightliner is a road/rail container operator, with 430 32/38-tonne trucks, 1200 trailers, and 200 containers, working out of nearly 40 depots, but employing under 1850 people.

THE REPAIR SECTOR An important part of the industry is repairing both commercial vehicles and cars. Most firms that have fleets of any size (eg the Post Office, British Telecom) have their own repair workshops, but firms with only a few vehicles, and the vast majority of car owners, expect to use what is usually called a 'garage'. According to RTITB, numbers of firms increased between 1978 and 1984 – 'light vehicle' repairers numbered over 6000 in 1984 against under 5900 in 1978, and commercial vehicle repairers were up in numbers to 550 from 534. But the numbers employed fell sharply – to 26,300 in light vehicle repair (from over 30,300), and to 3750 in commercial vehicle repair from 6330.

OTHER SECTORS which involve work related to road transport include driving schools, car dealing and distribution, and managing parking facilities (dominated by one firm whose management team includes 40 SURVEYORS and site negotiators).

Working in the industry

Road transport is labour intensive, mainly at the 'operating' end, and since every vehicle needs at least one man/woman or woman to drive it, it is difficult to find ways of cutting staff past a certain level without cutting services too. Passenger transport is steadily cutting out the bus/coach 'conductor', simpler-to-maintain cars and trucks mean fewer workshop staff are needed, and numbers of managers, clerical staff have never been large. A high proportion of those working in the industry, then, are 'operatives' – drivers, craft workers, fork-lift truck operators, porters, packers etc. But the percentage of managers, professional, commercial, sales and clerical staff is going up – if only because the number of workshop staff and drivers etc is being trimmed so hard.

Working in the industry is often strenuous – even for managers – hectic, and demanding, often (as one graduate entrant said) with 'baffling but stimulating logistic problems to solve'. Business goes on round the clock, seven days a week, so shift work is necessary, and managerial/administrative staff as well as drivers may have to be mobile, ready to move for long-term prospects.

MANAGERIAL, PROFESSIONAL AND SUPERVISORY STAFF probably make up only about one in twenty of those working in the industry, mainly because there are so many small firms. Many firms are run by a single owner-manager.

Spurred by tougher trading conditions, rising costs, and the problems of making transport service of any kind economic, demand for more sophisticated managerial and professional skill is rising, if slowly outside the larger fleets. But in the major fleets, management skills are crucial.

Amongst the most 'professional' managers are probably those running distribution services for, eg large supermarkets, major manufacturers and other retailers – their costs can be some 3.5% of prices charged, and on turnovers of £1000 million or more this is a substantial sum. Effective and efficient distribution can save a great deal of money, and involves some sharp operational decision-making – just an hour's delay per vehicle per day, it is said, would mean £1 million a year to a major food manufacturer.

Distribution has become capital- and energy-intensive, and has always been labour intensive. Managers may have to use sophisticated computer-controlled systems to organise day-to-day operations, and try to cut delivery cycles to a minimum. While distribution managers do not have to make a direct profit, their operations must be cost-effective, and they may have to compete for their own firm's business with outside contractors.

Many of the managerial jobs are in 'line' management, especially in independent contractors and passenger firms. Large firms are increasingly pushing as much responsibility as possible down into garages and depots. Each is usually a semi-independent unit, with its own administrative and clerical staff. The work is day-to-day transport administration, managing people, making schedules and timetables work, planning routes, allocating people to jobs (and loads to trucks), dealing with all the – usually extensive – paperwork and complex legal regulations, costing contracts, seeing that buses and trucks are properly maintained and serviced and so spend the maximum time on the road. Some managers specialise, as eg service, or parts/stores.

In larger organisations, promotion is to managerial and professional posts at district, regional and national levels. Work will include planning, for instance forecasting demand, setting timetables or schedules, fares or charges, planning routes, developing new business. Larger firms employ people in MARKETING, FINANCE, PURCHASING, but the industry employs comparatively few specialist managers in PERSONNEL, MANAGEMENT SERVICES (including COMPUTING). Many firms use computers in some form now, though, and the larger firms quite sophisticated systems.

ENGINEERS are employed in a professional capacity by comparatively few organisations, although they may be taken on as general managers. Transport services with 'metro' systems (London, Glasgow and Newcastle) employ the largest numbers, in multidisciplinary teams, especially where new rail systems (eg for London docklands) are being developed. Most of the work is though, maintenance and improvement – CIVIL ENGINEERS work on stations, bridges etc, ELECTRICAL/ELECTRONIC ENGINEERS on eg signalling, power generation and communication networks.

MECHANICAL ENGINEERS may also be employed to organise and manage fleet development, vehicle maintenance and overhaul etc for larger firms, but overall numbers are comparatively small – in the hundreds. London Regional Transport probably employs about 1000 professional and technical staff in engineering departments and labs.

Supervisory staff in the industry are mainly garage/workshop foremen and foremen fitters, PSV inspectors, office/depot supervisors, and chargehands.

Recruitment and entry A high proportion of managers, administrators, supervisors etc, work their way up from from, eg clerical work or driving. Direct entry to administrative work, with the possibility of managerial training is mainly for school leavers at 18-plus with GCE/GCSE passes including A-levels, an appropriate BTEC award, or the equivalent. Only the largest organisations specifically recruit graduate trainees. In passenger transport, this is now down mainly to London Regional Transport. In the haulage industries, RTITB encourages firms to recruit and train graduates. The Board expects (1987) companies to recruit some 200-250 a year, but they have not so far reached anything like that level. The National Freight Consortium recruits about 50 annually and BR's Freightliner a number, and it may be possible to train in the distribution divisions of larger manufacturers.

Older people may be recruited, but may be asked for a certificate of professional competence (below) pre-entry.

Qualifications and training Formal management training is only given by larger companies, although the amount of training being done throughout the industry is rising – and RTITB is pushing hard to improve standards via eg modular and distance learning. All managers must now (under EEC rules) have a certificate of professional competence (awarded on the basis of a written test set by the RSA or an exempting professional qualification). It is useful to gain a relevant qualification, eg of the Chartered Institute of Transport (see Background – to the industry generally – above), or –

The Institute of Road Transport Engineers (1986 membership 14,500) sets a three-part qualifying exam 'to improve the technical, commercial and management skill, knowledge and competence of all whose occupation is the operation of vehicles used to transport goods, passengers and equipment'.

DRIVERS make up well over half of all 'operatives' in the industry. These are the bus and coach (some train) drivers in passenger transport, van and truck drivers in the haulage business.

Bus and coach drivers work either within a restricted town or country area, or on long distance routes either just on mainland Britain, or on European coach tours. There is taxi- or hire-car driving.

Haulage drivers may drive vans for local deliveries and collections, deliver for large stores. They may collect milk from farms, doing a regular daily run, or take petrol from depot to petrol stations, ferry builders' materials to and from suppliers and yards, carry bulk goods from manufacturer to warehouse, or food from warehouse to supermarket.

The job is rarely just driving. Bus and coach drivers now also collect fares, and cope with passenger problems etc. Delivery and haulage drivers must load and deliver goods, make sure their vehicles are properly and safely loaded, must be able to couple and uncouple trailers, operate tipping gear, or tail lifts etc. They must all keep the vehicle's documentation in order, make detailed reports, be able to check their vehicles and recognise faults, and be able to find their way through complex transport and freight regulations in other countries. Most driving jobs mean irregular hours and shiftworking, but actual hours on the road are strictly limited. Driving is an active, outdoor life, with a practical bent.

Recruitment and entry Since it is not possible to hold a PSV (bus/coach), taxi or HGV (commercial vehicle) licence under the age of 21 (and in practice employers prefer 25 because the insurance is cheaper), the main entry requirement is age. A 'young driver' scheme gives training to a small number of 16-21-year-olds, and the ARMED FORCES train under-21s. Bus operators used to recruit all prospective drivers as conductors first, but 'one-person' operating means firms look either for people who already have licences, or they take on trainees, as and when needed.

Other qualifications include physical fitness (but strength is no longer so important as modern commercial vehicles are easier to drive if rather more complex), good sight (but glasses can be worn), the ability to concentrate, reasonable literacy and numeracy, and practical/mechanical aptitude.

Qualifications and training Larger passenger-transport companies and road haulage firms train, in their own schools, the larger ones with sophisticated equipment like simulators.

Trainees in approved companies can take a test at 18 for a class 3 HGV licence (to drive four-wheel rigid vehicles); a year later the class 2 test can be taken (covering heavy vehicles with more than four wheels), but for the class 1 test, to drive heavy articulated vehicles, the age limit is still 21. This scheme allows younger people to learn to drive increasingly large and heavy vehicles over a period of years, and also to learn about the haulage industry, repair and maintenance, loading techniques, records etc. YTS trainees can take a linked scheme.

For smaller haulage and firms, some 68 group training schemes country-wide cater for 92,000 employees in 1740 firms.

Taxi drivers have to gain a local licence, and the regulations for these can be strict. Before a licence is granted, drivers have to pass a special driving test, and also a test of knowledge of the area concerned – in large cities like London, this can take between a year and four years. Some firms run training schemes, and in London there are a few schools.

DRIVING INSTRUCTION AND EXAMINATION are closely linked to driving. However, although instructors must be good drivers, they must be able to teach both practical skills and road sense/rules to people from all kinds of backgrounds, however much (or little) intelligence or common sense they may have, without talking down, or up, to them, being patronising, over-critical, or too sympathetic. Costs keep the bulk of all driving instruction on the roads – use of classroom and/or simulator teaching has not developed as expected. It is teaching by example and practice, although instructors also have to make sure their pupils are learning the highway code. The hours can be 'unsocial' since most people have to learn to drive in out-of-work times.

Instructors must know – and work out – where to take their pupils to give them driving experience that matches their skill level, arrange driving tests, keep efficient paper work (including a diary) and self-employed instructors have to keep their own accounts.

Most instructors spend a relatively short time working for a school before becoming self-employed. Large transport firms and training associations employ instructors to teach for passenger and heavy goods vehicle licences.

Driving examiners are civil servants, working (at least at present) for the Department of the Environment. After initial training, the examiners work in teams, under the supervision of a senior examiner, at one of several hundred test centres sited throughout the country. Each examiner takes eight or nine examinations daily, and is solely responsible for deciding whether or not to pass or fail a driver.

Recruitment and entry Driving instructors must have held a full (and 'clean') driver's licence for four years of the preceding six, and must pass the Department of the Environment's driving instructor's examination. It is not, then, possible to become an instructor younger than 21, and in practice schools prefer to recruit at 25-plus, when the insurance premium is lower. Some schools recruit people with 'trainee licences' which are given by the DoT to give them a chance to gain practical experience. Personal qualities, such as patience and ability to keep calm, are important.

Driving examiners must be at least 28 years of age, have at least eight years' driving experience on several different types of vehicle and have had particularly wide experience in the preceding five years (eg, as a driving instructor). They must know the highway code extremely well, are expected to have an active interest in motoring, traffic, road sense and safety problems, and some mechanical knowledge of the vehicles with which they are familiar. Selection is by competitive exams (although there has been a severe shortage of examiners for some years now), and interview followed by a special driving test except where the applicant holds an approved instructor's licence.

Qualifications and training Instructors must pass an examination and practical test set by the Department of Transport. It is possible to study for these at an instructors' school (one- to three-week courses) – but standards vary. The National Joint Council of Approved Driving Instructors has a list of qualified tutors.

Examiners are trained after recruitment, but must pass a further test.

VEHICLE MECHANICS AND TECHNICIANS Mechanics/technicians are employed in substantial numbers by every road-vehicle fleet operator, and in independent garages. Numbers have, however, been falling steeply – RTITB estimates suggest they fell by about 15,000 to some 90,000 over the five or six years to 1984-5. Developments in vehicle technology are the main contributory factor, says RTITB.

The job is becoming increasingly 'technical' as car systems get more sophisticated, and modern diagnostic systems are introduced, especially in eg auto-electrical work where fault diagnosis, car tuning, in-car entertainment systems and fitting accessories, is increasingly complex. But while the newest cars and trucks need less frequent checks, and are mechanically simpler to repair, many older cars – which inevitably need more work on them – will be on the road for years to come.

Most mechanics/technicians specialise in light (cars) or heavy (goods) vehicles, motorcyles or 'performance' cars, coach body-building, body-repairing or electrical/electronic systems, but there is nothing to prevent good mechanics/technicians from adding to their skills and changing to another specialised area. After basic training most continue to add to their skills.

Some, for example, become new-style, highly-skilled technicians who diagnose what is wrong and specify what has to be done (the actual work is then done by workshop staff with more limited skills).

Others train as reception engineers, the link between garage and car-owner – finding out what the customer wants done, trying to estimate its cost, telling the workshop about the job, and returning the car (with account) to the owner. They may become foremen/women, then supervisors, and may go on to management, perhaps running a garage of their own.

Recruitment and entry is picking up after some very poor years, but is nowhere near the levels RTITB think necessary. Annual recruitment of young trainees is down to at most 1000 a year, mainly by larger firms, from the 9-10,000 a year in the later 1970s.

While no formal entry requirements are set, the best training schemes will probably want at least some passes at 16-plus†, especially maths and physics. Vehicle systems are changing, so mechanics and technicians have to be capable of keeping up with developing technologies. Practical aptitude for dealing with machinery and/or electrical/electronic systems is needed, as well as reasonable physical fitness. Mechanics/technicians have to appreciate the care needed to ensure vehicles are safe to drive.

YTS schemes, run both by RTITB and individual firms, are widely available (14,000 trainees were taken on in 1985-6).

Qualifications and training Training should be under RTITB schemes and standards. Traditional-style training schemes/apprenticeships for school-leavers lasted up to four years, but have been accelerated recently to just over two years, including release to study for the appropriate CGLI or BTEC awards. But the industry believes its needs have changed – time-serving craft training does not produce people good enough to be diagnosticians but they are too good to be operatives. RTITB has therefore produced a modular scheme, which lets trainees take tests in individual skills when they are ready. JTS schemes may also be shorter. YTS trainees can take a 'bridging' course to get them on to second-stage training.
See also RETAILING.

Further information from the Institute of Road Transport Engineers, the Freight Transport Association, the Road Haulage Association, the Road Transport Industry Training Board, and individual transport firms.

THE SEA AND INLAND WATERWAYS
Merchant navy (including working at sea and on shore) — inland waterways
It is common to think of all occupations that involve the sea, and waterways, together, probably because the skills involved in 'driving' ships are similar whatever purposes the ships themselves may have. In fact, the choice is (theoretically) between three distinct careers – the waterborne defence forces, mainly the ROYAL NAVY. in FISHING, and in providing passenger and freight services, through the Merchant Navy. While only the merchant navy is dealt with here, as transport, all three have very many common features. Also dealt with here are the support services, such as ports and pilotage.

THE MERCHANT NAVY
Working at sea — pilots (and lighthouse keepers) — working on shore
The world shipping industry has been in deepening trouble more or less since the oil-price crisis of 1973, and the subsequent fall in the volume of world trade, with a 1985 level only just above that of 1974. Too much tonnage has been chasing too little traffic for far too long – in all over 24% of the world's merchant ships are surplus to needs.

For the British fleet, the effects have been near catastrophic. Before world war II 40% of the world's merchant fleet was UK-registered. Today it is just 3%, and is only eighth in world ranking. The size of the fleet has fallen to 16.6 million (deadweight) tonnes in 1985, from a peak of over 53 million ten years earlier, and the number of British owned ships to 640 from 1614. The only remaining passenger services are the busy, but not profitable enough, ferry services to Europe, Scandinavia, Ireland and UK islands, and holiday cruise ships. The industry also includes support vessels for the North Sea rigs.

To survive in these conditions, shipping companies have been rationalising hard – a large tonnage, especially tankers, has been scrapped or sold. Costs have been slashed – a third of all ships in British ownership have been 'flagged out', to operate under 'open' registers of countries other than Britain because this is cheaper, allowing (amongst other things) companies to employ cheaper crews. They have modernised engines to cut fuel costs and staffing levels, and developed new services – major shipping lines now operate scheduled container-ship services round the globe for instance. Some shipping companies are 'diversifying' into other businesses. Larger ships, ships purpose-built for the commodities they are intended to carry, and containers – easier to load and unload straight on/off road trailers – are the norm.

Ships are increasingly technologically sophisticated. In the most modern the wheel – and so the helmsman – have gone. The modern 'bridge' is enclosed, and the desk officer controls the ship through banks of instrument panels akin to the 'deck' of an airliner. The ship isn't steered in the traditional sense at all – it is controlled automatically. Deck officers don't 'ring down' any more to the engine room – they just press a button. Highly-sensitive electronic controls are needed to give these 'juggernauts' the necessary manoeuvrability. Deck officers navigate, monitor instruments, and control the ship rather like airline pilots.

Amongst the instrument banks are satellite-linked radar and radio navigation aids, and a micro-computer with a VDU on which the officer of the watch can do all kinds of calculations, such as checking on speed against load and weather conditions, to make sure the ship gets to port at the most convenient time of day. The officer can input navigation changes, and call up all kinds of information, for instance a detailed analysis of fuel consumption. Ship-to-shore communications increasingly use fast satellite systems, so that ships can be in continuous touch with the company's offices, however far away, and with ports on the route. Through the satellite data transmission systems, ships can get completely up-to-date facsimile weather charts, for example, which can save many hours of 'steaming', and a great deal of fuel.

Ownership of merchant shipping varies according to type. Foreign-going cargo liners and container ships are mostly operated by large groups, provide world-wide networks of scheduled cargo and container services, as well as being in the passenger and holiday-cruise liner business. Foreign-going tramp ships, on the other hand, are operated by private owners, some with large fleets, but many owning only a small number of ships, some even only one. Most of the tanker fleet is owned and operated by the oil companies themselves, with a few major independent British tanker-owners.

Working at sea
The number of people, and particularly seamen, employed in the merchant fleet has has fallen dramatically, partly as a result of lower manning requirements for today's ships, but mainly due to the recession linked to 'flagging out' – which allows shipping lines to recruit crews of any nationality at the lowest going rates. In 1939, merchant seamen numbered 150,000 – by 1986, numbers were down to just 14,700 officers and 19,000 ratings (and under 3000, under 16%, are not British residents against 30-40% in the 1970s). Many are unemployed, and companies have given up their permanent crews and now recruit on short-term contracts.

Technologically-advanced ships change long sea-going traditions. For instance, as one deck officer on watch (with a cadet) can 'handle' the ship, control its speed and direction from the 'bridge', engineer officers do not now need to keep round-the-clock 'watches', so halving the number of engineer officers a modern ship needs to carry. As a result, new ships' complements get smaller and smaller – down below the 23 which only recently was said to be the absolute minimum.

Going to sea in the merchant navy is, then, a mixture of the traditional and the new. However much the ships are improved, the sea and the elements stay the same, and they are still as dangerous and hostile as ever, just as capable of sinking a container ship – or a cross-channel ferry – as the *Titanic* or a tea clipper, still to be treated with great respect and caution. The way the sea behaves is still not properly understood, or the effects of some developments in ship size and structure. The sailor's life-style, though, has improved on most modern ships, with comfortable cabins, good food, TV and films, and on some, swimming pools. The isolation is still there (and with faster turn-round times a higher proportion of each voyage is spent at sea), although married couples may be able to sail together.

Deck officers' work has become much more technical. They have to be able to 'manage' highly-sophisticated automated systems, and the computer-based information and communication systems. Ships' masters and deck officers must do rather more than get the ship from port A to port B. They are now expected to be involved in the commercial 'management' of the ship, work to an annual 'budget', and use their information systems and flexible communications to meet their financial targets and improve their ships' profitability. They may negotiate the finer details of charters on the spot, for example, send the latest information to head office via satellite, use the satellite to find and exploit 'spot' fuel prices at ports on the way, use the computer to calculate weather-to-fuel-to-load ratios to the best advantage, find ways of speeding turnaround times etc. The shipping industry now treats ships' masters and officers as a management team, with similar responsibilities to a production management team in industry, and of course they also 'manage' a team of seamen.

Engineers also have more sophisticated modern machinery to monitor, again through electronic instruments, and watch out for and solve problems, as well as supervising necessary maintenance and immediate repairs. Today's engine room is clean, well lit and ventilated.

Radio/electronic officers use and look after highly-sophisticated radio and electronic equipment, including radio-telephone – including satellite – links, radar and other direction-finding equipment, in-ship closed-circuit TV, and depth-sounding (sonar) apparatus, data transmission systems and teleprinters, etc. While radio officers maintain much of the equipment, on the most highly-automated ships there may be enough work for an electronics officer also. Some shipping companies employ their own radio officers, but most now have contracts with one of the marine radio companies which both install the equipment and supply a radio officer.

Seamen now work both on deck and in the engine room, doing whatever job may be needed at the time.

On deck, ratings keep watch as do naval ratings, steering, on look-out duty, mooring and unmooring the ship, patrolling the ship, and on stand-by duties, which usually means maintenance work. In port, crew may also have to clean out holds or tanks ready for a new cargo.

In the engine room, ratings look after, operate, maintain and where possible repair machinery etc, monitor instruments, look after stores, watch keep.

The number of ratings a ship carries depends to some extent on how much maintenance (eg painting) the company decides to have done while the ship is at sea. There are rarely, though, now more than nine to a dozen, including bos'n and bos'n's mate on a cargo liner, petty officers on a container ship. Depending on the type of ship and/or cargo (which may include passengers), a ship may also carry a carpenter, one or two mechanic fitters, an electrician, a refrigeration engineer.

Catering and other crew Every ship carries its own catering crew, small on a tanker or cargo ship with a small crew to feed, much larger on cruise liners where the senior catering officer may be called a 'hotel services manager'. On larger ships, the job is often split with the purser, who generally looks after the passengers' comfort and entertainment, provides a banking service, deals with customs and immigration, and handles all the ship's accounts, leaving the catering officer to organise stores, see menus and meals are prepared, manage dining rooms and services.

Cruise liners also carry (for example), MEDICAL STAFF, HAIRDRESSERS, people to run shops – usually on a concessionary basis. Depending on the cruise, ships may contract ENTERTAINERS.

Recruitment and entry Recruitment has been at an all-time low for some years now, largely because of the state of the industry, manning reductions, and 'flagging out'. Total school-leaver recruitment has picked up somewhat, and has been running at about 4-500 a year since about 1984, but because large numbers of registered officers, ratings etc are unemployed, further registration of adult entrants and re-entrants has come to a virtual stop. UK nationals can compete for work for foreign-registered ships.

When UK shipping companies do recruit –

Deck and engineer officers normally start as shipping (or oil) company cadets at between 16 and $19\frac{1}{2}$. Minimum entry requirements are four O-level-equivalent passes including maths, English and a physical science – some companies offer faster training with maths and/or physics A level(s) and the level of competition for places means most people have rather more than the minimum. (A small experimental graduate entry ran for a while, but there is no advantage to starting with a degree.) There are now college-based alternatives (see below).

Radio/electronic officers are generally only recruited once fully trained (see below), and many are recruited by equipment manufacturers rather than shipping companies. Employment prospects are currently very limited.

Junior deck, engine room and catering ratings Entry is via the Gravesend National Sea Training College but company sponsorship is required. No academic qualifications are set formally, but companies will normally expect at least maths and English to at least CSE-grades-3/4-equivalent level. The normal maximum age is $17\frac{1}{2}$.

Employers are attempting to agree an industry-based YTS programme, but this had not been agreed on going to press.

Other passenger-ship crew Pursers (male and female), stewards/stewardesses, nurses etc are generally only recruited when fully trained and experienced in the particular type of work, so the minimum entry age is 21, and more usually 24 or 25.

Qualifications and training To work on UK-registered vessels in particular grades, all sea-going officers and ratings have to gain statutory certificates of competency and pass the relevant Department of Transport examinations. Modern, technologically-sophisticated, large ships need more highly-skilled and trained people. Training is still largely sea-based – on the job – via company training schemes, but longer periods are being spent at shore colleges, and the pattern of training is now more in line with other industries. The number of colleges training for the sea has been cut substantially.

Deck and engineer officers normally qualify via sandwich courses leading to BTEC awards at one of three nautical colleges – Liverpool: S Mersey C, S Shields: S Tyneside C, Southampton IHE.

For deck officers, these are in nautical studies, for engineering officers in marine engineering (with O-level-equivalent passes via a National Diploma followed by a Higher National Diploma, for which there is direct entry with A levels).

As an alternative, the three colleges now offer a full-time two-year BTEC National Diploma in maritime technology, which is more broadly based, and gives students the option of going on to the HND in nautical studies or marine engineering, or to try for shore-based employment in marine-related work, eg port operations, ship broking, freightforwarding/ship agency, offshore agency etc. The colleges try to arrange 'industrial' training afloat. Entry requirements as for other BTEC courses above.

Engineering officers can read for a degree (see under ACADEMIC AND VOCATIONAL STUDIES IN ENGINEERING), and it is possible to read for a degree in nautical studies pre-entry, but there is no advantage to starting with this – a degree is more useful as a post-experience qualification.

All these qualifications give some exemption from the statutory certificates of competency, issued by the Department of Transport. BTEC awards (and degrees) take entrants to class 3 (class 5 is the lowest), needed to work as a second or third officer. To work as a chief officer, and then master, officers have to pass further Department-of-Transport exams, and periods of study leave are usually given to study for these.

Radio/electronic officers now only via a three-year course leading to BTEC National and Higher National Diplomas in maritime telecommunications and the Department of Transport maritime radio communications general certificate (which requires six months' sea-going experience), which can be followed by a six-month course for the electronic navigational maintenance certificate. Minimum entry requirements are four O-level-equivalent passes including maths, a physics subject, and English, but direct entry to the BTEC Higher is possible with maths and physics studied to A level and a pass in either.

Junior deck, engineroom and catering ratings Entrants spend up to three months at the Gravesend National Sea Training College. They must then do at least twelve months' at sea. Entrants have to pass Department of Transport exams, but cannot be certificated until they are 18 years old.

Further information from the General Council of British Shipping, local Merchant Navy Establishment offices, the Department of Transport (for regulations), individual shipping lines.

Pilots, coastguards (and lighthouse keepers)

These are safety services. Historically, they help ships in coastal waters avoid dangerous rocks, etc, and guide them into port. Despite all the highly-sophisticated systems ships now have, it is generally considered these services are still essential, especially for the huge tankers and container ships. However,

THE LIGHTHOUSE SERVICE is now automating both lighthouses and lightships so quickly that no new staff are being recruited. There may, however, still be some opportunities to work on installation, maintenance and repair.

PILOTS navigate larger ships through coastal waters, estuaries and rivers into ports, and help them to berth safely, using their detailed knowledge of the area, and training in inshore navigation.

The pilot service is being reorganised, with de-regulating legislation passed in 1987, and completely new arrangements are expected to be in place by mid 1988. Details of these have yet to be finalised, but the existing pilotage authorities are being abolished, and their responsibilities transferred to individual harbour authorities. According to the new Act, individual harbour authorities can employ pilots on whatever terms they decide will suit them best, or to sub-contract the service.

Some 300 of the present (1987) 1200 working (1400 are qualified) pilots are expected to retire.

Recruitment, entry, training etc New arrangements have yet to be finalised, but the recruiting bodies will in future be harbour authorities. Despite the numbers who will be surplus to needs when the new arrangements are in place, it is feared there may be a shortage of pilots before very long. This is because for some years now pilots have been recruited mainly from experienced, but comparatively young (under 35) ships' masters, who are already trained navigators and so need comparatively little extra training. With the decline in the merchant navy, few experienced recruits of the right age are available. It is, therefore, probable that some form of traineeship for younger people will have to be started, perhaps by 1990.

Further information from individual harbour authorities.

THE COASTGUARD SERVICE initiates, directs and co-ordinates (civil) marine search and rescue action around the coast, and over 1000 miles out to sea. The service is organised in six regions, each run by a regional controller based at a (regional) 'maritime rescue co-ordination centre' (MRCC), with each region divided into sub-centres (MRSCs). All the centres are staffed around the clock with officers keeping constant watch on international distress frequencies, and with sophisticated radio, telephone and telex equipment receiving messages automatically on special consoles. New technology is being used to up-grade the search-and-rescue capability, with advanced communication systems, so that coastguards have information on the location of the caller immediately, cutting search time dramatically, and all MRCCs have search-planning computers which can resolve difficult problems quickly and accurately.

Regular as well as auxiliary officers staff other stations, and they help in cliff rescues, crew small boats etc, when necessary. All full-time coastguards must do shift work (watchkeeping periods normally last twelve hours), and be prepared to work anywhere in the UK. Promotion depends on passing a qualifying examination (which must be passed on the second attempt to stay in the service).

Recruitment, entry etc Coastguards are expected to have three O-level-equivalent passes including maths and English language, and six years' practical marine experience or three years' operational experience in search and rescue co-ordination. The age limits are 27-40. Entrants are expected to be (and stay) very fit, have good sight and hearing, and be able to cope with sudden emergencies and 'stressful' situations. A valid driving licence is also needed. Training is given.

Further information from the Coastguard Service.

Working on shore
Shore-based marine work includes –

SHIPPING COMPANIES are commercial organisations like any other – they manage ships and their crews, cargoes and passengers. An estimated 10,000 managers/professional people work for the companies ashore.

At senior managerial level, of course, the problems are strategic – possibly whether to stay in the business at all, whether or not to stay under the British flag, to lay up – or scrap – ships, how to stay 'afloat', whether or not to risk investing, how to be cost effective. On the more day-to-day level, when the ships are working though –

Managing ships is an expert, technical business, making sure that the right ships are in the right places at the right times – and are operated as cost-effectively as possible.

Maintenance/re-fitting and repairs have to be organised with minimal disruption to schedules and at lowest-possible cost. Management has to find the yards which can do particular jobs most efficiently and cheaply, and may find it more economic to fly out gangs to do some routine work while a ship is still at sea – or finish off a re-fit while the ship sails from yard to pick-up port. Ships have to be fuelled and stocked where it is most economic, and crew rosters have to take account of leave and training periods ashore.

Shore managers are the people masters and chief engineers report to, while at sea and when they return to their home port. Managerial staff are, then, usually people with sea-going or equivalent qualifications and experience – in marine engineering, telecommunications etc, although shipping lines also employ people for general administrative work too. Functions such as FINANCIAL MANAGEMENT/ACCOUNTING, PERSONNEL, PURCHASING/SUPPLY etc are as important as elsewhere.

Some shipping companies design their own ships, and so employ NAVAL ARCHITECTS, DRAUGHTSMEN/WOMEN, etc. When firms buy 'off the shelf', or use independent (consulting) naval architects/marine engineers, they must still have a few technically-qualified people to decide what is needed and to assess tenders, both for new ships and for maintenance and re-fitting.

Freight organising – to fill ships' holds and tanks – or bringing in passengers is a MARKETING operation with its own slant.

In freight work, this involves finding exporting firms, providing the service customers want at the right price, having ships where cargoes are, being 'slick' at getting cargoes – containers – on and off ships, through harbours, and arranging collection and delivery. Cruise companies work rather more like TOUR OPERATORS, although it is their own 'hotel' accommodation they are selling.

Traffic managers – for freight, ferry/hovercraft, other passenger ships – mastermind operations. They, or their staff, have to liaise with port authorities for berths, to co-ordinate sailings. Much depends on the company's port offices and agents, who must see that 'cargo' and ship come together at the right moment, do all the complex paper work – although much of this (eg preparing manifests) is going onto computer – get clearances, arrange loading and unloading at each end, see the ship has berths where and when needed, that tugs and pilots are available to bring ships in, and take them out again. That freight – or passengers – are speeded through port areas and customs, that parking is available for trucks or cars, etc.

Cargo staff have to work closely with the people who manage the ships, and feed back in to managers changes in customers' needs. The job can be complex, with many problems to solve, such as whether or not it is worth taking on a cargo from port A to port B if no cargo is in prospect at port B, whether or not a ship can take a 'dirty' (eg ore) cargo and have its holds cleaned fast and well enough to take on a waiting food cargo, how to crate an unusual cargo, whether or not containers can be off-loaded at out of the way third-world ports.

Selling and buying cargo space in ships is not always done directly between shipping firm and clients. Independent SHIPBROKERS work from the Stock Exchange in London (see FINANCE), both acting as middle men/women between owners and merchants and their chartering agents. Shipbrokers also buy and sell ships on behalf of owners.

See also FREIGHT FORWARDING.

Recruitment and entry Fleet managers are generally recruited from amongst sea-going officers who have the right aptitudes. On the commercial side, and for general administration, entry is still possible at 16-plus with reasonable O-level-equivalent passes, to start in clerical work. But promotion prospects into management are probably better with A levels, and some larger groups take graduates as trainee managers.

Qualifications and training Training for most commercial work in the shipping business is largely on the job, with release to study (or by correspondence/distance learning) for appropriate, mainly business, qualifications (see BUSINESS STUDIES).

THE PORTS have been going through considerable transformation and large-scale modernisation for some years, bringing in more efficient, technologically-based freight-handling methods both to deal with conventional forms of freight, for bulk handling, and as part of continuing development of integrated containerised and 'roll-on, roll-off' systems, as well as improving port layout, and berthing facilities that modern ships need. Reducing staffing levels is also a major consideration. The size and cost of improvement schemes has been considerable – Felixstowe's new (1986) container terminal, for example, cost £42 million – but the decline in trade means investment has fallen recently, to £68.1 million in 1985.

The ports suffer from the decline in world trade – and more recently from the fall in oil prices – just as does the shipping industry. Although all the cargoes coming into the UK must come into UK ports, they have found it difficult competing with European ports, and they now have a new potential competitor in the Channel Tunnel just when new ferry capacity is being developed at several ports. The changing balance of UK trade is demonstrated by the fact that most recent developments have been on the east- and south-east – Europe-facing – ports, and the ports from which ships traditionally sailed west to America, and which served the industrial areas of Wales, have declined most. The largest port (in terms of tonnes handled) is the Sullom Voe oil terminal, but London still handles most cargo.

Although some 300 places have port/harbour facilities, the number handling freight/oil in the size and quantity to provide employment is much smaller. Associated British Ports owns and operates 19 major ports – about a fifth of total capacity. Trusts control and manage about seven major ports, and local authorities many small ports but also two large ones and the Orkney/Shetland oil ports. Most oil-tanker terminals are owned by the oil companies and serve specific refineries.

Working in the ports No official figures have been given for the ports recently, but numbers are certainly well down on 1983's 60,000 (it was 130,000 in the 1960s) – the number of dockers alone is probably down to, or below, 10,000. Ports employ a full range of managerial, administrative, technical and 'blue-collar' workers, but numbers working for each are now comparatively small. A high proportion of managers are ENGINEERS, mainly CIVIL, but also MECHANICAL AND ELECTRICAL. Professional staff employed include –

mechanical engineers design, specify, commission, and maintain port equipment from cranes of all sizes including massive container carriers, vehicles (buses, road sweepers, fuel tankers), lock-gate and bridge controls, conveyors and elevators, roll-on/roll-off linkspans, pumping stations, floating craft machinery, etc;

electrical engineers deal with electrical/electronic controls for eg cranes, roll-on/roll-off berths, grain silos, pumping stations, petrol/chemical terminals, lighting systems, electronic control, radio communication and navigational aids;

civil engineers develop installations and container berth complexes, and associated structures (berths, locks, dock gates, sea-walls, jetties, roads, bridges, transit sheds, grain silos etc);

ACCOUNTANTS, LEGAL STAFF, SURVEYORS, PERSONNEL MANAGERS and MARINE experts.

Recruitment and entry Engineers are generally recruited with appropriate qualifications (see ENGINEERING). The largest port authorities have, in the past, recruited graduate management trainees, but only in one and twos – and this appears to have stopped altogether in 1986-7. Ports are probably just recruiting to fill vacancies from amongst suitably qualified people.

Further information from individual port authorities.

INLAND WATERWAYS

Canals, rivers and other inland waterways have been popular 'playgrounds' for many years – for cruising etc, fishing etc. A fairly significant amount of freight is still carried, and efforts are being made to increase this. Canals are being re-opened (with eg MSC aid).

Inland, some 2500 miles of rivers, canals etc are navigable, about 2000 of them owned by the British Waterways Board, and the rest by local authorities and private companies. About 400 miles of the waterways under BWB's control are in use commercially, mostly on 'canalised' rivers, and freight is also carried on, eg the Thames. Some 1200 miles are maintained for recreational and amenity use, and the Board also controls about 90 reservoirs (they supply water for the canals), many of them also used for sailing, fishing etc.

Both recreational and commercial facilities are being improved and developed, if fairly slowly. BWB carries freight itself (on some 400 craft), hires out canal boats for holidays etc, sells water for industrial and agricultural use, and provides docks, warehousing and terminal services.

Working for the waterways British Waterways is probably the largest employer, with other freight handlers, firms hiring out and operating boats, providing marina and other river- and canal-side facilities, amongst the others. The total number of jobs is probably well under 10,000.

BWB employs people in its specialist departments (in addition to the 'normal' commercial functions) –

ENGINEERS (civil, water, mining and bridge), SURVEYORS, with similarly qualified technicians, craftworkers etc, to maintain and further develop the waterways and installations (docks, warehouses etc), reservoirs, etc.

SURVEYORS, BUILDING INSPECTORS (and related staff) to 'manage' the fairly extensive land holdings and buildings other than those directly linked to the waterways – negotiating purchases, sales, wayleaves etc, selling water.

Staff in the commercial department 'manage' the carrying craft, dock and warehousing facilities, develop commercial traffic etc. The Board also employs people to run the canal craft, operate locks, work in the warehouses etc.

The 'leisure' department deals with holiday lettings of boats, and developing other recreational uses for the waterways.

Recruitment and entry BWB recruits mostly according to vacancy, and/or locally, but recruits trainees for some functions, and has a small graduate intake in some years.

Further information from British Waterways Board.

THE TRAVEL BUSINESS AND FREIGHTFORWARDING

Finally, firms also make an income out of matching people's transport needs to the most suitable form of transport, whether the 'cargo' is people or goods. The work employs people who have expert and up-to-the-minute knowledge of the transport business.

Freightforwarding

Freightforwarders are experts at finding the best way of getting goods from the UK to anywhere in the world, and vice versa, in good condition, and at an economic cost. 'Best' has to be a balance between how quickly the goods are needed, how valuable they are, how much they weigh, what shape and size they are, how easily the goods can be damaged. Valuable freight which doesn't weigh too much, expensive fruit which damages easily and goes off quickly, race horses, medicine and machinery needed in a hurry, might have to go by air. Other goods may go by sea, perhaps in containers, perhaps in bulk.

Freight has to be shifted from the factory, warehouse, market garden etc to the air or sea port, by road and/or rail, and similar arrangements made at the other end. Items may have to be stored for short, or longer, periods at some stage in their journey.

Freightforwarders have to keep themselves up-to-date on what is happening in the transport business. Which carriers are most efficient, which ports have what facilities – and fastest turnrounds – and what ships they can 'service', for example. They have to be expert in getting cargoes packed correctly for each type of transport. They must also be expert at the complexities of customs and excise requirements, licences, regulations and other documentation, and insurance, not just for the UK, but for other countries too.

Freightforwarders often provide a 'door-to-door' service, and can negotiate bulk discounts with the transport companies. They are particularly expert at minimising delays – which can be costly – in getting goods customs clearance, for instance. They can keep customers up to date on changes – in eg customs requirements or rates charged – new freight services, etc.

Over 2000 companies operate as freightforwarders, their Institute estimates, ranging in size from single-office operations to major national companies with widely-spread offices and representatives. While they have suffered to some extent from declining trade, over 50% of exporting/importing firms use freightforwarders to improve efficiency and cut costs – and the most successful freightforwarders are quick to spot new opportunities when markets fall off.

Most freightforwarding companies specialise, or have specialist divisions/ departments – in transporting goods by air or sea, in different types of freight, and/or in transporting to and/or from particular parts of the world. Firms then have offices, or representatives, permanently at air and/or sea ports in the UK and other countries – airfreight companies are normally based at eg Heathrow, for instance. Many freightforwarding companies have their own warehousing and packaging facilities, and may have some transport – especially where airfreighting is involved.

Much of the work involved in freightforwarding is clerical/administrative, and most people start with basic routine – although computer-based systems are increasingly being used. Clerks deal with (depending on training and experience), for example, choosing routes and carriers, rates and schedules; telex and telephoning; documentation (commercial, customs, transport, warehouse), getting freight through customs; finance (credit control, preparing invoices, quotations and tariffs, accounts). Experienced, trained, freightforwarders mainly deal with the negotiating, although firms may employ SALES staff. Firms may also send experienced staff to overseas offices. Promotion is to eg section leader, department or warehouse or branch manager, possibly senior management.

Freightforwarders also employ warehouse staff – managers, clerks, drivers (vans, trucks, forklift trucks), packers, porters etc.

See also SHIPBROKING under FINANCE.

Recruitment and entry No formal entry route. Most people start 'at the bottom', usually with at least four O-level-equivalent passes including English, maths, geography – higher qualifications are likely to help gain expertise and promotion faster. Languages may be useful. Occasional A-level/graduate traineeships with larger firms. Personal characteristics are said to count considerably, especially ability to communicate easily and clearly – especially on the telephone (although telex is on the increase), ability to cope with complex documentation, regulations, currency etc.

Qualifications and training mainly on-the-job, learning from more experienced staff – few formal training schemes.

It makes sense to gain, eg BTEC National and/or Higher National award(s) in business studies including appropriate options, if possible by release from work, or pre-entry.

Professional bodies include –

Institute of Freight Forwarders sets a two-part examination for membership, for which part 1 is the foundation course in overseas trade set jointly with the Institute of Export. The Institute also arranges training courses etc.

Further information from the Institute of Freight Forwarders.

The travel business

While there is nothing to stop people making their own travel arrangements directly with the air, rail, or shipping line, booking their own accommodation etc, in practice, a high proportion of people go to a travel agent because they can do it more efficiently, and because the industry can provide them with attractive 'packages' which are matched to what they can afford – taking advantage of the tour operators' 'bulk buying'. It is, though, a highly volatile and fiercely competitive business. Predicting travel and holiday business at least a year ahead usually means these days too many package holidays, and too many tour operators and travel agencies, chasing too few customers for everyone to make a profit. Computerised booking systems, allowing travel agencies to deal screen-to-screen with tour operators, has increased efficiency, but kept down staffing levels – and been expensive to put in.

TRAVEL AGENTS are the retailers, the 'shop windows' of the travel and transport business. They sell tickets for road, rail and air travel over the counter. They sell several million of 'packaged' holidays a year, mainly to British people going on holiday abroad. All this makes up the bulk of their sales. But they also make travel arrangements for business men and women going on (for instance), a sales tour. They 'sell' holiday lettings in French villas, and 'self-catering' accommodation elsewhere. They arrange more complicated tours and other travel arrangements for people either travelling on their own, or in a group. They work out travel arrangements so that people can spend as much or as little time as they wish in particular places, check all the connections, arrange hotels and sight-seeing trips etc.

The number of travel agencies has been growing steadily since the 1970s, reaching some 5500 at least. However, the level of competition, rising costs etc, give the advantage to larger chains, and computer-booking, -accounting etc, more centralisation of some functions, is probably holding down employment, estimated at around 15,000 – 80% work in branches, probably only 10% are managerial staff.

How the work is organised can depend on the size of the agency – in larger agencies it is often divided up, while one or two people may have to do everything in a smaller outlet. Most jobs in travel agencies are for clerical and counter staff. Most start at the bottom on 'back room' clerical work, checking availability of flights via a computer link, making simpler bookings, keeping records (in files and/or computer), dealing with documentation, checking timetables, and ordering currency. They may then move to more complex booking work, and into counter work. This can be on simpler services – like arranging a sleeper to Glasgow, or finding brochures for people. More experienced staff help people choose holidays, arrange more complicated journeys. Counter staff have to deal with payments, visas, currency, and be able to advise on eg vaccinations, insurance etc. Some staff may specialise in arranging travel arrangements for people going abroad on business and/or dealing with the travel companies etc for them.

Trained and experienced counter staff have fair chances of going on to supervisory and managerial work in the office/branch. 'Managing' a travel agency outlet is very like RETAIL MANAGEMENT – meeting budgets, deciding which 'products' – ie holiday packages – will sell in the area and 'marketing' them, being aware of what is on offer (eg the latest TV advertising campaign) and preparing to deal with demand, coping with staffing, accounts, problems with computer links and telephones, etc. Promotion, for a few, may be to head office of a travel-agency chain, in eg MARKETING, planning – but specialist qualifications are needed for functions such as FINANCE.

Recruitment and entry Most people start at the bottom, as clerks at 16-plus – prospects are best with O-level-equivalent passes in English language, maths, geography and (preferably) at least one European language. The personality to deal with people, communicate effectively – on the telephone and face-to-face, ability to cope with detail, and accuracy are wanted. It is worthwhile starting with an ABTA (Association of British Travel Agencies) member committed to providing training.

ABTA runs a country-wide two-year YTS scheme (about 1250 places on 65 courses). Recruitment is via travel agents, and some of the larger groups are taking on young staff only via ABTA YTS. Some 95% of trainees gain full-time employment in the industry – competition is just as great as for employment, with up to 15 applications for every place, so school-leaving qualifications etc are just as important.

Larger travel agencies may recruit a very small number of graduate and other trainees for eg MARKETING, ACCOUNTANCY, and people with relevant professional qualifications are recruited for specific vacancies.

Qualifications and training Training is largely on the job, but the better recruiters give release to study, although evening and correspondence courses, and other 'distance learning' packages are available.

ABTA's YTS scheme includes a residential course and a flight to Europe – it trains for COTAC level I exams (below).

Qualifications (some leading to membership of the Institute of Travel and Tourism) include –

CGLI/ABTA certificate of travel agency competence – COTAC (CGLI 495) is the basic qualification, and can be taken at level I and level II. Local FE colleges put on courses, but self-study training packages are available. No formal entry requirements are set, but to pass will probably take an educational background to O-level equivalent and relevant work experience (practical tests are included).

CGLI/ABTA certificate in travel studies (CGLI 499) is a one-year full-time scheme which is more broadly based than COTAC (it adds eg travel geography, information technology, office skills). No formal academic entry requirements, but again an O-level equivalent education is probably needed.

BTEC National Diploma in Business studies with five or six option modules in travel and tourism – at about 30 colleges countrywide.

BTEC Higher National Diploma in business studies with a bias to tourism – at Bournemouth IHE, London; Ealing CHE, Sheffield P.

CGLI/ABTA certificate in travel agency management – COTAM (CGLI 496): two written papers on financial and legal, and economic and environment aspects (including staff management and training, marketing, office administration) and assessment of four written assignments.

Postgraduate courses: at universities – Glasgow: Strathclyde, Guildford: Surrey; polytechnic – Manchester.

Further information from ABTA, and the Institute of Travel and Tourism.

TOUR COMPANIES AND OPERATORS put together 'packaged' holidays and tours mainly for mass travel markets, although some make a business of high-value tours etc with a 'specialist' slant (eg to archaeological sites led by an expert), or in the 'luxury' market. Some specialise, eg in winter skiing holidays, or school educational journeys. Some large holiday companies have their own travel agencies. The competition verges on 'cut-throat'.

The work of a tour company divides between 'designing', planning and negotiating packages, promoting and marketing them, and ensuring that the 'package' is delivered.

Holiday 'packages' are effectively 'sub contracts' to transport, accommodate and feed, and sometimes also entertain. Plans have to be made over a year in advance, on market-research-based estimates of what the market wants and might pay. Staff have to visit and check out what is available, and constantly find new places and ideas to attract customers. Detailed and complex costings have to be agreed, and negotiating the discounts with transport companies, hoteliers etc is a tough business, and drawing up contracts involves some LEGAL input.

MARKETING and promoting holidays ranges from producing brochures (which employs writers, photographers, designers, print production staff etc), through ADVERTISING campaigns to SALES staff going out to travel agencies to see that the company's products are getting full attention.

A considerable proportion of the work is clerical/basic administrative – sending out brochures, confirming bookings, invoicing and preparing travel documents, compiling costings, making up passenger lists and aircraft seat plans, collating and filing information on resorts and their facilities. Much of the routine work is now done on computers.

More senior and experienced staff plan, check out resorts, negotiate contracts, design marketing/advertising campaigns, brochures etc – they may come up through the office, but some may have been couriers and/or resort representatives. Larger companies have offices in the main tourist countries.

Although the holiday business has become a large industry, numbers employed have probably not risen in parallel. No industry-wide figures are available, but the largest tour operator organised and sold nearly three times more holidays (about 2 million) in 1986 as in 1980, with the same number (about 550) of staff. This is largely due to computerisation.

Tour companies of course employ people in FINANCE/ACCOUNTING, MARKETING, and also COMPUTING. Statutory rules apply in the industry, so LEGAL STAFF are also needed.

Couriers, and resort representatives are also employed by tour organisations, to look after tourists, but mostly only for the main holiday seasons, although this may be changing as firms are increasingly offering very cheap winter holidays in warm countries for retired people. They may travel with them over part or all of their route, or meet them at their destination. They have to cope with all the practical problems of customs, difficulties over food or rooms, lost papers or luggage; they take tourists on trips or round local sights. Some tour operators employ eg NURSERY NURSES for the resorts.

Recruitment and entry School-leavers need at least O-level-equivalent passes in English, maths, and geography, and larger firms recruit people with A-levels, and graduates, potentially for professional and managerial work. Couriers and resort representatives normally need to be fluent in at least one European language, and are normally recruited only in their twenties – representatives need some kind of prior work experience abroad.

Qualifications and training Mainly on the job. The qualifications listed under TRAVEL AGENCY are the most suitable.

Further information from ABTA and the Institute of Travel and Tourism.

Working Overseas

Introduction   1161
Working abroad permanently   1162
Short-term opportunities   1173

INTRODUCTION

Men and women have migrated from place to place in search of better conditions, food and work, fame and fortune, or simply adventure, something new and different, since prehistoric times. Motives for moving may change, but the 'greener grass' syndrome is still common. Around 300,000 people leave Britain to live elsewhere every year, and that figure excludes people moving to EEC countries. Amongst them, in 1985, were 1584 new university graduates, 436 university postgraduates, and 571 (first-degree and HND) graduates from polytechnics.

Unfortunately, despite all the talk of a 'global village' it is possibly getting more, rather than less, difficult to up stakes and earn an income elsewhere – most of the world welcomes tourists, and anyone with money to invest. There are real problems and pitfalls in either trying to make a new life and career overseas and even finding work abroad on a shorter-term basis.

Opportunities for British nationals to live and work in other countries change all the time, with political, economic and social changes. In general, fewer countries are prepared to welcome any Briton with unquestioning open arms. Unemployment is a world-wide phenomenon, and governments have to give priority in the job market to their own nationals. Most countries legislate for this, just as Britain has legislation which restricts the rights of both Commonwealth citizens and foreign nationals to live and work in Britain. The countries to which Britons have traditionally migrated, such as New Zealand, Australia and Canada, are increasingly selective in their choice of migrants and are equally unwilling to let visitors work except under agreed schemes. The United States has long had strict legislation along similar lines. Other former colonial and developing countries, mainly for nationalist, political and social reasons, are now equally reluctant to have people of European origin permanently holding senior positions.

The exception, of course, is that UK membership of the EEC makes it legally possible for British nationals to work freely in any member country (but not in Greece until 1988, or Spain and Portugal until 1993). To obtain reasonable work in a European country, though, usually means being completely fluent in the language, not something that the many who went out to English-speaking countries in the past had to worry about. And any Briton trying for a job in Europe still has to compete with nationals who will often be preferred by local employers.

As in Britain, opportunities in other countries are increasingly limited to people with expertise, skills, training and/or experience to sell, skills which countries, and employers there, may need to buy from abroad, including the UK, just as they buy goods. (The alternative is enough money to start a business and create jobs.) The skills may not always be the obvious ones, and each country's needs is likely to change over time. For example, recently Australia was accepting cabinet-makers, skilled waiters and upholsterers, but not architects. America's shortage of nurses has been well publicised. It is likely that, as in Britain, there will be more such shortages, since the fall in the birth rate since the 1960s affects most Western countries, and this may mean more opportunities in the future.

But without skills which are in short supply, the chances to work in other countries are few, except on a casual basis, or as a volunteer. Even countries which may be short of labour in particular industries are reluctant to import unskilled people because of the political and social problems this can bring, or they can't afford them. Except in special circumstances, it is not normally possible to be trained in foreign countries at the state's – or any organisation's – expense. Of course, within the EEC unskilled people may still work wherever they want to, provided work is available.

Most careers literature emphasises that the people who gain most from working in another countries are those who have thought through their reasons for wanting to do so, and have matched realistic opportunities to their own personal priorities. It is all too easy to be carried away by the excitement of jetting off into the unknown, or thinking personal or other problems can be solved just by going abroad, and to forget practicalities. Thoroughly researching the opportunities, thinking through what happens if plans don't work out, what the opportunities would be for returning to a career in the UK, etc are just as crucial – if not more so – for anyone who is considering going overseas as for finding a career/job in Britain.

It is fair to decide that living in South America (or wherever) is a good idea, but while professional practices may vary from country to country, actual daily life in a bank, as an accountant or a teacher, in construction or engineering, is fundamentally the same the world over. Someone who doesn't enjoy teaching in England is most unlikely to find the job itself any more congenial in another country, even if the climate or the income is better. Equally, it is wrong to assume that it is possible to gain experience of a wider range of occupations overseas than at home in Britain. In fact, the reverse is often the case, since in many countries there are just as likely to be the same kinds of restrictions – qualifications, nationality, for example – as in Britain.

Planning to work overseas for a finite period, and planning to make a career abroad permanently, either by a single move from Britain to another country, or by choosing work which involves working in other countries, or by working for an organisation which sends employees to work overseas, imply quite different sorts of motivation and intention. Moreover, the opportunities are quite different in each case.

WORKING ABROAD PERMANENTLY
Emigrating — working permanently overseas (including British Council, European Community, international organisations)

EMIGRATING implies a decision to make a total change of life style, and not just the work situation. People seldom decide to move to another country solely on the basis of work – but of course unemployment may force some to look for permanent work abroad even though they would prefer to live in Britain. Permanent emigration suggests wanting to live in a different political, economic, social or even physical climate – to look for a differently structured society, to earn more money, to escape from a situation.

Emigrants need marketable training and skills, and usually fairly extensive experience of the work too. Countries accepting permanent immigrants as such are now relatively few – with the exception of Europe, the opportunities for English-speaking nationals to go to and live permanently in the traditional places such as Australia, New Zealand, and Canada, are now very restricted. Permanent residence in the United States is difficult, but not impossible, although it usually means having a job to go to. In general, it has to be assumed that immigration quotas are being reduced, although any organisation seriously short of people with specific skills is unlikely to have problems in getting round them.

While in theory a trial period working in the country in question is a good idea, in practice this is not always possible, since there are also very strict limitations on short-term work permits in many non-EEC countries including, for example, Australia. Many countries now also expect immigrants to have jobs before entry, and some (eg New Zealand) that they also have somewhere to live (and this does not mean having enough money to buy or rent property after arrival). It is, therefore, extremely important to use the most up-to-date information on the details of immigration laws and regulations from the appropriate authorities, before making any plans.

Further information The high commissions/embassies in the UK should have both information on immigration regulations and on the skills currently in short supply.

WORKING PERMANENTLY OVERSEAS for organisations which employ people in countries other than Britain is an alternative to emigrating. These are opportunities, however, which rarely offer the chance to spend an entire working career in a single place, and are therefore not ideal for those who want a settled life in one place. It means being happy to move from place to place fairly often, enjoying new experiences, change, and differing surroundings, over an entire working life. There are other disadvantages to this kind of life – choice of country is not always up to the individual, and may mean unpleasant climatic conditions, political instability, and so on. As with any nomadic existence, organising family life, even with substantial support from the employing organisation, can be difficult, especially when it comes to children's schooling.

Many of the traditional opportunities to work permanently or regularly abroad are declining, with economic, political, social or technological change, although others are opening up.

The decline of the merchant fleet, for example, means fewer opportunities to travel the world in the MERCHANT NAVY. The ARMED FORCES, including the ROYAL NAVY, do not, generally, go so far afield so often or for so long now (with the exception of the Falklands). The media, generally, has fewer foreign correspondents stationed permanently in individual countries, because jet travel makes it much easier to send people out to where the news is at any one time, but this does make some JOURNALISTS more peripatetic.

However,

INTERPRETING AND TRANSLATING still takes people to other countries, on a permanent or semi-permanent basis, for short stays or single events.

THE DIPLOMATIC SERVICE continues to give a comparatively small number of people the opportunity to work overseas for a large part of their careers.

PROFESSIONAL SPORTSMEN/WOMEN live international lives, on world circuits, playing for foreign clubs, or just competing in the growing number of international events.

The ENTERTAINMENT BUSINESS allows people to spend a proportion of their working lives working abroad.

TEACHING is still a major way of working abroad, especially teaching English as a foreign language (TEFL), in both state and private schools, in language schools and in (the equivalent of) higher and further education, in a wide range of countries, but usually on contract rather than in permanent employment.

The CONSTRUCTION INDUSTRY is increasingly international, with major British firms competing for business building, eg airports, industrial plant, power stations, roads, hospitals, and schools, world wide, and sending out managers, engineers etc, often for the length of a contract, which may be years. Such contracts also involve the firms which make equipment, machinery, etc.

MINING, MINERAL AND OIL EXPLORATION search for and exploit reserves in more and more remote parts of the world, which gives work for, eg GEOLOGISTS, MINING and DRILLING EXPERTS. Opportunities, though, fluctuate with the price and demand for oil, minerals etc.

Some multi-national companies give appropriately qualified UK personnel the chance to work elsewhere. Mostly, though, they are committed to employing people in the countries where they are based. Exceptions are, for example, large internationals which may concentrate research and development operations in particular countries, and therefore scientists of all nationalities are recruited for these units, and some large multi-nationals do move around production staff. It is always worth asking firms if they have the kind of organisational structure which allows employees to transfer from one country to another, or whether it is possible to apply direct to subsidiaries in other countries.

UK-based industrial and commercial firms giving the best opportunities to work abroad on a long-term basis are mainly those whose operations are international because their business demands it rather than because they happen to have subsidiaries or branches in a large number of countries. Firms selling internationally – particularly heavy capital equipment, aircraft, telecommunications – have international sales teams. FREIGHTFORWARDERS, and firms in the TRAVEL/TOURIST BUSINESS may also send trained, experienced staff to work in overseas offices, or on trips/tours abroad. Tourist firms also employ, but mainly on a seasonal basis, couriers and resort representatives.

The EEC is slowly turning more occupations into 'European' careers, and qualifications are being harmonised.

PATENT WORK, for example, is becoming a European profession.

LAWYERS and ACCOUNTANTS/FINANCIAL EXPERTS qualified professionally and linguistically to work in more than one European country are in demand. European institutions employ nationals of all member states, including the UK (see below).

SCIENTISTS are recruited Europe-wide for a still fairly small number of collaborative ventures, eg CERN – the European Organisation for Nuclear Research in Geneva (physicists, computer scientists, electrical engineers), and labs working for the European Space Agency.

POLITICIANS can make a career in the European parliament.

Developing countries may recruit – either directly or via, eg ODA (below), charities – for development and/or research, agricultural experts, people with qualifications in construction and surveying, teachers and other education specialists, engineers, business experts, qualified medical and paramedical people.

Overseas development, the relatively small number of international organisations, and bodies like the British Council, provide work for a comparatively small number of people.

The British Council (founded 1934), promotes understanding and appreciation of Britain in other countries, through cultural, educational and technical co-operation. The Council's activities are adapted to meet changing needs and conditions at home and abroad, and recently it has become increasingly responsible for planning and implementing programmes for educational development. The Council is funded largely by grants (about £71 million in 1986-7 out of a total budget of over £221 million) from the Foreign and Commonwealth Office and the Overseas Development Administration (ODA), down to 32% of the total (but this may increase as some of the funds withdrawn from UNESCO may go to the Council). The Council runs a number of British government programmes (eg higher and technical education, and technical co-operation schemes) for which it is paid some £101.6 million. The Council earns nearly £50 million from eg English language teaching and paid educational services.

According to the Council's recruiting literature, education in its broadest sense forms the largest element in its general cultural work, overseas representatives normally acting as education advisers (some as cultural attachés) to British embassies and high commissions, and in the 'third world' they act as agents for ODA in educational activities.

The Council also employs teachers and other educationalists for a wide variety of posts in overseas universities, colleges, schools and ministries of education, as well as helping British-style schools, conducting British examinations where appropriate, and providing information and advice on all aspects of British educational life. The Council is also significantly involved in designing and implementing educational projects funded by, eg the World Bank, and other multilateral aid sources.

The Council uses a variety of approaches and activities to meet world-wide demand for English language teaching. It co-operates with local ministries of education in training local English teachers, and in advising on syllabuses, textbooks, multi-media learning resources and evaluation, employing qualified ELT specialists. ODA funds a key English language teaching scheme which employs more specialists to work within the educational systems of third-world countries and gives them professional support at post, in helping to develop the potential of local teaching cadres and helping students who need English to gain relevant professional qualifications.

The Council also spends a substantial proportion of its income on promoting scientific contacts and, in developing countries, helping with scientific and technical education. The Council has specialist staff and libraries in London, and scientifically-qualified officers overseas who help develop scientific contacts, provide information and advice on training in Britain and on the provision of British experts overseas.

The Council has, or is associated with, some 110 libraries (against 130 in the late 1970s), ranging from small reference collections to lending libraries of up to 80,000 volumes, some with sizeable collections of audio-visual material. They provide lending, reference and information services, which increasingly have access to computerised data bases. The emphasis is on training programmes for overseas librarians, information scientists and archivists, and on advisory visits overseas by British specialists. Through ODA's books presentation programme the Council helps develop local library services. The Council also promotes British books overseas through some 250 book exhibitions yearly, and produces a monthly journal on books, and specialist bibliographies mainly on English literature, education, science and medicine.

In promoting the arts, the Council helps the best and most appropriate drama, dance and opera companies, orchestras and soloists to perform in Europe and elsewhere. Work by British artists (including photographers and film-makers) is sent for showing overseas in co-operation with local museums and art galleries.

The Council works to improve personal contacts between Britain and other countries outside normal commercial and diplomatic spheres, including, for example, arranging for leading British representatives in education, science, the professions and the arts to go overseas on tours or advisory visits, and providing services for overseas visitors and students coming to Britain.

Working for the British Council The Council had (1986-7) a (planned) staff of 4230 (against 4460 in 1979-80 but up from 3848 in 1981-2), of whom 1572 were working in Britain, mostly at London headquarters (the number of regional offices offices has been cut to fourteen), of whom about 776 are 'career' staff. Some 2658 were working overseas, but most (2355) were local people, and only 303 UK nationals. The increase in staff has been mainly amongst local staff, partly because of the increase in client-funded work, and partly because of security problems.

The home and overseas services are separate.

In the home service, most posts are in general administration – looking after people to come to the UK to study or train, in personnel and other services (eg arranging tour programmes overseas or recruiting teachers for special projects) supporting work in Britain and abroad, and managing the Council's finances. Finance is now an important function. Career administrative staff can transfer from one kind of work to another after two or three years in a first post. They have the support of administrative assistants. With fewer posts, promotion prospects may be limited.

LIBRARIANS, ACCOUNTANTS, and ARTS ADMINISTRATORS are also employed.

Overseas career staff do all kinds of different work, both in each post and throughout their Council careers, regardless of specialist qualifications. They may, for example, take part in the cultural life of the countries where they work, and advise London on whom and what to send there; organise concerts; administer direct teaching of English; deal with people going to Britain and with official visitors from Britain; look after the local VSO programme and the volunteers; run a technical co-operation programme; and deal with general administration.

Overseas staff move to different countries and even different parts of the world every three or four years, spending about two-thirds of their working lives abroad and a third in London. They are expected to go wherever posted, although preferences are taken into account. There are posts in about 80 countries, with numbers ranging from one in the Yemen, and two each in, eg Czechoslovakia, Hungary, Romania, and Venezuela, to 12 or more in Nigeria and India.

Promotion depends mainly on ability and performance, but mobility, length of service, age and special aptitudes are taken into account, and all members of each grade are considered for vacancies in the grade above. Most senior posts are filled by people from the overseas career service.

Recruitment and entry Recruitment for the home and overseas services is separate.

For the home service, general administrators need a degree or an appropriate professional qualification. All entrants should, ideally. have about two years' experience in relevant work. Administrative assistants need a good general education, preferably to A level (but graduates with little administrative experience are recruited); relevant office experience is useful, and some posts also need typing, book-keeping or driving. Qualified secretaries are also recruited.

For overseas service, a degree or higher degree is normally required, followed by several years' relevant experience, in eg research, library/information work, teaching or industry (the preferred age range is 26-early 30s) and/or a qualification in eg TEFL, or accountancy. Suggested degree subjects are librarianship, information science, science, engineering, agriculture or a related subject. Aptitude for learning languages is essential.

The Council also recruits teachers on contract for its own teaching institutes, and acts as recruiting agent for people to work on contract overseas, teaching and in educational advisory posts. Since those on contract service are recruited for specific posts, it is possible to be sure of working in a particular area or country, or of going overseas for only a limited period. It is often possible to move from one contract appointment to another. Most contracts are initially for two years, but may be renewed.

Training The Council pays for language courses, and has been upgrading staff finance, computer and management skills (1600 staff had specialist training in 1985-6).

Further information from the British Council.

INTERNATIONAL ORGANISATIONS The main international organisations which employ British nationals are the United Nations and its agencies. These include the Food and Agricultural Organisation (FAO) in Rome, UNESCO in Paris, and the Industrial Development Organisation (UNIDO). Other bodies include the General Agreement on Tariffs and Trade (GATT) in Geneva, the International Maritime Organisation in London, the International Atomic Energy Agency (IAEA) in Vienna, the World Bank Group (which includes the International Bank for Reconstruction and Development, the International Development Association, and the International Finance Corporation), and the International Monetary Fund), in Washington, the International Civil Aviation Organisation based in Montreal, the International Labour Organisation (ILO) in Geneva, the International Telecommunication Union also in Geneva, the Universal Postal Union in Berne, the World Health Organisation (WHO) and the World Meteorological Organisation, both in Geneva, and the Organisation for Economic Cooperation and Development (OECD) with its HQ in Paris.

Most posts in international organisations are either administrative, in the organisation's secretariat (and this normally includes eg TRANSLATORS and INTERPRETERS), or in professional, highly expert work carrying out the aims of the organisation. With few exceptions (mainly amongst linguistic staff and, in some organisations, secretarial personnel), international organisations try to keep a balance of staff among the member states of the organisation, as far as possible.

The United Nations has few professional posts, and these take considerable expertise in fields related to the work of the UN. Junior professional staff normally have an honours degree or its equivalent, and for higher-level professional posts they generally have recognised standing in their fields.

The UN administers its own development programme and also participates in a joint programme with twelve specialised agencies. The UN itself deals with industrial and economic development, social services (including housing and community development) and natural-resource development (other than agriculture). Demand is always for senior expert advisers, who are normally expected to have the highest professional standing and at least fifteen years' experience in their fields; more junior candidates are seldom nominated.

ECONOMISTS, with substantial governmental experience at home or overseas, are employed to advise on economic planning, programming and development problems.

In development of mineral resources, experts employed include GEOLOGISTS, MINING ENGINEERS, seismologists, geophysicists, geochemists, hydrologists and hydrogeologists.

In public finance, experts help to eg set up government accounts, establish central banks, with taxation and insurance problems, in fiscal aspects of trade policy and ways of attracting capital investment.

DATA PROCESSING experts advise on using computers in government organisational, financial, management and personnel administration.

STATISTICIANS advise on the organisation of, for example, population surveys.

Other experts and advisers are employed on TRANSPORT, electric power, PLANNING (especially low-cost housing), social welfare, community development, public administration, and promoting and developing tourism. The UN employs a few specialists in energy conservation, land survey and mapping, CARTOGRAPHERS, and MUSEUM and LIBRARY staff.

Administrative vacancies in the UN are few and far between, and are normally filled by reassigning existing staff. Posts in the office of public information take substantial professional experience in the use of the media even for junior posts, with preference for people able to work in more than one language. Some posts in the office are filled on a rotating basis through secondment from professional services in member states.

The office of LEGAL affairs has only a small staff (with a low turnover), all of whom have specialised in public international law.

TRANSLATORS/précis-writers translate into their mother tongues (English, French, Spanish, Russian or Chinese) – English translators have to be able to work in French with a sound background in one other language, and the few Arabic translators must translate from English and French into Arabic. All translators are graduates of a university where the language of instruction was their mother tongue. INTERPRETERS must have a university degree and a thorough knowledge of at least three of the above languages.

The UN also has a few social welfare workers, a number of posts for computer programmers (with degrees in economics or accounting plus at least three years' experience), qualified librarians (with a reading knowledge of several languages).

The UN field service personnel working in the field missions include security officers, vehicle mechanics, radio technicians and operators, and male secretaries. They may have to move from mission to mission in any part of the world at any time. Clerical and secretarial staff are generally recruited locally, except for the headquarters staff, who are chosen from among successful competitors in examinations held in New York (minimum requirements are a typing speed of about 50 wpm and a shorthand speed of about 100 wpm in the candidate's mother tongue, and secretaries and typists should preferably be at least bilingual). UN guides are recruited in New York (candidates from other countries must pay their own travel expenses), and all are female, under the age of 30, with a good secondary education and attractive speaking voices, fluent in English and preferably other languages as well.

It is believed that UN permanent staff totals in the region of 2400, of whom about 125 are UK nationals, with a linguistic staff of about 700, of whom under 100 are British (Britain tends to be over quota).

UN agencies recruit more closely to specialist interests, which are fairly obvious from their titles.

UNESCO, for example, had a headquarters staff in the region of 2200 of whom under 800 are classed as 'professionals' – but the UK has given up its membership, and it is not clear if staff numbers will change, or whether UK nationals will be employed in future.

The Food and Agricultural Organisation employs highly qualified technical personnel specialising in various fields of AGRICULTURE, IRRIGATION ENGINEERING, FORESTRY, FISHERIES, NUTRITION, ECONOMICS, and STATISTICS.

The list of experts needed by the UN agencies is endless, but it is emphasised that some skills are not suitable – there is little demand for industrial executives, for example, and very few posts for civil and mechanical engineers except in eg dam or highway design, and it is extremely rare for the UN to employ retired officers from the ARMED FORCES, however extensive their foreign experience.

The World Bank Group (made up of the International Bank for Reconstruction and Development, the International Development Association, and the International Finance Corporation) provides both financial and technical help to improve the living standards of developing member countries. Some 134 countries are members of the Bank.

The Washington-based Bank has a common administrative staff, but operational staff work either for IBRD and IFC or for the IDA. Most posts are permanent, calling for a combination of good academic and technical qualifications, and several years' professional experience (preferably in less developed countries), often with specialisation in depth across a broad range of related activities.

Project officers are professionally qualified specialists who handle the investigation of schemes put forward for loan approval – increasingly these are agriculturalists, agricultural engineers (including irrigation engineers) and agricultural credit specialists, although there are also posts for power, telecommunications and water-supply engineers, road, ports and railway engineers, specialists in education (agricultural, technical and general secondary), school-building architects. Economists (with an advanced degree and appropriate applied experience) are also employed in substantial numbers, in the projects departments, in the five area departments which handle the Bank's day-to-day relations with its member countries, and in the economics department itself, which makes special economic and financial studies on general and specific problems of interest to the Bank. Specialists in promoting and analysing new investment proposals, company legislation and finance, raising new issues and so on, are also in demand.

The Bank recruits young professionals who have little or no professional experience as such under a special programme – the upper age limit is 30 and a first- or good second-class honours degree (in theory in any discipline, although there is in fact a preference for economics), and some (preferably relevant) experience in finance, economics or development are required.

The Organisation for Economic Co-operation and Development has some long-term posts in its Paris secretariat, for people fluent in French. Posts for experts in the OECD technical assistance programmes are generally only for two or three months, although some can last a year.

Recruitment Technical personnel for most of these organisations are recruited in Britain via the International Recruitment Unit of the Overseas Development Administration. Exceptions are more general posts in the UN (for which application must be made direct to the New York headquarters).

THE EUROPEAN COMMUNITIES are made up of a number of semi-independent 'bodies', each with separate responsibilities (and recruiting separately). However, the great majority of jobs are with

The Commission, which sees that the provisions of the European Treaties are observed and carried out properly, and is also the 'executive' body of the Communities, initiating policy. Headquarters are in Brussels and Luxembourg. Most scientific and technical work is done in joint research centres located at Ispra (Italy), Karlsruhe (Germany), Petten (the Netherlands), Geel (Belgium), with the 'Jet' project at Culham in the UK.

The Commission employs 14,000 officials. About 2500 are administrative staff, about 1000 are linguistic staff, and over 2000 are scientific/technical staff. AGCAS estimates they include some 400 UK graduates.

The Commission is divided into a number of services, and about 30 'directorates', and these indicate the scope of the work.

The services include legal, interpreting/conference, statistical, customs union, and 'spokesman'.

The directorates cover – external relations; economic and financial affairs; internal market and industrial affairs (including the information and telecommunications technologies); competition; employment, social affairs and education; agriculture; transport; development; personnel and administration; information; environment, consumer protection and nuclear safety; science, research and development; information, market and innovation; fisheries; financial institutions and taxation; regional policy; energy; credit and investments; budgets; financial control.

All posts are tightly graded and classified –

Category A officials have a university education, deal with policy formation and administration, and advisory work, often political in character. The category divides into 'career brackets' running from A3 (head of division), A4 or 5 (head of specialised service) through the main career brackets A4 to 7. A8 is a new assistant-administrator grade for trainees.

Administrators and principal administrators assist directors, and heads of division in making proposals for policy, preparing background papers, developing the decisions or recommendations of the Council etc. They 'often' include lawyers and economists, staff with professional qualifications and experience in the sector for which the division is responsible. Whatever their specialisation, staff are expected to develop a 'deep level' of expertise in relation to their own specialised areas, as well as to help with the division's routine paperwork (briefs, correspondence, parliamentary business, in-house correspondence), and take initiatives and assume responsibility for some of the division's duties. In some cases they may also have management or supervisory duties for the work of category B staff. In areas where policy is already developed (eg agriculture, trade policy and development), they often have considerable autonomy and responsibility for carrying out Community legislation.

Translators and interpreters are on a parallel structure to category A.

Translation (with a few exceptions) is a self-contained unit in personnel and administration. Each division translates into one language, and is further divided into groups specialising in translating material in specified fields. Translators work exclusively into their mother tongue. A 'reviser's' main function is to check translations produced by less-experienced staff. One group deals with terminology and computer applications, and the legal service has its own team of legally-qualified translators.

The interpretation-conferences services provides interpreters for all meetings held by the Brussels Commission, the Council of Ministers, the economic and social committee, and the European Investment Bank – which involves servicing over 8000 meetings a year.

Category B officials have at least an 'advanced secondary education', and have 'executive'/administrative-assistant type duties. They help with the 'smooth running' of the division, 'often' collect and analyse detailed information needed for policy formation or monitoring and/or enforcing Community legislation. They work mostly where policy is already well developed, and in eg personnel, office administration, and accounting. There is a growing need for staff with specialised computer training.

Category C officials do secretarial/clerical type work. They either work for one or more A or B grade officials, look after the orderly flow of paperwork, for typing (word processors are being introduced), and for keeping files. The larger directorates and the translating services also have typing pools. A directorate has to be organised so it can, with the help of the translation service, type and duplicate complex documents in all nine Community languages, often to demanding timescales.

Category D officials do manual or support work. The most important functions are running the internal mail systems, transport, duplicating and printing, and housekeeping, security, and catering services.

Recruitment and entry The Commission recruits via open competitions to fill existing or future vacancies as and when needed. The Commission has said recently (1986) that there is a shortfall of British applicants.

All staff must have a thorough working knowledge of one Community 'working language' (which can be their 'mother tongue'), and a satisfactory knowledge of another as needed for the specific post.

For category A posts – a university degree is required, preferably in the subject area of the post(s) in question, eg economics, law, finance, administration, agriculture, social science, statistics, computer science or languages. For eg scientific posts, the requirement may be more specific, eg in nuclear sciences. Interpreters must be able to work in at least three Community languages. Entry to A7 requires at least two years' relevant experience after graduating, with an upper age limit of 35. For A8, no experience is required but candidates must have graduated within the previous three years, and be under 32.

Category B posts need proof of advanced secondary education as well as some relevant experience, normally in administration, accounting, 'archives', documentation, computing, or statistics. Upper age limit 35.

Category C posts need proof of secondary education, with training and/or experience in typing/secretarial work, general office/clerical assistant work, child-care or telex/telephone work. Upper age limit 35.

The Commission also recruits graduates as temporary trainees – called 'stagiaires' – to work for 3-5 months, which can help in gaining a permanent post later on.

Training Throughout their careers, staff can take advantage of extensive training opportunities – courses in economics, law, computing, word processing, negotiating techniques, management development, seminars for secretaries are examples. Translators and interpreters are given additional training as and when needed. Almost all training helps with career development, preparing staff for possible future moves.

The other 'bodies', which have far fewer posts, include –
The council of ministers which co-ordinates policies and activities of the member states and of the Community.
The European parliament is the directly elected body, considering and giving opinion on Commission proposals. It has (some) control over the Commission and can influence the Community budget.
The court of justice sees Community law is implemented, checks the legality of Community actions, and deal with references by national courts for preliminary rulings on matters of Community law.
The court of auditors examines Community accounts and expenditure for 'inefficiency and waste' [*sic*].
The economic and social committee is made up of representatives of the various areas of economic and social activity throughout the Community, giving opinion on Commission proposals in its area of responsibility.

Further information The European Commission, and the other institutions listed above.

SHORT-TERM OPPORTUNITIES

This may simply be a way of financing an extended working vacation 'to see the world', a way of having an enjoyable time before settling down to a 'serious' career or before starting a full-time course (eg for a degree). International work camps, working on an Israeli kibbutz (perhaps also learning Hebrew), taking a 'working holiday' in Australia, or seasonal tourist-based work are all possibilities.

Or this may be part of a career plan – gaining extra experience, faster promotion, fluent use of one or more languages. Another choice is to do some form of service to an underdeveloped country, although this now usually means having a needed skill.

Making sure that a period abroad will be a career advantage, and that it will not mean missing opportunities – just by coming back to the UK at the wrong time of year, for instance – is very important, though.

One alternative is to choose a career in which regular, if short, periods abroad are usual or can be arranged relatively easily. They range from SELLING to FILM-MAKING, and also include, eg academic work – university staff regularly spend periods abroad, studying, doing research, on sabbatical leave, advising developing countries, external examining, lecturing, on British Council business. Some opportunities exist to work for overseas governments on short-term contracts to fill particular gaps in their services, and for which local candidates with the right qualifications are not yet available. The international and other institutions and organisations described above also have limited numbers of openings for people to work on short-term contracts. These vary from year to year, often according to demand.

Other organisations recruiting on a short-term basis include –
The British Volunteer Programme Under this, four independent voluntary societies send suitably qualified volunteers overseas in response to requests from developing countries. The main areas of work are education, health, technical trades, crafts and engineering, agriculture, social, community and business development. All volunteers are now skilled and/or qualified people – teachers, doctors, nurses (including nurse tutors), electricians, accountants, civil engineers, builders and building craftworkers, technical education trainers, agricultural experts, water engineers, mechanics, medical lab technicians, small enterprise managers, etc.

They are International Voluntary Service (mainly southern Africa, some West Africa and Asia), the United Nations Association International Service (mainly Latin America, Africa and the Middle East), the Catholic Institute for International Relations (same areas as UN), and Voluntary Service Overseas (mainly Africa, Asia, the Caribbean, Papua New Guinea, and the Pacific).

The minimum period of service is normally two years, and some people stay for three or four. While people are recruited for specific work, they usually get involved in many other activities. Volunteers are generally expected to train local people to take over their work and keep the project going after volunteers go home.

Other organisations sending volunteers abroad – again mainly appropriately qualified people in fairly small numbers (mostly they recruit local people or spend through local organisations) – include Oxfam, Save the Children Fund, and Christian Aid.

Overseas Development Administration with the Crown Agents, recruits on behalf of overseas governments and para-government organisations, for short-term executive posts. ODA also recruits people to specific projects under the British overseas aid programme, working mainly in an advisory capacity. The total number of British experts employed is falling though.

ODA lists as still needed – accountants, agricultural experts (improving farming systems and methods, land-use planning, experimental projects, disease control, education), air transport experts (airfield management, traffic control, radio and mechanical technicians), architects and planners, broadcasting engineers and programme planners, civil engineers, computing staff, co-operative development experts, customs staff (including immigration), economists (development planning and more specialised work on, eg manpower, trade, transport), teachers (for secondary schools, training and technical colleges, polytechnics and universities), electrical engineers (design and production of specifications, estimates and contract documents, supervising installation and maintenance), fire control experts, fisheries experts, forestry staff (field and research work), geologists (field/economic geologists, mining geologists, petrologists, hydrogeologists etc, mainly with postgraduate experience), lawyers (for the judiciary, prosecution, litigation advice, and drafting), marine engineers, mechanical engineers, medical experts, meteorologists, mining experts, police, printers, scientists (mainly biologists and chemists), statisticians, surveyors, telecommunications experts, and vets (field and lab work, control and inspection).

Further information from the organisations mentioned above.

Appendix I

The organisations listed below (in key-word alphabetical index) are those able to provide information useful to readers. This is not, therefore, a comprehensive list of professional, examining or training organisations, but includes only those who can genuinely help anyone writing to them. The list does, though, include (almost) all professional and other bodies which are widely accepted as being the main representatives of the particular occupation or area of employment. A number of organisations have, however, asked us not to include them in this list, as they are unable to deal with correspondence and have no relevant literature available. Employers are only included if they are the sole or major source of information in the area of employment.

The list includes changes of title, address etc received up to September 1987.

Two points must be made – at the request of a number of organisations.

First – readers are asked to include a stamped addressed envelope (large enough to take a pamphlet or pamphlets) when requesting information.

Second – readers are asked to note that, except for employers and organisations managing training schemes (eg YTS), few if any of the organisations listed can directly help people to find jobs or training places. They can provide *information* only. Some may be able to provide lists of possible employers and/or training organisations, but this is not guaranteed.

Accepting Houses Committee	Granite House, 101 Cannon Street, London EC4N 5BA *Telephone:* 01-283 7332
Chartered Institute of Public Finance and **Accountancy** (CIPFA)	3 Robert Street, London WC2N 6BH *Telephone:* 01-930 3456
The Chartered Association of Certified **Accountants** (ACA)	29 Lincoln's Inn Fields, London WC2A 3EE *Telephone:* 01-242 6855
Institute of Chartered **Accountants** in England and Wales (ICAEW)	Chartered Accountants' Hall, PO Box 433, Moorgate Place, London EC2P 2BJ *Telephone:* 01-628 7060
Institute of Chartered **Accountants** of Scotland (ICAS)	27 Queen Street, Edinburgh EH2 1LA *Telephone:* 031-225 5687
Chartered Institute of Management **Accountants** (CIMA)	63 Portland Place, London W1N 4AB *Telephone:* 01-580 2311
Institute of Administrative **Accounting**	Burford House, 44 London Road, Sevenoaks, Kent TN13 1AS *Telephone:* 0732 458080

Association of **Accounting** Technicians (AAT)	21 Jockey's Fields, London WC1R 4BN *Telephone:* 01-405 4961
British **Actors'** Equity Association	8 Harley Street, London W1N 2AB *Telephone:* 01-636 6367
Faculty of **Actuaries**	23 St Andrew's Square, Edinburgh EH2 1AQ *Telephone:* 031-537 1575
Institute of **Actuaries**	Staple Inn Hall, High Holborn, London WC1V 7QJ *Telephone:* 01-242 0106
The British **Acupuncture** Association and Register	34 Alderney Street, London SW1V 4EU *Telephone:* 01-834 1012
Association of Average **Adjusters**	Irongate House, Duke's Place, London EC3A 7LP *Telephone:* 01-283 9033
Chartered Institute of Loss **Adjusters**	Manfield House, 376 Strand, London WC2R 0LR *Telephone:* 01-240 1496
Advertising Association	Abford House, 15 Wilton Road, London SW1V 1NJ *Telephone:* 01-828 2771
Institute of Practitioners in **Advertising**	44 Belgrave Square, London SW1X 8QS *Telephone:* 01-245 9904
Faculty of **Advocates**	Advocates' Library, Parliament House, Edinburgh EH1 1RF *Telephone:* 031-226 5071
The Royal **Aeronautical** Society	4 Hamilton Place, London W1V 0BQ *Telephone:* 01-499 3515
Society of British **Aerospace** Companies	29 King Street, London SW1Y 6RD *Telephone:* 01-839 3231
Institute of **Agricultural** Secretaries	National Agricultural Centre, Stoneleigh, Kenilworth, Warwicks CV8 2LZ *Telephone:* 0203 20623
Agricultural and Food Research Council	160 Great Portland Street, London W1N 6DT *Telephone:* 01-580 6655

British **Agricultural** and Garden Machinery Association Ltd

Church Street, Rickmansworth, Herts WD3 1RQ
Telephone: Rickmansworth 0923 77241

Agricultural Training Board

Bourne House, 32/34 Beckenham Road, Beckenham, Kent BR3 4PB
Telephone: 01-650 4890

National Examination Board for **Agriculture**, Horticulture and Allied Industries (NEBAHAI)

c/o City and Guilds (see below)

BAA plc (British **Airports** Authority)

Gatwick Airport, Gatwick, West Sussex RH6 0HZ

Institute of **Animal** Technicians

5 South Parade, Summertown, Oxford 0X2 2JL

Royal **Anthropological** Society

56 Queen Anne Street, London W1
Telephone: 01-486 6832

British **Antique Dealers** Association

20 Rutland Gate, London SW7 1BD
Telephone: 01-589 4128

Society of **Apothecaries**

The Apothecaries Hall, Black Friars Lane, London EC4V 6EJ
Telephone: 01-236 1189

Arboricultural Association

Ampfield House, Ampfield, Nr Romsey, Hants SO51 9PA
Telephone: Braishfield (0794) 68717

British **Archaeological** Trust (Rescue)

15A Bull Plain, Hertford, Herts SG14 1DX
Telephone: Hertford (0992) 553377

Council for British **Archaeology**

112 Kennington Road, London SE11 6RE
Telephone: 01-582 0494

Royal Institute of British **Architects** (RIBA)

66 Portland Place, London W1N 4AD
Telephone: 01-580 5533

Royal Incorporation of **Architects** in Scotland

15 Rutland Square, Edinburgh EH1
Telephone: 031-229 7205

Architects' Registration Council of the UK

73 Hallam Street, London W1N 6EE
Telephone: 01-580 5861

Faculty of **Architects** and Surveyors (FAS)

15 St Mary Street, Chippenham, Wilts SN15 3JN
Telephone: (0249) 55398

Incorporated Association of **Architects** and Surveyors (IAAS)

Jubilee House, Billing Brook Road, Weston Favell, Northampton NN3 4NW
Telephone: (0604) 404121

British Institute of **Architectural** Technicians

397 City Road, London EC1 1NE
Telephone: 01-278 2206

Society of **Archivists**

J F Watson, Hon Assistant Secretary, South Humberside Area Record Office, Town Hall Square, Grimsby DN31 1HX
Telephone: 0472 53481

Armed Forces: Army

Directorate of Army Recruiting, Ministry of Defence, Empress State Building, Lillie Road, London SW6 1TR
Telephone: 01-386 1244
or see local telephone directory for nearest recruiting office

Armed Forces: RAF

Directorate of Recruiting, Adastra House, Theobalds Road, London WC1X 8RY
Telephone: 01-430 7350
or see local telephone directory for nearest recruiting office

Armed Forces: Royal Navy

See local telephone directory for nearest recruiting office

Society of Industrial **Artists and Designers** (SIAD)

12 Carlton House Terrace, London SW1Y 5AH
Telephone: 01-930 1911

Arts Administration Training

The Arts Council of Great Britain, 105 Piccadilly, London W1V 0AU
Telephone: 01-629 9495

Royal Society of **Arts**

8 John Adam Street, London WC2N 6EZ
Telephone: 01-930 5115

Astronomy

See Science and Engineering Research Council

Incorporated Society of **Auctioneers and Valuers** (ISVA)

3 Cadogan Gate, London SW1X 0AS
Telephone: 01-235 2282

Audio Visual Association

46 Manor View, London N3 2SR
Telephone: 01-349 2429

Society of Hearing Aid **Audiologists**	54 Crobham Manor Road, South Croydon, Surrey CR2 7BE
British Society of **Audiology**	c/o Hearing Services, General Hospital, Nottingham NG1 6HA
Civil **Aviation** Authority (CAA)	CAA House, 45-59 Kingsway, London WC2B 6TE *Telephone:* 01-379 7311
The National Council for **Baking** Education	c/o Federation of Bakers, 20 Bedford Square, London WC1B 3HF *Telephone:* 01-580 4252
The British **Ballet** Organization	39 Lonsdale Road, London SW13 9JP *Telephone:* 01-748 1241
Baltic Mercantile and Shipping Exchange	St Mary Axe, London EC3A 88U *Telephone:* 01-623 5501
Bank of England	Threadneedle Street, London EC2R 8AH
Institute of **Bankers** and Banking Information Service Education and Careers Section	10 Lombard Street, London EC3V 9AT *Telephone:* 01-623 3531 (Inst) 01-626 8486 (BISECS)
Institute of **Bankers** in Scotland	20 Rutland Square, Edinburgh EH1 2BB *Telephone:* 031-229 9869
Bar Council of England and Wales/ Senate of the Inns of Court	11 South Square, Gray's Inn, London WC1R 5EL *Telephone:* 01-242 0082
Barristers' Clerks' Association	2 Crown Office Row, Temple, London EC4 7AS
British Association/Confederation of **Beauty Therapy and Cosmetology**	Suite 5, Wolseley House, Oriel Road, Cheltenham, Glos GL50 1TH
International Health and **Beauty** Council (Division of Vocational Training Charitable Trust)	109a Felpham Road, Felpham, W Sussex PO22 7PW
Billiards and Snooker Control Council	Coronet House, Queen Street, Leeds LS1 2TN *Telephone:* 0532 440586
World Professional **Billiards** and Snooker Association	27 Oakfield Road, Clifton, Bristol BS8 2AT

The **Biochemical** Society	7 Warwick Court, Holborn, London WC1R 5DP *Telephone:* 01-242 1076
Association of Clinical **Biochemists**	30 Russell Square, London WC1B 5D1
Biological Engineering Society	c/o Royal College of Surgeons, Lincoln's Inn Fields, London WC2A 3PN *Telephone:* 01-242 7750
Institute of **Biology**	20 Queensberry Place, London SW7 2DZ *Telephone:* 01-581 8333
The Unwin Foundation **Book House** Training Centre	45 East Hill, London SW18 2QZ *Telephone:* 01-874 2718
Booksellers Association	154 Buckingham Palace Road, London SW1W 9TZ *Telephone:* 01-730 8214
British **Boot** and Shoe Institution	see Clothing and Footwear Institute
Incorporated **Brewers'** Guild	8 Ely Place, Holborn, London EC1N 6SD *Telephone:* 01-405 4565
The **Brewers'** Society	42 Portman Square, London W1H 0BB *Telephone:* 01-486 4831
Institute of **Brewing**	33 Clarges Street, London W1Y 8EE *Telephone:* 01-499 8144
The **British** Council	65 Davies Street, London W1Y 2AA *Telephone:* 01-499 8011
Independent **Broadcasting** Authority (IBA)	70 Brompton Road, London SW3 1EY *Telephone:* 01-584 7011
British **Broadcasting** Corporation (BBC)	Broadcasting House, Portland Place, London W1A 1AA *Telephone:* 01-580 4468
Broadcasting: Independent Television Companies Association Training Adviser	Knighton House, 56 Mortimer Street, London W1 8AN *Telephone:* 01-636 6866

Builders' Merchants Federation Education and Training Department	Parnall House, 5 Parnall Road, Staple Tye, Harlow CM18 7PP *Telephone:* 0279 39654
Building Industry Careers Service	See Construction Industry Training Board
Chartered Institute of **Building**	Englemere, King's Ride, Ascot, Berks SL5 8BJ *Telephone:* Ascot (0990) 23355
Chartered Institution of **Building Services** Engineers (CIBSE)	Delta House, 222 Balham High Road, London SW12 9BS *Telephone:* 01-675 5211
Chartered **Building Societies** Institute	19 Baldock Street, Ware, Herts SG12 9DH *Telephone:* Ware (0920) 5051
Business in the Community	227A City Road, London EC1V 1LX 25 St Andrews Square, Edinburgh EH2 1AF
Business Systems and Office Stationery Federation (BOSSF)	6 Wimpole Street, London W1M 8AS *Telephone:* 01-637 7696
Business and Technician Education Council (BTEC)	Central House, Upper Woburn Place, London WC1H 0HH *Telephone:* 01-388 3288
Scottish **Business** Education Council (SCOTBEC)	See under Vocational (SCOTVEC)
The Society of **Cardiological** Technicians	214 Loughborough Road, Ruddington, Nottingham NG11 6NX *Telephone:* 0602 212377
National Association of **Careers** and Guidance Teachers (NACGT)	c/o Membership Secretary, 46 Fairfield Road, Penarth, S Glam CF6 1SL
Institute of **Careers** Officers	27a Lower High Street, Stourbridge, W Midlands DY8 1TA *Telephone:* Stourbridge (038 43) 76464
Institute of **Carpenters**	45 Sheen Lane, London SW14 8AB
British **Cartographic** Society	c/o Roger Anson, Department of Construction, Oxford Polytechnic, Headington, Oxford OX3 0BP

Catholic Institute for International Relations (CIIR)

Overseas Volunteer Department, 22 Coleman Fields, London N1 7AF
Telephone: 01-354 0883

Ceramics Industry Training Organisation

41a High Street, Newcastle-under-Lyme, Staffs
Telephone: 0782 638755

Institute of **Ceramics**

Shelton House, Stoke Road, Stoke-on-Trent ST4 2DR
Telephone: 0782 202116

Chemical Industry Association

Alembic House, Albert Embankment, London SE1
Telephone: 01-735 3001

Royal Society of **Chemistry** (RSC)

30 Russell Square, London WC1B 5DT
Telephone: 01-631 1355

Society of **Chiropodists**

8 Wimpole Street, London W1H 3PE
Telephone: 01-580 3228

British **Chiropractic** Association

5 First Avenue, Chelmsford, Essex CM1 1RX

Christians Abroad Ltd

15 Tufton Street, London SW1
Telephone: 01-222 2165

Church: Baptist Union of Great Britain and Ireland

Baptist Church House, 4 Southampton Row, London WC1B 4AB
Telephone: 01-405 9803

Church: Catholic

Diocesan Vocations Directors (address etc from any parish priest in the diocese)

Church: Congregational Federation

Ministerial Training Board, Congregational Centre, 4 Castle Gate, Nottingham NG1 7AS
Telephone: 0602 413801

Church of England

Vocations Adviser, Advisory Council for the Church's Ministry, Church House, Dean's Yard, London SW1P 3NZ
Telephone: 01-222 9011

Church: Methodist

Ministerial Training Departments, 1 Central Buildings, Matthew Parker Street, London SW1H 9NH
Telephone: 01-223 3176

Church of Scotland	Department of Education, 121 George Street, Edinburgh EH2 4YN *Telephone:* 01-247 1696
United Free **Church** of Scotland	11 Newton Place, Glasgow G3 7PR *Telephone:* 041-332 3435
Unitarian and Free Christian **Church(es)**	General Assembly, Essex Hall, 1-6 Essex Street, London WC2R 3HY *Telephone:* 01-240 2384
United Reformed **Church**	86 Tavistock Place, London WC1H 9RD *Telephone:* 01-837 7661
City and Guilds of London Institute	76 Portland Place, London W1N 4AA *Telephone:* 01-580 3050
Civil Service Commission	Alencon Link, Basingstoke, Hants RG21 11B *Telephone:* Basingstoke (0256) 29222
British Institute of **Cleaning Science**	Suite 76/7, Central Buildings, 24 Southwark Street, London SE1 1TY *Telephone:* 01-407 2304
Institute of **Clerks of Works**	41 The Mall, London W5 3TJ *Telephone:* 01-579 2917
Clothing and Allied Products Industry Training Board	Tower House, Merrion Way, Leeds LS2 8NY *Telephone:* 0532 41331
Clothing and Footwear Institute	71 Brushfield Street, London E1 6AA *Telephone:* 01-247 2697
British **Coal** (National Coal Board)	Hobart House, Grosvenor Place, London SW1X 7AE *Telephone:* 01-235 2020
HM **Coastguard**	Sunley House, 90 High Holborn, London WC1V 6LP *Telephone:* 01-405 6911
London Chamber of **Commerce and Industry** Examinations Board	Marlowe House, Station Road, Sidcup, Kent DA15 7BJ *Telephone:* 01-302 0261
United **Commercial** Travellers' Association (UCTA) Section (ASTMS)	Bexton Lane, Knutsford, Ches WA16 9DA *Telephone:* Knutsford 4136

Federation of **Commodity** Associations

Plantation House, Mincing Lane, London EC3
Telephone: 01-626 1745

London **Commodity** Exchange

1 Commodity Quay, Katherine Docks, London E1 9AX
Telephone: 01-481 2080

Communication, Advertising and Marketing Education Foundation Ltd (CAM)

Abford House, 15 Wilton Road, London SW1V 1NJ
Telephone: 01-828 7506

British **Computer** Society (BCS)

13 Mansfield Street, London W1M 0BP
Telephone: 01-637 0471

Computing Services Industry Training Committee (COSIT)

Victoria House, Vernon Place, London WC1B 4DP
Telephone: 01-278 8058

National **Computing** Centre

Bracken House, Charles Street, Manchester M1 7BD
Telephone: 061-228 6333

UK Institute for **Conservation**

c/o Conservation Department, Tate Gallery, Millbank, London SW1P 4RG

Construction Industry Training Board Careers Advisory Service

Bircham Newton, Nr King's Lynn PE31 6RH
Telephone: 0553 776677

Council for Licensed **Conveyancers**

Golden Cross House, Duncannon Street, London WC2N 4JF
Telephone: 01-210 4604

Co-operative Advisory Group

Antonia House, 262 Holloway Road, London N7 6NE
Telephone: 01-609 7017

Co-operative Development Agency

Broadmead House, 21 Panton Street, London SW1Y 4DR
Telephone: 01-839 2985

Association of **Corporate Treasurers**

16 Park Crescent, London W1N 3PA
Telephone: 01-631 1991

Council for National Academic Awards (CNAA)

344 Gray's Inn Road, London WC1X 8BP
Telephone: 01-278 4411

British Association for **Counselling**	37a Sheep Street, Rugby CV21 3BX *Telephone:* 0788 78328
Craft Council	12 Waterloo Place, London SW1Y 4AU *Telephone:* 01-930 4811
Institute of **Credit** Management	Easton House, Easton on the Hill, Stamford, Lincs PE9 3NZ *Telephone:* 0780 56777
HM **Customs** and Excise	PDA2, Dorset House, Stamford Street, London SE1 9PS *Telephone:* 01-283 8911
National **Dairy** Council	National Dairy Centre, 5 John Prince's Street, London W1M 0AP *Telephone:* 01-499 7822
Council for **Dance** Education and Training	5 Tavistock Place, London WC1H 9SN *Telephone:* 01-388 5770
International **Dance** Teachers Association	76 Bennett Road, Brighton BN2 5JL *Telephone:* 0272 685652
Incorporated Imperial Society of Teachers of **Dancing**	Euston Hall, Birkenhead Street, London WC1 8BE *Telephone:* 01-837 9967
Institute of **Data Processing** Management	Henrietta House, 18 Henrietta Street, London WC2E 8NU *Telephone:* 01-240 3304
British **Dental** Association (BDA)	64 Wimpole Street, London W1M 8AL *Telephone:* 01-935 0875
General **Dental** Council	37 Wimpole Street, London W1M 8DQ *Telephone:* 01-486 2171
British **Dental Hygienists** Association	c/o British Dental Association, 64 Wimpole Street, London W1M 8AL *Telephone:* 01-935 0875
Association of British **Dental Surgery** Assistants	DSA House, 29 London Street, Fleetwood, Lancs FY7 6JY *Telephone:* 039 17 78631

National Joint Council for the Craft of **Dental Technicians**

Employers' Side Secretary, 64 Wimpole Street, London, W1M 8AL
Telephone: 01-935 0875

Design Council

The Design Centre, 28 Haymarket, London SW1Y 4SU
Telephone: 01-839 8000

British **Dietetic** Assocation

305 Daimler House, Paradise Circus Queensway, Birmingham B1 2BJ
Telephone: 021-643 5483

British **Display** Society

Guardian House, 92-4 Foxberry Road, London SE4 2SH
Telephone: 01-692 8943

National Council for **Drama** Training

5 Tavistock Place, London WC1H 9SS
Telephone: 01-837 3650

Economic and Social Research Council (ESRC)

160 Great Portland Street, London W1N 6BA
Telephone: 01-637 1499

British Association of Industrial **Editors** (BAIE)

3 Locks Yard, High Street, Sevenoaks, Kent TN13 1LT
Telephone: 0732 459331

Scottish **Education** Department

St Andrew's House, Edinburgh EH1 3DB
Telephone: 031-556 8501

Department of **Education** and Science (DES)

Elizabeth House, York Road, London SE1 7PH
Telephone: 01-934 9000

Joint Industry Board for the **Electrical Contracting** Industry

Kingswood House, 47-51 Sidcup Hill, Sidcup, Kent DA14 6HP
Telephone: 01-302 0031

Central **Electricity** Generating Board (CEGB)

Sudbury House, 15 Newgate Street, London EC1A 7AU
Telephone: 01-248 1202

Electricity Council

30 Millbank, London SW1 4RD
Telephone: 01-834 2333

Society of **Electronic** and Radio Technicians

57-61 Newington Causeway, London SE1 6BL
Telephone: 01-403 2351

Electrophysiological Technologists Association (EPTA)

Department of Clinical Neurophysiology, Hospital for Sick Children, Great Ormond Street, London WC1N 3JH

Institute of **Energy**	18 Devonshire Street, London W1N 2AU *Telephone:* 01-580 7124
Engineering Careers Information Service (ECIS)	as EITB below
Society of Civil **Engineering** Technicians	1-7 Great George Street, London SW1P 3AA *Telephone:* 01-232 7722
Engineering Council	Canberra House, 10-16 Maltravers Street, London WC2R 3ER *Telephone:* 01-240 7891
Institution of **Engineering Designers**	Courtleigh, Westbury Leigh, Westbury, Wilts BA13 3TA *Telephone:* Westbury (0373) 822801
Engineering Industry Training Board (EITB)	54 Clarendon Road, Watford WD1 1LB *Telephone:* Watford (0923) 38441
Institute of **Domestic Heating and Environmental Engineering**	93 High Road, Benfleet, Essex *Telephone:* 03745 54266
Council of **Engineering** Institutions (CEI)	See Engineering Council
Institution of **Agricultural Engineers**	West End Road, Silsoe, Bedford MK45 4DU *Telephone:* Silsoe (0525) 61096
The Society of Licensed **Aircraft Engineers** and Technologists (amalgamating with the Royal Aeronautical Society)	Grey Tiles, Kingston Hill, Kingston upon Thames, Surrey KT2 7LW *Telephone:* 01-546 1843
Institution of **Chemical Engineers** Careers Office	12 Gayfere Street, London SW1P 3HP *Telephone:* 01-222 2681/2
Institution of **Civil Engineers**	1-7 Great George Street, London SW1P 3AA *Telephone:* 01-222 7722
Institution of **Electrical Engineers**	Savoy Place, London WC2R 0BS *Telephone:* 01-240 1871
Institution of Incorporated **Electrical and Electronics Engineers**	2 Savoy Hill, London WC2R 0BS *Telephone:* 01-240 3357

Institution of **Electronic and Radio Engineers**	99 Gower Street, London, WC1E 6AZ *Telephone:* 01-388 3071
Institute of **Marine Engineers**	76 Mark Lane, London EC3R 7JN *Telephone:* 01-481 8493
Institution of **Mechanical Engineers**	PO Box 23, Northgate Avenue, Bury St Edmunds IP32 6BN *Telephone:* Bury St Edmunds (0284) 63277
Institution of Technician Engineers in **Mechanical Engineering**	8-12 Old Queen Street, London SW1H 9HP *Telephone:* 01-222 0778
Institution of **Mechanical and General Technician Engineers**	33 Ovington Square, London SW3 1LL *Telephone:* 01-589 9648
Institution of **Mining Engineers**	Hobart House, Grosvenor Place, London SW1X 7AE *Telephone:* 01-235 3691
Institution of **Municipal Engineers**	See Institution of Civil Engineers
Institution of **Plant Engineers** (IPlantE)	138 Buckingham Palace Road, London SW1W 9SG *Telephone:* 01-730 0469
Institution of **Production Engineers**	Rochester House, 66 Little Ealing Lane, London W5 4XX *Telephone:* 01-579 9411
Institution of **Public Health Engineers**	See Institute of Water and Environment Management
Institute of **Road Transport Engineers**	1 Cromwell Place, London SW7 2JF *Telephone:* 01-589 3744
Institution of **Structural Engineers**	11 Upper Belgrave Street, London SW1 8EH *Telephone:* 01-235 4535
Institution of **Water Engineers and Scientists**	See Institute of Water and Environmental Management
Natural **Environment** Research Council	Polaris House, North Star Avenue, Swindon SN2 1EU *Telephone:* 0793 40101

Institution of **Environmental Health** Officers and Education Board	Chadwick House, Rushworth Street, London SE1 0RB
National Association of **Estate Agents**	Arbon House, 21 Jury Street, Warwick CV34 4EH *Telephone:* 0926 496800
Commission of the **European** Economic Communities (EEC)	Recruitment Division, 200 rue de la Loi, B-1049, Brussels, Belgium
Institute of **Export**	World Trade Centre, London E1 9AA *Telephone:* 01-488 2400
Farriers Registration Council	4 Royal College Street, London NW1 0TU *Telephone:* 01-387 9729
Joint Board for **Film Industry** Training (JOBFIT)	Fourth Floor, 5 Dean Street, London W1V 5RN *Telephone:* 01-734 5141
Finance Houses Association	18 Upper Grosvenor Street, London W1X 9PB *Telephone:* 01-491 2783
Fire Service Department	Home Office, Queen Anne's Gate, London SW1H 9AT *Telephone:* 01-213 3000
Institute of **Fisheries Management**	Balmaha, Coldwells Road, Holmer, Hereford
Society of **Florists**	Old Schoolhouse, Payford, Redmarley, Glos GL19 3HY *Telephone:* 0531 820809
Food Manufacturers' Council for Industrial Training	6 Catherine Street, London WC2B 5JJ *Telephone:* 01-836 2460
Institute of **Food Science and Technology**	20 Queensberry Place, London SW7 2DR *Telephone:* 01-581 0798
Football Association	16 Lancaster Gate, London W2 3LW *Telephone:* 01-262 4542
Professional **Footballers** Association	124 Corn Exchange Buildings, Manchester M4 3BN *Telephone:* 061-834 7554

British **Footwear** Manufacturers Federation

Royalty House, 72 Dean Street, London W1V 5HB
Telephone: 01-437 5573

Forestry Commission and Training Council

231 Corstorphine Road, Edinburgh EH12 7AT
Telephone: 031-334 0303 (Commission) 8083 (FTC)

The Institute of British **Foundrymen**

8th Floor, Bridge House, 121 Smallbrook Queensway, Birmingham B5 4JP
Telephone: 021-643 4523

British **Franchise** Association

75a Bell Street, Henley-on-Thames
Telephone: 0491 578049

Institute of **Freight Forwarders/** Freight Forwarding Training Council

Suffield House, 9 Paradise Road, Richmond TW9 1SA
Telephone: 01-948 3141

British **Furniture** Manufacturers' Training Division

9 Amersham Hill, High Wycombe
Telephone: 0494 23021

British **Gas**

Personnel Division, Rivermill House, 152 Grosvenor Road, London SW1V 3JL
Telephone: 01-821 1444

Institute of **Geological Sciences**

Exhibition Road, London SW7 2DE

Institution of **Geologists**

2nd Floor, Geological Society Apartments, Burlington House, London W1V 9HG

Glass Manufacturers' Federation

19 Portland Place, London W1N 4BH
Telephone: 01-580 6952

Glass Training Ltd

BGIRA Building, Northumberland Road, Sheffield S10 2UA
Telephone: 0742 601494

Society of **Glass Technology**	20 Hallam Gate Road, Sheffield S10 5BT *Telephone:* 0742 663168
British Society of Scientific **Glassblowers**	21 Grebe Avenue, Eccleston Park, St Helens WA10 3QL *Telephone:* 051-709 1438
Professional **Golfers'** Association: PGA European Tour	Wentworth Club, Wentworth Drive, Virginia Water, Surrey GU25 4LS *Telephone:* Wentworth (099 04) 2881
Government Communications Headquarters (GCHQ)	Oakley, Priors Road, Cheltenham GL52 5AJ *Telephone:* 0242 22912
Institute of **Grocery** Distribution	Careers Information Service, Freepost, Letchmore Heath, Watford WD1 8FP *Telephone:* Radlett (779) 7141
Institute of **Groundsmanship**	The Pavilion, Woughton on Green, Milton Keynes MK6 3EA *Telephone:* 0908 663600
Guide Dogs for the Blind Association	Alexandra House, 9-11 Park Street, Windsor, Berks SL4 1JR *Telephone:* Windsor (0753) 855711
Incorporated Guild of **Hairdressers**, Wigmakers and Perfumers	24 Woodbridge Road, Guildford GU1 1DY *Telephone:* 0483 67922
Hairdressing Training Board	17 Silver Street, Doncaster DN1 1HL *Telephone:* 0302 342837
National Institute of **Hardware**	10 Leam Terrace, Leamington Spa CV31 1BD *Telephone:* Leamington Spa (0926) 21284
Association of **Health Care Information and Medical Record** Officers	16 Beacon Hill, Dormansland, Lingfield, Surrey RH7 6RH
Health and Safety Executive	St Hugh's House, Stanley Precinct, Bootle L20 3QY
Institute of **Health Services Management**	75 Portland Place, London W1N 4AN *Telephone:* 01-580 5041

National **Health Service**	See telephone directory for address of nearest Regional Authority
Health Visitors	See Nursing
Highway and Traffic Technicians Association (HTTA)	3 Lygon Place, London SW1W 0JR *Telephone:* 01-730 5245
Institution of **Highways and Transportation**	3 Lygon Place, Ebury Street, London SW1W 0JS *Telephone:* 01-730 5245
Historic Buildings and Monuments Commission	Fortress House, Savile Row, London W1X 2HE *Telephone:* 01-734 6010
Institute of **Home Economics**	Aldwych House, 71-91 Aldwych, London WC2B 4HN *Telephone:* 01-0404 5532
British **Horological** Institute	Upton Hall, Upton, Newark, Notts NG23 5TE *Telephone:* Southwell (0636) 813795
Horse racing: National Trainers Federation	42 Portman Square, London W1H 0AP
British **Horse** Society (BHS)	British Equestrian Centre, Stoneleigh, Kenilworth, Warwicks CV8 2LR *Telephone:* 0203 52241
Royal **Horticultural** Society (RHS)	Wisley, Woking, Surrey GU23 6QB
Hotel and Catering Training Board Careers Information Service	International House, High Street, Ealing, London W5 5DB *Telephone:* 01-579 2400
Hotel, Catering and Institutional Management Association (HCIMA)	191 Trinity Road, London SW17 7HN *Telephone:* 01-672 4251
Institute of **Housing**	9 White Lion Street, London N1 9XJ *Telephone:* 01-278 2705
Institute of **Information Scientists**	44 Museum Street, London WC1A 1LY *Telephone:* 01-631 8633
Information Technology Training Accreditation Council (ITTAC)	London WC1N 3XX *Telephone:* 01-404 5011

British Institute of **Innkeeping**	121 London Road, Camberley, Surrey GU15 3LF *Telephone:* 0276 684449
British **Insurance** Association	Aldermary House, Queen Street, London EC4N 1TU *Telephone:* 01-248 4477
British Association of **Insurance Brokers**	BIBA House, 14 Bevis Marks, London EC3A 7NT *Telephone:* 01-623 9043
Chartered **Insurance** Institute (CII)	20 Aldermanbury, London EC2V 7HY *Telephone:* 01-606 3835
Insurance: Lloyd's of London	Lime Street, London EC3M 7HA *Telephone:* 01-623 7100
British Institute of **Interior Design**	1c Devonshire Avenue, Beeston, Nottingham NG9 1BS *Telephone:* Nottingham (0602)
The Society of **Investment Analysts**	211-3 High Street, Bromley, Kent BR1 1NY *Telephone:* 01-464 0811
Issuing Houses Association	Granite House, 101 Cannon Street, London EC4N 5BA *Telephone:* 01-283 7334
Jewish Community (orthodox)	Director of Education, London Board of Jewish Religious Education, Woburn House, Upper Woburn Place, London WC1H 0EP
Jewish Community (liberal)	Leo Baeck College, Manor House, 80 East End Road, London N3 2SY
National Council for the Training of **Journalists**	Carlton House, Hemnall Street, Epping, Essex CM16 4NL *Telephone:* Epping (0378) 72395
National Union of **Journalists** (NUJ)	Acorn House, 314-20 Gray's Inn Road, London WC1X 8DP *Telephone:* 01-278 7916
Justices' Clerks' Assistants	Home Office, C2 Division, Queen Anne's Gate, London SW1H 9AX *Telephone:* 01-213 3000
Knitting & Lace Industries Training Resources Agency	7 Gregory Boulevard, Nottingham NG7 6LD *Telephone:* 0602 623311

Landscape Institute

12 Carlton House Terrace, London SW1Y 5AH
Telephone: 01-839 4044

Association of British **Laundry, Cleaning** and Rental Services (ABLCRS)

319 Pinner Road, Harrow, Middx HA1 4HX
Telephone: 01-863 7755

Law Society

113 Chancery Lane, London WC2A 1PL
Telephone: 01-242 1222

Law Society of Scotland

26-27 Drumsheugh Gardens, Edinburgh EH3 7YB
Telephone: 021-226 7411

Lawn Tennis Association

Palliser Road, London W14
Telephone: 01-385 2366

National **Leathersellers** Centre

Nene College, Moulton Park, Northampton NN2 7AL
Telephone: 0604 715000

Council of **Legal Education**

4 Gray's Inn Place, London WC1R 5DX
Telephone: 01-404 5787

Institute of **Legal Executives**

Kempston Manor, Kempston, Bedford MK42 7AB
Telephone: 0234 857711

Association of **Legal Secretaries**

The Mill, Clymping Street, Clymping, Nr Littlehampton, W Sussex BN17 5RN
Telephone: Littlehampton (0903) 714276

Institute of **Leisure & Amenity Management**

Lower Basildon, Reading RG8 9NE
Telephone: Goring on Thames (0491) 873558

Library Association (LA)

7 Ridgmount Street, London WC1E 7AE
Telephone: 01-636 7543

Institute of **Linguists**

24a Highbury Grove, London N5
Telephone: 01-359 7445

Institute of **Local Government** Administrators

See Institute of Chartered Secretaries and Administrators

Local Government Training Board

Arndale House, The Arndale Centre, Luton LU1 2TS
Telephone: 0582 451166

London Visitor and Convention Bureau	26 Grosvenor Gardens, London SW1 *Telephone:* 01-730 3450
Lord Chancellor's Department	Trevelyan House, 30 Great Peter Street, London SW1V
Machine Tool Trades Association	62 Bayswater Road, London W2 3PH *Telephone:* 01-402 6671
Institute of **Administrative Management**	40 Chatsworth Parade, Petts Wood, Orpington, Kent BR5 1RW *Telephone:* Orpington (0689) 75555
Management Consultants' Association	11 West Halkin Street, London SW1X 8JL *Telephone:* 01-235 3897
Institute of **Management Services**	1 Cecil Court, London Road, Enfield EN2 6DD *Telephone:* 01-363 7452
Market Research Society	175 Oxford Street, London W1R 1TA *Telephone:* 01-439 2585
Institute of **Marketing**	Moor Hall, Cookham, Maidenhead, Berks SL6 9QH *Telephone:* Bourne End (062 85) 24922
Mathematical Association	20 Hazel End, Swanley, Kent BR8 8NU
Institute of **Mathematics** and Its Applications (ICIA)	Maitland House, Warrior Square, Southend-on-Sea SS1 2JY *Telephone:* Southend-on-Sea (0702) 612177
Institute of **Measurement and Control**	87 Gower Street, London WC1E 6AA *Telephone:* 01-387 4949
Institute of **Meat**	56/60 St John Street, London EC1M 4DT *Telephone:* 01-253 2971
General **Medical** Council (GMC)	44 Hallam Street, London W1N 6AE *Telephone:* 01-580 7642
Institute of **Medical Laboratory Sciences**	12 Queen Anne Street, London W1M 0AU *Telephone:* 01-636 8192

Association of **Medical Records** Officers

See Health Care Information

Medical Research Council

20 Park Crescent, London W1N 4AL
Telephone: 01-636 5422

Association of **Medical Secretaries**, Practice Administrators and Receptionists

Tavistock House South, Tavistock Square, London WC1 9LN
Telephone: 01-387 6005

Institute for **Complementary Medicine**

21 Portland Place, London W1N 3AF
Telephone: 01-636 9543

Council for Professions Supplementary to **Medicine**

184 Kennington Park Road, London SE11 4BY
Telephone: 01-582 0866

Institute of **Metallurgical** Technicians

See Institute of Metals

Royal Institution of **Metallurgists**

See Institute of Metals

The Institute of **Metals**

1 Carlton House Terrace, London SW1Y 5DB
Telephone: 01-839 4071

Metals Society

See Institute of Metals

Meteorological Office

London Road, Bracknell, Berks RG12 2SZ
Telephone: Bracknell (0344) 20242

Society for General **Microbiology**

Harvest House, 62 London House, Reading RG1 5AS
Telephone: 0734 861345

Milk Marketing Board

Thames Ditton KT7 0EL
Telephone: 01-398 4101

Mineral Industry Manpower and Careers Unit

Royal School of Mines Building, Prince Consort Road, London SW7 2BP
Telephone: 01-584 7397

The Institution of **Mining and Metallurgy**	44 Portland Place, London W1N 4BR *Telephone:* 01-580 3802
Motor Agents Association	201 Great Portland Street, London W1N 6AB *Telephone:* 01-580 9122
Institute of the **Motor Industry** (IMI)	Fanshaws, Brickendon, Hertford *Telephone:* Bayford (099 286) 282
Society of **Motor Manufacturers and Traders**	Forbes House, Halkin Street, London SW1X 7DS *Telephone:* 01-235 7000
Museums Association	34 Bloomsbury Way, London WC1A 2SF *Telephone:* 01-404 4767
Association of Independent **Museums**	c/o Museum of East Anglian Life, Stowmarket, Suffolk IP14 1DL *Telephone:* 0449 612229
British Society for **Music Therapy**	48 Lanchester Road, London N10
Incorporated Society of **Musicians**	10 Stratford Place, London W1N 9AE *Telephone:* 01-629 4413
Nature Conservancy Council	Recruitment Section, PO Box 6, George House, George Street, Huntingdon PE18 6BU *Telephone:* Huntingdon (0480) 56191
British **Naturopathic and Osteopathic** Association	6 Netherhall Gardens, London NW3 5RR *Telephone:* 01-435 7830
Royal Institution of **Naval** Architects	10 Upper Belgrave Street, London SW1X 8BQ *Telephone:* 01-235 4622
Newspaper Publishers Association Ltd	6 Bouverie Street, London EC4Y 8AY *Telephone:* 01-583 8132

The **Newspaper** Society	Whitefriars House, Carmelite Street, London EC4Y 0BL *Telephone:* 01-583 3311
National **Nursery Nurses** Examination Board (NNEB)	Argyle House, 29-31 Euston Road, London NW1 2SD *Telephone:* 01-837 5458
English National Board for **Nursing**, Midwifery and Health Visiting	Victory House, 170 Tottenham Court Road, London W1P 0HA *Telephone:* 01-388 3131 Careers Advisory Centre, 26 Margaret Street, London W1N 7LR *Telephone:* 01-631 0979
National Board for **Nursing**, Midwifery and Health Visiting for Northern Ireland	210 Belmont Road, Belfast BT4 2AT *Telephone:* 0232 246333
Scottish National Board for **Nursing**, Midwifery and Health Visiting	22 Queen Street, Edinburgh EH2 1JX *Telephone:* 031 226 7371
Welsh National Board for **Nursing**, Midwifery and Health Visiting	Floor 13, Pearl Assurance House, Greyfriars Road, Cardiff CF1 3RT *Telephone:* 0222 395535
Institution of, and National Examination Board in, **Occupational Safety and Health**	222 Uppingham Road, Leicester LE5 0QG *Telephone:* 0533 768424
British Association, and College, of **Occupational Therapists**	20 Rede Place, London W2 4TU *Telephone:* 01-229 9738
Institute of **Oceanographic Sciences**	Brook Road, Godalming, Surrey GU8 5UB *Telephone:* (042) 879 4141
Office Machines and Equipment Federation	See Business Systems and Office Stationery Federation
Operational Research Society	6th Floor, Neville House, Waterloo Street, Birmingham B2 5TX *Telephone:* 021-643 0236

General **Optical** Council	41 Harley Street, London W1N 2DJ *Telephone:* 01-580 3898
British Association of **Dispensing Opticians**	22 Nottingham Place, London W1M 4AT *Telephone:* 01-935 7411
British College of **Optometrists** (Ophthalmic Opticians)	10 Knaresborough Place, London SW5 0TG *Telephone:* 01-373 7765
Ordnance Survey	Romsey Road, Maybush, Southampton SO9 4DH *Telephone:* 0703 775555
British **Orthoptic** Council	Manchester Royal Eye Hospital, Oxford Road, Manchester M13 9WH *Telephone:* 061-832 5861
British **Orthoptic** Society	Tavistock House North, Tavistock Square, London WC1H 9HX *Telephone:* 01-273 5280
Orthotic and Prosthetic Training and Education Council	Centre Point, 103 New Oxford Street, London WC1A 1DU *Telephone:* 01-240 5906
British School of **Osteopathy** (and General Council and Register)	1 Suffolk Street, London SW1Y 4HG *Telephone:* 01-930 9254
Overseas Development Administration	Eland House, Stag Place, London SW1E 5DH *Telephone:* 01-213 3000
Institute of **Packaging**	Fountain House, 1a Elm Park, Stanmore, Middx HA7 4BZ *Telephone:* 01-954 6277
Institute of **Park and Recreation** Administration	See Leisure
Chartered Institute of **Patent Agents**	Staple Inn Buildings, London WC1V 7PZ *Telephone:* 01-405 9450
The **Patent** Office	66-71 High Holborn, London WC1 4TP *Telephone:* 01-831 2525

Pensions Managment Institute

Prudential House, Wellesley House, Croydon CR0 2AD
Telephone: 01-681 3580

Periodical Training Trust Ltd

c/o Periodical Publishers'Association, Imperial House, 15-19 Kingsway, London WC2B 6UN
Telephone: 01-836 8798

Institute of **Personnel Management**

IPM House, 35 Camp Road, Wimbledon, London SW19 4VW
Telephone: 01-949 9100

Institute of **Petroleum**

61 New Cavendish Street, London W1M 8AR
Telephone: 01-636 1004

Association of the British **Pharmaceutical** Industry

162 Regent Street, London W1R 6DP
Telephone: 01-930 3477

Pharmaceutical Society of Great Britain

1 Lambeth High Street, London SE1 7JN
Telephone: 01-735 9141

British Institute of Professional **Photography** (BIPP)

2 Amwell End, Ware, Herts
Telephone: Ware (0920) 4011

Institute of **Physics** and Hospital Physicists' Association

47 Belgrave Square, London SW1X 8QX
Telephone: 01-235 6111

Chartered Society of **Physiotherapy**

14 Bedford Row, London WC1R 4ED
Telephone: 01-242 1941

Pianoforte Tuners' Association

10 Reculver Road, Herne Bay, Kent CT6 6LD
Telephone: Herne Bay (0227) 368808

Pitman's Examination Institute

Catteshall Manor, Godalming, Surrey GU7 1UU
Telephone: Godalming (048 68) 5311

Royal Institute of Town **Planning**	26 Portland Place, London W1N 4BE *Telephone:* 01-636 9107
Plastics Industry Education Service	University of Technology, Loughborough LE11 3TU *Telephone:* 0509 232065
Plastics and Rubber Institute	11 Hobart Place, London SW1W 0HL *Telephone:* 01-245 9555
Plastics Processing Industry Training Board	Coppice House, Halesfield 7, Telford TS7 4NA *Telephone:* 0982 587121
Police Recruiting Department	Home Office, Queen Anne's Gate, London SW1H 9AT *Telephone:* 01-213 4074
Metropolitan **Police** Careers Information and Selection Centre	6 Harrow Road, London W2 1XH *Telephone:* 01-723 4237
British **Ports** Assocation	Commonwealth House, 1-19 New Oxford Street, London WC1A 1DZ *Telephone:* 01-242 1200
Post Office Management Recruitment Centre	Freepost, Calcon House, Rugby CV23 CBR *or* Local head postmaster (see telephone directory)
British **Printing** Industries Federation	11 Bedford Row, London WC1R 4DX *Telephone:* 01-242 6904
Institute of **Printing**	8 Lonsdale Gardens, Tunbridge Wells TW1 1NV *Telephone:* 0892 38118
Prison Service	Home Office, 50 Queen Anne's Gate, London SW1H 9AT *Telephone:* 01-213 3000
Scottish **Prison** Service	St Margaret's House, London Road, Edinburgh EH8 7TQ *Telephone:* 031-661 6181
Probation Service Division	Home Office, 50 Queen Anne's Gate, London SW1H 9AT *Telephone:* 01-213 3000

Institute of **Production Control**

Beaufort House, 46 Rother Street, Stratford upon Avon CV37 6LT
Telephone: 0789 5266

Property Services Agency (Department of Environment)

Lambeth Bridge House, Albert Embankment, London SE1 7SB
Telephone: 01-211 3000

British **Psycho-Analytical** Society

Mansfield House, 63 New Cavendish Street, London W1
Telephone: 01-580 4952

British **Psychological** Society

St Andrews House, 48 Princess Road East, Leicester LE1 7DR
Telephone: 0533 549568

Society of **Analytical Psychology**

1 Daleham Gardens, London NW3

British Association of **Psychotherapists**

121 Hendon Lane, London N3 3P
Telephone: 01-346 1747

Association of Child **Psychotherapists**

Burgh House, New End Square, London NW3 1LT

Institute of **Public Relations**

Gate House, St Johns Square, London EC1M 4DH
Telephone: 01-253 5151

Publishers Association

19 Bedford Square, London WC1B 3HJ
Telephone: 01-580 6321

Periodical Publishers Association

See under Periodical

Publishing

See also Book House Training Centre

Institute of **Purchasing and Supply**

Easton House, Easton-on-the-Hill, Stamford, Lincs PE9 2NZ
Telephone: Stamford (0780) 56777

Institute of **Quality Assurance**

54 Princes Gate, Exhibition Road, London SW7 2PG
Telephone: 01-584 8556/9

Institute of **Quarrying**

7 Regent Street, Nottingham NG1 5BY

Society and College of **Radiographers**

14 Upper Wimpole Street, London W1M 8BN
Telephone: 01-935 5726

British **Railways** Board

Euston House, 24 Eversholt Street, PO Box 100, London NW1 1DZ
Telephone: 01-922 6374

Rating and Valuation Association	115 Ebury Street, London SW1W 9QT *Telephone:* 01-730 7258
Institute of Baths and **Recreation Management**	Giffard House, 36-38 Sherrard Street, Melton Mowbray, Leics LE13 1XJ *Telephone:* 0664 65531
Recreation Managers Association	See Leisure and Amenity Management
Refractories, Clay Pipes & Allied Industries Training Council	c/o Dept of Ceramics, Glasses and Polymers, The University, Elmfield, Northumberland Road, Sheffield S10 2TZ *Telephone:* Sheffield (0742) 78555
Institute of **Refrigeration**	272 London Road, Wallington, Surrey SM5 2JR *Telephone:* 01-647 7033
National **Retail** Training Council	c/o Retail Consortium, Commonwealth House, 1-19 New Oxford Street, London WC1A 1PA *Telephone:* 01-404 4622
Road Haulage Association	104 New King's Road, London SW6 *Telephone:* 01-736 1183
Road Transport Industry Training Board (RTITB)	Capitol House, Empire Way, Wembley Middx HA9 0NG *Telephone:* 01-902 8880
Institution of the **Rubber** Industry	See Plastics and Rubber Institute
Council for Small Industries in **Rural** Areas (COSIRA),	4 Castle Street, Salisbury SP1 3TP *Telephone:* 0722 336255
Society of Master **Saddlers**	9 St Thomas's Street, London SE1 9SA *Telephone:* 01-407 1582
Institute of **Sales** and Marketing Management	Georgian House, George Street, Luton LU1 2RD *Telephone:* 0582 411130
The **Salvation Army**	101 Queen Victoria Street, London EC4P 4EP *Telephone:* 01-236 5222
Science and Engineering Research Council (SERC)	Polaris House, North Star Avenue, Swindon SN2 1ET *Telephone:* 0793 26222

Institute of **Science** Technology

Staple Inn Buildings South, 3rd Floor South, 335 High Holborn, London WC1V PX
Telephone: 01-837 2207

Scientific Instrument Manufacturers Assocation (SIMA)

Sima House, 20 Peel Street, London W8 7PD
Telephone: 01-727 2614

Sea Fish Industry Authority/ Training Council

Industrial Development Unit, St Andrew's Dock, Hull HU3 4QE
Telephone: 0482 27837

Institute of Chartered **Secretaries and Administrators** (ICSA)

16 Park Crescent, London W1N 4AH
Telephone: 01-580 4741

International Professional **Security** Association

292A Torquay Road, Paignton TQ3 2ET
Telephone: 0803 554849

National Inspectorate of **Security** Guard, Patrol and Transport Services

British Security Industry Association, The River House, Vicarage Crescent, London SW11 3JY

Ship and Boat Builders' National Federation

Boating Industry House, Vale Road, Oatlands, Weybridge, Surrey KT13 9NJ
Telephone: 0932 45411

Institute of Chartered **Shipbrokers**

24 St Mary Axe, London EC3A 8DE
Telephone: 01-283 1361

Shipbuilding and Allied Industries National Training Association

c/o Cammell Laird Shipbuilders Ltd, New Chester Road, Birkenhead L41 83P

General Council of British **Shipping**

30-32 St Mary Axe, London EC3A 8ET
Telephone: 01-283 2922

Central Council for Education and Training in **Social Work** (CCETSW)

Derbyshire House, St Chad's Street, London WC1H 8AD
Telephone: 01-278 2455

British **Sociological** Association

10 Portugal Street, London WC2A 2HU
Telephone: 01-405 7686 ext 3090

Worshipful Company of **Spectacle Makers**

Apothecaries' Hall, Blackfriars Lane, London EC4V 6EL
Telephone: 01-236 8645

College of **Speech Therapists**

56 Lechmere Road, London NW2 5BU
Telephone: 01-459 8521

Sports Council Information Centre

16 Upper Woburn Place, London WC1H 0QP
Telephone: 01-388 1277

British **Stationery and Office Products** Federation

See Business Systems and Office Stationery Federation

Royal **Statistical** Society

25 Enford Street, London W1H 2BH
Telephone: 01-723 5882

Institute of **Statisticians**

36 Church Gate Street, Bury St Edmunds, Suffolk IP33 1LP
Telephone: 0284 63660

British **Steel** Corporation (BSC)

8 Albert Embankment, London SW1 7SN
Telephone: 01-735 7654

The **Stock Exchange**

Old Broad Street, London EC2N 1HP
Telephone: 01-588 2355

British Institute of **Surgical Technologists**

Centre Point, 103 Oxford Street, London WC1A 1DU
Telephone: 01-240 5906

Society of **Surveying** Technicians

Drayton House, 30 Gordon Street, London WC1H 0BH
Telephone: 01-388 8008

Royal Institute of Chartered **Surveyors** (RICS)

12 Great George Street, London SW1P 5AD
Telephone: 01-222 7000

The Construction **Surveyors** Institute

Wellington House, 203 Lordship Lane, London SE22 8HA
Telephone: 01-693 0219

Institute of **Taxation**

12 Upper Belgrave Street, London SW1X 8BB
Telephone: 01-235 8847

The Centre for British **Teachers**

Quality House, Quality Court, London WC2A 1HP
Telephone: 01-242 2892

British **Telecommunications**

Education Service, British Telecom Centre, 81 Newgate Street, London EC1A 7AJ
Telephone: 01-356 5674

Textile Institute	10 Blackfriars Street, Manchester M3 5DR *Telephone:* 061-834 8457
British **Textile** Employers' Association	Second floor, Royal Exchange, Manchester M2 7ED *Telephone:* 061 834 7871
Confederation of British **Wool Textiles** Ltd (Training Department)	60 Toller Lane, Bradford BD8 9BZ *Telephone:* 0274 491241
British **Timber Merchants'** Association	Ridgeway House, 6 Ridgeway Road, Long Ashton, Bristol BS16 9UE *Telephone:* 0272 394022
Timber Trade Training Association	Stocking Lane, Hughendon Valley, High Wycombe HP14 4NB *Telephone:* 024 024 (Naphill) 4201
British **Tourist** Authority	Queen's House, 64 St James's Street, London SW1A 1NF *Telephone:* 01-629 9191
Royal **Town Planning** Institute	See Planning
Institute of **Trading Standards** Administration	Department of Trading Standards, Cumbria County Council, Kendal, Cumbria LA9 4RQ *Telephone:* 0539 21000 e327
Institute of **Training** and Development	Marlow House, Institute Road, Marlow, Bucks SL7 1BN *Telephone:* 0628 890123
Institute of **Translating and Interpreting**	318A Finchley Road, London NW3 5HT *Telephone:* 01-794 9931
Translators Association	84 Drayton Gardens, London SW10 9SD *Telephone:* 01-373 6642
Institute of **Transport Administration**	32 Palmerston Road, Southampton SO1 1LL *Telephone:* 0703 31380
Chartered Institute of **Transport** (CIT)	80 Portland Place, London W1N 4DP *Telephone:* 01-636 9952
Department of **Transport** (Marine Division)	Sunley House, 90 High Holborn, London WC1V 013 *Telephone:* 01-405 6911

London Regional **Transport**

55 Broadway, London SW1H 0BD
Telephone: 01-222 5600

Association of British **Travel Agents**
(ABTA)

53/54 Newman Street, London W1P
4JJ
Telephone: 01-580 8281
National Training Board, 7
Chertsey Road, Woking, Surrey
GU21 5AB
Telephone: 048 62 27321

Institute of **Travel and Tourism**

113 Victoria Street, St Albans AL1
3TJ

United Nations Information Centre

14-15 Stratford Place, London W1N
9AF

Incorporated Society of **Valuers and
Auctioneers**

3 Cadogan Gate, London SW1X
0AS
Telephone: 01-235 2282

British **Veterinary** Association

7 Mansfield Street, London W1M
0AT
Telephone: 01-636 6541

British **Veterinary Nursing**
Association

Mandeville Veterinary Hospital, 15
Mandeville Road, Northolt, Middx
UB5 5HD
Telephone: 01-845 5677

The Royal College of **Veterinary
Surgeons**

32 Belgrave Square, London SW1X
8QP
Telephone: 01-235 4971

National Council for **Vocational
Qualifications** (NCVQ)

222 Euston Road, London NW1
Telephone: 01-287 9898

Scottish **Vocational** Education
Council (SCOTVEC)

22 Great King Street, Edinburgh
EH3 6QH
Telephone: 031-557 4555

International **Voluntary Service**

Ceresole House, 53 Regent Road,
Leicester LE1 6YL
Telephone: 0533 541862

Voluntary Service Overseas (VSO)

9 Belgrave Square, London SW1X
8PW
Telephone: 01-235 5191

Institution of **Water and
Environmental Management**
(IWEM) (Formed 1987 by the
Institutes of Public Health
Engineers and Water Pollution
Control, and the Institution of
Water Scientists and Engineers)

Ledson House, 53 London Road,
Maidstone ME16 8JH
Telephone: 0622 62034

Institute of **Water Pollution Control**	See Institute of Water and Environmental Management
British **Waterways** Board	Willow Grange, Church Road, Watford WD1 3QA *Telephone:* 0923 26422
Institute of **Weights and Measures Administration**	See Institute of Trading Standards Administration
Welding Institute	54 Princes Gate, London SW7 2PG *Telephone:* 01-584 8556
Institute of **Wood Sciences**	Premier House, 150 Southampton Row, London WC1B 5AL *Telephone:* 01-837 8291
The **Zoological** Society of London	Regent's Park, London NW1 4RY *Telephone:* 01-722 3333

Appendix II: Higher and Further Education Institutions

This appendix lists universities, polytechnics, college/institutions of higher education and other major colleges/institutions providing courses given in the main text. Unless they offer unusual or higher-level courses, further education colleges are not listed (see local telephone directory, or the *Directory of Further Education* published by Hobsons Press for addresses etc).

Institutions are listed alphabetically by location/town. The list is includes changes notified up to September 1987, but further changes are in the pipeline.

Admissions

Applications for more and more courses must be made via *clearing houses*. These act simply as 'post offices' for their member institutions and do not take part in the selection of students. It is crucial to apply through the right clearing house, and to do so using the correct handbook and application form. They are (as of 1987)

University first degrees – Universities Central Council on Admissions (UCCA), PO Box 28, Cheltenham GL50 1HY

Polytechnic and some C/IHE first degrees (excl art/design, BEd) – Polytechnics Central Admissions System (PCAS), PO Box 67, Cheltenham GL50 3AP

Polytechnic and C/IHE BEd courses (optionally for other C/IHE degree courses) – Central Register and Clearing House (CRCH), 3 Crawford Place, London W1H 2BN

Art and design CNAA first degrees – Art and Design Admissions Registry (ADAR), Imperial Chambers, 24 Widemarsh Street, Hereford HR4 9EP

Nursing training (England only) – Nurses' Central Clearing House (ENB NCCH), PO Box 346, Bristol BS99 7FB

Occupational therapy – c/o College of Occupational Therapists (see Appendix I)

Physiotherapy – c/o Chartered Society of Physiotherapy (see Appendix I)

Social work (CQSW) – most postgraduate and non-graduate courses (first degree courses via appropriate clearing house above) – CQSW Clearing House, Fourth Floor, Myson House, Railway Terrace, Rugby CV21 3HT

Aberdeen

College of Education

(may amalgamate with Dundee below)

Hilton Place, Aberdeen AB9 1FA
Telephone: 0234 42341

Robert Gordon's Institute of Technology (RGIT)

Schoolhill, Aberdeen AB9 1FR
Telephone: 0224 633611

The University

Regent Walk, Aberdeen AB9 1FX
Telephone: 0224 272000

Aberystwyth

College of Librarianship

Llanbadarn Fawr, Aberystwyth
SY23 3AS
Telephone: 0970 2181

University College

PO Box 2, Aberystwyth SY23 2AX
Telephone: 0970 3177

Welsh Agricultural College

Llanbadarn Fawr, Aberystwyth
SY23 3AL
Telephone: 0970 4471

Ambleside

Charlotte Mason College

Ambleside, Cumbria LA22 9BB
Telephone: 05394 33066

Ayr

Craigie College of Education

Ayr KA8 0SR
Telephone: 0292 260321

Bangor

University College of North Wales

Bangor, Gwynedd LL57 2DG
Telephone: 0248 351151

Y Coleg Normal

Bangor, Gwynedd LL57 2PX
Telephone: 0248 370171

Bath

Academy of Art

See Bath CHE

College of Higher Education

Newton Park, Bath BA2 9BN
Telephone: 0225 873701

The University

Claverton Down, Bath BA2 7AY
Telephone: 0225 826826

Beaconsfield

National Film and TV School

Station Road, Beaconsfield HP9
1LG
Telephone: 04946 71233

Bedford

College of Higher Education

37 Lansdown Road, Bedford MK40 2BZ
Telephone: 0234 51966

London College of Dance

10 Linden Road, Bedford MK40 2DA
Telephone: 0234 213331

Belfast

Queen's University

University Road, Belfast BT7 1NN
Telephone: 0232 245133

Ulster Polytechnic

See University of Ulster under Coleraine

Birmingham

City of Birmingham Polytechnic

Perry Bar, Birmingham B42 2SU
Telephone: 021-331 5000

Newman/Westfield Colleges

Newman: Genners Lane, Bartley Green, Birmingham B32 3NT
Telephone: 021-476 1181
Westhill: Hamilton Building, Weoley Park Road, Selly Oak, Birmingham B29 6LL
Telephone: 021-472 7245

The University

PO Box 363, Birmingham B15 2TT
Telephone: 021-472 1301

University of Aston

Aston Triangle, Birmingham B4 7ET
Telephone: 021-359 3611

Bolton

Institute of Higher Education

Deane Road, Bolton BL3 5AB
Telephone: 0204 28851

Bournemouth

Dorset Institute of Higher Education

Wallisdown Road, Poole, Dorset BH12 5BB
Telephone: 0202 524111

Bradford

Bradford & Ilkley Community College

Great Horton Road, Bradford BD7 1AY
Telephone: 0274 753026

The University

Bradford BD7 1DP
Telephone: 0274 733166

Brighton

The Polytechnic

Mouslecoomb, Brighton BN2 4AT
Telephone: 0273 693655

University of Sussex

Sussex House, Falmer, Brighton
BN1 9RH
Telephone: 0273 606755

Bristol

The Polytechnic

Coldharbour Lane, Frenchay,
Bristol BS16 1QY
Telephone: 0272 656261

The University

Senate House, Bristol BS8 1TH
Telephone: 0272 303030

Buckingham

The University

Buckingham MK18 1EG
Telephone: 0280 814080

Buckland

University College

Buckland, Farringdon, Oxon SB7
8QX
Telephone: 036-787 202

Camborne

School of Mines

Pool, Redruth, Cornwall TR15 3SE
Telephone: 0209 714866

Cambridge

Cambridgeshire College of Arts and
Technology

East Road, Cambridge CB1 1PT
Telephone: 0223 63271

The University

Inter-Collegiate Applications
Office, Kellett Lodge, Tennis Court
Road, Cambridge CB2 1QJ
Telephone: 0223 333308

Canterbury

Christ Church College

North Holmes Road, Canterbury
CT1 1QU
Telephone: 0227 65548

College of Art

See Maidstone: Kent Institute of
Art and Design

University of Kent

Canterbury CT2 7NZ
Telephone: 0227 66822

Cardiff

South Glamorgan Institute of
Higher Education

Cyncoed, Cardiff CF2 6XD
Telephone: 0222 551111

University College

PO Box 78, Cardiff CF1 1XL
Telephone: 0222 874932

University of Wales Institute of
Science and Technology (UWIST)

PO Box 68, Cardiff CF1 3XA
Telephone: 0222 42588

(University College and UWIST are
amalgamating, probably with
practical effect from 1987-8, but the
title of the new college was not
decided as of September 1987)

(University) College of Medicine

Heath Park, Cardiff CF4 4XN
Telephone: 0222 755944

Welsh College of Music and Drama

Castle Grounds, Cathays Park,
Cardiff CF1 3ER
Telephone: 0222 42854

Carmarthen
Trinity College

Carmarthen, Dyfed SA31 3EP
Telephone: 0267 237971

Chelmsford
Essex Institute of Higher Education

Victoria Road South, Chelmsford
CM1 1LL
Telephone: 0245 354491

Cheltenham
College of St Paul and St Mary

The Park, Cheltenham GL50 2RH
Telephone: 0242 513836

Chester
Chester College

Cheyney Road, Chester CH1 4BJ
Telephone: 0244 375444

Chichester
West Sussex Institute of Higher
Education

College Lane, Chichester PO19 4PE
Telephone: 0243 78791
The Dome, Upper Bognor Road,
Bognor Regis PO21 1HR
Telephone: 0243 865581

Chislehurst
Ravensbourne College of Design
and Communication

Walden Road, Chislehurst BR7
5SN
Telephone: 01-468 7071

Cirencester
Royal Agricultural College

Cirencester GL7 6JS
Telephone: 0285 2531

Colchester

Colchester Institute
Sheepen Road, Colchester CO3 3LL
Telephone: 0206 570271

University of Essex
Wivenhoe Park, Colchester CO4 3SQ
Telephone: 0206 873333

Coleraine

University of Ulster
Coleraine, Northern Ireland BT52 1SA
Telephone: 0265 4141

Coventry

Lanchester Polytechnic
Priory Street, Coventry CV1 5FB
Telephone: 0203 24166

University of Warwick
Coventry CV4 7AL
Telephone: 0203 523523

Cranfield

Cranfield Institute of Technology
Cranfield, Bedford MK43 0AL
Telephone: 0234 750111

Crewe

Crewe and Alsager College of Higher Education
Crewe, Cheshire CW1 1DU
Telephone: 0270 500661

Derby

Derbyshire College of Higher Education
Kedleston Road, Derby DE3 1GB
Telephone: 0332 47181

Doncaster

Metropolitan Institute of Higher Education
Waterdale, Doncaster DN1 3EX
Telephone: 0302 22122

Dundee

Northern College of Education
Gardyne Road, Broughy Ferry, Dundee DD5 1NY
Telephone: 0382 453433

College of Technology
Bell Street, Dundee DD1 1HG
Telephone: 0382 27225

Duncan of Jordanstone College of Art
Perth Road, Dundee DD1 4HT
Telephone: 0382 23261

The University
Dundee DD1 4HN
Telephone: 0382 23181

Durham

New College

Framwellgate Moor, Durham DH1 5ES
Telephone: 0385 27225

The University

Old Shire Hall, Durham DH1 3HP
Telephone: 091 375 2000

Edinburgh

College of Art

Launston Place, Edinburgh EH3 9DF
Telephone: 031-229 9311

Dunfermline College of Physical Education

Cramond Road North, Edinburgh EH4 6JD
Telephone: 031-336 6001

(will probably merge with Moray House below)

Heriot-Watt University

Riccarton, Edinburgh EH14 4A
Telephone: 031-449 5111

Moray House College of Education

Holyrood Road, Edinburgh EH8 8AQ
Telephone: 031-556 8455

Napier College

Information Office, Freepost, Edinburgh EH14 0PA
Telephone: 031-444 2266

Queen Margaret College

Clerwood Terrace, Edinburgh EH12 8TS
Telephone: 031-339 8111

The University

Old College, South Bridge, Edinburgh EH8 9YL
Telephone: 031-667 1011

Exeter

College of Art and Design

Earl Richards Road North, Exeter EX2 6AS
Telephone: 0392 273519

The University

Northcote House, The Queen's Drive, Exeter EX4 4QJ
Telephone: 0392 263263

Exmouth

Rolle College

Exmouth EX8 2AT
Telephone: 0395 265344

Falkirk

College of Technology

Grangemouth Road, Falkirk FK2 9AD
Telephone: 0324 24981

Falmouth
School of Art

Woodlane, Falmouth TR11 4RA
Telephone: 0326 313269

Farnham
West Surrey College of Art and
Design

Falkner Road, The Hart, Farnham
GU9 7DS
Telephone: 0252 722441

Galashiels
Scottish College of Textiles

Netherdale, Galashiels TD1 3HF
Telephone: 0896 3351

Glasgow
Academy of Music and Drama

St George's Place, Glasgow G2 1BS
Telephone: 031-332 4101

College of Building and Printing

60 North Hanover Street, Glasgow
G1 2BP
Telephone: 041-332 9969

Glasgow College of Technology

Cowcaddens Road, Glasgow G4
0BA
Telephone: 041-332 7090

Jordanhill College of Education

Southbrae Drive, Glasgow G13 1PP
Telephone: 041-959 1232

Queen's College

1 Park Drive, Glasgow G3 6LP
Telephone: 041-334 8141

Royal Scottish Academic of Music
and Drama

St George's Place, Glasgow G2 1BS
Telephone: 041-332 4101

St Andrew's College of Education

Bearsden, Glasgow G61 4QA
Telephone: 041-943 1424

School of Art

167 Renfrew Street, Glasgow G3
6RQ
Telephone: 041-332 9797

The University

Glasgow G12 8QQ
Telephone: 041-339 8855

University of Strathclyde

16 Richmond Street, Glasgow G1
1XQ
Telephone: 041-552 4400

Gloucester
Gloucestershire College of Arts and
Technology

Oxtalls Lane, Gloucester GL2 9HW
Telephone: 0452 426700

Guildford
University of Surrey

Guildford, Surrey GU2 5XH
Telephone: 0483 571281

Hatfield
The Polytechnic

PO Box 109, College Lane, Hatfield
AL10 9AB
Telephone: 07072 79000

High Wycombe
Buckinghamshire College of Higher
Education

Queen Alexandra Road, High
Wycombe HP11 21Z
Telephone: 0494 22141

Huddersfield
The Polytechnic

Queensgate, Huddersfield HD1
3DH
Telephone: 0484 22288

Hull
Humberside College of Higher
Education

Cottingham Road, Hull HU6 7RT
Telephone: 0482 41451

The University

Hull HU6 7RX
Telephone: 0482 41451

Keele
The University

Keele, Staffs ST5 5BG
Telephone: 0782 712000

Kidderminster
College of Further Education

Hoo Road, Kidderminster DY10
1LX
Telephone: 0562 66311

Lampeter
St David's University College

Lampeter, Dyfed SA48 7ED
Telephone: 0570 422351

Lancaster
S Martin's College

Bowerham, Lancaster LA1 3JD
Telephone: 0524 63446

The University

University House, Lancaster LA1
4YW
Telephone: 0524 65201

Leeds
The Polytechnic

Calverley Street, Leeds LS1 3HE
Telephone: 0532 462903

Trinity and All Saints' College

Brownberrie Lane, Leeds LS18
5HD
Telephone: 0532 584341

The University

Leeds LS2 9JT
Telephone: 0532 431751

Leicester

The Polytechnic

PO Box 143, Leicester LE1 9BH
Telephone: 0533 551551

The University

University Road, Leicester LE1 7RH
Telephone: 0533 522295

Lincoln

Bishop Grosseteste College

Lincoln LN1 3DY
Telephone: 0522 27347

Liverpool

Institute of Higher Education

PO Box 6, Stand Park Road, Liverpool L16 9JD
Telephone: 051-722 2361

The Polytechnic

Rodney House, 70 Mount Pleasant, Liverpool L3 5UX
Telephone: 051-207 3581

The University

PO Box 147, Liverpool L69 3BX
Telephone: 051-709 7919

London (area)
[1] part of the London Institute

Architectural Association School

34-6 Bedford Square, London WC1B 3ES
Telephone: 01-636 0974

Avery Hill College

See Thames Polytechnic

Brunel University

Uxbridge, Middx UB8 3PH
Telephone: 0895 74000

Camberwell School of Arts and Crafts[1]

Peckham Road, London SE5 8UF
Telephone: 01-703 0987

Polytechnic of Central London

209 Regent Street, London W1R 8AL
Telephone: 01-580 2020

Central School of Art and Design[1]

Southampton Row, London WC18 4AP
Telephone: 01-405 1825

Central School of Speech and Drama

Embassy Theatre, Eton Avenue, London NW3 3HY
Telephone: 01-722 8183

Chelsea School of Art[1]

Manresa Road, London SW3 6LS
Telephone: 01-351 3844

City of London Polytechnic

117 Houndsditch, London EC3A 7BU
Telephone: 01-283 1030

City University	Northampton Square, London EC1V 0HB *Telephone:* 01-253 4399
College for the Distributive Trades	30 Leicester Square, London WC2H 7LE *Telephone:* 01-839 1547
Ealing College of Higher Education	St Mary's Road, London W5 5RF *Telephone:* 01-578 4111
Guildhall School of Music and Drama	Barbican, London EC2Y 8DT *Telephone:* 01-628 2571
Harrow College of Higher Education	Watford Road, Northwick Park, Harrow HA1 3TP *Telephone:* 01-864 5422
Jews' College	Albert Road, Hendon, London NW4 *Telephone:* 01-203 6427
Kingston Polytechnic	Kingston Hill, Kingston upon Thames KT2 7LB *Telephone:* 01-549 1366
Laban Centre of Movement and Dance	Goldsmiths' College, New Cross, London SE14 6NW *Telephone:* 01-692 4070
London Bible College	Green Lane, Northwood, Middx HA6 2UW *Telephone:* 092 74 26061
London College of Fashion	20 John Prince's Street, London W1M 9HE *Telephone:* 01-629 9401
London College of Furniture	41-71 Commercial Road, London E1 1LA *Telephone:* 01-247 1953
London College of Printing[1]	Elephant and Castle, London SE1 6SB *Telephone:* 01-735 8484
Middlesex Polytechnic	Admissions Office, 114 Chase Side, London N14 5PN *Telephone:* 01-886 6599
North East London Polytechnic	Admissions, Longbridge Road, Dagenham RM8 2AS *Telephone:* 01-590 7722
Polytechnic of North London	Holloway Road, London N7 8DB *Telephone:* 01-607 2789

Oak Hill College	Chase Side, Southgate, London N14 4PS *Telephone:* 01-449 0467
Roehampton Institute of Higher Education	Roehampton Lane, London SW15 5PU *Telephone:* 01-878 5751
Royal Academy of Dancing	48 Vicarage Crescent, London SW11 3LT *Telephone:* 01-223 0091
Royal Academy of Dramatic Art (RADA)	62-4 Gower Street, London WC1E 6ED *Telephone:* 01-636 7076
Royal Academy of Music	Marylebone Road, London NW1 5HT *Telephone:* 01-935 5461
Royal College of Art (RCA)	Kensington Gore, London SW7 2EU *Telephone:* 01-584 5020
Royal College of Music	Prince Consort Road, London SW7 2BS *Telephone:* 01-589 3643
St Martin's School of Art[1]	107 Charing Cross Road, London WC2H 0DU *Telephone:* 01-437 0611
St Mary's College	Strawberry Hill, Twickenham, Middx TW1 4SX *Telephone:* 01-892 0051
South Bank Polytechnic	Borough Road, London SE1 0AA *Telephone:* 01-928 8989
Spurgeon's College	South Norwood Hill, London SE25 6DJ *Telephone:* 01-653 0850
Thames Polytechnic	Wellington Street, Woolwich, London SE18 6PF *Telephone:* 01-854 2030
Trinity College of Music	11-13 Mandeville Place, London W1M 6AQ *Telephone:* 01-935 5773
West London Institute of Higher Education	Gordon House, 300 St Margaret's Road, Twickenham, Middx TW1 1PT *Telephone:* 01-891 0121

Wimbledon School of Art	Merton Hall Road, London SW19 3QA *Telephone:* 01-540 0231
London University The University	Senate House, Malet House, London WC1E 7HU *Telephone:* 01-636 8000
Courtauld Institute of Art	20 Portman Square, London W1H 0BE *Telephone:* 01-935 9292
Goldsmiths' College	New Cross, London SE14 6NW *Telephone:* 01-692 7171
Heythrop College	11-13 Cavendish Square, London W1M 0AN *Telephone:* 01-580 6941
Imperial College of Science and Technology	London SW7 2AZ *Telephone:* 01-589 5111
Institute of Archaeology	See University College London
King's College (KQC)	Strand, London WC2R 2LS *Telephone:* 01-836 5454
London School of Economics and Political Science	Houghton Street, London WC2A 2AE *Telephone:* 01-405 7686
Queen Mary College	Mile End Road, London E1 4NS *Telephone:* 01-980 4811
Royal Holloway and Bedford New College	Egham Hill, Egham, Surrey TW20 0EX *Telephone:* 0784 34455
Royal Veterinary College	Royal College Street, London NW1 0TU *Telephone:* 01-387 2898
School of Oriental and African Studies	Malet Street, London WC1E 7HP *Telephone:* 01-637 2388
School of Pharmacy	29-39 Brunswick Square, London WC1N 1AX *Telephone:* 01-837 7651
School of Slavonic and E European Studies	Senate House, Malet Street, London WC1E 7HU *Telephone:* 01-637 4934

| University College London | Gower Street, London WC1E 6BT
Telephone: 01-387 7050 |

Westfield College (to merge with Queen Mary College) — Kidderpore Avenue, London NW3 7ST
Telephone: 01-435 7141

Wye College — Ashford, Kent TN25 5AH
Telephone: 0233 812401

London University Medical and Dental Schools

Charing Cross and Westminster Medical School — The Reynolds Building, St Dunstan's Road, London W6 8RP
Telephone: 01-748 2040

King's College School of Medicine and Dentistry — Denmark Hill, London SE5 8RX
Telephone: 01-274 6222

London Hospital Medical College — Turner Street, London E1 2AD
Telephone: 01-377 7000

Middlesex Hospital Medical School — See University College London

Royal Free Hospital School of Medicine — Rowland Hill Street, London NW3 2PF
Telephone: 01-794 0500

St Bartholomew's Hospital Medical School — West Smithfield, London EC1A 7BE
Telephone: 01-606 7404

St George's Hospital Medical School — Cranmer Terrace, London SW17 0RE
Telephone: 01-672 1255

St Mary's Hospital Medical School — Norfolk Place, London W2 1PG
Telephone: 01-723 1252

United Medical and Dental Schools of Guy's and St Thomas's Hospitals — St Thomas's Campus, Lambeth Palace Road, London SE1 7EH
Telephone: 01-928 9292

Loughborough

College of Art and Design — Radmoor, Loughborough LE11 3BT
Telephone: 0509 261515

University of Technology — Loughborough LE11 3TU
Telephone: 0509 263171

Luton

College of Higher Education — Park Square, Luton LU1 3JU
Telephone: 0582 34111

Maidstone
Kent Institute of Art and Design

Oakwood Park, Oakwood Road,
Maidstone ME16 8AG
Telephone: 0622 52786

Manchester
The Polytechnic

All Saints, Manchester M15 6BH
Telephone: 061-228 6171

Royal Northern College of Music

124 Oxford Road, Manchester M13
9RD
Telephone: 061-273 6283

The University

Manchester M13 9PL
Telephone: 061-273 3333

University of Manchester Institute
of Science and Technology
(UMIST)

PO Box 88, Sackville Street,
Manchester M60 1QD
Telephone: 061-236 3311

Middlesbrough
Teesside Polytechnic

Borough Road, Middlesbrough,
Cleveland TS1 3BA
Telephone: 0642 218121

Milton Keynes
Open University

PO Box 48, Milton Keynes MK7
6AL
Telephone: 0908 653983

Newcastle
The Polytechnic

Ellison Place, Newcastle upon Tyne
NE1 8ST
Telephone: 0632 326002

The University

6 Kensington Terrace, Newcastle
upon Tyne NE1 7RU
Telephone: 091-232 8511

Newport (Gwent)
Gwent College of Higher Education

College Crescent, Caerleon,
Newport NP6 1XJ
Telephone: 0633 421292

Newport (Shropshire)
Harper Adams Agricultural College

Edgmont, Newport TF10 8NB
Telephone: 0952 811280

Newton Abbot
Seale-Hayne College

Newton Abbot TQ12 6NQ
Telephone: 0626 2323

Northampton

Nene College

Moulton Park, Northampton NN2 7AL
Telephone: 0604 715000

Norwich

College of Further and Higher Education

Ipswich Road, Norwich NR2 2LJ
Telephone: 0603 660011

School of Art

St George Street, Norwich NR3 1BB
Telephone: 0603 610561

University of East Anglia

University Plain, Norwich, Norfolk NR4 7TJ
Telephone: 0603 56161

Nottingham

Trent Polytechnic

Burton Street, Nottingham NG1 4BU
Telephone: 0602 418248

The University

University Park, Nottingham NG7 2RD
Telephone: 0602 506101

Ormskirk

Edge Hill College of Higher Education

St Helens Road, Ormskirk L39 4QP
Telephone: 0695 75151

Oxford

The Polytechnic

Headington, Oxford OX3 0BP
Telephone: 0865 819000

The University

Colleges Admissions Office, University Offices, Wellington Square, Oxford OX1 2JD
Telephone: 0865 270207

Westminster College

Harcourt Hill, North Hinksey, Oxford OX2 9AT
Telephone: 0865 247644

Paisley

College of Technology

High Street, Paisley PA1 2BE
Telephone: 041-887 1241

Plymouth

College of St Mark and St John

Derriford Road, Plymouth PL6 8BH
Telephone: 0752 777188

The Polytechnic

Drake Circus, Plymouth PL4 8AA
Telephone: 0752 221312

Royal Naval Engineering College

Manadon, Plymouth PL5 3AG
Telephone: 0752 553740

Pontypridd

Polytechnic of Wales

Pontypridd, Mid-Glam CF37 1DL
Telephone: 0443 480480

Portsmouth

Highbury College of Technology

Cosham, Portsmouth PO6 2SA
Telephone: 0705 383131

The Polytechnic

Museum Road, Portsmouth PO1 2QQ
Telephone: 0705 827681

Preston

Lancashire Polytechnic

Corporation Street, Preston PR1 2TQ
Telephone: 0772 22141

Reading

Bulmershe College of Higher Education

Woodlands Avenue, Reading RG6 1HY
Telephone: 0734 663387

The University

Whiteknights, Reading RG6 2AH
Telephone: 0734 875123

Redruth

Cornwall College of Further and Higher Education

Redruth TR15 3RD
Telephone: 0209 712911

St Andrews

The University

College Gate, St Andrews KY16 9AJ
Telephone: 0334 76161

Salford

The University

Salford M5 4WT
Telephone: 061-736 5843

Scarborough

North Riding College

Filey Road, Scarborough YO11 3AZ
Telephone: 0723 362392

Sheffield

City Polytechnic

Pond Street, Sheffield S1 1WB
Telephone: 0742 720911

The University

Western Bank, Sheffield S10 2TN
Telephone: 0742 768555

Shrivenham

Royal Military College of Science
(RMCS)

Shrivenham, Swindon SM6 8LA
Telephone: 0793 782551

Sidcup

Rose Bruford College of Speech
and Drama

Lamorbey Park, Sidcup DA15 9DF
Telephone: 01-300 3024

Silsoe

Silsoe College (Cranfield Institute
of Technology)

Silsoe, Bedford MK45 4DT
Telephone: 0525 60428

Southampton

Institute of Higher Education

East Park Terrace. Southampton
SO9 4WW
Telephone: 0703 229381

La Sainte Union College of Higher
Education

The Avenue, Southampton SO9
5HB
Telephone: 0703 228761

The University

Highfield, Southampton SO9 5NH
Telephone: 0703 559122

Stirling

The University

Stirling FK9 4LA
Telephone: 0786 73171

Stoke-on-Trent

North Staffordshire Polytechnic

College Road, Stoke-on-Trent ST4
2DE
Telephone: 0782 745531

Stourbridge

College of Technology and Art

Hagley Road, Oldwinsford,
Stourbridge DY8 1QU
Telephone: 03843 78531

Sunderland

The Polytechnic

Langham Tower, Ryhope Road,
Sunderland SR2 7EE
Telephone: 091 567 6231

Swansea
University College — Singleton Park, Swansea SA2 8PP
Telephone: 0792 205678

West Glamorgan Institute of Higher Education — Townhill Road, Swansea SA2 0UT
Telephone: 0792 203482

Totnes
Dartington College of Arts — Totnes, Devon TQ9 6EWJ
Telephone: 0803 862224

Wakefield
Bretton Hall College of Higher Education — Wakefield WF4 4LG
Telephone: 092485 261

Walsall
West Midlands College of Higher Education — Gorway, Walsall WS1 38D
Telephone: 0922 720141

Warrington
North Cheshire College — Padgate Campus, Warrington WA2 0DB
Telephone: 0925 814343

Watford
Hertfordshire College of Higher Education — See Hatfield Polytechnic

Watford College — Hempstead Road, Watford WD1 3EZ
Telephone: 0923 57500

Winchester
King Alfred's College — Sparkford Road, Winchester SO22 4NR
Telephone: 0962 62281

School of Art — Park Avenue, Winchester SO23 8DL
Telephone: 0962 61891

Wolverhampton
The Polytechnic — Molineux Street, Wolverhampton WV1 1SB
Telephone: 0902 313000

Worcester
Worcester College of Higher Education — Henwick Grove, Worcester WR2 6AJ
Telephone: 0905 428080

Wrexham

North East Wales Institute of
Higher Education

Connah's Quay, Clwyd CH5 4BR
Telephone: 0244 817531

York

College of Ripon and York St John

Lord Mayor's Walk, York YO3
7EX
Telephone: 0904 56771

The University

Heslington, York YO1 5DD
Telephone: 0904 430000

Index to Advertisers

Association of Accounting Technicians	434
Association of Cost and Executive Accountants	435
Career Analysts	xvi
Clothing and Allied Products Industry Training Board	890
Construction Industry Training Board	685
ECCTIS	xx
Engineering Careers Information Service	96
Incorporated Association of Architects and Surveyors	700
Independent Assessment & Research Centre	ix
Institute of Chartered Secretaries and Administrators	407
London Chamber of Commerce and Industry	414
Lucie Clayton Model School	615
Lucie Clayton Secretarial College	420
Napier College	46
Royal Academy of Dramatic Art	608
St Aldates College	*inside back cover*
St Helens College	27
S Martin's College	918
Shaw College	1096
Southampton Institute of Higher Education	39
Vocational Guidance	xii
West London College	*facing front cover*

Index

Abnormal psychology, 325
Academic qualifications,
  vocational qualifications/studies &,
  1-62
  where they lead &, 63-333
Account executive, advertising, 494
Accountancy/accounting, 432-48
  management, 439-40
  professional, working in, 434-40
  technician, working as, 447-8
Accountant, legal, qualification, 319
Acting, 606-10
Actuarial work, 468-70
Acupuncture, 1000
Adjusting (insurance), 470-1
Administration,
(see also specific forms of
  administration, eg Arts)
  commerce, finance and, 397-526
  management and, 400-28
Administrative
  management, 412-5
  work, company secretarial work and,
  406-9
Advertising, 491-7
  account executives/planners, 494
  agencies/departments, 492-5
  creative staff, 494-5
  design, 538-9
  media departments, 495
  photography, 554
  working in, 492
Aerial photography, 556
Aeronautical engineering, 135-40
Aerospace industry, 904-9
Agency see individual forms, eg Estate,
  Literary
Agricultural
  advisory services/work, 660
  contractors, 661
  economics, 225
  engineering, 140-3
  machinery, working with, 659
  research, 660
  sciences, horticultural/forest sciences
    and, 220-5
  secretarial work, 660
  surveying, 714
Agriculture, 655-65
  industry, 655-8

Ministry of, 765
  working in, 658-61
Air
  Force, Royal, 748-53
  stewarding/cabin crew, 1124-5
  traffic control, 1128-30
  transport industry, 1120-31
Aircraft
  cabin crew, 1124-5
  engineering (maintenance etc), 1125-6
  manufacturing, 904-9
Airline(s), 1121-2
  airport operations, 1127
  commercial management, 1127-8
  flight operations, 1127
  working in, 1122-8
Airports, 1130-1
Alternatives to employment, 351-5
Ambulance work, 1016-7
Amenity horticulture, 672-3
Animal
  husbandry, 659
  nursing, 648
  research, 648
  sciences courses, 243
  technician, 649
  welfare, 649
Animals, work with, 648-53
Anthropology, 298-9
Antiquarian bookselling, 511?
Antique dealing, 509-10
Arable farming, 55?
Arboriculture, 669
Archaeological surveying, 717
Archaeology, 65-71
Architectural
  photography, 556
  technician, 701
Architecture,
  landscape, 705-7
  naval, see Naval architecture
  profession, 698-702
  qualifications etc, 207-8
Archive work, 596-8
Area studies, 82
Armed Forces, 735-63
  teaching in, 938-9
Army, 739-48

Women's Royal Corps, 747
Art,
    dealing, 509-10
    design (etc) and, 529-59
        qualifications and careers, 85-7
    director, advertising, 494
    fine, 552-3
    galleries/museums, work in, 558
    journalism, 557
    qualifications and careers, 84-93
    sales, 558
    teaching, 558
    therapy, 559
Arts
    administration, 642-5
    creative/performing, qualifications and
        careers, 84-93
    qualifications and careers, 63-83
    Royal Society of, 34
Astronomy, 225-7
Athletics, professional, 627
Auctioneering, 712-3
Audio typing, see Secretarial work
Audiological scientists, 1004
Audiology technician, 1010
Automobile
    engineering, 143-5
    manufacturing, 909-12
Average adjusting, 470-1
Aviation, civil, 1120-31

Ballet dancing, 611-3
Banking, 448-61
    system, 450-3
    working in, 454-8
Baptist Union, 1041-2
Bar (the), 1021-3
    professional/vocational training, 317-8
Barrister, 1021-3
    professional/vocational training, 317-8
Barristers' clerk, 1028
Beauty care/culture/therapy, 1095-7
Billiards/snooker, professional, 627-8
Biochemistry, 229-30
    courses, 241-2
Biochemists, clinical, 1004-5
Biological sciences,
    biology and, 227-45
    studying, 240-5
Biologists,
    medical, 1005
    opportunities for, 236-40
Biology,
    biological sciences and, 227-45

branches of, 228-36
    marine, 234
        courses, 242
    molecular, 230
        courses, 141
    plant, 232-3
        courses, 242
Biomedical engineering, 145-7
Biophysics, 230
    courses, 242
Biotechnology,
    as applied biological science, 231
    courses, 242
    employment in, 835
    industry, 833-5
Blacksmiths, 661
Book
    design, 586
    production, 586-7
    publishing, 584-8
    sales (publishing), 587
Bookselling, 509-11
Botany, 323-3
Boxing, professional, 628-9
Brewing industry, 662-7
Brick
    laying, see Building crafts/trades
    making industry, 836-7
Broadcasting, 563-74
    administration, 570
    designers, 569
    employers, 564-5
    engineering, 569
    film crews, 568
    monitoring service, 570
    production/producer's assistants, 567
    programme
        contributors, 567
        making, 565-7
        producers/editors, 566
    recruitment/entry, 570-3
    researchers, 566-7
    studio/floor managers, 567-8
    technical operations, 568
    working in, 565-70
Broking,
    insurance, 475-6
    ship, 1153
Builders' merchants, 686-7
Building
    crafts and trades, 693-4
    industry, see Construction
    materials industry, 836-7
    public sector, 686

services engineering, 147-52
societies, 461-3
surveying, 713-4
technicians, 693
technology, 152-5
Bus, see Road transport
Business
    education/studies/qualifications in,
        300-8
    (and) Technician Education Council
        (BTEC), 30-3
Butchers, 511-2
Buying, purchasing, supply, 504-7

Cabinet Office, 765-6
Camera work,
    film, 575
    television, see Broadcasting
Car
    maintenance, 1145-6
    making/manufacture, 904-12
    selling, 512
Cardiology technicians, 1010
Careers advisory/information work,
    942-5
Carpenters, see Building crafts/trades
Cartographer, 702-3
Cartographic draughtsmanship, 702-3
Cartography, 702-3
Catering,
    hotels and, see Hotel
    restaurant and, management, 1087
Catholic Church, 1042-3
Cement making, 856-7
Ceramic design, 544-7
Ceramics industry, 837-9
Charity Commission, 766
Chef, 1088-9
Chemical
    engineering, 155-62
    industry, 841-5
Chemistry, 245-52
    studying and qualifying in, 249-52
Chemists,
    professional, opportunities for, 246-9
    retail, 512-3
    technician, opportunities for, 249
Children's nurses, 1100-1
Chiropodists, 970-2
Christian
    Churches, 1039-47
    missionary work, 1047
Churches, Christian, 1039-47

City and Guilds of London Institute
    (CGLI), 26-30
Civil
    aviation, 1120-31
    engineering, structural engineering
        and, 162-70
    Service, 763-800
        administration, 779-84
        recruitment/entry (general), 778-9
        specialist/other grades, 784-800
        structure: general, 777-8
        working in, 779
Claims work (insurance), 472-3
Classics, 71-2
Cleaning, dry, 1099-1100
Clearing banks, 450-1
    working in, 455-6
Clerical work, 419-28
Clerk of Works, 691-2
Clinical (see also Medical)
    biochemistry, 1004-5
    psychology, 328
Clothing,
    industry, 890-4
    retail selling, 513
Coaching, sports, 645-7
Coal mining, 721-31
Coastguards, 1151-2
Commerce, administration, finance, 397-
    526
Commercial horticulture, 671-2
Commodity
    markets, 478-86
    research, 484
    traders, 482
Communication
    design, 537-41
    media studies and, 89-91
    visual, 537-41
Communications
    HQ, Government, 772
    network management, 379
    systems/services, 1070-81
Community
    medicine, 964-5
    work (social), 1002-3
Company secretarial/administrative
    work, 406-9
Composing,
    music, 617-8
    print, see Printing industry
Computer
    engineering/technology, 170-5
    maintenance/servicing, 381

operations management, 379
  science, 252-7
  studying, 254-7
scientists, opportunities for, 253-6
selling, 381-2
systems development/design, 372
unit management/operations, 379
Computing/IT, 357-87
  employers, 364-70
  professional/technical functions, 371-8
  qualifications/training, 384-7
  recruitment/entry, 382-4
  related work, 381-2
  systems design/development, 372
  training/qualifications, 384-7
  working in, 370-82
Conducting, orchestral, 618
Confectioners, newsagents, etc, 513-4
Conservation,
  (environmental), 675-82
    working in, 675-81
  environment and, 675-83
  museum, 602-4
Construction
  companies (employers), 684-6
  crafts/trades, 693-4
  industry, 683-97
  professional/managerial staff, 691-2
  technician grades, 693
  working in/for, 690-4
Consumer protection, 806
Control engineering, measurement,
  instrumentation and, 173-6
Conveyancing, 1028-9
Cooking, professional, 1088-9
Co-operatives, 352-3
Copywriting, advertising, 494
Corporate treasury management, 428-9
Council for
  National Academic Awards (CNAA),
    49-51
  Vocational Qualifications, National
    (NCVQ), 25-7
Courts (law),
  legally-qualified staff, 1025-6
  other work, 1029
Craft
  based design, 544
  courses & qualifications, see City and
    Guilds
Creative
  arts, qualifications and careers, 84-93
  cultural, and entertainment work, 527-
    653

departments, advertising, 494-5
Credit accumulation and transfer scheme
  (CATS), 49
Cricket, professional, 629
Crown Estate Office, 766
Curators (museum), 599-602
Curriculum, national, proposals for, 8
Customs and Excise, 766-7
Cycling, professional, 629

Dairy
  farming, see Farming
  industry, see Food manufacturing
Dance qualifications, 87
Dancing, 611-3
Darts, professional, 629-30
Data processing, see Computing/IT
Database management, 380
Decorator, construction,
Defence,
  industry, 845-6
  Ministry of, 767
Degrees
  (as HE qualifications), 47-51
  occupations requiring, 57-8
  subject choice and careers, 56-8
  vocational preparation and, 51-6
Dental
  auxiliary work, 972
  hygiene, 972
  surgery assistant, 972-3
  technician's work, 973-4
  therapy, 974-5
Dentistry,
  academic qualifications in, 278-9
  profession, 965-7
Design (see also Art, design and),
  536-59
  advertising, 538-9
  book, 539
  craft based, 544-7
  engineering,
    art based, 547-8
    engineering based, 108-12
  exhibition, 551-2
  fashion/textile, 541-4
  graphic, 537-41
  industrial, 547-8
  interior, 548-50
  magazine, 539
  museum, 604
  packaging, 539
  product, 547-8
  retail, 551-2

textile/fashion, 541-4
theatrical/set, 550-1
three-dimensional, 544-52
TV, 569
Developmental psychology, 324
Dietetics, 258-61
Diplomatic Service, 787-8
Direct marketing, 507
Directing,
  film, 575
  television, 568
  theatre, 578
Dispensing optician, 987-9
Distribution, 507-21
DIY/hardware stores, 514
Doctor,
  community, 964
  general practitioner, 962-3
  hospital, 959-62
  working as a, 958-65
Dogs, working with, 649-50
Drama, qualifications etc, 87-9
  (see also Acting)
Draughtsmanship, 113-5
Dress
  design, see Fashion
  making, 892
Drink industry, see Food manufacturing
Driving, 1143-4
  examining/instruction, 1144-5
Dry cleaning, laundries and, 1099-1100

Earth sciences, see Geology
Ecology, 235
  courses, 242
Economics, 308-12
  home, 313-5
Editing,
  book, 586
  newspaper, 592
  radio/TV, 566
  sub-, 592
Education(al),
  administration, 940-2
  advisory work, 947
  broadcasting, 945-6
  careers in, 915-50
  colleges of (higher), 44-5
  curriculum development, 946
  further, see Further education
  health/welfare services, 946-7
  physical/sports, 645-7
  psychology, 327-8
  publishing, 945-6

research, 946
Science and, Department of, 767-8
studies in, 312-3
Electrical engineering,
  electronic engineering and, 177-87
  manufacturing industry, 846-8
Electricity supply, 854-8
Electronic
  engineering, electrical engineering
    and, 177-87
  manufacturing industry, 849-53
Emigrating, see Overseas, working
Employment,
  alternatives to, 352-5
  Department of, 768
  future of, 334-47
  impact of technological development
    on, 339-44
  self, 353-5
Energy,
  Department of, 769
  engineering/technology 188-90
  production, 853-62
Engine driving, see Railways
Engineering (and other technologies) see
  also individual branches, eg
  Agricultural engineering
  as a career, 97-108
  branches of, 134-205
  courses and qualifications, 117-34
  craft
    courses, education, training, 133-4
    worker, 100-1
  definitions, 97-101
  design,
    art based, 547-8
    engineering based, 108-12
  draughtsmanship, 113-5
  functions, 108-17
  future of, 102-8
  in broadcasting, 569
  in Civil Service, 788-91
  in local government, 805
  production planning/management,
    115-7
  professional/graduate, 97-8
    courses and qualifications, 120-8
  qualifications and careers in, 94-205
  research and development, 112-3
  technician (engineering-technician/
    technician-engineer),
    courses and qualifications, 128-33
    work, 98-100
Engineers, where they work, 101-2

England, Church of, 1043-4
English, 72-3
Entertainment, light, 613-4
Environment,
    conservation and, 675-83
    Department of, 769
    related work, 654-733
Environmental
    control, 681-2
    health work, 805-6
Ergonomics, 257-8
Estate agency/management, 712
Examining bodies, vocational, 27-35
Exhibition design, 551-2
Experimental psychology, 324
Export
    Credits Guarantee department, 770
    selling, 521-5
Extractive industries, see Mining

Fabric
    design, see Textile/fashion
    manufacture, see Textile industry
Factory inspectors, 791
Fair Trading, Office of, 770
Farm
    machinery, see Agricultural
        engineering
    management etc, 658-9
    secretaries, 660
    stock men/women, 659
    workers, skilled, 659
Farming, 655-64
    fish, 666-7
Farrier, 661
Fashion
    design, textile design and, 541-4
    modelling, 614-6
    photography, 554
Film
    crews, 575
        television, 568
    directing, 575
    editing, 575-6
    industry, working in, 574-6
    making, 574-7
    producers, 574-5
Finance, 428-86
    working in, 430-1
Financial management, 432-47
Fine art, 552-3
Fire services, 1102-5
Fish farming, 666-7
Fishing, 664-5

Flight
    controller (military), 749
    engineer
        (civil), 1124
        (military), 749
Florists, 514-5
Flying,
    commercial/civil, 1122-5
    military, 748-9
Food
    manufacturing, 862-7
    preparation, 1088-9
    retailing, 515
    science/technology, 258-61
    service, 1089
Football, professional, 630-1
Footwear
    manufacture, 894-6
    retail selling, 513
Forces, Armed, 735-63
Foreign/Commonwealth Office, 771-2
Forensic
    photography, 555-6
    science, see Police
Forest sciences, agricultural and
    horticultural sciences and, 220-5
Forestry, 667-70
Foundry industry, 875-6
Franchising, 353
Freightforwarding, 1156-7
Fuel engineering/technology, 188-90
Furnishing, retail, 516
Furniture
    design, 544-7
    manufacture, 902-4
    retailing, 516
Further education,
    educational/vocational provision, 35-9
    working/teaching in, 932-4

Gamekeepers/wardens, 647
Gas
    engineering/technology, 188-9
    exploration/recovery, 721-31
    supply industry, 858-61
Geneticist, 1005
Genetics, 235-6
    courses, 242
Geochemistry, 261-6
Geography, 208-11
Geology, 261-6
Geophysics, 261-6
Glass,
    blowing, 840-1

design, 544-7
manufacture, 839-41
science/technology, 266-71
Golf, professional, 631-2
Government,
    central (see also Civil Service), 763-800
    Communications HQ, 772
    departments, 764-77
    local, 800-12
Graphic design, 537-41
Groundsmanship/maintenance, 647-8

Hairdressing, 1097-9
Health,
    care/alternative, 999-1001
        other, 999-1002
        private sector, 955-6
        working in, 953-4
    Safety and, Commission/Executive, 769
    Service
        administration/management, 1012-6
        National, 954-5
    services, 950-1019
        occupational, 956-7
        organisation of, 954-7
        scientists/technicians in, 1002-11
        support/auxiliary services, 1016-9
    Social Security and, Department of, 772
    visitors, 975-6
Heating and ventilating engineering, see Building services
Higher education, 39-62
    awards and awarding bodies, 46-51
    colleges/institutes of, 44-45
    institutions, 42-6
        Scottish, 45-6
    qualifications other than degrees, 51
    working/teaching in, 934-8
Highway engineering see Civil engineering
History, 73-6
Home
    economics, 313
    Office, 772-3
Homoeopathic medicine, 1000
Horse(s)
    racing, 633-4
    riding/working with, 650-2
Horticultural sciences, agricultural and forest sciences and, 220-5
Horticulture, 670-5

amenity, 672-3
commercial, 671-2
Hotel and catering, 1081-95
    administration/management, 1085-8
    craft/supervisory work, 1088-91
    front office/reception, 1090
    industry, 1081-4
    qualifications/training, 1092-4
    recruitment/entry, 1091-2
    uniformed staff, 1090
    working in, 1084-91
Housekeeping, 1090
Housing management, 703-5
Human movement studies, 87
Hunting, horse, 650-2
Hydrographic surveying, 715

Ice skating, professional, 634
Illustrating, 537-41
Industrial
    design, 547-8
    photography, 555
Industry,
    (manufacturing), see Manufacturing
    Trade and, Department of, see Trade
Information,
    Central Office of, 766
    engineering/technology, 170-5
    scientist, working as, 392-4
    society, the, 356-96
    systems design/development, 372
    technology, computing and, 357-88
        employers, 364-70
        managing in, 378-81
        professional/technical functions, 371-8
        qualifications/training, 384-7
        recruitment/entry, 382-4
        related work, 381-2
        working in, 370-82
    work, library work and, 388-96
Inland
    Revenue, 773, 791-2
    waterways, 1155
Institutional management, 1082-95
Instrumental (musical) playing, see Music
Instrumentation, control and measurement engineering and, 173-6
Insurance, 463-78
    adjusting, 478-9
    agency
        inspecting, 471-2
        work, 472

branch management, 472
broking, 473-4
business, 464-5
claims work, 472-3
management, 476
qualifications/training (general), 467-8
recruitment/entry (general), 466-7
specialists, 468-77
surveying, 476-7
underwriting, 477-8
working in, 465-6
Interior design/decoration, 548-50
International
   banking, 454
      working in, 457-8
   organisations, work in1168-73
Interpreting, 1062-4
Investment
   analysts, 483
   banking, 453-4
      working in, 457
   fund managers, 483
   management, 478-86

Jewellery,
   making/design, 544-7
   retail, 516-7
Jewry, 1047-8
Jockey, professional, 833-4
Journalism, 590-5
Judiciary, 1025

Kennel work, 649-50
Keyboard (musical) playing, see Music
Knitting industry, see Textile industry
Knowledge engineering, 374

Labour market, size and shape of, 335-9
Lace making, see Textile industry
Land
   agency, 714
   Registry, 773-4
   related work, 654-733
   surveying, 714-5
   use
      professions, 694-721
      studies, qualifications and careers,
         205-13
Landscape architecture, 705-7
Language Service, Joint Technical, 772
Languages,
   qualifications in, 76-81
   teaching, 1066
   working with, 1061-8
Laundries, dry cleaners and, 1099-1100

Law, 315-20
   academic, 1025
   professional/vocational training, 317-9
   studying, 315-9
Lawyers,
   other careers for qualified, 1025-7
   professional, 1020-5
Leather/leather goods industry, 896-7
Legal
   accountant, qualifications, 319
   executive, 1029-30
      qualifications, 319
   profession, 1020-5
   services, community, 1025
   studies, 315-9
   system, 1019-30
Legally-related work, 1028-30
Leisure/recreation industries, see
   Recreational
Librarian, working as, 392-4
Libraries, information centres and,
   389-92
Library work, information work and,
   388-96
Licensed trade, see Hotel/catering
Light entertainment, 613-4
Lighthouse service, 1151
Literary
   agency, 579-80
   translating, 1064-5
Livestock farming, 659
Lloyd's (insurance), 474-5
Local government/authorities, 800-12
Lord Chancellor's Department, 774
Loss adjusting, 470-1

Machine tool industry, 867-70
Machinery, manufacture, 867-70
Magazine design, see Graphic design
Mail order (selling), 507
Make-up, television, 569
Management (see also individual
   subjects),
   accounting, see Accountancy
   administration and, 400-6
   consultancy, 409-12
   qualifications/training, 404-6
   services, 1030-9
   studies, 300-8
Manpower Services Commission, 768
Manufacturing (industry), 813-912
   changing shape of, 815-7
   employment in, 824-32
   how it works, 819-24

problem, 817-9
sectors, 832-912
working in, 825-9
Map work, 702-3
Marine
  biology, 234
    courses, 242
  engineering, naval architecture etc,
    199-204
Marines, Royal, 753-5
Market research, 497-500
Marketing
  direct, 507
  (general), 487-91
Materials science/technology, 266-71
Mathematics, statistics and, 272-6
Measurement, control engineering,
  instrumentation and, 173-6
Mechanic, vehicle, 1145-6
Mechanical engineering,
  branch of engineering profession,
    190-6
  industry, 867-70
Media
  agents, 579-80
  careers, 560-95
  communication studies and, 89-91
  working for the, 562-3
Medical,
  biology, 1005
  electronics/engineering, see
    Biomedical
  laboratory work, 1007-9
  photography, 555
  physicists, 1005-6
  technicians, 1009-11
  profession, 957-65
  records work, 1014-5
  research, 276, 964-5
  sciences, 276-9
  services, 950-1019
  social work, 1053-4
  teaching, 965
Medicine,
  academic qualifications in, 278-9
  alternative/complementary, 999-1001
  community, 964-5
  professions supporting/supplementary
    to, 967-98
Merchandising, retail, 518
Merchant
  banking, 453-4
    working in, 457
  Navy, 1146-51

Metal manufacture, 870-6
Metallurgy, 266-71
Meteorology, 278-9
Methodist Church, 1045-6
Microbiology, 234-5
  courses, 242
Microelectronics, see Electronic
Mineral
  engineering, mining engineering and,
    196-7
  surveying, 715
Mining
  engineering, mineral engineering and,
    196-9
  industry, 721-31
  surveying, 715
Ministry, Church, 1039-48
Missionary work, 1048
Model making, 559
Modelling, fashion/photographic, 614-6
Molecular biology, 230
Money markets, 478-86
Motor
  cycling, professional, 634
  industry, 9909-12
  racing, 634
  servicing, 1145-6
Municipal engineering, see Civil
  engineering
Museum
  conservation, 602-4
  design, 604
  keeping, 599-602
  work, 598-604
Music,
  academic qualifications, 91-3
  administration, 621
  broadcasting, 621
  careers in, 616-24
  instrumental playing, 618-20
  journalism, 621
  library work, 621
  pop/rock, 620
  publishing, 622
  record business, 622
  retail trade, 517
  teaching, 622
  therapy, 622
Musician, working as 617-23

National Council for Vocational
  Qualifications, 25-7
Natural gas, extraction/prospecting, see
  Mining etc

Naturopathy, 1000
Nautical careers,
    civil, 1146-51
    military, 755-63
Naval architecture, marine engineering
    etc, 199-203
Navy,
    Merchant, 1146-51
    Royal, 755-63
    Women's Service, 761-2
Neurophysiology technican, 1011
New Training Initiative, 3
News agencies, 582
Newsagents, 423-4
Newspaper publishing, 580-2
Nuclear engineering, see Energy
Nurse,
    children's, 1100-1
    working as a, 977-80
Nursery nurse, 1100-1
Nursing, 976-85
    Air Force (PMRANS), 753
    animal, 648
    Army (QARANC), 747-8
    dental, 972-3
    Naval (QARNNS), 762-3
    nursery, 1100-1
    psychiatric, 979
Nutrition, 258-61

Occupational
    health services, 956-7
    psychology, 328-9
    therapists, 985-7
Oceanography, 281-2
Office
    administration/management, 412-5
    machinery, retail trade in,
    work, 419-28
Oil
    extraction/processing, 721-31
    refining, 861-2
Opera, see Singing
Operational research, 1031-3
Ophthalmic
    optician, 987-9
    optics, 282-3
Optician,
    dispensing/ophthalmic, 987-9
    retail, 517
Optometrist, see Ophthalmic
Orchestral playing, see Music
Ordnance Survey, 774-5
Organ playing, see Music

Organisation and methods, work study
    and, 1037-9
Orthoptics, 989-90
Orthotists, 990-2
Osteopathy, 1000
Overseas, working, 1160-74

Packaging
    design, 877
    industry, 876-7
Painting (fine art), 552-3
Paper making/merchandising, 877-80
Parasitology, 235
Parliament, Members of, 810-1
Patent
    agents, 1034-6
    examiners, 1036-7
    officer, 1037
    work, 1033-7
Pensions management, 476
Performing
    arts, qualifications and careers, 84-93
    careers, 604-35
Periodical publishing, 582-4
Personal service, 1095-1105
Personnel management, 415-9
Pharmaceutical
    industry, 841-5
    science/technology, 283-7
Pharmacists,
    community. 512-3
    health service, 1006
    opportunities for, 284-5
Pharmacologists, opportunities for,
    284-5
Pharmacology, 283-7
Pharmacy, 283-7
    technician, 1010
Philosophy, 81-2
Photographic technician, 556
Photography, 554-8
Photo-journalism, 554-5
Physicists, medical, 1005-6
Physics, 287-92
Physiological
    measurement technican, 1010-1
    psychology, 324
Physiology, 236
    courses, 243
Physiotherapists, 992-4
Piano playing, see Music
Pilot,
    air – civil, 1122-4
    air – military, 748-9

sea, 1151
Planning,
   surveying, 717
   (town/country), 707-10
Plant biology/sciences, 234-5
   courses, 242
Plastics processing industry, 880-2
Police, 1105-13
Political
   careers, 810-2
   party work, 811-2
   science/politics, 320-3
Polymer science/technology, see
   Materials
Polytechnics, 43-4
Population Censuses/Surveys, Office of,
   775
Portering, hotel, 1090
Ports, working in, 1153-5
Postal services, 1072-5
Postgraduate qualifications, 60-2
Pottery
   design, 544-7
   manufacturing, see Ceramics industry
Poultry farming/husbandry, 659
Power supply, electrical, see Electricity
Press (see also Newspapers)
   photography, 554-8
Pre-vocational
   Education, Certificate of (CPVE),
      19-20
   preparation, choosing and, 347-52
   qualifications, school qualifications &,
      6-23
Primary school teaching, 520-2
Printing industry, 882-7
Prison service, 1113-5
Probation service/work, 1054-5
Product design, 547-8
Production
   broadcasting, see Broadcasting
   engineering, 203-5
   industrial, 821-3
   planning/management, as engineering
      function, 115-7
   theatrical, 577-9
Professional
   qualifications, 34-5
   services (see also individual
      professions), 913-1068
Programme production, broadcasting,
   see Broadcasting
Programming, computer/IT, 374-8
Prosecutions, Department of Public, 775

Prospecting, mineral, 721-31
Prosthetists, 990-2
Psychiatric social work, 1054
Psychoanalysis/therapy, 1001-2
Psychology,
   abnormal, 325
   animal, 325
   as a career, 326-30
   as a discipline, 323-6
   clinical, 328
   comparative, 325
   developmental, 324
   educational, 327-8
   experimental, 324
   occupational, 328-9
   physiological, 324
   research, 327
   social, 324
   studying, 325-6
Psychotherapy/analysis, 1001-2
Public
   administration, studies in, 320-3
   health engineering, see Civil
      engineering
   health services, 805-6
   house management, 1088
   Prosecutions, Department of, 775
   Records Office, 775
   relations, 500-3
Publishing,
   book, 584-8
   newspaper, 581-2
   periodical, 582-4
Purchasing, buying, supply, 504-7

Qualifications,
   academic/vocational, 1-62
   National Council for Vocational
      (NCVQ), 25-7
   vocational, examining bodies, 27-35
Quantity surveying, 715-6
Quarrying, 721-31

Racing, horse, 633-4
Radio/electronic work, naval, 1148
Radio/television broadcasting, see
   Broadcasting
Radiographers, 994-7
Railways, 1131-8
Reception work,
   commercial, 419-29
   hotel, 1090
Records Office, Public, 775
Recreational/leisure industries, 635-53
   administering/managing, 637-42

Refrigeration engineering, see Building services
Regional studies, 82
Religious
  organisations/services, 1039-48
  studies, 82-3
Reporting, see Journalism
Research, development and,
  engineering, 112-3
  industrial, 823-4
  scientific, 213-4
Restaurant management/work, 1087
Retail
  banking, 450-2
    working in, 455-6
  display/design, 551-2
  managers, 518
Retailing,
  distribution and, 507-21
  sectors, 509-17
  working in, 517-9
Riding, horse, 650-2
Risk management (insurance), 476
Road
  haulage, 1139-40
  passenger services, 1138-9
  transport, 1138-46
    management, professional work,
      1141-3
    repair, 1140-1
    working in, 1141-46
Rugby, professional, 634

Saddlery, see Leather goods industry
Sales promotion, display and, 518-9
Salvation Army, 1046
Savings,
  Bank, Trustee, see Retail banking
  National Department, 774
Scenic design, see Theatrical design
School
  health services, 946-7
  inspectors, 947
  library work, 947-8
  qualifications, pre-vocational
    qualifications &, 6-23
  teaching, 917-32
Science,
  as a career, 212-7
  technicians in, 216-7
Sciences,
  qualifications and careers in, 211-94
  social, see Social sciences
  studying, 217-20

Scientific
  Civil Service, 796-9
  laboratory work, 216-7
  photography, 555-6
  writing/journalism, 595
Scientists,
  professional, 213-6
    in health services, 1002-11
Scotland, Church of, 1045
Scottish
  higher education institutions, 44-5
  Office, 776
  Vocational Education Council
    (SCOTVEC), 33-4
Sculpture, 552-3
Sea,
  working at, 1137-41
  working on shore, 1152-5
Seamen,
  merchant, 1141
  Royal Navy, 755-63
Secondary school teaching, 922-4
Secretarial work, 419-28
  as a route to other careers, 425-6
Secretary, company, 406-9
Security operations, private, 1115-6
Self-employment, 353-5
Selling, 521-5
Service
  industries, 1069-160
  technical, 525
Set design, see Theatrical design
Sheep husbandry/production, 659
Ship
  broking, 1153
  building,
    industry, 887-9
    naval architecture, marine
      engineering and, 199-204
Shipping companies, 1152-4
Shoe manufacturing/retailing, see
  Footwear
Shop work, see Retailing
Shorthand-typing, see Secretarial work
Sign design, see Graphic design
Silver design/smithing, 544-7
Singing, 620-1
Site management, construction, see
  Construction
Sixteen- to eighteen-plus school & pre-
  vocational qualifications, 12-23
Skating, professional, 630
Snooker, billiards and, 627

Social
  administration, 299-300
  sciences,
    applied, 299-300
    qualifications and careers in, 294-333
    studying, 296-8
  services,
    community, 1052-3
    hospital, 1053-4
  work, 1048-61
    areas of, 1051-58
    community, 1056-7
    employers, 1051-2
    medical, 1053-4
    psychiatric, 1054
    residential, 1055-6
    semi/non-professional, 1057-8
    youth/youth/community, 1056-7
Sociology, 330-3
Software
  engineering, 375
  professional work, 374-8
Soil science, see Agricultural sciences
Soldiers, 739-48
Solicitors, 1023-5
  professional/vocational training, 318-9
Speech therapists, 997-8
Sport,
  coaching/instructing/teaching, 645-7
  professional, 624-35
Stage
  design, see Theatrical design
  management, 578-9
  technicians, 579
Stationery Office, HM, 776
Statistics, mathematics and, 272-6
Steel industry,
Steward/stewardessing,
  air, 1124-5
  sea, 1141
Stock exchange/markets, 478-86
  agency brokers, 483
  dealers/traders, 482
  regulatory/compliance officers, 484
  sales staff, 482-3
  traders/dealers, 482
Structural engineering, see Civil engineering
Studio management (broadcasting), 567-8
Supply, purchasing, buying and, 504-7
Surveying, 710-21
  agricultural, 714

archaeological, 717
building, 713-4
general practice, 712-4
hydrographic, 715
insurance, 476-7
land, 714-5
main divisions of, 712-7
mining/mineral, 715
planning/development, 717
quantity, 715-6
technician, 717-8
Systems
  analysis/design, 372-4
  programming, 374-5

Tailoring, see Clothing industry
Tax
  inspectorate, 791-2
  management, 439
Taxi driving, 1143-4
Taxidermy, 604
Teacher, working as, 919-25
Teaching,
  creative and vocational subjects, 940
  in Armed Forces, 938-9
  in custodial institutions, 93940
  in further education, 932-4
  in higher education, 934-8
  languages, 1066
  nursery/pre-school, 920
  other opportunities, 938-40
  physical education/sports, 645-7
  primary/preparatory school, 920-2
  qualifications/training, 926-32
  recruitment/entry, 925-6
  school, 917-32
  secondary school, 922-4
  sixth-form/tertiary college, 924
  special school, 924-5
Technical
  authorship/writing, 595
  photography, 555-6
  (and) Vocational Education Initiative (TVEI), 10-12
Technician
  (and) Business Education Council (BTEC), 30-3
  level qualifications, 30-4
Technological development, impact on employment, 339-44
Technology Group, Civil Service, 795-6
Telecommunications, 1075-81
Television, see Broadcasting
Tennis, professional, 634-5

Textile
  design, fashion design and, 541-4
  industry, 897-900
Theatrical
  administration/production, 577-9
  costume design, see Fashion etc
  design, set design and, 548-51
  director, 578
  technicians, 579
Theology, 82-3
Three-dimensional design, 544-52
Timber trade, 900-2
Tour companies/operators, 1159-60
Tourist
  guides, 1117
  industry, 1116-7
Town/country planning, 707-10
Trade, Industry and, Department of,
  776-7
Trading standards, 806
Traffic engineering, see Civil
  engineering
Training,
  boards/organisations, 35
  Initiative, New, 3-6
  officers, advisers, instructors, 948-9
  Scheme, Youth (YTS), 15-8
Translating, 1064-5
Transport,
  Department of, 776-7
  industry, 1117-55
  working in, 1119-20
Travel
  agencies, 1157-9
  business, 1157-60
Treasury,
  corporate, management, 438-9
  HM, 778
Tree specialists, 669
Typing, see Secretarial work
Typographic design, see Graphic design

Underwriting (insurance), 477-8
United Reformed Church, 1046-7

Universities,
  educational/vocational provision, 42-4
  teaching/research in, 934-8

Valuation surveying/valuing, 713
Vehicle
  maintenance/mechanics/technicians,
    1145-6
  manufacture, 904-12
Veterinary science, 292-4
Visual communication, see Graphic
  design
Vocational
  Education Council, Scottish
    (SCOTVEC), 33-4
  qualifications, 24-35
    academic qualifications &, 1-62
    national council for, 25-7
    where they lead &, 63-333

Waiting, 1089
Wardrobe work (theatrical/television),
  579
Warehousing, wholesaling and, 525-6
Water
  engineering, see Civil engineering
  industry, 731-3
  ways, inland, 1155
Welsh Office, 777
Wholesaling, warehousing and, 525-6
Wild life 'safari' parks, 652-3
Work,
  changing pattern of, 344-7
  study, O&M and, 1037-9
  world of, 334-55
Wrestling, professional, 635
Writing, for a living/professionally,
  588-95

Youth
  Training Scheme (YTS), 14-8
  work (social), 1056-7

Zoology, 236
  courses, 243
Zoos, 652-3